Oracle Press™

Oracle8 Certified Professional™ DBA Certification Exam Guide

Jason S. Couchman

Osborne **McGraw-Hill**

Berkeley New York St. Louis
San Francisco Auckland Bogotá Hamburg London Madrid
Mexico City Milan Montreal New Delhi Panama City
Paris São Paulo Singapore Sydney Tokyo Toronto

Osborne/**McGraw-Hill**
2600 Tenth Street
Berkeley, California 94710
U.S.A.

For information on translations or book distributors outside the U.S.A., or to arrange bulk purchase discounts for sales promotions, premiums, or fund-raisers, please contact Osborne/**McGraw-Hill** at the above address.

Oracle8 Certified Professional DBA Certification Exam Guide

1234567890 DOC DOC 90198765432109

ISBN 0-07-212087-8

Publisher
Brandon A. Nordin

Associate Publisher and Editor in Chief
Scott Rogers

Acquisitions Editor
Jeremy Judson

Project Editor
Ron Hull

Editorial Assistant
Monika Faltiss

Technical Editor
Ulrike Schwinn

Copy Editor
Andy Carroll

Proofreader
Rhonda Holmes

Indexer
Irv Hershman

Computer Designers
Jani Beckwith
Roberta Steele
Ann Sellers

Illustrators
Brian Wells
Beth Young

Series Design
Jani Beckwith

Cover Design
Lisa Schultz

This book was composed with Corel VENTURA.

To Stacy

Date Functions 29
Conversion Functions 31
Chapter Summary 33
Two-Minute Drill 36
Chapter Questions 37
Answers to Chapter Questions 42

2 Advanced Data Selection in Oracle 47
Displaying Data from Multiple Tables 48
select Statements That Join Data from More Than One Table . . . 50
Creating Outer Joins 53
Joining a Table to Itself 55
Group Functions and Their Uses 57
Identifying Available Group Functions 57
Using Group Functions 58
Using the group by Clause 60
Excluding Group Data with having 63
Using Subqueries 64
Nested Subqueries 64
Subqueries in Other Situations 66
Putting Data in Order with Subqueries 71
Using Runtime Variables 72
Entering Variables at Run Time 73
Automatic Definition of Runtime Variables 75
accept: Another Way to Define Variables 76
Chapter Summary 79
Two-Minute Drill 81
Chapter Questions 83
Answers to Chapter Questions 86

3 Creating Oracle Database Objects 89
Data Modeling and Database Design 90
Stages of System Development 91
Basic Types of Data Relationships 94
Relational Database Components 95
Reading an Entity-Relationship Diagram 96
Creating the Tables of an Oracle Database 100
Creating a Table with Integrity Constraints 100
Using Table-Naming Conventions 105
Datatypes and Column Definitions 108
Indexes Created by Constraints 110
Creating One Table with Data from Another 112

The Oracle Data Dictionary ... 113
Available Dictionary Views ... 114
Querying the Data Dictionary ... 116
Manipulating Oracle Data ... 119
Inserting New Rows into a Table ... 120
Making Changes to Existing Row Data ... 122
Deleting Data from the Oracle Database ... 123
The Importance of Transaction Control ... 124
Chapter Summary ... 127
Two-Minute Drill ... 130
Chapter Questions ... 131
Answers to Chapter Questions ... 135

4 Creating Other Database Objects in Oracle ... 139
Table and Constraint Modifications ... 140
Adding and Modifying Columns ... 141
Modifying Integrity Constraints ... 143
Enabling and Disabling Constraints ... 145
Dropping Tables ... 149
Truncating Tables ... 151
Changing Names of Objects ... 151
Viewing Dictionary Comments on Objects ... 152
Sequences ... 153
Role of Sequences ... 153
Creating Sequences ... 154
Using Sequences ... 156
Modifying Sequence Definitions ... 158
Removing Sequences ... 159
Views ... 160
Data Dictionary Views ... 160
Creating Simple and Complex Views ... 162
Creating Views That Enforce Constraints ... 167
Modifying Views ... 168
Removing Views ... 169
Indexes ... 169
Manual and Automatic Indexes ... 170
Uses for Indexes ... 171
Index Structure and Operation ... 171
Creating Indexes ... 174
Removing Indexes ... 175
Guidelines for Creating Indexes ... 176

User Access Control 177
Oracle Database Security Model 177
Granting System Privileges 178
Available Object Privileges 179
Using Roles to Manage Database Access 180
Changing Passwords 182
Granting and Revoking Object Privileges 182
Using Synonyms for Database Transparency 183
Chapter Summary 186
Two-Minute Drill 188
Chapter Questions 193
Answers to Chapter Questions 196

5 Introducing PL/SQL 201
Overview of PL/SQL 202
Using PL/SQL to Access Oracle 203
PL/SQL Program Constructs 204
Developing a PL/SQL Block 211
Declaring and Using Variables 211
Variable Value Assignment 214
Controlling PL/SQL Process Flow 215
Conditional Statements and Process Flow 215
Using Loops 217
Interacting with the Oracle Database 220
Using SQL Statements in PL/SQL 220
Using Implicit Cursor Attributes 222
Transaction Processing in PL/SQL 225
Explicit Cursor Handling 225
Implicit versus Explicit Cursors 226
Declaring and Using Explicit Cursors 228
Parameters and Explicit Cursors 231
Writing cursor for Loops 233
Error Handling 235
Three Basic Types of Exceptions 235
Identifying Common Exceptions 239
Coding the Exception Handler 240
Chapter Summary 241
Two-Minute Drill 244
Chapter Questions 246
Answers to Chapter Questions 250

UNIT II
Preparing for OCP DBA Exam 2: Database Administration

6 Basics of the Oracle Database Architecture 255
Oracle Architectural Components 256
Structures That Connect Users to Oracle Servers 257
Stages in Processing Queries 261
Stages in Processing DML Statements 263
Stages in Processing commit Statements 266
Using Administration Tools 267
Using Server Manager Line Mode 267
Identifying Administration Applications in Oracle Enterprise Manager 269
Using Oracle Enterprise Manager Components 271
Managing an Oracle Instance 274
Setting Up OS and Password File Authentication 275
Creating Your Parameter File 279
Starting an Instance and Opening the Database 281
Closing a Database and Shutting Down the Instance 284
Getting and Setting Parameter Values 286
Managing Sessions 287
Monitoring ALERT and Trace Files 288
Creating an Oracle Database 289
Preparing the Operating System 290
Preparing the Parameter File 291
Creating a Database in Oracle 293
Chapter Summary 296
Two-Minute Drill 299
Chapter Questions 303
Answers to Chapter Questions 307

7 Managing the Physical Database Structure 311
Data Dictionary Views and Standard Packages 312
Constructing the Data Dictionary Views 313
Using the Data Dictionary 314
Preparing the PL/SQL Environment with Admin Scripts 315
Administering Stored Procedures and Packages 317
Managing Control Files 318
How Control Files Are Used 319
Examining Control File Contents 320

Obtaining Information About Control Files 321
Multiplexing Control Files 323
Maintaining Redo Log Files 324
How Online Redo Log Files Are Used 325
Obtaining Log and Archive Information 325
Controlling Log Switches and Checkpoints 328
Multiplexing and Maintaining Redo Log Files 330
Planning Online Redo Log Files 332
Troubleshooting Common Redo Log File Problems 334
Managing Tablespaces and Datafiles 335
Describing the Logical Structure of the Database 336
Creating Tablespaces 337
Changing Tablespace Size Using Various Methods 339
Changing Tablespace Status and Storage Settings 340
Relocating Tablespaces 342
Preparing Necessary Tablespaces 343
Storage Structures and Relationships 345
Different Segment Types and Their Uses 345
Controlling the Use of Extents by Segments 348
Using Block Space Utilization Parameters 350
Obtaining Information About Storage Structures 352
Locating Segments with Consideration for Fragmentation and Lifespan 353
Chapter Summary 355
Two-Minute Drill 357
Chapter Questions 359
Answers to Chapter Questions 363

8 Managing Database Objects I 367
Managing Rollback Segments 368
Planning the Number and Size of Rollback Segments 369
Creating Rollback Segments with Appropriate Storage Settings 374
Maintaining Rollback Segments 376
Obtaining Rollback Segment Information from Dictionary Views 378
Troubleshooting Rollback Segment Problems 380
Managing Temporary Segments 383
Distinguishing Different Types of Temporary Segments 383
Allocating Space for Temporary Segments in the Database 385
Obtaining Temporary Segment Information from Oracle 386
Managing Tables 387
Distinguishing Oracle Datatypes 388
Creating Tables with Appropriate Storage Settings 393

Controlling the Space Used by Tables 397
Analyzing Tables to Check Integrity and Migration 400
Retrieving Data Dictionary Information About Tables 401
Converting Between Different ROWID Formats 402
Chapter Summary 404
Two-Minute Drill 405
Chapter Questions 407
Answers to Chapter Questions 411

9 Managing Database Objects II 415
Managing Indexes 416
Different Index Types and Their Use 417
Creating B-tree and Bitmap Indexes 421
Reorganizing Indexes 424
Dropping Indexes 425
Getting Index Information from the Data Dictionary 426
Managing Data Integrity 427
Describing Integrity Constraints and Triggers 428
Implementing Data-Integrity Constraints and Triggers 433
Maintaining Integrity Constraints and Triggers 436
Obtaining Constraint and Trigger Information from Oracle 439
Using Clusters and Index-Organized Tables 440
Creating and Maintaining Clusters 441
Using Index-Organized Tables 447
Dictionary Information About Clusters and IOTs 450
Chapter Summary 450
Two-Minute Drill 451
Chapter Questions 454
Answers to Chapter Questions 458

10 Managing Database Use 463
Managing Users 464
Creating New Database Users 465
Altering and Dropping Existing Users 468
Monitoring Information About Existing Users 470
Managing Resource Use 471
Creating and Assigning Profiles to Control Resource Use 472
Altering and Dropping Profiles 475
Administering Passwords Using Profiles 476
Obtaining Profile Information from the Data Dictionary 480
Managing Privileges 480
Identifying System Privileges 481
Identifying Object Privileges 484

Granting and Revoking Privileges 485
Controlling OS or Password Authentication 489
Managing Roles 490
Creating and Modifying Roles 490
Controlling Availability of Roles 492
Removing Roles 493
Using Predefined Roles 494
Displaying Role Information from the Data Dictionary 495
Auditing the Database 496
Differentiating Between Database and Value-Based Auditing ... 497
Using Database Auditing 498
Viewing Enabled Auditing Options 501
Retrieving and Maintaining Auditing Information 502
Chapter Summary 504
Two-Minute Drill 505
Chapter Questions 510
Answers to Chapter Questions 514

11 Data Loads and National Language Support 519
Loading and Reorganizing Data 520
Loading Data Using Direct-Path insert 520
Using SQL*Loader Conventional
and Direct Path 522
Reorganizing Data with EXPORT and IMPORT 534
Using National Language Support 543
Choosing a Character Set for a Database 543
Specifying Language-Dependent Behavior 545
Obtaining Information about NLS Settings 546
Chapter Summary 547
Two-Minute Drill 548
Chapter Questions 550
Answers to Chapter Questions 552

UNIT III

Preparing for OCP DBA Exam 3: Backup and Recovery Workshop

12 Overview of Backup and Recovery 557
Backup and Recovery Considerations 558
Business, Operational, and Technical Considerations 559
Components of a Disaster-Recovery Plan 560
The Importance of Testing Backup and Recovery Strategy 561

Oracle Recovery Structures and Processes 563
Architectural Components for Backup and Recovery 563
Importance of Redo Logs, Checkpoints, and Archives 566
Synchronizing Files During Checkpoints 569
Multiplexing Control Files and Redo Logs 571
Oracle Backup and Recovery Configuration 574
Recovery Implications of Not Archiving Redo Logs 575
Configuring Oracle for Redo Log Archiving 577
Multiplexing Archived Redo Log Files 583
Physical Backups in Oracle Without RMAN 585
Using OS Commands for Database Backup 585
Recovery Implications for Offline and Online Backups 586
Performing Offline and Online Backups 587
Backup Implications of logging and nologging Modes 590
Taking Backups of Your Control File 591
Backing Up Read-Only Tablespaces 593
Dictionary Views for Database Backup 594
Chapter Summary 595
Two-Minute Drill 596
Chapter Questions 600
Answers to Chapter Questions 605

13 Using Recovery Manager for Backups 609
Oracle Recovery Manager Overview 610
Determining When to Use RMAN 610
Backup Manager Uses 614
RMAN Advantages, With or Without a Recovery Catalog 615
Creating the Recovery Catalog 617
Connecting to RMAN 619
Oracle Recovery Catalog Maintenance 620
Registering, Resynchronizing, and Resetting the Database 621
Maintaining the Recovery Catalog 623
Generating Reports and Lists 625
Creating, Storing, and Running RMAN Scripts 626
Physical Backups Using Recovery Manager 629
Identifying Types of RMAN Backups 629
Describing Backup Concepts Using RMAN 632
Performing Incremental and Cumulative Backups 637
Troubleshooting Backup Problems 639
Viewing Information from the Data Dictionary 640

Chapter Summary . . . 641
Two-Minute Drill . . . 642
Chapter Questions . . . 645
Answers to Chapter Questions . . . 649

14 Database Failure and Recovery . . . 653
Types of Failure and Troubleshooting . . . 654
Types of Failure in an Oracle Database . . . 655
Structures for Instance and Media Recovery . . . 656
Using the DBVERIFY Utility . . . 659
Configuring Checksum Operations . . . 661
Using Log and Trace Files to Diagnose Problems . . . 663
Oracle Recovery Without Archiving . . . 666
Implications of Media Failure in noarchivelog Mode . . . 666
Recovering noarchivelog Databases . . . 667
Restoring Files to Different Locations . . . 668
Recovering noarchivelog Databases with RMAN . . . 669
Oracle Recovery with Archiving . . . 671
Implications of Instance Failure in archivelog Mode . . . 672
Complete Recovery Operation . . . 673
Pros and Cons of Recovering archivelog Databases . . . 674
Recovering archivelog Databases After Media Failure . . . 675
Using RMAN and Backup Manager . . . 683
Chapter Summary . . . 688
Two-Minute Drill . . . 689
Chapter Questions . . . 692
Answers to Chapter Questions . . . 696

15 Advanced Topics in Data Recovery . . . 701
Incomplete Recovery with Archiving . . . 702
When to Use Incomplete Recovery . . . 703
Performing an Incomplete Recovery . . . 706
Recovering after Losing Current and Active Redo Logs . . . 709
Using RMAN in Incomplete Recovery . . . 711
Working with Tablespace Point-in-Time Recovery . . . 713
Additional Oracle Recovery Issues . . . 714
Methods for Minimizing Downtime . . . 715
Diagnosing and Recovering from Database Corruption Errors . . . 719
Reconstructing Lost or Damaged Control Files . . . 719
Recovery Issues for Offline and Read-Only Tablespaces . . . 721
Recovering from Recovery Catalog Loss . . . 722

Oracle EXPORT and IMPORT Utilities 722
Using EXPORT to Create Complete Logical Backups 723
Using EXPORT to Create Incremental Logical Backups 725
Invoking EXPORT on the Direct Path 727
Using IMPORT to Recover Database Objects 728
Chapter Summary 730
Two-Minute Drill 731
Chapter Questions 736
Answers to Chapter Questions 740

UNIT IV

Preparing for OCP DBA Exam 4: Performance Tuning Workshop

16 Introducing Database Tuning **747**
Business Requirements and Tuning 748
Roles Associated with Tuning 749
Steps Associated with Tuning 751
Different Tuning Goals 753
Oracle ALERT Logs, Trace Files, and Events 754
Location and Use of the ALERT Log 754
Location and Use of Trace Files 757
Retrieving and Displaying Wait Events 759
Setting Predefined Events Using OEM 762
Utilities and Dynamic Performance Views 765
Using Dynamic Performance Views 765
Using the UTLBSTAT/UTLESTAT Output Report 768
Using Appropriate OEM Tools 777
Chapter Summary 778
Two-Minute Drill 779
Chapter Questions 781
Answers to Chapter Questions 784

17 Tuning Database Applications **789**
Tuning for Differing Application Requirements 790
Using Data-Access Methods to Tune Logical Database Design 791
Demands of Online Transaction Processing Systems 793
Demands of Decision Support Systems 795
Configuring Systems Temporarily for Particular Needs 796

SQL Tuning ... 799
Role of the DBA in Application Tuning ... 799
Using Oracle Tools to Diagnose SQL Performance ... 801
Using Different Optimizer Modes ... 809
Using Star Queries and Hash Joins ... 812
Tracking and Registering Module Use for PL/SQL Blocks ... 817
Identifying Alternative SQL Statements to Enhance Performance ... 820
Chapter Summary ... 828
Two-Minute Drill ... 829
Chapter Questions ... 833
Answers to Chapter Questions ... 837

18 Tuning Memory and Operating System Use ... 841
Generic Operating System Tuning ... 842
The Primary Steps for OS Tuning ... 843
Similarities Between OS and Database Tuning ... 845
The Difference Between Processes and Threads ... 846
Describing Paging and Swapping ... 848
Tuning the Shared Pool ... 849
Tuning the Library Cache and Dictionary Cache ... 849
Measuring Shared-Pool Hit Percentage ... 852
Sizing the Shared Pool ... 854
Pinning Objects in the Shared Pool ... 855
Tuning Shared-Pool Reserved Space ... 857
Listing the UGA and Session Memory ... 858
Tuning the Buffer Cache ... 859
How Oracle Manages the Buffer Cache ... 860
Calculating the Buffer-Cache Hit Ratio ... 861
Assessing the Impact of Adding or Removing Buffers ... 863
Creating Multiple Buffer Pools ... 867
Sizing Multiple Buffer Pools ... 870
Monitoring the Buffer Cache ... 872
Using Table Caching ... 873
Tuning Redo Mechanisms ... 873
Determining Contention for the Redo Log Buffer ... 874
Sizing the Redo Log Buffer ... 875
Reducing Redo Operations ... 875
Chapter Summary ... 876
Two-Minute Drill ... 877
Chapter Questions ... 881
Answers to Chapter Questions ... 886

19 Tuning Disk Utilization **891**
Database Configuration and I/O Issues 892
Identifying Inappropriate Use of Different Tablespaces 893
Detecting I/O Problems 896
Distributing Files to Reduce I/O Contention 898
Using Striping Where Appropriate 901
Tuning Checkpoints 902
Tuning Background Process I/O 903
Tuning Rollback Segments 904
Using V$ Views to Monitor Rollback-Segment Performance 905
Modifying Rollback-Segment Configuration 907
Determining Number and Size of Rollback Segments 909
Allocating Rollback Segments to Transactions 911
Using Oracle Blocks Efficiently 911
Determining Appropriate Block Size 912
Optimizing Space Usage Within Blocks 913
Detecting and Resolving Row Migration 915
Monitoring and Tuning Indexes 917
Sizing Extents Appropriately 918
Chapter Summary 921
Two-Minute Drill 922
Chapter Questions 925
Answers to Chapter Questions 929

20 Tuning Other Areas of the Oracle Database **933**
Monitoring and Detecting Lock Contention 934
Levels of Locking in Oracle 935
Identifying Possible Causes for Contention 938
Using Tools to Detect Lock Contention 940
Resolving Contention in an Emergency 941
Preventing Locking Problems 942
Identifying and Preventing Deadlocks 943
Resolving Latch and Contention Issues 945
Using Oracle Tools to Resolve Freelist Contention 945
Identifying Latch-Contention Situations 947
Resolving Redo Allocation-Latch and Copy-Latch Contention . . . 951
Resolving LRU Latch Contention 955
Tuning Sort Operations 956
Identifying SQL Operations That Use Sorts 957
Ensuring That Sorts Happen in Memory 958
Allocating Temporary Disk Space for Sorts 960
Using Direct Writes for Sorts 960

Tuning with Oracle Expert 961
Oracle Expert Features 962
Creating a Tuning Session 964
Gathering, Viewing, and Editing Input Data 964
Analyzing Collected Data Using Rules 966
Reviewing Tuning Recommendations 967
Implementing Tuning Recommendations 967
Chapter Summary 968
Two-Minute Drill 969
Chapter Questions 971
Answers to Chapter Questions 974

PART V

Preparing for OCP Exam 5: Network Administration

21 Overview of Net8 for Client and Server 979
Net8 Overview 980
Identifying Networking Trends and Problems 980
Describing Oracle Networking Solutions 984
Basic Net8 Architecture 985
The Procedure Net8 Uses to Establish Server Connections 986
Components of Net8 Architecture 989
Basic Net8 Server-Side Configuration 991
Configuring the Listener with Net8 Assistant 991
Starting the Listener Using LSNRCTL 998
Stopping the Listener Using LSNRCTL 999
Additional LSNRCTL Commands 1001
Setting Up Multiple Listeners on the Same Node 1003
Basic Net8 Client-Side Configuration 1009
Establishing Connections Using Host Naming Method 1009
Configuring Net8 Files and Using the Local Naming Method 1011
Using Net8 Assistant to Identify Client Preferences 1017
Chapter Summary 1020
Two Minute Drill 1021
Chapter Questions 1025
Answers to Chapter Questions 1030

22 Names, Intelligent Agent, and MTS 1035
Use and Configuration of Oracle Names 1036
Using Net8 Assistant to Configure Centralized Naming 1037
Storing Network Configuration on the Local File System 1044
Storing Network Configuration on a Regional Database 1047
Managing the Names Server with NAMESCTL 1049

Use and Configuration of Oracle Intelligent Agent for OEM 1057
The Purpose of Intelligent Agent 1057
Using LSNRCTL to Start and Stop Intelligent Agent 1058
Intelligent Agent Configuration Files 1060
Use and Configuration of Multithreaded Server (MTS) 1061
The Components of MTS 1061
Configuring Dispatchers Using initsid.ora 1063
Configuring Shared Servers Using initsid.ora 1065
Specifying a Listener Address for MTS 1066
Setting Up Connection Pooling Using MTS 1067
Chapter Summary 1068
Two Minute Drill 1069
Chapter Questions 1072
Answers to Chapter Questions 1077

23 Connection Manager, Troubleshooting, and Security 1081
Using and Configuring Connection Manager 1082
Connection Manager Capabilities 1083
Configuring Connection Concentration 1086
Configuring Multiprotocol Functionality 1088
Enabling Network Access Control 1091
Troubleshooting Network Environments 1093
Setting Log and Trace Parameters 1094
Analyzing and Troubleshooting Network Problems 1101
Formatting Trace Files Using Trace Assistant 1107
Security in Network Environments 1111
Network Security Risks During Data Transmission 1111
Security Features in Oracle Networking Products 1112
Features of Advanced Networking Option 1114
Configuring Components of Advanced Networking Option 1115
Chapter Summary 1123
Two-Minute Drill 1124
Chapter Questions 1130
Answers to Chapter Questions 1135

PART VI

Preparing for OCP Exam 6: Oracle8*i* New Features for Administrators

24 Oracle8*i* New Features Topics 1141
Chapter 25: Oracle8*i* Database Management 1143
Installation and Configuration 1143
Migrating Server and Applications 1144
Oracle Enterprise Manager 1144

ROWID Format in Oracle8*i* 1145
Tablespace Management 1146
Password Management 1146
Other Security Enhancements 1147
Chapter 26: Oracle8*i* Internals 1147
SQL*Plus, PL/SQL, and NLS Enhancements 1148
Memory Management 1148
Parallel Query Enhancements 1149
Database Resource Manager 1149
Optimizer and Query Improvements 1150
Materialized Views 1150
Chapter 27: Oracle8*i* Object Management I 1151
Constraints 1151
Other Manageability Enhancements 1152
Index Enhancements 1152
Index-Organized Tables 1153
Managing Large Objects 1153
Object Relational Databases 1154
Chapter 28: Oracle8*i* Object Management II 1154
Partitioning Tables 1155
Partitioning Indexes 1155
Parallel DML and Queries 1156
Partitioning Techniques 1157
Partitioned IOTs, LOBs, and Objects 1157
Chapter 29: Oracle8*i* Recoverability Enhancement 1158
Introducing Recovery Manager 1158
Using RMAN Catalog Commands and Reports 1159
Using RMAN run Commands and Scripts 1159
Oracle8i Availability and Recoverability Enhancements 1160
Standby Databases 1160
Chapter 30: Oracle8*i* Advanced New Features 1161
Advanced Queuing 1161
Net8 1162
Java in the Database 1162

Index 1165

Preface

My interest in Oracle certification began in 1996 when I read about the Oracle DBA certificate offered by the Chauncey Group. I found it difficult to prepare for that certification exam for two reasons. First, there was an absence of practice questions readily available. Second, preparation for the exam involved reviewing six or seven different manuals and Oracle Press books, none of which were particularly suited to the task. Judging from the response to this book so far, it would seem others have had similar experiences.

This book is divided into six units, the first five of which cover each exam in the Oracle8 DBA certification track from Oracle. The remaining unit, found exclusively in the electronic edition on the book's CD-ROM, is dedicated to covering Oracle8*i* new features for the upgrade exam on that topic. Each unit has several chapters covering the material you need to know in order to pass the exam. Each chapter follows the format described in this preface.

Within each chapter, there are several discussion sections. These discussions correspond directly to subject areas tested in the OCP exams. Each discussion presents facts about the Oracle database. Commands and keywords that the user enters are presented in `Courier`, while new terms or emphasized facts are presented in italics. Particularly important facts and suggestions are set apart from regular text. They are preceded by the word "tip" or "note," and an icon appears in the margin next to them.

At the end of each section are some exercises. Designed to reinforce the material you just read, these exercises are short-answer questions. You should try to do *all* the exercises at the end of each discussion. If you can, try to answer the questions without reviewing the chapter material, and write the answers in the book for later review.

A summary of the material presented appears near the end of each chapter. This digest information is designed for quick review after reading the chapter and doing the exercises. In the days prior to your OCP exam, you can re-read the chapter summary to familiarize yourself with the information covered.

After the chapter summary, you'll find a short list of the key facts about Oracle presented in the chapter. This list, called a "two-minute drill," is designed to be your final review for the OCP exam in the subject area covered in the chapter. Go over the two-minute drill for each chapter in the unit covering your OCP exam the night before you take the test as a memory jogger and memorization list.

The chapter also contains multiple-choice questions patterned after the actual exam. These questions will familiarize you with the style of OCP questions. They will also test your knowledge of the Oracle material presented in the chapter. You should attempt to answer these questions after reviewing the chapter. Finally, to help you understand the test material, each chapter contains the answers to the chapter questions, along with an explanation of each answer.

In order to get the most from this book, you need to answer the following question: What is your level of Oracle experience? There are two ways to use this book. If you are a professional with a beginner or intermediate level of Oracle experience, you should use the standard method of studying this book. Start at the beginning of each chapter, read it from start to finish, and *do the exercises.* Review the material by reading the chapter summary and two-minute drill, and then answer the practice questions. The standard method should give you the facts you need in order to pass the OCP exams. If you have reviewed the material thoroughly—answering the exercise questions and studying the chapter summary and the drill for all chapters in the unit—you should do well on the OCP exam.

However, advanced users of Oracle seeking to prepare for OCP exams quickly can also use the book's *accelerated reading method.* Skip directly to the chapter summary and read it to review the chapter's content. Then go over the two-minute drill and try the chapter questions. If you find yourself getting most of the questions right, you may be ready to take the test. Even if you are missing questions, you will probably have a better idea of the areas you need review. You can then flip back to the specific part of the chapter to help refresh your memory. Given the introduction of Oracle8 topics and concepts that may be unfamiliar to readers, however, I discourage all but the most advanced users of Oracle from using the accelerated reading method.

Finally, a note about errata. Because OCP covers such vast ground in a short time, this has become a living text. If you feel you have encountered difficulties due to errors, you can either check out **www.exampilot.com** to find the latest errata, or send me an email directly at **jcouchman@mindspring.com**.

Good luck!

Acknowledgments

There are many people I would like to thank for their help with writing this book. My first and most heartfelt thanks goes to the dedicated readers of my other book and first edition of this one, who took time out of their busy schedules to send feedback on the book. I have listened to your praise and constructive criticism, and made every effort to correct and amplify my work based on the points you made. Please, keep the email coming—it is by far the most effective way to make the book better!

Next, a note of gratitude to the folks at Oracle who make the book possible. Thanks to Rob Pedigo, Brad Saffer, Julia Johnson, Chris Pirie, Ulrike Schwinn, Geoff McDonald, and Andrea Ward of Oracle and Oracle Education for their feedback and assistance with the technical content review and with the material covering Oracle8 Oracle8*i*. Thanks also to the fine folks at Osborne—Scott Rogers, Jeremy Judson, and Monika Faltiss. Special thanks to the folks in editorial and production and to Ron Hull for accommodating some important last-minute changes. A heartfelt thanks to Andy Carroll as well, for his dedication to the work and to painstaking details.

Most of all, thanks to my wonderful wife who tended to numerous details while I wrote. Stacy, you really are the greatest thing that ever happened to me.

About the Author . . .

Jason S. Couchman is a database consultant and the co-author of *Oracle Certified Professional Application Developer Exam Guide,* also from Oracle Press. He is a regular presenter on Oracle and OCP-related topics at international Oracle user conferences and meetings. His work has been published by *Oracle Magazine,* Harvard Business School Publishing, and Gannett Newspapers, among others.

Introduction

The Oracle Certified Professional DBA certification exam series is the latest knowledge good from Oracle Corporation. Called OCP, it represents the culmination of many people's request for objective standards in one of the hottest markets in the software field, Oracle database administration. The presence of OCP on the market indicates an important reality about Oracle as a career path. Oracle is mature, robust, and stable for enterprise-wide information management. However, corporations facing a severe shortage of qualified Oracle professionals need a measurement for Oracle expertise.

The OCP certification core track for DBAs consists of five tests in the following areas of Oracle8: SQL and PL/SQL, database administration, performance tuning, network administration, and backup/recovery. As of this printing, each test consists of about 60 multiple choice questions pertaining to the recommended usage of Oracle databases. You have about 90 minutes to take each exam. The current content of those five exams covers Oracle through version 8.0. A sixth exam is in the works to test DBAs on the new features available in Oracle8*i*. Obtaining certification for Oracle8 through the core track is contingent on taking and passing *all five* core examinations, while certification on the upgrade track for Oracle8 and Oracle8*i* requires passing the Oracle8 and Oracle8*i* new features exams.

Why Get Certified?

If you are already an Oracle professional, you may wonder, "Why should I get certified?" Perhaps you have a successful career as an Oracle DBA, enjoying the instant prestige your résumé gets with that one magic word on it. With market forces currently in your favor, you're right to wonder. While no one is saying you don't know Oracle if you're not certified, can you prove how well you *do* know Oracle without a technical interview? I started asking myself that question when Oracle certification began to emerge. I was surprised to find out that, after years of using Oracle, developing Oracle applications, and administering Oracle databases for Fortune 500 companies, there were a lot of things about Oracle I *didn't* know. And the only reason I know them now is because I took the time and effort to become certified.

If you're looking for another reason to become certified in Oracle, consider the example of computer professionals with Novell NetWare experience in the late 1980s and early 1990s. It seemed that anyone with even a little experience in Novell could count on a fantastic job offer. Then Novell introduced its CNE/CNA programs. At first, employers hired professionals with or without the certificate. As time went on, however, employers no longer asked for computer professionals with Novell NetWare experience—they asked for CNEs and CNAs. A similar phenomenon can be witnessed in the arena of Microsoft Windows NT, where the MCSE has already become the standard by which those professionals are measuring their skills. If you want to stay competitive in the field of Oracle database administration, your real question shouldn't be *whether* you should become certified, but *when*.

If you are not in the field of Oracle database management, or if you want to advance your career using Oracle, there has never been a better time to do so. OCP is altering the playing field for DBAs by changing the focus of the Oracle skill set from "How many years have you used it?" to "*How well* do you know how to use it?"

Managers who are faced with the task of hiring Oracle professionals benefit from OCP as well. By seeking professionals who are certified, managers can spend less time trying to determine if the candidate knows Oracle well enough to do the job, and more time assessing the candidate's work habits and compatibility with the team.

How Should You Prepare for the Exam?

If you spend your free time studying things like the name of the dynamic performance view that helps a DBA estimate the effect of adding buffers to the buffer cache, you are probably ready to take the OCP DBA exams right now. For the rest of us, there are many training options available to learn Oracle, such as classroom and computer-based training from Oracle Education. Those classes can be useful—their content forms the basis of the OCP exams, after all—but not everyone has an employer willing to pay for instructor-led training. Now, users have another option—this book! By selecting this book, you demonstrate two excellent characteristics—that you are committed to a superior career in the field of Oracle database administration, and that you care about preparing for the exam correctly and thoroughly. And by the way, the name of the dynamic performance view that helps a DBA estimate the effect of adding buffers to the buffer cache is V$RECENT_BUCKET, and it is on the OCP DBA exam. That fact, along with thousands of others, is covered extensively in this book to help you prepare for, and pass, the OCP DBA certification exam.

DBA Certification Past and Present

Oracle certification started in the mid 1990s with the involvement of the Chauncey Group International, a division of Educational Testing Service. With the help of many Oracle DBAs, Chauncey put together an objective, fact-based and scenario-based examination on Oracle database administration. This test did an excellent job of measuring knowledge of Oracle7, versions 7.0 to 7.2. Consisting of 60 questions, Chauncey's exam covered several different topic areas, including backup and recovery, security, administration, and performance tuning, all in one test.

Oracle Corporation has taken DBA certification several giant leaps ahead with the advent of OCP. Their certification examination is actually five tests, each consisting of about 60 questions. By quintupling the number of questions you must answer, Oracle requires that you have unprecedented depth of knowledge in Oracle database administration. Oracle has also committed to including scenario-based questions on the OCP examinations, and preparation material for these new questions is included in this book as well. Scenario-based questions require you not only to know the facts about Oracle, but also to understand how to apply those facts in real-life situations.

Oracle's final contribution to the area of Oracle certification is a commitment to reviewing and updating the material presented in the certification exams. Oracle-certified DBAs will be required to maintain their certification by retaking the certification exams periodically—meaning that those who certify will stay on the cutting edge of the Oracle database better than those who do not.

Taking the Oracle Assessment Test

It is essential that you begin your preparation for the OCP DBA certification exams by taking the Oracle assessment test. The Oracle assessment test is a mock-up of the real exam, with questions designed to help you identify your personal areas of strength and weakness with Oracle. You can download the Oracle assessment test from the Oracle Education website at **http://education.oracle.com/certification**. You should load it onto your Windows-based computer and take the exams to determine which areas you need to study. You should also download the OCP *Candidate Guide* for the DBA 8.0 track. It lists the topic areas for each exam corresponding to chapters and discussion sections in this book.

Figure 1 is a diagram of the assessment test graphical user interface. The features of the interface are indicated in the figure. Several of the main features of the assessment test interface are explained here. The assessment test interface is very similar to the actual Sylvan Prometric OCP DBA test driver, with a few exceptions as noted. At the top of the assessment test, you can see how much time has elapsed and the number of questions you have answered. On the actual OCP exam only, there is also a checkbox in the upper left-hand corner of the window. You can use this checkbox to mark questions you would like to review later. In the main window of the interface is the actual question, along with the choices. The interface allows the user to select only one answer, unless the question directs you to select more

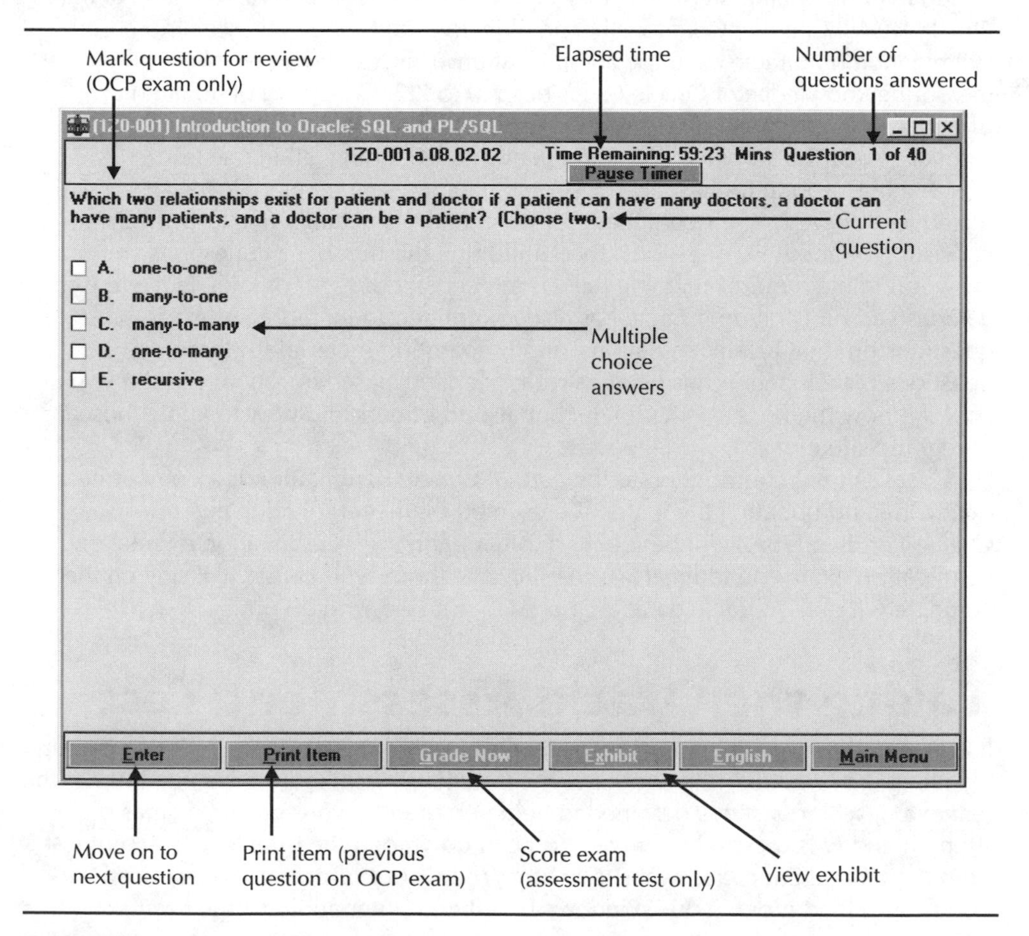

FIGURE 1. *The Oracle assessment test user interface*

answers. In this case, the interface will allow you to select only as many answers as the question requests. After answering a question, or marking the question for later review, the candidate can move onto the next question by clicking the appropriate button in the lower left-hand corner. The next button allows you either to print out the assessment test or to return to the previous question on the OCP exam. Next, in the assessment test only, you can score your questions at any time by clicking the Grade Test button on the lower right-hand side. Another feature worth noting is the Exhibit button. In some cases, you may need to view an exhibit to answer a question. If the question does not have an exhibit, the button will be grayed out.

The assessment test indicates your performance in a Grade Report window, like the one shown in Figure 2. It details the number of questions you answered correctly, along with your percentage score based on 100 percent. Finally, a bar graph indicates how your score compares to the maximum score possible on the exam. The OCP exam reports your score immediately after you exit the test, so you will know right then whether you pass or not in a similar fashion as the assessment test. Both interfaces offer the ability to print a report of your score.

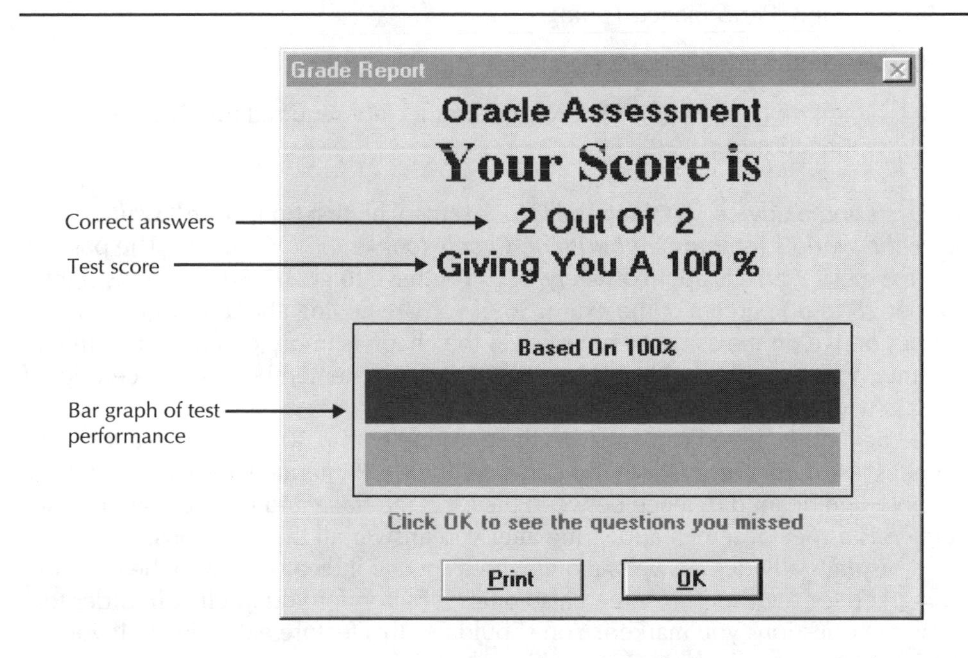

FIGURE 2. *Grading your test performance*

Taking the OCP Exams

The score range for each OCP Exam is between 200 and 800. Since there is a 600-point range for potential scores, and typically there are 60 questions, each question is worth about 10 points. Given the recent use of questions with two or even three correct answers on OCP exams, the scoring method for actual OCP exams may differ somewhat from my explanation . There is no penalty for wrong answers. The OCP DBA certification exam is administered at Sylvan Prometric test centers. To schedule your OCP Exam in the United States, call Sylvan Prometric at 1-800-891-EXAM. For contact information outside the USA, refer to the assessment test software. For Oracle's official information about OCP certification, visit **http://education.oracle.com/certification**. The exams in the OCP DBA series are as follows:

- Oracle8: SQL and PL/SQL
- Oracle8: Database Administration
- Oracle8: Backup and Recovery
- Oracle8: Performance Tuning
- Oracle8: Network Administration
- Oracle8*i*: New Features for Administrators (not required for Oracle8 certification)

Here's some advice on taking the OCP exams. The first tip is, *don't wait until you're the world's foremost authority on Oracle to take the OCP Exam.* The passing score for most exams is approximately 650. You have to get 45-50 questions right, or about 75 to 80 percent of the exam. So, if you are getting about four questions right out of five on the assessment test or in the chapters (more on chapter format in a minute), you should consider taking the OCP exam. Remember, you're certified if you pass with a 650 or an 800.

The next tip is, if you can't answer the question within 30 seconds, mark it with the checkbox in the upper left-hand corner of the OCP interface for review later. The most significant difference between the OCP interface and the assessment test interface is a special screen appearing after you answer all the questions. This screen displays all your answers, along with a special indicator next to the questions you marked for review. This screen also offers a button for you to click in order to review the questions you marked. You should use this feature extensively. If you spend only 30 seconds answering each question in your first pass on the exam, you will have at least an hour to review the questions you're unsure of, with the added bonus of knowing you answered all the questions that were easiest to you first.

Third, *there is no penalty for guessing.* If you answer the question correctly, your score goes up ten points, if not, your score does not change. If you can eliminate any choices on a question, you should take the chance in the interest of improving your score. In some questions, the OCP exam requires you to specify two or even three choices—this can work in your favor, meaning you need to eliminate fewer choices to get the question right.

Finally, unless your level of expertise with Oracle is high in a particular area, *it is recommended that you take the exams in the sequential order listed earlier.* This is especially recommended for readers whose background in Oracle is more on the beginner/intermediate level, and even more important if you are using this book to prepare for the exam. This is because each subsequent chapter of the book builds on information presented in the previous chapters. As such, you should read the book from beginning to end, and take the test accordingly. Taking the exams in this manner will maximize your results on the tests.

The Scenario-Based Questions on the OCP Exam

Oracle Corporation has begun including scenario-based questions in the OCP DBA certification exam series. These questions require you to take the facts about Oracle and apply those facts to real-life situations portrayed on the exam—complete with exhibits and documents to substantiate the example—and determine the correct answer based on those exhibits and documents. In order to assist you better in preparation for these test questions, the questions in this book have been designed to replicate scenario-based exam questions.

Finally, if you have comments about the book or would like to contact me about it, please do so by email at **jcouchman@mindspring.com**. You can also find related information such as posted corrections and amplifications at **www.exampilot.com**.

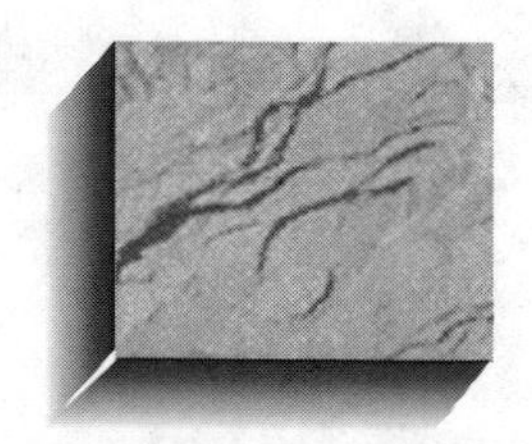

UNIT I

Preparing for OCP DBA Exam 1: SQL and PL/SQL

CHAPTER 1

Selecting Data from Oracle

n this chapter, you will learn about and demonstrate knowledge in the following areas:

- Selecting rows
- Limiting and refining selected output
- Using single-row functions

The first exam in the OCP series covers basic areas of database usage and design. Every Oracle user, developer, and DBA should have complete mastery in these areas before moving on into other test areas. This unit assumes little or no prior knowledge of Oracle in order to help you go from never having used Oracle to having enough expertise in the Oracle server product to maintain and enhance existing applications and develop small new ones. The five chapters in this unit will function as the basis for understanding the rest of the book. This chapter will cover several aspects of data retrieval from the Oracle database, including selecting rows, limiting the selection, and using single-row functions. This chapter covers 17 percent of the test content of OCP Exam 1.

Selecting Rows

This section will cover the following areas related to selecting rows:

- Writing `select` statements
- Performing arithmetic equations
- Handling NULL values
- Changing column headings with column aliases
- Putting columns together with concatenation
- Editing SQL queries within SQL*Plus

Experience with Oracle for many developers, designers, DBAs, and power users begins with using an existing Oracle application in an organization. The first tool many people see for selecting data directly from the Oracle relational database management system is SQL*Plus. When users first start SQL*Plus, in most cases they must enter their Oracle username and password in order to begin a session with the Oracle database. There are some exceptions to this rule that utilize the password authentication provided with the operating system. The following examples show how you might begin a session with Oracle from a command line operating system, such as UNIX. From Windows, you can instead click on Start | Programs | Oracle for Windows | SQL*Plus, or double-click the SQL*Plus icon on your desktop if one appears there.

```
$> sqlplus jason/athena
```

or

```
$> sqlplus /
```

A *session* is an interactive runtime environment in which you enter commands to retrieve data and Oracle performs a series of activities to obtain the data you ask for. Think of it as a conversation, which in turn implies language. You communicate with Oracle using structured query language, or SQL for short. (SQL can be pronounced either as three individual letters or as "sequel.")

SQL is a "functional" language, which means that you specify the types of things you want to see happen in terms of the results you want. Contrast this approach to other languages you may have heard about or programmed in, such as C++ or COBOL, which are often referred to as "procedural" programming languages because the code written in these languages implies an end result by explicitly defining the means, or the procedure, by which to get there. In contrast, SQL explicitly defines the end result, leaving it up to Oracle to determine the method by which the data is obtained. Data selection can be accomplished using the following code listing:

```
SELECT *
FROM emp
WHERE empid = 39334;
```

This SQL statement asks Oracle to provide all data from the EMP table where the value in a certain column called EMPID equals 39334. The following block of code from an imaginary procedural programming language similar to C illustrates how the same function may be handled by explicitly defining the means to the end:

```
Include <stdio.h>
Include <string.h>
Include <rdbms.h>

Int *empid;
Char *statement;

Type emp_rec is record (
Int             empid;
Char[10]        emp_name;
Int             salary; )
```

```
Void main()

  Access_table(emp);
  Open(statement.memaddr);
  Strcpy("SELECT * FROM EMP WHERE EMPID = 39334",statement.text);
  parse(statement);
  execute(statement);
  for (I=1,I=statement.results,I+1)
    fetch(statement.result[I],emp_rec);
    printf(emp_rec);

  close(statement.memaddr);
```

Of course, this C-like block of code would not compile anywhere but in your imagination, but the point of the example is clear—other languages define a process, while SQL defines the result.

Writing select Statements

The most common type of SQL statement executed in most database environments is the *query*, or `select` statement. A `select` statement pulls requested data from a table in a database. A table in Oracle is similar in concept to Table 1-1. (For more information about tables, see Chapter 3.) You can issue a simple `select` statement to pull all data from the table shown in Table 1-1.

The following code block demonstrates a `select` statement used to obtain data from a table called EMP, owned by a user called JASON. Sometimes Oracle developers and DBAs refer to database objects as being part of something called a "schema." A schema is a logical grouping of database objects, such as tables, specified by owner. Thus, the EMP table you will see is part of the JASON schema.

Empid	**Lastname**	**Fname**	**Salary**
39334	Smith	Gina	75,000
49539	Qian	Lee	90,000
60403	Harper	Rod	45,000
02039	Walla	Rajendra	60,000
49392	Spanky	Stacy	100,000

TABLE 1-1. *EMP*

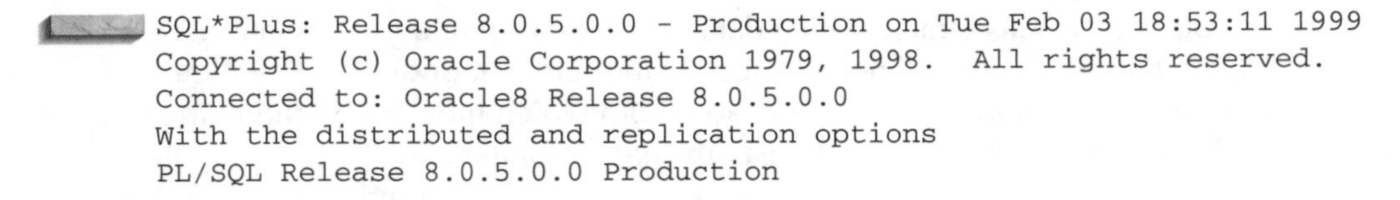

```
SQL*Plus: Release 8.0.5.0.0 - Production on Tue Feb 03 18:53:11 1999
Copyright (c) Oracle Corporation 1979, 1998.  All rights reserved.
Connected to: Oracle8 Release 8.0.5.0.0
With the distributed and replication options
PL/SQL Release 8.0.5.0.0 Production

SQL> SELECT * FROM JASON.EMP;

EMPID    LASTNAME     FIRSTNAME     SALARY
-----    --------     ---------     ------
39334    SMITH        GINA           75000
49539    QIAN         LEE            90000
60403    HARPER       ROD            45000
02039    WALLA        RAJENDRA       60000
49392    SPANKY       STACY         100000
```

The first part of this code block, containing the copyright information, is a "welcome" message from SQL*Plus. If you wanted, you could suppress this information in your call to SQL*Plus from the operating system command line by entering (in UNIX) **`sqlplus -s`** and pressing ENTER, where the `-s` extension indicates SQL*Plus should run in silent mode. The line in bold in the preceding excerpt illustrates the entry of a simple SQL statement. The query requests Oracle to return all data from all columns in the EMP table. Oracle replies with the contents of the EMP table shown in Table 1-1. Note that you did not tell Oracle how to retrieve the data; you simply specified the data you wanted using SQL syntax and Oracle returned it.

For now, make sure you understand how to specify a schema owner, the table name, and the column name in a `select` statement in SQL*Plus. The following code block demonstrates proper usage:

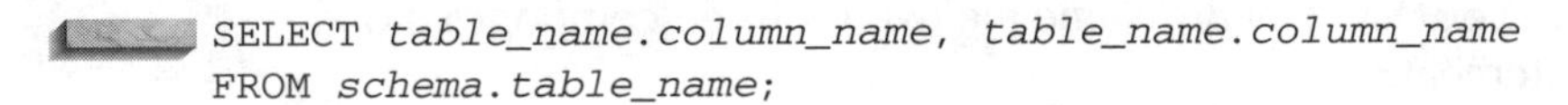

```
SELECT table_name.column_name, table_name.column_name
FROM schema.table_name;
```

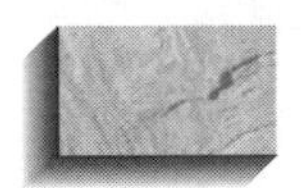

TIP
*Always use a semicolon (;) to end SQL statements when entering them directly into SQL*Plus. You can use a slash in some situations, such as for SQL*Plus batch scripts, as well.*

The main components of a `select` statement are the `select` clause and the `from` clause. A `select` clause contains the list of columns or expressions containing data you want to see. The first statement used a *wildcard* (*) character, which indicates to Oracle that you want to view data from every column in the table. The `from` clause tells Oracle which database table to pull the information from. Often, the database user will need to specify the schema, or owner, to which the table belongs, in addition to naming the table from which the data should come, as we do in this next example with a *schema.tablename* notation:

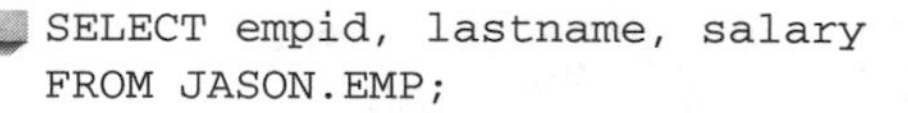

```
SELECT empid, lastname, salary
FROM JASON.EMP;

EMPID     LASTNAME      SALARY
-----     --------      ------
39334     SMITH          75000
49539     QIAN           90000
60403     HARPER         45000
02039     WALLA          60000
49392     SPANKY        100000
```

Just to review, the statement issued in the code block gets its information from the table called JASON.EMP. This means that Oracle should pull data from the EMP table in the JASON schema. When you are granted the ability to create database objects, the objects you create will belong to you. Ownership creates a logical grouping of the database objects by owner, and that grouping is called a *schema*.

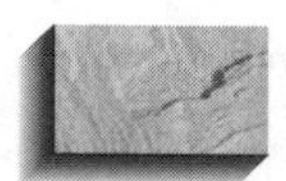

TIP
A schema is a logical grouping of database objects based on the user that owns the objects.

Exercises

1. What is a `select` statement? Name the two required components of a `select` statement.
2. How should you end a `select` statement in SQL*Plus?
3. What is a schema?

Performing Arithmetic Equations

In addition to doing simple data selection from a table, Oracle allows you to perform different types of activities using the data. For example, all basic arithmetic operations are available in Oracle. The operators used to denote arithmetic in

Oracle SQL are the same as in daily use (+ for addition, – for subtraction, * for multiplication, and / for division). The order of precedence for these arithmetic equations is *, /, +, –. Thus, 6 * 8 + 3 equals 51. If you want the expression to evaluate to 66, you must use 6 * (8 + 3).

Assume, for example, that you are performing a simple annual review that involves giving each user a cost-of-living increase in the amount of 8 percent of their salary. The process would involve multiplying each person's salary by 1.08. Oracle makes this sort of thing easy with the use of arithmetic expressions, as shown below:

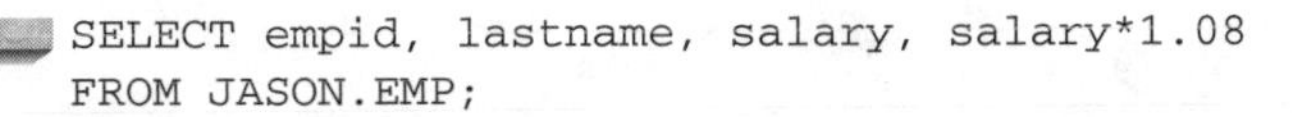

```
SELECT empid, lastname, salary, salary*1.08
FROM JASON.EMP;

EMPID     LASTNAME      SALARY     SALARY*1.08
-----     --------      ------     -----------
39334     SMITH          75000           81000
49539     QIAN           90000           97200
60403     HARPER         45000           48600
02039     WALLA          60000           64800
49392     SPANKY        100000          108000
```

Performing Arithmetic on Numeric Expressions

`Select` statements in Oracle require you specify columns or expressions following the `select` keyword and a table name after the `from` keyword. However, you may not always want to perform arithmetic calculations on data from a table. For example, say you simply want to add two fixed values together. Every `select` statement must have a `from` clause, but since you are specifying fixed values, you don't want Oracle to pull data from a real table. So why not pull data from a fake one? A special table called DUAL can be used in this query to fulfill the `from` clause requirement. Execute a `select * from DUAL` statement and see for yourself that there is no data stored here. Now issue the following statement, and see results from the DUAL table:

```
SELECT 64+36
FROM DUAL;

64+36
-----
  100
```

There is no meaningful data actually in DUAL; it simply exists as a SQL construct to support the requirement of a table specification in the `from` clause. The DUAL table contains only one column called DUMMY and one row with a value of "X."

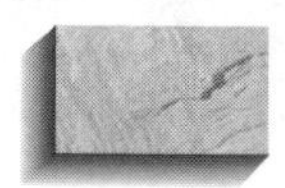

TIP
DUAL is used to satisfy the SQL syntax requiring that all SQL statements contain a `from` *clause that names the table from which the data will be selected. When you do not want to pull data from any table, but rather want simply to use an arithmetic operation on a constant value, include the values, operations, and the* `from DUAL` *clause.*

Exercises

1. How can you perform arithmetic on selected columns in Oracle?
2. What is the DUAL table? Why is it used?
3. How do you specify arithmetic operations on numbers not `selected` from any table?

Handling NULL Values

Sometimes, a query for some information will produce a nothing result. In database terms, *nothing* is called *NULL*. In set theory (the mathematical foundation for relational databases), NULL represents the value of an empty dataset, or a dataset containing no values. Unless specified otherwise, a column in a table is designed to accommodate the placement of nothing into the column. An example of retrieving NULL is listed in the SPOUSE column of the following code block:

```
SELECT empid, lastname, firstname, spouse
FROM JASON.EMP;

EMPID     LASTNAME     FIRSTNAME     SPOUSE
-----     --------     ---------     ------
39334     SMITH        GINA          FRED
49539     QIAN         LEE
60403     HARPER       ROD           SUSAN
02039     WALLA        RAJENDRA      HARPREET
49392     SPANKY       STACY
```

However, there arise times when you will not want to see nothing. You may want to substitute a value in place of NULL. Oracle provides this functionality with a special function called `nvl( )`. Assume that you do not want to see blank spaces for spouse information. Instead, you want the output of the query to contain the word "unmarried." The query in the next code block illustrates how you can obtain the desired result.

```
SELECT empid, lastname, firstname,
NVL(spouse,'unmarried')
FROM JASON.EMP;

EMPID     LASTNAME     FIRSTNAME     NVL(spous
-----     ---------    ---------     ---------
39334     SMITH        GINA          FRED
49539     QIAN         LEE           unmarried
60403     HARPER       ROD           SUSAN
02039     WALLA        RAJENDRA      HARPREET
49392     SPANKY       STACY         unmarried
```

If the column specified in `nvl( )` is not NULL, the value in the column is returned; when the column is NULL, the special string is returned. The `nvl( )` function can be used on columns of all datatypes, but remember that the value specified to be returned if the column value is NULL must be the same datatype as the column specified. The basic syntax for `nvl( )` is as follows:

```
NVL(column_name, value_if_null)
```

Exercises

1. What does NULL mean in the context of Oracle SQL?
2. What is the `nvl( )` function? How is it used?

Changing Column Headings with Column Aliases

When Oracle returns data to you, it creates headings for each column so that you know what the data is. Oracle bases the headings it creates on the name of the column passed to Oracle in the `select` statement:

```
SELECT empid, lastname, firstname, NVL(spouse,'unmarried')
FROM JASON.EMP;

EMPID    LASTNAME     FIRSTNAME     NVL(spous
-----    ---------    ---------     ---------
39334    SMITH        GINA          FRED
49539    QIAN         LEE           unmarried
60403    HARPER       ROD           SUSAN
02039    WALLA        RAJENDRA      HARPREET
49392    SPANKY       STACY         unmarried
```

By default, Oracle reprints the column name exactly as it was included in the `select` statement, including functions, if there are any. Unfortunately, this method usually leaves you with a bad description of the column data, compounded by the fact that Oracle truncates the expression to fit a certain column length corresponding to the datatype of the column returned. Fortunately, Oracle allows column aliases to be used in the `select` statement to solve this problem. You can give any column another name when the `select` statement is issued. This feature gives you the ability to fit more descriptive names into the space allotted by the column datatype definition.

```
SELECT empid, lastname, firstname,
NVL(spouse,'unmarried') spouse
FROM JASON.EMP;

EMPID    LASTNAME    FIRSTNAME    SPOUSE
-----    --------    ---------    ---------
39334    SMITH       GINA         FRED
49539    QIAN        LEE          unmarried
60403    HARPER      ROD          SUSAN
02039    WALLA       RAJENDRA     HARPREET
49392    SPANKY      STACY        unmarried
```

As indicated in bold, the SPOUSE column is again named SPOUSE, even with the `nvl( )` operation being performed on it. In order to specify an alias, simply name the alias after identifying the column to be selected, with or without an operation performed on it, separated by a space.

Alternately, you can issue the `as` keyword to denote the alias. The SPOUSE column with the `nvl( )` operation shows the use of the `as` keyword to denote the alias in the following code block:

```
SELECT empid, lastname, firstname,
NVL(spouse,'unmarried') AS spouse
FROM JASON.EMP;

EMPID    LASTNAME    FIRSTNAME    SPOUSE
-----    --------    ---------    ---------
39334    SMITH       GINA         FRED
49539    QIAN        LEE          unmarried
60403    HARPER      ROD          SUSAN
02039    WALLA       RAJENDRA     HARPREET
49392    SPANKY      STACY        unmarried
```

Column aliases are useful for adding meaningful headings to output from SQL queries. As shown, aliases can be specified in two ways: either by naming the alias after the column specification separated by a space, or with the use of the `as` keyword to mark the alias more clearly. Here's the general rule:

```
SELECT column_with_or_without_operation  alias, ...;
```

or

```
SELECT column_with_or_without_operation  AS alias, ...;
```

Exercises

1. What is a column alias? In what situations might column aliases be useful?
2. What are two ways to define aliases for columns?

Putting Columns Together with Concatenation

Changing a column heading in a `select` statement and using the `nvl( )` operation are not the only things that can be done to change the output of a query. Entire columns can be glued together to produce more interesting or readable output. The method used to merge the output of two columns into one is called *concatenation*. The concatenation operator is two pipe characters put together: `||`. You can also use the `concat( )` operation, passing it the two column names. In the following example, the name output is changed to the format *lastname, firstname* using the two methods:

```
SELECT empid, lastname||', '||firstname full_name,
NVL(spouse,'unmarried') spouse
FROM JASON.EMP;

EMPID    FULL_NAME            SPOUSE
-----    ----------------     ---------
39334    SMITH, GINA          FRED
49539    QIAN, LEE            unmarried
60403    HARPER, ROD          SUSAN
02039    WALLA, RAJENDRA      HARPREET
49392    SPANKY, STACY        unmarried

SELECT empid, concat(concat (lastname, ','), firstname)
NVL(spouse,'unmarried') spouse
FROM JASON.EMP;
```

```
EMPID    FULL_NAME          SPOUSE
-----    ----------------   ---------
39334    SMITH, GINA        FRED
49539    QIAN, LEE          unmarried
60403    HARPER, ROD        SUSAN
02039    WALLA, RAJENDRA    HARPREET
49392    SPANKY, STACY      unmarried
```

By using the concatenation operator in conjunction with a text string enclosed in single quotes, the output of two or more columns can become one column to express new meaning. For good measure, the use of column aliases is recommended in order to make the name of the concatenated columns more meaningful.

Exercises

1. What is column concatenation?
2. What special character sequence is used to concatenate columns?

Editing SQL Queries Within SQL*Plus

The SQL*Plus environment works well when you don't make mistakes, but it is unforgiving to the fat-fingered once they've pressed ENTER to move to the next input line. So far, this limitation of the SQL command line hasn't presented much difficulty. However, as the queries you write get more and more complicated, you will grow frustrated. SQL*Plus does allow some correction of entered statements with a special command called `change`, abbreviated as c. Consider the following example, which illustrates this point:

```
SELECT empid, lastname||', '||firstname full_name,
NVL(sppuse,'unmarried') spouse
FROM JASON.EMP;

NVL(sppuse,'unmarried') spouse
         *
ERROR at line 2:
ORA-00904: invalid column name

SQL> 2

2> NVL(sppuse,'unmarried') spouse, FROM JASON.EMP;

SQL> c/sppuse/spouse
```

```
2> NVL(spouse,'unmarried') spouse, FROM JASON.EMP;

SQL> /

EMPID   FULL_NAME           SPOUSE
-----   ----------------    ---------
39334   SMITH, GINA         FRED
49539   QIAN, LEE           unmarried
60403   HARPER, ROD         SUSAN
02039   WALLA, RAJENDRA     HARPREET
49392   SPANKY, STACY       unmarried
```

In this example, the `select` statement contained a typographical error, `sppuse`. Oracle notices the error and alerts you to it with `ORA-00904`. Other error messages that may be produced include:

```
ORA-00923: FROM keyword not found where expected
```

The preceding error indicates that the `from` keyword was not included or was misspelled. The following error indicates that the table or view typed in does not exist:

```
ORA-00942: table or view does not exist
```

Usually, the `ORA-00942` indicates a typo in the name of the table or view, or that the schema owner was not specified in front of the table name. This error is fixed either by correcting the typing problem or by adding the schema owner onto the front of the table name. (An alternative solution for the latter case involves creating synonyms for tables that are accessible to other users. This solution will be discussed later.)

In any case, the method used to correct the typing problem is to first type the line number containing the error, in the example above with the number 2. Then use the `change` command with the following syntax:

```
c/old_value/new_value
```

After making the change to the *first* appearance of *`old_value`* in the current line, Oracle redisplays the current line with the change made. Note that the change will be made to the first appearance of *`old_value`* only. If the change must be made to a specific place in the line, more characters can be added to the *`old_value`* parameter as appropriate. Finally, the corrected text can be reexecuted by entering a slash (/) at the prompt as indicated.

Oracle makes provisions for you to use your favorite text editor to edit the statement created in `afiedt.buf`, the file in which SQL*Plus stores the most recently executed SQL statement. You simply type `edit` (abbreviated ed). This action causes Oracle to bring up the SQL statement from afiedt.buf into the operating system's default text editor. On UNIX systems, that text editor is usually VI or EMACS, while Windows environments use Notepad. To change the text editor used, issue the `define _editor="`*`youreditor`*`"` command from the SQL*Plus prompt.

Using a text editor rather than the line editor native to SQL*Plus offers many benefits. First and foremost is that you can use a text editor you know well, creating a familiarity with the application that is useful in adapting to SQL*Plus quickly. Second, it is helpful with large queries to have the entire block of code in front of you and immediately accessible.

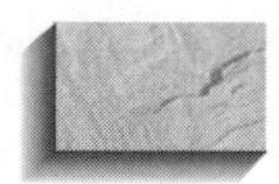

TIP

When running SQL statements from scripts, do not put a semicolon (;) at the end of the SQL statement. Instead, put a slash (/) character on the line following the script. Do this if Oracle gives you error messages saying it encountered an invalid character (the semicolon) in your script.

It is possible to write your entire query in a text editor first and then load it into SQL*Plus. If you do this, be sure you save the script with a `.sql` extension so that SQL*Plus can read it easily. Three commands are available to load the file into SQL*Plus. The first is `get`. The `get` command opens the text file specified and places the contents in `afiedt.buf`. Once the script is loaded, you can execute the command using the slash (/) command. Or, you can use the @ command, which loads SQL statements from the named file into `afiedt.buf` and executes them in one step. Both methods are shown in the following example.

```
SQL*Plus: Release 8.0.5.0.0 - Production on Tue Feb 03 18:53:11 1999
Copyright (c) Oracle Corporation 1979, 1998.  All rights reserved.
Connected to Oracle8 Release 8.0.5.0.0
With the distributed and replication options
PL/SQL Release 8.0.5.0.0 - Production

SQL> GET select_emp
SELECT * FROM emp
SQL> /
```

```
EMPID    LASTNAME    FIRSTNAME    SALARY
-----    --------    ---------    ------
39334    SMITH       GINA          75000
49539    QIAN        LEE           90000
60403    HARPER      ROD           45000
02039    WALLA       RAJENDRA      60000
49392    SPANKY      STACY        100000

5 rows selected;

SQL> @select_emp

SELECT * FROM emp
/

EMPID    LASTNAME    FIRSTNAME    SALARY
-----    --------    ---------    ------
39334    SMITH       GINA          75000
49539    QIAN        LEE           90000
60403    HARPER      ROD           45000
02039    WALLA       RAJENDRA      60000
49392    SPANKY      STACY        100000

5 rows selected;
```

Notice that the `.sql` extension was left off the end of the filename in the line with the `get` command. SQL*Plus assumes that all scripts containing SQL statements will have the `.sql` extension, so it can be omitted in the get and the @ command. Notice also that after the file is brought in using `get`, it can then be executed using the slash (/) command.

In the second case illustrated, the same file is read into `afiedt.buf` using the @ command and it is executed in one step, eliminating the need for the slash (/) command. Again, the `.sql` extension is omitted. When using the `get` or @ command, if a full pathname is not specified as the filename, Oracle SQL*Plus assumes the file is in the local directory.

Exercises

1. What two mechanisms are available to enter and modify SQL statements within SQL*Plus?
2. What is the edit command in the SQL*Plus command line? How can SQL scripts be loaded from files into SQL*Plus? How are they run?
3. What command is used to define a text editor for SQL*Plus to use?

Limiting and Refining Selected Output

In this section, you will cover the following areas related to limiting and refining selected output:

- The `order by` clause
- The `where` clause

Obtaining all output from a table is great, but usually you must be more selective in choosing output. Most database applications contain a lot of data. How much data can a database contain? Some applications contain tables with a million rows or more, and the most recent release of Oracle8i will store up to 512 petabytes ($512*1024^5$ bytes) of data. Of course, this is only a theoretical limit; the real amount of data you can store with Oracle depends on how much disk space you give Oracle to use. But, needless to say, manipulating vast amounts of data like that requires you to be careful. Always ask for *exactly* what you want, and no more.

The order by Clause

Data within a table need not have any order. Another quick look at the output from the EMP table will demonstrate this:

```
SQL> /

EMPID     LASTNAME     FIRSTNAME     SALARY
-----     --------     ---------     ------
39334     SMITH        GINA           75000
49539     QIAN         LEE            90000
60403     HARPER       ROD            45000
02039     WALLA        RAJENDRA       60000
49392     SPANKY       STACY         100000
```

Notice that the data returned is in no particular order on any column, either numeric or alphabetical. That's fine for the database, but not always fine for people. Oracle allows you to order the output from `select` statements using the `order by` clause in `select` statements. The general syntax for the `order by` clause is to include both the clause and the column(s) or column alias(es) by which Oracle will order the results, optionally followed by a special clause defining the direction of the order. Possible directions are `asc` for ascending and `desc` for descending. The default value is `asc`, and the output for `desc` is as shown here:

```
SQL> SELECT *
  2> FROM emp
  3> ORDER BY empid DESC;
```

```
EMPID     LASTNAME     FIRSTNAME      SALARY
-----     --------     ---------      ------
60403     HARPER       ROD             45000
49539     QIAN         LEE             90000
49392     SPANKY       STACY          100000
39334     SMITH        GINA            75000
02039     WALLA        RAJENDRA        60000
```

The `order by` clause can impose a sort order on one or many columns in ascending *or* descending order in each of the columns specified. For this reason, the clause can be useful in simple reporting. It can be applied to columns that are of NUMBER, text (VARCHAR2 and CHAR), and DATE datatypes. You can even use numbers to indicate the column on which Oracle should order the output from a statement. The use of numbers depends on the positioning of each column. For example, if you issue a statement similar to the one in the following code block, the order for the output will be as shown. The number *2* indicates that the second column specified in the statement should be used to define order in the output.

```
SELECT empid, lastname FROM emp ORDER BY 2 DESC;

EMPID     LASTNAME
-----     --------
02039     WALLA
49392     SPANKY
39334     SMITH
49539     QIAN
60403     HARPER

SELECT lastname, empid FROM emp ORDER BY 2 DESC;

LASTNAME EMPID
-------- -----
HARPER   60403
QIAN     49539
SPANKY   49392
SMITH    39334
WALLA    02039
```

Exercises

1. How can a user put row data returned from a `select` statement into order? What are the various sort orders that can be used with this option?
2. What are the two ways to specify the column on which sort order should be defined?

The where Clause

The `where` clause in Oracle `select` statements is where the really interesting things begin. This important clause in `select` statements allows you to single out a few rows from hundreds, thousands, or even millions like it. The `where` clause operates on a basic principle of comparison:

```
SELECT * FROM emp WHERE empid = 49392;

EMPID     LASTNAME      FIRSTNAME      SALARY
-----     --------      ---------      ------
49392     SPANKY        STACY          100000
```

Assuming the EMPID column contains all unique values, instead of pulling all rows from EMP, Oracle pulls just one row for display. To determine what row to display, the `where` clause performs a comparison operation as specified by the query—in this case, the comparison is an equality operation, `where empid = 49392`. However, equality is not the only means by which Oracle can obtain data. A complete list of comparison operations is provided here:

`x = y`	Comparison to see if *x* is equal to *y*
`x > y`	Comparison to see if *x* is greater than *y*
`x >= y`	Comparison to see if *x* is greater than or equal to *y*
`x < y`	Comparison to see if *x* is less than *y*
`x <= y`	Comparison to see if *x* is less than or equal to *y*

`x <> y`
`x != y`
`x ^= y`
	Comparison to see if *x* is not equal to *y*

`like`	A special comparison used in conjunction with the character wildcards (`% or _`) to find substrings in text variables.
`soundex`	A special function used to introduce "fuzzy logic" into text string comparisons by allowing equality based on similarly spelled words.
`between`	A range comparison operation that allows for operations on dates, numbers, and characters that are similar to the following numeric comparison: *y* "is between" *x* and *z*.
`in`	A special comparison that allows you to specify multiple equality statements by defining a set of values, any of which the value can be equal to; an example of its usage may be `x in (1,2,3,4,5)`.

Every comparison between two values in Oracle boils down to one or more of these operations. Multiple comparisons can be placed together using the following list of operations. The operator is listed, along with the result that is required to fulfill the criteria based on the presence of this operator.

`x and y`	Both comparisons in *x* and *y* must be true.
`x or y`	One comparison in *x* or *y* must be true.
`not x`	The logical opposite of *x*.

Note that the order of precedence for the operators listed above is `not`, `and`, `or`. Thus, the expression "`not TRUE and FALSE`" evaluates to FALSE. If you want the expression to evaluate as TRUE, you must use `not (TRUE and FALSE)` instead. For more information on logic operations and set theory, consult a textbook on discrete mathematics.

Exercises

1. What is a `where` clause? On what principle does this clause operate to determine which data is selected?
2. What are some operations available to assist in the purpose of comparison? What are some operations that allow you to specify more than one comparison in the `where` clause?

Using Single-Row Functions

In this section, you will cover the following areas related to using single-row functions:

- Explanations of various single-row functions
- Using functions in `select` statements
- Date functions
- Conversion functions

There are dozens of functions available in Oracle that can be used for many purposes. Some functions in Oracle are designed to alter the data returned by a query, such as the `nvl( )` function already presented. The functions in this category are designed to work on columns of any datatype to return information in different ways. One commonly used function of this type is `decode( )`. The `decode( )` function works on the same principle as an `if-then-else` statement works in many common programming languages, including PL/SQL.

```
SELECT DECODE(column, val1, return1, val2, return2,...,return_default)
...
```

The `decode( )` function allows for powerful transformation of data from one value to another. Some examples of `decode( )` in action will appear later in the chapter.

Various Single-Row Functions Explained

From this point on, all the functions described will have limitations on the datatypes on which they can perform their operations.

Several functions in Oracle manipulate text strings. These functions are similar in concept to `nvl( )` and `decode( )` in that they can perform a change on a piece of data, but the functions in this family can change only one type of data—text. Some are as follows.

`lpad(x,y[,z])` `rpad(x,y[,z])`	Returns the column padded on the left or right side of the data in the column passed as *x* to a width passed as *y*. The optional passed value *z* indicates the character(s) that `lpad( )` or `rpad( )` will insert into the column. If no character is specified, a space will be used.

`lower(x)`
`upper(x)`
`initcap(x)`
	Returns the column value passed as *x* into all lowercase or uppercase characters, or changes the initial letter in the string to a capital letter.

`length(x)`	Returns a number indicating the number of characters in the column value passed as *x*.
`substr(x,y[,z])`	Returns a substring of string *x*, starting at the character in position number *y* to the end, which is optionally defined by the character appearing in position *z* of the string.

Other functions are designed to perform specialized mathematical functions, such as those used in scientific applications, like sine and logarithm. These operations are commonly referred to as math or number operations. The functions falling into this category are listed next. These functions are not all that are available in Oracle. But they are the most commonly used ones—the ones that will likely appear on OCP Exam 1.

`abs(x)`	Obtains the absolute value for a number. For example, the absolute value of -1 is 1, while the absolute value of 6 is 6.
`ceil(x)`	Similar to executing `round` on an integer (for example, `round(x,0)`, except `ceil` always rounds up. For example, `ceil(1.4) = 2`. Note that rounding "up" on negative numbers produces a value closer to zero (for example, `ceil(-1.6) = -1, not -2)`.

`floor(x)`	Similar to `ceil`, except `floor` always rounds down. For example, `floor(1.6)` = 1. Note that rounding "down" on negative numbers produces a value further away from zero (for example, `floor(-1.6)` = –2, not –1).
`mod(x,y)`	The modulus of *x*, defined in long division as the integer remainder when *x* is divided by *y* until no further whole number can be produced. For example `mod(10,3) = 1`, and `mod(10,2) = 0`.
`round(x,y)`	Rounds *x* to the decimal precision of *y*. If *y* is negative, rounds to the precision of *y* places to the left of the decimal point. For example, `round(134.345,1)` = 134.3, `round(134.345,0) = 134`, and `round(134.345,-1)` = 130.
`sign(x)`	Displays an `integer` value corresponding to the sign of *x*: 1 if *x* is positive, –1 if *x* is negative.
`sqrt(x)`	The square root of *x*.
`trunc(x,y)`	Truncates the value of *x* to the decimal precision of *y*. If *y* is negative, then truncates to *y* number of places to the left of the decimal point.
`vsize(x)`	The storage size in bytes for value *x*.

The final category of number functions discussed here is the set of list functions. These functions are actually used for many different datatypes, including text, numeric, and date.

`greatest(x,y,...)`	Returns the highest value from the list of text strings, numbers, or dates (*x*,*y*...).
`least(x,y,...)`	Returns the lowest value from the list of text strings, numbers, or dates (*x*,*y*...).

Another class of data functions available in Oracle correspond to the DATE datatype. The functions that perform operations on dates are known as date functions. There is a special keyword that can be specified to give Oracle users the current date. This keyword is called `sysdate`. In the same way that you calculated simple arithmetic in an earlier part of the chapter using the DUAL table, so too can you execute a `select` statement using `sysdate` to produce today's date:

```
SELECT sysdate FROM DUAL;

SYSDATE
---------
15-MAY-99
```

The functions that can be used on DATE columns are listed in the following definitions:

`add_months(x,y)`	Returns a date corresponding to date *x* plus *y* months.
`last_day(x)`	Returns the date of the last day of the month that contains date *x*.
`months_between(x,y)`	Returns a number of months between dates *x* and *y* as produced by *x–y*. This function can return a decimal value.
`new_time(x,y,z)`	Returns the current date and time for date *x* in time zone *y* as it would be in time zone *z*.

The functions available in Oracle are very useful for executing well-defined operations on data in a table or on constant values, and they often save time and energy. Make sure you understand these functions for OCP.

Exercises

1. Identify some of the character, number, and date functions available in SQL. What are two functions that allow you to transform column values regardless of the datatype?
2. What are other types of functions that perform operations on columns of specific datatypes?

Using Functions in select Statements

The previous section introduced many of the functions available in Oracle. The definitions in that section should suffice for reference; however, there is no substitute for actual usage. This section shows the functions in action.

The first example details use of the `decode( )` function. Assume that you select data from the EMP table. The data in the SEX column of EMP is populated with *M* for male and *F* for female. Instead of displaying a letter, the following code block lets you write out the full word for each sex:

```
SELECT empid, lastname, firstname,
DECODE(sex,'M','MALE','F','FEMALE') sex FROM emp
ORDER BY empid DESC;

EMPID  LASTNAME   FIRSTNAME  SEX
-----  --------   ---------  ------
60403  HARPER     ROD        MALE
49539  QIAN       LEE        FEMALE
49392  SPANKY     STACY      FEMALE
39334  SMITH      GINA       FEMALE
02039  WALLA      RAJENDRA   MALE
```

The decode( ) command has six variables, the first of which is the name of the column. This must always be present. The second variable corresponds to the value that could be found in the SEX column, followed by the value that decode( ) should return if SEX in this row is equal to 'M'. The next set of variables answers the question of what decode( ) should return if the value in the column is 'F'. This matching of column values with appropriate return values can continue until you have identified all cases you would like decode( ) to handle. The last variable, which is optional, is used for the default return value.

Now look at some text or character function examples. The first of these examples is for rpad( ) and lpad( ). As shown in the following code, these two functions can be used to place additional filler characters on the right or left side of data in a column out to a specified column width:

```
SELECT empid, lastname, firstname,
RPAD(DECODE(sex,'M','MALE','F','FEMALE'),10,'-') sex FROM emp
ORDER BY empid DESC;

EMPID  LASTNAME   FIRSTNAME  SEX
-----  --------   ---------  ----------
60403  HARPER     ROD        MALE------
49539  QIAN       LEE        FEMALE----
49392  SPANKY     STACY      FEMALE----
39334  SMITH      GINA       FEMALE----
02039  WALLA      RAJENDRA   MALE------
```

The output from one SQL function can be used as input for another, as demonstrated here. The rpad( ) operation will pad the decoded SEX column out to ten characters with dashes. If the lpad( ) operation had been used instead, the result would have been as follows:

```
SELECT empid, lastname, firstname,
LPAD(DECODE(sex,'M','MALE','F','FEMALE'),10,'-') sex FROM emp
ORDER BY empid DESC;
```

```
EMPID   LASTNAME    FIRSTNAME   SEX
-----   --------    ---------   ----------
60403   HARPER      ROD         ------MALE
49539   QIAN        LEE         ----FEMALE
49392   SPANKY      STACY       ----FEMALE
39334   SMITH       GINA        ----FEMALE
02039   WALLA       RAJENDRA    ------MALE
```

Some of the simpler character functions are next. Two straightforward examples of SQL queries are sometimes referred to as "case translators" because they perform a simple translation of case based on the text string passed:

```
SELECT LOWER(title) TITLE_NOQUOTE,
UPPER(artist) ARTIST1, INITCAP(artist) ARTIST2 FROM SONGS;

TITLE_NOQUOTE           ARTIST1     ARTIST2
-------------------     ---------   ---------
"happy birthday"        ANONYMOUS   Anonymous
"diamonds and rust"     ANONYMOUS   Anonymous
"amazing grace"         ANONYMOUS   Anonymous
```

Another straightforward and useful character function is the `length( )` function, which returns the length of a text string:

```
SELECT title, LENGTH(title) LENGTH
FROM SONGS;

TITLE                   LENGTH
-------------------     ------
"HAPPY BIRTHDAY"            16
"DIAMONDS AND RUST"         19
"AMAZING GRACE"             15
```

Note one interesting thing happening in this query—spaces and double quotes are all counted as part of the length!

Another extraordinarily useful function related to character strings is the `substr( )` function. This function is commonly used to extract data from a longer text string. The `substr( )` function takes as its first variable the full text string to be searched. The second variable contains an integer that designates the character number at which the substring should begin. The third parameter is optional and specifies how many characters to the right of the start of the substring will be included in the substring. Observe the following output to understand the effects of omitting the third parameter:

```
SQL> select lastname, substr(lastname,2,3)
  2  from emp;
LASTNAME                       SUB
------------------------------ ---
WALLA                          ALL
SMITH                          MIT
HARPER                         ARP
QIAN                           IAN
SPANKY                         PAN

SQL> select lastname, substr(lastname,2)
  2  from emp;
LASTNAME                       SUBSTR(LASTNAME,2)
------------------------------ -----------------------------
WALLA                          ALLA
SMITH                          MITH
HARPER                         ARPER
QIAN                           IAN
SPANKY                         PANKY
```

The number or math functions are frequently used in scientific applications. The first function detailed here is the `abs( )` or absolute value function, which calculates how far away from zero the parameter passed lies on the number line:

```
SELECT ABS(25), ABS(-12) FROM DUAL;

ABS(25)     ABS(-12)
-------     --------
     25           12
```

The next single-value function, the `ceil( )` function, automatically rounds the number passed as its parameter up to the next higher integer:

```
SELECT CEIL(123.323), CEIL(45), CEIL(-392), CEIL(-1.12) FROM DUAL;

CEIL(123.323)     CEIL(45)    CEIL(-392)     CEIL(-1.12)
-------------     --------    ----------     -----------
          124           45          -392              -1
```

The next single-value function is the `floor( )` function, which is the opposite of `ceil( )`. The `floor( )` function rounds the value passed down to the next lower integer:

```
SELECT FLOOR(123.323), FLOOR(45), FLOOR(-392), FLOOR(-1.12) FROM DUAL;

FLOOR(123.323)    FLOOR(45)    FLOOR(-392)    FLOOR(-1.12)
-------------     --------    ----------     -----------
          123           45          -392              -2
```

The next function covered in this section is related to long division. The function is called `mod( )`, and it returns the remainder or modulus for a number and its divisor:

```
SELECT MOD(12,3), MOD(55,4) FROM DUAL;

MOD(12,3)   MOD(55,4)
---------   ---------
        0           3
```

After that, look at `round( )`. This important function allows you to round a number off to a specified precision:

```
SELECT ROUND(123.323,2), ROUND(45,1), ROUND(-392,-1), ROUND (-1.12,0)
FROM DUAL;

ROUND(123.323,2)    ROUND(45,1)  ROUND(-392,-1)    ROUND(-1.12,0)
----------------    -----------  --------------    --------------
          123.32             45            -390                -1
```

The next function is called `sign( )`. It assists in identifying whether a number is positive or negative. If the number passed is positive, `sign( )` returns 1, and if the number is negative, `sign( )` returns -1. If the number is zero, `sign( )` returns 0:

```
SELECT SIGN(-1933), SIGN(55), SIGN(0) FROM DUAL;

SIGN(-1933)   SIGN(55)      SIGN(0)
----------    -----------   -------
        -1              1         0
```

The next example is the `sqrt( )` function. It is used to derive the square root for a number:

```
SELECT SQRT(34), SQRT(9) FROM DUAL;

SQRT(34)   SQRT(9)
---------  ----------
5.8309519           3
```

The next single-value number function is called `trunc( )`. Similar to `round( )`, `trunc( )` truncates a value passed into it according to the precision that is also passed in:

```
SELECT TRUNC(123.232,2), TRUNC(-45,1), TRUNC(392,-1), TRUNC(5,0)
FROM DUAL;
```

```
TRUNC(123.232,2) TRUNC(-45,1) TRUNC(392,-1) TRUNC(5,0)
---------------- ------------ ------------- ----------
          123.23          -45           390          5
```

The final single-row operation that is covered in this section is the `vsize( )` function. This function is not strictly for numeric datatypes. The `vsize( )` function gives the size in bytes of any value for text, number, date, ROWID, and other columns.

```
SELECT VSIZE(384838), VSIZE('ORANGE_TABBY'), VSIZE(sysdate) FROM DUAL;

VSIZE(384838)    VSIZE('ORANGE_TABBY')     VSIZE(SYSDATE)
-------------    ---------------------     --------------
            4                       12                  8
```

Exercises

1. What is the purpose of the `nvl( )` function? What datatypes does it accept? What is the purpose of a `decode( )` statement? What datatypes does it accept?
2. Name some character functions? Can two functions be combined? Why or why not?
3. Name some single-value number functions. What types of applications are these functions typically used in?
4. What function is used to determine the size in bytes of a given value or column?

Date Functions

There are several date functions in the Oracle database. The syntax of these functions has already been presented. This section will discuss each function in more detail and present examples of their usage. The Oracle database stores dates as integers, representing the number of days since December 21, 4713 B.C.E. This method allows for easy format changes and inherent millennium compliance.

The first function is the `add_months( )` function. This function takes as input a date and a number of months to be added. Oracle then returns the new date, which is the old date plus the number of months:

```
SELECT ADD_MONTHS('15-MAR-99',26)
FROM DUAL;
```

```
ADD_MONTHS('15
--------------
     15-MAY-01
```

The next date function, `last_day( )`, helps to determine the date for the last day in the month for the date given:

```
SELECT LAST_DAY('15-MAR-00') FROM DUAL;

LAST_DAY('15-M
--------------
     31-MAR-00
```

The next date function determines the number of months between two different dates given. The name of the function is `months_between( )`. The syntax of this command is tricky, so it will be presented here. The syntax of this command is `months_between(x,y)`, and the return value for this function is *x–y*:

```
SELECT MONTHS_BETWEEN('15-MAR-99','26-JUN-98') FROM DUAL;

MONTHS_BETWEEN
--------------
     8.6451613
```

The last example of a date function is `new_time( )`. It accepts three parameters, the first being a date and time, the second being the time zone the first parameter belongs in, and the last parameter being the time zone you would like to convert to. Each time zone is abbreviated in the following way: *X*ST or *X*DT, where *S* or *D* stands for standard or daylight saving time, and where *X* stands for the first letter of the time zone (such as *A*tlantic, *B*ering, *C*entral, *E*astern, *H*awaii, *M*ountain, *N*ewfoundland, *P*acific, or *Y*ukon). There are two exceptions: Greenwich mean time is indicated by GMT, while Newfoundland standard time does not use daylight saving.

So far, none of the queries used to demonstrate the date functions have required that much precision, but the following example will. In order to demonstrate the full capability of Oracle in the `new_time( )` function, the format Oracle displays date information (also known as the National Language Set (NLS) date format) can be changed to display the full date and time for the query. The following example demonstrates both the use of `nls_date_format` to change the date format and the `new_time( )` function to convert a timestamp to a new time zone:

```
ALTER SESSION
SET NLS_DATE_FORMAT = 'DD-MON-YYYY HH24:MI:SS';

SELECT NEW_TIME('15-MAR-1999 14:35:00','AST','GMT')
FROM DUAL;

NEW_TIME('15-MAR-199
--------------------
15-MAR-1999 18:35:00
```

Exercises

1. What is `nls_date_format`? How is it set? How is it used?
2. Which date functions described in this section return information in the DATE datatype? Which one returns information in a datatype other than DATE?
3. How are dates stored in Oracle?

Conversion Functions

Other functions are designed to convert columns of one datatype to another type. These functions do not actually modify the data itself; they just return the converted values. Several different conversion functions are available in the Oracle database, as listed below:

`to_char(x)`	Converts noncharacter value *x* to character
`to_number(x)`	Converts nonnumeric value *x* to number
`to_date(x[,y])`	Converts nondate value *x* to date, using format specified by *y*
`to_multi_byte(x)`	Converts single-byte character string *x* to multibyte characters according to national language standards
`to_single_byte(x)`	Converts multibyte character string *x* to single-byte characters according to national language standards
`chartorowid(x)`	Converts string of characters *x* into an Oracle ROWID
`rowidtochar(x)`	Converts a ROWID *x* into a string of characters
`hextoraw(x)`	Converts hexadecimal (base-16) value *x* into raw (binary)format

`rawtohex(x)`	Converts raw (binary) value *x* into hexadecimal (base-16) format
`convert(x[,y[,z]])`	Executes a conversion of alphanumeric string *x* from the current character set optionally specified as *z* to the one specified by *y*
`translate(x,y,z)`	Executes a simple value conversion for character or numeric string *x* into something else based on the conversion factors *y* and *z*

The following text illustrates the most commonly used procedures for converting data in action. These are the `to_char( )`, `to_number( )`, and `to_date( )` functions.

The first one demonstrated is the `to_char( )` function. In the example of `new_time( )`, the date function described earlier, the `alter session set nls_date_format` statement was used to demonstrate the full capabilities of Oracle in both storing date information and converting dates and times from one time zone to another. That exercise could have been accomplished with the use of the `to_char( )` conversion function as well. Using `to_char( )` in this manner saves you from converting `nls_date_format`, which, once executed, is in effect for the rest of your session, or until you execute another `alter session set nls_date_format` statement. Rather than using this method, you may want to opt for a less permanent option offered by the `to_char( )` function, as shown below:

```
SELECT TO_CHAR(NEW_TIME(TO_DATE('15-MAR-1999 14:35:00',
'DD-MON-YYYY HH24:MI:SS'),'AST','GMT'))
FROM DUAL;

NEXT_DAY('15-MAR-9
------------------
15-MAR-99 18:35:00
```

Note that this example also uses the `to_date( )` function, another conversion function in the list to be discussed. The `to_date( )` function is very useful for converting numbers, and especially character strings, into properly formatted DATE fields.

The next function to consider is `to_number( )`, which converts text or date information into a number:

```
SELECT TO_NUMBER('49583') FROM DUAL;

TO_NUMBER('49583')
------------------
             49583
```

Although there does not appear to be much difference between the output of this query and the string that was passed, the main difference is the underlying datatype. Even so, Oracle is intelligent enough to convert a character string consisting of all numbers before performing an arithmetic operation using two values of two different datatypes, as shown in the following listing:

```
SELECT '49583' + 34 FROM DUAL;

'49583'+34
----------
     49617
```

Exercises

1. Identify some conversion functions. Which conversion functions are commonly used?
2. What is `nls_date_format`? How is it used?

Chapter Summary

This chapter provides an introduction to using Oracle by demonstrating basic techniques for using `select` statements. The areas discussed in this chapter are selecting row data from tables using the `select from` statement, limiting the rows selected with the `where` clause of the `select from` statement, and using the single-row functions available in Oracle to manipulate selected data into other values, formats, or meanings. This chapter is the cornerstone for all other usage in Oracle, as well as for passing the OCP Exam 1. Material covered in this chapter comprises 17 percent of test content on OCP Exam 1.

The first area covered in this chapter is selecting data from Oracle. The most common manipulation of data in the Oracle database is to `select` it, and the means by which data is selected from Oracle is the `select` statement. The `select` statement has two basic parts: the `select` clause and the `from` clause. The `select` clause identifies the column(s) of the table that you would like to view the contents of. The `from` clause identifies the table(s) in which the data selected is stored. In this chapter, data from only one table at a time was considered. In the next chapter, the concept of pulling or "joining" data from multiple tables is considered.

Often, users will want to perform calculations involving the data selected from a table. Oracle allows for basic, intermediate, and complex manipulation of data selected from a database table through the use of standard arithmetic notation. These operators can be used to perform math calculations on the data selected from a table or to perform math operations on numbers in calculator-like fashion. In order to perform calculations on numbers that are not selected from any table, you must utilize the DUAL table. DUAL is simply a table with one column that fulfills the syntactic requirements of SQL statements like `select`, which need a table name in the `from` clause in order to work.

When manipulating data from a table, you must remember to handle cases when column data for a particular row is nonexistent. Nonexistent column data in a table row is often referred to as being NULL. These NULL values can be viewed either as blank space by default, or you can account for the appearance of NULL data by using a special function that will substitute NULL fields with a data value. The name of this special function is `nvl( )`. The `nvl( )` function takes two parameters: the first is the column or value to be investigated for being NULL, and the second is the default value that `nvl( )` will substitute if the column or value is NULL. The `nvl( )` function operates on all sorts of datatypes, including CHAR, VARCHAR2, NUMBER, and DATE.

When performing special operations on columns in a `select` statement, Oracle often displays hard-to-read headings for the column name because Oracle draws the column name directly from the `select` clause of the `select` statement. You can avoid this problem by giving a column alias for Oracle to use instead. For example, the following `select` may produce a cryptic column heading: `select nvl(LASTNAME,'DOE')...`, while a column alias would allow Oracle to provide a more meaningful heading: `select nvl(LASTNAME,'DOE') LASTNAME...`. Column aliases are specified as character strings following the function and/or column name the alias will substitute. Be sure to include a space between the function and/or column name and the alias.

Concluding the introduction to SQL `select` statements, the use of concatenation and entering the actual statements was discussed. Columns can be concatenated using two pipe (||) characters. This operation is useful for making two columns into one, or for using special characters, such as commas or others, to separate the output. The SQL statement itself is entered using the SQL*Plus tool. If you make an error while typing a line of SQL, you can use the BACKSPACE key to erase characters until you reach the mistake; however, this approach only works if you are still on the same line in the SQL entry buffer. If you have already proceeded to another line, or if you tried to execute the command, you can type in the number corresponding to the line to be corrected in order to select that line for editing. Then, you can type in the `change` command, abbreviated `c/`*`old`*`/`*`new`*, where *`old`* is the existing version of the string containing the mistake, and *new* is the correction. If this all sounds complicated, you can simply type `edit`, or `ed`, from the prompt in SQL*Plus, and Oracle will immediately bring up your favorite text editor. The text editor used can be specified or changed with the `define _editor="`*`youreditor`*`"` command.

The number or order of rows selected from the database can be limited or refined with various options. The option discussed for refining data is `order by`. This is a clause that allows you to specify two things—the first is a column on which to list the data in order, and the second is whether Oracle should use ascending or descending order. Using the `order by` clause can make output from an Oracle `select` statement more readable, since there is no guarantee that the data in Oracle will be stored in any particular order.

The means of limiting selected output is the `where` clause. Properly using this clause is key to successfully using Oracle and SQL. In the `where` clause, you can specify one or more comparison criteria that must be met by the data in a table in order for Oracle to `select` the row. A comparison consists of two elements that are compared using a comparison operator, which may consist of a logic operator such as equality (=), inequality (<>,!=, or ^=), less than (<) or greater than (>), or a combination of less or greater than and equality. Alternatively, you can also utilize special comparison operators: pattern matches using `like %`, range scans using `between` *x* `and` *y*, or fuzzy logic with the `soundex(`*x*`) = soundex(`*y*`)` statement. In addition, one or more comparison operations may be specified in the where clause, joined together with the `and` or the `or` operator, or preceded by `not`.

Data selected in Oracle can be modified with several functions available in Oracle. These functions may work on many different types of data, as is the case with `nvl( )`, `decode( )`, `greatest( )`, or `least( )`. Alternatively, their use may be limited to a particular datatype. These functions may be divided into categories based on the types of data they can handle. Typically, the functions are categorized into text or character functions, math or number functions, and date functions.

Using Oracle built-in functions, you can perform many different operations. In general, to use a function you need to specify the name of the function and pass one or more variables to the function. For example, to change the characters in a text string, you would identify the function that performs this task and pass the function a value, for example, `upper(`*lowercase*`)`.

The chapter also detailed the use of all the functions available in Oracle, and provided examples for most of them. It should be noted that many of the functions *can* be used together and in conjunction with the multitype functions, such as `decode( )`. For example, the use of `decode(sqrt(`*x*`), 4, 'HARVEY',5,'JILL', 'BRAD')` is permitted. In essence, this functionality allows you to incorporate the output from one function as the input for another. An entire set of conversion functions is also available to change the datatypes of values, or to create ciphers, or even to change the character sets used in order to move data onto different machines. The conversion functions can be used in conjunction with many of the other functions already named.

Two-Minute Drill

- Data is retrieved from Oracle using `select` statements.
- Syntax for a `select` statement consists of `select ... from ...;`.
- When entering a `select` statement from the prompt using SQL*Plus, a semicolon (`;`) or slash (`/`) must be used to end the statement.
- Arithmetic operations can be used to perform math operations on data selected from a table, or on numbers using the DUAL table.
- The DUAL table is a table with one column and one row used to fulfill the syntactic requirements of SQL `select` statements.
- Values in columns for particular rows may be empty or NULL.
- If a column contains the NULL value, you can use the `nvl( )` function to return meaningful information instead of an empty field.
- Aliases can be used in place of the actual column name or to replace the appearance of the function name in the header.
- Output from two columns can be concatenated together using a double-pipe (| |).
- SQL commands can be entered directly into SQL*Plus on the command line.
- You can edit mistakes in SQL*Plus with the `change` command. If a mistake is made, the change (`c/`*`old`*`/`*`new`*) command is used
- Alternatively, the edit (`ed`) command can be used to make changes in your favorite text editor.
- You can specify a favorite text editor by issuing the `define _editor` command at the prompt.
- The `order by` clause in a `select` statement is a useful clause to incorporate sort order into the output of the file.
- Sort orders that can be used are `ascending` or `descending`, abbreviated as `asc` and `desc`. The order is determined by the column identified in the `order by` clause.

- The `where` clause is used in SQL queries to limit the data returned by the query.
- The `where` clauses contain comparison operations that determine whether a row will be returned by a query.
- There are several logical comparison operations, including =, >, >=, <, <, <=, <>, !=, ^=.
- In addition to the logical operations, there is a comparison operation for pattern matching called `like`. The % and _ characters are used to designate wildcards.
- There is also a range operation called `between`.
- There is also a fuzzy logic operation called `soundex`.
- The `where` clause can contain one or more comparison operations linked together by using `and`, `or`, and preceded by `not`.
- Several SQL functions exist in Oracle.
- SQL functions are broken down into character functions, number functions, and date functions.
- A few functions can be used on many different types of data.
- There are also several conversion functions available for transforming data from text to numeric datatypes and back, numbers to dates and back, text to ROWID and back, and so on.

Chapter Questions

1. Which of the following statements contains an error?

A. `select * from EMP where EMPID = 493945;`

B. `select EMPID from EMP where EMPID = 493945;`

C. `select EMPID from EMP;`

D. `select EMPID where EMPID = 56949 and LASTNAME = 'SMITH';`

2. Which of the following correctly describes how to specify a column alias?

A. Place the alias at the beginning of the statement to describe the table.

B. Place the alias after each column, separated by a space, to describe the column.

C. Place the alias after each column, separated by a comma, to describe the column.

D. Place the alias at the end of the statement to describe the table.

3. The `nvl( )` function

A. Assists in the distribution of output across multiple columns

B. Allows you to specify alternate output for non-NULL column values

C. Allows you to specify alternate output for NULL column values

D. Nullifies the value of the column output

4. Output from a table called PLAYS with two columns, PLAY_NAME and AUTHOR, is shown next. Which of the following SQL statements produced it?

```
PLAY_TABLE
-------------------------------------
"Midsummer Night's Dream", SHAKESPEARE
"Waiting For Godot", BECKETT
"The Glass Menagerie", WILLIAMS
```

A. `select PLAY_NAME|| AUTHOR from PLAYS;`

B. `select PLAY_NAME, AUTHOR from PLAYS;`

C. `select PLAY_NAME||', ' || AUTHOR from PLAYS;`

D. `select PLAY_NAME||', ' || AUTHOR play_table from PLAYS;`

5. Issuing the command `define _editor="emacs"` will produce which outcome?

A. The EMACS editor will become the SQL*Plus default text editor.

B. The EMACS editor will start running immediately.

C. The EMACS editor will no longer be used by SQL*Plus as the default text editor.

D. The EMACS editor will be deleted from the system.

6. Which function can best be categorized as similar in function to an `if-then-else` statement?

A. `sqrt( )`

B. `decode( )`

C. `new_time( )`

D. `rowidtochar( )`

7. Which of the following are number functions? (Choose three of the four)

A. `sinh( )`

B. `to_number( )`

C. `sqrt( )`

D. `round( )`

8. You issue the following statement. What will be displayed if the EMPID selected is 60494?

```
select DECODE(empid,38475, 'Terminated',60494, 'LOA',
'ACTIVE')
from emp;
```

A. 60494

B. LOA

C. Terminated

D. ACTIVE

9. Which of the following is a valid SQL statement?

A. `select to_char(nvl(sqrt(59483), '0')) from dual;`

B. `select to_char(nvl(sqrt(59483), 'INVALID')) from dual;`

C. `select (to_char(nvl(sqrt(59483), '0')) from dual;`

D. `select to_char(nvl(sqrt(59483), 'TRUE')) from dual;`

10. The appropriate table to use when performing arithmetic calculations on values defined within the `select` statement (not pulled from a table column) is

A. EMP

B. The table containing the column values

C. DUAL

D. An Oracle-defined table

11. Which of the following keywords are used in `order by` clauses? (Choose two)

A. `abs`

B. `asc`

C. `desc`

D. `disc`

12. Which of the following statements are *not true* about `order by` clauses?

A. Ascending or descending order can be defined with the `asc` or `desc` keywords.

B. Only one column can be used to define the sort order in an `order by` clause.

C. Multiple columns can be used to define sort order in an `order by` clause.

D. Columns can be represented by numbers indicating their listed order in the `select` clause within `order by`.

13. Which lines in the following `select` statement contain errors?

```
select decode(EMPID, 58385, 'INACTIVE', 'ACTIVE')
empid
from EMP
where substr(LASTNAME,1,1) > to_number('S')
and EMPID > 02000
order by EMPID desc, lastname asc;
```

A. `select decode(EMPID, 58385, 'INACTIVE', 'ACTIVE') empid`

B. `from EMP`

C. `where substr(LASTNAME,1,1) > to_number('S')`

D. `and EMPID > 02000`

E. `order by EMPID desc, lastname asc;`

F. There are no errors in this statement.

Answers to Chapter Questions

1. D. `select EMPID where EMPID = 56949 and LASTNAME = 'SMITH';`

Explanation There is no `from` clause in this statement. Although a `select` statement can be issued without a `where` clause, no `select` statement can be executed without a from clause specified. For that reason, the DUAL table exists to satisfy the `from` clause in situations where you define all data needed within the statement.

2. B. Place the alias after each column, separated by a space, to describe the column.

Explanation Aliases do not describe tables, they describe columns, which eliminates choices A and D. Commas in the `select` statement separate each column selected from one another. If a column alias appeared after a column, Oracle would either select the wrong column name based on information provided in the alias or return an error.

3. C. Allows you to specify alternate output for NULL column values

Explanation The `nvl( )` function is a simple `if-then` operation that tests column value output to see if it is NULL. If it is, `nvl( )` substitutes the specified default value for the NULL value. Since this function only operates on one column per call to `nvl( )`, choice A is incorrect. Choice B is incorrect because it is the logical opposite of choice C. Choice D is incorrect because `nvl( )` is designed to substitute actual values for situations where NULL is present, not nullify data.

4. D. `select PLAY_NAME||', ' || AUTHOR play_table from PLAYS;`

Explanation This question illustrates the need to read carefully. Since the output specified for the question contained a column alias for the output of the statement, choice D is the only one that is correct, even though choice C also performed the correct calculation. Choice A is incorrect because it specified an inaccurate concatenation method, and choice B is wrong because it doesn't specify concatenation at all.

5. A. The EMACS editor will become the SQL*Plus default text editor.

Explanation The `define _editor` statement is designed to define the default text editor in SQL*Plus. Changing the definition will not start the specified editor or stop it from running, which eliminates B and D. Choice C is the logical opposite of choice A and therefore is incorrect.

6. B. `decode( )`

Explanation The `decode( )` function is a full-fledged `if-then-else` statement that can support manipulation of output values for several different cases, along with a default. The `sqrt( )` statement simply calculates square roots, eliminating choice A. Choice C is incorrect because `new_time( )` is a date function that converts a time in one time zone to a time in another time zone. Choice D is incorrect because it is a simple conversion operation.

7. A, C, and D. `sinh( )`, `sqrt( )`, and `round( )`

Explanation The only nonnumber function in this list is the `to_number( )` function, which is a conversion operation. Several questions of this type appear throughout the OCP exams, whereby the test taker will choose multiple answers. For more information about number functions, refer to the discussion or examples of their usage.

8. B. LOA

Explanation The `decode( )` statement has a provision in it that will return LOA if the EMPID in the row matches the EMPID specified for that case, which also eliminates choice D. Also, since a default value is specified by the `decode( )` statement, there will never be an EMPID returned by this query. Therefore, choice A is incorrect. Choice C is also eliminated because Terminated is only displayed when 38475 is the column value.

9. A. `select to_char(nvl(sqrt(59483), '0')) from dual;`

Explanation Functions such as these can be used in conjunction with one another. Though usually the datatype of the value inserted if the column value is NULL and the column specified for `nvl( )` must match, Oracle performs many datatype conversions implicitly, such as this one.

10. C. DUAL

Explanation When all data to be processed by the query is present in the statement, and no data will be pulled from the database, users typically specify the DUAL table to fulfill the syntactic requirements of the `from` clause.

11. B and C. `asc` and `desc`

Explanation The `abs( )` function is the absolute value function, which eliminates choice A. The `disc` keyword is not an actual option either, eliminating choice D.

12. B. Only one column can be used to define the sort order in an `order by` clause.

Explanation Notice first that there is a logical difference between B and C, meaning you can eliminate one of them on principle. Multiple columns can be used to define order in `order by` statements, thereby eliminating choice C automatically. Choice A is incorrect because you can use `asc` or `desc` to specify ascending or descending order in your order by clause. Finally, choice D is incorrect because you can use numbers to represent the column you want to place order on, based on how the columns are listed in the `select` statement.

13. C. `where substr(LASTNAME,1,1) > to_number('S')`

Explanation Characters that are alphabetic, such as *S*, cannot be converted into numbers. When this statement is run, it will produce an error on this line.

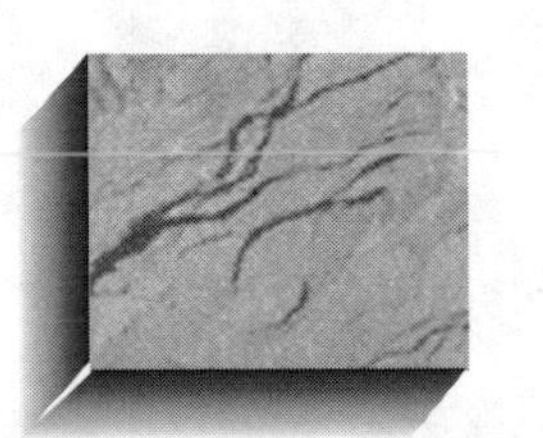

CHAPTER 2

Advanced Data Selection in Oracle

In this chapter, you will learn about and demonstrate knowledge in the following areas:

- Displaying data from multiple tables
- Group functions and their uses
- Using subqueries
- Using runtime variables

This chapter covers the advanced topics of Oracle data selection, and the first topic discussed is the table join. The chapter will cover how you can write `select` statements to access data from more than one table, how you can create joins that display data from different tables even when the information in the two tables does not correspond completely, and how to use table self joins. The chapter also introduces the `group by` clause used in `select` statements and group functions, the use of the subquery, and the specification and use of variables. The material in this chapter will complete the user's knowledge of data selection and comprises 22 percent of OCP Exam 1.

Displaying Data from Multiple Tables

In this section, you will cover the following areas related to displaying data from multiple tables:

- Using `select` statements to join data from more than one table
- Creating outer joins
- Joining a table to itself

The typical database contains many tables. Some smaller databases may have only a dozen or so tables, while other databases may have hundreds. The common factor, however, is that no database has just one table that contains all the data you need. Oracle recognizes that you may want data from multiple tables drawn together in some meaningful way. In order to show data from multiple tables in one query, Oracle allows you to perform *table joins.* A table join is when data from one table is associated with data from another table according to a common column in both tables.

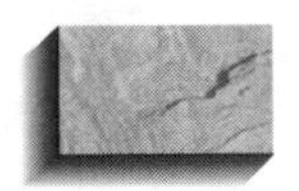

TIP
There must be at least one column shared between two tables in order to join the two tables in a `select` *statement.*

If a column value appears in two tables, and one of the columns appears as part of a primary key in one of the tables, a relationship can be defined between the two tables. A *primary key* is used in a table to identify the uniqueness of each row in a table. The table in which the column appears as a primary key is referred to as the *parent table* in this relationship, while the column that references the other table in the relationship is often called the *child table*. The common column in the child table is referred to as a *foreign key*. Figure 2-1 demonstrates how the relationship may work in a database.

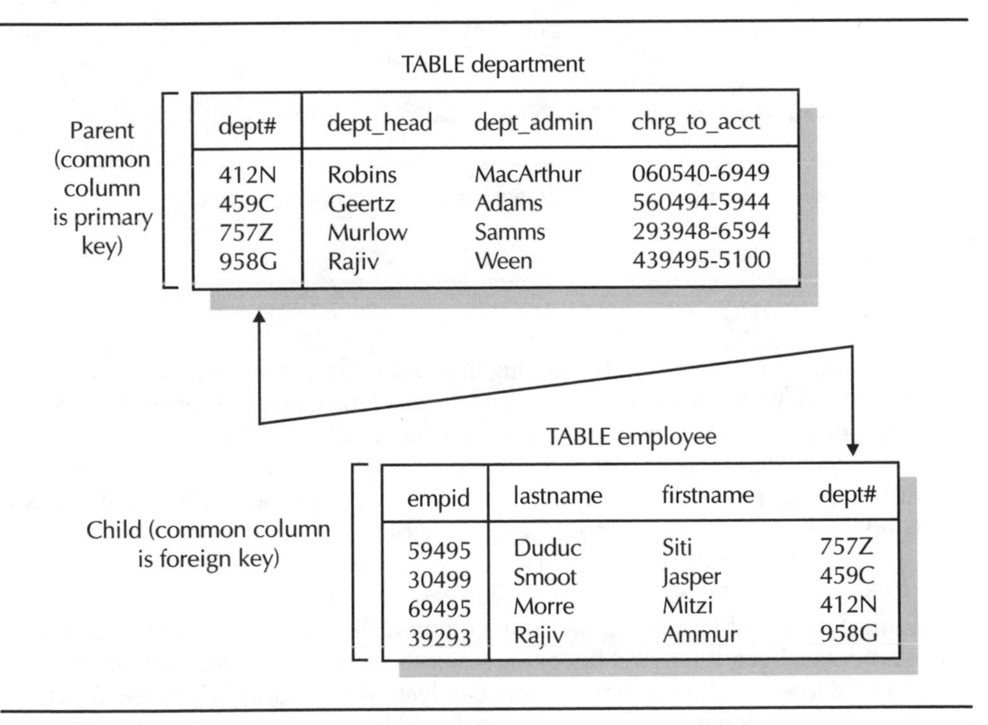

FIGURE 2-1. *Parent and child tables*

select Statements That Join Data from More Than One Table

When a primary- or foreign-key relationship exists between several tables, it is possible to join their data. As described in the Chapter 1, a `select` statement can have three parts: the `select` clause, the `from` clause, and the `where` clause. The `select` clause is where you list the column names you want to view data from, along with any single-row functions and/or column aliases. The `from` clause gives the names of the tables where the data is stored. In a table join, two or more tables are named as sources for data. The final clause is the `where` clause, which contains comparison operations that will filter out the unwanted data from what you want to see. The comparison operations in a table join statement also have another purpose—to describe how the data between two tables should be joined together, as shown in the following code:

```
SELECT a.antique_name, a.antique_cost,
a.storage_box_number, b.box_name, b.box_location
FROM antique a, storage_box b
WHERE a.antique_name in ('VICTROLA','CAMERA','RADIO')
AND a.storage_box_number = b.storage_box_number;

A.ANTIQUE_N  A.ANTIQ  A.STOR  B.BOX_NAME  B.BOX_LOCATION
-----------  -------  ------  ----------  --------------
VICTROLA      150.00       3  ALPHA-3     ALPHA BLDG
CAMERA         75.00       4  ALPHA-4     ALPHA BLDG
RADIO         200.00       4  ALPHA-4     ALPHA BLDG
```

Many important things are happening in this sample statement, the most fundamental of which is the table join. The `from` clause in this statement is the clearest indication that a table join is taking place. In this statement, the `from` clause contains two table names, each of which is followed by a letter. Table ANTIQUE in this example is followed by the letter `a`, while table STORAGE_BOX is followed by the letter `b`. This display demonstrates an interesting concept in Oracle—not only can the columns in a `select` statement have aliases, but the tables named in the `from` clause can have aliases as well.

In most cases, tables with columns in common should have the same name for those columns, because then it becomes easier to identify that they contain the same data. However, this common name can lead to ambiguity when the Oracle SQL processing mechanism (also known as the RDBMS) attempts to parse the statement and resolve all database object names. If each column isn't linked to the particular tables identified in the `from` clause, Oracle will return an error. By specifying an alias for each table in the `from` clause, and then prefixing each column name in the `select` statement with the alias, you avoid ambiguity in the

SQL statements while also avoiding the need to type out a table name each time a column is specified. The following code block illustrates the extra coding necessary when referencing columns if table aliases aren't used:

```
SELECT antique_name, antique_cost,
antique.storage_box_number, box_name, box_location
FROM antique, storage_box
WHERE antique_name in ('VICTROLA','CAMERA','RADIO')
AND antique.storage_box_number = storage_box.storage_box_number;

ANTIQUE_NAM  ANTIQUE  ANTIQU  BOX_NAME  BOX_LOCATION
-----------  -------  ------  --------  ------------
VICTROLA      150.00       3  ALPHA-3   ALPHA BLDG
CAMERA         75.00       4  ALPHA-4   ALPHA BLDG
RADIO         200.00       4  ALPHA-4   ALPHA BLDG
```

Notice something else. Neither the alias nor the full table name need be specified before a column that appears in only one table specified by the `from` clause. Ambiguity is only produced when the column appears in two or more of the tables specified in the `from` clause.

The next topic to cover in creating queries that join data from one table to data from another table is the use of comparison operations in the `where` clause of the statement. The `where` clause must include one comparison that links the data of one table to the data in the other table. Without this link, the output includes all data from both tables and is referred to as a *Cartesian product*. A Cartesian product is when Oracle joins one row in a table with every row in another table because the SQL statement joining the two tables has a malformed `where` clause or lacks one altogether. Thus, an attempt to join two tables with 3 rows each using a `select` statement with no `where` clause results in output with 9 rows. The following code block illustrates:

```
SQL> select a.col1, b.col_2
  2  from example_1 a, example_2 b;
     COL1 COL_2
--------- ------------------------------
        1 one
        2 one
        3 one
        1 two
        2 two
        3 two
        1 three
        2 three
        3 three
```

There are two comparison possibilities available in order to link the data from one table to another: *equality* comparisons and *inequality* comparisons. Joins between tables that are based on equality statements in the `where` clause are referred to as an "inner" joins, or equijoins. An *equijoin* will return data where the value in one column in one table equals the value in the column of the other table. In the situation where the tables are being joined based on an inequality statement in the where clause, typically the data returned will have less meaning unless a range of data is specified and the actual link between the two tables is an equality statement.

```
SELECT antique_name, antique_cost,
antique.storage_box_number, box_name, box_location
FROM antique, storage_box
WHERE antique_name IN ('VICTROLA','CAMERA','RADIO')
AND antique.storage_box_number < storage_box.storage_box_number;
ANTIQUE_NAM  ANTIQUE  ANTIQU  BOX_NAME  BOX_LOCATION
-----------  -------  ------  --------  ------------
VICTROLA      150.00       3  ALPHA-1   ALPHA BLDG
VICTROLA      150.00       3  ALPHA-2   ALPHA BLDG
VICTROLA      150.00       3  ALPHA-3   ALPHA BLDG
VICTROLA      150.00       3  ALPHA-4   ALPHA BLDG
CAMERA         75.00       4  ALPHA-1   ALPHA BLDG
CAMERA         75.00       4  ALPHA-2   ALPHA BLDG
CAMERA         75.00       4  ALPHA-3   ALPHA BLDG
CAMERA         75.00       4  ALPHA-4   ALPHA BLDG
RADIO         200.00       4  ALPHA-1   ALPHA BLDG
RADIO         200.00       4  ALPHA-2   ALPHA BLDG
RADIO         200.00       4  ALPHA-3   ALPHA BLDG
RADIO         200.00       4  ALPHA-4   ALPHA BLDG
```

This is junk data. It illustrates that when an inequality operation is specified as part of the `where` clause joining data from one table to another, there is no way to guarantee that the inequality operation will be satisfied for *all* values in the column for *both* tables. There is also a high possibility that the data returned by an inequality join will look suspiciously like a Cartesian product. A better alternative for drawing data from a table that satisfies an inequality operation but does not produce a Cartesian product is to specify the inequality operation outside the comparison that produces the join, as shown here:

```
SELECT antique_name, antique_cost,
antique.storage_box_number, box_name, box_location
FROM antique, storage_box
WHERE antique_name in ('VICTROLA','CAMERA','RADIO')
AND antique.storage_box_number = storage_box.storage_box_number
AND antique.storage_box_number > 3;
```

```
ANTIQUE_NAM  ANTIQUE  ANTIQU  BOX_NAME  BOX_LOCATION
-----------  -------  ------  --------  ------------
CAMERA         75.00       4  ALPHA-4   ALPHA BLDG
RADIO         200.00       4  ALPHA-4   ALPHA BLDG
```

This `select` statement will produce all results joined properly using the equality operation to link the rows of two tables in an inner join, while also satisfying the comparison needed to obtain data for only those storage boxes greater than box number three. In general, it is best to specify an equality operation for the two columns linking the tables for the join, followed by an inequality operation on the same column in *one* of the tables to filter the number of rows that will be linked in the join.

The query used to produce a table join must contain the right number of equality operations to avoid a Cartesian product. If the number of tables to be joined equals *N*, the user should remember to include at least *N*–1 equality conditions in the `select` statement so that each column in each table that exists in another table is referenced *at least once.*

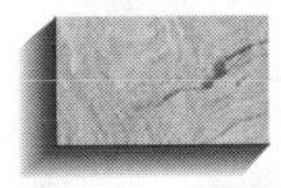

TIP

For N joined tables, you need at least N–1 join conditions in the `select` *statement in order to avoid a Cartesian product.*

Exercises

1. What is a table join? How is a table join produced?
2. Why is it important to use equality operations when creating a table join?
3. How many equality conditions are required to join three tables? Six tables? Twenty tables?

Creating Outer Joins

In some cases, however, you need some measure of inequality on the joined columns of a table-join operation in order to produce the data required in the return set. Say, for example, that you want to see all Victrolas not in storage boxes, as well as those that are boxed. One limitation of inner join or equijoin statements is that they will not return data from either table unless there is a common value in both columns for both tables on which to make the join.

```
SELECT antique_name, antique_cost,
antique.storage_box_number, box_name, box_location
FROM antique, storage_box
WHERE antique_name = 'VICTROLA'
AND antique.storage_box_number = storage_box.storage_box_number;

ANTIQUE_NAM  ANTIQUE  ANTIQU  BOX_NAME  BOX_LOCATION
-----------  -------  ------  --------  ------------
VICTROLA      150.00       3  ALPHA-3   ALPHA BLDG
```

Notice, only Victrolas that have corresponding storage box entries in the STORAGE_BOX table are included in the return set. In an attempt to obtain a list of Victrolas that are not boxed, the user then issues the following nonjoin query:

```
SELECT antique_name, antique_cost
FROM antique
WHERE antique_name = 'VICTROLA';

ANTIQUE_NAM ANTIQUE
----------- -------
VICTROLA     150.00
VICTROLA      90.00
VICTROLA      45.00
```

This query is a little closer to the mark, returning data on antique Victrolas regardless of whether or not they are boxed, but the user still needs to see storage box information for those Victrolas that are boxed.

In order to force the join to return data from one table even if there is no corresponding record in the other table, the user can specify an *outer join* operation. The previous inner join statement can be modified in the following way to show records in the ANTIQUE table that have no corresponding record in the STORAGE_BOX table:

```
SELECT antique_name, antique_cost,
antique.storage_box_number, box_name, box_location
FROM antique, storage_box
WHERE antique_name = 'VICTROLA'
AND antique.storage_box_number = storage_box.storage_box_number (+);

ANTIQUE_NAM  ANTIQUE  ANTIQU  BOX_NAME  BOX_LOCATION
-----------  -------  ------  --------  ------------
VICTROLA      150.00       3  ALPHA-3   ALPHA BLDG
VICTROLA       90.00
VICTROLA       75.00
```

Outer join statements such as these produce result sets that are "outside" the join criteria as well as inside it. Notice the special `(+)` character string called the *outer join operator* at the end of the comparison that forms the join. This marker denotes which column can have NULL data corresponding to the non-NULL values in the other table. In the previous example, the outer join marker is on the side of the STORAGE_BOX table, meaning that data in the ANTIQUE table can correspond either to values in STORAGE_BOX or to NULL if there is no corresponding value in STORAGE_BOX.

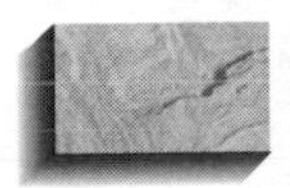

TIP
For inner joins, there must be shared values in the common column in order for the row in either table to be returned by the `select` *statement.*

Exercises

1. How does an outer join remedy the situation where a lack of corresponding values in the shared column of two tables causes rows from neither table to be selected?
2. What is the special character used to denote outer joins?

Joining a Table to Itself

In special situations, it may be necessary for you to perform a join using only one table. Well, you really are using two copies of the tables—you join the table to itself. This task can be useful in certain cases where there is a possibility that some slight difference exists between two rows that would otherwise be duplicate records. If you want to perform a self join on a table, you should utilize the table alias method, described earlier in the chapter, to specify the same table so that Oracle understands that a self join is being performed.

The following example of a self join shows how to use this technique properly. Assume that there is a table called TEST_RESULTS on which users at various locations administer a test for employees of a large corporation. The test is designed to determine whether a given employee is ready for promotion. If an employee fails the test, he or she must wait a full year before taking the test again. It is discovered that there is a bug in the system that allowed some employees to circumvent the rule by taking the test at a different location. Now, management wants to find out which employees have taken the test more than once in the past year. The columns in the TEST_RESULTS table are listed as follows: EMPID, LOCATION, DATE, and

SCORE. In order to determine whether an employee has taken the test twice in the last year, you could issue the following SQL `select` that uses self-join techniques:

```
SELECT a.empid, a.location, a.date, b.location, b.date
FROM test_results a, test_results b
WHERE a.empid = b.empid
AND a.location <> b.location
AND a.date > trunc(sysdate-365)
AND b.date > trunc(sysdate-365);

A.EMPID  A.LOCATION  A.DATE     B.LOCATION  B.DATE
-------  ----------  ---------  ----------  ---------
94839    St. John    04-NOV-98  Wendt       03-JAN-98
04030    Stridberg   27-JUN-98  Wendt       03-AUG-97
59393    St. John    20-SEP-98  Wendt       04-OCT-97
```

The output from this self join shows that three employees took the test in different locations within the last 12 months. The clause used to determine DATE highlights the flexibility inherent in Oracle's internal method for storing both DATE datatypes and `sysdate` as numbers representing the number of days since December 21, 4713 B.C.E. The storage method Oracle uses allows you to perform simple mathematical operations on dates to obtain other dates without worrying about taking into account factors like the number of days in months between the old date and new, whether the year in question is a leap year, and so on.

Those users who must perform self joins on tables should be extremely cautious about doing so in order to avoid performance issues or Cartesian products. The required number of equality operations is usually at least *two* in the situation of self joins, simply because using only one equality condition does not usually limit the output of a self join to the degree necessary to produce meaningful information.

TIP
The number of equality operations usually needed in the `where` clause of a self join should be two or more.

It should be stated that a self join typically requires a long time to execute, because Oracle must necessarily read all table data twice sequentially. Ordinarily, Oracle will read data from two different tables to perform the join, but since the operation in this case is a self join, all data comes from one table. Without a proper comparison operation set up in the `where` clause, you may wind up with many copies of every row in the table returned, which will certainly run for a long time and produce a lot of unnecessary output.

Exercises

1. What is a self join? How might a self join be used?
2. How many equality operations should be used to create a self join?
3. What performance issues do self joins present?

Group Functions and Their Uses

In this section, you will cover the following topics related to group functions and their uses:

- Identifying available group functions
- Using group functions
- Using the `group by` clause
- Excluding group data with the `having` clause

A group function allows you to perform a data operation on several values in a column of data as though the column were one collective group of data. These functions are also called group functions, because they are often used in a special clause of `select` statements called a `group by` clause. A more complete discussion of the `group by` clause appears later in this section.

Identifying Available Group Functions

An important difference between group functions and single-row functions is that group functions can operate on several rows at a time. This allows functions to calculate figures like averages and standard deviation. The list of available group functions appears here:

`avg(x)`	Averages all *x* column values returned by the `select` statement
`count(x)`	Counts the number of non-NULL values returned by the `select` statement for column *x*
`max(x)`	Determines the maximum value in column *x* for all rows returned by the `select` statement
`min(x)`	Determines the minimum value in column *x* for all rows returned by the `select` statement
`stddev(x)`	Calculates the standard deviation for all values in column *x* in all rows returned by the `select` statement

`sum(x)`	Calculates the sum of all values in column *x* in all rows returned by the `select` statement
`variance(x)`	Calculates the variance for all values in column *x* in all rows returned by the `select` statement

Exercises

1. What is a group function? How do they differ from single-row functions?
2. Name several group functions.

Using Group Functions

Examples of the several of these group functions appear over the next few pages. Since these functions require the use of several rows of data, the EMP table from the previous chapter (shown as Table 2-1) will be used frequently.

The `avg( )` function takes the values for a single column on all rows returned by the query and calculates the average value for that column. Based on the data from the previous table, the `avg( )` function on the SALARY column produces the following result:

```
SELECT AVG(salary)FROM EMP;

AVG(salary)
-----------
      74000
```

The second grouping function illustrated is `count( )`. This function is bound to become the cornerstone of any Oracle professional's repertoire. The `count( )`

Empid	Lastname	Firstname	Salary
39334	Smith	Gina	75,000
49539	Qian	Lee	90,000
60403	Harper	Rod	45,000
02039	Walla	Rajendra	60,000
49392	Spanky	Stacy	100,000

TABLE 2-1. *The EMP Table*

function returns a row count for the table, given certain column names, `select` criteria, or both. Note that the fastest way to execute `count( )` is to pass a value that resolves quickly in the SQL processing mechanism. Some values that resolve quickly are integers and the ROWID pseudocolumn.

```
SELECT COUNT(*), -- Slow
       COUNT(1), -- Fast
       COUNT(rowid) -- Fast
FROM EMP;

COUNT(*)  COUNT(1) COUNT(rowid)
-------- -------- ------------
       5        5            5
```

The asterisk (*) in the previous query is a wildcard variable that indicates all columns in the table. For better performance, this wildcard should not generally be used because the Oracle SQL processing mechanism must first resolve all column names in the table, a step that is unnecessary if one is simply trying to count rows. Notice that one of these examples uses the special pseudocolumn called ROWID. A ROWID is a special value that uniquely identifies each row. Each row in a table has one unique ROWID. The ROWID is not actually part of the table; rather, ROWID is a piece of information stored internally within Oracle indexes, not the table. This is why it is considered a pseudocolumn. Note that index-organized tables in Oracle 8.0 do not have a ROWID, although this is changing in Oracle8*i*.

TIP
Do not use `count(*)` to determine the number of rows in a table. Use `count(1)` or `count(ROWID)` instead. These options are faster because they bypass some unnecessary operations in Oracle's SQL processing mechanism.

The next pair of grouping functions to be covered are the `max( )` and `min( )` functions. The `max( )` function determines the largest value for the column passed, while `min( )` determines the smallest value for the column passed, as shown here:

```
SELECT MAX(salary), MIN(salary) FROM EMP;

MAX(salary)  MIN(salary)
-----------  -----------
     100000        45000
```

The final group function is used commonly in simple accounting reports. The `sum( )` function gives the total of all values in a column.

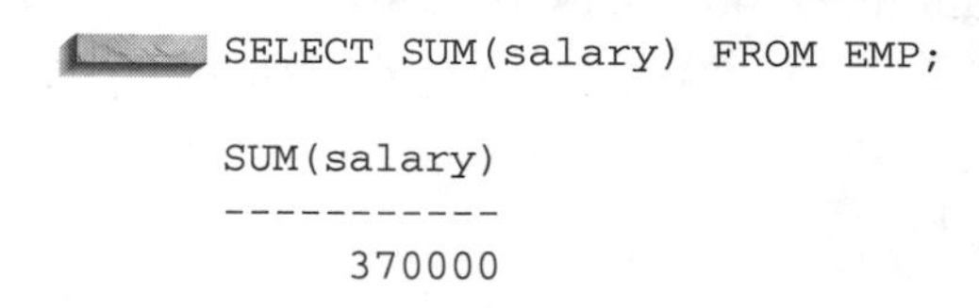

```
SELECT SUM(salary) FROM EMP;

SUM(salary)
-----------
     370000
```

In general, the group functions will operate on columns of datatypes NUMBER and DATE because many of the functions they represent in mathematics are numeric operations. For example, it makes little sense to take the standard deviation for a set of 12 words, unless the user wants to take the standard deviation of the length of those words by combining the use of the `length( )` function with the `stddev( )` function. There is one notable exception to this general rule, though—that exception is the `count( )` function. The `count( )` function will operate on a column of any datatype.

TIP
Group functions ignore NULL values by default. This is an essential piece of information you should know for OCP.

Exercises

1. How are group functions incorporated into `select` statements? How many rows of output can usually be expected from a query using a group function?
2. What is ROWID? Is ROWID stored in a table?

Using the group by Clause

Sometimes it gives more meaning to the output of a `select` statement to collect data into logical groupings. For example, to perform calculations on the populations of several cities in America, you might issue a query against all records in the CITIES table. A `select` statement containing `order by` may work well for specific queries against particular cities in this table; it could list data in order based on an alphabetized list of cities and states, as the SQL statement here shows:

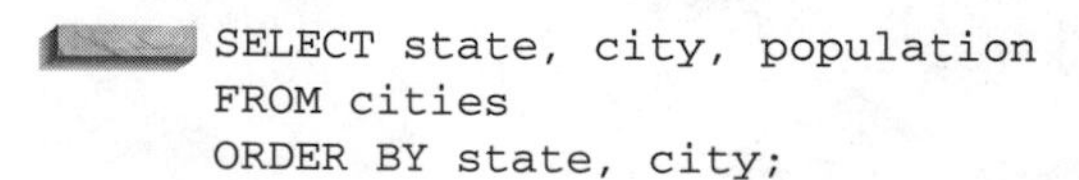

```
SELECT state, city, population
FROM cities
ORDER BY state, city;
```

```
STATE              CITY              POPULATION
---------------    --------------    ----------
ALABAMA            AARDVARK              12,560
ALABAMA            BARNARD              176,000
...
```

However, suppose you want to perform specific calculations on the cities in each state separately. For example, you want to find out the average city population for each of the states listed on the table. The preceding `select` statement works fine for producing the raw data you need in order to calculate the average city population for each state, but there is an easier way for you to make Oracle return the average city population you seek by using the `group by` clause in SQL statements.

```
SELECT state, AVG(population)
FROM CITIES
GROUP BY state;

STATE               AVG(POPULA
-----------------   ----------
ALABAMA                  49494
ALASKA                   14349
NEW YORK                 85030
ARIZONA                  35003
CALIFORNIA               65040
...
```

The `group by` clause in this example saves you from performing a great deal of work by hand. Instead, Oracle shoulders most of the work and shows only the results you need. The `group by` clause works well in many situations where you want to report calculations on data according to groups or categories.

There are some common error messages with `group by` operations. The first is shown in the following code block. The problem with this statement is that you are using a group function in a `select` statement that lacks the `group by` clause:

```
SQL> select lastname, avg(salary), empid
  2  from emp;
select lastname, avg(salary), empid
       *
ERROR at line 1:
ORA-00937: not a single-group group function
```

However, notice what happens when you add the `group by` clause:

```
SQL> select lastname, avg(salary), empid
  2  from emp
```

```
  3* group by lastname;
select lastname, avg(salary), empid
                              *
ERROR at line 1:
ORA-00979: not a GROUP BY expression
```

To solve the problem with this statement's execution, you should add the EMPID column to the `group by` clause, so that all nonaggregate columns in the `select` statement are part of the grouping expression, as shown in this code block:

```
SQL>  select lastname, avg(salary), empid
  2   from emp
  3   group by lastname, empid;
LASTNAME                       AVG(SALARY) EMPID
------------------------------ ----------- --------------------
HARPER                               45000 60403
QIAN                                 90000 49539
SMITH                                75000 39334
SPANKY                              100000 49392
WALLA                                60000 02039
```

In this situation, however, the `group by` expression lacks meaning, because all the "groups" are really just individuals with different last names. Thus, the average salary by last name and EMPID is simply an individual person's salary. To demonstrate the use of `group by` in a meaningful way, let's assume that you want to calculate the average salary for all employees in a corporation by department. The EMP table is altered to contain the following columns: EMPID, LASTNAME, FIRSTNAME, SALARY, and DEPT. There are only two departments, 504A and 604B. Harper and Qian are part of 504A; the rest are in 604B. The following code block illustrates how you can obtain the average employee salary by department, ordering the output from highest average salary to lowest:

```
SQL> select dept, avg(salary)
  2  from emp
  3  group by dept
  4  order by avg(salary) desc;
DEPT       AVG(SALARY)
---------- -----------
604B         78333.333
504A             67500
```

In this example, the `order by` clause was combined with the `group by` clause to create a special order for the output. This order gives the data some additional meaning. You're not limited to grouping data by only one selected column, either. If you want, more than one column can be used in the `group by` statement—provided that the same nonaggregate columns specified in the `select` clause of the query match the columns specified in the `group by` clause.

Exercises

1. How is the `group by` clause of a `select` statement used?
2. Identify some situations where statements containing the `group by` clause return errors.

Excluding Group Data with having

One initial problem encountered when using the `group by` statement is that once the data is grouped, you must then analyze the data returned by the `group by` statement in order to determine which groups are relevant and which are not. It is sometimes useful to *weed out* unwanted data. For example, in the final query from the previous section, suppose you only wanted to see which departments paid an average salary of $80,000 or more per year. In effect, you would be attempting to put a `where` clause on the `group by` clause. This effect can be achieved with the use of a special clause in Oracle called `having`. This clause acts as a modified where clause that only applies to the resultant rows generated by the `group by` expression.

Consider the previous query of employee salary by department. If you want to view only those departments whose employees make an average of $70,000 or more, you could issue the following query. The `having` clause in this case is used to eliminate the departments whose average salary is $70,000 or less. Notice that this selectivity cannot easily be accomplished with an ordinary `where` clause, because the `where` clause selects individual rows whereas this example requires that groups of rows be selected. In this query, you successfully limit output on the `group by` rows by using the `having` clause:

```
SQL> select dept, avg(salary)
  2  from emp
  3  group by dept
  4  having avg(salary) > 70000
  5  order by avg(salary) desc;
DEPT        AVG(SALARY)
---------- -----------
604B          78333.333
```

Exercises

1. What is the having clause, and what function does it serve?
2. How can the user specify values to fulfill having criteria without actually knowing what the values themselves are?

Using Subqueries

In this section, you will cover the following topics related to using subqueries:

- Nested subqueries
- Subqueries in other situations
- Putting data in order with subqueries

A subquery is a "query within a query," a select statement nested within a select statement designed to limit the selected output of the parent query by producing an intermediate result set of some sort. There are several different ways to include subqueries in where statements. The most commonly used method is the equality comparison operation, or the in comparison, which is similar to the case statement offered in many programming languages because the equality can be established with one element in the group. Another way of including a subquery in the where clause of a select statement is the exists clause. When you specify the exists operation in a where clause, you must include a subquery that satisfies the exists operation. If the subquery returns data, the exists operation returns TRUE. If not, the exists operation returns FALSE. These subquery options will be discussed shortly.

Nested Subqueries

Subqueries can be used to obtain search criteria for select statements, as follows. The where clause in a select statement has one or more comparison operations. Each comparison operation can contain the name of a column on the left side of the equality operator and a given search method to obtain unknown data on the right side of the equality operator by means of a subquery.

```
SELECT empid, dept, salary
FROM emp
WHERE dept =
  (select dept
from emp
where empid = 78483);
```

The portion of the SQL statement that is highlighted is the subquery portion of the statement. On one side is the DEPT column, on which a comparison will be based to determine the result set. On the other side is the unknown search criteria, defined by the subquery. At the time this `select` statement is submitted, Oracle will process the subquery *first* in order to resolve all unknown search criteria, then feed that resolved criteria to the outer query. The outer query then can resolve the dataset it is supposed to return.

The subquery itself can contain subqueries, referred to as nested subqueries. Consider the following example. An employee has submitted an expensive invoice for payment on the company's relocation expenditure system, and you are trying to determine the salary of employees in the same department as that employee. The tables involved in this `select` statement are the EMP table, which has been described, and the INVOICE table, which consists of the following columns: INVOICE_NUMBER, EMPID, INVOICE_AMT, and PAY_DATE. The only information you have about the employee you are looking for is the invoice number the employee submitted for relocation expenses, which is 5640.

```
SELECT e.empid,
       e.salary
FROM emp e
WHERE e.dept =
 (SELECT dept
FROM emp
WHERE empid =
   (SELECT empid
FROM invoice
WHERE invoice_number = 5640));
```

In this statement, there are two subqueries: the subquery to the main `select` statement highlighted in bold, and the nested subquery in italics. Each subquery produces criteria that are crucial for completing the `select` statement, yet the actual criteria are unknown at the time the `select` statement is issued. The first subquery produces the department information and the second produces the employee ID for the person submitting the invoice. Oracle must first resolve the innermost nested subquery in italics to resolve the next level. Then Oracle will resolve the subquery in bold to resolve the outermost level of the `select` statement.

Subqueries can be nested to a surprisingly deep level. The rule of thumb used to be that you could nest 16 or more subqueries in a `select` statement. In reality, the number of nested subqueries can be far higher. However, if you need to nest more than five subqueries, you may want to consider writing the query in PL/SQL or in a programming language like PRO*C or PRO*COBOL, or some other programming language that allows embedded SQL statements and cursors. At the very least, you may want to consider changing a query that makes heavy use of subqueries into a query that performs extensive join operations as well. Database performance degrades substantially after about five levels of subqueries on all but the most powerful database servers and mainframes.

Exercises

1. What is a subquery? When might a user want to incorporate a subquery into a database `select` statement?
2. What are some situations in which a `where` clause may be sufficient in place of a subquery?
3. What performance issues might revolve around the use of subqueries?

Subqueries in Other Situations

Subqueries are quite powerful, and this discussion barely scratches the surface. A subquery can be used for complicated step-by-step joins of data that use data from one subquery to feed into the processing of its immediate parent. However, subqueries also allow you to "jump" subquery levels to perform incredibly complex, almost counterintuitive processing that necessarily must involve some discussion of a programming concept known as *variable scope*. Variable scope refers to the availability or "viewability" of data in certain variables at certain times.

Sometimes a variable has a *local* scope. That is to say that the variable can only be seen when the current block of code is being executed. You can consider the columns in subquery comparison operations to be variables whose scope is *local* to the query. There is also *global* scope. In addition to a variable having local scope within the subquery where it appears, the variable also has *global* scope, meaning that it is available in all subqueries to that query. In the previous `select` statement example, all variables or columns named in comparison operations in the outermost `select` operation are local to that operation and global to all the nested subqueries (the ones showing in bold and italics. Additionally, all columns in the subquery shown in bold are local to that query and global to the subquery shown in italics. Columns named in the query in italics are local to that query, and since there are no subqueries to it, the columns in that query cannot be global. The nested query example from the previous discussion is featured in Figure 2-2.

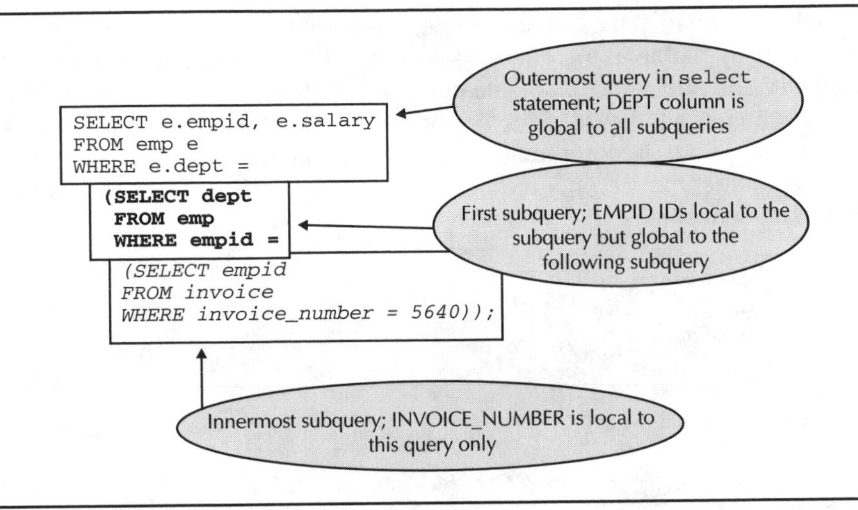

FIGURE 2-2. *Nested subqueries and variable scope*

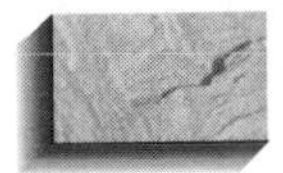

TIP
The scope of a variable defines which code blocks will have the variable and its defined value available to it. There are two different types of variable scope—local and global. If a variable has global scope, then it and its value are available everywhere in the code block. If a variable has local scope, then it and its value are available only in the current code block running in the memory stack.

Example 1: Subqueries to Derive Valid Values

Assume that there is a recruiter for a national consulting firm who wants to find people in Minneapolis who are proficient in Oracle SQL skills. Furthermore, the recruiter only wants to see the names and home cities for people who are certified Oracle professionals. The recruiter has at her disposal a nationwide resume search system with several tables. These tables include one called CANDIDATE, which contains the candidate ID, candidate name, salary requirement, and current employer. Another table in this example is called SKILLS, where the candidate ID is matched with the skill(s) the candidate possesses. A third table, called COMPANIES, contains the names and home cities for companies that the consulting firm tries to draw their talent from. In order to find the names and locations of people who possess the abilities the recruiter requires, the recruiter may issue the following `select` statement against the national recruiting database:

```
SQL> SELECT candidate_id,
  2>        name,
  3>        employer
  4> FROM   candidate
  5> WHERE  candidate_id IN
  6> (SELECT candidate_id
  7>  FROM   skills
  8>  WHERE  skill_type = 'ORACLE SQL'
  9>  AND    certified = 'YES')
 10> AND    employer IN
 11> (SELECT employer
 12>  FROM   companies
 13>  WHERE  city = 'MINNEAPOLIS');
CANDIDATE_ID  NAME       EMPLOYER
------------  --------   --------------
60549         DURNAM     TransCom
```

This query produces the result set the recruiter is looking for. Notice in the last subquery the use of the `in` keyword. Recall from Chapter 1 that the `in` operation allows you to identify a column and a set of values, and that the column can equal any of the values in order to be part of the result set. You must use the `in` keyword here because multiple values will be returned from the subquery. Thus, if the `where` clause of the `select` statement contains `and` NUMBER `in (1,2,3)`, all rows whose value in the NUMBER column are equal to 1, 2, or 3 will be part of the result set.

Example 2: Using Correlated Subqueries

In certain cases, it may be useful for a subquery to refer to a global column value rather than a local one to obtain result data. The subquery architecture of Oracle allows you to refer to global variables in subqueries as well as local ones to produce more powerful queries. A subquery using this type of global scope is sometimes referred to as a *correlated subquery*. Oracle performs a correlated subquery when the subquery references a column from a table referred to in the parent statement. A correlated subquery is evaluated once for each row processed by the parent statement, according to the following syntax:

```
SELECT select_list
FROM table1 t_alias1
WHERE expr operator
 (SELECT column_list
  FROM table2 t_alias2
  WHERE t_alias1.column = t_alias2.column);
```

Here is an example:

```
SELECT e.empid, e.lastname, e.firstname
FROM emp e
WHERE e.salary < (SELECT sum(i.invoice_total)
                  FROM invoice i
                  WHERE i.empid = e.empid)
ORDER BY e.empid;
```

Example 3: Keywords that Require Subqueries

Another complicated possibility offered by subqueries is the use of the `exists` operation. Mentioned earlier, `exists` allows the user to specify the results of a `select` statement according to a special subquery operation. This `exists` operation returns TRUE or FALSE based on whether or not the subquery obtains data when it runs. An example of a use for the `exists` subquery is the relocation expenditure tracking system. The tables involved in this system are the EMP table, which has been described, and the INVOICE table, which consists of the following columns: INVOICE_NUMBER, EMPID, INVOICE_AMT, and PAY_DATE. Let's assume that you want to identify all the departments that have employees who have incurred relocation expenses in the past year:

```
SELECT distinct e.dept
FROM emp e
WHERE EXISTS
 (SELECT i.empid
  FROM invoice i
  WHERE i.empid = e.empid
  AND i.pay_date > trunc(sysdate-365));
```

There are a couple of things that are worthy of note in this `select` statement. First, this example is a correlated subquery. Second, note that global scope variables are incorporated into the subquery to produce meaningful results from that code.

The third point concerns the general nature of exists statements. Oracle will go through every record in the EMP table to see if the EMPID matches that of a row in the INVOICE table. If there is a matching invoice, then the exists criteria are met and the department ID is added to the list of departments that will be returned. If not, the exists criteria are not met and the record is not added to the list of departments that will be returned. This can sometimes be a slow process, so be patient.

Example 4: having Clauses and Subqueries

The having clause need not be limited by some arbitrary number that you key in manually. In addition to performing a comparison operation on a constant value, the having clause can perform a special operation to derive the required data by using a subquery. Subqueries are useful when you need for valid data that you don't know the value of, but you do know how to obtain it. In the following example, the subquery is used to specify the salary of employee 60403, though the actual value of the salary is not known.

```
SQL> select dept, avg(salary)
  2  from emp
  3  group by dept
  4  having avg(salary) > (select salary
  5                        from emp
  6                        where empid=60403);
DEPT       AVG(SALARY)
---------- -----------
504A             67500
604B         78333.333
```

Using the distinct Keyword

Notice that there is one other aspect of the select distinct query in Example 3 that has not been explained—the distinct keyword highlighted in bold in the select clause of the outer portion of the query. This special keyword identifies a filter that Oracle will put on the data returned from the exists subquery. When distinct is used, Oracle will return only one row for a particular department, even if there are several employees in that department that have submitted relocation expenses within the past year. This distinct operation is useful for situations when you want a list of unique rows but anticipate that the query may return duplicate rows. The distinct operation removes duplicate rows from the result set before displaying the result to the user.

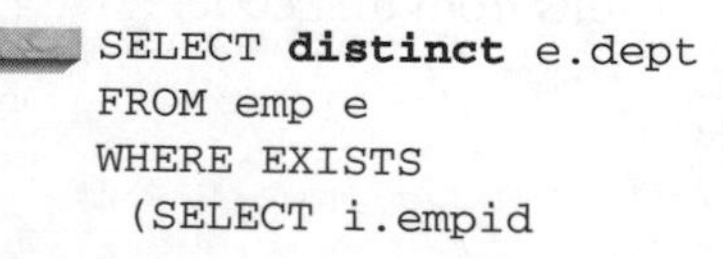

```
SELECT distinct e.dept
FROM emp e
WHERE EXISTS
 (SELECT i.empid
```

```
FROM invoice i
WHERE i.empid = e.empid
AND i.pay_date > trunc(sysdate-365));
```

Exercises

1. Name a TRUE/FALSE operation that depends on the results of a subquery to determine its value.
2. What is variable scope? What is a local variable? What is a global variable?
3. What is the `distinct` keyword, and how is it used?

Putting Data in Order with Subqueries

As with other types of `select` statements, those statements that involve subqueries may also require some semblance of order in the data that is returned to the user. In the subquery examples in the previous discussion, you might need to return the data in a particular order based on the columns selected by the outermost query. In this case, you might simply want to use the `order by` clause. The previous example of selecting departments containing relocated employees could be modified, as follows, to produce the required department data in a particular order:

```
SELECT distinct e.dept
FROM emp e
WHERE EXISTS
 (SELECT i.empid
  FROM invoice i
  WHERE i.empid = e.empid
  AND i.pay_date > trunc(sysdate-365))
ORDER BY dept;
```

By using the `order by` clause in the outermost statement, the data returned from the outermost statement can be sorted into ascending or descending order. You cannot, however, incorporate `order by` into the data returned by the subquery, meaning that `order by` clauses must be applied at the global level in `select` statements containing subqueries, not within the local level of the subquery itself. The following sample will not work:

```
SELECT distinct e.dept
FROM emp e
WHERE EXISTS
 (SELECT i.empid FROM invoice i
  WHERE i.empid = e.empid
  AND i.pay_date > trunc(sysdate-365)
  ORDER BY i.empid); -- WILL NOT WORK!
```

In the following example, the recruiter from the national consulting firm mentioned earlier tries to issue the following select statement, similar to the original one discussed with that example:

```
SELECT candidate_id,
       name,
       employer
FROM candidate
WHERE candidate_id IN
( SELECT candidate_id
  FROM skills
  WHERE employer IN
   ( SELECT employer
     FROM companies
     WHERE city = 'MINNEAPOLIS'))
ORDER BY salary_req;
```

Oracle will execute this statement without error because the column specified by the order by clause need not be part of the column list in the select column list of the outermost select statement, though it must be part of the table in the from clause of the outermost query.

Exercises

1. Can you use the order by clause within select statement with subqueries? Why or why not?
2. Can you use the order by clause within the subquery itself? Explain.

Using Runtime Variables

In this section, you will cover the following topics related to using runtime variables:

- Entering variables at run time
- Automatic definition of runtime variables
- The accept command

SQL is an interpreted language. That is, there is no executable code other than the statement you enter into the command line. At the time that statement is entered, Oracle's SQL processing mechanism works on obtaining the data and returning it to you. When Oracle is finished returning the data, it is ready for you to enter another statement. This interactive behavior is typical of interpreted programming languages.

```
SQL> SELECT name, salary, dept
  2> FROM emp
  3> WHERE empid = 40539;
NAME        SALARY   DEPT
--------    -------  ----
DURNAP        70560  450P
```

In the preceding statement, the highlighted comparison operation designates that the data returned from this statement must correspond to the EMPID value specified. If you run this statement again, the data returned would be exactly the same, provided that no portion of the record had been changed by anyone on the database. However, Oracle's interpretive RDBMS mechanism need not have everything defined for it at the time you enter a SQL statement. In fact, there are features within the SQL processing mechanism of Oracle that allow you to identify a specific value to be used for the execution of the query as a runtime variable. This feature permits some flexibility and reuse of SQL statements.

Entering Variables at Run Time

Consider, for example, the situation where you pull up data for several different employees manually for the purpose of reviewing some aspect of their data. Rather than rekeying the entire statement with the EMPID value hard-coded into each statement, you can substitute a variable specification that forces Oracle to prompt you to enter a data value in order to let Oracle complete the statement. The earlier statement that returned data from the EMP table based on a hard-coded EMPID value can now be rewritten as follows to allow you to reuse the same code again and again with different values set for EMPID:

```
SELECT name, salary, dept
FROM emp
WHERE empid = &empid;

Enter value for empid: 40539
Old 3: WHERE empid = &empid;
New 3: WHERE empid = 40539;

NAME      SALARY   DEPT
------    -------  ----
DURNAP      70560  450P
```

After completing execution, you now have the flexibility to rerun that same query, except now you can specify a different EMPID without having to reenter the entire statement. Notice that a special ampersand character (&) precedes the name of the variable that will be specified at run time. This combination of ampersand and identifier creates a *substitution variable.*

```
Enter value for empid: 99706
Old 3: WHERE empid = &empid;
New 3: WHERE empid = 99706;

NAME      SALARY   DEPT
-------  -------   ----
MCCALL    103560   795P
```

This time, you enter another value for the EMPID, and Oracle searches for data in the table based on the new value specified. This activity will go on as listed above until you enter a new SQL statement. Notice that Oracle returns additional information to you after a value is entered for the runtime variable. The line as it appeared before is listed as the old value, and the new value is presented as well. This presentation lets you know what data was changed by your input. Finally, if you don't want to use the ampersand to create the substitution variable, the input can be changed with the `set define` command at the SQL prompt in SQL*Plus. You can reexecute the statement containing a runtime variable declaration by using the slash (/) command at the prompt in SQL*Plus. The following code block illustrates:

```
SQL> set define ?
SQL> select * from emp where
  2  empid = '?empid';
Enter value for empid: 60403
old   2: empid = '?empid'
new   2: empid = '60403'
EMPID      LASTNAME     FIRSTNAME   DEPT
---------- ------------ ----------- ----------
60403      HARPER       ROD         504A
SQL> /
Enter value for empid: 49392
old   2: empid = '?empid'
new   2: empid = '49392'
EMPID      LASTNAME     FIRSTNAME   DEPT
---------- ------------ ----------- ----------
49392      SPANKY       STACY       604B
```

Exercises

1. What special character is used to specify a runtime variable?
2. How does Oracle prompt for runtime variable change?
3. What special character is used to reexecute a statement in SQL*Plus if the statement is stored in the current buffer? Can you recall the name of the file in which the SQL*Plus statement buffer is stored?

Automatic Definition of Runtime Variables

In some cases, it may not be useful to enter new values for a runtime variable every time the statement executes. For example, assume that there is some onerous reporting process that you must perform weekly for every person in a company. A great deal of value is added to the process by having a variable that can be specified at run time because you can then simply execute the same statement over and over again, with new EMPID values each time.

However, even this improvement does not streamline the process as much as you would like. Instead of running the statement over and over again with new values specified, you could create a script that contains the SQL statement, preceded by a special statement that defines the input value automatically and triggers the execution of the statement automatically. Some basic reporting conventions will be presented in this example, such as `spool`. This command specifies to SQL*Plus that all output generated by the following SQL activity should be redirected to an output file named after the parameter that follows `spool`:

```
SPOOL emp_info.out;
DEFINE VAR_EMPID = 34093
SELECT lastname, firstname, salary
FROM emp
WHERE empid = &var_empid;
UNDEFINE VAR_EMPID
DEFINE VAR_EMPID = 50292
SELECT lastname, firstname, salary
FROM emp
WHERE empid = &var_empid;
```

When run in SQL*Plus, this script would produce the following output, both to the screen and in the `emp_info.out` file:

```
SQL> @emp.txt
old   3: WHERE empid = &var_empid
new   3: WHERE empid = 34093
```

```
LASTNAME     FIRSTNAME      SALARY
------------ -------------- ---------
TABACCO      ANTHONY         40000
old   3: WHERE empid = &var_empid
new   3: WHERE empid = 50292

LASTNAME     FIRSTNAME      SALARY
------------ -------------- ---------
TABACCO      DEBORAH         45000
```

When you execute the script, the time spent actually keying in values for the variables named in the SQL `select` statement is eliminated with the `define` statement. Notice, however, that in between each execution of the SQL statement there is a special statement using a command called `undefine`. In Oracle, the data that is defined with the `define` statement will remain defined for the variable for the entire session unless the variable is undefined. By *undefining* a variable, the user allows another `define` statement to reuse the variable in another execution of the same or a different statement.

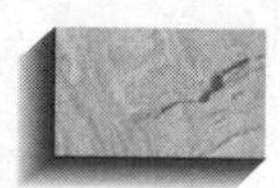

TIP
You can also use the `define` command if you want to reuse substitution variables over different SQL statements, allowing you to pass a value from one statement to another.

Exercises

1. How are variables defined within the SQL*Plus session to be used by `select` statements?
2. How can the user change a value set for a defined variable?

accept: Another Way to Define Variables

After executing a few example SQL statements that incorporate runtime variables, you may notice that Oracle's method for identifying input, though not exactly cryptic, is fairly nonexpressive.

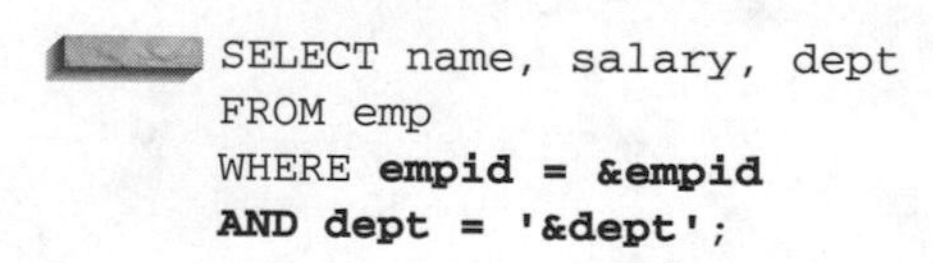

```
SELECT name, salary, dept
FROM emp
WHERE empid = &empid
AND dept = '&dept';
```

```
Enter value for &empid: 30403
Old 3: WHERE empid = &empid
New 3: WHERE empid = 30403

Enter value for &dept: 983X
Old 4: WHERE dept = '&dept';
New 4: WHERE dept = '983X';

NAME       SALARY     DEPT
--------   --------   ----
TIBBINS       56700   983X
```

You need not stick with Oracle's default messaging to identify the need for input. Instead, you can define a more expressive message that the user will see when Oracle prompts for input data. The name of the command that provides this functionality is the `accept` command. In order to use the `accept` command in a runtime SQL environment, you can create a script as follows. Assume for this example that you have created a script called `emp_sal_dept.sql`, into which the following SQL statements are placed:

```
ACCEPT var_empid PROMPT 'Enter the Employee ID Now:'
ACCEPT var_dept PROMPT 'Enter the Employee Department Now:'

SELECT name, salary, dept
FROM emp
WHERE empid = &var_empid
AND dept = '&var_dept';
```

At this point, the user can run the script at the prompt using the following command syntax:

```
SQL> @emp_sal_dept
```

or

```
SQL> start emp_sal_dept.sql
```

Oracle will then execute the contents of the script. When Oracle needs to obtain the runtime value for the variables that the user identified in the SQL statement and with the `accept` statement, Oracle will use the prompt the user defined with the `prompt` clause of the `accept` statement.

```
SQL> @emp_sal_dept
Enter the Employee ID Now: 30403
```

```
SELECT name, salary, dept
FROM emp
WHERE empid = &var_empid
AND dept = '&var_dept';

Old 3: WHERE empid = '&var_empid'
New 3: WHERE empid = 30403

Enter the Employee Department Now: 983X

SELECT name, salary, dept
FROM emp
WHERE empid = 30403
AND dept = '&var_dept';

Old 4: WHERE dept = '&var_dept'
New    4: WHERE dept = '983X'

NAME        SALARY   DEPT
--------   -------   ----
TIBBINS      56700   983X
```

Using the `accept` command can be preferable to Oracle's default output message in situations where you want to define a more accurate or specific prompt, or you want more output to display as the values are defined. In either case, the `accept` command can work well. Oracle offers a host of options for making powerful and complex SQL statements possible with runtime variables. These options can be used for both interactive SQL data selection and for SQL scripts.

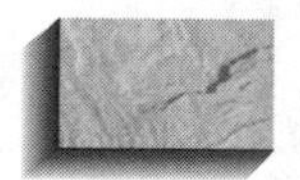

TIP

By default, the datatype for a variable defined with the `accept` command is CHAR. You can also explicitly specify the datatype in the `accept` command.

Exercises

1. What is the `accept` command and how is it used? What benefits does using the `accept` command offer?
2. What is the `start` command? Identify the purposes of the `define`, `undefine`, and `spool` commands.

Chapter Summary

This chapter continues the discussion presented last chapter of using the `select` statement to obtain data from the Oracle database. The `select` statement has many powerful features that allow the user to accomplish many tasks. Those features include joining data from multiple tables, grouping data output together and performing data operations on the groups of data, creating `select` statements that can use subqueries to obtain criteria that is unknown (but for which the method of obtaining it is known), and using variables that accept values at run time. Together, these topics comprise the advanced usage of SQL `select` statements. The material in this chapter comprises 22 percent of the information questioned on OCP Exam 1.

The first area discussed in this chapter is how data from multiple tables can be joined together to create new meaning. Data in a table can be linked if there is a common or shared column between the two tables. This shared column is often referred to as a foreign key. Foreign keys establish a relationship between two tables that is referred to as a parent/child relationship. The parent table is typically the table in which the common column is defined as a primary key, or the column by which uniqueness is identified for rows in the table. The child table is typically the table in which the column is not the primary key, but refers to the primary key in the parent table.

There are two types of joins. One of those types is the inner join, also known as an equijoin. An equijoin is a data join based on equality comparisons between common columns of two or more tables. An outer join is a join operation not based on equality of column values that allows you to obtain output from a table even if there is no corresponding data for that record in the other table.

Joins are generated by using `select` statements in the following way. First, the columns desired in the result set are defined in the `select` clause of the statement. Those columns may or may not be preceded with a table definition, depending on whether or not the column appears in more than one table. If the common column is named differently in each table, then there is no need to identify the table name along with the column name, as Oracle will be able to distinguish which table the column belongs to automatically. However, if the column name is duplicated in two or more tables, then you must specify which table you would like to obtain data from, because Oracle must be able to resolve any ambiguities clearly at the time the query is parsed. The tables from which data is selected are named in the `from` clause, and may optionally be followed by a table alias. A table alias is similar in principle to a column alias, which was discussed in Chapter 1. The `where` clause of a join statement specifies how the join is performed. An inner join is created by specifying the two shared columns in each table in an equality comparison. An outer join is created in the same way, with an additional marker placed by the column specification of the "outer" table—the table in which there need not be data corresponding to rows in the other table for that data to be returned. That special marker is indicated by `(+)`. Finally, a table may be joined to itself with the use of table aliases. This is often done to determine whether there are records in a table with slightly different information from rows that are otherwise duplicate rows.

Another advanced technique for data selection in Oracle databases is the use of grouping functions. Data can be grouped together in order to provide additional meaning to the data. Columns in a table can also be treated as a group in order to perform certain operations on them. These grouping functions often perform math operations, such as averaging values or obtaining the standard deviation of the dataset. Other group functions available on groups of data are `max( )`, `min( )`, `sum( )`, and `count( )`.

One common grouping operation performed on data for reporting purposes is a special clause in `select` statements called `group by`. This clause allows the user to segment output data and perform grouping operations on it. The `having` keyword is another special operation associated with grouping that acts like a `where` clause and limits the output produced by the selection. The criteria for including or excluding data using the `having` clause can be identified in one of two ways. A criterion can be a hard-coded value or it can be based on the results of a `select` statement embedded into the overarching `select` statement. This embedded selection is called a subquery.

Another advanced function offered by `select` statements is the use of subqueries in the `where` clause of the `select` statement. There is no theoretical limit to the number of queries that can be nested in `select` statements, but it is not generally advisable to use more than half a dozen, for performance reasons. Subqueries allow the user to specify unknown search criteria for the comparisons in the `where` clause as opposed to using strictly hard-coded values. Subqueries also illustrate the principle of data scope in SQL statements; the user can specify columns that appear in the parent query, even when those columns do not appear in the table used in the subquery.

Another special operation that can be used in the `where` clause of a `select` statement is `exists`. This operation produces a TRUE or FALSE value based on whether or not the related subquery produces data. The `exists` clause is a popular option in their `select` statements.

Output from a query can be placed into an order specified by the user with the assistance of the `order by` clause. However, the user must make sure that the columns in the `order by` clause are the same as those actually listed by the outermost `select` statement. The `order by` clause can also be used in subqueries; however, since the subqueries of a `select` statement are usually used to determine a valid value for searching or as a part of an `exists` clause, the user should be more concerned about the existence of the data than the order in which data is returned from the subquery. Therefore, there is not much value added to using the `order by` clause in subqueries.

One final advanced technique covered in this chapter is the specification of variables at run time. This technique is especially valuable in providing reusability in a data-selection statement. In order to denote a runtime variable in SQL, the user should place a variable name in the comparison operation for which the runtime value is to be specified. The name of that variable in the `select` statement should be preceded with a special character to denote it as a variable. By default, this character is an ampersand (`&`). However, the default variable specification character can be changed with the use of the `set define` command at the prompt.

Runtime variables can be specified for SQL statements in other ways, as well. The `define` command can be used to identify a runtime variable for a `select` statement automatically. After being specified in the `define` command, a variable is specified for the entire session or until it is altered with the `undefine` command. In this way, the user can avoid the entire process of having to input values for the runtime variables. The final technique covered in this chapter on `select` statements is the use of `accept` to redefine the text displayed for the input prompt. More cosmetic than anything else, `accept` allows the user to display a more helpful message than the Oracle default message for data entry.

Two-Minute Drill

- `Select` statements that obtain data from more than one table and merge the data together are called joins.
- In order to join data from two tables, there must be a common column.
- A common column between two tables can create a foreign key, or link, from one table to another. This condition is especially true if the data in one of the tables is part of the primary key—the column that defines uniqueness for rows on a table.
- A foreign key can create a parent/child relationship between two tables.
- One type of join is the inner join, or equijoin. An equijoin operation is based on an equality operation linking the data in common columns of two tables.
- Another type of join is the outer join. An outer join returns data in one table even when there is no data in the other table. The "other" table in the outer join operation is called the outer table.

- The common column that appears in the outer table of the join must have a special marker next to it in the comparison operation of the `select` statement that creates the table.
- The outer join marker is as follows: `(+)`.
- If the column name is the same in both tables, common columns in tables used in join operations must be preceded either with a table alias that denotes the table in which the column appears, or the entire table name.
- The data from a table can be joined to itself. This technique is useful in determining whether there are rows in the table that have slightly different values but are otherwise duplicate rows.
- Table aliases must be used in self join `select` statements.
- Data output from table `select` statements can be grouped together according to criteria set by the query.
- A special clause exists to assist the user in grouping data together. That clause is called `group by`.
- There are several grouping functions that allow you to perform operations on data in a column as though the data were logically one variable.
- The grouping functions are `max( )`, `min( )`, `sum( )`, `avg( )`, `stddev( )`, `variance( )`, and `count( )`.
- These grouping functions can be applied to the column values for a table as a whole or for subsets of column data for rows returned in `group by` statements.
- Data in a `group by` statement can be excluded or included based on a special set of `where` criteria defined specifically for the group in a `having` clause.
- The data used to determine the `having` clause can either be specified at run time by the query or by a special embedded query, called a subquery, which obtains unknown search criteria based on known search methods.
- Subqueries can be used in other parts of the `select` statement to determine unknown search criteria, as well. Subqueries are generally included in this fashion in the `where` clause.
- Subqueries can use columns in comparison operations that are either local to the table specified in the subquery or use columns that are specified in tables named in any parent query to the subquery. This use is based on the principles of variable scope as presented in this chapter.

- Variables can be set in a `select` statement at run time with use of runtime variables. A runtime variable is designated with the ampersand character (&) preceding the variable name.
- The special character that designates a runtime variable can be changed using the `set define` command.
- A command called `define` can identify a runtime variable value to be picked up by the `select` statement automatically.
- Once defined, the variable remains defined for the rest of the session or until undefined by the user or process with the `undefine` command.
- A user can modify the message that prompts the user to input a variable value. This activity is performed with the `accept` command.

Chapter Questions

1. Which of the following is not a group function?

A. `avg( )`

B. `sqrt( )`

C. `sum( )`

D. `max( )`

2. In order to perform an inner join, which criteria must be true?

A. The common columns in the join do not need to have shared values.

B. The tables in the join need to have common columns.

C. The common columns in the join may or may not have shared values.

D. The common columns in the join must have shared values.

3. Once defined, how long will a variable remain defined in SQL*Plus?

A. Until the database is shut down

B. Until the instance is shut down

C. Until the statement completes

D. Until the session completes

4. You want to change the prompt Oracle uses to obtain input from a user. Which two of the following choices are used for this purpose? (Choose two)

A. Change the prompt in the `config.ora` file.

B. Alter the `prompt` clause of the `accept` command.

C. Enter a new prompt in the `login.sql` file.

D. There is no way to change a prompt in Oracle.

5. No search criteria for the EMP table are known. Which of the following options are appropriate for use when search criteria is unknown for comparison operations in a `select` statement? (Choose two)

A. `select * from emp where empid = &empid;`

B. `select * from emp where empid = 69494;`

C.
```
select * from emp where empid =
(select empid from invoice where invoice_no =
4399485);
```

D. `select * from emp;`

6. The default character for specifying substitution variables in `select` statements is

A. Ampersand

B. Ellipses

C. Quotation marks

D. Asterisk

7. A user is setting up a join operation between tables EMP and DEPT. There are some employees in the EMP table that the user wants returned by the query, but the employees are not assigned to department heads yet. Which `select` statement is most appropriate for this user?

A. `select e.empid, d.head from emp e, dept d;`

B.
```
select e.empid, d.head from emp e, dept d where
e.dept# = d.dept#;
```

C. `select e.empid, d.head from emp e, dept d where e.dept# = d.dept# (+);`

D. `select e.empid, d.head from emp e, dept d where e.dept# (+) = d.dept#;`

8. Which of the following uses of the `having` clause are appropriate? (Choose three)

A. To put returned data into sorted order

B. To exclude certain data groups based on known criteria

C. To include certain data groups based on unknown criteria

D. To include certain data groups based on known criteria

9. A Cartesian product is

A. A group function

B. Produced as a result of a join `select` statement with no `where` clause

C. The result of fuzzy logic

D. A special feature of Oracle server

10. The default character that identifies runtime variables is changed by

A. Modifying the `init`*`sid`*`.ora` file

B. Modifying the `login.sql` file

C. Issuing the `define` *`variablename`* command

D. Issuing the `set define` command

11. Which line in the following `select` statement will produce an error?

A. `select dept, avg(salary)`

B. `from emp`

C. `group by empid;`

D. There are no errors in this statement.

Answers to Chapter Questions

1. B. `sqrt( )`

Explanation Square root operations are performed on one column value. Review the discussion of available group functions.

2. B. The tables in the join need to have common columns.

Explanation It is possible that a join operation will produce no return data, just as it is possible for any `select` statement not to return any data. Choices A, C, and D represent the spectrum of possibilities for shared values that may or may not be present in common columns. However, joins themselves are not possible without two tables having common columns. Refer to the discussion of table joins.

3. D. Until the session completes

Explanation A variable defined by the user during a session with SQL*Plus will remain defined until the session ends or until the user explicitly undefines the variable. Refer to the discussion of defining variables earlier in the chapter.

4. B and C. Alter the `prompt` clause of the `accept` command *and* enter a new prompt in the `login.sql` file.

Explanation Choice D should be eliminated immediately, leaving the user to select between A, B, and C. Choice A is incorrect because `config.ora` is a feature associated with Oracle's client/server network communications product. Choice C is correct, because you can use the set `sqlprompt` command within your `login.sql` file. This is a special file Oracle users can incorporate into their use of Oracle that will automatically configure aspects of the SQL*Plus session, such as the default text editor, column and NLS data formats, and other items.

5. A and C.

Explanation Choice A details the use of a runtime variable that can be used to have the user input an appropriate search criteria after the statement has begun processing. Choice C details the use of a subquery that allows the user to select unknown search criteria from the database using known methods for obtaining the data. Choice B is incorrect because the statement simply provides a known search criteria; choice D is incorrect because it provides no search criteria at all. Review the discussion of defining runtime variables and subqueries.

6. A. Ampersand

Explanation The ampersand (&) character is used by default to define runtime variables in SQL*Plus. Review the discussion of the definition of runtime variables and the `set define` command.

7. C. `select e.empid, d.head from emp e, dept d where e.dept# = d.dept# (+);`

Explanation Choice C details the outer join operation most appropriate to this user's needs. The outer table in this join is the DEPT table, as identified by the (+) marker next to the DEPT# column in the comparison operation that defines the join.

8. B, C, and D. To exclude certain data groups based on known criteria, to include certain data groups based on unknown criteria, *and* to include certain data groups based on known criteria

Explanation All exclusion or inclusion of grouped rows is handled by the `having` clause of a `select` statement. Choice A is not an appropriate answer because sort order is given in a `select` statement by the `order by` clause.

9. B. Produced as a result of a join `select` statement with no `where` clause.

Explanation A Cartesian product is the result dataset from a `select` statement where all data from both tables is returned. Some potential causes of a Cartesian product include not specifying a `where` clause for the join `select` statement. Review the discussion of performing join `select` statements.

10. D. Issuing the `set define` command

Explanation Choice A is incorrect because a change to the `initsid.ora` file will alter the parameters Oracle uses to start the database instance. Use of this feature will be covered in the next unit. Choice B is incorrect because although the `login.sql` file can define many properties in a SQL*Plus session, the character that denotes runtime variables is not one of them. Choice C is incorrect because the `define` command is used to define variables used in a session, not an individual statement. Review the discussion of defining runtime variables in `select` statements.

11. C. `group by empid;`

Explanation Since the EMPID column does not appear in the original list of columns to be displayed by the query, it cannot be used in a `group by` statement. Review the discussion of using `group by` in `select` statements.

CHAPTER 3

Creating Oracle Database Objects

In this chapter, you will learn about and demonstrate knowledge in the following topics:

- Data modeling and database design
- Creating the tables of an Oracle database
- The Oracle data dictionary
- Manipulating Oracle data

The topics covered in this chapter include data modeling, creating tables, the data dictionary, and data manipulation. With mastery of these topics, the user of an Oracle system moves more into the world of application development. Typically, it is the application developer who creates database objects and determines how users will access those objects in production environments. The database administrator (DBA) is then the person who is responsible for migrating developed objects into production and then managing the needs of production systems. This chapter will lay the foundation for discussion of Oracle database object creation and other advanced topics, so it is important to review this material carefully. The OCP Exam 1 test questions in this subject area are worth 15 percent of the final score.

Data Modeling and Database Design

In this section, you will cover the following topics related to data modeling:

- The stages of system development
- The basic types of data relationships
- The relational database components
- Reading an entity-relationship diagram

Computer programs are the most animate of inanimate objects. Like the people who use, develop, and maintain them, software applications are dynamic creatures that are subject to the same constraints and realities as the very realities they try to model. Software applications are also subject to economic constraints, as any analyst who has spent months planning a project only to have the project's funds pulled at the last minute will attest. In so attempting to model reality, software applications become reality. This section will help you understand several areas of developing software applications that use databases. The first topic covers the stages of system development. The next section explains the basic types of data relationships in Oracle. After that, you will learn about the components of a relational database. Last, you learn how to read an entity-relationship diagram, also known as an ERD.

Stages of System Development

The first part of the software development life cycle is generally the one that most people pay attention to. This period of development is followed by a production phase, which may or may not involve the creation of enhancements. As time goes on, the users and developers of the project attempt to incorporate more features into the production system. After quite a long time, usually, advances in the industry or the emergence of new system requirements that the original technology cannot handle will cause the system's use to wane, until finally the data from the system will be archived or converted into a new system and the old system itself will be retired.

The steps involved in the software development life cycle are as follows:

- Needs assessment
- Database design
- Application development
- Performance tuning
- Database security
- Enhancements

Needs Assessment

A database system begins as an idea in someone's head. At this early stage in the game, a database application's possibilities can seem endless—however, this stage is as fraught with danger as other stages in the model. Many questions should be answered by the end of this planning stage.

The first question that can be asked about an application is "Will this application support large-volume data entry, or is the fundamental point of this application to make data viewable to users?" In many cases, the answer is both. By the end of needs assessment, the designer of an application should have clear answers to the following questions:

- Who will use the application?
- What use will the application fill in the organization?
- How do people plan on using the application?

Recent successes involving user-facilitated meetings show that the success of a project can often be improved with the early and frequent involvement of users in the project.

Once the users' needs have been assessed, the developers can determine what data and tools are available for use. In this phase of software development, the developers of a software application must assess many things, such as process flow for data within the system, and the ways data can be presented to the user both on the screen and in reports. Generally, a database software application involves three components, all of which should be planned before they are created: the user interface, the database, and the reports.

Database Design

The database design lays the groundwork for success in supporting the current and future needs of the application. The two steps of designing a database are these:

- Creating an entity-relationship diagram
- Translating an entity-relationship diagram into a logical data model

Creating an entity-relationship diagram and translating it into a logical data model is an involved process. The process is important, however, in ensuring correctly designed tables that can support both the user interface and the reports. Even though the users will interface with the database via the application in a controlled manner, it is still important to have a strong database design to ensure the success of the application. This process will be discussed again in this chapter's final section, "Reading an Entity-Relationship Diagram."

Application Development

Once the users' needs are assessed and the database design is in place, the building of the application logic can begin. Some components of the application can be placed within the database, such as integrity constraints, triggers, stored procedures, packages, and tuned SQL statements that take into account how Oracle optimizes its processing. Application development is often a task that involves stepwise refinement. As needs arise, or as hidden intricacies of a current process are uncovered, the application software that models business rules will undoubtedly grow more complex. PL/SQL is Oracle's procedural language extension to SQL. PL/SQL enables you to mix SQL statements with procedural constructs. With PL/SQL, you can define and execute PL/SQL program units, such as procedures, functions, and packages.

Performance Tuning

No application is harder to use than a slow one. The source of most performance issues in applications using Oracle databases is the application code itself. The application developers should, wherever possible, explore alternative methods for providing the same data to the user interface or reports in order to find the method that performs best. This step may involve developing alternative blocks of code that pull the same data from the database and executing benchmark tests to compare performance. This step may also involve the maintenance of two different databases, or at the very least, the ability to stop and restart a database with initialization parameters set to handle different periods of operation, such as daily production and weekend maintenance.

Database Security

Database security is an important factor in any database, allowing the developers and managers for the database system to handle large user populations, if necessary, and to limit database access to those users who require it. Early on in the development of an application the levels of data access that will be granted to each user or type of user in the system should be determined. Users should be divided into rough categories to determine what data they need to access to perform their tasks.

Once general access and usage levels for various users are established, there are features within the Oracle database that allow the developer or the DBA to limit users to only their access level or to restrict their usage of the database to only what they need. Some key terms to know here are *privileges* and *roles* for managing user access, and *resource profiles* for managing system hardware usage.

Enhancements

Enhancements are often as important as the actual application in the minds of the users, because they represent an evolution of the business process that must be modeled by the application supporting that business process. However, in some ways, developing enhancements is often riskier than developing the original application, itself. Some of the advantages of the initial application development, such as reduced production burden on the developers of the application, a structured project plan, funding, and management attention, are lost once the application sees its first few months of successful production life. When enhancements are requested, the developers often have to do double duty—they are both the enhancement developers who have to rework existing code *and* the analysts who have to handle the production issues of the application as they arise. However, these obstacles represent an opportunity for success as much as one for failure. Strong project management in these situations generally helps the enhancement development effort to succeed.

Exercises

1. What are the stages of the software development life cycle?
2. What important questions should be answered before the application is developed?

Basic Types of Data Relationships

The focus of this discussion is to present the areas of data modeling and database design. In order to model data, there must be relationships between the various components that make up a database design. These components are stored as data, while the relationships between data can be defined either explicitly, via the use of integrity constraints and/or database triggers that model business rules, or implicitly, by the data manipulation statements that select data for viewing or populate the database with new data. The following data relationships will be discussed in this section:

- Primary keys
- Functional dependency
- Foreign keys

One type of data relationship starts in the tables that comprise the Oracle database. So far, we have seen many tables containing data. One common element in all the tables shown is that they contain multiple columns that "hang off of" one main column, called a primary key. This primary key is one or more columns that determine the uniqueness of every row in the database. In the primary key, there can be no duplicate value for any row in the entire table. Each column that is not part of the primary key is considered to be *functionally dependent* on the primary key. This term simply means that the dependent column stores data that relates directly to or modifies directly the primary key value for that row. For example, suppose you have a table called APPLE_TABLE with two columns called APPLE_TYPE and COLOR. The APPLE_TYPE column would function well as the primary key because it uniquely identifies a type of apple you might store in the table. The COLOR column would function well as the functionally dependent column because color has little meaning taken by itself, but does a great job of enhancing your understanding of APPLE_TYPE.

One other relationship is the foreign key. This relationship is often referred to as a parent/child relationship because of where the data must appear in each table in order to create the foreign-key relationship. In the child table, the data can appear either as part of the primary key or as a functionally dependent column. However, in the parent table, the referenced column must appear in the primary key. The concept of a foreign key will be explained in detail later when we discuss constraints, where you will see some examples of this to round out your understanding.

Exercises

1. What are three types of data relationships?
2. What is functional dependency?
3. What is required of two tables in order for the tables to be related to one another?

Relational Database Components

A relational database consists of many components, some of which already have been covered. These components include objects that store data, objects that aid in accessing data quickly, and objects that manage user access to data. Additionally, there are objects in the database that contain the code that is used to manipulate and change data, to produce reports of data, and to otherwise use data to produce the desired result.

Some of the objects that are part of the relational database produced by Oracle and that are used in the functions just mentioned are as follows:

- **Tables, views, and synonyms** Used to store and access data
- **Indexes and the SQL processing mechanism** Used to speed access to data
- **Triggers and integrity constraints** Used to maintain the validity of data entered
- **Privileges, roles, and profiles** Used to manage database access and usage
- **Packages, procedures, and functions** Used to code the applications that will use the database

A relational database works on the principle of having relational data within tables. The relational data models real-world business situations through the use of datasets, called tables, that can contain different elements or columns. These columns then are able to relate to other columns in other tables, or simply to the primary key via functional dependency.

Exercises

1. What is a relational database model?
2. What are the components of a relational database? How are they used?

Reading an Entity-Relationship Diagram

Every database starts out as an entity-relationship diagram. In order to model a business process, the developers of an application must first map out the different components of a system. This map of a business process is often referred to as the *entity-relationship diagram,* or *ERD* for short. The ERD consists of two different components:

- **Entity** A person, place, thing, or idea involved in the business-process flow
- **Relationship** The ties that bind entities together

In order to explain the process of creating an ERD, we'll go through an example. This example is of a business process used by employees of an organization to obtain reimbursement for expenses that they may have incurred on behalf of their employer. Already in this description, a few entities have emerged in the description of the application to be created, namely *employee* (a person), *expenses* (things), and the *employer* (a person or group of people). A relationship has also been identified, *obtain reimbursement,* or "pay," which is an activity. Figure 3-1 shows an entity-relationship diagram for this example.

Often, a database application begins with looking at the process as it already exists. For this example, assume there is inefficiency in the current process. There may be several different points of entry of data, and there is the possibility that copies will get lost. Finally, there is the turnaround lag in paying employees. If there is a problem, the employee will not know about it for several weeks. On top of that, it may take several more weeks for the problem to be corrected. These reasons are enough to justify the need for a more automated process, and the ERD is the mechanism to model that process.

From ERD to LDM

An entity-relationship diagram helps in understanding the process flow of data through the system. Once an entity-relationship diagram is created, the developer must then create a special diagram that models the data stored in a database to represent the entities and relationships in the ERD. The name of this special diagram is *logical data model,* or *LDM* for short. The LDM will be used to display how all

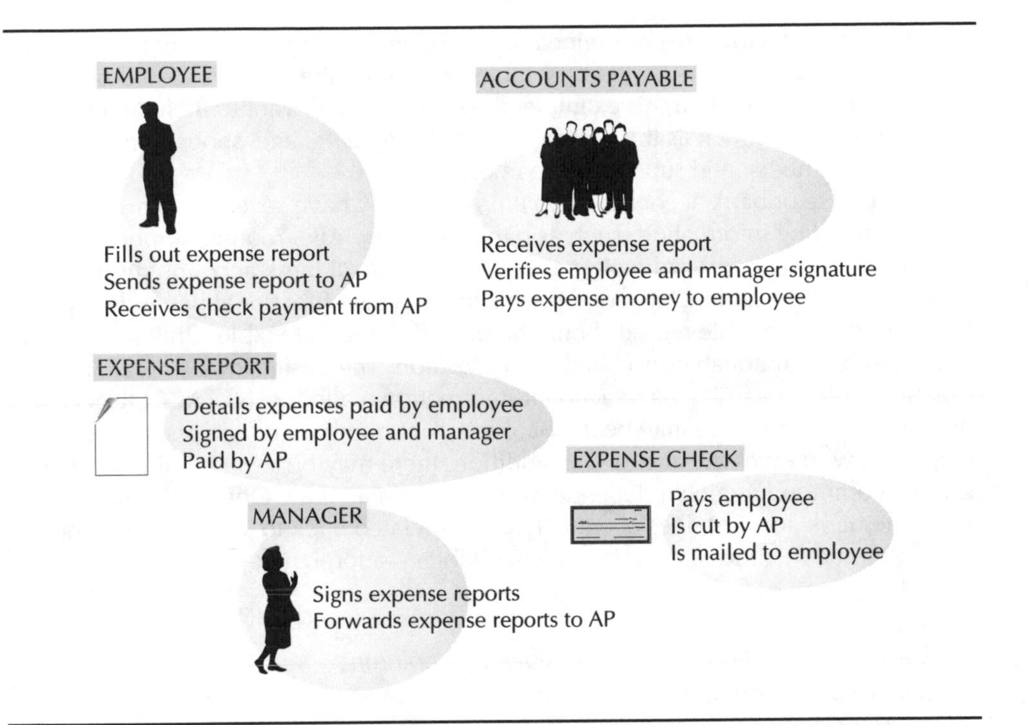

FIGURE 3-1. *An entity-relationship diagram of the employee expense system*

data relating to the business process being modeled is stored in the database. A logical data model consists of a diagrammatic representation of tables in a database. Some of the tables for this example are EMPLOYEE, EXPENSE, BANK_ACCOUNT, and PHONE_NUMBER.

The first step in creating a list of table columns is to determine what will be the unique characteristic of any row in the table. The unique identifier for all employees may be a social security number or some other unique integer assigned by the company to an employee for the term of that employee's employment.

The second step is determining what features about employees need to be included in the EMPLOYEE table, and which should be stored elsewhere in the database. The determination about whether to incorporate data as a column into the EMPLOYEE table should rest on two conditions:

- Is this data functionally dependent on the primary key?
- Will there be only one copy of this data per appearance of the primary key?

Once these factors are determined, the designer will know whether the column should be included in the EMPLOYEE table or whether the column should be used to define another table. In this example, the designer may want to include a few different elements, such as the person's name, hiring date, age, spouse's name, telephone numbers, and supervisor's name.

In the case of bank accounts, each employee may have several, each with a set of corresponding information, such as bank name and ABA routing number. The additional storage overhead makes it difficult to store all bank account information in the EMPLOYEE table. Data components that have no functional dependency on the other data in a table record should be placed in separate tables; this separation of data into separate tables is called *normalization*. The designer may create a separate table containing bank account information, called BANK_ACCOUNT. The primary key of this table may be the bank account number and the associated employee who owns the account. In addition, there may be several columns that share a common functional dependency on the primary key. One final point is that since the bank account does eventually get associated back to an employee, there must be some method to associate the two tables—a foreign key.

TIP
Data normalization is the act of separating column data into tables where each column in the table is functionally dependent on only one primary key. This process reduces data-storage costs by eliminating redundancy, and it minimizes the dependence of any column in the normalized database to only one primary key.

Role of Ordinality

Related to the discussion of foreign keys and table relationships is something called *ordinality*. The ordinality of a table relationship represents two important features about the relationship:

- Whether the relationship is mandatory or optional for these objects
- Whether one record in the table corresponds to one or to many records in the other table

The ordinality of a table relationship contains two elements and is generally represented in the logical data model as an "ordered pair," usually (0,*N*) or (1,1), or (1,*N*), or something similar. The first component in the ordered pair identifies whether the relationship is mandatory or optional. The number 1 indicates the relationship is mandatory, whereas 0 indicates the relationship is optional. The second component of the ordered pair indicates whether one row in this table relates to one or many rows in the other table. The number 1 indicates a one-to-one relationship, while *N* indicates a one-to-many relationship.

In some cases, the relationship between two entities may not be required. Consider the example of employees and expenses. This relationship works in two directions: from employees to expenses, and from expenses to employees. In the direction of employees to expenses, the relationship is optional. That is to say, an employee need not have ever incurred expenses on behalf of the company. However, in the other direction, from expenses to employees, the relationship is mandatory because each and every expense submitted to the employee expense system will correspond to an employee. In the direction of employees to expenses there is a one-to-many relationship, as each employee in the company may have submitted one or more expense reports in the course of their employment, or none at all. In contrast, in the other direction, each expense submitted will always have one and only one employee who submitted it, as shown in Figure 3-2. In this figure, each ordered pair describes the relationship between the table closest to that

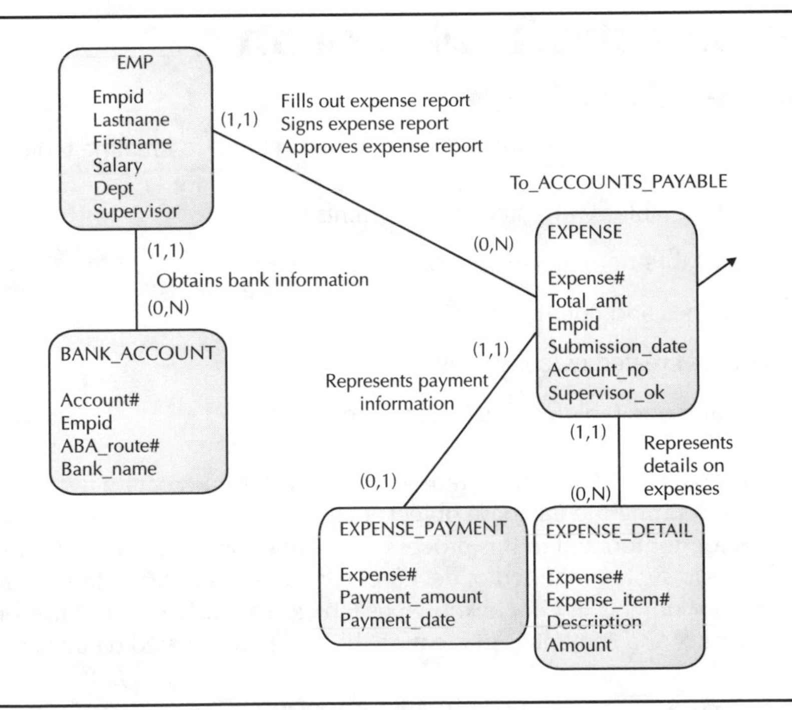

FIGURE 3-2. *The logical data model for the employee expense system*

ordered pair and the table at the other end of the connecting line. In the case of EMP and EXPENSE, the (1,1) ordered pair closest to table EMP indicates that mandatory one-to-one relationship of EMP rows to EXPENSE rows. The (0,N) ordered pair next to the EXPENSE table indicates that, in the other direction, EXPENSE rows have an optional one-to-many relationship to rows in table EMP. Note that you can use alternate notation to indicate relationships in ERDs and LDMs. Draw dotted lines between entities or tables for optional relationships and solid lines for mandatory relationships. "Crow's feet" indicate one-to-many data relationships between objects. The `erdnot.pdf` file on the CD-ROM illustrates use of this notation, which you need to understand for OCP Exam 1.

Exercises

1. What is an entity-relationship diagram, and how is it read?
2. What is a logical data model? Identify some methods used to translate an entity-relationship diagram into a data model.

Creating the Tables of an Oracle Database

In this section, you will cover the following topics related to creating tables:

- Creating tables with integrity constraints
- Using table-naming conventions
- Datatypes and column definitions
- Indexes created by constraints
- Creating one table with data from another

Once you have modeled the database, the next step in creating a database application is defining the database objects that will comprise the logical data model. A major component in this process is creating the tables. This discussion will explain the basic syntax required of developers and DBAs in order to produce the logical database objects in Oracle known as tables. The only material presented here is the syntax and semantics of creating the table and related database objects.

Creating a Table with Integrity Constraints

The basic creation of a table involves using the `create table` command. This statement is one of many database object creation statements known in Oracle as the data-definition language (DDL). Tables created can contain *integrity constraints*—rules that limit the type of data that can be placed in the table, row, or column. There are five types of integrity constraints: PRIMARY KEY, UNIQUE, FOREIGN KEY, CHECK, and NOT NULL. Two methods exist for defining constraints: the *table constraint method* and the *column constraint method*. The constraint is defined as a table constraint if the constraint syntax is part of the table definition, located away from the column datatype definition. The constraint is defined as a column constraint if the constraint definition syntax appears as part of a column definition. All constraints can be defined either as table constraints or as column constraints, except for NOT NULL constraints, which can only be defined as column constraints. The following code block displays two create table statements. The first shows definition of the primary key constraint defined as a table constraint, while the second shows definition of the primary key as a column constraint:

```
-- Table constraint definition
CREATE TABLE employee
(empid           NUMBER(10),
lastname         VARCHAR2(25),
firstname        VARCHAR2(25),
salary           NUMBER(10,4),
CONSTRAINT       pk_employee_01
PRIMARY KEY      (empid));

-- Column constraint equivalent definition
CREATE TABLE employee
(empid           NUMBER(10) primary key,
lastname         VARCHAR2(25),
firstname        VARCHAR2(25),
salary           NUMBER(10,4));
```

The main difference between use of table and column constraint definition methods is your ability to name your constraints yourself only when you define your constraint using the table constraint method. When you use the column constraint definition method, Oracle names the constraint for you. For simplicity sake throughout the rest of the chapter, you will work with constraint definitions defined as table constraints. Later in the book, you may see constraints defined both as table and column constraints.

The definition of a column as the primary key in a table produces a few noticeable effects within the database itself. The term *primary key* refers to a special designation for a constraint that says to Oracle, "don't let any row insert a column value for EMPID that is NULL or that is the same as a column value that already exists for another row." There are some special methods Oracle will use to enforce this integrity constraint. Column values that are part of primary keys have the following conditions enforced on them. Any value in the column for any row must be unique. Secondly, no row can define the value in a column as NULL if that column is part of the primary key. So, in this example, no employee in the EMPLOYEE table can have a NULL value defined for EMPID.

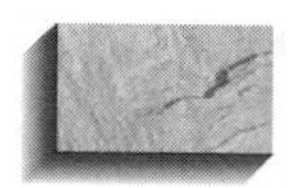

TIP
Integrity constraints are rules that are defined on table columns that prevent anyone from placing inappropriate data in the column. There are five types of integrity constraints: `PRIMARY KEY`, `FOREIGN KEY`, `UNIQUE`, `NOT NULL`, and `CHECK`.

Take another moment to review the definition that was determined for the BANK_ACCOUNT table. Remember that the BANK_ACCOUNT table was supposed to have the BANK_ACCT_NO column be its primary key, because that column defines the data that is unique about each row in the table. However, remember also that there is a special relationship between the BANK_ACCOUNT table and the EMPLOYEE table.

```
CREATE TABLE bank_account
(bank_acct_no          VARCHAR2(40),
empid                  NUMBER(10),
BANK_ROUTE_NO          VARCHAR2(40),
BANK_NAME              VARCHAR2(50),
CONSTRAINT             pk_bank_acct_01
PRIMARY KEY            (bank_acct_no),
CONSTRAINT             fk_bank_acct_01
FOREIGN KEY (empid) REFERENCES employee (empid));
```

Notice that in addition to the definition of a primary-key constraint, this table also has a foreign-key constraint. The syntax for the definition allows the column to reference another table's column, of either the same or a different name. In order for a foreign-key constraint to be valid, the columns in both tables must have exactly the same datatypes. (A discussion of datatypes and their significance will appear in the "Datatypes and Column Definitions" section, later in this chapter.) The designation `FOREIGN KEY` tells Oracle that the developer would like to create referential integrity between the EMPID columns in the BANK_ACCOUNT table and the EMPLOYEE table. This fact prevents a column in the child table (BANK_ACCOUNT) from containing a value that does not exist in the referenced column in the parent table (EMPLOYEE).

An option that can be specified along with the foreign key relates to the deletion of data from the parent. If someone attempts to `delete` a row from the parent table that contains a referenced value from the child table, Oracle will block the deletion unless the `on delete cascade` option is specified in the foreign-key definition of the `create table` statement. When the `on delete cascade` option is used,

Oracle will not only allow the user to `delete` a referenced record from the parent table, but the deletion will cascade into the child table as well.

```
CREATE TABLE bank_acct
(bank_acct_no          VARCHAR2(40),
empid                 NUMBER(10),
BANK_ROUTE_NO         VARCHAR2(40),
BANK_NAME             VARCHAR2(50),
CONSTRAINT            pk_bank_acct_01
PRIMARY KEY           (bank_acct_no),
CONSTRAINT            fk_bank_acct_01
FOREIGN KEY (empid) REFERENCES employee (empid)
ON DELETE CASCADE);
```

Other integrity constraints abound. There are five types of integrity constraints in all, including `PRIMARY` and `FOREIGN` keys, `UNIQUE` constraints, `NOT NULL` constraints, and `CHECK` constraints.

```
CREATE TABLE employee
(empid            NUMBER(10),
lastname          VARCHAR2(25),
firstname         VARCHAR2(25),
salary            NUMBER(10,4),
home_phone        number(15),
CONSTRAINT        pk_employee_01
PRIMARY KEY       (empid),
CONSTRAINT        uk_employee_01
UNIQUE            (home_phone));
```

The definition of a `UNIQUE` constraint on HOME_PHONE prevents anyone from defining a row that contains a phone number that is identical to the phone number of anyone else already in the table. There are two weaknesses in this definition. The first is that having a `UNIQUE` constraint on a home phone number makes it difficult to store records for employees who are spouses or roommates with the same telephone number. Another point to be made about `UNIQUE` constraints, and foreign-key constraints for that matter, is that there is no data integrity enforced if the column data value in a row is NULL. This is a special case scenario that applies only to NULL data in columns with foreign-key, `UNIQUE`, and `CHECK` constraints defined on them.

TIP
Foreign-key, `CHECK`, and `UNIQUE` integrity constraints for a column are not enforced on a row if the column data value for the row is NULL.

The final two types of constraints are NOT NULL constraints and CHECK constraints. The NOT NULL constraint prevents the data value defined by any row for the column from being NULL. By default, primary keys are defined to be NOT NULL. All other constraints are nullable unless the developer explicitly defines the column to be NOT NULL.

CHECK constraints allow Oracle to verify the validity of data being entered on a table against a set of constants that act as valid values. For example, you could specify that the SALARY column not contain values over $500,000. If someone tries to create an employee row with a salary of $1,000,000 per year, Oracle would return an error message saying that the record data defined for the SALARY column has violated the CHECK constraint for that column.

```
CREATE TABLE employee
(empid          NUMBER(10),
lastname        VARCHAR2(25)      NOT NULL,
firstname       VARCHAR2(25)      NOT NULL,
salary          NUMBER(10,4)      CHECK(salary<500000),
home_phone     number(15),
CONSTRAINT     pk_employee_01
PRIMARY KEY    (empid),
CONSTRAINT     uk_employee_01
UNIQUE         (home_phone));
```

Notice that in this table definition, there are *three* columns defined to be NOT NULL, including the primary key. The two others are the LASTNAME and FIRSTNAME columns. The NOT NULL table constraint will be applied to the columns, preventing anyone from creating a row for this table that does not contain a first and last name for the employee.

Notice also that the CHECK constraint has been created on this table. CHECK constraints have a number of limitations, all centering around the fact that the constraint can only refer to a specific set of constant values or operations on those values. A CHECK constraint cannot refer to another column or row in any table, including the one the constraint is defined on, and it cannot refer to special keywords that can have values in them, such as user, sysdate, or rowid. Thus, the CHECK constraint in the previous table definition is valid, but the one in the following excerpt from a table definition is not valid:

```
CREATE TABLE address
(...,
city    VARCHAR2(80)  check(city in (SELECT city FROM cities))
...);
```

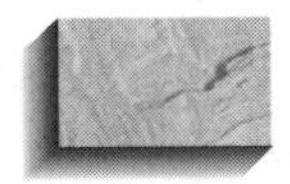

TIP

There are some special keywords that contain information about certain database conditions. These keywords, or pseudocolumns, are `user`, `sysdate`, and `rowid`. The `user` keyword gives the username of the owner of the current session. The `sysdate` keyword gives the current date and time at the time the statement is issued. The `rowid` keyword gives the ROWID of the row specified. These keywords cannot be used in conjunction with a `CHECK` constraint.

Exercises

1. Identify some table components that can be created when you issue the `create table` statement.
2. What is an integrity constraint? What are the five types of integrity constraints?

Using Table-Naming Conventions

There are many philosophies about the naming of variables, tables, columns, and other items in software that come from the early days of computing. Available memory and disk space was limited on those early machines, and so the names of variables in those environments were also small. This cryptic practice was born out of necessity. In many systems today, however, developers are not faced with that restriction. As a result, the names of variables, columns, and tables need not be bound by the naming rules of yesteryear. However, standards for naming tables and columns still have value, if only for the sake of readability. There are also rules about object names in Oracle.

Keep Names Short and Descriptive

Your naming convention in the Oracle database may be compact, but someone viewing variables in the database for the first time should also have some idea of what the variable is supposed to represent. For example, using the name EMP_LN_FN_SAL for the table created previously would not be as easily understood as simply calling the table EMPLOYEE, or even EMP. Also, most Oracle database object names can be between 1 and 30 characters long, except for databases (which have a maximum of 8 characters) and database links (with a maximum of 128 characters). Names are not case-sensitive.

Relate Names for Child Tables to Their Parent

In certain situations, the developers of an application may find themselves creating multiple tables to define a logical object. The developer may have a logical entity that is represented by several tables, which have a one-to-many relationship among them. Consider the EXPENSE table, which was defined to hold the expense summaries that employees submit in order to generate a feed to the AP system. The developer could define a second table in conjunction with the EXPENSE table called EXPENSE_ITEM, which stores detail information about each expense incurred. Both are descriptive names, and it is obvious from those names that there is some relationship between them.

Foreign-Key Columns Should Have the Same Name in Both Tables

If you are creating foreign-key relationships between columns in two different tables, it also helps if the referring and the referenced columns in both tables share the same name, making the potential existence of a foreign key a bit more obvious. However, you should make sure you use table aliases in your join statements when you reference columns that have the same name in both tables in order to avoid ambiguity, as in the following example:

```
SELECT A.EMPID, B.ACCTNO
FROM EMPL E, ACCT A
WHERE E.EMPID = A.EMPID;
```

Names of Associated Objects Should Relate to the Table

Other naming conventions include giving all integrity constraints, triggers, and indexes meaningful names that identify both the type of constraint created and the table to which the constraint belongs. Consider some of the names chosen in the previous examples. They include PK_EMPLOYEE_01, which is a primary key (PK) on the EMPLOYEE table; or FK_EMPLOYEE_01, which is a foreign key defined for the EMPLOYEE table. The name of the foreign key includes a reference to the table to which the foreign-key constraint belongs.

Avoid Quotes, Keywords, and Nonalphanumeric Characters

You can't use quotes in the name of a database object. Nor can you use a nonalphanumeric character, with three exceptions: the dollar sign ($), the underscore (_), and the hash mark (#), sometimes also called the pound sign. The dollar sign is most notable in naming dynamic performance views, while the hash mark is used in some data dictionary tables owned by a privileged user called SYS in Oracle. In general, you should steer clear of using $ or #. The underscore is useful for separating two words or abbreviations, such as EXPENSE_ITEM, or BANK_ACCOUNT.

Other Miscellaneous Naming Rules

Here are a few more naming rules to keep in mind:

- Do not use special characters from European or Asian character sets in a database name, global database name, or database link names. For example, characters with an umlaut (¨) are not allowed.
- An object name cannot be an Oracle reserved word, such as `select` or `from`, a datatype such as NUMBER, or a built-in function, such as `decode( )`. Oracle may not complain when you create the object, but it may give you an unpleasant surprise when you refer to the object in your SQL statement.
- Don't name a table DUAL, because, as you know, Oracle already a table called DUAL that is accessible by everyone.
- Do not use table names beginning with "SYS."
- A user cannot own or refer to two objects with the same name, so if you own a table called EMP, and user SPANKY owns a table called EMP, you must prefix the name of the table with the owner when referencing the table, as in YOU.EMP or SPANKY.EMP.
- Depending on the product you plan to use to access a database object, names might be further restricted by other product-specific reserved words. For a list of a product's reserved words, see the manual for that specific product.

Exercises

1. Describe some table-naming conventions.
2. What should be included in the name of a table that has a referential integrity constraint with another table, in which the table referring to the other table is the child table?

Datatypes and Column Definitions

The use of datatypes to identify the type of data a column can hold has been mentioned a few times in this chapter. At this point, it is necessary to discuss the available datatypes in the Oracle database. In the tables defined and discussed so far, we have used alphanumeric datatypes that store text strings, such as CHAR and VARCHAR2, the NUMBER datatype that stores numeric data only, and the DATE datatype.

Here is a list of datatypes and their descriptions:

Datatype	Description
VARCHAR2	Contains variable length text strings of up to 4,000 bytes in Oracle8
CHAR	Contains fixed text strings of up to 2,000 bytes in Oracle8
NUMBER	Contains numeric data
DATE	Contains date data
RAW	Contains binary data of up to 2,000 bytes in Oracle8
LONG	Contains text data of up to 2 gigabytes
LONG RAW	Contains binary data of up to 2 gigabytes
ROWID	Contains the row's address for table rows
BLOB	Large binary object (Oracle8 only)
CLOB	Large character-based object (Oracle8 only)
NCLOB	Large single- or multibyte character-based object (Oracle8 only)
BFILE	Large external file (Oracle8 only)

There are two alphanumeric datatypes—a CHAR datatype and a VARCHAR2 datatype. Both the CHAR and the VARCHAR2 variable datatypes can be defined to hold character strings, but there are some subtle differences. First, the CHAR datatype only supports character strings up to a length of 2,000 bytes for Oracle8, while the VARCHAR2 datatype supports character strings up to a length of 4,000 bytes for Oracle8. Second, and perhaps most important, when Oracle stores data in a CHAR datatype, it will pad the value stored in the column with blanks up to the declared length of the column. In contrast, Oracle will not store padded blank spaces if the same value is stored in a column defined as datatype VARCHAR2. To illustrate, if a column called LASTNAME was defined as CHAR(50) and the value "BRADY" was assigned to it, the value Oracle would store would actually be "BRADY" with 45 blank spaces to the right of it. That same value stored in a column defined as datatype VARCHAR2 would be stored simply as "BRADY".

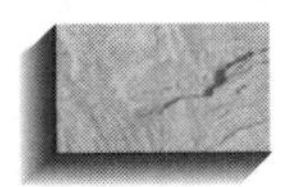

TIP

VARCHAR2 has the "2" on the end of the name because there may be a VARCHAR datatype defined in future releases of Oracle. Although VARCHAR and VARCHAR2 are currently synonymous, they may not be in the future, so Oracle recommends using VARCHAR2.

The NUMBER datatype that is used to store number data can be specified either to store integers or decimals with the addition of a parenthetical precision indicator. For example, if you had a column defined to be datatype `NUMBER(15,2)`, the number 49309.593 would be stored as 49309.59 because the number specified after the comma in the parenthetical precision definition of the datatype represents the number of places to the right of the decimal point that will be stored. The number on the left of the comma shows the total width of allowed values stored in this column, including the two places to the right of the decimal point. A column declared to be of type `NUMBER(9)` will not store any decimals at all. The number 49309.593 stored in a column defined in this way will appear as 49310, because Oracle automatically rounds up if the value is 5 or more in the precision area that the declared datatype will not support. You may also wonder what happens when you try to store 49309.593 in a column defined as a NUMBER(4) datatype. In this situation, Oracle returns an error—`ORA-01438: value larger than specified precision allows for this column.`

Another datatype that has already been discussed is the DATE datatype, which stores date values in a special Oracle format represented as the number of days since December 31, 4713 B.C.E. This datatype offers a great deal of flexibility to users who want to perform date manipulation operations, such as adding 30 days to a given date. In this case, all the user has to do is specify the column declared as a DATE datatype and add the number of days. Of course, there are also numerous functions that handle date operations more complex than simple arithmetic. Another nice feature of Oracle's method for date storage is that it is inherently millennium compliant. Beyond these datatypes, there is an entire set of important type declaration options available to the developer and DBA dedicated to storage of small and large amounts of text and unformatted binary data. These datatypes include LONG, RAW, and LONG RAW. RAW datatypes in Oracle store data in binary format up to 2000 bytes. It is useful to store graphics and sound files when used in conjunction with LONG to form the LONG RAW datatype, which can accommodate up to 2 gigabytes of data. The developer can declare columns to be of LONG datatype, which stores up to 2 gigabytes of alphanumeric text data. There can be only one column declared to be of type LONG in a table.

The entire operation of storing large blocks of data has been enhanced significantly as of Oracle8, in which BLOB, CLOB, and NCLOB objects, which can contain up to 4 gigabytes of data, are used to store binary, single-byte, and multibyte character-based objects in the Oracle database. Oracle8 stores this data outside of the table keeping pointers in the table to locate the object. This is in contrast to earlier versions of Oracle, where the actual LONG or LONG RAW data is stored inline with the rest of the table information. However, you should note that these older methods for large data storage are included in the current version of Oracle for backward compatibility.

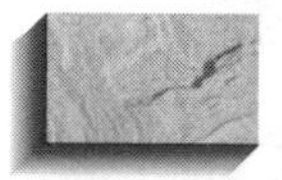

TIP
Storing data "inline" means that the data in a LONG datatype column is stored literally "in line" with the rest of the data in the row, as opposed to Oracle storing a pointer inline with row data, pointing to LONG column data stored somewhere else.

Finally, the ROWID datatype stores information related to the disk location of table rows. Generally, no column should be created to store data using type ROWID, but this datatype supports the ROWID virtual column associated with every table.

Exercises

1. Name several different datatypes available in Oracle. What are some differences between the LONG and CLOB datatypes with respect to where data is stored in relation to the overall table?
2. What are some of the differences between the CHAR and the VARCHAR2 datatypes?
3. How is data stored in the DATE datatype? What is the ROWID datatype?

Indexes Created by Constraints

Indexes are created automatically by Oracle to support integrity constraints that enforce uniqueness. The two types of integrity constraints that enforce uniqueness are `PRIMARY KEY` and `UNIQUE` constraints. Essentially, `UNIQUE` constraints in Oracle are the same as primary-key constraints, except for the fact that they allow NULL values. When the primary-key or the `UNIQUE` constraint is declared, the index that supports the uniqueness enforcement is also created, and all values in all columns that were defined as part of the primary key or UNIQUE constraint are placed into the index.

The name of the index depends on the name given to the constraint. For example, the following table definition statement creates one index on the primary-key column EMPID. EMPID cannot then contain any NULL values or any duplicates.

```
CREATE TABLE employee
(empid          NUMBER(10),
lastname        VARCHAR2(25)      NOT NULL,
firstname       VARCHAR2(25)      NOT NULL,
salary          NUMBER(10,4)      CHECK(salary<500000),
home_phone      number(15),
CONSTRAINT      pk_employee_01
PRIMARY KEY     (empid),
CONSTRAINT      uk_employee_01
UNIQUE          (home_phone));
```

The name of the index is the same as the name given to the primary key. Thus, the name given to the index created to support uniqueness on the primary key for this table is called PK_EMPLOYEE_01. There are performance benefits associated with indexes that will be discussed in the next chapter, but for now it is sufficient to say that the creation of an index in conjunction with the definition of a primary key is a handy feature of table declaration in Oracle.

Another important case to consider is the `UNIQUE` constraint index. If the `UNIQUE` constraint is defined in the manner detailed in the previous code example, then the name of the corresponding index in the database created automatically by Oracle to enforce the uniqueness of the column will be UK_EMPLOYEE_01. However, there is another method for declaring a `UNIQUE` constraint on a column such that the index created will remain somewhat anonymous, as shown below:

```
CREATE TABLE employee
(empid          NUMBER(10),
lastname        VARCHAR2(25)      NOT NULL,
firstname       VARCHAR2(25)      NOT NULL,
salary          NUMBER(10,4)      CHECK(salary<500000),
home_phone      number(15)        UNIQUE,
CONSTRAINT      pk_employee_01
PRIMARY KEY     (empid));
```

The `UNIQUE` constraint created in this situation will have the same properties as the `UNIQUE` constraint created in the previous code example. It will also enforce uniqueness on the HOME_PHONE column just as well as the constraint defined in the previous example. If you don't name your constraint, Oracle will name it for you. The name Oracle will generate in this situation is SYS_C*xxxxxx*, where *xxxxxx* is a six-digit number. The Oracle-generated name can also be less than six digits.

In summary, indexes are used to support the enforcement of unique integrity constraints, such as the primary-key and the `UNIQUE` constraints. If the constraint is explicitly named, the associated indexes can given a corresponding name, or the constraint can automatically be given a relatively anonymous name by Oracle when the UNIQUE index is created. It is important to bear in mind that with the creation of a table comes the creation of an associated primary-key index.

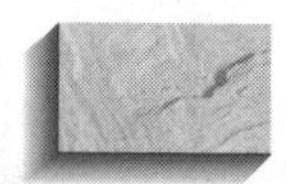

TIP
When a table is created, an index corresponding to the primary key of the table is created to enforce uniqueness and to speed performance on data selection that uses the primary key in the `where` clause of the `select` statement.

Exercises

1. Identify two constraints that create indexes.
2. What determines the name given to an index created automatically?
3. What two purposes does the index serve in the enforcement of its associated constraint?

Creating One Table with Data from Another

The final area of discussion in this section on creating tables is how to create a table with prepopulated data. In most cases, when a developer creates a table in Oracle, the table is empty—it has no data in it. Once created, the users or developers are then free to populate the table as long as proper access has been granted. However, there are some cases in which the developer can create a table that already has data in it. The general statement used to create tables in this manner is the `create table as select` statement, as shown here:

```
CREATE TABLE employee
(empid,
lastname,
firstname,
salary,
home_phone,
CONSTRAINT      pk_employee_01
PRIMARY KEY     (empid))
AS SELECT * FROM hrglobal.empl;
```

The final `as select` clause instructs Oracle to insert data into the table it just created from the table specified (HRGLOBAL.EMPL in this case). In order to use `select *`, the columns in the table from which data will be selected must be identical to the column specification made in the table just created. Alternatively, an exact copy of a table can be made without declaring any columns at all with the code block shown here:

```
CREATE TABLE employee
AS SELECT * FROM hrglobal.empl;
```

Finally, in the `select` statement that makes a copy of data, it is possible for the developer to specify any option, except `order by`, that the developer could use in any other `select` statement in the database. This feature includes the specification of column concatenation, selecting only a limited number of columns, limiting the number of rows returned with the `where` clause, or even using arithmetic and other single-row operations to modify data in virtually any way available on other `select` statements.

Exercises

1. How can a table be created with data already populated in it?
2. What limits are there on the data that can be selected in creating a table from existing data?

The Oracle Data Dictionary

In this section, we will cover the following topics related to the Oracle data dictionary:

- Available dictionary views
- Querying the data dictionary

Few resources in the Oracle database are as useful as the Oracle data dictionary. Developers, DBAs, and users will find themselves referring to the data dictionary time and time again to resolve questions about object availability, roles and privileges, and performance. Whatever the information, Oracle has it all stored in the data dictionary. This discussion will introduce the major components of the data dictionary in the Oracle database, pointing out its features and highlights in order to set the groundwork for fuller discussions on the data dictionary in later chapters. It is important to understand the major data dictionary concepts before moving on, as data dictionary views will be referred to in many other areas throughout this guide.

Available Dictionary Views

There are scores of dictionary tables available in the Oracle data dictionary, used to keep track of many of the database objects. The dictionary tells you just about anything you need to know about the database, including which objects can be seen by the user, which objects are available, the current performance status of the database, and so on.

There are a few basic facts about the data dictionary that you should know. First, the Oracle data dictionary consists of tables where information about the database is stored. The SYS user in Oracle is the only user allowed to `update` those dictionary tables. Oracle processes routinely do this as part of their processing, but a user such as the DBA should never do so except to periodically `update` and `delete` records from the SYS.AUD$ table, which stores audit trail records.

Rather than having users manipulate the dictionary tables directly, Oracle has several views on the dictionary tables through which users get a distilled look at the dictionary contents. A *view* is a database object somewhat like a "virtual table." The data in a view is pulled from a real table by way of a `select` statement and stored in memory. The Oracle data dictionary allows users to see the available database objects to various depths, depending on their needs as users.

The views of the data dictionary are divided into three general categories that correspond to the depth of the database users are permitted to view. The three general categories of views are as follows, with the text in capitals at the beginning of each point corresponding to text that is prefixed onto the name of the dictionary views in question.

- **USER_** These views typically allow the user to see all relevant database objects that are owned by the user accessing the view.
- **ALL_** These views typically allow the user to see all relevant database objects that are accessible to the user.
- **DBA_** This powerful set of views allows those who may access them to see all database objects appropriate to the view in the entire database.

The USER_ views are generally those views with the least scope. They only display a limited amount of information about the database objects that the user created in his or her own schema. One way that tables can be referred to is by their schema owner. For example, assume there is a database with a user named SPANKY. Suppose SPANKY creates some tables in her user schema, one of which is called PRODUCTS, and then grants access to those tables to another user on the database called ATHENA. User ATHENA can then refer to SPANKY's tables as SPANKY.PRODUCTS, or SPANKY.*tablename* for a more general format. However,

if user ATHENA attempts to look in the USER_TABLES view to gather more information about table PRODUCTS, she will find nothing in that view about it. Why? Because the table belongs to user SPANKY.

The next level of scope in dictionary views comes with the ALL_ views. The objects whose information is displayed in the ALL_ views correspond to any database object that the user can look at, change data in, or access in any way. In order for a user to be able to access a database object, one of three conditions must be true. The user must have created the object, the user must have been granted access by the object owner to manipulate the object or data in the object, or the owner of the object must have granted access privileges on the object to the PUBLIC user. The PUBLIC user in the database is a special user who represents the access privileges every user has. Thus, when an object owner creates a table and grants access to the table to user PUBLIC, then every user in the database has access privileges to the table created.

The final category of data dictionary views available on the database is the DBA_ views. These views are incredibly handy for DBAs, who need to be able to find out information about every database object. Thus, the DBA_TABLES view displays information about every table in the database. Developers should note that this view allows the user to see objects in the database that the user may not even have permission to use. It can be a violation of security to allow certain users to be aware of the existence of certain tables. Usually, the developer will not have access to DBA_ views.

The name of each view normally has two components: the scope or depth to which the user will be able to see information about the object in the database (USER_, ALL_, DBA_), followed by the name of the object type itself. For example, information about tables in the database can be found in the USER_TABLES, ALL_TABLES, or DBA_TABLES views. Some other views that correspond to areas that have been or will be discussed are listed here:

- **USER_, ALL_, DBA_OBJECTS** Gives information about various database objects
- **USER_, ALL_, DBA_TABLES** Displays information about tables in the database
- **USER_, ALL_, DBA_INDEXES** Displays information about indexes in the database
- **USER_, ALL_, DBA_VIEWS** Displays information about views in the database
- **USER_, ALL_, DBA_SEQUENCES** Displays information about sequences in the database; a sequence is a database object that generates numbers in sequential order

- **USER_, ALL_, DBA_USERS** Displays information about users in the database
- **USER_, ALL_, DBA_CONSTRAINTS** Displays information about constraints in the database
- **USER_, ALL_, DBA_CONS_COLUMNS** Displays information about table columns that have constraints in the database
- **USER_, ALL_, DBA_IND_COLUMNS** Displays information about table columns that have indexes in the database
- **USER_, ALL_, DBA_TAB_COLUMNS** Displays information about columns in tables in the database

Exercises

1. What is the data dictionary?
2. What are the three categories of views that a user may access in the dictionary? How much information about the database is available in each view?
3. Who owns the data dictionary? Are users allowed to access the tables of the dictionary directly? Why or why not?

Querying the Data Dictionary

We'll now look at ways for you to select data from the dictionary so you can better understand how useful the data dictionary is in Oracle. (For the purposes of this section, the ALL_ views will be used, except where noted.) Consider first the need to get information about tables. Every user should learn how to list the columns available in a table. A listing of the columns in a table can be obtained from the dictionary with the use of the `describe` command, often abbreviated as `desc`. Note that this is a SQL*Plus command, so you cannot use it in PL/SQL code.

```
DESC spanky.products

NAME                 NULL?        TYPE
---------            -----        ------
PRODUCT              NOT NULL     NUMBER
PRODUCT_NAME         NOT NULL     VARCHAR2(30)
QUANTITY                          NUMBER
```

The user can find out any information about the database tables that are available for their use with the ALL_TABLES view. ALL_TABLES displays information about who owns the table, where the table is stored in the database, and what storage parameters a table is using.

TIP
In order to apply the description of any of these ALL_ views to its counterparts in the USER_ and DBA_ families, substitute the scope "available to the user" with "created by the user" or "all those created in the database" for USER_ or DBA_, respectively.

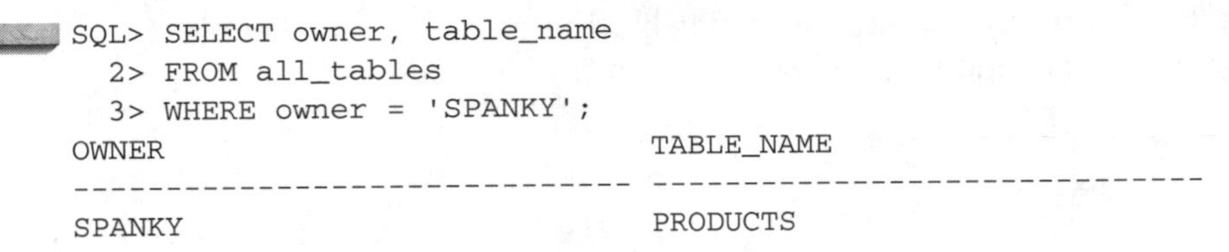

```
SQL> SELECT owner, table_name
  2> FROM all_tables
  3> WHERE owner = 'SPANKY';
OWNER                          TABLE_NAME
------------------------------ ------------------------------
SPANKY                         PRODUCTS
```

Some of the other object views are similar to ALL_TABLES. For example, ALL_INDEXES contains information about the indexes on tables that are available to the user. Some of the information listed in this view details the features of the index, such as whether or not all values in the indexed column are unique. Other information in the view identifies the storage parameters of the index and where the index is stored.

```
SQL> SELECT owner, index_name, table_name, uniqueness
  2> FROM all_indexes
  3> WHERE owner = 'SPANKY';
OWNER      INDEX_NAME     TABLE_NAME UNIQUENESS
---------- -------------- ---------- --------------
SPANKY     PKY_PRD_01     PRODUCTS   UNIQUE
```

The next data dictionary view represents a slight departure from the previous pattern. The ALL_VIEWS data dictionary view gives information about all the views in the database available to the user. It lists the schema owner, the view name, and the query that was used to create the view. The column containing the text that created the view is stored in LONG format. To obtain data from this column of the view, the user may need to issue the `set long` command to set the formatting that SQL*Plus uses to display a LONG column to be large enough to display the entire query used to create the view. Typically, `set long 5000` will suffice. More information about creating views in Oracle will be covered in the next chapter.

```
SQL> SET LONG 5000
SQL> SELECT owner, view_name, text
  2> FROM all_views
  3> WHERE owner = 'SPANKY';
OWNER      VIEW_NAME   TEXT
---------- ----------- ----------------------
SPANKY     PRD_VW      select * from products
```

The next view is the USER_USERS view. This view is used to give the current user of the database more information about his or her environment. Contained in this view are the default locations where objects created by the user will be stored, along with the user profile this user will abide by. There are several other pieces of information that will be more useful to DBAs than to developers.

```
SQL> SELECT *
  2> FROM user_users;
USERNAME                         USER_ID ACCOUNT_STATUS   LOCK_DATE
------------------------------ --------- ---------------- ---------
EXPIRY_DA DEFAULT_TABLESPACE   TEMPORARY_TABLESPACE          CREATED
--------- -------------------- ------------------------------ ---------
EXTERNAL_NAME
----------------------
SPANKY                                25 OPEN
          SPANKY               TEMPORARY                      30-MAR-99
```

The next few views are related to constraints. The first one is the ALL_CONSTRAINTS view. This view is used to display information about the constraints that have been defined in the database. It is particularly useful in determining the referenced column in cases where referential integrity constraints have been created on a table. This view gives the name of the constraint, the owner of the constraint, the name of the table the constraint is created on, and the name of the referenced table and column if the constraint created is a `FOREIGN KEY`.

```
SQL> SELECT constraint_name, table_name, r_owner, r_constraint_name
  2> FROM all_constraints
  3> WHERE table_name = 'PRODUCTS' and owner = 'SPANKY';
CONSTRAINT_NAME    TABLE_NAME R_OWNER  R_CONSTRAINT_NAME
------------------ ---------- -------- -----------------
FK_PRD_01          PRODUCTS   JASON    PK_PRD_MASTER_01
PK_PRD_01          PRODUCTS
```

The next view, ALL_CONS_COLUMNS, presents information about the columns that are incorporated into constraints on a table. For example, it is possible to create a primary key for a table that uses two or more columns from the table as its unique identifier. This definition of the primary key is sometimes referred to as a *composite primary key*. The ALL_CONS_COLUMNS view gives information about the columns that are in the primary key, and in which order they appear in the composite index.

```
SQL> SELECT constraint_name, table_name, column_name, position
  2> FROM all_cons_columns
  3> WHERE table_name = 'PRODUCTS' and owner = 'SPANKY';
CONSTRAINT_NAME    TABLE_NAME   COLUMN_NAME     POSITION
------------------ ------------ --------------- --------
FK_PRD_01          PRODUCTS     PRODUCT_NAME           1
PK_PRD_01          PRODUCTS     PRODUCT                1
```

The final dictionary view discussed in this section, ALL_IND_COLUMNS, is related to the ALL_CONS_COLUMNS view, but extends the scope of that view by providing information about all the indexed columns on the database.

```
SQL> SELECT index_name, table_name, column_name, column_position
  2> FROM all_ind_columns
  3> WHERE table_name = 'PRODUCTS' and index_owner = 'SPANKY';
INDEX_NAME    TABLE_NAME    COLUMN_NAME      COLUMN_POSITION
------------- ------------- ---------------- ---------------
PK_PRD_01     PRODUCTS      PRODUCT                        1
```

Exercises

1. Describe the use of object views. What purpose do the constraint views serve?
2. What is a composite index?
3. What purpose does the COLUMN_POSITION column serve in some of the dictionary views?

Manipulating Oracle Data

In this section, you will cover the following topics related to manipulating Oracle data:

- Inserting new rows into a table
- Making changes to existing row data
- Deleting data from the Oracle database
- The importance of transaction control

This section will introduce you to all forms of data-change manipulation. The three types of data-change manipulation in the Oracle database are updating, deleting, and inserting data. These statements are collectively known as the *data-manipulation language* of Oracle, or *DML* for short. We'll also look at *transaction processing*. Transaction processing is a mechanism that the Oracle database provides in order to facilitate the act of changing data. Without transaction-processing mechanisms, the database would not be able to guarantee that the users would not overwrite one another's changes in mid-process, or select data that is in the process of being changed by another user.

Inserting New Rows into a Table

The first data-change manipulation operation that will be discussed is the act of inserting new rows into a table. Once a table is created, there is no data in the table, unless the table is created and populated by rows selected from another table. Even in this case, the data must come from somewhere. This "somewhere" is from users who enter data into the table via `insert` statements.

An `insert` statement has a different syntax from a `select` statement. The general syntax for an `insert` statement is listed in the following code block, which defines several rows to be added to the PRODUCTS table owned by SPANKY. This table has three columns, titled PRODUCT#, PRODUCT_NAME, and QUANTITY. User SPANKY now wants to put some data in her table, so she executes the following statement designed to place one new row into the PRODUCTS table:

```
INSERT INTO products (product#, product_name, quantity)
VALUES (7848394, 'KITTY LITTER', 12);
```

Notice a few general rules of syntax in this statement. The `insert` statement has two parts: In the first part, the table to receive the inserted row is defined, along with the columns of the table that will have the column values inserted into them. The second portion of the statement defines the actual data values for the row to be added. This latter portion of the statement is denoted by the `values` keyword.

Oracle is capable of handling several variations on the `insert` statement. For example, the user generally only needs to define explicit columns of the table when data is not going to be inserted in all columns of the table. For example, if user SPANKY only wanted to define the product number and the name at the time the row was inserted, then SPANKY would be required to list the PRODUCT# and PRODUCT_NAME columns in the `into` clause of the `insert` statement. However, since she named column values for all columns in the table, the following statement would be just as acceptable as the previous one for inserting the row into the PRODUCTS table:

```
INSERT INTO products
VALUES (7848394, 'KITTY LITTER', 12);
```

One important question to ask in this situation is "how does Oracle know which column to populate with what data?" Suppose that the column datatypes are defined to be NUMBER for PRODUCT# and QUANTITY, and VARCHAR2 for PRODUCT_NAME. What prevents Oracle from placing the 12 in the PRODUCT# column? The answer is position. Position can matter in tables on the Oracle database; the position of the data in the `insert` statement must correspond to the position of the columns in the table. The user can determine the position of each column in a table by using the `describe` command or the output from the USER_TAB_COLUMNS dictionary view using COLUMN_ID to indicate position as part of the `order by` clause. The order in which the columns are listed in the output from the `describe` command is the same order in which values should be placed to `insert` data into the table without explicitly naming the columns of the table. The following code block shows two ways to glean positional information for table columns from the Oracle database:

```
SQL> select table_name, column_name
  2  from user_tab_columns
  3  where table_name = 'PRODUCTS'
  4  order by column_id;
 TABLE_NAME                      COLUMN_NAME
------------------------------ ------------------------------
PRODUCTS                        PRODUCT#
PRODUCTS                        PRODUCT_NAME
PRODUCTS                        QUANTITY
SQL> describe products
 Name                            Null?    Type
 ------------------------------- -------- ----
 PRODUCT#                        NOT NULL NUMBER
 PRODUCT_NAME                             VARCHAR2(30)
 QUANTITY                                 NUMBER
```

Another variation on the `insert` theme is the option to populate a table using data obtained from other tables using a `select` statement. This method of populating table data is similar to the method used by the `create table as select` statement, which was discussed earlier in the chapter. In this case, the `values` clause can be omitted entirely. However, the rules regarding column position of the inserted data still apply in this situation, meaning that if the user can `select` data for all columns of the table having data inserted into it, then the user need not name the columns in the `insert into` clause.

```
INSERT INTO products
(SELECT product#, product_name, quantity
 FROM MASTER.PRODUCTS);
```

In order to put data into a table, a special privilege must be granted from the table owner to the user who needs to perform the `insert`. A more complete discussion of object privileges will appear in the next chapter.

Exercises

1. What statement is used to place new data into an Oracle table?
2. What are the three options available with the statement that allows new data to be placed into Oracle tables?

Making Changes to Existing Row Data

Often, the data rows in a table will need to be changed. In order to make those changes, the `update` statement can be used. Updates can be made to any row in a database, except in two cases. One case is where you don't have enough access privileges to `update` the data. (You will learn more about access privileges in Chapter 4.) The other case is where some other database user is making changes to the row you want to change. You will learn more about data change control later in this chapter under the heading "The Importance of Transaction Control." If neither exception applies, the user changes data when an `update` statement is issued, as shown below:

```
UPDATE spanky.products
SET quantity = 54
WHERE product# = 4959495;
```

Notice that the typical `update` statement has three clauses. The first is the actual `update` clause, where the table that will be updated is named. The second clause is the `set` clause. In the `set` clause, all columns that will be changed by the `update` statement are named, along with their new values. The final clause of the `update` statement is the `where` clause. The `where` clause in an `update` statement is the same as the `where` clause in a `select` statement: it provides one or more comparison operations that determine which rows Oracle will `update` as a result of this statement being issued.

The `update` and `set` clauses are mandatory in an `update` statement. However, the `where` clause is not. Omitting the `where` clause in an `update` statement has the effect of applying the data change to every row that presently exists in the table. Consider the following code block that issues a data change without a `where` clause specified. The change made by this statement will apply to every row in the table.

```
UPDATE spanky.products
SET quantity = 0;
```

Every operation that was possible in the `where` clauses of a `select` statement are possible in the `where` clauses of an `update`. The `where` clause in an `update` statement can have any type of comparison or range operation in it and can even handle the use of the `exists` operation and subqueries.

Exercise

What statement is used to change data in an Oracle table? What clauses in this statement are mandatory?

Deleting Data from the Oracle Database

The removal of data from a database is as much a fact of life as putting the data there in the first place. The `delete` statement in SQL*Plus is used to remove database rows from tables. The syntax for the `delete` statement is detailed in the following code block. Note that in this example there is no way to `delete` data from selected columns in a row in the table; this act is accomplished with the `update` statement with the columns that are to be "deleted" being set to NULL by the `update` statement.

```
DELETE FROM spanky.products
WHERE product# = 4959394; -- all column values removed
```

As in the case of database updates, `delete` statements use the `where` clause to help determine which rows are meant to be removed. Like an `update` or `select` statement, the `where` clause in a `delete` statement can contain any type of comparison operation, range operation, subquery, or any other operation acceptable for a `where` clause. Like an `update` statement, if the `where` clause is left off the `delete` statement, the deletion will be applied to all rows in the table.

Data deletion should be undertaken with care. It can be costly to replace data that has been inappropriately deleted from the database, which is why the privilege of deleting information should only be given out to those users who really should be able to delete records from a table.

Exercises

1. What statement is used to remove data from an Oracle table? What clauses in this statement are mandatory?
2. When can a user not remove data in a table?

The Importance of Transaction Control

One of the first realities that a user of the Oracle database must understand is that a change to data made in the Oracle database is not saved immediately. Oracle allows users to execute a series of data-change statements together as one logical unit of work, terminated by either saving the work in the database or discarding it. This logical unit of work is called a transaction, and it begins with the user's first executable SQL statement. A transaction ends when it is explicitly committed or rolled back (both terms are discussed later in this section) by that user.

Transaction processing consists of a set of controls that allow a user issuing an `insert`, `update`, or `delete` statement to declare a beginning to the series of data change statements he or she will issue. When the user has finished making the changes to the database, the user can save the data to the database by explicitly ending the transaction. Alternatively, if a mistake is made at any point during the transaction, the user can have the database discard the changes made to the database in favor of the way the data existed before the transaction.

Transactions are created with the use of two different elements in the Oracle database. The first element is the set of commands that define the beginning, breakpoint, and end of a transaction. The second element is the special locking mechanisms designed to prevent more than one user at a time from making a change to row information in a database. Locks will be discussed after the transaction control commands are defined.

The commands that define transactions are as follows:

- **`set transaction`** Initiates the beginning of a transaction and sets key features. This command is optional. A transaction will be started automatically when you start SQL*Plus, commit the previous transaction, or rollback the previous transaction.
- **`commit`** Ends the current transaction by saving database changes and starts a new transaction.
- **`rollback`** Ends the current transaction by discarding database changes and starts a new transaction.
- **`savepoint`** Defines breakpoints for the transaction to allow partial rollbacks.

set transaction

This command can be used to define the beginning of a transaction. If any change is made to the database after the `set transaction` command is issued but before the transaction is ended, all changes made will be considered part of that transaction. The `set transaction` statement is not required, because a transaction begins as soon as you log onto Oracle via SQL*Plus and execute the first command, or immediately after issuing a `rollback` or `commit` statement to end a transaction.

By default, a transaction is `read write` unless you override this default by issuing `set transaction read only`. Finally, you can set the transaction isolation level with `set transaction` as well. The `set transaction isolation level serializable` command specifies serializable transaction isolation mode as defined in SQL92. If a serializable transaction contains data-manipulation language (DML) that attempts to update any resource that may have been updated in a transaction uncommitted at the start of the serializable transaction, then the DML statement fails. The `set transaction isolation level read committed` command is the default Oracle transaction behavior. If the transaction contains DML that requires row locks held by another transaction, then the DML statement waits until the row locks are released.

```
SET TRANSACTION READ ONLY;
SET TRANSACTION READ WRITE;
SET TRANSACTION ISOLATION LEVEL SERIALIZABLE;
SET TRANSACTION ISOLATION LEVEL READ COMMITTED;
```

commit

The `commit` statement in transaction processing represents the point in time where the user has made all the changes he or she wants to have logically grouped together, and since no mistakes have been made, the user is ready to save the work. The `work` keyword is an extraneous word in the `commit` syntax that is designed for readability. Issuing a `commit` statement also implicitly begins a new transaction on the database because it closes the current transaction and starts a new one.

It is important also to understand that an implicit `commit` occurs on the database when a user exits SQL*Plus or issues a data-definition language (DDL) command, such as a `create table` statement used to create a database object or `alter table` to alter it.

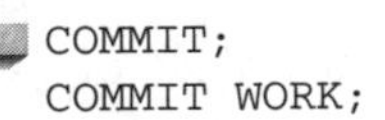

```
COMMIT;
COMMIT WORK;
```

rollback

If you have at any point issued a data-change statement you don't want, you can discard the changes made to the database with the use of the `rollback` statement. After the `rollback` command is issued, a new transaction is started implicitly by the database session. In addition to rollbacks executed when the `rollback` statement is issued, there are implicit `rollback` statements conducted when a statement fails for any reason or if the user cancels a statement with the CTRL-C cancel command.

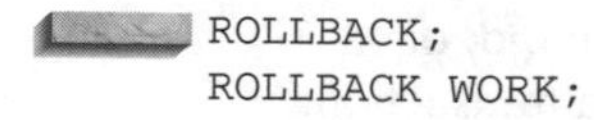

```
ROLLBACK;
ROLLBACK WORK;
```

savepoint

In some cases involving long transactions or transactions that involve many data changes, you may not want to scrap all your changes simply because the last statement issued contains unwanted changes. Savepoints are special operations that allow you to divide the work of a transaction into different segments. You can execute rollbacks to the savepoint only, leaving prior changes intact. Savepoints are great for situations where part of the transaction needs to be recovered in an uncommitted transaction. At the point the `rollback to savepoint so_far_so_good` statement completes in the following code block, only changes made before the savepoint was defined are kept when the `commit` is issued:

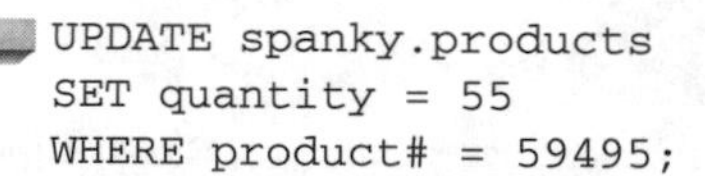

```
UPDATE spanky.products
SET quantity = 55
WHERE product# = 59495;

SAVEPOINT so_far_so_good;

UPDATE spanky.products
SET quantity = 504;

ROLLBACK TO SAVEPOINT so_far_so_good;
COMMIT;
```

Locks

The final aspect of the Oracle database that allows the user to have transaction processing is the lock, the mechanism by which Oracle prevents data from being changed by more than one user at a time. There are several different types of locks, each with its own level of scope. Locks available on a database are categorized into table-level locks and row-level locks.

A table-level lock allows only the user holding the lock to change any piece of row data in the table, during which time no other users can make changes anywhere on the table. A table lock can be held in any of several modes: row share (RS), row exclusive (RX), share (S), share row exclusive (SRX), and exclusive (X). The restrictiveness of a table lock's mode determines the modes in which other table locks on the same table can be obtained and held.

A row-level lock is one that allows the user the exclusive ability to change data in one or more rows of the table. However, any row in the table that is not held by the row-level lock can be changed by another user.

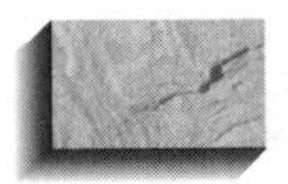

TIP

An `update` statement acquires a special row-level lock called a "row-exclusive" lock, which means that for the period of time the `update` statement is executing, no other user in the database can view or change the data in the row. The same goes for `delete` or `insert` operations. Another `update` statement, the `select for update` statement, acquires a more lenient lock called the "share row" lock. This lock means that for the period of time the `update` statement is changing the data in the rows of the table, no other user may change that row, but users may look at the data in the row as it changes.

Exercises

1. What is transaction processing?
2. Identify the mechanisms that support transactions.

Chapter Summary

This chapter covered the foundational material for understanding the mechanics of creating an Oracle database. The material in this chapter corresponds to 15 percent of the test material in OCP Exam 1 and represents the foundation on which other exams will build. This material will turn the casual user who understands how to select data from an Oracle database into a full-fledged expert on the Oracle database server product. Understanding this material is crucial to understanding several areas in the rest of this guide, including the management of tables, the use of transaction processing, locks and the contention issues they often produce, and proper management of the data dictionary.

The first portion of this chapter discussed the concepts of data modeling. In order to create a database in Oracle, it is important that all stages of system development be executed carefully. Some of the stages covered include needs assessment, requirements definition, database design, application development, performance tuning, security enforcement, and enhancements development. The enhancement stage in that life cycle is really a miniature version of the first several stages rolled into one.

The needs assessment stage is a critical one. It is the period of time where the users of the system are identified and the desired and required features of the system are documented. After needs assessment, a full list of requirements should be agreed upon and documented so as to avoid costly rework later. Once the requirements of the system are completely understood, the developers of the database portion of the application should model the required business process in an entity-relationship diagram, which consists of entities (persons, places, things, or ideas) involved in the process flow, and the relationships between each entity. This entity-relationship diagram will then be used to create a logical data model—a pictorial diagram of the tables that will represent each entity and the referential integrity constraints that will represent each relationship. Ordinality is a key point here. Ordinality is represented by the ordered pair appearing in your data model, such as (0,0), (0,1), and others. The numbers in the ordered pair defines two items. The first number, 0 or 1, defines whether the relationship is optional (0) or mandatory (1) for the entities partaking of the relationship. The second number in the ordered pair specifies the record-to-record correspondence of one record in a database. There are two types of record-to-record correspondence—one-to-one (1), and one-to-many (N). A one-to-one correspondence means that one record of one table corresponds to one record in another. One-to-many correspondence means that one record from one table can correspond to one or more records of another table.

Once the planning is complete, then developers can move forward with the process of actually creating the database. The syntax for creating a table with column definitions and constraints was covered in this chapter. A table can be created with several different columns, and the allowed datatypes for these columns are VARCHAR2, CHAR, NUMBER, DATE, RAW, LONG, LONG RAW, ROWID, BLOB, CLOB, NCLOB, and BFILE. One or more of these columns is used to define the primary key, or element in each row that distinguishes one row of data from another in the table.

A `PRIMARY KEY` is one type of integrity constraint. Another type of integrity constraint is the `FOREIGN KEY`, which defines referential integrity on the table, creating table relationships and often modeling the relationships between entities from the entity-relationship diagram. Referential integrity produces a parent/child relationship between two tables. Sometimes it is useful to name tables according to conventions that have the child objects take on the name of the parent object as part of their own name. The three other constraints available on the database are `UNIQUE`, `CHECK`, and `NOT NULL`. `UNIQUE` constraints prevent duplicate non-NULL values from appearing in a column for two or more rows. `CHECK` constraints verify data in a column against a set of constants defined to be valid values. `NOT NULL` constraints prevent the entry of NULL data for a column on which the `NOT NULL` constraint is defined. Two of the five constraints create indexes to help enforce the integrity they are designed to enforce. Those two constraints are the ones designed to enforce uniqueness: the `UNIQUE` constraint and the `PRIMARY KEY`. Finally, a table is created with no data in it, except in the case of the `create table as select` statement. This statement allows the user to create a table with row data prepopulated from another table. All options available for regular `select` statements are available in this statement as well.

The next portion of this chapter discussed the Oracle data dictionary. The data dictionary contains information about all objects created in the database. It also contains a listing of available columns in each object created in the database. Information about table columns can be obtained using the `describe` command, followed by the name of the table you want to view the columns on. Information is kept in data dictionary tables about the objects created in Oracle, their locations, and their performance statistics. However, you will not usually access the tables of the data dictionary directly. Rather, you generally will look at that data using data dictionary views. Data can be selected from views in the same way it can be selected from tables. No user is able to `delete` data from the data dictionary, because doing so could permanently damage the Oracle database. All tables and views in the Oracle data dictionary are owned by SYS.

Several data dictionary views are available for finding out information about the objects discussed in this unit. Those views are divided into three general categories that correspond to the scope of data availability in the view. The USER_ views show information on objects owned by the user, the ALL_ views show information on all the objects accessible by the user, and the DBA_ views show information on all objects in the database. Data dictionary views are available on every type of object in the database, including indexes, constraints, tables, views, synonyms, sequences, and triggers. Additionally, information is available to help the user understand which columns are available in indexes or primary-key constraints. Several views exist to show the position of columns in composite indexes, which are indexes that contain several columns.

The remainder of the chapter discussed the use of SQL statements for the purpose of changing data in a database. There are three types of data-change statements available in the Oracle database. They are `update`, `insert`, and `delete`. The `update` statement allows you to change row data that already exists in the database. The `insert` statement allows you to add new row data records to the tables of a database. The `delete` statement allows you to remove records from the database. The various data-change operations are supported in Oracle with the use of transaction-processing control. There are several different aspects to transaction processing. These include the commands used to set the beginning, breakpoint, and end of transactions and the locking mechanisms that allow one and only one user at a time to make changes to the data in the database.

Two-Minute Drill

- The stages of system development include needs assessment, requirements definition, database design, application development, performance tuning, database security enforcement, and enhancement development.
- The basic types of data relationships in Oracle include primary keys and functional dependency within a table, and foreign-key constraints from one table to another.
- A relational database is composed of objects that store data, objects that manage access to data, and objects that improve performance when accessing data.
- Within database planning, it is necessary to create an entity-relationship diagram that acts as a visual representation of the business process being modeled. The diagram consists of people, places, things, and ideas, all called *entities*, which are related to one another by activities or process flow called *relationships*.
- Once an entity-relationship diagram has been created for an application, it must be translated into a logical data model. The logical data model is a collection of tables that represent entities and referential integrity constraints that represent relationships.
- A table can be created with five different types of integrity constraints: `PRIMARY KEY`, `FOREIGN KEY`, `UNIQUE`, `NOT NULL`, and `CHECK`.
- Referential integrity often creates a parent/child relationship between two tables, the parent being the referenced table and the child being the referring table. Often, a naming convention that requires child objects to adopt and extend the name of the parent table is useful in identifying these relationships.
- The datatypes available for creating columns in tables are CHAR, VARCHAR2, NUMBER, DATE, RAW, LONG, LONG RAW, ROWID, BLOB, CLOB, NCLOB, and BFILE.
- Indexes are created automatically in conjunction with primary-key and `UNIQUE` constraints. These indexes are named after the constraint name given to the constraint in the definition of the table.
- Tables are created without any data in them, except for tables created with the `create table as select` statement. These tables are created and prepopulated with data from another table.

- There is information available in the Oracle database to help users, developers, and DBAs know what objects exist in the Oracle database. The information is in the Oracle data dictionary.
- To find the positional order of columns in a table, or what columns there are in a table at all, the user can issue a `describe` command on that table. The Oracle data dictionary will then list all columns in the table being described.
- Data dictionary views on database objects are divided into three categories based on scope of user visibility: USER_, for what is owned by the user; ALL_, for all that can be seen by the user; and DBA_, for all that exists in the database, whether the user can see it or not.
- New rows are put into a table with the `insert` statement. The user issuing the `insert` statement can `insert` one row at a time with one statement, or do a mass insert with `insert into` *`table_name`* `(select` ...).
- Existing rows in a database table can be modified using the `update` statement. The update statement contains a `where` clause similar in function to the `where` clause of select statements.
- Existing rows in a table can be deleted using the `delete` statement. The `delete` statement also contains a `where` clause similar in function to the `where` clause in update or `select` statements.
- Transaction processing controls the change of data in an Oracle database.
- Transaction controls include commands that identify the beginning, breakpoint, and end of a transaction, and locking mechanisms that prevent more than one user at a time from making changes in the database.

Chapter Questions

1. Which of the following integrity constraints automatically create an index when defined? (Choose two)

A. Foreign keys

B. `UNIQUE` constraints

C. `NOT NULL` constraints

D. Primary keys

2. **Which of the following dictionary views gives information about the position of a column in a primary key?**

   A. ALL_PRIMARY_KEYS

   B. USER_CONSTRAINTS

   C. ALL_IND_COLUMNS

   D. ALL_TABLES

3. **Developer ANJU executes the following statement:**

   ```
   create table ANIMALS as select * from MASTER.ANIMALS;
   ```

   What is the effect of this statement?

   A. A table named ANIMALS will be created in the MASTER schema with the same data as the ANIMALS table owned by ANJU.

   B. A table named ANJU will be created in the ANIMALS schema with the same data as the ANIMALS table owned by MASTER.

   C. A table named ANIMALS will be created in the ANJU schema with the same data as the ANIMALS table owned by MASTER.

   D. A table named MASTER will be created in the ANIMALS schema with the same data as the ANJU table owned by ANIMALS.

4. **User JANKO would like to insert a row into the EMPLOYEE table that has three columns: EMPID, LASTNAME, and SALARY. The user would like to enter data for EMPID 59694, LASTNAME Harris, but no salary. Which statement would work best?**

   A. `insert into EMPLOYEE values (59694,'HARRIS', NULL);`

   B. `insert into EMPLOYEE values (59694,'HARRIS');`

   C. `insert into EMPLOYEE (EMPID, LASTNAME, SALARY) values (59694,'HARRIS');`

   D. `insert into EMPLOYEE (select 59694 from 'HARRIS');`

5. Which components are parts of an entity-relationship diagram? (Choose two)

A. Referential integrity constraints

B. Entities

C. Relationships

D. Triggers

6. Which of the following choices is the strongest indicator of a parent/child relationship?

A. Two tables in the database are named VOUCHER and VOUCHER_ITEM, respectively.

B. Two tables in the database are named EMPLOYEE and PRODUCTS, respectively.

C. Two tables in the database were created on the same day.

D. Two tables in the database contain none of the same columns.

7. Which of the following are valid database datatypes in Oracle? (Choose three)

A. CHAR

B. VARCHAR2

C. BOOLEAN

D. NUMBER

8. Omitting the `where` clause from a `delete` statement has which of the following effects?

A. The `delete` statement will fail because there are no records to delete.

B. The `delete` statement will prompt the user to enter criteria for the deletion.

C. The `delete` statement will fail because of syntax error.

D. The `delete` statement will remove all records from the table.

9. Which line of the following statement will produce an error?

A. `create table GOODS`

B. `(GOODNO number,`

C. `GOOD_NAME varchar2(20) check(GOOD_NAME in (select NAME from AVAIL_GOODS)),`

D. `constraint PK_GOODS_01`

E. `primary key (GOODNO));`

F. There are no errors in this statement.

10. The transaction control that prevents more than one user from updating data in a table is which of the following?

A. Locks

B. Commits

C. Rollbacks

D. Savepoints

Answers to Chapter Questions

1. B and D. `UNIQUE` constraints and primary keys

Explanation Every constraint that enforces uniqueness creates an index to assist in the process. The two integrity constraints that enforce uniqueness are `UNIQUE` constraints and primary keys. Refer to the discussion of creating a table with integrity constraints.

2. C. ALL_IND_COLUMNS

Explanation This view is the only one listed that provides column positions in an index. Since primary keys create an index, the index created by the primary key will be listed with all the other indexed data. Choice A is incorrect because no view exists in Oracle called PRIMARY_KEYS. Choice B is incorrect because although ALL_CONSTRAINTS lists information about the constraints in a database, it does not contain information about the index created by the primary key. Choice D is incorrect because ALL_TABLES contains no information related to the position of a column in an index.

3. C. A table named ANIMALS will be created in the ANJU schema with the same data as the ANIMALS table owned by MASTER.

Explanation This question requires you to look carefully at the `create table` statement in the question and to know some things about table creation. First, a table is always created in the schema of the user who created it. Second, since the `create table as select` clause was used, choices B and D are both incorrect because they identify the table being created as something other than ANIMALS, among other things. Choice A identifies the schema into which the ANIMALS table will be created as MASTER, which is incorrect for the reasons just stated. Refer to the discussion of creating tables for more information.

4. A. `insert into EMPLOYEE values (59694,'HARRIS', NULL);`

Explanation This choice is acceptable because the positional criteria for not specifying column order is met by the data in the values clause. When you would like to specify that no data be inserted into a particular column, one method of doing so is to insert a `NULL`. Choice B is incorrect because not all columns in the table have values identified. When using positional references to populate column data, there must be values present for every column in the table. Otherwise, the columns that will be populated should be named explicitly. Choice C is incorrect because when a column is named for data insert in the `insert into` clause, then a value must definitely be specified in the `values` clause. Choice D is incorrect because using the multiple row insert option with a `select` statement is not appropriate in this situation. Refer to the discussion of `insert` statements for more information.

5. B and C. Entities *and* Relationships

Explanation There are only two components to an entity-relationship diagram: entities and relationships. Choices A and D are incorrect because referential integrity constraints and triggers are part of database implementation of a logical data model. Refer to the discussion of entity-relationship diagrams.

6. A. Two tables in the database are named VOUCHER and VOUCHER_ITEM, respectively.

Explanation This choice implies the use of a naming convention similar to the one discussed. Although there is no guarantee that these two tables are related, the possibility is strongest in this case. Choice B implies the same naming convention, and since the two tables' names are dissimilar, there is little likelihood that the two tables are related in any way. Choice C is incorrect because the date a table is created has absolutely no bearing on what function the table serves in the database. Choice D is incorrect because two tables can *not* be related if there are no common columns between them. Refer to the discussion of creating tables with integrity constraints, naming conventions, and data modeling.

7. A, B, and D. CHAR, VARCHAR2, *and* NUMBER

Explanation BOOLEAN is the only invalid datatype in this listing. Although BOOLEAN is a valid datatype in PL/SQL, it is not a datatype available on the Oracle database, meaning that you cannot create a column in a table that uses the BOOLEAN datatype. Review the discussion of allowed datatypes in column definition.

8. D. The `delete` statement will remove all records from the table.

Explanation There is only one effect produced by leaving off the `where` clause from any statement that allows one—the requested operation is performed on all records in the table.

9. C. `GOOD_NAME varchar2(20) check(GOOD_NAME in (select NAME from AVAIL_GOODS)),`

Explanation A `CHECK` constraint cannot contain a reference to another table, nor can it reference a virtual column, such as ROWID or SYSDATE. The other lines of the `create table` statement contain correct syntax.

10. A. Locks

Explanation Locks are the mechanisms that prevent more than one user at a time from making changes to the database. All other options refer to the commands that are issued to mark the beginning, middle, and end of a transaction. Review the discussion of transaction controls.

CHAPTER 4

Creating Other Database Objects in Oracle

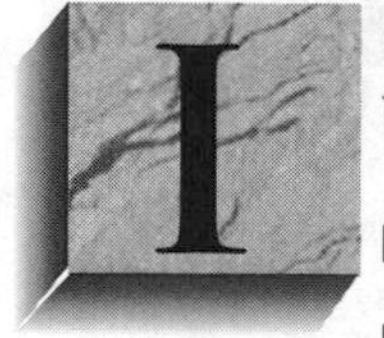

In this chapter, you will learn about and demonstrate knowledge in the following areas:

- Altering tables and constraints
- Creating sequences
- Creating views
- Creating indexes
- Controlling user access

At this point, you should already know how to `select` data from a database, model a business process, design a set of database tables from that process, and populate those tables with data. These functions represent the cornerstone of functionality that Oracle can provide in an organization. However, the design of a database does not stop there. There are features in the Oracle architecture that can make data "transparent" to some users but not to others, that can speed access to data, or that can generate primary keys for database tables automatically. These are the advanced database features of the Oracle database. This chapter covers material in several different areas tested in the OCP Exam 1. The material in this chapter comprises 17 percent of the material covered on the exam.

Table and Constraint Modifications

In this section, you will cover the following topics related to altering tables and constraints:

- Adding and modifying columns
- Modifying integrity constraints
- Enabling or disabling constraints
- Dropping tables
- Truncating tables
- Changing names of objects
- Dictionary comments on objects

Once a table is created, the needs of the database may change such that the table must be changed. The database developer will need to understand how to implement changes on the database in an effective and *nondisruptive* manner. For example, there are two ways to cure an ingrown toenail. One is to go to a podiatrist and have the toenail removed. The other is to chop off the toe. Although both approaches work, the second one produces side effects that most people can safely do without. The same concept applies to database changes. The developer can do one of two things when a request is made to add some columns to a table. One is to add the columns, and the other is to re-create the entire table from scratch. Obviously, there is a great deal of value in knowing the right way to take the first approach.

Adding and Modifying Columns

Columns can be added and modified in the Oracle database with ease, using the `alter table` statement and its many options for changing the number of columns in the database. When adding columns, a column added with a `NOT NULL` constraint must have data populated for that column in all rows before the `NOT NULL` constraint is enabled, and only one column of the LONG datatype can appear in a table in Oracle. The following code block shows an example of the `alter table` statement:

```
SQL> alter table products add (color varchar2(10));

Table altered.
```

If the developer or the DBA needs to add a column that will have a `NOT NULL` constraint on it, then several things need to happen. The column should first be created without the constraint, and then values for all rows should be entered in the column. After all column values are not NULL, the `NOT NULL` constraint can be applied to it. If the user tries to add a column with a `NOT NULL` constraint on it, the developer will encounter an error stating that the table must be empty.

Only one column in the table may be of type LONG within a table. That restriction includes the LONG RAW datatype. However, many columns of datatype BLOB, CLOB, NCLOB, and BFILE can appear in one table, as of Oracle8. It is sometimes useful to emulate Oracle8 in Oracle7 databases by having a special table that contains the LONG column and a foreign key to the table that would have contained the column; this reduces the amount of data migration and row chaining on the database.

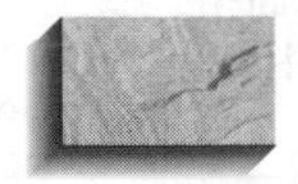

TIP
Row chaining and row migration is when the Oracle RDBMS has to move row data around or break it up and save it in pieces inside the files on disk that comprise an Oracle database. This activity is a concern to DBAs because it hurts database performance.

Another important aspect of table columns is the configuration of the datatype that can be stored in the column. Suppose that on a table called PRODUCTS, you have the PRODUCT_NAME column of type VARCHAR2(30). The retailer has just begun to carry a new line of products whose name is substantially longer than the names of other products the store carries. You are called in to determine whether the longer name will present a problem to the database. In order to resolve the situation, you can issue a statement that will make the column length longer.

```
SQL> alter table products modify (product_name varchar2(45));

Table altered.
```

Several conditions apply when you are modifying the existing columns' datatypes or adding columns to a table in the database. The general rule of thumb is that increases are generally okay, but decreases are usually a little trickier. Here are some examples of increases that are generally acceptable:

- Increasing the size of a VARCHAR2 or CHAR column
- Increasing the size of a NUMBER column
- Adding new columns to a table

Decreasing the size of various aspects of the table, including some of the column datatypes or the actual number of columns in the table, requires taking special steps. Usually, the effort involves making sure that the relevant column (or columns) has all NULL values in it before executing the change. In order to execute these types of operations on columns or tables that contain data, the developer must find or create some sort of temporary storage place for the data in the column. One acceptable method is creating a table using the `create table as select` statement, with the `select` statement drawing data from the primary key and the column(s) that will be altered. Another method is spooling the data from the table to a flat file, and reloading it later using SQL*Loader, a utility provided with Oracle for loading data into tables from flat files.

Here are some allowable operations that decrease various aspects of the database. Note that in all the following situations, the change can only be made when you have an empty column for all rows in the table. This means that all rows that currently exist in the table must have NULL defined as the value for the column you are making this change to, or else the table must itself be empty. The operations are:

- Reducing the size of a NUMBER column (empty column for all rows only)
- Reducing the length of a VARCHAR2 or CHAR column (empty column for all rows only)
- Changing the datatype of a column (empty column for all rows only)

Exercises

1. What statement is used to change the definition of a table?
2. What process is used to change a nullable column to one with a NOT NULL constraint?
3. What are some of the rules and guidelines for changing column definitions?

Modifying Integrity Constraints

There are several changes that can be made to constraints. These changes include altering the constraint and disabling, enabling, or removing the constraint from the column or table of the database. These processes allow the developer to create, modify, or remove the business rules that constrain data.

The first constraint-related activity that a developer may need to do is add constraints to a database. This process can be easy or difficult, depending on the circumstances. If a constraint cannot be created with the database, the simplest scenario for adding the constraint is to add it to the database before data is inserted.

```
SQL> alter table products modify (color not null);
Table altered.
SQL> create table avail_colors
  2  (color varchar2(10) primary key);
Table created.
SQL> alter table products add
  2  (constraint fk_products_02 foreign key (color)
  3  references avail_colors (color));
Table altered.
SQL> alter table products add (unique (product_name));
Table altered.
SQL> alter table products add (prod_size varchar2(10) check
  2  (prod_size in ('P','S','M','L','XL','XXL','XXXL')));
Table altered.
```

Notice that in the first statement in the preceding list of examples, the modify clause is used to add a NOT NULL constraint as a column constraint to the column, while the add clause is used to add all other types of integrity constraints as table constraints to the table. The column on which the constraint is added must already exist in the database table; no constraint can be created for a column that does not exist in the table.

Some of the restrictions on creating constraints are listed here:

- **Primary keys** Columns cannot contain NULL values, and all values must be unique.
- **Foreign keys** Referenced columns in other tables must contain values corresponding to all values in the referring columns or the referring columns values must be NULL.
- **UNIQUE constraints** Columns must contain all unique values or NULL values.
- **CHECK constraints** The new constraint will only be applied to data added or modified after the constraint is created.
- **NOT NULL** Columns cannot contain NULL values.

Constraints That Fail on Creation

If any of the conditions for the constraints just listed are not met for the constraint to which the rule applies, then creation of the constraint *will fail*. You will need to correct the problem before attempting to create the constraint again. The following code block demonstrates a situation where you attempt to add a primary key to a table when one already exists for that table:

```
SQL> alter table products add
  2  (constraint pk_products_01 primary key (product#))
(constraint pk_products_01 primary key (product#))
 *
ERROR at line 2:
ORA-02260: table can have only one primary key
```

The following code block illustrates another situation where your constraint fails on creation, using an example of CHECK constraints. Here, you also see that if Oracle cannot create the constraint properly, the constraint will not exist in disabled state — in other words, it simply won't exist at all:

```
SQL> create table example_1
  2  (col1 number);
Table created.
SQL> insert into example_1 values (1);
1 row created.
SQL> insert into example_1 values (10);
1 row created.
SQL> commit;
Commit complete.
```

```
SQL> alter table example_1 add
  2  (constraint ck_01 check (col1 in (1,2,3)));
(col1 in (1,2,3)))
 *
ERROR at line 2:
ORA-02293: cannot enable (JASON.CK_01) - check constraint violated
SQL> alter table example_1 enable constraint ck_01
  2  exceptions into exceptions;
alter table example_1 enable constraint ck_01
*
ERROR at line 1:
ORA-02430: cannot enable constraint (CK_01) - no such constraint
```

Exercises

1. What are some of the ways integrity constraints can be changed on a table?
2. What are some rules that must be adhered to when modifying each type of constraint?

Enabling and Disabling Constraints

Think of a constraint as a switch that can be turned on or off. When the switch is enabled, the constraint will do its job in enforcing business rules on the data entering the table; when the switch is disabled, the rules defined for the constraint are not enforced, rendering the constraint as ineffective as if it had been removed.

Disabling Constraints

The following code block demonstrates some sample statements for disabling constraints:

```
SQL> ALTER TABLE products DISABLE PRIMARY KEY;
Table altered.
SQL> ALTER TABLE emp DISABLE CONSTRAINT pk_emp_01;
Table altered.
SQL> ALTER TABLE products DISABLE UNIQUE (product_name);
Table altered.
```

In some cases, you may have a problem if you attempt to disable a primary key when existing foreign keys depend on that primary key. This problem is shown in the following situation:

```
SQL> alter table avail_colors disable primary key;
alter table avail_colors disable primary key
*
```

```
ERROR at line 1:
ORA-02297: cannot disable constraint (JASON.SYS_C001913) -
dependencies exist
```

If you try to drop a primary key when there are foreign keys depending on it, the `cascade` option is required as part of the `alter table disable` *`constraint`*, as shown in the following code block:

```
SQL> alter table avail_colors disable primary key cascade;
Table altered.
```

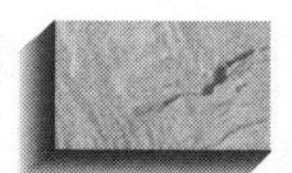

TIP
Disabling a constraint leaves the table vulnerable to inappropriate data being entered. Care should be taken to ensure that the data loaded during the period the constraint is disabled will not interfere with your ability to enable the constraint later.

Enabling a Disabled Constraint

You can enable a disabled constraint as follows:

```
SQL> alter table products enable primary key;
Table altered.
SQL> alter table products enable unique (product_name);
Table altered.
SQL> alter table avail_colors enable primary key;
Table altered.
```

Note that only constraints that have been defined and are currently disabled can be enabled by this code. A constraint that fails on creation will not exist in disabled state, waiting for you to correct the problem and re-enable it.

Using the EXCEPTIONS Table

There are situations where you may want to disable a constraint for some general purpose, such as disabling a primary key in order to speed up a large number of `insert` statements. *Be careful when using this approach, however!* If you disable a constraint and then load data that violates the integrity constraint into a table while the constraint is disabled, your attempt to enable the constraint later with the `alter table` *`TABLE_NAME`* `enable constraint` statement will fail. You will need to use a special table called EXCEPTIONS (created by running the `utlexcpt.sql` script in `rdbms/admin` under the Oracle software home directory) to identify and correct the offending records. The following example involving a primary key constraint should give you an idea of how this works:

```
SQL> @D:\ORANT\RDBMS80\ADMIN\UTLEXCPT
Table created.
SQL> alter table example_1 add (constraint pk_01 primary key (col1));
Table altered.
SQL> select * from example_1;
COL1
---------
       10
        1
SQL> alter table example_1 disable constraint pk_01;
Table altered.
SQL> insert into example_1 values (1);
1 row created.
SQL> alter table example_1 enable constraint pk_01
  2  exceptions into exceptions;
alter table example_1 enable constraint pk_01
*
ERROR at line 1:
ORA-02437: cannot enable (JASON.PK_01) - primary key violated
SQL> desc exceptions
 Name                            Null?    Type
 ------------------------------- -------- ----
 ROW_ID                                   ROWID
 OWNER                                    VARCHAR2(30)
 TABLE_NAME                               VARCHAR2(30)
 CONSTRAINT                               VARCHAR2(30)
SQL> select e.row_id, a.col1
  2  from exceptions e, example_1 a
  3  where e.row_id = a.rowid;
ROW_ID                 COL1
------------------ --------
AAAAvGAAGAAAAPWAAB        1
AAAAvGAAGAAAAPWAAD        1
```

At this point of execution in the code block, you have identified the offending rows in the EXAMPLE_1 table that break the rules of the primary key constraint. You also know their ROWIDs, which you can use to either modify the value of one of these rows or to remove one of them so the primary key can be unique. To ensure that the enabling of the constraint will be a smooth process, precautions should be taken to make sure that any data loaded into a table with has disabled constraints does not violate the constraint rules.

Removing Constraints

Usually, there is little about a constraint that will interfere with the ability to remove it, so long as the person attempting to do so is either the owner of the table or has been granted the appropriate privilege to do so. When a constraint is dropped, any index associated with that constraint (if there is one) is also dropped.

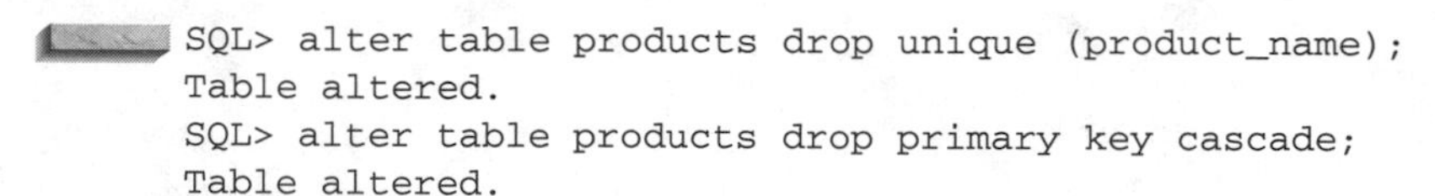

```
SQL> alter table products drop unique (product_name);
Table altered.
SQL> alter table products drop primary key cascade;
Table altered.
```

TIP
Several anomalies can be found when adding, enabling, disabling, or dropping NOT NULL *constraints. Generally, the* `alter table modify` *clause must be used in all situations where the* NOT NULL *constraints on a table must be altered.*

Using the validate and novalidate Options for Enabling Constraints

There is another pair of options you can specify when enabling constraints. They are `enable validate` and `enable novalidate`. If you try to enable your constraint without specifying one of these options, Oracle will use `enable validate` by default. The `enable validate` option when enabling constraints forces Oracle to validate all the data in the constrained column to ensure that data meets the constraint criteria. As you might imagine, this is the default behavior you would want when a constraint is created and/or enabled. However, Oracle also allows you to use the `enable novalidate` option when you want to enforce the constraint for new data entering the table but don't care about data that already exists in the table. Assuming first that the PRODUCTS table has no primary key, the following code block illustrates how to create, disable, and enable a primary key constraint using `enable validate` and `enable novalidate`:

```
SQL> select * from products;
PRODUCT# PRODUCT_NAME     QUANTITY COLOR       PROD_SIZE
--------- ------------ --------- ---------- ----------
        1 FLIBBER               34 GREEN      XXL
        1 blobber                4 GREEN      P
SQL> update products set product# = 2
  2  where product_name = 'blobber';
1 row updated.
SQL> commit;
Commit complete.
SQL> alter table products add
  2  (constraint pk_products_01 primary key (product#));
Table altered.
```

```
SQL> alter table products disable primary key;
Table altered.
SQL> update products set product# = 1
  2  where product_name = 'blobber';
1 row updated.
SQL> commit;
Commit complete.
SQL> alter table products enable validate primary key;
alter table products enable validate primary key
*
ERROR at line 1:
ORA-02437: cannot enable (JASON.PK_PRODUCTS_01) - primary
key violated
SQL> alter table products enable novalidate primary key;
Table altered.
SQL> select * from products;
PRODUCT# PRODUCT_NAME     QUANTITY COLOR      PROD_SIZE
--------- ------------- --------- ---------- ----------
        1 FLIBBER              34 GREEN      XXL
        1 blobber               4 GREEN      P
SQL> insert into products
  2  (product#, product_name, quantity, color, prod_size)
  3  values (1,'FLOBBER',23,'GREEN','L')
insert into products
*
ERROR at line 1:
ORA-00001: unique constraint (JASON.PK_PRODUCTS_01) violated
```

Exercises

1. How do you enable a disabled constraint? What are some restrictions on enabling constraints?
2. What is the EXCEPTIONS table ,and how is it used?
3. Explain use of the `validate` and `novalidate` options for enabling constraints.

Dropping Tables

Sometimes, the "cut off your toe" approach to database alteration is required to make sweeping changes to a table in the database. All the tools for taking that approach have been discussed so far, except one—eliminating the offending table. There are usually some associated objects that exist in a database along with the table. These objects may include the index that is created by the primary key or the `UNIQUE` constraint that is associated with columns in the table. If the table is dropped, Oracle automatically drops any index associated with the table as well. In order to delete a table from the database, the `drop table` command must be executed.

```
SQL> DROP TABLE test_1;
Table dropped.
```

However, dropping tables may not always be that easy. Recall from the earlier in this chapter that when you disable constraints such as primary keys that have foreign-key constraints in other tables depending on their existence, you may have some errors. The same thing happens when you try to drop a table that has a primary key referenced by enabled foreign keys in another table. If you try to drop a table that has other tables' foreign keys referring to it, the following error will ensue:

```
SQL> drop table avail_colors;
drop table avail_colors
           *
ERROR at line 1:
ORA-02449: unique/primary keys in table referenced by foreign keys
```

When there are foreign-key constraints on other tables that reference the table to be dropped, you can use `cascade constraints`. The constraints in other tables that refer to the table being dropped are also dropped with `cascade constraints`.

```
SQL> drop table avail_colors cascade constraints;
Table dropped.
```

Alternatively, you can disable or drop the foreign key in the other table first, by using `alter table drop constraint` *`fk_constraint_name`* syntax, and then issue the `drop table` statement without the `cascade constraints` option. However, with this method you run the risk that many other tables having foreign keys that relate back to the primary key in the table you want to drop will each error out, one at a time, until you disable or drop every foreign-key constraint referring to the table. If there are several, your `drop table` activity may be extremely frustrating.

Exercises

1. How is a table dropped?
2. What special clause must be used when dropping a table when other tables have foreign-key constraints against it?
3. What happens to associated objects, such as indexes, when a table is dropped?

Truncating Tables

There is a special option available in Oracle that allows certain users to delete information from a table quickly. Remember, in Chapter 3 the `delete` statement was discussed. One limitation of the `delete` statement is that it uses the transaction-processing controls that were also covered in the Chapter 3. When the DBA or privileged developer needs to remove the data in a large table, the `delete` option is an inefficient one for accomplishing the job because subsequent `count` operations will perform poorly.

As an alternative, the DBA or developer may use the `truncate` statement. The `truncate` statement is a part of the data-definition language (DDL) of Oracle, like the `create table` statement (unlike the `delete` statement, which is part of the data-manipulation language, the DML). Truncating a table removes all row data from a table quickly, while leaving the definition of the table intact, including the definition of constraints and indexes on the table. The `truncate` statement is a high-speed data deletion statement that bypasses the transaction controls available in Oracle for recoverability in data changes. Truncating a table is almost always faster than executing the `delete` statement without a `where` clause, but once it has been completed, the data cannot be recovered unless you have a backed up copy of the data.

```
TRUNCATE TABLE products;
```

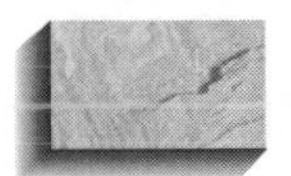

TIP

Truncating tables affects a characteristic about them that Oracle calls the highwatermark. This characteristic is a value Oracle uses to keep track of the largest size the table has ever grown to. When you truncate the table, Oracle resets the highwatermark to zero.

Exercises

1. What are two options for deleting data from a table?
2. Is the `truncate` statement a part of DML or DDL? Explain.
3. What is a highwatermark, and how does it work?

Changing Names of Objects

You can change object names in Oracle by using the `rename` command or with the `alter table rename` command. These commands allow you to change the name of a table without actually moving any data physically within the database. The following code block demonstrates the use of these commands:

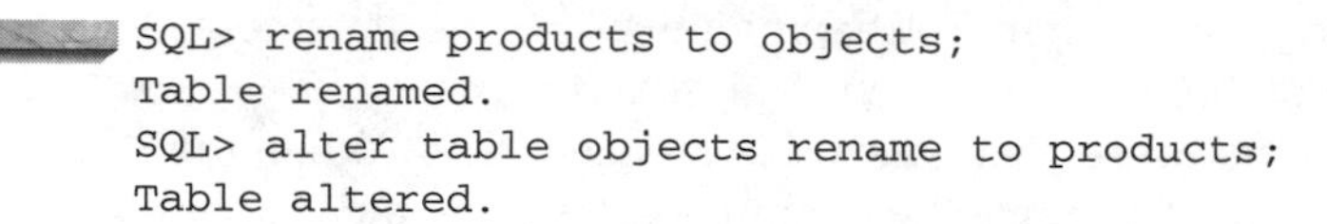

```
SQL> rename products to objects;
Table renamed.
SQL> alter table objects rename to products;
Table altered.
```

Exercise

How is a database object name changed? What are some of the effects of renaming a table?

Viewing Dictionary Comments on Objects

The Oracle data dictionary carries information about tables, including descriptions of the columns in tables. This information can be retrieved from the data dictionary by using the `describe` command.

Comments can also be found in the data dictionary. Comments are useful for recording data-modeling information or any other information about database objects and storing it within the data dictionary. To add a comment to a table or column, use the `comment on` statement, as demonstrated in the following code block.

```
SQL> COMMENT ON TABLE product IS 'I am a teenage werewolf';
Comment created.
SQL> COMMENT ON COLUMN product.serial# IS 'I am a teenage werewolf';
Comment created
```

To view these comments, query the ALL_TAB_COMMENTS view for tables, or the ALL_COL_COMMENTS view for columns on tables.

```
SQL> select a.table_name, a.comments, b.column_name, b.comment
  2  from all_tab_comments a, all_col_comments b
  3  where a.table_name = 'PRODUCTS'
  4  and a.table_name = b.table_name;
TABLE_NAME COMMENTS                COLUMN_NAME COMMENTS
---------- ----------------------- ----------- -----------------------
PRODUCTS   I am a teenage werewolf PRODUCT#    I am a teenage werewolf
PRODUCTS   I am a teenage werewolf COLOR
PRODUCTS   I am a teenage werewolf PROD_SIZE
PRODUCTS   I am a teenage werewolf PRODUCT_NAME
PRODUCTS   I am a teenage werewolf QUANTITY
```

Exercises

1. How can table remarks be entered, and where are they stored?
2. How can you reference comments on a database object?

Sequences

In this section, we will cover the following topics related to sequences:

- The role of sequences
- Creating sequences
- Using sequences
- Modifying sequence definitions
- Removing sequences

In database development, sometimes it becomes necessary to populate a column with a series of integers on an ongoing basis. These integers may be used to uniquely identify the records being entered. For example, a doctor's office may have a client tracking system that assigns each new patient a unique integer ID to identify their records. There are several ways to produce this integer ID through programmatic means, but the most effective means in Oracle is to use sequences.

Role of Sequences

A sequence is a special database object that generates integers according to rules specified at the time the sequence is created. Sequences have many purposes in database systems, the most common of which is to generate primary keys automatically. This task is common in situations where the primary key is not generally used for accessing data in a table. The common use of sequences to create primary keys has one main drawback; because it is simply a sequential number, the primary key itself and the index it creates are somewhat meaningless. But, if you only need the key to guarantee uniqueness, and don't care that you're creating a nonsense key, it is perfectly alright to do so.

Sequences are used as follows. Users `select` data from the sequence with two special keywords that denote virtual columns or *pseudocolumns* in the database. The first pseudocolumn is CURRVAL. This column can be used to see what the current value generated by the sequence is. The second pseudocolumn is NEXTVAL. This column contains the next value that the sequence will generate, according to the rules developed for it. Selecting NEXTVAL on the sequence effectively eliminates whatever value is stored in CURRVAL. Data may only be drawn from a sequence, never placed into it. These pseudocolumns are available for `select` access, but users can incorporate a call on the sequence's CURRVAL or NEXTVAL in insert or update statements so that the value in either of the two columns can be used on a row of another table.

Some restrictions are placed on the types of statements that can draw on CURRVAL and NEXTVAL. Any `update` or `insert` statement can make use of the data in a sequence. References to sequences can *not* be used in subqueries of select statements (including those with having), views, select statements using set operations (such as union or minus), or any select statement that requires a sort to be performed.

Exercises

1. What is a sequence? What are some ways a sequence can be used?
2. What are CURRVAL and NEXTVAL? What happens to CURRVAL when NEXTVAL is selected?

Creating Sequences

Many rules can be applied to sequences, allowing the developer to specify how the sequence generates integers. These rules are useful for defining sequences that produce integers in a special order, or with certain increments. There is even a feature that allows the developer to improve performance on a sequence.

Sequences are created with the **create sequence** statement. Each clause in the **create sequence** statement, and some options for configuring those clauses, are explained in the following list:

- **`start with n`** Allows the creator of the sequence to specify the first value generated by the sequence. Once created, the sequence will generate the value specified by `start with` the first time the sequence's NEXTVAL virtual column is referenced.
- **`increment by n`** Defines the number by which to increment the sequence every time the NEXTVAL virtual column is referenced. The default for this clause is 1 if it is not explicitly specified. You can set *n* to be positive for incrementing sequences, or negative for decrementing or countdown sequences.

- **minvalue *n*** Defines the minimum value that can be produced by the sequence. If no minimum value is specified, Oracle will assume the default, `nominvalue`.
- **maxvalue *n*** Defines the maximum value that can be produced by the sequence. If no maximum value is desired or specified, Oracle will assume the default, `nomaxvalue`.
- **cycle** Allows the sequence to recycle values produced when the `maxvalue` or `minvalue` is reached. If cycling is not desired or not explicitly specified, Oracle will assume the default, `nocycle`. You cannot specify `cycle` in conjunction with `nomaxvalue` or `nominvalue`. If you want your sequence to `cycle`, you must specify maxvalue for incrementing sequences or minvalue for decrementing or countdown sequences.
- **cache *n*** Allows the sequence to cache a specified number of values to improve performance. If caching is not desired or not explicitly specified, Oracle will assume the default, `nocache`.
- **order** Allows the sequence to assign values in the order in which requests are received by the sequence. If order is not desired or not explicitly specified, Oracle will assume the default, `noorder`.

Consider now an example for defining sequences. The integers that can be specified for sequences can be negative as well as positive. Consider the following example of a decrementing sequence. The `start with` integer in this example is positive, but the `increment by` integer is negative, which effectively tells the sequence to decrement instead of increment. When zero is reached, the sequence will start again from the top. This sequence can be useful in programs that require a countdown before an event will occur.

```
CREATE SEQUENCE countdown_20
START WITH 20
INCREMENT BY -1
MAXVALUE 20
MINVALUE 0
CYCLE
ORDER
CACHE 2;
```

If you use the `cycle` option, you must specify a `maxvalue` for incrementing sequences or `minvalue` for decrementing sequences so that Oracle knows when it has reached the maximum or minimum value for the sequence and is supposed to cycle. If you choose to use the `nomaxvalue` and/or `minvalue` options in your sequence (or exclude them from your sequence definition, thereby making them the defaults), then you must also use the `nocycle` option or Oracle will return an error.

Exercises

1. What statement is used for creating a sequence?
2. What are the options used for sequence creation?

Using Sequences

Once the sequence is created, it is referenced using the CURRVAL and NEXTVAL pseudocolumns. The users of the database can view the current value of the sequence by using a `select` statement. Similarly, the next value in the sequence can be generated with a `select` statement. Because sequences are not tables—they are only objects that generate integers via the use of virtual columns—the DUAL table acts as the "virtual" table from which the virtual column data is pulled. As stated earlier, values cannot be placed into the sequence, only selected from the sequence.

The following example demonstrates how COUNTDOWN_20 cycles when the `minvalue` is reached.

```
SQL> select countdown_20.nextval from dual;
  NEXTVAL
---------
       20
SQL> /
  NEXTVAL
---------
       19

...

SQL> /
NEXTVAL
---------
        1
SQL> /
NEXTVAL
---------
        0
SQL> /
NEXTVAL
---------
       20
```

Once the NEXTVAL column is referenced, the value in CURRVAL is updated to match the value in NEXTVAL, and the prior value in CURRVAL is lost. The next code block illustrates this point:

```
SQL> select countdown_20.currval from dual;
  CURRVAL
---------
       20
SQL> select countdown_20.nextval from dual;
  NEXTVAL
---------
       19
SQL> select countdown_20.currval from dual;
  CURRVAL
---------
       19
```

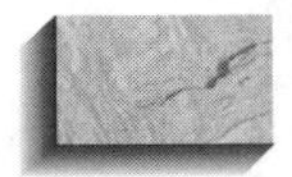

TIP

CURRVAL is set to the `start with` value until NEXTVAL is referenced for the first time after sequence creation. After that, CURRVAL is set to the value for NEXTVAL. Every time NEXTVAL is referenced, CURRVAL changes. Interestingly, the first time you reference NEXTVAL, it gets set to the `start with` value also, so that effectively, the value for CURRVAL doesn't change!

Referencing Sequences in Data Changes

Sequence-value generation can be incorporated directly into data changes made by `insert` or `update` statements. This direct use of sequences in `insert` and `update` statements is the most common use for sequences in a database. In the situation where the sequence generates a primary key for all new rows entering the database table, the sequence would likely be referenced directly from the `insert` statement. Note, however, that this approach sometimes fails when the sequence is referenced by triggers. Therefore, it is best to reference sequences within the user interface or within stored procedures. The following statements illustrate the use of sequences directly in changes made to tables:

```
INSERT INTO expense(expense_no, empid, amt, submit_date)
VALUES(countdown_20.nextval, 59495, 456.34, '21-NOV-99');

UPDATE product
SET product_num = countdown_20.currval
WHERE serial_num = 34938583945;
```

Exercises

1. Identify a way to refer to a sequence with the `select` statement. Why is the DUAL table important in this method?
2. Identify a way to refer to a sequence with the `update` and `insert` statements.

Modifying Sequence Definitions

There may come a time when the sequence of a database will need its rules altered in some way. For example, you may want COUNDOWN_20 to decrement by a different number. Any parameter of a sequence can be modified by issuing the `alter sequence` statement.

```
SQL> select countdown_20.nextval from dual;
NEXTVAL
-------
     16
SQL> alter sequence countdown_20
  2  increment by -4;
Sequence altered.
SQL> select countdown_20.nextval from dual
  2  ;
  NEXTVAL
---------
       12
SQL> /
  NEXTVAL
---------
        8
```

The effect is immediate. In this example, the statement will change the COUNTDOWN_20 to decrement each NEXTVAL by 4 instead of 1.

Any parameter of a sequence that is not specified by the `alter sequence` statement will remain unchanged. Thus, by altering the sequence to use `nocycle` instead of `cycle`, the COUNTDOWN_20 sequence in the following listing will run through one countdown from 20 to 0 only. After the sequence hits 0, no further references to COUNTDOWN_20.NEXTVAL will be allowed:

```
SQL> alter sequence countdown_20
  2  nocycle;
Sequence altered.
SQL> select countdown_20.nextval from dual;
```

```
  NEXTVAL
---------
        4
SQL> /
  NEXTVAL
---------
        0
SQL> /
select countdown_20.nextval from dual
*
ERROR at line 1:
ORA-08004: sequence COUNTDOWN_20.NEXTVAL goes below MINVALUE
and cannot be instantiated
```

Beware of Effects of Modifying Sequences

Modifying sequences is a simple process. However, the impact of the changes can be complex, depending on how an application uses the sequence. The main concern with changing sequences is monitoring the effect on tables or other processes that use the values generated by the sequence.

For example, resetting the value returned by a sequence from 1,150 to 0 is not difficult to execute. However, if the sequence was being used to generate primary keys for a table, for which several values between 0 and 1,150 had already been generated, you would encounter problems when the sequence began generating values for `insert` statements that depend on the sequence to create primary keys. This problem won't show up when the sequence is altered, but later `inserts` will have primary-key constraint violations on the table. The only way to solve the problem (other than deleting the records already existing in the table) is to alter the sequence again.

Exercises

1. What statement is used to modify a sequence definition?
2. When do changes to a sequence take effect?

Removing Sequences

When a sequence is no longer needed, it can be removed. To do so, the DBA or owner of the sequence can issue the `drop sequence` statement. Dropping the sequence renders its virtual columns CURRVAL and NEXTVAL unusable. However, if the sequence was being used to generate primary-key values, the values generated by the sequence would continue to exist in the database. There is no cascading effect on the values generated by a sequence when the sequence is removed.

```
SQL> DROP SEQUENCE countdown_20;
Sequence dropped.
SQL> select countdown_20.currval from dual;
select countdown_20.currval from dual
       *
ERROR at line 1:
ORA-02289: sequence does not exist
```

Exercises

1. How are sequences dropped?
2. What are the effects of dropping a sequence?

Views

In this section, you will cover the following topics concerning views:

- Data dictionary views
- Creating simple and complex views
- Creating views that enforce constraints
- Modifying views
- Removing views

It has been said that eyes are the windows to the soul. While this may or may not be true, it is true that eyes can be used to view the data in a table. In order to make sure the right eyes see the right things, however, some special "windows" on the data in a table can be created. These special windows are called *views*.

A view can be thought of as a virtual table. In reality, a view is nothing more than the results of a `select` statement stored in a memory structure that resembles a table. To the person using the view, manipulating the data from the view is just like manipulating the data from a table. In some cases, it is even possible for the user to insert data into a view as though the view *were* a table. The relationship between tables and views is illustrated in Figure 4-1.

Data Dictionary Views

Data dictionary views prevent you from referring to the tables of the data dictionary directly. This safeguard is important for two reasons. First, it underscores the sensitivity of the tables that store dictionary data. If something happened to the

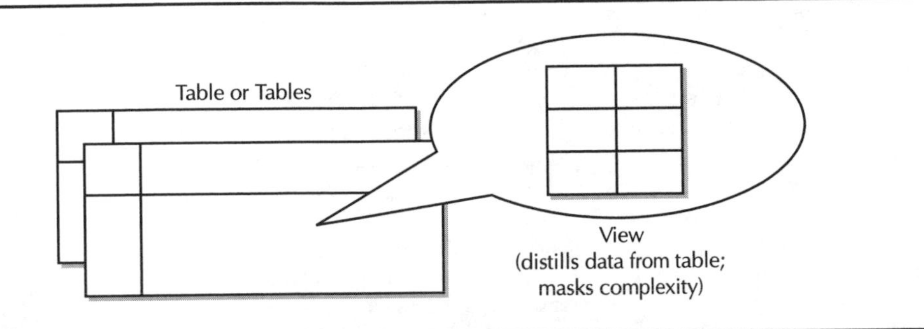

FIGURE 4-1. *Tables and views*

tables that store dictionary data causing either the data to be lost or the table to be removed, the effects could seriously damage the Oracle database, possibly rendering it completely unusable. Second, the dictionary views distill the information in the data dictionary into highly understandable and useful formats. These views divide information about the database into neat categories based on viewing scope and the objects referred to.

Dictionary views are useful for drawing data from the data dictionary. Some of the following examples illustrate selecting data from the data dictionary views identified in Chapter 3:

```
SELECT * FROM all_sequences;
SELECT * FROM dba_objects;
SELECT * FROM user_tables;
```

Other dictionary views provide information about the views themselves. Recall that a view is simply the resultant dataset from a `select` statement, and that the data dictionary actually contains the `select` statement that creates the view. As shown next, view definitions can be quite complex. There are several functions specified in the `select` statement that produces the ALL_TABLES view. Don't worry if you don't understand the structure of this view, you won't need to know the meanings of these columns for OCP Exam 1.

```
SET LONG 9999;
SELECT text FROM all_views WHERE view_name = 'ALL_TABLES';

TEXT
----------------------------------------
select u.name, o.name, ts.name, co.name,
t.pctfree$, t.pctused$,
t.initrans, t.maxtrans,
```

```
s.iniexts * ts.blocksize, s.extsize * ts.blocksize,
s.minexts, s.maxexts, s.extpct,
decode(s.lists, 0, 1, s.lists), decode(s.groups, 0, 1, s.groups),
decode(bitand(t.modified,1), 0, 'Y', 1, 'N', '?'),
t.rowcnt, t.blkcnt, t.empcnt, t.avgspc, t.chncnt, t.avgrln,
lpad(decode(t.spare1, 0, '1', 1, 'DEFAULT', to_char(t.spare1)), 10),
lpad(decode(mod(t.spare2, 65536), 0, '1', 1, 'DEFAULT',
to_char(mod(t.spare2, 65536))), 10),
lpad(decode(floor(t.spare2 / 65536), 0, 'N', 1, 'Y', '?'), 5),
decode(bitand(t.modified, 6), 0, 'ENABLED', 'DISABLED')
from sys.user$ u, sys.ts$ ts, sys.seg$ s,
 sys.obj$ co, sys.tab$ t, sys.obj$ o
where o.owner# = u.user#
and o.obj# = t.obj#
and t.clu# = co.obj# (+)
and t.ts# = ts.ts#
and t.file# = s.file# (+)
and t.block# = s.block# (+)
and (o.owner# = userenv('SCHEMAID')
or o.obj# in
(select oa.obj#
from sys.objauth$ oa
where grantee# in ( select kzsrorol from x$kzsro))
or /* user has system privileges */
exists (select null from v$enabledprivs
where priv_number in (-45 /* LOCK ANY TABLE */,
-47 /* SELECT ANY TABLE */,
-48 /* INSERT ANY TABLE */,
-49 /* UPDATE ANY TABLE */,
-50 /* DELETE ANY TABLE */)))
```

Exercises

1. Why are views used by Oracle in the data dictionary?
2. What are two reasons for using views, both in the data dictionary and elsewhere?

Creating Simple and Complex Views

One example statement for creating a view has already been identified—the one for creating the ALL_VIEWS dictionary view in the Oracle database. Again, though, don't worry about understanding the minutiae of creating every Oracle data dictionary view. The most important things to remember about views can be summarized in the following points:

- Views add extra security to data (for example, a view on the EMP_SALARY table that only shows salary information for the user performing the `select` against the view).
- Views can hide data complexity by combining appropriate information from multiple tables, as discussed under "Creating Complex Views" later in this section.
- Views can hide real column names that may be hard to understand and display simpler names.

Views are created by using the `create view` statement. Once created, views are owned by the user who created them. They cannot be reassigned by the owner unless the owner has the `create any view` system privilege. Privileges will be covered in the "User Access Control" section of this chapter.

Creating Simple Views

There are different types of views that can be created in Oracle. The first type of view is a *simple view*. This type of view is created from the data in one table. Within the simple view, all single-row operations are permitted. Options that are not allowed in a simple view include: `order by` clauses, references to more than one table via a table join, grouping or set operations, `group by` clauses, hierarchical queries (those queries containing a connect by clause), and queries with the `distinct` keyword. The following code block demonstrates the creation of a simple view:

```
CREATE VIEW employee_view
AS (SELECT empid, lastname, firstname, salary
FROM employee
WHERE empid = 59495);
```

Users of a simple view can `insert` data in the underlying table of the view if the creator of the view allows them to do so, subject to the restrictions discussed next. First, though, this statement demonstrates data change via a view:

```
UPDATE employee_view
SET salary = 99000
WHERE empid = 59495;
```

Changing Data in Underlying Tables Through Simple Views: Restrictions

Users can `insert` data in the table underlying a simple view, subject to several restrictions. First, users may have problems inserting data into views if the underlying table has `NOT NULL` constraints on it. This problem can be solved by using a default value for the `NOT NULL` column in the table definition.

The other restrictions on inserting or updating data to a table underlying a simple view are listed here:

- If the `with check option` is used, the user may not `insert`, `delete`, or `update` data on the table that the simple view is not able to `select` for the user.
- The user may not `insert`, `delete`, or `update` data on the table underlying the simple view if the `select` statement creating the view contains `group by`, or `order by`, or a single-row operation.
- No data may be inserted on the table underlying a simple view that contains references to any virtual column, such as ROWID, CURRVAL, NEXTVAL, and ROWNUM.
- No data may be inserted into tables underlying simple views that are created with the `read only` option.

Creating Complex Views

Complex views have some major differences from simple views. Complex views draw data from more than one table and can contain single-row operations and references to virtual columns. Complex views can also contain `group by` clauses. However, `insert`, `update`, and `delete` statements are not permitted on the underlying tables for complex views under most circumstances. Complex views allow complicated data models and conversion operations to be hidden behind a simple view name for the user.

The following complex view presents data from multiple tables:

```
CREATE VIEW employee_view
AS (SELECT e.empid empid, e.lastname lastname, e.firstname firstname,
e.salary salary, a.address, a.city, a.state, a.zipcode
FROM employee e, employee_address a
WHERE e.empid = a.empid);
```

Updatable Join Views

Complex views usually do not allow data to be changed on the underlying table because of the join that is performed in order to obtain the result set displayed in the view. However, in some cases, you may set up a complex view that allows underlying tables to be updated, which is referred to as an *updatable join view*. (A *join view* is simply a view that contains a join.)

Fundamental to the discussion of updatable join views is the concept of a *key-preserved table*. A key-preserved table is a table in a complex view whose primary key columns are all present in the view, and whose values are all unique and not NULL in the view. Views containing outer joins generally won't contain key-preserved tables unless the outer join generates no NULL values. Even in such a case, the updatability is dependant on your data, so for all intents and purposes you should just assume that outer join views are not updatable. If you define a complex view that permits data changes in the underlying tables, but you don't want the underlying tables to be changed, you must specify the `read only option` on the view.

You can execute data change statements on a complex view only where all of the following conditions are met:

- The statement must affect only one of the tables in the join.
- For `update` statements, all columns changed must be extracted from a key-preserved table. In addition, if the view is created `with check option`, join columns and columns taken from tables that are referenced more than once in the view can not be part of the `update`.
- For `delete` statements, there may only be one key-preserved table in the join. This table may be present more than once in the join, unless the view has been created `with check option`.
- For `insert` statements, all columns in which values are inserted must come from a key-preserved table, and the view must not have been created `with check option`.

Updatable Join Views: Some Examples

The easy way to determine whether you can make data changes to a complex view is by issuing the following statement: `select * from USER_UPDATABLE_COLUMNS where TABLE_NAME = '`*`your_complex_view`*`'`. This view will inform you whether the data in the updatable join view's columns can be changed based on considering the key-preserved table criteria. However, even this method isn't foolproof, as demonstrated in the following code block. Also, notice in following block that even though you can add data to the underlying table, you won't necessarily be able to see the data in the view if there is no matching information in the other table in the join. For this example, EXAMPLE_1 is the same table used earlier in this chapter, with its one column, COL1:

```
SQL> create table example_2
  2   (col_2 varchar2(30) primary key,
  3    col_3 varchar2(30),
  4    col_4 varchar2(30),
  5*   col_1 number)
Table created.
SQL>  create view example_vw as
  2  (select col1, col_3, col_4, col_1
  3  from example_1, example_2
View created.
SQL> insert into example_vw (col1) values (3);
insert into example_vw (col1) values (3)
                         *
ERROR at line 1:
ORA-01779: cannot modify a column which maps to a non
key-preserved table
SQL> SELECT column_name, updatable
  2   FROM user_updatable_columns
  3   WHERE table_name = 'EXAMPLE_VW'
COLUMN_NAME                    UPD
------------------------------ ---
COL1                           NO
COL_3                          YES
COL_4                          YES
COL_1                          YES
SQL> insert into example_vw (col_3, col_4, col_1) values ('f','g',1);
insert into example_vw (col_3, col_4, col_1) values ('f','g',1)
            *
ERROR at line 1:
ORA-01400: cannot insert NULL into ("JASON"."EXAMPLE_2"."COL_2")
SQL> create or replace view example_vw as
  2  ((select col1, col_3, col_4, col_1
  3  from example_1, example_2
  4  where col1 = col_1);
View created.
SQL> SELECT column_name, updatable
  2  FROM user_updatable_columns
  3  WHERE table_name = 'EXAMPLE_VW';
```

```
COLUMN_NAME                    UPD
------------------------------ ---
COL1                           NO
COL_2                          YES
COL_3                          YES
COL_4                          YES
COL_1                          YES
SQL> insert into example_vw (col_2, col_3, col_4, col_1)
  2  values ('r','s','t',1);
1 row created.
SQL> select * from example_vw;
No rows selected.
```

Exercises

1. What is a simple view? How does it differ from a complex view? Which view allows the user to `insert` data into the view's underlying table? Explain.
2. What is a complex view? What are the rules that determine when a complex view can be used to modify data in an underlying table?

Creating Views That Enforce Constraints

Tables that underlie views often have constraints that limit the data that can be added to a table. Views have the same limitations on data that can enter the table. In addition, the view can define special constraints for data entry. The option used to configure view constraints is `with check option`. This special constraint forces the view to review the data changes made to see if the data being changed is data the view can `select`. If the data being changed will not be selected by the view, then the view will not let the user make the data change.

The following view will now guarantee that any user who tries to `insert` data into EMPLOYEE_VIEW for an employee other than EMPID# 59495 will not be able to do so:

```
CREATE VIEW employee_view
AS (SELECT empid, lastname, firstname, salary
FROM employee
WHERE empid = 59495)
WITH CHECK OPTION;
```

Exercises

1. How can constraints be created and enforced on views?
2. On what principle does a view constraint operate?

Modifying Views

Sometimes, the creator of a view may need to change the view. However, views don't follow the syntax conventions of other database objects. There is an `alter view` statement in the Oracle SQL language for recompiling or revalidating all references in the view *as it exists already*, but the statement used to alter the definition of a view is the `create or replace view` statement. When a `create or replace view` statement is issued, Oracle will disregard the error that arises when it encounters the view that already exists with that name, and overwrite the definition for the old view with the definition for the new. The following code block illustrates the use of the `create or replace view` statement:

```
CREATE OR REPLACE VIEW employee_view
AS (SELECT empid, lastname, firstname, salary
FROM employee
WHERE empid = user)
WITH CHECK OPTION;
```

A view is made invalid when the underlying table is removed; this illustrates an example of object dependency in the Oracle database. That is to say, certain objects in Oracle depend on others in order to work. Some examples of object dependency that have been presented so far are indexes depending on the existence of the corresponding tables, and views depending on the existence of underlying tables.

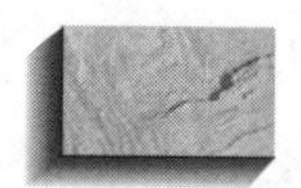

TIP
To fix a view that has become invalid due to the redefinition or deletion of a table that underlies it, the creator of the view must either re-create the underlying table and issue the `alter view` *command, or modify the view with the* `create or replace view` *statement.*

Exercises

1. What statement is used to recompile or revalidate an existing view definition?
2. What statement is used to alter the definition of a view?
3. What is object dependency?

Removing Views

Like other database objects, there may come a time when the view creator needs to remove the view. The command for executing this function is the `drop view` statement. The following statement illustrates the use of `drop view` for deleting views from the database:

```
DROP VIEW employee_view;
```

Exercise

How are views dropped?

Indexes

In this section, we will cover the following topics related to indexes:

- Manual and automatic indexes
- Uses for indexes
- Index structure and operation
- Creating indexes
- Removing indexes
- Guidelines for creating indexes

Indexes are synonymous with performance on the Oracle database. Especially on large tables, indexes make the difference between an application that drags its heels and an application that runs with efficiency. However, there are many performance considerations that must be weighed before making the decision to create an index.

Some uses of indexes have already been presented in the discussion of constraints. However, the indexes that are created along with constraints are only the beginning. In Oracle, indexes can be created on any column in a table except for columns of the LONG datatype. However, performance is not improved simply by throwing a few indexes on the table and forgetting about it. This section will discuss the use of indexes.

Manual and Automatic Indexes

So far, the indexes that have been presented have been ones that are created automatically via the `PRIMARY KEY` or `UNIQUE` constraints on tables. These indexes are identified in the data dictionary in the DBA_INDEXES view. Their names correspond to the name of the `PRIMARY KEY` or `UNIQUE` constraint that can be given if the creator of the table chooses to name indexes. Alternatively, if the creator of the table chooses to use unnamed constraints, then the name given to the constraint and the index will be something akin to SYS_C*xxxxx*, where *xxxxx* is an integer.

However, there are many more indexes that can exist on a database. These other indexes are the manual indexes that are created when the table owner or the developer issues the `create index` command to bring indexes into existence. Once created, there is little to distinguish an index that was created automatically by Oracle from an index that was created manually.

The most common way to distinguish automatic indexes from manual indexes is through naming conventions. Take, for example, the table EMPLOYEE. The primary-key constraint on this table might be named EMPLOYEE_PKEY_01, while an index created on some other column in the table might be called EMPLOYEE_INDX_01. In this fashion, it is easier for the DBA or creator of the database objects to distinguish which objects are which when selecting dictionary data.

Another way for the developer to distinguish manually created indexes from automatically created ones is by looking at the actual columns in the index. The information about the columns in an index can be found in the ALL_CONS_COLUMNS data dictionary view. To someone who is familiar with the design of the database tables, the columns in an index can give some indication as to whether the index was created automatically or manually. Finding indexes that were automatically created for columns that have unique constraints can be trickier, however. This may require an in-depth knowledge of the application or an additional call to the ALL_CONSTRAINTS table to verify the name of the constraint generated automatically by Oracle, if not named explicitly by the creator of the table.

Exercises

1. What are some differences between manual and automatic indexes?
2. How can you distinguish between indexes created manually and those created automatically?

Uses for Indexes

Indexes have multiple uses on the Oracle database. Indexes can be used to ensure uniqueness on a database, and indexes can also boost performance when searching for records in a table. The improvement in performance is gained when the search criteria for data in a table includes a reference to the indexed column or columns.

So far, all the uses we have discussed for indexes have involved unique indexes, where all the values in the indexed column are unique. However, data need not be in this form to create an index on the table. Although the best performance improvement can be seen when a column containing all unique values has an index created on it, similar performance improvements can be made on columns containing some duplicate values or NULL values. However, there are some guidelines for ensuring that the traditional index produces the performance improvements desired. The guidelines for evaluating performance improvements given by traditional indexes and some consideration of the performance and storage trade-offs involved in creating the index will be presented later in this section of the chapter.

Exercises

1. Identify two reasons for using indexes.
2. Must all the data in an index be unique? Explain.

Index Structure and Operation

When data in a column is indexed, a special structure is created that allows Oracle to search for values in that column quickly. This discussion will highlight the features of the index structure, explaining why it works and what it works best with. This discussion covers traditional indexes and bitmap options that are available in Oracle.

B-Tree Index Structure

The traditional index in the Oracle database is based on a highly advanced algorithm for sorting data, called a *B-tree*. A B-tree contains data placed in layered, branching order, from top to bottom, resembling an upside-down tree. The midpoint of the entire list is placed at the top of the "tree" and is called the *root node*. The midpoints of each half of the remaining two lists are placed at the next level, and so on, as illustrated in Figure 4-2.

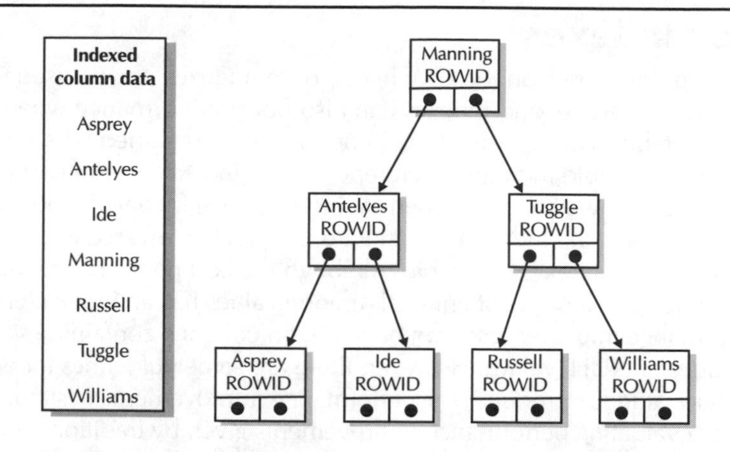

FIGURE 4-2. *A simple B-tree index, displayed pictorially*

By using a "divide and conquer" method for structuring and searching for data, the values of a column are only a few hops away on the tree, rather than several thousand sequential reads through the list away. However, traditional indexes work best when there are many distinct values in the column, or when the column is unique.

The algorithm works as follows:

1. Compare the given value to the value in the halfway point of the list. If the value at hand is greater, discard the lower half the list. If the value at hand is less, then discard the upper half of the list.
2. Repeat step 1 for the remaining part of the list until a value is found or the list exhausted.

Along with the data values of a column, the individual nodes of an index also store a piece of information about the column value's row location on disk. This crucial piece of lookup data is called a *ROWID*. The ROWID for the column value points Oracle directly to the disk location of the table row corresponding to the column value. A ROWID consists of three components that identify the location of a row: the row in the data block in the datafile on disk. With this information, Oracle can then find all the data associated with the row in the table.

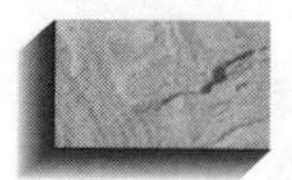

TIP
The ROWID for a table is an address for the row on the disk. With the ROWID, Oracle can find the data on the disk rapidly.

Bitmap Index Structure

The other type of index available in Oracle is the bitmap index. Try to conceptualize a bitmap index as being a sophisticated lookup table, having rows that correspond to all unique data values in the column being indexed. Thus, if the indexed column contains only three distinct values, the bitmap index can be visualized as containing three rows. Each row in a bitmap index contains four columns. The first column contains the unique value for the column being indexed. The next column contains the start-ROWID for all rows in the table. The third column in the bitmap index contains the end-ROWID for all rows in the table. The last column contains a bitmap pattern, in which there will be one bit for every row in the table. Thus, if the table being indexed contains 1,000 rows, there will be 1,000 corresponding bits in this last column of the bitmap index. Each bit in the bitmap index will be set to 0 (off) or 1 (on), depending on whether the corresponding row in the table has that distinct value for the column. In other words, if the value in the indexed column for that row matches this unique value, then the bit is set to 1, otherwise, the bit is set to 0. Figure 4-3 displays a pictorial representation of a bitmap index containing three distinct values.

Each row in the table being indexed adds only a bit to the size of the bitmap pattern column for the bitmap index, so growth of the table won't affect the size of the bitmap index too much. However, each distinct value adds another row to the bitmap index, which adds another entire bitmap pattern with one bit for each row in the table. Be careful about adding distinct values to a column with a bitmap index,

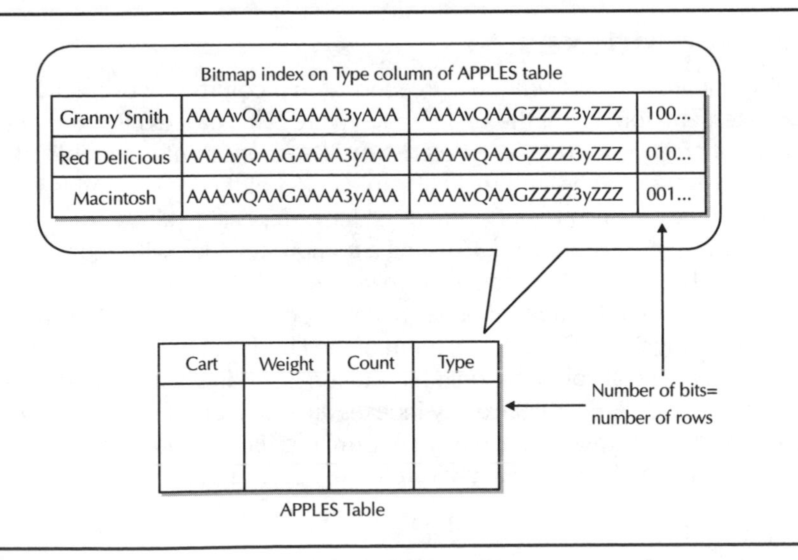

FIGURE 4-3. *A bitmap index, displayed pictorially*

because these indexes work better when there are few distinct values allowed for a column. The classic example of using a bitmap index is where you want to query a table containing employees based on a GENDER column indicating whether the employee is male or female. This information rarely changes about a person, and there are only two distinct possibilities, so a traditional B-tree index is not useful here. However, these are exactly the conditions where a bitmap index would aid performance. Thus, the bitmap index improves performance in situations where traditional indexes are not useful, and vice-versa.

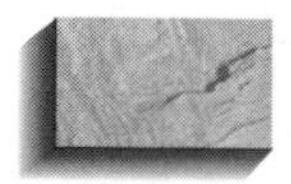

TIP
Up to 32 columns from one table can be included in a single B-tree index on that table, while a bitmap index can include a maximum of 30 columns from the table.

Exercises

1. What is a B-tree index? How does it work? In what situations does it improve performance?
2. What is a bitmap index? How does it work? In what situations does it improve performance?

Creating Indexes

You can manually create a unique B-tree index on a column by using the `create index` statement containing the `unique` keyword. This process is the manual equivalent of creating a `UNIQUE` or `PRIMARY KEY` constraint on a table. (Remember, unique indexes are created automatically in support of those constraints.)

You can index a column that contains NULL or repeated values, as well, simply by eliminating the `unique` keyword. Creating a composite index with more columns named is possible as well. You can also create a *reverse key index* where the contents of the index correspond to a reversed set of data from the indexed column. For example, if you are indexing the LASTNAME column of the EMPLOYEE table, a row containing "COUCHMAN" in that column would have a corresponding value in the reverse key index for "NAMHCOUC." Reverse key indexes are often found in Oracle Parallel Server environments to improve parallel query performance. Finally, you can create a bitmap index by substituting the `bitmap` keyword for the `unique` keyword.

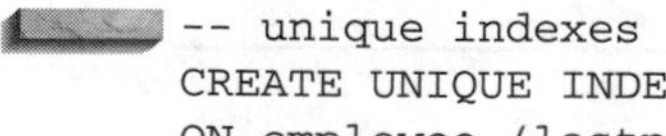

```
-- unique indexes
CREATE UNIQUE INDEX employee_lastname_indx_01
ON employee (lastname);
```

```
-- nonunique indexes
CREATE INDEX employee_lastname_indx_01
ON employee (lastname);

-- composite indexes
CREATE UNIQUE INDEX employee_last_first_indx_01
ON employee (lastname, firstname);

-- reverse key indexes
CREATE INDEX emp_lastname_reverse_indx
ON employee (lastname) REVERSE;

-- bitmap indexes
CREATE BITMAP INDEX employee_status_indx_01
ON employee (empl_status);
```

Once created, little can be altered about an index other than some storage parameters, which you will learn more about in Unit II. In order to replace the definition of the index, the entire index must be dropped and re-created.

Once the index is created, there are several different ways to find information about it. The ALL_INDEXES dictionary view displays storage information about the index, along with the name of the table with which the index is associated. The ALL_OBJECTS dictionary view displays object information about the index, including the index status. The ALL_IND_COLUMNS view displays information about the columns that are indexed on the database. This last view is especially useful for determining the order of columns in a composite index.

Exercises

1. What method is used to create a unique index? A nonunique index?
2. How do you create a bitmap index? A reverse-key index?
3. In unique indexes containing more than one column, how do you think uniqueness is identified? Explain.

Removing Indexes

When an index is no longer needed in the database, the developer can remove it with the `drop index` command. Once an index is dropped, it will no longer improve performance on searches using the column or columns contained in the index. No mention of that index will appear in the data dictionary any more, either. You cannot drop an index that is used for a primary key.

The syntax for the `drop index` statement is the same, regardless of the type of index being dropped (unique, bitmap, or B-tree). If you wish to rework the index in any way, you must first drop the old index and then create the new one.

```
DROP INDEX employee_last_first_indx_01;
```

Exercises

1. How is a bitmap index dropped? How is a unique index dropped?
2. What are the effects of dropping an index?

Guidelines for Creating Indexes

Using indexes for searching tables for information can provide incredible performance gains over searching tables using columns that are not indexed. However, care must be taken to choose the right index. Although a completely unique column is preferable for indexing with a B-tree index, a nonunique column will work almost as well if only about 10 percent of its rows, or even less, have the same values. "Switch" or "flag" columns, such as ones for storing the sex of a person, are not appropriate for B-tree indexes. Neither are columns used to store a few "valid values," or columns that store a token value representing valid or invalid, active or inactive, yes or no, or any such types of values. Bitmap indexes are more appropriate for these types of columns. Finally, you will typically use reverse key indexes in situations where Oracle Parallel Server is installed and running and you want to maximize parallelism in the database.

TIP
The uniqueness of the values in a column is referred to as "cardinality." Unique columns or columns that contain many distinct values have "high cardinality," while columns with few distinct values have "low cardinality." Use B-tree indexes for columns with high cardinality and bitmap indexes for columns with low cardinality.

Exercises

1. What is cardinality?
2. When might the DBA use a B-tree index to improve performance? When might the DBA use a bitmap index to improve performance?

User Access Control

In this section, we will cover the following topics related to controlling user access:

- The Oracle database security model
- Granting system privileges
- Available object privileges
- Using roles to manage database access
- Changing passwords
- Granting and revoking object privileges
- Using synonyms for database transparency

The most secure database is one with no users, but take away the users of a database and the whole point of creating a database is lost. In order to address the issues of security within Oracle, a careful balance must be maintained between providing access to necessary data and functions, while preventing unnecessary access. Oracle provides a means of doing this with its security model, which consists of several options for limiting connect access to the database and for controlling what a user can and cannot see once a connection is established. This section will focus on security on the Oracle database, from creating users to administering passwords to administering security on individual objects in the database.

Oracle Database Security Model

The Oracle database security model consists of two parts. The first part consists of password authentication for all users of the Oracle database. Password authentication is available either directly from the Oracle server or from the operating system supporting the Oracle database. When Oracle's own authentication system is used, password information is stored in Oracle in an encrypted format. The second part of the Oracle security model consists of controlling which database objects a user may access, the level of access a user may have to the object, and whether a user has the authority to place new objects into the Oracle database. At a high level, these controls are referred to as privileges.

The key to giving database access is creating users. Users are created in Oracle with the `create user` command. Along with a password, several storage and database usage options are set up when a user is created. The following statement for creating new users can be issued by a user with the `create user` privilege in Oracle:

```
CREATE USER athena IDENTIFIED BY greek#goddess
```

Security in the database is a serious matter. In most organizations, it consists of a set of functions handled either by the DBA or, more appropriately, by a *security administrator*. This person is the one with the final say over creating new users and determining the accessibility of objects in the database. As a general rule, the larger the organization is and the more sensitive the information, the more likely it is that security will be handled by a special security administrator. However, it is important that developers, DBAs, and users all understand the options available in the Oracle security model for the version of Oracle the organization uses.

Exercises

1. What are the two parts of database security?
2. Who should manage database security, such as user and password administration?

Granting System Privileges

System privileges grant the user the ability to create, modify, and eliminate database objects in Oracle that store data for the application. In fact, in order to do anything in the Oracle database, the user must have a system privilege called `create session`. Within the scope of system privileges, there are two categories. The first is the set of system privileges that relate to object management. These objects include tables, indexes, triggers, sequences and views, packages, stored procedures, and functions. The three actions on objects that are managed by system privileges are defining or creating the object, altering the definition, and dropping the object.

The other category of system privileges refers to the ability of a user to manage special system-wide activities. These activities include functions such as auditing database activity, generating statistics to support the cost-based optimizer, and setting up Oracle to allow access to the database only to users with a special system privilege called `restricted session`. These privileges should generally be granted only to the user or users on the database who will be performing high-level database administration tasks.

All granting of system privileges is managed with the `grant` command. In order to grant a system privilege, the grantor must have either of two privileges: `with admin option` or `grant any privilege`. Granting a privilege `with admin option` signifies that the grantee may further grant or revoke that system privilege to any user on the database, with or without the `with admin option`. Users can create objects in their own schema with a system privilege such as `create table`. However, the user can create objects in any schema if the `any` keyword is added to the system privilege when it is granted, as in `create any table`.

```
GRANT CREATE PROCEDURE, CREATE FUNCTION, CREATE PACKAGE TO spanky;
GRANT CREATE TABLE, CREATE VIEW, CREATE TRIGGER TO athena;
GRANT CREATE TABLE TO athena WITH ADMIN OPTION;
```

Revoking System Privileges

Revoking system privileges is handled with the `revoke` command. In general, there are no cascading concerns related to revoking system privileges. For example, user ATHENA created 17 tables with the `create table` privilege while she had it. Another user revokes the privilege from her, but ATHENA's tables will still exist in Oracle. As another example, user JONES grants the `create table` privilege `with admin option` to user ATHENA, who grants the same to user SPANKY. User JONES then revokes the privilege from user ATHENA. User SPANKY will still have the privilege, in this case.

```
REVOKE SELECT ON EMP FROM ATHENA;
```

Exercises

1. What is a system privilege? What abilities do system privileges manage?
2. How are privileges granted and revoked?
3. What does `with admin option` mean, and how is it used?

Available Object Privileges

Once an object in the Oracle database has been created, its privileges can be administered by the creator of the object. Administration of a database object consists of granting privileges that will allow users to manipulate the object by adding, changing, removing, or viewing data in the database object. Object privileges include:

- **`select`** Permits the grantee of this object privilege to access the data in a table, sequence, view, or snapshot
- **`insert`** Permits the grantee of this object privilege to `insert` data into a table or, in some cases, a view
- **`update`** Permits the grantee of this object privilege to `update` data in a table or view
- **`delete`** Permits the grantee of this object privilege to `delete` data from a table or view

- **alter** Permits the grantee of this object privilege to `alter` the definition of a table or sequence *only*; the `alter` privileges on all other database objects are considered system privileges
- **index** Permits the grantee of this object privilege to create an index on a table already defined
- **references** Permits the grantee of this object privilege to `create` or `alter` a table in order to create a foreign-key constraint against data in the referenced table
- **execute** Permits the grantee of this object privilege to run a stored procedure or function

The object privileges for any database object belong to the user who created that object. Object privileges can be granted to other users for the purpose of allowing them to access and manipulate the object, or to administer the privileges to other users. Giving some other user administrative abilities over object privileges is accomplished via a special parameter on the privilege called `with grant option`.

Exercises

1. What are object privileges? Name some of the object privileges.
2. What option is used to grant an object privilege with the ability to grant the privilege further to others?

Using Roles to Manage Database Access

When databases get large, privileges can become unwieldy and hard to manage. You can simplify the management of privileges with the use of a database object called a *role*. Roles act in two capacities in the database. First, the role can act as a focal point for grouping the privileges to execute certain tasks. The second capacity is to act as a "virtual user" of a database, to which all the object privileges required to execute a certain job function can be granted, such as data entry, manager review, batch processing, and so on.

In order to use roles, you must do three things. First, you must logically group certain privileges together, such as the ability to create tables, indexes, triggers, and procedures. You can further restrict use of the privileges granted to a role by adding password protection to that role, using the `identified by` clause during role creation.

```
CREATE ROLE create_procs IDENTIFIED BY creator;
GRANT create any procedure TO create_procs WITH ADMIN OPTION;
```

Second, you must logically group the users of a database application together according to their similar needs. The most effective way to manage users is to identify the various types of users that will be using the database. Determine the activities each type of user will carry out, and list the privileges that each activity will require. These types or categories will determine the access privileges that will then be granted to roles on the database.

The third step is to create roles that correspond to each activity, and to grant the privileges to the roles. Once this architecture of using roles as a "middle layer" for granting privileges is established, the administration of user privileges becomes a simple matter of granting the appropriate role or roles to the users that need them.

```
CREATE ROLE ofc_developer;

GRANT CREATE TABLE TO ofc_developer;
GRANT SELECT ANY TABLE TO ofc_developer;
GRANT DROP USER TO ofc_developer;

GRANT ofc_developer TO athena;
GRANT ofc_developer TO spanky;
```

Roles can be altered to require a password by using the `alter role identified by` statement. Roles can be deleted with the `drop role` statement. These two options may only be executed by those users with the `create any role`, `alter any role`, or `drop any role` privileges, or by the owner of the role. Privileges can be revoked from a role in the same way as they can be revoked from a user. When a role is dropped, the associated privileges are revoked from the users granted the role. Figure 4-4 shows how privileges can be managed with roles.

In order to use the privileges granted to a user via a role, the role must be enabled for that user. In order for the role to be enabled, it must be the default role for the user, or one of the default roles. The status of a role is usually enabled, unless for some reason the role has been disabled. To change the status of a role for the user, the `alter user default role` statement can be issued. Some of the keywords that can be used in conjunction with defining roles are `all`, `all except`, and `none`; these keywords limit the roles defined for the `alter user` statement.

```
ALTER USER spanky DEFAULT ROLE ALL;
ALTER USER spanky DEFAULT ROLE ALL EXCEPT sysdba;
ALTER USER spanky DEFAULT ROLE app_dev, sys_aly, unit_mgr;
ALTER USER spanky DEFAULT ROLE NONE;
```

Finally, a role can be revoked using the `revoke` statement, much like revoking privileges:

```
REVOKE APP_DEV FROM SPANKY;
```

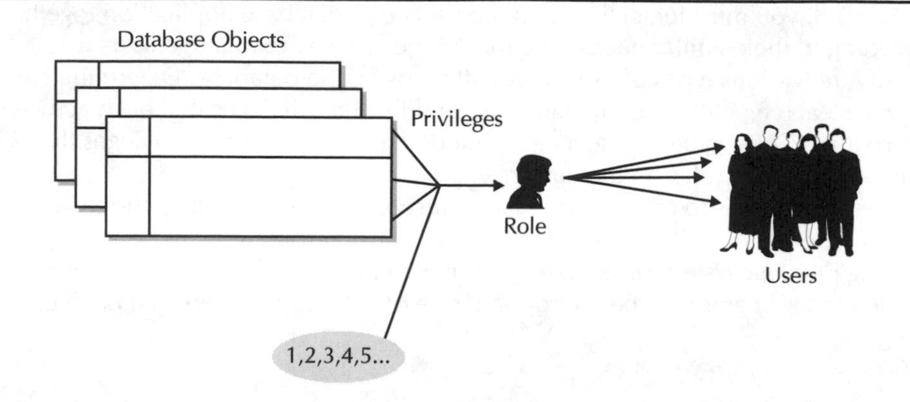

FIGURE 4-4. *Using roles to manage privileges*

Exercises

1. What is a role? How are privileges granted to a role?
2. What is a default role? Can a user exercise privileges granted through a role if the role is disabled? Explain.

Changing Passwords

Once usernames are created, the users can change their own passwords by issuing the following statement:

```
ALTER USER athena IDENTIFIED BY blackcat;
```

Exercise

How is the user password changed?

Granting and Revoking Object Privileges

All granting of object privileges is managed with the `grant` command. In order to `grant` an object privilege, the grantor must either been granted the privilege with the `with grant option` privilege, or must own the object. To grant an object privilege, the grantor of the privilege must determine the level of access a user requires on the object. Then, the privilege must be granted.

Granting object privileges can also allow the grantee of the privilege the ability to administer a privilege if the `with grant option` privilege is used. Administrative ability over an object privilege includes the ability to `grant` the privilege or revoke it from anyone, as well as the ability to grant the object privilege to another user with administrative ability over the privilege.

```
GRANT select, update, insert ON employee TO howlett;
GRANT references ON employee.empid TO athena;
GRANT select, update, insert ON employee TO howlett WITH GRANT OPTION;
```

Revoking object privileges is handled with the `revoke` command. If the user has a privilege granted with the `with grant option` privilege, then the `revoke` command takes away the ability to perform the action managed by that privilege and the ability to administer that privilege. In general, there are many cascading concerns related to revoking object privileges in addition to the removal of a user's ability to use the privilege. For example, suppose user HOWLETT creates the EMPLOYEE table and inserts several rows in it. She then grants the `select` privilege along with the `with grant option` on the EMPLOYEE table to user ATHENA. User ATHENA then grants the same to user SPANKY. If user HOWLETT then revokes the privilege from user ATHENA, that action will also revoke the privilege from user SPANKY. Also, if you drop a table, all object privileges granted to users for that table will also be removed.

Exercises

1. Describe some cascading effects of revoking object privileges from users. Are these effects the same as the cascading effects of revoking system privileges from users? Why or why not?
2. User JONES has `select` privileges on YOU.EMP granted to her with the `with grant option`. You then issue `revoke select on EMP from JONES`. Can JONES still administer the privilege? Why or why not?

Using Synonyms for Database Transparency

Database objects are owned by the users who create them. The objects are available only in the user's schema unless the user grants access to the objects explicitly to other users or to roles granted to other users. However, even when a user is granted permission to use the object, the user must be aware of the boundaries created by schema ownership in order to access the data objects in Oracle. For example, assume the EMPLOYEE table exists in user SPANKY's schema, and user ATHENA attempts to access the table. The following code block shows what happens:

```
SQL> SELECT * FROM employee
  2  WHERE empid = 96945;
SELECT * FROM employee
              *
ORA-00942: table or view does not exist.
```

Instead of returning the data associated with EMPID 96945, Oracle tells the user that the object does not exist. The reason that ATHENA could not see the table in the SPANKY schema is because ATHENA did not refer to the table as being in the schema owned by SPANKY. The following code block shows the successful `select`:

```
SQL> SELECT * FROM spanky.employee
  2  WHERE empid = 96945;
EMPID LASTNAME FIRSTNAME SALARY
----- -------- --------- ------
96945 AHL      BARBARA   45000
```

If remembering which user owns which table seems unnecessarily complicated , synonyms can be used on the database for schema transparency. A synonym gives users an alternate method referring to an existing table. Synonyms allow users to access a database object either by a different name or without having to refer to the owner of the object. The synonym doesn't alter the details of the table's definition, however. Thus, the synonym can allow users to access a table without prefixing the name of the owner of the object.

Synonyms can be public or private. If the synonym is private, it can only be accessed by the user who creates and owns it. If a synonym is public, it will be accessible by any user in the database. The following code block demonstrates the statements used to create private and public synonyms, respectively:

```
CREATE SYNONYM objects FOR products;
CREATE PUBLIC SYNONYM objects FOR products;
```

A public synonym can be created by a privileged user to allow other users of the database to access a particular table without having to prefix the schema name to the table reference. For example, user SPANKY can create a synonym on the EMPLOYEE table, as shown here:

```
-- Executed by SPANKY
SQL> CREATE PUBLIC SYNONYM employee FOR spanky.employee;
```

After the synonym has been created, user ATHENA can access the table with it:

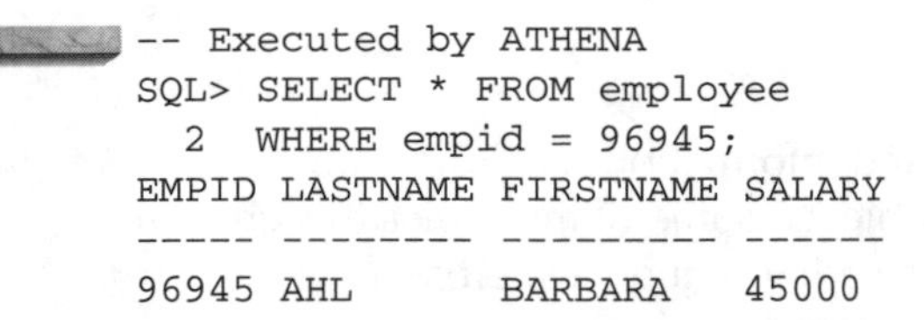

```
-- Executed by ATHENA
SQL> SELECT * FROM employee
  2  WHERE empid = 96945;
EMPID LASTNAME FIRSTNAME SALARY
----- -------- --------- ------
96945 AHL      BARBARA   45000
```

TIP
To create a public synonym, the DBA must first grant you the special `create public synonym` privilege. More information about privileges can be found earlier in this chapter.

The other type of synonym is the private synonym. This is a synonym you create for yourself that allows only you to refer to a table in another schema by the table name only. No other user can access the table via your private synonym—they must create their own. The following code block illustrates ATHENA's use of private synonyms to achieve the same result as before:

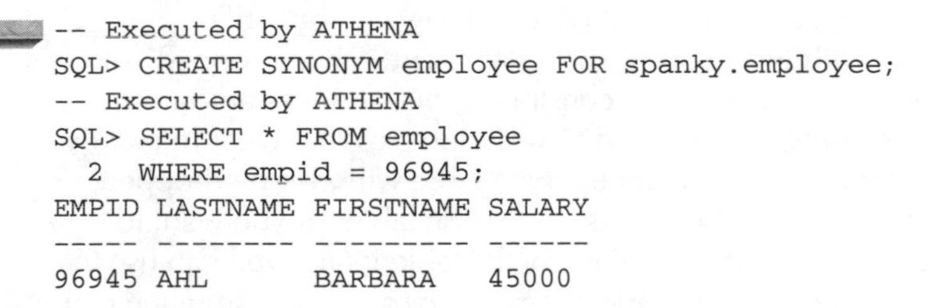

```
-- Executed by ATHENA
SQL> CREATE SYNONYM employee FOR spanky.employee;
-- Executed by ATHENA
SQL> SELECT * FROM employee
  2  WHERE empid = 96945;
EMPID LASTNAME FIRSTNAME SALARY
----- -------- --------- ------
96945 AHL      BARBARA   45000
```

TIP
Synonyms do not give users access to data in a table that they do not already have access to. Only privileges can do that. Synonyms simply allow you to refer to a table without prefixing the schema name to the table reference.

Exercises

1. What is schema transparency?
2. How are synonyms used to facilitate schema transparency? What is a public synonym? What is a private synonym? How do they differ, and how are they the same?

Chapter Summary

This chapter covered several sections of required information for OCP Exam 1 related to the advanced creation of database objects. Some of the topics this chapter covered were altering tables and constraints, creating sequences, creating views, creating indexes, and controlling user access. The material in this chapter comprises about 17 percent of OCP Exam 1.

The first area of discussion in this chapter was altering tables and constraints. There are several ways a developer or DBA can alter tables and constraints. Some of these include adding columns or constraints, modifying the datatypes of columns, or removing constraints. Adding and modifying columns is accomplished with the `alter table` command, as are adding or modifying constraints on the table. There are several restricting factors on adding constraints, all centering around the fact that adding a constraint to a column means that the data already in the column must conform to the constraint being placed upon it.

When adding columns or changing the datatype of a column, there are some general rules to remember. It is easy to increase the size of a datatype for a column, and to add columns to a table. More difficult is changing the datatype of a column from one type to another. Generally, the column whose datatype is being altered must have NULL values for that column specified for all rows in the table.

A table can be dropped with the `drop table` statement. Once dropped, all associated database objects, such as triggers, constraints, and indexes automatically created to support the constraints, are dropped as well. Indexes that were manually generated by the DBA to improve performance on the table will also be dropped.

The chapter also covered several other tricks for altering tables. If you want to delete all data from a table but leave the definition of the table intact, you can use the `truncate` command. Alternately, the `delete from` *`table_name`* command can be used, but on large tables you may see a noticeable difference in performance between these two commands. Also, you cannot issue the `rollback` statement to get all your data back after a truncate the way you can after a `delete` statement. A database object can be renamed with the rename command. Alternatively, you can create a synonym, which allows users to reference a database object using a different name. One final option offered to you is to make notes in the database about objects by adding comments. Comments are added with the `comment on` statement.

The creation of sequences is another important area of advanced Oracle object creation. A sequence is an object that produces integers on demand, according to rules that are defined for the sequence at sequence creation time. One use for a sequence is to generate primary keys for a table. A sequence is created with the `create sequence` command in Oracle. To use a sequence, you must reference two pseudocolumns in the sequence, known as CURRVAL and NEXTVAL. The CURRVAL column stores the current value generated by the sequence; referencing

NEXTVAL causes the sequence to generate a new number and replace the value in CURRVAL with that new number. Several rules can be used to govern how sequences generate their numbers. These rules include specifying the first number the sequence should generate, how the sequence should increment, maximum and minimum values, whether values can be recycled, and so on. The rules that govern sequence integer generation can be modified with the `alter sequence` statement. The sequence can be removed with the `drop sequence` statement.

Creating views is another area of database object creation covered in this chapter. Views are used to distill data from one or more tables that may be inappropriate or too complex for some users to access. One common example of view use is the data dictionary, which stores all data about the Oracle database in tables but disallows direct access to the tables in favor of providing views through which the user can `select` data.

There are two categories of views: simple and complex. A simple view is one that draws data from only one table. A complex view is one that draws data from two or more tables. Simple views sometimes allow the user to `insert, update,` or `delete` data from the underlying table, while complex views allow this to occur only in certain situations as described earlier in the chapter. (There are some other differences between simple and complex views covered in the chapter, and you should be sure you understand the differences before taking OCP Exam 1.) A view can also have the option of enforcing a check on the data being inserted. This means that if you try to make a change, insertion, or deletion to the underlying table, the view will not allow it unless that view can then select the row being changed. Modifying the definition of a view requires dropping the old view and re-creating it or, alternatively, creating the view again with the or replace option. The alter view statement is used for recompiling an existing view following a problem with the object dependencies of the database. Views can be removed from the database with the drop view statement.

The creation of indexes is another area covered in this chapter. There are several indexes created automatically to enforce uniqueness constraints, such as the `PRIMARY KEY` or the `UNIQUE` constraint. However, the DBA can also create nonunique indexes to support performance improvements on the database application. The traditional index consists of a B-tree structure. The search algorithm supported by this structure is similar to a binary search tree, the operation of which was explained in the chapter. In order for a column to be indexed and used effectively using the B-tree index, the cardinality—number of distinct values in the column—should be high. To change the number of columns in an index, the index must be dropped, using the `drop index` statement, and rebuilt. Another index available in Oracle is the bitmap index, also explained in this chapter, and you should understand its use before taking OCP Exam 1. Bitmap indexes work well for improving performance on columns with few distinct values.

Controlling user access on the database is the final area covered by this chapter. The Oracle database security model contains three major areas—user authentication, system privileges, which control the creation of database objects, and object privileges, which control the use of database objects. To change a password, the user can issue the `alter user identified by` statement, specifying the person's username and the desired password. System privileges govern the creation of new database objects, such as tables, sequences, triggers, and views, as well as the execution of certain commands for analyzing and auditing database objects. Three general object maintenance activities are governed by system privileges, and they are the creation, change, and dropping of database objects. Object privileges govern access to an object once it is created, such as `select`, `update`, `insert`, and `delete` statements on tables, execution of packages or procedures, and reference of columns on tables made by foreign-key constraints.

In situations where there are many users and many privileges governing database usage, the management of granting privileges to users can be improved by using roles. Roles act as "virtual users" of the database system, which you can then assign to users. You first define the privileges a user may need, group them logically by function or job description, and then create an appropriate role with those privileges. Then, the role is granted to the users who need those privileges. Roles help to alleviate the necessity of granting several privileges each time a user is added to an application.

Finally, the use of synonyms for data transparency was discussed. Database objects are owned by users and are accessible to their schema only, unless permission is explicitly granted by the owner to another user to view the data in the table. Even then, the schema owning the object must be included in the statement the user issues to reference the object. Public synonyms can eliminate that requirement, making the schema ownership of the database object transparent. A public synonym is created with the `create public synonym` statement, while a private synonym is created with the `create synonym` statement.

Two-Minute Drill

- A table column can be added or modified with the `alter table` statement.
- Columns can be added with little difficulty if they are nullable, using the `alter table add (`*`column_name datatype`*`)` statement. If a `NOT NULL` constraint is desired, add the column, populate the column with data, and then add the `NOT NULL` constraint separately.

- Column datatype size can be increased with no difficulty by using the `alter table modify (`*`column_name datatype`*`)` statement. Column size can be decreased, or the datatype can be changed, only if the column contains NULL for all rows.
- Constraints can be added to a column only if the column already contains values that will not violate the added constraint.
- `PRIMARY KEY` constraints can be added with a table constraint definition by using the `alter table add (constraint` *`constraint_name`* `primary key (`*`column_name`*`))` statement, or with a column constraint definition by using the alter table modify `(`*`column_name`* `constraint` *`constraint_name`* `primary key)` statement.
- `UNIQUE` constraints can be added with a table constraint definition by using the `alter table add (constraint` *`constraint_name`* `unique (`*`column_name`*`))` statement, or with a column constraint definition by using the `alter table modify (`*`column_name`* `constraint` *`constraint_name`* `unique)` statement.
- `FOREIGN KEY` constraints can be added with a table constraint definition by using the `alter table add (constraint` *`constraint_name`* `foreign key (`*`column_name`*`) references` *`OWNER.TABLE`* `(`*`column_name`*`) [on delete cascade])` statement, or with a column constraint definition by using the `alter table modify (`*`column_name`* `constraint` *`constraint_name`* `references` *`OWNER.TABLE`* `(`*`column_name`*`) [on delete cascade])` statement.
- `CHECK` constraints can be added with a table constraint definition by using the `alter table add (constraint` *`constraint_name`* `check (`*`check_condition`*`))` statement, or with a column constraint definition by using the `alter table modify (`*`column_name`* `constraint` *`constraint_name`* `check (`*`check_condition`*`))` statement.
- The check condition cannot contain subqueries, references to certain keywords (such as `user, sysdate, rowid`), or any pseudocolumns.
- `NOT NULL` constraints can be added with a column constraint definition by using the `alter table modify (`*`column_name`* `NOT NULL)` statement.
- A named `PRIMARY KEY, UNIQUE, CHECK,` or `FOREIGN KEY` constraint can be dropped with the `alter table drop constraint` *`constraint_name`* statement. A `NOT NULL` constraint is dropped using the `alter table modify (`*`column_name`* `NULL)` statement.

- If a constraint that created an index automatically (primary keys and `UNIQUE` constraints) is dropped, then the corresponding index is also dropped.
- If the table is dropped, all constraints, triggers, and indexes created for the table are also dropped.
- Removing all data from a table is best accomplished with the `truncate` command rather than the `delete from table_name` statement because `truncate` will reset the table's highwatermark and deallocate all the table's storage quickly, improving performance on `select count( )` statements issued after the truncation.
- An object name can be changed with the `rename` statement or with the use of synonyms.
- A comment can be added to the data dictionary for a database object with the `comment on` command. The comment can subsequently be viewed in DBA_TAB_COMMENTS or DBA_COL_COMMENTS.
- A sequence generates integers based on rules that are defined by sequence creation.
- Options that can be defined for sequences are the first number generated, how the sequence increments, the maximum value, the minimum value, whether the sequence can recycle numbers, and whether numbers will be cached for improved performance.
- Sequences are used by selecting from the CURRVAL and NEXTVAL virtual columns.
- The CURRVAL column contains the current value of the sequence.
- Selecting from NEXTVAL increments the sequence and changes the value of CURRVAL to whatever is produced by NEXTVAL.
- The rules that a sequence uses to generate values can be modified using the `alter sequence` statement.
- A sequence can be deleted with the `drop sequence` statement.
- A view is a virtual table defined by a `select` statement.
- Views can distill data from tables that may be inappropriate for some users, and can hide the complexity of data from several tables or on which many operations have been performed.
- There are two types of views: simple and complex.

- Simple views are those that have only one underlying table.
- Complex views are those with two or more underlying tables that have been joined together.
- Data may be inserted into simple views except in the following cases:
  - If the `with check option` is used, the user may not `insert`, `delete`, or `update` data on the table underlying the simple view if the view itself is not able to `select` that data for the user.
  - The user may not `insert`, `delete`, or `update` data on the table underlying the simple view if the `select` statement creating the view contains `group by`, `order by`, or a single-row operation.
  - No data may be inserted in simple views that contain references to any virtual column, such as ROWID, CURRVAL, NEXTVAL, and ROWNUM.
  - No data may be inserted into simple views that are created with the `read only` option.
- Data may be inserted into complex views when all of the following conditions are true:
  - The statement affects only one of the tables in the join.
  - For `update` statements, all columns changed are extracted from a key-preserved table. In addition, if the view is created with the `with check option` clause, join columns and columns taken from tables that are referenced more than once in the view are not part of the update.
  - For `delete` statements, there is only one key-preserved table in the join. This table may be present more than once in the join, unless the view has been created with the `with check option` clause.
  - For `insert` statements, all columns where values are inserted must come from a key-preserved table, and the view must not have been created with the `with check option` clause.
- The `with check option` clause on creating a view allows the simple view to limit the data that can be inserted, or otherwise changed, on the underlying table by requiring that the data change be selectable by the view.
- Modifying the data selected by a view requires re-creating the view with the `create or replace view` statement, or dropping the view first and issuing the `create view` statement.

- An existing view can be recompiled by executing the `alter view` statement if for some reason it becomes invalid due to object dependency.
- A view is dropped with the `drop view` statement.
- Some indexes in a database are created automatically, such as those supporting the `PRIMARY KEY` and the `UNIQUE` constraints on a table.
- Other indexes are created manually to support database performance improvements.
- Indexes created manually are often on nonunique columns.
- B-tree indexes work best on columns that have high cardinality— a large number of distinct values and few duplicates in the column.
- B-tree indexes improve performance by storing data in a binary search tree, and then searching for values in the tree using a "divide and conquer" methodology outlined in this chapter.
- Bitmap indexes improve performance on columns with low cardinality—few distinct values and many duplicates on the column.
- Columns stored in the index can be changed only by dropping and re-creating the index.
- Indexes can be deleted by issuing the `drop index` statement.
- The Oracle database security model consists of two parts: limiting user access with password authentication and controlling object use with privileges.
- Available privileges in Oracle include system privileges for maintaining database objects and object privileges for accessing and manipulating data in database objects.
- Changing a password can be performed by a user with the `alter user identified by` statement.
- Granting system and object privileges is accomplished with the `grant` command.
- Taking away system and object privileges is accomplished with the `revoke` command.
- Creating a synonym is accomplished with the `create public synonym` command.

Chapter Questions

1. **Dropping a table has which of the following effects on a nonunique index created for the table?**

   A. No effect.

   B. The index will be dropped.

   C. The index will be rendered invalid.

   D. The index will contain NULL values.

2. **Which of the following statements about indexes is true?**

   A. Columns with low cardinality are handled well by B-tree indexes.

   B. Columns with low cardinality are handled poorly by bitmap indexes.

   C. Columns with high cardinality are handled well by B-tree indexes.

3. **To increase the number of nullable columns for a table:**

   A. Use the `alter table` statement.

   B. Ensure that all column values are NULL for all rows.

   C. First, increase the size of adjacent column datatypes, and then add the column.

   D. Add the column, populate the column, and then add the `NOT NULL` constraint.

4. **To add the number of columns selected by a view:**

   A. Add more columns to the underlying table.

   B. Issue the `alter view` statement.

   C. Use a correlated subquery in conjunction with the view.

   D. Drop and re-create the view with references to select more columns.

5. A user issues the statement `select count(*) from EMPLOYEE`. The query takes an inordinately long time and returns a count of zero. The most cost-effective solution is

A. Upgrade the hardware.

B. Truncate the table.

C. Upgrade the version of Oracle.

D. Delete the highwatermark.

6. Which of the following choices are valid parameters for sequence creation?

A. `identified by`

B. `using temporary tablespace`

C. `maxvalue`

D. `on delete cascade`

7. The following statement is issued against the Oracle database. Which line will produce an error?

A. `create view EMP_VIEW_01`

B. `as select E.EMPID, E.LASTNAME, E.FIRSTNAME, A.ADDRESS`

C. `from EMPLOYEE E, EMPL_ADDRESS A`

D. `where E.EMPID = A.EMPID`

E. `with check option;`

F. This statement contains no errors.

8. The following statement is issued on the database: `comment on table EMPL is 'Do not use this table.'` How can this data be viewed?

A. Using the `describe` command

B. Issuing a `select * from empl` statement

C. Selecting from ALL_COMMENTS

D. Selecting from ALL_TAB_COMMENTS

9. Which system privilege allows the user to connect to a database in restricted session mode?

A. `create table`

B. `create user`

C. `restricted session`

D. `create session`

10. Which of the following statements is true about roles? (Choose three)

A. Roles can be granted to other roles.

B. Privileges can be granted to roles.

C. Roles can be granted to users.

D. Roles can be granted to synonyms.

11. User MANN has granted the `create any view with admin option` privilege to user SNOW. User SNOW granted the same privilege `with admin option` to user REED. User MANN revokes the privilege from user SNOW. Which statement is true about privileges granted to users REED, MANN, and SNOW?

A. REED and MANN have the privilege, but SNOW does not.

B. REED and SNOW have the privilege, but MANN does not.

C. MANN and SNOW have the privilege, but REED does not.

D. MANN has the privilege, but SNOW and REED do not.

12. After referencing NEXTVAL, the value in CURRVAL

A. Is incremented by one

B. Is now in PREVVAL

C. Is equal to NEXTVAL

D. Is unchanged

Answers to Chapter Questions

1. B. The index will be dropped.

Explanation Like automatically generated indexes associated with a table's primary key, the indexes created manually on a table to improve performance will be dropped if the table is dropped. Choices A, C, and D are therefore invalid. Refer to the discussion of dropping indexes in the chapter summary.

2. C. Columns with high cardinality are handled well by B-tree indexes.

Explanation Columns with low cardinality are the bane of B-tree indexes, eliminating choice A. Furthermore, bitmap indexes are primarily used for performance gains on columns with low cardinality, eliminating choice B. The correct answer is C. Review the discussion of how B-tree indexes work if you do not understand.

3. A. Use the `alter table` statement.

Explanation The `alter table` statement is the only choice offered that allows the developer to increase the number of columns per table. Choice B is incorrect because setting a column to all NULL values for all rows does simply that. Choice C is incorrect because increasing the adjacent column sizes simply increases the sizes of the columns, and choice D is incorrect because the listed steps outline how to add a column with a `NOT NULL` constraint, something not specified by the question.

4. D. Drop and re-create the view with references to select more columns.

Explanation Choice A is incorrect because adding columns to the underlying table will not add columns to the view, but will likely invalidate the view. Choice B is incorrect because the `alter view` statement simply recompiles an existing view definition, whereas the real solution here is to change the existing view definition by dropping and re-creating the view. Choice C is incorrect because a correlated subquery will likely worsen performance and underscores the real problem—a column must be added to the view. Review the discussion of altering the definition of a view.

5. B. Truncate the table.

Explanation Choices A and C may work, but an upgrade of hardware and software will cost far more than truncating the table. Choice D is partly correct, as there will be some change required to the highwatermark, but the change is to reset, not eliminate entirely, and the method used is to `truncate` the table.

6. C. `maxvalue`

Explanation The `maxvalue` option is a valid option for sequence creation. Choices A and B are both part of the `create user` statement, while choice D is a part of a constraint declaration in an `alter table` or `create table` statement. Review the discussion on creating sequences.

7. F. This statement contains no errors.

Explanation Even though the reference to `with check option` is inappropriate, considering that inserts into complex views are not possible, the statement will not actually produce an error when compiled. Therefore, there are no errors in the view. This is not something that can be learned; it requires hands-on experience with Oracle.

8. D. Selecting from ALL_TAB_COMMENTS

Explanation Choice A is incorrect because comments will not appear in the description of the table from the data dictionary. Instead, the user must select comments from the ALL_, USER_, or DBA_TAB_COLUMNS views. Choice C is incorrect because ALL_COMMENTS is not a view in the Oracle data dictionary, while choice B is incorrect because selection of data from the table commented yields only the data in that table, not the comments. Refer to the discussion of adding comments to tables.

9. C. `restricted session`

Explanation Choice A is incorrect because the `create table` privilege allows the user to create a table, while choice B is incorrect for a similar reason—create user allows the user to create new users. Choice D is required for establishing connection to an open database, while choice C is the only privilege listed that allows the user to connect to a database in restricted session mode. Refer to the discussion and review of roles and privileges.

10. A, B, and C.

Explanation Choice D is the only option not available to managing roles. Roles cannot be granted to synonyms. Refer to the discussion of roles and privileges in this chapter.

11. A. REED and MANN have the privilege, but SNOW does not.

Explanation The only result of revoking a system privilege in Oracle is that the user the privilege is revoked from is the only user who loses it. If the user has granted the privilege to someone else, that other user will still have the privilege. Review the discussion of cascading effects of granting privileges.

12. C. Is equal to NEXTVAL

Explanation Once NEXTVAL is referenced, the sequence increments the integer and changes the value of CURRVAL to be equal to NEXTVAL. Refer to the discussion of sequences for more information.

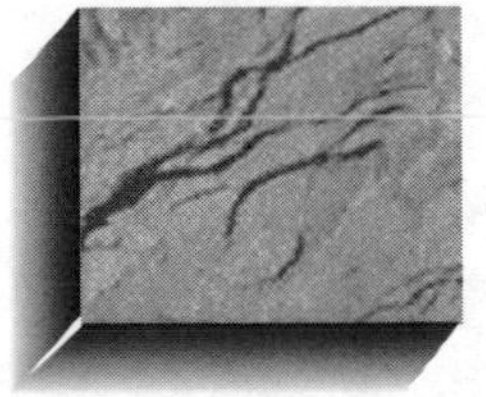

CHAPTER 5

Introducing PL/SQL

n this chapter, you will learn about and demonstrate knowledge in the following areas:

- Overview of PL/SQL
- Developing a PL/SQL block
- Controlling PL/SQL process flow
- Interacting with the Oracle database
- Explicit cursor handling
- Error handling

In Oracle, there is a special language available for developers to code stored procedures that seamlessly integrate with database object access via SQL, the language of database objects. However, the language known as PL/SQL, offers far more execution potential than simple `update`, `select`, `insert`, and `delete` statements. PL/SQL offers a procedural extension that allows for modularity, variable declaration, loops and other logic constructs, and advanced error handling. This chapter will present an overview of PL/SQL syntax, constructs, and usage. This information is tested on OCP Exam 1, and comprises 22 percent of the test material. Since PL/SQL is used extensively in Oracle development, it is crucial that you understand this language.

Overview of PL/SQL

In this section, you will cover the following topics:

- Using PL/SQL to access Oracle
- PL/SQL program constructs

PL/SQL offers many advantages over other programming languages for handling the logic and enforcement of business rules in database applications. It is a straightforward language with all the common logic constructs associated with a programming language, and it has many things other languages don't have, such as robust error handling and modularization of code blocks. The PL/SQL code used to interface with the database is also stored directly on the Oracle database, and is the only programming language that interfaces with the Oracle database natively and within the database environment. This overview will cover the benefits associated with using PL/SQL in the Oracle database and the basic constructs of the PL/SQL language.

Using PL/SQL to Access Oracle

Many applications that use client/server architecture have one thing in common—a difficulty in maintaining the business rules for an application. When business rules are decentralized throughout the application, the developers must make changes throughout the application and implement system testing to determine whether the changes are sufficient. However, in tight scheduling situations, the first deployment item to get left off is almost invariably testing. One logical design change that should be implemented in this scenario is to centralize the logic in the application to allow for easier management of change. In systems that use the Oracle database, a "middle layer" of application logic can be designed with PL/SQL. The benefits of doing so are as follows:

- PL/SQL is managed centrally within the Oracle database. You manage source code and execution privileges with the same syntax used to manage other database objects.
- PL/SQL communicates natively with other Oracle database objects.
- PL/SQL is easy to read and has many features permitting code modularity and error handling.

Decentralized computing has increased the capacity of organizations to provide fast, easy-to-use applications to their customers. However, when business logic is stored in the client application, making changes to the business logic involves coding the changes, recompiling the client application (potentially on several different platforms), and installing the new executable versions of the client on every user's desktop. There is also overhead for communication and support to make sure all users of the application are on the right version.

Some centralization improves the job by allowing the application development shop the ability to eliminate distribution channels for business-logic changes and to focus the client-side developers' efforts on the client application. Storing application logic centrally, as PL/SQL stored procedures allow, means only having to compile a change once to make it immediately accessible to all users of the application.

Figure 5-1 shows an example of the difference between centralized and decentralized business logic code management.

Exercises

1. What are some advantages of using PL/SQL to access the database?
2. Where is PL/SQL compiled and stored?

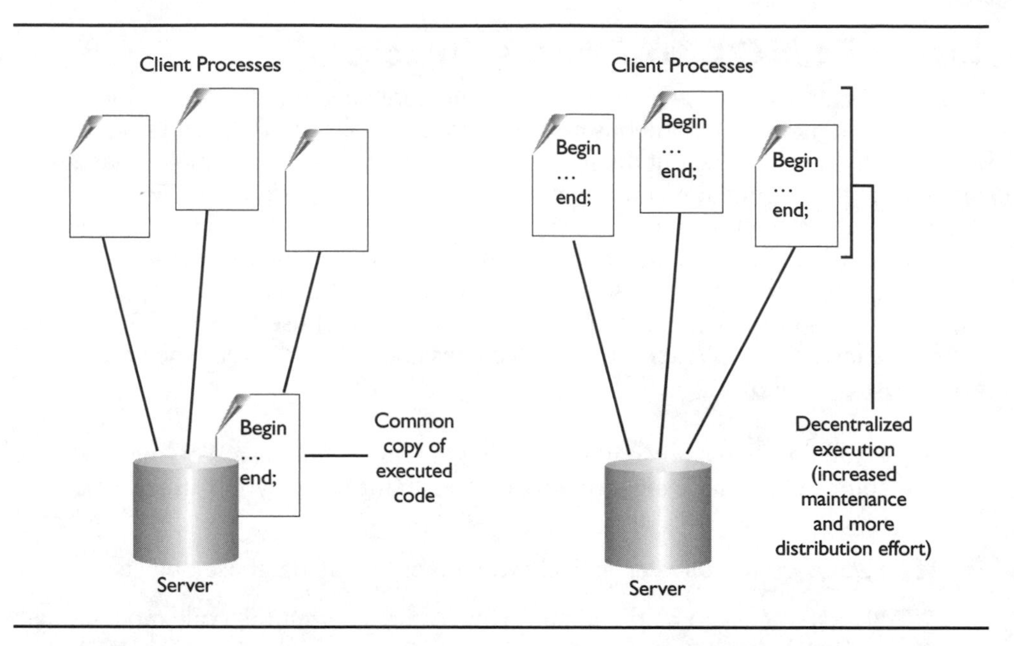

FIGURE 5-1. *Centralized versus decentralized business-logic code management*

PL/SQL Program Constructs

There are many different programming constructs available to PL/SQL—from various types of modules, to the components of a PL/SQL block, to the logic constructs that manage process flow. This section will identify each component of the PL/SQL language and give some highlights about each.

Modularity

PL/SQL allows the developer to create program modules to improve software reusability and to hide the complexity of the execution of a specific operation behind a name. For example, there may be a complex process involved in adding an employee record to a corporate database, which requires records to be added to several different tables for several different applications. Stored procedures may handle the addition of records to each of the systems, making it look to the user that the only step required is entering data on one screen. In reality, that screen's worth of data entry may call dozens of separate procedures, each designed to handle one small component of the overall process of adding the employee. These components may even be reused data entry code blocks from the various pension, health care, day-care, payroll, and other Human Resources applications, which have simply been repackaged around this new data entry screen. Figure 5-2 shows how modularity can be implemented in PL/SQL blocks.

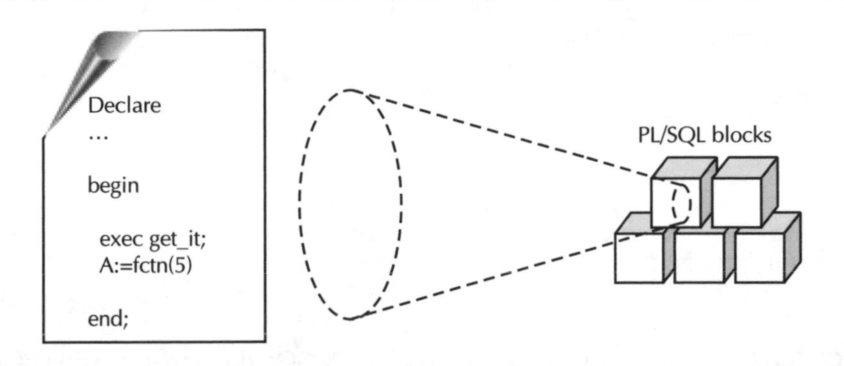

FIGURE 5-2. *Modularity and PS/SQL blocks*

Named PL/SQL—Procedures, Functions, Triggers, and Packages

There are two basic types of PL/SQL code available in Oracle. The first is *named PL/SQL blocks.* Named blocks or modules of PL/SQL code are blocks of code that can be stored and referenced by name by other PL/SQL blocks—or by a user from the SQL*Plus command line. When you submit a named block of code to Oracle, the database will parse and compile the block and store it with the name you have given the block. You can run the block later by referencing it by name using the `execute` command. For example, if you had a named PL/SQL procedure called `money_converter( )`, you could execute it as follows:

```
SQL> execute money_converter;
```

Named blocks of PL/SQL code are divided into four categories. Those categories are stored procedures, functions, packages, and triggers. The four types of named PL/SQL code blocks are described in the following paragraphs, and examples are given to show you what these different code blocks look like.

PROCEDURE A *procedure* is a named block of PL/SQL code that consists of a series of statements accepting and/or returning zero or more variables.

```
PROCEDURE money_converter
(amount          IN NUMBER,
from_currency    IN VARCHAR2,
to_currency      IN VARCHAR2,
return_val       IN OUT NUMBER
) IS   /* denotes beginning of declaration section. */
   my_new_amt number(10) := 0;
   bad_data exception;
```

```
BEGIN   /* begins the executable section of a code block. */
    IF my_new_amt > 3 THEN
      DBMS_OUTPUT.PUT_LINE('Do this');
    ELSE
      DBMS_OUTPUT.PUT_LINE('Do that');
    END IF;
    return_val := my_new_amt;
EXCEPTION   /*Begins the Exception Handler */
    WHEN bad_data THEN
      DBMS_OUTPUT.PUT_LINE('Error condition');
END;
```

FUNCTION A *function* is a named block of PL/SQL code that consists of a series of statements accepting zero or more variables and returning one value.

```
FUNCTION convert_money
(amount          IN NUMBER,
from_currency    IN VARCHAR2,
to_currency      IN VARCHAR2
) RETURN NUMBER IS    /* denotes beginning of declaration section. */
   my_new_amt number(10) := 0;
   bad_data exception;
BEGIN   /* begins the executable section of a code block. */
    IF my_new_amt > 3 THEN
      DBMS_OUTPUT.PUT_LINE('Do this');
    ELSE
      DBMS_OUTPUT.PUT_LINE('Do that');
    END IF;
    RETURN my_new_amt;
EXCEPTION   /*Begins the Exception Handler */
    WHEN bad_data THEN
      DBMS_OUTPUT.PUT_LINE('Error condition');
END;
```

PACKAGE A *package* is a named block of PL/SQL code that consists of a collection of named procedures and functions that has two parts. The first part is a *specification,* listing available procedures and functions and their parameters, constants, and user-defined type declarations. The second part is a *body,* containing the actual code for the procedures and functions.

```
-- Package Specification
CREATE OR REPLACE PACKAGE money_pkg IS
/************/
  EOF constant varchar2(30) := '~~+~~+~~';
/************/
```

```
  FUNCTION convert_money
  (amount          IN NUMBER,
   from_currency   IN VARCHAR2,
   to_currency     IN VARCHAR2
  ) RETURN NUMBER;
/************/
  PROCEDURE money_converter
  (amount          IN NUMBER,
   from_currency   IN VARCHAR2,
   to_currency     IN VARCHAR2,
   return_val      IN OUT NUMBER
  );
/************/
END;

-- Package Body
CREATE OR REPLACE PACKAGE BODY money_pkg IS
/************/
 FUNCTION convert_money
  (amount          IN NUMBER,
   from_currency   IN VARCHAR2,
   to_currency     IN VARCHAR2
  ) RETURN NUMBER
 IS   /* denotes beginning of declaration section. */
     my_new_amt number(10) := 0;
     bad_data exception;
  BEGIN  /* begins the executable section of a code block. */
    IF my_new_amt > 3 THEN
      DBMS_OUTPUT.PUT_LINE('Do this');
    ELSE
      DBMS_OUTPUT.PUT_LINE('Do that');
    END IF;
    RETURN my_new_amt;
  EXCEPTION  /*Begins the Exception Handler */
    WHEN bad_data THEN
      DBMS_OUTPUT.PUT_LINE('Error condition');
 END;
/**************/
  PROCEDURE money_converter
  ( amount           IN NUMBER,
    from_currency    IN VARCHAR2,
    to_currency      IN VARCHAR2,
    return_val       IN OUT NUMBER
  ) IS   /* denotes beginning of declaration section. */
   my_new_amt number(10) := 0;
   bad_data exception;
```

```
  BEGIN   /* begins the executable section of a code block. */
    IF my_new_amt > 3 THEN
      DBMS_OUTPUT.PUT_LINE('Do this');
    ELSE
      DBMS_OUTPUT.PUT_LINE('Do that');
    END IF;
    return_val := my_new_amt;
  EXCEPTION  /*Begins the Exception Handler */
    WHEN bad_data THEN
      DBMS_OUTPUT.PUT_LINE('Error condition');
  END;
/************/
END;
```

TRIGGER A *trigger* is a named block of PL/SQL code that consists of a series of PL/SQL statements attached to a database table. Whenever a triggering event (`update`, `insert`, or `delete`) occurs, the event's corresponding trigger will occur. For example, an update trigger will fire whenever an `update` statement occurs, but not when an `insert` statement occurs. Triggers can be defined to fire once for an entire table when the triggering event occurs, or for each row modified by the triggering event. Triggers can also be set to fire only when one column in a row changes.

```
CREATE OR REPLACE TRIGGER rate_hist_trigger_01
BEFORE delete ON exch_rate
BEGIN
   INSERT INTO exch_rate_hist (chg_user, chg_date_time, comment)
   VALUES (user, to_char(sysdate,'YYYY-MM-DD HH:MIAM'),
           'Exchange rates removed from table on this date');
END;
```

Anonymous PL/SQL Blocks

In addition to named blocks of PL/SQL, you can have *unnamed,* or *anonymous,* PL/SQL blocks. An anonymous PL/SQL block is the second type of code block, consisting of several PL/SQL commands that are submitted to Oracle for parsing and execution all at the same time. Anonymous blocks are not stored in the Oracle database the way named blocks are. Instead, Oracle parses and executes the statements when you submit the block. The following code listing contains an anonymous PL/SQL block:

```
DECLARE /* begins the declaration section in an anonymous block */
    my_convert_amt          NUMBER(10);
    my_convert_currency     VARCHAR2(5);
```

```
    my_old_currency         VARCHAR2(5);
    bad_data                EXCEPTION;
BEGIN /* begins the executable section of a code block. */
    IF my_convert_amt=6 THEN
     . . .
    ELSE
     . . .
    END IF;
EXCEPTION  /*Begins the Exception Handler */
    WHEN bad_data THEN
      DBMS_OUTPUT.PUT_LINE('Error condition');
END;
```

Components of a PL/SQL Block

There are three components of named or anonymous PL/SQL blocks from the previous sections. The components are the *variable declaration section*, the *executable section*, and the *exception handler*. The declaration section, which is optional, identifies all variable constructs that will be used in the code block. A variable can be of any datatype available in the Oracle database, as well as of some other types exclusive to PL/SQL. The executable section of a PL/SQL block is mandatory and starts with the `begin` keyword and ends either with the `end` keyword for the entire code block or with the `exception` keyword. The final component of a PL/SQL block is the exception handler. This code portion defines all errors that may occur in the block and specifies how they should be handled. The exception handler is optional in PL/SQL.

It is easier to identify the declaration section of an anonymous PL/SQL block because the declaration section is preceded by the `declare` keyword. It too contains a declaration section, an executable section, and an exception handler. Look at the preceding anonymous code block again, and identify the declaration, execution, and exception section, denoted by the appropriate keywords. In a named PL/SQL block, the declaration section is found between the `is` keyword and the `begin` keyword. Take another look at the `money_converter( )` procedure, this time looking for the named block's declaration, execution, and exception handler sections:

```
PROCEDURE money_converter
(amount           IN NUMBER,
from_currency     IN VARCHAR2,
to_currency       IN VARCHAR2,
return_val        IN OUT NUMBER
) IS   /* denotes beginning of declaration section. */
   my_new_amt number(10) := 0;
   bad_data exception;
```

```
BEGIN   /* begins the executable section of a code block. */
    IF my_new_amt > 3 THEN
      DBMS_OUTPUT.PUT_LINE('Do this');
    ELSE
      DBMS_OUTPUT.PUT_LINE('Do that');
    END IF;
    return_val := my_new_amt;
EXCEPTION  /*Begins the Exception Handler */
    WHEN bad_data THEN
      DBMS_OUTPUT.PUT_LINE('Error condition');
END;
```

TIP
*The call to `DBMS_OUTPUT.put_line( )` in the code blocks is used to write a line of output to the SQL*Plus interface. In order to view the line of output produced, use the `set serveroutput on` command.*

Process Flow and Logic Constructs

PL/SQL offers logic constructs such as `for` loops, `while` loops, `if-then-else` statements, assignments, and expressions. Other logic constructs include PL/SQL tables and records. These "procedural" constructs are the items in PL/SQL that allow it to be both a programming language for supporting business rules and a functional language for providing data.

Cursors

One of the real strengths of PL/SQL is its ability to handle cursors. A cursor is a handle to an address in memory that stores the results of an executed SQL statement. They are extremely useful for performing operations on each row returned from a `select` statement. Therefore, PL/SQL programmers often use the looping procedural constructs of PL/SQL in conjunction with cursor manipulation operations.

Error Handling

Errors are called *exceptions* in PL/SQL, and they are checked implicitly anywhere in the code block. If at any time an error occurs in the code block, the exception corresponding to that error can be raised. At that point, execution in the executable code block stops, and control is transferred to the exception handler. There are many different types of exceptions in Oracle, some of which are user-defined. Others are defined by Oracle.

Exercises

1. What is PL/SQL? Name some benefits to accessing the Oracle database with PL/SQL.
2. What are the three parts of a PL/SQL code block? Name four different types of code blocks in Oracle. What are some program constructs available in PL/SQL?
3. What is the difference between a named and an anonymous code block?

Developing a PL/SQL Block

In this section, you will cover the following topics related to developing a simple PL/SQL block:

- Declaring and using variables
- Variable value assignment

A couple of sample PL/SQL blocks have already been offered. This section will cover in more detail some of the technical aspects of creating PL/SQL blocks. The topics that will be covered in this section include advanced use and declaration of variables and constants in the declarative section of the PL/SQL block, and a refresher on assigning values to variables in the executable section.

Declaring and Using Variables

PL/SQL offers a great deal of flexibility in variable declaration. So far, two examples of variable declaration in different code blocks have been presented. Both of these examples used simple declaration of datatypes that have been presented as valid datatypes on the Oracle database.

Database Datatypes

There are several datatypes that can be used in PL/SQL that correspond to the datatypes used on the database. These types are as follows:

- **NUMBER(*size*[,*precision*])** Used to store any number.
- **CHAR(*size*), VARCHAR2(*size*)** Used to store alphanumeric text strings. The CHAR datatype pads the value stored to the full length of the variable with blanks.

- **DATE** Used to store dates.
- **LONG** Stores large blocks of text, up to 2 gigabytes in length.
- **LONG RAW** Stores large blocks of data in binary format.
- **RAW** Stores smaller blocks of data in binary format.
- **MLSLABEL** Used in Trusted Oracle.
- **ROWID** Used to store the special format of ROWIDs on the database.
- **BLOB, CLOB, NCLOB, BFILE** Large object datatypes from Oracle8.

Nondatabase Datatypes

There are also several other PL/SQL datatypes that are not designed for use in storing data to a table:

- **DEC, DECIMAL, REAL, DOUBLE_PRECISION** These numeric datatypes are a subset of the NUMBER datatype that is used for variable declaration in PL/SQL.
- **INTEGER, INT, SMALLINT, NATURAL, POSITIVE, NUMERIC** These numeric datatypes are a subset of the NUMBER datatype that is used for variable declaration in PL/SQL.
- **BINARY_INTEGER, PLS_INTEGER** These datatypes store integers. A variable in either format cannot be stored in the database without conversion first.
- **CHARACTER** Another name for the CHAR datatype.
- **VARCHAR** Another name for the VARCHAR2 datatype.
- **BOOLEAN** Stores a TRUE/FALSE value.
- **TABLE/RECORD** Tables can be used to store the equivalent of an array, while records store variables with composite datatypes.

%type

In general, the variables that deal with table columns should have the same datatype and length as the column itself. Rather than look it up, you can use PL/SQL's special syntactic feature that allows you simply to identify the table column to which this variable's datatype should correspond. This syntax uses a special keyword known as `%type`. When using the `%type` keyword, all you need to know is the name of the column and the table to which the variable will correspond. Additionally, a variable can be declared with an initialization value by setting it equal to the value in the declaration section. Notice the characters used to set the variable to a value:

```
DECLARE
   my_employee_id      employee.empid%TYPE;
BEGIN ...

DECLARE
   my_salary        employee.salary%TYPE   := 0;
   my_lastname      employee.lastname%TYPE:= 'SMITH';
BEGIN ...
```

%rowtype

There is another variable declaration method that uses the same reference principle described in the previous text. It is called `%rowtype`, and it permits the developer to create a composite datatype in which all the columns of a row are lumped together into a record. For example, if the EMPLOYEE table contains four columns—EMPID, LASTNAME, FIRSTNAME, and SALARY—and you want to manipulate the values in each column of a row using only one referenced variable, the variable can be declared with the `%rowtype` keyword. Compare the use of `%rowtype`, shown here:

```
DECLARE
   my_employee       employee%ROWTYPE;
BEGIN ...
```

to manual record declaration:

```
DECLARE
   TYPE t_employee IS RECORD (
     my_empid       employee.empid%TYPE,
     my_lastname    employee.lastname%TYPE,
     my_firstname   employee.firstname%TYPE,
     my_salary      employee.salary%TYPE);

     my_employee    t_employee;
BEGIN ...
```

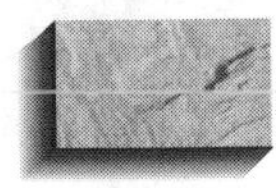

TIP

Blocks of PL/SQL code can be nested, that is to say that a procedure can have subprocedures. In this case, the principles of variable scope discussed in Chapter 2 also apply to nested PL/SQL blocks.

Constant Declaration

It may be useful for you to declare constants in the declaration section of the PL/SQL blocks. Constants make a good substitute for the use of hard-coded values, or "magic numbers." A magic value in programming is a value that is required to perform an operation or calculation but does not have any sort of meaning in the code block to help others identify why the value is there.

For example, consider a function that calculates the area of a circle, which is the number pi times radius squared. The number pi is well known to most people, but imagine if it were not, how difficult it would be to understand the reason for having the number 3.14159265358 in the middle of the function. Declaring pi as a constant makes the purpose of the value clearer in the code block. Assume that in the Oracle database there is a table called CIRCLE with a column called RADIUS, whose datatype you want to refer to in the function as `circle.radius%TYPE`:

```
CREATE FUNCTION find_circle_area (
    p_radius    IN    circle.radius%TYPE
) RETURN NUMBER IS
    my_area        number(10) := 0;
    pi             constant number(15,14)    := 3.14159265358;
BEGIN
    my_area := (p_radius*p_radius)* pi;
    Return (my_area);
END;
```

Note that OCP Exam 1 may ask questions about declaring PL/SQL table types using the `type` *`tabletype`* `is table of` *`datatype`* statement and then declaring variables using the defined types. In addition, PL/SQL tables have attributes you should be aware of. To find out more about PL/SQL table types and their attributes, consult the *PL/SQL Users Guide and Reference* section on collections and records.

Exercises

1. Identify some of the database and nondatabase datatypes that can be used in PL/SQL.
2. How can you declare PL/SQL variables without explicitly identifying the datatype?
3. How do you declare a variable with an initialized value?

Variable Value Assignment

As noted, it is possible to assign an initial value to a variable in the declaration section of the code block, and it is also possible to assign a value to a variable at any point during execution by using the assignment character: the colon followed by an equals sign. Note that the use of the equality (=) operator is for comparison only. Note also that variable assignment can be accomplished in a variety of ways in the executable section, such as using the return value from a function call to populate a variable or using the current value in a variable in an arithmetic equation to produce a new value.

```
DECLARE
    my_area     circle.area%TYPE := 0;
BEGIN
    my_area := find_circle_area(493);
    my_area := my_area + 45;
END;
```

Exercises

1. Where can a variable be assigned a value?
2. What is the assignment operator? How does it differ from the equality operator?

Controlling PL/SQL Process Flow

In this section, you will cover the following topics related to controlling PL/SQL process flow:

- Conditional statements and process flow
- Using loops

No programming language is complete without the use of semantic devices to control the processing flow of its code. Some mention has already been made of the two categories of PL/SQL process flow statements, which are conditional expressions and loops. This section will cover the details of using both conditions and loops to moderate the processing of a PL/SQL block. As these concepts are fairly standard among procedural programming languages, such as COBOL or C, most developers with programming experience should have no problem with the concepts. The more specific subject of the chapter, and the one that will be tested in OCP Exam 1, is the subject of syntax and appropriate usage. You should focus on these areas to gain the best background in preparation for the test.

Conditional Statements and Process Flow

A condition in a program equates directly with the idea of making a decision. The fundamental idea behind conditional processing is that of applying Boolean (TRUE or FALSE) logic to certain types of statements called *comparison operations*. Comparison operations can all be evaluated for their validity, that is, whether they are TRUE or FALSE. For example, the statement 3 + 5 = 8 is TRUE because the sum of 3 and 5 equals 8. In another example, 4 = 10, 4 definitely does not equal 10, so the statement is FALSE. A final example is today = Tuesday, which illustrates an interesting principle about comparison operations; sometimes today is Tuesday (thus the statement is TRUE), but sometimes today is not Tuesday (thus the statement is FALSE). The validity of the statement, then, depends on when the comparison is made.

Conditional statement-processing mechanisms allow you to structure code such that certain statements may or may not execute based on the validity of a comparison operation. The general syntax for conditional statements is "`if` the comparison is TRUE, `then` do the following." PL/SQL also offers an optional add-on, called `else`, which essentially says "otherwise, do whatever the `else` clause says."

```
BEGIN
    IF to_char(to_date('26-JAN-99'),'DAY') = 'SATURDAY' THEN
       find_hypotenuse(56,45,my_hypotenuse);
    ELSE
       My_hypotenuse := derive_hypotenuse(56,45);
    END IF;
END;
```

Note that single-row operations are allowed in comparison statements, so long as they resolve to a datatype that can be compared properly. If, for example, one side of the comparison operation resolves to a number and the other side is a text string, that will be a problem. Additionally, note that the `else` statement can contain another `if` statement, allowing for nested `if` statements that amount to a `case` operation.

```
BEGIN
 IF to_char(to_date('26-JAN-99'), 'DAY') = 'SATURDAY' THEN
      find_hypotenuse(56,45,my_hypotenuse);
 ELSIF
  TO_CHAR(sysdate,'DAY') = to_char(to_date('28-JAN-99'),'DAY') THEN
      my_hypotenuse := derive_hypotenuse(56,45);
 ELSE
      my_hypotenuse := 0;
 END IF;
END;
```

Once again, if the first condition is TRUE, the first block of PL/SQL will execute. If the second condition is TRUE, the second block of PL/SQL code will execute. If neither of the preceding code blocks is TRUE, then the third PL/SQL block will execute. To end an `if` statement, the `end if` keywords must be used. Otherwise, the code after the conditional expression will be treated as part of the `else` clause, which will cause the PL/SQL compiler to error out.

Exercises

1. What statement allows you to handle conditional statement processing?
2. What is a comparison operation? What is Boolean logic?

Using Loops

Another situation that arises in programming is the need to execute a set of statements repeatedly. The repetitions can be controlled in two ways: the first is to repeat the code for a specified number of times, and the second is to repeat the code until some condition is met, thus rendering a comparison operation TRUE. The types of loops that are available in PL/SQL are as follows:

- `loop-exit` statements, also called basic loops
- `while-loop` statements
- `for-loop` statements

loop-exit Statements

The `loop-exit` statement is the simplest type of loop that can be written in PL/SQL. The `loop` keyword denotes the beginning of the code block that will be repeated, and the `end loop` keywords denote the end of the code block that will be repeated. The `exit` keyword specified by itself denotes that the process should break out of the loop, while the `exit when` keywords denote a comparison operation that will test whether the statement is finished executing.

```
DECLARE
    my_leg              NUMBER(10) := 0;
    my_hypotenuse       NUMBER(10) := 0;
BEGIN
    LOOP
      my_leg := my_leg + 1;
      find_hypotenuse(my_leg,my_leg,my_hypotenuse);
      IF my_leg = 25 THEN
        EXIT;
      END IF;
    END LOOP;
END;
```

The `if-then` statement is designed to determine whether the conditions within the loop are such that the loop should terminate. The `exit` statement instructs the PL/SQL execution mechanism to leave the loop. An alternative to setting up an `if-then` statement to determine whether the loop should end is to add a `when` condition to the exit statement. The when condition contains the comparison operation that the if-then statement would have handled. An example of a simple loop statement that uses an exit when statement is listed in the following code block. Note that the code is essentially a revision of the simple loop block.

```
DECLARE
    my_leg              NUMBER(10)  := 0;
    my_hypotenuse       NUMBER(10)  := 0;
BEGIN
    LOOP
      my_leg := my_leg + 1;
      find_hypotenuse(my_leg,my_leg,my_hypotenuse);
      EXIT WHEN my_leg = 25;
    END LOOP;
END;
```

The when clause is very useful for the developer because it offers an elegant solution to defining when the loop will end, as opposed to hiding an exit statement inside an if-then statement. However, there are other possibilities for developing loops to handle repetition in coding.

while loop Statements

The next type of loop that approximates the usage of a loop-exit when statement is the while loop statement. The code in the previous block can be rewritten to include the while loop. The only difference between the while loop statement and the loop-exit when statement is where PL/SQL evaluates the exit condition. In a while loop statement, the exiting condition is evaluated at the beginning of the statement, while in the loop-exit when statement, the exit condition is evaluated wherever the exit when statement is placed. In one sense, the loop-exit when statement offers more flexibility than the while loop statement does because loop-exit when allows the developer to specify the exit condition at any place in the statement. However, the flexibility that the while loop statement may lack is made up for by its comparative elegance, in that there is no need for an exit statement.

```
DECLARE
    my_leg              NUMBER(10)  := 0;
    my_hypotenuse       NUMBER(10)  := 0;
BEGIN
    WHILE my_leg <= 25 LOOP
      my_leg := my_leg + 1;
      find_hypotenuse(my_leg,my_leg,my_hypotenuse);
    END LOOP;
END;
```

for loop Statements

The final example of looping constructs to be presented is the `for loop` statement. This type of loop allows the developer to specify exactly the number of times the code will execute before PL/SQL will break out of it. To accomplish this process, the `for loop` statement specifies a loop counter and a range through which the counter will circulate. Optionally, you can circulate through the loop counter in reverse order, or in numeric descending order. The loop counter is then available for use by the statements in the `for loop` statement.

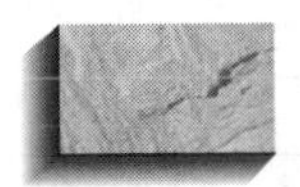

TIP

`for loop` statements have a built-in counter, which automatically increments itself by 1. Other options for incrementing the counter are also available.

```
DECLARE
    My_leg            NUMBER(10) := 0;
    My_hypotenuse     NUMBER(10) := 0;
BEGIN
    FOR my_leg IN 1..25 LOOP
      find_hypotenuse(my_leg,my_leg,my_hypotenuse);
    END LOOP;
END;
```

Notice that the use of a `for loop` statement made this code block even more elegant. No longer is the statement that increments the *my_leg* variable necessary, since the `for loop` statement handles the incrementation automatically.

There is another type of `for loop` statement related to cursor handling that offers the same elegance and utility as the `for loop` statement detailed in the previous code block. Its use, as well as the more general use of cursors, will be covered in the next section of this chapter. The following code block shows the previous anonymous PL/SQL block again, this time with the `for loop` statement executing in reverse order. Notice that you don't need to assign the beginning and end values any differently; Oracle handles everything properly with the `reverse` keyword.

```
DECLARE
    My_leg            NUMBER(10) := 0;
    My_hypotenuse     NUMBER(10) := 0;
BEGIN
    FOR my_leg IN REVERSE 1..25 LOOP
      find_hypotenuse(my_leg,my_leg,my_hypotenuse);
    END LOOP;
END;
```

PL/SQL does not natively allow you to increment or decrement your counter in the `for loop` statement by anything other than one. You can build this functionality with the use of a `mod( )` function in your `for loop` statement, as shown in this following code block:

```
DECLARE
    My_leg             NUMBER(10) := 0;
    My_hypotenuse      NUMBER(10) := 0;
BEGIN
    FOR my_leg IN 1..25 LOOP
      IF mod(my_leg,2) = 0 THEN
         find_hypotenuse(my_leg,my_leg,my_hypotenuse);
      END IF;
    END LOOP;
END;
```

Exercises

1. How is nested conditional-statement processing handled?
2. What are three different types of loops? What is an `exit when` statement? What is a loop counter, and for which type of loop is it most commonly used? Which type of loop doesn't require an explicit `exit` statement?

Interacting with the Oracle Database

In this section, you will cover the following topics related to interacting with Oracle:

- Using `select`, `insert`, `update`, and `delete` in PL/SQL code
- Using implicit cursor attributes
- Transaction processing in PL/SQL

No use of PL/SQL is complete without presenting the ease of use involved in interacting with the Oracle database. Any data manipulation or change operation can be accomplished within PL/SQL without the additional overhead typically required in other programming environments. There is no ODBC interface, and no embedding is required for database manipulation with PL/SQL.

Using SQL Statements in PL/SQL

The integration of PL/SQL and the Oracle database is seamless. There are no special characters that must precede the PL/SQL variables in SQL statements; the one concession PL/SQL must make is the `into` clause, which places the return values from the `select` statement into the `%rowtype` record created in the declaration section. You are not forced to use `%rowtype`; a manual record declaration or even three stand-alone variables declared as the same datatypes as the columns you use in your `select` statement will suffice. Even so, the utility for declaring a complex record with `%rowtype` has already been proven to be more efficient than manual record declaration.

The same ease of use can be seen in `update` statements. The *record.element* notation is used to refer to the components of a record variable. Similarly, using the `insert`, `update`, and `delete` statements in PL/SQL is as straightforward as the other statements.

```
DECLARE
   my_employee        employee%ROWTYPE;
   my_lastname        VARCHAR2(30)    := 'SAMSON';
   my_firstname       VARCHAR2(30)    := 'DELILAH';
   my_salary          NUMBER(10)      := 49500;
BEGIN
   SELECT *
   INTO my_employee
   FROM employee
   WHERE empid = 49594;

   UPDATE employee
   SET salary = my_employee.salary + 10000
   WHERE empid = my_employee.empid;

   INSERT INTO employee (empid, lastname, firstname, salary)
   VALUES (emp_sequence.nextval,
           my_lastname,
           my_firstname,
           my_salary);

   my_employee.empid := 59495;

   DELETE FROM employee
   WHERE empid = my_employee.empid;
END;
```

Exercises

1. What special characters are required for using data manipulation statements in PL/SQL?
2. Explain how Oracle assigns values to elements in a record.

Using Implicit Cursor Attributes

Every SQL statement in an Oracle PL/SQL block executes in what Oracle calls an *implicit cursor*. After a SQL statement executes, several things can happen that a developer may care about. For example, assume that a block of code is designed to change data in a table. If an `update` statement does not change any row data, you can assume the record doesn't exist in the table, and thus you will want to add the record using an insert statement. There are two ways to handle this situation.

The first option is to use a `select into` statement to retrieve the record you plan to update. If no data is returned, Oracle will automatically raise an *exception* called `no_data_found`. This exception is a special error condition you will learn more about later in the chapter. For now, simply understand that it happens automatically when Oracle detects that a `select into` statement didn't get any data fetched into it (and therefore the `update` statement didn't work). You must add code in the exception handler of the code block to tell you the exception was raised, and to do something about it with the `insert` command. The following code block illustrates this:

```
SQL>  create table error_table
  2  (err_code varchar2(10),
  3  err_date date,
  4* err_msg varchar2(100));
Table created.
SQL>  CREATE OR REPLACE PROCEDURE add_chg_errors
  2  ( p_code   IN VARCHAR2,
  3    p_date   IN DATE,
  4    p_error  IN VARCHAR2
  5  ) IS
  6    my_error ERROR_TABLE%ROWTYPE;
  7  BEGIN
  8    DBMS_OUTPUT.PUT_LINE('selecting data');
  9    SELECT * INTO my_error
 10    FROM error_table WHERE err_code = p_code;
 11    DBMS_OUTPUT.PUT_LINE('found data, now changing');
 12    UPDATE error_table SET err_msg = p_error, err_date  = p_date
 13    WHERE err_code = p_code;
 14  EXCEPTION
 15    WHEN NO_DATA_FOUND THEN
 16       DBMS_OUTPUT.PUT_LINE('found nothing, now inserting');
 17       INSERT INTO error_table (err_code, err_date, err_msg)
 18       VALUES (p_code, p_date, p_error);
 19* END;
Procedure created.
SQL> set serveroutput on;
SQL> exec add_chg_errors('MY_ERROR',sysdate,'THE THING DID NOT WORK');
selecting data
```

```
found nothing, now inserting
PL/SQL procedure successfully completed.
SQL> exec add_chg_errors('MY_ERROR',sysdate-40,
  2 'IT STILL DID NOT WORK');
selecting data
found data, now changing
PL/SQL procedure successfully completed.
SQL> select * from error_table;
ERR_CODE   ERR_DATE  ERR_MSG
---------- --------- --------------------
MY_ERROR   09-MAR-99 IT STILL DID NOT WORK
```

However, it's not very effective to program in this way if you have several different tables you will `update` and/or `insert` from the same code block. You also add overhead by `selecting` the data first, and frequently your code block will be processing changes out of the exception handler, which isn't exactly what the exception handler is designed to do. Instead, you should use implicit cursor attributes to provide a more powerful and elegant solution.

Cursor attributes are a set of built-in "checks" on the implicit cursor that you can use to identify when certain situations occur during SQL statement processing in PL/SQL blocks. The following code block shows a rewrite of procedure `add_chg_errors( )` using implicit cursor attributes to eliminate the extra `select` statement and the exception handler, which makes the code much shorter and easier to understand:

```
SQL> CREATE OR REPLACE PROCEDURE add_chg_errors
  2    ( p_code  IN VARCHAR2,
  3      p_date  IN DATE,
  4      p_error IN VARCHAR2
  5    ) IS
  6  BEGIN
  7      DBMS_OUTPUT.PUT_LINE('Looking for data to change');
  8      UPDATE error_table
  9      SET err_msg = p_error, err_date  = p_date
 10      WHERE err_code = p_code;
 11      IF SQL%NOTFOUND THEN -- Implicit cursor attribute
 12         DBMS_OUTPUT.PUT_LINE('found nothing, now inserting');
 13         INSERT INTO error_table (err_code, err_date, err_msg)
 14         VALUES (p_code, p_date, p_error);
 15      END IF;
 16* END;
Procedure created.
SQL> exec add_chg_errors('NEW_ERROR',sysdate,
  2  'IT IS MUCH SMALLER NOW');
looking for data to change
found nothing, now inserting
```

```
PL/SQL procedure successfully completed.
SQL> exec add_chg_errors('NEW_ERROR',sysdate-25,
  2  'IT IS STILL SMALLER');
looking for data to change
PL/SQL procedure successfully completed.
SQL> select * from error_table;
ERR_CODE   ERR_DATE  ERR_MSG
---------- --------- --------------------
MY_ERROR   09-MAR-99 IT STILL DID NOT WORK
NEW_ERROR  24-MAR-99 IT IS STILL SMALLER
```

Valid Implicit Cursor Attributes

When you want to test the attributes on an implicit cursor, precede the implicit cursor attribute with SQL, as in `SQL%notfound`, which was used in the preceding code block. This syntax is similar to that used for the `%type` and `%rowtype` variable declaration attributes. You can also use implicit cursor attributes to test the status of *explicit*, or *named*, cursors, which you will learn about later in the chapter. For example, if you wanted to see whether an explicit cursor called EMPLOYEES is open, you can do it with EMPLOYEES`%isopen` in your PL/SQL block, which will return TRUE if the cursor is open or FALSE if the cursor is closed. More details about general cursor processing and using cursor attributes are discussed later in this chapter. The implicit cursor attributes you can use are as follows:

- **`%notfound`** Identifies whether the executed SQL statement obtained, changed, or removed any row data. If not, this attribute evaluates to TRUE; otherwise, it evaluates to FALSE.
- **`%rowcount`** Identifies the number of rows that were processed by the statement. Returns a numeric value.
- **`%found`** Identifies whether the SQL statement processed any row data. If data was processed, this attribute evaluates to TRUE; otherwise, it evaluates to FALSE.
- **`%isopen`** Identifies whether the cursor referred to is opened and ready for use. Returns TRUE if the cursor is open, and FALSE if the cursor is not.

Exercises

1. What value can implicit cursor attributes serve in PL/SQL code?
2. What are some of the implicit cursor attributes a developer can use in PL/SQL?

Transaction Processing in PL/SQL

The same options for transaction processing that are available in SQL statement processing are available in PL/SQL processing. Those options include specifications that name the beginning, logical breakpoint, and end of a transaction. The database options that provide lock mechanisms to ensure that only one user at a time has the ability to change a record in the database are still available within the database, regardless of whether SQL or PL/SQL is used to reference the database objects.

The three transaction specifications available in PL/SQL are `commit`, `savepoint`, and `rollback`. An important distinction to make between executing SQL statements in PL/SQL blocks and the iterative entering of SQL statements with SQL*Plus is that the beginning and end of a PL/SQL block does not generally denote the beginning or end of a transaction. The beginning of a transaction in the PL/SQL block is the execution of the first SQL data-change statement. In general, in order to guarantee that statements executed that make changes in the database have those changes saved, the PL/SQL code block should explicitly contain a `commit` statement. Likewise, to discard changes made or to specify a breakpoint in a transaction, the developer should code in `rollback` and `savepoint` operations appropriately. Also, since the `set transaction` statement is not available in PL/SQL to denote the beginning of the transaction or to set the transaction's database access to `read only`, Oracle provides the DBMS_TRANSACTION package. Within this package, there are several different functions that allow the user to start, end, and moderate the transaction processing within PL/SQL blocks.

Exercises

1. What transaction-processing features are available in PL/SQL?
2. What is DBMS_TRANSACTION?

Explicit Cursor Handling

In this section, you will cover the following topics related to using cursors in PL/SQL:

- Implicit versus explicit cursors
- Declaring and using explicit cursors
- Parameters and explicit cursors
- Writing `cursor for` loops

The definition of an implicit cursor has already been presented. It is an address in memory where a SQL statement is processed. Implicit cursors are used every time you issue a standalone SQL statement in a PL/SQL block. Explicit (named) cursors are frequently used in PL/SQL to handle loop processing for a set of values returned by a `select` statement, and they have other uses, as well. This discussion will present the uses for cursors, the different types of cursors available in Oracle, guidelines for creating all types of cursors, and a more detailed discussion of creating the `cursor for` loop for cursor data handling.

Implicit versus Explicit Cursors

Every time a user executes SQL statements of any sort, there is activity on the database that involves cursors. There are two types of cursors in PL/SQL: implicit and explicit cursors. The implicit cursor is an unnamed address where the SQL statement is processed by Oracle and/or the PL/SQL execution mechanism. Every SQL statement executes in an implicit cursor, including `update`, `insert`, and `delete` statements, and `select` statements that do not execute in explicit cursors.

TIP
Every SQL statement executed on the Oracle database is an implicit cursor, and any implicit cursor attribute can be used in conjunction with them.

An explicit cursor is one that is named by the developer. The cursor is little more than a `select` statement that has a name. Any sort of `select` statement can be used in an explicit cursor using the `cursor` *`cursor_name`* `is` syntax. When a `select` statement is placed in an explicit cursor, the developer has more complete control over the statement's execution.

```
DECLARE
   CURSOR employee_cursor IS
      SELECT * FROM employee;
   END;
BEGIN ...
```

There is really no such thing as determining "the best time" to use an implicit cursor, but the developer can determine the best time to use an explicit one. Every time a SQL operation is requested, an implicit cursor is used. When the developer wants to perform some manipulation on each record returned by a `select` operation, an explicit cursor will be used.

Most serious processing of data records is done with explicit cursors; however, there are some operations that work with implicit cursors, as well. For example, many of the cursor attributes identified in an earlier section of this chapter can be applied to implicit cursors with useful results. To refresh the discussion, the cursor attributes available are `%notfound`, `%found`, `%rowcount`, and `%isopen`. The `%notfound` attribute identifies whether the `select` executed did not return a row. The return value is the opposite of that which is returned by `%found`, which identifies whether the `select` executed returned a row. These two attributes return a TRUE or FALSE value. The `%rowcount` attribute identifies the number of rows that were processed by this cursor and returns a numeric value. The `%isopen` attribute identifies whether the cursor referred to is opened and ready for use, and it returns a TRUE or FALSE value.

Using an implicit cursor in conjunction with cursor attributes may consist of executing some statement and then finding out if the results were successful. In the following example, a user attempts to update an employee salary record. If there are no employees in the EMPLOYEE table that correspond with the EMPID to be modified, then the process should add an employee record.

```
DECLARE
   my_empid     employee.empid%TYPE := 59694;
   my_salary    employee.salary%TYPE := 99000;
   my_lastname employee.lastname%TYPE := 'RIDDINGS';
BEGIN
     UPDATE employee
     SET salary = my_salary
     WHERE empid = my_empid;

     IF SQL%NOTFOUND THEN
          INSERT INTO EMPLOYEE (empid, lastname, salary)
          VALUES(my_empid, my_lastname, my_salary);
     END IF;
END;
```

There are two implicit cursors in this example. The first is the `update` statement, and the second is the `insert` statement. If the `update` statement produces a change on no rows, the `if sql%notfound then` statement will trap the error and force some operation to happen as a result of the condition. Note that in the situation of an implicit cursor, "SQL" is the name you use to refer to the most recent implicit cursor. In this situation, the developer should specify `sql%notfound`, or `sql%found`, or use "SQL" followed by the cursor attribute. That "SQL" represents the most recently executed SQL statement producing an implicit cursor.

Exercises

1. What is an implicit cursor, and what is the syntax for creating one?
2. What is an explicit cursor? Why might a developer use an explicit cursor rather than an implicit one?
3. What is the syntax for creating an explicit cursor?

Declaring and Using Explicit Cursors

Most of the time, developers spend their efforts working with explicitly defined cursors. These programming devices allow the developer to control processing outcome based on the manipulation of individual records returned by a `select` statement. As stated, a cursor is defined with the syntax `cursor` *`cursor_name`* `is`, which is then followed by a `select` statement. Once defined, the cursor allows the developer to step through the results of the query in a number of different ways.

```
DECLARE
   /* extract from a salary review program */
   high_pctinc  constant   number(10,5)      := 1.20;
   med_pctinc   constant   number(10,5)      := 1.10;
   low_pctinc   constant   number(10,5)      := 1.05;
   my_salary    employee.salary%TYPE;
   my_empid     employee.empid%TYPE;
   CURSOR employee_crsr IS
       SELECT empid, salary
       FROM employee;
BEGIN ...
```

Consider the definition of EMPLOYEE_CRSR. The two keywords used are `cursor` and `is`. Note that the syntactic requirements of the `select` statement are fairly standard. The declaration of a cursor does not actually produce the cursor, however. At this point, the cursor definition simply stands ready for action. The cursor will not actually exist in memory until it is opened and parsed by the SQL execution mechanism in Oracle. Data will not populate the cursor until the cursor is executed.

Now consider the process of invoking the cursor in memory. In the following example, the employees of the company will be selected into the cursor for the purpose of salary review. Once selected, the review will be conducted as follows. Every employee of the company will obtain a midlevel raise as defined by the percentage increase listed for *med_pctinc*. There are four exceptions: two employees will get a large raise as defined by the percentage increase listed for *high_pctinc*, while two other employees will get low performance increases as defined by *low_pctinc*. The process flow will be governed by a conditional statement, along with a loop.

```
DECLARE
   /* extract from a salary review program */
   high_pctinc  constant   number(10,5)      := 1.20;
   med_pctinc   constant   number(10,5)      := 1.10;
   low_pctinc   constant   number(10,5)      := 1.05;
   my_salary    employee.salary%TYPE;
   my_empid     employee.empid%TYPE;
    CURSOR employee_crsr IS
       SELECT empid, salary
       FROM employee;
BEGIN
   /* The following statement creates and */
   /* executes the cursor in memory */
   OPEN employee_crsr;

   LOOP  /* sets a loop that allows program to step through */
         /* records of cursor */
      FETCH employee_crsr INTO my_empid, my_salary;
      EXIT WHEN employee_crsr%NOTFOUND;  /* stop looping when no */
                                         /* records found */
      IF my_empid = 59697 OR my_empid = 76095 THEN
         UPDATE employee SET salary = my_salary*high_pctinc
         WHERE empid = my_empid;
      ELSIF my_empid = 39294 OR my_empid = 94329 THEN
         UPDATE employee SET salary = my_salary*low_pctinc
         WHERE empid = my_empid;
      ELSE
         UPDATE employee SET salary = my_salary*mid_pctinc
         WHERE empid = my_empid;
      END IF;
   END LOOP;
END;
```

The main cursor manipulation operations are the `open`, `loop-exit when`, `fetch`, and *`cursor`*`%notfound` statements. The cursor is first opened with the `open` command, which implicitly parses and executes the statement as well. The loop is defined such that it should run until all records from the cursor are processed. The `exit` condition uses the `%notfound` attribute, preceded by the name of the explicit cursor.

Pay particular attention to the `fetch` statement. This operation can only be performed on explicit cursors that are `select` statements. When a call to `fetch` is made, PL/SQL will obtain the next record from the cursor and populate the variables specified with values obtained from the cursor. If the `fetch` produces no results, then the `%notfound` attribute is set to TRUE. The cursor `fetch` statement can handle variables of two sorts. The `fetch` command in the preceding code block illustrates the use of stand-alone variables for each column value stored in the cursor. The `fetch` statement depends on positional specification to populate the variables if this option is used. Alternatively, the use of a record that contains the same attributes as those columns defined by the cursor is also handled by `fetch`. Positional specification is used here as well, so it is required for the order of the variables in the declared record to match the order of columns specified in the cursor declaration.

```
DECLARE
   /* extract from a salary review program */
   high_pctinc  constant   number(10,5)    := 1.20;
   med_pctinc   constant   number(10,5)    := 1.10;
   low_pctinc   constant   number(10,5)    := 1.05;
   TYPE t_emp IS RECORD (
       t_salary    employee.salary%TYPE,
       t_empid     employee.empid%TYPE);
   my_emprec  t_emp;
   CURSOR employee_crsr IS
       SELECT salary, empid
       FROM employee;
BEGIN
   /* The following statement creates
      and executes the cursor in memory */
   OPEN employee_crsr;
   LOOP  /* sets a loop that allows program to step */
       /* through records of cursor */
      FETCH employee_crsr INTO my_emprec;
      EXIT WHEN employee_crsr%NOTFOUND;  /* stop looping when no */
                                         /* records found */
      IF my_emprec.t_empid = 59697 OR
         my_emprec.t_empid = 76095 THEN
         UPDATE employee SET salary = my_emprec.t_salary*high_pctinc
         WHERE empid = my_emprec.t_empid;
      ELSIF my_emprec.t_empid = 39294 OR
            my_emprec.t_empid = 94329 THEN
         UPDATE employee SET salary = my_emprec.t_salary*low_pctinc
         WHERE empid = my_emprec.t_empid;
      ELSE
         UPDATE employee SET salary = my_emprec.t_salary*mid_pctinc
         WHERE empid = my_emprec.t_empid;
      END IF;
   END LOOP;
END;
```

The additional code required to support records in this case may well be worth it if there are many variables in the PL/SQL block. Records give the developer a more object-oriented method for handling the variables required for cursor manipulation.

Exercises

1. What must be done in order to make a cursor exist in memory?
2. What step must be accomplished to put data in a cursor?
3. How is data retrieved from a cursor?

Parameters and Explicit Cursors

At times, there may be an opportunity to reuse a cursor definition. However, the cursors demonstrated thus far either `select` every record in the database or, alternatively, may be designed to `select` from a table according to hard-coded "magic values." There is a way to configure cursors such that the values from which data will be selected can be specified at the time the cursor is opened. Parameters are used to create this cursor setup.

Parameters allow for reuse of cursors by passing in the "magic" value. For example, assume the developer wanted the cursor to select a subset of values from the database, based on the first letter of the last name. This process could be accomplished with the use of cursor parameters. The developer could allow the cursor to accept a low and high limit, and then `select` data from the table for the cursor using that range.

```
DECLARE
/* extract from a salary review program */
   high_pctinc  constant  number(10,5)   := 1.20;
   med_pctinc   constant  number(10,5)   := 1.10;
   low_pctinc   constant  number(10,5)   := 1.05;
   TYPE t_emp IS RECORD (
       t_salary   employee.salary%TYPE,
       t_empid    employee.empid%TYPE);
       my_emprec  t_emp;
   CURSOR employee_crsr(low_end in VARCHAR2,
          high_end in VARCHAR2) IS
       SELECT empid, salary
       FROM employee
       WHERE substr(lastname,1,1)
       BETWEEN UPPER(low_end) AND UPPER(high_end);
BEGIN ...
```

With the parameter passing defined, the developer can set up the cursor with more control over the data that is processed. For example, if the developer wants only to process salary increases for employees whose last names start with A through M, the following code block could be used:

```
DECLARE
/* extract from a salary review program */
   high_pctinc  constant   number(10,5)    := 1.20;
   med_pctinc   constant   number(10,5)    := 1.10;
   low_pctinc   constant   number(10,5)    := 1.05;
   TYPE t_emp IS RECORD (
      t_salary   employee.salary%TYPE,
      t_empid    employee.empid%TYPE);
      my_emprec  t_emp;
   CURSOR employee_crsr(low_end in VARCHAR2, high_end in VARCHAR2) IS
      SELECT empid, salary
      FROM employee
         WHERE UPPER(substr(lastname,1,1))
         BETWEEN UPPER(low_end) AND UPPER(high_end);
BEGIN
/* The following statement creates
   and executes the cursor in memory */
   OPEN employee_crsr('A','M');
   LOOP  /* sets a loop that allows program to step */
         /* through records of cursor */
      FETCH employee_crsr INTO my_emprec;
      EXIT WHEN employee_crsr%NOTFOUND;  /* stop looping when no */
                                         /* records found */
      IF my_emprec.t_empid = 59697 OR my_emprec.t_empid = 76095 THEN
         UPDATE employee SET salary = my_emprec.t_salary*high_pctinc
         WHERE empid = my_emprec.t_empid;
      ELSIF my_emprec.t_empid = 39294 OR
          my_emprec.t_empid = 94329 THEN
         UPDATE employee
         SET salary = my_emprec.t_salary*low_pctinc
         WHERE empid = my_emprec.t_empid;
      ELSE
         UPDATE employee
         SET salary = my_emprec.t_salary*mid_pctinc
         WHERE empid = my_emprec.t_empid;
      END IF;
   END LOOP;
END;
```

Notice that this code block—the open statement that opens, parses, and executes the cursor—now contains two values passed into the cursor creation as parameters. This parameter passing is required for the cursor to resolve into a set of data rows.

Exercises

1. What value does passing parameters to a cursor provide?
2. How can a cursor be defined to accept parameters?

Writing cursor for Loops

Quite a bit of cursor use involves selecting data and performing operations on each row returned by the cursor. The code examples presented thus far illustrate how to perform this activity. However, each one of the examples also illustrates that there is some overhead for handling the looping process correctly. Depending on the type of loop used, the overhead required can be substantial. Take, for example, the use of a simple `loop-exit` statement. Not only must the code that will execute repeatedly be enclosed in the `loop` syntax construct, but the test for the `exit` condition must be defined explicitly. Other looping statement examples do simplify the process somewhat.

There is one loop that is ideal for the situation where a developer wants to pull together some rows of data and perform a specified set of operations on them. This loop statement is the `cursor for` loop. The `cursor for` loops handle several loop creation activities implicitly, including the opening, parsing, executing, and fetching of row data from the cursor, and the check to determine whether there is more data (and thus whether the loop should exit). Moreover, the declaration of a record variable to handle the data fetched from the cursor by the `cursor for` loop is also handled implicitly. The following PL/SQL block uses a `cursor for` loop statement to handle all cursor processing:

```
DECLARE
/* extract from a salary review program */
   high_pctinc  constant   number(10,5)    := 1.20;
   med_pctinc   constant   number(10,5)    := 1.10;
   low_pctinc   constant   number(10,5)    := 1.05;
   CURSOR employee_crsr(low_end in VARCHAR2, high_end in VARCHAR2) IS
       SELECT empid, salary
       FROM employee
```

```
        WHERE UPPER(substr(lastname,1,1))
        BETWEEN UPPER(low_end) AND UPPER(high_end);
BEGIN
/* The following statement creates
   and executes the cursor in memory */
/* sets a loop that allows program to
   step through records of cursor */
  FOR my_emprec IN employee_crsr('A','M') LOOP
    IF my_emprec.empid = 59697 OR my_emprec.empid = 76095 THEN
       UPDATE employee SET salary = my_emprec.salary*high_pctinc
       WHERE empid = my_emprec.empid;
    ELSIF my_emprec.empid = 39294 OR my_emprec.empid = 94329 THEN
       UPDATE employee SET salary = my_emprec.salary*low_pctinc
       WHERE empid = my_emprec.empid;
    ELSE
       UPDATE employee SET salary = my_emprec.salary*mid_pctinc;
       WHERE empid = my_emprec.empid;
    END IF;
  END LOOP;
END;
```

Take an extra moment to review this code block detailing a `cursor for` loop and confirm the following features that the loop handles implicitly. Note that the benefit of using a `cursor for` loop is that there are fewer requirements for setting up the loop, resulting in fewer lines of code, fewer mistakes, and easier-to-read programs. The features that `cursor for` loops handle implicitly are listed here:

- The `cursor for` loop opens, parses, and executes the cursor automatically.
- The `cursor for` loop fetches row data implicitly for each iteration of the loop.
- The `cursor for` loop notes when the end of the records in the cursor is reached and appropriately terminates the loop when the attribute is TRUE.
- The `cursor for` loop defines a record to store the row values returned by the cursor `fetch` automatically, resulting in a smaller declaration section.

Exercises

1. What steps in cursor loop handling does a `cursor for` loop handle implicitly?
2. How is the `exit` condition defined for a `cursor for` loop?

Error Handling

In this section, you will cover the following areas related to error handling:

- The three basic types of exceptions
- Identifying common exceptions
- Coding the exception handler

The handling of errors in PL/SQL is arguably the best contribution PL/SQL makes to commercial programming. Errors in PL/SQL need not be trapped and handled with `if` statements directly within the program, as they are in other procedural languages, like C. Instead, PL/SQL allows the developer to *raise exceptions* when an error condition is identified and switch control to a special program area in the PL/SQL block, called the *exception handler*. The code for handling an error does not clutter the executable program logic in PL/SQL, nor is the programmer required to terminate programs with `return` or `exit` statements. The exception handler is a cleaner way to handle errors.

Three Basic Types of Exceptions

The three types of exceptions in Oracle PL/SQL are *predefined* exceptions, *user-defined* exceptions, and *internal* exceptions. Exception handling in PL/SQL is simple and flexible. Predefined exceptions offer the developer several built-in problems that can be checked. User-defined and internal exceptions allow for additional flexibility in supporting errors defined by the developer.

Predefined Exceptions

In order to facilitate error handling in PL/SQL, Oracle has designed several "built-in" or predefined exceptions, including `no_data_found`, a predefined exception you have already seen. These exceptions are used to handle common situations that may occur on the database. For example, there is a built-in exception that can be used to detect when a statement returns no data, or when a statement expecting one piece of data receives more than one piece of data. There is no invoking a predefined exception—they are tested and raised automatically by Oracle. However, in order to have something done when the predefined error occurs, there must be code in the exception handler both to identify the error and to define a response. Later, in the "Identifying Common Exceptions" section, several of the most common exceptions will be presented.

You have already seen an example of a predefined exception in a PL/SQL block. Notice that you didn't need to declare or explicitly raise a predefined exception because Oracle does this for you. All you need to do is code support for the predefined exception in your exception handler, as the following code block shows:

```
CREATE OR REPLACE PROCEDURE add_chg_errors
  ( p_code  IN VARCHAR2,
    p_date  IN DATE,
    p_error IN VARCHAR2
  ) IS
    my_error ERROR_TABLE%ROWTYPE;
BEGIN
   DBMS_OUTPUT.PUT_LINE('selecting data');
   SELECT * INTO my_error
   FROM error_table WHERE err_code = p_code;
   DBMS_OUTPUT.PUT_LINE('found data, now changing');
   UPDATE error_table SET err_msg = p_error, err_date  = p_date
   WHERE err_code = p_code;
EXCEPTION
   WHEN NO_DATA_FOUND THEN
      DBMS_OUTPUT.PUT_LINE('found nothing, now inserting');
      INSERT INTO error_table (err_code, err_date, err_msg)
      VALUES (p_code, p_date, p_error);
END;
```

TIP
In order to trap a predefined exception, there must be an exception handler coded for it in the exceptions section of the PL/SQL block.

User-Defined Exceptions

In addition to predefined exceptions, you can create a whole host of user-defined exceptions to handle situations that may arise in the code. A user-defined exception may not produce an Oracle error; instead, user-defined exceptions may enforce business rules in situations where an Oracle error would not necessarily occur. Unlike predefined exceptions, which are implicitly raised when the associated error condition arises, a user-defined exception must have explicit code in the PL/SQL block designed to raise it. There is code required for all three sections of a PL/SQL block if the developer plans on using user-defined exceptions, as follows:

- **Exception declaration** In the declaration section of the PL/SQL block, the exception name must be declared. This name will be used to invoke, or *raise*, the exception in the execution section if the conditions of the exception occur.

- **Exception testing** In the execution section of the PL/SQL block, there must be code that explicitly tests for the user-defined error condition, which raises the exception if the conditions are met.
- **Exception handling** In the exception handler section of the PL/SQL block, there must be a specified `when` clause that names the exception and the code that should be executed if that exception is raised. Alternatively, there should be a `when others` exception handler that acts as a catchall.

The following code block provides an example for coding a user-defined exception. In the example, assume that there is some problem with an employee's salary record being NULL. The following code will select a record from the database, and if the record selected has a NULL salary, the user-defined exception will identify the problem with an output message. Note that code must appear for user-defined exceptions in all three areas of the PL/SQL block. Without one of these components, the exception will not operate properly and the code will produce errors.

```
DECLARE
    my_empid          employee.empid%TYPE := 59694;
    my_emp_record     employee%ROWTYPE;
    my_salary_null    EXCEPTION;
BEGIN
    SELECT * FROM employee
    INTO my_emp_record
    WHERE empid = my_empid;

    IF my_emp_record.salary IS NULL THEN
       RAISE my_salary_null;
    END IF;
EXCEPTION
    WHEN my_salary_null THEN
       DBMS_OUTPUT.PUT_LINE('Salary column was null for employee');
END;
```

Internal Exceptions

The list of predefined exceptions is limited, and overall they really do nothing other than associate a named exception with an Oracle error. You can extend the list of exceptions associated with Oracle errors within your PL/SQL code by using the `pragma exception_init` keywords. The `pragma exception_init` statement is a compiler directive that allows the developer to declare the Oracle-numbered error to be associated with a named exception in the block. This allows the code to handle errors that it might not have handled previously, without requiring the developer to program an explicit `raise` statement for the exception. For example, assume that the developer is inserting data into the EMPLOYEE table, and this table defined a `NOT NULL` constraint on SALARY. Instead of allowing the PL/SQL block to terminate with an `ORA-01400` error if an `insert` occurs that does not name a value for the SALARY column, the declaration of an exception allows the PL/SQL block to handle the error programmatically.

```
DECLARE
    my_emp_record       employee%ROWTYPE;
    my_salary_null exception;
    PRAGMA EXCEPTION_INIT(my_salary_null, -1400);
BEGIN
    my_emp_record.empid := 59485;
    my_emp_record.lastname := 'RICHARD';
    my_emp_record.firstname := 'JEAN-MARIE';
    my_emp_record.salary := 65000;

    INSERT INTO employee(empid,lastname,firstname,salary)
    VALUES(my_emp_record.empid, my_emp_record.lastname,
           my_emp_record.firstname, my_emp_record.salary);
EXCEPTION
  WHEN NO_DATA_FOUND THEN
  DBMS_OUTPUT.PUT_LINE('No Data Found');
  WHEN my_salary_null THEN
DBMS_OUTPUT.PUT_LINE('Salary column was null for employee');
END;
```

An advantage to using `pragma exception_init` when the user-defined error produces some Oracle error is that there is no need for an explicit condition test that raises the exception if the condition is met. Exceptions defined with `pragma exception_init` enjoy the same implicit exception handling as predefined exceptions do.

Exercises

1. What is a predefined error? How are predefined errors invoked?
2. What is a user-defined error? Where must code be defined in order to create a user-defined exception?
3. What can be used to associate an Oracle error with a user-defined error?

Identifying Common Exceptions

There are many common exceptions that Oracle PL/SQL allows developers to define and handle in their programs. Some of the predefined exceptions are:

- **invalid_cursor** Occurs when an attempt is made to close a cursor that is already closed
- **cursor_already_open** Occurs when an attempt is made to open a cursor that is already open
- **dup_val_on_index** Unique or primary-key constraint violation
- **no_data_found** No rows were selected or changed by the SQL operation
- **too_many_rows** More than one row was obtained by a single-row subquery, or in another SQL statement operation where Oracle was expecting one row
- **zero_divide** An attempt was made to divide by zero
- **rowtype_mismatch** The datatypes of the record to which data from the cursor is assigned are incompatible
- **invalid_number** An alphanumeric string was referenced as a number

Of these operations, the developer may expect to use the `no_data_found` or `too_many_rows` exceptions most frequently. In fact, the user can incorporate checks for these using cursor attributes.

As mentioned previously, in order to use an exception, the developer must *raise* it. Raising an exception requires using the `raise` statement. However, one of the best features about the predefined exceptions is that there is no need to `raise` them. They must simply be included in the exception handler for the PL/SQL block, and if a situation arises in which the error occurs, the predefined exception will be raised automatically. The following code block illustrates the use of an exception handler, along with a predefined exception:

```
DECLARE
    my_empid   number(10);
    my_emprec employee%rowtype;
BEGIN
```

```
    my_empid := 59694;
    SELECT * FROM employee INTO my_emprec
    WHERE empid = my_empid;
EXCEPTION
    WHEN NO_DATA_FOUND THEN
        DBMS_OUTPUT.PUT_LINE('No Data Found');
END;
```

Notice that there is no code that explicitly tells PL/SQL to write the output message if no data is found in the particular `select` statement in the executable portion of the block. Instead, the exception is implicitly raised when a predefined exception condition occurs. This layer of abstraction is useful, because the additional `if` statement required for checking this condition manually is unnecessary.

Exercises

1. What predefined exception is used to identify a situation in which no data is returned by a `select` statement?
2. What predefined exception is used to identify when the datatype of the information returned is not the same datatype as the declared variable?

Coding the Exception Handler

Special attention should be paid to the actual code of the exception handler. The exceptions handled in previous code blocks have had simple routines that display an error message. There are more advanced options than those, of course. This discussion will focus on a few of the options.

A named or user-defined exception in the declaration and executable section of the PL/SQL block should have an associated exception handler written for it. The way to handle an exception is to name it specifically using the `when` clause in the exceptions block of the PL/SQL program. Following the `when` clause, there can be one or several statements that define the events that will happen if this exception is raised. If there is no code explicitly defined for the exception raised, then PL/SQL will execute whatever code is defined for a special catchall exception called `others`. If there is no explicit code defined for a particular exception and no code defined for the `others` exception, then control passes to the exception handler of the procedure that called the PL/SQL code block. If the program was called by a user, such as from SQL*Plus, then the error returns directly to the user's SQL*Plus session. The exception handler is perhaps the greatest achievement gained by using

PL/SQL to write stored procedures in Oracle. Its flexibility and ease of use make it simple to code robust programs.

```
EXCEPTION
   WHEN NO_DATA_FOUND THEN …
       /* does some work when the NO_DATA_FOUND predefined
          exception is raised implicitly. */
   WHEN OTHERS THEN …
       /* this code will execute when any other exception
          is raised, explicitly or implicitly. */
END;
```

TIP
Once an exception is raised, PL/SQL flow control passes to the exception handler. Once the exception is handled, the PL/SQL block will be exited. In other words, once the exception is raised, the execution portion of the PL/SQL block is over.

Exercises

1. What are the components of an exception handler?
2. What is the `others` exception, and how is it used?

Chapter Summary

PL/SQL programming is the topic of this chapter. The subject areas discussed include an overview of PL/SQL, modular coding practices, developing PL/SQL blocks, interacting with Oracle, controlling process flow with conditional statements and loops, cursors, and error handling. The PL/SQL areas of OCP Exam 1 comprise about 22 percent of the overall test.

PL/SQL is the best method available for writing and managing stored procedures that work with Oracle data. PL/SQL code consists of three sub-blocks: the declaration section, the executable section, and the exception handler. In addition, PL/SQL can be used in four different programming constructs—procedures, functions, packages, and triggers. Procedures and functions are similar in that they both contain a series of instructions that PL/SQL will execute. However, the main difference is that a function will always return one value. Procedures can return more than that number as output parameters. Packages are collected libraries of PL/SQL procedures and functions that have an interface to tell others what procedures and functions are available as well as their parameters, and the package body contains the actual code executed by those procedures and functions. Triggers are special PL/SQL blocks that execute when a triggering event occurs. Events that fire triggers include any SQL statement.

The declaration section allows for the declaration of variables and constants. A variable can have either a simple or "scalar" datatype, such as NUMBER or VARCHAR2. Alternatively, a variable can have a referential datatype that uses a reference to a table column to derive its datatype. Constants can be declared in the declaration section in the same way as variables, but with the addition of a `constant` keyword and with a value assigned. If a value is not assigned to a constant in the declaration section, an error will occur. In the executable section, a variable can have a value assigned to it at any point using the assignment expression (`:=`).

Using PL/SQL allows the developer to produce code that can seamlessly access the Oracle database. Examples of using all SQL statements, including data selection, data change, and transaction-processing statements appeared in the chapter. There are no special characters or keywords required to "embed" SQL statements into PL/SQL, because SQL is an extension of PL/SQL. As such, there really is no embedding at all. Every SQL statement executes in a cursor. When a cursor is not named, it is called an implicit cursor. PL/SQL allows the developer to investigate certain return status features in conjunction with the implicit cursors that run. These implicit cursor attributes include `%notfound` and `%found` to identify whether records were found or not found by the SQL statement; `%rowcount`, which tells the developer how many rows were processed by the statement; and `%isopen`, which determines whether the cursor is open and active in the database.

Conditional process control is made possible in PL/SQL with the use of `if-then-else` statements. The `if` statement uses a Boolean logic comparison to evaluate whether to execute the series of statements after the `then` clause. If the comparison evaluates to TRUE, the `then` clause is executed. If it evaluates to FALSE, the code in the `else` statement is executed. Nested `if` statements can be placed in the `else` clause of an `if` statement, allowing for the development of code blocks that handle a number of different cases or situations.

Process flow can be controlled in PL/SQL with the use of loops, as well. There are several different types of loops, from simple `loop-exit` statements to `loop-exit when` statements, `while loop` statements, and `for loop` statements. A simple `loop-exit` statement consists of the `loop` and `end loop` keywords enclosing the statements that will be executed repeatedly, with a special `if-then` statement designed to identify whether an `exit` condition has been reached. The `if-then` statement can be eliminated by using an `exit when` statement to identify the `exit` condition. The entire process of identifying the `exit` condition as part of the steps executed in the loop can be eliminated with the use of a `while loop` statement. The `exit` condition is identified in the `while` clause of the statement. Finally, the `for loop` statement can be used in cases where the developer wants the code to execute repeatedly for a specified number of times.

Cursor manipulation is useful for situations where a certain operation must be performed on each row returned from a query. A cursor is simply an address in memory where a SQL statement executes. A cursor can be explicitly named with the use of the `cursor` *`cursor_name`* is statement, followed by the SQL statement that will comprise the cursor. The cursor *`cursor_name`* is statement is used to define the cursor in the declaration section only. Once declared, the cursor must be opened, parsed, and executed before its data can be manipulated. This process is executed with the open statement. Once the cursor is declared and opened, rows from the resultant dataset can be obtained if the SQL statement defining the cursor was a `select` using the `fetch` statement. Both individual variables for each column's value or a PL/SQL record may be used to store fetched values from a cursor for manipulation in the statement.

Executing each of the operations associated with cursor manipulation can be simplified in situations where the user will be looping through the cursor results using the `cursor for` loop statement. The `cursor for` loops handle many aspects of cursor manipulation explicitly. These steps include opening, parsing, and executing the `cursor` statement, fetching the value from the statement, exiting the loop when no data is found, and even implicitly declaring the appropriate record type for a variable, identified by the loop, in which to store the fetched values from the query.

The exception handler is arguably the finest feature PL/SQL offers. In it, the developer can handle certain types of predefined exceptions without explicitly coding error-handling routines. The developer can also associate user-defined exceptions with standard Oracle errors, thereby eliminating the coding of an error check in the executable section. This step requires defining the exception using the `pragma exception_init` and coding a routine that handles the error when it occurs in the exception handler. For completely user-defined errors that do not raise Oracle errors, the developer can declare an exception and code a programmatic check in the execution section of the PL/SQL block, followed by some routine to execute when the error occurs in the exception handler. A special predefined exception called `others` can also be coded into the exception handler to function as a catchall for any exception that has no exception-handling process defined. Once an exception is raised, control passes from the execution section of the block to the exception handler. Once the exception handler has completed, control is passed to the process that called the PL/SQL block.

Two-Minute Drill

- PL/SQL is a programming environment that is native to the Oracle database. It features seamless integration with other database objects in Oracle and with SQL.
- There are three parts to a PL/SQL program: the declaration area, the execution area, and the exception handler.
- There are two categories of PL/SQL blocks: named and anonymous blocks. Named blocks include procedures, functions, packages, and triggers.
- Procedures allow the developer to specify more than one output parameter, while functions only allow one return value. Other than that, the two PL/SQL blocks are similar in function and use.
- Variables are defined in the declaration section.
- Variables can have a scalar datatype, such as NUMBER or VARCHAR2, or a referential datatype defined by a table and/or column reference followed by `%type` or `%rowtype`.
- Constants are declared the same way as variables, except for the fact that the `constant` keyword is used to denote a constant and the constant must have a value assigned in the declaration section.
- Variables can have values assigned anywhere in the PL/SQL block using the assignment operator, which is a colon followed by an equal sign (`:=`).
- Any SQL statement is valid for use in PL/SQL. This includes all SQL statements, such as `select` and `delete`, and transaction control statements, such as `commit` and `rollback`.
- Conditional processing is handled in PL/SQL with `if-then-else` statements.
- `If-then-else` statements rely on Boolean logic to determine which set of statements will execute. If the condition is TRUE, the statements in the `then` clause will execute. If the condition is FALSE, the statements in the `else` clause will execute.
- The `if` statements can be nested into `else` clauses.
- Several loops control the repetition of blocks of PL/SQL statements.
- The `loop-exit` statement is a simple definition for a loop that marks the beginning and end of the loop code. An `if-then` statement tests to see whether conditions are such that the loop should exit. An `exit` statement must be specified explicitly.

- The `if-then` statement can be replaced with an `exit when` statement, which defines the `exit` condition for the loop.
- The `while` statement eliminates the need for an `exit` statement by defining the `exit` condition in the `while loop` statement.
- If the programmer wants the code to execute a specified number of times, the `for loop` can be used.
- Every SQL statement executes in an implicit cursor. An explicit cursor is a named cursor corresponding to a defined SQL statement.
- An explicit cursor can be defined with the `cursor` *`cursor_name`* `is` statement. Cursors can be defined to accept input parameters that will be used in the where clause to limit the data manipulated by the cursor.
- Once declared, a cursor must be opened, parsed, and executed in order to have its data used. This task is accomplished with the `open` statement.
- In order to obtain data from a cursor, the programmer must `fetch` the data into a variable. This task is accomplished with the fetch statement.
- The variable used in the `fetch` can either consist of several loose variables for storing single-column values or a record datatype that stores all column values in a record.
- A special loop exists to simplify use of cursors: the `cursor for` loop.
- The `cursor for` loop handles the steps normally done in the open statement, and implicitly fetches data from the cursor until the `%notfound` condition occurs. This statement also handles the declaration of the variable and associated record type, if any is required.
- The exception handler in PL/SQL handles all error handling.
- There are user-defined exceptions, predefined exceptions, and pragma exceptions in PL/SQL.
- Only user-defined exceptions require explicit checks in the execution portion of PL/SQL code to test to see if the error condition has occurred.
- A named exception can have a `when` clause defined in the exception handler that executes whenever that exception occurs.
- The `others` exception is a catchall exception designed to operate if an exception occurs that is not associated with any other defined exception handler.

Chapter Questions

1. Developer Janet receives an error due to the following statement in the declaration section:

```
pi constant number;
```

Which of the following caused this problem?

A. There is not enough memory in the program for the constant.

B. There is no value associated with the constant.

C. There is no datatype associated with the constant.

D. Pi is a reserved word.

2. You are designing your PL/SQL exception handler. Which statement most accurately describes the result of not creating an exception handler for a raised exception?

A. The program will continue without raising the exception.

B. There will be a memory leak.

C. Control will pass to the PL/SQL block caller's exception handler.

D. The program will return a `%notfound` error.

3. You are determining which types of cursors to use in your PL/SQL code. Which of the following statements is true about implicit cursors?

A. Implicit cursors are used for SQL statements that are not named.

B. Developers should use implicit cursors with great care.

C. Implicit cursors are used in `cursor for` loops to handle data processing.

D. Implicit cursors are no longer a feature in Oracle.

4. You are constructing PL/SQL process flow for your program. Which of the following is not a feature of a `cursor for` loop?

A. Record-type declaration

B. Opening and parsing of SQL statements

C. Fetches records from cursor

D. Requires `exit` condition to be defined

5. A developer would like to use a referential datatype declaration on a variable. The variable name is EMPLOYEE_LASTNAME, and the corresponding table and column is EMPLOYEE and LASTNAME, respectively. How would the developer define this variable using referential datatypes?

A. Use `employee.lname%type.`

B. Use `employee.lname%rowtype.`

C. Look up datatype for EMPLOYEE column on LASTNAME table and use that.

D. Declare it to be type LONG.

6. After executing an `update` statement, the developer codes a PL/SQL block to perform an operation based on `sql%rowcount`. What data is returned by the `sql%rowcount` operation?

A. A Boolean value representing the success or failure of the `update`

B. A numeric value representing the number of rows updated

C. A VARCHAR2 value identifying the name of the table updated

D. A LONG value containing all data from the table

7. You are defining a check following a SQL statement to verify that the statement returned appropriate data. Which three of the following are implicit cursor attributes? (Choose three)

A. `%found`

B. `%too_many_rows`

C. `%notfound`

D. `%rowcount`

E. `%rowtype`

8. You are constructing PL/SQL process flow into your program. If left out, which of the following would cause an infinite loop to occur in a simple loop?

A. `loop`

B. `end loop`

C. `if-then`

D. `exit`

9. You are coding your exception handler. The `others` exception handler is used to handle all of the following exceptions, except one. Which exception does the `others` exception handler not cover?

A. **no_data_found**

B. **others**

C. **rowtype_mismatch**

D. **too_many_rows**

10. You are defining a cursor in your PL/SQL block. Which line in the following statement will produce an error?

A. `cursor` *`action_cursor`* `is`

B. `select` *`name, rate, action`*

C. `into` *`action_record`*

D. `from` *`action_table;`*

E. There are no errors in this statement.

11. You are developing PL/SQL process flow into your program. Which of the following keywords is used to open a `cursor for` loop?

A. `open`

B. `fetch`

C. `parse`

D. None, `cursor for` loops handle cursor opening implicitly.

12. You are determining the appropriate program flow for your PL/SQL application. Which one of the following statements about `while` loops is true?

A. Explicit `exit` statements are required in `while` loops.

B. Counter variables are required in `while` loops.

C. An `if-then` statement is needed to signal when a `while` loop should end.

D. All `exit` conditions for `while` loops are handled in the `while` conditional clause.

Answers to Chapter Questions

1. B. There is no value associated with the constant.

Explanation A value must be associated with a constant in the declaration section. If no value is given for the constant, an error will result.

2. C. Control will pass to the PL/SQL block caller's exception handler.

Explanation If the exception raised is not handled locally, then PL/SQL will attempt to handle it at the level of the process that called the PL/SQL block. If the exception is not handled there, then PL/SQL will attempt to keep finding an exception handler that will resolve the exception. If none is found, then the error will be returned to the user..

3. A. Implicit cursors are used for SQL statements that are not named.

Explanation Implicit cursors are used for all SQL statements except for those statements that are named. They are never incorporated into `cursor for` loops, nor is much care given to using them more or less, which eliminates choices B and C. They are definitely a feature of Oracle, eliminating choice D.

4. D. Requires `exit` condition to be defined

Explanation A `cursor for` loop handles just about every feature of cursor processing automatically, including exit conditions.

5. A. Use `employee.lname%type`

Explanation The only option in this question that allows the developer to use referential type declaration for columns is choice A. Choice B uses the `%rowtype` referential datatype, which defines a record variable and is not what the developer is after.

6. B. A numeric value representing the number of rows updated

Explanation `%rowcount` returns the numeric value representing the number of rows that were manipulated by the SQL statement.

7. A, C, D. `%found`, `%notfound`, `%rowcount`

Explanation These three are the only choices that are valid cursor attributes. The %too_many_rows attribute does not exist in PL/SQL. The %rowtype is a keyword that can be used to declare a record variable that can hold all column values from a particular table.

8. D. `exit`

Explanation Without an `exit` statement, a simple loop will not stop. Although the `loop` and `end loop` keywords are needed to define the loop, you should assume these are in place, and you are only trying to figure out how to end the loop. The `if-then` syntax might be used to determine a test condition for when the loop execution should terminate, but is not required in and of itself to end the loop process execution.

9. B. `others`

Explanation There is no `others` exception. The `others` exception handler handles all exceptions that may be raised in a PL/SQL block that do not have exception handlers explicitly defined for them. All other choices identify Oracle predefined exceptions that are caught by the `others` keyword when used in an exception handler. If there is no specific handler for another named exception, the `others` exception handler will handle that exception.

10. C. `into` *`action_record`*

Explanation The `into` clause is not permitted in cursors, nor is it required. Your `fetch` operation will obtain the value in the current cursor record from the cursor.

11. D. None, `cursor for` loops handle cursor opening implicitly.

Explanation The `cursor for` loops handle, among other things, the opening, parsing, and executing of named cursors.

12. D. All `exit` conditions for `while` loops are handled in the `while` conditional clause.

Explanation There is no need for an `exit` statement in a `while` loop, since the exiting condition is defined in the `while` statement, eliminating choice A. Choice B is also wrong because you don't specifically need to use a counter in a `while` loop the way you do in a `for` loop. Finally, choice C is incorrect because even though the `exit` condition for a while loop evaluates to a Boolean value (for example, `exit when (`*`this_condition_is_true`*`)`, the mechanism to handle the exit does not require an explicit `if-then` statement.

UNIT II

Preparing for OCP DBA Exam 2: Database Administration

CHAPTER 6

Basics of the Oracle Database Architecture

n this chapter you will learn about, and demonstrate knowledge in, the following areas:

- Oracle architectural components
- Using administration tools
- Managing an Oracle instance
- Creating an Oracle database

To be a successful Oracle DBA and to pass OCP Exam 2, you must understand the Oracle database architecture. About 16 percent of OCP Exam 2 is on this topic. An Oracle database in action consists of several elements, including memory structures, special processes that make things run faster, and recovery mechanisms that allow the DBA to restore systems after seemingly unrecoverable problems. Whatever the Oracle feature, it's all here. Review this chapter carefully, as these concepts form the foundation for the material covered in the rest of this book.

Oracle Architectural Components

In this section, you will cover the following topics related to the Oracle architecture:

- Structures that connect users to Oracle servers
- Stages in processing queries
- Stages in processing DML statements
- Stages in processing `commit` statements

The Oracle database server consists of many different components. Some of these components are memory structures, while others are processes that execute certain tasks behind the scenes. There are also disk resources that store the applications used to track data for an entire organization, and special resources designed to allow for recovering from problems ranging from incorrect data entry to disk failure. All these structures of the Oracle database server, running together to allow users to read and modify data, are referred to as an Oracle *instance*. This section will explain what each component of the Oracle instance is, as well as what Oracle does when users issue queries, data changes, or DML statements, and then save their work to Oracle by issuing `commit` commands.

Structures That Connect Users to Oracle Servers

Figure 6-1 demonstrates the various disk, memory, and process components of the Oracle instance. Every Oracle database, from the smallest Oracle application running on a handheld device to terabyte data warehouses that run on mainframes and supercomputers, has these features working together to manage data. They allow for applications, ranging from online transaction processing (OLTP) applications to *N*-tier applications to data marts to data warehouses, to process their data efficiently and effectively.

The SGA: Oracle's Primary Memory Component

Focus first on the memory components of the Oracle instance. There are two basic memory structures in Oracle. The first and most important is the System Global Area, or SGA. When DBAs talk about most things related to memory, they usually mean the SGA. The SGA consists of several different items: the *buffer cache, shared pool,* and *redo log buffer,* as well as a few other items that will be discussed later in this unit. The following subtopics explain the primary components of the Oracle SGA.

BUFFER CACHE This memory structure consists of buffers the size of database blocks that store data needed by SQL statements issued in user processes. A database block is the most granular unit of information storage in which Oracle can place several rows of table data. The buffer cache has two purposes: to improve performance for subsequent repeated `select` statements on the same data, and to allow Oracle users to make data changes quickly in memory. Oracle writes such data changes to disk later.

SHARED POOL There are two mandatory structures and one optional structure in the Oracle shared pool. The first required component is the *library cache,* used for storing parsed SQL statement text and the statement's execution plan for reuse. The second is the *dictionary cache,* sometimes also referred to as the *row cache,* which is used for storing recently accessed information (table and column definitions, usernames, passwords, and privileges) from the Oracle data dictionary. (If you don't know what the data dictionary is, you'll find more out about it later in this chapter.) These two components are designed to improve overall Oracle performance in multiuser environments. The optional shared pool structure contains session information about user processes connected to Oracle. When will Oracle include this optional component in the SGA? You'll find out shortly.

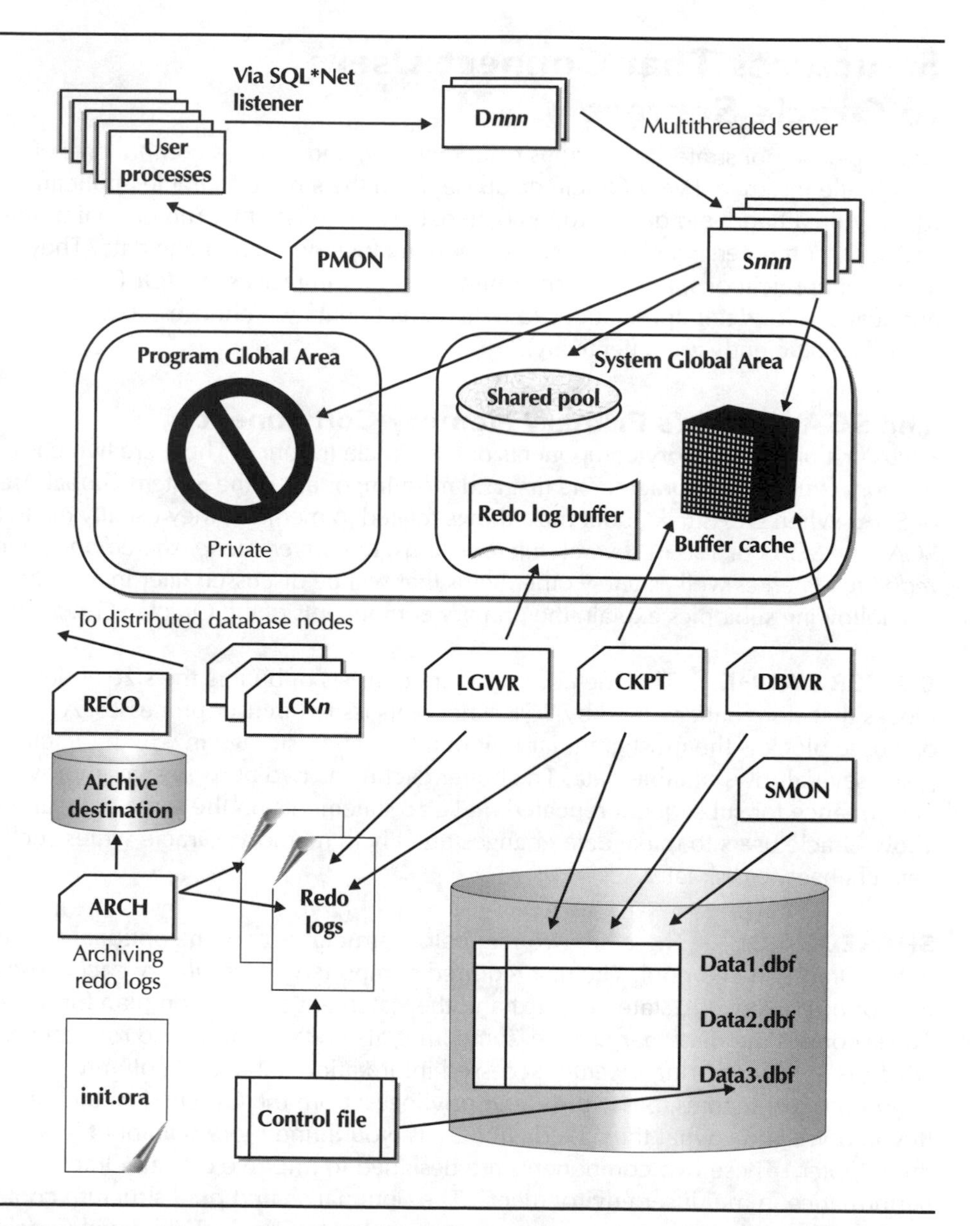

FIGURE 6-1. *The Oracle database architecture*

REDO LOG BUFFER This SGA component temporarily stores in memory the redo entry information generated by DML statements run in user sessions until Oracle writes the information to disk. DML statements include `update`, `delete`, and `insert` statements run by users. What is a redo entry? It is a small amount of information produced and saved by Oracle to reconstruct, or redo, changes made to the database by `insert`, `update`, `delete`, `create`, `alter`, and `drop` statements. If some sort of failure occurred, the DBA can use redo information to recover the Oracle database to the point of the database failure.

The PGA: The Oracle User's Memory Area

The other memory structure in the Oracle instance is called the Program Global Area, or PGA. The PGA helps user processes execute by storing information like bind variable values, sort areas, and other aspects of cursor handling. Why do users need their own area to execute? Even though the parse information for SQL or PL/SQL may already be available in the library cache of the shared pool, the values upon which the user wants to execute the `select` or `update` statement cannot be shared. The PGA is used to store real values in place of bind variables for executing SQL statements.

Reading Data from Disk for Users: The Server Process

Let's move on to quickly cover Oracle background processes. There are several types of processes running all the time in Oracle. These types are *background, server,* and *network* processes. The most important one from your users' perspectives is the server process. This process acts on the user's behalf to pull Oracle data from disk into the buffer cache, where the user can manipulate it. There are two ways DBAs can set up Oracle to run server processes: *shared servers* and *dedicated servers.* The following subtopics identify the primary differences between these two configurations.

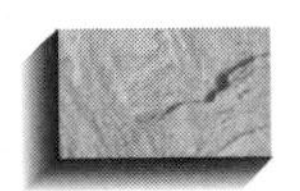

TIP

Think of the Oracle server process as a genie—the magical being from the story of Aladdin—because your wish for Oracle data is the server process's command!

DEDICATED SERVERS: ONE GENIE, ONE MASTER In this setup, every single user connecting to Oracle will have a personal genie handling data retrieval from disk into the buffer cache. If there are 150 users connected to Oracle, there will also be 150 genies out there grabbing data from disk and putting it in the buffer cache for those users. This architectural setup means that every user gets their data retrieval requests acted upon immediately. It also means that there will be additional memory and CPU overhead on the machine running the Oracle database, and that each dedicated server process will, depending on the workload and the access method, sit idle most of the time. Still, this is the setup chosen by many DBAs for overall performance when hardware resources are readily available.

SHARED SERVERS: ONE GENIE, MANY MASTERS In this setup, there is a small pool of server processes running in Oracle that support data retrieval requests for a large number of users. Several users are served by one server process. Oracle manages this utilization by means of a network process called the *dispatcher*. User processes are assigned to a dispatcher, and the dispatcher puts the user requests for data into one queue, and the shared server process fulfills all the requests, one at a time. This configuration can reduce memory and CPU burden on the machine that hosts Oracle, as well as limiting server process idle time, but during periods of high database use, the user processes may have to wait for attention from the genie with many masters.

Locating User Session Info: Shared Pool or PGA?

Let's return to the point raised earlier about the optional component of the shared pool, where user session information is stored in Oracle. Oracle will store session information in the shared pool only if the DBA configures Oracle to use shared servers to handle user data retrieval requests. This option is known as *multithreaded server*, or *MTS*, architecture. Otherwise, if dedicated servers are used, user session information is housed in the PGA.

And Finally, How Users Connect to the Server Process

Before answering this final question, let's spend just another quick moment covering a few other important Oracle network processes. The first is called the *listener process*. The Oracle listener process does just that—it listens for users trying to connect to the Oracle database via the network. When a user connects to the machine hosting the Oracle database, the listener process will do one of two things. If dedicated server processes are being used, the listener tells Oracle to generate a new dedicated server and then assigns the user process to that dedicated server. If MTS is being used, the listener sends the user process to another process called the *dispatcher process*, which has already been mentioned.

A request from a user is a single program-interface call that is part of the user's SQL statement. When a user makes a call, its dispatcher places the request on the request queue, where it is picked up by the next available shared server process. The request queue is in the SGA and is common to all dispatcher processes of an instance. The shared server processes check the common request queue for new requests, picking up new requests on a first-in-first-out basis. One shared server process picks up one request in the queue and makes all necessary calls to the database to complete that request. When the server completes the request, it places the response on the calling dispatcher's response queue. Each dispatcher has its own response queue in the SGA. The dispatcher then returns the completed request to the appropriate user process. And that is the magic behind how users are connected to an Oracle server.

TIP
Here's a quick summary of server, background, and network processes. The server process handles user requests for data. Background processes are Oracle processes that handle certain aspects of database operation behind the scenes. Network processes are used for network connectivity between user processes running on other machines to server processes running on the machine hosting the Oracle database.

Exercises

1. What is the name of the main memory structure in Oracle, and what are its components? What is the function of the PGA?
2. Where is user session information stored in memory on the Oracle instance? How is its location determined?
3. How do user processes get connected to a server when dedicated servers are used? When MTS is used? What are the performance implications of using shared versus dedicated servers?

Stages in Processing Queries

Now that you know how Oracle connects a user process with a server process, it's time for you to learn how Oracle behaves when the user wants to do something with the server, such as selecting Oracle data. You already know most of the main players, including the server process, user process, buffer cache, and library cache of the shared pool. You know all players, that is, except one—the Oracle *RDBMS*, or *relational database management system*. Recall from Unit I that SQL is a functional programming language, as opposed to a procedural language like

COBOL or C. You write your code in terms of your desired outcome, not the process by which Oracle should get there. The relational database management system translates the outcome defined in your SQL statement into a process by which Oracle will obtain it.

With all of the components in the world of processing Oracle queries established, let's look now at how Oracle processes queries. There are several steps for processing an Oracle `select` statement. The operations involved in executing both `select` statements and DML statements fall into a general pattern shown in Figure 6-2. The specific flow of operation in processing a `select` statement is as follows:

1. **Parse statement** The RDBMS creates a *parse tree*, or *execution plan*, for the statement, and places it in the library cache. This is a list of operations the RDBMS uses to obtain data. If a parse tree already exists for this statement, the RDBMS can omit this step.
2. **Execute statement** The RDBMS performs all processing to execute the `select` statement. At this point, the server process will retrieve data from disk into the buffer cache.
3. **Fetch values from cursor** Once the `select` statement has been executed, all data returned from Oracle is stored in the cursor. The data is then placed into bind variables, row by row, and returned to the user process.

When complete, both the statement execution plan and the data in blocks retrieved from disk stick around in the library cache and buffer cache, respectively, for a variable length of time, just in case that user or another one wants to execute the same `select` statement. In multiuser application environments, a performance gain is achieved every time user processes execute the same `select` statement because the RDBMS spends less time parsing the statement, and the server process spends less time retrieving data.

Exercises

1. Does SQL allow the user to define procedures or desired data for information retrieval? Explain.
2. What are the general tasks Oracle accomplishes to process `select` statements? At what point in processing does the server process actually retrieve data into the buffer cache?

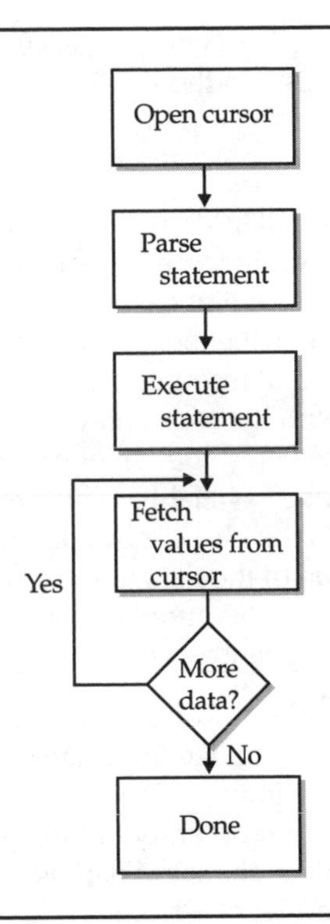

FIGURE 6-2. *Steps in Oracle SQL statement processing*

Stages in Processing DML Statements

At this point, it's time to meet yet another "behind-the-scenes" player in Oracle transaction processing—the *rollback segment*. The rollback segment is a database object in Oracle that stores old versions of data being changed by DML statements issued by the user process. Rollback segments only store the old values, not the new values—the new values are stored in the object itself.

With this in mind, return to the processing of DML statements. There are several differences between how Oracle processes `select` statements and how it processes DML statements such as `update`, `insert`, and `delete`. Though the operations involved in executing DML statements fall into the same general pattern as those for select statements shown in Figure 6-2, the specific flow of operation in processing DML statements is as follows:

1. **Parse statement** The RDBMS creates a *parse tree,* or *execution plan,* for the statement and places it in the library cache. The parse tree is a list of operations the RDBMS uses to process the data change. If a parse tree already exists for this statement, the RDBMS can omit this step.
2. **Execute statement** The RDBMS performs all processing to execute the DML statement. For `update` or `delete` statements, the server process will retrieve the data from disk into the buffer cache, implicitly acquire a lock on the data to be changed, and then make the specified data change in the buffer cache. A *lock* is an Oracle internal resource that one user process acquires before updating or deleting existing data to prevent other users from doing the same thing. For `insert` statements, the server process will retrieve a block from disk that has enough space available to house the new row of data, and will place that new row into the block. Also, part of executing the DML statement is writing the old version of the data to the rollback segment acquired for that transaction. A lock must be acquired on the rollback segment to write changes to a rollback segment as well.
3. **Generate redo information** Recall from the prior lesson that the redo log buffer stores redo or data change information produced as the result of DML operations running in user sessions. After issuing DML statements, the user process must write a redo entry to the redo log buffer. In this way, Oracle can recover a data change if damage is later done to the disk files containing Oracle data.

TIP
Acquiring a lock is how one Oracle user says to the other users "Hey! Hands off this data! I'm changing it now, so that means you can't have it until I let go of my lock!" Locks can be acquired at the row level implicitly as part of `update` *or* `delete` *statements, or at the table level through explicit methods described later in the book.*

Moving Data Changes from Memory to Disk

Once the DML statement has been executed, there is no further need to fetch values, as there was for `select` statements. However, as with `select` statements, the execution plan for the DML statement sticks around in the library cache for a variable period of time in case another user tries to execute the same statement. The changed blocks in the buffer cache are now considered "dirty" because the version in the buffer cache and on disk are no longer identical. Those dirty buffers stick around in the buffer cache as well, but they will need to be copied to disk eventually in order for Oracle not to lose the data change that has been made. Also, new information appears in the redo log buffer as the result of the data changes made by the DML statement. By having all the data changes happening in memory, Oracle is in a position to relieve user processes from having to wait for the data changes to be written to disk. Oracle does this by running two other background processes called *DBWR* and *LGWR* that write the data changes from the buffer cache and the redo log buffer to disk; these processes are asynchronous, meaning that they occur sometime after the user actually makes the change. The following subtopics explain the role of each background process.

ROLE OF DBWR Called the *database writer* process, the DBWR background process writes dirty data blocks from buffer cache to disk. The writes are done when the server process needs to make room in the buffer cache to read more data in for user processes, when DBWR is told to write data to disk by the LGWR process, or every three seconds due to a timeout. The event that causes LGWR to tell DBWR to write to disk is called a *checkpoint*. You will learn more about checkpoints in Chapter 7. Because Oracle8 allows multiple database writers to run on the host machine, the DBWR process is sometimes referred to as *DBW0*, where *0* can be a digit between 0 and 9, representing one of several DBWR processes running in Oracle.

ROLE OF LGWR Called the *log writer* process, the LGWR background process writes redo log entries from the redo log buffer to online redo log files on disk. LGWR has some other specialized functions related to the management of redo information that you will learn about in Chapter 7. LGWR also tells DBWR to write dirty buffers to disk at checkpoints, as mentioned earlier.

Exercises

1. How does the processing of DML statements differ from processing queries?
2. What are rollback segments? What are locks? How are these objects involved in DML processing?
3. How is changed data moved from memory to disk? What background processes and memory structures are involved?

Stages in Processing commit Statements

As discussed in Unit I, issuing a `commit` statement ends the current transaction by making permanent any data change the user process may have issued to the Oracle database. A `rollback` statement discards the data change in favor of how the data appeared before the change was made. The rollback segment is how Oracle manages to offer this functionality. By keeping a copy of the old data in the rollback segment for the duration of the transaction, Oracle is able to discard any change made by the transaction before the `commit` statement was issued.

Before proceeding any further, make sure you understand the following important point—issuing `commit` has no effect on when Oracle copies a data change in the buffer cache to disk. Thus, a `commit` statement does not somehow trigger DBWR activity. Only a checkpoint, a timeout, or a need for room in the buffer cache for blocks requested by users will make DBWR write dirty blocks to disk. With that fact in mind, what exactly does processing a `commit` statement consist of? The following list tells all:

- **Release table/row locks acquired by transaction** All row locks (or even table locks, if any were acquired) are released by issuing `commit` statements. Other users can then modify the rows (or tables) previously locked by this user.
- **Release rollback segment locks acquired by transaction** Changes to rollback segments are subject to the same locking mechanisms as other objects. Once the change is committed, the space to hold both old and new versions of data for that transaction in the rollback segment is available for another user's transaction.
- **Generate redo for committed transaction** Once the `commit` takes place, a redo entry is generated by the user process stating that all the changes associated with that transaction have now been committed by the user.

Note that Oracle takes no special action related to redo information as the result of a `commit`, other than to indicate that the transaction has been committed. How does Oracle know which DML statement redo entries to associate with each transaction? The answer is the *system change numbers* (*SCN*s). An SCN is an ID that Oracle generates for each and every transaction that a user process engages. Every redo entry for every data change lists the change made and the SCN the change is associated with. The redo entry for the `commit` also identifies the SCN and simply notes that the SCN has been committed. Thus, Oracle can keep easy track of the status of every transaction via the SCN.

Exercises

1. What events occur as part of a `commit` statement?
2. What does a redo entry for `commit` statements consist of? What is an SCN?

Using Administration Tools

In this section, you will cover the following topics related to using administration tools:

- Using Server Manager line mode
- Identifying administration applications in Oracle Enterprise Manager
- Using Oracle Enterprise Manager components

In the past few years, there has been an explosion in the use of administrative tools for Oracle databases. These tools are designed to simplify many aspects of Oracle database administration, including tablespace, instance, storage, object, and backup and recovery management. However, OCP certification on Oracle7 did not focus on using administrative tools. Instead, it focused on the importance of understanding server internals, such as V$ views and issuing commands from the command line. Though the importance of these Oracle components can hardly be diminished, administrative tools such as Oracle Enterprise Manager matured and expanded their functionality, and these areas have risen to take similar levels of importance in the repertoire of every DBA. Plus, they make your job a heck of a lot easier.

Using Server Manager Line Mode

The workhorse database administrative tool on Oracle is Server Manager. This tool has been around in one form or another for the last few releases of Oracle, and it rendered SQL*DBA obsolete as of Oracle 7.3. Many functions in Oracle are accomplished easily with Server Manager, including database startup and shutdown, database creation, and management of key aspects of the database, such as redo log creation and control file backup.

Server Manager is usually started from the command line on the machine hosting the Oracle database. In UNIX, the executable is called `svrmgrl`. You can access the host machine command line either via Telnet or an X terminal. You can execute Server Manager from any place in your file system if the `$ORACLE_HOME/bin` directory is part of your path environment setting. If this directory is not part of your path, you should add it. The following code block demonstrates the execution of Server Manager in line mode from the UNIX command line.

```
[ oracle80 : orgdbux01 ] > svrmgrl
Oracle Server Manager Release 3.0.5.0.0 - Production
(c)Copyright 1997, Oracle Corporation. All Rights Reserved.
Oracle8 Enterprise Edition Release 8.0.5 - Production
With the Partitioning and Objects options
PL/SQL Release 8.0.5 - Production
SVRMGR> connect internal
Connected.
SVRMGR>
```

Running Server Manager line mode in Windows environments is slightly different, since most people don't work directly from the DOS prompt as they do with the UNIX command prompt. Again, however, you must somehow access the DOS prompt on the machine hosting Oracle. One method for starting Server Manager line mode in Windows can be accomplished by choosing Start | Programs | DOS Prompt, and issuing the following commands from within DOS:

```
D:\>svrmgr30
Oracle Server Manager Release 3.0.5 - Production
(c) Copyright 1997, Oracle Corporation. All Rights Reserved.
Oracle8 Enterprise Edition Release 8.0.5.0.0 - Production
With the Partitioning and Objects options
PL/SQL Release 8.0.5 - Production
SVRMGR>
```

Unfortunately, the Oracle installation on Windows does not add Server Manager to the list of menu options available under the Start | Programs | Oracle Enterprise Manager menu. Another way to execute Server Manager in Windows is to double-click My Computer on your desktop, double-click the drive containing the Oracle software home directory, double-click the `bin` subdirectory, and double-click the executable called `svrmgr30`. Figure 6-3 shows Server Manager in action. Shortly, you will explore the use of Server Manager for startup and shutdown of the Oracle database, in the "Managing an Oracle Instance" section.

Exercises

1. What is Server Manager? Where is its executable found? What functionality does it offer?

2. How is Server Manager accessed in UNIX environments? In Windows environments?

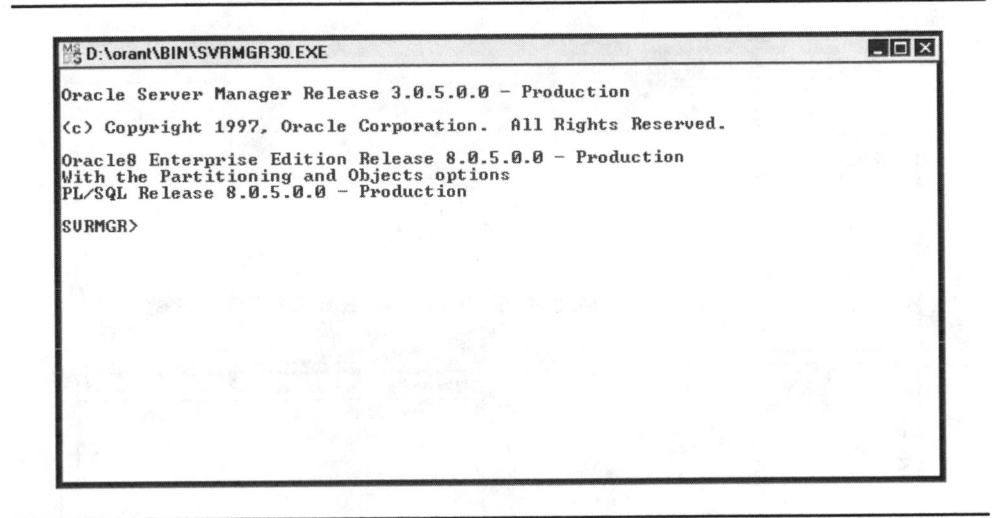

FIGURE 6-3. *Server Manager line mode*

Identifying Administration Applications in Oracle Enterprise Manager

Fortunately, your administrative capabilities for Oracle don't end at Server Manager line mode. Oracle Enterprise Manager (OEM) is a suite of applications that allows you to manage your Oracle database in a graphical user interface. Anything you can do from Server Manager, you can do from Oracle Enterprise Manager—provided you have set up a password file for remote database administration. More about how to do this appears in the next section. If you do not have a password file set up for administering your Oracle database remotely, then you cannot start up and shut down the Oracle database using OEM, but you can do most anything else.

There is no such thing as easy database administration, but using the administrative tools available in Oracle Enterprise Manager can simplify many areas of managing your database. Oracle Enterprise Manager is usually run from your desktop. Assuming you use Windows, you can identify the tools at your disposal as part of OEM either by looking under Start | Programs | Oracle Enterprise Manager, or under the Tools | Applications menu within the Enterprise Manager application itself. Figure 6-4 illustrates Enterprise Manager, the Tools | Applications menu, and the Applications button bar, both of which can be used to access any of the administrative applications available in OEM. The following list identifies the

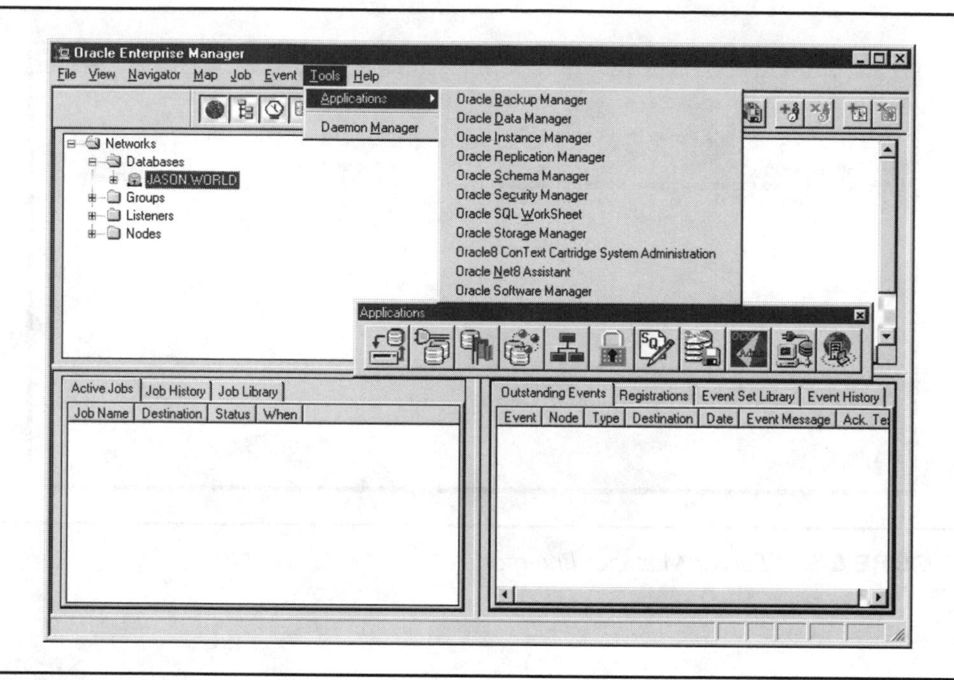

FIGURE 6-4. *Oracle Enterprise Manager administrative applications*

applications available for Oracle Enterprise Manager, along with a brief description of their use:

- **Backup Manager** Handles automation of backup operations
- **Data Manager** Manages import, export, and loading of data into tables of an Oracle database
- **Instance Manager** Handles management of an Oracle instance, including session, in-doubt transaction, and initialization parameter information
- **Replication Manager** Manages configuration, scheduling, and administrative functions of replication between nodes on a network running Oracle databases
- **Schema Manager** Manages table, index, cluster, and other object creation and management in an Oracle database
- **Security Manager** Handles user access privileges and role administration

- **SQL Worksheet** Used to execute SQL statements from scripts in a graphical interface more advanced than SQL*Plus
- **Storage Manager** Handles configuration and management of logical and physical disk resources for the Oracle database
- **Software Manager** Used as part of an enterprise-wide management of Oracle software application design, distribution, and asset management
- **Repository Manager** Used to create, validate, and drop OEM repositories

TIP
In addition to the administrator tools listed above, other applications are available for different cartridges you may have installed on your Oracle database, such as ConText Cartridge System Administrator. Administrative tools accompany add-ins like the Tuning Pack as well, including Lock Manager, Performance Manager, and others.

Exercises

1. Identify the functionality provided by the Storage, Instance, and Schema Manager administrative tools that are part of OEM.
2. What are some other administrative tools that OEM might use, and where/how might the DBA get them?

Using Oracle Enterprise Manager Components

To show you everything that each of the manager tools is capable of would take quite a bit of space in this book—as it is, you will cover some serious territory! Instead, we will look at how one of the manager tools works in OEM, and from there we will extrapolate some general rules that all the manager tools abide by. Because so much of your effort in this chapter will focus on managing the Oracle instance and opening and closing the Oracle database, the tool we will focus on here is Instance Manager.

The basic purpose of Instance Manager is—you guessed it—managing the Oracle instance. You can start and stop the instance with this tool (provided you've set up your password file—more information on how to do this in a moment); view and modify `initsid.ora` parameters; view current sessions, in-doubt transactions, and apply database configuration information you have available on your desktop. Figure 6-5 displays the Instance Manager login prompt. To open this

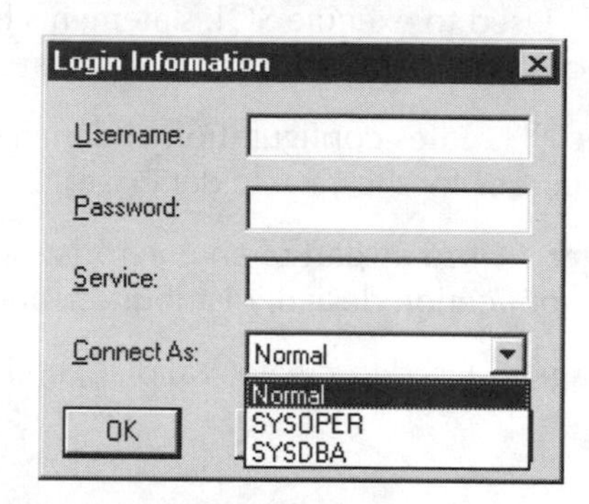

FIGURE 6-5. *Instance Manager tool in OEM*

tool, either click on the Tools | Applications | Instance Manager menu item from OEM, or click on Start | Programs | Oracle Enterprise Manager | Instance Manager from the Windows console. After providing the appropriate username, password, and TNS connect information, notice the fourth text box, where the tool prompts you to choose how you want to connect. The options are Normal, `sysdba`, and `sysoper`. The first option allows you to connect as the username you provided, but gives you no administrative abilities on the database. Thus, you can view database initialization parameters, but cannot start up or shut down the database. Use of the other two options is for administrative authentication, and both will be explained in the next section.

TIP
Instance Manager will not prompt you for login information if you run it from OEM. It will instead use the login info you provided when you started OEM.

After login, you will see the Instance Manager interface. The left-hand window is the navigator window. On it, there are several nodes you can drill down into to find information. You drill into each node by clicking on the plus sign (+) to the left of the node. The names of each node are self-explanatory. For example, if you drill into the Sessions node as shown in Figure 6-6, you will see all the sessions currently happening in Oracle listed below the node. On the right side is the work interface. If you click on the name of the node or the file folder icon to the left of that name, the relevant information will be displayed in the work window. As

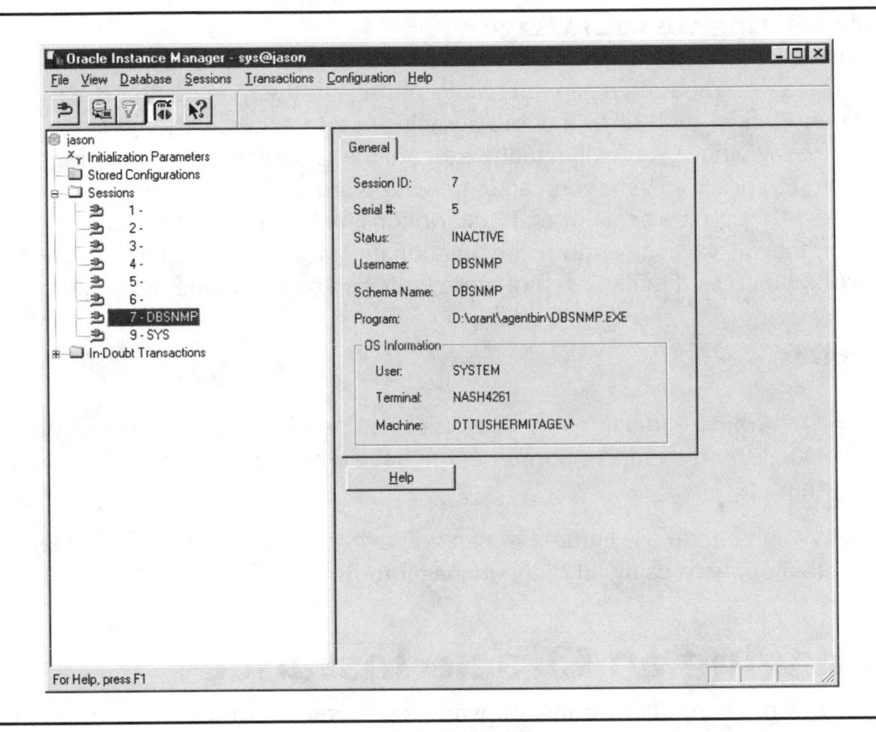

FIGURE 6-6. *Instance Manager interface*

another example, if you click on the name of one of the connected sessions in the navigator window, you will see some additional information about that session appearing in the work window.

Along the top of the interface is a set of menus. From left to right, they are File, View, Database, Sessions, Transactions, Configuration, and Help. The options under the File menu allow you to change database connection, enable roles, or exit the application. The options under the View menu allow you to modify the tools available in Instance Manager and expand or collapse nodes in the left window. The Database menu permits startup and shutdown operations, archiving, and other things. The Sessions menu permits management of sessions, including the ability to disconnect a session, restrict access to the database to only those users with `restricted session` privileges, or allow all users to access the database. The Transactions menu allows the DBA to force `commit` and `rollback` operations to happen in the database. The Configuration menu allows you to change or remove database configurations from the database to the desktop. Finally, the Help menu gives you access to online help.

Extrapolating General Usage

After using Instance Manager, as well as some of the other manager tools, you should be able to see some general patters of use. All the manager tools have both a navigator window with several nodes allowing you to access various things, and a work window where you will actually execute the tasks that the manager tool allows you to do. For each, you can login with Normal, `sysdba`, or `sysoper` privileges. Though the actual menus and options for each manager tool are different, they all basically mirror the functionality you have through the navigator and work windows. Finally, each of these tools can be run alone or as part of OEM.

Exercises

1. Describe the functionality and general use of the Instance Manager tool. What three connect options do you have when logging into Oracle via the tool?
2. What general use guidelines can you extract from using Instance Manager that apply to using all of the manager tools?

Managing an Oracle Instance

In this section, you will cover the following topics related to starting and stopping an Oracle instance:

- Setting up OS and password file authentication
- Creating your parameter file
- Starting an instance and opening the database
- Closing a database and shutting down the instance
- Getting and setting parameter values
- Managing sessions
- Monitoring ALERT and trace files

After installing the Oracle software, the DBA should master the management of an Oracle instance. There are several important things that should be done to manage the Oracle instance before even thinking about setting up the Oracle database. Important questions about authentication must be answered, and the parameter file must be developed and managed. This parameter file is generically referred to as `initsid.ora` by many DBAs. Starting up and shutting down the instance, and opening and closing the database are key areas both before and after the database is created. Finally, the management of sessions and places to look for information about the Oracle instance in action are covered in this section.

Setting Up OS and Password File Authentication

How you plan to support the Oracle database you create determines, to a large extent, how you will set up Oracle to handle *administrative authentication*. Authentication requires the DBA to provide a password in order to gain entry for administrative tasks onto the machine hosting Oracle, the database itself, or both. There are two methods of providing administrative authentication: operating system and password file authentication. If the DBA will administer the database directly from the machine hosting the Oracle database by means of Telnet and Server Manager line mode, operating system authentication should suffice. But, if the DBA plans to manage the site from software running on a desktop computer, such as OEM, then the DBA should set up a password file. Another nice feature about a password file is that it allows many DBAs to manage databases, each with varying levels of control. For example, the organization might want the junior DBA to handle backups and user creation, but not startup and shutdown of the instance. Password files work well to support organizations wanting a team of DBAs to have a range of capabilities on the machine.

More Introductions: SYS, SYSTEM, and the Data Dictionary

Another round of introductions is in order. *SYS* and *SYSTEM* are two users Oracle creates when you install your database. Each has their own default password. The default password for SYS is CHANGE_ON_INSTALL, and for SYSTEM it is MANAGER. Be careful to protect the passwords for both these users by changing them after installing Oracle. These two privileged users have the power to administer most any feature of the Oracle database. SYS is more important than SYSTEM because SYS will wind up owning all Oracle system tables from which the data dictionary is derived.

The Oracle data dictionary is the system resource you will turn to in order to find out just about anything about your database, from which users own what objects, to the initialization parameter settings, to performance monitoring, and more. There are two basic categories for Oracle database views: those that show information about database objects and those that show dynamic performance. The views showing information about objects are the data dictionary views. The views showing information about performance are dynamic performance views.

Using OS Authentication

Operating system authentication offers the comfort of a familiar face to old-school UNIX folks, in the same way that using the VI text editor and Kornshell does. Because of this, the discussion of OS authentication will focus primarily on its implementation in UNIX. However, OS authentication has few real advantages and many disadvantages compared to the password file method of authentication. The main benefit OS authentication offers is easy login to Oracle via the slash (/) character, as shown here:

```
UNIX® SYSTEM V TTYP01 (23.45.67.98)
Login: bobcat
Password:
User connected. Today is 12/17/99 14:15:34
[companyx] /home/bobcat/> sqlplus /
SQL*PLUS Version 8.0.5.0.0
(c) 1979,1998 Oracle Corporation(c) All rights reserved.
Connected to Oracle8 Enterprise Edition 8.0.5 - Production
PL/SQL Version 8.0.5 - Production
SQL>
```

The disadvantages of OS authentication are many. For one thing, you must have a machine login to use Oracle. When might this pose a problem? You may not want to make the host machine's command prompt accessible to your 10,000+ user base for a production system, for example. For development and test environments, however, OS authentication may be fine.

To use OS authentication, a special group called `dba` must be created on the operating system before you even install your Oracle software. Later, when Oracle is installed and configured, you can log into the OS via Telnet as a user belonging to the `dba` group (such as the Oracle software owner) run Server Manager in line mode, and perform startup and shutdown operations after issuing the `connect internal` command. This command has been around for several versions of Oracle and continues to be provided for backward compatibility. The DBA can connect to the database by using the `connect` *name* `as sysdba` command and then providing the appropriate password, as well. The `sysdba` keyword denotes a collection of privileges that are akin to those privileges granted to `internal`. The following block illustrates simple usage:

```
SVRMGR> connect internal
Connected.
```

Or,

```
SVRMGR> connect sys as sysdba
Password:
Connected.
```

Oracle creates some other OS roles as part of its UNIX installation that must be granted to the DBA, such as `osoper` and `osdba`. These OS roles are given to the Oracle software owner, and must be granted to other OS users who would be DBAs via operating system commands. These roles cannot be revoked or granted from within Oracle. However, there are two equivalent Oracle privileges used when you authenticate with a password file—`sysoper` and `sysdba`, respectively.

There are some small differences between the `osoper` and `sysoper`, and `osdba` and `sysdba`, which you may use to your advantage for breaking out DBA roles and responsibilities. The `osoper` role and `sysoper` privilege allow you to start and stop the instance, mount or open the database, back up the database, initiate archiving redo logs, initiate database recovery, and change database access to `restricted session` mode. The `osdba` and `sysdba` roles offer the same privileges as `osoper` and `sysoper`, and add the ability to execute and administer all Oracle system privileges, the `create database` privilege, and all privileges required for time-based incomplete database recovery. Obviously, `osdba` or `sysdba` is given to the DBA ultimately responsible for the operation of the database.

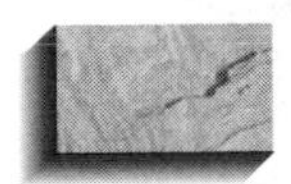

TIP
The implementation of operating system authentication in Oracle depends heavily on the operating system you use. Since operating system–specific issues are not part of OCP Exam 2, they will not be covered here. If you need more information on operating system authentication, consult the appropriate operating system–specific Oracle administrative manual.

Authentication with the Password File

Oracle's other method of authenticating DBAs is the *password file*. The DBA creates the password file, and passwords for all others permitted to administer Oracle are stored in the file. The password file is created with the ORAPWD utility. The name of this executable varies by operating system. For example, it is `orapwd` on UNIX, but `orapwd80` on Windows.

When executing ORAPWD, you will pass three parameters: `FILE`, `PASSWORD`, and `ENTRIES`. To determine what to specify for `FILE`, you usually place the password file in $ORACLE_HOME/dbs, and name it `orapw`*`sid`*`.pwd`, substituting the name of your database for *`sid`*. For PASSWORD, be aware that as you define the password for your password file, you are also simultaneously assigning the password for logging into Oracle as `internal` and SYS. Later, if the DBA connects as `internal` or SYS and issues the `alter user` *name* `identified by` *`password`* command, the passwords for `internal`, SYS, and the password file are all changed. The final parameter is `ENTRIES`, specifying the number of user entries allowed for the password file. Be careful, because you can't add more later without deleting and re-creating the password file, which is risky. The actual execution of ORAPWD in Windows may look something like this, from the command line:

```
D:\orant\bin\>orapwd80 FILE=D:\orant\dbs\orapworgdb01.pwd
PASSWORD=jason ENTRIES=5
```

In UNIX, it may look something like this:

```
/home/oracle80> orapwd \
FILE=app/oracle/product/8.0.5/dbs/orapwdorgdb01.pwd \
 PASSWORD=jason ENTRIES=5
```

After creating the password file, you must do a few other things to allow administrative access to the database while simultaneously preventing the use of `internal`. First, set the value for the `REMOTE_LOGIN_PASSWORDFILE` parameter in the `init`*`sid`*`.ora` parameter file. This parameter accepts none, shared, and exclusive as its values. The `none` setting means the database won't allow privileged sessions over unsecured connections. When OS authentication is used, the `REMOTE_LOGIN_PASSWORDFILE` is set to `none` to disallow remote database administration. Setting `REMOTE_LOGIN_PASSWORDFILE` to shared means that only SYS and `internal` can log into Oracle to perform administrative functions remotely. Finally, setting `REMOTE_LOGIN_PASSWORDFILE` to exclusive means that a password file exists and any user/password combination in the password file can log in to Oracle remotely and administer that instance. If this setting is used, the DBA should use the `create user` command in Oracle to create the users that are added to the password file, and grant `sysoper` and/or `sysdba` system privileges to those users. After that, users can log into the database as themselves with all administrator privileges.

After creating the password file with the ORAPWD utility and setting the `REMOTE_LOGIN_PASSWORDFILE` parameter to exclusive in order to administer a database remotely, the DBA can then connect to the database as a user with sysdba privileges as shown here:

```
SVRMGR>  CONNECT sys AS SYSDBA;
Password:
Connected.
```

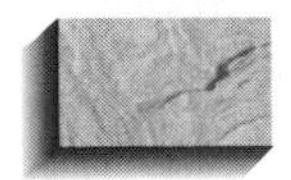

TIP
Remember two important points about password files. First, to find out which users are in the database password file, use the V$PWFILE_USERS dynamic performance view. (More on the data dictionary will be presented in Chapter 7.) Second, any object created by anyone logging in as `sysdba` *or* `sysoper` *will be owned by SYS.*

Exercises

1. What two methods of user authentication are available in Oracle? Explain some advantages and disadvantages for each.
2. What is the name of the utility used to create a password file? Describe its use, parameters, and the related parameter that must be set in `initsid.ora` in order to use a password file for authentication.
3. What are the two Oracle roles granted to DBAs in order to perform database administration?
4. Who is SYS, and how is it used? Who is SYSTEM?

Creating Your Parameter File

How well or poorly your database performs is determined to a great extent by how you configure your Oracle instance. You configure your instance dynamically when you start it, using a parameter file. This parameter file is commonly referred to by DBAs as the `initsid.ora` file. The real name of the parameter file for your database is arbitrary and completely up to you; however, when you install Oracle and create your first database, Oracle will generate a parameter file for you named after the database. Thus, if your database is named ORGDB01, your default name for the `initsid.ora` file will be `initORGDB01.ora`.

You can create your parameter file from scratch, but why bother when Oracle creates one for you? The parameter file Oracle creates for you will contain several different options for the most essential initialization parameters you need to include when creating a new database. However, Oracle has literally hundreds of initialization parameters, documented and undocumented. The following code block shows a sample parameter file in use on a small Oracle database running under Windows. The pound sign (#) is used to denote comments in the parameter file.

```
db_name = ORGDB01
db_files = 1020
control_files = (D:\orant\DATABASE\ctl1orgdb01.ora,
D:\orant\DATABASE\ctl2orgdb01.ora)
db_file_multiblock_read_count = 16
db_block_buffers = 1000
shared_pool_size = 1048576
log_checkpoint_interval = 8000
processes = 100
dml_locks = 200
log_buffer = 32768
sequence_cache_entries = 30
sequence_cache_hash_buckets = 23
#audit_trail = true
#timed_statistics = true
background_dump_dest = D:\orant\RDBMS80\trace
user_dump_dest = D:\orant\RDBMS80\trace
core_dump_dest = D:\orant\RDBMS80\trace
db_block_size =2048
sort_area_size = 65536
log_checkpoint_timeout = 0
remote_login_passwordfile = shared
max_dump_file_size = 10240
rollback_segments = (RB0_ORGDB01, RB1_ORGDB02)
global_names=false
open_cursors=400
```

In general, when working with parameter files, it is best not to start from scratch. Use the Oracle default, or borrow one from another DBA. But be sure that you alter the parameters in the file to reflect your own database, including `DB_NAME`, `DB_BLOCK_SIZE`, `CONTROL_FILES`, and others. You should remember where you store your parameter file on the machine hosting the Oracle database. *Do not leave multiple copies in different directories.* This could lead you to make a change to one but not the other. Then if you start your instance with the old parameter file later, you could have problems. However, it can be useful to have a few different copies of a parameter file for various administrative purposes, such as one for production environments, and one for running the database in restricted mode for DBA maintenance operations.

Exercises

1. What is the typical name for the parameter file in Oracle? By what name do most DBAs refer to their parameter file?
2. Is it wise to create parameter files from scratch? Why or why not?

Starting an Instance and Opening the Database

There is an important distinction between an Oracle instance and an Oracle database. The Oracle database is a set of tables, indexes, procedures, and other objects used for storing data. More precisely, an Oracle database, identified by the database name (DB_NAME), represents the physical structures and is composed of operating system files. Although it is possible to use a database name that is different from the name of the instance, you should use the same name for ease of administration. The Oracle instance is the memory structures, background processes, and disk resources, all working together to fulfill user data requests and changes.

With that distinction made, let's consider starting the Oracle instance. You must do this before creating a new database, or before allowing access to an existing database. To start the instance, follow these steps:

1. From the command line on the host machine, start Server Manager and log in either as `sysdba` or `internal`:

```
[ oracle80 : orgdbux01 ] > svrmgrl
Oracle Server Manager Release 3.0.5.0.0 - Production
(c)Copyright 1998, Oracle Corporation. All Rights Reserved.
Oracle8 Enterprise Edition Release 8.0.5 - Production
With the Partitioning and Objects options
PL/SQL Release 8.0.5 - Production
SVRMGR> connect internal
Connected.
SVRMGR>
```

2. From within Server Manager, use the `startup` *`start_option dbname`* `pfile=`*`init.ora`* command to start the instance. Several options exist for *`start_option`*, including `nomount`, `mount`, `open`, and `open force`. The PFILE parameter should be used to identify the exact `init`*`sid`*`.ora` file you want to use. An example of `startup nomount` is shown in the following code block:

```
SVRMGR> startup nomount pfile=initORGDB01.ora
ORACLE instance started.
Total System Global Area                    227174560 bytes
Fixed Size                                      42764 bytes
Variable Size                                93999104 bytes
Database Buffers                             81920000 bytes
Redo Buffers                                 51208192 bytes
SVRMGR>
```

Options for Starting Oracle

You can also start a database with OEM Instance Manager. All the options discussed for Server Manager are available via Instance Manager, except through a graphical user interface. You may also want to note that starting Oracle databases in Windows is not necessarily handled with Server Manager or even OEM, but instead may be handled as a *service*. A service in Windows is similar to a *daemon* in UNIX. Both of these operating system functions allow Oracle to start automatically when the machine boots. (We're getting a little off the topic here, but if you're interested in more information, consult the *Oracle8 Installation Guide for Windows NT*, which comes with that distribution of Oracle.) There are several different options for starting Oracle instances, with or without opening the database.

STARTUP NOMOUNT This option starts the instance without mounting the database. That means all the memory structures and background processes are in place, but no database is attached to the instance. You will use this option later for creating the Oracle database. You can specify this option with or without specifying an `init`*`sid`*`.ora` file for the `PFILE` parameter. If you do not specify `PFILE`, Oracle uses its own built-in default settings for initialization parameters specific to each operating system.

STARTUP MOUNT This option starts the instance and attaches the database, but does not open it. You can't mount a database you haven't created yet. This option is useful in situations where you have to move physical database files around on the machine hosting Oracle, or when database recovery is required. You should specify an `init`*`sid`*`.ora` file for the `PFILE` parameter when using this option; otherwise, Oracle will not use values you may have specified in your `init`*`sid`*`.ora` file. If the instance is already started but the database is not mounted, use `alter database mount` instead.

STARTUP OPEN This option starts your instance, attaches the database, and opens it. This is the default option for starting Oracle. It is used when you want to make your database available to users. You can't open a database you haven't created yet. The file you specify for the `PFILE` parameter must be an `init`*`sid`*`.ora` file. If the instance is started and the database is mounted, use `alter database open` instead.

STARTUP FORCE This option forces the instance to start and the database to open. It is used in situations where other `startup` options are met with errors from Oracle, and no `shutdown` options seem to work either. This is an option of last resort, and there is no reason to use it generally unless you cannot start the database with any other option.

TIP
Two other cases for database startup include `startup recover` for handling database recovery, and `startup restrict` to open the database while simultaneously preventing all users but the DBA from accessing database objects. You'll learn about using `startup restrict` when we talk about the EXPORT utility in Chapters 11 and 15.

Exercises

1. What tools can be used for starting Oracle instances and databases? What connection must be used for the task?
2. What are some options for database startup?

Closing a Database and Shutting Down the Instance

Shutdown of the Oracle instance works in much the same way as starting the instance. You must either be logged onto Oracle as `internal` or as a user with `sysdba` privileges. The task can be accomplished from Server Manager or OEM Instance Manager, or as a Windows service. The steps for shutting down an Oracle database from Server Manager are as follows:

1. From the command line on the host machine, start Server Manager, and log in either as `sysdba` or `internal`:

```
[ oracle80 : orgdbux01 ] > svrmgrl
Oracle Server Manager Release 3.0.5.0.0 - Production
(c)Copyright 1998, Oracle Corporation. All Rights Reserved.
Oracle8 Enterprise Edition Release 8.0.5 - Production
With the Partitioning and Objects options
PL/SQL Release 8.0.5 - Production
SVRMGR> connect internal
Connected.
SVRMGR>
```

2. From within Server Manager, use the `shutdown` *`stop_option`* command to start the instance. Several options exist for *`stop_option`*, including `immediate`, `normal`, or `abort`. An example of `shutdown immediate` is shown in the following code block:

```
SVRMGR> shutdown immediate
ORA-01507: database not mounted
ORACLE instance shut down.
SVRMGR>
```

Options for Stopping Oracle

There are four priorities that can be specified by the DBA for shutting down the database. They include `shutdown normal`, `shutdown immediate`, `shutdown abort`, and `shutdown transactional`. The next four subtopics will explain each of these options and give cases where their use might be appropriate.

SHUTDOWN NORMAL This is the lowest priority shutdown. When `shutdown normal` is issued, Oracle will wait for users to log out before actually shutting down the instance and closing the database. There are three rules Oracle follows during `shutdown normal`. First, Oracle will not let new users access the database. Second, Oracle will not force users already logged on to the system to log off in order to complete the shutdown. Third, under normal shutdown situations, there is no need for instance recovery.

SHUTDOWN IMMEDIATE This is a higher-priority shutdown that the DBA can use when `shutdown normal` would take too long. The `shutdown immediate` command shuts down a database as follows. No new users will be able to connect to the database once the `shutdown` command is issued. Oracle will not wait for a user to log off as it does for `shutdown normal`; instead, it will terminate user connections immediately and roll back uncommitted transactions. Immediate database shutdown, though more drastic than `shutdown normal`, does not require any instance recovery.

SHUTDOWN ABORT This is the highest priority database shutdown command. In all cases where this priority is used, the database will shut down immediately. All users are immediately disconnected, no transactions are rolled back, and recovery will be required when the database starts up again. You will use this option only when media or disk failure has taken place on the machine hosting Oracle.

SHUTDOWN TRANSACTIONAL A transactional shutdown prevents clients from losing work. A transactional database shutdown proceeds with the following conditions: no client can start a new transaction on this particular instance, a client is disconnected when the client ends the transaction that is in progress, and a `shutdown immediate` occurs when all transactions have finished. The next startup will not require an instance recovery.

Exercises

1. What connection must be used for the task of database shutdown?
2. What are the four options for database shutdown?

Getting and Setting Parameter Values

Once your instance is started, several different ways exist for obtaining the values set for the instance on initialization. The first and least effective way to view parameter values in your database is to look at the `initsid.ora` file. This choice does not give you all parameters, and what's more, the parameters in your parameter file may have changed since the last time you started Oracle. A much better way to obtain parameter values is to `select` them from a special view in Oracle called V$PARAMETER. Still another effective way for obtaining parameter values in Oracle is to use Server Manager. The `show parameter` command will list all parameters for the instance. Finally, you can use the OEM Instance Manager to display instance parameters, as shown in Figure 6-7. Can you guess where Instance Manager and Server Manager draw their initialization parameter information from? If you said V$PARAMETER, you were right!

Setting parameters is done in one of two ways. By far, the most effective way to set a database parameter is to add the name of the parameter and the value to the `initsid.ora` file for your instance. After that, shut down and start up your instance using the `initsid.ora file`. Unfortunately, in the world of multiuser

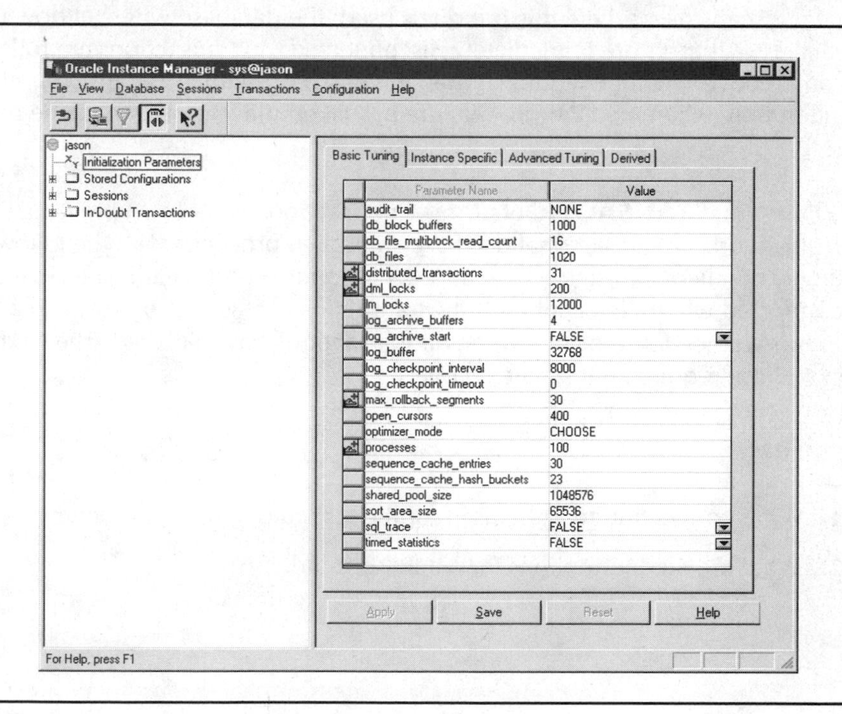

FIGURE 6-7. *Instance parameters in Instance Manager*

database environments, DBAs do not always have the luxury of bouncing the database whenever they want. You can always try to schedule this sort of thing, or if the need is not critical, wait until the weekend. Another method for setting parameters is with the `alter system` command. However, this is not an effective method for changing parameters, because not all initialization parameters can be changed using this command. The ones that can be changed include `RESOURCE_LIMIT, GLOBAL_NAMES, AUDIT_TRAIL, TIMED_STATISTICS,` some of the MTS parameters, and some of the licensing parameters.

Exercises

1. Identify some ways you can obtain instance parameters. Which of these ways is least effective? Which are most effective?
2. What methods are available for changing instance parameters before the instance is started? What about after the instance is started?

Managing Sessions

Each user process that connects to Oracle maintains a session with the Oracle database. The user has the ability to do whatever they have been granted privileges to do within their session. User sessions are managed with the `alter session` statement. Several things can be changed about a user session, including national language settings like `NLS_LANGUAGE`, `NLS_DATE_FORMAT`, and so on, in the form `alter session set NLS_DATE_FORMAT = 'date_format'`. In addition, if the user wants to enable tracing on the session to determine performance statistics for the SQL they execute, the `alter session set SQL_TRACE = TRUE` command can be used.

In order to connect to the database, the user must be granted the `create session` privilege. Note that this privilege only allows the user to connect to Oracle—they must be granted further privileges to actually see anything once connected! Although privileges will be covered in more detail in Chapter 10, this privilege is mentioned because it is useful in managing sessions to know how to continue and discontinue a user's ability to create sessions with Oracle.

There are a few basic ways the DBA can manage sessions. One is to disconnect a session, another is to restrict access to an open database to only those users with a special privilege called `restricted session`. You have already seen how to open the database from Server Manager in restricted mode with the `startup restrict` command. You can restrict database access with the `alter system enable restricted session` command after the database is open. To disconnect a session, you must issue the `alter system kill session 'sid, serial#'` command. The values for *sid* and *serial#* come from the V$SESSION dynamic performance view columns of the same name.

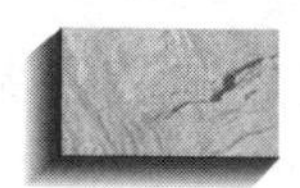

TIP
The V$SESSION dictionary view contains information about every session currently connected to Oracle. It forms the basis of information displayed in the Instance Manager tool.

Exercises

1. What command is used to manage a user session? What tasks can actually be accomplished with that command?
2. What privileges must be granted in order for a user to connect to Oracle?
3. How do you restrict access to an open Oracle database to only those users with the `restricted session` privilege? What two pieces of information are required to disconnect a session from Oracle with the `alter system kill session` command?

Monitoring ALERT and Trace Files

The background processes of the Oracle database each maintain a log file of their execution if an error occurs in the background process during the life of the instance. This log file is called a trace file. If something goes wrong, the background process will write error information to the trace file, enabling you to figure out what happened. The types of things that get written to trace files include abnormal errors and process termination messages. A special trace file called the ALERT log is maintained by the Oracle instance. This file gets written in several situations. Oracle writes to the ALERT log whenever the database is started or shut down, whenever the control file is modified (for example, by creating a new tablespace), whenever a severe error occurs or an Oracle internal error occurs, and when Oracle starts writing to a new redo log file.

There are other times in Oracle execution when the ALERT log is written to, as well. The ALERT log can grow quite large, so it makes sense to clear it out once in a while and allow Oracle to start generating a new one, particularly if nothing eventful has happened on your database in a long time. Sometimes, when the ALERT log is written, the message must be addressed. As such, it is important for you as the DBA to check the ALERT log regularly for things like internal errors or other anomalies in database behavior. And if you have some kind of problem with your Oracle software and need to open a trouble ticket with Oracle Support, you may be requested to supply them with a copy of your ALERT log.

The location of your ALERT log and background trace files depends on the directory specified for the `BACKGROUND_DUMP_DEST` parameter for your instance. Both the background process trace files and the ALERT log will be found in this directory. If you are unsure of the location of your ALERT log, simply use the methods defined for getting parameter values, and look up the value for `BACKGROUND_DUMP_DEST`.

TIP
If you start getting really weird errors in your database, and your ALERT log contains `ORA-00600` *errors, you should call Oracle Support ASAP!*

Exercises

1. What is the ALERT log? What is a trace file? What is the difference between the two?
2. Where are ALERT logs and trace files stored in Oracle?

Creating an Oracle Database

In this section, you will cover the following topics related to creating an Oracle database:

- Preparing the operating system
- Preparing the parameter file
- Creating the database

Once the DBA has set up some necessary preliminary items for running the Oracle instance, such as password authentication, the DBA can then create the database that users will use for data management. Creating a database involves three activities that will be discussed in this section. The first activity for creating a database is mapping a logical entity-relationship diagram that details a model for a process to the data model upon which the creation of database objects like indexes and tables will be based. Second, the DBA will create physical data storage resources in the Oracle architecture, such as datafiles and redo log files. The final (and perhaps the most important) aspect of creating a database is creating the structures that comprise the Oracle data dictionary. Each element in the database creation process will be discussed in detail.

Preparing the Operating System

There are a few things you should do at the OS level before creating your database. Since every operating system is different, you'll be introduced to the general concepts here for the purpose of preparing for OCP. If you have further questions, refer to the operating system–specific Oracle installation guide that came with your software distribution. Some of these steps are things you should be aware of at the time you install the Oracle software on your host machine, while others can wait until you are ready to issue the `create database` statement. In general, the things you must do to prepare the operating system include: making sure your machine has the capacity to handle Oracle, ensuring you have at least three separately controlled disk resources, ensuring asynchronous I/O is possible for your operating system, configuring certain environment settings, shutting down and backing up any other Oracle databases running on the host, and making sure any appropriate operating system patches recommended by Oracle are installed on the machine. More details about each of these items follows:

- **Make sure your machine has the capacity to handle Oracle** Almost any machine made these days has the capacity to install Oracle successfully. However, not every machine has the guts to run a full-scale Oracle enterprise database application. Before creating an Oracle environment, be sure to assess whether your host machine has the CPU power, memory, and disk space it takes to run an Oracle database in a multiuser environment.
- **Ensure you have at least three separately controlled disk resources** A running Oracle database has many moving parts. Often, these parts are also moving at the same time. Putting every Oracle resource on the same hard drive is a recipe for slow performance on all but the smallest single-user database setups. Oracle recommends three separately controlled disk resources. An enterprise production installation of Oracle can require 20 or more controlled disk resources. Again, think before you create.
- **Configure certain environment settings** You may need to configure a few environment variables before creating your database, such as ORACLE_BASE, ORACLE_HOME, ORACLE_SID, ORACLE_LD_LIBRARY_PATH, and others. These are items that you will set up in your machine configuration files or user configuration files. Where possible, you should try to follow the optimal flexible architecture (OFA). This is Oracle's recommended guideline for file-system directory paths, and following it will help Oracle Support find files for you when you call in the inevitable emergency production-support issue.
- **Shut down and back up other Oracle databases running on the host** Unless you like long hours spent in a computer room handling

recovery, don't care about your data, or both, you should never install an Oracle database on a machine already hosting Oracle without shutting down and backing up that other database first. The `reuse` keyword in the `create database` command, as well as the `CONTROL_FILES` parameter in your `init`*`sid`*`.ora` file, make it possible for one Oracle database to overwrite the files of another database on the same machine. Avoid problems by taking the extra time to back up your data, and put different Oracle database files in different directories.

- **Install Oracle-recommended operating system patches on the machine** This final point is as much an Oracle software installation issue as it is a database creation issue. Since the exact OS version and required patches vary from operating system to operating system, you should consult the Oracle installation guide that came with your software for specifics, while being mindful for OCP that OS patches may need to be applied for Oracle to work properly.

Exercise

What are some items you may need to tend to at the OS level before creating your database?

Preparing the Parameter File

You've already learned about the parameter file, so now focus on the values that must be set in order to create a new Oracle database. As mentioned, Oracle provides a generic copy of the parameter file, `init`*`sid`*`.ora`, in the software distribution used to install Oracle server on the machine hosting Oracle. Generally, the DBA will take this generic parameter file and alter certain parameters according to his or her needs. Several parameters *must* be changed as part of setting up a new database. The following subtopics identify and describe the parameters you'll need to change.

DB_NAME The local name of the database on the machine hosting Oracle, and one component of a database's unique name within the network. If the value for this parameter is the same as another Oracle database running on the host, permanent damage may result in the event that a database is created. Try to limit this name to approximately eight characters. Do not leave the name as DEFAULT. There is a name for the database and a name for the instance, and they should be the same. `DB_NAME` is required for the creation of the database, and it should be unique among all Oracle databases running in your organization.

DB_DOMAIN Identifies the domain location of the database name within a network. It is the second component of a database's unique name within the network. This is usually set either to WORLD or to the domain name appearing in your e-mail address at your organization, such as EXAMPILOT.COM.

DB_BLOCK_SIZE The size in bytes of data blocks within the system. Data blocks are unit components of datafiles into which Oracle places the row data from indexes and tables. This parameter cannot be changed for the life of the database.

CONTROL_FILES A name or list of names for the control files of the database. The control files document the location of all disk files used by Oracle. If the name(s) specified for this parameter do not match filenames that exist currently, then Oracle will create a new control file for the database at startup only when you create a new database. Otherwise, Oracle simply tells you it won't start because it can't find the control files it needs to open your existing database. Only during creation of a new database will Oracle overwrite the contents of a file of the same name as the control file you specified in `init`*`sid`*`.ora` with the physical layout of the database being created. Beware of this feature, as it can cause a control file on an existing database to be overwritten if you are creating a second database to run on the same machine.

DB_BLOCK_BUFFERS The maximum number of data blocks that will be stored in the database buffer cache of the Oracle SGA. The size of the buffer cache in bytes is a derived value of `DB_BLOCK_SIZE` multiplied by `DB_BLOCK_BUFFERS`.

LOG_BUFFER The size of the redo log buffer in bytes. As stated earlier, the redo log buffer stores redo log entries in memory until LGWR can write the entries to online redo logs on disk. There will be more about this in Chapter 7.

ROLLBACK_SEGMENTS A list of named rollback segments that the Oracle instance will have to acquire at database startup. If there are particular segments the DBA wants Oracle to acquire, these can be named here.

PROCESSES The number of processes that can connect to Oracle at any given time. This value includes background processes (of which there are at least five) and server processes. This value should be set high in order to avoid errors that prevent users from connecting.

LICENSE_MAX_SESSIONS Used for license management. This number determines the number of sessions that users can establish with the Oracle database at any given time.

LICENSE_MAX_WARNING Used for license management. If set to less than LICENSE_MAX_SESSIONS, Oracle will issue warnings to users as they connect if the number of users connecting has exceeded LICENCE_MAX_WARNING.

LICENSE_MAX_USERS Used for license management. As an alternative to licensing by concurrent sessions, the DBA can limit the number of usernames created on the database by setting a numeric value for this parameter.

Exercises

1. Identify some parameters that should be unique in the init*sid*.ora file for your new database.
2. What happens if you have two databases on one machine, you borrow the parameter file from one database to create the other, and then forget to change the value set for CONTROL_FILES?

Creating a Database in Oracle

Creation of the Oracle database is accomplished with the create database statement. Oracle recommends a series of steps for creating new databases. They are as follows:

1. Back up the existing databases on the machine hosting the new database you want to create.
2. Create or edit the init*sid*.ora parameter file for your new instance.
3. Verify the instance name in any database creation script you have, as well as in the init*sid*.ora file.
4. Start Server Manager.
5. Start the instance, but do not mount any database.
6. Issue the create database statement manually, or run a script containing the create database statement.

7. Shut down your instance.
8. Back up your new database.
9. Open your new database again to make the database available to the users.

Following the creation of the appropriate initialization parameter file, the DBA will need to start the instance from Server Manager connected as `sysdba` or `internal`. The task of connecting to the database as `sysdba` has already been discussed. To start the instance, use the `startup nomount` command in order to run the instance without mounting a previously existing database. After starting the instance without mounting a database, the DBA can create the database with the `create database` command. In order to create a database, the user must have the `sysdba` privilege granted to them and enabled. The following code block contains a sample script for creating a new database in UNIX:

```
CONNECT INTERNAL;

CREATE DATABASE orgdb01
CONTROLFILE REUSE
LOGFILE
  GROUP 1 ('/oracle/disk_01/redo1a.log',
           '/oracle/disk_02/redo1b.log') SIZE 5M,
  GROUP 2 ('/oracle/disk_03/redo2a.log',
           '/oracle/disk_04/redo2b.log') SIZE 5M
MAXLOGFILES 40
DATAFILE '/oracle/disk_05/sys01.dbf' SIZE 30M,
         '/oracle/disk_05/sys02.dbf' SIZE 50M
         AUTOEXTEND ON NEXT 30M MAXSIZE 150M
MAXDATAFILES 240
CHARACTERSET US7ASCII;

EXIT;
```

The Datafiles of the SYSTEM Tablespace

The files created as part of the `datafile` clause of the `create database` command are SYSTEM tablespace datafiles. A *tablespace* is a logical collection of disk files collectively used to store data. The SYSTEM tablespace can be compared to the root directory of a machine's file system. The SYSTEM tablespace houses the tables comprising the basis for the Oracle data dictionary, as well as the system rollback segments. The tables of the data dictionary and system rollback segment will all be owned by user SYS. Oracle creates one system rollback segment in the SYSTEM tablespace at database creation for Oracle to acquire at database startup.

Without this system rollback segment, the database won't start. In the interests of preserving the integrity of the Oracle database, the DBA should ensure that only the data dictionary and system rollback segments are placed in the SYSTEM tablespace. No data objects owned by any user other than SYS should be placed in the SYSTEM tablespace. Instead, you will create other tablespaces to store the database objects. You will learn more about tablespaces and datafiles in Chapter 7.

Minimum Two Online Redo Log Groups

Redo logs are created with the `logfile` clause. Redo logs are entries for data changes made to the database. You must create at least two redo log groups for your new database, each with at least one member. In the database created with the preceding code block, redo log group 1 consists of two members, called `log1a.dbf` and `log1b.dbf`, respectively. If any file specified in the `create database` statement currently exists on the system, and the `reuse` keyword is used, Oracle will overwrite the file. Be careful when reusing files to prevent accidentally overwriting the files in your existing database on the host machine. You will learn more about redo logs in Chapter 7.

Other Items in create database Statements

Other options set when the database is created include `maxdatafiles` and `maxlogfiles`. The `maxdatafiles` option specifies the initial sizing of the data files section of the control file at `create database` or `create controlfile` time. An attempt to add a file whose number is greater than `maxdatafiles`, but less than or equal to `DB_FILES`, causes control file to expand automatically so that the data files section can accommodate more files. This clause can limit database size later, when new datafiles are added, if the `maxdatafiles` value would be exceeded. To work around this problem, use the `autoextend` option when defining datafiles. When `autoextend` is used, the datafiles will automatically allocate more space when the datafile fills, up to a total size specified by the `maxsize` keyword. However, you'll want to take care to ensure that Oracle does not try to extend the datafile to more space than the file system has available.

The final item in the `create database` statement, `characterset`, is used to identify the character set used in the Oracle database for information storage. More information about character sets appears in Chapter 10.

Another option you can use in `create database` commands is `archivelog`. When `archivelog` is used, Oracle archives the redo logs generated. More about archiving redo information will be presented in Unit III. Finally, the `create database` command uses several initialization parameters set in the `init`*`sid`*`.ora` file in database creation. These include `DB_BLOCK_SIZE`, and certain NLS environment settings.

Exercises

1. Name some of the steps in creating a new Oracle database. What resources are created as part of the creation of a database?
2. What is the SYSTEM tablespace? What is its significance?
3. What is a parameter file? What are some of the parameters a DBA must set uniquely for any database via the parameter file?

Chapter Summary

This chapter introduced you to Oracle database administration. It covered several topics, including an overview of the Oracle architecture, using administrative tools such as Server Manager and OEM, managing the Oracle instance, starting and stopping the instance, and creating an Oracle database. The material in this chapter comprises about 16 percent of the questions asked on OCP Exam 2.

The first area of discussion in this chapter was an overview of the various components of the Oracle database. Figure 6-1 gave an idea of the background processes, memory structures, and disk resources that comprise the Oracle instance, and how they act together to allow users to access information. Several memory structures exist on the Oracle database to improve performance on various areas of the database. They include the System Global Area (SGA) and the Program Global Area (PGA). The SGA, in turn, consists of several components: the buffer cache, the shared pool, and the redo log buffer. Behind the scenes, there are several memory processes that move data between disk and memory or handle activities on Oracle's behalf. The core background processes covered in this chapter were the database writer (DBWR or DBW0) for writing blocks to disk, the log writer (LGWR) for writing redo entries to disk, and the server for reading data from disk into the buffer cache for users.

You were introduced to the Oracle Relational Database Management System (RDBMS), and learned how `select` and DML statements are processed. The RDBMS translates SQL code, which defines results, into a step-by-step procedure for Oracle to use in obtaining that data. You also learned about how users are connected to server processes, the differences and tradeoffs involved in the dedicated server and the MTS architecture, and how listener processes and dispatchers are used to route user processes to servers. Finally, you learned how `commit` statements are processed and that a `commit` being issued does not automatically make Oracle run right out and copy changed data back to disk.

The next section covered using administrative tools. The Server Manager application was demonstrated in its line mode operation for various environments. You also learned about the administrative tools that are part of Oracle Enterprise

Manager, or OEM for short. The tools described were the Instance Manager, Data Manager, Schema Manager, Backup Manager, Software Manager, Storage Manager, as well as many others. A demonstration of using some of these tools was presented, as well, so that you could better grasp how Oracle allows you to perform the same functions in a graphical user interface that it allows you to execute using line mode commands in Server Manager.

The next area covered was managing the Oracle instance. Setting up operating system authentication for management of Oracle from the command line of the machine that hosts the database was demonstrated. The use of password file administrative authentication and the value of setting this up was also demonstrated. If you want to use OEM for things like starting up and shutting down your database from the client desktop, you must set up a password file. This is handled with the ORAPWD utility. An explanation of the various ways to connect to Oracle administratively, such as `connect internal`, `connect as sysdba`, and the differences between `sysdba` and `osdba`, and `sysoper` and `osoper` were covered, as well.

Creating a parameter file, also known as the `init`*`sid`*`.ora` file, was also covered. Oracle provides a generic parameter file with every software release, so it is easiest to reuse an initialization parameter file rather than creating one from scratch yourself. The various parameters that can be set were explained in some detail, along with how to find out what the current parameter values are using the V$PARAMETER dynamic performance view, the show parameter command in Server Manager, and from within the OEM Instance Manager. The requirement for changing parameter values by modifying the `init`*`sid`*`.ora` file and stopping and restarting the instance in most cases, as well as the special cases for changing parameter values with the `alter system` command, were shown in this discussion, too.

Starting up the instance and opening the database is described in this chapter. The use of Server Manager and the need for connecting as `internal` or `sysdba` was explained. The use of the startup command and its several different options for opening the database, such as `nomount`, `mount`, `open`, `restrict`, `recover`, and `force`, were all explained, along with their appropriate usage. Situations in which you shouldn't use each option for opening the database were also covered in some detail.

The shutdown of an instance and closing of the database was explained, as well. The DBA must again connect to the database as `internal` or `sysdba` using the Server Manager tool. The three options for closing the `Oracle` database are `normal`, `immediate`, `transactional`, and `abort`. When the DBA shuts down the database with the `normal` option, the database refuses new connections to the database by users and waits for existing connections to terminate. Once the last user has logged off the system, then the `shutdown normal` will complete. The DBA issuing a `shutdown immediate` causes Oracle to prevent new connections while also terminating current ones, rolling back whatever transactions were taking place in the sessions just terminated. The third option for shutting down a database is `shutdown abort`, which disconnects current sessions without rolling back their transactions and prevents new connections to the database as well. The last option is `shutdown transactional`, which disconnects current sessions after they complete their current transaction, but otherwise acts like shutdown immediate.

You learned about the management of sessions with the `alter session` command, and the create session privilege required for connecting to Oracle was also presented. Oracle's maintenance of special trace files for logging each background process's execution was also described. The location of these files is identified in the `init`*`sid`*`.ora` file by the `BACKGROUND_DUMP_DEST` parameter. The special trace file for the instance called the ALERT log was described in some detail, along with the events that cause the ALERT log to be written and the need for regular monitoring and cleanup of this file.

The final area covered in this chapter was creating a database. The steps required for preparing the OS were described, such as making sure the hardware capacity, such as CPU, memory, and disk space, were up to the task of managing the Oracle database you want to run. The required changes to be made to the parameter file were also described. The importance of changing `DB_NAME`, `DB_DOMAIN`, `DB_BLOCK_SIZE`, `DB_BLOCK_BUFFERS`, `PROCESSES`, `ROLLBACK_SEGMENTS`, `LICENSE_MAX_SESSIONS`, `LICENSE_MAX_WARNING`, and the `LICENSE_MAX_USERS` parameters to reflect the uniqueness of this database from others on the host machine or on the network in your organization was addressed.

Finally, the steps of database creation were discussed. First, the DBA should back up existing databases associated with the instance, if any, in order to prevent data loss or accidental deletion of a disk file resource. The next thing that should happen is that the DBA should create a parameter file that is unique to the database being created. Several initialization parameters were identified as needing to be set to create a database. After the parameter file is created, the DBA can execute the `create database` command, which creates disk files for a special resource called the SYSTEM tablespace, and other disk files for online redo logs. Oracle also uses the settings in the `init`*`sid`*`.ora` file to make appropriate changes to control files, database block size, and other things. The SYSTEM tablespace will contain at least one system rollback segment, which must be allocated in order for Oracle to start, and all the tables and views that comprise the Oracle data dictionary. After creating the database, the DBA should back up the new database to avoid needing to create it from scratch in the event of a problem later.

Two-Minute Drill

- Several structures are used to connect users to an Oracle server. They include memory structures like the System Global Area (SGA) and Program Global Area (PGA), network processes like listeners and dispatchers, shared or dedicated server processes, and background processes like DBW0 and LGWR.
- The SGA consists of the buffer cache for storing recently accessed data blocks, the redo log buffer for storing redo entries until they can be written to disk, and the shared pool for storing parsed information about recently executed SQL for code sharing.
- The fundamental unit of storage in Oracle is the data block.
- SQL `select` statements are processed in the following way: a cursor or address in memory is opened, the statement is parsed, bind variables are created, the statement is executed, and values are fetched.
- SQL DML statements such as `update`, `delete`, and `insert` are processed in the following way: a cursor or address in memory is opened, the statement is parsed, and the statement is executed.
- Several background processes manage Oracle's ability to write data from the buffer cache and redo log buffer to appropriate areas on disk. They are DBW0 for writing data between disk and buffer cache, and LGWR for writing redo log entries between the redo log buffer and the online redo log on disk.
- DBW0 writes data to disk in three cases. They are every 3 seconds (when a timeout occurs), when LGWR tells it to (during a checkpoint), and when the buffer cache is full and a server process needs to make room for buffers required by user processes.
- Server processes are like genies from the story of Aladdin because they retrieve data from disk into the buffer cache according to the user's command.
- There are two configurations for server processes: shared servers and dedicated servers. In dedicated servers, a listener process listens for users connecting to Oracle. When a listener hears a user, the listener tells Oracle to spawn a dedicated server. Each user process has its own server process available for retrieving data from disk.

- In shared server configurations (also called multithreaded server or MTS), a user process attempts to connect to Oracle. The listener hears the connection and passes the user process to a dispatcher process. A limited number of server processes, each handling multiple user requests, are monitored by a dispatcher, which assigns user processes to a shared server based on which has the lightest load at the time of user connection.
- The `commit` statement may trigger Oracle to write changed data in the buffer cache to disk, but not necessarily. It only makes a redo log buffer entry that says all data changes associated with a particular transaction are now committed.
- Two user authentication methods exist in Oracle: operating system authentication and Oracle authentication.
- There are two privileges DBAs require to perform their function on the database. In Oracle authentication environments, they are called `sysdba` and `sysoper`.
- To use Oracle authentication, the DBA must create a password file using the ORAPWD utility.
- To start and stop a database, the DBA must connect as `internal` or `sysdba`.
- The tool used to start and stop the database is called Server Manager. This tool is usually run in line mode.
- Another tool for managing database administration activity is Oracle Enterprise Manager (OEM). OEM has many administrative tools available, including Backup Manager, Data Manager, Daemon Manager, Instance Manager, Replication Manager, Schema Manager, Security Manager, SQL Worksheet, Storage Manager, Net8 Assistant, Software Manager.
- There are several options for starting a database:
    - **`startup nomount`** Starts the instance and does not mount a database.
    - **`startup mount`** Starts the instance and mounts but does not open the database.
    - **`startup open`** Starts the instance and mounts and opens the database.
    - **`startup restrict`** Starts the instance, mounts and opens the database, but restricts access to those users with `restricted session` privilege granted to them.

- **`startup recover`** Starts the instance, leaves the database closed, and begins recovery for disk failure scenario.
- **`startup force open`** Makes an instance start that is having problems either starting or stopping.

- When a database is open, any user with a username and password and the `create session` privilege can log into the Oracle database.
- Closing or shutting down a database must be done by the DBA while running Server Manager and while the DBA is connected to the database as `internal` or `sysdba`.
- There are three options for closing a database:
  - **`shutdown normal`** No new existing connections are allowed, but existing sessions may take as long as they want to wrap up.
  - **`shutdown immediate`** No new connections are allowed, existing sessions are terminated, and their transactions are rolled back.
  - **`shutdown abort`** No new connections are allowed, existing sessions are terminated, and transactions are not rolled back.
- Instance recovery is required after `shutdown abort` is used.
- You can obtain values for initialization parameters from several sources:
  - V$PARAMETER dynamic performance view
  - `show parameter` command in Server Manager
  - OEM Instance Manager administrative tool
- Several important runtime logging files exist on the machine hosting Oracle. Each background process, such as LGWR and DBWR, will have a trace file if some error occurs in their execution, and the instance has a special trace file called the ALERT log. Trace files are written whenever the background process has a problem executing. The ALERT log is written whenever the instance is started or stopped, whenever the database structure is altered, or whenever an error occurs in database.
- Trace files and ALERT logs are found in the directory identified by the `BACKGROUND_DUMP_DEST` parameter in the `init`*`sid`*`.ora` file.

- Before creating the database, assess whether several things exist on the OS level:
  - Are there enough individual disk resources to run Oracle without I/O bottlenecks?
  - Is there enough CPU, memory, and disk space for Oracle processing?
  - Are disk resources for different Oracle databases on the same host in separate directories?
  - Are environment settings correct for the database creation?
- The first step in creating a database is back up any existing databases already on the host machine.
- The second step in creating a database is for the DBA to create a parameter file with unique values for several parameters, including the following:
  - **DB_NAME** The local name for the database
  - **DB_DOMAIN** The network-wide location for the database
  - **DB_BLOCK_SIZE** The size of each block in the database
  - **DB_BLOCK_BUFFERS** The number of blocks stored in the buffer cache
  - **PROCESSES** The maximum number of processes available on the database
  - **ROLLBACK_SEGMENTS** Named rollback segments the database acquires at startup
  - **LICENSE_MAX_SESSIONS** The maximum number of sessions that can connect to the database
  - **LICENSE_MAX_WARNING** The sessions trying to connect above the number specified by this parameter will receive a warning message
  - **LICENSE_MAX_USERS** The maximum number of users that can be created in the Oracle instance
- LICENSE_MAX_SESSIONS and LICENSE_MAX_WARNING are used for license tracking or LICENSE_MAX_USERS is used, but usually not both.

- After creating the parameter file, the DBA executes the `create database` command, which creates the datafiles for the SYSTEM tablespace, an initial rollback segment, SYS and SYSTEM users, and redo log files. On conclusion of the `create database` statement, the database is created and open.
- The default password for SYS is CHANGE_ON_INSTALL.
- The default password for SYSTEM is MANAGER.
- The number of datafiles and redo log files created for the life of the database can be limited with the `maxdatafiles` and `maxlogfiles` options of the `create database` statement.
- The size of a datafile is fixed at its creation, unless the `autoextend` option is used.
- The size of a control file is directly related to the number of datafiles and redo logs for the database.

Chapter Questions

1. The user is trying to execute a `select` statement. Which of the following background processes will obtain data from disk for the user?

A. DBW0

B. LGWR

C. SERVER

D. USER

E. DISPATCHER

2. In order to perform administrative tasks on the database using Oracle password authentication, the DBA should have the following two privileges granted to them:

A. `sysdba` or `sysoper`

B. CONNECT or RESOURCE

C. `restricted session` or `create session`

3. Which component of the SGA stores parsed SQL statements used for process sharing?

A. Buffer cache

B. Private SQL area

C. Redo log buffer

D. Library cache

E. Row cache

4. Which of the following choices does not identify an aspect of shared server processing architecture?

A. Each user gets their own server process for data retrieval

B. A dispatcher process is involved

C. A listener process is involved

D. The server process sits idle infrequently

5. The `init`*`sid`*`.ora` parameter that indicates the size of each buffer in the buffer cache is the

A. DB_BLOCK_BUFFERS

B. BUFFER_SIZE

C. DB_BLOCK_SIZE

D. ROLLBACK_SEGMENTS

6. The datafiles named in a `create database` statement are used as storage for which of the following database components?

A. SYSTEM tablespace

B. `init`*`sid`*`.ora` file

C. Redo log member

D. ALERT log

7. Changing the password used to manage the password file changes the password for which of the following?

A. SYSTEM

B. RPT_BATCH

C. CONNECT

D. `internal`

E. `audit`

8. The default password for the SYS user is

A. CHANGE_ON_INSTALL

B. NO_PASSWORD

C. MANAGER

D. ORACLE

E. NULL

9. DBAs who are planning to administer a database remotely should use all of the following choices, except:

A. ORAPWD

B. `REMOTE_LOGIN_PASSWORDFILE` set to `shared`

C. `OS_AUTHENT_PREFIX` set to OPS$

D. A password file

10. Power will disconnect on the machine running Oracle in two minutes, but user JASON has left for the day while still connected to Oracle. His workstation is locked, so he cannot be logged out from his desktop. How should the DBA shut down the instance?

A. `shutdown normal`

B. `shutdown immediate`

C. `shutdown abort`

D. `shutdown force`

E. `shutdown recover`

11. Which of the following administrative tools in OEM can be used to view the initialization parameter settings for Oracle?

A. Schema Manager

B. Instance Manager

C. Security Manager

D. Data Manager

E. Software Manager

12. Which of the following items are required for killing a user session? (Choose two)

A. Username

B. SID

C. Serial number

D. Password

Answers to Chapter Questions

1. C. SERVER

Explanation The server process handles data access and retrieval from disk for all user processes connected to Oracle. Choice A, DBW0, moves data blocks between disk and the buffer cache, and therefore is not correct. Choice B, LGWR, copies redo entries from the redo log buffer to online redo logs on disk, and therefore is not correct. Choice D, USER, is the process for which the server process acts in support of. Choice E, DISPATCHER, is used in Oracle MTS architecture and routes user processes to a server, but does not handle reading data from disk on behalf of the user process.

2. A. `sysdba` or `sysoper`

Explanation Choices B and C are incorrect. Each privilege listed has some bearing on access, but none of them give any administrative ability. Refer to the discussion of choosing an authentication method.

3. D. Library cache

Explanation Choice A is incorrect because the buffer cache is where data blocks are stored for recently executed queries. Choice B is incorrect because the private SQL area is in the PGA where the actual values returned from a query are stored, not the parse information for the query. Choice C is incorrect because the redo log buffer stores redo entries temporarily until LGWR can write them to disk. Choice E is incorrect because the row cache stores data dictionary row information for fast access by users and Oracle. Refer to the discussion of Oracle architecture.

4. A. Each user gets their own server process for data retrieval

Explanation The shared server or MTS architecture uses several elements that correspond to the choices. A dispatcher process assigns users to a shared server, while the listener process routes user processes either directly to a server in the case of dedicated server processing or to a dispatcher in MTS. The final choice, D, indicates a benefit of the MTS architecture. Since many users utilize the same server process, that server process will sit idle less frequently than in the dedicated server architecture. Choice A indicates the dedicated server architecture only, and is therefore the correct answer to the question.

5. C. `DB_BLOCK_SIZE`

Explanation Since each buffer in the buffer cache is designed to fit one data block, the size of buffers in the database block buffer cache will be the same size as the blocks they store. The size of blocks in the database is determined by `DB_BLOCK_SIZE`. Refer to the discussion of initialization parameters to be changed during database creation.

6. A. SYSTEM tablespace

Explanation Since datafiles can only be a part of tablespaces (more on this in Chapter 7), all other choices must be eliminated immediately. Another reason to eliminate at least choices B and D is that neither the `init`*`sid`*`.ora` file nor the ALERT log are created in the `create database` statement. So, as long as you know that redo logs are composed of online redo log members, and tablespaces like SYSTEM are composed of datafiles, you should have no problem getting a question like this one right.

7. D. `internal`

Explanation Choice A is incorrect because the SYSTEM password has no affiliation with the password for the password file. SYS and internal do. Choice B is incorrect because RPT_BATCH is not a password created by Oracle in a create database statement. Choice C is incorrect because CONNECT is a role, not a user. Choice E is incorrect because `audit` is a command, not a user. Refer to the discussion of creating the password file as part of choosing user authentication.

8. A. CHANGE_ON_INSTALL

Explanation This is a classic piece of Oracle trivia. Memorize it, along with the SYSTEM password, which incidentally is MANAGER. This is all fine for OCP, but beware of others who may also have memorized these facts. Don't let a hacker use this information against you. Make sure you change the default passwords for SYS and SYSTEM after creating your database.

9. C. `OS_AUTHENT_PREFIX` set to OPS$

Explanation A DBA should use password file authentication when planning to administer a database remotely. This action consists of a password file, the ORAPWD utility, and setting the `REMOTE_LOGIN_PASSWORDFILE` parameter to shared. The `OS_AUTHENT_PREFIX` parameter is used to alter the prefix Oracle requires on Oracle users when operating system authentication is being used. This one, obviously, is not required for Oracle password authentication.

10. B. `shutdown immediate`

Explanation A power outage can cause damage to an Oracle instance if it is running when the power goes out. But choice C is just too drastic, given that you are basically treating the situation as if it required media recovery. After all, you know that JASON is not executing a transaction, so no additional time to finish the rollback will be required before shutdown. Choice A will not do it either, though, because shutdown normal will wait all night for JASON to come in and log off. Choice B is the logical choice. Choices D and E are not valid options for shutting down a database instance.

11. B. Instance Manager

Explanation The Instance Manager tool handles all instance-related tasks, including display and modification of initialization parameters set in the `init`*`sid`*`.ora` file. Schema Manager handles tasks involving database object creation and modification, eliminating choice A. Security Manager handles user privilege and role management, which eliminates choice C. Data Manager handles the loading and unloading of data from EXPORT binary or flat file format, eliminating choice D. Finally, Software Manager handles enterprise deployment of Oracle software, eliminating choice E.

12. B. and C. SID *and* serial number.

Explanation To disconnect a database user with the `alter system kill session` statement, you must have the SID and serial number. Both these pieces of information for the session you want to kill can be found in the V$SESSION dictionary view. You only need username and password information to establish the connection, not eliminate it, which in turn eliminates choices A and D.

CHAPTER 7

Managing the Physical Database Structure

n this chapter, you will understand and demonstrate knowledge in the following areas:

- Data dictionary views and standard packages
- Managing the control file
- Maintaining redo log files
- Managing tablespaces and datafiles
- Storage structures and relationships

In this chapter, you will examine Oracle's disk resources in detail. Oracle disk resources are broken into two categories: physical and logical. Oracle physical disk resources include *control files*, *datafiles*, and *redo log files*. Logical disk resources include *tablespaces*, *segments*, and *extents*. After reading this chapter, you will understand the differences between physical disk resources and logical disk resources, and how the two map into one another. In addition, you will wrap up your examination of the objects stored in the most important disk resource in an Oracle database—the SYSTEM tablespace. Those objects include the data dictionary and standard packages for PL/SQL programming. This chapter covers 16 percent of the OCP Exam 2 test content.

Data Dictionary Views and Standard Packages

In this section, you will cover the following points about dictionary views and standard packages:

- Constructing the data dictionary views
- Using the data dictionary
- Preparing the PL/SQL environment with admin scripts
- Administering stored procedures and packages

The data dictionary is the first set of database objects the DBA should create after issuing the `create database` command. Every object in the database is tracked in some fashion by the Oracle data dictionary. Oracle generally creates the data dictionary without any intervention from the DBA at database creation time with the use of the `catalog.sql` and `catproc.sql` scripts. This section will explain how Oracle creates the data dictionary using these different scripts, and exactly which components of database creation is handled by each of the scripts.

Constructing the Data Dictionary Views

The first script, `catalog.sql`, is used to create the objects that comprise the data dictionary. From Unit I and the discussion in Chapter 6, you should already understand that the data dictionary supports virtually every aspect of Oracle database operation, from finding information about objects to performance tuning, and everything in between. A related script, `cat8000.sql`, is used as part of migrating your Oracle database between versions, and will be discussed more in Unit VI.

To create a data dictionary, the DBA runs the `catalog.sql` script from within Server Manager, while connected as the administrative privilege `sysdba` or as the `internal` user. This script performs a laundry list of `create view` statements, as well as executing a series of other scripts in order to create other data dictionary views in special areas and special public synonyms for those views. Within the `catalog.sql` script, there are calls to several other scripts, which are listed here:

- **`cataudit.sql`** Creates the `SYS.AUD$` dictionary table, which tracks all audit trail information generated by Oracle when the auditing feature of the database is used
- **`catldr.sql`** Creates views that are used for the SQL*Loader tool, discussed later in this unit, which is used to process large-volume data loads from one system to another
- **`catexp.sql`** Creates views that are used by the IMPORT/EXPORT utilities, discussed in the unit covering OCP Exam 3, "Database Backup and Recovery"
- **`catsvrmg.sql`** Creates views used by the Server Manager utility, used in database administration. For more information on Server Manager, review Chapter 6
- **`catpart.sql`** Creates views that support Oracle8's partitioning option
- **`catadt.sql`** Creates views that support user-defined types and object components of Oracle8's new object features
- **`standard.sql`** Creates the STANDARD package, which stores all Oracle "scalar" or simple datatypes like VARCHAR2 and BLOB; STANDARD also contains built-in SQL functions like `decode( )` and others

It is important to remember that `catalog.sql` calls these other scripts automatically. All the scripts can be found in the `rdbms/admin` directory under the

Oracle software home directory. The following code block demonstrates the commands necessary to run the catalog.sql file on UNIX:

```
/home/oracle/app/oracle/product/8.0.5> cd rdbms/admin
/home/oracle/app/oracle/product/8.0.5/rdbms/admin> svrmgrl
Oracle Server Manager Release 3.0.5.0.0 - Production
(c)Copyright 1998, Oracle Corporation. All Rights Reserved.
Oracle8 Enterprise Edition Release 8.0.5 - Production
With the Partitioning and Objects options
PL/SQL Release 8.0.5 - Production
SVRMGR> connect internal
Connected.
SVRMGR> @catalog
```

Do not create the dictionary views unless you have created the database. Since you run the scripts while connected as internal or another user with sysdba privileges, the SYS user winds up owning the database objects that comprise the data dictionary, and these objects are stored in the SYSTEM tablespace, neither of which will exist until you issue the create database statement.

Exercises

1. How is the data dictionary created?
2. What two scripts are used as part of database creation?

Using the Data Dictionary

Since the catalog.sql script generates public synonyms for many of the data dictionary views, there is no need to log into Oracle as a special user to see dictionary data. Any user will be able to see the dictionary to the extent that they need it. Recall from Unit I that several categories of dictionary views exist for finding information about the various objects available to the user in Oracle. For example, if you wanted to see the tables owned by the user you logged into Oracle as, you would use USER_TABLES. If you wanted to see all the tables the user can see, use the ALL_TABLES view. If you are the DBA, and you want to see all the tables in the database, use DBA_TABLES.

Other views abound in Oracle, many of which are used mainly by DBAs. There are several views that start with the prefix V$ that offer performance information for the current run of the Oracle instance. You will work more directly with those views in Unit IV. Several other views exist, such as ROLE_TAB_PRIVS, which do not follow the naming convention of including scope (USER_, ALL_, or DBA_). These views are designed for DBA usage.

TIP
In a pinch, you can find out information about the views in the data dictionary by issuing `select` statements against the DICT dictionary view. It contains two columns: TABLE_NAME, the name of the dictionary view; and COMMENTS, which contains a short description of the view's contents.

Always `select` dictionary information from the dictionary views and not from the base tables. The base tables owned by SYS must be managed only by Oracle. If a change is made to the data in those base tables, or if a dictionary view is recompiled incorrectly, it can adversely affect the performance of your machine. Finally, Oracle recommends that you log into the Oracle database as the SYS user as infrequently as possible, in order to avoid potentially damaging the dictionary base tables.

Exercises

1. What is the scope of dictionary views like ROLE_SYS_PRIVS that do not have ALL_, USER_, or DBA_ prefixed to them? What dictionary view contains a listing of the other dictionary views?
2. What use do the V$ dictionary views have in Oracle? What user owns the dictionary objects?

Preparing the PL/SQL Environment with Admin Scripts

The second script generally run in the Oracle database when the data dictionary is created is the `catproc.sql` script. This script creates several different data dictionary components used in everything related to PL/SQL in the Oracle database. The code for creating these dictionary views is not contained in `catproc.sql`; the code is in several scripts called by this master script. Some of the objects created by these scripts are stored procedures, packages, triggers, snapshots, and certain utilities for PL/SQL constructs, such as alerts, locks, mail, and pipes.

There are two different types of scripts that are run by `catproc.sql`. If you look in the script, you will see references to other scripts in the `rdbms/admin` directory, such as `dbmsutil.sql` and `dbmssql.sql`. These scripts ending in `.sql` are package specifications for the various Oracle server packages. Recall from Unit I that the package specification contains the procedure, function, type, and constant definitions that are available in the package, but which are not in actual code. The other type of script is a `.plb` script, such as `prvtutil.plb` and `prvtpipe.plb`. This extension denotes PL/SQL code that has been encrypted using a wrapper program to prevent you from seeing the application code logic.

It is important to remember that `catproc.sql` calls these other scripts automatically. All the scripts can be found in the `rdbms/admin` directory under the Oracle software home directory. The following code block demonstrates the commands necessary to run the `catproc.sql` file on UNIX:

```
/home/oracle/app/oracle/product/8.0.5> cd rdbms/admin
/home/oracle/app/oracle/product/8.0.5/rdbms/admin> svrmgrl
Oracle Server Manager Release 3.0.5.0.0 - Production
(c)Copyright 1998, Oracle Corporation. All Rights Reserved.
Oracle8 Enterprise Edition Release 8.0.5 - Production
With the Partitioning and Objects options
PL/SQL Release 8.0.5 - Production
SVRMGR> connect internal
Connected.
SVRMGR> @catproc
```

Do not run this script unless you have created the database. Since you run the scripts while connected as `internal` or another user with `sysdba` privileges, the SYS user winds up owning the database objects that comprise the data dictionary, and these objects are stored in the SYSTEM tablespace, neither of which will exist until you issue `create database`.

TIP

If users complain that certain Oracle-supplied packages are not available on the server, such as DBMS_PIPE, DBMS_ALERT, or DBMS_SQL, the problem most likely is that the `catproc.sql` script has not been run.

Exercises

1. What Oracle database components are created by running the `catproc.sql` script? As what user (or connected with what privileges) should you run the `catproc.sql` script?
2. What filename extension is used to denote files containing package specifications? What filename extension denotes package bodies? Can you see the actual application code in the package bodies of Oracle-supplied packages? Explain.

3. BONUS: Try to figure out which Oracle-supplied packages are created by the `dbmsutil.sql`, `dbmsotpt.sql`, and `dbmsjob.sql` scripts. If necessary, look at their source code in your Oracle software release.

Administering Stored Procedures and Packages

After creating your Oracle-supplied stored procedures and packages, the door is wide open in terms of administering access to the packages. In order for a user to run a stored procedure or package, the user must be granted execute privileges for that procedure or package. You can do this either by logging in as SYS and issuing a grant statement, or by creating a role, granting the privilege to the role, and then granting the role to the user. Oracle creates a role called EXECUTE_CATALOG_ROLE, and this role has certain privileges to execute Oracle-supplied packages. To grant this role to user SPANKY, run the following statement from SQL*Plus while logged into Oracle as user SYS :

```
SQL> grant execute_catalog_role to spanky;
```

Roles will be covered extensively in Chapter 10, so for now we'll talk about granting appropriate privileges directly to users. The appropriate privilege used for running Oracle-supplied procedures and packages is the `execute` privilege. As shown in the prior block, the appropriate statement for giving a privilege or role to a user is `grant` *`priv_or_role`* `to` *`user`*. In the following block, user SYS grants `execute` privileges to SPANKY on DBMS_SQL:

```
SQL> grant execute on DBMS_SQL to SPANKY;
```

When you are executing a procedure, you do so with the privileges granted to the owner of that procedure, not with your own. For example, user SPANKY may not have been given access to perform `select` statements on the CAT_FOOD table, but may have `execute` privileges on the `eat_cat_food( )` procedure, owned by ATHENA, who has been given `select` access to CAT_FOOD. Thus, user SPANKY can see the CAT_FOOD table to the extent that the `eat_cat_food( )` procedure permits, but only by running the `eat_cat_food( )` procedure.

An important point must be made here—since Oracle-supplied packages are usually owned by SYS, you will execute these procedures and packages as if you had the privileges of SYS granted to you. There is one exception to this rule, related to the DBMS_SQL package. Since this package allows the user to dynamically generate and execute SQL statements, Oracle will execute the SQL statement the user generates only if that user has permission to run the generated statement. Thus, if user SPANKY had `execute` privileges on DBMS_SQL, and tried to generate a `select` statement on the CAT_FOOD table, Oracle would still return the "insufficient privileges" error, even if SYS can `select` from that table.

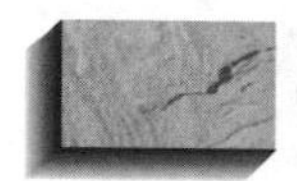

TIP
Most Oracle-supplied packages are automatically installed when the database is created and the `catproc.sql` *script is run. For example, to create the DBMS_ALERT package, the* `dbmsalrt.sql` *and* `prvtalrt.plb` *scripts must be run when you are connected as the user SYS. These scripts, however, are run automatically by the* `catproc.sql` *script. Certain packages are not installed automatically. Special installation instructions for these packages are documented in the individual scripts.*

Exercises

1. What role in the database has the ability to run certain Oracle-supplied packages? BONUS: which packages can that role run (hint: look in OEM Security Manager)?
2. What is the name of the privilege that allows a user to run a stored procedure? Which user must be granted privileges for operations specified in the procedure, the procedure owner or user? Which Oracle-supplied package is the exception to this rule?

Managing Control Files

In this section, you will cover the following points about managing control files:

- How control files are used
- Examining control file contents
- Obtaining information about control files
- Multiplexing control files

Control files are to the physical structure of the Oracle database what the data dictionary is to the logical structure. The control files keep track of all the files Oracle needs and where they are on the host machine. The control files also contain information about the redo log member filenames and where they are located in the file system. Without control files, the Oracle database server would be unable to find its physical components. The names of the control files are specified in the `init`*`sid`*`.ora` file for each Oracle instance.

In this section, we will talk about how Oracle uses control files, what is stored in the control files, where to obtain information about your control files, and the importance of storing multiple copies of control files on separate disks.

How Control Files Are Used

When you enter Server Manager to bring the database online, Oracle looks in the control file to find all the components it needs in order to bring that database online. For example, if the control file on your database has three files associated with it, and only two are available, Oracle will complain that the third file was missing, and it won't start your database. After database startup, control files will be modified or used by Oracle when a new physical disk resource (such as a tablespace) is created, when an existing disk resource is modified in some way (for example, when a datafile is added to a tablespace), and when LGWR stops writing to one online redo log and starts writing to another.

Control files in Oracle8 are considerably larger than their Oracle7 counterparts because they store many additional components of information. However, the purpose of control files in Oracle8 is largely unchanged—they document the overall layout of the Oracle database.

Recall from Chapter 6 the presence of the `CONTROL_FILES` parameter in the `init`*`sid`*`.ora` file. This parameter defines the location of your control files on the machine hosting Oracle, and indicates where Oracle will look on instance startup to find its control files. When you start the instance before creating the database, when you are migrating from one version of Oracle to another, Oracle will create control files based on the filenames and locations you provide in the `CONTROL_FILES` `init`*`sid`*`.ora` parameter. In subsequent instance startups, if Oracle does not find the control files it expects to find based on the content of the `CONTROL_FILES` parameter, Oracle won't start.

By default, Oracle will create three control files and put them in the `dbs` directory under the Oracle software home directory, giving them the name `cntrl`*`ndbname`*`.dbf`, where *`n`* is a number between 1 and 3 (the number could be operating-system specific) and *`dbname`* is the name of your database as indicated by the DB_NAME parameter. You can follow whatever naming convention you like when you define your own control files; you're not restricted to placing the control files in `$ORACLE_HOME/dbs`, either.

For reasons we will explore shortly, Oracle recommends using multiple control files placed on separate disks. Be sure to include the absolute pathname for the location of your control file when defining values for the `CONTROL_FILES` parameter.

Exercises

1. What is a control file, and what purpose does it serve in Oracle?
2. How does Oracle know where to find its control file? If the database has not been created yet, or if you are migrating from one database version to another, what does Oracle do if the control files it expects to find are not present?

Examining Control File Contents

Control files have several items contained in them. But, you can't just open a control file in your favorite text editor and see what it holds. If you want to see the contents of a control file, you must generate a control-file creation script. This is done by issuing the `alter database backup controlfile to trace` statement. The `trace` keyword in this statement indicates that Oracle will generate a script containing a `create controlfile` command and store it in the trace directory identified in the `init`*`sid`*`.ora file` by the USER_DUMP_DEST parameter. A sample control file creation script generated by this command is displayed in the following code block:

```
# The following commands will create a new control file and use it
# to open the database.
# Data used by the recovery manager will be lost. Additional
# logs may be required for media recovery of offline data
# files. Use this only if the current version of all online
# logs are available.
STARTUP NOMOUNT
CREATE CONTROLFILE REUSE DATABASE "ORGDB01" NORESETLOGS
NOARCHIVELOG
    MAXLOGFILES 16
    MAXLOGMEMBERS 2
    MAXDATAFILES 240
    MAXINSTANCES 1
    MAXLOGHISTORY 113
LOGFILE
  GROUP 1 ('/oracle/disk_01/log1a.dbf',
'/oracle/disk_02/log1b.dbf') SIZE 30M,
  GROUP 2 ('/oracle/disk_03/log2a.dbf','/oracle/disk_04/log2b.dbf')
  SIZE 30M
DATAFILE
  '/oracle/disk_05/system01.dbf',
  '/oracle/disk_05/system02.dbf'
;
```

```
# Recovery is required if any of the datafiles are restored
# backups, or if the last shutdown was not normal or immediate.
RECOVER DATABASE
# Database can now be opened normally.
ALTER DATABASE OPEN;
```

From this script, you can guess what the correct syntax for a `create controlfile` statement would be. In general, you won't need to create many new control files this way, but in case you do, you'll know how to do it. Plus, you should understand how to do this for the OCP exam.

Exercises

1. What are the contents of a control file? How can you view the contents of your control file?
2. How does the size of Oracle8 control files compare to the size of Oracle7 control files? What is the reason for this difference?

Obtaining Information About Control Files

The main view available in the Oracle data dictionary for control file use and management is the V$CONTROLFILE view. This view has only two columns, STATUS and NAME.

- **STATUS** Displays INVALID if the control filename cannot be determined; otherwise, it will be NULL
- **NAME** Gives the absolute path location of the file on your host machine as well as the control filename

The information in the V$CONTROLFILE view corresponds to the values set for the initialization parameter `CONTROL_FILES`. The following code block shows the SQL statement used to obtain information from the V$CONTROLFILE view about the control files for Oracle on a Windows machine, as well as the output:

```
SQL> select * from v$controlfile;
STATUS   NAME
------   ----------------------------------------
         D:\ORANT\DATABASE\CTL1D704.ORA
         E:\ORANT\DATABASE\CTL2D704.ORA
         F:\ORANT\DATABASE\CTL3D704.ORA
```

You can find other information about your control files from the V$DATABASE dictionary view. Several columns in this view give information about your control file.

- **CONTROLFILE_TYPE** The section type in the control file
- **CONTROLFILE_CREATED** Indicates when the current control file was created
- **CONTROLFILE_SEQUENCE#** The current sequence number for the database, recorded in the control file
- **CONTROLFILE_CHANGE#** The current system change number for the database, recorded in the control file
- **CONTROLFILE_TIME** The last time the control file was updated

```
SQL> select * from v$database;

      DBID NAME      CREATED   RESETLOGS_CHANGE# RESETLOGS
---------- --------- --------- ----------------- ---------
PRIOR_RESETLOGS_CHANGE# PRIOR_RES LOG_MODE     CHECKPOINT_CHANGE#
----------------------- --------- ------------ ------------------
ARCHIVE_CHANGE# CONTROL CONTROLFI CONTROLFILE_SEQUENCE#
--------------- ------- --------- ---------------------
CONTROLFILE_CHANGE# CONTROLFI OPEN_RESETL VERSION_T
------------------- --------- ----------- ---------
1674500680 ORGDB01   21-JAN-99             33409 21-JAN-99
                      1 06-OCT-98 NOARCHIVELOG             736292
         716268 CURRENT 21-JAN-99                  4412
             736292           NOT ALLOWED 21-JAN-99
```

A final view available for displaying control file information is the V$CONTROLFILE_RECORD_SECTION view. A working control file is divided into several sections, each storing different information about the database in action. For example, there is a section in the control file that keeps track of the sequence number of the current online redo log, a section that contains information about the physical disk file layout of the Oracle database, and so on. This view displays information about each of those sections, such as the size of each record in the control file for that section, the total number of records allocated to each section, and so on. The following code block shows output from this view:

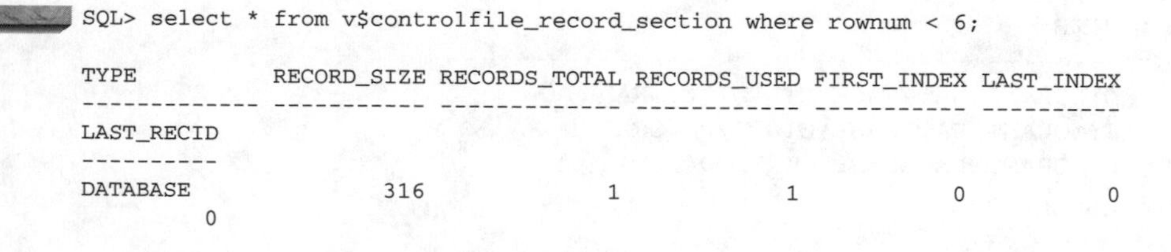

```
SQL> select * from v$controlfile_record_section where rownum < 6;

TYPE          RECORD_SIZE RECORDS_TOTAL RECORDS_USED FIRST_INDEX LAST_INDEX
------------- ----------- ------------- ------------ ----------- ----------
LAST_RECID
----------
DATABASE              316             1            1           0          0
         0
```

```
CKPT PROGRESS              2036            1            0            0            0
         0
REDO THREAD                 228            1            1            0            0
         0
REDO LOG                     72           30            5            0            0
         5
DATAFILE                    428          400           18            0            0
        20
```

TIP

You can also find the names of your control files by issuing `select VALUE from V$PARAMETER where NAME = 'control_files'`*. Be sure that the parameter name is in lowercase.*

Exercise

What dictionary views store information about control files?

Multiplexing Control Files

Depending on the availability of multiple disk drives, the DBA should store multiple copies of the control files to minimize the risk of losing these important physical disk resources. If you stick with the default creation of control files, Oracle recommends that you copy these control files to different disk resources and set the `CONTROL_FILES` parameter to let Oracle know that there are multiple copies of the control file to be maintained. This is called *multiplexing* or *mirroring* the control file. Multiplexing control files reduces Oracle's dependence on any one disk available on the host machine. In the event of a failure, the database is more recoverable because multiple copies of the control file have been maintained. In no case should you ever use only one control file for an Oracle database, because of the difficulty in recovering a database when the control file is lost. Having a copies of the control file and parameter file on different disks will minimize the possibility of one disk failure rendering your database inoperable.

Making additional copies of your control file and moving them to different disk resources is something you handle outside of Oracle. You can create a duplicate copy of the control file by simply using the operating system copy command. In Windows, that command is `copy`, while in UNIX it is `cp`. However, that file will be unusable unless you follow these steps:

1. In Server Manager, execute the `shutdown normal`, `shutdown immediate`, or `shutdown transactional` command to shut down the instance and close the database.

2. Copy the control file to another disk using your operating system's file copy command.
3. Modify the `CONTROL_FILES` parameter in `initsid.ora` to include the additional control file.
4. Restart the instance in Server Manager with the `startup open` command. Oracle will now maintain an additional copy of the control file.

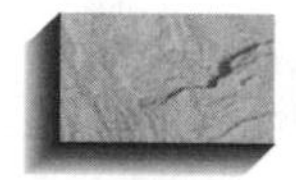

TIP
By specifying multiple control files in the `initsid.ora` file before database creation, you will start your database administration on that database on the right foot, making the database easy to maintain.

Exercises

1. What is multiplexing control files? Why is it important to do?
2. Which initialization parameter tells Oracle where to find its control files?

Maintaining Redo Log Files

In this section, you will cover the following points about maintaining redo log files:

- How online redo log files are used
- Obtaining log and archive information
- Controlling log switches and checkpoints
- Multiplexing and maintaining redo log files
- Planning online redo log files
- Troubleshooting common redo log file problems

Redo logs are disk resources that store data changes made by users on Oracle. In this section, you'll look at how redo logs are used in Oracle, and where you can look to find information about redo log status. The special role of the LGWR background process in maintaining redo logs, and its behavior, will be examined. You will learn more about the importance of maintaining two or more copies of each redo log on your machine, in the same way you do for control files. Finally, you will cover important information about redo log planning and pointers on how to troubleshoot common redo log problems.

How Online Redo Log Files Are Used

Oracle uses redo logs to track data changes users make to the database. Each user process that makes a change to a table must write a small record, called a *redo log entry*, that identifies the change that was made. This redo log entry is placed in the area of the SGA called the redo log buffer, which you learned about in Chapter 6. The LGWR process writes the changes to files on disk called redo log files. Generally, there are at least two redo logs (called online redo logs) available to LGWR for storing redo information. Each of these online redo logs is also referred to as a redo log group. A redo log group can consist of one or more redo log files, referred to as members of the group. Each of the members of the group is the same size and contains an identical copy of one another's data.

The operation of online redo logs occurs as follows. As the redo log buffer fills with redo entries from user processes, LGWR writes copies of the entry to each member of the group. The group being written is considered the current group because LGWR is currently maintaining it. LGWR writes redo log entries to the active group until the group is full, at which point LGWR switches to writing redo entries to the other redo log group. When the other group fills, LGWR will start writing to the next group, or switch back to the original group if there are only two groups.

After creating your database, issue the `alter database archivelog` command. It indicates whether your database will archive its redo log information. This feature of Oracle means that, after the active redo log fills, that group will be copied and archived for safekeeping, either manually by the DBA or automatically with a background process called ARCH. If there is a problem with loss of data from a disk later, archived redo log entries allow you to recover the database from backup to the moment the database failed. When LGWR finishes writing redo entries to the last online redo log group in the sequence, it will return to the first group and begin overwriting the contents of the members in that group.

Exercises

1. What is an online redo log? What is its importance in Oracle?
2. Which background process writes redo information to disk?

Obtaining Log and Archive Information

During the course of database operation, you may want to find out how your redo logs are doing. There are several dictionary views that offer information about redo logs. The first view you will examine is V$LOG. This view gives comprehensive information about the current status of your redo log. Its columns include the following:

- **GROUP#** Displays the group number
- **THREAD#** Shows the database thread for this redo log
- **SEQUENCE#** Identifies how many redo logs have been generated since the last time `resetlogs` was issued to reset the redo log sequence number
- **BYTES** Shows the size of your redo log
- **MEMBERS** Indicates how many members are in the group
- **ARCHIVED** Displays whether the redo log info has been archived or not
- **STATUS** Indicates the current status of the online redo log
- **FIRST_CHANGE#** Indicates the oldest transaction SCN stored in the redo log
- **FIRST_TIME** Indicates the age of the oldest redo log entry in that group

The following code block demonstrates output from an Oracle database running on Windows:

```
SQL> select * from v$log;
GROUP#  THREAD# SEQUENCE# BYTES   MEMBERS ARC STATUS
------- ------- --------- ------- ------- --- --------
FIRST_CHANGE# FIRST_TIM
------------- ---------
     1        1         66  204800        1 NO  CURRENT
       736292 15-FEB-99
     2        1         65  204800        1 NO  INACTIVE
       736283 15-FEB-99
```

The next view for finding information about your redo logs is called V$LOGFILE. This view allows you to see the status of each individual member of each redo log group in the database. V$LOGFILE holds three columns: GROUP#, STATUS, and MEMBER.

- **GROUP#** Gives the redo log group number
- **STATUS** Shows the status of the member
- **MEMBER** Lists the path and filename of each member in the online redo log

The following code block demonstrates the SQL statement and result of a `select` operation against V$LOGFILE for an Oracle database running in Windows:

```
SQL> SELECT * FROM V$LOGFILE;

GROUP# STATUS      MEMBER
------ -------     -----------------------------------
     1 CURRENT     D:\ORANT\DATABASE\LOG1.ORA
     2 INACTIVE    D:\ORANT\DATABASE\LOG2.ORA
```

Information about your online redo logs is not the only type of information you will want to view. You will also want to see information about the archived redo logs in your database. The dictionary view V$ARCHIVED_LOG shows information about the redo logs that have been archived in the database. You should note that this view will contain no information if archiving is not enabled for your database. You can check the archiving status of the database by issuing `select LOG_MODE from V$DATABASE`.

Getting Information About Archived Logs

Several dictionary views offer information about archived redo logs. V$LOG_HISTORY shows a listing of all archived redo logs, listed by THREAD# and SEQUENCE#. The view also lists the lowest and highest SCN of transactions having redo entries in this log. V$LOG_HISTORY is meant to supercede the V$LOGHIST view. V$ARCHIVE stores information about the archive status of online redo logs. This is the same information stored in the ARCHIVED column of V$LOG, and given that V$LOG offers a more complete picture of your online redo logs, you might want to consider using that log instead. Finally, V$ARCHIVED_LOG displays archived log information from the control file, including archive log names.

An archive log record is inserted after the online redo log is successfully archived or cleared (the name column is NULL if the log was cleared). If the log is archived twice, there will be two archived log records with the same THREAD#, SEQUENCE#, and FIRST_CHANGE#, but with different names. An archive log record is also inserted when an archive log is restored from a backup set or a copy. More information about archiving your redo logs is offered in Unit III.

Exercises

1. From which view can you obtain information about the online redo logs, including whether the log has been archived and whether the log is currently being written by LGWR?

2. Identify some views that contain information about archived redo logs.

Controlling Log Switches and Checkpoints

A *log switch* is the point at which LGWR fills one online redo log group with information. At every log switch, a checkpoint occurs.

A checkpoint (CKPT) is when LGWR tells DBWR to write all changes made to data blocks in memory to disk, and DBWR does it. Checkpoints occur at least as frequently as log switches, and they can (and probably should) occur more frequently. If an instance experiences failure, the dirty blocks that haven't been written to disk must be recovered from redo logs. Though this task is handled automatically when the instance is restarted by the *system monitor* or *SMON* background process, it may take a long time if checkpoints happened infrequently and transaction volumes are large.

The events that occur at a log switch are as follows. First, LGWR stops writing the redo log it filled. Second, CKPT is responsible for signaling DBW0 at checkpoints and updating all the database's datafiles and control files to indicate the most recent checkpoint. Finally, when these changes have been made to the database, LGWR will continue writing redo entries to the next online redo log group in the sequence.

The DBA has only a small amount of control over log switches. Since users will always change data, there is little the DBA can do to stop redo information from being written. With that said, you *can* control how often a log switch will occur by changing the size of the online redo log members. Larger member files make log switches less frequent, while smaller member files make log switches more frequent.

Specifying Checkpoint Frequency

If your database redo logs are very large, you should set up the database so that checkpoints happen more often than just at log switches. You can specify more frequent checkpoints with `LOG_CHECKPOINT_INTERVAL` or `LOG_CHECKPOINT_TIMEOUT` in the `init`*`sid`*`.ora file`. These two parameters reflect two different principles on which checkpoint frequency can be based—volume-based intervals and time-based intervals.

`LOG_CHECKPOINT_INTERVAL` sets checkpoint intervals to occur on a volume basis. When LGWR writes as much information to the redo log as is specified by `LOG_CHECKPOINT_INTERVAL`, the checkpoint occurs, and dirty blocks are written to the database. Periods of high transaction volume require flushing the dirty buffer write queue more often; conversely, periods of low transaction volume require fewer redo log entries to be written, and fewer checkpoints are needed. The effect of using `LOG_CHECKPOINT_INTERVAL` is much the same as using smaller redo logs, but it also eliminates the additional overhead of a log switch, such as the archiving of the redo log.

The value you set for `LOG_CHECKPOINT_INTERVAL` is the number of operating system blocks LGWR should write to the redo log (after a log switch) before a checkpoint should occur. If you want checkpoints to occur only at log switches, set

LOG_CHECKPOINT_INTERVAL larger than the size of the redo log. If you want checkpoints at various intervals while writing the current redo log, first divide the size of the redo log in bytes by the size of each Oracle block as specified by DB_BLOCK_SIZE. Then, multiply the result by the number of operating system blocks that fit in an Oracle block. This value, of course, is specific to your operating system. Finally, divide the result by the number of checkpoints you want to occur between the log switch checkpoints.

The formula in Figure 7-1 demonstrates the calculation. Thus, if the size of the redo log is 1,048,576 bytes (1MB), the size of Oracle blocks is 2048 bytes, operating system blocks are 512 bytes in size, and you want 5 checkpoints to occur between log switches, your result is ((1,048,576 / 2048) * 4) / 5, or about 410.

The other way of specifying checkpoint frequency is to use a time-based interval. This is defined with the `LOG_CHECKPOINT_TIMEOUT` init*sid*.ora parameter. Time-based checkpoint intervals are far simpler to configure than volume-based ones, though they make checkpoints occur at uniform intervals, regardless of the transaction volume on the system. You can set the `LOG_CHECKPOINT_TIMEOUT` value to the number of seconds that should pass before another checkpoint occurs. To disable time-based checkpoints, set the `LOG_CHECKPOINT_TIMEOUT` to zero.

One concern you may have when specifying checkpoints to occur at regular intervals is that a checkpoint may occur just before a log switch. In order to avoid log switches causing checkpoints to occur in rapid succession, determine the average time it takes the redo log to fill, and specify a time interval that factors in the checkpoint that happens at log switches. To do so, review the trace file generated by LGWR in the directory specified by the `BACKGROUND_DUMP_DEST` directory.

Finally, you can force checkpoints to occur either by forcing a log switch or by forcing a checkpoint. Both can be done with the `alter system` command. To force a log switch, issue the `alter system switch logfile` command. To force a checkpoint, issue the alter `system checkpoint` command. Checkpoints that occur without a corresponding log switch are called *fast* checkpoints, while checkpoints involving log switches are *full* or *complete* checkpoints.

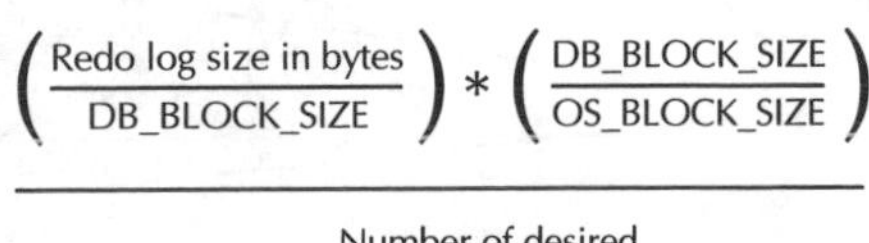

FIGURE 7-1. *Use this formula to calculate checkpoint interval*

Exercises

1. What is a checkpoint? When do checkpoints always occur?
2. What are two principles on which the DBA can specify more frequent checkpoints to occur regularly on the database? What parameters are used in this process?
3. What are two ways the DBA can force a checkpoint to occur? How does the DBA configure the database to have checkpoints occur only at log switches?

Multiplexing and Maintaining Redo Log Files

There are several important details involved in configuring the redo log files of a database. The first and most important detail is that of *multiplexing* your redo logs. In order to improve recoverability in the event of disk failure, the DBA should configure Oracle to multiplex, or store each redo log member in a group on different disk resources. This means that Oracle will maintain two or more members for each redo log group. Figure 7-2 illustrates the concept of multiplexing redo log members.

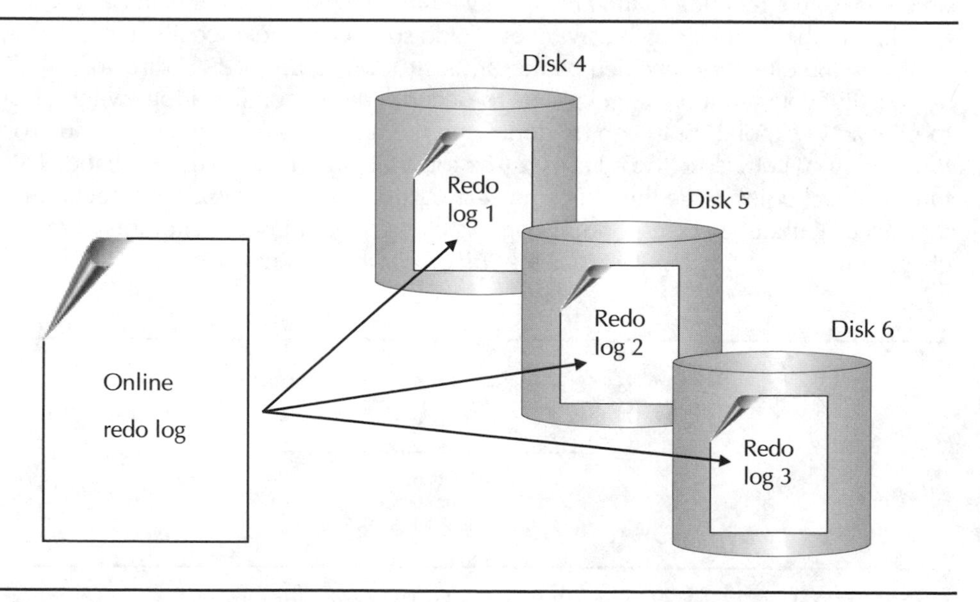

FIGURE 7-2. *Mirroring online redo logs*

By multiplexing redo log members, you keep multiple copies of the redo log available to LGWR. If LGWR has a problem with a disk that holds the redo log (for example, if the disk controller fails), the entire instance will continue running because another redo log member is available on a different disk. If the redo log group has only one member, or if multiple online redo log members are not multiplexed, and the same failure occurs, LGWR will not be able to write redo log entries, and the Oracle instance will fail. This is because LGWR must write redo log entries to disk in order to clear space in the redo log buffer so that user processes can continue making changes to the database. If LGWR cannot clear the space in memory by writing the redo log entries to disk, no further user changes are allowed.

Multiplexing redo logs on separate disks benefits the database in other ways, too. The *archiver process* (*ARCH*) handles the archiving of redo logs automatically when it is enabled. When the database is run in `archivelog` mode, ARCH can be set up to run. When ARCH is running, it automatically moves archived redo logs to an archive destination specified by the LOG_ARCHIVE_DEST parameter in the `initsid.ora` file, every time a log switch occurs. If redo log groups are on one disk, contention can arise at log switch time when ARCH tries to copy the filled redo log to the archive destination at the same time that LGWR tries to write to the next redo log group. If redo log members and the archive log destination are on different disks, there is little possibility for ARCH and LGWR to contend, because ARCH can work on one disk while LGWR continues on another.

Adding and Removing Redo Logs and Members

A redo log group must have at least one member. To add additional members, use the `alter database add logfile member 'filename' to group grpnum`, where `filename` is the name of the file with the absolute path that the group will now have, and *grpnum* is the number of the group to which you are adding the member. You can also add new online redo log groups with the `alter database add logfile group grpnum 'filename'` statement. Finally, if you have more than two redo log groups, you can remove redo logs, provided at least two logs will remain and the one you want to remove is not currently being written by LGWR. The statement used to remove an online redo log from Oracle is `alter database drop logfile group grpnum`. Note that dropping the redo log group does not remove the actual file from your host machine.

TIP
Group number and status information for online redo logs can be obtained from V$LOG, as described previously in this chapter.

Exercises

1. What is multiplexing redo logs, and how is it accomplished?
2. What performance issues are associated with archiving redo logs? How does multiplexing serve to resolve this issue?
3. What statement is used to remove online redo logs? What constraints surround its use?

Planning Online Redo Log Files

Given the importance of multiplexing redo log members on your database for recoverability and performance, and the heavy use of online redo logs overall in your database, you can see that some planning is required for optimal performance of online redo logs. Take the following situation. If you plan to use two online redo logs for your database and simply switch back and forth, you should consider multiplexing members across separate disks. If you use two members per group, you ideally should have 4 disks at Oracle's disposal—one for each redo log member. Realistically, however, you may not have much flexibility for purchasing additional hardware, so you need practical approaches to maximize what you have.

Suppose you have three disks, and you want to multiplex. Archiving is enabled, and your database uses two or three online redo logs. You can multiplex this in several different ways, with different consequences. First, consider using three redo logs, each with two members. In order to avoid contention between ARCH and LGWR, you could put the two members from each group on the same disk. That way, LGWR and ARCH will always be using different disks. However, this architecture violates the fundamental layout principle of multiplexing—that you put the members on different drives. So that configuration is out. Next, consider using three redo log groups, each with three members. For placement, you could put each member on a separate disk. This setup makes each redo log member available on a separate drive for both groups, satisfying the distribution requirement for multiplexing. What's more, although LGWR will need to write to members on each of the three drives, one of which will be in use by ARCH, the two processes will have less of a tendency to conflict with one another because if LGWR cannot write to one of the members for whatever reason, it will write to another instead, and so will ARCH. This feature of both processes makes this configuration a better bet for you. If you're pressed to give up a disk, you can even drop the third set of members from the arrangement, and not sacrifice too much performance.

Planning Redo Logs for Speedy Recovery

Although a slow recovery is better than no recovery at all, a fast recovery distinguishes the superb recovery plan from a passable one. In order to enhance the recovery time of a database, the size of the redo log members should be kept as small as possible without causing excessive performance degradation due to frequent log switches. If redo logs are too small, LGWR frequently switches from one log to another. If the redo log buffer is also small, it may fill to capacity during the switch, causing user processes to wait until LGWR starts clearing out redo entries again. Remember that no user process can make a data change if a corresponding redo log entry cannot be written.

However, while increasing the size of each redo log might seem like the best solution, resulting in less frequent switches (because each redo log takes longer to fill), this also results in longer database recovery time (because more logged changes need to be applied to the database). The better alternative is to increase the number of online redo logs available in Oracle.

The number of online redo log groups is an important factor in smooth redo log operation. You must have at least two redo log groups, but you may want to consider adding more for a couple of reasons. For example, LGWR cannot start writing to a new group if ARCH has not archived that group yet. If you notice that ARCH does not finish archiving a redo log before LGWR is ready to start using it again, you may want to add log groups. You may also need to add groups if you notice that all your redo logs consistently show a status of ACTIVE (meaning that the online log is needed for crash recovery) when LGWR attempts to switch from the last log in the sequence back to the first. Additional redo log groups can be set up at database creation time, or new redo log groups can be added after database creation with the `alter database add logfile group` statement. The only restrictions on this statement are options set by the `create database` command, specifically `MAXLOGFILES`, which limits the number of redo log groups that can be associated with a database, and `MAXLOGMEMBERS`, which limits the size of each member or copy in the group. The only way to alter these settings is to re-create the control file. In emergency situations only, and only for the lifetime of the current instance, the DBA can *decrease* the number of redo log groups that can be set by changing the LOG_FILES initialization parameter. However, this does not solve the problem of wanting to *add* more redo log groups than `MAXLOGFILES` allows.

Exercises

1. An Oracle database has three online redo logs and three available disks for housing redo logs. How might you use multiplexing to reduce contention and maximize uptime in this situation?

2. How should the DBA plan redo logs in order to recover the database quickly? What two parameters may restrict your ability to add more redo logs to your database in the future? How can this limitation be avoided?

Troubleshooting Common Redo Log File Problems

Finally, here are a few tidbits on identifying, resolving, and avoiding common redo log problems. By far the biggest headache with an easy solution that you will encounter as a DBA is when the disk resource that houses the archive log fills to capacity. If your archive destination won't hold any more archived redo logs, the ARCH process will no longer archive the online redo logs, which means that eventually your online redo logs will fill. Since archiving is enabled in this situation (obviously, or you wouldn't be archiving!), LGWR will not overwrite an online redo log that hasn't been archived, and redo entries will eventually back up in the log buffer, filling it. When that happens, Oracle will accept no more data changes, and the entire database will enter a paralyzing wait state. To resolve the issue, either move archived redo logs to a different destination, add more disk space to the archive log destination, or empty out that directory on your file system.

Another problem that may arise on your database that is actually a miniature version of the preceding problem is when the database enters a protracted wait state during a log switch. This is often due to all online redo logs being active when LGWR wants to roll over from the last redo log in the sequence to the first, which cannot be done until that redo log is inactive. The solution is to add more online redo logs.

Also, you may encounter situations in which a redo log member is inaccessible for some reason, and the STATUS column in the V$LOGFILE view for that member shows INVALID status. This could be due to disk failure, and it must be resolved. One solution is to create additional log groups on other disks, issue the `alter system switch logfile` command to get LGWR writing to a different redo log, and remove the redo log group with the invalid member. However, the better solution is to prevent the problem by multiplexing.

Finally, it is possible for your Oracle database to be unrecoverable, even if you are archiving your redo logs, due to some low-level data block corruption in an archived redo log. In order to determine if this low-level corruption exists, you can set the `LOG_BLOCK_CHECKSUM` `init`*`sid`*`.ora` parameter to TRUE to make Oracle use checksums to detect corruption in your online redo logs before they are archived. If LGWR finds corruption in the online redo log it is trying to archive, LGWR will attempt to archive the same block from a different member in the group. If they are all corrupted, the log cannot be archived. Instead, the DBA must clear the online redo log with the `alter database clear unarchived logfile group` *`grpnum`* statement. Afterward, it is a good idea for the DBA to shut down the database and do a cold backup to avoid recovery problems later due to the missing redo log.

Exercises

1. Identify a problem that may occur if archiving is enabled on your database and the ARCH process is turned off. Is adding more redo logs an effective solution for this problem?
2. How is data block corruption in redo logs cleared? How is it detected?

Managing Tablespaces and Datafiles

In this section, you will cover the following points about managing tablespaces and datafiles:

- Describing the logical structure of the database
- Creating tablespaces
- Changing tablespace size using various methods
- Changing tablespaces status and storage settings
- Relocating tablespaces
- Preparing necessary tablespaces

Tablespaces and *datafiles* are the last disk structure to be analyzed in this chapter. These two disk resources are used to house data from Oracle tables, indexes, rollback segments, and the like, which you will learn more about in Chapter 8. Tablespaces and datafiles are great examples of the overlap between physical and logical disk resources in Oracle. From the logical perspective, Oracle sees its storage areas as tablespaces—vast areas that can house the objects mentioned. From the physical perspective, the host machine sees one or several files called datafiles. In this section, you will learn about the logical structure of Oracle tablespaces and how that logical structure maps to the physical world of files on your host machine. The creation and changing of tablespaces is also covered, as well as Oracle's requirements for preparing necessary tablespaces to make the database operate properly.

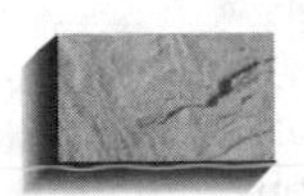

TIP
In some places on OCP Exam 2, Oracle may refer to the Oracle Enterprise Manager tool for managing tablespaces as the Tablespace Manager. This tool is synonymous with Storage Manager.

Describing the Logical Structure of the Database

Meet three more players in the world of logical Oracle disk resources: tablespaces, segments, and extents. A *tablespace* is a logical database structure that is designed to store other logical database structures. Oracle sees a tablespace as a large area of space into which Oracle can place new objects. Space in tablespaces is allocated in segments. A *segment* is an allocation of space used to store the data of a table, index, rollback segment, or temporary object. When the database object runs out of space in its segment and needs to add more data, Oracle allows it to allocate more space in the form of an extent. An *extent* is similar to a segment in that the extent stores information corresponding to a table, index, rollback segment, or temporary object. You will learn more about segments and extents in the last section of this chapter on storage structures and relationships, so for now we will focus on tablespaces. When you are logged into Oracle and manipulating storage factors, you are doing so with the logical perspective of tablespaces.

The other perspective you will have on your Oracle database is that provided by the operating system of the host machine. Underlying the logical storage in Oracle is the physical method your host system uses to store data, the cornerstone of which is the *block*. Segments and extents are composed of data blocks, and in turn, the blocks are taken together to comprise a *datafile*. Recall that you specified a value in bytes for an initialization parameter called `DB_BLOCK_SIZE`. This parameter determined the size of each Oracle block. Block size is typically specified as a multiple of operating system block size. Oracle blocks are usually 2K, 4K, 8K, and sometimes 16K. You can size your Oracle blocks larger, depending on your operating system. A tablespace may consist of one or many datafiles, and the objects in a tablespace can be stored by Oracle anywhere within the one or multiple datafiles comprising the tablespace. And while a tablespace may have many datafiles, each datafile can belong to only one tablespace. Figure 7-3 shows you the glasses through which you can view logical and physical disk storage in your Oracle database.

Managing Space Within Tablespaces

Within tablespaces, Oracle manages free space by coalescing it into contiguous segments. This coalescing activity is handled automatically by the system monitor or SMON background process in Oracle, a process that has already been introduced. When new database objects are created, Oracle will acquire the requested amount of contiguous storage space in the form of a segment for the new object, based either on the object's own storage clause or on the default storage clause for that tablespace. For OCP, remember that SMON is the process that handles this coalescing of free space into contiguous chunks on an ongoing basis while Oracle is running.

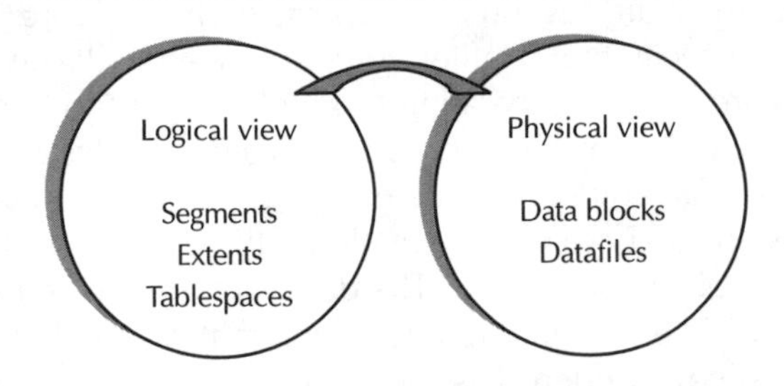

FIGURE 7-3. *The logical and physical views of a database*

Exercises

1. What items comprise the logical disk storage resources in Oracle? What items comprise the physical disk storage resources in Oracle?
2. How do physical disk storage resources map to logical disk storage resources in your Oracle database?
3. What process coalesces free space in your tablespace?

Creating Tablespaces

Tablespaces are created in two ways. The first way is by creating a database. Recall that in the `create database` statement you named a few datafiles. These files comprised the SYSTEM tablespace, which contains a bunch of important resources in your database, such as dictionary tables and the system rollback segment. Unfortunately, creating tablespaces in this way is a one-shot deal. After that, you can create tablespaces with the `create tablespace` statement, as shown for Windows in the following code block:

```
CREATE TABLESPACE ORGDBDATA DATAFILE
'E:\Oracle\orgdata01.dat' SIZE 20M,
'F:\Oracle\orgdata02.dat' SIZE 30M AUTOEXTEND ON NEXT 10M MAXSIZE 50M
MINIMUM EXTENT 150K
DEFAULT STORAGE
( INITIAL 750K NEXT 250K MINEXTENTS 1
  MAXEXTENTS 25 PCTINCREASE 0 )
ONLINE;
```

As you can see, there are several components to the `create tablespace` statement. First, you specify the datafiles your tablespace will own, using absolute pathnames. (If you are using an operating system like UNIX to host your Oracle database, be sure the pathnames you specify for your datafiles are ones Oracle can actually write.) After that, you specify the `default storage` clause to set options that will be applied to database object creation if the `create` statement does not have storage parameters defined for it. (The details of these storage parameters will be explained shortly.) There is one storage option that, when defined in a tablespace, cannot be overridden. That option is `minimum extent`, which ensures that every extent size used in the tablespace is a multiple of the specified integer value. Finally, you request that Oracle put your tablespace in the online and available state after creating it. If you omit the `online` keyword from your `create tablespace` statement, you can ensure it is online later by issuing `alter tablespace` *`tblspc_name`* `online` (the default is `online`).

TIP
You can also add tablespaces to your database through the Storage Manager administrative tool in Oracle Enterprise Manager.

Default Storage Options Defined

The `default storage` clause defines storage options that will be applied to newly created database objects if the `create` statement does not have storage parameters defined for it. The `initial` and `next` options specify the size of the object's initial segment and next allocated extent, respectively. If `minimum extent` is defined for the tablespace you put your object in, and the value specified for `next` on your database object is less than `minimum extent`, Oracle rounds up to the next highest multiple for `minimum extent` and creates the initial or next extent as that size. This feature can reduce the amount of fragmentation in a tablespace.

The `minextents` and `maxextents` options specify the minimum and maximum number of extents the object can allocate in the tablespace. If you specify `minextents` greater than one and the tablespace has more than one datafile, Oracle will tend to spread extents over multiple datafiles, which can improve performance if those datafiles are also located on different disk resources.

Finally, `pctincrease` allows you to specify a percentage increase in the amount of space allocated for the next extent in the object. For example, if `next` is set to 200K, and `pctincrease` is 50, the second extent would be 200K in size, the third extent would be 300K (50 percent more than the second extent), the fourth extent would be 450K (50 percent more than the third extent), and so on. The minimum value is 0, and the default value is 50. The calculated value is rounded up to the next data block, which is a multiple of 5 times DB_BLOCK_SIZE. To make all extents the same size, specify `pctincrease` to be zero.

Exercises

1. Identify two ways that tablespaces are created in Oracle.
2. Name some different aspects of tablespaces you can define with the `create tablespace` statement. Describe the meaning of each storage option. How are tablespace default storage options used?

Changing Tablespace Size Using Various Methods

There are a few different ways to modify the size of a tablespace. The first is by adding new datafiles to the tablespace. This task is accomplished with the `alter tablespace add datafile` statement. You can add as many datafiles to your tablespace as you want, subject to two restrictions. First, you cannot add datafiles that will exceed the physical size of your disk resources (that one's pretty straightforward). Increasing the size of your tablespace by adding datafiles is accomplished with the statement in the following code block:

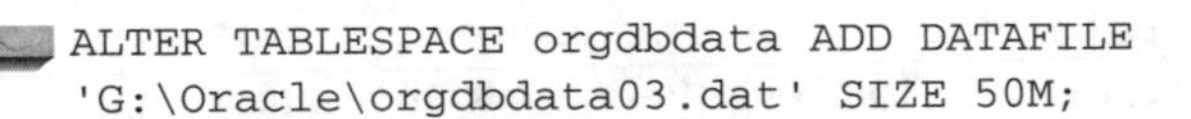

```
ALTER TABLESPACE orgdbdata ADD DATAFILE
'G:\Oracle\orgdbdata03.dat' SIZE 50M;
```

Second, consider the following point about `MAXDATAFILES` for a moment. If you have added the maximum number of datafiles permitted for your database as specified by this parameter, and you *still* need more room, you can increase the size of your tablespace either with the `resize` keyword or by activating the autoextend feature on your datafile. Resizing a datafile upward rarely meets with difficulty (unless there is not enough space in the file system). To resize a datafile, issue the following statement:

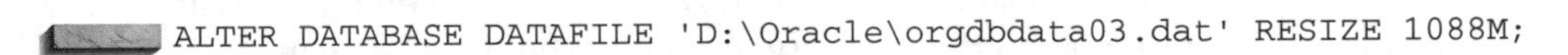

```
ALTER DATABASE DATAFILE 'D:\Oracle\orgdbdata03.dat' RESIZE 1088M;
```

To enable automatic extension of your datafile, execute the following statement:

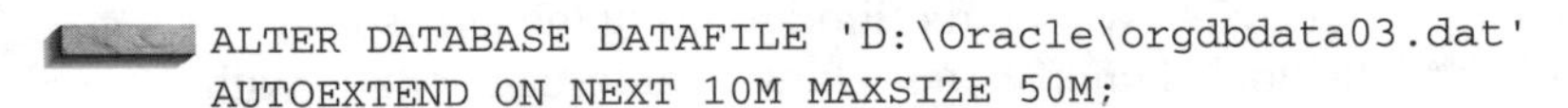

```
ALTER DATABASE DATAFILE 'D:\Oracle\orgdbdata03.dat'
AUTOEXTEND ON NEXT 10M MAXSIZE 50M;
```

TIP
You can set up autoextend on your datafiles and add new datafiles to your tablespaces with the Storage Manager administrative tool that is part of Oracle Enterprise Manager.

Usually, you can also resize a tablespace to be smaller, either through dropping datafiles with `alter database datafile` *`filename`* `offline drop` or by resizing a datafile to be smaller. This is not always safe, however, especially if the datafile contains segments or extents owned by database objects. Be careful when attempting this sort of activity.

Exercises

1. Identify some ways that the size of a tablespace can be changed in Oracle.
2. Issuing the `alter database datafile` *`filename`* `offline drop` statement has what effect on your tablespace size?

Changing Tablespace Status and Storage Settings

Your `create tablespace` code block from the previous lesson describes how to create the tablespace so that it is online and available for use as soon as it's created. Recall also that the `alter tablespace` *`tblspc_name`* `online` statement allows you to bring a tablespace online after creation. You can also take a tablespace offline using the `alter tablespace` *`tblspc_name`* `offline` statement. You might do this if you were trying to prevent access to the data in that tablespace while simultaneously leaving the rest of the database online and available for use. Individual datafiles can be taken online and offline as well, using the `alter database datafile` *`filename`* `online` or `alter database datafile` *`filename`* `offline` statements.

A tablespace can be taken offline with one of several priorities, including `normal`, `temporary`, and `immediate`. Depending on the priority used to take the tablespace offline, media recovery on that tablespace may be required. A tablespace taken offline with normal priority will not require media recovery, but a tablespace taken offline with immediate priority will. A tablespace taken offline with temporary priority will not require media recovery if none of the datafiles were offline prior to taking the tablespace offline. However, if any of the datafiles were offline before the tablespace was taken offline temporarily due to read or write errors, then media recovery will be required to bring the tablespace back online. The following code block demonstrates taking a tablespace offline with each of the three possible priorities. Note that if you leave off a priority specification, normal priority is assumed.

```
ALTER TABLESPACE orgdbdata OFFLINE;
ALTER TABLESPACE orgdbdata OFFLINE NORMAL;
```

```
ALTER TABLESPACE orgdbdata OFFLINE IMMEDIATE;
ALTER TABLESPACE orgdbdata OFFLINE TEMPORARY;
```

On occasion, you may also have situations that make use of Oracle's ability to specify tablespaces to only be readable. To do this, three conditions must be true: there must be no active transactions in Oracle, the tablespace you want to prevent write access to must be online, and no active rollback segments may be present in the tablespace. The following code block demonstrates both the code required to make a tablespace readable but not writeable, and then to change it back to being writeable again.

```
ALTER TABLESPACE orgdbdata READ ONLY;
ALTER TABLESPACE orgdbdata READ WRITE;
```

Now, consider again the default storage parameters you set for a tablespace when you create it. They have no bearing on the tablespace itself, but rather are used as default settings when users issue `create table`, `create index`, or `create rollback segment` statements that have no storage parameter settings explicitly defined. You can change the default settings for your tablespace by issuing the `alter tablespace` command, as shown in the following block:

```
ALTER TABLESPACE orgdbdata DEFAULT STORAGE ( INITIAL 2M NEXT 1M );
```

You needn't specify all the default storage parameters available—only the ones for which you want to change values. However, keep in mind that changing the default storage settings has no effect on existing database objects in the tablespace. It only affects storage settings on new database objects, and only when those new database objects do not specify their own storage settings explicitly.

Finally, if you want to eliminate a tablespace, use the `drop tablespace` command. This command has a few additional clauses, such as `including contents` for removing all database objects contained in the tablespace as well as the tablespace itself, and the `cascade constraints` keyword to remove any constraints that may depend on database objects stored in the tablespace being dropped. The following code block demonstrates a `drop tablespace` command:

```
DROP TABLESPACE orgdbdata INCLUDING CONTENTS CASCADE CONSTRAINTS;
```

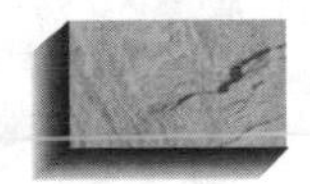

TIP
Tablespace management can also be handled with Oracle Enterprise Manager's Storage Manager administrative application.

Exercises

1. What are some of the statuses a tablespace can have, and how can you change them?
2. How are default storage values for a tablespace changed? If they are changed, what effect does this have on database objects already existing in the tablespace? If a new table is created that has no storage settings of its own, where will the table get its storage settings from? Explain.

Relocating Tablespaces

"Relocating tablespaces" is something of a misnomer. You can't actually *relocate* a tablespace in Oracle—a tablespace is always part of the same database, and as a logical storage resource, it has no location as far as the database is concerned. You can, however, move or relocate the datafiles underlying the tablespace from within Oracle, which offers some value, particularly when you are trying to eliminate "hotspots" in the database or distribute I/O load or disk use more evenly across the host machine.

Relocating datafiles in a tablespace is handled with the `alter database rename file` command. The idea is that you move the datafile by specifying a new path or filename as part of the command. This command renames datafiles as well as redo log file members. However, within Oracle, the command only renames files by changing control file information; the command does not actually rename them on your operating system.

To relocate data files, execute the following steps:

1. Shut down the database.
2. Use an operating system command to move the files.
3. Mount the database.
4. Execute the `alter database rename file` command.
5. Open the database.

The following code block illustrates these steps in Windows:

```
D:\ORANT\DATABASE\> SVRMGR30
Oracle Server Manager Release 3.0.5.0.0 - Production
(c)1997, Oracle Corporation. All Rights Reserved.
Oracle8 Enterprise Edition Release 8.0.5.0.0 - Production
With the Partitioning and Objects options
PL/SQL Release 8.0.5.0.0 - Production
```

```
SVRMGR> connect internal
Password:
Connected.
SVRMGR> shutdown immediate
Database closed.
Database dismounted.
ORACLE instance shut down.
SVRMGR> !move tmp1jsc.ora temp1jsc.ora
        1 file(s) moved.
SVRMGR> startup mount pfile=initjsc.ora
Total System Global Area                    14442496 bytes
Fixed Size                                     49152 bytes
Variable Size                               13193216 bytes
Database Buffers                             1126400 bytes
Redo Buffers                                   73728 bytes
Database mounted.
SVRMGR> alter database rename file
     2> 'D:\ORANT\DATABASE\TMP1JSC.ORA'
     3> to
     4> 'D:\ORANT\DATABASE\TEMP1JSC.ORA';
Statement Processed.
SVRMGR> alter database open;
Statement processed.
```

Exercises

1. Can tablespaces be moved? Explain.
2. What command is issued in order to move datafiles of a tablespace from one location to another in the file system? What constraints are there on Oracle's operation when this command is run?

Preparing Necessary Tablespaces

When an Oracle database is created, the SYSTEM tablespace is created automatically. Though the SYSTEM tablespace can store any database object, it is not recommended that you put objects in it other than the dictionary objects and the system rollback segment. To avoid problems with your database, you will need to prepare a few other tablespaces to store types of database objects that you will learn about in Chapter 8. By placing these objects in other databases designed to fit their storage needs, the DBA prevents a number of potential storage problems.

One of your first database activities should be to create separate tablespaces to store tables, indexes, rollback segments, temporary segments, and segments associated with database administrative tools such as Oracle Enterprise Manager.

The tablespaces necessary for your Oracle database can be created with statements like the following ones:

```
CREATE TABLESPACE orgdbrbs datafile '/oracle/disk_6/rbs01.dbf'
SIZE 300M DEFAULT STORAGE ( INITIAL 1M NEXT 1M MINEXTENTS 1
 MAXEXTENTS 200) ONLINE;

CREATE TABLESPACE orgdbdata datafile '/oracle/disk_7/data01.dbf'
SIZE 300M DEFAULT STORAGE ( INITIAL 1M NEXT 1M MINEXTENTS 1
MAXEXTENTS 200) ONLINE;

CREATE TABLESPACE orgdbindex datafile '/oracle/disk_8/index01.dbf'
SIZE 300M DEFAULT STORAGE ( INITIAL 1M NEXT 1M MINEXTENTS 1
MAXEXTENTS 200) ONLINE;

CREATE TABLESPACE orgdbtools datafile '/oracle/disk_9/tools01.dbf'
SIZE 300M DEFAULT STORAGE ( INITIAL 1M NEXT 1M MINEXTENTS 1
MAXEXTENTS 200) ONLINE;

CREATE TABLESPACE orgdbtemp datafile '/oracle/disk_10/temp01.dbf'
SIZE 300M DEFAULT STORAGE ( INITIAL 1M NEXT 1M MINEXTENTS 1
MAXEXTENTS 500) TEMPORARY;
```

Each of these different types of database objects has its own unique behavior, and sometimes the behavior of one type of object conflicts with another. In the next section, on storage structures and relationships, you will learn more about the various types of segments that exist in Oracle and why it is important to put them in their own tablespaces. When identifying default storage parameters for these tablespaces, the DBA should attempt to set parameters that work well for the type of database object that will be stored in this tablespace. Chapter 8 presents more information related to this task.

Special Note on Creating Temporary Tablespaces

Most of your tablespaces on the database will house permanent objects, or objects that will stick around in your database for a long time. However, remember that you will also want a special tablespace for housing temporary segments. You can use a special keyword to distinguish your temporary tablespace from permanent tablespaces, to prevent anyone from creating a permanent database object, such as a table or index with data, in the tablespace used for temporary segments. Review the following code block, and note the replacement of the keyword `online` with `temporary` for creating the temporary tablespace. You don't need to specify this keyword in order to use this tablespace as your temporary tablespace, but it adds some protection against users trying to put tables and other permanent objects in an area where permanent objects are not meant to go.

```
CREATE TABLESPACE orgdbtemp datafile '/oracle/disk_9/temp01.dbf' SIZE 300M
DEFAULT STORAGE ( INITIAL 1M NEXT 1M MINEXTENTS 1 MAXEXTENTS 500)
TEMPORARY;
```

Exercises

1. Which tablespace is created with every Oracle database?
2. What additional tablespaces are necessary for correct Oracle operation? What sorts of database objects will these tablespaces eventually support?
3. Which keyword is used to denote temporary tablespaces?

Storage Structures and Relationships

In this section, you will cover the following topics concerning storage structures and relationships:

- Different segment types and their uses
- Controlling the use of extents by segments
- Using block space utilization parameters
- Obtaining information about storage structures
- Locating segments with consideration for fragmentation and lifespan

The storage of database objects in Oracle can often become a cantankerous matter, because each of the different types of database objects have their own storage needs and typical behavior. What's more, the behavior of one type of database object often interferes with the behavior of other objects in the database. As the Oracle DBA, your job is to make sure that all objects "play well together." To help you with OCP and in being a DBA, this section will discuss the different segment types and their uses, how to control Oracle's use of extents, the management of space at the block level, where to go for information about your database storage allocation, and how to locate segments by considering fragmentation and lifespan.

Different Segment Types and Their Uses

Earlier, you saw that different types of objects need different types of tablespaces to store them. At a minimum, in addition to the SYSTEM tablespace, you will have separate tablespaces for your tables, indexes, rollback segments, and temporary segments. In order to understand the different types of tablespaces, and also why it is a bad idea to ever try to store all your database objects in the SYSTEM tablespace, you must understand the different types of objects that a tablespace may store. Every database object, such as tables or rollback segments, ultimately consists of segments and extents. For this reason, the discussion focuses on the different types of segments available on the Oracle database, and how they are used.

Table and Index Segments and Their Usage

The first type of segment is the table segment. Each segment contains data blocks that store the row data for that table. The rate at which the table fills and grows is determined by the type of data that table will support. For example, if a table supports an application component that accepts large volumes of data insertions (sales order entries for a popular brand of wine, for example), the segments that comprise that table will fill at a regular pace and rarely, if ever, reduce in size. Therefore, the DBA managing the tablespace that stores that segment will want to plan for regular growth. If, however, this table is designed for storing validation data, the size requirements of the table may be a bit more static. In this case, the DBA may want to focus more on ensuring that the entire table fits comfortably into one segment, thus reducing the potential fragmentation that extent allocation could cause. More complete discussions of how these different goals can be achieved will appear later in the chapter.

Another type of segment is the index segment. As with table segments, index segment growth is moderated by the type of role the index supports in the database. If the table to which the index is associated is designed for volume transactions (as in the wine example mentioned previously), the index also should be planned for growth. However, the index will almost invariably be smaller than the database.

What does an index consist of, exactly? An index consists of a list of entries for a particular column (the indexed column) that can be easily searched for the values stored in the column. Corresponding to each value is the ROWID for the table row that contains that column value. The principle behind index growth is the same as the growth of the corresponding table. If an index is associated with a table that rarely changes, the size of the index may be relatively static. But if the index is associated with a table that experiences high `insert` activity, then plan the index for growth, as well.

Rollback and Temporary Segment Usage

Rollback segments are different from the table and index segments just discussed. Rollback segments store data changes from transactions to provide read consistency and transaction concurrency. The segments used to store data for tables and indexes are generally for ongoing use, meaning that once data is added to a table or index segment, it generally stays there for a while. Rollback segments aren't like that. Instead, once a user process has made its database changes and `commits` the transaction, the space in the rollback segment that held that user's data is released for reuse. Oracle's rollback segment architecture is designed to allow the rollback segment to reuse that space. Usually, a rollback segment has some extents allocated to it at all times to store uncommitted transaction information.

As the number of uncommitted transactions rises and falls, so, too, does the amount of space used in the rollback segment. Where possible, the rollback segment will try to place uncommitted transaction data into space it already has allocated to it. For example, if a rollback segment consists of five extents, and the entire initial extent contains old data from committed transactions, the rollback segment will reuse that extent to store data from new or existing uncommitted transactions once it fills the fifth extent. But, if the rollback segment fills the fifth extent with data from a long uncommitted transaction, and the first extent still has data from uncommitted transactions in it, the rollback segment will need to allocate a new extent. Various long- and short-running transactions on your Oracle database can cause rollback segments to allocate and deallocate dozens of extents over and over again throughout the day, which can adversely affect the growth of other database objects because of tablespace fragmentation. Thus, it is wise to keep rollback segments out of data tablespaces, and vice versa.

Next, consider the temporary segment. True to its name, the temporary segment is allocated to store temporary data for a user transaction that cannot all be stored in memory. One popular use for temporary segments in user processes is for sorting data into a requested order. These segments are allocated on the fly and dismissed when their services are no longer required. Their space utilization is marked by short periods of high storage need followed by periods of no storage need. Because you have no idea when a temporary segment could come in and use all the available space in a tablespace, you can't make an adequate plan to accommodate the growth of other database objects—you really need to keep temporary segments in their own tablespace, as separate from other database objects as possible.

Beyond the Basics: LOB, Cluster, and IOT Segments

The final types of segments that may be used in your Oracle database are LOB segments, cluster segments, and IOT segments. LOB stands for large object, and a large object in Oracle will use a special sort of segment to house its data. If your database uses large objects frequently, you may want to create a separate tablespace to hold these objects. Otherwise, don't bother with creating the extra tablespace.

You may have heard of clustered tables—a physical grouping of two or more tables around a common index. Cluster segments support the use of clusters on the database. The sizing of cluster segments and planning for their growth is complex and should be performed carefully, as each segment will essentially be storing data from two different tables in each block. A more complete discussion of cluster segments appears in the next chapter.

Finally, IOT stands for index-organized table, in which essentially the entire table is stored within the structure historically reserved for an index. These segments have specific storage needs. However, your use of cluster and IOT segments will probably be so limited that you won't need to worry about any potential conflict between these objects and your other database objects.

A Note about Database Tools

Database administrative tools like Oracle Enterprise Manager operate based on a set of tables, indexes, and other database objects that collect data about your database. This set of database objects is often called a *repository*. Although the segments that house repository objects are the same as those segments that house your data, you should create a separate tablespace to store repository objects for several reasons. One reason is that this will keep a logical division between your organization's data and the tool's data. Another reason is that, though it is not likely, the repository may have a table or other object with the same name as an object in your database, causing a conflict. By using a special TOOLS tablespace to store objects used by your database administrative tools, you will ease your own efforts later.

Exercises

1. Identify several types of segments available for storing database objects.
2. Why is it important not to put all database objects in the SYSTEM tablespace?
3. Should different types of database segments be stored in the same tablespace or in different tablespaces? Why or why not? What is the purpose of a TOOLS tablespace, and why is it necessary?

Controlling the Use of Extents by Segments

Growth in a data segment is generally handled with extents. If the segment runs out of space to handle new record entries for the object, then the object will acquire an extent from the remaining free space in the tablespace. A logical database object, such as a table or index, can have many extents, but all those extents (plus the original segment) must all be stored in the same tablespace.

When a database object is created, Oracle allocates it a finite amount of space in the tablespace, based on the database object's storage parameters. Usually, the object is initially created with only one segment of space allocated. As new rows are added to tables, the space of the segment is used to store that new data. When the segment storing the table data is full and more data must be added to the table, the table must allocate another extent to store that data in. Figure 7-4 illustrates an extent being acquired on an Oracle database.

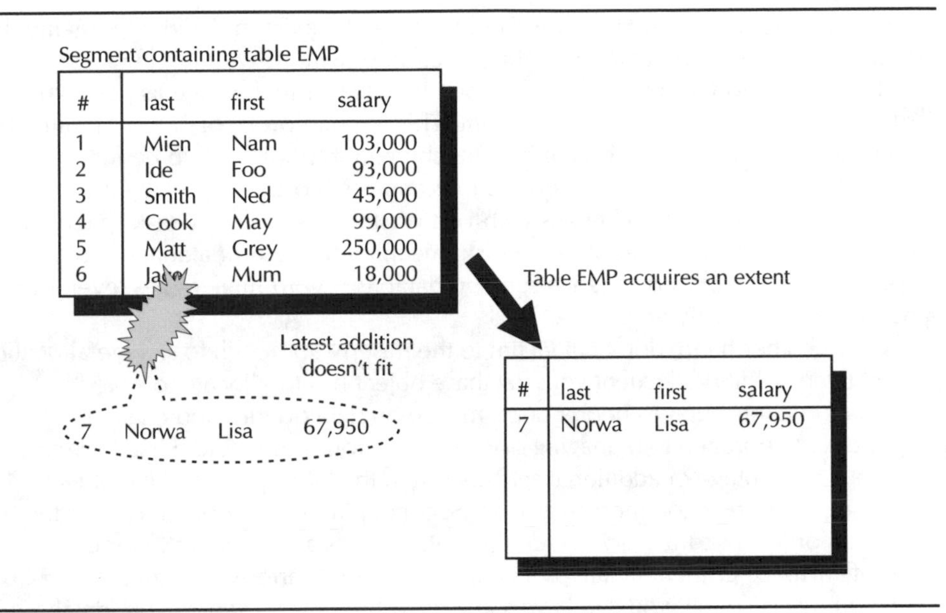

FIGURE 7-4. *Acquiring extents*

A new extent will be acquired for a database object only if there is no room in any of the object's current segments or extents for the new data. Once acquired, an extent will only be relinquished if the DBA truncates or drops and re-creates the table.

The size of an acquired extent is based on the value specified for the next clause if there is only one extent on the database. If the object is acquiring its third or greater extent, the size of the extent will equal next multiplied by pctincrease. If you want to specify a different size, you should issue the `alter` *`object`* `storage (next` *`nextval`*`)` statement, where *object* is the name of the object and *`nextval`* is the size of the next extent in K or MB. Or, you can change the value for `pctincrease`. If you do this, Oracle will multiply future extents allocated by a larger percentage increase factor, thereby increasing the storage allocation rate for the object on an ongoing, rather than a fixed, basis. The two following statements are examples of these two approaches to modifying extent sizes:

```
ALTER TABLE employee STORAGE (NEXT 10M);
ALTER TABLE employee STORAGE (PCTINCREASE 50);
```

In general, you will get the best performance from a database object, such as a table or index, if all the data for that object is housed in only one segment, or in a set of contiguous blocks. However, certain trade offs exist in deciding how much space to allocate, particularly for tables you know will grow quickly.

The temptation for every DBA is to preallocate as much space as possible, in order to keep all the data in one segment. This temptation is, of course, limited by two factors—limited space on the host machine, and poor backup performance because of the excessive time required to compress mostly empty objects for storage on tape. Also, having many tables with vast wastelands of empty disk space puts tables far away from one another on disk, meaning that your database could experience the poor performance seen on databases with huge tables, even though your tables are mostly empty.

On the other hand, don't fall victim to the miserly approach to storage allocation either. Every additional extent your database object has to allocate to store its information contributes to poorer performance on data queries and changes.

The best approach to managing storage allocation is threefold. First, leave a generous percentage of additional space, both in the tablespace and the object's initial segment, to accommodate growth. Second, plan for disk purchases for the host machine, or leave extra space to add new tablespaces and datafiles in order to alleviate a space crunch. Finally, set up a monthly or quarterly maintenance schedule with your users so that you can have some downtime to reorganize your database and avert those potential database sizing issues before they become headaches.

Exercises

1. What must happen in order for Oracle to allocate an extent to a database object?
2. On what parameters does the size of the extent allocated to a database object depend?
3. Which statement can be used to change the size of the next extent allocated to a database object?

Using Block Space Utilization Parameters

In addition to overall storage allocation for objects in the database, Oracle allows you to manage how the objects use the space they are given. Space usage is determined at the block level with the `pctfree` and `pctused` options. There are several ways to configure block space usage, depending on how the object itself is utilized by the application. If the database object experiences a high `update` activity that increases the size of rows in the table, the block space allocation for that database object should allow for additional growth per row. If data change activity on the object consists of lots of `insert` statements entering rows mostly the same size, then the space usage goal within each block should be to place as many rows as possible into each block before allocating another one. This same approach may work if a table's size is static and rows are infrequently added to the table.

TIP
When determining values for `pctfree` and `pctused`, do not assign values for these space utilization options that exceed 100 when added together. In fact, you should not set values for these options that even approach 90, because this causes Oracle to spend more time managing space utilization than is necessary.

Review first the `pctfree` option. It is used to specify the amount of space left free in each block to accommodate the growth of existing rows in the block. For example, if a table has `pctfree` specified to be 10 percent, Oracle will stop inserting new rows in the block when there is 10 percent free space left in the block. You should use the following general approach when deciding how to set `pctfree`. Set this value high if rows in your table will be updated often and each update will add to the size in bytes of the row. Setting `pctfree` high prevents performance killers such as row migration (where Oracle moves an entire row to another block because the original block doesn't have the room to store it anymore). Conversely, if the rows in the block will not be updated frequently, or if the updates that will occur will not affect the size of each row, set the value for `pctfree` low on that database object.

The `pctused` option specifies the threshold by which Oracle will determine if it is acceptable to add new rows to a block. Oracle fills the block with inserted rows until reaching the cutoff set by `pctfree`. Later, as data is deleted from a table, its space utilization may fall. When the space used in a data block falls below the threshold limit set by `pctused`, Oracle adds the block to a *freelist* maintained for that table. A freelist is a list of data blocks that are currently accepting new data rows. Oracle incurs some performance overhead by marking a block free and adding it to a freelist for that database object. Thus, there is a trade off inherent in specifying `pctused` that you should understand for OCP and beyond. You must temper your interest in managing space freed by row removal as efficiently as possible against that overhead incurred by each block. To prevent the block from making its way to the freelist when only one or two rows can even be added to the block, you should set the `pctused` option relatively low.

Chapter 8 has more thorough coverage of table creation and management, but to give you the opportunity to see pctfree and pctused in action, the following code block contains a create table statement with pctfree and pctused specified.

```
CREATE TABLE FAMILY
( NAME          VARCHAR2(10),
  RELATIONSHIP VARCHAR2(10))
 PCTFREE 20
 PCTUSED 40;
```

Exercises

1. How is space usage within data blocks managed?
2. What are chaining and row migration? Which parameter should be set in order to prevent them from occurring? How should that parameter be set?

Obtaining Information About Storage Structures

You can determine storage information for database objects from many sources in the data dictionary. There are several data dictionary views associated with tracking information about structures for storage in the database, such as tablespaces, extents, and segments. In addition, there are dictionary views for the database objects that offer information about space utilization settings. The names of dictionary views are usually taken from the objects represented by the data in the dictionary view, preceded by classification on the scope of the data. Each segment has its own data dictionary view that displays the storage information. Assuming that the DBA wants to know the storage parameters set for all objects on the database, the DBA may use the following views to determine storage information for the segment types already discussed:

- **DBA_SEGMENTS** This summary view contains all types of segments listed by the data dictionary views and their storage parameters.
- **DBA_TABLESPACES** You can use this view to see the default storage settings for the tablespaces in the database.
- **DBA_TS_QUOTAS** You can use this view to identify the tablespace quotas assigned for users to create objects in their default and temporary tablespaces.

- **V$TABLESPACE** This gives a simple listing of the tablespace number and name.
- **DBA_EXTENTS** You use this view to see the segment name, type, owner, name of tablespace storing the extent, ID for the extent, file ID storing the extent, starting block ID of the extent, total bytes, and blocks of the extent.
- **DBA_FREE_SPACE** This view identifies the location and amount of free space, by tablespace name, file ID, starting block ID, bytes, and blocks.
- **DBA_FREE_SPACE_COALESCED** This view identifies the location of free space in a tablespace that has been coalesced, by tablespace name, total extents, extents coalesced, percent of extents that are coalesced, as well as other information about the space in the tablespace that SMON has coalesced.

TIP
Coalescing is the act of putting small chunks of free space in a tablespace into larger chunks of free space. The SMON process takes care of coalescing the tablespace on a regular basis. If you want to take care of coalescing the tablespace yourself, issue the `alter tablespace tblspc coalesce` *command.*

Exercises

1. Which dictionary view will tell the DBA the default settings for database objects in a tablespace? Which dictionary view tells the DBA the quotas for space on tablespaces each user has?
2. What views might be used to see how much space is free in a tablespace, and further, how much of that space has been coalesced?
3. How do you manually coalesce free space?

Locating Segments with Consideration for Fragmentation and Lifespan

As a wrap-up for this section, let's review the fragmentation potential for the different segments (and thus tablespaces) you may store in your database. This will help you understand why it is so important to store these different types of segments in different tablespaces. First, consider the following question: What makes fragmentation happen? A tablespace gets fragmented when objects stored in the tablespace are truncated or dropped and then recreated (or for rollback segments when extents the object has acquired are deallocated. The amount of time a segment or extent will stay allocated to a database object is known as its *lifespan*. The more frequently an extent is deallocated, the shorter the extent's lifespan. The shorter the lifespan, the more fragmented your tablespace can become. The SMON background process continuously looks for smaller fragments of free space left over by truncate or drop operations, and pieces or coalesces them together to create larger chunks of free space.

Now, consider the potential for tablespace fragmentation on different tablespaces. The SYSTEM tablespace houses the system rollback segment and the data dictionary. Oracle manages its SYSTEM tablespace effectively, and extents have a long lifespan, so you are likely to see very little or no fragmentation in this tablespace. Your TOOLS tablespace will likely have little fragmentation, either, because you won't (and shouldn't) typically go into your TOOLS tablespace and manage things yourself—your best bet is to let the administrative tool manage the repository itself. Again, extents have a long lifespan.

The next two tablespaces to consider are DATA and INDEX. The amount of fragmentation that may happen with these tablespaces will depend completely on how often you truncate or drop tables. In your production system, you may never, or hardly ever, do this, so extents will have a long lifespan, and fragmentation may be low. In development, however, you may do this all the time, potentially making extent lifespan very short and fragmentation in the tablespace very high. You are your own best judge for interpreting fragmentation for these tablespaces, based on how long or short the extent lifespan is in those systems.

The other two types of tablespaces, ROLLBACK for rollback segments and TEMPORARY for temporary segments (you can have more than one tablespace for sorting and temporary segments), will experience high to very high fragmentation. This is true in the ROLLBACK tablespace because rollback segments have potentially a very short lifespan, and Oracle can allocate and deallocate extents as necessitated by long-running transactions. In the next chapter, you will learn more about rollback segment extent allocation and deallocation. Finally, the lifespan of segments and extents in the TEMPORARY tablespace is incredibly short. Temporary segments are used to handle sort operations (a sort might be caused by issuing a `select … order by` statement) that manipulate too much data to be stored in memory. Oracle automatically allocates the space when needed. Once the sort operation is finished, Oracle again automatically deallocates the space. Thus, by definition of usage and lifespan, the TEMPORARY tablespace will have the highest amount of fragmentation of any tablespace on your database.

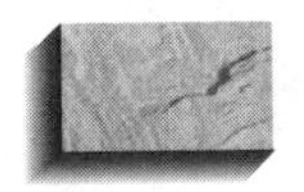

TIP
Extent lifespan and tablespace fragmentation are inversely proportional—the shorter the lifespan, the higher the potential for tablespace fragmentation.

Exercises

1. What is meant by the lifespan of an object's extent? How does this affect tablespace fragmentation?
2. Name several different types of tablespaces, and the expected lifespan of extents in each type of tablespace.

Chapter Summary

This chapter covered a great deal of information on Oracle database administration. The topics covered were the data dictionary views and standard packages in Oracle, maintaining the control file, maintaining redo log files, managing tablespaces and datafiles, and storage structures and relationships. These areas consist of 16 percent of material tested on OCP Exam 2 and are important for understanding both how the Oracle database works and how you can manage it.

The first section of the chapter covered the creation of the Oracle data dictionary and standard packages. The `catalog.sql` query and its cousin, `cat8000.sql`, are both used to create the Oracle data dictionary. The procedure for running these scripts involves logging into Oracle administratively via Server Manager and `connect internal`. Dictionary views can be used after you create them with the `create tablespace` command. They are stored along with the system rollback segment in the SYSTEM tablespace. The `catproc.sql` script is used to create the standard Oracle-supplied PL/SQL packages, including STANDARD, UTL_FILE, and DBMS_SQL. This script is processed in the same way as `catalog.sql`. Access is granted to the Oracle-supplied packages through the `execute` privilege, as in `grant execute on` *`pkg_name`* `to` *`user`*.

The second section of the chapter covered Oracle disk utilization and structures. The first topic was the management of control files. Control files store the physical file layout of the Oracle database so that when the instance starts it is able to find all the other files it needs for normal database operation. The control files' contents cannot be viewed as a text file because they are stored in binary. However, you can view a script that creates your existing control file by issuing `alter database backup controlfile to trace`. A script for creating your existing control file will then be created in the directory specified by the USER_DUMP_DEST `init`*`sid`*`.ora` parameter file. This script will display the other disk resources that exist on your system, in the syntax of the create controlfile statement in Oracle. You can find information about your control file, such as the names of the control files for the Oracle database on your host machine, from the V$CONTROLFILE or V$PARAMETER dictionary view. Oracle8 control files are considerably larger than their Oracle7 counterparts, and the Oracle8 control file is divided into many sections. More information about the sections can be found in the V$CONTROLFILE_RECORD_ SECTIONS dictionary view. Finally, to avoid dependency on any single disk resource on the host machine for housing your only copy of the control file, you can multiplex control files using the CONTROL_FILES `initsid.ora` parameter.

The next disk resource covered in this chapter was redo log files. Oracle tracks changes to the database with online redo logs. There are several components to the online redo logs. They are broken into groups, each of which may have one or many members. Redo entries produced by user processes making data changes are first written to the redo log buffer, and then written from buffer to the online redo log files by LGWR. You must have a minimum of two online redo log groups in the Oracle database, and you should multiplex redo logs, or put each redo log member in a group on separate disks to avoid the failure of one disk causing the failure of an entire Oracle instance. When LGWR finishes filling one online redo log, it starts writing to another. If you set up Oracle to archive redo logs, the recently filled redo log is then automatically archived, and LGWR will not write to that online redo log again until the archiving is complete. Archiving may have an impact on performance, as well. Checkpoints were also discussed in this section, and how LGWR tells DBWR to write dirty buffers from buffer cache to disk when a checkpoint occurs. Checkpoints occur at the time a log switches, and you can set checkpoints to occur more frequently with the initialization parameters LOG_CHECKPOINT_TIMEOUT and LOG_CHECKPOINT_INTERVAL in `initsid.ora`. Finally, some elementary troubleshooting guidelines for online redo logs were covered.

The next set of disk structures covered was tablespaces and datafiles. All Oracle data is stored in datafiles. One or many datafiles will make up a tablespace, such as the SYSTEM tablespace, used to hold the data dictionary and the initial rollback segment of the database. Database objects in Oracle are composed of segments and extents, which, in turn, are composed of data blocks, and the relationships between tablespaces, datafiles, segments, extents, and blocks were discussed. The use of the `create tablespace` statement to create tablespaces was also covered, and how to add space to a tablespace both by resizing existing datafiles and adding new ones. Tablespaces are either online (available for use) or offline (not available for use), and this section explained how to change the availability of the tablespace. This section also showed you the creation of storage parameters in tablespaces that can be used when objects are placed in those tablespaces and the object creation statements themselves don't have their own default storage parameters. The `alter database rename file` statement can be used for relocating any database file, including datafiles comprising your tablespace. In addition, because there are several different types of segments on the database corresponding to various types of database objects, each with unique (and sometimes conflicting) storage needs, it is usually best for them to be in separate tablespaces. The tablespaces you might need to create for your system include a DATA tablespace, an INDEX tablespace, a ROLLBACK tablespace, and a TEMPORARY tablespace, for each of these respective segments.

Finally, storage allocation in Oracle was covered. Database objects, as mentioned, are stored in segments, contiguous collections of data blocks in tablespaces. Several different types of segments exist in Oracle, such as table segments, index segments, rollback segments, temporary segments, cluster segments, and IOT segments. When the object contained by any of these segments fills its segment to capacity with data, an extent must be allocated to store the overflow. Each additional extent allocated to your object incurs additional performance overhead, so it is best to have as much of the data in your table in one segment as possible. It is important to balance that need with concern for the detrimental performance experienced when too much space is allocated and unused by database objects. Oracle also allows you to manage how space in each block is utilized with the `pctfree` and `pctused` storage options. You can get information on the configuration of your storage structures from the data dictionary, in the DBA_SEGMENTS, DBA_TABLESPACES, DBA_TS_QUOTAS, V$TABLESPACE, DBA_EXTENTS, DBA_FREE_SPACE, and DBA_FREE_SPACE_COALESCED views. The SMON process coalesces fragments of free space in your tablespaces into contiguous blocks at all times while Oracle is running. Keep in mind the inverse relationship between the lifespan of object extents and the fragmentation of the tablespace housing them.

Two-Minute Drill

- The `catalog.sql` script creates the data dictionary. Run it after creating a database, while connected to Oracle administratively through Server Manager.
- The `catproc.sql` script creates the Oracle-supplied packages used often in PL/SQL development. Run it after creating a database, while connected to Oracle administratively through Server Manager.
- Understand all Oracle physical disk resources, and they are control files, redo logs, and datafiles.
- Some logical disk resources map to Oracle physical disk resources, and they are tablespaces, segments, extents, and blocks.
- Control files are used to tell the Oracle instance where to find the other files it needs for normal operation.

- The contents of a control file can be found in the script to create it, which Oracle generates with an `alter database backup controlfile to trace`. This file is then found in the directory specified by the USER_DUMP_DEST initialization parameter.
- You will find information about control files, such as where they are located on your host machine, in V$CONTROLFILE, V$CONTROLFILE_RECORD_SECTION, and V$DATABASE.
- It is important to multiplex control files in order to reduce dependency on any single disk resource in the host machine. This is done using the CONTROL_FILES parameter in `init`*`sid`*`.ora`.
- The Oracle redo log architecture consists of the following components: redo log buffer to store redo entries from user processes, LGWR to move redo entries from memory onto disk, and online redo logs on disk to store redo entries taken out of memory.
- Online redo logs are referred to as groups. The group has one or more files, called members, where LGWR writes the redo log entries from memory. There must be at least two online redo log groups for the Oracle instance to start.
- Checkpoints are events in which LGWR tells DBWR to write all changed blocks to disk. They occur during log switches, which are when LGWR stops writing a full log and starts writing a new one. At this point, LGWR will also write the redo log file sequence change to datafile headers and to the control file.
- Understand the process LGWR uses to write redo data from one log to another and then back again, what happens when archiving is used, what the role of the ARCH process is, and how LGWR can contend with ARCH.
- Understand how to multiplex redo logs using both the `create database` and `alter database` statements, and why it is important to do so.
- Understand how tablespaces and datafiles relate to one another. A tablespace can have many datafiles, but each datafile can associate with only one tablespace.
- At database creation, there is one tablespace—SYSTEM. The DBA should *not* place all database objects into that tablespace, because often their storage needs conflict with each other. Instead, the DBA should create multiple tablespaces for the different segments available on the database and place those objects into those tablespaces.

- The different types of segments (and tablespaces you need) are: *table*, *index*, *rollback*, and *temporary*. Two other segment types, *cluster* and *IOT*, will not be used frequently, and thus can probably be placed into your data tablespace without interfering with the other objects.
- A final tablespace you should create to separate your application data from objects created in support of your Oracle database administrative tools, such as Oracle Enterprise Manager, is the TOOLS tablespace.
- When a segment containing a database object cannot store any more data for that table, Oracle will obtain an extent to store the data. This adversely affects performance. Understand the discussion of how to weigh segment preallocation against allowing Oracle to acquire new extents.
- Understand how Oracle allows the DBA to control space usage at the block level with `pctfree` and `pctused`.
- Know what dictionary views are used to find information about storage structures, including DBA_SEGMENTS, DBA_TABLESPACES, DBA_TS_QUOTAS, V$TABLESPACE, DBA_EXTENTS, DBA_FREE_SPACE, and DBA_FREE_SPACE_COALESCED.
- Understand the inverse proportional relationship between the lifespan of extents and fragmentation in the tablespace—the shorter the lifespan, the higher potential for fragmentation in the tablespace.

Chapter Questions

1. **The keyword that prevents you from creating a table in a tablespace marked for use when you run `select…order by` statements on millions of rows of output is which of the following choices?**

   A. `lifespan`

   B. `permanent`

   C. `online`

   D. `offline`

   E. `temporary`

   F. `read only`

2. When no storage options are specified in a `create table` command, what does Oracle use in order to configure the object's storage allocation?

A. The default options specified for the user in the tablespace

B. The options specified for the table in the tablespace

C. The default options specified for the user in the database

D. The default options specified for the table in the database

3. A high `pctused` has which of the following effects?

A. Increases performance costs by forcing Oracle to place the block on freelists frequently

B. Increases performance costs by forcing Oracle to place the block on freelists rarely

C. Decreases performance costs by forcing Oracle to place the block on freelists frequently

D. Decreases performance costs by forcing Oracle to place the block on freelists rarely

4. To control the allocation of additional extents for a table or index, which of the following choices is most appropriate?

A. Make the next extent be allocated as high as possible

B. Specify a high `pctused`

C. Specify a low `pctfree`

D. Make the initial segment allocated be large enough to accommodate all data plus growth

5. Flushing dirty buffers out of the buffer cache is influenced to the greatest extent by which of the following processes?

A. LGWR

B. SMON

C. ARCH

D. SERVER

6. **To decrease the number of checkpoints that occur on the database:**

   A. Set LOG_CHECKPOINT_INTERVAL to half the size of the online redo log.

   B. Set LOG_CHECKPOINT_INTERVAL to twice the size of the online redo log.

   C. Set LOG_CHECKPOINT_TIMEOUT to the number of bytes in the online redo log.

   D. Set LOG_CHECKPOINT_TIMEOUT to half the number of bytes in the online redo log.

7. **The following strategies are recommended when customizing the redo log configuration:**

   A. Store redo log members on the same disk to reduce I/O contention.

   B. Run LGWR only at night.

   C. Store redo log members on different disks to reduce I/O contention.

   D. Run DBWR only at night.

8. **By allowing user processes to write redo log entries to the redo log buffer, how does Oracle affect I/O contention for disks that contain redo log entries?**

   A. It increases I/O contention because user processes have to wait for disk writes

   B. It decreases I/O contention because user processes have to wait for disk writes

   C. It increases I/O contention because user processes do not have to wait for disk writes

   D. It decreases I/O contention because user processes do not have to wait for disk writes

9. **At which point during database execution is the data change from an `update` statement actually made in the datafile?**

   A. Parse step

   B. Execution step

   C. Commit step

   D. Checkpoint step

10. Which of the following choices identifies a database component that will be used for multiplexing control files?

A. `init`*`sid`*`.ora`

B. V$CONTROLFILE

C. V$DATABASE

D. DBA_DATAFILES

11. By default, checkpoints happen at least as often as

A. Redo log switches

B. `update` statements are issued against the database

C. The SYSTEM tablespace is accessed

D. SMON coalesces free space in a tablespace

12. To determine the space allocated for temporary segments, the DBA can access which of the following views?

A. DBA_TABLESPACES

B. DBA_TABLES

C. DBA_SEGMENTS

D. DBA_FREE_SPACE

13. If a redo log member becomes unavailable on the database,

A. The instance will fail.

B. The instance will continue to run, but media recovery is needed.

C. The database will continue to remain open, but instance recovery is needed.

D. The system will continue to function as normal.

14. Which of the following choices will decrease segment lifespan in the Oracle tablespace? (Choose two)

A. Frequent `truncate table` operations

B. Frequent `insert` operations

C. Frequent `drop table` operations

D. Frequent `alter table` operations

Answers to Chapter Questions

1. E. `temporary`

Explanation Oracle enforces the intended use of a temporary tablespace through the use of the `temporary` keyword. There is no `lifespan` keyword, although the concept of a lifespan is very important in understanding tablespace fragmentation, eliminating choice A. Choices C, D, and F are incorrect because the tablespace availability status is not the factor that is being tested in this situation. Finally, although there is a difference between permanent and temporary tables, `permanent` is not an actual keyword used anywhere in the definition of your tablespace.

2. B. The default options specified for the table in the tablespace

Explanation All default storage parameters for table objects are specified as part of the tablespace creation statement. A default tablespace can be named for a user on username creation, along with a maximum amount of storage in a tablespace for all objects created by the user. However, there are no default storage parameters on a table-by-table basis either in the database or for a user. Refer to the discussion of tablespace creation.

3. A. Increases performance costs by forcing Oracle to place the block on freelists frequently

Explanation A high value for `pctused` means that Oracle must keep a high percentage of each block used at any given time. Choice B is incorrect because the block will make its way to the freelist frequently, not rarely, if rows are frequently removed from the block. Choices C and D are incorrect because performance costs are increased by high `pctused`, not lowered. Refer to the discussion of space usage in the Oracle database.

4. D. Make the initial segment allocated be large enough to accommodate all data plus growth

Explanation In order to reduce the number of extents allocated to an object, the DBA should attempt to make all the data fit into the initial segment. The `pctfree` and `pctused` options may make more data fit into the initial segment. But the cost of cramming too much data into one block could be felt in terms of performance if the rows in your block start to chain or if Oracle has to migrate them due to `update` activity, making B and C wrong choices.

5. A. LGWR

Explanation At a checkpoint, LGWR signals DBWR to write changed blocks stored in the dirty buffer write queue to their respective datafiles. Choice B is incorrect because SMON handles instance recovery at instance startup and periodically coalesces free space in tablespaces. Choice C is incorrect because ARCH handles automatic archiving at log switches, and even though checkpoints happen at log switches, the overall process is not driven by ARCH. Choice D is incorrect because the server process retrieves data from disk in support of user processes.

6. B. Set LOG_CHECKPOINT_INTERVAL to twice the size of the online redo log.

Explanation The other three choices are incorrect because each of them actually increases the number of checkpoints that will be performed by Oracle. In addition, choices C and D indicate that values set for LOG_CHECKPOINT_TIMEOUT depend on the size of the redo log in bytes, which is not true. LOG_CHECKPOINT_TIMEOUT is a numeric value that determines the timed intervals for checkpoints. Refer to the discussion on checkpoints.

7. C. Store redo log members on different disks to reduce I/O contention.

Explanation Choice A is incorrect because storing all redo log members on the same disk increases I/O contention when log switches occur. Choices B and D are incorrect because DBWR and LGWR should be running at all times on the database. Refer to the discussion on redo logs.

8. D. It decreases I/O contention because user processes do not have to wait for disk writes

Explanation Allowing users to write redo entries to the redo memory buffer while LGWR handles the transfer of those entries to disk does reduce I/O dependency for user processes. This means that choice D is correct. Choices B and C are paradoxical statements—how can increased wait times lead to better throughput, or vice versa? Choice A is the logical opposite of choice D, meaning that choice A is the wrong answer.

9. D. Checkpoint step

Explanation This is one of the most difficult questions in the section. At the parse step, Oracle simply develops an execution plan for the query. At the execution step, Oracle makes the change to the row in a data block *that is stored in the buffer cache*. That block is then transferred to the dirty buffer write queue. At the time the transaction is committed, an entry is simply made to the redo log that relates to the system change number (SCN) for the transaction stating that this transaction is committed. An SCN is a unique identifier for every transaction that takes place in the database. Only when the checkpoint occurs and the dirty buffer write queue is flushed is the change to the data block written to disk.

10. A. `initsid.ora`

Explanation Choice A is the `initsid.ora` file, which contains the CONTROL_FILES parameter. This parameter is where you would define whether you wanted to use multiple copies of the control file, and where Oracle should look for them. All other choices are incorrect. They refer to places where you can look for data about your control file, but remember this—the data dictionary can only inform you of the database configuration, never modify it.

11. A. Redo log switches

Explanation Choice A is the only choice that relates to checkpoints. Refer to the discussion of checkpoints. Working with the SYSTEM tablespace and SMON's coalescing behavior have nothing whatsoever with the behavior of checkpoints. You might be able to make a small case for `update` statements, but even then you have little indication of whether the data change is frequent, infrequent, heavy, or light, and these are the things you'd need to know in order to determine checkpoint intervals. And, `update` activity still won't determine checkpoints if you are using LOG_CHECKPOINT_TIMEOUT.

12. C. DBA_SEGMENTS

Explanation Choices A and D are incorrect because they are not actual views in the data dictionary. Choice B is incorrect because DBA_TABLES only lists information about the tables in the database, not the temporary segments created as part of a sort operation. Refer to the discussion of viewing storage information in Oracle.

13. A. The instance will fail.

Explanation If a disk becomes unavailable that contains all redo log members for the redo log currently being written, the instance will fail. All other choices are incorrect because they depend on the instance being fully available, which is not the case in this situation. Refer to the discussion of redo log components.

14. A and C. Frequent `truncate table` operations *and* frequent `drop table` operations

Explanation Segment lifespan is defined as the length of time the segment will exist in a tablespace. By truncating or dropping a table, you decrease the lifespan of the segment because `truncate table` and `drop table` deallocate segments and return them to the pool of free space in the tablespace for Oracle to use.

CHAPTER 8

Managing Database Objects I

n this chapter, you will learn about and demonstrate knowledge in the following areas:

- Managing rollback segments
- Managing temporary segments
- Managing tables

As a DBA, part of your daily job function is to create database objects. This is especially true for database administrators who manage development and test databases. But even DBAs working on production systems will find that a good deal of their time is spent exploring the depths of setting up database objects. In this chapter, you will cover what you need to know for creating tables, rollback segments, and temporary segments. Chapter 9 will cover related material on creating indexes, integrity constraints, clusters, and index-organized tables (IOTs), finishing the overall discussion of managing database objects for OCP Exam 2. The types of database objects covered in these chapters are found in most database environments. This chapter covers material that will comprise about 16 percent of OCP Exam 2.

Managing Rollback Segments

In this section, you will cover the following topics related to managing rollback segments:

- Planning the number and size of rollback segments
- Creating rollback segments with appropriate storage settings
- Maintaining rollback segments
- Obtaining rollback segment information from dictionary views
- Troubleshooting rollback segment problems

Often, the DBA spends part of any given day "fighting fires." Many times, these emergencies involve rollback segments. As discussed in Chapter 7, rollback segments store the old data value when a process is making changes to the data in a database. It stores data and block information, such as file and block ID, as it existed before being modified. This copy of data changes made to the database is used by other statements running in Oracle until the change is `committed`. The rollback segment stores the changes after the `commit`, as well, but Oracle will eventually and systematically overwrite the rollback data from committed transactions whenever it needs room in the rollback segment to store data for uncommitted transactions.

Rollback segments serve three purposes: providing transaction-level read consistency of data to all processes in the database; permitting transactions to roll back, or discard, changes that have been made, in favor of the original version; and allowing transaction recovery in case the instance fails while a user is making a data change. Rollback segments are probably the most useful database objects in data processing, but they can be troublesome for the DBA to maintain. You are well advised to master the management of these fussy objects. This section will cover how to plan and create your rollback segments, how to maintain them, where to go for information about them, and how to troubleshoot common problems with them.

Planning the Number and Size of Rollback Segments

Let's start with a quick refresher on the types of rollback segments. These objects can be broken into two categories: the system rollback segment and non-SYSTEM rollback segments. As you know, the system rollback segment is housed by the SYSTEM tablespace and handles transactions made on objects in the SYSTEM tablespace. The other type of rollback segments, non-SYSTEM rollback segments, handle transactions made on data in non-SYSTEM tablespaces in the Oracle database. These non-SYSTEM rollback segments are housed in a non-SYSTEM tablespace, such as the ROLLBACK tablespace you created in Chapter 7. In order for Oracle to start when the database has one or more non-SYSTEM tablespaces, there must be at least one non-SYSTEM rollback segment available for the instance to acquire outside the SYSTEM tablespace.

Non-SYSTEM rollback segments come in two flavors—private and public. A *private* rollback segment is one that is only acquired by an instance explicitly naming the rollback segment to be acquired at startup via the `ROLLBACK_SEGMENTS` parameter in `init`*`sid`*`.ora`, or via the `alter rollback segment` *`rollback_seg`* `online` statement issued manually by you, the DBA. *Public* rollback segments are used when Oracle Parallel Server is running, and they are acquired by Oracle automatically using a calculation of `TRANSACTIONS_ PER_ROLLBACK_SEGMENT` and `TRANSACTIONS` `init`*`sid`*`.ora` parameters, from a pool of rollback segments available on the database.

How Transactions Use Rollback Segments

Transactions occurring on the Oracle database need rollback segments to store their uncommitted data changes. Transactions are assigned to rollback segments in one of two ways. You can assign a transaction to a rollback segment explicitly with the `set transaction use rollback segment` *`rollback_seg`* statement. Or, if no rollback segment is explicitly defined for the transaction, Oracle assigns the transaction to the rollback segment that currently has the lightest transaction load in round-robin fashion. Thus, more than one transaction can use the same rollback segment, but each block in the rollback segment houses data from one and only one transaction.

Rollback segments are used as follows. A rollback segment usually has several extents allocated to it at any given time, and these extents are used sequentially. After the database is started, the first transaction will be assigned to the first rollback segment, and it will store its data changes in extent #1 of the rollback segment. As the transaction progresses (a long-running batch process with thousands of `update` statements, let's say), it places more and more data into rollback segment extent #1. An extent containing data from a transaction in progress is called an *active* extent. As more and more transactions start on the database, some of the other transactions may be assigned to this rollback segment. Each transaction will fill extent #1 with more and more change data until the transactions commit.

If extent #1 fills with data changes before the transactions `commit`, the transactions will begin filling extent #2 with data. Transactions with data changes "spilling over" to a new extent are said to be performing a *wrap*. A special marker called a rollback segment *head* moves from extent #1 to extent #2 to indicate the extent where new and existing transactions assigned to the rollback segment can write their next data change. As soon as the transaction `commits` its data changes, the space in extent #1 used to store its data changes is no longer required. If extent #1 is filled with data change information from only committed transactions, then extent #1 is considered *inactive*. Figure 8-1 displays the rollback segment behavior as described here.

To effectively use rollback segment space, the rollback segment allocates only a few extents, which are reused often. The ideal operation of a rollback segment with five extents is as follows: Transactions assigned to the rollback segment should fill extent #5 a little after transactions with data changes in extent #1 commit. Thus, extent #1 becomes inactive just before transactions in extent #5 need to wrap into it. However, this behavior is not always possible. If a transaction goes on for a long time without committing data changes, it may eventually fill all extents in the rollback segment. When this happens, the rollback segment acquires extent #6, and wraps data changes from the current transaction into it. The rollback segment head moves into extent #6, as well. Figure 8-2 illustrates how Oracle obtains or allocates more extents for a rollback segment.

If a transaction causes the rollback segment to allocate many extents for storing the long transaction's data changes—as determined by the `maxextents` storage option defined when the rollback segment is created—the rollback segment becomes enormously stretched out of shape. Oracle has an `optimal` option available in rollback segment storage that permits rollback segments to deallocate

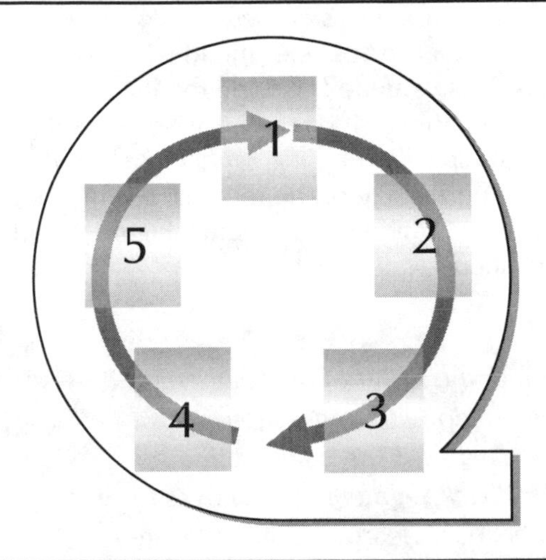

FIGURE 8-1. *A rollback segment containing five reusable extents*

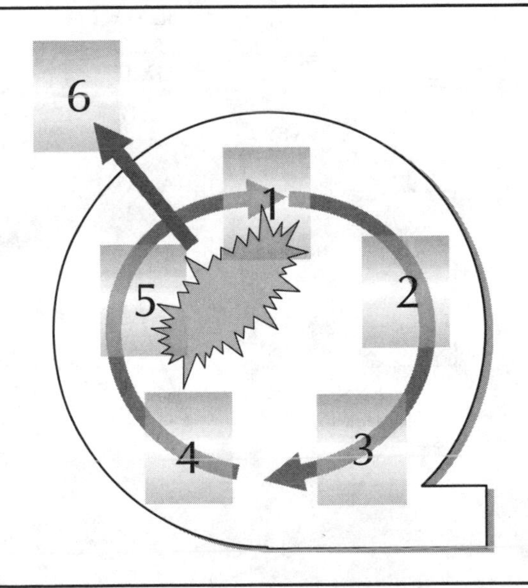

FIGURE 8-2. *How a rollback segment acquires more extents*

extents after long-running transactions cause them to acquire more extents than they really need. The `optimal` clause specifies the ideal size of the rollback segment in kilobytes or megabytes. This value tells Oracle the ideal number of extents the rollback segment should maintain. If `optimal` is specified for a rollback segment, that object will deallocate space *when the rollback segment head moves from one extent to another,* if the current size of the rollback segment exceeds `optimal` and if there are contiguous adjoining inactive extents. Figure 8-3 illustrates rollback segment extent deallocation.

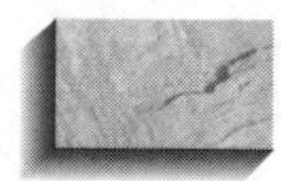

TIP
Extent deallocation as the result of `optimal` has nothing whatsoever to do with transactions committing on the database. The deallocation occurs when the rollback segment head moves from one extent to another. Oracle does not deallocate extents currently in use (even if the total size exceeds `optimal`), and always attempts to deallocate the oldest inactive extents first.

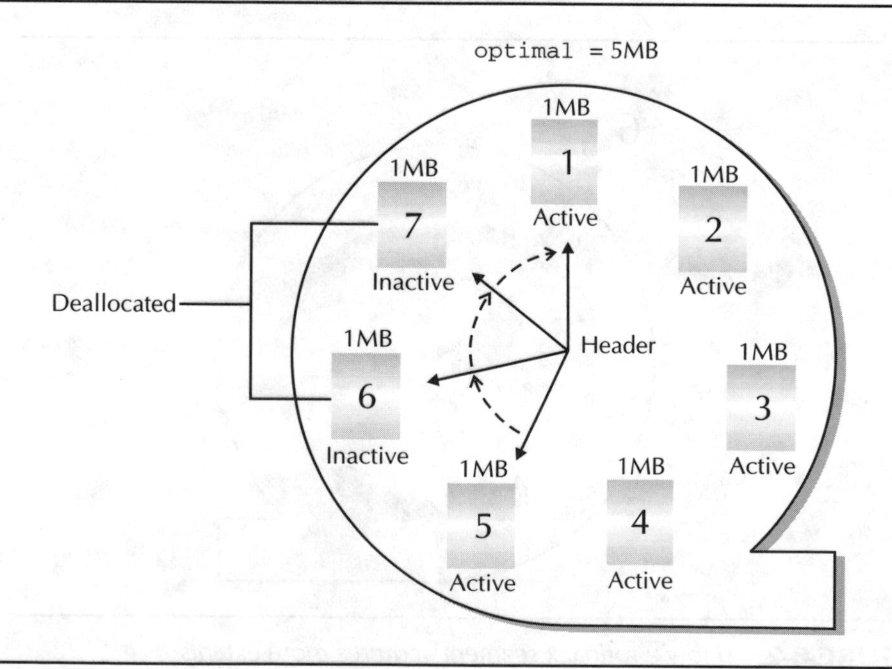

FIGURE 8-3. *Rollback segment extent deallocation*

The Rule of Four to Plan Rollback Segment Numbers for OLTP Systems

Oracle's recommended strategy for planning the appropriate number of rollback segments for most online transaction processing (OLTP) systems is here called the *Rule of Four,* for easy recollection. Take the total number of transactions that will hit the database at any given time, and divide by 4 to decide how many rollback segments to create. Consider this example. You have a database that will be used for a small user rollout of an OLTP application. About 25 concurrent transactions will happen on the database at any given time. By applying the Rule of Four, you determine that about 6 rollback segments are required. Shortly, you will see the additional calculation required for determining rollback segment size.

Two exceptions exist to the Rule of Four. The first is if the quotient is less than 4 + 4, round the result of the Rule of Four up to the nearest multiple of 4 and use that number of rollback segments. In this case, the result would be rounded from 6 to 8. The second exception to the Rule of Four is that Oracle generally doesn't recommend more than 50 rollback segments for a database. If the Rule of Four determines that more than 50 rollback segments are needed, the DBA should start by allocating 50 and spend time monitoring the rollback segment wait ratio to determine whether more should be added later.

Planning Rollback Segment Numbers for Batch System Processing

When planning the number of rollback segments required on the batch transaction processing system, you need to make a small number of large rollback segments available to support long-running processes that make several data changes. You should monitor the database to see how many transactions your batch processes execute concurrently and apply the Rule of Four to determine the number of rollback segments needed, just as you would with an OLTP application. The next topic demonstrates how to calculate the size for rollback segments supporting both OLTP and batch transactions.

Sizing OLTP and Batch Rollback Segments

There are two components to determining rollback segment size, and the first is the overall size of the rollback segment. The size of your rollback segments, in turn, depends on two main factors: the type of DML statement used to perform the data change and the volume of data being processed. Different DML statements that change data require different amounts of data storage; in the order from least amount of data change information stored in a rollback segment to greatest is `insert` (stores new ROWID in rollback segment only), `update` (stores ROWID plus old column values), and `delete` (stores ROWID and all row/column data). Incidentally, data change information stored in a rollback segment is called *undo*.

So, if your transactions primarily `insert` data, your rollback segments would be smaller than if your transactions primarily `delete` data.

The second component involved in rollback segment size is the number of extents that will comprise the rollback segment. Bigger is often better in determining the number of extents to have in your rollback segment. By using more extents in the initial rollback segment allocation—determined by the `minextents` storage option—you reduce the probability of your rollback segment extending. Oracle recommends 20 (or more) extents as part of the initial rollback segment allocation.

Exercises

1. What happens to database performance if Oracle has to allocate extents to its rollback segments frequently without giving them up? What storage option can be used to minimize this occurrence?
2. How are `minextents` and `maxextents` used in sizing rollback segments? What is the Rule of Four? What is the Rule of Batch? Why is it important to use many extents in your rollback segment?
3. How are extents of a rollback segment deallocated?

Creating Rollback Segments with Appropriate Storage Settings

Rollback segments are created with the `create rollback segment` statement. *All* extents in the rollback segments of an Oracle database should be the same size. Commit this fact to memory—it's on the OCP exam in one form or another. To partially enforce this recommendation, Oracle disallows the use of `pctincrease` in the `create rollback segment` statement. (The `pctincrease` option is available for other objects, such as tables, to increase the size of subsequent extents that may be allocated to the object in order to reduce the overall number of extents allocated.) Size for rollback segments and their included extents is determined by the options in the storage clause.

The following list of options is available for setting up rollback segments:

- **`initial`** The size, in K or MB, of the initial rollback segment extent.
- **`next`** The size, in K or MB, of the next rollback segment extent to be allocated. Ensure that all extents are the same size by specifying `next` equal to `initial`.

- **minextents** Minimum number of extents on the rollback segment. The value for `minextents` should be 2 or greater.
- **maxextents** Maximum number of extents the rollback segment can acquire. Be sure to set this to a number and not to `unlimited;` this will prevent runaway transactions from using all your available tablespace. This is especially important if your ROLLBACK tablespace has datafiles using the `autoextend` feature.
- **optimal** Optimally, the total size, in K or MB, of the rollback segment. Assuming `initial` equals `next`, the value for optimal cannot be less than `initial * minextents.`

The following code block demonstrates the creation of a non-SYSTEM private rollback segment in your database, according to the guidelines Oracle recommends. For OCP questions in this area, you should base your answers on the Oracle guidelines.

```
CREATE ROLLBACK SEGMENT rollseg01
TABLESPACE orgdbrbs
STORAGE ( INITIAL    10K
          NEXT       10K
          MINEXTENTS 20
          MAXEXTENTS 450
          OPTIMAL    300K );
```

In the code block, notice that the `public` keyword was not used. Rollback segments are private unless you create them with the `create public rollback segment` command. After creating your rollback segment, you must bring it online so it will be available for user transactions. This is accomplished with the `alter rollback segment` *rollback_seg* `online` command. The number of rollback segments that can be brought online can be limited at instance startup by setting the `MAX_ROLLBACK_SEGMENTS` `init`*sid*`.ora` parameter to 1 + the number of non-SYSTEM rollback segments you want available in Oracle.

TIP
*You can create rollback segments using the Storage Manager administrative utility in Oracle Enterprise Manager, as well as from within SQL*Plus or Server Manager.*

Bringing Rollback Segments Online at Instance Startup

Once you issue the `shutdown` command, any rollback segments you created, or brought online while the database was up, are now offline as well. They can only be brought back online in two ways. The first is if you issue the `alter rollback segment` *`rollback_seg`* `online` command again for every rollback segment you want online.

The other way is through a multistep process engaged by Oracle at instance startup. Oracle first acquires any rollback segments at instance startup named by you in the `ROLLBACK_SEGMENTS` `init`*`sid`*`.ora` parameter, specified as `ROLLBACK_SEGMENTS = (`*`rollseg01`*`,`*`rollseg02...`*`)`. Then, Oracle performs a calculation of the rollback segments required for the proper operation of the database, based on values set for the `TRANSACTIONS` and `TRANSACTIONS_PER_ROLLBACK_SEGMENT` and `init`*`sid`*`.ora` parameters. The calculation performed is `TRANSACTIONS / TRANSACTIONS_PER_ROLLBACK_SEGMENT`. Thus, if `TRANSACTIONS` is 146 and `TRANSACTIONS_PER_ROLLBACK_SEGMENT` is 18, then Oracle knows it needs to acquire 8 rollback segments. If 8 rollback segments were named, Oracle brings the private rollback segments online. If there weren't 8 rollback segments named, then Oracle attempts to acquire the difference from the pool of public rollback segments available. If there are enough public rollback segments available in the pool, Oracle acquires the difference, and brings all its acquired rollback segments online. Note, however, that the calculation step is required primarily for public rollback segments where Oracle Parallel Server is being used.

TIP
If too few public rollback segments are available for Oracle to acquire, the Oracle instance will start, and the database will open anyway, with no errors reported in trace files or the ALERT log.

Exercises

1. Identify the options available for the rollback segment storage clause, and describe their general use. How does Oracle attempt to enforce equal sizing of all extents in rollback segments?
2. How are rollback segments brought online after creation? At instance startup?

Maintaining Rollback Segments

Several statements are available in Oracle for maintaining rollback segments. The first is the `alter rollback segment` statement. You have already seen this statement used to bring the rollback segment online, as in `alter rollback segment` *`rollback_seg`* `online`. You can bring a rollback segment offline in this way also, with alter rollback segment *`rollback_seg`* `offline`. However, you can only bring a rollback segment offline if it contains no active extents supporting transactions with uncommitted data changes. This statement is used to change any option in the storage clause as well, except for the size of the `initial` extent. However, note that changing the next extent size will alter the size of the next extent the rollback segment acquires, not the size of any extent the rollback segment has already acquired, and furthermore doing this is not recommended for reasons already explained.

```
ALTER ROLLBACK SEGMENT rollseg01
STORAGE ( MAXEXTENTS 200
          OPTIMAL    310K );
```

The `alter rollback segment` statement has one additional clause for you to use, and that clause is `shrink to`. This clause allows you to manually reduce the storage allocation of your rollback segment to a size not less than that specified for `optimal` (if `optimal` is specified). As with `optimal`, Oracle will not reduce the size of the rollback segment if extents over the size specified are still active. If no value is specified, Oracle will attempt to shrink the rollback segment to the value specified for `optimal`. Finally, Oracle will ignore the `alter rollback segment` *`rollback_seg`* `shrink [to` *`x`*`[K|M]]` statement if the value specified for *x* is greater than the current rollback segment allocation. The following code block shows an appropriate use of the `shrink to` clause:

```
ALTER ROLLBACK SEGMENT rollseg01 SHRINK;
ALTER ROLLBACK SEGMENT rollseg01 SHRINK TO 220K;
```

Finally, once brought offline, a rollback segment can be dropped if you think it is no longer needed, or if you need to re-create it with different extent `initial`, `next`, and `minextents` size settings. The statement used for this purpose is `drop rollback segment` *`rollback_seg`*.

```
DROP ROLLBACK SEGMENT rollseg01;

CREATE ROLLBACK SEGMENT rollseg01
TABLESPACE orgdbrbs
STORAGE ( INITIAL    12K
          NEXT       12K
          MINEXTENTS 25
          MAXEXTENTS 400
          OPTIMAL    300K )
```

Exercises

1. Which storage option cannot be modified by the `alter rollback segment` statement? How might you manually make a rollback segment unavailable for transaction usage, and what might prevent you from doing so?
2. What is the `shrink to` clause of the `alter rollback segment` statement, and how is it used? When is it appropriate (or possible) to eliminate a rollback segment, and which statement is used to do it?

Obtaining Rollback Segment Information from Dictionary Views

There are several views available for obtaining information about your instance's use of rollback segments. The views displaying rollback segment information base their content either on rollback segments that exist in the database, or on dynamic performance information about rollback segments collected while the instance is running. The views you should remember for viewing rollback segment information include the following list:

- **DBA_ROLLBACK_SEGS** Gives information about the name, tablespace location, owner, and current status of every rollback segment in the Oracle database, regardless of whether the rollback segment is online or offline.
- **V$ROLLSTAT** Gives information about the size of the rollback segment currently used by the instance, its current number of extents, highwatermark, optimal size if one is specified, status, current extent and block location of rollback segment head, and number of active transactions using that rollback segment.
- **V$ROLLNAME** Gives the name of the rollback segment and its associated rollback segment number, corresponding to records from V$ROLLSTAT.
- **V$TRANSACTION** Gives the session address and use of rollback segments by transactions that are currently taking place. The information given includes the total number of blocks storing data changes for this transaction, and other information about specific extent, file, and block location where the transaction started writing data-change information.
- **V$SESSION** Gives the username, SID, and serial number for session address corresponding to session address in V$TRANSACTION.

Typically, all rollback segments will be owned by user SYS, but public rollback segments will be owned by user PUBLIC. The SYSTEM rollback segment will be stored in that tablespace, while other rollback segments should be stored in the tablespace you created to house them. The following code block demonstrates the use of DBA_ROLLBACK_SEGS to find information about rollback segments:

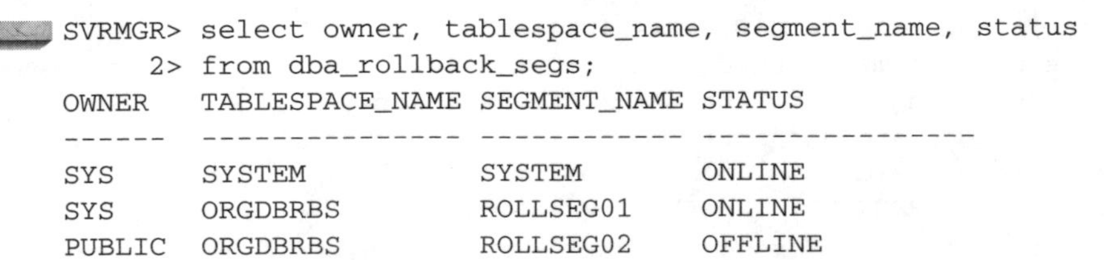

```
SVRMGR> select owner, tablespace_name, segment_name, status
     2> from dba_rollback_segs;
OWNER   TABLESPACE_NAME SEGMENT_NAME STATUS
------  --------------- ------------ ----------------
SYS     SYSTEM          SYSTEM       ONLINE
SYS     ORGDBRBS        ROLLSEG01    ONLINE
PUBLIC  ORGDBRBS        ROLLSEG02    OFFLINE
```

Other information about the rollback segments is offered from the V$ views, based on statistics collected by Oracle since the instance last started. You can find information about the extents a rollback segment has acquired, the number of transactions using that rollback segment from the XACTS column, and current size, optimal size, highwatermark size, and extended status information using the V$ROLLSTAT view. You may want to join this view with V$ROLLNAME to read output from V$ROLLSTAT corresponding to the names you gave to each rollback segment. The following code block demonstrates this:

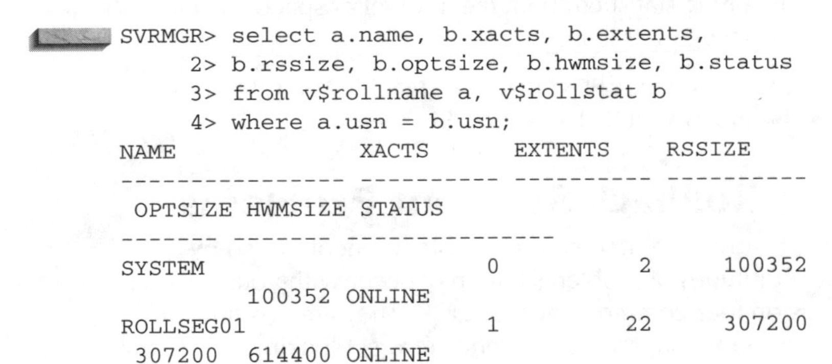

```
SVRMGR> select a.name, b.xacts, b.extents,
     2> b.rssize, b.optsize, b.hwmsize, b.status
     3> from v$rollname a, v$rollstat b
     4> where a.usn = b.usn;
NAME                 XACTS      EXTENTS    RSSIZE
---------------- ---------- ---------- ----------
 OPTSIZE HWMSIZE STATUS
------- ------- ---------------
SYSTEM                    0          2     100352
         100352 ONLINE
ROLLSEG01                 1         22     307200
 307200  614400 ONLINE
```

TIP
The same rollback segment showing status ONLINE in DBA_ROLLBACK_SEGS may show status PENDING OFFLINE in V$ROLLSTAT. This happens when you issue the `alter rollback segment offline` *statement against a rollback segment.*

Finally, you can find current transaction information about the amount of undo generated by transactions on the database from the USED_UBLK column in

V$TRANSACTION, as well as the rollback segments being used by those user transactions, with the following query:

```
SVRMGR> select a.username, a.sid, a.serial#,
     2> b.name as rbsname, c.used_ublk
     3> from v$session a, v$rollname b, v$transaction c
     4> where a.saddr = c.ses_addr
     5> and b.usn = c.xidusn;
USERNAME SID SERIAL# RBSNAME    USED_UBLK
-------- --- ------- ---------- ---------
SPANKY     4      34 ROLLSEG01         43
ATHENA     4      35 ROLLSEG01          2
```

Exercises

1. Identify the view containing statistics about rollback segment size generated since the time the instance last started. What column in that view contains the number of transactions currently using that rollback segment?
2. Identify the view containing statistics about the amount of space used in rollback segments by active transactions.
3. If a rollback segment shows status PENDING OFFLINE in V$ROLLSTAT, what will its status be in DBA_ROLLBACK_SEGS?

Troubleshooting Rollback Segment Problems

You may be called upon to resolve certain common problems encountered by rollback segments. Of the multitudes of problems that may occur with your rollback segments, you should focus on four common ones for OCP. They are: insufficient space for transaction undo information, read-consistency errors, blocking transactions, and problems taking tablespaces containing rollback segments offline.

Insufficient Space for Transactions

The first of these problems is insufficient space for the transaction undo information in the rollback segment. Some errors indicating insufficient space for the transaction's data change information include those shown in the following code block:

```
ORA-01562 - insufficient space in rollback segment
ORA-01560 - insufficient space in the tablespace
ORA-01628 - MAXEXTENTS has been reached
```

There are several possible solutions to the problem of insufficient space. If the problem is that there isn't enough space in the rollback segment, you can add more space by increasing the value set for `maxextents` or by dropping the rollback segment and creating new rollback segments with larger extents. If there isn't enough space in the tablespace, you can add more datafiles to the tablespace, `resize` datafiles to be larger, or turn on the `autoextend` option for datafiles in the tablespace.

Read Consistency Errors

Recall that rollback segments allow transaction-level read consistency for all statements running on the database. A long-running query in one session that starts before a change on that data is `committed` by another session will see the data as it existed pre-`commit`. If Oracle cannot provide a read-consistent view of data, the following error will ensue:

```
ORA-01555 - snapshot too old (rollback segment too small)
```

The solution to this problem is to re-create the rollback segments with a higher minimum number of extents, larger extents, or a higher `optimal` rollback segment size. You cannot simply increase `maxextents` to resolve this problem.

Blocking Sessions

Recall the principle of extent reuse in rollback segments. When a transaction fills the current extent, the transaction attempts to wrap its undo into the next extent. However, the next extent must be inactive, or the transaction will not be able to reuse the extent. Even if the extent after next is inactive, the rollback segment must allocate a new extent to preserve its sequential behavior in using extents. Sometimes, a session making a data change may inadvertently leave a transaction open, either through the application issuing a data change where one wasn't expected, or by the user making a data change and then forgetting to `commit` it. In any event, the rollback segment is forced to compensate by allocating too many extents because the one containing undo for that long-running transaction remains active. The following query will show blocking session/transaction information for all rollback segments:

```
SVRMGR> select a.username, a.sid, a.serial#,
    2> to_char(b.start_time,'MM/DD/YY HH24:MI:SS')
    3> as start_time, c.name
    4> from v$session a, v$transaction b, v$rollname c, v$rollstat d
    5> where a.saddr = b.ses_addr
    6> and b.xidusn = c.usn
    7> and c.usn = d.usn
    8> and ((d.curext = b.start_uext-1) or
    9> ((d.curext = d.extents-1) and b.start_uext=0))
USERNAME SID SERIAL# START_TIME        NAME
-------- --- ------- ----------------- ---------
ATHENA     4      35 10/30/99 22:30:33 ROLLSEG01
```

The resolution in this situation is DBA intervention. You can kill the session using the `alter system kill session` command, and the output from the query above will give you the SID and SERIAL# information you need to accomplish this task. Killing a session makes Oracle roll back its data change. Alternatively, you can have the user `commit` the change.

You Cannot Take a Tablespace Offline

Recall that you cannot take a rollback segment offline if it contains active transactions. The same restriction applies to tablespaces that contain those active rollback segments. You will receive the following error if you attempt to do so:

```
ORA-01546 - cannot take tablespace offline
```

To resolve the problem, follow these steps:

1. Find out which rollback segments are in that tablespace by issuing the DBA_ROLLBACK_SEGS query (shown in the previous lesson on dictionary views for rollback segments).
2. Determine the active transactions that are using the rollback segment(s) with the query on V$SESSION, V$TRANSACTION, and V$ROLLNAME (from the previous lesson). This query gives you the SID and SERIAL# information you need to kill the session.
3. Use `alter system kill session` to force Oracle to roll back the data changes and release the rollback segment. Finally, take the tablespace offline.

Exercises

1. Identify four problems you might encounter related to rollback segment use. Describe the situation around the problem of blocking transactions/sessions and how to resolve it.
2. What activity occurring as part of `alter system kill session` helps Oracle to release a rollback segment? From what view can you obtain this information?

Managing Temporary Segments

In this section, you will cover the following points on managing temporary segments:

- Distinguishing different types of temporary segments
- Allocating space for temporary segments in the database
- Obtaining temporary segment information from Oracle

Your Oracle database should offer users temporary space to support certain operations they might engage in. Typically, your users will need temporary disk space if they perform sort operations on enormous amounts of data that may be associated with `select` statements containing the `group by`, `order by`, `distinct`, or `union` clauses, or the `create index` statement. Where possible, Oracle will try to sort data for these statements in the sort area in memory for the session, the size of which is determined with the `SORT_AREA_SIZE` `init`*`sid`*`.ora` parameter. But, if the space needed for the sort exceeds `SORT_AREA_SIZE`, Oracle allocates temporary segments and does a disk sort.

Distinguishing Different Types of Temporary Segments

There are two types of temporary segments in Oracle, stored in the two types of tablespaces in Oracle, temporary tablespaces and permanent tablespaces. (The creation of both tablespace types was covered in Chapter 7. A permanent tablespace is one created using the `create tablespace` statement, while a temporary tablespace is created using the `create tablespace ... temporary` statement.) Permanent tablespaces can contain only permanent database objects, such as tables, indexes, and temporary segments, while a temporary tablespace can only contain temporary segments and sort segments, but not permanent database objects such as tables and indexes. The main difference between temporary and permanent tablespaces is that temporary tablespaces are designed to store temporary segments exclusively, while permanent tablespaces are designed to store every type of segment in Oracle.

Thus, you can place a temporary segment in a permanent tablespace, but you cannot put a permanent database object (a table, for example) in a temporary tablespace. You can switch a tablespace between being permanent and temporary, provided the permanent tablespace does not contain permanent database objects when you try to switch it to a temporary tablespace. The following code block illustrates this:

```
SVRMGR> create tablespace test01 datafile 'D:\ORANT\test01.dat'
     > size 1M default storage ( initial 10K
     > next 10K pctincrease 0
     > minextents 1 maxextents 5 ) temporary;
Tablespace created.
SVRMGR> create table dummy3 (dummy varchar2(10)) tablespace test01;
create table dummy3 (dummy varchar2(10)) tablespace test01;
ERROR at line 1:
ORA-02195: Attempt to create PERMANENT object in a TEMPORARY
tablespace
SVRMGR> alter tablespace test01 permanent;
Command completed successfully;
SVRMGR> create table dummy3 (dummy varchar2(10)) tablespace test01;
Table created.
SVRMGR> alter tablespace test01 temporary;
alter tablespace test01 temporary
ERROR at line 1:
ORA-01662: tablespace 'TEST01' is non-empty and cannot be made
temporary
```

Temporary Segments in Permanent Tablespaces

A user may be assigned to either a permanent or temporary tablespace for sorting. Users create temporary segments in a tablespace when a disk sort is required to support their use of `select` statements containing the `group by`, `order by`, `distinct`, or `union` clauses, or the `create index` statement, as mentioned earlier. Users can be assigned to either permanent or temporary tablespaces for creating temporary segments. If the user is assigned to a permanent tablespace for creating temporary segments, the temporary segment will be created at the time the disk sort is required. When the disk sort is complete, the SMON (system monitor) process drops the temporary segment automatically to free the space for other uses. Since this activity causes high fragmentation, the permanent tablespace used for storing temporary segments should be used for this purpose.

Temporary Segments in Temporary Tablespaces

Temporary space is managed differently in temporary tablespaces. Instead of allocating temporary segments on the fly, only to have them dropped later by SMON, the Oracle instance allocates one sort segment for the first statement requiring a disk sort. All subsequent users requiring disk sorts can share that segment. There is no limit to the number of extents that can be acquired by the sort segment, either. The sort segment is released at instance shutdown. Because less space is deallocated during normal database operation with temporary tablespaces, disk sorts are more efficient in temporary tablespaces than in their permanent counterparts. All space management for the sort segment in a temporary tablespace is handled in a new area of the SGA called the *sort extent pool*. A process needing space for disk sorts can allocate extents based on the information in this area.

Exercises

1. Identify four problems you might encounter related to rollback segment use. Describe the situation around the problem of blocking transactions/sessions, and how to resolve it.
2. What activity occurring as part of `alter system kill session` helps Oracle to release a rollback segment? From what view can you obtain this information?
3. Which area of the SGA is used to obtain information about storage allocation in the temporary tablespace?

Allocating Space for Temporary Segments in the Database

Temporary tablespaces offer improved performance for disk sorts and better multiuser space management. Like other tablespaces, the `default storage` clause governs how sort segments and extents are sized in this tablespace. There are some special rules you should use when defining values for these storage options. Since by the definition of a disk sort, the data written to disk will equal `SORT_AREA_SIZE`, your extents must be at least that large. Size your `initial` sort segment according to the formula *num* * `SORT_AREA_SIZE + DB_BLOCK_SIZE`, where *num* is a small number of your choice used as a multiplier of `SORT_AREA_SIZE`. This sizing formula allows for header block storage as well as multiple sort run data to be stored in each extent. Next, as with rollback segments, sort segments should acquire extents that are all the same size, so set `initial` equal to `next`. Also, `pctincrease` should be 0. Finally, the `maxextents` storage option is not used in temporary tablespaces.

You can create multiple temporary tablespaces to support different types of disk sorts required by your users. For example, you might have an extremely large temporary tablespace for long-running `select order by` statements in report batch processes, or for the creation of an index on a large table that is periodically reorganized. In addition, you might include a smaller temporary tablespace for disk sorts as the by-product of ad hoc queries run by users. Each of these temporary tablespaces can then be assigned to users based on their anticipated sort needs.

Exercises

1. How do you determine the appropriate size for extents in the temporary tablespace? Why is it important that this size be a multiple of SORT_AREA_SIZE?
2. What is the importance of creating multiple temporary tablespace for different sorting needs?

Obtaining Temporary Segment Information from Oracle

There are several data dictionary views available for obtaining information about temporary segments. The views in the dictionary displaying this information base their content either on temporary segments that exist in the database or on dynamic performance information about temporary segments collected while the instance is running. The views you should remember for viewing temporary segment information include the following:

- **DBA_SEGMENTS** Gives information about the name, tablespace location, and owner of both types of temporary segments in Oracle. Note that you will only see information on temporary segments in permanent tablespaces while those segments are allocated, but you will see information about temporary segments in temporary tablespaces for the life of the instance.
- **V$SORT_SEGMENT** Gives information about size of the temporary tablespaces, current number of extents allocated to sort segments, and sort segment highwatermark information.
- **V$SORT_USAGE** Gives information about sorts that are happening currently on the database. This view is often joined with V$SESSION, described earlier in the chapter.

You can obtain the name, segment type, and tablespace storing sort segments using the DBA_SEGMENTS view. Note that this segment will not exist until the first disk sort is executed after the instance starts. The following code block is an example:

```
SVRMGR> select owner, segment_name, segment_type, tablespace_name
     2> from dba_segments;
OWNER SEGMENT_NAME SEGMENT_TYPE TABLESPACE_NAME
----- ------------ ------------ ----------------
SYS   13.2         TEMPORARY    TEST01
```

You can get the size of sort segments allocated in temporary tablespaces by issuing queries against V$SORT_SEGMENT, which you will find useful in defining the sizes for your temporary tablespaces on an ongoing basis. The following query illustrates how to obtain this sort segment highwatermark information from V$SORT_SEGMENT:

```
SVRMGR> select tablespace_name, extent_size,
     2> total_extents, max_sort_blocks
     3> from v$sort_segment;
TABLESPACE_NAME EXTENT_SIZE TOTAL_EXTENTS MAX_SORT_SIZE
--------------- ----------- ------------- -------------
TEST01              3147776            14      44068864
```

Finally, you can see information about sorts currently taking place on the instance by joining data from the V$SESSION and V$SORT_USAGE views. The following code block displays an example:

```
SVRMGR> select a.username, b.tablespace,
     2> b.contents, b.extents, b.blocks
     3> from v$session a, v$sort_usage b
     4> where a.saddr = b.session_addr;
USERNAME TABLESPACE  CONTENTS  EXTENTS BLOCKS
-------- ----------- --------- ------- ------
SPANKY   TEST01      TEMPORARY      14  21518
```

Exercise

What views are available for obtaining information about temporary and sort segments?

Managing Tables

In this section, you will cover the following topics related to managing tables:

- Distinguishing Oracle datatypes
- Creating tables with appropriate storage settings
- Controlling space used by tables
- Analyzing tables to check integrity and migration
- Retrieving data dictionary information about tables
- Converting between different ROWID formats

There are four basic table types in Oracle8. They are regular tables, partitioned tables, cluster tables, and index-organized tables (IOTs). Further discussion of clusters and IOTs will be offered in Chapter 9. For now, focus on the two main Oracle8 table types—regular tables and partition tables. These are the main types of tables in Oracle. In keeping with E. F. Codd's original definition of relations, or tables (in his landmark work on relational database theory), Oracle does not guarantee that row data will be stored in a particular order. Partitioned tables give more control over data distribution for the purposes of scaling extremely large tables, such as those found in data warehouses. In a partitioned table, data is stored in each partition according to a partition key, or column, that defines which range of row data goes into which partition. Each partition can then be stored in different tablespaces. Several added benefits are seen with partitions, including increased data availability and the potential for parallel data-change operations operating on different partitions simultaneously.

Distinguishing Oracle Datatypes

The cornerstone of storage management is managing the data block. There are several different components to a data block, divided loosely into the following areas: block header and directory information, row data, and free space. Each block has a *block header* containing information about the block, including information about the table that owns the block and the row data the block contains. *Row data* consists of the actual rows of each data table. The *column data* is stored in the order in which the columns were defined for the table. A special *length* field is stored along with non-NULL column data as well. If a column value is NULL, no length field or column value is stored in the block for that row column, and thus no bytes are used for storage of NULL column values. The column length field is 1 byte if the column length is under 250 bytes, and it is 3 bytes if the column length is 250 bytes or more. In both cases, Oracle stores a number identifying the length of the non-NULL column value in the length field. Finally, Oracle leaves a certain amount of space free in the block for each row to expand via `update` statements issued on the row. Figure 8-4 illustrates block and row structure in Oracle8.

Oracle8 Scalar Datatypes

Oracle substantially reorganized the available datatypes between versions 7.3 and 8.0. There are two basic categories of datatypes in Oracle8, and they are *built-in types* and *user-defined types*. Within the built-in types, there are three basic classes of datatypes available, and they are *scalar*, *collection*, and *relationship* datatypes. Within the user-defined types, the classes of datatype you can define for your own

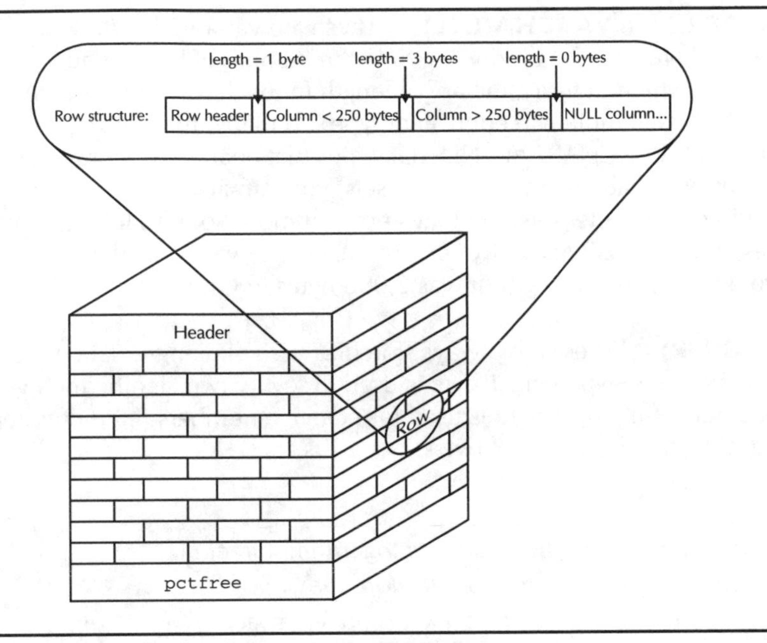

FIGURE 8-4. *Block and row structure in Oracle8*

application uses are endless. The following subtopics explain each of the Oracle8 datatypes in some detail.

CHAR(L), NCHAR(L) These are fixed-length text string datatypes, where the data is stored with blanks padded out to the full length specified in bytes for the column or variable (represented here by *L*). NCHAR is CHAR's NLS multibyte equivalent type. NLS stands for National Language Set, and it is used for making Oracle available in languages other than American English. Some world languages with large character sets (such as Japanese, Chinese, or Korean) or other substantial differences from English (such as being read from right to left, like Arabic or Hebrew), and thus need multiple bytes to store one character. English, on the other hand, requires only one byte to store a character, such as the letter A. Both NCHAR and CHAR columns or variables can be up to 2,000 bytes in length in Oracle8. In Oracle7, the limit was 255 bytes.

VARCHAR2(L), NVARCHAR2(L) These are variable-length text string datatypes, where data is stored using only the number of bytes required to store the actual value, which in turn can vary in length for each row. NVARCHAR2 is VARCHAR2's NLS multibyte equivalent type. (Actually, that's not quite correct: NCHAR and NVARCHAR2 are NLS datatypes that enable the storage of either fixed-width or variable-width character sets; you can also use them for non-multibyte character sets, but that's not common. So, for all intents and purposes, NVARCHAR2 is VARCHAR2's NLS multibyte equivalent type.) These can be up to 4,000 bytes in length (it was 2,000 bytes in Oracle7).

NUMBER(L,P) These are always stored as variable-length data, where 1 byte is used to store the exponent, 1 byte is used for every two significant digits of the number's mantissa, and 1 byte is used for negative numbers if the number of significant digits is less than 38 bytes.

TIP
A mantissa is the decimal part of a logarithm. Oracle uses the logarithm of a number to store the binary version of the number so that it takes up less space.

DATE This is stored as a fixed-length field of 7 bytes. The Oracle DATE format actually includes time as well as date.

RAW(L) This datatype holds small binary data. There are no conversions performed on raw data in Oracle, the raw data is simply stored "as is."

Comparing LONG, LONG RAW, and LOB Datatypes

There are several key differences between how Oracle7 handled large data objects and how Oracle8 handles them. For backward compatibility, Oracle8 offers both sets of datatypes, but encourages you to use the Oracle8 LOB datatypes. The large object datatypes available in Oracle8 are:

- **LONG** Stores up to 2GB of text data
- **LONG RAW** Stores up to 2GB of binary data
- **BLOB** Stores up to 4GB binary data
- **CLOB, NCLOB** Stores up to 4GB text data; NCLOB is a large fixed-width NLS datatype
- **BFILE** Stores up to 4GB unstructured data in operating system files

Several key differences between LONG and LOB types make LOB types more versatile and helpful for large object management. First, there can be only one LONG column in a table, because the LONG column data is stored inline. In contrast, there can be many LOB columns in a table, because when the LOB value is over 4,000 bytes, only a locator for the LOB type is stored inline with the table data—in other words, no LOB will ever require more than 4,000 bytes of space inline with other table data. Thus, `select` statements on LONG columns return the actual data, while the same statement on an LOB column returns only the locator. Oracle supports the use of the LOB types in object types except NCLOB, while LONG does not. LOBs can also be larger than LONGs—4GB for LOBs versus 2GB for LONGs. LOB data can also be accessed piecewise while LONG access is sequential; only the entire value in the LONG column can be obtained, while parts of the LOB can be obtained.

Oracle7 versus Oracle8 ROWIDs

Another area of significant difference between Oracle7 and Oracle8 is the way ROWID information is stored. An Oracle8 ROWID is a unique identifier for every row in the Oracle database. However, ROWIDs are not addresses in memory or on disk; rather, they are identifiers that can be computed to locate a table row, and this is the fastest way to find a row in a table. Though ROWID information can be queried like other columns in a table, a ROWID is not stored explicitly as a column value. In Oracle8, ROWID data needs 80 bits (10 bytes) for storage. Oracle8 ROWIDs consist of four components, an object number (32 bits), a relative file number (10 bits), a block number (22 bits), and a row number (16 bits). Oracle8 ROWIDs are displayed as 18-character representations of the location of data in the database, with each character represented in a base-64 format consisting of A–Z, a–z, 0–9, +, and /. The first 6 characters correspond to the data object number, the next 2 are the relative file number, the next 5 are the block number, and the last 3 are the row number. The following code block demonstrates ROWID format in Oracle8:

```
SVRMGR> select name, ROWID from employee;
NAME       ROWID
---------- ------------------
DURNAM     AAAA3kAAGAAAAGsAAA
BLANN      AAAA3kAAGAAAAGsAAB
```

Oracle7's ROWID format is now considered a "restricted" format because it does not store the object number. This format was acceptable in Oracle7 because the database required all datafiles to have a unique file number, regardless of the tablespace they belonged to. In contrast, Oracle8 numbers datafiles relative to the tablespace they belong to. Oracle7 ROWIDs require 6 bytes and are displayed as 18 characters in base-16 format, where the first 8 characters represent the block number, characters 10–13 are the row number, and characters 15–18 are the (absolute) file number. Characters 9 and 14 are static separator characters.

Restricted ROWID format is still used to locate rows in nonpartitioned indexes for nonpartitioned tables where all index entries refer to rows within the same segment, thus eliminating any uncertainty about relative file numbers, because a segment can be stored in one and only one tablespace.

TIP
You might think it silly, but here's how I remember the components of Oracle ROWIDs. In Oracle7, the components are block ID, row number, and file number, which shorten to the acronym "BRF." In Oracle8, the components are object ID, block ID, row number, and relative file number, which shorten to "OBRRF." To remember the acronyms, I imagine how little dogs sound when they bark.

Collection, Reference, and User-Defined Types

A collection is a gathering of like-defined elements. The two types of collection types available in Oracle8 are variable-length arrays with the VARRAY type and nested tables with the TABLE type.

A VARRAY can be thought of as an ordered list of objects, all of the same datatype. The VARRAY is defined to have two special attributes (in addition to those attributes within the objects the VARRAY contains). These attributes are a *count* for the number of elements in the VARRAY and the *limit* for the maximum number of elements that can appear in a VARRAY. Although the VARRAY can have any number of elements, the limit must be predefined. Each element in the VARRAY has an index, which is a number corresponding to the position of the element in the array. Constraints and default values may not be created for elements in a VARRAY, and once the VARRAY is created, the user only refers to an individual element in a VARRAY with PL/SQL (although SQL can be used to access the entire VARRAY).

The other collection type, the nested table, is a table within a table. The nested table architecture is exceptionally suited for applications that in Oracle7 have parent/child tables with referential integrity. A nested table is an unordered list of row records, each having the same structure. These rows are usually stored away from the table, with a reference pointer from the corresponding row in the parent table to the child table. Like VARRAYs, nested tables can have any number of elements, with the added bonus that you don't need to predetermine a maximum limit.

Finally, consider the reference type and user-defined types. Developers can use the reference type to define a foreign-key relationship between two objects. The reference type can reference all columns in the table for a particular row—it is a pointer to a particular object, not the object itself. User-defined types are abstract datatypes defined by you, that are composed either of scalar, collection, or other user-defined types.

Exercises

1. Identify two general categories of datatypes. Within one of the categories, there are three classes of datatypes. What are they?
2. Describe the four LOB types in Oracle8, and the two large object types held over from Oracle7. What are some differences between them?
3. Identify the changes in ROWID format from Oracle7 to Oracle8. Describe collection, reference, and user-defined types.

Creating Tables with Appropriate Storage Settings

Recall from Chapter 3 that you create tables with the `create table` statement. There, you learned about the restrictions around defining column names, their datatypes, and so on. What you didn't see was the other two-thirds of the equation. The rest of the story on table creation is defining integrity constraints and table storage allocation. The following code block revisits a `create table` statement from Chapter 3:

```
CREATE TABLE SPANKY.EMPLOYEE
(empid          NUMBER(10),
lastname        VARCHAR2(25),
firstname       VARCHAR2(25),
salary          NUMBER(10,4),
CONSTRAINT      pk_employee_01
PRIMARY KEY     (empid))
TABLESPACE orgdbdata
PCTFREE    20  PCTUSED    50
INITRANS   1   MAXTRANS   255
NOCACHE        LOGGING
STORAGE ( INITIAL 100K  NEXT  150K
MINEXTENTS 4  MAXEXTENTS  300
PCTINCREASE 20 );
```

Let's examine the areas of the `create table` statement marked in bold, starting with the username in the first line. Recall that in Oracle, every object is owned by the user who created it. This ownership creates a logical grouping, or schema, to which the object belongs. In this case, table EMPLOYEE is part of user SPANKY's schema. Skipping down to the `tablespace` clause, this keyword indicates which tablespace Oracle should create the table in. If you do not specify this clause, Oracle will put the table in the default tablespace you were assigned to when your user was created. (More discussion on default tablespaces and user creation is offered in Chapter 10.) The next two clauses are for space utilization.

`pctfree` specifies space that Oracle leaves free when inserting rows, to accommodate growth later via updates. The `pctused` option specifies a threshold percentage of a block that the actual contents of row data must fall below before Oracle will consider the block free for new row inserts.

The next two space utilization clauses, `initrans` and `maxtrans`, control Oracle's ability to make concurrent updates to a data block. The `initrans` option specifies the initial number of transactions that can update the rows in a data block concurrently, while `maxtrans` specifies the maximum number of transactions that can that can update the rows in a data block concurrently. For the most part, the default values for each of these options should not be changed. For `initrans`, the default for tables is 1, while for clustered tables the default is 2. For `maxtrans`, the default for tables is 255.

The `nocache` clause specifies that Oracle should not make these blocks persistent in the buffer cache if a `select` statement on the table results in a full table scan. In this case, `select * from EMPLOYEE` would have Oracle load blocks into the buffer cache so that those blocks will not persist for very long. If you wanted the table to stay cached in the buffer cache when `select * from EMPLOYEE` was issued, you would specify the `cache` keyword instead.

The next clause, `logging`, tells Oracle to track table creation in the redo log so that, in the event of disk failure, the table could be recovered. This is the default. If you didn't want the table to be recoverable, you would substitute the `nologging` keyword instead. Finally, you can specify `storage` clauses for table creation that will override the default storage settings of the tablespace you create the object in. The only tablespace default that your `storage` clause will not override is `minimum extent`.

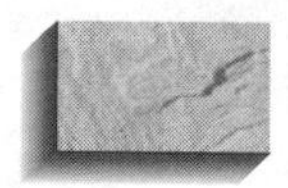

TIP
Schema Manager in Enterprise Manager is used for table creation. You can create a table either using menu options or with the Table Creation Wizard.

Observe the following rules of thumb when creating tables, and remember them for OCP Exam 2:

- Your tables should not go in the same tablespace as your rollback segments, temporary segments, index segments, or into the SYSTEM tablespace.
- In order to make sure there is as little fragmentation in the tablespace as possible, have a collection of standard extent sizes that are complementary for your tables, that are all multiples of 5 * `DB_BLOCK_SIZE` in size. For example, for small tables you might use 50 * `DB_BLOCK_SIZE`, and for large tables you might use 250 * `DB_BLOCK_SIZE`.

- To improve performance on full table scans like `select * from EMPLOYEE` relates to the `DB_FILE_MULTIBLOCK_READ_COUNT` `initsid.ora` parameter. This parameter specifies the number of blocks the server process will read when performing full table scans. Set it to the number of blocks in extents on your database for tables most likely to be accessed via `select` statements without where clauses (these are the statements that will likely result in full table scans), up to the maximum value permitted, which is operating system–specific.

- Recall that the `cache` statement will make blocks read into the buffer cache via full table scans persist for much longer than they otherwise would. If you have a small lookup table accessed frequently, you may want to keep it in memory by specifying the cache clause, or by issuing `alter table lookup_tblname cache`.

Specifying pctfree and pctused

Depending on the types of changes being made to data in a table, you may want to manage space inside each Oracle data block accordingly. The `pctfree` and `pctused` options are sized in tandem. When added together, they should not exceed or even be close to 100. Setting these options in different ways has different effects on the database. A high `pctfree` will keep a great deal of space free in the database for updates to increase the size of each row. However, this configuration also means that some space in each block will lie dormant until the data updates to the rows utilize the space. Setting the value of `pctfree` low will maximize the number of rows that can be stored in a block. But, if a block runs out of space to store row data when the row is updated, then Oracle will have to migrate the row data to another block. We'll look more at chaining and row migration later in this chapter. Oracle recommends using the formula ((*avg_row_size* – *init_row_size*) * 100) / *avg_row_size* to calculate `pctfree`, where the value for *avg_row_size* is obtained using the analyze command, described later in this section.

Settings for `pctused` create different effects on storage, too. A high value for `pctused` will ensure that whenever a few rows are removed from a data block, the block will be considered free and repopulated in a timely manner. However, this configuration degrades performance by requiring Oracle to keep track of blocks whose utilization falls below pctused, placing the block on a freelist, and then taking the block off the freelist after inserting relatively few records into the block. Although space is managed effectively, the database as a whole pays a price in performance. A low `pctused` changes this situation by putting blocks on freelists only when a lot of row data can be put into the block. However, even this situation has a trade-off, which is that if a lot of data is removed from the blocks, but enough to put utilization below `pctused`, that block will sit underused until enough rows are removed to place it on a freelist. Oracle recommends using the formula 100 – `pctfree` – ((*avg_row_size* * 100) / *avail_space*).

You may want to specify a high pctfree value and a low pctused for online transaction processing systems experiencing many update, insert, and delete commands. This approach is designed to make room in each block for increased row lengths as the result of frequent update commands. In contrast, consider a data warehouse where a smaller number of users execute long-running query statements against the database. In this situation, the DBA may want to ensure that space usage is maximized. A low pctfree and high pctused configuration may be entirely appropriate.

Row Migration and Chaining

If pctfree is too low for blocks in a table, update statements may increase the size of that row, only to find there is not enough room in the block to fit the change. Thus, Oracle has to move the row to another block in which it will fit. Row migration degrades performance when the server process attempts to locate the migrated row, only to find that the row is in another location.

Chaining is also detrimental to database performance. Chaining is when data for one row is stored in multiple blocks. This is a common side-effect in tables with columns defined to be datatype LONG, because the LONG column data is stored inline with the rest of the table. The server process must piece together one row of data using multiple disk reads. In addition, there is performance degradation by DBWR when it has to perform multiple disk writes for only one row of data.

Copying Existing Tables

There is one last situation in which you can create tables easily based on data from existing table definitions, using the create table as select statement. This statement will create the table with the same columns, datatype definitions, and NULL and NOT NULL column constraints that existed on the original table. You can specify your own storage clause for this object, or accept the defaults from the tablespace you create the new table in. Related database objects, such as table constraints or triggers, are not copied as part of the create table as select statement; if you want those objects, you must add them with alter table add constraint or create trigger later. Further uses for the alter table statement will be described in the next lesson. The following code block demonstrates use of the create table as select statement:

```
CREATE TABLE EMPLOYEE_A_to_N
AS SELECT *
FROM EMPLOYEE
WHERE upper(substr(last_name,1,1)) BETWEEN 'A' AND 'N';
```

Exercises

1. Identify the meaning and usage of the `tablespace`, `initrans`, `maxtrans`, `pctfree`, and `pctused` storage options in the `create table` statement.
2. What is row migration and chaining? Which statement creates a table from the contents of another table?

Controlling the Space Used by Tables

As mentioned, changing many aspects of table definition, such as adding constraints or modifying certain space or storage allocation options, is accomplished with the `alter table` statement. Because so much of the table's definition can be changed with the `alter table` statement, let's focus instead on what you can't change.

You can't resize the table's first segment with the `initial` storage option in the `alter table` command. Also, you can't change what tablespace the table exists in with the `alter table` statement. You can't allocate less than a full block for any table extent, either. For example, you can issue the `alter table EMPLOYEE storage ( next 31K )` if `DB_BLOCK_SIZE` is 4096, but if you do, Oracle simply rounds up the size of the next extent allocated to 32K.

Next, consider the changes that you can make, but that won't have an immediate effect. If you change the value for `next`, `pctincrease`, `pctfree`, `pctused`, or `initrans`, the change is applied only to new extents or blocks allocated or used, not to existing extents or blocks. However, a change to `maxtrans`, `maxextents`, or `pctused` will immediately benefit and impact the table.

Finally, you can't change `minextents` in the `alter table` statement to be greater than the value you set in the `create table` statement, but if you alter the `minextents` to be less than that value, Oracle will make the change the next time the `truncate table` statement is issued. You will learn more about `truncate table` shortly.

Adding to the Table's Storage Allocation

Now, let's consider how to allocate extents. Oracle allocates them automatically when a data change adds more data to the table than the current allocation will hold. You can add more extents manually with the `alter table allocate extent (size` *`num`*`[K|M] datafile '`*`filename`*`')` statement, where *num* is the size of the extent you want to allocate (subject to the tablespace limit set by `minimum extent)` and *`filename`* is the absolute path and filename of the datafile you want the extent stored in. Both the `size` and `datafile` clauses are optional. If `size` is not used, Oracle uses the size specified in the next storage option for the table. If `datafile` is excluded, Oracle manages placement itself. You would use this command to control the distribution of extents before performing bulk data loads.

```
ALTER TABLE EMPLOYEE ALLOCATE EXTENT;
ALTER TABLE EMPLOYEE ALLOCATE EXTENT ( SIZE 200K );
ALTER TABLE EMPLOYEE ALLOCATE EXTENT ( DATAFILE '/Oracle/disk_08/
                                        orgdbdata05.dbf' );
```

Table Highwatermarks and Unused Space

Now, consider how Oracle maintains knowledge about table size. A special marker called the *highwatermark* is used by Oracle to indicate the last block used to hold the table's data. As `insert` statements fill data blocks, Oracle moves the highwatermark further and further out to indicate the last block used. The highwatermark is stored in a table segment header and is used to determine where to stop reading blocks during full table scans. You can find the highwatermark for your table using the `unused_space()` procedure from the DBMS_SPACE Oracle-supplied package, or in the DBA_TABLES dictionary view after the `analyze` command has been run on your table. (There is more about `analyze` and the dictionary views housing table information later in this section.) Finally, if you want to eliminate the unused space allocated to your table, you can issue the `alter table` *`tblname`* `deallocate unused keep` *`num`* `[K|M]` statement, where `keep` is an optional clause that lets you retain *num* amount of the unused space.

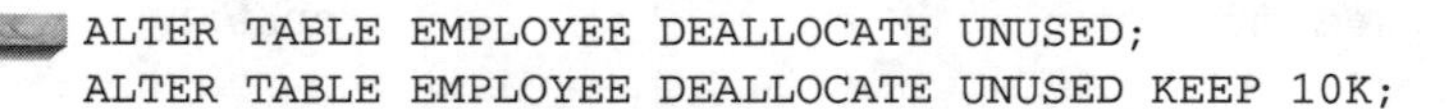

```
ALTER TABLE EMPLOYEE DEALLOCATE UNUSED;
ALTER TABLE EMPLOYEE DEALLOCATE UNUSED KEEP 10K;
```

Truncating and Dropping Tables

Now, consider a favorite tidbit from the archives of Oracle minutiae. You issue a `delete` statement on a table with many hundreds of thousands or millions of rows, and `commit` it. Feeling smug with your accomplishment, you issue a `select count(*)` statement. A few minutes later, you get a count of zero rows. What happened? Oracle didn't reset the highwatermark after the `delete` statement, and what's more, it never does! To get rid of the extents allocated that are now empty, and reset the highwatermark while still preserving the table definition, the `truncate table` command (with the optional `drop storage` clause) is used. Note that this is a DDL operation, not DML, thus meaning that once the table is truncated, you cannot issue a `rollback` command to magically get the data back.

Recall that any change made to `minextents` after table creation will now be applied to the table, unless you specify the optional `reuse storage` clause, which preserves the current storage allocation and does not reset the highwatermark. A final note—any associated indexes will also be truncated, and any optional `drop storage` or `reuse storage` clauses will also be applied to associated indexes. More about indexes in Chapter 9.

```
TRUNCATE TABLE EMPLOYEE;
TRUNCATE TABLE EMPLOYEE DROP STORAGE;
TRUNCATE TABLE EMPLOYEE REUSE STORAGE;
```

TIP

Here's an interesting fact about `truncate table` that may or may not find its way to OCP Exam 2. Despite your inability to `rollback` a table truncation, Oracle does acquire a rollback segment for the job. Why? Because if you terminate the `truncate table` command, or if some failure occurs, the rollback segment stores the changes made for the duration of the truncate operation to enable crash recovery.

Finally, to rid yourself of the table entirely, and give all allocated space back to the tablespace, issue the `drop table` statement. There is an optional clause you must include to handle other tables that may have defined referential integrity constraints into this table, called `cascade constraints`. The following code block demonstrates this command:

```
DROP TABLE EMPLOYEE;
DROP TABLE EMPLOYEE CASCADE CONSTRAINTS;
```

Exercises

1. At what point do changes made to the `maxextents` storage option take effect? What about `minextents`? How can you allocate more storage to a table?
2. What is a highwatermark, and how is it used? Where can you find information about it? How do you reset it without getting rid of the table definition? How do you get rid of the table definition?

Analyzing Tables to Check Integrity and Migration

Typically, Oracle automatically handles validation of the structure of every data block used whenever the block is read into the buffer cache for user processes. However, there are two things you can do to validate the structural integrity of data blocks. The first is to use the `init`*`sid`*`.ora` parameter `DB_BLOCK_CHECKSUM`. Setting this parameter to TRUE makes the DBWR process calculate a checksum on every block it writes, as a further measure protecting the integrity of blocks in the database. However, this parameter also makes your database run poorly, so Oracle doesn't really recommend you do this except when you feel it's imperative and you are willing to (potentially) sacrifice performance in a big way. The second method for checking integrity can be performed at any time using the `analyze table` *`tblname`* `validate structure` command. The optional `cascade` clause in this statement further validates the structure of blocks in indexes associated with the table, and will be discussed more in Chapter 10. The `analyze` command is issued from Server Manager on one table at a time.

Using analyze to Detect Row Migration

The main use of the `analyze` command is determining performance statistics for cost-based optimization of how Oracle processes SQL statements. An added benefit of the `analyze` command is that it will also detect row migration on your table. There are two basic clauses for this command: `estimate statistics` and `compute statistics`. The former will estimate statistics collection for the table, based on a sample size of data that you can optionally specify with the `sample` *`num`* `[rows|percent]` clause. If you don't specify a sample clause, Oracle uses 1064 rows. The `compute statistics` clause will calculate statistics collection for the table based on every row in the table. Oracle suggests you use `estimate statistics` rather than `compute statistics` because the former is almost as accurate and takes less time.

Once statistics are generated, the CHAIN_CNT column in the DBA_TABLES dictionary view will contain the number of chained and migrated rows estimated or found in the table. If you think this number is high, you might want to save the table data, drop the table, re-create it, and reload the data to eliminate the problem. Remember, some chaining is to be expected especially when your rows are wide (for example, if you have lots of VARCHAR2(4000) columns or a LONG column). Finally, if you want to validate integrity on an ongoing basis as part of a PL/SQL application, you can develop code that calls the `analyze_schema( )` procedures in the DBMS_UTILITY package, or the `analyze_object` procedure in DBMS_DDL. The scope of these procedures should be self-evident.

Exercises

1. Identify two uses of the `analyze` command. Which clauses are used to support these two options?
2. What is the difference between computing and estimating statistics? Which packages and procedures can also be used to perform `analyze` operations on a database?

Retrieving Data Dictionary Information About Tables

There are several data dictionary views available for obtaining information about tables. The views in the dictionary displaying this information base their content either on tables that exist in the database or on dynamic performance information about tables collected while the instance is running. The views you should remember for viewing table information include the following:

- **DBA_SEGMENTS** Gives information about the name, tablespace location, and owner of segments containing table data in Oracle.
- **DBA_OBJECTS** Gives information about the object ID number used in part to determine ROWID for rows in the table, as well as the table creation timestamp for determining dependencies.
- **DBA_TABLES** Gives information about all storage settings for the table, as well as the statistics collected as part of the `analyze` operation on that table.
- **DBA_EXTENTS** Gives information about the number of extents allocated to a table, the datafiles in which they are stored, and how large each extent is.
- **DBA_TAB_COLUMNS** Gives information about every column in every table, including datatype, size, precision, column position in each row, and nullability.
- **DBA_TAB_COMMENTS** Gives comment information for every table, if any comment information is stored.
- **DBA_COL_COMMENTS** Gives comment information for every column in every table, if any comment information is stored.

Since the possibilities for combining this data are vast, no example SQL statements will be shown here. Instead, consider the possible match-ups. For example, if you wanted to determine whether an extremely large table was "clumped" in one datafile, you could query the DBA_EXTENTS view to find out. If you wanted to determine what rows were chained or migrated in your table, you could query the DBA_TABLES view to find out. If you are looking to see if there is a great deal of unused space in a table, you could query the DBA_TABLES view as well. Be aware that the columns you would query from DBA_TABLES in these cases will only be populated if `analyze` has been run on that table. If these columns are NULL, run `analyze` to tabulate the data you need.

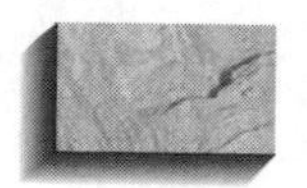

TIP
Before taking OCP Exam 2, check out the actual columns in each of these views using the `describe` *command from Server Manager. The column names are fairly descriptive, so you should be able to get a sense of what data is stored where.*

Exercises

1. Which view can you use to find out the date/time a table was created? What about where you would look to see if there were rows chained or migrated in the table?
2. How can you determine whether there are a substantial number of unused blocks under the table's highwatermark? Which command can be used to populate NULL columns in the DBA_TABLES view that you may want to use?

Converting Between Different ROWID Formats

The last topic you will cover in defining tables in Oracle is converting between Oracle7 restricted ROWID format and Oracle8 format. This may be required in cases where your tables in Oracle7 contained columns you defined explicitly to use the ROWID datatype, because you wanted to specify a pointer to a row in another table. For example, in Oracle7 you may have declared a column of type ROWID to store a pointer to a table row where you were storing LONG column data to approximate the design characteristics of LOB datatypes in Oracle8. Since there were such significant changes between ROWID formats in Oracle7 and Oracle8, you will need to run some sort of conversion on your ROWID data.

TIP

Do not concern yourself with converting the ROWID pseudocolumn of every table in your Oracle7 database when upgrading, or when converting the ROWID column in the Oracle EXCEPTIONS table. Oracle converts data in the ROWID pseudocolumn of every table automatically, and you can drop and re-create EXCEPTIONS in Oracle8 using scripts provided with that software release. This discussion only applies if you have defined real columns in your tables to be type ROWID.

You can convert between restricted and extended ROWID formats in Oracle with functions in the DBMS_ROWID Oracle-supplied package. There are functions you can use to find out information about the components of your ROWID and how they convert to object ID number, relative file number, and all the rest. The two functions for converting ROWIDs between Oracle versions are `ROWID_to_restricted( )` (O8 to O7) and `ROWID_to_extended( )` (O7 to O8). The following code block shows an interesting use of some other ROWID functions you can use to break a ROWID into its various components and display them:

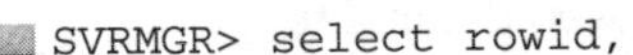

```
SVRMGR> select rowid,
     2> dbms_rowid.rowid_object(rowid) as obj_id,
     3> dbms_rowid.rowid_block_number(rowid) as block_num,
     4> dbms_rowid.rowid_row_number(rowid) as row_num,
     5> dbms_rowid.rowid_relative_fno(rowid) as relative_fno
     6> from repos.candidate;
ROWID                  OBJ_ID  BLOCK_NUM    ROW_NUM RELATIVE_FNO
------------------ ---------- ---------- ---------- ------------
AAAA3kAAGAAAAGsAAA       3556        428          0            6
AAAA3kAAGAAAAGsAAB       3556        428          1            6
```

Exercises

1. Which package contains functions that assist in converting Oracle7 ROWIDs to Oracle8 format? In what situations do you not need to worry about ROWID conversion?
2. Identify the functions you would use to display a ROWID as its object, block, row, and file components.

Chapter Summary

This is the first of two chapters covering the administration of objects in the Oracle database. The areas you've covered include management of rollback segments, temporary segments, and tables, which comprise material representing 16 percent of questions asked on the OCP Exam 2.

You learned what a rollback segment is, and how to plan the number and size of them according to various usage factors on your database. You also covered the storage options for rollback segments and their appropriate storage settings. The use of the `alter rollback segment` command was also shown for maintaining rollback segments. You learned about the appropriate views in the Oracle data dictionary for finding information about your rollback segments, such as DBA_ROLLBACK_SEGS and V$ROLLSTAT, and ended up examining how to troubleshoot the most common problems you may see with rollback segment use.

The next section covered temporary segments. This is an expanded area of Oracle that was enhanced for Oracle8. You learned about the two types of temporary segments—those in temporary tablespaces and those in permanent tablespaces—and the difference between how they are allocated in permanent tablespaces and temporary tablespaces. You learned about the performance improvements associated with disk sorts using temporary tablespaces in Oracle, and how to allocate space for your temporary segments in both types of tablespaces. The role of SMON in deallocating temporary segments in permanent tablespaces, and the inherent fragmentation issues associated with this activity were also covered. Finally, you learned about the different dictionary views associated with finding information about temporary segments.

The last area covered in this chapter was table creation and management. The different datatypes available in Oracle8 were introduced and described, and the use of the `create table` statement was covered, as well. Special attention was given to the various storage and table configuration options presented, such as tablespace placement, block space usage, as well as overall storage allocation in the tablespace for that table. You learned how to determine appropriate values for the `pctfree` and `pctused` space usage options, and dealt with how to use the `analyze` command to discover row migration, chaining, and block structural integrity. Using the data dictionary to find information about tables, and the available views for this purpose, was also covered. Finally, you learned about the DBMS_ROWID package, and the functions from that package that allow you to convert columns of ROWID datatype from the Oracle7 restricted format to the Oracle8 extended format, and then back again. Functions that break the extended ROWID into its various components were also presented.

Two-Minute Drill

- Rollback segments allow transaction processing to occur by storing the old version of data that has been changed, but not committed, by the users.
- Rollback segments should consist of equally sized extents.
- The `pctincrease` option is not permitted on rollback segments.
- Rollback segments must be brought online in order to use them.
- A rollback segment cannot be taken offline until all active transactions writing rollback entries have completed. This same restriction applies to tablespaces containing active rollback segments.
- Entries are associated with transactions in the rollback segment via the use of a system change number (SCN).
- When Oracle Parallel Server is used, the number of public rollback segments allocated by Oracle when the database is started is equal to the quotient of `TRANSACTIONS / TRANSACTIONS_PER_ROLLBACK_SEGMENT`.
- Specific private rollback segments can be allocated at startup if they are specified in the `ROLLBACK_SEGMENTS` parameter in `init`*`sid`*`.ora`.
- The number of rollback segments required for an instance is determined by the Rule of Four—divide concurrent user processes by 4; if the result is less than 4 + 4, round up to the nearest multiple of 4. Use no more than 50 rollback segments.
- Monitor performance in rollback segments with V$ROLLSTAT and V$WAITSTAT.
- There are two types of temporary segments: temporary segments for permanent tablespaces and temporary segments for temporary tablespaces.
- Oracle's use of temporary segments was reworked to make disk sorts more efficient. Sort segments in temporary tablespaces are allocated for the first disk sort and then persist for everyone's use for the duration of the instance. The result is less fragmentation than is the case in temporary segments in permanent tablespaces.
- A new memory area called the sort extent pool manages how user processes allocate extents for disk sorts in temporary tablespaces.
- SMON handles deallocation of temporary segments in permanent tablespaces when the transaction no longer needs them.

- You cannot create permanent database objects, such as tables, in temporary tablespaces. You also cannot convert permanent tablespaces into temporary ones unless there are no permanent objects in the permanent tablespace.
- You can get information about temporary segments and sort segments from the DBA_SEGMENTS, V$SORT_SEGMENT, V$SESSION, and V$SORT_USAGE dictionary views.
- A sort segment exists in the temporary tablespace for as long as the instance is available. All users share the sort segment.
- The size of extents in the temporary tablespace should be set to a multiple of `SORT_AREA_SIZE`, plus one additional block for the segment header, in order to maximize disk sort performance.
- There are four types of tables: regular tables, partitioned tables, cluster tables, and index-organized tables.
- There are two categories of datatypes: user-defined and built-in.
- There are three classes of built-in types: scalar, collection, and relationship types.
- The "regular size" scalar types include: CHAR, NCHAR, VARCHAR2, NVARCHAR2, DATE, RAW, ROWID, and NUMBER.
- The "large size" scalar types include: LONG and LONG RAW from Oracle7, and CLOB, NCLOB, BLOB, and BFILE.
- The collection types include VARRAY or variable-length array, and TABLE, which is a nested table type.
- The relationship type is REF, and it is a pointer to other data in another table.
- Collection and relationship types require the object option installed on your Oracle database.
- To remember the components of a ROWID, think of the BRF and OBRRF acronyms (and a little dog barking).
- Remember how to use each of the options for defining storage and table creation. They are as follows:
  - **`initial`** First segment in the table
  - **`next`** Next segment allocated (not simply the second one in the table)
  - **`pctincrease`** Percentage increase of next extent allocated over `next` value
  - **`minextents`** Minimum number of extents allocated at table creation

- **`maxextents`** Maximum number of extents the object can allocate
- **`pctfree`** How much of each block stays free after `insert` for row update
- **`pctused`** Threshold that usage must fall below before a row is added
- **`initrans`** Number of concurrent changes that can happen per block
- **`maxtrans`** Maximum number of transactions that can perform the same function
- **`logging/nologging`** Whether Oracle will store redo for the `create table` statement
- **`cache/nocache`** Whether Oracle allows blocks to stay in the buffer cache after full table scans

- Row migration is when an `update` makes a row too large to store in its original block.
- Chaining is when a row is broken up and stored in many blocks. Both require multiple disk reads/writes to retrieve/store, and therefore are bad for performance.

Chapter Questions

1. When determining the number of rollback segments in a database, which of the following choices identifies a factor to consider?

A. Concurrent transactions

B. Size of typical transactions

C. Size of rows in table most frequently changed

D. Number of anticipated disk sorts

2. Which of the following choices is the process that most directly causes fragmentation in a tablespace storing temporary segments because it deallocates segments used for disk sorts?

A. Server

B. DBWR

C. SMON

D. LGWR

3. Which of the following choices best describes the methodology for sizing extents for the sort segments on your Oracle database?

A. TRANSACTIONS / TRANSACTIONS_PER_ROLLBACK_SEGMENT

B. X * SORT_AREA_SIZE + DB_BLOCK_SIZE

C. (*avg_row_size* – *init_row_size*) * 100 / *avg_row_size*

D. 100 – `pctfree` – (*avg_row_size* * 100) / *avail_data_space*

4. Each of the following choices identifies an event in a series of events that are run from Server Manager. If A is the first event, and D is the last event, which of the following choices identifies the event that will cause an error?

A.
```
create tablespace TB01 datafile '/oracle/tb01.dbf'
default storage
(initial 10K next 10K pctincrease 0 minextents 4
maxextents 20) temporary;
```

B.
```
create table my_tab (my_col varchar2(10))
tablespace TB01;
```

C.
```
alter tablespace TB01 permanent;
```

D.
```
create table my_tab (my_col varchar2(10))
tablespace TB01;
```

5. You want to compute statistics for cost-based optimization on all rows in your EMPLOYEE table, using Oracle default settings. Which of the following choices contains the statement you will use?

A. `analyze table EMPLOYEE validate structure;`

B. `analyze table EMPLOYEE compute statistics;`

C. `analyze table EMPLOYEE estimate statistics;`

D.
```
analyze table EMPLOYEE estimate statistics sample
10 percent;
```

6. You are trying to determine how many disk sorts are happening on the database right now. Which of the following dictionary tables would you use to find that information?

A. V$SESSION

B. V$SESSTAT

C. DBA_SEGMENTS

D. V$SORT_USAGE

7. How many rollback segments will be required if the value set for `TRANSACTIONS` is 20 and the value set for `TRANSACTIONS_PER_ROLLBACK_SEGMENT` is 4?

A. 2

B. 4

C. 8

D. 9

8. When a rollback segment is created, its availability status is automatically set, by Oracle, to which of the following?

A. Online

B. Pending online

C. Offline

D. Stale

9. The DBA suspects there is some chaining and row migration occurring on the database. Which of the following choices indicates a way to detect it?

A. `select CHAIN_CNT from DBA_SEGMENTS`

B. `select CHAIN_CNT from DBA_TABLES`

C. `select CHAIN_CNT from DBA_OBJECTS`

D. `select CHAIN_CNT from DBA_EXTENTS`

10. All of the following choices indicate a way to resolve the `ORA-1555 Snapshot too old (rollback segment too small)` error, except one. Which choice is it?

A. Create rollback segments with a higher `optimal` value.

B. Create rollback segments with higher `maxextents`.

C. Create rollback segments with larger extent sizes.

D. Create rollback segments with high `minextents`.

11. Which datatype is used in situations where you want an ordered set of data elements, in which every element is the same datatype, and where you predefine the number of elements that will appear in the set?

A. REF

B. TABLE

C. CLOB

D. VARRAY

12. Using the `nologging` clause when issuing `create table as select` has which of the following effects?

A. Slows performance in creating the table

B. Ensures recoverability of the table creation

C. Improves performance in creating the table

D. Makes blocks read into memory during full table scans persistent

13. Entries in a rollback segment are bound to a transaction by

A. Number of `commit` operations performed

B. Number of `rollback` operations performed

C. ROWID

D. System change number

14. The largest size a table has ever reached is identified by which one of the following items stored in the segment header for the table?

A. ROWID

B. Highwatermark

C. Session address

D. None of the above

Answers to Chapter Questions

1. A. Concurrent transactions

Explanation The number of concurrent transactions is used in part to determine the number of rollback segments your database should have. Had the question asked for which choice played a role in determining the size of extents or total rollback segment size, then choices B or C would have been correct. Since disk sorts have little to do with rollback segments, under no circumstances should you have chosen D.

2. C. SMON

Explanation The SMON process automatically drops temporary segments from the permanent tablespace as soon as they are no longer needed by the transaction. The server process can only retrieve data from disk, eliminating choice A. DBWR handles writing data changes to disk, but does not drop the temporary segment, eliminating choice B. Choice D is also incorrect because LGWR handles writing redo log entries to disk, as explained in Chapter 7.

3. B. X * `SORT_AREA_SIZE` + `DB_BLOCK_SIZE`

Explanation If the data to be sorted was any smaller than the `init`*`sid`*`.ora` `parameter SORT_AREA_SIZE`, then the sort would take place in memory. Thus, you can be sure that all disk sorts will write data at least as great as `SORT_AREA_SIZE` to disk, so you should size your sort segment to be a multiple of that parameter. Since the sort segment will need a header block, adding in `DB_BLOCK_SIZE` is required to make the extra room for the header. Choices C and D are formulas for determining `pctfree` and `pctused`, respectively, so they are wrong. Choice A is used to determine the number of rollback segments your database needs, making it wrong as well.

4. B.

```
create table my_tab (my_col varchar2(10))
tablespace TB01;
```

Explanation Since tablespace TB01 is temporary, you cannot create a permanent object like a table in it, making choice B correct. Incidentally, if the tablespace created in choice A had been permanent, then choice C would have been the right answer because an error occurs when you try to convert a permanent tablespace into a temporary one when the tablespace contains a permanent object. Choice D could be correct in that scenario, too, because your MY_TAB table would already exist.

5. B. `analyze table EMPLOYEE compute statistics;`

Explanation The tip-off in this question is that you are being asked to compute statistics for all rows in the table. In this situation, you would never estimate, because you are processing all rows in the table, not just some of them. Thus, choices C and D are both incorrect. Also, because the `validate structure` clause only verifies structural integrity of data blocks, choice A is incorrect.

6. D. V$SORT_USAGE

Explanation The V$SORT_USAGE view shows the sessions that are using sort segments in your database. Although you may want to join that data with the data in choice A, V$SESSION, to see the username corresponding with the session, V$SESSION by itself gives no indication about current disk sorts. Nor do V$SESSTAT or DBA_SEGMENTS, eliminating those choices as well.

7. C. 8

Explanation Refer to the Rule of Four in creating rollback segments. Remember, the equation is `TRANSACTIONS / TRANSACTIONS_PER_ROLLBACK_SEGMENT`. In this case, the result is 5. This is a special case in the Rule of Four that gets rounded up to 8.

8. C. Offline

Explanation Once created, a rollback segment status is offline and must be brought online in order to be used. Refer to the discussion of rollback segments. In order to bring it online, you must issue the `alter rollback segment online` statement, eliminating choice A. Pending online is not a valid status for rollback segments in Oracle, eliminating choice B. Stale is a valid status for redo logs, but not rollback segments, eliminating choice D.

9. B. `select CHAIN_CNT from DBA_TABLES`

Explanation The CHAIN_CNT column is found in the DBA_TABLES dictionary view, making choice B correct. The trick of this question is identifying not where the data comes from, for it obviously comes from the CHAIN_CNT column, which is populated by the `analyze` command. The trick is knowing where to look for in the dictionary for information. Before taking OCP Exam 2, be sure you go through each of the dictionary views identified in the chapter, and run the `describe` command on them to get a feel for which columns show up where.

10. B. Create rollback segments with higher `maxextents`.

Explanation Refer to the discussion of indexes created in conjunction with integrity constraints.

11. D. VARRAY

Explanation The content in the question, namely that you want an ordered set of data elements, where every element is the same datatype, and where you predefine the number of elements that will appear in the set, describes the features available in a VARRAY. A nested table is not correct because the nested table is an unordered set, eliminating choice B. Choice A, REF, is a relationship type that stores a pointer to data, not data itself, and is therefore wrong. Finally, a CLOB is a text large object, eliminating choice C.

12. C. Improves performance in creating the table

Explanation Since `nologging` causes the `create table as select` statement to not generate any redo information, performance is improved somewhat for the overall operation. This is the logical opposite of Choice A, and given these other facts, choice A is wrong. Choice B is also wrong, because disabling redo generation means your operation is not recoverable. Finally, choice D is wrong because the `cache` option is used to make blocks read into memory for full table scans persistent, not `nologging`.

13. D. System change number

Explanation SCNs are identifiers that group data-change statements together as one transaction both in rollback segments and redo logs. The number of `commit` operations or `rollback` operations performed simply reduces the number of active transactions on the database, and thus the amount of active undo in a rollback segment. Thus, choices A and B are incorrect. Finally ROWIDs correspond to the location on disk of rows for a table, and have little to do with grouping transactions, so choice C is incorrect.

14. B. Highwatermark

Explanation ROWID information simply is a locator for rows in a table. It does nothing to determine the size of that table. Thus, choice A is incorrect. Choice C is incorrect because the session address is dynamic information about the user processes currently connected to Oracle. This has nothing to do with the size of any table anywhere in the database. Since choice B is correct, choice D is logically wrong as well.

CHAPTER 9

Managing Database Objects II

In this chapter, you will cover the following areas of Oracle database administration:

- Managing indexes
- Managing data integrity
- Managing clusters and IOTs

This chapter will finish the discussion, started in Chapter 8, of managing database objects. Here, you will learn about managing indexes, data integrity, clusters, and index-organized tables (IOTs). Of these topics, you will most likely find yourself using information from the section on indexes and data integrity the most, because indexes are important tools for performance tuning, and integrity is key to successfully managing data stored in Oracle. Clusters and IOTs are sometimes of limited use, but you may still find them useful and therefore should understand how they work. Together, these subject areas comprise about 16 percent of OCP Exam 2 content.

Managing Indexes

In this section, you will cover the following topics on managing indexes:

- Different index types and their use
- Creating B-tree and bitmap indexes
- Reorganizing indexes
- Dropping indexes
- Getting index information from the data dictionary

Tables can grow quite large, and when they do, it becomes difficult for users to quickly find the data they need. For this reason, Oracle offers indexes as a method of speeding database performance when accessing tables with a lot of data. Oracle provides different types of indexes for different uses, and you will learn about them here. You will also learn about the specific procedures for creating B-tree and bitmap indexes, and what sorts of situations may cause you to choose one over the other. The methods used to reorganize and drop indexes are shown here as well. Finally, you will learn where to look in the data dictionary for information about your indexes.

Different Index Types and Their Use

An index in Oracle can be compared to the card catalogs once found in all libraries. When you want to find a book, you go to the card catalog (or computer) and look up the book under author, title, or subject. When you find the card for that book, it lists the location of the book in the library according to a classification system. Looking for a book in this way reduces the time you'd spend looking, say, for a book on fly-fishing in the section where autobiographies are kept. Oracle indexes work the same way. You find row data that matches your search criteria in the index first, and then use the ROWID for that row from the index to get the entire row quickly from the table.

Several criteria are used to determine what kind of index you're looking at. The first criterion is how many columns the index has. *Simple* indexes contain only one column of data through which you can search, plus the ROWID of the corresponding row in the table. *Composite* indexes store more than one column of data for you to search, plus the ROWID of the corresponding row in the table. You can put up to 32 columns in a composite index, but you may be restricted from including that many if the total size of all the columns you want in the index exceeds `DB_BLOCK_SIZE / 3`. Other criteria for identifying indexes is whether the indexed column(s) contains all unique (composite) values, whether an index is partitioned or nonpartitioned and whether it is a traditional B-tree or a bitmap index, or whether the data in the index is stored in reverse order.

Oracle maintains indexes whenever user processes make data changes to tables. For example, if you `insert` a new row in a table, an associated entry is made in the index for that row's indexed column. That entry is not made to the last leaf block of the index, but, rather, the appropriate leaf block is located according to index sort order, and the entry is made there. When data is removed from the table, the corresponding index entry is marked for removal. Later, when all other rows corresponding to all index entries in the leaf node are removed, then and only then is the entire block purged of index entries. Thus, the structure of the index is preserved. An `update` statement that changes the value of a row's indexed column value is treated as a marked removal followed by an `insert`. Finally, index entries can be added to a block even past the `pctfree` threshold.

Nonpartitioned B-Tree Indexes

The B-tree index is the traditional indexing mechanism used in Oracle. It stores data in a treelike fashion, as displayed in Figure 9-1. At the base of the index is the *root node*, which is an entry point for your search for data in the index. The root node contains pointers to other nodes at the next level in the index. Depending on the value you seek, you will be pointed in one of many directions. The next level in the index consists of *branch nodes*, which are similar to the root node in that they, too, contain pointers to the next level of nodes in the index. Again, depending on the value you seek, you will be pointed in one of many directions. Branch nodes point to the highest level of the index, the *leaf nodes*. In this highest level, *index entries* contain indexed column values and the corresponding ROWIDs of rows storing those column values. Each leaf node is linked both to the leaf node on its left and right, in order to make it possible to search up and down through a range of entries in the index.

Within a single index entry, there are several elements, some of which have already been covered. The first is the *index entry header*, containing the number of columns in the entry. Following that, the entry stores the values for the column(s) in the index. Preceding each column value is a length byte that follows the same rules that length bytes follow in row entries, as described in Chapter 8. Finally, the index entry stores the ROWID. No length byte is needed for this value, because all ROWIDs are the same length.

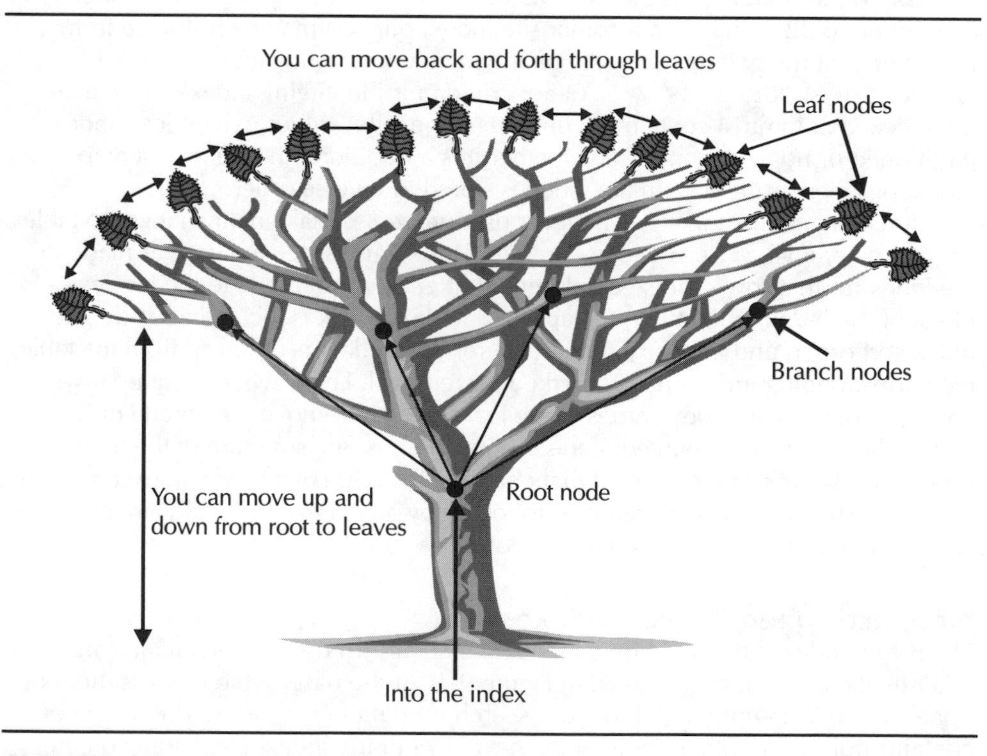

FIGURE 9-1. *B-tree index structure*

There are a few special cases of data stored in index entries that you should understand:

- If the index is nonunique, and several rows contain the same value for the column, then each row with that value will have its own index entry to store each unique ROWID.
- If a row has a NULL value for the column(s) being indexed, there will be no corresponding index entry for that row.
- For non-partitioned indexes only, since the index stores data for only one table, and since all tables can be stored in only one tablespace, the object ID number is not required to locate the row from the index. Thus, nonpartitioned B-tree indexes use restricted ROWIDs to point to row data.

B-tree indexes are used most commonly to improve performance on `select` statements using columns of unique or mostly distinct values. It is relatively easy and quick for Oracle to maintain B-tree indexes when data is changed in an indexed column, too, making this type of index useful for online transaction processing applications. However, these indexes do a bad job of finding data quickly on `select` statements with `where` clauses containing comparison operations joined with `or`, and in situations where the values in the indexed column are not very distinct.

Bitmap Indexes

Although all indexes in Oracle are stored with the root-branch-leaf structure illustrated in Figure 9-1, bitmap indexes are conceptualized differently. Instead of storing entries for each row in the table, the bitmap index stores an entry containing each distinct value, the start and end ROWID to indicate the range of ROWIDs in this table, and a long binary string with as many bits as there are rows in the table.

For example, say you are looking at a representation of a bitmap index for a table such as the one in Figure 9-2. The APPLE_TYPE column indexed has only three distinct values. The bitmap index would have three entries as you see in the figure. The start and end ROWID for the object are also shown, so that you know what the potential ROWID range is. Finally, you see a binary string representing a bitmap. A position will be set to 1 for the entry if the column for that row contains the associated value ; otherwise, the bit is set to 0. If an entry contains a bit set to 1, the corresponding bit in every other entry will always be set to 0.

Bitmap indexes improve performance in situations where you `select` data from a column whose values are repeated often, as is the case with employee status

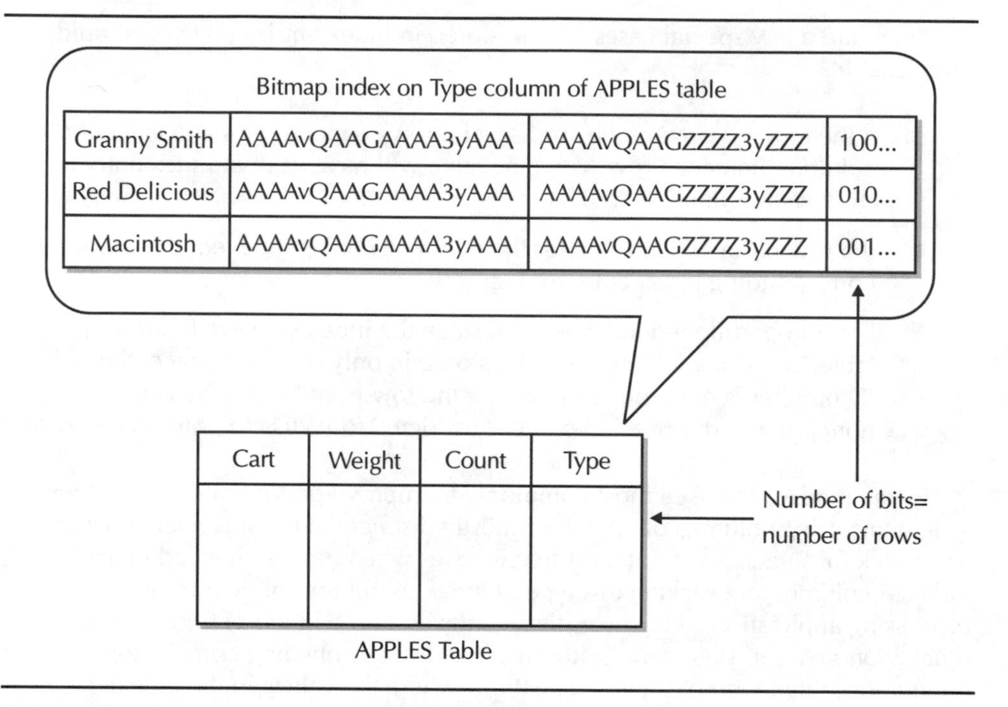

FIGURE 9-2. *Logical representation of bitmap index*

(for example, active, LOA, or retired). They also improve performance on `select` statements with multiple `where` conditions joined by `or`.

Bitmap indexes improve performance where data in the column is infrequently or never changed. By the same token, it is a somewhat arduous process to change data in that column. This is because changing the value of a column stored in a bitmap index requires Oracle to lock the entire segment storing the bitmap index to make the change.

Reverse-Key Indexes

Finally, consider the use of reverse-key indexes. This type of index is the same as a regular B-tree index, except for one thing—the data from the column being indexed is stored in reverse order. Thus, if the column value in a table of first names is JASON, the reverse-key index column will be NOSAJ. Typically, users of Oracle Parallel Server see the most benefit from reverse-key indexes when their `select` statements contain `where` clauses that use equality comparisons, such as `where X = 5`, but not in situations where range comparisons are used, such as `where X` `between 4 and 6`. The benefit of reverse-key indexes is that they enhance performance in Oracle Parallel Server environments.

Exercises

1. What is a unique index, and how does it compare with a nonunique index? What is the difference between a simple and composite index?
2. What is a B-tree index, and in what situations does it improve performance? When does it not improve performance? How does it compare to a bitmap index?
3. What is a reverse-key index, and when does it improve performance?

Creating B-tree and Bitmap Indexes

Recall from Chapter 4 that the `create index` statement is used to create all types of indexes. To define special types of indexes, you must include various keywords, such as `create unique index` for indexes on columns that enforce uniqueness of every element of data, or `create bitmap index` for creating bitmap indexes. If you want to see the basic syntax again, flip back to Chapter 4. The following code block shows the statement for creating a unique B-tree index repeated from Chapter 4, only this time the statement also includes options for data storage and creation.

```
CREATE UNIQUE INDEX employee_lastname_indx_01
ON employee (lastname ASC)
TABLESPACE ORGDBIDX
PCTFREE 12
INITRANS 2 MAXTRANS 255
LOGGING
NOSORT
STORAGE ( INITIAL 900K
          NEXT 1800K
          MINEXTENTS 1
          MAXEXTENTS 200
          PCTINCREASE 0 );
```

There are several items in the storage definition that will look familiar, such as `pctfree`, `tablespace`, `logging`, and the items in the `storage` clause. Other than `pctfree`, these options have the same use as they do in `create table` statements; if you need review, flip back to Chapter 8. Oracle uses `pctfree` only during the creation of the index to reserve space for index entries that may need to be inserted into the same index block.

There are a few other items that may look unfamiliar, such as `unique`, `asc`, and `nosort`. You specify `unique` when you want the index to enforce uniqueness for values in the column. The `asc` keyword indicates ascending order for this column in the index, and `desc` (descending) can be substituted for this clause. The `nosort` keyword is for when you have loaded your table data in the proper sort order on the column you are indexing. In this case, it would mean that you have loaded data into the EMPLOYEE table sorted in ascending order on the LASTNAME column. By specifying `nosort`, Oracle will skip the sort ordinarily used in creating the index, thereby increasing performance on your `create index` statement. You might use this option if your operating system offered a procedure for sorting that was more efficient than Oracle's. Finally, `pctused` is not used in index definitions. Since all items in an index must be in the right order for the index to work, Oracle must put an index entry into a block, no matter what. Thus, `pctused` is not used.

You can create bitmap indexes with several storage specifications, as well, but remember that they are used to improve search performance for low cardinality columns, so bitmap indexes may not be unique. The following code block creates a bitmap index:

```
CREATE BITMAP INDEX employee_lastname_indx_01
ON employee (lastname)
TABLESPACE ORGDBIDX
PCTFREE 12
INITRANS 2 MAXTRANS 255
LOGGING
NOSORT
STORAGE ( INITIAL 900K
          NEXT 1800K
          MINEXTENTS 1
          MAXEXTENTS 200
          PCTINCREASE 0 );
```

The performance of commands that use bitmap indexes is heavily influenced by an area of memory specified by the `CREATE_BITMAP_AREA_SIZE` `init`*`sid`*`.ora` parameter. This area determines how much memory will be used for storing bitmap segments. You need more space for this purpose if the column on which you are creating the bitmap index has high cardinality. For a bitmap index, high cardinality might mean a dozen or so unique values out of 500,000 (as opposed to B-tree indexes, for which high cardinality might mean 490,000 unique values out of

500,000). So, in this situation you might stick with the Oracle default setting of 8MB for your `CREATE_BITMAP_AREA_SIZE` initialization parameter.

An example of low cardinality for a column would be having two distinct values in the entire table, as is the case for a column indicating whether an employee is male or female. In this case, you might size your initialization parameter considerably lower than the Oracle default, perhaps around 750K.

Sizing and Other Index-Creation Issues

Searching a large table without the benefit of an index takes a long time because a full table scan must be performed. Indexes are designed to improve search performance. Unlike full table scans, whose performance worsens as the table grows larger, the performance of table searches that use indexes gets exponentially better as the index (and associated table) gets larger and larger. In fact, on a list containing one million elements, a binary search tree algorithm similar to the one used in a B-tree index finds any element in the list within 20 tries; in reality, the B-tree algorithm is actually far more efficient.

However, there is a price for all this speed, paid in the additional disk space required to store the index and the overhead required to maintain it when DML operations are performed on the table. To minimize the trade-off, you must weigh the storage cost of adding an index to the database against the performance gained by having the index available for searching the table. The performance improvement achieved by using an index is exponential over the performance of a full table scan, but there is no value in the index if it is never used by the application. You should also consider the volatility of the data in the table before creating an index. If the data in the indexed column changes regularly, you might want to index a more static column.

Also, consider how you are sizing `pctfree` for your index. Oracle only uses `pctfree` to determine free space when the index is first created. After that, the space is fair game, because Oracle has to keep all the items in the index in order. So, after creation, Oracle will put index records in a block right down to the last bit of space available. To determine the best value for `pctfree` on your index, consider the following. If the values in the column you are indexing increase sequentially, such as column values generated by sequences, you can size `pctfree` as low as 2 or 3. If not, you should calculate `pctfree` based on rowcount forecasts for growth over a certain time period (12 months, for example) with the following formula:

((max_#_rows_in_period – initial_#_rows_in_period) / max_#_rows_in_period) * 100

Finally, you should also follow the space allocation guidelines outlined in Chapter 8 for tables, such as using standard sizes for your extents that are multiples of 5 * DB_BLOCK_SIZE, and put your indexes in a tablespace separate from your tables, ideally on a separate disk resource. Also, make sure `initrans` is higher on the index than it is for the table, since index entries in a block take up less space, yielding more index entries per block. Finally, where you can, try to sort your data before initially loading the table and before creating the index. This way, you can utilize the `nosort` option, and substantially increase performance on the `create index` operation.

Exercises

1. Identify some of the storage clauses used for creating indexes that are not used for creating tables. How is `pctfree` used in indexes?
2. Can you define a bitmap index that is unique? Why or why not? How is the `CREATE_BITMAP_AREA_SIZE` parameter used?

Reorganizing Indexes

Reorganizing indexes is handled with the `alter index` statement. The `alter index` statement is useful for redefining storage options, such as `next`, `pctincrease`, `maxextents`, `initrans`, or `maxtrans`. You can use the `alter index` statement to change the `pctfree` value for new blocks in new extents allocated by your index, as well.

Other Index-Reorganization Options

Oracle8 offers many new index-reorganization options. You can add extents manually to an index much like you do for tables, with the `alter index allocate extent` statement (specifying `size` and `datafile` optionally was covered in Chapter 8). You can also rid yourself of unused space below the index highwatermark with the `alter index deallocate unused` statement, optionally reserving a little extra space with the `keep` clause (also covered in Chapter 8).

Another option for reorganizing your index is to rebuild it. This operation allows you to create a new index using the data from the old one, resulting in fewer table reads while rebuilding, tidier space management in the index, and better overall performance. This operation is accomplished with the `alter index` *`idxname`* `rebuild tablespace` *`tblspcname`* statement. All the storage options you can specify in a `create index` statement can be applied to `alter index rebuild`, as well. You would rebuild an index in situations where you want to move the index to another tablespace, or when a great many rows have been `deleted` from the table, causing index entries to be removed, as well. Finally, you may want to rebuild an index as a reverse-key index in Oracle Parallel Server environments to take advantage of performance gains offered by this new type of index.

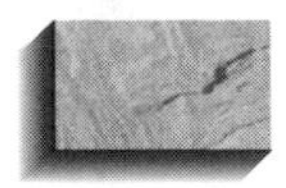

TIP
You can use the `analyze index validate structure` *command as you would with tables, to check for block corruption. The INDEX_STATS dictionary view will then show you the number of index entries in leaf nodes in the LF_ROWS column compared to the number of deleted entries in the DEL_LF_FOWS column. Oracle recommends that, if the number of deleted entries is over 30 percent, you should rebuild the index.*

Exercises

1. In what situations would you want to rebuild an index, and what is the statement for doing so?
2. Which storage parameters cannot be changed as part of the `alter index` command?
3. Describe the usage of the INDEX_STATS dictionary table, and how it relates to the `analyze` command.

Dropping Indexes

What happens when you want to expand your index to include more columns, or to get rid of columns? Can you use `alter index` for that? Unfortunately, the answer is no. You must drop and re-create the index to modify column definitions or change column order from ascending to descending (or vice-versa). This is accomplished with the `drop index` *`idxname`* statement.

You may want to get rid of an index that is used only for specific purposes on an irregular basis, especially if the table has other indexes and volatile data. You may also want to drop an index if you are about to perform a large load of table data, perhaps preceded by purging all data in the table. In this way, your data load runs faster, and the index created later is fresh and well-organized. You may have to recreate your index if it has a status of INVALID in the DBA_OBJECTS view, or if you know the index is corrupt from running DBVERIFY on the tablespace housing the index or the `analyze` command on the index itself.

Exercise

Identify some reasons for dropping an index. Do you need to drop an index to add more columns to the index? Why or why not?

Getting Index Information from the Data Dictionary

You may find yourself looking for information about your indexes, and the Oracle data dictionary can help. The DBA_INDEXES view offers a great deal of information about indexes, such as the type of index (normal or bitmap), its current status (valid, invalid, and others), and whether the index enforces uniqueness or not. You can also get information about which table is associated with the index. Another view that contains information about the columns that are stored in an index is called DBA_IND_COLUMNS. The most valuable piece of information this view can give you (in addition to telling you which columns are indexed) is the order in which the columns of the index appear. This is a crucial factor in determining whether the index will improve performance in selecting data from a table. For example, if you were to issue `select * from EMPLOYEE where LASTNAME = 'SMITH'`, and a composite index existed in which LASTNAME was the first column in the index order, then that index would improve performance. But, if the index listed FIRSTNAME as the first column, then the index would not help. Figure 9-3 illustrates this concept.

Finally, a note on finding information about reverse-key indexes. You might notice, if you have reverse-key indexes in your database, that there is no information in the DBA_INDEXES view telling you specifically that the index is reverse key. To see this information, you must execute a specialized query that uses a SYS-owned table called IND$, as well as the DBA_OBJECTS view. The following code block shows the query:

```
SELECT object_name FROM dba_objects
WHERE object_id IN (SELECT obj#
FROM ind$
WHERE BITAND(property,4) = 4);
```

Exercises

1. Identify some dictionary views and tables that contain information about indexes.
2. What is the significance of column position in a composite index? Where can you find this information about an index?

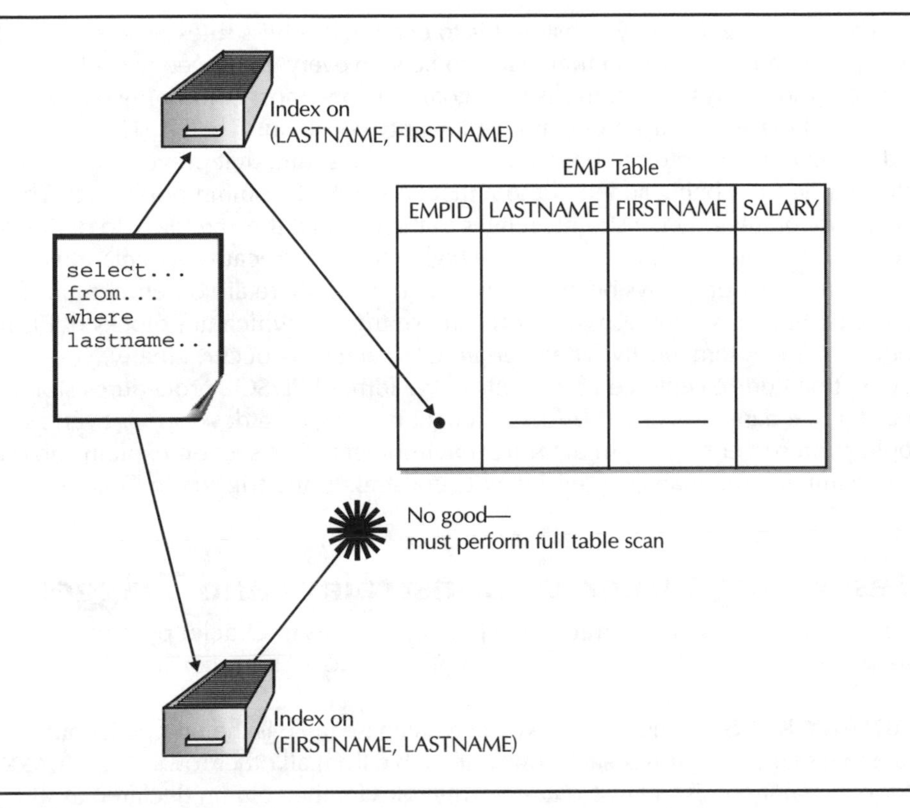

FIGURE 9-3. *The effect of column position in composite indexes*

Managing Data Integrity

In this section, you will cover the following four topics related to managing data-integrity constraints:

- Describing integrity constraints and triggers
- Implementing data-integrity constraints and triggers
- Maintaining integrity constraints and triggers
- Obtaining constraint and trigger information from Oracle

The goal of an integrity constraint is to enforce business rules of some kind. For example, in an organization that wants to be sure every employee has a last name, there are three ways to accomplish the goal. The one most commonly employed in Oracle databases is using a declarative integrity constraint. The LASTNAME column of the EMPLOYEE table can have a NOT NULL constraint that prevents any row of information from being added without that LASTNAME column populated. The popularity of integrity constraints relates to the fact that they are easy to define and use, they execute quickly, and they are highly flexible. Because a declarative constraint may not always be able to handle the job, there are other methods for enforcing business rules, as well. You can use *triggers*, which are blocks of PL/SQL code that fire automatically when certain DML activities occur. Finally, you can use application code to enforce constraints in the form of PL/SQL procedures stored in your Oracle database, as a robust GUI client running on a desktop, or even as an application server running in an N-tier environment. This section explains how to use, maintain, and manage your integrity constraints and triggers in Oracle.

Describing Integrity Constraints and Triggers

There are five types of declarative integrity constraints in Oracle: primary keys, foreign keys, unique keys, check constraints, and NOT NULL constraints.

PRIMARY KEYS The primary key of a database table is the unique identifier for that table that distinguishes each row in the table from all other rows. A PRIMARY KEY constraint consists of two data-integrity rules for the column declared as the primary key. First, every value in the primary key column must be unique in the table. Second, no value in the column declared to be the primary key can be NULL. Primary keys are the backbone of the table. You should choose the primary key for a table carefully. The column or columns defined to be the primary key should reflect the most important piece of information that is unique about each row of the table.

FOREIGN KEYS The creation of a FOREIGN KEY constraint from one table to another defines a special relationship between the two tables that is often referred to as a parent-child relationship, illustrated in Figure 9-4. The parent table is the one referred to by the foreign key, while the child table is the table that actually contains the foreign key. The DBA should ensure that foreign keys on one table refer only to primary keys on other tables. Unlike PRIMARY KEY constraints, a FOREIGN KEY constraint on a column does not prevent user processes from setting the value in the foreign key column of the child table to NULL. In cases where the column is NULL, there will be no referential integrity check between the child and the parent.

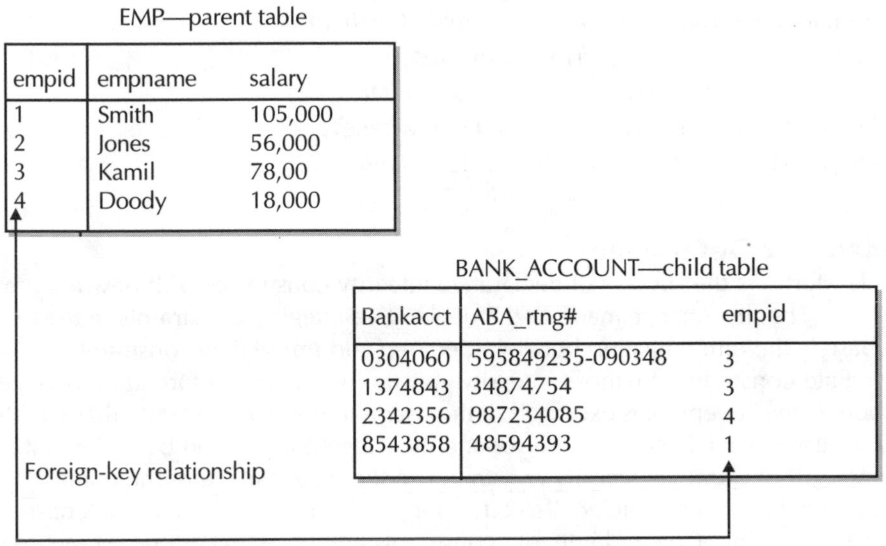

EMP—parent table

empid	empname	salary
1	Smith	105,000
2	Jones	56,000
3	Kamil	78,00
4	Doody	18,000

BANK_ACCOUNT—child table

Bankacct	ABA_rtng#	empid
0304060	595849235-090348	3
1374843	34874754	3
2342356	987234085	4
8543858	48594393	1

Foreign-key relationship

FIGURE 9-4. *Creating parent-child table relationships using foreign keys*

UNIQUE KEYS Like the primary key, a unique key or `UNIQUE` constraint ensures that values in the column on which the unique constraint is defined are not duplicated by other rows. In addition, the `UNIQUE` constraint is the only type of constraint (other than the `PRIMARY KEY` constraint) that has an associated index created with it when the constraint is named.

NOT NULL CONSTRAINTS NULL cannot be specified as the value for a column on which the `NOT NULL` constraint is applied. Often, the DBA will define this constraint in conjunction with another constraint. For example, the `NOT NULL` constraint can be used with a `FOREIGN KEY` constraint to force validation of column data against a "valid value" table.

CHECK CONSTRAINTS `CHECK` constraints allow the DBA to specify a set of valid values for a column, which Oracle will check automatically when a row is inserted with a non-NULL value for that column. This constraint is limited to hard-coded valid values only. In other words, a `CHECK` constraint cannot "look up" its valid values anywhere, nor can it perform any type of SQL or PL/SQL operation as part of its definition.

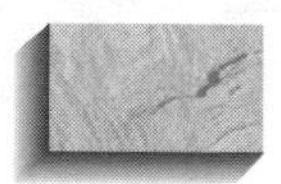

TIP
Primary keys and unique keys are created with an associated unique index. This index preserves uniqueness in the column(s) and also facilitates high-performance searches on the table whenever the primary key is named in the `where` *clause.*

Constraint Deferability

Oracle8 furthers the success of declarative integrity constraints with new features for their use. The first change made to the declarative integrity constraints in the Oracle database is the differentiation between *deferred* and *immediate* constraints. Immediate constraints are those integrity constraints that are enforced immediately, as soon as the statement is executed. If the user attempts to enter data that violates the constraint, Oracle signals an error and the statement is rolled back. Up until Oracle8, all declarative integrity constraints in the database were immediate constraints. However, Oracle8 also offers the DBA an option to defer database integrity checking. Deferred integrity constraints are those that are not enforced until the user attempts to `commit` the transaction. If, at that time, the data entered by statements violates an integrity constraint, Oracle will signal an error and roll back the entire transaction.

The user can defer any and all constraints that are deferrable during the entire session using the `alter session set constraints=deferred` statement. Alternatively, the user can defer named or all constraints for a specific transaction, using the `set constraint` *`name`* `deferred` or `set constraint all deferred`. This form of "lazy evaluation" temporarily allows data to enter the database that violates integrity constraints. For example, in Oracle7 there was no way to insert data into a child table for which there wasn't also data in the parent. In Oracle8, the user can conduct the insert on the child table before inserting data into the parent simply by deferring the FOREIGN KEY constraint. The user may also set constraints for immediate enforcement, using the `set constraint` *`name`* `immediate` or `set constraint all immediate statement`. You can define constraints as either deferrable or not deferrable, and either initially deferred or initially immediate. These attributes can be different for each constraint. You specify them with keywords in the `constraint` clause, as described next.

DEFERRABLE OR NOT DEFERRABLE The definition of a constraint will determine whether the constraint is deferrable by users. Two factors play into that determination. The first is the overall deferability of the constraint. If a constraint is created with the `deferrable` keyword, the constraint is deferrable by user processes until the time the transaction is committed. In contrast, if the constraint is created with the `not deferrable` keywords, then user process statements will always be bound by the integrity constraint. The `not deferrable` status is the default for the constraint. If a constraint has been created with the `not deferrable` status, then the `alter session` and `set` statements for deferring integrity constraints, mentioned previously, cannot be used.

INITIALLY DEFERRED OR INITIALLY IMMEDIATE The second factor is the default behavior of the constraint. The first option is to have the constraint deferred, defined with the `initially deferred` keywords. This option, and the `not deferrable` keyword option, described previously, are mutually exclusive. The other option is to have the integrity constraint enforced unless explicitly deferred by the user process, specified by the `initially immediate` keywords.

```
CREATE TABLE employees
(empid      NUMBER(10)      NOT NULL,
 name       VARCHAR2(40)    NOT NULL,
 salary     NUMBER(10)      NOT NULL,
 CONSTRAINT pk_employees_01
 PRIMARY KEY (empid) NOT DEFERRABLE);
```

Constraint Statuses

The other new features for integrity constraints are a new status for constraints and the use of nonunique indexes to enforce unique constraints. In versions earlier than Oracle8, there are two statuses for the integrity constraints: `enable` and `disable`. Oracle8 changes the `enable` status to `enable validate` and adds a third status for integrity constraints, `enable novalidate`. The new status allows Oracle to enforce the constraint on new data entering the table (enabling), but not on data that already exists on the table (no validating). These statuses can be used by issuing the `alter table` *`table_name`* `enable novalidate constraint` *`constraint_name`* statement, or `alter table` *`name`* `enable validate constraint` *`constraint_name`* statement.

Also, Oracle can support `UNIQUE` constraints being enforced with nonunique indexes. The columns indexed as part of the `UNIQUE` constraint should be the first columns in the nonunique index, but as long as those columns are the leading columns of the index, they may appear in any order. Other columns can also be present in the index to make it nonunique. This feature speeds the process of enabling `PRIMARY KEY` or `UNIQUE` constraints on the table. The nonunique index supporting the `UNIQUE` or `PRIMARY KEY` constraint cannot be dropped.

Using Triggers to Enforce Business Rules

A trigger is a database object directly associated with a particular table that fires whenever a specific statement or type is issued against that table. The types of statements that fire triggers are data manipulation statements: `update`, `delete`, and `insert` statements.

The basic type of database trigger is a statement trigger. It will fire every time a triggering statement occurs on the table to which the trigger is attached. Let's assume you want to monitor the EMPLOYEE table's `delete` activity to identify when employees are removed from the table. You create a history table that logs the user that changes the EMPLOYEE table, along with the date/time information and a comment in VARCHAR2 format for tracking when data is removed. Then you set up a trigger to populate the new EMPLOYEE_REC_HIST table either before or after the triggering event occurs. Trigger SQL code is sort of a hybrid between a database object creation statement (like `create table`) and straight PL/SQL code. A statement trigger will fire once whenever the triggering event occurs, no matter how many records are affected by the triggering event.

Sometimes when developing triggers, you want to have more precision over the work the trigger will accomplish than over a statement trigger allows. A row trigger gives this functionality. A row trigger adds some syntax to the statement trigger for accessing row data in the trigger's own table, both before the triggering statement executes and after. For example, say you have an EXCH_RATE table that lists the "from" and "to" currency, along with an exchange rate. Your batch process will come in and update the exchange rate every day—let's pretend it does so with only one `update` statement. Then, you decide later you want a history table that gives "from" currency, "to" currency, an old rate, a new rate, and the date the rate changed. However, these requirements may be beyond what a statement trigger provides. Remember, your statement trigger fires once for the `update` of the entire table, but you want a trigger that does something for every row.

The following code block shows a row trigger creation statement. When you issue this statement, Oracle will compile the trigger and store it in the database. The actions defined by the trigger code itself (in this case, an `insert` into the EXCH_RATE_HIST table) will not actually occur until the triggering event (in this case, an `update` issued on the EXCH_RATE table) occurs.

```
CREATE OR REPLACE TRIGGER exch_rate_trig
AFTER UPDATE ON exch_rate
FOR EACH ROW
BEGIN
  INSERT INTO exch_rate_hist (from_currency, to_currency,
   old_rate, new_rate, chg_date)
  VALUES (:old.from_currency, :old.to_currency,
   :old.exch_rate, :new.exch_rate, sysdate);
END;
```

TIP
Triggers may be enabled or disabled, meaning that they will either fire or not fire when the triggering event occurs.

Exercises

1. What is declarative data integrity? Name the five types of integrity constraints used on the Oracle database. What are some uses for each? How is each defined?
2. Which integrity constraints have indexes associated with them?
3. What are two other ways to enforce data integrity and business rules? What do you think are the advantages and disadvantages of each?

Implementing Data-Integrity Constraints and Triggers

Constraint definitions are handled at the table-definition level, either in a `create table` or in an `alter table` statement. Whenever a constraint is created, it is enabled automatically unless a condition exists on the table that violates the constraint. If the constraint condition is violated, Oracle will create the constraint with disabled status and the rows that violated the constraint are optionally written to a special location. Alternatively, you can specify your constraint to be disabled on creation with the `disable` clause, or force the constraint to be created and enabled by not validating the data with the `novalidate` clause. Some general guidelines for creating constraints are as follows:

- Put indexes associated with constraints in a tablespace separate from table data
- Disable constraints before loading tables with lots of row data, then re-enable the constraints afterward
- Make constraints deferrable when using self-referencing foreign key constraints

Creating Primary Keys and NOT NULL Constraints

The primary key is defined with the `constraint` clause. A name should be given to the primary key in order to name the associated index. The type of constraint is defined on the next line; it will either be a `PRIMARY KEY`, `FOREIGN KEY`,

UNIQUE, or CHECK constraint. For indexes associated with primary and unique keys, the tablespace used for storing the index is named in the using tablespace clause. You should specify a separate tablespace for indexes and the tables, for performance reasons. The code block here illustrates the creation of a table with constraints defined:

```
CREATE TABLE emp
( empid        NUMBER            NOT NULL,
  empname      VARCHAR2(30)      NOT NULL,
  salary       NUMBER            NOT NULL,
  CONSTRAINT pk_emp_01
PRIMARY KEY (empid)
NOT DEFERRABLE
USING INDEX TABLESPACE indexes_01 DISABLE)
TABLESPACE data_01;
```

The preceding example displays a create table statement defining constraints after the columns are named. This is called *out-of-line* constraint definition because the constraints are after the columns. You must do this if you plan to use two or more columns in your primary or unique keys. A different way to use create table with inline constraint definitions is shown here, but remember that if you use inline constraint definition, your constraint can only apply to the column it is inline with. Also, remember that NOT NULL constraints must always be defined inline:

```
CREATE TABLE emp
( empid        NUMBER
   CONSTRAINT pk_emp_01
PRIMARY KEY NOT DEFERRABLE
USING INDEX TABLESPACE indexes_01 ENABLE NOVALIDATE,
  empname      VARCHAR2(30)      NOT NULL,
  salary       NUMBER            NOT NULL )
TABLESPACE data_01;
```

Creating Foreign Keys

A foreign key is also defined in the create table or alter table statement. The foreign key in one table refers to the primary key in another, which is sometimes called the parent key. Another clause, on delete cascade, is purely optional. When included, it tells Oracle that if any deletion is performed on EMP that causes a bank account to be orphaned, the corresponding row in BANK_ACCOUNT with the same value for EMPID will also be deleted. Typically, this relationship is desirable, because the BANK_ACCOUNT table is the child of the EMP table. If the on delete cascade option is not included, then deletion of a record from EMP that has a corresponding child record in BANK_ACCOUNT with the EMPID defined will not be allowed. Additionally, in order to link two columns via a FOREIGN KEY constraint, the names do not have to be the same, but the datatype for each column must be identical.

```
CREATE TABLE bank_account
(bank_acct      VARCHAR2(40)       NOT NULL,
 aba_rtng_no    VARCHAR2(40)       NOT NULL,
 empid          NUMBER             NOT NULL,
 CONSTRAINT pk_bank_account_01
 PRIMARY KEY (bank_acct)
 USING INDEX TABLESPACE indexes_01,
 CONSTRAINT fk_bank_account_01
 FOREIGN KEY (empid) REFERENCES (emp.empid)
 ON DELETE CASCADE)
TABLESPACE data_01;
```

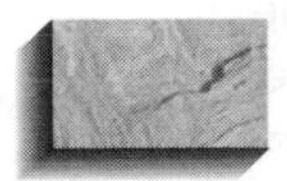

TIP

In order for a foreign key to reference a column in the parent table, the datatypes of both columns must be identical.

Creating UNIQUE and CHECK Constraints

Defining a UNIQUE constraint is handled as follows. Suppose the DBA decides to track telephone numbers in addition to all the other data tracked in EMP. The alter table statement can be issued against the database to make the change. As with a primary key, an index is created for the purpose of verifying uniqueness on the column. That index is identified with the name given to the constraint.

```
alter table emp
add (home_phone varchar2(10)
constraint ux_emp_01 unique
using index tablespace indexes_01);
```

The final constraint considered is the CHECK constraint. The fictitious company using the EMP and BANK_ACCOUNT tables places a salary cap on all employees of $110,000 per year. In order to mirror that policy, the DBA issues the following alter table statement, and the constraint takes effect as soon as the statement is issued. If a row exists in the table whose column value violates the check constraint, the constraint remains disabled.

```
ALTER TABLE emp
ADD CONSTRAINT ck_emp_01
CHECK (salary < 110000);
```

Exercises

1. What datatype condition must be true when defining `FOREIGN KEY` constraints?
2. Which statement is used to create integrity constraints on a new table and on an existing table?

Maintaining Integrity Constraints and Triggers

Constraints perform their intended operation when enabled, but do not operate when they are disabled. The `alter table` *`tblname`* `enable constraint` command enables a constraint. You can use the optional `validate` or `novalidate` keywords to have Oracle validate or not validate data currently in the constrained column for compliance with the constraint. Using validate means Oracle will check the data according to the rules of the constraint. If Oracle finds that the data does not meet the constraint's criteria, Oracle will not enable the constraint. Using `novalidate` causes Oracle to enable the constraint automatically without checking data, but users may later have trouble committing their changes if the changes contain data that violates the deferred constraint.

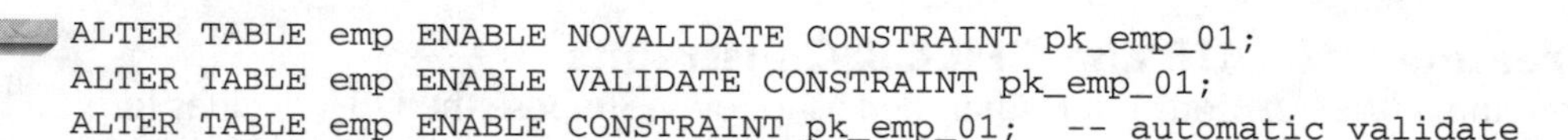

```
ALTER TABLE emp ENABLE NOVALIDATE CONSTRAINT pk_emp_01;
ALTER TABLE emp ENABLE VALIDATE CONSTRAINT pk_emp_01;
ALTER TABLE emp ENABLE CONSTRAINT pk_emp_01;  -- automatic validate
```

Disabling a constraint is much simpler—just use the `alter table` *`tblname`* `disable constraint` command. If you want to remove a constraint from the table, use the alter table *`tblname`* `drop constraint` statement. If you want to remove a table from your database that is referenced by foreign keys in other tables, use the drop table *`tblname`* `cascade constraints` statement.

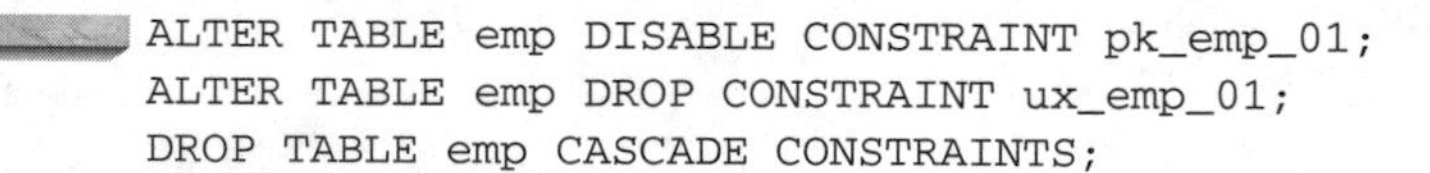

```
ALTER TABLE emp DISABLE CONSTRAINT pk_emp_01;
ALTER TABLE emp DROP CONSTRAINT ux_emp_01;
DROP TABLE emp CASCADE CONSTRAINTS;
```

TIP
When using `novalidate` to enable or `deferrable` to defer a primary or unique key, your associated index must be nonunique to store the potential violator records for a short time while the transaction remains uncommitted.

Using the EXCEPTIONS Table

The only foolproof way to create a constraint without experiencing violations on constraint creation is to create the constraint before any data is inserted. Otherwise, you must know how to manage violations using the EXCEPTIONS table, which is created by running a script provided with the Oracle software distribution called `utlexcpt.sql`. This file is usually found in the `rdbms/admin` subdirectory under the Oracle software home directory. You can alternatively use a table you name yourself, so long as the columns are the same as those created by the `utlexcpt.sql` script for the EXCEPTIONS table. This table contains a column for the ROWID of the row that violated the constraint and the name of the constraint it violated. In the case of constraints that are not named explicitly (such as `NOT NULL`), the constraint name listed is the one that was automatically created by Oracle at the time the constraint was created. The `exceptions into` clause also helps to identify those rows that violate the constraint you are trying to enable.

The following code block demonstrates a constraint violation being caused and then resolved using the EXCEPTIONS table. First, you create the problem:

```
SQL> truncate table exceptions;
Table truncated.
SQL> alter table emp disable constraint ux_emp_01;
Table altered.
SQL> desc emp
 Name                            Null?    Type
 ------------------------------- -------- ----
 EMPID                           NOT NULL NUMBER
 EMPNAME                         NOT NULL VARCHAR2(30)
 SALARY                          NOT NULL NUMBER
 HOME_PHONE                               VARCHAR2(10)
SQL> insert into emp (empid, empname, salary, home_phone)
  2  values (3049394,'FERRIS',110000,'1234567890');
1 row created.
SQL> insert into emp (empid, empname, salary, home_phone)
  2  values(40294932,'BLIBBER',50000,'1234567890');
1 row created.
SQL> commit;
Commit complete.
SQL> alter table emp enable validate constraint ux_emp_01
  2  exceptions into exceptions;
alter table emp enable validate constraint ux_emp_01
*
ERROR at line 1:
ORA-02299: cannot enable (SYS.UX_EMP_01) - duplicate keys found
```

Once you come up against a problem like this, you can use the EXCEPTIONS table to resolve it. Note that EXCEPTIONS will show you every row that violates the constraint. You could have simply deleted the offending data, and then added it after enabling the constraint:

```
SQL> select rowid, home_phone from emp
  2  where rowid in (select row_id from exceptions);
ROWID              HOME_PHONE
------------------ ----------
AAAA89AAGAAACJKAAA 1234567890
AAAA89AAGAAACJKAAB 1234567890
SQL> update emp set home_phone = NULL where rowid =
  2  chartorowid('AAAA89AAGAAACJKAAB');
1 row updated.
SQL> commit;
Commit complete.
SQL> select * from emp;
     EMPID EMPNAME                            SALARY HOME_PHONE
---------- ------------------------------ ---------- ----------
   3049394 FERRIS                             110000 1234567890
  40294932 BLIBBER                             50000
SQL> alter table emp enable validate constraint ux_emp_01;
Table altered.
SQL> truncate table EXCEPTIONS;
Table truncated.
```

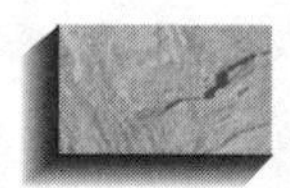

TIP
Remember to clean up the EXCEPTIONS table before and after you use it to avoid being confused by rows violating constraints from different tables.

Enabling, Disabling, and Dropping Triggers

Triggers will fire after they are created, meaning that they are enabled. You can change the status of a trigger from enabled to disabled and back again. If the trigger is disabled, it will not fire. The trigger will also not fire after it has been dropped. You may want to disable a trigger if you want to perform some large DML operation on the table to which the trigger belongs, but have the trigger not fire. The `alter trigger` *`trigname`* `enable` and `alter trigger` *`trigname`* `disable` statements enable and disable triggers, respectively. The `drop trigger` *`trigname`* statement removes the trigger.

Exercises

1. The DBA defines an integrity constraint associated with a table, which fails on creation. What can be done to determine which rows in a table violate an integrity constraint?
2. What does it mean for a constraint or trigger to be enabled or disabled?

Obtaining Constraint and Trigger Information from Oracle

There are several ways to access information about constraints. Many of the data dictionary views present various angles on the constraints. Although each of the views listed are prefixed with DBA_, the views are also available in the ALL_ or USER_ versions, with data limited in the following ways. ALL_ views correspond to the data objects, privileges, and so on, that are available to the user who executes the query, while the USER_ views correspond to the data objects, privileges, and so on, that were created by the user.

DBA_CONSTRAINTS This view lists detailed information about all constraints in the system. The constraint name and owner of the constraint are listed, along with the type of constraint it is, the status, and the referenced column name and owner of the parent key, if the constraint is a `FOREIGN KEY` constraint. One weakness lies in this view—if trying to look up the name of the parent table for the `FOREIGN KEY` constraint, the DBA must try to find the table whose primary key is the same as the column specified for the referenced column name. Some important and/or new columns in this view for Oracle8 include:

- **CONSTRAINT_TYPE** Displays *p* for `PRIMARY KEY`, *r* for `FOREIGN KEY`, c for `CHECK` constraints (including checks to see if data is NOT NULL), and *u* for `UNIQUE` constraints.
- **SEARCH_CONDITION** Displays the `CHECK` constraint criteria.
- **R_OWNER** Displays the owner of the referenced table, if the constraint is `FOREIGN KEY`.
- **R_CONSTRAINT_NAME** Displays the name of the primary key in the referenced table if the constraint is `FOREIGN KEY`.

- **GENERATED** Indicates whether the constraint name was defined by the user creating a table, or if Oracle generated it.
- **BAD** Indicates whether the `CHECK` constraint contains a reference to 2-digit years, a problem for millennium compliance.

DBA_CONS_COLUMNS This view lists detailed information about every column associated with a constraint. The view includes the name of the constraint and the associated table, as well as the name of the column in the constraint. If the constraint is composed of multiple columns, as can be the case in `PRIMARY KEY`, `UNIQUE`, and `FOREIGN KEY` constraints, the position or order of the columns is specified by a 1,2,3,...*n* value in the POSITION column of this view. Knowing the position of a column is especially useful in tuning SQL queries to use composite indexes when there is an index corresponding to the constraint.

Dictionary Views for Triggers

Though DBA_OBJECTS will display status information for triggers, the best dictionary views to access for trigger information are DBA_TRIGGERS and DBA_TRIGGER_COLS. The DBA_TRIGGERS view shows the name of the trigger, whether the trigger fires before or after its triggering statement, the trigger status, the triggering event, and the PL/SQL code that executes when the trigger fires. DBA_TRIGGER_COLS lists columns the trigger monitors to determine when to fire.

Exercises

1. Where in the data dictionary can the DBA look to find out whether a constraint's status is enabled or disabled?
2. Where in the dictionary can you find the PL/SQL source code for a trigger?

Using Clusters and Index-Organized Tables

In this section, you will cover the following topics related to managing clusters and IOTs (index-organized tables):

- Creating and maintaining clusters
- Using index-organized tables
- Dictionary information about clusters and IOTs

For the most part, the users and the DBA on an Oracle database system will find the use of standard tables effective in most situations. In this format, row data in standard tables is organized randomly, and Oracle cannot guarantee any order in the way row data is stored. This is usually fine, but other table objects offer the ability to guarantee structure in the way row data is stored. These other objects are clusters and index-organized tables (IOTs). Clusters guarantee grouping of related row data from different tables together, while IOTs store row data in sorted order similar to the structure of an index. Both of these options have advantages for use in certain, specialized situations. However, compared to standard tables and indexes, they are both somewhat complex to set up. It is important to know when clusters and IOTs will assist performance.

Creating and Maintaining Clusters

Clustered tables contain row data from two or more related tables, where the different tables are stored in the same segment and the related row data is stored in the same data blocks. This close physical proximity on disk improves performance for SQL join statements on those tables. Figure 9-5 illustrates the idea behind clustering. The three tables that are clustered in the figure are INVOICE, which

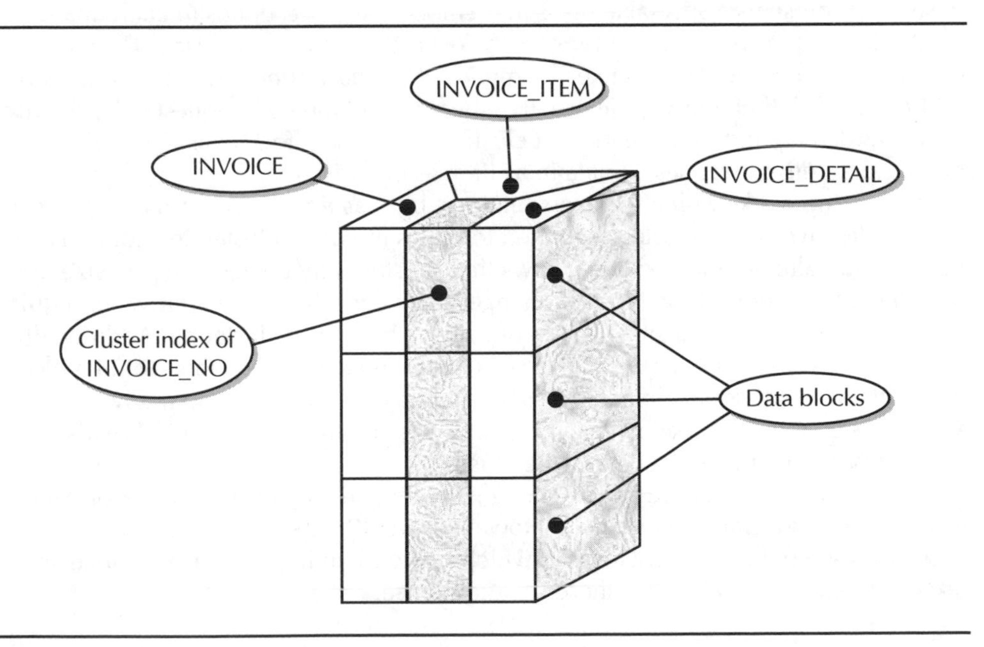

FIGURE 9-5. *Cluster keys and table distribution in cluster blocks*

stores general information about invoices for each purchase order; INVOICE_ITEM, which stores each line item of the purchase order; and INVOICE_DETAIL, which stores detailed information about each INVOICE_ITEM record, including part number, color, and size.

To cluster tables, all tables must contain at least one common column. This common column shared by the tables is the basis for a special index, called the *cluster key,* that references rows in every table. The cluster key can consist of more than one column. It may also be the primary key for each table, but it doesn't have to be. Although the cluster key column or columns are stored only once for all tables, yielding some storage benefit, clustered tables require more space for storage than would be required for the tables individually, for reasons discussed shortly. Even though the tables in a cluster are stored as one object, each table looks logically separate to the application.

Two types of clusters in Oracle are *index clusters* and *hash clusters.* Index clusters work on the principle of hanging the data from several different tables together with one common index, and then searching the index when data from the cluster is needed. The performance improvement it offers is on disk I/O. Hashing is designed to enhance performance even more. The implementation of hashing adds two new items to the creation of a cluster—a *hash key* and a *hash function.* The hash key represents a special address in memory that corresponds to each unique cluster-key value. When a user process looks for data in a hash cluster, the required data is converted into the hash key by means of the hash function. The result is an address on disk that tells Oracle exactly where to find the data requested by the user process. Ideally, performance in hash clusters can be so effective as to enable the database to retrieve requested data in as little as one disk read.

Clustering works well in certain situations, but has limited performance gains in others. Effective use of clusters is limited to tables in which cluster key columns are infrequently altered and updates to rows that substantially change the row size are uncommon. Either of these types of changes can cause the clustered rows to require relocation, potentially negating any performance benefit of clustering. Additionally, the cluster works best when enough rows of data in each of the tables to fill a block hang off each individual element in the cluster key. If too few or too many rows share cluster keys, the space in each block is wasted, and additional I/O reads may be necessary to retrieve the data in the cluster.

On the whole, cluster segments offer a fairly limited way to achieve performance gains in a few special circumstances. However, the DBA should have a full understanding of the circumstances in which clusters can improve performance and use clustering effectively when those situations arise.

TIP
The point of an index cluster is to improve performance for join operations accessing rows of all tables in the cluster. The SQL statements that reference tables in a cluster ideally should do so on the cluster key. Full table scans of clustered tables on columns other than the primary or cluster key are generally slower than if the tables were not part of a cluster.

Creating Index Clusters

Configuring and using clusters can be tricky. An important calculation to remember is the one used to determine how much space should be allocated for all the rows from all clustered tables that will be associated with a particular entry in the cluster key. This space allocation is determined with the `size` option at cluster creation. The formula for determining the appropriate value for `size` is as follows:

(est#_rows_in_tbl1 * size_of_tbl1_row) + (est#_rows_in_tbl2 * size_of_tbl2_row) + ... (est#_rows_in_tblN * size_of_tblN_row)

Review Figure 9-5 to see how `size` is calculated in this example.

Although the cluster key columns appear in several different tables, the data for the key is stored only once. However, it is acceptable to factor this additional space in as part of each row, because you want to make sure that there is enough space reserved in the block for each cluster-key entry. If a data change is made that makes the cluster entry larger than the current block can handle, then Oracle must migrate the entry to another block, reducing performance because of the additional disk reads required to retrieve the cluster. Thus, you will find yourself overestimating storage for clusters and wasting disk space constantly in order to preserve the cluster's performance gains. Once the required space has been determined and the `size` value determined, the DBA can then go about creating the cluster in the database. The first step is to create the actual cluster segment for the tables to reside in. This step is accomplished with a `create cluster` statement:

```
CREATE CLUSTER invoices_items_details
(invoice_id VARCHAR2(20))
PCTUSED 90  PCTFREE 5
SIZE 400
TABLESPACE clustered_data_02
STORAGE  ( INITIAL 1M  NEXT 1M
           MINEXTENTS 2 MAXEXTENTS 100
           PCTINCREASE 0 );
```

TIP
The default value for `size`, if none is specified, is 1 data block.

Storage options, such as `pctfree`, `pctused`, and the `storage` clause, are not available for the individual tables in the cluster, but they *are* available for the cluster as a whole. All `storage` definitions and `pctfree/pctused` options for tables in the cluster default to the values set for the cluster, which makes sense, because all tables being stored in a cluster are treated as one object. Attempts to issue alter table statements that assign values for storage options for the table, such as `pctfree`, `initrans`, or `pctincrease`, will result in an error.

After creating the cluster segment, you add tables with the `create table` statement:

```
CREATE TABLE invoice (
Invoice_id        VARCHAR2(20) PRIMARY KEY,
User_account      VARCHAR2(9),
Pmt_dttm          DATE)
CLUSTER invoices_items_details (invoice_id);

CREATE TABLE invoice_item (
Invoice_id        VARCHAR2(20) PRIMARY KEY,
Part_id           VARCHAR2(4),
Item_amount       NUMBER)
CLUSTER invoices_items_details (invoice_id);

CREATE TABLE invoice_detail (
Invoice_id        VARCHAR2(20) PRIMARY KEY,
Prchs_address     VARCHAR2(20),
Purchaser_zip     VARCHAR2(10))
CLUSTER invoices_items_details (invoice_id);
```

The final step is to create the cluster-key index. This is crucial to the placement of data into the cluster. Without completing this step, the cluster is unusable, even if the table definitions and cluster definitions are in place. In order to place data in the cluster, the DBA must create the cluster-key index:

```
CREATE INDEX invoices_items_details_01
ON CLUSTER invoices_items_details
TABLESPACE  data_clusters_02
STORAGE ( INITIAL 1M  NEXT 1M
          MINEXTENTS 2  MAXEXTENTS 50
          PCTINCREASE 50)
PCTFREE 5;
```

After the index is created, the DBA can load data into the table with SQL*Loader or with some other mechanism for batch `update`. At that point, you may consider some form of control for limiting the amount of user `update` to the cluster-key column or other columns in tables in the cluster, to prevent user data changes from migrating cluster entries and degrading performance. This task can be accomplished either by issuing `alter tablespace read only` on the tablespace housing the cluster, or by revoking user `update` privileges to the tables in the cluster and managing all database changes to clustered tables via an application designed for the purpose.

TIP
The tables in the cluster cannot be populated until the cluster-key index is created by the DBA.

Creating Hash Clusters

Creating hash clusters is much like creating index clusters, with a few differences. The first difference is an option called `hashkeys`, which is used to determine the exact number of cluster-key entries that will be allowed in the object. Set `hashkeys` to a prime number, or else Oracle will simply round up your `hashkeys` specification to the nearest prime. The second difference is the `hash is` clause, which determines the hashing function Oracle uses on the hash cluster. When a user process looks for data in a hash cluster, the required data is converted into the hash key by means of the hash function. The result is an address on disk that tells Oracle exactly where to find the data requested by the user process.

```
CREATE CLUSTER invoices_items_details
(invoice_id VARCHAR2(20))
PCTUSED 90  PCTFREE 5
SIZE 400 HASHKEYS 1003
TABLESPACE clustered_data_02
STORAGE  ( INITIAL 1M  NEXT 1M
           MINEXTENTS 2 MAXEXTENTS 100
           PCTINCREASE 0 );
```

TIP
Beware of collisions when using hash clusters. A collision occurs if several key values are evaluated to the same result by the hashing function. Additional disk reads will be required when collisions occur. Additional disk reads will also be required when there is insufficient space to accommodate all rows in a cluster block because Oracle will place some data into an overflow block.

Maintaining Clusters

When used properly, clusters and hashing can dramatically improve performance in your database application. However, when mismanaged, they can severely impact the performance of an application. You should understand the following points about proper and improper use of clusters and hashing for both the OCP Exam 2 and for general database administration:

- Do not use clusters or hashing in situations where updates increase the size of rows in the table dramatically or where the cluster-key column is updated frequently.
- Use clusters and hashing when you have master and detail tables joined frequently. This mainly applies to index clusters.
- Do not use hash clusters when application comparisons in the `where` clause don't use an equality operator on the cluster-key column. Another index can be used for performance gains in hash clusters when this situation occurs, however.
- Clusters work best when the distribution of data is uniform. In the invoice example, this would mean that there are about the same number of items and details associated with each invoice.

Changing and Removing Clusters

The `alter cluster` command is used to change `storage`, `pctfree`, `pctused`, ad `size` options, or to allocate and deallocate space for a cluster. You cannot change the `size`, `hash is`, or `hashkeys` options for hash clusters with the `alter cluster` command. Other commands like `analyze` or `truncate cluster` have the same uses here as they do for regular tables.

```
ALTER CLUSTER invoices_items_details SIZE 1024;
ANALYZE CLUSTER invoices_items_details ESTIMATE STATISTICS;
TRUNCATE CLUSTER invoices_items_details;
```

To rid yourself of the cluster, you can do one of two things. The first is issuing the `drop cluster` *`clustername`* `including tables` statement to drop the cluster and tables at once, as shown here:

```
DROP CLUSTER invoices_items_details INCLUDING TABLES;
```

Or, issue a `drop table` command for all tables in the cluster, and then issue the `drop cluster` command to drop the cluster, as shown here:

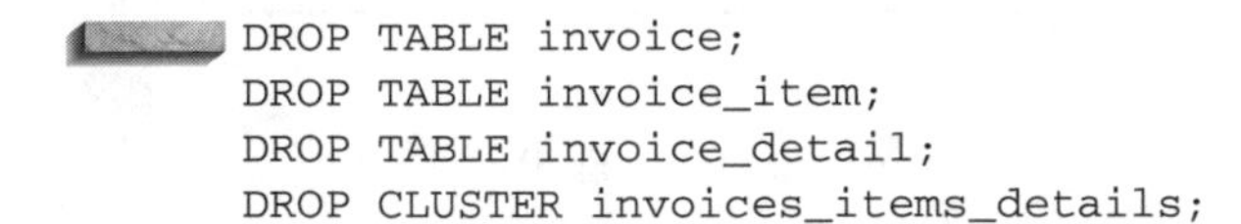

```
DROP TABLE invoice;
DROP TABLE invoice_item;
DROP TABLE invoice_detail;
DROP CLUSTER invoices_items_details;
```

TIP
Truncating an index cluster releases its storage allocation and returns it to the tablespace. This command only removes table data for hash clusters; it does not release storage allocation or return extents to the tablespace.

Exercises

1. What are the two types of cluster? What advantages do clusters offer over nonclustered tables? What is the `size` clause, and what does it indicate? What is the `hashkeys` clause, and what does it indicate?
2. What are the limitations of clusters? Which type of DML activity is particularly detrimental to clusters?

Using Index-Organized Tables

Another new feature available in Oracle that builds on the use of indexes is the *index-organized table* (IOT). Consider the following scenario: In Oracle7, the DBA can create a table with few columns and index all columns in the table, effectively creating a table that is easier to search but that requires significant storage for the combined size of table and index. In Oracle8, those two objects can be combined to minimize storage requirements. The resultant object is the index-organized table, an object with the structure of a B-tree index, but with all data of all columns of the table stored in it, accessible quickly by the primary key with Oracle's index scan operation. Figure 9-6 illustrates the concept of an index-organized table. Since the data in an index-organized table is stored by the indexed primary key, no SQL statement searching for data on an index-organized table will ever use a full table scan.

Index-organized tables store all data in a B-tree structure. In traditional B-tree indexes, the column data would be stored in the index, along with a ROWID for accessing the data in the table. Since the data is actually stored in the tree, however, there is no need for a correlated ROWID between table and index. Thus, row data in index-organized tables do not have ROWIDs. It is not possible to create another index on an index-organized table in Oracle 8.0, so users must remember to use the primary key for all data searches on the index-organized table. Other restrictions include the inability to cluster, partition, or use LONG columns or `UNIQUE` constraints in index-organized tables. These database objects work best in applications that store

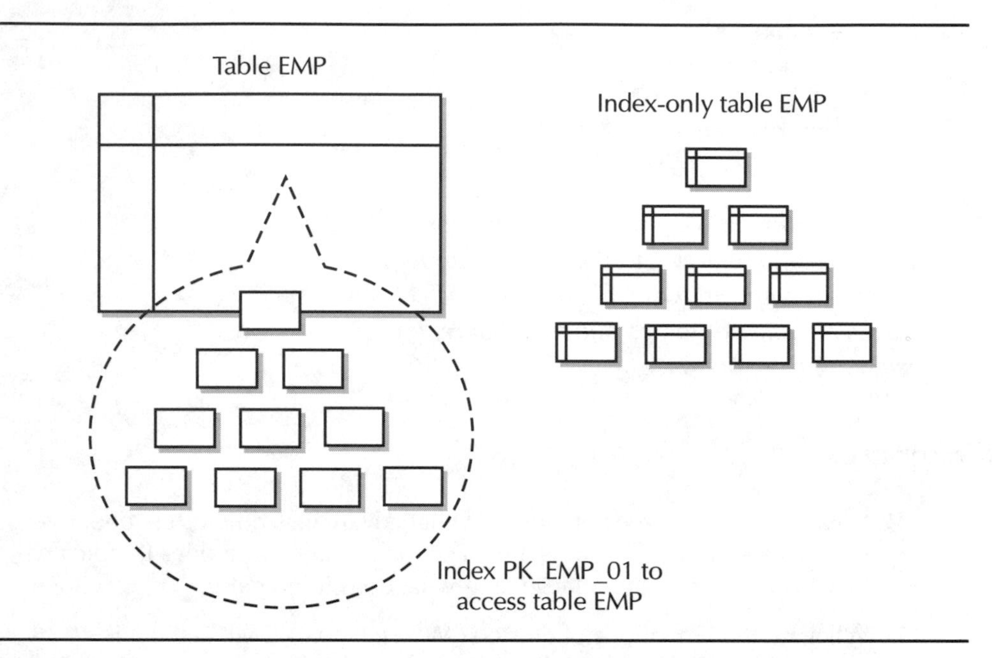

FIGURE 9-6. *Table/index relationships and the index-organized table*

spatial data. A good example of the use of index-organized tables is for improving text searches, because the location of all copies of a particular word can be stored together in one index node for that word. An example of the `create table` statement used to create an index-organized table appears in the following code block:

```
CREATE TABLE prglang_keywords
(keyword VARCHAR2(30) CONSTRAINT pk_manual_keywords_01 PRIMARY KEY,
 page_number NUMBER(10))
ORGANIZATION INDEX
PCTTHRESHOLD 25
OVERFLOW TABLESPACE data_oflow_01;
```

There are several new keywords in this `create table` statement to discuss. First, the use of the `organization index` keywords is perhaps the most important component in defining an index-organized table, because it is the component that actually defines the table as index-organized. Prior to Oracle8, this parameter was set implicitly for all tables as `organization heap`. In Oracle8, the DBA can define the method used to organize data in regular tables using the `organization heap` keywords, but this behavior is the one Oracle uses by default. Only when `organization index` is used does Oracle create an index-organized table.

The next parameter used in defining an index-organized table is the `pctthreshold` *num* clause. This clause is optional. When specified, `pctthreshold` indicates a threshold limit that any row of data can occupy in an index-organized table block. In the example, the value set for this clause is 25, which means that any row in the table that takes up 25 percent *or more* of its data block for storage will have non-key column data moved into an overflow tablespace defined using the overflow tablespace keywords. If `overflow tablespace` is specified without defining a `pctthreshold`, the default `pctthreshold` of 50 will be used. Any data manipulation or load operation can be performed on index-organized tables, including `alter table`, `drop table`, truncation, EXPORT/IMPORT, and direct path data loads, with the exception of operations based on ROWID, as mentioned earlier.

TIP
Rows in an index-organized table have no ROWID.

Comparing Regular Tables with IOTs

Obviously, there are some significant differences between IOTs and regular tables. The following list identifies the differences at a glance:

- IOTs store all row data in a B-tree structure, while regular tables store table data in table segments and index data in indexes.
- IOT rows have no ROWID, whereas regular table rows do.
- Uniqueness for IOT data is determined by primary key, rather than by ROWID.
- A full table scan on a regular table guarantees no return order on row data, while index scans on IOTs return data in primary key order.
- In Oracle 8.0, IOTs cannot be partitioned, replicated, or participate in a distributed transaction, because ROWIDs are not used.
- There can be no index on an IOT, other than the implicit IOT index structure. This restriction includes indexes created as part of unique keys, so unique keys other than the primary key are not supported in IOTs, either.

Exercises

1. What is an IOT? What advantages do IOTs offer over other kinds of tables?
2. What are the limitations of IOTs? What special identifier used in all other types of tables is not used in IOTs?

Dictionary Information About Clusters and IOTs

Several views are useful for finding information about clusters in your database; they include DBA_CLUSTERS, DBA_CLU_COLUMNS, DBA_TAB_COLUMNS, and DBA_CLUSTER_HASH_EXPRESSIONS. The DBA_CLUSTERS dictionary view gives the cluster owner, name, tablespace, value set for `size`, type of cluster (index or hash), and value for `hashkeys`. DBA_CLU_COLUMNS identifies the table name and columns in all tables in the cluster, which is approximately the same information you would find in DBA_TABLES. Finally, the DBA_CLUSTER_HASH_EXPRESSIONS dictionary view shows the hashing expression specified for hash clusters.

Information about index-organized tables created in the database can be found with the use of the USER_, ALL_, and DBA_TABLES dictionary views. A new column called IOT stores information about index-organized tables. Data in rows for this column can have three values—IOT for index-organized tables, IOT_OVERFLOW for overflow segments, or NULL for any table that is not index-organized.

Exercises

1. Which views can be used to find information about clusters in a database? Where would you look to find the value set for the `size` clause in a cluster?
2. Which views are used to find information about IOTs? Have you already used these views? Explain?

Chapter Summary

This chapter covers the remainder of database object management started in Chapter 8. The objects covered here include indexes, declarative integrity constraints, triggers, clusters, and index-organized tables. The part of OCP Exam 2 that focuses on management of these database objects is worth about 16 percent of your overall grade on this test.

The first area you covered was managing indexes. There are three types of indexes in Oracle8: bitmap indexes, B-tree indexes, and reverse-key indexes. You learned how each of these indexes is used in Oracle and the various situations in which each type of index will improve application performance. The use of the `create index` statement for creating bitmap and B-tree indexes was discussed, along with the use of the `alter index` statement for reorganizing indexes and the `drop index` statement for removing indexes. Finally, the dictionary views that show information about the indexes was covered in this section.

The next section discussed how to manage data integrity on your database. The three methods for managing integrity were introduced; they are declarative integrity constraints, application code, and triggers. Since the use of declarative integrity constraints is the preferred method for managing data integrity, the section focused on the five types of integrity constraints you may use on your tables, and how to create them. However, for complex situations, you may not be able to rely solely on declarative integrity constraints. In such a case, you should consider using triggers. This section covered creating, maintaining, and dropping triggers. You also learned how to obtain constraint and trigger information from the Oracle data dictionary.

The final area covered in this chapter was managing clusters and IOTs (index-organized tables). The performance benefits of these two objects was explained, along with how they each differ from regular tables, and how clusters and IOTs differ from one another. The differences between index and hash clusters was explained, along with the methods used to create each of them. The methods used for creating IOTs was explained, as well. Finally, the dictionary views that will help you see information about each of the different objects were identified.

Two-Minute Drill

- Indexes are used to improve performance on database objects in Oracle. The three types of indexes in Oracle are bitmap, B-tree, and reverse-key.
- Bitmap indexes are best used for improving performance on columns containing static values with low cardinality, or few unique values in the column.
- B-tree indexes are best used for improving performance on columns containing values with high cardinality.
- The decision to create an index should weigh the performance gain of using the index against the performance overhead produced when DML statements change index data.
- Reverse-key indexes store the index values in reverse sort order, which can improve performance in Oracle Parallel Server environments.
- The `pctused` parameter is not available for indexes, because every index block is always available for data changes as the result of Oracle needing to keep data in order in an index.
- DBA_INDEXES and DBA_IND_COLUMNS are dictionary views that store information about indexes.
- Data integrity constraints are declared in the Oracle database as part of the table definition.

- There are five types of integrity constraints:
    - **PRIMARY KEY** Identifies each row in the table as unique
    - **FOREIGN KEY** Develops referential integrity between two tables
    - **UNIQUE** Forces each non-NULL value in the column to be unique
    - **NOT NULL** Forces each value in the column to be not NULL
    - **CHECK** Validates each entry into the column against a set of valid value constants.
- There are different constraint states in Oracle8, including deferrable constraints or non-deferrable constraints.
- In addition, a constraint can be enabled on a table without validating existing data in the constrained column using the `enable novalidate` clause.
- Oracle uses unique indexes to enforce `UNIQUE` and `PRIMARY KEY` constraints when those constraints are not deferrable. If the constraints are deferrable, then Oracle uses nonunique indexes for those constraints.
- When a constraint is created, every row in the table is validated against the constraint restriction.
- The EXCEPTIONS table stores rows that violate the integrity constraint created for a table.
- The EXCEPTIONS table can be created by running the `utlexcpt.sql` script.
- The DBA_CONSTRAINTS and DBA_CONS_COLUMNS data dictionary views display information about the constraints of a database.
- Triggers are PL/SQL programs that allow you to define a DML statement event that causes the code to execute.
- There are two types of triggers: row triggers and statement triggers.
- Triggers and constraints can be enabled or disabled. If enabled, constraints will be enforced and triggers will fire. If disabled, constraints will not be enforced and triggers will not fire.
- Index clusters improve performance on queries that join two or more tables with static data by storing related data from the tables in the same physical data blocks. This reduces the number of I/O reads required to retrieve the data.

- Determining space requirements for clusters is accomplished by doing the following:

  1. Determining the number of rows that will associate with each individual cluster entry.
  2. Determining the number of cluster entries that will fit into one block.
  3. Determining the number of blocks required for the cluster.

- Clusters should not be used to store tables whose data is dynamic or volatile.
- The steps to create a cluster, once proper sizing has taken place, are as follows:

  1. Create the cluster with the `create cluster` statement.
  2. Place tables in the cluster with the `create table` command with the `cluster` option.
  3. Create the cluster index with the `create index on cluster` command.
  4. Populate tables with data. This step cannot be done until step 3 is complete.

- Hash clustering is similar to regular clusters because data from multiple tables are stored together in data blocks. However, there is an additional key to search for data, called a hash key.
- Data is retrieved from a hash cluster by Oracle applying a hash function to the value specified in equality operations in the `where` clause of the table join. Ideally, this allows for data retrieval in one disk read.
- Hash clusters only improve performance on queries when the data is static, and the `select` statements contain equality operations *only*. Range queries are not allowed.
- Index-organized tables (IOTs) are tables that are stored in B-tree index structures.
- ROWID information is not stored in IOTs because the row data is stored along with the index.
- IOTs store all row data in a B-tree structure, while regular tables store table data in table segments and index data in indexes.

- IOT rows have no ROWID; regular table rows do.
- Uniqueness for IOT data is determined by the primary key, rather than by ROWID.
- A full table scan on a regular table guarantees no return order on row data, while index scans on IOTs return data in primary key order.
- IOTs cannot be partitioned, replicated, or participate in a distributed transaction, because ROWIDs are not used.
- There can be no index on an IOT in Oracle 8.0, other than the implicit IOT index structure. This restriction includes indexes created as part of unique keys, so unique keys other than the primary key are not supported in IOTs, either.

Chapter Questions

1. The DBA is designing the data model for an application. Which of the following statements are not true about primary keys?

A. A primary key cannot be NULL.

B. Individual or composite column values combining to form the primary key must be unique.

C. Each column value in a primary key corresponds to a primary-key value in another table.

D. A primary key identifies the uniqueness of that row in the table.

E. An associated index is created with a primary key.

2. Developers of an application have turned to the DBA to determine an appropriate database architecture. After presenting their model, one developer who is studying for her OCP exam suggests table clusters. Index clusters are appropriate when

A. The tables in the cluster are frequently joined

B. The tables in the cluster are frequently updated

C. The tables in the cluster have fewer than 60 rows

D. The tables in the cluster have no primary key

3. In working with developers of an application, the DBA might use the POSITION column in DBA_CONS_COLUMNS for which of the following purposes?

A. To indicate the position of the constraint on disk

B. To relate to the hierarchical position of the table in the data model

C. To improve the scalability of the Oracle database

D. To identify the position of the column in a composite index

4. The DBA is evaluating the type of index to use in an application. Bitmap indexes improve database performance in which of the following situations?

A. `select` statements on column indicating employee status, which has only four unique values for 50,000 rows

B. `update` statements where the indexed column is being changed

C. `delete` statements where only one or two rows are removed at a time

D. `insert` statements where several hundred rows are added at once

5. The DBA is considering the best method for enforcing data integrity according to some business rules. The requirement is that when a row is added to a table, the data in one column STATUS is checked. If the STATUS column is 1, then the data in column VALUE is validated against table VAL_1; otherwise, the data in column VALUE is validated against table VAL_2. Based on these requirements, which of the following choices would be best for enforcing business rules?

A. Unique keys

B. Foreign keys

C. Triggers

D. Views

6. The DBA is developing an index creation script. Which of the following choices best explains the reason why indexes do not permit the definition of the `pctused` storage option?

A. Indexes have a preset `pctused` setting of 25.

B. Oracle must keep index entries in order, so index blocks are always being updated.

C. Indexes are not altered unless they are recreated.

D. Indexes will not be modified after the `pctfree` threshold is crossed.

7. The DBA is designing an architecture to support a large document-scanning and cross-referencing system used for housing policy manuals. The architecture will involve several tables that will contain an excess of 30,000,000 rows. Which of the following table designs would be most appropriate for this architecture?

A. Partitioned tables

B. Index-organized tables

C. Clustered tables

D. Regular tables

8. In order to design a table that enforces uniqueness on a column, which of the following choices are appropriate? (Choose three)

A. `UNIQUE` constraint

B. Bitmap index

C. Primary key

D. Foreign key

E. `NOT NULL` constraint

F. Partitioned index

G. Unique index

H. `CHECK` constraint

9. In designing a database architecture that maximizes performance on database `select` statements, each of the following would enhance performance, except for:

A. Using indexes on columns frequently used in `where` clauses

B. Using bitmap indexes on frequently updated columns

C. Putting indexes in a separate tablespace from tables on a different disk resource

D. Designing index-organized tables around `select` statements used in the application

10. When attempting to re-enable the primary key after a data load, the DBA receives the following error: "ORA-02299: cannot enable (SYS.UX_EMP_01) - duplicate keys found." Where might the DBA look to see what rows caused the violation?

A. DBA_CONS_COLUMNS

B. DBA_CONSTRAINTS

C. DBA_CLU_COLUMNS

D. EXCEPTIONS

11. The DBA is trying to make sure that database performance is not degraded by Oracle spending too much time managing space usage due to data blocks making short frequent visits to the freelist for more data. What combination of space utilization settings would most effectively allow this to happen?

A. `pctfree = 20, pctused = 75`

B. `pctfree = 5, pctused = 90`

C. `pctfree = 5, pctused = 60`

D. `pctfree = 20, pctused = 30`

12. The DBA notices that the system-generated indexes associated with integrity constraints in the Oracle database have been defined to be nonunique. Which of the following choices accurately describes the reason for this?

A. Non-deferrable `PRIMARY KEY` constraints

B. Deferrable `UNIQUE` constraints

C. Internal error

D. Incomplete data load

13. The DBA is comparing IOTs to regular tables for use in a particular portion of the application. Which of the following statements is not true about IOTs?

A. IOTs allow no additional indexes to be created on table columns

B. IOTs allow partitioning

C. IOT rows have no ROWIDs

D. IOTs use a B-tree structure to store table data

Answers to Chapter Questions

1. C. Each column value in a primary key corresponds to a primary-key value in another table.

Explanation All other statements made about primary keys are true. They must be not NULL and unique, in order to allow them to represent each row uniquely in the table. An associated index is also created with a primary key. Refer to the discussion of primary keys as part of integrity constraints.

2. A. The tables in the cluster are frequently joined

Explanation Choice B is incorrect because data in tables that are clustering candidates should not grow as the result of updates, and the columns in the cluster key should ideally be completely static. Choice C is incorrect because there is no limit on the number of rows a table can have in order to be clustered. Choice D is incorrect because a table without a primary key is inappropriate for general use in Oracle, including for use in clusters. Refer to the discussion of clustering.

3. D. To identify the position of a column in a composite index

Explanation Constraints are stored with the data definition of a table, without regard to the value stored in POSITION. Therefore, choice A is incorrect. POSITION also has nothing to do with parent/child hierarchies in the data model or with scalability, thereby eliminating choices B and C. Refer to the discussion on using dictionary views to examine constraints.

4. A. `select` statements on column indicating employee status, which has only four unique values for 50,000 rows

Explanation Bitmap indexes are designed to improve performance on a table whose column contains relatively static data of low cardinality. This means there are very few unique values in a large pool of rows. Four unique values out of 50,000 definitely qualifies. Choice B is incorrect because of the point made about the column values being relatively static. Since it is a relatively processor-intensive activity to change a value in a bitmap index, you should use bitmap indexes mainly on column values that are static.

5. C. Triggers

Explanation The requirements are fairly complex and require a data check to even determine how to validate. Declarative integrity constraints usually don't work in this situation. Therefore, triggers are the best method.

6. B. Oracle must keep index entries in order, so index blocks are always being updated.

Explanation Recall from the discussion of how an index works that, in order for Oracle to maintain the index order, all blocks are always available for update. Thus, choice B is the correct answer to this question. Besides, there is no default `pctused` value for indexes.

7. A. Partitioned tables

Explanation 30,000,000 rows is a lot of data to manage in an ordinary table. Thus, you should eliminate Choice D immediately. A smart DBA will want to maximize data availability by ensuring that the table is partitioned and that the partitions are spread across multiple drives to make it possible to use parallel processing. Though IOTs are designed for text scanning, they *cannot* be partitioned, making them a poor candidate for storing this much data. Thus, eliminate choice B. Finally, since no mention of table joins is made, you have no reason to choose choice C.

8. A, C, G. `UNIQUE` constraint, primary key, unique index

Explanation Unique indexes enforce uniqueness of values in a column or columns. They are used by Oracle as the underlying logic for primary keys and unique keys. This fact makes A, C, and G the correct answers. Choices D and E are eliminated because neither of these declarative integrity constraints have unique indexes or any other mechanism to support uniqueness. Bitmap indexes cannot be unique, either, eliminating choice B.

9. B. Using bitmap indexes on frequently updated columns

Explanation Bitmap indexes should never be used on columns that are frequently updated, because those changes are very costly in terms of maintaining the index. Using indexes on columns frequently used in `where` clauses, putting indexes in a separate tablespace from tables on a different disk resource, and designing index-organized tables around `select` statements used in the application are all good methods for performance enhancement.

10. D. EXCEPTIONS

Explanation When a constraint fails upon being enabled, you would not look in the data dictionary at all. This fact eliminates choices A, B, and C. Instead, you look in the EXCEPTIONS table. Recall that the `exceptions into EXCEPTIONS` clause in the `alter table enable constraint` statement allows you to put the offending records into the EXCEPTIONS table for review and later correction.

11. D. `pctfree = 20, pctused = 30`

Explanation A high value set for `pctused` forces a data block into being placed on a freelist frequently. This activity is the opposite of the criteria in the question, so you should know right away to eliminate the answers where `pctused` is set highest. These choices include A and B. For choice C, `pctused` is still high relative to choice D, so you should eliminate choice C, as well.

12. B. Deferrable `UNIQUE` constraints

Explanation The entire rationale behind the situation described in this question, namely that the system-generated indexes associated with integrity constraints in the Oracle database have been defined to be nonunique, is completely a product of deferrable integrity constraints. Since the constraint is deferrable, the index cannot be unique, because it must accept new record input for the duration of the transaction. The user's attempted `commit` causes the transaction to roll back if the constraints are not met.

13. B. IOTs allow partitioning

Explanation Choices A, C, and D, that IOTs allow no additional indexes to be created on table columns, IOT rows have no ROWIDs, and IOTs use a B-tree structure to store table data, are all true about IOTs. Only the statement about IOTs allowing partitioning is incorrect. They, in fact, do not allow the DBA to use partitions.

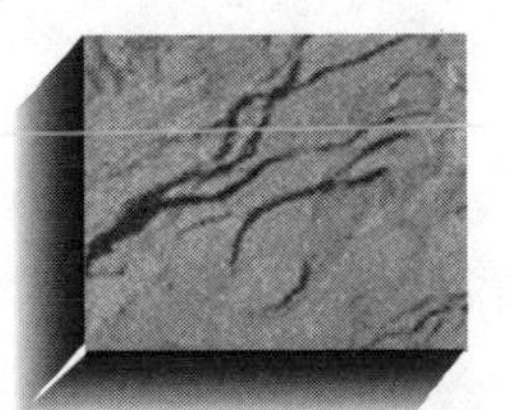

CHAPTER 10

Managing Database Use

In this chapter, you will learn about and demonstrate knowledge in the following areas:

- Managing users
- Managing resource use
- Managing privileges
- Managing roles
- Auditing the database

This chapter focuses on the functionality Oracle provides for limiting database access. There are several different aspects to limiting database use. In many larger organizations, you may find that security is handled by a security administrator—the functionality provided by Oracle for security is not handled by the DBA at all. As the resident expert on Oracle software, it helps to familiarize yourself with this subject in order to better manage the Oracle database. Bear in mind that this discussion will use the terms *DBA* and *security administrator* interchangeably, and that the main reason it is covered here is that there will be questions about security on the OCP Exam 2. Approximately 16 percent of test content on this exam focuses on database security.

Managing Users

In this section, you will cover the following topics related to managing users:

- Creating new database users
- Altering and dropping existing users
- Monitoring information about existing users

There are many activities involved in managing users in the Oracle database. First, new users must be created, and then their identification methods and default database use can be altered by the DBA or security administrator in many ways. There are many aspects of user management that the DBA or security administrator can control with the Oracle database.

Database-use management is sometimes referred to as Oracle's *security domain*. You covered the beginning of that security domain in Chapter 6 when you learned about operating system and Oracle password file authentication. Oracle8 adds several new features over Oracle7 for user authentication and security, including features such as account locking, password expiry, and others that will be covered in the section.

Creating New Database Users

One of the primary tasks early on in the creation of a new database is adding new users. However, user creation is an ongoing task. As users enter and leave the organization, so too must the DBA keep track of access to the database granted to those users. When using Oracle's own database authentication method, new users are created with the `create user` statement:

```
CREATE USER spanky
IDENTIFIED BY first01
DEFAULT TABLESPACE users_01
TEMPORARY TABLESPACE temp_01
QUOTA 10M ON users_01
PROFILE app_developer
PASSWORD EXPIRE
ACCOUNT UNLOCK;
```

This statement highlights several items of information that comprise the syntax and semantics of user creation, and these areas will be covered in the following subtopics:

CREATE USER The user's name in Oracle. If the DBA is using operating system authentication to allow users to access the database, then the usernames should by default be preceded with OPS$. In no other case is it recommended that a username contain a nonalphanumeric character, although both _ and # are permitted characters in usernames. The name should also start with a letter. On single-byte character sets, the name can be from 1 to 30 characters long, while on multibyte character sets, the name of a user must be limited to 30 bytes. In addition, the name should contain one single-byte character according to Oracle recommendations. The username is not case sensitive and cannot be a reserved word.

IDENTIFIED BY The user's password in Oracle. This item should contain at least three characters, and preferably six or more. Generally, it is recommended that users change their password once they know their username is created. Oracle enforces this with the `password expire` clause. Users should change their passwords to something that is not a word or a name that preferably contains a numeric character somewhere in it. As is the case with the username, the password can be a maximum length of 30 bytes and cannot be a reserved word. If operating system authentication is being used, you would use the keywords `identified externally`.

DEFAULT TABLESPACE Tablespace management is a crucial task in Oracle. The `default tablespace` names the location where the user's database objects are created by default. This clause plays an important role in protecting the integrity of the SYSTEM tablespace. If no `default tablespace` is named for a user, objects that the user creates may be placed in the SYSTEM tablespace. Recall that SYSTEM contains many database objects, such as the data dictionary and the SYSTEM rollback segment, that are critical to database use. Users should not be allowed to create their database objects in the SYSTEM tablespace.

TEMPORARY TABLESPACE If `temporary tablespace` is not explicitly specified by the DBA when the username is created, the location for all temporary segments for that user will be the SYSTEM tablespace. SYSTEM, as you already know, is a valuable resource that should not be used for user object storage.

QUOTA A `quota` is a limit on the amount of space the user's database objects can occupy within the tablespace. If a user attempts to create a database object that exceeds that user's `quota` for that tablespace, then the object creation script will fail. Quotas can be specified either in kilobytes (K) or megabytes (M). A `quota` clause should be issued separately for every tablespace other than the temporary tablespace on which the user will have access to create database objects. If you want a user to have the ability to use all the space in a tablespace, `quota unlimited on` *`tblspcname`* can be specified.

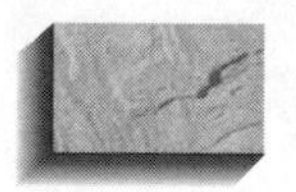

TIP
Users need quotas on tablespaces to create database objects only. They do not need a quota on a tablespace to `update`, `insert`, or `delete` data in an existing object in the tablespace, so long as they do have the appropriate privilege on the object for data being inserted, updated or deleted.

PROFILE Profiles are a bundled set of resource-usage parameters that the DBA can set in order to limit the user's overall host machine utilization. A driving idea behind their use is that many end users of the system only need a certain amount of the host machine's capacity during their session. To reduce the chance that one user could affect the overall database performance with, say, a poorly formulated ad hoc report that drags the database to its knees, you may assign profiles for each user that limit the amount of time they can spend on the system.

PASSWORD EXPIRE This clause enforces the requirement that a user change his or her password on first logging into Oracle. This extra level of password security guarantees that not even you, the DBA, will know a user's password. If this clause is not included, then the user will not have to change the password on first logging into Oracle.

ACCOUNT UNLOCK This is the default for user accounts created. It means that the user's account is available for use immediately. The DBA can prevent users from using their accounts by specifying `account lock` instead.

Guidelines for User-Account Management

The following list identifies several new guidelines to follow when managing user accounts. In many cases, these items are new for Oracle8 and enhance the management of user accounts:

- Use a standard password for user creation, such as `123abc` or `first1`, and use `password expire` to force users to change this password to something else the first time they log into Oracle.
- Avoid OS authentication unless all your users will access Oracle while connected directly to the machine hosting your database (this second part is also not advised).
- Be sure to always assign `temporary tablespace` and `default tablespace` to users with the ability to create database objects, such as developers.
- Give few users `quota unlimited`. Although it's annoying to have users asking for more space, it's even more annoying to reorganize tablespaces carelessly filled with database objects.
- Become familiar with the user-account management and other host machine limits that can be set via profiles. These new features take Oracle user-account management to new levels of security.

Exercises

1. What statement is used to create users? Explain the need for tablespace quotas. Do users need tablespace quotas to `insert` data in existing tables? Explain.
2. What is the purpose of a temporary tablespace? What clause is designed to force users to change their password after initial login?

Altering and Dropping Existing Users

Once a user is created, there are a few reasons you'll need to modify that user. One is to expire the password if a user forgets it, so that the next time the user logs in, the password can be changed by the user. The `alter user identified by` statement is used to change the user's password:

```
ALTER USER athena
IDENTIFIED BY forgotpassword
PASSWORD EXPIRE;
```

In certain situations, as the result of user profiles, a user's account may become locked. This may occur if the user forgot his or her password and tried to log in using a bad password too many times. To unlock a user's account while also making it possible for the user to change the password, the following `alter user` statement can be used:

```
ALTER USER athena
IDENTIFIED BY forgotpassword
ACCOUNT UNLOCK
PASSWORD EXPIRE;
```

Other situations abound. In an attempt to prevent misuse, you may want to lock an account that has been used many times unsuccessfully to gain access to Oracle, with the following statement:

```
ALTER USER athena
ACCOUNT LOCK;
```

TIP
You should remember that changes to password, account lock status, or password expiration are applied only to subsequent user sessions, not the current one.

Changing User Tablespace Allocation

You may want to reorganize tablespaces to distribute I/O load and make more effective use of the hardware running Oracle. Perhaps this effort involves dropping some tablespaces and creating new ones. If the DBA wants to change a user's default tablespace, the `alter user default tablespace` statement can be used. As explained earlier, this change is good for preserving integrity of the SYSTEM tablespace. Only newly created objects will be affected by this statement. Existing objects created in other tablespaces by that user will continue to reside in those tablespaces until they are dropped. Additionally, if the user specifies a tablespace in which to place a database object, that specification will override the default tablespace.

```
ALTER USER spanky
DEFAULT TABLESPACE overflow_tabspc01;
```

By the same token, you may want to reorganize the tablespace used for disk sorts as you move from permanent tablespaces to temporary tablespaces, and this is done using `alter user temporary tablespace`. Only the DBA can make these changes; the users cannot change their own temporary or default tablespaces.

```
ALTER USER spanky
TEMPORARY TABLESPACE temp_overflow_01;
```

A tablespace accessible to the user at user creation can have a quota placed on it. A quota can be altered by the DBA with the `alter user quota` statement. For example, the DBA may want to reduce the quota on the USERS_01 tablespace from 10MB to 5MB for user SPANKY. If the user has already created over 5MB worth of database objects in the tablespace, no further data can be added to those objects and no new objects can be created. Only the DBA can change a user's tablespace quota; the users cannot change their own quotas.

```
ALTER USER spanky
QUOTA 5M ON users_01;
```

TIP
Specifying `quota 0 on` SYSTEM for a user will prevent him from creating any object in the SYSTEM tablespace, even if that user still has his `default tablespace` set to SYSTEM. However, this restriction does not include the creation of packages, stored procedures, and functions.

Aspects of User Accounts Changeable by Users

All aspects of the user's account covered already are the components that can be modified by the DBA. However, the aspects of the account that can be changed by the actual user are far more limited. A situation may arise in regular database use where a user wants to change his or her password. This is accomplished with the following:

```
ALTER USER athena
IDENTIFIED BY mynewpassword;
```

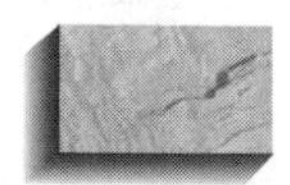

TIP
Except for altering the password, the user can change nothing about their own user account, except in certain situations where the `alter any user` privilege has been granted to that user.

Dropping User Accounts

As users come and go, their access should be modified to reflect their departure. To drop a user from the database, you execute the `drop user` statement. If a user has created database objects, the user cannot be dropped until the objects are dropped, as well. In order to drop the user and all related database objects in one fell swoop, Oracle provides the `cascade` option.

```
DROP USER spanky CASCADE;
```

TIP
If you want to remove a user but assign the user's table(s) to another user, you should use the EXPORT tool to dump the user's, then use IMPORT with the FROMUSER and TOUSER parameters to import the tables as that other user. More information on these tools appears in Chapters 11 and 15.

Exercises

1. What statement is used for altering users?
2. What are the features of a user that the users themselves can change? What features can only the DBA change?
3. What statement is used to drop a database user? How can the objects created by the user be eliminated at the same time?

Monitoring Information About Existing Users

The DBA may periodically want to monitor information about users. Several data dictionary views may be used for the purpose of obtaining information about users. Some information a DBA may want to collect includes default and temporary tablespace information, objects created by that user, and what the current account status for that user account is. The following data dictionary views can be used to determine this information.

- **DBA_USERS** Contains username, Oracle-generated ID number, encrypted password, default and temporary tablespace information, and the user profile that was specified in the ID creation statements or any alteration that may have followed. Also, the view offers ACCOUNT_STATUS, which may be locked, open, or expired; GRACE_DATE, which identifies the date by which the user must change the password or the account will be locked; LOCK_DATE, which is the date the account was locked (NULL for open accounts); and EXPIRY_DATE, which is the date for account expiration.
- **DBA_OBJECTS** Contains the specific information about every object in the database. The DBA can determine which objects belong to which users by using the OWNER column of this view.
- **DBA_TS_QUOTAS** Names all users and any tablespace quotas that have been created for them.

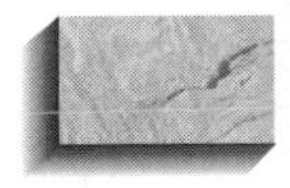

TIP
A value of –1 in the MAX_BYTES or MAX_BLOCKS column of the DBA_USERS view means that the user has unlimited space quota for that tablespace.

Exercises

1. How can the DBA determine which users own which objects?
2. How can the DBA determine whether there are any quotas on tablespaces that a user has been granted access to?
3. What view contains user-account status and other account information?

Managing Resource Use

In this section, you will cover the following topics related to managing resource use:

- Creating and assigning profiles to control resource use
- Altering and dropping profiles
- Administering passwords using profiles
- Obtaining profile information from the data dictionary

Oracle's use of the host machine on behalf of certain users can be managed by creating specific user profiles to correspond to the amount of activity anticipated by average transactions generated by those different types of users. The principle of user profiles is not to force the user off the system every time an artificially low resource-usage threshold is exceeded. Rather, resource-usage thresholds should allow the users to do everything they need to do on the Oracle database, while also limiting unwanted or unacceptable use. When users make mistakes, or try to do something that hurts database performance, profiles can stop them short, helping to reduce problems.

Creating and Assigning Profiles to Control Resource Use

A special user profile exists in Oracle at database creation called DEFAULT. If no profile is assigned with the `profile` clause of the `create user` statement, the DEFAULT profile is assigned to that user. DEFAULT gives users unlimited use of all resources definable in the database. However, any of its resource-usage settings can be changed to ensure that no user can issue SQL statements that arbitrarily consume database resources. You might create a user profile like the one in the following code block:

```
CREATE PROFILE developer LIMIT
SESSIONS_PER_USER 1
CPU_PER_SESSION 10000
CPU_PER_CALL 20
CONNECT_TIME 240
IDLE_TIME 20
LOGICAL_READS_PER_SESSION 50000
LOGICAL_READS_PER_CALL 400
PRIVATE_SGA 1024;
```

This code block is a good example of using profiles to set *individual resource limits.* All other resources that are not explicitly assigned limits when you create a profile will be assigned the default values specified in the DEFAULT profile. Thus, if you change the value for a resource limit in the DEFAULT profile, you may be making changes to other profiles on your system as well. Notice also that some of the resource-limit names refer to limits at the *session level,* while others refer to limits at the *call level.* Thus, you can limit resource use at both levels if you want to.

Once profiles are created, they are assigned to users with the `profile` clause in either the `create user` or `alter user` statement. The following code block contains examples:

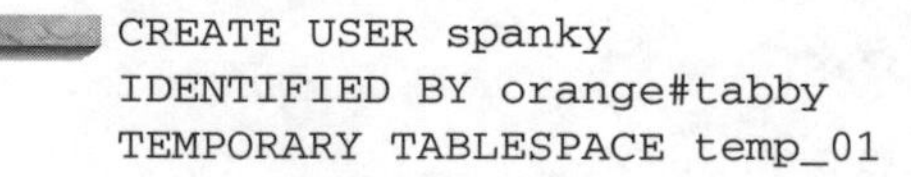

```
CREATE USER spanky
IDENTIFIED BY orange#tabby
TEMPORARY TABLESPACE temp_01
```

```
QUOTA 5M ON temp_01
PROFILE developer;

ALTER USER athena
PROFILE developer;
```

Setting Individual Resource Limits: Session Level

The following resource-usage areas can have limits assigned for them within the profiles you create. If a session-level resource limit is exceeded, the user gets an error and the session is terminated automatically. At the session level, the resource limits are as follows:

- **`sessions_per_user`** The number of sessions a user can open concurrently with the Oracle database.
- **`cpu_per_session`** The maximum allowed CPU time in 1/100 seconds that a user can utilize in one session.
- **`logical_reads_per_session`** The maximum number of disk I/O block reads that can be executed in support of the user processing in one session.
- **`idle_time`** The time, in minutes, that a user can issue no commands before Oracle times out their session.
- **`connect_time`** The total amount of time in minutes that a user can be connected to the database.
- **`private_sga`** The amount of private memory in kilobytes or megabytes that can be allocated to a user for private storage. This is only used when MTS is in use on your Oracle database.

Individual Resource Limits: Call Level

At the call level, the resource-usage areas can have limits assigned for them within the profiles you create. If the user exceeds the call-level usage limits they have been assigned, the SQL statement that produced the error is terminated, any transaction changes *made by the offending statement only* are rolled back, previous statements remain intact, and the user remains connected to Oracle. Call-level usage limits are identified as follows:

- **`logical_reads_per_call`** The maximum number of disk I/O block reads that can be executed in support of the user's processing in one session.
- **`cpu_per_call`** The maximum allowed CPU time, in 1/100 seconds, that any individual operation in a user session can use.

Setting Composite Limits and Resource Costs

In some cases, the DBA may find individual resource limits inflexible. The alternative is setting composite limits on the principle of resource cost. Resource cost is an arbitrary number that reflects the relative value of that resource based on the host machine's capabilities. For example, on a host machine with few CPUs and many disk controllers, you might consider `cpu_per_session` more "valuable" than `logical_reads_per_session`. The statement used for assigning a resource cost is `alter resource cost`. Resource costs only apply to the `cpu_per_session`, `logical_reads_per_session`, `connect_time`, and `private_sga` resources. The default value for each resource cost is zero. Resource costs are not necessarily monetary costs. Cost is specified as an abstract unit value, not a monetary resource price. For example, setting the resource cost of CPU cycles per session equal to 1.5 does not mean that each CPU cycle costs a user process $1.50 to run.

```
ALTER RESOURCE COST
CPU_PER_SESSION 10
LOGICAL_READS_PER_SESSION 2
PRIVATE_SGA 6
CONNECT_TIME 1;
```

Once resource costs are set, you assign composite limits to your users. Composite limits restrict database use by specifying a limit of how much host machine resource can be used per session. Each time the session uses a resource, Oracle tallies the total resource use for that session. When the session hits the `composite_limit`, the session is terminated. Profiles are altered to include a `composite_limit` with the `alter profile` statement.

```
ALTER PROFILE developer LIMIT
COMPOSITE_LIMIT 500;
```

Enabling Resource Limits

To use resource limits, you must first change the `RESOURCE_LIMIT` init*sid*.ora parameter to TRUE on your Oracle database. However, the change there will not take effect until the database is shut down and restarted. To enable resource restriction to be used in conjunction with profiles on the current database session, the DBA should issue the following statement:

```
ALTER SYSTEM
SET RESOURCE_LIMIT = TRUE;
```

Exercises

1. What are user profiles? How can they be used to prevent excessive use of the database system?
2. What must happen before resource use can be limited with user profiles? What are the parameters that can be set to restrict database use for individual resources?
3. What are resource costs and composite limits? How do these two features work together?
4. What is the DEFAULT profile? What are the default values for resource limits in the DEFAULT profile? What profile is assigned to a user if one is not explicitly set by the `create user` statement?

Altering and Dropping Profiles

Changing a user profile may be required if user profiles in the database rely on default values set in the DEFAULT profile. If the resource limit `cpu_per_session` in DEFAULT is changed from `unlimited` to 20,000, then `cpu_per_session` in any user profile that didn't explicitly set one for itself will also be affected. Only by explicitly setting its own value for `cpu_per_session` will the profile not depend on the DEFAULT profile for the `cpu_per_session` limit. Any option in any profile can be changed at any time; however, the change will not take effect until the user logs out and logs back in. You issue the following statement to change a resource limit in a profile:

```
ALTER PROFILE developer LIMIT
CPU_PER_SESSION UNLIMITED;
```

If you want to drop a user profile from the database, do so by executing the `drop profile` statement. A profile cannot be eliminated without using the `cascade` option if the profile has already been assigned to users. After issuing the `drop profile cascade` command, any user who had the dropped profile will use the DEFAULT profile instead.

```
DROP PROFILE developer CASCADE;
```

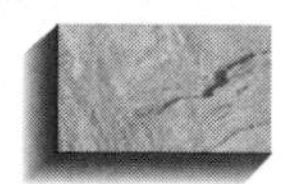

TIP
To gather information about how users are utilizing the host machine in database sessions to set resource limits properly, use the `audit session` command. Resource limits you can gather information for include `connect_time`, `logical_reads_per_session`, and `logical_reads_per_call`.

Exercises

1. How are user profiles changed? If a resource limit value is not set when the profile is created, where does the profile get the value for the resource limit?
2. What happens if you change the value for a resource limit in the DEFAULT profile?
3. How are user profiles dropped? If a profile that was granted to a user is dropped, what profile will the user use?

Administering Passwords Using Profiles

Four new features exist in Oracle8 to handle password management more effectively. These features are *account locking, password aging and expiration, password history*, and *password complexity requirements*. These new features are designed to make it harder than ever to hack the Oracle8 database as an authorized user without knowing the user's password. This protects the integrity of assigned usernames, as well as the overall data integrity of the Oracle database.

Though not required to enable password management in Oracle8, the DBA can run the `utlpwdmg.sql` script as SYS to support the functionality of password management. This script can be found in the `rdbms/admin` subdirectory under the Oracle software home directory. This script makes some additions to the DEFAULT profile, identified earlier in the chapter, for use with password management. When the password management script is run, all default password management settings placed in the DEFAULT profile are enforced at all times on the Oracle8 database. This is unlike other resource limits, which still require that `RESOURCE_LIMIT` be set to TRUE before the instance starts.

Account Management

Account locking allows Oracle8 to lock out an account when users attempt to log into the database unsuccessfully on several attempts. The maximum allowed number of failed attempts is defined per user or by group. The number of failed attempts is specified by the DBA or the security officer in ways that will be defined shortly, and tracked by Oracle such that if the user fails to log into the database in the specified number of tries, Oracle locks out the user automatically. In addition, a time period for automatic user lockout can be defined such that the failed login attempt counter will reset after that time period, and the user may try to log into the database again. Alternatively, automatic lockout can be permanent, disabled only by the security administrator or DBA. User accounts can also be locked manually if the security administrator or DBA so desires. In this situation, the only way to unlock the account is manually.

Password Aging and Rotation

A password is also aged in the Oracle8 database. The DBA or security administrator can set a password to have a maximum lifetime in the Oracle database. Once a threshold time period passes, the user must change his or her password or be unable to access the Oracle database. A grace period can be defined, during which the user must change the password. If the time of the grace period passes and the user doesn't change the password, the account is then locked and only the security administrator can unlock it. A useful technique for creating new users is to create them with expired passwords, such that the user enters the grace period on first login and must change the password during that time.

A potential problem arises when users are forced to change their passwords. Sometimes users try to "fool" the system by changing the expired password to something else, and then immediately changing the password back. To prevent this, Oracle8 supports a password history feature that keeps track of recently used passwords and disallows their use for a specified amount of time or number of changes. The interval is defined within the user profile, and information on how to set it will be presented shortly.

Password Complexity Verification

Finally, and perhaps most important to the integrity of an Oracle user's account, is the feature of password complexity verification. There are many commonly accepted practices in creating a password, such as making sure it has a certain character length, that it is not a proper name or word in the dictionary, that it is not all numbers or all characters, and so on. Too often, however, users don't heed these mandates and create passwords that are easy to decode using any of a number of products available for decoding encrypted password information. To prevent users from unwittingly subverting the security of the database, Oracle8 supports the automatic verification of password complexity with the use of a PL/SQL function that can be applied during user or group profile creation to prevent users from creating passwords of insufficient complexity. The checks provided by the default function include making sure the minimum password length is four characters and is not the same as the username. Also, the password must contain at least one letter, number, and punctuation character, and the password must be different from the previous password defined by at least three characters.

If this level of complexity verification provided by the given PL/SQL function is not high enough, a PL/SQL function of sufficient complexity may be defined by the organization, subject to certain restrictions. The overall call syntax must conform to the details in the following code listing. In addition, the new routine must be assigned as the password verification routine in the user's profile or the DEFAULT profile. In the `create profile` statement, the following must be present: `password_verify_function` *`user_pwcmplx_fname`*, where *`user_pwcmplx_fname`* is the name of the user-defined password complexity function. Some other constraints on the definition of this function include that an appropriate error must be returned if the routine raises an exception or if the verification routine becomes invalid, and that the verification function will be owned by SYS and used in system context. The call to the PL/SQL complexity verification function must conform to the following parameter-passing and return-value requirements:

```
USER_PWCMPLX_FNAME
( user_id_parm        IN VARCHAR2,
  new_passwd_parm     IN VARCHAR2,
  old_passwd_parm     IN VARCHAR2
) RETURN BOOLEAN;
```

To show the coding used in a password-complexity function, the following example is offered. This example is a simplified and modified block of code similar to the password verification function provided with Oracle8. The function will check three things: that the new password is not the same as the username, that the new password is six characters long, and that the new password is not the same as the old one. When the DBA creates a username, the verification process is called to determine whether the password is appropriate. If the function returns TRUE, then the DBA will be able to create the username. If not, the user creation will fail. This example is designed to give you some groundwork for coding your own password complexity function; bear in mind, however, that the function in the following listing is greatly simplified for example purposes only.

```
CREATE OR REPLACE FUNCTION my_pwver (
x_user       IN  VARCHAR2,
x_new_pw     IN  VARCHAR2,
x_old_pw     IN  VARCHAR2
)RETURN BOOLEAN IS
BEGIN
   IF LENGTH(x_new_pw) < 6 THEN
     RAISE_APPLICATION_ERROR(-20001, 'New password too short.');
   ELSIF x_new_pw = x_user THEN
     RAISE_APPLICATION_ERROR(-20002, 'New password same as username');
   ELSIF x_new_pw = x_old_pw THEN
     RAISE_APPLICATION_ERROR(-20003, 'New password same as old');
   ELSE
     RETURN(TRUE);
   END IF;
END;
```

Password Management Resource Limits in the DEFAULT Profile

After the `utlpwdmg.sql` script is run, default values will be specified for several password-management resource limits. An explanation of each option is listed below, along with its default value:

- **failed_login_attempts** Number of unsuccessful attempts at login a user can make before account locks. Default is 3.
- **password_life_time** Number of days a password will remain active. Default is 60.
- **password_reuse_time** Number of days before the password can be reused. Default is 1,800 (approximately 5 years).
- **password_reuse_max** Number of times the password must be changed before one can be reused. Default is `unlimited`.
- **password_lock_time** Number of days after which Oracle will unlock a user account locked automatically when the user exceeds `failed_login_attempts`. Default is 1/1,440 (1 minute).
- **password_grace_time** Number of days during which an expired password must be changed by the user or else Oracle permanently locks the account. Default is 10.
- **password_verify_function** Function used for password complexity verification. The default function is called `verify_function( )`.

Exercises

1. Define and describe the four new features for user-account protection in Oracle8.
2. What process is used to enable account protection?
3. On what Oracle feature for managing resource use do the new account protection features depend?

Obtaining Profile Information from the Data Dictionary

The following dictionary views offer information about the resource-usage limits defined for profiles, and about the profiles that have been assigned to users:

- **DBA_PROFILES** Contains specific information about the resource-usage parameters specified in conjunction with each profile.
- **RESOURCE_COST** Identifies all resources in the database and their corresponding cost, as defined by the DBA. Cost determines a resource's relative importance of use.
- **USER_RESOURCE_LIMITS** Identifies the system resource limits for individual users, as determined by the profiles assigned to the users.
- **DBA_USERS** Offers information about the profile assigned to a user, current account status, lock date, and password expiry date.

Exercises

1. What dictionary view is used to find out what profile has been assigned to a user?
2. What dictionary view is used to find out what values have been assigned to different resource limits?

Managing Privileges

In this section, you will cover the following topics related to managing privileges:

- Identifying system and object privileges
- Granting and revoking privileges
- Controlling OS or password authentication

All access in an Oracle database requires database privileges. Access to connect to the database, the objects the user is permitted to see, and the objects the user is allowed to create are all controlled by privileges. Use of every database object and system resource is governed by privileges. There are privileges required to create objects, to access objects, to change data within tables, to execute stored procedures, to create users, and so on. Since access to every object is governed by privileges, security in the Oracle database is highly flexible in terms of what objects are available to which users.

Identifying System Privileges

There are two categories of privileges, and the first is *system privileges*. System privileges control the creation and maintenance of many database objects, such as rollback segments, synonyms, tables, and triggers. Additionally, the ability to use the `analyze` command and the Oracle database `audit` capability is governed by system privileges.

Generally speaking, there are several categories of system privileges that relate to each object. Those categories determine the scope of ability that the privilege grantee will have. The classes or categories of system privileges are listed here. In the following subtopics, the privilege itself gives the ability to perform the action against your own database objects, while the `any` keyword refers to the ability to perform the action against any database object of that type in Oracle.

ADMIN FUNCTIONS These privileges relate to activities typically reserved for and performed by the DBA. Privileges include `alter system`, `audit system`, `audit any`, `alter database`, `analyze any`, `sysdba`, `sysoper`, and `grant any privilege`. You must have the `create session` privilege to connect to Oracle. More information about `sysdba` and `sysoper` privileges, and the activities they permit you to do, will appear in the last lesson.

DATABASE ACCESS These privileges control who accesses the database, when they can access it, and what they can do regarding management of their own session. Privileges include `create session`, `alter session`, and `restricted session`.

TABLESPACES You already know that tablespaces are disk resources used to store database objects. These privileges determine who can maintain these disk resources. These privileges are typically reserved for DBAs. Privileges include `create tablespace`, `alter tablespace`, `manage tablespace`, `drop tablespace`, and `unlimited tablespace`. Note that you cannot grant `unlimited tablespace` to a role. More information on roles appears in the next section.

USERS These privileges are used to manage users on the Oracle database. Typically, these privileges are reserved for DBAs or security administrators. Privileges include `create user`, `become user`, `alter user`, and `drop user`.

ROLLBACK SEGMENTS You already know that rollback segments are disk resources that make aspects of transaction processing possible. The privileges include `create rollback segment`, `alter rollback segment`, and `drop rollback segment`.

TABLES You already know that tables store data in the Oracle database. These privileges govern which users can create and maintain tables. The privileges include `create table`, `create any table`, `alter any table`, `backup any table`, `drop any table`, `lock any table`, `comment any table`, `select any table`, `insert any table`, `update any table`, and `delete any table`. The `create table` or `create any table` privilege also allows you to drop the table. The `create table` privilege also bestows the ability to create indexes on the table, and run the `analyze` command on the table. To be able to truncate a table, you must have the `drop any table` privilege granted to you.

CLUSTERS You already know that clusters are used to store tables commonly used together in close physical proximity on disk. The privileges include `create cluster`, `create any cluster`, `alter any cluster`, and `drop any cluster`. The `create cluster` and `create any cluster` privileges also allow you to alter and drop those clusters.

INDEXES You already know that indexes are used to improve SQL statement performance on tables containing lots of row data. The privileges include `create any index`, `alter any index`, and `drop any index`. You should note that there is no `create index` system privilege. The `create table` privilege also allows you to alter and drop indexes that you own and that are associated with the table.

SYNONYMS A synonym is a database object that allows you to reference another object by a different name. A public synonym means that the synonym is available to every user in the database for the same purpose. The privileges include `create synonym`, `create any synonym`, `drop any synonym`, `create public synonym`, and `drop public synonym`. The `create synonym` privilege also allows you to alter and drop synonyms that you own.

VIEWS You already know that a view is an object containing a SQL statement that behaves like a table in Oracle, except that it stores no data. The privileges include `create view`, `create any view`, and `drop any view`. The `create view` privilege also allows you to alter and drop views that you own.

SEQUENCES You already know that a sequence is an object in Oracle that generates numbers according to rules you can define. Privileges include `create sequence`, `create any sequence`, `alter any sequence`, `drop any sequence`, and `select any sequence`. The `create sequence` privilege also allows you to drop sequences that you own.

DATABASE LINKS Database links are objects in Oracle that, within your session connected to one database, allow you to reference tables in another Oracle database without making a separate connection. A public database link is one available to all users in Oracle, while a private database link is one that only the owner can use. Privileges include `create database link`, `create public database link`, and `drop public database link`. The `create database link` privilege also allows you to drop private database links that you own.

ROLES Roles are objects that can be used for simplified privilege management. You create a role, grant privileges to it, and then grant the role to users. Privileges include `create role`, `drop any role`, `grant any role`, and `alter any role`.

TRANSACTIONS These privileges are for resolving in-doubt transactions being processed on the Oracle database. Privileges include `force transaction` and `force any transaction`.

PL/SQL You have already been introduced to the different PL/SQL blocks available in Oracle. These privileges allow you to create, run, and manage those different types of blocks. Privileges include `create procedure`, `create any procedure`, `alter any procedure`, `drop any procedure`, and `execute any procedure`. The `create procedure` privilege also allows you to alter and drop PL/SQL blocks that you own.

TRIGGERS You know that triggers are PL/SQL blocks in Oracle that execute when a specified DML activity occurs on the table to which the trigger is associated. Privileges include `create trigger`, `create any trigger`, `alter any trigger`, and `drop any trigger`. The `create trigger` privilege also allows you to alter and drop triggers that you own.

PROFILES You know that profiles are objects in Oracle that allow you to impose limits on resources for users in the machine hosting Oracle. Privileges include `create profile`, `alter profile`, `drop profile`, and `alter resource cost`.

SNAPSHOTS Snapshots are objects in Oracle that allow you to replicate data from a table in one database to a copy of the table in another. Privileges include `create snapshot`, `create any snapshot`, `alter any snapshot`, and `drop any snapshot`.

DIRECTORIES Directories in Oracle are objects that refer to directories on the machine hosting the Oracle database. They are used to identify a directory that contains objects Oracle keeps track of that are external to Oracle, such as objects of the BFILE type. Privileges include `create any directory` and `drop any directory`.

TYPES Types in Oracle correspond to user-defined types you can create using Oracle8's Objects option. Privileges include `create type`, `create any type`, `alter any type`, `drop any type`, and `execute any type`. The `create type` privilege also allows you to alter and drop types that you own.

LIBRARIES A library is an object that allows you to reference a set of procedures external to Oracle. Currently, only C procedures are supported. Privileges include `create library`, `create any library`, `alter any library`, `drop any library`, and `execute any library`.

Exercises

1. Name some system privileges on database objects. What are some objects that do not use system privileges to let users change the object definition or create the object?
2. What are some other system privileges used to manage certain operations on any database object? What is the `unlimited tablespace` privilege? What is the `restricted session` privilege?

Identifying Object Privileges

The other category of privileges granted on the Oracle database is the set of *object privileges*. Object privileges permit the owner of database objects, such as tables, to administer access to those objects according to the following types of access. The eight types of object privileges are as follows:

- **select** Permits the grantee of this object privilege to access the data in a table, sequence, view, or snapshot.
- **insert** Permits the grantee of this object privilege to `insert` data into a table or, in some cases, a view.
- **update** Permits the grantee of this object privilege to `update` data into a table or view.
- **delete** Permits the grantee of this object privilege to `delete` data from a table or view.
- **alter** Permits the grantee of this object privilege to `alter` the definition of a table or sequence *only*. The `alter` privileges on all other database objects are considered system privileges.
- **index** Permits the grantee of this object privilege to create an index on a table already defined.
- **references** Permits the grantee to `create` or `alter` a table in order to create a `FOREIGN KEY` constraint against data in the referenced table.
- **execute** Permits the grantee to run a stored procedure or function.

TIP
A trick to being able to distinguish whether something is a system or object privilege is as follows. Since there are only eight object privileges, memorize them. If you see a privilege that is not one of the eight object privileges, it is a system privilege.

Exercise

What are some object privileges? What abilities to these privileges bestow?

Granting and Revoking Privileges

Giving privileges to users is done with the `grant` command. System privileges are first given to the SYS and SYSTEM users, and to any other user with the `grant any privilege` permission. As other users are created, they must be given privileges, based on their needs, with the `grant` command. For example, executing the following grant statements gives access to create a table to user SPANKY, and object privileges on another table in the database:

```
GRANT CREATE TABLE TO spanky;                              -- system
GRANT SELECT, UPDATE ON athena.emp TO spanky;              -- object
```

Giving Administrative Ability Along with Privileges

At the end of execution for the preceding two statements, SPANKY will have the ability to execute the create table command in her user schema and to select and update row data on the EMP table in ATHENA's schema. However, SPANKY can't give these privileges to others, nor can she relinquish them without the help of the DBA. In order to give user SPANKY some additional power to administer to other users the privileges granted to her, the DBA can execute the following queries:

```
GRANT CREATE TABLE TO spanky WITH ADMIN OPTION;
GRANT SELECT, UPDATE ON emp TO SPANKY WITH GRANT OPTION;
```

The with admin option clause gives SPANKY the ability to give or take away the system privilege to others. Additionally, it gives SPANKY the ability to make other users administrators of that same privilege. Finally, if a role is granted to SPANKY with admin option, SPANKY can alter the role or even remove it. The with grant option clause for object privileges gives SPANKY the same kind of ability as with admin option for system privileges. SPANKY can select and update data from EMP, and can give that ability to others, as well. Only privileges given with grant option or with admin option can be administered by the grantee. Additionally, there is a consolidated method for granting object privileges using the keyword all. Note that all in this context is not a privilege, it is merely a specification for all object privileges for the database object.

```
GRANT ALL ON emp TO spanky;
```

There may also come a time when users must have privileges revoked as well. This task is accomplished with the revoke command. Revoking the create table privilege also takes away any administrative ability given along with the privilege or role. No additional syntax is necessary for revoking either a system privilege granted with admin option or an object privilege granted with grant option.

```
REVOKE CREATE TABLE FROM spanky;
REVOKE SELECT, UPDATE ON emp FROM spanky;
```

In the same way, roles can be revoked from users, even if the user created the role and thus has the `admin option`. The ability to revoke any role comes from the `grant any role` privilege, while the ability to grant or revoke certain system privileges comes from being granted the privilege with the `admin option`. When a system privilege is revoked, there are no cascading events that take place along with it. Thus, if SPANKY created several tables while possessing the `create table` privilege, those tables are not removed when the privilege is revoked. Only the `drop table` command will remove the tables.

TIP

Understand the following scenario completely before continuing: User X has a system privilege granted to her `with admin option`. User X then grants the privilege to user Y, with the administrative privileges. User Y does the same for user Z. Then X revokes the privilege from user Y. User Z will still have the privilege. Why? Because there is no cascading effect to revoking system privileges other than the fact that the user no longer has the privilege.

When an object privilege is revoked, there are some cascading events. For example, if you have the `update` privilege on SPANKY's EMP table and SPANKY revokes it, then you will not be able to change records in the table. However, the rows you've already changed don't get magically transformed back the way they were before. There are several considerations to make when revoking object privileges. For instance, if a privilege has been granted on two individual columns, the privilege cannot be revoked on only one column—the privilege must be revoked entirely and then regranted, if appropriate, on the individual column. Also, if the user has been given the `references` privilege and used it to create a `FOREIGN KEY` constraint to another table, then there is some cascading that must take place in order to complete the revocation of the `references` privilege.

```
REVOKE REFERENCES ON emp FROM spanky CASCADE CONSTRAINTS;
```

In this example, not only is the privilege to create referential integrity revoked, but any instances where that referential integrity was used on the database are also revoked. If a `FOREIGN KEY` constraint was created on the EMP table by user SPANKY, and the prior statement was issued without the `cascade constraints` clause, then the `revoke` statement would fail. Other cascading issues may appear after object privileges are revoked, as well. In general, if an object privilege is revoked, then any item created by the user that relied on that object privilege may experience a problem during execution.

In order to grant a privilege to a user, the appropriate privilege administrator or the DBA can issue the following statement:

```
GRANT privilege ON object TO user;
```

To grant object privileges to others, you must own the database object, you must have been given the object privilege `with grant option`, or you must have the `grant any privilege` ability given to you.

In addition to granting object privileges on database objects, privileges can also be granted on columns within the database object. The privileges that can be administered on the column level are the `insert`, `update`, and `references` privileges. However, the grantor of column privileges must be careful when administering them, in order to avoid problems—particularly with the `insert` privilege. If a user has the `insert` privilege on several columns in a table but not all columns, the privilege administrator must ensure that none of the columns that do not have the `insert` privilege granted are `NOT NULL` columns. Consider the following example. Table EMP has two columns, NAME and EMPID. Both columns have `NOT NULL` constraints on them. The `insert` access is granted for the EMPID column to SPANKY, but not the NAME column. When SPANKY attempts to `insert` an EMPID into the table, Oracle generates a NULL for the NAME column, and then produces an error stating that the user cannot `insert` a NULL value into the NAME column because the column has a `NOT NULL` constraint on it. Administration of `update` and `insert` object privileges at the column level must be handled carefully, whereas using the `references` privilege on a column level seems to be more straightforward.

Some special conditions relate to the use of the `execute` privilege. If a user has the ability to execute a stored procedure owned by another user, and the procedure accesses some tables, the object privileges required to access those tables must be granted *to the owner of the procedure*, and not the user to whom `execute` privileges were granted. What's more, the privileges must be granted directly to the user, not through a role. When a user executes a stored procedure, the user is able to use whatever privileges are required to `execute` the procedure. For example, execute privileges are given to SPANKY on procedure `process_deposit( )` owned by ATHENA, and this procedure performs an update on the BANK_ACCOUNT table using an `update` privilege granted to ATHENA. SPANKY will be able to perform that `update` on BANK_ACCOUNT via the process_deposit( ) procedure even though the `update` privilege is not granted to SPANKY. However, SPANKY will *not* be able to issue an update statement on table BANK_ACCOUNT from SQL*Plus, because the appropriate privilege was not granted to SPANKY directly.

Open to the Public

Another aspect of privileges and access to the database involves a special user on the database. This user is called PUBLIC. If a system privilege, object privilege, or role is granted to the PUBLIC user, then every user in the database has that privilege. Typically, it is not advised that the DBA should grant many privileges or roles to PUBLIC, because if the privilege or role ever needs to be revoked, then every stored package, procedure, or function will need to be recompiled.

Dictionary Information on Privileges

You can find information about system privileges granted to all users in the DBA_SYS_PRIVS view and the privileges available to you as the current user in the session using the SESSION_PRIVS dictionary view. You can also find information about the object privileges granted in the database with the DBA_TAB_PRIVS and DBA_COL_PRIVS dictionary views. Spend some extra time before OCP Exam 2 querying these views to get a feel for the information stored in them.

Exercises

1. What command is used to give privileges to users?
2. What special options are required for system and object privileges if the user is to have administrative capability along with the privilege?
3. What cascading issues exist related to the `references` object privilege and the user PUBLIC? What views are available for finding information about the system and object privileges granted in the database?

Controlling OS or Password Authentication

You have already used the `sysoper` and `sysdba` privileges in Oracle for password authentication setup in Chapter 6. These are special privileges that allow you to do a great many things. For example, `sysoper` enables you to start and stop the Oracle instance, and open, mount, and unmount the database. It also permits you to back up the control file, back up tablespaces, execute full database recovery, and change archiving status on your database. The `sysdba` privilege gives you every privilege `sysoper` gives `with admin option`, and adds the ability to create the database and execute point-in-time recovery. These privileges cannot be given to roles, and cannot be given unless the DBA connects `as sysdba` or `as sysoper`.

Exercises

1. What is password authentication?
2. What are the capabilities given with the `sysdba` or `sysoper` privileges?

Managing Roles

In this section, you will cover the following points on managing roles:

- Creating and modifying roles
- Controlling availability of roles
- Removing roles
- Using predefined roles
- Displaying role information from the data dictionary

Roles take some of the complexity out of administrating user privileges. A role in the database can be thought of as a virtual user. The database object and system privileges that are required to perform a group of user functions are gathered together and granted to the role, which then can be granted directly to the users. In this section, you will learn how to create and change roles, control their availability, remove roles, use roles that are predefined in Oracle, and display information about roles from the data dictionary.

Creating and Modifying Roles

As users add more objects to the database, privilege management can become a nightmare. This is where roles come in. Roles are named logical groupings of privileges that can be administered more easily than the individual privileges. Roles are created on databases in the following manner. The DBA determines what types of users exist on the database and what privileges on the database can be logically grouped together. In order to create a role that will support user privilege management, one of the following statements can be executed. Once the role is created, there are no privileges assigned to it until you explicitly do grant them.

```
CREATE ROLE role_name;

CREATE ROLE role_name NOT IDENTIFIED;
```

```
CREATE ROLE role_name IDENTIFIED BY role_password;

CREATE ROLE role_name IDENTIFIED EXTERNALLY;
```

The Role-User Relationship

Using a password to authenticate usage of a role is optional. If used, however, the password provides an extra level of security over the authentication process at database login. For OS authentication, the `identified externally` clause is used in roles in the same way it is used for users. For heightened security when using roles with passwords, set the role authenticated by a password to be a nondefault role for that user. That way, if the user tries to execute a privilege granted via the role, he or she will first have to supply the role's password. Like users, roles have no owner, nor are they part of a schema. The name of a role must be unique among all roles and users of a database.

Privileges are granted to roles in the following manner. At the same time that the DBA determines the resource use of various classes of users on the database, the DBA may also want to determine what object and system privileges each class of user will require. Instead of granting the privileges directly to users on an individual basis, however, the DBA can grant the privileges to the roles, which then can be granted to several users more easily.

```
GRANT SELECT, INSERT, UPDATE ON cat_food TO cat_privs;
GRANT SELECT, INSERT, UPDATE ON litter_box TO cat_privs;
GRANT SELECT ON fav_sleeping_spots TO cat_privs;
GRANT cat_privs TO spanky;
```

Roles allow dynamic privilege management, as well. If several users already have a role granted to them, and you create a new table and grant `select` privileges on it to the role, then all the users who have the role will be able to `select` data from your table. Once granted, the ability to use the privileges granted via the role is immediate. Roles can be granted to other roles, as well. However, you should take care not to grant a role to itself (even via another role) or else Oracle will return an error.

Altering Roles

Later on, you may want to change a role using the `alter role` command. All items that are definable in `create role` are also definable using `alter role`, as shown in the following code examples:

```
ALTER ROLE role_name NOT IDENTIFIED;

ALTER ROLE role_name IDENTIFIED BY role_password;

ALTER ROLE role_name IDENTIFIED EXTERNALLY;
```

Exercises

1. What is a role? How are privileges managed using roles? Explain.
2. Describe the relationship between roles and users, covering points about ownership, uniqueness, and password authentication.

Controlling Availability of Roles

As mentioned earlier, a user may have several roles granted when he or she logs on. Some, all, or none of these roles can be set as a default role, which means that the privileges given via the role will be available automatically when the user logs on to Oracle. There is no limit to the number of roles that can be granted to a user; however, if there are privileges granted to a user through a nondefault role, the user may have to switch default roles in order to use those privileges.

All roles granted to a user are default roles unless another option is specified by the username creation, or the user is changed with the `alter user` statement. The `alter user default role all` statement sets all roles granted to SPANKY to be the default role. Other options available for specifying user roles include physically listing one or more roles that are to be the default, or specifying all roles except for the ones named using `all except (`*`role_name`*` [, …])`, or `none`.

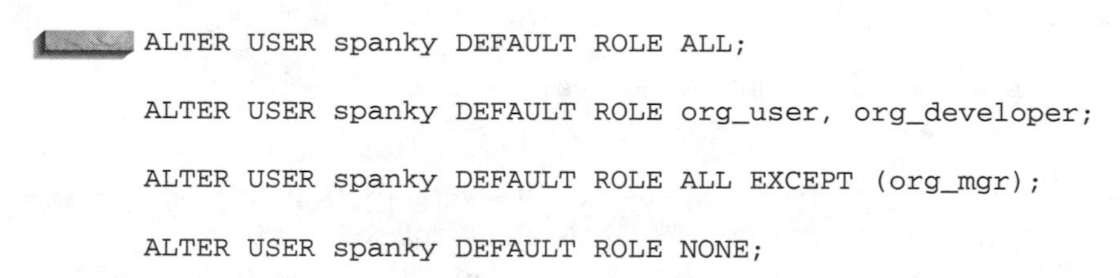

```
ALTER USER spanky DEFAULT ROLE ALL;

ALTER USER spanky DEFAULT ROLE org_user, org_developer;

ALTER USER spanky DEFAULT ROLE ALL EXCEPT (org_mgr);

ALTER USER spanky DEFAULT ROLE NONE;
```

TIP
Note that `default role` is only an option used for the `alter user` statement. You do not define a default role in `create user` because no roles have been granted to the user yet.

Enabling or Disabling Roles

A role can be enabled or disabled for use with the `set role` command. If this command is used, all roles granted to the user other than the one(s) specified will be activated or deactivated until the end of the session or until the `set role` command is issued again. This command is issued by the user and emulates the alter user default role command, which can only be executed by privileged users, such as the DBA.

```
SET ROLE cat_privs;

SET ROLE ALL;

SET ROLE ALL EXCEPT cat_privs;

SET ROLE NONE;
```

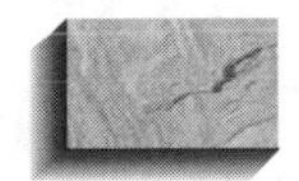

TIP
The DBMS_SESSION package contains a procedure called set_role( ) which is equivalent to the set role statement. It can enable or disable roles for a user and can be issued from Oracle Forms, Reports, anonymous blocks, or any other tool that allows PL/SQL, except for stored PL/SQL functions, procedures, and packages.

Exercises

1. What procedure in Oracle emulates the set role statement, and where can't this procedure be executed?
2. What is a default role? Why must a separate command be used for DBAs and the user to change the roles that the user can use in a session?

Removing Roles

Another way to restrict role use is to revoke the role from the user. This is accomplished with the revoke command in the same way that a privilege is revoked. The effect is immediate—the user will no longer be able to use privileges associated with the role. You can drop a role to restrict its use as well. You don't need to revoke the role from users before dropping it—Oracle handles that task for you. However, you must have the drop any role privilege or have been granted the role with admin option in order to drop it.

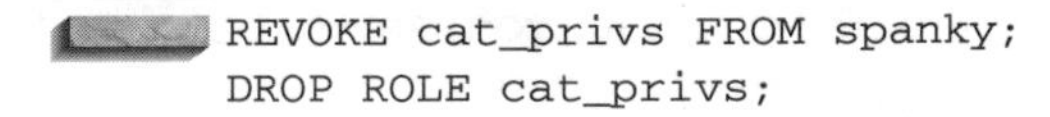

```
REVOKE cat_privs FROM spanky;
DROP ROLE cat_privs;
```

Exercises

1. Identify how roles are taken away from users.
2. Do you have to take roles away from users before removing them from the database? Explain.

Using Predefined Roles

There are some special roles available to the users of a database. The roles available at database creation from Oracle7 onward include the CONNECT, RESOURCE, DBA, EXP_FULL_DATABASE, and IMP_FULL_DATABASE roles. Additionally, Oracle8 adds the DELETE_CATALOG_ROLE, EXECUTE_CATALOG_ROLE, and SELECT_CATALOG_ROLE roles to the mix. The use of each role is described in the following list:

- **CONNECT** Allows the user extensive development capability within their own user schema, including the ability to perform `create table`, `create cluster`, `create session`, `create view`, and `create sequence`, but does not allow the creation of stored procedures.
- **RESOURCE** Allows the user moderate development capability within their own user schema, such as the ability to execute `create table`, `create cluster`, `create trigger`, and `create procedure`.
- **DBA** Allows the user to administer and use all system privileges.
- **EXP_FULL_DATABASE** Allows the user to export every object in the database using the EXPORT utility.
- **IMP_FULL_DATABASE** Allows the user to import every object from an export dump file using the IMPORT utility.
- **DELETE_CATALOG_ROLE** Extends `delete` privileges on SYS-owned dictionary tables, in response to the new restriction on `delete any table` privileges that prevent grantees from removing rows from SYS-owned dictionary tables.
- **EXECUTE_CATALOG_ROLE** Allows the user `execute` privileges on any SYS-owned package supplied with the Oracle software.
- **SELECT_CATALOG_ROLE** Allows the user to `select` data from any SYS-owned dictionary table or view.

Exercises

1. Identify some predefined roles that give you the ability to create some, but not all, types of database objects in Oracle?
2. What predefined privileges were added in Oracle8, and why?
3. If you were about to load a lot of data using the IMPORT utility, what predefined role might you want to have?

Displaying Role Information from the Data Dictionary

You can find information about the roles created in your Oracle database in the data dictionary. The following list describes the various views available for finding information about your created roles:

- **DBA_ROLES** Names all the roles created on the database and whether a password is required to use each role.
- **DBA_ROLE_PRIVS** Names all users and the roles granted to them in the database.
- **ROLE_ROLE_PRIVS** Identifies all the roles and the roles that are granted to them in the database.
- **DBA_SYS_PRIVS** Identifies all the role and user grantees and granted system privileges to those roles and users.
- **ROLE_SYS_PRIVS** Identifies all the system privileges granted only to roles in Oracle.
- **ROLE_TAB_PRIVS** Identifies all the object privileges granted only to roles in Oracle.
- **SESSION_ROLES** Identifies all the roles available in the current session of Oracle.

Exercises

1. What view will show you the roles available to your session while you are logged into the database?
2. Which dictionary view will tell you all the roles requiring a password for use in the database?

Auditing the Database

In this section, you will cover the following topics related to auditing the database:

- Differentiating between database and value-based auditing
- Using database auditing
- Viewing enabled auditing options
- Retrieving and maintaining auditing information

Securing the database against inappropriate activity is only one part of the total security package Oracle offers the DBA or security administrator on an Oracle database. The other major component of the Oracle security architecture is the ability to monitor database activity to uncover suspicious or inappropriate use. Oracle provides this functionality via the use of database auditing. This section will cover differentiating between database and value-based auditing, using database auditing, using the data dictionary to monitor auditing options, and viewing and managing audit results.

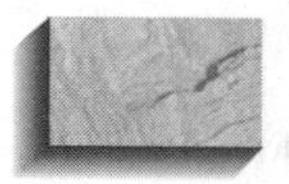

TIP
Auditing your database requires a good deal of additional space allocated to the SYSTEM tablespace for storing the audit data generated.

Several things about your database are always audited. They include privileged operations that DBAs typically perform, such as starting and stopping the instance and logins with `as sysdba` or `as sysoper`. You can find information about these activities in the ALERT log on your database, along with information about log switches, checkpoints, and tablespaces taken offline or put online.

Audit information is stored in a few different places in Oracle, depending on whether you specify your audit trail to be maintained within Oracle or in an operating system file. You specify the location of your audit trail with the `AUDIT_TRAIL` `init`*`sid`*`.ora` parameter as *DB*, *OS*, or *NONE*. Each of these values corresponds to the method by which the audit will be conducted. *DB* indicates that the database architecture will be used to store audit records. *OS* indicates that the audit trail will be stored externally to Oracle, using some component of the operating system, and *NONE* indicates that no database auditing will be conducted at all. After changing the value set for this parameter, the instance must be shut down and started again.

Differentiating Between Database and Value-Based Auditing

There is a difference between *database auditing* and *value-based auditing*. Database auditing pertains to audits on database object access, user session activity, startup, shutdown, and other database activity. The information about these database events is stored in the audit trail, and the information can then be used to monitor potentially damaging activities, such as rows being removed from tables. The data can also be used by the DBA for statistical analysis of database performance over time. Value-based auditing pertains to audits on actual column/row values that are changed as the result of database activity. The Oracle audit trail does not track value-based audit information, so instead you must develop triggers, tables, PL/SQL code, or client applications that handle this level of auditing in the database.

A good example of value-based auditing in a package delivery application would be to track status changes on existing deliveries from the time the order is received to the time it is delivered. Customers can then call in or access the system via the Web to find out what the package delivery status is. Each time the package reaches a certain milestone, such as picked up at local office or signed over to recipient, the delivery status is updated and a historical record is made of the old status, time of status change, and username of person making the change. However, as you might imagine, value-based auditing is specific to an application. Thus, the DBA will focus much of his or her time managing database auditing with Oracle's audit features.

TIP

In UNIX, your OS audit trail information will be stored in the directory named by your AUDIT_FILE_DEST `initsid.ora` *file, which is set to the* `rdbms/audit` *directory under your Oracle software home directory. Your DB audit trail information is stored in the AUD$ table owned by SYS.*

Exercises

1. Where is audit data stored in the Oracle database? In the OS?
2. What is the difference between database auditing and value-based auditing? Which one does the audit feature in Oracle support?

Using Database Auditing

A database audit is most effective when the DBA or security administrator knows what he or she is looking for. The best way to conduct a database audit is to start the audit with a general idea about what may be occurring on the database. Once the goals are established, set the audit to monitor those aspects of database use and review the results to either confirm or disprove the hypothesis.

Why must an audit be conducted this way? Database auditing generates *lots* of information about database access. If the DBA tried to audit everything, the important facts would get mixed into a great deal of unnecessary detail. With a good idea about the general activity that seems suspicious, as well as knowledge of the types of statements or related objects on the database that should be looked at, the DBA can avoid having to sort through excess detail.

Using the Audit Command for Privilege or Statement Audits

After deciding what to audit, you must begin auditing by setting the `AUDIT_TRAIL` `init`*`sid`*`.ora` parameter appropriately. After that, you must use the audit command to set up the auditing options you want to use. Once the database is prepared for an audit, you can set auditing features to monitor database activities including starting, stopping, and connecting to the database. Or, you can set up audits on statements involving the creation or removal of database objects. Additionally, you can set up audits on direct database use, such as table updates or inserts.

The general syntax for setting up auditing on statements or system privileges is as follows. State the name of the statement (such as `update`) or system privilege (such as `create table`) that will be audited. Then, state which users will be monitored, either by *`username`*, `by session`, or `by access`. Finally, state whether or not the audit should record successful or unsuccessful executions of the activity in question. The following code block shows an example of an `audit` statement:

```
AUDIT CREATE TABLE, ALTER TABLE, DROP TABLE
BY spanky
WHENEVER SUCCESSFUL;
```

The following statement demonstrates how you can record the data change operations that happen on particular tables:

```
AUDIT UPDATE, DELETE
ON spanky.cat_toys
BY ACCESS
WHENEVER NOT SUCCESSFUL;
```

Consider some other unique features in the `audit` syntax. The person setting up audits need not name particular users on which to monitor activity. Rather, the activities of this sort can be monitored every time the statement is issued with the by access clause. Additionally, when the not successful option is specified, audit records are generated only when the command executed is unsuccessful. The omission of clauses from the audit syntax causes audit to default to the widest scope permitted by the omission. For example, an audit can be conducted on all inserts on table PRODUCTS, regardless of user and completion status, by omitting the by and whenever clauses:

```
AUDIT INSERT ON products;
```

You can use the default option of the audit command to specify auditing options for objects that have not yet been created. Once you have established these default auditing options, any subsequently created object is automatically audited with those options. The following code block demonstrates use of the default keyword:

```
AUDIT INSERT
ON DEFAULT
WHENEVER SUCCESSFUL;
```

Using the audit Command for Object Audits

Any privilege that can be granted can also be audited. However, since there are nearly 100 system and object privileges that can be granted on the Oracle database, the creation of an audit statement can be an excessively long task. As an alternative to naming each and every privilege that goes along with a database object, Oracle allows the administrator to specify the name of an object to audit, and Oracle will audit all privileged operations. Instead of listing all privileged operations related to the type of object that would be audited, the security administrator could instead name the type of object and achieve the desired result.

```
AUDIT TABLE
BY spanky
WHENEVER SUCCESSFUL;
```

Finally, the person setting up auditing can also specify that audit records are to be compiled by session. This means that audit will record data for audited activities in every session, as opposed to by access. Eliminating the when successful clause tells audit to record every table creation, alteration, or drop activity for every session that connects to the database, regardless of whether or not they were successful.

```
AUDIT TABLE
BY SESSION;
```

Using Audit Definition Shortcuts

There are other options available for consolidating the specification of database activities into one easy command for auditing. These commands are:

- **`connect`** Audits the user connections to the database. Can be substituted with `session` for the same effect. Audits the login and logout activities of every database user.
- **`resource`** Audits detailed information related to the activities typically performed by an application developer or a development DBA, such as creating tables, views, clusters, links, stored procedures, and rollback segments.
- **`dba`** Audits activities related to "true" database administration, including the creation of users and roles, and granting system privileges and system audits.
- **`all`** Is the equivalent of an "on/off" switch, where all database activities are monitored and recorded.

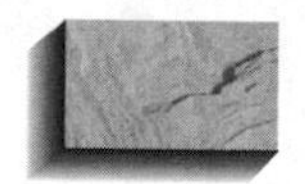

TIP
A PL/SQL procedure or SQL statement may reference several different objects or statements being audited. Thus, many audit trail entries can be produced by one single statement.

Disabling Audit Configuration

There are two methods used to disable auditing. The first method is to change the initialization parameter `AUDIT_TRAIL` to NONE. On database shutdown and restart, this option will disable the audit functionality on the Oracle database. The other, less drastic, option used for changing the activities `audit` will record is called `noaudit`. This option can be executed in two ways. The first is used to turn off selective areas that are currently being audited.

```
NOAUDIT INSERT ON application.products;
```

In some cases, however, the person conducting the audit may want to shut off all auditing processes going on, and simply start auditing over again. Perhaps the auditor has lost track of what audits were occurring on the database. This statement can be further modified to limit turning off auditing to a particular database object.

```
NOAUDIT ALL;

NOAUDIT ALL PRIVILEGES;

NOAUDIT ALL ON application.products;
```

Remembering to Protect the Audit Information

Above all else in handling database audits for inappropriate activity is the importance of protecting the evidence. The DBA must ensure that no user can remove records from the audit logs undetected. Therefore, a key step in auditing is to audit the audit trail.

```
AUDIT delete ON sys.aud$;
```

Exercises

1. How is auditing set in Oracle? If you wanted to set up an audit that tracks all users in Oracle that drop tables, what statement would you use?
2. What does the `by access` clause mean in the `audit` statement context? What about the `whenever` clause?
3. What is the difference between object auditing and statement/privilege auditing?

Viewing Enabled Auditing Options

The following views offer information about the enabled audit options configured in the Oracle database:

- **DBA_OBJ_AUDIT_OPTS** A list of auditing options for views, tables, and other database objects.
- **DBA_PRIV_AUDIT_OPTS** A list of auditing options for all privileges on the database.
- **DBA_STMT_AUDIT_OPTS** A list of auditing options for all statements executed on the database.
- **ALL_DEF_AUDIT_OPTS** A list of all default options for auditing database objects.

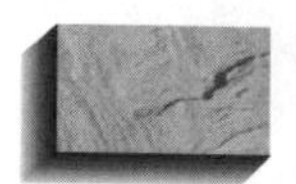

TIP
Perform some `select` statements to see what kinds of database audit information is contained in each of these views before taking OCP Exam 2.

Exercises

1. Where is audit data stored in the data dictionary?
2. What data dictionary views are available for viewing audit data? What data dictionary views are available for viewing `audit` options and parameters?

Retrieving and Maintaining Auditing Information

The following data dictionary views are used to find results from audits currently taking place in the Oracle database. These views are created by the `cataudit.sql` script found in `rdbms/admin` off the Oracle software home directory. This script is run automatically at database creation by the `catalog.sql` script. Some additional audit information is stored in the ALERT log as explained earlier, and more audit information will be stored in an OS file if operating system auditing is used:

- **DBA_AUDIT_EXISTS** A list of audit entries generated by the `exists` option of the `audit` command.
- **DBA_AUDIT_OBJECT** A list of audit entries generated for object audits.
- **DBA_AUDIT_SESSION** A list of audit entries generated by session connects and disconnects.
- **DBA_AUDIT_STATEMENT** A list of audit entries generated by statement options of the `audit command`.
- **DBA_AUDIT_TRAIL** A list of all entries in the AUD$ table collected by the `audit command`.

Managing Audit Information

Once created, all audit information will stay in the AUD$ table owned by SYS. In cases where several auditing options are used to gather information about database activity, the AUD$ table can grow to be large. In order to preserve the integrity of other tables and views in the data dictionary, and to preserve overall space in the SYSTEM tablespace (where all data dictionary objects are stored), the DBA or security administrator must periodically remove data from the AUD$ table, either by deleting, or by archiving and then removing the records. Additionally, in the event that audit records on an Oracle database are being kept to determine whether there is suspicious activity, the security administrator must take additional steps to ensure that the data in the AUD$ table is protected from tampering.

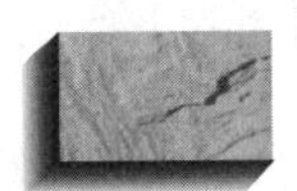

TIP
You may want to move the AUD$ table outside the SYSTEM tablespace because of the volatile and high-growth nature of audit data. To do so, create another table with AUD$ data, using the `create table as select` statement. Next, drop AUD$ and rename your other table AUD$. Next, index the new AUD$ table on the SESSIONID and SES$TID columns (storing the index outside of SYSTEM, of course). Finally, grant `delete` on the new AUD$ table to DELETE_CATALOG_ROLE.

In order to prevent a problem with storing too much audit data, the general guideline in conducting database audits is to record enough information to accomplish the auditing goal without storing a lot of unnecessary information. The amount of information that will be gathered by the auditing process is related to the number of options being audited and the frequency of audit collection (namely, `by` *`username`*, `by access`, `by session`).

What if problems occur because too much information is collected? To remove records from AUD$, a user with the `delete any table` privilege, the SYS user, or a user to whom SYS has granted `delete` access to AUD$ must log onto the system and remove records from AUD$. Before doing so, however, it is generally advisable for archiving purposes to make a copy of the records being deleted. This task can be accomplished by copying all records from AUD$ to another table defined with the same columns as AUD$, spooling a select statement of all data in AUD$ to a flat file, or using EXPORT to place all AUD$ records into a database dump file. After this step is complete, all or part of the data in the AUD$ table can be removed using either `delete from AUD$` or `truncate table AUD$`. But, remember to protect the audit trail, using methods already outlined.

Exercises

1. How can the security administrator remove data from the audit trail?
2. What problems can arise when the audit trail fills? How can data in the audit trail be protected?

Chapter Summary

This chapter covered several aspects of managing database use that are critical to database administration. The areas discussed were creating and managing users, managing profiles, managing privileges, managing roles, and monitoring database activity with the `audit` command. The content discussion provided by this chapter comprises 16 percent of the material covered in OCP Exam 2.

Managing users is the first important area of database administration covered in this chapter. You learned how to create new database users, and what all the clauses mean in the `create user` statement. You also learned how to change user settings and remove existing users from the Oracle database. Special attention was paid to identifying which features of a user's account can be changed by the user, and which ones must be changed by the DBA. Finally, the dictionary views that can be used to find information about users in the Oracle database were presented.

The next area you learned about was how to manage profiles to limit the use of host machine resources by the Oracle database on a user basis. You learned how to create user profiles and assign them to actual users in your database. The topics of controlling the use of resources with profiles and of altering and dropping profiles were also covered. New features of Oracle8 for password administration using profiles were covered, as were the dictionary views where you can find information about your profiles in the Oracle database.

In terms of the management of privileges, you learned about the system and object privileges available in Oracle, along with how to grant and revoke privileges from users. Special attention was paid to administrative power that can be granted along with a system or object privilege, and what cascading effects may be caused if the privilege is revoked. You also reviewed information presented in Chapter 6 on how to manage the privileges required for password file or operating system authentication.

The next section discussed the use of roles in your database. You learned how to create and modify roles, and how to limit their availability by setting default roles for users and using password authentication for roles. You also learned how to remove roles from the Oracle database. The use of several predefined roles that Oracle creates when you create the database were covered, as well. The views are available for finding out information about your roles in the Oracle data dictionary were also discussed.

The final section of this chapter covered the setup and use of auditing in the database. You learned about the differences between value-based auditing and database auditing, and that value-based auditing is handled by developing application code, while Oracle database auditing is handled with the `audit` command. You learned how to set up database auditing with the `audit` command, and covered the features available in Oracle for database auditing using this command. Finally, you learned how to view the enabled audit options in your database, and where to go to find the information collected in the Oracle audit.

Two-Minute Drill

- New database users are created with the `create user` statement.
- A new user can have the following items configured by the `create user` statement:
  - Password
  - Default tablespace for database objects
  - Temporary tablespace
  - Quotas on tablespaces
  - User profile
  - Account lock status
  - Whether the user must specify a new password on first logging on
- User definitions can be altered with the `alter user` statement and dropped with the `drop user` statement. Users can issue the `alter user` statement only to change their password and default roles.
- Information about a database user can be found in the following data dictionary views:
  - DBA_USERS
  - DBA_PROFILES
  - DBA_TS_QUOTAS
  - DBA_OBJECTS
  - DBA_ROLE_PRIVS
  - DBA_TAB_PRIVS
  - DBA_SYS_PRIVS
- Users in operating system authenticated database environments generally have their usernames preceded by OPS$ at user-creation time.
- User profiles help to limit resource usage on the Oracle database.

- The DBA must set the `RESOURCE_LIMIT` parameter to TRUE in order to use user profiles.
- The resources that can be limited via profiles include the following:
  - Sessions connected per user at one time
  - CPU time per call
  - CPU time per session
  - Disk I/O per call
  - Disk I/O per session
  - Connection time
  - Idle time
  - Private memory (only for MTS)
  - Composite limit
- Profiles should be created for every type or class of user. Each parameter has a resource limit set for it in a user profile, which can then be assigned to users based on their processing needs.
- Oracle installs a special profile granted to a user if no other profile is defined. This special profile is called DEFAULT, and all values in the profile are set to `unlimited`.
- Any parameter not explicitly set in another user profile defaults in value to the value specified for that parameter in DEFAULT.
- New Oracle8 features in password administration are also available:
  - **`failed_login_attempts`** Number of unsuccessful attempts at login a user can make before the account locks. Default is 3.
  - **`password_life_time`** Number of days a password will remain active. Default is 60.
  - **`password_reuse_time`** Number of days before the password can be reused. Default is 1,800 (approximately 5 years).
  - **`password_reuse_max`** Number of times the password must be changed before one can be reused. Default is `unlimited`.

  - **`password_lock_time`** Number of days after which Oracle will unlock a user account locked automatically when the user exceeds `failed_login_attempts`. Default is 1/1,440 (1 minute).
  - **`password_grace_time`** Number of days during which an expired password must be changed by the user or else Oracle permanently locks the account. Default is 10.
  - **`password_verify_function`** Function used for password complexity verification. The default function is called `verify_function( )`.
- Database privileges govern access for performing every permitted activity in the Oracle database.
- There are two categories of database privileges: *system privileges* and *object privileges*.
- System privileges allow for the creation of every object on the database, along with the ability to execute many commands and connect to the database.
- Object privileges allow for access to data within database objects.
- There are three basic classes of system privileges for some database objects: `create`, `alter`, and `drop`. These privileges give the grantee the power to create database objects in their own user schema.
- Some exceptions exist to the preceding rule. The `alter table` privilege is an object privilege, while the `alter rollback segment` privilege is a system privilege. The `create index` privilege is an object privilege as well.
- Three oddball privileges are `grant`, `audit`, and `analyze`. These privileges apply to the creation of all database objects and to running powerful commands in Oracle.
- The `any` modifier gives the user extra power to create objects or run commands on any object in the user schema.
- The final system privilege of interest is the `restricted session` privilege, which allows the user to connect to a database in `restricted session` mode.

- Object privileges give the user access to place, remove, change, or view data in a table or one column in a table, as well as to alter the definition of a table, create an index on a table, and develop `FOREIGN KEY` constraints.
- When system privileges are revoked, the objects a user has created will still exist.
- A system privilege can be granted `with admin option` to allow the grantee to administer others' ability to use the privilege.
- When object privileges are revoked, the data placed or modified in a table will still exist, but you will not be able to perform the action allowed by the privilege anymore.
- An object privilege can be granted `with grant option` to another user in order to make them an administrator of the privilege.
- The `grant option` cannot be used when granting a privilege to a role.
- Roles are used to bundle privileges together and to enable or disable them automatically.
- A user can create objects and then grant the nongrantable object privileges to the role, which then can be granted to as many users as require it.
- There are roles created by Oracle when the software is installed:
  - **CONNECT** Can connect to the database and create clusters, links, sequences, tables, views, and synonyms. This role is good for table schema owners and development DBAs.
  - **RESOURCE** Can connect to the database and create clusters, sequences, tables, triggers, and stored procedures. This role is good for application developers. It also has unlimited tablespace.
  - **DBA** Can use any system privilege `with admin option.`
  - **EXP_FULL_DATABASE** Can export all database objects to an export dump file.
  - **IMP_FULL_DATABASE** Can import all database objects from an export dump file to the database.
  - **DELETE_CATALOG_ROLE** Extends `delete` privileges on SYS-owned dictionary tables, in response to the new restriction on `delete any table` privileges that prevent grantees from removing rows from SYS-owned dictionary tables.

  - **EXECUTE_CATALOG_ROLE** Allows grantee `execute` privileges on any SYS-owned package supplied with the Oracle software.
  - **SELECT_CATALOG_ROLE** Allows grantee to `select` data from any SYS-owned dictionary table or view.

- Roles can have passwords assigned to them to provide security for the use of certain privileges.
- Users can alter their own roles in a database session. Each role requires four bytes of space in the program global area (PGA) in order to be used. The amount of space each user requires in the PGA can be limited with the `MAX_ENABLED_ROLES` initialization parameter.
- When a privilege is granted to the user PUBLIC, then every user in the database can use the privilege. However, when a privilege is revoked from PUBLIC, then every stored procedure, function, or package in the database must be recompiled.
- Auditing the database can be done either to detect inappropriate activity or to store an archive of database activity.
- Auditing can collect large amounts of information. In order to minimize the amount of searching, the person conducting the audit should limit the auditing of database activities to where they may think a problem lies.
- Any activity on the database can be audited, either by naming the privilege or by naming an object in the database.
- The activities of one or more users can be singled out for audit; or every access to an object or privilege, or every session on the database, can have their activities audited.
- Audits can monitor successful activities surrounding a privilege, unsuccessful activities, or both.
- In every database audit, starting and stopping the instance, and every connection established by a user with DBA privileges as granted by SYSDBA and SYSOPER, are monitored regardless of any other activities being audited.
- Audit data is stored in the data dictionary in the AUD$ table, which is owned by SYS.

- Several dictionary views exist for seeing data in the AUD$ table. The main ones:
  - DBA_AUDIT_EXISTS
  - DBA_AUDIT_OBJECT
  - DBA_AUDIT_SESSION
  - DBA_AUDIT_STATEMENT
  - DBA_AUDIT_TRAIL
- If auditing is in place and is monitoring session connections, and if the AUD$ table fills, then no more users can connect to the database until the AUD$ table is (archived and) emptied.
- The AUD$ table should be audited, whenever in use, to detect tampering with the data in it.

Chapter Questions

1. The DBA is considering restricting her users' use of the host machine via the Oracle database. If the DBA wishes to use resource costs to limit resource usage, the first thing she must do is

A. Change the value of `RESOURCE_LIMIT to TRUE.`

B. Change the value of `composite_limit` in the user profile to zero.

C. Change the value of `composite_limit` in the DEFAULT profile to zero.

D. Change the value of the resource costs for the resources to be limited.

2. The DBA is eliminating some foreign key dependencies from the Oracle database prior to removal of some tables. When revoking the `references` privilege, the DBA must use which option to ensure success?

A. `with admin option`

B. `with grant option`

C. `cascade constraints`

D. `trailing nullcols`

3. **The DBA is using operating system authentication for his Oracle database. He is creating a user for that database. Which line of the following statement will produce an error?**

   A. `create user OPS$ELLISON`

   B. `identified externally`

   C. `default tablespace USERS_01`

   D. `default role CONNECT;`

   E. There are no errors in this statement.

4. **The DBA is about to enable auditing on the Oracle database in an attempt to discover some suspicious database activity. Audit trail information is stored in which of the following database objects?**

   A. SYS.SOURCE$

   B. SYS.AUD$

   C. DBA_SOURCE

   D. DBA_AUDIT_TRAIL

5. **The creator of a role is granted which of the following privileges with respect to the role she has just created?**

   A. `grant any privilege`

   B. `create any role`

   C. `with admin option`

   D. `with grant option`

   E. `sysdba`

6. **In order to find out how many database objects a user has created, which view would the DBA query in the Oracle data dictionary?**

   A. DBA_USERS

   B. DBA_OBJECTS

   C. DBA_TS_QUOTAS

   D. DBA_TAB_PRIVS

7. **The DBA is considering which settings to use for profiles in the Oracle database. On database creation, the value of the `CONNECT_TIME` parameter in the DEFAULT profile is set to which of the following choices?**

   A. 1

   B. 10

   C. 300

   D. `unlimited`

   E. None, the DEFAULT profile hasn't been created yet.

8. **A user cannot change aspects of his or her account configuration with the exception of one item. Which of the following choices identifies an area of the user's account that the user can change himself, using an `alter user` statement?**

   A. `identified by`

   B. `default tablespace`

   C. `temporary tablespace`

   D. `quota on`

   E. `profile`

   F. `default role`

9. **The DBA is considering implementing controls to limit the amount of host machine resources a user can exploit while connected to the Oracle database. Which of the following choices accurately describes a resource cost?**

   A. A monetary cost for using a database resource

   B. A monetary cost for using a privilege

   C. An integer value representing the importance of the resource

   D. An integer value representing the dollar cost for using the resource

10. The DBA gets a production emergency support call from a user trying to connect to Oracle, saying that the database won't let her connect and that she gets a message saying that the audit log is full. Which of the following choices accurately describes what is happening on the Oracle database?

A. The database is up and running.

B. The AUD$ table has been filled and `session` is being audited.

C. Restricted session has been disabled.

D. Operating system authentication is being used.

11. The DBA needs to keep track of when the database is started, due to a reported problem with Oracle being available after the host machine reboots. When auditing instance startup, the audit records are placed in which of the following locations?

A. SYS.AUD$

B. DBA_AUDIT_TRAIL

C. `ARCHIVE_DUMP_DEST`

D. `AUDIT_FILE_DEST`

12. In determining resource costs for defining user profiles, the DBA will assign a high resource cost to a resource in order to indicate which of the following?

A. A less expensive resource

B. A lower amount of resource used per minute

C. A more expensive resource

D. A higher amount of resource used per minute

Answers to Chapter Questions

1. A. Change the value of `RESOURCE_LIMIT` to TRUE.

Explanation In order for any value set for a resource cost to be effective, and in order to use any user profile, the `RESOURCE_LIMIT` initialization parameter must be set to TRUE. Refer to the discussion of user profiles.

2. C. `cascade constraints`

Explanation If a `FOREIGN KEY` constraint is defined as the result of a references privilege being granted, then in order to revoke the `references` privilege, the `cascade constraints` option must be used. Choices A and B are incorrect because the `admin option` and `grant option` relate to the granting of system and object privileges, respectively, while this question is asking about the revocation of an object privilege. Choice D is incorrect because `trailing nullcols` refers to an option in the SQL*Loader control file covered in the next chapter. Refer to the discussion of administering object privileges.

3. D. `default role CONNECT;`

Explanation The user creation statement will error out on line D. This is because no privileges or roles have been granted to the user yet. After creating the user and granting some privileges and/or roles to him or her, you can issue the `alter user default role` statement. Refer to the section on user creation.

4. B. SYS.AUD$

Explanation AUD$ holds all audit trail records. It is owned by user SYS. Choice A is incorrect because SOURCE$ contains source code for all stored procedures, functions, and packages. Choices C and D are dictionary views that provide access to the underlying data dictionary tables named in choices A and B. While they allow viewing of the data, the views themselves store nothing, because they are views. Refer to the discussion of auditing.

5. D. `with grant option`

Explanation Choice D is the correct answer because it is the appropriate administrative clause offered to the creator of a role in Oracle. The creator of a role can do anything he or she wants to with the role, including remove it. Choice C is incorrect because with `admin option` refers to the administrative clause for system privileges. Choices A, B, and E are incorrect because no privileges are given to a role on creation. Refer to the discussion of roles and the with grant option.

6. B. DBA_OBJECTS

Explanation The DBA_OBJECTS view lists all objects that are in the Oracle database, as well as the owners of those objects. Choice A is incorrect because DBA_USERS contains the actual user-creation information, such as encrypted password, default and temp tablespace, user profile, and default role. Choice C is incorrect because DBA_TS_QUOTAS identifies all the tablespace quotas that have been named for the user. Choice D is incorrect because DBA_TAB_PRIVS names all the table object privileges that have been granted and to whom they have been given. Refer to the discussion of monitoring information about existing users.

7. D. `unlimited`

Explanation All resource limits in the DEFAULT user profile created when Oracle is installed are set to `unlimited`. You can change them later using the `alter profile` command. Refer to the discussion of the DEFAULT profile in the managing resource usage discussion.

8. A. `identified by`

Explanation There is only one user creation option that the created user can modify. All others are managed either by a security administrator or the DBA. Although users can change the current role from the roles currently granted to them using the `set role` statement, they cannot issue the `alter user` statement to get the same result. Refer to the discussion of user creation.

9. C. An integer value representing the importance of the resource

Explanation The resource cost is an integer that measures relative importance of a resource to the DBA. Its value is completely arbitrary, and has nothing to do with money. Therefore, choices A, B, and D are all incorrect. Refer to the discussion of assessing resource costs in the section on user profiles.

10. B. The AUD$ table has been filled and `session` is being audited.

Explanation If user connections are being audited and the AUD$ table fills, then no user can connect until the AUD$ table is cleared. Choice A is incorrect because the database is open for everyone's use when it is up and running. By the same token, choice C is incorrect as well, because when a restricted session is disabled, the database is open for general access. Choice D is incorrect because operating system authentication is simply another means of verifying user passwords; it doesn't cut users off from accessing the database. Refer to the discussion of managing the audit trail.

11. D. AUDIT_FILE_DEST

Explanation This is a difficult question. For instance startup, `audit` places the information collected in this action into a special file that is placed where background process trace files are written. The location where background processes place their trace files is identified at instance startup with the `AUDIT_FILE_DEST` initialization parameter. Since the database has not started yet, the AUD$ table cannot be the location to which instance startup information is written, eliminating choice A. Since DBA_AUDIT_TRAIL is a view on AUD$, choice B is wrong, too. Choice C is the location where archive logs are written, which is closer to the spirit of the answer but still not correct. Refer to the discussion of auditing system-level database activity.

12. C. A more expensive resource

Explanation The higher the value set for resource cost, the more valued the resource is to the database system, increasing its relative "expense." Choice A is incorrect because the exact opposite is true. Choices B and D are incorrect because, although the DBA can track resource use on a per-minute basis, there is no value added by doing so. Nor does doing so indicate the relative expense of using the resource.

CHAPTER 11

Data Loads and National Language Support

n this chapter, you will learn about and demonstrate knowledge in the following areas:

- Loading and reorganizing data
- Using National Language Support

This chapter covers the remainder of the OCP Exam 2 material. The first topic is loading mass quantities of data into your Oracle database, and how to manage it quickly as a DBA. The second topic is Oracle's National Language Support, or NLS. This feature allows you to deploy Oracle in languages other than English. These topics comprise 16 percent of the actual test material on OCP Exam 2. Learning SQL*Loader, IMPORT, EXPORT, and NLS features have a big payoff in the career of a DBA. The data loading, unloading, and manipulation tools are useful both for loading data and for managing existing data.

Loading and Reorganizing Data

In this section, you will cover the following three points on loading and reorganizing data:

- Loading data using direct-path `insert`
- Using SQL*Loader conventional and direct path
- Reorganizing data with EXPORT and IMPORT

The role of the DBA comes down to managing data. The objects you are learning how to manage in this section have one main purpose—to manage the data your users put into the system. In your career as an Oracle DBA, you may manage databases of only a few hundred megabytes or VLDB systems expanding into the terabytes, or larger. It quickly becomes impossible to manage data transfer, data saves, or tablespace reorganization through the use of flat files. This is true both because of the size of the flat file produced when you dump a table with millions of rows to file, and because data loads and extractions using flat files take forever! So, this section teaches you data management techniques you will need to know using SQL*Loader, IMPORT, and EXPORT, both for OCP, and beyond.

Loading Data Using Direct-Path insert

First, I'll take a minute to teach you how to speed up big `insert` statements you may run on your database. Recall from Unit I that you can specify an `insert` statement that populates a table with multiple rows of data from another table, such as:

```
INSERT INTO spanky.employees
(SELECT * FROM athena.employees);
```

This statement is fine, and if you have time to wait, it will load all of your data. However, you may not have time to wait. Oracle makes it possible for you to speed performance of `insert` statements using a few different techniques for setting up a direct path to disk for your inserted data. You will see the term *direct path* is used a lot in the chapter. A direct path is a method for loading data in Oracle that bypasses certain aspects of the Oracle relational database management system (RDBMS) in order to improve the performance of your data load.

The way to use the direct path for inserting data into Oracle is by using *hints*. A hint is a directive you pass to the RDBMS along with your SQL statement to "encourage" Oracle to perform your SQL statement in one way as opposed to another. In this case, to hint to Oracle that you want to use the direct path for an `insert` statement, you should use the `append` hint, as shown syntactically in the following code block:

```
INSERT /*+APPEND */ INTO spanky.employees NOLOGGING
(select * from athena.employees);
```

First, notice that the direct-path hint consists of placing the `append` keyword inside a comment, with no space after the first comment indicator character string. Second, notice the use of the `nologging` keyword. This means that Oracle should not log any redo information to the redo log buffer in the SGA as part of making the data change. Of course, some space in the buffer cache will still be required for the `select`. Oracle simply adds data starting at the highwatermark, and since no blocks are being changed, no space is required in the SGA for this insert. From a data-change standpoint, this speeds things up considerably. From a data-recovery standpoint, this is the bane of your existence, because you are basically making a data change that is unrecoverable unless you have a backup. Thus, only use `nologging` when you are prepared to take the database offline to make a backup of your datafiles after you are done with your loads. There is also an outside chance that your database performance may degrade later, particularly if the users perform many full table scans on this table, and the highwatermark has been set too high because of substantial deletes.

In Oracle, you have the power of parallel DML and query to speed your direct path along, as well. In the code block that follows, notice the `select` statement has an embedded parallel query hint. Query and DML operation allows parallelism by generating multiple I/O processes that either draw more data into memory or write more data to disk. This hint can be used both on the `insert` statement and the query. It requires that you first enable parallel DML in your session, using the `alter session enable parallel DML` statement, which must be executed at the beginning of the transaction if it is to be used at all during the transaction.

The following code block demonstrates how you can mix and match hints in your direct-path `insert` statements:

```
ALTER SESSION ENABLE PARALLEL DML;

INSERT /*+APPEND */ INTO spanky.employees NOLOGGING
(select /*+PARALLEL(athena.employees,4)*/ *
 from athena.employees);

INSERT /*+PARALLEL(spanky.employees,4)*/INTO spanky.employees NOLOGGING
(select /*+PARALLEL(athena.employees,4)*/ *
 from athena.employees);
```

Exercises

1. What is the direct path in the context of `insert` statements?
2. What is the syntax of the hint used to identify a direct path insert?

Using SQL*Loader Conventional and Direct Path

SQL*Loader is a tool used by DBAs and developers to populate Oracle tables with data from flat files. It allows the DBA to selectively load certain columns but not others, or to exclude certain records entirely. SQL*Loader has some advantages over programming languages that allow embedded SQL statements, as well. Although a programmer could duplicate the functionality of SQL*Loader by writing a separate load program, SQL*Loader offers flexibility, ease of use, and good performance. It allows the developer to think more about loading the data than the details of opening files, reading lines, executing embedded SQL, and checking for end-of-file markers, and it dramatically reduces the need for debugging.

Before using SQL*Loader, you should understand its elements. The first is the data to be loaded, which is stored in a *datafile*. The SQL*Loader datafile is not to be confused with Oracle server datafiles, which store database objects. The next is a set of controls for data loading that are defined in a file called the *control file* (not to be confused with Oracle server's control file). These controls include specifications of how SQL*Loader should read records and parse them into columns, which columns should be loaded by data appearing in each position, and other features.

The Control File

The control file provides the following information to Oracle:

- Datafile name(s) and format

- Character sets used in the datafiles
- Datatypes of fields in those files
- How each field is delimited
- Which tables and columns to load

You must provide the control file to SQL*Loader so that it knows about the data it is about to load. Data and control file information can be provided in the same file or in separate files. Some items in the control file are mandatory, such as which tables and columns to load and how each field is delimited.

Example 1: A Combined Data and Control File

The following example is of a combined control file and datafile. It illustrates basic usage and syntax for control files and the effects of those specifications.

```
--variable-length, terminated enclosed data formatting
LOAD DATA
INFILE *
APPEND INTO TABLE address
FIELDS TERMINATED BY "," OPTIONALLY ENCLOSED BY '"'
(global_id, person_lname, person_fname,
 area_code,phone_number, load_order SEQUENCE(MAX,1))
BEGINDATA
83456, "Smith","Alfred",718,5551111
48292, "Smalls","Rebeca",415,9391000
34436, "Park","Ragan",919,7432105
15924,"Xi","Ling",708,4329354
49204,"Walla","Praveen",304,5983183
56061,"Whalen","Mark",407,3432353
```

Comments can appear anywhere in the control file, and need only be delimited by two dashes. Care should be taken not to place comments in either the datafile or the data portion of the control file.

The `load data` clause generally indicates the beginning of the contents of the control file. For all control files, the `infile` clause is required. It denotes where SQL*Loader can find the input data for this load. Using an asterisk (*) denotes that the data is in the control file.

The next line of the control file is the `into table` clause. It tells SQL*Loader the table to which the data will be loaded and the method by which it will be loaded. The `append` keyword denotes that these records can be inserted even if the table has other data. Other options include insert, which allows records to enter the table only if the table is empty; and `replace` and `truncate`, which delete all rows from the table before loading the new records.

The `fields terminated by` clause defines how columns will be delimited in the variable-length data records. The character that separates each data element is enclosed in double-quotes. Also, an optional enclosure character is defined with the `optionally enclosed by` clause.

The next line begins with a parenthesis, and within the parentheses the columns in the table to be loaded are specified. If a column from the table is not listed in this record, it will not be loaded with data from the datafile. The data loaded in each column will be selected from the data record positionally, with the first item in the record going into the first column, the second item in the second column, and so on. (Example 2 contains one special case in which an exception is made—a column is denoted by SEQUENCE(MAX,1), corresponding to a column in the table that will be populated with a sequence number that is not present in the datafile. SQL*Loader supports the generation of special information for data loads, such as sequences and datatype conversions.)

Finally, in cases where the data is included in the control file, the `begindata` clause is mandatory for denoting the end of the control file and the beginning of the data. This clause need not be present if the data is in a separate file.

TIP
Only put data in your control file if you are doing a small data load.

Example 2: A Control File for Fixed-Width Data

Usually, the control file and datafile are separate. For this example, the direct-path option has been set by the `options` clause, which can be used for setting many command-line parameters for the load. In a direct-path load, SQL*Loader bypasses most of Oracle's SQL-statement processing mechanism, turning flat file data directly into data blocks. The `load data` clause indicates the actual beginning of the control file. The `infile` clause specifies a datafile called `datafile1.dat`. The `badfile` clause specifies a file into which SQL*Loader can place datafile records that cannot be loaded into the database. The `discardfile` clause specifies a file containing records that were filtered out of the load because they did not match any record-selection criteria specified in the control file. The discard file, therefore, contains records that were not inserted into any table in the database. A `replace` load has been specified by the `into table` clause, so all records in the tables named will be deleted, and data from the file will be loaded. The column specifications in parentheses indicate, by the `position` clause, that the records in the datafile are of fixed width. Multiple `into table` clauses indicate that two files will be loaded.

```
OPTIONS (direct=true)
LOAD DATA
INFILE 'datafile1.dat'
BADFILE 'datafile1.bad'
DISCARDFILE 'datafile1.dsc'
REPLACE INTO TABLE phone_number
(global_id      POSITION(1:5)       INTEGER EXTERNAL,
 people_lname   POSITION(7:15)      CHAR,
 people_fname   POSITION(17:22)     CHAR,
 area_code      POSITION(24:27)     INTEGER EXTERNAL,
 phone_number   POSITIONAL(29:36)   INTEGER EXTERNAL)
INTO TABLE address
WHEN global_id != '     '
(global_id      POSITION(1:5)       INTEGER EXTERNAL,
 city           POSITION(38:50)     CHAR,
 state          POSITION(52:54)     CHAR,
 zip            POSITION(56:61)     INTEGER EXTERNAL)
```

The contents of `datafile1.dat` are listed as follows:

```
14325 SMITH    ED     304 3924954 MILLS         VA 20111
43955 DAVISON  SUSAN  415 2348324 PLEASANTON    CA 90330
39422 MOHAMED  SUMAN  201 9493344 HOBOKEN       NJ 18403
38434 MOUSE    MIKE   718 1103010 QUEENS        NY 10009
```

Datafiles

Datafiles can have two formats. The data Oracle will use to populate its tables can be in fixed-length fields or in variable-length fields delimited by a special character. Additionally, SQL*Loader can handle data in binary format or character format. If the data is in binary format, then the datafile must have fixed-length fields. Figure 11-1 gives a pictorial example of records that are fixed in length.

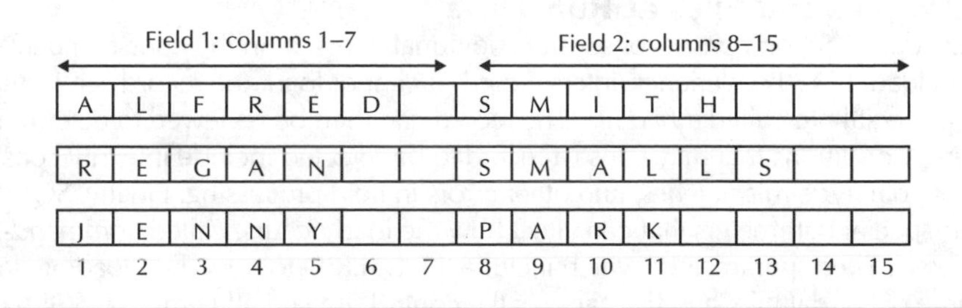

FIGURE 11-1. *Fixed-length records*

In contrast to fixed-length data fields, variable-length data fields are only as long as is required to store the data. Unlike in Figure 11-1, a variable-length record will have only four characters for the second field of the third record. Typically, data fields in variable-length records are terminated by a special character or enclosed by special characters. These options are called terminated fields and enclosed fields, respectively. The following list shows the differences between terminated and enclosed fields:

Terminated Fields (Delimiter Is ,)	Enclosed Fields (Delimiter Is |)
SMITH,ALFRED	|SMITH|ALFRED|
SMALLS,REGAN	|SMALLS|REGAN|
PARK,JENNY	|PARK|JENNY|

The final thing to know about data records is the difference between physical and logical data records. In a datafile, each row of the file may be considered a record. This type of record is called a *physical record*. A physical record in a datafile can correspond either to a row in one table or several tables. Each row in a table is also considered a record—a *logical record*. In some cases, the logical records or rows of a table may correspond to several physical records of a datafile. In these cases, SQL*Loader supports the use of continuation fields to map two or more physical records into one logical record. A continuation field can be defined in one or more of the ways listed below:

- A fixed number of physical records always are concatenated to form a logical record for table loading.
- Physical records are appended if a continuation field contains a special string.
- Physical records are concatenated if a special character appears as the last nonblank character.

Additional Load Files at Run Time

SQL*Loader in action consists of several additional items. If, in the course of performing the data load, SQL*Loader encounters records it cannot load, the record is rejected and put in a special file called a *bad file*. The record can then be reviewed to determine the problem. Conditions that may cause a record to be rejected include integrity constraint violation, datatype mismatches, and other errors in field processing. Finally, SQL*Loader accepts special parameters that can affect how the load occurs, called *command-line parameters*. These parameters, which include the USERID to use when loading data, the name of the datafile, and the name of the control file, are all items that SQL*Loader needs to conduct the data load. These parameters can be passed to SQL*Loader on the command line or in a special parameter file called a *parfile*.

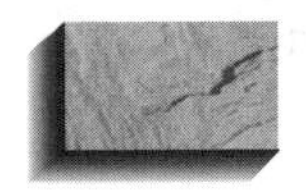

TIP
Use a parameter file to specify the command-line options you frequently use, in order to avoid unnecessary keystrokes.

Additionally, SQL*Loader gives the user options to reject data, based on special criteria. These criteria are defined in the control file as part of the `when` clause. If the tool encounters a record that fails a specified `when` clause, the record is placed in a special file called the *discard file*. The second example in the previous control file discussion describes this type of load. In both cases, SQL*Loader writes the bad or discarded record to the appropriate file in the same format as was fed to the tool in the datafile. This feature allows for easy correction and reloading, with reuse of the original control file. Figure 11-2 represents the process flow of a data record from the time it appears in the datafile of the load to the time it is loaded in the database.

The execution of SQL*Loader is recorded in the log file. If, for any reason, the tool cannot create a *log file*, the execution terminates. The log file consists of six elements: header section, global information section, table information section, datafile section, table load information section, and summary statistics section. The elements are described in the following list:

- **Header section** Details the SQL*Loader version number and date of the run

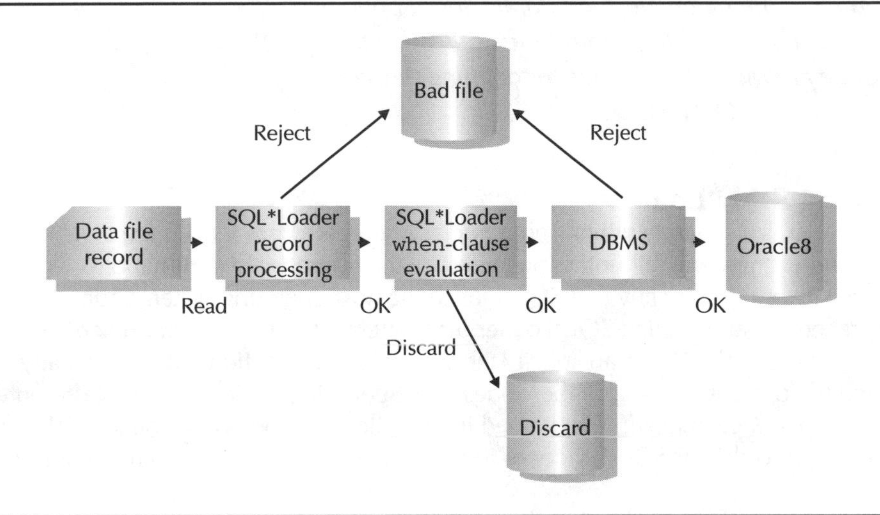

FIGURE 11-2. *Control flow for record filtering*

- **Global information section** Gives names for all input and output files, the command-line parameters, and a continuation character specification if one is required
- **Table information section** Lists all tables being loaded by the current run, and load conditions, and whether data is being inserted, appended, or replaced
- **Datafile section** Contains details about any rejected records
- **Table load information section** Lists the number of tables loaded and the number of records that failed table requirements for loading, for reasons such as integrity constraints
- **Summary statistics section** Describes the space used for the bind array, cumulative load statistics, end time, elapsed time, and CPU time

SQL*Loader Command-Line Parameters

The parameters described in Table 11-1 are accepted by SQL*Loader on the command line. These options can be passed to SQL*Loader as parameters on the command line in the format `PARAMETER=value`. Alternatively, parameters can be passed to SQL*Loader in another component, called the *parfile*. The parameters can be identified in the parfile as `option=value`.

NOTE
*Some of the parameters are duplicates of options that can be set in the control file, indicating that there are multiple methods for defining the same load using SQL*Loader.*

Running SQL*Loader

SQL*Loader is a separate utility from Oracle. Attempts to run it from the SQL*Plus command prompt will fail unless preceded by the appropriate command to temporarily or permanently exit SQL*Plus to the host operating system prompt. The preceding table, listing SQL*Loader parameters, presents the parameters in a special order—the DBA can specify the values for each option without actually naming the options, so long as the values correspond in position to the list presented. Thus, the parameters needn't be named in the following code block because they are in the proper order for SQL*Loader to interpret them correctly according to position:

```
Sqlldr spanky/fatcat load.ctl load.log load.bad load.dat
```

Parameter	Description
USERID *name/pass*	Oracle username and password
CONTROL *filename*	Control filename
LOG *filename*	Log filename
BAD *filename*	Bad filename
DATA *filename*	Datafile name
DISCARD *filename*	Discard filename
DISCARDS *n*	Number of discards to terminate the load (default: all)
SKIP *n*	Number of logical records to skip (default: 0)
LOAD *n*	Number of logical records to load (default: all)
ERRORS *n*	Number of errors to terminate the load (default: 50)
ROWS *n*	Number of rows in the conventional-path bind array or between direct-path data saves (conventional path: 64; direct path: all)
BINDSIZE *n*	Size of conventional-path bind array in bytes
SILENT *option*	Suppress messages between run (*option* is set to header, feedback, errors, or discards)
DIRECT *boolean*	Use direct-path load (default: FALSE)
PARFILE *filename*	Parameter filename
PARALLEL *boolean*	Perform parallel load (default: FALSE)
FILE *filename*	Datafile to allocate extents

TABLE 11-1. *SQL*Loader Command-Line Parameters*

However, in the following code block, the parameters must be identified because they are not in proper order for SQL*Loader to interpret them by position:

```
Sqlldr USERID=scott/tiger CONTROL=load.ctl DATA=load.dat
```

Additionally, a mixture of positional and named parameters can be passed. One issue to remember is that positional parameters can be placed on the command line before named parameters, but not after them. Thus, the first of the following statements is acceptable, but the second is not:

```
sqlldr spanky/fatcat load.ctl DATA=load.dat /* OK */
sqlldr DATA=load.dat spanky/fatcat load.ctl /* ERROR */
```

As mentioned previously, another option for specifying command-line parameters is placing the parameters in a parfile. The parfile can then be referenced on the command line, as follows:

```
Sqlldr parfile=load.par
```

The contents of `load.par` may look like the following:

```
DATA=load.dat
USERID=scott/tiger
CONTROL=load.ctl
LOG=load.log
BAD=load.bad
DISCARD=load.dsc
```

A final alternative to specifying SQL*Loader load parameters on the command line is specifying the command-line parameters in the control file. In order to place command-line parameters in the control file, the `options` clause must be used. This clause should be placed at the beginning of the control file, before the `load` clause. Command-line parameters specified in the `options` clause should be named parameters, and they can be overridden by parameters passed on the command line or in the parfile. The control file in the second example of the previous section details the use of parameters in the control file.

Performance Tuning and Problem Resolution

Your data loads can fail for several reasons, the first being insufficient space allocation for a table or index. To improve performance and reduce load failure rates, be sure to preallocate enough space for the load to finish. In this case, the data adds up until the failure will likely be committed to Oracle. You may want to use the `skip` command in your control file to have Oracle ignore the data that's already there. However, you may encounter fragmentation issues if SQL*Loader has already caused many extents to allocated to your partially-loaded table . You could instead truncate the table and try loading it again, or simply use the `truncate` or `replace` keywords for loading data into the table in the SQL*Loader control file.

Another way to improve performance on your database is to sort the data on the largest index your table will have before loading the data. This allows you to create the index using the `nosort` option, which was explained in Chapter 7. If you do use the nosort option, however, be sure your data is sorted properly. If not, another error will ensue, and you'll have to allow Oracle to perform its sort to create the index.

A related problem is that of duplicate column data in a column that expected unique values, such as in a primary key. To resolve this issue, you can use the EXCEPTIONS table in enabling integrity constraints explained in Chapter 9. One good point to note here is that you most likely won't need to reload your data.

SQL*Loader may leave an index in a state called the *direct load state* if a direct load is unsuccessful. This means that the index is unusable and must be dropped and re-created for the data currently in the table. A query on INDEX_NAME and status against the DBA_INDEXES data dictionary view will show whether an index was left in direct load state. Reasons for this failure include SQL*Loader running out of space for the index, instance failure while creating an index, duplicate values in a unique or primary key, or presorted data not being in the order specified by the sorted indexes clause of the control file. To correct the problem, drop and recreate the index.

You also may find yourself encountering problems if your table has very large rows or your BINDSIZE load parameter is set too low. In this situation, the SQL*Loader bind array might not be able to fit one row of data. To resolve this, simply increase the value set for BINDSIZE (being sensitive to the amount of memory available on the machine running SQL*Loader), and rerun the load. Finally, SQL*Loader dumps data records that generate errors to a discard file. You can specify a limit on the number of records that may be discarded before the SQL*Loader run terminates.

Conventional-Path and Direct-Path Data Loads

SQL*Loader provides two data paths for loading data. They are the *conventional* path and the *direct* path. Whereas the conventional path uses a variant of the SQL insert statement, with an array interface to improve data load performance, the direct path avoids the RDBMS altogether by converting flat file data into Oracle data blocks and writing those blocks directly to the database. Conventional-path data loads compete with other SQL processes, and also require DBWR to perform the actual writes to the database.

Figure 11-3 pictorially displays the differences between conventional and direct-path loads. In a conventional load, SQL*Loader reads multiple data records from the input file into a bind array. When the array fills, SQL*Loader passes the data to the Oracle SQL-processing mechanism or optimizer for insertion. In a direct load, SQL*Loader reads records from the datafile, converts those records directly into Oracle data blocks, and writes them to disk, bypassing most of the Oracle database processing. Processing time for this option is generally faster than for a conventional load.

The direct-load option is specified as a command-line parameter, and like other parameters, it can be specified in three different ways—on the command line as a named or positional parameter, in a parameter file, or in the control file as part of the options clause. At the beginning of the direct-path load, SQL*Loader makes a call to

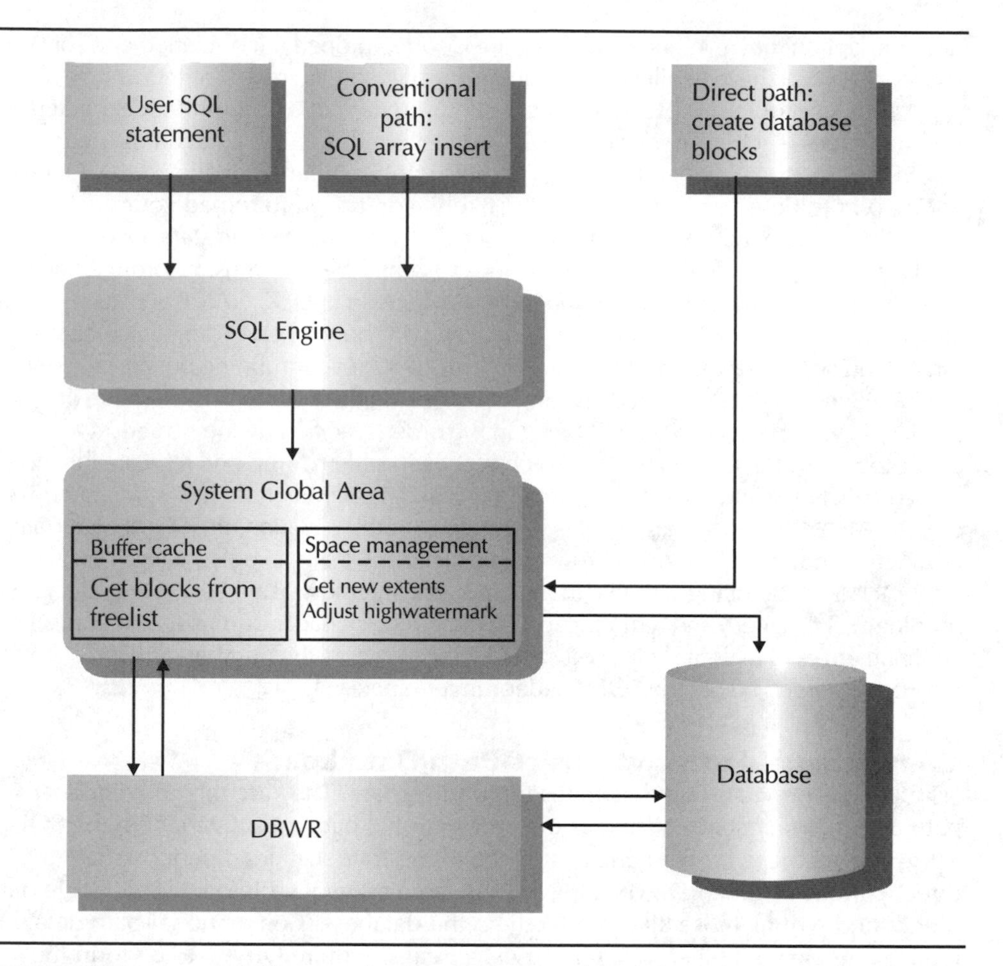

FIGURE 11-3. *Database paths for conventional and direct loads*

Oracle to put a lock on the tables being inserted, and it makes another call to Oracle again at the end to release the lock. During the load, SQL*Loader makes a few calls to Oracle to get new extents when necessary and to reset the highwatermark when data saves are required. A data save is the direct-path equivalent to a `commit`. A list of behaviors and actions the SQL*Loader direct path assumes and takes is given here:

- Partial blocks are not used, so the server process is never required to do a database read.
- No SQL `insert` commands are used.

- The bind array is not used; SQL*Loader creates database blocks and writes them directly to storage. This feature allows the tool to avoid contending with other SQL statements for database buffer cache blocks.
- The direct path allows for presorting options, which enables the use of operating system high-speed sorting algorithms, if they are available. This speeds the creation of indexes and primary keys.
- Since SQL*Loader writes data directly to disk, in the event of instance failure, all changes made up to the most recent data save will be stored on disk, limiting the need for recovery.

Prior to executing the data load using SQL*Loader, the DBA must determine the type of load to use. There are two paths available for use: conventional and direct. The following list describes the situations for using each load type. Generally speaking, the conventional path is slower than the direct path because it handles all the constraints and indexing in an Oracle database as the data is loaded, essentially paying all its dues up front. The direct-path load can make some substantial performance gains over the conventional-path load in certain situations by deferring payment of all its dues by managing constraint and index updates after the load completes.

Use the direct path in the following cases:

- When loading a large amount of data in a short time frame
- When increasing load performance by using parallel loading
- When loading a character set not supported in the current session (or when the conventional load of that character set produces errors)

Use the conventional path in the following cases:

- When loading data across a network
- When loading data into a clustered table
- When loading a small amount of data into a large indexed table or a large table with many integrity constraints (it takes longer to drop and re-create a large index than insert a few rows to the table and index)
- When applying single-row operations or SQL functions to data being loaded

The advantages of conventional-path loading result from it being relatively nondisruptive to the underpinnings of a database table. Conventional-path loads work on the same principles that normal data inserts work, only much faster. Records in a conventional-path load pay their dues to the Oracle database as the records load; that is to say, the records loaded on the conventional path will update the associated indexes with a table, and generally have the look and feel of normal online transaction processing.

In contrast, direct-path loading helps when a great deal of data must be loaded in a short period of time. Direct-path loads bypass the "customs inspectors" of the Oracle database—namely, integrity constraints, as well as the "post office," or table indexes, of the database. Unfortunately, the safety and performance conditions provided by indexes and integrity constraints must be met at some point. Therefore, the direct path operates on a "pay me later" principle; the index updates have to happen at some point, so after the DBA completes the direct-path load, he or she will need to reapply the constraints and rebuild the indexes so as to put the Oracle database back together before users can access the data loaded in the direct path.

Exercises

1. Name and describe the two types of delimited fields. What is a continuation record and how is one defined?
2. What is the bad file? How is it produced, and what does it contain? In what format are the bad records written?
3. What are the functions and contents of the log file? What is the discard file? What clause in the control file determines its contents? In what format are the discard records written?
4. Why does a direct-path load usually take less time to execute than a conventional load? When will a direct-path load take longer than a conventional load?

Reorganizing Data with EXPORT and IMPORT

EXPORT is a command-line tool that you can use to extract data from your tablespace into a *dump file* using special binary format. You can read the data back into Oracle with the use of IMPORT. You run these utilities outside of SQL*Plus, on the operating system command line, using a series of parameters specified either in a parameter file, on the command line, or even interactively. There is some overlap between the discussion of EXPORT and IMPORT here and in Unit III, where you will learn about the use of these tools for backup and recovery at the logical tablespace level.

How Are EXPORT and IMPORT Used?

Why would you want to dump your data out of Oracle into binary files? Well, for one thing, your data and index tablespaces may get fragmented as the result of volatile data changes. Database changes that substantially increase the size of rows may also cause row migration. This combination of migration and fragmentation degrades performance. To resolve the problem, you must reorganize your tables with EXPORT and IMPORT on an as-needed basis. Other reasons for using EXPORT and IMPORT include moving data between different users, moving data between Oracle databases (from development to production, from OLTP to warehouse, and so on). These tools are useful for migrating from one version of Oracle to another or from Oracle on one platform to Oracle on another. Dump files are useful for testing data-change processes repeatedly—you use EXPORT to get a "gold" copy of your data, run the test, then revert to the "gold" backup for the next test run.

Command-Line Parameters for EXPORT

The EXPORT parameters and values can be given either at the command line or in the parameter file, and they determine several things about the database export. The objects that will be exported in this execution of EXPORT, the name and location of the exported data file, and the name and password for the username EXPORT will use for execution, are all options that can be defined by command-line parameters. A sample listing of the parameters EXPORT can handle appears in Table 11-2.

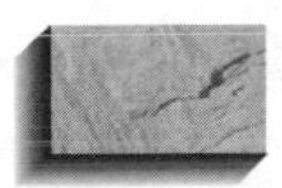

TIP
Only use the `CONSISTENT` parameter if you are exporting a small amount of data. EXPORT must allocate a rollback segment if this parameter is used, and you may encounter problems if you try to dump a lot of data with `CONSISTENT=Y` should the space in your allocated rollback segment be exceeded.

EXPORT Runtime Modes

There are three modes for using EXPORT. The first is `user` mode. This mode makes it possible to copy data in tables and indexes owned by a particular user, as well as other objects, such as procedures and triggers, also owned by that user. EXPORT will not make copies of indexes and triggers that this user owns for tables owned by another user, however. Triggers and indexes owned by another user on tables owned by this user will not be exported either. In order to set up EXPORT to export the objects that are owned by a user, the DBA should provide a list of one or more users whose objects will be taken in the export.

If no value is specified for a parameter, then EXPORT uses the default value for that parameter. Exporting in `user` mode is useful in database situations where the DBA has configured several applications within the same database that use different usernames as schema owners for the database objects. Exporting in `user` mode is

Parameter	Description
USERID (*name/pass*)	The username and password under which EXPORT will execute.
BUFFER (*number*)	Defines a buffer size EXPORT will use to fetch rows for the export file.
FILE (*filename*)	Identifies the name and location of the export file produced.
GRANTS (Y/N)	Indicates whether table grants should be included in the export.
INDEXES (Y/N)	Indicates whether table indexes should be included in the export.
ROWS (Y/N)	Indicates whether table rows should be included in the export.
CONSTRAINTS (Y/N)	Indicates whether table constraints should be included in the export.
COMPRESS (Y/N)	Indicates whether EXPORT will place all rows of the table into one initial extent in the export file. This is useful for reducing fragmentation, but you may allocate too much space if your table has lots of deleted rows. It is important to note here that Oracle does not actually reduce space use; it merely recalculates the existing data so that it fits into one big initial extent, which can still cause space problems later.
FULL (Y/N)	Indicates whether EXPORT should export the entire database.
OWNER (*name*)	Indicates a list of users whose database objects should be exported (user mode).
TABLES (*list*)	Specifies a list of tables that should be exported (table mode).
RECORDLENGTH (*number*)	Lists the size of each data record in the export file. If the DBA wants to import the exported file onto a database in another operating system, this value must be modified to the proper value for that operating system.

TABLE 11-2. *Examples of Parameters EXPORT Can Handle*

Parameter	Description
`INCTYPE` *(keyword)*	Accepts the keywords complete, cumulative, or `incremental` to indicate the type of EXPORT executed.
`HELP (Y/N)`	Displays a help message with all the features of EXPORT described.
`RECORD (Y/N)`	Will specify information about the export in one of the following SYS tables used to track export information: INCVID, INCFIL, INCEXP.
`LOG` *(filename)*	Specifies the name of a file containing runtime details and error messages for the given export.
`CONSISTENT (Y/N)`	Allows EXPORT to obtain a read-consistent view of all data exported. This requires a large rollback segment. The effect can be duplicated by the DBA enabling `restricted session` mode before beginning the export.
`FEEDBACK` *(number)*	When set, displays a dot to indicate progress on rows exported per table.
`STATISTICS` *(keyword)*	Accepts the `estimate, compute,` or `none` keywords. This is used to generate statistics for cost-based optimization on the database.
`MLS (Y/N)`	Used for Trusted Oracle. Stores the multilayer security label for tables and rows in the export.
`MLS_LABEL_FORMAT`	Used for Trusted Oracle. Redefines the default format for multilayer security labels.
`DIRECT (Y/N)`	Allows the DBA to run faster exports using the direct path. This is similar in function to direct-path loading in SQL*Loader.

TABLE 11-2. *Examples of Parameters EXPORT Can Handle* (continued)

also useful when you want to move data from one user to another. The following is a sample issuance of the export command from your UNIX command line that causes EXPORT to run in `user` mode:

```
/home/oracle80/> exp userid=DBA/password owner=HRAPL \
 > file='/oracle/export/hrapl10298.dmp'
```

The next mode is `table` mode. With `table` mode, the DBA can specify very selective exports that only draw data from a few different tables. You can use the `table` mode EXPORT for the purpose of highly supplemental, highly selective exports for restoring a specific table or other object to the database. This mode is also handy for extracting table definitions with or without data, all indexes or triggers for the table when EXPORT is run by the DBA (or other user granted the EXP_FULL_DATABASE role), constraints, grants, and statistics from an `analyze` run.

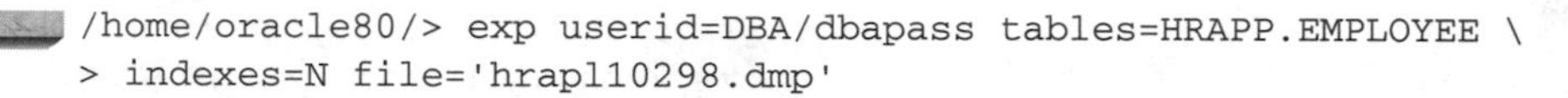

```
/home/oracle80/> exp userid=DBA/dbapass tables=HRAPP.EMPLOYEE \
> indexes=N file='hrapl10298.dmp'
```

The final option for running EXPORT is to do so in `full` mode. This mode will export all tables from all user schemas except SYS. In order to use `full` mode, the `FULL` parameter must be set to `Y` either at the command line or in the parameter file. Unlike `table` or `user` mode, `full` mode for database export is used in order to provide a full database backup and recovery option with logical methods. One other important use is when you migrate to a different platform.

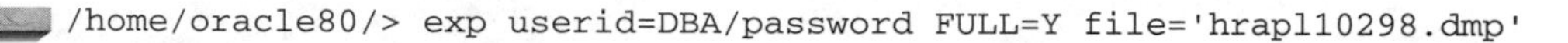

```
/home/oracle80/> exp userid=DBA/password FULL=Y file='hrapl10298.dmp'
```

TIP
Use of the `FULL`, `OWNER`, and `TABLES` parameters in your EXPORT run are mutually exclusive. If your parameter file defines more than one of these parameters, EXPORT will terminate with an error.

EXPORT Conventional Path and Direct Path

There are two unload paths for EXPORT to use: the conventional path and the direct path. The conventional-path export uses much the same mechanisms for extracting data as a SQL `select` statement would. Data is read into the buffer cache from disk, evaluated, passed over to a user process (the EXPORT client, in this case), and written to file. Direct-path exports, on the other hand, run faster because the data is extracted from Oracle datafiles and passed directly to the EXPORT client for processing, bypassing many steps in Oracle SQL-statement processing entirely. The IMPORT tool has no problem with data extracted using either the conventional-path or direct-path EXPORT.

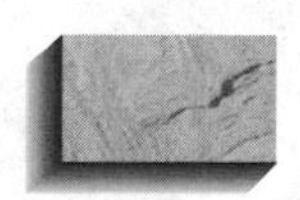

TIP
For best performance of EXPORT, run it with `DIRECT=Y`, and set `BUFFER` as high as your operating system and host machine will allow.

Command-Line Parameters for IMPORT

The IMPORT tool is designed to complement the functionality of EXPORT by allowing the DBA to take data stored in an EXPORT file and draw it back into the database. The only program that can read exported data is the IMPORT tool. In general, IMPORT allows the DBA to import data from an export file either into the same database or a different one, depending on the needs of the DBA.

```
Imp userid=DBA/password full=y file='/oracle/export/010199exp.dmp'
```

IMPORT works much like EXPORT. The DBA issues the command to run IMPORT, either from the command line, interactively, or with the use of a graphical user interface. IMPORT supports the use of many of the same parameters that EXPORT supports, with a few differences. All of the parameters supported by IMPORT are listed in Table 11-3.

Running IMPORT in Various Modes

Like EXPORT, IMPORT has the ability to run in `user` and `table` modes. The parameter for table mode is `TABLES=(`*`list_of_tables`*`)`. The DBA can provide a list of tables that IMPORT should draw from the export dump file into the database. However, the parameter must contain listed tables that are part of the export file, or else the tables in the TABLES parameter listing will not be imported.

```
imp userid=DBA/password file='010199exp.dmp' tables=EMPLOYEE
```

There are some slight differences in the way IMPORT handles `user` mode. The parameters used in IMPORT `user` mode are called `FROMUSER` and `TOUSER`. `FROMUSER` identifies the owner of the objects in the dump file that will be extracted.

Parameter	Description
`USERID (`*`user/pass`*`)`	The username and password used to run the IMPORT
`BUFFER (`*`number`*`)`	Parameter that defines the number of rows inserted into a database at one time
`FILE (`*`filename`*`)`	Determines the name of the export file to use for the input
`SHOW (Y/N)`	Displays the contents of the export file but doesn't actually cause IMPORT to import anything
`IGNORE (Y/N)`	Specifies whether to ignore errors that occur during import

TABLE 11-3. *Parameters Supported by IMPORT*

Parameter	Description
GRANTS (Y/N)	Specifies whether grants in the export file should be imported
INDEXES (Y/N)	Specifies whether indexes in the export file should be imported
ROWS (Y/N)	Specifies whether rows in the export file should be imported
FULL (Y/N)	Determines whether the import will be in `full` mode
FROMUSER (*name*)	The names of schema user database object owners for the objects in the export file that should be imported
TOUSER (*name*)	Identifies the user schema into which database objects should be placed if the IMPORT is running in `user` mode
TABLES (*list*)	Specifies whether tables in the export file should be imported
RECORDLENGTH (*number*)	Identifies the length in bytes of each record in the export dump; only necessary when data was exported on an OS with a different record size
INCTYPE (*keyword*)	Defines the type of import that will occur—valid values are `system` and `restore`.
COMMIT (Y/N)	Specifies whether IMPORT should `commit` each time a buffer's worth of data is written to the database
HELP (Y/N)	Indicates whether IMPORT should display help information about the parameters and their meanings
LOG (*filename*)	Indicates the name of a file into which all IMPORT runtime information and errors will be stored
DESTROY (Y/N)	Indicates whether IMPORT should reuse the datafiles that exist in the database for storing imported objects
INDEXFILE (Y/N)	Indicates whether IMPORT should create a file containing a script that will create a table's index rather than creating the index itself
FEEDBACK (Y/N)	Specifies whether IMPORT should give the dot notation to indicate progress in the importation of data
MLS	Used in conjunction with importing data into Trusted Oracle
MLS_LISTLABELS	Used in conjunction with importing data into Trusted Oracle
MLS_MAPFILE	Used in conjunction with importing data into Trusted Oracle

TABLE 11-3. *Parameters Supported by IMPORT* (continued)

TOUSER identifies who will own the objects when they are imported. The value for TOUSER must already exist in Oracle, because IMPORT will not create that user for you.

```
Imp userid=DBA/password file='010199exp.dmp' fromuser='MILON'
touser='SHUG'
```

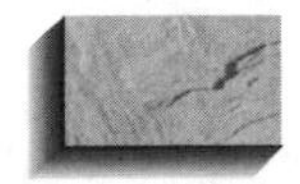

TIP

IMPORT can run in `table` or `user` mode to import database objects from dump files made by EXPORT running in `full` mode. IMPORT cannot run in `full` mode, however, when the dump file was made with EXPORT running in `table` or `user` mode.

Running IMPORT in `full` mode is also an option. In this situation, Oracle will import all objects in the dump file. Note, however, that the export dump file may not contain all objects in the Oracle database from which the dump file was produced. For example, your export may run in `table` mode, and your import can run in `full` mode to import all the tables in the dump file.

Order of Objects Imported

Data is imported from the export dump file in the following sequence:

1. Table definitions
2. Row data
3. B-tree indexes
4. Constraints, bitmap indexes, and triggers

Troubleshooting IMPORT Runs

One of the biggest data-inconsistency problems a DBA may encounter in a database relates to statement triggers. If a statement trigger populates data or applies some business rule as a result of the change of data in a table, then that change may not occur during an import. This is because the statement trigger is imported last, and therefore will not fire when the row data is imported. There are ways to circumvent this problem, such as importing the table definitions, index definitions, constraints, and triggers, but not row data, and then running IMPORT a second time to import the row data. Another problem you might see is invalid procedures or views when the job is finished, because of object or procedure dependencies, such as when imported PL/SQL program units or views look for objects that aren't there.

Row triggers present an interesting situation for IMPORT. As IMPORT loads data, any row triggers that exist on the object will actually fire. Thus, if you want the trigger to fire, perhaps because rows in another table are populated for each row populated in this table, you should run the entire import first with `ROWS=N`. Then, run a second execution of IMPORT parameters set in the following way: `IGNORE=Y`, `ROWS=Y`, `INDEXES=N`, `CONSTRAINTS=N`, and `TRIGGERS=N`.

EXPORT, IMPORT, and Character Sets

The character set used in your dump file is determined in the following way. When you run EXPORT using conventional path, it produces a dump file using whatever character set is specified for the session in which EXPORT runs. This may or may not be the same as the database character set, because the intermediate layers of processing required for conventional-path exports performs character conversions. However, if you run EXPORT in direct path, it produces a dump file in the specified character set for the database, no matter what. The dump file itself contains information about the character set of the contents.

IMPORT can convert the contents of a dump file in one character set to that of the target database, but this process lengthens the time it takes the import to run. Also, if there is no equivalent character in the character set of the target database, a default character will be substituted, leading to potential meaning loss in translation. Where possible, you should try to import data in the same character set it was exported in, or at least ensure that the target character set contains all characters used in the source character set.

Exercises

1. Identify the overall purpose of EXPORT and IMPORT. How are runtime parameters specified for these tools?
2. What are the different modes that EXPORT and IMPORT can run in? What happens when you specify parameters for two different modes at the same time?
3. What is the difference between a conventional-path and a direct-path export? Why is direct-path export faster? In what situations might use of the `CONSISTENT` parameter be a bad idea?
4. In what order are objects imported from a dump file?

Using National Language Support

In this section, you will cover the following three points on using National Language Support (NLS) in Oracle:

- Choosing a character set for a database
- Specifying language-dependent behavior
- Obtaining information about NLS settings

In order to produce a product that is usable worldwide, Oracle supports many different language-encoding schemes. There are four different classes supported, including single-byte character sets (both 7-bit and 8-bit), varying-width multibyte character set, fixed-width multibyte character set, and the Unicode character set. Since you are reading this book, you are probably already familiar with the single-byte character set US7ASCII, the 7-bit ASCII character set used in America. Several 8-bit character sets are used throughout Europe to represent the characters found in those languages, in addition to those used in English. Both the varying- and fixed-width character sets are commonly used in support of Japanese, Chinese, Korean, and other languages that use complex characters to represent language, and for Arabic and Hebrew, which add the complexity of being read from right to left. Unicode is a standard for encoding all characters usable in computers, including all characters in all languages, plus specialized print media, math, and computer characters. In this section, you will learn about choices in character sets for the database; how to specify NLS behavior in different scenarios, NLS parameters, and NLS usage; and what influence language-dependent application behavior may have.

TIP
There is slight variation from the OCP Candidate Guide in the coverage of this topic. This is meant to eliminate redundancy and to streamline your learning process. You should also consider that NLS usage comprises only a small amount of OCP content.

Choosing a Character Set for a Database

Two character sets can be defined for your database: a *database character set* and the *national character set*. Both database and national character sets are defined when you create your database, and cannot be changed after the fact. So, any choice you want to make in this area should happen before you create your database, or you should be prepared to drop and re-create it. The database character set is used for Oracle SQL and PL/SQL source code storage, whereas the national character set is used to represent your table data. SQL and PL/SQL must be stored in a language containing all characters in US 7-bit ASCII or EBCDIC, whichever is supported by your host machine. So, even if you speak Korean, and want to store Korean in your database, you still need to know enough English to type in the SQL and PL/SQL commands.

Some special conditions apply to national character sets and text or large object variables. The CLOB, CHAR, and VARCHAR2 datatypes can store database character sets, and each has national character set equivalents, called NCLOB, NCHAR, and NVARCHAR2, respectively. The LONG datatype can only store character sets that are allowed to be database character sets. Note also that the terms "fixed length" and "variable length" have different meanings for CHAR and VARCHAR2 datatypes than "fixed width" and "variable width" in the CHAR and NCHAR or VARCHAR2 and NVARCHAR2 context. In the first case, fixed width means that the data stored in a CHAR(3) will always be three characters long, even if you specify only one character of data. The one character will be padded with two extra spaces. VARCHAR2 columns will not be padded with extra blanks, so the same one character of data in a VARCHAR2(3) column will be only one character long. In the second case, fixed and variable width refers to the number of bytes used to store each character in the string.

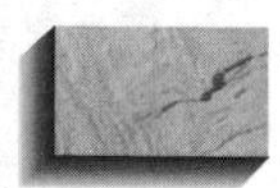

TIP

For best results, your database and national character sets should be closely related. Also, the tradeoff between fixed-width and variable-width character sets is that fixed-width sets permit better performance in string operations, such as `length( )` and `substr( )`, but variable-width sets are better for managing space.

Exercises

1. Compare fixed-length and variable-length datatypes to fixed-width and variable-width character sets. What is meant by each?

2. Compare database and national character sets. What is meant by, and permitted by, each?

Specifying Language-Dependent Behavior

There are several different areas where language-dependent behavior can be specified. The first of these is on the Oracle server. As you might predict, the way you specify language-dependent behavior on the Oracle server is to set `initsid.ora` parameters. Those parameters, and the information in the database those parameters identify, are listed here:

- **NLS_LANGUAGE** Indicates the language for error messages, the names of days and months, the symbols for 12-hour time of day and calendar era; this parameter also defines the sort mechanism Oracle will use
- **NLS_DATE_LANGUAGE** Changes the language for day and month names, and other language components of date information
- **NLS_SORT** Changes the sort mechanism Oracle uses; for example, you can override the default sort order of the national character set to use the sort order of another character set
- **NLS_TERRITORY** Indicates numbering for day of the week, default date format, currency symbols, decimal symbol
- **NLS_CURRENCY** Identifies a new currency symbol
- **NLS_ISO_CURRENCY** Identifies a new territory whose ISO currency symbol should be used
- **NLS_DATE_FORMAT** Identifies a new date format
- **NLS_NUMERIC_CHARACTERS** Identifies a new decimal (0.00) and group (0,000) separator

In addition, you can use certain environment variables to change NLS settings in your session. `NLS_LANG` overrides default NLS settings for the user, using the following format: *language_territory.characterset*. Altering NLS parameters within the session is accomplished in two ways: either by using the `alter session set` *parm_name* = *value* command, where *parm_name* is the name of the NLS parameter and *value* is what you want to set the parameter to; or, you can use the `set_nls( )` procedure in the DBMS_SESSION package, which accepts two values, *parm_name* and *value*.

Exercises

1. Identify two ways for changing NLS parameters in your session.
2. Identify the parameter that changes the information format in the DATE datatype.

Obtaining Information about NLS Settings

You can get NLS information from your database in two ways—information about your data in various NLS formats, and information about the general NLS setup for your database. The first set of information can be obtained through the standard SQL functions `to_char( )`, `to_number( )`, and `to_date( )`. These functions accept various NLS parameters and return information based on the NLS parameter you gave them.

In addition, several NLS functions are available for use that utilize the `NLS_SORT` parameter. The following code block shows output from a table with NLS parameters used to assist in providing meaningful formatting in a simple report. For this example, note the use of `L`, `G`, and `D` as the local currency, group (or thousands), and decimal separator character markers in your formatting mask:

```
SQL> select year,
to_char(gnp,'L9G999G999G999D99','NLS_NUMERIC_CHARACTERS=''.,$''')
  2> as GNP
  3> from us_gnp;
     YEAR GNP
--------- ---------------------------
     1997             $5,948,399,939.34
     1998             $6,043,345,223.34
     1999             $6,143,545,453.80
```

TIP
Experiment with the order of characters specified for the `NLS_NUMERIC_CHARACTERS` `initsid.ora` parameter above, and see what happens with your output. The appropriate order for specifying them is `D`, `G`, `L`, and `C` (which represents the local ISO currency symbol, such as USD for American dollars).

Dictionary Views Containing NLS Parameters

In addition to the V$PARAMETER view, you can find information about settings for your NLS parameters in Oracle by looking at several dictionary views, which are listed below:

- **NLS_DATABASE_PARAMETERS** All NLS database-wide parameters are stored in this view.
- **NLS_INSTANCE_PARAMETERS** All NLS instance-wide parameters are stored in this view.
- **NLS_SESSIONS_PARAMETERS** All NLS parameters for the active session are stored in this view.
- **V$NLS_PARAMETERS** This is a superset of the previous three views.
- **V$NLS_VALID_VALUES** This is a listing of all valid values for all parameters.

Exercises

1. Identify the view that contains all NLS parameters for your instance, session, and database.
2. Identify a way you might use an NLS parameter in a SQL conversion function. What other ways might this be a useful feature in Oracle?

Chapter Summary

This chapter covered the two remaining topic areas for Oracle database administration, which were loading and reorganizing data, and managing NLS considerations for your Oracle database. Though these are not areas covered too intensely in OCP Exam 2, they represent 16 percent of exam questions and are relatively easy points to score if you understand these areas. The first area covered was loading data quickly with direct-path `insert` statements. Next came a discussion of using SQL*Loader, and all the files used by this tool. The differences between conventional-path and direct-path data loads in SQL*Loader were also examined. Finally, this section covered the use of IMPORT and EXPORT. The parameters were identified, and you learned about the differences between direct and conventional path EXPORT processing.

The second section in the chapter covered National Language Support (NLS). You learned the difference between a database and national character set, and how to define each. You also learned about the parameters you can define in the `init`*`sid`*`.ora` file for NLS. You covered the use of those parameters in conversion functions, such as `to_char( )`, `to_date( )`, and `to_number( )` to change the output appearance of your data. Finally the Oracle data dictionary views where you can look to find information about your language settings were covered.

Two-Minute Drill

- A hint is a directive you pass to the Oracle RDBMS telling it to process your statement in a certain way.
- Direct-path `insert` is accomplished using hints. They are specified as follows:
    - **`/*+append */`** Add records to the end of the table, above the highwatermark.
    - **`/*+parallel(`*`tablename, integer`*`) */`** Add records in parallel, using multiple I/O processes.
- SQL*Loader loads data from a flat file to a table.
- There are several file components:
    - **Datafile** Contains all records to be loaded into the database
    - **Control file** Identifies how SQL*Loader should interpret the datafile
    - **Parameter file** Gives runtime options to be used by SQL*Loader
    - **Discard file** Holds records that SQL*Loader might reject, based on when conditions defined in the control file

- **Bad file** Holds records that SQL*Loader might reject, based on constraint violations defined in your database
- **Log file** Stores information about the execution of a SQL*Loader run, such as record counts and why records were rejected

- Data in the datafiles can be structured into fixed- or variable-length fields.
- The positional specifications for fixed-length fields are contained in the control file, along with other specifications for the data load.
- For variable-length data fields, appropriate delimiters must be specified.
- The two types of delimiters used are terminating delimiters and enclosing delimiters.
- There are two data load paths: *conventional* and *direct*.
- Conventional loads use the same SQL interface and other Oracle RDBMS processes and structures that other processes use.
- Conventional-path loading updates indexes as rows are inserted into the database, and also validates integrity constraints and fires triggers at that time.
- Direct-path loads bypass most of the Oracle RDBMS, writing full database blocks directly to the database.
- Direct-path loading disables indexes, `insert` triggers, and constraints until all data is loaded. Constraints and indexes are rechecked and built after data load.
- The direct-path load may occasionally leave an index in direct-path state. This often is due to load failure or the loading of a data record that violates the table's integrity constraints.
- EXPORT pulls data out of your Oracle database and puts it into a file in binary format. The IMPORT tool is used to read files produced by EXPORT into the database. (Review the use of these tools in the chapter.)
- A database has two character sets: a database character set for storing your SQL and PL/SQL code, and a national character set for storing table data. These ideally should be related. (Review the chapter to better understand how to define and use NLS parameters in the Oracle database.)
- The database character set must be US 7-bit ASCII, or contain those characters as a subset.

Chapter Questions

1. **After loading data into Oracle, you notice that several rows are missing. Where would you look to find the data discarded by SQL*Loader when performing the load of data into the database?**

   A. Datafile

   B. Control file

   C. Command line

   D. Discard file

   E. Parameter file

2. **Which of the following would you do in order to improve performance on an `insert` statement that places lots of data into a table?**

   A. Create triggers before the load

   B. Enable `PRIMARY KEY` constraints before the load

   C. Specify `DIRECT=TRUE` in the SQL*Loader control file

   D. Run the load across a database link

   E. Use optimizer hints

3. **After running SQL*Loader with the conventional path, which file contains the records that could not be loaded due to violating integrity constraints?**

   A. The parameter file

   B. The bad file

   C. The discard file

   D. The log file

4. **After completing a database import, you notice that several procedures in the database are marked invalid. Which two of the following methods would you use to correct this problem? (Choose two)**

   A. Drop and re-create the database

   B. Drop and re-create the procedures

   C. Recompile the procedures

   D. Grant `execute` privileges on the procedure to SYS

5. The DBA is considering improving performance for a database export. In which of the following operations does EXPORT use the SGA when the direct path is chosen?

A. Obtaining data to write to file

B. Adjusting the highwatermark

C. Updating the indexes

D. Never, direct-path EXPORT gives data directly to export process

E. Verifying integrity constraints

6. Users of an Oracle database are accustomed to time settings in the 24-hour format. Which of the following choices best illustrates the method you can use to set this up for them in Oracle?

A. Change the value for `NLS_LANG in initsid.ora`, and restart the instance.

B. Issue the `alter session set NLS_DATE_FORMAT` statement.

C. Query the V$NLS_PARAMETER view.

D. Change the value for `NLS_DATE_FORMAT` in `initsid.ora`, and restart the instance.

7. A SQL report in the Oracle database produces output in monetary format. If the users are getting .5$948,34 when they should be getting $5,948.34, which of the following choices identify how to resolve the problem?

A. Change the value for `NLS_CURRENCY` in `initsid.ora`, and restart the instance.

B. Change the format mask in the conversion procedure to 'L9G999D99'.

C. Change the order of items in the `NLS_NUMERIC_CHARACTERS` assignment in the conversion procedure.

D. Query the V$NLS_PARAMETER view.

Answers to Chapter Questions

1. D. Discard file

Explanation The discard file contains records that you specified the SQL*Loader to reject because of the `when` clause. Choice A is incorrect because the datafile can only contain data used for input. Choice B is incorrect because the control file actually contains the restriction, not the discarded records. Choice C is incorrect because the command line is used to define your parameters for the run. Choice E is incorrect because the parameter file is used for basically the same thing as choice C.

2. E. Use optimizer hints

Explanation Optimizer hints, such as `/*+append */` will cause Oracle to `insert` data over the highwatermark, taking the direct path and improving performance. Choice A is incorrect because firing a trigger on every record `insert` slows down the overall processing. The same is true with integrity constraints, thereby eliminating choice B. Running a load across a database link will cause the `insert` to perform poorly as well, eliminating choice D. Though choice C improves performance for SQL*Loader, the question actually pertains to direct-path inserts.

3. B. The bad file

Explanation The parameter file for SQL*Loader contains runtime parameters used to control the data load, eliminating choice A. The discard file is similar in function to the bad file, but contains data rejected by user-defined reasons as part of the `when` clause, while the bad file contains rejected data for database-definition reasons, such as violating integrity constraints. This difference eliminates choice C. The log file contains information about the SQL*Loader run, such as the start and stop times and the number of records rejected, but not the records themselves. This eliminates choice D.

4. B *and* C. Drop and recreate the procedures *and* recompile the procedures

Explanation Either of these choices will cause the procedure to be recompiled. Chances are there was some object or procedural dependency not satisfied when the procedures were loaded, which caused their source code to load fine, but the procedures themselves were marked invalid. Simply granting `execute` privileges to SYS will not make these procedures valid, eliminating choice D. Finally, dropping and re-creating the database may work, but it is more trouble than the solution is worth.

5. D. Never, direct-path EXPORT gives data directly to export process

Explanation When direct-path EXPORT is used, EXPORT never uses the SGA. That's why it runs so much faster than a conventional-path export. Choice A indicates when EXPORT uses the SGA in conventional-path loading. You will not adjust the highwatermark when exporting data because EXPORT does not put data into Oracle, eliminating Choice B. The same reasoning applies to why choices D and E are incorrect.

6. D. Change the value for `NLS_DATE_FORMAT` in `init`*`sid`*`.ora`, and restart the instance.

Explanation Time is specified as part of the date in Oracle, and the parameter governing this is `NLS_DATE_FORMAT`. Choice B would have been correct if users wanted to specify the date format for themselves, but since you are doing it for them, the change must be made to the parameter in the `init`*`sid`*`.ora` file.

7. C. Change the order of items in the `NLS_NUMERIC_CHARACTERS` assignment in the conversion procedure.

Explanation The problem is that the local currency, group (thousands) separator, and decimal character are most likely improperly assigned. If you simply change the order values are assigned for `NLS_NUMERIC_CHARACTERS` in the `to_char( )` conversion function, you will likely see the problem go away.

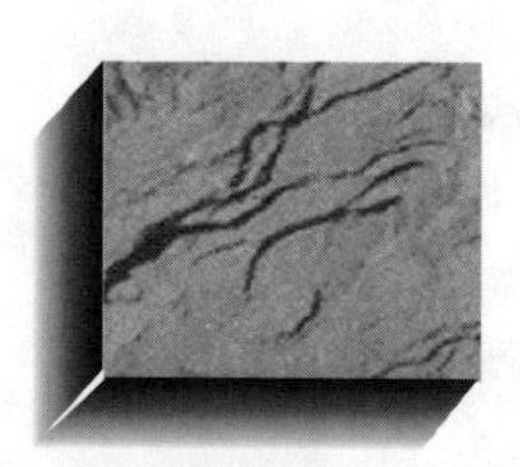

UNIT III

Preparing for OCP DBA Exam 3: Backup and Recovery Workshop

CHAPTER 12

Overview of Backup and Recovery

In this chapter, you will learn about and demonstrate knowledge in the following four areas:

- Backup and recovery considerations
- Oracle recovery structures and processes
- Oracle backup and recovery configuration
- Physical backups in Oracle without RMAN

Mastering the art of backup and recovery is perhaps the most important area of Oracle database administration. However, while the concept of ensuring that you have a recoverable database by taking backups and archiving redo logs is very straightforward, its implementation is often far more complex; it is often neglected, as well. Too often, recoverability, like testing, falls by the wayside during system development, especially for a project that is behind schedule.

The importance of backups to allow database recovery is something no one will dispute. It's like having gas in your car. However, when you're in a rush to get somewhere and your tank is on empty, you might be tempted to think of the time you'll save by not stopping for gas. Unfortunately, five minutes on foot after you run out of gas is not like five minutes by car—similarly, it is too late to develop a great backup strategy when a disk on your host machine crashes, taking with it your company's only copy of information about the most lucrative clients. So, make sure you take good backups (and fill your gas tank) regularly, before you need them.

This chapter covers backup and recovery considerations in Oracle, the structures and processes required for recovery, how to configure Oracle for backup and recovery, and how to take backups of your database in Oracle without the use of RMAN. You will learn more about RMAN in the next chapter. Approximately 25 percent of the material in OCP Exam 3 is covered in this chapter.

Backup and Recovery Considerations

In this section, you will cover the following topics related to backup and recovery considerations:

- Business, operational, and technical considerations
- Components of a disaster-recovery plan
- Importance of testing backup and recovery strategy

Backups are copies of a database that can be used in the event of an emergency. Restoring an Oracle database depends on the existence of these backups. You, the DBA, are responsible for maintaining the recoverability of your Oracle database in three ways. First, you need to keep the number of database failures to a minimum, *maximizing database availability*. Second, you need to keep the time spent in recovery to a minimum when the database inevitably does fail, *maximizing recovery performance*. Third, you need to ensure that little or no data is lost in a database failure, *maximizing data recoverability*.

Business, Operational, and Technical Considerations

"Seek first to understand, then to be understood." This famous adage used by Stephen R. Covey in his *Seven Habits for Highly Effective People* is as relevant to database recovery as it is to interpersonal relationships. First, the DBA needs to understand the business use of the system and the availability needs as they relate to maximizing overall database availability, recovery performance, and data recoverability. Once this is understood, then the DBA needs to make the system owners and management understand the cost of maintaining that system availability. For example, the ideal way to assess how much an organization should spend on putting together a system with maximum database availability is to determine the cost of downtime spent in recovery—or even better, the cost of losing data.

TIP
A great database backup and recovery process is one that evolves with the system. Mechanize change by establishing an ongoing change-schedule in which new requirements may be evaluated.

After the costs have been assessed, the logistics of backup and recovery processing can be discussed. Define the overall availability requirements and assign work priorities according to their impact on database availability. For example, does the database need to be up and available 24 × 7? If so, the costs associated with maximizing uptime will be higher than those for a system that runs in batch once a month. The decision to go with 24 × 7 availability should have everything to do with business needs, and nothing to do with the "cool" factor. In other words, don't fall prey to the "coolness" of being able to do something just for the sake of doing it. Smart DBAs (like you) are those who can align technology with business goals.

Finally, the logistics of your backup and recovery strategy should factor in the amount of change that occurs on your database. For example, databases that frequently have data changes, new data or datafiles added, or significant changes to table structure should be backed up frequently, while databases with static data or read-only user access may only need to be backed up once in a while. Remember the golden rule: If you're in doubt about the recoverability of your database, take a backup.

Exercises

1. What are some issues surrounding backup and recovery?
2. How might the DBA identify solutions to these issues?

Components of a Disaster-Recovery Plan

There are many issues surrounding disaster recovery that must be addressed for any computer system. What disaster recovery scenarios can occur on the system? What disaster recovery scenarios involve recovery from data loss? How volatile is the data stored on the system? How quickly does the system need to be made available? How does the cost of providing a recovery strategy for any scenario evaluate against the cost of losing time to reenter the data? The answers to these questions comprise a disaster recovery plan.

Computers are fragile machines. Consider the cornerstone of any computer—the motherboard and CPU. They are vulnerable to moisture, sudden jarring movements, dust, and even the electricity fed to a computer is particularly important. The damage these factors may cause includes memory loss, damage to memory chips, or damage to the circuitry of the motherboard. Though doing so is annoying, memory cards and CPUs can be replaced, and damage to them will not cause lasting damage to the applications that use the machinery. However, special attention should be paid to the permanent disks used to store information on the machine. If data on disk is ruined, you are dependent upon your backups to recover that data.

The most crucial step that can be taken for disaster recovery is to devise sufficiently frequent procedures for backing up hard disks. The backup procedures should be designed to provide the recoverability that is required, based on the needs of the system. For example, if your database can stand some downtime, you might be able to get away with making cold backups weekly with archived redo logs. However, if your system can spare only small amounts of downtime, you may want to consider backup and recovery approaches at the hardware level, such as disk mirroring or the Oracle standby database architecture. Determining and providing the best backup strategy depends on the cost of losing data in a situation versus the cost of ensuring that data is not lost.

It would be nice if every Oracle database could have daily backups to tape, which could then be replicated and delivered to an offsite location for warehousing. It might also be great to have a full replica of the system waiting for the need for its use to arise . The reality of many organizations, though, is to stretch the budget as much as possible, meaning that there could be neither the money nor the staff to maintain the "best" option for a system. Furthermore, with careful planning and an eye on the bottom line, success can be attained for less money than you might think.

Create a Level of Service

An important step is for DBAs, and users alike, to defined quantifiable standards for recoverability and availability in a level-of-service agreement. This agreement should be documented and looked upon as a means of discussing the services provided by DBAs, and as a means of determining whether or not that service meets the original expectations. This approach ensures that everyone involved will enter a potential crisis with the same set of expectations. Service-level agreements are as much about maintaining good business relationships, and sending a message of customer service commitment, as they are about meeting the standards they define.

Exercises

1. What are the components of a disaster recovery plan?
2. What role might a level-of-service agreement for database recoverability and availability serve in improving the support available for systems in your organization?

The Importance of Testing Backup and Recovery Strategy

Another key facet for DBAs to consider is testing. Taking backups without having any idea whether those backups support an adequate recovery is almost as pointless as taking no backups at all. It takes only a few short practice runs of the recovery strategy to determine whether the backups are adequate. Don't let the first time you test your recovery strategy be the day that several disks crash.

Consider also your own procedural dependencies as part of the recovery strategy, and commit only to a level of service that you yourself can expect from those you depend upon. Find out what level of support your vendors are committed to. For example, if a disk fails on your host machine, will the manufacturer deliver you a new one and install it the same day? Will your system administrator field pager support calls at 4 A.M. to reboot the server if necessary?

Another big consideration is whether your database stands up to the threat of natural disaster. For example, if your work site were leveled by a tornado overnight, would you be able to partially recover your data on another machine in another office with backups stored offsite, or are all your backups stored in a drawer in the computer lab, right next to the host machine? Here's a hint: think about offsite backup archives.

Finally, what if a disaster happened to your superstar Oracle DBA overnight? Would your backup DBA be able to handle the backup strategy? Would he or she know where to find support documents? Do such documents exist?

Nothing is worse than taking the hard work of many people to develop good plans for database backups, and then squandering it by failing to perform system tests to determine whether the plan is adequate for the needs of the application. A good backup strategy accommodates user errors, too, particularly for development environments, where a user might accidentally drop a table. Extra backup coverage provides a value-added service that achieves additional recognition both for the DBA and for the entire IT shop. The ideal test plan consists of several elements, including a set of test case scenarios, the steps for resolving those scenarios, and a set of criteria for measuring the success or failure of the test. Only after the initial test plans are developed and executed successfully should the DBA consider implementing the backup strategy in production.

The testing of backup strategies should not stop once the database hits production, either. Spot-checks ensure that the strategy meets ongoing needs. And, as the focus of a database matures, so too should the backup strategy. When changes to the service-level agreement are made, the backup strategy should be tested to ensure that the new requirements are met. If they are not met, then the strategy should be rethought, reworked, and retested. However, just as the DBA may consider taking out some added "insurance" with special backups, the organization may also want to contemplate the power of random "audits" to ensure that the systems can be backed up adequately in a variety of different circumstances. Testing backup strategy has some other benefits as well. The testing of a manual backup strategy may uncover some missing steps in the manual process, and may prompt the DBA to consider automating the backup process. There is no harm in automation, as long as the process is tested and accommodates changes that occur in the database. Otherwise, the automated scripts will systematically "forget" to save certain changes made to the database, such as the addition of tablespaces and datafiles after the scripts are created.

Another benefit of testing the backup strategy is its ability to uncover data corruption. If one or several data blocks are corrupted in a datafile, and the physical database backup method is used for database backup, the corrupted data will be copied into the backups, resulting in backup corruption as well as corruption in the database. There is no way to verify whether this is happening if the backups are not tested, so without testing, a DBA would only discover that the backups contain corrupted data when it is too late. Systematic data-integrity checks can be done with the `DB_BLOCK_CHECKSUM` `init`*`sid`*`.ora` parameter and the DBVERIFY utility, both of which were discussed in Unit II. Data integrity checking is also handled by RMAN.

Exercises

1. What role should testing have in backup and recovery?
2. Name two reasons why testing the validity of backups is important.

Oracle Recovery Structures and Processes

In this section, you will cover the following topics concerning Oracle's recovery structures and processes:

- Architectural components for backup and recovery
- Importance of redo logs, checkpoints, and archives
- Synchronizing files during checkpoints
- Multiplexing control files and redo logs

This section covers the architectural components for backup and recovery, and the importance of several structures for this purpose. Furthermore, you will read about Oracle's behavior during a checkpoint, and how this activity supports data recovery. Finally, you will learn what multiplexing means for control files and redo logs, and how to set Oracle up to use this feature.

You may find a lot of this discussion to be a review of database administration topics covered in Unit II. You are right. Oracle structures OCP Exam 3 to review Exam 2 content and thus reinforce your understanding of these areas, because your ability to handle database backup and recovery will make or break your Oracle DBA career. Be sure you understand these areas before taking OCP Exam III.

Architectural Components for Backup and Recovery

We'll start with a review of Oracle's architectural components supporting backup and recovery—Figure 12-1 identifies the Oracle backup and recovery architecture and related database views. Recall that Oracle lives in three areas of your host machine. The first of these areas is the disk drives containing datafiles, online redo logs, archived redo logs, control files, `initsid.ora` files, and password files.

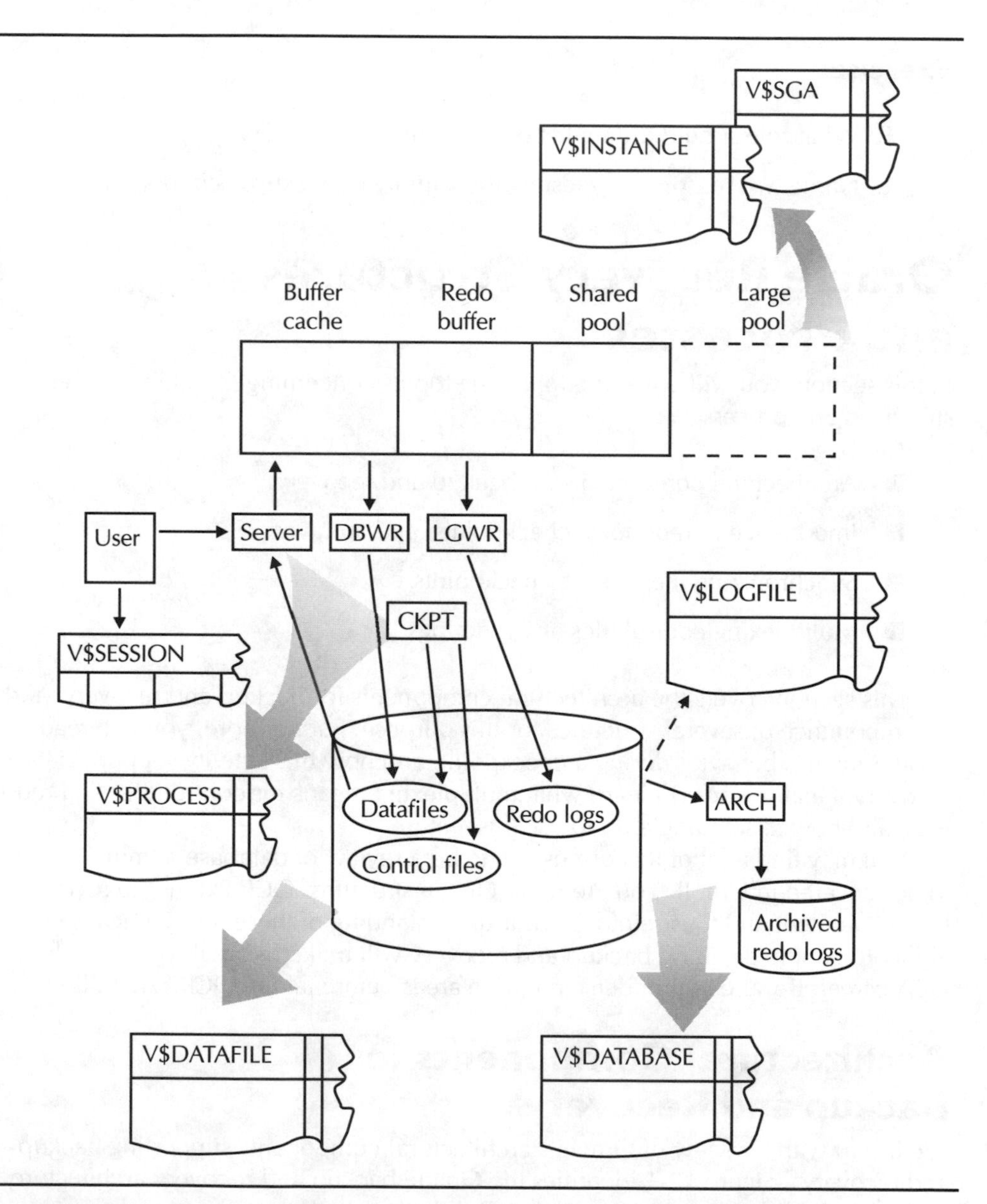

FIGURE 12-1. *Oracle backup and recovery architecture and related views*

The second area in which Oracle lives is memory, which contains your buffer cache, redo log buffer, shared pool, and an area of memory (introduced in this Unit) called the *large pool*. The large pool is used, at the request of the DBA, by *Recovery Manager* (RMAN) for disk I/O during database recovery, and is also used in the multithreaded server architecture and for parallel query processing. More about this area in Oracle memory later in this Unit.

Oracle also lives in your CPU, running certain background processes all the time. These processes include DBWR for writing changed data blocks out of the buffer cache and into datafiles, and LGWR for writing redo entries from the redo buffer to online redo logs. Another Oracle background process you should pay attention to include the *system monitor* (SMON), which handles instance recovery after database startup if necessary, and periodically coalesces smaller chunks of free space in tablespaces into larger chunks. A function of SMON in Oracle8 is to deallocate space in temporary segments no longer in use. Another background process that always exists in Oracle is the *checkpoint process* (CKPT). This process supports LGWR in several ways during checkpoints, and it will be discussed in more detail when checkpoints are discussed.

The *process monitor* (PMON) is another recovery process. Recall that when Oracle runs in dedicated server mode, each user process (such as SQL*Plus) connecting to Oracle has its own dedicated server obtaining data on the user's behalf. If the user process were to cease running unexpectedly (for example, if the user's desktop hangs), the dedicated server would still be left hanging on the host machine, waiting for more instructions from the user session that will never come. The PMON process is designed to clean up messes left by dedicated servers with no user sessions attached to them—it rolls back changes and silently kills the dedicated server in order to release its memory and CPU usage.

Finally, recall the optional background *archiver process* (ARCH) for data recovery, which you first learned about in Unit II. ARCH archives redo logs only when the database runs in `archivelog` mode and automatic redo log archiving is enabled.

Exercises

1. Identify the memory structures in Oracle that support backup and recovery. What memory structure is used to support database recovery using RMAN?
2. What are the disk resources Oracle uses? Of these resources, can you determine which one is readable using a text editor?
3. What are the background processes Oracle uses to support backup and recovery. Which of these processes would handle a situation in which a user reboots a desktop computer that froze unexpectedly while conducting a transaction?

Importance of Redo Logs, Checkpoints, and Archives

The dynamic performance views shown in Figure 12-1 can retrieve backup information about your database during regular operation, and can help when recovering the database, as well. These views include the following:

- **V$DATABASE** Identifies current database status, and provides information about redo log checkpoint and recovery performed in the database
- **V$SGA** Shows the values set for fixed and variable sizes of your database SGA, as well as the sizes of various SGA components
- **V$INSTANCE** Displays instance name and status, the name of the machine hosting Oracle, and the time the instance was most recently started
- **V$DATAFILE** Identifies information about datafiles, such as the tablespace the datafile is associated with, the recoverability of data in the file, whether the file is online or offline, whether users can change data in the file, and so on
- **V$LOGFILE** Shows information about online redo log files, such as their creation date and their current status
- **V$LOG** Identifies the number of redo log members in each logfile group, which is useful for determining multiplexing status for the database
- **V$LOG_HISTORY** Shows historical information about log switches that is stored in the control file
- **V$PROCESS** Presents pertinent information about processes and resource use for server and background processes running in Oracle
- **V$SESSION** Offers information about user processes connected to Oracle

Online redo logs are also very important. Without these disk resources, Oracle is unable to perform instance crash recovery, regardless of whether you are archiving your redo logs or not. Furthermore, if you are not archiving your redo logs, then you can only recover your Oracle database up to the time you took your last full offline backup of the database. However, if you are archiving your redo logs, you can recover the database up to the last committed transaction before a critical error, such as disk failure, crashes your database. Thus, online (and archived) redo logs are critical database-recovery elements of your Oracle database.

Using the Large Pool

The large pool is a new area in the Oracle SGA that supports the Recovery Manager tool in recovering the Oracle database. This memory area is optional, and when it is configured, it will improve RMAN performance by offering buffer space in memory for I/O slave processes to use when backing up the database or restoring file components from tape. Multiple I/O slave processes are used when BACKUP_TAPE_IO_SLAVES is set to TRUE and when BACKUP_DISK_IO_SLAVES is greater than 0. I/O slaves can be used for archiving redo logs, as well, by setting the `ARCH_IO_SLAVES` parameter to a value greater than 0. The large pool supports these slaves with buffer space as well. However, be prepared to see all these parameters become obsolete within Oracle8*i*.

You can set the large pool size with two `initsid.ora` parameters, as well. They are `LARGE_POOL_SIZE` and `LARGE_POOL_MIN_ALLOC`. The first parameter is set in bytes. If `LARGE_POOL_SIZE` is 0 or not set, there will be no large pool in your Oracle database, and Oracle will use the shared pool in place of the large pool to support RMAN and archiving activity. If the large pool is set but not large enough to support archiving or RMAN I/O slave processes, however, you may encounter errors with the archiving of redo logs, and RMAN will not use I/O slaves. The `LARGE_POOL_MIN_ALLOC` parameter defines the least amount of space in the large pool that will be allocated to an I/O slave.

TIP

An LRU list is a list of the least recently used *resources in a particular area of memory. Both the shared pool and buffer cache have associated LRU lists that Oracle uses to determine which execution plans and blocks are the least recently used and therefore candidates for elimination. Unlike the shared pool and buffer cache, the large pool does not maintain an LRU list. This list records the time an object in memory was last used, so that the least recently used objects can be eliminated when space is required in either of those memory areas.*

How the ARCH Process Works

When you enable the `archivelog` feature in Oracle, the database will make a copy of every online redo log after that log fills, for the purpose of data recovery to the point in time of database failure. Archiving redo logs is critical for production databases in order to prevent data loss. When a redo log fills, Oracle switches to writing the next online log in the sequence. The most recently filled log should then be copied to the archive destination location identified by the `initsid.ora` `LOG_ARCHIVE_DEST` parameter. This can be handled manually by the DBA or automatically by Oracle. The key point to remember when archiving redo logs is that if all your online logs fill and the next online log in the sequence has not been archived, Oracle will not allow users to make any data changes. To prevent this from happening, it is usually best to set up Oracle to archive redo logs automatically using the ARCH process. The following code block shows how to put the database into `archivelog` mode:

```
SVRMGR> alter database archivelog;
Database altered.
```

The following code block will start the ARCH background process for the current session only, so that archiving will be handled automatically:

```
SVRMGR> alter system archive log start;
```

If you don't set LOG_ARCHIVE_DEST to TRUE in your `initsid.ora` file, you will need to perform this statement every time you restart your database, or else you will have to archive your redo logs manually whenever a log switch occurs, using the following statement:

```
SVRMGR> alter system archive log all;
```

Finally, a note about the importance of checkpoints. A checkpoint is when LGWR tells DBWR to write all the dirty buffers in the buffer cache from memory to disk. This feature is important because it keeps the datafiles consistent with the changes made to blocks in memory by users. By default, checkpoints happen as frequently as log switches, but they can happen more frequently if you appropriately configure the `LOG_CHECKPOINT_INTERVAL` and `LOG_CHECKPOINT_TIMEOUT` `initsid.ora` parameters, or in other situations you will learn about shortly.

Exercises

1. Why are online redo logs so important to Oracle database recovery? Where can you look in the dictionary to find information about the recoverability of your datafiles?
2. What is the large pool, and what processes or utilities use it? How is it configured?
3. What is a checkpoint, and what is its significance in the processing of an Oracle database?

Synchronizing Files During Checkpoints

A checkpoint is when Oracle writes all dirty buffers in the buffer cache to disk. Behind the scenes, Oracle's CKPT process marks the datafile header as current, and records the sequence number for the current checkpoint in the control file(s). Checkpoints are used to ensure that, at some point, all of the information in both the buffer cache and redo log buffer are copied to disk, which synchronizes write activities performed by LGWR and DBWR.

Now, consider the CKPT process. This is a process that handles certain aspects of checkpoint processing. Oracle8 has CKPT running all the time, unlike Oracle7, in which CKPT was optional. At specific times, all modified database buffers in the system global area are written to the datafiles by DBW0; this event is called a checkpoint. The checkpoint process is responsible for signaling DBW0 at checkpoints and updating all the datafiles and control files of the database to indicate the most recent checkpoint.

A checkpoint will occur at least as often as a log switch, but can occur more frequently, depending on several factors:

- If a value is set for `LOG_CHECKPOINT_TIMEOUT`, then checkpoints will occur at time intervals, specified in seconds, for that `init`*`sid`*`.ora` parameter
- If a value is set for `LOG_CHECKPOINT_INTERVAL`, a checkpoint will occur when that number of operating system blocks (usually a multiple of Oracle blocks) have been written to an online redo log
- When the instance is shut down in any way other than `shutdown abort`
- When tablespace status is brought offline or backed up while online
- When you manually force a checkpoint with the `alter system checkpoint` command

A certain tradeoff is inherent in specifying checkpoints. More frequent checkpoints will make instance recovery run faster because datafiles, redo logs, and control files are synchronized more often. But, with frequent checkpoints, you also run the risk of degrading performance for online database use. You can optionally record, in the ALERT log, the time at which checkpoints occur by setting the `LOG_CHECKPOINTS_TO_ALERT` `init`*`sid`*`.ora` parameter to TRUE.

Datafiles can store both committed and uncommitted data changes. If DBWR writes a dirty buffer to a datafile for a transaction that is not committed, and the instance fails later, then Oracle will ensure the datafile is properly changed by applying redo log changes and then rolling back any uncommitted transactions to the point in time of the database failure. The main example of when a datafile will not contain uncommitted data is when the database is closed, or when the last active user on the database commits his or her last transaction. Otherwise, it is fair game for Oracle datafiles to contain uncommitted data.

How Disk Files Are Synchronized

Oracle synchronizes all of its disk resources at database startup through the use of checkpoints. Every time a checkpoint is performed, Oracle notes the system change number for the most recently committed transaction. The system change number (SCN) is an ever-increasing value that uniquely identifies a committed version of the database. Every time a user commits a transaction, Oracle records a new SCN. You can obtain SCNs in a number of ways, including from the ALERT log. You can then use the SCN as an identifier for purposes of recovery. For example, you could perform an incomplete recovery of a database up to SCN 1030.

Oracle uses SCNs in control files, datafile headers, and redo records. Every redo log file has both a log sequence number and low and high SCN. The low SCN records the lowest SCN recorded in the log file, while the high SCN records the highest SCN in the log file. CKPT writes those numbers to the datafiles and to the control file. The checkpoint number is also written to the redo log file. When the database starts, all checkpoint sequence numbers in all datafiles, redo log files, and control files must match. If they do not, Oracle will not start, and you must perform media recovery on your database to get the files synchronized and in a consistent state.

Tablespaces and Recoverability

To understand the backup requirements for the different types of tablespaces you will have in your Oracle database, you need to know something about them. Recall that there are several different types of tablespaces in Oracle, such as SYSTEM, RBS, DATA, and TEMP. The following subtopics identify each type of tablespace and the recoverability for each.

SYSTEM This is the most important tablespace in your database because it contains vital dictionary and operative information. You should never store table, index, or temporary data in this tablespace. To do so not only jeopardizes database performance, it also makes backup and recovery of your table data difficult.

RBS These tablespaces are challenging to recover if they contain online rollback segments. Recall that you cannot take a tablespace containing rollback segments offline or into a backup state until all the rollback segments are also offline. In many cases, you can recover by recreating the tablespaces and then the rollback segments, provided you can recover your other tablespaces.

TEMPORARY These tablespaces contain data required only for a short time, and usually can be recovered simply by recreating the temporary tablespace. Thus, there is little need to back up these tablespaces.

READ ONLY DATA These tablespaces can be backed up once after putting the tablespace into read-only state. These tablespaces will not need redo information to be applied to them, because none of the data in a read-only tablespace can be changed.

READ/WRITE DATA You must back up these tablespaces and archive redo logs in order to make them recoverable to the point in time of database failure. More frequent backups speed recovery because fewer archived redo logs must be applied to restore the data changed after the most recent backup.

INDEX The recovery of index tablespaces is complex, due to the need to keep data synchronized between tables and their respective indexes. Thus, you might be better off when recovering index tablespaces to simply restore the tablespace and then recreate the indexes.

Exercises

1. What is a checkpoint? How are the datafiles of your database synchronized during normal database operation? Why does this occur?
2. Explain the recoverability considerations posed by several major tablespace types.

Multiplexing Control Files and Redo Logs

At the risk of seeming like a broken record, you should be sure to multiplex your control files and redo logs in the Oracle databases you administer. This lesson recounts material covered in Unit II to underscore the importance of multiplexing redo logs and control files. If you feel you understand this material thoroughly, go ahead and skip to the exercises. However, if you find you cannot answer the questions, or if you haven't already read Unit II, you should be sure to review this content.

Multiplexing Control Files

Depending on the availability of multiple disk drives, the DBA should store multiple copies of the control files on separate devices to minimize the risk of losing these important physical disk resources. If you stick with the default naming convention and creation of your control files, Oracle recommends that you move these control files to different disk resources, and set the CONTROL_FILES parameter to let Oracle know there are multiple copies of the control file that should be maintained. This is called *multiplexing* or *mirroring* the control file.

Multiplexing control files reduces the dependency Oracle has on any one disk available on the host machine. In the event of a failure, your chances of successful recovery will be improved because multiple copies of the control file have been maintained. In no case should you ever use only one control file for an Oracle database, because of the difficulty in recovering a database when the control file is lost. Having a copy of the control file and parameter file on different disks available to the database will minimize the possibility of one disk failure rendering your database inoperable.

Making additional copies of your control file and moving them to different disk resources is something you handle outside of Oracle. You can create a duplicate copy of the control file by simply using the operating system's copy command. In Windows, the command is `copy`, while in Unix it is `cp`. However, the copied file will be unusable unless you follow these steps:

1. In Server Manager, execute the `shutdown normal`, `shutdown immediate`, or `shutdown transactional` command to shut down the instance and close the database.
2. Copy the control file to another disk, using your operating system's file copy command.
3. Modify the CONTROL_FILES parameter in init*sid*.ora to include the additional control file.
4. Restart the instance in Server Manager with the `startup open` command. Oracle now maintains an additional copy of the control file.

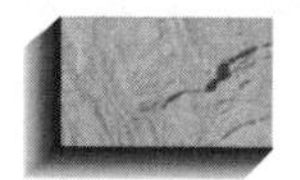

TIP
By specifying multiple control files in the initsid.ora file before database creation, you start on the right administrative foot with the database, making it easy to maintain.

Multiplexing Online Redo Logs

Several important details are involved in configuring the redo log files of a database. The first and most important detail is that of *multiplexing* your redo logs. In order improve recoverability in the event of disk failure, the DBA should configure Oracle to multiplex redo logs—store each redo log member in a group on a different disk resource. This means that Oracle will maintain two or more members for each redo log group. Figure 12-2 illustrates the concept of multiplexing redo log members.

Multiplexing redo log members keeps multiple copies of the redo log available to LGWR. In the event that LGWR has a problem with a disk that holds the redo log (for example, if the disk controller fails), the entire instance will continue running because another member is available on a different disk. If the redo log group has only one member, or if multiple online redo log members are not multiplexed, and the same failure occurs, LGWR would not be able to write redo log entries and the Oracle instance would fail. This is because LGWR must write redo log entries to disk in order to clear space in the redo log buffer so that user processes can continue making changes to the database. If LGWR cannot write the redo log entries to disk, it cannot clear the space in memory, and the entire instance fails.

Multiplexing redo logs on separate disks benefits the database in other ways. When the database is run in `archivelog` mode, ARCH can be set up to run. When ARCH is running, it automatically moves archived redo logs to an archive destination specified by the `LOG_ARCHIVE_DEST` parameter in the `init`*`sid`*`.ora` file every time a log switch occurs. If redo log groups are on one disk, contention can arise at log switch time when ARCH tries to copy the filled redo log to the archive destination at the same time that LGWR tries to start writing redo to the next group. If redo log members and the archive log destination are on different disks, there is little possibility for ARCH and LGWR to contend, because ARCH can work on what it needs to do using one disk while LGWR continues on another.

Adding and Removing Redo Logs and Members

A redo log group must have at least one member. To add additional members, use the `alter database add logfile member '`*`filename`*`' to group`

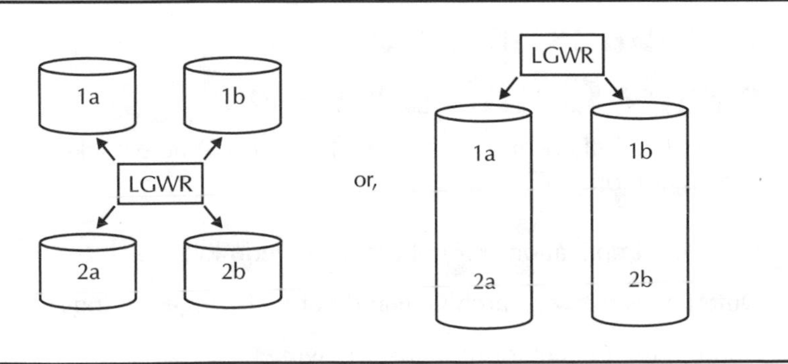

FIGURE 12-2. *Multiplexing online redo logs*

grpnum statement, where `filename` is the name of the file with the absolute path that the group will now have, and *grpnum* is the number of the group to which you are adding the member. You can also add new online redo log groups with the `alter database add logfile group` *grpnum* '*filename*' statement. Finally, if you have more than two redo log groups, you can remove redo logs, provided at least two logs will remain, and the one you want to remove is not currently being written by LGWR. The statement used to remove an online redo log from Oracle is `alter database drop logfile group` *grpnum*. Note that dropping the redo log group does not remove the actual file from your host machine.

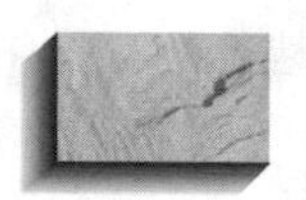

TIP
Group number and status information for online redo logs can be obtained from V$LOG, as described earlier.

Exercises

1. What is multiplexing redo logs, and how is it accomplished? What is multiplexing control files? Why is it important to do?
2. What performance issues are associated with archiving redo logs? How does multiplexing serve to resolve this issue?
3. What statement is used to remove online redo logs? What constraints surround its use?
4. What initialization parameter tells Oracle where to find its control files?

Oracle Backup and Recovery Configuration

In this section, you will cover the following topics on Oracle backup and recovery configuration:

- Recovery implications for not archiving redo logs
- Differences between archiving and not archiving redo logs
- Configuring Oracle for redo log archiving
- Multiplexing archived redo log files

Now that you understand Oracle backup and recovery in concept, let's dig into how to set these things up in practice. You will need to understand several factors when configuring Oracle for backup and recovery. The first is what sort of impact you might have if you don't archive your online redo logs. Then you will learn about the differences in Oracle when redo logs are and are not being archived. After that, you will learn how to actually set up redo log archiving in Oracle. Last, you will learn that multiplexing is not just for online redo logs and control files anymore. You can multiplex your archived redo logs, and the last lesson will show you how.

Recovery Implications of Not Archiving Redo Logs

Your Oracle database needs its online redo logs to handle data recovery to points in time after the most recent backup was taken. For example, if the instance fails, Oracle needs a certain amount of online redo information to handle recovery from the crash. If you lose a disk six hours after you take your most recent backup, archived redo logs can help you recover your data from the point of failure on the database. Because LGWR writes redo to one online log, to another, and so on, until the end of the sequence is reached, and then starts overwriting the first online redo log in the series and the process begins all over again. Not archiving redo logs means that, in the event of a system disaster, you will not be able to recover any data changes after your most recent backup.

If you don't specify a particular archiving mode for your database on creation, Oracle will create your database in `noarchivelog` mode. You can change this using the `alter database archivelog` statement. Doing so is useful not only for production support of mission-critical database applications; it is useful for less critical database applications as well. If you do not archive redo information, you should make sure the user community is aware that data is recoverable only to the point in time of the most recent complete database backup. You must have a complete database backup, or your database is not recoverable.

Running Oracle in noarchivelog Mode

So, as alluded to previously, running Oracle in `noarchivelog` mode means your redo information is overwritten every time LGWR returns to the first online redo log in the series. Each online redo log is immediately reused, provided its status is inactive, meaning that the contents are not required for crash recovery of your instance. In general, you will not be able to recover data changes made to the Oracle database after the most recent backup was taken.

Here's a preview of what is to come regarding database backup. There are two main forms of backups, online backups and offline backups. Online backups can be taken while the Oracle database is open and available to users, usually with a combination of Oracle and operating system commands. Offline backups are taken when the Oracle database is closed, using operating system commands. If you choose not to run Oracle in `archivelog` mode, you will not be able to take online backups. This is because online backups rely on archived redo logs to supplement the changes users may make to Oracle data while the backup is in progress. What's more, when you take your offline backups, you must be sure to make a backup of *every file* in your Oracle database, including all datafiles, redo log files, and control files. So, if you run Oracle in `noarchivelog` mode, be sure also that your users can tolerate frequent periods of database unavailability.

Another factor to consider when running Oracle in `noarchivelog` mode is what happens when a disk containing datafiles for a particular tablespace crashes. This event is called *media failure*. When media failure occurs and Oracle is running in `noarchivelog` mode, you have two options. First, you can drop the tablespace and recreate it, which works when the tablespace lost is a temporary tablespace, or in some cases it's an index tablespace. Your second option is to shut down Oracle and restore all datafiles for all tablespaces, all redo logs, and all control files from your most recent backup, losing all data changes made to Oracle after that backup. This is what you will have to do if the disk that crashed took your SYSTEM or data tablespace along with it. For this reason, you must make a copy of all your Oracle database files when you take a backup while offline.

Running Oracle in archivelog Mode

There are several changes in Oracle's behavior when `archivelog` mode is used. First, after filling an online redo log, Oracle will not overwrite the data in that log until a checkpoint has taken place. This ensures that all redo information for transactions corresponds to actual changes made in datafiles. Recall that a checkpoint happens at least as often as a log switch, which is the event that occurs when LGWR fills one online redo log and starts writing to another. The log must also be archived. There are two ways that online redo logs will be archived: either manually, with the `alter system archive log` statement, or automatically by ARCH (when it has been configured for use). You will learn more about configuring Oracle to run in `archivelog` mode in the next lesson.

If you run your Oracle database in `archivelog` mode, consider these two golden rules. First, be sure your filled online redo logs are archived in a timely manner. You can do this by enabling the ARCH background process for the tasks. If all your online redo logs fill before a filled one can be archived, then all of your Oracle database users will experience a massive wait until that redo log has been archived so that LGWR can overwrite its contents. Second, archived redo logs are stored in an archive location specified by the `init`*`sid`*`.ora` parameter `LOG_ARCHIVE_DEST`. If you archive your redo logs, be sure you have enough space on the disk resource you specify for `LOG_ARCHIVE_DEST`, because if that disk fills, then no more redo logs can be archived to that location. If archiving cannot take place, all online redo logs will fill, and then LGWR will not be able to write any more redo information. Again, users will experience a massive wait, only this time the wait will not stop until you clear out enough space in your `LOG_ARCHIVE_DEST` location to make room for more archived redo logs.

When you use Oracle in `archivelog` mode, you can do many things that you can't do when archiving is not used. For example, you can take online backups, meaning that 24 × 7 database operation is only possible when redo logs are archived. You also will not need to restore your entire database if a disk containing datafiles for a non-SYSTEM tablespace crashes. Finally, and perhaps most importantly, you can recover your database to the point of disk failure occurring after your most recent backup. What's more, you can conduct forms of *incomplete recovery*, or recovery to a point other than your most recent backup or the time of the failure. More information about incomplete recovery will be offered later in this Unit.

Exercises

1. What does it mean to run your database in `noarchivelog` mode versus running it in `archivelog` mode? How does the recoverability of your database change as the result of using this option?
2. What is the default archiving setting for an Oracle database if none is specified at database creation?
3. If `noarchivelog` mode is used for your database, can you recover data changes made after your most recent backup was taken? Why or why not? What type of database backups can you not take when Oracle runs in this way?

Configuring Oracle for Redo Log Archiving

There are five steps involved in configuring Oracle for archiving of redo logs. The first step is to shut down the database using `shutdown immediate`, `shutdown normal`, or `shutdown transactional`. The second step is to set up `init`*`sid`*`.ora` parameters for the archiving destination, format, and ARCH process. The third step is to start up and mount, but not open, the database. Fourth, set the database mode to `archivelog`. Last, open the database. After you are done, you should backup your database. The following explanations detail each of the five steps.

Step 1: Close Database, Shut Down Instance

This is easily accomplished using the `shutdown immediate`, `shutdown normal`, or `shutdown transactional` commands in Server Manager:

```
SVRMGR> shutdown immediate;
Database closed.
Database dismounted.
ORACLE instance shut down.
```

Step 2: Specifying Initialization Parameters

First, you should seriously consider using the ARCH process to avoid archiving problems. This process will be started if you set `LOG_ARCHIVE_START` to TRUE. Next, the location Oracle uses to store archived redo logs is specified with `LOG_ARCHIVE_DEST`, an `init`*`sid`*`.ora` parameter. Note an interesting difference between Unix and Windows for this parameter. In Unix, you specify `LOG_ARCHIVE_DEST` by identifying both the absolute path for the archive destination directory and a prefix for the archived log filenames, as listed in the following code block:

```
LOG_ARCHIVE_DEST='/disk_11/archive'
```

But, for Windows, this parameter only specifies the directory name:

```
LOG_ARCHIVE_DEST='H:\ORANT\ARCHIVE'
```

Finally, the naming convention Oracle will use when automatically generating and naming archiving redo logs is specified with the `LOG_ARCHIVE_FORMAT` parameter in the `init`*`sid`*`.ora` file. The format for archived redo log names is arbitrary, and it is dependent on the filename formats supported by the host machine's operating system. However, since the archived redo logs will be created in a particular sequence, there are some format conventions you can use to identify your archived redo logs according to the data the logs contain. There are four formatting conventions usable with `LOG_ARCHIVE_FORMAT: %S, %s, %T`, and `%t`. Some examples appear a little later in this chapter. The formatting conventions are as follows:

- **%S** Log sequence number, a sequential number representing the number of redo logs that have been written and archived since archiving began, the instance started, or the sequence was reset by `resetlogs`. When capitalized, the sequence number used to name the file will padded to the left with zeros.
- **%s** Log sequence number, a sequential number representing the number of redo logs that have been written and archived since archiving began, instance started, or sequence reset by `resetlogs`, as in the preceding description. However, in this case the value will not be padded to the left with zeros.

- **%T** Thread number for the redo logs of that instance within the Oracle Parallel Server architecture. When the format convention is capitalized, the thread number used in file naming will be padded with zeros to the left. A thread is a running set of redo log information for one instance within a parallel database server.
- **%t** Thread number for the redo logs of that instance within the Oracle Parallel Server architecture, not padded to the left with zeros. Again, a thread is a running set of redo log information for one instance within a parallel database server.

Step 3: Start Up Instance, Mount Database

This is accomplished easily with the following command in Server Manager:

```
SVRMGR> startup mount pfile=initjsc.ora
Total System Global Area                       14442496 bytes
Fixed Size                                        49152 bytes
Variable Size                                  13193216 bytes
Database Buffers                                1126400 bytes
Redo Buffers                                      73728 bytes
Database mounted.
```

Step 4: Enable archivelog Mode

Now, set the archiving mode for the entire database in the control file. You can first determine the archiving status on your database using several different methods, such as the `archive log list` command in Server Manager:

```
SVRMGR> ARCHIVE LOG LIST
Database log mode                      NOARCHIVELOG
Automatic archival                     DISABLED
Archive destination                    /DISK01/Oracle/home/arch/
Oldest online log sequence             20
Next log sequence to archive           21
Current log sequence                   21
```

Another option is to query the V$DATABASE view, as shown here:

```
SVRMGR> SELECT name, log_mode FROM v$database;
NAME       LOG_MODE
---------  --------------------------
ORGDB01    NOARCHIVELOG
```

You enable archiving with the `alter database archivelog` statement. Oracle defaults to `noarchivelog` mode when you create your database if archivelog mode is not specified in the create database statement. You can switch the archiving status of a database after the database has been created. The following example illustrates putting your database into archivelog mode:

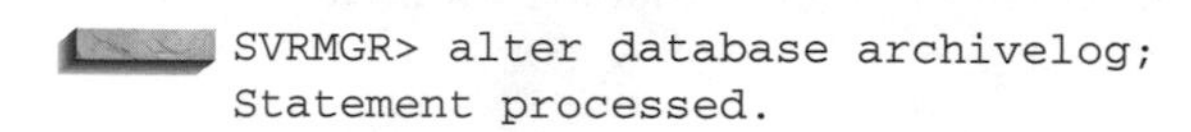

```
SVRMGR> alter database archivelog;
Statement processed.
```

Step 5: Open Your archivelog Database

Open your database using the alter database open command, shown here:

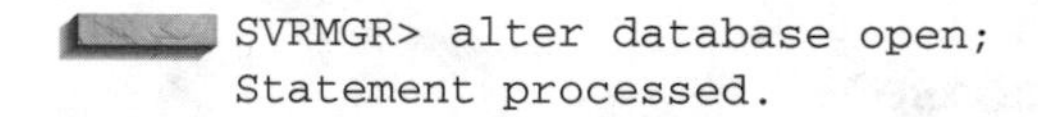

```
SVRMGR> alter database open;
Statement processed.
```

TIP
Always shut down the database and take a backup of it after enabling or disabling archivelog mode, because the contents of the control file will have changed. If you don't perform this step and you have to perform a complete recovery of your database using a cold backup taken when Oracle was running in noarchivelog mode, you will be unable to recover your database, even if you have the archived redo information.

LOG_ARCHIVE_FORMAT Examples

Note that in Unix, the files you will see in your directories will also have the prefix you specify for LOG_ARCHIVE_FORMAT. The results of some different combinations of these four naming conventions are shown in the following code block. They will give you a better idea of how you might want to use them in your own Oracle databases. The first example incorporates the LOG_ARCHIVE_DEST parameter setting for Unix, shown earlier in this lesson:

```
LOG_ARCHIVE_FORMAT = Log%S.arc
archiveLog0023.arc
archiveLog0024.arc
archiveLog0025.arc
```

In this example from Windows, you can see that the entire filename is based only on LOG_ARCHIVE_FORMAT:

```
LOG_ARCHIVE_FORMAT = Arch-%t-%S.arc
Arch-3-0001.arc
Arch-3-0002.arc
Arch-3-0003.arc
```

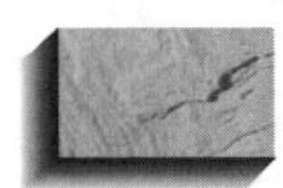

TIP
During database recovery, the suggestions that Oracle formulates for you to confirm are based on the value of the `LOG_ARCHIVE_FORMAT` parameter.

Displaying Information About Archived Redo Logs

Once the redo logs are archived, you can identify which redo logs exist and what their contents are, using several different dictionary views besides V$DATABASE, and using the `archive log list` command in Server Manager. The other views are:

- **V$LOG_HISTORY** Lists archived redo logs for the database and detailed information about the system change numbers of the contents. The ARCHIVE_NAME column identifies the filename of the archived redo log.
- **V$ARCHIVED_LOG** Shows information about your archived redo logs, such as archive status and size.
- **V$ARCHIVE_DEST** Identifies information about archive log destinations used in your database.

TIP
Experiment with archiving, and look at the contents of these dynamic views before taking OCP Exam 3.

Selectively Archiving Redo Logs

The options for manually archiving redo logs include seq, `change`, `current`, `group`, `logfile`, `all`, and `next`. These options are explained here.

ALL Used to manually archive all online redo logs not yet archived. It is used as follows:

```
ALTER SYSTEM ARCHIVE LOG ALL;
```

SEQ Used to manually archive online redo logs according to sequence number. The sequence number for a given current log group can be obtained by using `archive log list` in Server Manager, or using the V$LOG view:

```
ALTER SYSTEM ARCHIVE LOG SEQ 39;
```

CHANGE Used to manually archive logs according to a system change number (SCN) obtained from the V$LOG dynamic performance view. The column that defines the first SCN available on the redo log is FIRST_CHANGE#. The following statement can be used for that purpose:

```
ALTER SYSTEM ARCHIVE LOG CHANGE 450394;
```

CURRENT This option is used to manually archive the redo log that is currently being written by the instance, forcing Oracle to do an implicit log switch. Its use is straightforward:

```
ALTER SYSTEM ARCHIVE LOG CURRENT;
```

GROUP This option is used to manually archive redo log information according to redo log group number. The DBA can obtain group information from the GROUP# column in the V$LOG performance view. The use of this option is as follows:

```
ALTER SYSTEM ARCHIVE LOG GROUP 3;
```

LOGFILE This option manually archives the redo log containing the member identified by the filename specified. The value specified for `logfile` must be a filename for one of the members of a log file group, without an absolute pathname specified. Its use appears in this code block:

```
ALTER SYSTEM ARCHIVE LOG LOGFILE 'LOG1A';
```

NEXT This option manually archives the oldest online redo log that has filled but not been archived. If all online redo logs have been filled, nothing happens. Its use is as follows:

```
ALTER SYSTEM ARCHIVE LOG NEXT;
```

TO This option overrides the automatic archiving destination specified by LOG_ARCHIVE_DEST. However, the automatic archiving destination will still default to the LOG_ARCHIVE_DEST location. This option is used in conjunction with other options listed previously:

```
ALTER SYSTEM ARCHIVE LOG NEXT TO '/disk_16/archive/alt';
```

Turning Off Archiving

If you no longer want to archive your redo logs, you should take the following steps. First, issue the `alter system archive log stop` statement to stop ARCH from processing. Second, change the archiving status of Oracle in the control file with the `alter database noarchivelog` statement. Be sure the instance is started and the database mounted but not opened before you do so. Also, don't forget this second step, or else your users will eventually experience massive wait problems due to the fact that Oracle still expects to archive redo logs but the ARCH process is stopped.

Exercises

1. What are the four steps for archiving redo logs? Describe the process involved in each step. How do you turn archiving off?
2. What `init`*`sid`*`.ora` parameters are involved in setting up archive redo logs, and what purpose does each serve? What views are available for finding information about archived redo logs?
3. What options for the `alter system statement` are used for manually archiving redo logs in Oracle?

Multiplexing Archived Redo Log Files

The final area covered in setting up Oracle for backup and recovery redo log archiving is a new feature in Oracle8 that allows you to multiplex (sometimes also referred to as *duplex*) your archived redo logs. Why might this feature be handy? If the disk resource storing your archived redo logs were to fail, you would lose the archived redo logs you need to restore your database. Of course, the workaround for this situation is to shut down the database, take a cold backup, fix the archive disk resource or switch to a new one, and open the database, starting your use of archived redo logs from scratch. But, for 24 × 7 database operation, this option simply will not work.

Oracle allows you to multiplex your archived redo logs by specifying a few new `init`*`sid`*`.ora` parameters. The first is `LOG_ARCHIVE_DUPLEX_DEST`, and it is used to identify the second location where Oracle will store copies of archived redo logs. You can set this parameter to a directory in your file system other than the one specified for LOG_ARCHIVE_DEST, or to a device name. Do not use this option in Oracle Parallel Server to point your multiplexing destination to a raw device. The second new init*sid*.ora parameter is the LOG_ARCHIVE_MIN_SUCCEED_DEST parameter. This is set to a number indicating how many archive log copies Oracle should maintain. It will be set to 1 if you do not plan to use multiplexing for your archived redo logs, and to 2 if you do plan to use multiplexing. You can only set this parameter to 1 or 2. The following code block illustrates the contents of your init*sid*.ora file for these parameters:

```
LOG_ARCHIVE_DEST = 'D:\ORANT\DATABASE\ARCHIVE'
LOG_ARCHIVE_DUPLEX_DEST = 'Z:\ORANT\DATABASE\ARCHIVE_DUPLEX'
LOG_ARCHIVE_MIN_SUCCEED_DEST = 2
```

You can determine how Oracle will behave regarding archive duplexing based on the contents of the V$ARCHIVE_DEST view. Assuming you run Oracle with the parameters set as shown in the preceding code block, the following code block shows the output you will see in V$ARCHIVE_DEST:

```
SVRMGR> select * from v$archive_dest;
ARCMODE      STATUS    DESTINATION
------------ --------- ---------------------------
MUST-SUCCEED NORMAL    D:\ORANT\DATABASE\ARCHIVE
MUST-SUCCEED NORMAL    Z:\ORANT\DATABASE\ARCHIVE_DUPLEX
```

However, look at the output from that same view when you set the initialization parameter LOG_ARCHIVE_MIN_SUCCEED_DEST to 1 instead of 2, while still leaving the parameter LOG_ARCHIVE_DUPLEX_DEST set to a valid destination:

```
SVRMGR> select * from v$archive_dest;
ARCMODE      STATUS    DESTINATION
------------ --------- ---------------------------
MUST-SUCCEED NORMAL    D:\ORANT\DATABASE\ARCHIVE
BEST-EFFORT  NORMAL    Z:\ORANT\DATABASE\ARCHIVE_DUPLEX
```

The difference between the output for the ARCMODE column indicates Oracle's requirement for success in duplexing archived redo logs. If that requirement is "must-succeed," then duplexing is mandatory, but if that requirement is "best-effort," Oracle does not guarantee that you will have two sets of functional archived redo logs.

Exercises

1. Which init*sid*.ora parameters are used to support archived redo log multiplexing?

2. Describe a situation where you might want to multiplex your archived redo logs. What column in what V$ view can tell you whether Oracle will guarantee the production of two redo log sets?

Physical Backups in Oracle Without RMAN

In this section, you will cover the following points about physical backups in Oracle without using Recovery Manager (RMAN):

- Using OS commands for database backup
- Recovery implications for offline and online backups
- Performing offline and online backups
- Backup implications of `logging` and `nologging` modes
- Taking backups of your control file
- Backing up read-only tablespaces
- Dictionary views for database backup

The final area covered in this chapter is the actual process of taking database backups. This topic is relatively complex, so you should read carefully. In this section, you will learn a few of the general operating system commands for taking backups on the most popular platforms for Oracle—Windows and Unix. This section also covers the recovery implications of offline and online backups, which are sometimes referred to as closed or open backups. This section also covers the steps required for taking those two types of backups. You will also learn about the recoverability of data when operations such as index creation are performed using the `logging` and `nologging` options. Taking backups of your control files is also covered, as is backing up read-only tablespaces. Finally, you will learn which dictionary views are helpful for backing up databases.

Using OS Commands for Database Backup

As mentioned earlier in this chapter, there are two types of backups: online (or open) and offline (or closed). These backups are usually referred to as physical backups because they involve making physical copies of the actual files Oracle uses to do its job. Oracle cannot make these physical copies for you. You must have some knowledge of the operating system's file copy commands, such as `copy` for

Windows and cp for Unix, in order to make physical backups of your Oracle database files.

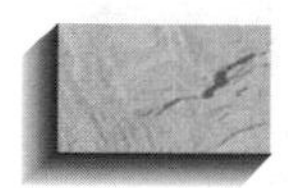

TIP
Another type of backup is the logical backup. These backups are copies of data in Oracle stored in some format other than as the files Oracle uses to do its job. For example, EXPORT makes logical backup copies of Oracle data in a binary format readable by IMPORT. You will learn more about the use of EXPORT and IMPORT in Chapter 15.

As an aside, you may also use third-party products for your database backups. Some examples of these products include ADSM from IBM, ArcServe from Computer Associates, and Backup Exec from Seagate. If you do use a third-party product, you will need to understand how it works, either with Oracle, or in its own right. Most likely it will have its own command set, syntax, and other rules. However, in some cases Oracle offers interfaces between RMAN and other tools (for example, ADSM). Using RMAN in conjunction with third-party tools is not tested in OCP Exam 3, however, so a discussion of this topic is beyond the scope of this book. The RMAN tool offers several new options for backup and recovery in Oracle; these will be explained in the next chapter.

Exercises

1. What role does the operating system play in Oracle database backup?
2. What is a logical backup?

Recovery Implications for Offline and Online Backups

The amount of data you can actually recover in the event of media failure depends on your backup strategy. The discussion of archiving versus not archiving redo logs showed that you will not be able to recover data changes made after the most recent backup if you don't archive your redo logs. In this lesson, you will learn about data recovery as it relates to online and offline backups.

First, consider the recoverability provided by offline backups. The offline backup is very simple and easy to manage. You simply close your database using `shutdown immediate`, `shutdown normal`, or `shutdown transactional`, and then copy your database files and bring everything back online again. If you're in a pinch, an offline backup will almost always make your database recoverable—simply copy the files back to their respective places, and start up the database. The flip side of offline backups is that you always lose any changes made to the data after the backup was taken. Thus, your recovery is only as current as your most recent backup. The actual recovery of data may take a while too, particularly if your database has lots of datafiles that are very large, or if you must first restore your files from tape instead of disk. Finally, offline backups require downtime—something that may not be possible if your organization is counting on 24 × 7 database system availability.

Second, consider the recoverability provided by online backups. The online backup is conceptually a bit more of a challenge, because you have to put each tablespace into backup mode one by one, jump out to the operating system to copy the datafiles, and then return to Oracle to take the tablespace out of backup mode. As if that were not enough, you have to be very careful to ensure you have all redo logs archived so that any data changes made while you were backing up can be recovered. You can't take online backups if you don't archive the redo logs. This is a tricky operation, and one with many points of potential failure. Depending on how heavy the transaction volume is when you back up the tablespaces, your database may suffer performance degradation because more redo continues to be produced when a tablespace is being backed up. Still, this is the backup method of choice for organizations that need to have their databases available 24 × 7.

Exercises

1. Describe the advantages and disadvantages of online backups. In what scenario must you use online backups?
2. Describe the advantages and disadvantages of offline backups. Do you have to archive your redo logs? Why or why not? If not, what might be the consequences of not archiving redo logs?

Performing Offline and Online Backups

To ensure that all data is captured in an offline backup, the DBA should close the database and make copies of all database files. All the files of the database that store application data should be copied and archived using the methods for file copy made available by the operating system. You can first check the database layout by querying V$DATAFILE, V$CONTROLFILE, and V$LOGFILE, and perhaps you should execute the `archive log list` command in Server Manager to note the date of the backup. The following steps explain how to take an offline backup.

1. Take the database offline using the `shutdown normal`, `shutdown immediate`, or `shutdown transactional` statement.
2. Note the file system layout of your host machine. This will need to be preserved in the event of media failure.
3. Make copies of all datafiles for all tablespaces using the operating system commands.
4. Make copies of all online redo logs using the operating system commands. Though it is not always required to have copies of your online redo logs, you are better off having them.
5. Make copies of all control files using the operating system commands.
6. Make copies of your `init`*`sid`*`.ora` and password files (if used) with the operating system commands.

The DBA should back up the copies of the datafiles, online redo log files, control files, password file, and parameter file to another disk, and keep copies on that backup disk, if possible, to improve recovery time. Later, these backups can be moved to tape when the database is back online. The offline backup, by itself, provides a good means of recovery to the point in time of database backup. Offline backups with archived redo logs allow recovery to virtually any point in time—from the time the offline backup took place, right up to the time the database experienced disk failure, or to any point in between.

Procedure for Taking Online Backups

In order to guarantee that the changes made to the tablespace while the online backup was in progress are kept, the DBA must archive redo logs that were taken during the operation of online backups. Prior to taking the online backup, the DBA should issue the `archive log list` command from Server Manager in order to determine the oldest online redo log sequence that should be saved with the online backups. Once the tablespace backups are complete, the `archive log list` command should be issued again, followed by a log switch to ensure that the current redo log entries made for the backed-up tablespaces are archived properly for use by the backups, should recovery be necessary. The steps of this process are:

1. Execute `archive log list` from Server Manager. Note the value for "Oldest online log sequence." This is the oldest redo log required for using the online backup.

```
SVRMGR> ARCHIVE LOG LIST
Database log mode                 ARCHIVELOG
automatic archival                ENABLED
```

```
Archive destination              /u01/oracle/home/arch
Oldest online log sequence       21
Next log sequence to archive     25
Current log sequence             25
```

2. Execute `alter tablespace` *name* `begin backup` from Server Manager. This step prepares the tablespace for online backup.

```
SVRMGR> ALTER TABLESPACE users BEGIN BACKUP;
```

3. Copy the datafiles for that tablespace using the operating system commands or a third-party product. Be sure the copy resides on a disk other than the production datafiles themselves.

4. Execute `alter tablespace` *name* `end backup` from Server Manager. This step completes the online backup process for that tablespace.

```
SVRMGR> ALTER TABLESPACE users END BACKUP;
```

5. Repeat steps 2–4 for all tablespaces to be backed up.

6. Execute `archive log list` again from Server Manager. Note the value given for "Current log sequence" this time. This is the last redo log required for using the online backup.

```
SVRMGR> ARCHIVE LOG LIST
Database log mode                ARCHIVELOG
automatic archival               ENABLED
Archive destination              /u01/oracle/home/arch
Oldest online log sequence       21
Next log sequence to archive     33
Current log sequence             33
```

7. Issue an `alter system switch logfile` to cause Oracle to create an archive of the current redo log. This archive should then be stored in the `LOG_ARCHIVE_DEST` area. If desired, copy the archives associated with the backup to tape.

```
SVRMGR> ALTER SYSTEM SWITCH LOGFILE;
```

8. Create a copy of the control file using the `alter database backup controlfile` statement.

TIP

A control file must be backed up whenever a change is made to the structure of a database. For example, after the creation of a new tablespace, or an addition or removal of a datafile, the control file for the database must be backed up.

It is possible to perform parallel online backups of the tablespaces of the database. The following code block illustrates parallel online tablespace backup. However, this method *is not recommended*. Taking tablespace backups iteratively allows less time between the beginning and the end of a tablespace backup. Minimizing backup time is important, because less time for backup means there is less time when the database is exposed to the danger of database failure during backup. The second reason for taking online tablespace backups iteratively is that the amount of redo information written is larger and more extensive during online backups than during normal operation of the database.

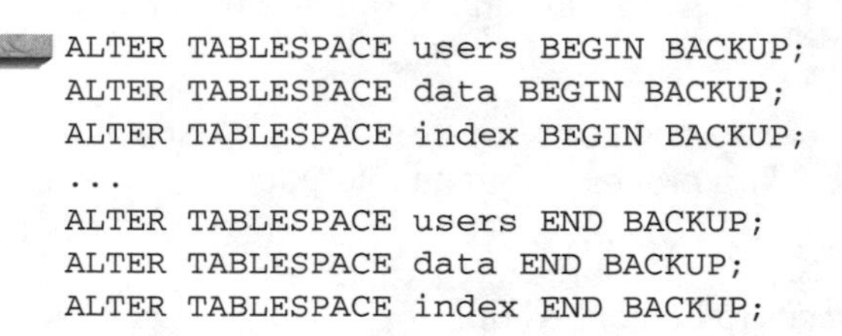

```
ALTER TABLESPACE users BEGIN BACKUP;
ALTER TABLESPACE data BEGIN BACKUP;
ALTER TABLESPACE index BEGIN BACKUP;
...
ALTER TABLESPACE users END BACKUP;
ALTER TABLESPACE data END BACKUP;
ALTER TABLESPACE index END BACKUP;
```

Exercises

1. What are the steps required for taking an online backup? What are the steps involved for offline backups?
2. What is the difference between taking online backups in an iterative fashion and taking them in a parallel fashion?
3. What are the advantages and drawbacks for parallel tablespace backups?

Backup Implications of logging and nologging Modes

Recall from Unit II that several types of statements such as `create table` or `create index` allow you to include the `logging` or `nologging` clause to put the object in those respective modes. The `logging` clause is the default in Oracle, and it means that the object created and any data loaded into that object will generate redo information. This option is good for data recoverability, but in some cases you might see slow performance as a result of redo being generated. Specifying the `nologging` clause means that the creation of the table or index, as well as data loaded into the table or index, will not generate any redo information. This enhances performance of data load or object creation operations, but leaves you with a dilemma later if the database fails and you haven't taken a backup. Even if you archive your redo logs, you still will not be able to recover data, because no redo was generated for operations related to that object. Use `nologging` very sparingly, and only with table data load or index creation operations when you plan to take a backup very soon anyway.

Exercises

1. What are the implications of `logging` versus `nologging` in Oracle?
2. What should you do immediately after a data load operation in which you specified `nologging` in Oracle?

Taking Backups of Your Control File

You need to back up the control file when you add or remove tablespaces, datafiles, or online redo log groups or members, or when you rename any file in your Oracle database. You also need to take a backup of your control file if you change the archiving status of your database. Furthermore, you should back up the control file whenever you drop tablespaces or change them from read-write to read-only state, or vice-versa.

TIP
To stay on the safe side, back up your control file every time you issue the `alter database`, `create tablespace`, `alter tablespace`, or `drop tablespace` statements.

A backup copy of your control file can be made while the database is offline by simply using operating system commands. Taking an online backup of the control file is accomplished in two different ways. The first way provides the DBA with a backup of the actual database control file, which is then used if there is a media failure that causes damage to a control file on the database. The method used to handle backup of this control file is the `alter database backup controlfile` statement. An example of using this statement appears in the following code block:

```
SVRMGR> ALTER DATABASE BACKUP CONTROLFILE TO 'flibber.dbf';
Statement processed.
```

There is another method available for database backup of control files, as well, using the same syntax with the addition of a special keyword called `trace`, which is used in place of *name*. In this situation, Oracle creates the script required to create the control file. This file is created in the trace file directory specified by the

BACKGROUND_DUMP_DEST parameter of the init*sid*.ora file. An example of using the trace option is shown in the following code block:

```
SVRMGR> ALTER DATABASE BACKUP CONTROLFILE TO TRACE;
Statement processed.
```

After using the trace option, you will have a new trace file in the directory specified by BACKGROUND_DUMP_DEST on your machine. The output is shown here:

```
SVRMGR> !dir D:\ORANT\RDBMS80\TRACE\*.trc
ORA00117.TRC
SVRMGR> !type ORA00117.TRC
Dump file D:\orant\rdbms80\trace\ORA00117.TRC
Tue Apr 20 09:34:23 1999
ORACLE V8.0.5.0.0 - Production vsnsta=0
vsnsql=c vsnxtr=3
Windows NT V4.0, OS V5.101, CPU type 586
Oracle8 Enterprise Edition Release 8.0.5.0.0 - Production
With the Partitioning and Objects options
PL/SQL Release 8.0.5.0.0 - Production
Windows NT V4.0, OS V5.101, CPU type 586
Instance name: orgdb01
Redo thread mounted by this instance: 1
Oracle process number: 10
pid: 75
*** SESSION IDSYMBOL 76 \f "Wingdings" \s 1111.49)
1999.04.20.09.34.23.285
*** 1999.04.20.09.34.23.285
# The following commands will create a new control file and use it
# to open the database.
# Data used by the recovery manager will be lost. Additional logs may
# be required for media recovery of offline data files. Use this
# only if the current version of all online logs are available.
STARTUP NOMOUNT
CREATE CONTROLFILE REUSE DATABASE "ORGDB01" NORESETLOGS ARCHIVELOG
    MAXLOGFILES 32
    MAXLOGMEMBERS 2
    MAXDATAFILES 254
    MAXINSTANCES 1
    MAXLOGHISTORY 112
LOGFILE
  GROUP 1 'D:\ORANT\DATABASE\LOGJSC1.ORA'  SIZE 4M,
  GROUP 2 'E:\ORANT\DATABASE\LOGJSC2.ORA'  SIZE 4M
DATAFILE
  'F:\ORANT\DATABASE\SYSJSC1.ORA',
  'G:\ORANT\DATABASE\RBS1JSC.ORA',
```

```
  'H:\ORANT\DATABASE\TEMP1JSC.ORA',
  'I:\ORANT\DATABASE\INDX1JSC.ORA',
  'J:\ORANT\DATABASE\DRJSC.ORA',
  'K:\ORANT\DATABASE\RMAN01.DBF',
  'L:\ORANT\DATABASE\TBLSPC.DBF'
;
# Configure snapshot controlfile filename
EXECUTE SYS.DBMS_BACKUP_RESTORE.CFILESETSNAPSHOTNAME(
'D:\ORANT\DATABASE\SNCFJSC.ORA');
# Recovery is required if any of the datafiles are restored backups,
# or if the last shutdown was not normal or immediate.
RECOVER DATABASE
# All logs need archiving and a log switch is needed.
ALTER SYSTEM ARCHIVE LOG ALL;
# Database can now be opened normally.
ALTER DATABASE OPEN;
# Files in read only tablespaces are now named.
ALTER DATABASE RENAME FILE 'MISSING00003'
  TO 'D:\ORANT\DATABASE\USR1JSC.ORA';
# Online the files in read only tablespaces.
ALTER TABLESPACE "USR" ONLINE;
SVRMGR>
```

Exercises

1. How do you take offline backups of your control file?
2. What are the two options for backing up control files?

Backing Up Read-Only Tablespaces

There are special considerations that should be considered for backing up the least frequently changed database objects. In cases where special "valid values" data is kept in lookup tables on the Oracle database, the tables that contain this data can be placed into special tablespaces called *read-only tablespaces*. The data in the tables of a read-only tablespace may not be changed.

Data that is read-only in a database requires little maintenance and backup. When database data is defined as read-only, the DBA needs to back up the read-only tablespace once, after the status of the tablespace is changed to read-only. The mechanics of setting a tablespace to read-only status is handled with the `alter tablespace` *`tblspace`* `read only` statement. Once the tablespace status is changed, you can rest assured that the data will not change.

Exercises

1. What is a read-only tablespace?
2. How often should you back up read-only tablespaces? Why?

Dictionary Views for Database Backup

There are several views you might use in support of your database backups. You might use these views in a script that helps you make offline or online backups of your database. These views are identified and described in the following list:

- **V$CONTROLFILE** You can identify the names and file system locations of all your database control files using this view, as part of offline or online database backup scripts.
- **V$DATAFILE** You can identify the names and file system locations of all your datafiles using this view, as part of online or offline database backup scripts.
- **V$LOGFILE** You can identify the names and file system locations of all your online redo log file members using this view, as part of offline database backup scripts.
- **V$TABLESPACE** You can join this view with the V$DATAFILE view to determine which tablespace each datafile belongs to, as part of online backup scripts.

TIP
The Backup Manager utility in OEM handles database backups. Because OEM is a big component of OCP exams, you should experiment with this utility to find out its capabilities.

In addition, there are several views that assist in determining actual backups in progress on your database, or in determining information about datafile headers:

- **V$BACKUP** This view identifies the datafiles in your database that belong to tablespaces that are currently being backed up. Active status in the STATUS column means the file is being backed up; not active means the datafile is not being backed up.
- **V$DATAFILE_HEADER** Recall that during checkpoints the new online redo log sequence number is written to the headers of every datafile in Oracle, as well as to the control file. In addition to this information, the V$DATAFILE_HEADER view indicates that the datafile is currently being backed up if the FUZZY column contains the word "yes."

Chapter Summary

This chapter ambitiously covered a great deal of material for your preparation for OCP Exam 3. You learned about four different topic areas for database backup, comprising 25 percent of OCP test content. The first area covered was backup and recovery considerations. You learned about the business, operational, and technical requirements for planning a backup and recovery strategy. The three objectives for database recovery, namely maximizing uptime, reducing the time it takes to recover, and ensuring maximum recoverability of data in your database, were each covered in some detail. You also learned how to identify the required components of a backup and recovery plan. And there was a discussion regarding the importance of testing your backup and recovery strategy to ensure the recoverability of your Oracle database.

The next section explained the Oracle architectural components that support database backup and recovery. The SMON, PMON, CKPT, LGWR, ARCH, and DBWR processes were all explained in detail, as were the disk resources involved in backups, such as datafiles, redo logs, control files, password files, and `init`*`sid`*`.ora` files. The SGA memory structures, such as the large pool and redo log buffer, which are involved in database backup and recovery, were also explained in detail. You learned about the importance of archived redo logs in database recovery, and the use of online redo logs in this architecture. The special importance of and process involved in checkpoints was explained from the perspective of how Oracle uses checkpoints to synchronize the state of online redo logs and datafiles in general processing. This section wrapped up with a discussion of how to multiplex your control files and online redo logs, and why it is important to do so. This content is largely a repeat of content from Unit II because both OCP exams will test you on this content—the extra review should help you in your ultimate goal of becoming a better Oracle DBA.

The chapter then covered backup and recovery configuration, beginning with all the recovery implications of running your database in `noarchivelog` mode. This section might as well have been titled "Why You Shouldn't Run Your Database in `noarchivelog` Mode," because Oracle strongly recommends that you archive your redo logs for the sake of ensuring database recoverability. With that in mind, the section compared Oracle in `noarchivelog` and in `archivelog` modes, and then discussed the five-step process for configuring Oracle to run in `archivelog` mode. The steps are: (1) shut down the database; (2) set up `init`*`sid`*`.ora` parameters for the archiving destination, format, and ARCH process; (3) start up and mount, but do not open, the database; (4) set the database mode to `archivelog`; and (5) open the database. You should take a backup of your database after changing mode as well. The last area of this section discussed the new Oracle8 feature for multiplexing archived redo logs to two destinations, and the `initsid.ora` parameters that support this functionality.

The last section in this chapter covered how to actually execute your backups. You learned about the difference between a physical backup and a logical one, as well as the differences between online and offline backups. The operating system commands used in physical backups were also discussed, along with the implications on recoverability of both online and offline backups. Another lesson included in this section was the implications on recoverability of running data loads or having your tables or indexes in `nologging` mode, and why backups are essential after performing load activities with `nologging` enabled. You also learned when you need to back up your control file, and which of the two online and one offline methods you would use to perform this task. The chapter also covered an explanation of backing up tablespaces set to read-only status, and concluded with a listing of the Oracle dictionary views that you might use for backing up your database.

Two-Minute Drill

- The three axioms of database backup and recovery for a DBA are: maximize database availability, maximize recovery performance, and maximize data recoverability.
- Without backups, database recovery is not possible in the event of a database failure that destroys data.
- Three factors that should be considered when developing a backup strategy are the business requirements that affect database availability, whether the database should be recoverable to the point in time of the database failure, and the overall volatility of data in the database.
- Disaster recovery for any computer system can have the following impact: loss of time spent recovering the system, loss of user productivity correcting data errors or waiting for the system to come online again, the threat of permanent loss of data, and the cost of replacing hardware.
- The final determination of the risks an organization is willing to take with regard to their backup strategy should be handled by management. The DBA should advise management of any and all risks and the impact of any plan that management wants to enact regarding recovery.

- Complete recovery of data is possible in the Oracle database, but it depends on a good backup strategy.
- Testing backup and recovery strategy has three benefits: weaknesses in the strategy can be found and corrected, data corruption in the database that is being copied into the backups can be detected, and the DBA can improve his or her own skills resulting in the ability to tune the overall process to save time.
- The background processes involved in Oracle database backup and recovery are as follows:
  - SMON, which handles instance recovery at database startup and periodically coalesces free space in tablespaces
  - PMON, which performs process recovery on dedicated servers when associated user processes crash
  - CKPT, which handles aspects of checkpoint processing
  - ARCH, which handles automatic archiving of redo logs
  - LGWR, which writes redo entries from memory to disk
  - DBWR, which writes dirty buffers from memory to disk
- File structures for Oracle database recovery include online and archived redo logs, and backup copies of datafiles, control files, `initsid.ora` files, and password files
- Memory structures for Oracle database backup and recovery include the redo log buffer, buffer cache, and large pool.
- Checkpoints are opportunities for Oracle to synchronize the data stored in redo logs with data stored in datafiles.
- Multiplexing online redo logs and control files reduces the dependency on any one disk, which could crash and make your database unrecoverable.
- The difference between logical and physical backups is the same as the difference between the logical and physical view of Oracle's use of disk resources on the machine hosting the database.
- Logical backups are used to copy the data from the logical Oracle database objects, such as tables, indexes, sequences.

- The EXPORT and IMPORT tools are used for logical database object export and import.
- Physical backups are used to copy Oracle database files that are present from the perspective of the operating system. This includes datafiles, redo log files, control files, the password file, and the parameter file.
- To determine what datafiles are present in the database, use the V$DATAFILE dictionary view.
- To determine what control files are present in the database, use the `show parameters control_files` command from Server Manager, or look in the V$CONTROLFILE view.
- To determine what redo log files are available in the database, use the V$LOGFILE dictionary view.
- There are two types of physical backups: offline backups and online backups.
- Offline backups are complete backups of the database taken when the database is closed. In order to close the database, use the `shutdown normal`, `shutdown transactional`, or `shutdown immediate` command.
- Online backups are backups of tablespaces taken while the database is running. This option requires that Oracle be archiving its redo logs. To start an online backup, the DBA must issue the `alter tablespace` *`name`* `begin backup` statement from Server Manager. When complete, the DBA must issue the `alter tablespace` *`name`* `end backup` statement.
- Archiving redo logs is crucial for providing complete data recovery to the point in time that the database failure occurs. Redo logs can only be used in conjunction with physical backups.
- When the DBA is not archiving redo logs, recovery is only possible to the point in time when the last backup was taken.
- Databases that must be available 24 hours a day generally require online backups because they cannot afford the database downtime required for logical backups or offline backups.
- Database recovery time consists of two factors: the amount of time it takes to restore a backup, and the amount of time it takes to apply database changes made after the most recent backup.

- If archiving is used, then the time spent applying the changes made to the database since the last backup consists of applying archived redo logs. If not, then the time spent applying the changes made to the database since the last backup consists of users identifying and manually reentering the changes they made to the database since the last backup.
- The more changes made after the last database backup, the longer it generally takes to provide full recovery to the database.
- Shorter recovery time can be achieved with more frequent backups.
- Each type of backup has varied time implications. In general, offline physical database backups require database downtime.
- Only online database backups allow users to access the data in the database while the backup takes place.
- The more transactions that take place on a database, the more redo information that is generated by the database.
- An infrequently backed-up database with many archived redo logs is just as recoverable as a frequently backed-up database with few online redo logs. However, the time spent handling the recovery is longer for the first option than the second.
- Read-only tablespaces need to be backed up only once, after the database data changes and the tablespace is set to read only.
- `initsid.ora` parameters involved in archiving include the following:
    - `LOG_ARCHIVE_DEST`, which identifies primary archive destination
    - `LOG_ARCHIVE_START`, which makes ARCH start running
    - `LOG_ARCHIVE_FORMAT`, which determines format conventions for archived redo logs
    - `LOG_ARCHIVE_DUPLEX_DEST`, which identifies the multiplexed archive destination
    - `LOG_ARCHIVE_MIN_SUCCEED_DEST`, which identifies in how many locations an archived redo log will need to be stored
- The five steps for setting up archiving of redo logs are:

1. Shutting down the database using `immediate`, `normal`, or `transactional` options.
2. Configuring `LOG_ARCHIVE_DEST`, `LOG_ARCHIVE_START`, and `LOG_ARCHIVE_FORMAT` init*sid*.ora parameters
3. Mounting the database
4. Changing archiving status with `alter database archivelog`
5. Opening the database

- Take control-file backups whenever you issue the `alter database` command or `create`, `alter`, or `drop tablespace` commands. This is done with the `alter database backup controlfile to [trace|`*`filename`*`]` command.
- Review the chapter to make sure you know how to take online and offline database backups.
- Never take an online backup of multiple tablespaces at the same time. Instead, take tablespace backups serially.
- Dictionary views to use for database backup include V$DATABASE, V$TABLESPACE, V$DATAFILE, V$LOGFILE, V$CONTROLFILE, V$BACKUP, and V$DATAFILE_HEADER.

Chapter Questions

1. **The DBA is planning a backup and recovery strategy. Which of the following situations will produce the longest recovery time if daily online backups in conjunction with archiving is the method used for database backup?**

   A. Unusually low transaction volumes

   B. Batch `update` processing occurring at the same time as the backup

   C. A broken disk controller

   D. An application that locks users out of the database when backups occur

2. **When `nologging` is used as part of data loads, which of the following activities should the DBA strongly consider doing when the load is complete?**

A. Dropping and recreating the index

B. Switching the database to `noarchivelog` mode

C. Issuing the `alter system archive log switch command`

D. Backing up the database

3. A disk has just crashed, taking with it all archived redo logs for the database. Which of the following steps should the DBA take to ensure recoverability of the database in the future?

A. Issue the `alter database noarchivelog` command.

B. Take an offline backup of the database.

C. Modify the `LOG_ARCHIVE_DEST` parameter.

D. Modify the `LOG_ARCHIVE_FORMAT` parameter.

4. The DBA is planning a backup strategy for read-only tablespaces. A good plan for backups of a read only tablespace may include which of the following?

A. Weekly offline backups and nightly online backups

B. Weekly online backups and monthly offline backups

C. Backing up the read-only tablespace once

D. Backing up the read-only tablespace once daily

5. The DBA has disabled archiving of redo logs in Oracle. Which of the following choices identifies the only recovery option available if the disk containing a data tablespace crashed?

A. Recovery to point of failure

B. Recovery to a point in time after the most recent offline backup

C. Recovery of data up to the point of the most recent offline backup

D. Recovery of data to the point of the most recent online backup

6. A disk controller for the disk resource associated with `LOG_ARCHIVE_DEST` fails, making the disk inaccessible. Which of the following is not a behavior Oracle displays as the result of this situation?

A. Oracle will eventually not allow users to make data changes

B. The Oracle instance will fail

C. ARCH will not be able to archive redo information

D. All online redo logs will eventually fill

7. **The DBA is evaluating backup and recovery strategies for a user population spread across 12 time zones. Which of the following backup strategies best accommodates the needs of this application?**

   A. Offline backups with archiving enabled and archive log multiplexing in place

   B. Online backups with archiving disabled and redo log multiplexing in place

   C. Online backups with archiving enabled and archive log multiplexing in place

   D. Offline backups with archiving disabled and control file multiplexing in place

8. **Which of the following choices best identifies the task an Oracle DBA should perform before changing the archiving mode of an Oracle database?**

   A. Start the instance and mount but do not open the database

   B. Back up the database

   C. Take the tablespace offline

   D. Issue the `archive log list` command from Server Manager

9. **The database is operating in `noarchivelog` mode. LGWR has just filled the last online redo log in the series, and is about to cycle back to the first. Which of the following best describes the availability of the first online redo log for LGWR's use?**

   A. The first online redo log is unavailable for new redo information until it has been archived.

   B. The first online redo log is unavailable for new redo information until the checkpoint to write all data in the buffer cache is complete.

   C. The first online redo log is offline.

   D. No users will be able to make data changes to the database.

10. In order to improve performance for backup and file restoration using RMAN, which of the following memory areas should be utilized?

- **A.** Buffer cache
- **B.** Shared pool
- **C.** Log buffer
- **D.** Large pool
- **E.** Dictionary cache

11. After several months of production operation, a disk on the host machine fails. Several datafiles are lost. After 27 hours of effort, the DBA is able to manage only partial recovery of data due to corruption in an archived redo log. Which of the following choices might have prevented the problem?

- **A.** Management concurrence
- **B.** Backup and recovery testing
- **C.** Using the ARCH process
- **D.** Reducing the number of users

12. In evaluating a backup plan for a database with few users and minimal data change, which of the following options would most likely be considered?

- **A.** Online backups with archiving disabled and redo log multiplexing in place
- **B.** Online backups with archiving enabled and archive log multiplexing in place
- **C.** Offline backups with archiving disabled and no archive log multiplexing
- **D.** Offline backups with archiving disabled and control file multiplexing in place

13. In order to actually make the backup of datafiles as part of the online backup, which of the following commands is most appropriate?

- **A.** Operating system copy command
- **B.** `alter tablespace begin backup` command

C. `alter tablespace end backup` command

D. `shutdown immediate` command

14. If 24 × 7 operation is required for an organization's mission-critical database system, which of the following choices best identifies what will be necessary in order to prevent downtime and give the highest performance recoveries when a disk containing the system's only archived redo logs crashes?

A. More frequent tape backup of archived redo logs

B. Use of archive log multiplexing

C. Use of redo log multiplexing

D. Use of control file multiplexing

15. You are asked to analyze a backup and recovery strategy for an Oracle database. The system recently crashed, and data was not recoverable beyond the most recent offline backup. Which of the following strategies would you suggest?

A. Take more frequent offline backups

B. Multiplex the online redo logs

C. Enable the CKPT process

D. Archive redo logs

Answers to Chapter Questions

1. B. Batch `update` processing occurring at the same time as the backup

Explanation Batch `update` processing will likely generate a lot of redo information, which will generate more archived redo logs to apply in order to recover changes made between backups. Locking users out of the database, as in choice D, will likely reduce the amount of redo generated, as in choice A, which will reduce the overall time spent in database recovery, not increase it. Finally, a bad disk controller is a relatively easy fix requiring only a small amount of database downtime to replace the controller, and little, if any, data recovery time.

2. D. Backing up the database

Explanation The DBA should always back up the database after loading data with the `nologging` option set for the table because otherwise the data change will not be recoverable. Although dropping and recreating the index may be useful, particularly if the index is dropped before data is loaded and recreated after data is loaded, this is not the most important consideration in this question—the `nologging` clause is. Choices B and C can be eliminated for the same reason.

3. B. Take an offline backup of the database.

Explanation Since the archived redo logs are lost, your ability to recover the database with current backups is in jeopardy. Thus, you must take an offline backup to ensure the recoverability of your database. Although you may need to change the archiving destination in order to continue database operation, as noted in choice C, your most immediate priority in this situation is to ensure recoverability of your database. The other two choices are incorrect.

4. C. Backing up the read-only tablespace once

Explanation Since data cannot change in them, read-only tablespaces need to be backed up only once. All other backup strategies are recommended for more volatile databases.

5. C. Recovery of data up to the point of the most recent offline backup

Explanation Recovery to the point of your offline backup is the only option you have, because the only type of physical backup available to you when redo logs are not archived is offline backups. Thus, choice C is right. All other choices require that you archive your redo logs in Oracle.

6. B. The Oracle instance will fail

Explanation The instance will not fail as the result of the archive log destination not being available. However, all other options indicate activities that Oracle will perform as the result of the archive destination disk resource not being available.

7. C. Online backups with archiving enabled and archive log multiplexing in place

Explanation A database with users in 12 time zones must be available 24 hours a day. With a user base so globally defined, the best option in this situation usually involves online backups. This narrows you down to choices B and C. However, choice C is correct because choice B is logically impossible—you cannot take online backups if redo logs are not archived.

8. A. Start the instance and mount but do not open the database

Explanation In order to change the archiving status of the database, the database must not be open. The instance has to be started and the database mounted, however, because the DBA is making a change to the control file. Choice B might be correct if the question asked for a task to complete after the archiving status is changed, but that's another question entirely. The other choices are simply wrong.

9. B. The first online redo log is unavailable for new redo information until the checkpoint to write all data in the buffer cache is complete.

Explanation This is not to say that the redo log will not be available for LGWR to use. It most likely will be. However, the important item to remember is that the most recently filled online redo log is available only after DBWR writes dirty buffers to disk as part of the checkpoint that occurs as part of the log switch.

10. D. Large pool

Explanation The large pool is used as buffer space to support RMAN I/O slave processes running during backup and restore operations. All other choices are incorrect. The shared pool is incorrect because if the large pool exists and is too small, RMAN will not generate I/O slaves for processing.

11. B. Backup and recovery testing

Explanation This situation is your basic database administration nightmare. The whole point of recovery testing is to ensure that situations such as this one are avoided. No amount of anything identified in choices A, C, or D will make this situation avoidable.

12. D. Offline backups with archiving disabled and control file multiplexing in place

Explanation Since there is little data change taking place on this system, archiving redo logs is probably overkill. Instead, you can disable archiving and simply perform offline backups, leaving you with choices C and D. Now, to narrow the choice to one, you can eliminate choice C because it makes no sense to consider the value of disabling archive log multiplexing if you aren't even archiving redo logs. In contrast, multiplexing control files adds value to the recoverability of the database, making it the better choice.

13. A. Operating system copy command

Explanation Remember, you cannot make copies of online redo logs using Oracle commands. You must use the operating system's copy commands, whatever they may be for the operating system on your host machine.

14. B. Use of archive log multiplexing

Explanation The whole point of archive log multiplexing is to reduce the chance that your database will require downtime for an offline backup in the event that a disk containing your archived redo logs crashes. Although choice A may ensure you have a copy of the archived redo log somewhere, you will need to restore those files from tape before being able to use them in a recovery. Faster recovery is ensured if you already have the files you need on disk.

15. D. Archive redo logs

Explanation Of all the choices, choice D allows you to recover past the most recent offline backup, which is a problem indicated in the question. Taking more frequent offline backups may increase the amount of data recovered, but will not allow you to recover past the point of the backup. Only archiving redo logs allows you to do that. Multiplexing online redo logs does not improve recoverability, it only reduces the chance of instance failure if a disk containing a redo log member fails, eliminating choice B. Enabling the CKPT process is a moot point in Oracle—CKPT runs all the time in Oracle8!

CHAPTER 13

Using Recovery Manager for Backups

n this chapter, you will learn about and demonstrate knowledge in the following areas:

- Oracle Recovery Manager overview
- Oracle recovery catalog maintenance
- Physical backups using Recovery Manager

Until Oracle8, the DBA required knowledge of the underlying operating system and the available Oracle tools in order to perform database backup and recovery. With the release of Oracle8 comes the introduction of a new tool to assist the DBA with the backup and recovery strategy for the Oracle database. This new tool is called Recovery Manager, or RMAN. The purpose of this chapter is to cover the use and features of this new tool, the language constructs it possesses, and the advantages it offers for backup and recovery strategy.

Oracle Recovery Manager Overview

In this section, you will cover the following points on RMAN:

- Determining when to use RMAN
- Backup Manager uses
- RMAN advantages with or without a recovery catalog
- Creating the recovery catalog
- Connecting to RMAN

Recovery Manager (RMAN) possesses many features that ease the job of backup and recovery. This section will introduce you to the architecture, benefits, and appropriate times to use RMAN. You will learn that RMAN can be run as its own utility, or as part of other utilities, such as Backup Manager in the Oracle Enterprise Manager tool set. The use of RMAN with and without another new feature called the *recovery catalog* will also be presented. An in-depth discussion of the recovery catalog, plus how to configure it, will also be offered. Finally, the methods used to connect to and run RMAN will be discussed.

Determining When to Use RMAN

RMAN is used to manage the creation of database backups for the purpose of recovery. RMAN can be run as its own utility, or the functionality of RMAN in the form of a set of library functions can be embedded into another program or script. RMAN interfaces directly with Oracle8 to handle backup and recovery operations using a PL/SQL interface. The actual work of producing the backup or applying the recovery is done within Oracle8. RMAN also maintains a *recovery catalog,* a collection of backups taken to improve the DBA's ability to provide fast and effective recovery, which is stored as a separate database from the primary database housing your application data.

You don't have to use RMAN to handle backup and recovery in Oracle8. The tried and true method of operating system commands and Server Manager that has been available since Oracle7 is still available. However, there are some advantages to using RMAN. The entire database can be backed up using RMAN, or you can back up individual tablespaces and datafiles. You've already covered how to perform these tasks using operating system commands, and this chapter will explain how to do the same thing with RMAN. In addition, RMAN supports backup to the granularity of changed data blocks, a function not provided in Oracle7. This new feature permits backup time to be proportional to the amount of change made to a database rather than to the size of the database. Consider the impact of this change—instead of backups on infrequently changed large databases, such as data warehouses, taking hours because the database stores a lot of data, RMAN can complete the backup task quickly by targeting only the changed blocks for backup.

RMAN also eases the task of automating overall database backup and recovery. If there is a backup operation that is executed repeatedly, the DBA can create a backup script in an Oracle-supported utility. This utility also lets the DBA generate logs of backup and recovery activity. RMAN is well integrated with the Oracle8 database architecture, and the backup and recovery operations take advantage of several of the database's new features. These features include parallel backup and recovery, definition of conditions for backing up datafiles and targeting locations (rather than simply listing the datafiles to back up and their correlated storage devices), and even compression of unused blocks.

RMAN and Media Management

When performing your database backups, RMAN will not necessarily interface directly with your tape drive. Nor will you necessarily want it to. By making backup copies of datafiles, archived redo logs, and other database files to disk, RMAN allows you to keep a set of backups available for speedy recovery in the event of an emergency. This can reduce the amount of time you spend restoring files that would otherwise be on tape. However, if you want to use RMAN to interface directly with your tape drive, you need to add a media management layer (MML) of software to do so. If this software is available, you can get it from the maker of your tape drive or from the software maker that supports the tape backup software you use.

When Not to Use RMAN

You shouldn't use RMAN to handle backup and recovery on Oracle7 databases. Enterprise Backup Utility (EBU) is available for that. You shouldn't use RMAN to back up files other than Oracle files on your operating system, either. Also, you don't need to manage a recovery catalog in order to use RMAN, but it is a good idea to do so.

RMAN Features and Components

RMAN has several important features and components. It allows you to develop scripts for database backup and recovery that are stored in Oracle and executable from within PL/SQL. Although you can write backup scripts using your operating system scripting language, these scripts cannot be run from within the Oracle database. RMAN also allows incremental block-level datafile backups and does not take backups of blocks in your datafiles not currently storing used information. Another important feature of RMAN is its ability to detect block corruption while taking backups. This is something that would otherwise require the use of DBVERIFY or LOG_BLOCK_CHECKSUM or DB_BLOCK_CHECKSUM. RMAN also supports Oracle Parallel Server with backup and recovery parallel-processing enhancements. In addition, RMAN does not cause additional redo log overhead when performing online tablespace backups.

So much for features—there are several RMAN components to be mentioned. There is the RMAN executable program that you will run either from a command line, a GUI, PL/SQL, or OCI calls in your own application. Behind the scenes is a runtime interpreter, an engine that translates your RMAN commands into step-by-step instructions in the same way that Oracle translates SQL statements into instructions that manipulate data on disks and in memory. There is the primary production database being backed up, which is called a *target* in RMAN's terms. There is the *recovery catalog*, which is a database that contains information about datafile and control file copies, backup sets, archived redo logs, and other things to help you recover your database in times of need. The final component you should understand is the RMAN *channel*. A channel is a line of communication that RMAN opens with Oracle (via a server process) and with your operating system to handle backups, restores, and recoveries.

There are also several Oracle server-supplied packages that are part of RMAN, which you may consider to be part of the program, as well. They are particularly useful if you plan to handle backup and recovery activities using PL/SQL programs and the Oracle job scheduler. These packages are generated automatically when the `catproc.sql` script is run as part of database installation. The packages include DBMS_RCVCAT, DBMS_RCVMAN, and DBMS_BACKUP_RESTORE.

DBMS_RCVCAT This package maintains recovery catalog information for RMAN, including tasks such as registering databases, resetting databases, and other procedures you will cover in the next section. The `dbmsrman.sql` and `prvtrmns.plb` scripts are used to generate this package, and these scripts are called automatically when `catproc.sql` is run.

DBMS_RCVMAN This package handles activities that correspond to RMAN commands such as the `set` command. You will learn more about these commands in the section on handling backups using RMAN and in later chapters where recovery using RMAN is covered. The `dbmsrman.sql` and `prvtrmns.plb` scripts are used to generate this package, and these scripts are called automatically when `catproc.sql` is run.

DBMS_BACKUP_RESTORE This package works with Oracle and your operating system to produce backups of your database, and to perform restoration and recovery activities. The `dbmsbkrs.sql` and `prvtbkrs.plb` scripts are used to generate this package, and these scripts are called automatically when `catproc.sql` is run.

RMAN Setup and Modes

In order to set up RMAN, you must perform the following activities. First, determine whether you need a recovery catalog. The next thing you should determine is whether you need a password file so that RMAN can connect to the primary and recovery catalog databases using TNS. You may also need a password file if you plan to administer backup and recovery from a remote console, such as your desktop, using the Backup Manager tool in Oracle Enterprise Manager.

TIP
The `initsid.ora` file is not backed up by RMAN. When you use Backup Manager, you may be prompted to save copies of your parameter configurations. You should make copies of the `initsid.ora` file using either this method or some other file copying method of your own devising.

Finally, RMAN can run in a few different modes. You can process backup and recovery operations in RMAN from the command line, which should be pretty familiar to most Unix users. A nice benefit to using the command-line interface is that RMAN backup and recovery scripts can be run in batch mode. In addition, you can run RMAN through a GUI, such as Backup Manager. There is even an application programming interface (API) available to allow other programming languages to use RMAN to manage Oracle backup and recovery.

Exercises

1. What is RMAN? How can DBAs interface with RMAN?
2. What new category of backup does RMAN provide?
3. Identify some benefits of using RMAN in backup and recovery.

Backup Manager Uses

As mentioned in the previous lesson, you can use Backup Manager to handle backup and recovery with RMAN through a GUI instead of via the command line. Figure 13-1 displays the Backup Manager interface. You can only run Backup Manager from the Oracle Enterprise Manager (OEM) console, so first you need to

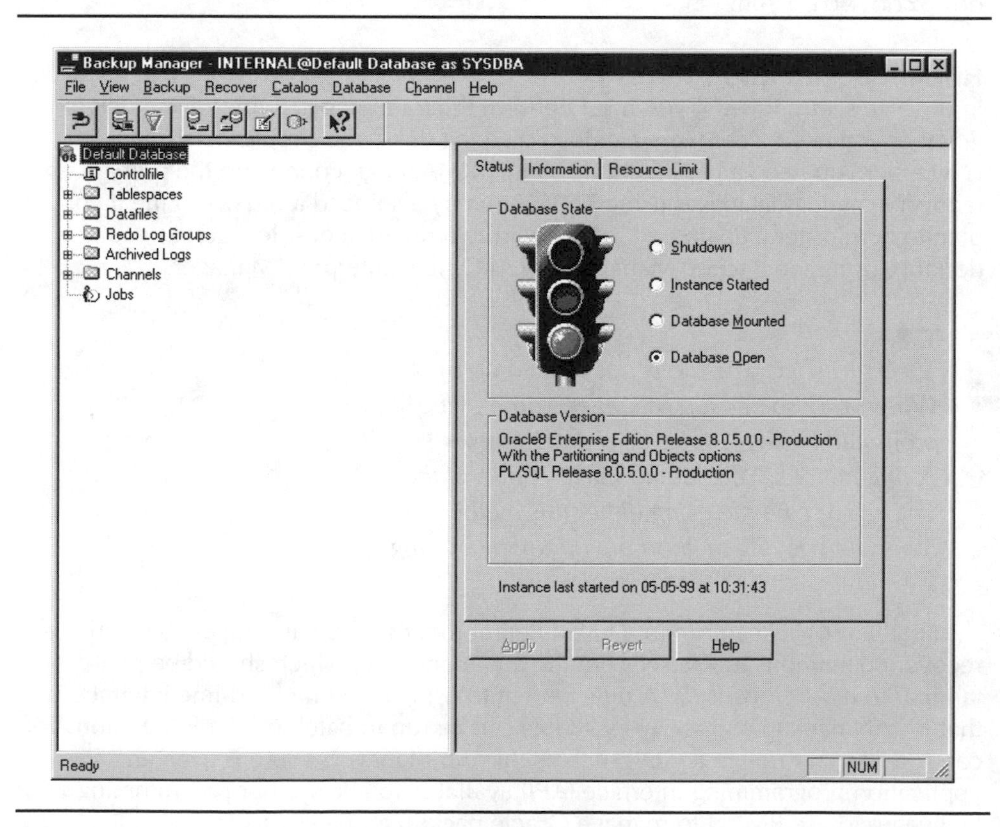

FIGURE 13-1. *Backup Manager interface*

install OEM. Furthermore, Backup Manager is available mainly on certain Windows platforms, so you may not have access to this tool.

Backup Manager provides a few main benefits. First, it is fairly easy to use, and it offers all the functionality RMAN provides on the command line. It allows you to extend your use of Enterprise Manager for backup and recovery, in addition to tablespace creation, schema management, and other tasks you may use Enterprise Manager for already. Backup Manager gives you the ability to set up backup, restore, and recovery jobs using a GUI interface rather than through scripts. Because of this feature, you don't need a lot of operating system–specific know-how when setting up backup and recovery operations. Given the acute shortage of knowledgeable Oracle professionals, expanded use of GUI interfaces should make database administration an easier and more accessible profession.

Exercise

What is Recovery Manager? How is it installed? Where does it typically run?

RMAN Advantages, With or Without a Recovery Catalog

RMAN works in conjunction with another new feature: the recovery catalog. The recovery catalog is a collection of information about the backup and recovery operations, along with the actual backups taken with RMAN. Ideally, it is stored in a separate database from the production system whose backup and recovery processing is being handled by RMAN.

The recovery catalog is optional; it is not created automatically when Oracle8 is installed. The DBA must create it separately with the `catrman.sql` script provided with the Oracle database distribution software; the script is found in the `rdbms/admin` subdirectory of the Oracle software home directory. You should also create a schema owner other than SYS for recovery catalog objects, in order to manage the scripts and other information generated by RMAN effectively. After creating the recovery catalog in a separate database, the DBA makes the other database available to RMAN via remote links. Once created, the recovery catalog is its own database, and must be backed up as such. Thus, a symbiotic relationship is formed between the production or "target" database and the recovery catalog "backup" database—just as the backup supports recovery for the production database, the production database can act as the backup for the recovery catalog database.

The recovery catalog includes several components. The physical structure of the production database is stored in the recovery catalog, including locations of datafiles, redo logs, and control files. Information about datafile copies, datafile backup sets, archived redo logs, and database backups are also stored in the recovery catalog. If you don't know what these things are, you can review the set of definitions at the end of this lesson. However, note that the files themselves are *not* stored in the recovery catalog—the files themselves are stored on disk or on tape. The recovery catalog is a repository of information useful to and maintained by RMAN, and should never be directly accessed by the production database itself.

Any structural changes to the production database should be maintained in the recovery catalog by RMAN. (Instructions on how to perform this task will be covered shortly.) Since a great deal of information about the structure of the database is taken from control files and rollback segments, the production database must be open in order to use RMAN to execute its processing. If for some reason RMAN attempts to execute something improperly, or attempts to use a corrupt file, there are integrity checks built into the Oracle database to prevent RMAN from causing inadvertent damage.

Recovery Catalog Component Definitions

The following list contains definitions of all the specialized terms you'll need to understand in order to use RMAN and a recovery catalog for backup and recovery.

- **Backup sets and backup pieces** A backup set, which is a logical construction, contains one or more physical backup pieces. Backup pieces are operating system files that contain the backed up datafiles, control files, or archived redo logs. You cannot split a file across different backup sets or mix archived redo logs and datafiles into a single backup set.
- **Datafile copies** A datafile copy is a physical copy of a datafile. This is similar to the offline backup datafile copies you make using operating system commands, but the difference is that RMAN tracks when the copy was made.
- **Archived redo log copies** A datafile copy is a physical copy of an archived redo log. This is similar to the archived redo logs made using database operation, but the difference is that RMAN tracks when the archive copy was made.
- **Database structure** This is the physical layout of your database, similar to the information stored in the control file.
- **RMAN scripts** These scripts execute RMAN backup, restore, and recovery activities.

Pros and Cons of the Recovery Catalog

Oracle can also operate RMAN in the absence of the recovery catalog under certain conditions. These conditions include the maintenance of small databases, where the use of an additional database to store the recovery catalog would be more trouble than it is worth. Since much of the structural information about the Oracle database maintained in the recovery catalog is taken from the control file anyway, RMAN can go directly to the source for structural information about the database it maintains.

There are, however, some limitations when using RMAN without the recovery catalog. The following operations are not supported without the recovery catalog:

- Using of automated RMAN scripts for executing routine backup operations
- Recovering a tablespace to a particular point in time through RMAN operations
- Taking incremental backups that save data changes at the block level
- Recovering the database when the control file doesn't reflect the current structure of the Oracle database

These limits can be mild or severe, depending on the level of failure encountered on the production database.

Exercises

1. What is the recovery catalog? What are the components of the recovery catalog?
2. Under what situations might the DBA not want to use the recovery catalog? What are the limitations of doing so?

Creating the Recovery Catalog

Before you create the recovery catalog, you should consider the following points.

- Your recovery catalog should be managed as a separate database outside your primary database, which means it needs a backup and recovery strategy.
- Not every primary database needs its own recovery catalog; however, when you do not use a recovery catalog with RMAN you lose some of its functionality.

- Your recovery catalog will not require a great deal of space, and it may even be run on the same host machine as your primary database. However, you should be prepared to offer around 100MB for its use on disks not used by the primary database so that the failures of the target are not mimicked by the recovery catalog.

Procedure for Creating a Recovery Catalog

To create a recovery catalog, follow these steps:

1. Either pick an existing database or create a new database to be the recovery catalog for your primary database. Do not use your primary database.
2. Create a tablespace for the objects that RMAN will maintain in the recovery catalog. Do not simply use the SYSTEM tablespace. Your RMAN tablespace can be relatively small, perhaps 50MB or less.
3. Create user RMAN, and set the RMAN tablespace you created in step 2 to be the default for this user.
4. Grant the RECOVERY_CATALOG_OWNER role to user RMAN to give RMAN the privileges to maintain the recovery catalog.
5. Give the DBA, CONNECT, and RESOURCE Oracle-supplied roles to user RMAN so that RMAN has enough privileges to perform its work. Also, give the `sysdba` privilege to RMAN to allow it to perform backup and recovery operations.
6. Connect to the recovery catalog as RMAN, and run the `catrman.sql` script to create the appropriate recovery catalog objects.

TIP

The recovery catalog gains most of its information from the control file. When you first create the recovery catalog and register the database with RMAN, the required information is read from the control file. But, when the control file changes, the recovery catalog does not change and will need to be resynchronized by the DBA.

New Control File Features

There are several new features that are present in the Oracle8 control file, so it is significantly changed from, and larger than, the Oracle7 control file. The Oracle8 control file stores information that is of use to RMAN. Some of this information is recycled, while other information is permanent. The new CONTROL_FILE_RECORD_KEEP_TIME init*sid*.ora parameter allows the DBA to specify the period of time after which data in recyclable portions of the control file expire and the space in the control file occupied by that data is reused. If more RMAN information needs to be stored, and the old information has not expired, then the control file will expand to accommodate the new data as well as the old. The value for CONTROL_FILE_RECORD_KEEP_TIME is specified as an integer representing the number of days recyclable data will be stored before it expires. When this parameter is set to 0, the control file will not expand, allowing Oracle to expire the recyclable data as needed to make room for new data.

Exercises

1. What must you consider before creating your recovery catalog? Describe the overall procedure you must follow to create your recovery catalog.
2. What are some of the considerations involving recovery catalogs and the control file? What are some of the new features of the control file?

Connecting to RMAN

There are four types of commands available in RMAN: recovery catalog maintenance, script maintenance and execution, report and list generation, and run commands. To start the RMAN utility, type **rman** at the operating system command line, followed by the **target** keyword, followed by the connect string for the production database on which RMAN will operate (in single or double quotes) and press ENTER.

Optionally, at the command line, four other things can be specified. First, the connect string location of the recovery catalog can be specified, preceded by the rcvcat keyword. Second, the pathname and location of a script containing commands that RMAN will process, and the keyword cmdfile can be specified. If a command file is used, RMAN runs in batch; otherwise, RMAN runs interactively. Third, a name and path for a message log for the execution of RMAN can be specified at the operating system command line, preceded with the msglog keyword. Fourth, RMAN can maintain an ongoing message log with the specification of the append keyword. An example of running RMAN in batch mode in Unix with these specifications is shown here:

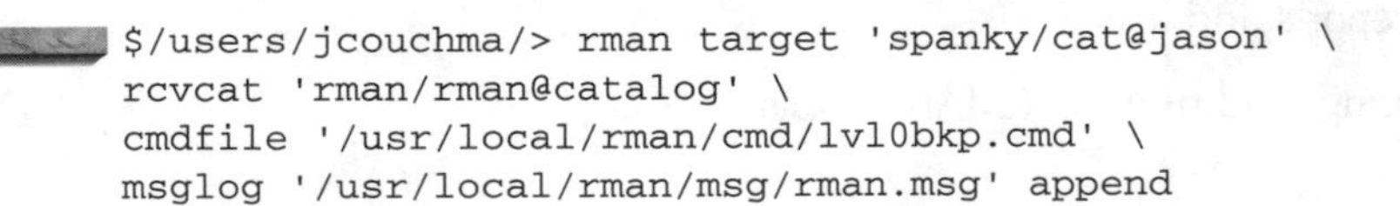

```
$/users/jcouchma/> rman target 'spanky/cat@jason' \
rcvcat 'rman/rman@catalog' \
cmdfile '/usr/local/rman/cmd/lvl0bkp.cmd' \
msglog '/usr/local/rman/msg/rman.msg' append
```

An example of running RMAN interactively when connecting to the primary database from the recovery catalog is listed here:

```
$/users/jcouchma/> rman rcvcat 'rman/rman@catalog'
Recovery Manager: Release 8.0.5.0.0 Production
RMAN> connect target
```

An example of running RMAN interactively when connecting to both the primary database and recovery catalog from a remote machine follows:

```
$/users/jcouchma/> rman target spanky/cat@jason \
rcvcat 'rman/rman@catalog'
Recovery Manager: Release 8.0.5.0.0 Production
```

RMAN terminates if it encounters an error at any point. Upon exit, RMAN will provide a return code according to its execution. If the entire operation was successful, RMAN returns `ex_succ`. If some commands succeeded, but the most recent one did not, then `ex_warn` will result. If no command processed was successful, `ex_fail` will be returned. The results of each command processed will be stored in the message file if one is defined; otherwise, the return codes will be displayed on the screen if RMAN is running interactively.

Exercises

1. What is the difference between running RMAN in batch mode and in interactive mode? What command line options can be specified for RMAN? Which one must always be specified?
2. What conditions cause RMAN to exit? What are the three return statuses given by RMAN, and what do they mean?

Oracle Recovery Catalog Maintenance

In this section, you will cover the following topics concerning recovery catalog maintenance:

- Registering, resynchronizing, and resetting the database
- Maintaining the recovery catalog
- Generating reports and lists
- Creating, storing, and running RMAN scripts

If you plan to use the recovery catalog in conjunction with RMAN, you need to understand a few important points before you proceed. RMAN will not maintain the recovery catalog automatically for you whenever you, for example, issue the `create tablespace` command to add more datafiles. Instead, the accuracy of the recovery catalog with respect to the control file on your primary database depends on your own ability to perform maintenance activities on the recovery catalog. You will learn several aspects of recovery catalog maintenance in this section. The commands for registering, resynchronizing, and resetting the database will be introduced, along with commands for backing up, restoring, and recovering the files listed in the recovery catalog. You will also learn how to generate reports and lists to determine the recoverability of your database. Finally, you will learn how to create `run` scripts that can automate many of the tasks of backup and recovery.

Registering, Resynchronizing, and Resetting the Database

There are several commands for maintaining the recovery catalog with RMAN. These commands allow the DBA to do many things, such as registering the target database with the recovery catalog, resetting information in the recovery catalog, and synchronizing information in the recovery catalog with the status of the target database. Other commands allow the DBA to change availability on a backup set or image copy, access the operating system for a backup or recovery operation using channels (information about what a channel is appears shortly), and to catalog image copies of datafiles made outside RMAN.

The register database Command

This process must be executed the first time RMAN is run. When executed, RMAN obtains data from the targeted production database and places necessary information into the recovery catalog. The production instance must be started and the database mounted for this operation. There are no parameters or additional clauses for this operation. The following code block shows the execution of this procedure in a Windows environment:

```
D:\> rman80 target internal/jason@primary rcvcat rman/rman@catalog
Recovery Manager Release 8.0.5.0.0 - Production
RMAN> REGISTER DATABASE;
RMAN-03022: compiling command: register
RMAN-03023: executing command: register
RMAN-08006: database registered in recovery catalog
RMAN-03023: executing command: full resync
RMAN-08029: snapshot controlfile name set to default value:
```

```
%ORACLE_HOME%\DATABASE\SNCF%ORACLE_SID%.ora
RMAN-08002: starting full resync of recovery catalog
RMAN-08004: full resync complete
```

The reset database Command

If you ever need to perform an *incomplete recovery* on your database, or recovery to a point in time in the past, the database will be opened with the `resetlogs` option to reset the sequence number of the online redo logs. A new *incarnation*, or version, of the target database information in the recovery catalog must be created with the `reset database` command in RMAN. This must be done, or RMAN will not allow further access to the recovery catalog.

In the situation of point-in-time recovery, the DBA may want to reinstate a prior incarnation of the database. This is done by adding the `to incarnation` *`num`* clause to the `reset database` command. To obtain the value to substitute for num, use the list incarnation of database command and take the value from the column with the "Inc Key" header in the resultant output. If you have registered your database, and that registration is current with the current control file, you will not need to reset your database. If this discussion seems difficult to understand, you might want to review it after you read Chapter 15 and learn about the `resetlogs` option that is used when opening a database after incomplete recovery.

The following code block displays what will happen if you try to reset your database when the incarnation is already registered:

```
RMAN> RESET DATABASE;
RMAN-03022: compiling command: reset
RMAN-03023: executing command: reset
RMAN-03026: error recovery releasing channel resources
RMAN-00569: ========error message stack follows==========
RMAN-03006: non-retryable error occurred during execution of command
RMAN-07004: unhandled exception during command execution on channel
RMAN-10032: unhandled exception during execution of job step 1:
RMAN-20009: database incarnation already registered
```

The following code block demonstrates how to revert to a prior incarnation of your database and how to use the `list incarnation of database` command:

```
RMAN> LIST INCARNATION OF DATABASE;
RMAN-03022: compiling command: list
RMAN-06240: List of Database Incarnations
RMAN-06241: DB Key Inc Key DB Name DB ID  CUR Reset SCN Reset Time
RMAN-06242: ------ ------- ------- ------ --- --------- ----------
RMAN-06243: 1      2       Jason   158474 YES 1         19-MAR-99
RMAN-06244: 1      12      Jason   158474 NO  2093      12-MAR-99
RMAN> RESET DATABASE TO INCARNATION 12;
```

The resync catalog Command

The recovery catalog is not updated when a log switch occurs, when a log file is archived, or when datafiles or redo logs are added. Thus, the `resync catalog` command must periodically be executed to keep the recovery catalog in line with the production database. This command is executed automatically when a database is registered and after a backup, recovery, or restoration. You may want to set up a job that automatically executes at defined intervals to perform resynchronization. The default is for the recovery catalog to `resync` against the current control file.

```
RMAN> RESYNC CATALOG;
RMAN-03022: compiling command: resync
RMAN-03023: executing command: resync
RMAN-08002: started full resync of recovery catalog
RMAN-08004: full resync complete
```

Alternatively, a backup control file may be named for the process. The following code block shows the appropriate command:

```
RMAN> RESYNC CATALOG
  > FROM CONTROLFILECOPY 'D:\orant\database\jsc01.ctl';
```

Exercises

1. Identify the use of the `register database` command. What purpose does it serve?
2. Identify the use of the `reset database` command. What is a database incarnation? What command can be used to determine incarnations on your database?
3. What is the `resync database` command used for? This command's activities are performed during the activity of which other command?

Maintaining the Recovery Catalog

You will learn how to maintain your recovery catalog in this lesson. There are many commands used for recovery catalog maintenance because there are many areas of the recovery catalog to maintain. These commands include `change` and `catalog`. Another set of commands are required for communication between RMAN and the operating system. Lines of communication of this sort are referred to as *channels* in Oracle.

The allocate channel and release channel Commands

These commands are used in conjunction with all major backup, restore, and recovery operations to allow communication between RMAN and the operating system for the purpose of manipulating files. The `allocate channel` *`channel_name`* command opens the line of communication, while the `release channel` *`channel_name`* command closes it.

A channel can be named by adding a name in place of *`channel_name`*. The channel can be allocated with specific purposes in mind, such as with the `for delete` clause to delete files. Channels with specific resources in the file system can also be opened, either by name with the name `"`*`resource_name`*`"` clause or by type with the `type disk` clause. Parameters for allocating the channel and the connect string for doing so can also be identified as part of the `allocate channel` command. Only one option is allowed for the `release channel` command—the name of the channel. Some examples of the use of these commands are listed in the following code block:

```
RMAN> ALLOCATE CHANNEL my_channel FOR DELETE TYPE DISK;
RMAN> ALLOCATE CHANNEL channel1 NAME "BKPTAPE:TAPE1";
RMAN> ALLOCATE CHANNEL c1 TYPE DISK;
```

The `release channel` command is used as follows:

```
RMAN> RELEASE CHANNEL channel1;
```

The change Command

The `change` command alters the availability status of a specified backup item. For backups, the `backuppiece` keyword is used. For archived redo logs, the `archivelog` keyword is used. For an image copy, the `datafilecopy` keyword is used. For a control file backup, the `controlfilecopy` keyword is used. The availability statuses that can be specified are `delete`, `unavailable`, `available`, and `uncatalog`.

To delete a backup object, the DBA must first issue the `allocate channel` command, because the `change` command will issue a signal to the operating system to tell it to delete the backup file. Marking a backup object as `unavailable` identifies the backups that are missing or offsite, and that are therefore not allowed for use in a recovery or restoration operation. Marking the object `available` means it has been found or is onsite and available again. The `uncatalog` option removes the backup permanently from the control file if it has been deleted from your database manually or accidentally. Both the target and the recovery catalog must be defined for this operation to work. The following code block demonstrates deleting a backup object:

```
RMAN> ALLOCATE CHANNEL channel1 FOR DELETE TYPE DISK;
RMAN> CHANGE CONTROLFILECOPY
    > '/oracle/home/bkp/orgdb01bkp.ctl' DELETE;
RMAN> RELEASE CHANNEL channel1;
```

The catalog Command

A datafile image copy, backup control file, or archived redo log taken using methods other than RMAN can be used by RMAN if it is identified to the recovery catalog with the `catalog` command. Only files that are part of the database can be part of the recovery catalog for that database. Only Oracle8 files can be cataloged, and both the target database and the recovery catalog must be defined for this operation to work. The `backuppiece` keyword is used for backups, the `archivelog` keyword for archived redo logs, the `datafilecopy` keyword for image copies, and the `controlfilecopy` keyword for a control file backup. The following code block contains an example of the use of `catalog`:

```
RMAN> CATALOG CONTROLFILECOPY '/oracle/home/bkp/orgdb01bkp.ctl';
```

Exercises

1. Identify the commands used for the maintenance of the recovery catalog.
2. Which command must be issued in conjunction with the `change...delete` command?

Generating Reports and Lists

Another series of commands available in RMAN includes the commands used to define reports. Reports identify the database files that require backup. In addition, reports may help to identify which components of the database have not been backed up recently, and also to identify the backups that are no longer necessary for database recovery. Reports are generated with the `report` command. The following code block illustrates use of the `report` command:

```
RMAN> REPORT NEED BACKUP INCREMENTAL 5 DATABASE;
RMAN> REPORT NEED BACKUP DAYS 3 DATABASE;
RMAN> REPORT NEED BACKUP DAYS 2 DATABASE;
RMAN> REPORT OBSOLETE REDUNDANCY 3;
RMAN> REPORT UNRECOVERABLE DATABASE;
```

Options for Report Generation

There are several common options for report generation. Their use and functionality is given in the following list. These points refer back to the commands you just saw in the previous code listing.

- **need backup** Tells RMAN to list all datafiles that are in need of a backup. The backup needed can be defined with three keywords. The `incremental` *num* keyword is for datafiles that require *num* or more incremental backups to be restored to the current state. The `days` *num* keyword identifies datafiles that have not been backed up in any way for *num* or more days. The `redundancy` *num* keyword identifies datafiles that require *num* backups to fulfill a minimum *num* number of redundancy.

- **`obsolete`** Identifies backups that are no longer necessary.
- **`unrecoverable`** Identifies the datafiles in the database that are not recoverable with backups currently available.

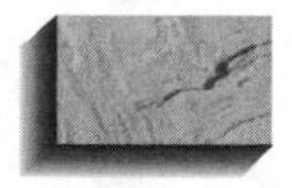

TIP
You will usually need to give Oracle an idea of the scope of your report by adding the `database` or `tablespace` keyword to the `report` command.

Lists provide a complementary function of showing the available backups for specified datafiles, available copies for certain datafiles, and available backup sets or image copies for datafiles belonging to a specified list of tablespaces. Lists also provide information about backup sets of archived redo logs and incarnations of the database. Lists are created with the `list` command. The clauses available are `copy of` *name*, `backupset of` *name*, and `incarnation of database` *dbname*, where *name* is the name of a datafile or tablespace, and *dbname* is the name of the database. Some example uses of the `list` command appear in the following code block:

```
RMAN> LIST COPY OF TABLESPACE DATA01;
RMAN> LIST COPY OF DATAFILE '/oracle/home/dbf/data01.dbf';
RMAN> LIST BACKUPSET OF SYSTEM;
RMAN> LIST INCARNATION OF DATABASE orgdb01;
```

Exercises

1. What is the `report` command, and what are its uses? What are its options?
2. What is the `list` command and what are its uses? What are its options?

Creating, Storing, and Running RMAN Scripts

RMAN backup, restore, and recovery activities are performed via `run` commands. To execute most `run` commands, the DBA must first allocate a channel. This step establishes a connection between RMAN and the operating system so that RMAN can create operating system files for backups and copies, or retrieve files for restores and recoveries.

As mentioned earlier in the chapter, channels can be allocated by type or by name. The syntax is `allocate channel` *`channel_name`*, where *`channel_name`* is a name the DBA assigns to the channel to use in referring to it later. If a channel is allocated by type, such as with the `type disk` clause, then a specific device shouldn't be named by the DBA. Alternatively, if the DBA allocates a channel with a specific device by name, such as with the `name 'device_name'` clause, then the `type` clause shouldn't be used. When `name` `'`*`device_name`*`'` is used, an additional option called parms can be specified to allow port-specific parameters to be defined to allocate the channel.

To operate a `run` command in parallel, the DBA must allocate a channel for each process working on the `run` command. An example for `allocate channel` is shown next:

```
RMAN> RUN { ALLOCATE CHANNEL my_channel TYPE DISK }
```

Two related commands for channel allocation are `release channel` and `setlimit channel`. A channel can be released after the `backup, copy, restore`, or `recover` operation is complete. The syntax is straightforward, requiring only the specification of a *`channel_name`*. The `setlimit channel` *`channel_name`* command allows the DBA to set certain options on the activity of the channel. The parameters include the size of each backup piece with `kbytes` *`num`*, the number of blocks read per second by `backup or copy commands with readrate` *`num`*, and the number of files that can be open at one time by the channel with `maxopenfiles` *`num`*. Examples of both statements appear in the following code block:

```
RMAN> RUN { SETLIMIT CHANNEL my_channel
    >  KBYTES 2048 READRATE 100 MAXOPENFILES 50 }
RMAN> RUN { RELEASE CHANNEL my_channel }
```

Creating Scripts

Scripts are created in RMAN using the `create script` command. Once created, the script is an object stored in the recovery catalog, and it will be backed up as part of the recovery catalog. The following code block shows a `create script` command and an associated script. The example shows a full backup. All blocks in the datafiles, except for those never used by an Oracle object to store data, will be stored in this backup. Note in the last line that the `sql` keyword can be used to denote a SQL statement you would like RMAN to process as part of the script:

```
RMAN> CREATE SCRIPT daily_backup {
    >   ALLOCATE CHANNEL channel1 TYPE DISK;
    >   BACKUP FULL (DATABASE 'orgdb01');
    >   RELEASE CHANNEL channel1;
    >   SQL 'alter system archive log current'; }
```

Running Scripts

The run command can be used to execute scripts you create. RMAN can execute the script in batch using run commands. It can be executed with the run command using the execute script command. To alter the commands in the script, the replace script command can be used. Deleting and printing scripts is possible with the delete script and print script commands, respectively. Examples of these statements appear in the following code block:

```
RMAN> RUN { PRINT SCRIPT daily_backup }
RMAN> RUN { EXECUTE SCRIPT daily_backup }
RMAN> RUN { REPLACE SCRIPT daily_backup WITH daily_backup_new }
RMAN> RUN { DELETE SCRIPT daily_backup }
```

Attributes for the entirety of a run command can also be set using the set command. The attributes that can be defined include three clauses. The maxcorrupt *num* option defines a maximum number of corrupted blocks allowed in a datafile or list of datafiles extracted in a backup or copy command before RMAN terminates the run command. The newname *name* option can be used to change the name of the datafile being restored or switched. The archivelog destination *path* option changes the location where RMAN will look for restored redo log archives from the location specified in LOG_ARCHIVE_DEST to the location specified for *path*. The following code block illustrates the use of the set command:

```
RMAN> RUN { SET MAXCORRUPT 0;
    >  SET ARCHIVELOG DESTINATION '/DISK1/oracle/home/arch/alt';
    > ... }
```

Exercises

1. What statement is used to set up lines of communication between RMAN and the operating system? What statement is used to close that line of communication? What statement defines certain features of that line of communication?
2. What statement defines an object that can be executed to process backup and recovery operations? How is the object modified and eliminated? Where is that object stored?
3. What statement defines options used throughout the run command?

Physical Backups Using Recovery Manager

In this section, you will cover the following points on physical backups using Recovery Manager:

- Identifying types of RMAN backups
- Describing backup concepts using RMAN
- Performing incremental and cumulative backups
- Troubleshooting backup problems
- Viewing information from the data dictionary

Now you will focus on the practical usage of RMAN for handling backup processing, and there are a set of different areas this section will cover. You will learn how to identify different types of RMAN backups and how to describe different backup concepts using RMAN. You will also learn to perform incremental and cumulative backups of your data in datafiles at the block level. This is a new feature in Oracle8. Finally, you will learn how to troubleshoot backup problems, and where to look for information about your RMAN backups in the data dictionary.

Identifying Types of RMAN Backups

RMAN supports a set of commands that perform its core functionality—`backup`, `restore`, and `recover` operations. The `backup`, `restore`, and `recover` commands can be used whenever the production database needs any of these operations performed, either with the use of the `run` command, which executes them immediately, or through the creation of a script. For your purposes here, you will learn how to use RMAN for backing up a database. Chapters 14 and 15 will cover the use of RMAN for `restore` and `recover` operations.

Database backup and recovery operations may also run in parallel. RMAN allows backup and recovery operations to run in parallel internally to improve backup and recovery performance by running multiple sessions that have the ability to communicate with one another. Parallelism is when multiple processes, sessions, or users all perform a portion of a larger job at the same time to speed performance. Parallelism is used for the execution of only one command at a time in RMAN. In other words, two commands (for example, a `backup` on one part of the database and a `recover` on another part) cannot be run in parallel, but a `backup` operation can run in parallel, followed by a `recover` operation running in parallel.

Using Backup Sets

There are two basic types of backups supported by RMAN. The first is called *backup sets*, of which there are two types: *archivelog backup sets* and *datafile backup sets*. Each type of backup set consists either of datafiles for database recovery or archived redo logs for recovery, but not both. Usually backup sets can be written to offline storage, such as tape, or online storage, such as a backup disk. You can develop or purchase a backup management system whereby backup sets are placed on disk and copied to tape periodically, to improve recovery time in certain situations by eliminating the time-consuming step of retrieving backup sets from tape. RMAN also manages the segmented movement of backup sets from disk to tape, and vice versa, during backup and recovery. This process is called *staging*.

NOTE
The rest of the discussion focuses mainly on datafile backup sets because the features RMAN offers in conjunction with datafile backup sets are more complex than those offered for archivelog backup sets.

Datafile backup sets have several features. The first is a user-specified parameter that limits the number of datafiles backed up at the same time to the same backup set. Moderating this activity allows the DBA to strike a good balance between backing up datafile information to tape efficiently, without causing undue burden on a particular datafile and thereby limiting online performance. The datafile backup set can be created from a production datafile or from a backup datafile. Full backups of datafiles, as well as incremental backups of datafiles where only the changed blocks are saved, are both supported with RMAN. In either case, RMAN will never store empty blocks from datafiles in the backup set. More information about incremental and full backups using RMAN will be covered shortly.

Backup sets can also be multiplexed. Multiplexed backup sets contain data from many datafiles stored together. Recall that the server process reads data from datafiles into the buffer cache for use in user SQL statements. The server process also retrieves data blocks for RMAN to use in creating backup sets. Since multiple datafiles and tablespaces can be accessed at the same time by one server process, the server process can retrieve blocks from one datafile when the datafile is less active, and then switch to another datafile when online processing activity on the first one picks up. The data will then be ported into the backup set in a nonsequential manner, as illustrated in Figure 13-2, which can keep the stream of

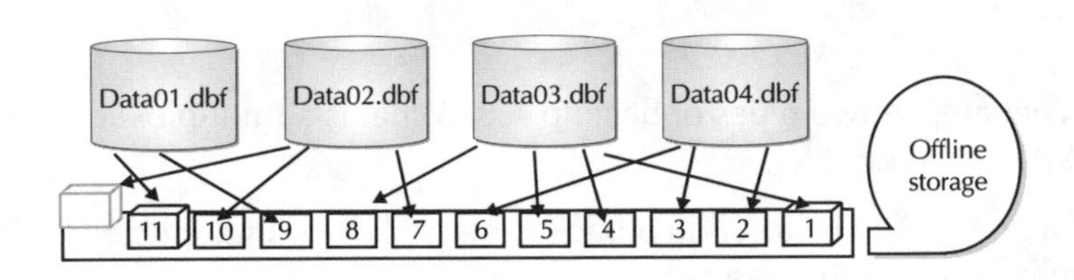

FIGURE 13-2. *Backup set streaming*

data flowing smoothly from the production database onto offline storage. The only impediment to a smooth backup in this scenario is the need to change the tape, which is still the responsibility of the DBA or systems administrator. Control files can be included in a datafile backup set; however, the control file information will not be multiplexed with datafile information.

Once the backup set is completed, each component file of a backup set is called a *piece*. When RMAN creates the backup set out of datafiles or archived redo logs, it produces a single file of sequentially stored blocks from all datafiles or archive logs stored in the backup set for each tape volume used in the backup. If multiplexing is used, the piece will contain blocks from multiple datafiles with each file stored in nonsequential order. In order to recover a database, the necessary datafiles must first be restored from pieces of the backup set. Datafile information can be distributed to different pieces on different tapes explicitly by the DBA or automatically by RMAN.

Making Image Copies

The second type of backup strategy RMAN supports is file *image copies*. RMAN also supports the backup of individual datafiles in the database by creating image copies of these files. An image copy cannot be placed on offline storage, but it can be made to disk. Unlike datafiles in backup sets, image-copy datafiles needn't be restored before they are used in database recovery.

Using Tags

RMAN allows the DBA to define a special name to be used in conjunction with an image copy or a backup set. This name is called a *tag*. The tag may be up to 30 characters in length and has similar naming restrictions to other database objects. The tag can then be used in conjunction with restoring the backup set or image copy. Multiple backup objects can have the same tag. If a tag is specified for use in recovery, and more than one object corresponds to that tag, then the most recent object that is fit to use for the recovery will be the one RMAN uses.

Exercises

1. What are the two types of backup sets? What is a multiplexed backup set? What is a piece?
2. If a control file is stored in a backup set, will it be multiplexed? What is an image copy? What is a tag?

Describing Backup Concepts Using RMAN

Backups for the database are created with the `backup` command. This command produces one or more backup sets into which backup copies of datafiles, archived redo logs, or control files may be placed. Password files and `initsid.ora` files are backed up separately. The number of backup sets created depends on the number of files backed up, the number of tapes required for the backup, the parallelism of the backup, and other factors. The parallelism of a backup depends on the number of channels allocated to the backup; several backup sets will be the result of multiple channeled backups.

Types of Backups

There are several different types of backups you can take using RMAN. Some correspond to types of backups available in Oracle before RMAN was introduced, such as the backup types presented in Chapter 12. Others are new to RMAN. With RMAN, you can take backups of all or selected datafiles, the control file, and all or selected archived redo logs. The first two types of backups are open and closed backups. A closed backup is one taken while Oracle is offline. With RMAN, the primary database must be mounted but not open, and the recovery catalog must be open. For open database backups, RMAN does not require you to use the `alter tablespace [begin|end] backup` statement. Instead, RMAN has its own way of taking online backups that creates less online redo log information during the backup. Datafile backup sets can consist of either full or incremental backups. A full backup of a datafile consists of all blocks in a datafile, while an incremental backup of a datafile consists only of the datafile's blocks that changed since the last backup was taken. Thus, the DBA can reduce both the time it takes to obtain a backup of the database and the amount of storage that the backup will take. The DBA also has the option of taking cumulative backups, which will consolidate the information stored in several incremental backups into one cumulative incremental backup of all changes made since the last full backup.

Multiple-level incremental backup strategies are also supported. Each level of incremental backup will capture data changes made according to specified time intervals. RMAN running in GUI mode has four levels of multiple-level incremental backup strategy, numbered 1 through 4. Although a level-0 incremental backup also exists, it is logically similar to a full database backup. RMAN in line mode offers eight levels of incremental backup, which simply extends to a higher granularity than Backup Manager. Level 0 is a full backup of the datafile, level 1 is a monthly incremental, level 2 is a weekly incremental, level 3 is a daily incremental, and so on. The incremental backup strategy a DBA chooses to implement can take into account these different levels. Consider the following backup strategy. The baseline level-0 backup is made, followed by level-1 backups once a month, level-2 backups once a week, and level-3 backups once a day. Recovery of a datafile then consists of applying the most recent level-0 backup, then any level-1 backups occurring since then. The next step is to apply all level-2 backups made since the most recent level-1 backup, followed by all level-3 backups made since the most recent level-2 backup. This process continues until the supply of backups made is exhausted, at which point archived redo information taken after the most recent backup can be applied for full recovery to the point of failure.

BACKUP Command Syntax

The general syntax of the `backup` command consists of two parts, options and scope, and it looks like `backup` *`options`* `(`*`scope`*`)`. The `backup` options that can be specified include `full, incremental level` *`num`*, `tag, cumulative, skip, parms, filesperset`, and `maxcorrupt`. The `backup` scope can be `database, tablespace, datafile, archivelog, controlfilecopy`, and `current controlfile`. The following code block illustrates an example backup:

```
RMAN> RUN { ALLOCATE CHANNEL bkp_chan NAME 'tape_reel_1';
    >  BACKUP FULL FILESPERSET 5 SKIP OFFLINE
    >  ( DATABASE FORMAT 'bkp_full_orgdb01.%s.%p' );
    >  RELEASE CHANNEL bkp_chan; }
```

In this example, the DBA wants to create a full backup of the database. Remember that "full" in this context means that the entire datafile, not just the changed blocks, will be backed up. The fact that the full database is backed up is specified with the `database` clause. The DBA explicitly defines the number of datafiles to multiplex into each backup set with the `filesperset` parameter and defines a naming convention for the `backup` pieces in the backup command with the `format` option. Offline datafiles for the database will be skipped in the backup.

SPECIFYING OPTIONS The clauses that can be specified as *options* for the `backup` statement include the following:

- **`full`** Specifies a full backup, which is similar to an incremental level-0 backup, in which the full datafile will be copied to the backup set. The main difference is that a full backup will save every block in a datafile (except for datafile blocks that have never been used), while an incremental level-0 backup will skip empty blocks.
- **`incremental level`** ***`num`*** Specifies a level 0–4 backup, in which only the blocks changed since the last full backup will be taken. There must be an associated level-0 backup for the database with `available` status in the recovery catalog in order to define the baseline for the incremental.
- **`tag`** ***`name`*** Gives a name to the backup set for identification later. It cannot be a reserved word and is usually a meaningful identifier.
- **`cumulative`** Specifies that this incremental backup will accumulate all changes recorded in peer- or lesser-level incremental backups since the last level-0 full backup.
- **`nochecksum`** Specifies that no block checksum will be used in this backup to detect block corruption. It should only be used in conjunction with the `DB_BLOCK_CHECKSUM` initialization parameter being TRUE for the instance.
- **`filesperset`** ***`num`*** Defines the number of datafiles that can be multiplexed into individual backup sets.
- **`maxcorrupt`** ***`num`*** Defines the maximum number of corrupt data blocks that will be backed up before the process fails.
- **`skip`** ***`option`*** Defines datafile classes that will be skipped. Three options are available: `offline,` `readonly`, and `inaccessible.`
- **`channel`** ***`name`*** Names the channel that should be used when creating backup sets for this process.
- **`delete input`** Deletes input files after creating backup sets for them. Usable only when backing up archived redo logs.

SPECIFYING SCOPE The clauses available for defining the *scope* of the backup are the following:

- **`database`** Backs up all datafiles and the control file.
- **`tablespace`** ***`name`*** Backs up all datafiles for named tablespaces.

- **datafile** Backs up all datafiles named by name or by datafile number. If named, the name must be a datafile named in the current control file.
- **datafile copy** Backs up all datafiles named by name or by datafile number. If named, the name must not be a datafile named in the current control file. This option simply makes another copy of backup datafiles, minimizing your dependence on only one backup.
- **archivelog** Backs up archived redo logs according to a filename pattern, sequence range, or date/time range.
- **include current controlfile** Backs up the current control file.
- **controlfilecopy** Backs up a backup control file.
- **backupset** Backs up the primary key of a backup set on disk.
- **format** Identifies the file-naming format RMAN should use when naming backup files. It can contain text strings or expressions. Valid expressions are `%p` for backup piece number, `%s` for backup set number, and `%d` or `%n` for target database name.

copy Command Syntax

RMAN allows the DBA to create backup copies of the datafiles on the database. These copies are called image copies, and they are created with the `copy` command. The image copy can only be put onto a disk. Image copies can be made of current datafiles, datafile copies made using any method, archived redo logs, and the current or backup control file. Once created, the image copy is immediately usable for a recovery without executing a `restore` command. RMAN also can interact with image copies of datafiles made without its assistance, such as in the case of mirrored datafiles on multiple disks used to provide highly fault-tolerant databases. However, these copies must be catalogued.

General syntax for the `copy` command is `copy` *`file`* `to` *`location`*. The `allocate channel` command must precede the `copy` command, and the level of parallelism that can be used with the `copy` command relates directly to the number of channels allocated to the `copy`. Only full copies of datafiles are permitted with the `copy` command. An example of the `copy` command appears in the following code block. In this example, one copy of a single datafile is made.

```
RMAN> RUN { ALLOCATE CHANNEL my_channel TYPE DISK;
    >  COPY DATAFILE '/DISK1/oracle/home/dbs/data01.dbf'
    >  TO '/DISK2/oracle/home/bkp/data01bkp.dbf';
    >  RELEASE CHANNEL my_channel; }
```

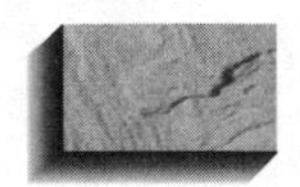

TIP
The `copy` command only allows channels to be allocated that specify `type disk`. All other `allocate channel` commands will be ignored for the `copy` command.

SPECIFYING FILE Several clauses are available for use in place of `file`. These clauses are as follows:

- **`datafile`** Copies the current datafile.
- **`datafilecopy` *`name`*** Copies an existing copy of the datafile.
- **`archivelog` *`name`*** Copies a named archived redo log.
- **`current controlfile`** Copies the current control file. Alternatively, the `current` keyword can be dropped to copy an existing control file copy, either by name or tag.

SPECIFYING LOCATION The filename and path where the image copy will be placed is usually specified by location. Alternately, a couple of clauses are available for use as part of *location*. These clauses are listed here:

- **`tag` *`name`*** The name of a tag assigned to the image copy.
- **`level 0`** Treat this datafile copy as a level-0 backup. Subsequent incremental backups will use this image copy as a baseline.

TIP
RMAN does not skip blocks in `copy` operations as it does in incremental backups. The `copy` operation will also use checksums to detect block corruption. If you make a datafile copy using operating system commands, it is a valid copy that is usable by RMAN, but you will need to catalog it first.

Exercises

1. What command is used to perform backups? What are two categories of options or clauses that can be specified with this command? What are the categories based on? What are some of the clauses in each?

2. What does `full` clause mean? What does `incremental level` clause mean?
3. What command is used to create duplicates of database files? What is the only option allowed in the channel allocation statement when this command is issued?
4. What is the difference between a full and incremental backup? What is a multiple-level backup? Does Oracle8 support point-in-time tablespace recovery? Explain.

Performing Incremental and Cumulative Backups

In this lesson, you'll cover the mechanics of performing backups using RMAN. Although the title indicates that incremental and cumulative backups are the only topics, the lesson will also discuss using RMAN for taking full backups. This is done to show you the mechanics of taking all types of backups with this tool, so that you will be able to recognize the differences when taking OCP Exam 3. The following code block demonstrates an RMAN script that will make a full datafile backup set:

```
RMAN> RUN { ALLOCATE CHANNEL BKP1 TYPE DISK;
    >       BACKUP FULL
    >        FORMAT 'D:\ORANT\BACKUP\DF_%S%P.%D'
    >       ( DATABASE FILESPERSET = 5
    >          INCLUDE CURRENT CONTROLFILE ); }
```

Or, for archived log backup sets, you might use a script similar to the following:

```
RMAN> RUN { ALLOCATE CHANNEL BKP1 TYPE DISK;
    >       BACKUP FILESPERSET = 5
    >        FORMAT 'D:\ORANT\BACKUP\LOG_%S%P.%D'
    >       ( ARCHIVELOG FROM LOGSEQ=19 UNTIL LOGSEQ=25
    >          THREAD=1 DELETE INPUT ); }
```

Your backup strategy must start with a level-0 or full backup as a benchmark for applying incremental backups taken later. There is one major difference between an incremental level-0 backup and a full backup. The full backup saves all blocks in a datafile, while the level-0 incremental saves only blocks with data in them. So, although they are logically the same and you can use either as your baseline backup in a database recovery, full backups and incremental level-0 backups are physically different because one contains empty blocks and the other does not. There is no reason to take both full and incremental level-0 backups, and there is obviously no reason to make your backups larger than they need to be by backing up empty blocks.

Incremental and Cumulative Backups

The next example is of an incremental backup. Although the preceding code block displays a backup containing the `incremental` keyword, the backup that is actually taken is logically close in form and content to a full backup. Incremental level-1 backups will only save blocks that have changed since the last level-0 or full backup was run. A level-2 backup will save only those blocks that have changed since the last level-0 and level-1 backup, and so on. Incremental backups can be processed using scripts similar to the one in the following code block:

```
RMAN> RUN { ALLOCATE CHANNEL BKP1 TYPE DISK;
    >       BACKUP INCREMENTAL LEVEL = 1
    >        FORMAT 'D:\ORANT\BACKUP\DF_%S%P.%D'
    >       ( DATABASE FILESPERSET = 5
    >          INCLUDE CURRENT CONTROLFILE ); }
```

The first time you run this script, RMAN will save all data blocks that have changed in datafiles since the last full or incremental level-0 backup. If no full or incremental level-0 backups are run in between, the next time you run the level-1 backup script, RMAN will only save the data blocks that have changed since the last time you ran the level-1 script. The preceding script may also be considered a cumulative backup, because it will store blocks that may have been backed up already in incremental level-2 or higher backups.

Figure 13-3 demonstrates a backup strategy mapped out over a 2-week period. Level-0 backups are taken every other Saturday to provide the benchmark for cumulative and incremental backups taken in the next cycle. Level-1 backups are taken about every 4 days to roll up all changes saved in incremental backups. Level-2 backups are taken every night that a cumulative or complete backup is not taken, to save changes made that day. The following script shows a level-2 backup script that, if used, would be the lowest level of incremental backup:

```
RMAN> RUN { ALLOCATE CHANNEL BKP1 TYPE DISK;
    >       BACKUP INCREMENTAL LEVEL = 2
    >        FORMAT 'D:\ORANT\BACKUP\DF_%S%P.%D'
    >       ( DATABASE FILESPERSET = 5
    >          INCLUDE CURRENT CONTROLFILE ); }
```

Exercises

1. Using the framework outlined in this lesson, describe the data that will be backed up in a level-3 backup. Given the backup strategy in Figure 13-3, what purpose might level-3 backups serve?

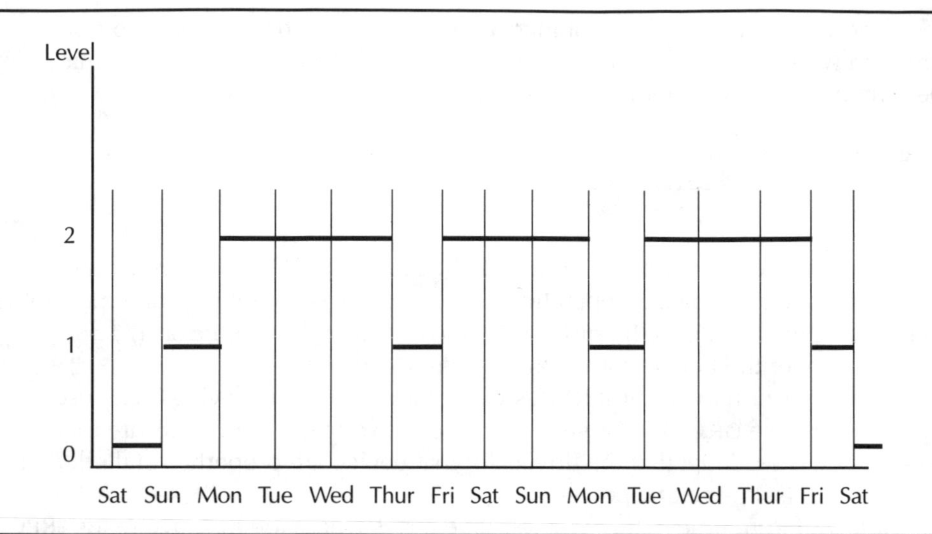

FIGURE 13-3. *A backup strategy using RMAN*

2. Consider an Oracle database in your organization that does not currently use RMAN. How might you apply the use of RMAN to provide a backup strategy for your database?

Troubleshooting Backup Problems

In the course of running your database backups using RMAN, you may find yourself trying to figure out problems that may arise. For example, a backup may seem to take a long time, leaving you wondering if something may have gone wrong. To observe the backup in progress, use the V$SESSION_LONGOPS dynamic performance view. This view has several columns, but in terms of job progress, the two most important columns are SOFAR and TOTALWORK. The values in these two columns, where the value in the COMPNAM column is equal to "DBMS_BACKUP_RESTORE," can be used to calculate the percentage of work completed in the backup process. Repeated execution of the statement in the following code block can assist in this task:

```
SVRMGR> select round(sofar/totalwork*100,2) as pct_complete
     > from v$session_longops
     > where compnam = 'dbms_backup_restore';
```

If the value returned does not increase steadily, then there is some sort of problem with waits on the database. Query your V$SESSION_WAIT dynamic performance view to determine the source of the wait event:

```
SVRMGR> select event, p1test, seconds_in_wait
     > from v$session_wait
     > where wait_time = 0;
```

If there is no output from the query on V$SESSION_WAIT, you may be observing a delay in backup operation as the result of some other problem. Another place you can check is in the `sbtio.log` log file found in the `rdbms/log` directory under the Oracle software home directory.

Another error may occur if RMAN cannot identify a tape device it can use, as evidenced by the `ORA-07004` error. In this case, you will need to ensure that your tape device is working, that the drivers for that device are properly installed, and that the unit itself is getting power.

Finally, if from time to time you observe errors where the message reads "RPC call failed to start on channel . . .," don't worry. These errors are red herrings and will most likely disappear. They simply indicate that your primary database being backed up is running slow.

Exercises

1. What are some problems you might encounter when using RMAN? With "RPC call failed to start on channel" errors, what is the appropriate course of action?
2. What dynamic performance views can help you identify the progress of your RMAN backup, and what view helps to determine wait events?

Viewing Information from the Data Dictionary

Several dynamic performance views exist in the data dictionary to support RMAN, some of which are new. Both the old and new dictionary views available are listed here:

- **V$ARCHIVED_LOG** Displays name and information in the control file about archived redo logs
- **V$BACKUP_CORRUPTION** Displays information in the control file about corrupt datafile backups
- **V$BACKUP_DATAFILE** Offers information from the control file about backup datafiles and control files

- **V$BACKUP_DEVICE** Offers operating-system-specific information about supported third-party vendors for RMAN in Oracle8
- **V$BACKUP_REDOLOG** Displays information about archived redo logs in backup sets
- **V$BACKUP_SET** Displays information from the control file about all backup sets
- **V$BACKUP_PIECE** Displays information from the control file about all pieces in all backup sets
- **V$DATAFILE** Lists information about datafiles in the Oracle8 database
- **V$DATAFILE_HEADER** Lists information about datafile headers in the Oracle8 database

Exercises

1. Which of the V$ performance views are used to store information about backup sets?
2. Which of the V$ performance views are used to store information about datafiles?
3. Which of the V$ performance views are used to store information about redo logs?

Chapter Summary

Three main topics concerning the use of Recovery Manager were the subject of this chapter. The topics were: an overview of Recovery Manager (RMAN), recovery catalog maintenance, and physical backups using RMAN. These Oracle backup and recovery concepts comprise 16 percent of OCP Exam 3 test content.

The first topic was an overview of using RMAN. You learned how to determine when to use RMAN, and what different methods you have available for doing so. Both RMAN for the command line and for batch processing were shown. Some explanation of Backup Manager, a GUI tool that interfaces with RMAN, was offered as well. You also learned about the advantages RMAN offers when running both with and without a recovery catalog. You learned what a recovery catalog is and how to create one, as well. This first section concluded with an explanation of how to run RMAN and how to connect to the target and recovery catalog databases.

The next section covered maintaining your recovery catalog. The use of RMAN to `register`, `reset`, and `resync` your recovery catalog with data stored in the control file of your target database was presented. You also learned how to maintain the recovery catalog using the `change` and `catalog` commands. The use of RMAN reports and lists to determine the recoverability of the database was also described. You also learned how to create and execute RMAN scripts to perform backup and recovery operations

The last section in this chapter explained how to take backups with RMAN. The different types of RMAN backups were presented, along with a description of the backup concepts involved in using RMAN. You learned the how-to of performing incremental and cumulative backups using RMAN, and how to troubleshoot backup problems that occur while RMAN is running. Finally, you learned where you could find information about RMAN in your Oracle data dictionary and in dynamic performance views.

Two-Minute Drill

- The new architecture for backup and recovery in Oracle8 consists of Recovery Manager (RMAN) and a recovery catalog.
- Recovery Manager is a utility that allows DBAs to manage all aspects of backup and recovery using an Oracle-supported tool.
- A recovery catalog runs on a database other than the production database containing all your user data, and it tracks all backup and archived redo logs produced for the production database.
- There are some enhancements to the control file, which is much larger in Oracle8 to support RMAN. RMAN information is stored for a period of time corresponding to the `CONTROL_FILE_RECORD_KEEP_TIME` initialization parameter.
- RMAN is created with the `catrman.sql` script, found in the `rdbms/admin` directory under the Oracle software home directory.
- RMAN has four sets of commands: recovery catalog maintenance commands, reporting commands, scripting commands, and `run` commands.
- To run RMAN, type `rman` at the OS command prompt. One mandatory option and four optional ones are used:
  - **`target`** **(Mandatory)** Used to identify the production or target database

- **rcvcat** Used to identify the recovery catalog database
- **cmdfile** Used to execute RMAN in `batch` mode with a command script
- **msglog** Used to keep a log of all activity
- **append** Permits RMAN to append information to an old log file for the current RMAN session

- Communication with the operating system is possible in RMAN with the `allocate channel` command.
- Recovery catalog management commands include the following:
  - **register database** Used to register a target database
  - **reset database** Used when the target database is opened and the redo log sequence needs to be reset
  - **resync catalog** Used after log switches in target database
  - **change** Used to alter the control file or other database filenames used
  - **list incarnation** Used to show the current database data version
  - **catalog** Used to identify copies of files made outside of RMAN
- RMAN reporting and listing commands give information about the current database and its recovery status.
- Reports show information about database files and recoverability. One of the reports that can be used is `report need backup` to show the files of the database that need to be backed up. Options for this report `include incremental` *num* to show the files that need num incremental backups to be recovered, and days *num* to show the files that haven't been backed up in *num* days. Another report includes `report unrecoverable` to show files that are not recoverable.
- Lists show information about the backups that are available in the database. Some lists that can be used are `list copy of tablespace`, `list copy of datafile`, `list backupset`, and `list incarnation of database`.
- There are several commands available in RMAN for script creation. They are `create script`, `replace script`, `delete script`, and `print script`.

- The final set of commands in RMAN are `run` commands. These commands handle most of the processing in RMAN, such as execution of scripts, SQL, and backup and recovery operations.
- The `backup` command runs backups. RMAN creates incremental or full copies of files for the entire database, the files of a tablespace, or individual datafiles.
- The backups of files and archived redo logs are placed into collections called backup sets. A backup can contain only archived redo logs or only datafiles and control files.
- Datafiles can be multiplexed into a backup set, meaning that the blocks of datafiles are stored noncontiguously on the sequential offline storage media, such as tape.
- Backup sets are composed of backup pieces. The number of pieces in a backup set depends on the parallelism of the backup, the number of tapes required for the backup, and other factors.
- Oracle8 and RMAN support the incremental backup of datafiles, which store only the blocks of a datafile that have been changed since the last full backup. A full backup is one containing all blocks of datafiles.
- There are four levels of incremental backup available in RMAN GUI mode, as well as a level-0 backup, which is a full backup. RMAN line mode offers eight levels of incremental backup.
- To recover a database component from backup, the component must first be restored.
- The `copy` command will create an image copy of a database file component. This component is immediately usable for recovery.
- The `copy` command only produces image copies to disk, while backup can send database file components directly to tape.
- The `switch` command will substitute a datafile copy for a current file. The switched datafile will then need media recovery.
- The `restore` command will retrieve files from the backup copy and put them where the DBA specifies.
- The `recover` command will conduct media recovery using backups restored in combination with archived redo logs.
- Several old and new dictionary views exist in Oracle8 to support RMAN.

- V$ARCHIVED_LOG displays names and information from the control file about archived redo logs.
- V$BACKUP_CORRUPTION displays information from the control file about corrupt datafile backups.
- V$BACKUP_DATAFILE offers information from the control file about backup datafiles and control files.
- V$BACKUP_DEVICE offers operating-system-specific information about supported third-party vendors for RMAN in Oracle8.
- V$BACKUP_REDOLOG displays information about archived redo logs in backup sets.
- V$BACKUP_SET displays information from the control file about all backup sets.
- V$BACKUP_PIECE displays information from the control file about all pieces in all backup sets.
- V$DATAFILE lists information about datafiles in the Oracle8 database.
- V$DATAFILE_HEADER lists information about datafile headers in the Oracle8 database.

Chapter Questions

1. The `allocate channel` command used in conjunction with `copy` must

A. Name the resource explicitly

B. Use the `disk` clause

C. Use the `for delete` clause

D. Be run after the `copy` is complete

2. Which of the following maintenance operations should the DBA run after adding a datafile?

A. `register database`

B. `reset database`

C. `catalog`

D. `resync catalog`

3. **A full backup consists of which of the following elements?**
   - **A.** All blocks in a datafile except those that never have been used
   - **B.** Changed blocks in a datafile
   - **C.** All datafiles in the database
   - **D.** Changed datafiles in the database
4. **In the absence of the recovery catalog, where can RMAN find most of the information it needs?**
   - **A.** Backup sets
   - **B.** Datafiles
   - **C.** Password file
   - **D.** Control file
5. **The DBA issues the `alter database backup controlfile to '/DISK1/Oracle/home/dbcontrol.ctl'` statement. What can the DBA do to use this control file backup in conjunction with RMAN?**
   - **A.** Issue the `catalog` command.
   - **B.** Copy the file to tape.
   - **C.** Issue the `copy` command.
   - **D.** Nothing, the control file backup can be used as is.
6. **What effect does setting `CONTROL_FILE_RECORD_KEEP_TIME` to 0 have?**
   - **A.** Forces Oracle8 to keep no information for RMAN
   - **B.** Decreases backup and recovery performance
   - **C.** Limits growth of the control file size
   - **D.** Has no effect on control file size
7. **The DBA identifies that the backups necessary for media recovery are on tape. What command should be executed first to perform the recovery?**
   - **A.** `copy`
   - **B.** `switch`

C. `allocate channel`

D. `restore`

8. Once the DBA defines attributes in a `run` command, how long will they be defined?

A. Permanently

B. For the duration of the instance

C. For the duration of the session

D. For the duration of the `run` command

9. By default, how many errors will occur in a `run` command before RMAN terminates?

A. 1

B. 5

C. 25

D. Operating-system specific

10. The DBA finishes an incomplete recovery to a system change number and then opens the database. What recovery catalog maintenance command must be executed?

A. `register database`

B. `reset database`

C. `resync catalog`

D. `change database`

11. Which command can the DBA issue to determine which datafiles in the database are in the most serious need of backup?

A. `report unrecoverable`

B. `report need backup`

C. `list incarnation`

D. `list copy of datafile`

12. Which of the following best describes multiplexing in backup sets?

A. One archive log in one backup set with file blocks stored contiguously

B. Multiple control files in one backup set with file blocks for each stored noncontiguously

C. Multiple datafiles in one backup set with file blocks for each stored noncontiguously

D. One datafile in multiple backup sets with file blocks stored contiguously

Answers to Chapter Questions

1. B. Use the `disk` clause

Explanation The `copy` command can only work in conjunction with the `disk` specification because an image copy can be made only to disk. Review the discussion of the `copy` command. Naming the resource explicitly will not work in situations where the DBA names a tape resource, eliminating choice A. The `for delete` clause is mainly used to allocate a channel to delete a backup, eliminating choice C. The channel must be allocated before issuing the `copy` command, eliminating choice D.

2. D. `resync catalog`

Explanation The catalog must be synchronized with the database every time the control file changes. This includes changes made by the log switch and changes made by adding or removing datafiles or redo logs. Choice A is incorrect because the database need only be registered when RMAN is first run. Choice B is incorrect because the database needs to be reset only when the redo log sequence is reset, as after incomplete recovery. Choice C is incorrect because `catalog` is used to include copies of database components with the recovery catalog if the copy was made using a method other than RMAN.

3. A. All blocks in a datafile except those that never have been used

Explanation Full backup means the full datafile will be backed up, while incremental refers to the backup of only those blocks in a datafile that have changed. Thus, other choices are incorrect. Review the discussion of full and incremental backups.

4. D. Control file

Explanation The control file contains a great deal of information to support RMAN. If the maintenance of the recovery catalog is not possible, the next best thing is to let RMAN use the control file. Review the introduction to RMAN and the recovery catalog.

5. A. Issue the `catalog` command

Explanation To include a backup file in the recovery catalog that has been created using tools other than RMAN, the DBA can issue the `catalog` command. Simply copying the file to tape will not record its existence in the recovery catalog, eliminating choice B. Executing the `copy` command on the current version of the file that the DBA has already made a copy of externally is fine, but does nothing to include the first copy made by the DBA in the recovery catalog. Choice D is simply incorrect.

6. C. Limits growth of the control file size

Explanation The `CONTROL_FILE_RECORD_KEEP_TIME` initialization parameter determines how long certain time-sensitive information will be kept to support RMAN in the control file. If set to 0, Oracle will eliminate this information from the control file as often as necessary to make room for new information, thereby limiting the control file size. Review information about the enhanced Oracle8 control file's support for backup and recovery.

7. C. `allocate channel`

Explanation The first step on almost all `run` commands is to allocate a channel to communicate with the operating system.

8. D. For the duration of the `run` command

Explanation The `set` statements issued during a `run` command are valid for the entire `run` command, but no longer than that.

9. A. 1

Explanation RMAN has low error tolerance. As soon as it encounters an error of any sort, it will terminate. This is default behavior and it can't be changed.

10. B. `reset database`

Explanation Incomplete recovery requires the DBA to recover the database to a point in time in the past. After completing that recovery, the DBA must discard all archived redo logs that contained changes made after that point in time by opening the database with the `resetlogs` option. After opening the database in this way, the recovery catalog must be reset with the `reset database` command in RMAN.

11. A. `report unrecoverable`

Explanation This report will list all datafiles that are not recoverable with the current backups and archived redo information—the files that are in most dire need of backup.

12. C. Multiple datafiles in one backup set with file blocks for each stored noncontiguously

Explanation Multiplexing is when multiple datafiles are stored noncontiguously in a backup set to prevent the backup of any datafile from reducing online performance on that datafile. Choices A and B are incorrect because archived redo logs and control files are not multiplexed in backup sets. Choice D doesn't describe multiplexing either.

CHAPTER 14

Database Failure and Recovery

In this chapter, you will learn about and demonstrate knowledge in the following three areas:

- Types of failure and troubleshooting
- Oracle recovery without archiving
- Oracle recovery with archiving

This chapter presents Oracle's capacity to handle database recovery. The first portion of the chapter focuses on the types of failure that may occur, ways to address them, and the methods at your disposal to identify problems when they occur. The chapter also presents the methods for database recovery when you do not archive your redo logs. You will learn how to perform several variations on database recovery. The chapter then covers how to perform recovery when you do archive your redo logs. Implicit in this discussion is the rationale for why you should almost always archive your redo logs. Approximately 25 percent of the OCP Exam 3 content is presented in this chapter.

Types of Failure and Troubleshooting

In this section, you will cover the following topics related to types of failure and troubleshooting:

- Types of failure in an Oracle database
- Structures for instance and media recovery
- Using the DBVERIFY utility
- Configuring checksum operations
- Using log and trace files to diagnose problems

This first portion of the chapter focuses on the types of failure that may occur, and ways to address them, along with the need for you to communicate effectively in this time of crisis. The architectural components for database recovery available in Oracle are discussed, and you will also learn about methods that can assist you in identifying corruption in your datafiles and redo logs. Finally, you will examine Oracle's logging mechanisms, in an effort to learn how to use them to diagnose and resolve problems.

Types of Failure in an Oracle Database

There are several different scenarios for failure in the Oracle database. These scenarios can be divided into five general categories, three of which will be discussed in this and the next lesson. The five categories include statement failure, user-process failure, instance failure, user error, and media failure. Each of these categories has different implications for DBA intervention in recovering from the situation. Statement failure, user-process failure, and user error are discussed in this lesson.

TIP
It is beyond the scope of OCP exams and this text to discuss the ways you can manage the human aspects of database failure situations. However technically adept you may become with your database administration, there is still the issue of customer service that every DBA must address in making crisis situations more manageable. Depending on how high-stakes your organization's databases are, you might consider taking some training on effective communication as a means to round out your abilities in this area.

Statement Failure

When Oracle cannot process a statement issued by a user, this situation is generally known as *statement failure*. There are several causes for statement failure. First of all, a user may be attempting to issue a statement referencing a table that does not exist, or to which they do not have permission to use. In this case, Oracle will issue the user an error that details both the area of the statement that contained the error and a reference to the Oracle error message code. Other types of statement failure include situations where the statement is flawed, such as when a `select` statement has no from clause, or when the user tries to `insert` data into a table that exceeds his or her quota for doing so. Recovering from this error situation consists of Oracle immediately (and automatically) rolling back any changes made by the statement. The user may have to reissue the statement that failed with the proper syntax or table reference. The DBA may have to alter the user's tablespace quotas or permissions, as well.

User-Process Failure

The failure of a user process requires more intervention from the Oracle server. In some cases, the user may cancel or terminate the statement or process he or she is running with a CTRL-C command from SQL*Plus. Another cause might be if the client PC hangs while connected to Oracle. If a user process terminates, then the process monitor (PMON) background process intervenes, which saves the DBA some time and effort. PMON is there to handle automatic process recovery for the database: when PMON detects the process failure, PMON rolls back the failed process and releases locks on the tables.

User Error

Users occasionally make mistakes. Sometimes they accidentally delete data or drop database objects. This situation tests the limits of your backup and recovery strategy. If the problem is related to data change, the user may be able to recover using the `rollback` command. However, dropped tables or other objects may require DBA intervention and the use of EXPORT, IMPORT, and other backup and recovery strategies. Usually, the DBA will need to recover the entire database to another machine, export the dropped or deleted object data, and restore the object to the appropriate environment. You may see this situation occur quite a bit in development environments where the developers are their own DBAs. You may want to consider informal or formal training (such as this book) for your developers if a situation gets aggravating. To avoid this problem in production, only the DBA should be allowed to create, alter, or drop database objects. By controlling the introduction, change, or removal of database objects in your production system, you reduce the likelihood that users become dependant upon an unrecoverable database object.

Exercises

1. Describe the causes of statement failure. How might statement failure be resolved?
2. Describe the causes of process failure. How might process failure be resolved?
3. Describe the causes of user error. How might user-error problems be resolved?

Structures for Instance and Media Recovery

Instance and media recoveries are the two last types of database failure discussed in this lesson. They are considered the most complex because several things must happen in order for the recovery to be completed. Several concepts, structures, and processes are involved in completing each type of recovery, as well.

Instance Failure

There are many possible causes of instance failure, including problems with the memory of the host system running Oracle, power outages, or background process failures. Although instance failure requires the DBA to restart the database, the actual recovery is handled by Oracle via the system monitor (SMON) background process. After the DBA issues the `startup open` command, SMON engages in the following steps to recover the instance:

1. SMON detects that instance recovery is required because checkpoint sequence numbers in the datafile headers are not synchronized.
2. DBW0 uses redo log information to write both uncommitted and committed data to datafiles. This is called the *roll-forward* process.
3. The database opens.
4. Either Oracle or user processes roll back all uncommitted work in progress at the time the instance failed, depending on who attempts to access the uncommitted data first.
5. After all uncommitted data is rolled back, the datafiles are again synchronized.

It was mentioned in Chapter 7 that Oracle needs to keep certain online redo logs active after LGWR switches to a new one for the purpose of crash recovery. This situation is the crash you were learning about. After you start Oracle, SMON restores the instance to full operational capacity. It may take a while to recover the instance, depending on the transaction volumes on the database at the time of database failure. When instance recovery is complete, the users should be advised to re-enter any transactions not committed at the time of database failure. As the DBA, you may also want to check the ALERT log to see what caused the failure. If the ALERT log contains an `ORA-00600` internal error, listing several numbers in square brackets (`[`), call Oracle Worldwide Support.

TIP
When recovering an instance, Oracle opens after the roll-forward process is complete in order to speed access to the database. Thus, uncommitted transactions may still be rolling back after the database is open and available for users.

Media Failure

Media failure means the loss of access to information on a disk due to data corruption, disk-head hardware failure, other types of I/O hardware failure, or accidental datafile deletion. There are two types of media failure that may occur on the database: temporary and permanent. If data on disk is temporarily unavailable (perhaps because a disk controller card failed), the problem can be corrected easily and quickly with a hardware replacement. If data on disk is permanently unavailable (perhaps because of physical or magnetic damage to the casing in which the disk is stored), the DBA must do two things:

1. The file(s) lost must be restored from backup copies of the database.
2. Any database changes made after the most recent backup must be applied using archived redo log information, if archiving is used.

Your backup and recovery strategy is an insurance policy against problems in the database rendering it unusable. Recovery usually requires a good understanding of both operating system–specific commands for physical file manipulation and of Oracle's recovery mechanisms. The amount of time spent recovering the database depends on four factors:

- **Accessibility of backups** Both the physical location of backups (onsite or offsite) *and* the accessibility of backups on hardware storage media are factors. Disk is the fastest medium; tape is slower.
- **Frequency of backups** More frequent backups mean faster recovery, because fewer archived redo logs need to be applied for the same amount of recovered data.
- **Type of failure** Some types of failure are easier to fix and less time consuming than others. For example, if the database lost one disk drive that contained only a few read-only tablespaces, the DBA would spend less time recovering than if the database lost several disks of volatile data that were backed up infrequently.
- **Type of backups** Physical backups provide better recoverability than logical exports, because archived redo can be applied to handle the changes made after the most recent backup was taken.

What Is Synchronization?

A point was made earlier that SMON will perform instance recovery if it detects that the datafiles are not synchronized. Recall that part of the work done in a checkpoint is to write the SCN to datafile headers and copy data in the buffer cache and log buffer to their respective disk files. This process synchronizes all Oracle files. If the instance crashes, these files will not be synchronized because Oracle did not have the opportunity to synchronize them before the instance failed. SMON will synchronize them for you automatically.

If media failure occurs, you will restore the lost datafiles from an earlier backup, and the headers for those files will have a different sequence number than the undamaged files. You will have to synchronize these datafiles yourself, through the use of archived redo logs. Oracle will not open the database unless all datafiles are synchronized, except where the datafiles that are not synchronized are either offline or part of a read-only tablespace.

Exercises

1. What are the five types of failure that may occur on an Oracle database? How is instance failure detected? How is it resolved?
2. What is the difference between temporary media failure and permanent media failure? How is media failure resolved?
3. What is database synchronization? Why is it so important in detecting and resolving instance failure?

Using the DBVERIFY Utility

Verification of structural integrity of Oracle database files is done with the DBVERIFY utility. DBVERIFY is a utility that verifies the integrity of a datafile backup or production file. It can be used either to verify that a backup is usable, to verify the usability of a production database, or to diagnose a situation where corruption is suspected on a datafile or backup. The rest of this lesson focuses on its use by the DBA.

DBVERIFY Parameters

DBVERIFY is usually run from the operating system's command line, and it is a stand-alone utility. It operates on a datafile or datafiles of a database that is currently offline. As such, it usually runs with good performance. Like other Oracle utilities, it runs from the command line according to the parameters that are identified for it. There are several parameters that can be specified. They are `FILE`, `START`, `END`, `BLOCKSIZE`, `LOGFILE`, `FEEDBACK`, `HELP`, and `PARFILE`:

- **`FILE`** This parameter specifies the name of the datafile that DBVERIFY will analyze. Without this parameter, the utility can do nothing.

- **START** This parameter specifies the start address in the Oracle blocks where DBVERIFY will begin its analysis. If no value for `START` is specified, the utility will assume the start of the file.
- **END** This parameter specifies the address in the Oracle blocks where DBVERIFY will end its analysis. If no value is specified, the utility will assume the end of the file.
- **BLOCKSIZE** This parameter specifies the database block size for the database. It should be specified explicitly for all cases in which the block size for the Oracle database is not 2K (2,048 bytes). The value should be specified in bytes. If the database block size is not 2K, and a value is not specified for this parameter, an error will occur and the run of DBVERIFY will terminate.
- **LOGFILE** This parameter identifies a file to which all output from DBVERIFY will be written. If no filename is specified, then DBVERIFY will write all output to the screen.
- **FEEDBACK** This parameter allows the DBA to use an indicator method built into the utility that indicates the progress made by the utility. The indicator works as follows: An integer value is assigned to the FEEDBACK parameter, which represents the number of pages that must be read of the datafile before DBVERIFY will display a period (.) on the output method—either the terminal or the log file. If `FEEDBACK=0`, then the function is disabled.
- **HELP** When DBVERIFY is run with `HELP=Y`, the utility will print out a help screen containing information about the parameters that can be set for this tool.
- **PARFILE** As with other Oracle utilities, all parameters can be included in a parameter file that is named by the `PARFILE` parameter. This parameter identifies a parameter file for use by the utility in this run.

The DBVERIFY tool is a stand-alone program that, again, should be run from the command line. The name for the command that runs the utility varies from one operating system to the next, but the functionality is the same. If the DBA encounters any errors when running DBVERIFY, it is recommended that the DBA contact Oracle Worldwide Support. On many systems, the utility is referred to on the command line as `dbv`. The following code block demonstrates using this utility from a Unix prompt:

```
$ dbv file=users01.dbf blocksize=4096 logfile=users01.log feedback=0
```

Alternatively, the DBA can execute the utility by using a parameter file. An example of doing so in Windows is as follows:

```
D:\orant> dbverf80 parfile=users01.par
```

The contents of the parameter file are listed here:

```
file=users01.dbf
blocksize=4096
logfile=users01.log
feedback=0
```

Typically, the DBVERIFY utility is only used when the DBA is trying to identify corruption problems with the data in a datafile. Aside from situations where no corruption exists in the datafile, DBVERIFY's output should be interpreted with the assistance of Oracle Worldwide Support. In fact, it is often used under the guidance of Oracle Worldwide Support. However, it, like all other troubleshooting methods identified herein, can be quite useful in resolving database problems.

Exercises

1. Describe the use of DBVERIFY.
2. What parameters can be used in conjunction with DBVERIFY?

Configuring Checksum Operations

Normal redo log operation consists of LGWR writing redo log buffer information to the online redo log. (Archiving redo log information is optional but highly recommended.) One situation that Oracle may encounter in the process of writing redo log information is the corruption of a data block containing redo information within the online redo log. This scenario is highly detrimental to the recoverability of a database, because if it goes undetected, redo block corruption will be propagated silently to the archived redo logs. Only when the archived redo log is used for recovery will Oracle discover that the archived redo information is corrupt. However, by then it is too late—the database has failed and complete recovery is questionable.

For added protection, the DBA can specify redo log checksums to ensure that data block corruption does not occur within archived redo logs. This feature verifies each block by using checksums of values for each data block. If Oracle encounters unexpected values in this operation, Oracle will read the data in the corrupted data block of one online redo log member from another member in the redo log group. Hence, the benefit of multiplexing redo log groups is twofold—Oracle is more likely to obtain good archived redo log information, and it is not likely to have instance failure occur as a result of a media failure taking with it the only copy of an online redo log.

Checking redo log file blocks for data corruption is conducted only when the checksum operation is active. To activate this feature, the DBA must set the `LOG_BLOCK_CHECKSUM` initialization parameter to TRUE. This parameter is set by default to FALSE, rendering redo block checksum inactive by Oracle's default behavior. When set to TRUE, Oracle checks every redo log block at archive time, substituting copies of corrupted blocks in one member with the same uncorrupted blocks from another redo log member. As long as the data block is not corrupted in every redo log member, the process will complete. If the block is corrupted in all members, however, Oracle will not be able to archive the redo log.

There are some points to be made about this feature. First of all, the use of log block checksums is irrelevant unless archiving is enabled. If you are not archiving redo logs, don't use the checksum feature. Second, performance degradation may be experienced as a result of checking sums. The checksum process occurs at each log switch, at the same time the archiving of redo logs takes place, and the performance loss would occur at this point. If online redo logs are filling fast, due to heavy database use, there might be some overall impact on performance. For the most part, however, the benefit of using `LOG_BLOCK_CHECKSUM` outweighs any performance hit. It is recommended that this feature be used on the Oracle database.

Clearing Corruption in Online Redo Logs

If data block corruption is detected in an online redo log, Oracle will automatically try to obtain the same block from a different member of the online redo log group. If for some reason the same redo data block is corrupt in all members of the online redo log (or if there is only one member in the online redo log), then Oracle cannot archive the redo log. Furthermore, the DBA must manually correct the problem. Recall the discussion about archiving redo logs manually in Chapter 13. If a redo log does not get archived manually, and all online redo logs fill with redo information, Oracle will not accept any database transaction activity until the redo logs are archived. Since the redo log containing block corruption cannot be archived, an alternate step must be taken promptly by the DBA. That alternative is clearing the online redo log.

To clear an online redo log, the DBA must issue an `alter database clear logfile group` statement. In order to clear an *unarchived* redo log, the DBA must remember to specify the `unarchived` keyword in the statement. Issuing this statement will eliminate all redo information in the database redo log group specified. An example of the statement is shown in the following code block

```
ALTER DATABASE orgdb01
CLEAR UNARCHIVED LOGFILE GROUP 5;
```

In the event that a redo log is found to be corrupt by the checksum process, the DBA must back up the database. If a database backup is not done, the DBA will not have a complete set of archives from which to conduct a complete database recovery—the DBA would have only enough data to conduct an incomplete recovery in the event of a database failure, which results in a loss of data. The best method for handling the situation is simply to take a new backup after clearing the corrupted redo log, and then start archiving again.

Only redo logs that have a status of inactive can be cleared. For example, if the DBA would like to clear the redo log that was just archived, he or she can issue the `alter database clear logfile group` statement to do so. If the redo log being cleared has already been archived, then the DBA should *not* use the `unarchived` keyword used in the previous example. The following code block demonstrates the use of this statement. Assume in this example that Oracle is currently writing to online redo log group 5, having just finished on group 4. An archive of group 4 is then created, and afterward, the DBA decides to clear the redo log group. This can be done with the following statement:

```
ALTER DATABASE orgdb01 CLEAR LOGFILE GROUP 4
```

Exercises

1. How does the DBA remove corruption from the online redo logs?
2. How can the DBA identify corruption in data blocks in the online redo logs to prevent propagation of block corruption to archives?

Using Log and Trace Files to Diagnose Problems

Trace files can be used to identify many different things about the runtime activities of user, server, background, and network processes in the Oracle database. Trace files for network and background processes are generated when the process experiences a problem of some kind. Trace files for server processes are generated when either the user or the DBA requests them. Trace files collect different things for different processes. A background process trace file will list any errors that the process may have encountered during execution. Server process trace files will list performance information and execution plans for every statement issued by the user.

A special trace file for the entire Oracle database exists and is called the ALERT log. The ALERT log contains runtime information about the execution of the Oracle database, and it can be used to identify many different types of problems in the Oracle database. Several different things are recorded in the ALERT log, including startup and shutdown times, initialization parameter values, information about `create database`, `create` and `drop tablespace`, `create`, `alter`, and `drop rollback segment` statements, database errors, and database-wide events.

The location of trace information and the ALERT log vary by database instance. The DBA can control where the files are placed with two `initsid.ora` parameters: `BACKGROUND_DUMP_DEST` and `USER_DUMP_DEST`. These parameters can be specified in the init*sid*.ora file and will be set at the time the instance is started. The path and file locations specified for the parameters must conform to the operating system. The location specified by `BACKGROUND_DUMP_DEST` identifies where Oracle will place trace files for background processes like LGWR, DBW0, SMON, and PMON, and where Oracle places the ALERT log. `USER_DUMP_DEST` is where server processes write session trace files.

The following code block illustrates the contents of an Oracle database ALERT log. Notice that each item in the ALERT log contains a time stamp for its activity. This ALERT log illustrates a startup and shutdown of an Oracle database, with no problems encountered. Notice that all activities associated with startup and shutdown are listed, along with the specified values of the initialization parameters for the database, and the activities of archiving on the database, as well.

```
Fri Feb 5 09:45:03 1999
Starting ORACLE instance (normal)
LICENSE_MAX_SESSION = 0
LICENSE_SESSIONS_WARNING = 0
LICENSE_MAX_USERS = 0
Starting up ORACLE RDBMS Version: 8.0.5.0.0.
System parameters with non-default values:
 processes            = 500
 shared_pool_size         = 9000000
 control_files          = ('/oracle/disk_1/control01.dbf',
'/oracle/disk_2/control03.dbf, /oracle/disk_3/control02.dbf')
 db_block_buffers         = 10000
 log_buffer          = 10485760
 log_checkpoint_interval = 10000
 db_files            = 1000
 db_file_multiblock_read_count= 8
 rollback_segments   = (ROLLBACK01, ROLLBACK02, ROLLBACK03, ROLLBACK04,
 ROLLBACK05)
 sequence_cache_entries   = 100
 sequence_cache_hash_buckets= 89
 db_domain           = exampilot.com
 global_names           = TRUE
 db_name            = JSC
 sql_trace           = TRUE
 utl_file_dir           = /FTP
 parallel_max_servers    = 16
 background_dump_dest    = /home/oracle80/app/oracle/admin/jsc/bdump
```

```
 user_dump_dest        = /home/oracle80/app/oracle/admin/jsc/udump
 max_dump_file_size     = 10240
 core_dump_dest        = /home/oracle80/app/oracle/admin/jsc/cdump
PMON started with pid=2
DBW0 started with pid=3
LGWR started with pid=4
CKPT started with pid=5
SMON started with pid=6
RECO started with pid=7
Fri Feb 5 09:45:04 1999
alter database mount
Fri Feb 5 09:45:08 1999
Successful mount of redo thread 1, with mount id 3383172772.
Fri Feb 5 09:45:08 1999
Database mounted in Exclusive Mode.
Completed: alter database mount
Fri Feb 5 09:45:08 1999
alter database open
Fri Feb 5 09:45:08 1999
Thread 1 opened at log sequence 6
 Current log# 1 seq# 6 mem# 0: /oracle/disk_4/logfile01.dbf
Successful open of redo thread 1.
Fri Feb 5 09:45:08 1999
SMON: enabling cache recovery
SMON: enabling tx recovery
Fri Feb 5 09:45:09 1999
Completed: alter database open
Mon Feb 8 14:22:00 1999
create tablespace data datafile
'/oracle/disk_5/data01.dbf' size 1800M,
'/oracle/disk_5/data02.dbf' size 1800
default storage ( initial 750K next 250K
minextents 1 maxextents 450 pctincrease 0) online
Completed: create tablespace data datafile
'/oracle/disk
Mon Feb 8 14:39:51 1999
Thread 1 advanced to log sequence 7
 Current log# 2 seq# 7 mem# 0: /oracle/disk_6/logfile02.dbf
Mon Feb 8 14:44:48 1999
Thread 1 advanced to log sequence 8
 Current log# 3 seq# 8 mem# 0: /oracle/disk_7/logfile03.dbf
Tue Feb 9 11:59:46 1999
Thread 1 advanced to log sequence 9
 Current log# 4 seq# 9 mem# 0: /oracle/disk_8/logfile04.dbf
Tue Feb 9 12:58:40 1999
ORA-1652: unable to extend temp segment by 512000 in tablespace DATA
```

Exercises

1. What is a trace file?
2. What is the name of the special trace file for database-wide error messages? Can you identify several items that are recorded in this file?

Oracle Recovery Without Archiving

In this section, you will cover the following topics about Oracle recovery without archiving:

- Implications of media failure in `noarchivelog` mode
- Recovering `noarchivelog` databases after media failure
- Restoring files to different locations
- Recovering `noarchivelog` databases using RMAN

You must understand database recovery in order to perform as an Oracle DBA. This section covers several topics about database recovery when you run your database in `noarchivelog` mode. First, you will learn about the implications of running Oracle in this mode, and what the limitations are in terms of database recovery when doing so. The next topic covers recovery of a database in this mode after some media failure has occurred. Next, you will learn how to restore files to different locations, and why this might be necessary. Last, you'll learn how to recover your `noarchivelog` mode database using RMAN.

Implications of Media Failure in noarchivelog *Mode*

Running a database in `noarchivelog` mode has advantages and disadvantages. When you don't save your redo logs, you cannot recover your data past the point of the most recent database backup. Thus, media failure for databases that are not archiving redo logs has the impact of wiping out all data changes made after the most recent backup. This is bad for production databases that experience heavy data-change activity. In some situations, however, this condition might be acceptable. For example, on a development environment where you are testing the execution of a particular batch file by running it over and over again, you probably don't care about restoring data to the point in time of media failure. In fact, just the opposite might be true—you might only want to restore the database to the point when the last backup was taken, so that you can rerun the batch process for the next test.

An advantage of running Oracle in noarchivelog mode is that database backup and recovery is simple. All you need to do is shut down the database and copy the datafiles to an offline storage medium, such as tape. The only time constraint for recovery is the speed at which the offline storage medium can restore the files to their proper locations. You run few risks with this method—restoring from the wrong backup or restoring before shutting down the database, for example. Even so, you can easily correct the damage by running the recovery again.

Running your database in noarchivelog mode also means that your database must be taken offline in order to make backups of your data. If your database experiences some form of media failure that causes Oracle datafiles to become corrupt or unreadable, you must have a valid offline backup of all necessary datafiles, log files, and control files in order to recover your database. You don't need to have a copy of the password file or the init*sid*.ora file unless these files were lost. If no offline backup is available, then your database is unrecoverable.

When media failure occurs, you must restore all datafiles, redo log files, and control files from your backup in order to recover the database, even if only one file on one disk was lost. This is because all datafiles, redo logs, and control files must be synchronized in order for the database to open. One exception to this rule is when your database experiences media failure and no online redo log has been overwritten by LGWR. In this case, you need only restore the datafile lost by media failure and let Oracle handle crash recovery.

Exercises

1. Identify some advantages of running Oracle in noarchivelog mode when media failure occurs. What sorts of database environments would be appropriate for this use?
2. Identify some disadvantages of running Oracle in noarchivelog mode when media failure occurs. What sorts of database environments would be inappropriate for this use?

Recovering noarchivelog Databases

The term "restoring" is really more accurate than "recovering" when discussing the method used for database recovery when you operate your database runs in noarchivelog mode. For noarchivelog databases, you must recover from full backup to resolve media failure. The database cannot be open for use during complete recovery. If the database is not shut down already, you can use any shutdown option you want, including shutdown abort to shut it down. At the command line within Server Manager, the following statement can be executed by the DBA while connected as `internal` or as a user with the `sysdba` privilege granted:

```
SVRMGR> SHUTDOWN ABORT;
```

Media failure usually requires some sort of hardware repair or replacement. In order to restore the database to its full functionality, the DBA should ensure that the disk hardware that was damaged—the initial cause for the media failure—is fixed. Alternatively, the DBA may choose to circumvent the problem by restoring the database using another disk to store the different files of the database. The following steps are necessary for performing complete recovery:

1. Shut down the database with the `shutdown abort` statement.
2. Replace any damaged hardware.
3. Restore all datafiles, redo log files, and control files from appropriate offline backup using operating system copy commands or third-party offline storage media methods. All files must be restored, not just the damaged ones. To issue operating system commands from within Server Manager, prefix the OS command with an exclamation mark (!), sometimes called a "bang."
4. Open the database.

   ```
   SVRMGR> STARTUP OPEN PFILE=init_orgdb01.ora;
   ```

Exercises

1. What steps are required when recovering from a full physical backup?
2. What shutdown method causes Oracle to require media recovery after shutdown is complete? Identify the importance of resetting the redo log sequence number after recovery using full backups.

Restoring Files to Different Locations

If the disk cannot be replaced, then the DBA may need to move the files to other disks and update the control file accordingly. The following steps can be used for this purpose:

1. Close the database using the `alter database offline` command. You could also use the `shutdown` command using any shutdown option, but this is not strictly necessary.

2. Restore datafiles, redo log files, and control files from appropriate offline backups using operating system copy commands or third-party offline storage media methods. All files must be restored, not just the damaged ones.

3. Move the control file specification as noted by the `CONTROL_FILES` parameter of the `initsid.ora` file. The path and filename may be changed to reflect a new location for the control file of the Oracle database if the control file was lost in the disk failure.

4. Start up and mount the database, but do not open it. If you are using Oracle Parallel Server, mount the database in exclusive mode to one instance only.

5. Update the control file to reflect new locations of datafiles or redo log files. To move a datafile or redo log file, the DBA must use the `alter database` statement with the `rename file` option from Server Manager. Full pathnames for the datafile at old and new locations should be specified. Examples of executing this operation appear in the following code block:

```
ALTER DATABASE orgdb01
RENAME FILE '/u01/oracle/data/data_301a.dbf'
TO '/u02/oracle/data/data_301b.dbf';

ALTER DATABASE orgdb01
RENAME FILE '/u01/oracle/ctl/rdorgdb01'
TO '/u02/oracle/ctl/rdorgdb01';
```

6. Open the database.

```
SVRMGR> STARTUP OPEN PFILE=init_orgdb01.ora;
```

7. Shut down the database using the `normal` or `immediate` option, and take a backup. Though not required, this step is recommended for safety's sake.

Exercises

1. What steps are required in moving files to different locations on the machine, in addition to those involved in regular database recovery?

2. If you are using Oracle Parallel Server, in what mode should you mount your database when preparing to recover it?

Recovering noarchivelog Databases with RMAN

Since database backup and recovery is a straightforward process that is handled with the database offline, you may not feel you need to use RMAN for recovering a database running in `noarchivelog` mode. In fact, for reasons you will learn shortly, using RMAN in conjunction with backup and recovery on `noarchivelog` databases is slightly more cumbersome than managing this backup and recovery method using operating system commands. However, there are some compelling reasons to do so. RMAN allows you to write scripts to handle database recovery automatically, which are slightly less complicated than the ones you would have to write to automate these tasks using whatever operating system scripting language is offered on the host machine. RMAN also allows you to store the scripts you write in the recovery catalog. When recovery is processed via RMAN, you also have the benefit of those backup datafile copies tracked in the recovery catalog, as well.

Like its operating system command–based counterpart, recovery of a `noarchivelog` database running in RMAN offers the ability to use fewer commands to restore all the datafiles and control files in your database from backup. This is opposed to operating systems, where you most likely would need to issue a command for every single datafile that needs to be replaced. The command used in RMAN to restore all datafiles and control files from backup copies is `restore` *`object options`*. For *`object`* in the `restore` command syntax, you can substitute `controlfile` to *`filename`*, `archivelog all` (not used when `noarchivelog` is used), `tablespace "`*`tablespace`*`"`, `datafile "`*`datafile`*`"`, or `database`. For *`options`* in the `restore` command syntax, you can substitute `channel=`*`channel`*, from `tag=`*`tag`*, `parms="`*`parms_string`*`"`, or from `[`*`backupset`*`|`*`datafilecopy`*`]`.

The following steps can be used to recover a `noarchivelog` database using RMAN:

1. Shut down the database with whatever option you want. This is required for complete recovery on the primary database, because you are discarding the unsynchronized datafiles and control files, anyway.
2. Start up, mount, but do not open, the primary database. The recovery catalog database should be open.
3. Start RMAN by connecting to both the primary database and the recovery catalog.
4. Develop your `run` script for restoring the datafiles and control files from offline backups, allocating appropriate channels. This will require two separate commands, because the `restore database` command only restores datafiles. Since you will not be using archived redo logs, you don't need to add the `recover database` command into your RMAN `run` script.
5. Execute the script.

6. When RMAN finishes running the script, open the database. Also, add support for deallocating the channel when completed.

7. Shut down the database and take a full offline backup. This seems like a mistake, but you really do have to perform this task when restoring your database with RMAN. For this reason, using RMAN in conjunction with backup and recovery on `noarchivelog` databases is slightly more cumbersome than managing this backup and recovery method using operating system commands.

8. Open the database and make it available to users, telling them to re-enter any changes made after the most recent backup.

In order to use RMAN, your datafile and control-file backups must either have been taken with RMAN, or been registered with RMAN after being taken with operating system commands. The following code block demonstrates an RMAN script running in Windows that can be used to restore all your database files when your database runs in `noarchivelog` mode:

```
D:\orant\bin> rman80 target user/pass@proddb rcvcat user/pass@catdb
RMAN> run { allocate channel c1 type disk;
  >     restore controlfile to 'E:\database\jscctl1.ctl';
  >     restore database;
  >     sql 'alter database open';
  >     release channel c1; }
```

Exercises

1. What database backup files will RMAN restore if you use the `restore database` command? Is this acceptable for recovery of `noarchivelog` databases? Why or why not?

2. What step is required after restoring your database with RMAN that is not required after restoring your database with operating system commands?

Oracle Recovery with Archiving

This section covers the following topics about Oracle recovery with archiving:

- Implications of instance failure in `archivelog` mode
- Complete recovery operation

- Pros and cons of recovering archivelog databases
- Recovering archivelog databases after media failure
- Using RMAN and Backup Manager

This section continues to round out your understanding of Oracle recovery when archiving redo logs. The first topic covered in this section is the implications of instance failure when you archive your online redo logs. The next section describes the operations involved in recovering a database where redo logs are archived, and you will learn about the pros and cons of recovering databases running in archivelog mode. After that, you will learn how to recover a database running in archivelog mode after media failure. Finally, you will learn how to use RMAN and the Backup Manager for these purposes, as well.

Implications of Instance Failure in archivelog *Mode*

There are many situations in which media failure for databases running in noarchivelog mode will be damaging. If your database is characterized by heavy data-change activity by users, your recovery needs would be best served by archiving redo logs, because recreating all the changes made by those users will be a time-consuming and frustrating process for them and you. Archiving your redo logs allows you to restore all data changes made to the database up to the point in time of the failure, in best-case situations, saving your users a great deal of time and aggravation.

There are some implications for database failure associated with 24 × 7 database operation, as well. You should not use noarchivelog mode if you cannot shut down your database for cold backups, because you cannot take an online backup of a database running in noarchivelog mode. Only when the database runs in archivelog mode can you use the online backup feature that archived redo logs support. Thus, the needs of 24 × 7 database operations are best served if you archive your online redo logs.

Usually, you will use archivelog mode for production databases, while using noarchivelog mode for development or test environments. However, your Oracle database will be in noarchivelog mode by default when you first create it. In order to get the database into the appropriate mode so that your redo logs are archived, you must shut down, restart, and mount (but do not open) the database, and issue the alter database archivelog command to set archiving status in the control file. After that, you must issue the alter system archive log start command to activate the ARCH process so that your redo logs are automatically archived when log switches occur.

Exercises

1. What are some reasons to use archiving versus not archiving redo logs in your Oracle database? In what situations would you have to use archiving?
2. What are the steps for setting up archiving on the Oracle database?

Complete Recovery Operation

You have to have several items in order to manage a complete recovery up to the point of your most recent database failure. These items include a backup set of database files that contains the file(s) lost or damaged by the media failure. Another set of items required is a complete set of all archived redo logs taken since the backup was performed, as well as those taken while the backup was performed, if the backup was an online backup.

After ensuring that you have the appropriate files available for the recovery, you can then perform a series of steps to handle recovery (these steps will be described in more detail shortly).

1. Ensure that the files damaged in the failure are not currently open by shutting down the database with the `shutdown abort` option, taking the tablespace containing the datafile(s) to be overlaid offline, or simply taking the datafile to be overlaid offline.
2. Restore the file(s) that have been damaged. You don't want to restore all the files from the backup, however, because doing so will return your database to the state it was in at the time the backup was made.
3. Mount the database if you plan to perform a closed recovery, or open the database if you plan to perform an open recovery.
4. Recover the backup files to be synchronized with the other database files by applying redo information from the archived redo logs to those backup files. This is handled with the `recover` command.

Exercises

1. Identify the items required for database recovery to the point in time of media failure.
2. What steps are involved in recovering a database to the point in time of failure?

Pros and Cons of Recovering archivelog Databases

There are several advantages to recovering databases running in `archivelog` mode over recovering databases running in `noarchivelog` mode. Not the least important of these benefits is the ability to recover past the point of your most recent backup. You cannot recover past your most recent backup if you are not running your database in `archivelog` mode. Thus, the major benefit of this setup is that no committed data need ever be lost in the event of media failure.

Another nice recovery benefit of `archivelog` databases is that the recovery in most cases can be performed while the database is open and available to your users. The only exceptions to this are when your database experiences media failure to the datafiles of the SYSTEM tablespace or a tablespace containing online rollback segments. In general, you only need to restore those files that were damaged by the media failure when recovering `archivelog` databases. Recall that you needed to restore all database files from backup when recovering your `noarchivelog` database.

When recovering your database in `archivelog` mode there are a couple of limitations. First, recovery time will be longer than the time it takes to recover `noarchivelog` databases, because recovery time is a factor of the time it takes to restore the backup database files and archived redo logs from tape and the time it takes to apply those archived redo logs to the lost database files. This isn't really an advantage or disadvantage, because although it generally takes less time to recover a `noarchivelog` database than an `archivelog` database, your recovery of an `archivelog` database yields greater data recoverability and user satisfaction.

The main disadvantage of recovering an `archivelog` database is the fact that you need to have every single archived redo log taken between the most recent backup and the present time in order to have complete recovery. If even one is missing, the best you can hope for is recovery to the point in time prior to the missing archived redo log.

Exercises

1. What are some advantages to recovering your database running in `archivelog` mode?
2. What are some advantages to recovering your database running in `noarchivelog` mode?

Recovering archivelog Databases After Media Failure

Database recovery happens in the following way. First, you must restore the database files and archived redo logs from backup. After that, the recovery can take place. Oracle will look for archived redo logs in the location specified by the LOG_ARCHIVE_DEST parameter of the init*sid*.ora file. An alternate location for the archived redo logs can be specified manually by the DBA using the from clause in the alter database recover statement.

You do not need to specify the alter database clause before the recover keyword. If you choose to recover your entire database, the database must be closed. An example of the use of recover in which an alternate location for archived redo log files is specified is as follows:

```
ALTER DATABASE RECOVER DATABASE FROM '/u03/archive/alt';
```

Or, simply:

```
RECOVER FROM '/u03/archive/alt' DATABASE;
```

There are some other elements of recover syntax. First, it is possible to recover only a tablespace in the database, or even a datafile. To do so, replace the recover database syntax with recover tablespace or recover datafile, respectively. Oracle also allows you to specify automatic application of archived and online redo logs as part of recovery. Oracle will decide which redo logs to apply based on the values of the LOG_ARCHIVE_DEST and LOG_ARCHIVE_FORMAT init*sid*.ora parameters. The database can be closed or open during tablespace or datafile recovery. The following code block illustrates the appropriate syntax:

```
RECOVER TABLESPACE data01;
RECOVER AUTOMATIC DATAFILE '/oracle/disk_8/data01.dbf';
```

There are many database situations that you should know how to recover from. Each situation has a set of rules that apply to how the DBA handles the recovery. You will now learn about each failure scenario and a small amount about the database recovery required. In the next set of lessons, you will examine each scenario in more detail.

Scenario 1: Recovery for SYSTEM or ROLLBACK Tablespace Datafiles

The loss of SYSTEM tablespace datafiles or datafiles from tablespaces containing rollback segments may cause Oracle to stop running. In this situation, full recovery using backup copies of all database files is required. The database cannot be open during recovery. Media failure will most likely be accompanied by disk failure, which you will need to have fixed. The following steps are used to recover the database when media failure takes with it copies of datafiles for SYSTEM or ROLLBACK tablespaces:

1. Close your database using the `shutdown abort` command.
2. Repair or replace the hardware.
3. Restore damaged files only from the most recent complete backup. Operating system copy commands are used to handle this step.
4. Startup and mount, but do not open the database, using the `startup mount` command.
5. Recover the database using archived redo log information. The command syntax for this process is `alter database recover database`, or simply `recover database`. This statement will begin the interactive process of applying redo log information. Or, you could use the `automatic` keyword to allow Oracle to apply redo logs:

   ```
   SVRMGR> ALTER DATABASE RECOVER AUTOMATIC DATABASE;
   ```

   Or,

   ```
   SVRMGR> RECOVER AUTOMATIC DATABASE;
   ```

6. Shut down the database using the `normal` or `immediate` options, and take a full backup of the database using the methods described in Chapter 12.
7. Open the database for use.

   ```
   SVRMGR> STARTUP OPEN PFILE=initjsc.ora;
   ```

Scenario 2: Recovery for Deleted or Damaged Non-SYSTEM or Non-ROLLBACK Datafiles

Loss of datafile(s) from non-SYSTEM tablespaces or a tablespace not containing rollback segments will typically not cause your instance to fail. Instead, users will most likely only notice that occasionally they cannot access the data in those datafiles. In this situation, recovery using backup copies of only database files that were damaged is required.

Recovery can be performed on individual tablespaces or on the datafiles themselves. The DBA can execute a tablespace recovery using the `recover tablespace` statement, or a datafile recovery with the `recover datafile` statement. The database must be open in order to accomplish a tablespace or datafile recovery, so that Oracle can view the contents of the database while the tablespace recovery occurs. However, the tablespace must be offline for tablespace recovery, or the datafile itself must be offline while the tablespace remains online. A benefit of tablespace or datafile recovery is that the DBA can allow users to access other tablespaces while the offline tablespace or datafile is restored.

In this example, assume that the USERS01 tablespace or the associated datafile needs to be recovered.

1. If the database is open, do not shut it down, because you will have trouble opening it again with datafiles missing.
2. Take the tablespace or datafile on the disk(s) that failed offline. Remember, if you are doing datafile recovery, both the tablespace and the database must both be online. You should use the `immediate` option for bringing the tablespace or datafile offline because otherwise, Oracle will attempt to perform a checkpoint and try to write a new sequence number to datafile headers in files that don't exist or are inaccessible.

```
SVRMGR> ALTER TABLESPACE users01 OFFLINE IMMEDIATE;
```

   Or,

```
SVRMGR> ALTER DATABASE DATAFILE '/oracle/disk_22/users0101.dbf'
   > OFFLINE IMMEDIATE;
```

3. Repair or replace damaged disk hardware. Some host machines may not allow you to do this when the machine is running.
4. Restore damaged datafiles with their respective backup copies using operating system commands. You will soon learn how to do this with RMAN.
5. Recover the tablespace or datafile. To minimize interaction between the DBA and Oracle, use the `automatic` keyword in the `recover` statement, allowing Oracle to automatically apply its own suggestions for redo logs.

```
SVRMGR> RECOVER AUTOMATIC TABLESPACE users01;
```

   Or,

```
SVRMGR> RECOVER AUTOMATIC DATAFILE '/oracle/disk_11/users0101.dbf;
```

6. Bring the tablespace online using the `alter tablespace online` statement, or bring the datafile online with the `alter database datafile` *`filename`* `online` statement.

```
SVRMGR> ALTER TABLESPACE users01 ONLINE;
```

Or,

```
SVRMGR> ALTER DATABASE DATAFILE '/oracle/disk_11/users0101.dbf'
   > ONLINE;
```

7. Notify users that recovery is complete and that a backup is necessary. Then, shut down the database using `shutdown normal`, `shutdown transactional`, or `shutdown immediate`, take your offline backup, and open the database again for use.

Scenario 3: Datafile Recovery Without Backup Datafile

Recovering from loss of datafile(s) from non-SYSTEM tablespaces or tablespaces not containing rollback segments is slightly trickier when there is no backup datafile; you have to create a generic datafile, then recover the changes using archived redo logs. To do so, you must have ALL archived redo logs created by Oracle since you added the datafile to your database. You can find out whether your datafile is backed up or not by looking in the V$RECOVER_FILE dynamic performance view. If the status of the file you seek is "file not found," you do not have a backup copy. Assuming that you have all archived redo logs generated from the time the datafile was created, it is possible to recover this datafile even when there is no backup.

The database may or may not be open during recovery. If open, the datafile(s) or tablespace(s) containing them must be offline. This scenario can only occur if the lost datafile or tablespace is not part of a SYSTEM or ROLLBACK tablespace. The following steps are used to perform this type of recovery:

1. If the database is already open, do not shut it down, because you may have trouble trying to restart it with missing datafiles.

2. Take the tablespace or datafile on the disk(s) that failed offline. Remember, if you are doing datafile recovery, the tablespace and the database must both be online. You should use the `immediate` option for bringing tablespaces or datafiles offline because, otherwise, Oracle will attempt to perform a checkpoint and try to write a new sequence number to datafile headers in files that don't exist or are inaccessible.

```
SVRMGR> ALTER TABLESPACE users01 OFFLINE IMMEDIATE;
```

Or,

```
SVRMGR> ALTER DATABASE DATAFILE '/oracle/disk_22/users0101.dbf'
   > OFFLINE IMMEDIATE;
```

3. Regenerate datafiles you didn't have a backup of by creating your new datafile to be similar to an existing one with the `alter database create datafile` command, as shown here:

```
SVRMGR> ALTER DATABASE CREATE DATAFILE
   > '/oracle/disk_26/users0101.dbf'
   > AS '/oracle/disk_22/data0101.dbf';
```

4. Recover the tablespace or datafile using archived redo logs. To minimize the amount of interaction required between the DBA and Oracle, the DBA can include the `automatic` keyword in the `recover` statement, allowing Oracle to automatically apply its own suggestions for redo logs.

```
SVRMGR> RECOVER AUTOMATIC TABLESPACE users01;
```

   Or,

```
SVRMGR> RECOVER AUTOMATIC DATAFILE 'users0101.dbf';
```

5. Bring the tablespace or datafile online using the appropriate statement.

```
ALTER TABLESPACE users01 ONLINE;
```

   Or,

```
ALTER DATABASE DATAFILE '/oracle/disk_22/users0101.dbf' ONLINE;
```

6. Shut down the database using the `normal`, `transactional`, or `immediate` options, back up the database using procedures covered in Chapter 12, and open it again for your users.

TIP

You can refer to datafiles either by their absolute path and filename or by the datafile number associated with the datafile in the V$DATAFILE view.

Scenario 4: Recovery When Datafile Is Being Backed Up

Recovering a datafile that was in the process of being backed up is another important area of database recovery to understand for OCP. When the instance fails and a tablespace is in backup mode, the backups made are most likely unusable. What's more, you will have trouble opening the database. This is because when you issue the `alter tablespace begin backup` command, Oracle locks the headers on all the tablespace datafiles so that the sequence numbers won't be changed until the hot backup is complete. All the rest of the datafile headers in the database will continue to be updated, however. This means that the sequence numbers on the datafiles being backed up will be out of sync with the rest of the datafiles on your database.

Thus, if media failure causes the database to crash while a tablespace was being backed up, you will not be able to reopen your database unless you revert to an earlier backup for those datafiles and recover using archived redo logs. However, there is one shortcut you can take to avoid having to revert to an earlier version of the file. While the database is closed, you can perform a `select * from V$BACKUP` command and see all your datafiles for the tablespace still in hot backup mode. You can force Oracle to unlock the datafile header using the `alter database datafile end backup` statement, which will allow you to open the database. Assuming the USER tablespace has one datafile, which is datafile #6 on the database, the following code block illustrates this situation:

```
SVRMGR> alter tablespace user begin backup;
Statement processed.
SVRMGR> select file#, status, checkpoint_change#
   > from v$datafile_header;
  FILE# STATUS CHECKPOINT_CHANGE#
--------- ------- ------------------
    1 ONLINE       801738
    2 ONLINE       801738
    3 ONLINE       721651
    4 ONLINE       801738
    5 ONLINE       801738
    6 ONLINE       801748
SVRMGR> shutdown abort;
ORACLE instance shut down.
SVRMGR> startup open pfile=d:\orant\database\initjsc.ora
ORACLE instance started.
Total System Global Area    14442496 bytes
Fixed Size                  49152 bytes
Variable Size               13193216 bytes
Database Buffers            1126400 bytes
Redo Buffers                73278 bytes
Database mounted.
ORA-01113: file 6 needs media recovery
ORA-01110: data file 6: 'D:\ORANT\DATABASE\DRJSC.ORA'
SVRMGR> select * from v$backup;
FILE#  STATUS   CHANGE#  TIME
------- ---------- --------- ---------
   1 NOT ACTIVE     0
   2 NOT ACTIVE     0
   3 NOT ACTIVE     0
   4 NOT ACTIVE     0
   5 NOT ACTIVE     0
```

```
   6 ACTIVE    801748 31-MAR-99
SVRMGR> alter database datafile 2 end backup;
Statement processed.
SVRMGR> select * from v$backup;
FILE#  STATUS    CHANGE#  TIME
------- ---------- --------- ---------
   1 NOT ACTIVE      0
   2 NOT ACTIVE      0
   3 NOT ACTIVE      0
   4 NOT ACTIVE      0
   5 NOT ACTIVE      0
   6 NOT ACTIVE  785294 31-MAR-99
SVRMGR> alter database open;
Statement processed.
```

Scenario 5: Recovery When Inactive Redo Log is Lost

The final scenario considered here is database recovery when you lose an online redo log group that is not currently active. This may happen because of accidental removal or because of block corruption. In any event, the recoverability of your database might be in jeopardy unless three conditions are met:

- The lost redo log is not the current redo log being written by LGWR
- The lost redo log has already been archived
- There are more than the minimum of two online redo log groups

You can determine the gravity of this situation by viewing data in the V$LOG performance view. You can see in the STATUS column which redo log is currently being written by LGWR. If the FIRST_CHANGE column contains a value of 0 for any log group, then that log group might have some sort of problem. Also worthy of note is the ARCHIVED column, which tells you if the redo log has been archived or not. If this column says "yes," then you most likely don't have a problem with data loss, though you will still have to recreate the missing redo log file.

Creation of a new online redo log is accomplished in the following way:

1. Create a temporary online redo log with the `alter database add logfile` statement. (This step can be omitted if you have more than two online redo logs for your database.) You should determine the highest group number using the V$LOGFILE view, and specify the next highest group number to save space in the control file:

   ```
   SVRMGR> select max(group#) from v$logfile;
   ```

```
MAX(GROUP#)
-----------
      2
SVRMGR> alter database add logfile group 3
   2> '/oracle/disk_18/logtemp.dbf' size 2M;
```

2. Drop the redo log group that contains missing log file members with the `alter database drop logfile group` *n*, where *n* is the group number of the online redo log that is missing members.
3. Re-create that redo log group with the appropriate members by using the statement displayed in step 1.
4. Repeat step 2 to eliminate the temporary redo log group you created in step 1.
5. Remove the physical redo log file(s) you created in step 1 using operating system commands.
6. Open the database.
7. Multiplex your online redo log groups, if that hasn't been done already, using the `alter database add logfile member` *`filename`* `to group` *n* command.

TIP
If you have lost only one member of a group that has been multiplexed, you can add a new member using the `alter database add logfile member` command.

Observing Recovery Status in Progress

There are two views you can use to observe the status of your recovery in progress. They are V$RECOVERY_FILE_STATUS and V$RECOVERY_STATUS. These views are unique because their contents are stored in the PGA for the server process you are connected to while performing the recovery. Thus, only you can see the information in these views, and only within the session from which you actually perform the recovery. V$RECOVERY_FILE_STATUS gives detailed information about the status of particular database files currently being recovered. The V$RECOVERY_STATUS view gives detailed information about the redo SCNs that actually must be applied to the file being recovered in order to complete the recovery process.

Exercises

1. Identify the type of recovery that must be performed if a datafile associated with your SYSTEM tablespace is lost. Can the database be available? Why

or why not? What about the type of recovery if the DATA tablespace loses a datafile?

2. Can a datafile be recovered if there is no backup copy of it? If so, what items are required to handle this recovery?
3. Which command is used if the database crashes while you are taking an online backup?

Using RMAN and Backup Manager

RMAN can be used for the complete recovery of databases, tablespaces, and datafiles in a few ways: you can perform a complete database recovery, recover individual tablespaces, or recover datafiles and move them to new locations. The following discussions will identify the steps required for recovery in each of these situations because each situation is different. Only for the complete recovery of your entire database should the database be closed. For tablespace and datafile recovery, the unaffected parts of the Oracle database can be open and available to users.

Complete Database Recovery Procedures

Recovering your entire database in `archivelog` mode using RMAN is handled in the same way as recovering a `noarchivelog` database, except that with an `archivelog` database you also need to apply the archived redo logs with the `recover` command. The following procedures explain how to perform this type of recovery:

1. Complete recovery on the primary database requires that the database be shut down. So shut down the database with whatever option you prefer: `immediate`, `normal`, `transactional`, or `abort`. You are replacing the datafiles that were lost, thus leaving all Oracle files in an unsynchronized state, so the type of shutdown doesn't matter.
2. Start up and mount, but do not open, the primary database. The recovery catalog database should also be open.
3. Start RMAN by connecting to both the primary database and the recovery catalog.
4. Develop your `run` script for restoring the datafiles from offline backups, allocating appropriate channels. The `restore database` command only restores datafiles, but in this situation you don't want to use backup control files anyway.
5. Add the `recover database` command into your RMAN `run` script.

6. When RMAN finishes running the script, the database will need to be opened with the reset redo log sequence number. This allows the database to open by resetting LGWR to start at the beginning of the first redo log group in the database. Otherwise, the lack of synchronization between the online redo log copies and restored datafiles and control files prevents Oracle from starting. You need to include support for these areas in the development of your RMAN `run` script. Also, add support for deallocating the channel when the restoration is completed. When finished, your script should look like the following code block:

```
D:\orant\bin> rman80 target user/pass@proddb rcvcat
user/pass@catdb
RMAN> run { allocate channel c1 type disk;
  >     restore database;
  >     recover database;
  >     sql 'alter database open';
  >     release channel c1; }
```

7. Execute the script.
8. Shut down the database and take a full offline backup. This seems like a mistake, but you really do have to perform this task when restoring your database with RMAN. For this reason, using RMAN in conjunction with backup and recovery on `noarchivelog` databases is slightly more cumbersome than managing this backup and recovery method with operating system commands.
9. Open the database and make it available to users, telling them to re-enter any uncommitted changes they were making when the database went down.

Tablespace Recovery Procedures

RMAN can also help recover a single tablespace from your database that contains lost or damaged datafiles. The database can be open for this procedure, but the tablespace itself must be closed.

The steps of this procedure are as follows:

1. Identify the status of the database by issuing `select INSTANCE_NAME, STATUS from V$INSTANCE`. If the instance is stopped, you can start it and mount, but not open, the database.
2. Determine which of the datafiles in your tablespace must be recovered by issuing the `select NAME, TABLESPACE_NAME, STATUS from V$DATAFILE_HEADER where TABLESPACE_NAME = `*`tablespace`*` and ERROR is not NULL` command. This will give you the names of the datafiles that need to be recovered.

3. Develop your RMAN `run` script to contain support for allocating a channel and for taking the tablespace offline using the `immediate` option.

4. Code in some support for restoring the datafiles of the tablespace with the `restore tablespace` *`tablespace`* command. Also restore archived redo logs if necessary.

5. Add support for handling the actual recovery with the `recover tablespace` *`tablespace`* command.

6. Add support for bringing the tablespace back online with the `alter tablespace` *`tablespace`* `online` command, and for releasing your channel.

7. Run the script.

```
D:\orant\bin> rman80 target user/pass@proddb rcvcat user/pass@catdb
RMAN> run { allocate channel c1 type disk;
  >     sql 'alter tablespace users offline immediate';
  >     restore tablespace users;
  >     recover tablespace users;
  >     sql 'alter tablespace users online';
  >     release channel c1; }
```

8. Check to make sure your changes were made correctly, and then take an online or offline backup of the entire database.

9. Open the database without using the `resetlogs` option (if it's not open already) and give it back to the users.

Datafile Recovery Procedures When Files Must Move

When using RMAN, as when using operating system commands, you will occasionally need to move datafiles to different locations when you cannot wait for hardware replacements in order to recover the database. RMAN allows you to perform this task as part of your database recovery. The following set of procedures can be used for this purpose:

1. Determine which datafile has been lost on the disk that experienced media failure by checking the STATUS column of V$DATAFILE for datafiles that are not online or that are not part of the SYSTEM tablespace. These are the datafiles that will need to be recovered, so note their datafile numbers.

2. Develop your RMAN `run` script to contain support for allocating a channel and for taking offline the tablespace containing the datafile on the disk that experienced media failure.

3. Change the location of the datafile using the `set newname for datafile` *`filename`* `to` *`new_filename`* statement.

4. Code in some support for restoring the datafiles of the tablespace with the `restore tablespace` *`tablespace`* command. Also, restore archived redo logs if necessary.
5. Let Oracle know that the new file location should be recorded using the `switch datafile` *`num`* command, where *`num`* is the datafile number you retrieved in step 1.
6. Add support for handling the actual recovery with the `recover tablespace` *`tablespace`* command.
7. Add support for bringing the tablespace back online with the `alter tablespace` *`tablespace`* `online` command, and for releasing your channel.
8. Run the script.

```
D:\orant\bin> rman80 target user/pass@proddb rcvcat user/pass@catdb
RMAN> run { allocate channel c1 type disk;
  >     sql 'alter tablespace users offline immediate';
  >     set newname for datafile 'E:\database\users03.dbf' to
  >      'F:\database\users03.dbf';
  >     restore tablespace users;
  >     switch datafile 4;
  >     recover tablespace users;
  >     sql 'alter tablespace users online';
  >     release channel c1; }
```

9. Check to make sure your changes were made correctly, and then take an online or offline backup.
10. Open the database if it's not open already, and give it back to the users.

TIP
Overall, RMAN allows for more robust recovery than simply restoring backup datafiles and applying archived redo logs to them. Recall that you can take incremental backups using RMAN to the granularity level of changed blocks in datafiles. If you have these backups available on your system, RMAN will use them as part of the recovery.

Looking at Backup Manager

Finally, aspects of database recovery can also be handled using the Backup Manager tool in Oracle Enterprise Manager. In order to access Backup Manager, start Oracle Enterprise Manager and select Tools | Applications | Backup Manager from the menu bar. You will be prompted to log in, at which point you should enter a username and password that has the ability to shut down and start up your database. A good example is the INTERNAL user. Be sure also to log in to that user with the `sysdba` privilege activated. Once Backup Manager is running, you can perform all the RMAN tasks shown in these scripts interactively, using the Backup Manager GUI, which is displayed in Figure 14-1.

Exercises

1. What steps are necessary to perform tablespace or datafile recovery using RMAN? What commands are used to move a datafile from one disk to another using RMAN?

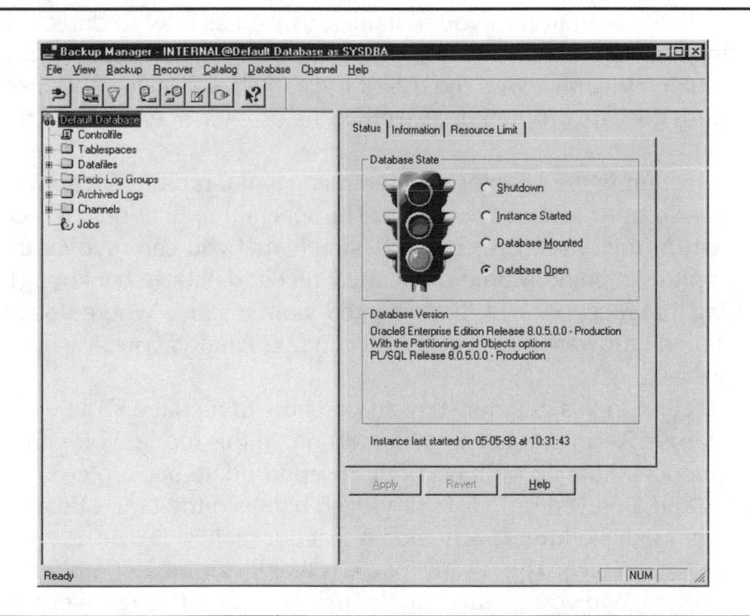

FIGURE 14-1. *Backup Manager*

2. Are you limited strictly to using datafile copies and archived redo logs with RMAN? Why or why not?

Chapter Summary

In this chapter, you learned about several areas of database failure and how to recover your database up to the point of the failure, or at least to the point of the most recent database backup. The topics this chapter covered included failure scenarios, database recovery when `noarchivelog` mode is used, and database recovery when `archivelog` mode is used. These topics comprise 25 percent of OCP Exam 3 test content.

The first area you covered was identifying the types of failure that can occur in Oracle. You learned about the causes and effects of user error, statement failure, process failure, instance failure, and media failure. You also learned about the memory structures and background processes that assist in media and instance recovery. The role of SMON and PMON were covered. You should also recall that the large pool memory area has some use when using RMAN, which is the tool that assists in media recovery. You learned how to use DBVERIFY, a utility for determining block corruption in your datafiles, as well as how to detect block corruption in your redo log files with the `LOG_BLOCK_CHECKSUM` `init`*`sid`*`.ora` parameter. Finally, you reviewed the use of trace files for background processes, and when those files are produced, as well as the use of a special trace file called the ALERT log.

The next section in the chapter covered managing Oracle recovery when the database is run in `noarchivelog` mode. The special implications of recoverability when Oracle runs this way were covered, namely that you can recover from media failure only up to the point in time of the most recent database backup. The method for performing that recovery was then covered, both in cases where you are able to replace the failed hardware and where you can not. Finally, you saw how to use RMAN in this task.

The last section in this chapter showed you how to manage Oracle recovery when the database is run in `archivelog` mode. In this mode, you can recover to the point of media failure if you have both the appropriate backup copies of lost database files and archived redo logs produced between the time of that backup and the time of media failure. It was shown that this feature is `archivelog` mode's biggest advantage. The disadvantage is that it can be a complicated operation to set up, and you always run the risk of incomplete recovery if you lose an archived redo log. The methods for performing complete recovery in six different situations were also covered. These situations ranged from loss of datafiles in SYSTEM and ROLLBACK tablespaces to loss of online redo logs currently not being used. The special tasks required for recovering from media failure that occurs when the tablespace datafiles are being backed up was also covered. Finally, you learned how to incorporate RMAN and Backup Manager in this process.

Two-Minute Drill

- The types of database failure are user error, statement failure, process failure, instance failure, and media failure.
- User error is when the user permanently changes or removes data from a database in error. Rollback segments give supplemental ability to correct uncommitted user errors, but usually the DBA will need to intervene for recovery.
- Statement failure occurs when there is something syntactically wrong with SQL statements issued by users in the database. Oracle rolls back these statements automatically and issues an error to the user indicating what the statement problem was.
- Process failure occurs when the user session running against the database is terminated abnormally. Statement rollback, release of locks, and other process cleanup actions are performed automatically by PMON.
- Instance failure occurs when the instance is forced to shut down due to some problem with the host machine or an aborted background process. Recovery from this problem occurs when the instance is restarted. Instance recovery is handled automatically by the SMON process.
- Media failure occurs when there is some problem with the disks that store Oracle data, and the data is rendered unavailable. The DBA must manually intervene in these situations to restore lost data from backups.
- Temporary media failure usually results from the failure of hardware other than the actual disk drive. After the problem is corrected, the database can access its data again.
- Permanent media failure is usually the result of damage to data itself. Usually, the drive will need to be replaced and the DBA will need to recover the data on the disk from backup.
- The DBVERIFY utility is helpful for identifying block corruption in datafiles on your database. The `LOG_BLOCK_CHECKSUM` parameter in your `init`*`sid`*`.ora` file is useful for identifying block corruption in your redo logs before they are archived.

- When operating, background processes like PMON and DBW0 produce trace files whenever an error occurs.
- A special trace file called the ALERT log contains information about several database-wide operations, including:
  - Database startup and shutdown
  - `initsid.ora` parameter values
  - Tablespaces being created, altered, and dropped
  - Databases being altered
  - Rollback segments being created, altered, and dropped
  - Internal errors
  - Log switch activities
- Recovery when the database runs in `noarchivelog` mode is only possible to the point in time at which the most recent backup was taken.
- The advantage of running your database in `noarchivelog` mode, from a recovery perspective, is simplicity of backup and recovery.
- The disadvantage of `noarchivelog` mode is that you lose any data changes made after the most recent backup. This database operation mode is effective for development and testing environments.
- Database recovery for `noarchivelog` mode databases must be accomplished from full offline backups. *All* files must be restored from backup, not just damaged ones, to ensure that the database is consistent at a single point in time.
- Review the step-by-step process for recovery of the database when running in `noarchivelog` mode, as it was outlined in the chapter.
- Recovery when the database runs in `archivelog` mode is possible to the point in time of media failure.
- The advantage of running your database in `archivelog` mode is that you have that additional level of recoverability, and can run your database 24 hours a day, 7 days a week, while still being able to take backups.
- The disadvantage of `archivelog` mode is that recovery is somewhat more complex, and you need to make sure you have all the archived redo logs—from the time your backup was taken to the time of media failure. This database operation mode is effective for production database operation.

- Two components of database recovery when archiving is enabled are the database file backups and archived redo logs that can be applied in order to restore data changes made after the most recent backup.
- Database recovery is performed in Server Manager with the `recover` command. You can perform database, tablespace, and datafile recovery.
- Automatic recovery can be used to reduce the amount of interaction required for database recovery and is specified with the `automatic` keyword. When enabled, Oracle will automatically apply its suggestions for archive logs.
- Automatic archiving needs the `LOG_ARCHIVE_DEST` and `LOG_ARCHIVE_FORMAT` parameters to be set in `init`*`sid`*`.ora` to help formulate and apply redo log suggestions:
  - `LOG_ARCHIVE_DEST` determines where redo log archives will be placed.
  - `LOG_ARCHIVE_FORMAT` determines the nomenclature for the archived redo information.
- When archiving is enabled and recovery is necessary, you only need to restore the damaged datafiles, except when the datafile damaged was part of the SYSTEM or a ROLLBACK tablespace, in which case database recovery will be accomplished from full offline backups.
- Recovery of an Oracle database running in `archivelog` mode can consist of the following six situations:
  - Recovery from damage to datafiles in SYSTEM or ROLLBACK tablespaces
  - Recovery from deleted datafiles in non-SYSTEM or non-ROLLBACK tablespaces
  - Recovery from damaged datafiles in non-SYSTEM or non-ROLLBACK tablespaces
  - Recovery from deleted datafiles in non-SYSTEM or non-ROLLBACK tablespaces when there is no backup datafile
  - Recovery from media failure occurring while the datafiles were being backed up; for this situation you can circumvent a long recovery using the `alter database datafile` *`num`* `end backup` statement
  - Recovery when an unused online redo log is removed accidentally

- Information about the status of a database recovery and the files you need can be found in the following views:
  - **V$RECOVER_FILE** Used for locating datafiles needing recovery
  - **V$LOG_HISTORY** Used for identifying the list of all archived redo logs for the database
  - **V$RECOVERY_LOG** Used for identifying the list of archived redo logs required for recovery
  - **V$RECOVERY_FILE_STATUS** Used for identifying the files that need recovery and the status of that recovery
  - **V$RECOVERY_STATUS** Used for identifying overall recovery information, such as start time, log sequence number needed for recovery, status of previous log applied, and reason recovery needs user input

Chapter Questions

1. An Oracle internal error causes the instance to abort. Which of the following choices correctly identifies the process or individual who will handle correcting the problem?

A. The user

B. The PMON process

C. The DBA

D. The SMON process

2. The DBA begins backup of the tablespace containing data tables for an application. While the backup is taking place, lightning strikes and a power outage occurs. Which of the following choices identifies the easiest method for recovering the database in this situation?

A. Issue the `alter tablespace end backup` statement

B. Issue the `alter database datafile end backup` statement

C. Restore all datafiles and apply all archived redo logs

D. Restore only damaged datafiles and apply all archived redo logs

3. The DBA is trying to describe the use of the ALERT log to diagnose failure issues and problems to a developer. Which of the following problems will the records in the ALERT log not give any information about?

A. Statement failure due to a tablespace running out of space

B. Oracle internal error

C. A tablespace being dropped

D. A user dropping a table

4. The DBA is attempting to determine the status of a recovery in progress. Which of the following database views offers information about the time the recovery operation started and the SCNs that still need to be applied to the damaged datafiles?

A. V$RECOVERY_FILE_STATUS

B. V$BACKUP

C. V$RECOVERY_STATUS

D. V$RECOVER_FILE

5. The DBA has just finished creating a database. Without putting the database into `archivelog` mode, the DBA can provide which of the following levels of service to users of the database in question?

A. 24-hour availability with guaranteed data recovery to the point of failure

B. Recoverability to the point of database failure

C. Recoverability to any point in time between the most recent backup and the failure

D. Recoverability to the point in time of the last backup

6. Use of the `alter database rename file` command is most appropriate in which of the following situations?

A. Recovery of unused damaged redo log files

B. Recovery when a disk cannot be replaced

C. Recovery when there is no backup datafile

D. Recovery when `noarchivelog` mode is used

7. The DBA is about to execute a complete recovery from media failure. Three datafiles were damaged. Which of the following choices indicates the files the DBA should restore to perform this recovery?

A. All datafiles in the database

B. All datafiles in tablespaces with damaged datafiles

C. All damaged datafiles only

D. All archived redo logs only

8. You suspect there is some block corruption in your datafiles. Which of the following tools would you use to detect it? (Choose two)

A. DBVERIFY

B. `LOG_BLOCK_CHECKSUM`

C. ORAPWD

D. EXPORT

E. IMPORT

F. RMAN

9. User MANNY is in the process of entering transactions when her machine hangs. She reboots her machine and re-enters the application to finish the transaction. After clicking the SUBMIT button to update Oracle, the application hangs. Why does this happen?

A. The instance most likely has crashed.

B. MANNY's prior session still holds necessary locks for that transaction.

C. The SMON process is busy cleaning up from the prior session.

D. The process is probably waiting for DBWR to finish a checkpoint.

10. When a user process disconnects abnormally from the server process, which Oracle background process will clean up any unfinished transactions that user processes may have generated?

A. SMON

B. LGWR

C. PMON

D. DBW0

11. You are recovering a tablespace using an RMAN script. Which of the following commands should be used to move your datafile to another disk if the old location can't be restored prior to recovery?

A. `restore tablespace`

B. `sql 'alter database rename file'`

C. `recover tablespace`

D. `set newname`

12. Media failure has just occurred on a disk containing datafiles of a tablespace that was in the process of being backed up. Which of the following options describes the easiest way for the DBA to recover?

A. Shut down the entire database and perform complete recovery from the most recent backup.

B. Start up, mount, but don't open the database, and issue the `alter database datafile end backup` command.

C. Start up, mount, but don't open the database, and issue the `alter tablespace end backup` command.

D. Take the tablespace offline, restore all datafiles, and recover the tablespace.

13. You have just deleted a datafile belonging to the SYSTEM tablespace on your `archivelog` database. Which of the following choices best identifies how to recover the database?

A. Take the tablespace offline, restore the missing datafile, and recover.

B. Shut down the database, restore all datafiles, and recover.

C. Shut down the database, restore the missing datafile, and recover.

D. Take the datafile offline, restore the missing datafile, and recover.

14. The interactive aspect of database recovery can be eliminated with the use of which of the following options to the `recover database` statement?

A. `archivelog`

B. `resetlogs`

C. `automatic`

D. `start`

Answers to Chapter Questions

1. D. The SMON process

Explanation The SMON process handles instance recovery automatically after the instance crashes. Though the DBA will have to restart the database, this is really the only intervention required, eliminating choice C. The users on the database will have nothing to do with recovery, eliminating choice A. Finally, the PMON process handles recovery after a user process terminates by rolling back uncommitted work, relinquishing locks, and killing the associated server process if dedicated servers are being used. PMON does not handle instance recovery, however, thus eliminating choice B.

2. B. Issue the `alter database datafile end backup` statement

Explanation By issuing the statement identified in choice B, you prevent yourself from having to recover the tablespace or datafile from restored backup copies or with archived redo logs. Although choice A seems like it says the same thing, you must remember that you cannot change tablespace status until the database has started, which is impossible in this situation. Choices C and D are the long, drawn-out options for recovery that you are trying to avoid with choice B.

3. D. A user dropping a table

Explanation Of the choices given, only when users drop a table will an associated message not be written to the ALERT log. Remember, the ALERT log records database-wide activities. These activities include internal errors, creation or removal of tablespaces, creation or removal of rollback segments, log switches, or any `alter database` statements. Be sure you understand how to use the ALERT log before taking OCP Exam 3.

4. C. V$RECOVERY_STATUS

Explanation The V$RECOVERY_STATUS view gives detailed information about the entire recovery operation, including files still needing recovery in this run, the time recovery started, and the SCNs that still need to be applied. Choice B is incorrect because V$BACKUP gives you information about the datafiles that are currently part of a tablespace in backup state on your database. Choice A is incorrect because V$RECOVERY_FILE_STATUS only shows the name of the file being recovered and its status. Choice D is incorrect because V$RECOVER_FILE gives information about files that need to be recovered.

5. D. Recoverability to the point in time of the last backup

Explanation Without putting the database into `archivelog` mode, you can guarantee recoverability only to the point of the last database backup. This fact should be sufficient for you to eliminate choice A, which can only be given if archiving is enabled. Choice B is eliminated as well, because the choice basically describes complete recovery. Choice C is eliminated because the choice describes incomplete recovery. You should know by now that these two things are only possible once you start archiving your redo logs.

6. B. Recovery when a disk cannot be replaced

Explanation When you need to move your datafiles, as is the case when you cannot wait for hardware replacement to recover your database, you can use the `alter database rename file` command to make the change in your control file. Choice A is incorrect because recovering unused online redo logs requires a different set of commands. Choice C is incorrect because there is a separate set of procedures for recreating your datafile for recovery when there is no backup. Choice D is incorrect because renaming files is neither appropriate or inappropriate in situations where you plan to recover a database that is not archiving its redo logs.

7. C. All damaged datafiles only

Explanation You would only restore damaged datafiles on databases running in `archivelog` mode, because the application of archived redo information will make the database read-consistent. Choices A and B are incorrect because although you can restore more datafiles than those that are damaged, your recovery will take longer because there will be more redo to apply. Choice D is incorrect because you don't just need archived redo logs on hand for the recovery, you need datafiles, too.

8. A *and* F. DBVERIFY *and* RMAN

Explanation The DBVERIFY and RMAN utilities handle identification of block corruption in datafiles. Choice B is not correct because `LOG_BLOCK_CHECKSUM` detects block corruption in your redo logs only. ORAPWD is incorrect because this utility is used to create your password file, and has no place in database recovery. Choices D and E are incorrect because although you might repopulate a table containing corrupted data using dump files, these utilities will not actually help you to identify the problem, only possibly to fix it.

9. B. MANNY's prior session still holds necessary locks for that transaction.

Explanation Recall from the discussion of process failure that PMON must detect server processes whose user processes have crashed and perform cleanup, such as releasing locks and rolling back uncommitted changes. MANNY's original session probably still holds locks on the rows she wants to make changes to, so she will wait until PMON forces her original server process to relinquish those locks and roll back the work. The instance does not crash when process failure happens, eliminating choice A. As mentioned, SMON doesn't handle the cleanup after process failure, PMON does, eliminating choice C. Choice D is wrong because DBWR handles its checkpoint activities fairly rapidly, so you won't necessarily see a delay in this situation as the result of choice D.

10. C. PMON

Explanation PMON must detect server processes whose user processes have crashed, and perform cleanup, such as releasing locks and rolling back uncommitted changes. SMON handles instance recovery after instance failure, eliminating choice A. LGWR writes redo from memory to disk, eliminating choice B. DBW0 writes data blocks from memory to disk, eliminating choice D, as well.

11. D. `set newname`

Explanation The command in choice D is used to rename a file in RMAN so that the change is tracked in the recovery catalog. Although choice B will update the control file in the primary database, the recovery catalog will still need the change made to it with another statement. Thus, choice D is more effective. Choice A and C are both incorrect—database restore and recovery operations must be performed after the filename changes are made; these commands don't actually perform the name changes.

12. B. Start up, mount, but don't open the database, and issue the `alter database datafile end backup` command.

Explanation By issuing the statement in choice B, you eliminate all the extra work required in restoring the datafiles from backup and then applying archived redo logs. This eliminates choices A and D. Though choice C appears to be the same thing as choice B at first glance, it's not because you can't take the tablespace out of backup state until you can get the database open, which can't be done without recovery. So, choice C must be eliminated as well.

13. C. Shut down the database, restore the missing datafile, and recover.

Explanation Datafiles belonging to the SYSTEM or a ROLLBACK tablespace can be restored, but the database must be shut down in order to do so. This eliminates choices A and D. However, the nice thing about archiving your redo logs is that you no longer need to restore all datafiles from backup in order to recover your database. Thus, choice B is also incorrect, leaving you with your correct answer, choice C.

14. C. `automatic`

Explanation The `automatic` keyword is used to have Oracle apply its own redo log suggestions as part of the recovery process. The `archivelog` keyword is not used in the `recover database` statement, therefore choice A is incorrect. The `resetlogs` keyword relates to discarding redo logs and resetting the sequence number after incomplete recovery, therefore choice B is incorrect. (Incomplete recovery is covered in the next chapter.) The `start` keyword is an option used in the `alter system archive log` statement to begin automatic archival of online redo logs, which doesn't relate to the disabling of interaction between the DBA and Oracle during database recovery. Therefore, choice D is incorrect.

15

Advanced Topics in Data Recovery

In this chapter, you will learn about and demonstrate knowledge in the following areas:

- Incomplete recovery with archiving
- Additional Oracle recovery issues
- Oracle EXPORT and IMPORT utilities

This chapter concludes your treatment of Oracle backup and recovery topics for OCP Exam 3. One of the areas left to cover includes how you can handle *incomplete database recovery*—recovery to a point in the past that is neither the point at which the backup was taken nor the time of the media failure. Another area left to cover is advanced topics in data recovery. These topics include how to minimize downtime and recover lost control files. The final area left to cover is how to use EXPORT and IMPORT to quickly save and restore copies of your data for various purposes. You first learned about EXPORT and IMPORT in Unit II, where they were introduced as a set of tools for performing tablespace reorganization and mass data-loading. Here, the tools will be reintroduced as potential alternatives to offline backups for database development and testing environments. These three main content areas comprise approximately 20 percent of OCP DBA Exam 3, and are critical for passing the test.

Incomplete Recovery with Archiving

In this section, you will cover the following topics related to incomplete recovery with archiving:

- When to use incomplete recovery
- Performing an incomplete recovery
- Recovering after losing current and active redo logs
- Using RMAN in incomplete recovery
- Working with tablespace point-in-time recovery

Archiving allows you to recover your Oracle database to a point in time in the past that is neither the point at which you took your backup nor the time the database experienced media failure. This type of recovery is called incomplete recovery. This section presents several aspects of incomplete recovery, from understanding what situations will require that you execute incomplete recovery, to the processes required for executing incomplete recovery, and many things in between. In addition, you will learn how to perform tablespace point-in-time incomplete recovery—something that was not possible in Oracle7.

When to Use Incomplete Recovery

Incomplete recovery is recovery to a point in time in the past, before a media failure occurred. A database recovery that doesn't involve application of archived redo logs could be considered a form of incomplete recovery because it is the application of archived redo information that brings the database to a state of complete recovery. However, archived redo logs also give a great deal of flexibility in allowing recovery up to any point between the most recent database backup and the point in time at which the database media failure occurred. Thus, recovery to a point after a backup was taken, and before the point that the database experienced media failure, is the more appropriate definition of incomplete recovery, and is the definition we will use as the basis for discussion of incomplete recovery in this chapter.

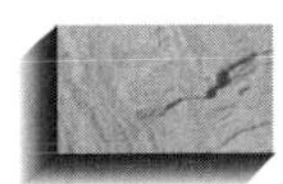

TIP
Understand an important factor in incomplete recovery—you will lose all data changes made to the database after the point to which you recover your data.

Incomplete recovery generally takes place only when the instance is started and the database is mounted, but not opened, in `exclusive` mode. You must be operating Oracle in `archivelog` mode or else you will not be able to perform incomplete recovery. Three types of incomplete database recovery exist in Oracle. They are *change-based recovery, time-based recovery,* and *cancel-based recovery.* These categories of database recovery are based on the mechanisms that Oracle offers for ending the recovery. These types of incomplete recovery are described next, and they will be covered in more detail later in this chapter.

Change-Based Incomplete Recovery

In change-based recovery, Oracle restores database changes up to the database change you specify in the `recover` command. For example, suppose somebody executes a data change inappropriately, and this data change forms the basis for changing several records in the database. If you know the SCN, you can use change-based recovery to recover Oracle to the last known good transaction that took place. Recall that SCN stands for *system change number,* which is the unique number Oracle assigns every transaction in the database. Every statement executing within the transaction has the SCN attached to it in the rollback segments and online redo logs, identifying all statements that make changes together as one transaction.

To find the last SCN archived by Oracle, or to find out what SCN was written at the last checkpoint, you can query the ARCHIVE_CHANGE# or CHECKPOINT_CHANGE# columns in the V$DATABASE dynamic performance view, respectively. The following statement illustrates the `recover` command you would use for change-based recovery. The number 4043 is the SCN for a transaction in the online redo log. When the recovery procedure reaches transaction number 4043, Oracle will apply the database changes that were committed as part of that transaction and then terminate the recovery automatically.

```
RECOVER AUTOMATIC DATABASE UNTIL CHANGE 4043;
```

TIP
To find the range of transaction SCNs in an archived redo log, look at the FIRST_CHANGE# and NEXT_CHANGE# columns in the V$LOG_HISTORY dynamic performance view.

WHEN TO USE IT You might use change-based recovery to recover your Oracle database in a distributed database environment.

Time-Based Incomplete Recovery

Rather than restoring to a system change number, which may be hard for the DBA to ascertain, the incomplete database recovery may be conducted to a certain point in time, instead. This type of recovery is considered to be a time-based recovery. Time-based and change-based recoveries are similar in that Oracle will restore data to the database to some point in the past. The big difference is that the DBA can identify a point in time rather than dig through the database to identify the SCN for the last transaction committed at a point in time. Once the recovery has applied redo information for *all committed* transactions through the time specified, the recovery will end automatically. If uncommitted data was written in order to supply the database with all committed information to the time named, then the uncommitted transaction data will be rolled back before the recovery ends.

WHEN TO USE IT You might use time-based recovery to resolve the following situations in your Oracle database:

- A user made unwanted data changes or you dropped a table, and you know approximately what time the mishap occurred

- A redo log that is not multiplexed is discovered to be corrupt, and you know what time the redo log was archived

Cancel-Based Incomplete Recovery

The final type of incomplete recovery to be considered is the cancel-based recovery, which allows the DBA to run a database recovery for an indefinite period, defined on the fly by the DBA as the recovery executes. During the course of the recovery, the DBA may choose to issue a `cancel` command, and the recovery will stop. The cancel-based recovery offers the DBA unmatched control over the execution of database recovery; however, it carries with that control the responsibility of the DBA to monitor the recovery process.

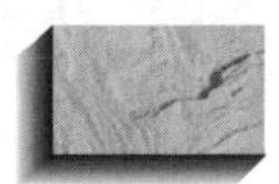

TIP
You can't run cancel-based recovery in conjunction with the `automatic` option to have Oracle automatically apply redo log suggestions to your recovery operation!

WHEN TO USE IT You might use cancel-based recovery to resolve the following situations in your Oracle database:

- The current redo log is damaged and not available for recovery
- You are missing an archive log required for complete recovery

Recovery with Backup Control Files

Another recovery activity you can use with the three types of database recovery just discussed is recovering your database when you are missing control files, or when (for whatever reason) you don't use the control files you do have. In this situation, you must use a backup control file in order to perform recovery. The command is `recover database using backup controlfile`. Recall that in Chapter 12 you learned how to make backup copies of your control file and how to generate a `create controlfile` script. You should review that material, if necessary, for better understanding.

WHEN TO USE IT You might recover using a backup control file to resolve the following situations in your Oracle database:

- You have no copies of the control file to revert to, and no way to regenerate the control file, but you have a backup copy

- When you want to recover to a prior point in time when the file structure of the database was different

Exercises

1. What are the types of incomplete recovery? Which type of incomplete recovery cannot be run in conjunction with automatic recovery?
2. Can the database be available during incomplete recovery? Why or why not?
3. Make a list of the incomplete recovery options for exercise 1. Next to each option, list situations in which this type of incomplete recovery might be used.

Performing an Incomplete Recovery

In Chapter 14, you saw the `recover` command from Server Manager in action. This lesson elaborates on the special requirements and syntax for performing incomplete recovery using this command, and the procedures required for the incomplete recovery. The database cannot be opened or available for use when performing incomplete recovery, and it must be mounted by only one instance. To perform an incomplete recovery, you must have an offline or online backup containing all datafiles for your database, and you must also have all archived redo logs up to the point to which you want to recover the database.

Incomplete Recovery Procedure

The following steps must be completed to perform the incomplete recovery of your Oracle database:

1. Shut down your database using `shutdown abort`.
2. Restore all datafiles from the prior backup (not from the backup you just took). Don't restore any of the control files, redo logs, password files, or parameter files, however. Remember that the datafiles must not be synchronized with the control or redo log files, or Oracle will not demand media recovery.
3. Start up and mount, but do not open Oracle.
4. Run your recovery using the appropriate statement options, shown in the following code block and elaborated upon in the rest of the lesson:

```
RECOVER DATABASE UNTIL CANCEL;
RECOVER DATABASE UNTIL CHANGE scn;
RECOVER DATABASE UNTIL TIME time;
```

5. Simultaneously open your database and discard your online redo logs with the `alter database open resetlogs` command. If this step is not accomplished, you might later apply your old archive logs from before the incomplete recovery and really screw things up. Remember, no data changes made after the point to which you recovered your database will be available.
6. Shut down the database using the `normal`, `transactional`, or `immediate` option, and take an offline backup. You never know what might happen between recovery and the next scheduled backup.
7. Open the database for your users.

Using the recover Command for Incomplete Recovery

The three incomplete recovery processes begin to differentiate after the `until` keyword. The specifications tell Oracle when and how to identify the moment recovery is finished. Recovery can be stopped after the application of a specific system change number (SCN), at a point in time in the past, or via an explicit `cancel` issued by the DBA during database recovery.

In change-based recovery where the `automatic` option is specified, Oracle restores database changes made up to a particular SCN, and then terminates the recovery automatically.

```
RECOVER AUTOMATIC FROM '/oracle/disk_28/archive' DATABASE
UNTIL CHANGE 39983;
```

Incomplete database recovery can also be conducted on a time basis, identified in the format *YYYY-MM-DD-HH24:MI:SS* enclosed in single quotes. Once the recovery has applied redo information for *all committed* transactions through the identified point in time, the recovery ends. Any transaction data written during the recovery that has not been committed at this time will be rolled back before the end of database recovery.

```
RECOVER AUTOMATIC DATABASE
UNTIL TIME '1999-04-15:22:15:00';
```

The final type of incomplete recovery being considered is the cancel-based recovery. This type of recovery allows you to run a database recovery for an indefinite period. During the course of the recovery, the DBA may choose to issue a `cancel` command, and the recovery will stop. This option offers unmatched control over recovery execution, and it is useful for situations where you know you are missing archived redo logs. However, with this control comes the obligation to monitor the recovery process. The following code block illustrates the command used to start cancel-based recovery. Note that you cannot use the `automatic` keyword in specifying cancel-based recovery.

```
RECOVER DATABASE UNTIL CANCEL;
```

Incomplete Recovery Using a Backup Control File

In some cases, you may need to use a backup copy of the control file to perform database recovery. For example, if you are recovering to a point where the physical layout of the database was different than its current layout, you will need to use backup copies of the control file containing that system layout. In the incomplete-recovery procedure listed previously, the syntax you should use in step 5 is `recover database until` *`option`* `using backup controlfile`:

```
RECOVER AUTOMATIC FROM '/oracle/disk_28/archive' DATABASE
UNTIL CHANGE 39983
USING BACKUP CONTROLFILE;
```

Or,

```
RECOVER DATABASE
UNTIL CANCEL
USING BACKUP CONTROLFILE;
```

Or,

```
RECOVER AUTOMATIC DATABASE
UNTIL TIME '1999-04-15:22:15:00'
USING BACKUP CONTROLFILE;
```

TIP
To perform incomplete recovery, you must have a database backup prior to the point to which you want to recover. This enables you to roll the redo logs forward. You cannot move backward through redo, systematically "unapplying" information, however.

Exercises

1. Describe in detail the incomplete-recovery process. What keywords are used to determine whether Oracle pursues change-based, cancel-based, or time-based recovery?
2. How does the DBA open the database while simultaneously discarding redo information?

3. What is the syntax for recovery using a control file backup? When might you need to perform this type of recovery?

Recovering after Losing Current and Active Redo Logs

In some situations, Oracle may hang because a redo log being written becomes unavailable. This may be due to media failure on the disk containing the log, or because the log file itself contains corrupt blocks. Perhaps, for some other reason, the LGWR process crashes. In any case, you will need to recover your database. The method you use for this task depends on whether the database is open or closed. If the database is open, you will perform the following tasks. First, look in the V$LOG view to see which group shows a current status, meaning that the log is being written currently by LGWR. This is the log you must clear, for by clearing the redo log, you might eliminate the problem. You can clear the redo log using the `alter database clear unarchived logfile group` *`num`* statement. The redo log will then be overwritten, meaning that database operation can continue, unless the problem is media failure and lack of access to the log file.

The other situation you might encounter is when your database fails because LGWR died. This will abort your instance. To recover, you must revert to your backup and apply redo logs up to the current one. You may need to create new redo logs, as well, particularly if a disk failure prevents Oracle from accessing the redo logs it needs. The following procedure should be used in this situation:

1. Start up your instance, but do not mount or open the database.
2. Select the sequence number for the current redo log. You will recover your database up to this redo log shortly. Use the following query on the V$LOG view:

```
SVRMGR> SELECT SEQUENCE# FROM V$LOG
     2> WHERE STATUS = 'CURRENT';
SEQ#
----
  23
```

3. Restore all your datafiles (but not control files, redo log files, password files, or `init`*`sid`*`.ora` files) from the most recent backup.
4. Perform your incomplete recovery. Cancel-based recovery is probably the easiest, although you'll have to baby-sit the recovery process. When Oracle tells you it's ready to apply the redo log sequence number you obtained in step 2, cancel the recovery.

5. Simultaneously open your database and discard redo log information by issuing the `alter database open resetlogs` command.
6. If you lost a disk containing redo logs, and you do not have the minimum number of logs necessary for Oracle to open, you must create some new redo log groups and drop the one whose files were lost. Use the appropriate combination of `alter database add logfile group` and `alter database drop logfile group` commands.
7. Take an offline backup of your database, and give it back to the users.

If You Don't Take Backups After Incomplete Recovery...

OK, so you've ignored the message thus far and didn't make a backup of your database after performing incomplete recovery, and now your database has crashed again. It is possible to recover when you have no new backup and after you've discarded redo log information, but you will need three things, and if you don't have them, you shouldn't even attempt this recovery. You need backup copies of your control file, to go with the most recent datafile backups; a copy of the ALERT log written when you performed the prior incomplete recovery; and all the archive logs from your prior incomplete recovery. The procedure that follows will guide you through the process and perhaps show you why you should always take an offline backup when you're done with incomplete recovery.

1. Use the `shutdown abort` command to stop Oracle, if it is still running.
2. Start up your instance, but do not mount or open the database.
3. Select the sequence number for the current redo log. You will soon recover your database up to this redo log. Use the following query on the V$LOG view:

```
SVRMGR> SELECT SEQUENCE# FROM V$LOG
     2> WHERE STATUS = 'CURRENT';
SEQ#
----
  23
```

4. Shut down the database and move your control files somewhere else.
5. Restore all datafiles and control files from your original backup.
6. In the ALERT log written when you performed the prior incomplete recovery, find where it contains either the SCN for the last change applied to Oracle in that recovery, or the log sequence number. This is the point to which you will recover your database.

7. Start up and mount the database, but do not open it.
8. Perform your incomplete cancel-based recovery. When Oracle tells you it's ready to apply the redo log sequence or SCN you obtained in step 6, cancel the recovery. When finished, shut down the database using the `normal` option.
9. Replace the backup copies of your control file with the control files you moved somewhere else in step 4.
10. Start up and mount the database, but do not open it.
11. Perform another incomplete recovery, this time up to the point you identified in step 2.
12. Start up, mount, and open Oracle. Check to see if the recovery restored the data you wanted it to. If so, you're ready to take your offline backup this time!

Exercises

1. What procedure is used to return Oracle to normal operation if your database has not stopped running?
2. What must you do to return Oracle to normal operation if your database has stopped running?
3. What extra sorts of things do you need if your database crashes again after incomplete recovery and you didn't take an offline backup?

Using RMAN in Incomplete Recovery

In RMAN, incomplete recovery is handled in the same way as in an operating system command-driven database recovery. You first recover all datafiles from your last complete backup. Then, you apply your redo log information up to either a point in time, an SCN, or interactively until a `cancel` command is issued. The main difference is that with RMAN you can do everything from within an Oracle command interface. The job is stored in your recovery catalog, as well.

NOTE
You cannot use a datafile or archived redo log that is not part of the recovery catalog in a recovery managed by RMAN.

Incomplete recovery using RMAN is managed as follows:

1. Shut down the primary database with the `transactional`, `immediate` or `normal` option.
2. Start up, mount, but do not open, the primary database. The recovery catalog database should also be open.
3. Set your `NLS_LANG` variable according to local specifications. In Nashville, TN, for example, you might use `NLS_LANG=american`. If you're planning to perform time-based incomplete recovery, set `NLS_DATE_FORMAT`, as well; for example, `NLS_DATE_FORMAT='YYYY-MM-DD:HH24:MI:SS'`.
4. Start RMAN by connecting to both the primary database and the recovery catalog.
5. Develop your `run` script for restoring the datafiles, allocating appropriate channels and setting the time-based or change-based recovery variables.
6. Add content to restore your archived redo logs for this recovery, if they do not exist on disk.
7. Add the `recover database` command into your RMAN `run` script.
8. When RMAN finishes running the script, the database will need to be opened with the redo log's sequence number reset. Also, add support for releasing the channel when completed.
9. Execute the script.

```
D:\orant\bin> rman80 target user/pass@proddb rcvcat user/pass@catdb
RMAN> run { allocate channel c1 type disk;
    >       set until time = '1999-08-24:15:30:00';
    >       restore database;
    >       recover database;
    >       sql 'alter database open resetlogs';
    >       release channel c1; }
```

10. Make sure the data was recovered as you expected it to be. If it was, register this as a new incarnation of your database using the `reset database` command.

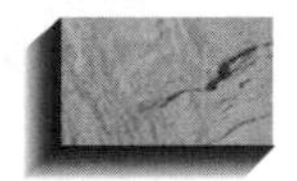

TIP
You should understand that the `restore database` command only restores datafiles, not any other type of Oracle database file or archived redo log, to the database. To restore other types of files, return to Chapter 14 and review the syntax offered in the discussion of using RMAN to recover databases running in `noarchivelog` mode.

Exercises

1. Describe the process of incomplete recovery using RMAN. How is it different from managing the incomplete recovery using only operating system commands?
2. What files are restored with the RMAN `restore` command? What files are specifically not restored?

Working with Tablespace Point-in-Time Recovery

Oracle didn't advertise that in Oracle7 you could perform incomplete tablespace recovery, but you could. You can in Oracle8, as well. It's just very tricky and risky. Say, for example, some data change was made a week ago in a table on one tablespace, and now it needs to be backed out. You don't want to back out of data changed in every tablespace, just this one. You can use incomplete recovery on a tablespace in order to revert to the version of data that existed just prior to the problem. For this task, you will need to create a second database on this or another machine, export the table on the second database, and import it back to the original. Creating this second database, sometimes referred to as a *clone*, is a main part of performing tablespace incomplete recovery.

To perform tablespace incomplete recovery, you need several things—if you don't have these things, don't perform this recovery. You need backup copies of all datafiles for the tablespace to be recovered, all archived redo logs up to the point you wish to recover to, enough disk space and memory on your machine (or another machine) to create and run the clone, and a backup copy of your current control file. Because of the complexity presented by incomplete recovery for a tablespace, you should only perform this task with the assistance of Oracle Worldwide Support. Loosely speaking, the procedure is as follows:

1. Use your backup to create a clone database.
2. Recover your clone to the point at which you can get the object(s) you need to restore on your production database.
3. Export from your clone the object(s) you need on your production database.
4. Import the object(s) you exported in step 3 to your production database.
5. Shut down, back up, and start your production Oracle database.

TIP
If you need help managing use of EXPORT and IMPORT for this procedure, review the coverage provided in Unit II, or the information about these tools offered later in this chapter.

Exercises

1. Identify the things you will need for incomplete tablespace recovery on your Oracle database.
2. What is the basic procedure for handling tablespace incomplete recovery?

Additional Oracle Recovery Issues

In this section, you will cover these additional Oracle recovery issues:

- Methods for minimizing downtime
- Diagnosing and recovering from database corruption errors
- Reconstructing lost or damaged control files
- Considerations for recovering offline and read-only tablespaces
- Recovering from Recovery Catalog loss

This section covers the final set of items you should know about Oracle physical database file recovery and the tasks you perform to handle it. Several issues are addressed. One of them is minimizing downtime. In this lesson, you'll learn about reducing the amount of time spent in database recovery. Another issue covered is diagnosing and recovering from database corruption errors. The methods used for reconstructing lost or damaged control files is a special issue covered here, as well. There are also some important recovery issues you need to know about for offline and read-only tablespaces. Finally, you will learn how to recover from recovery catalog loss.

Methods for Minimizing Downtime

Back in Chapter 12, you were introduced to the three-fold goal for an organization's backup and recovery strategy, which is *maximizing database availability, maximizing recovery performance,* and *maximizing data recoverability.* In this lesson, you will learn more about maximizing recovery performance using a few different methods. These methods include the way Oracle improves recovery by opening the database faster after failure occurs, how you can run recovery in parallel, and how to open your database even when datafiles are missing.

Using Fast Transaction Rollback

The Oracle database feature that allows it to start quickly after failure is called *fast transaction rollback,* sometimes also referred to in Oracle documentation as *fast warmstart.* The architecture of the Oracle database is set so that recovery occurs in two phases: *rolling forward* and *rolling back.* Figure 15-1 demonstrates Oracle during the roll-forward process, where archive redo log data is applied. It also demonstrates the second phase, when Oracle rolls back all transactions that were not committed when database activity terminated.

The fast warmstart feature of Oracle improves recovery performance by opening the database for use after Oracle completes the roll-forward process. What effect does this fast warmstart have on the rest of the database? As part of media recovery, Oracle applies all changes found in redo logs up to the point in time of the failure. When the process is complete, the database opens. Oracle will continue to roll some uncommitted transactions back. User processes will roll back uncommitted changes implicitly as they request blocks that contain that uncommitted data, as well. This feature slows down user-transaction processing a little, but the overall effect of making data available improves database recovery, so the performance hit is outweighed.

Starting Oracle with Datafiles Missing

You may need to make Oracle available when datafiles are missing. Say, for example, you have a database that supports many applications, each with database objects in their own schema. These schemas, in turn, have their own tablespace sets, each of which are on different disks. A media failure occurs, making tablespaces for the employee expense system unavailable for use. In this situation, all other applications

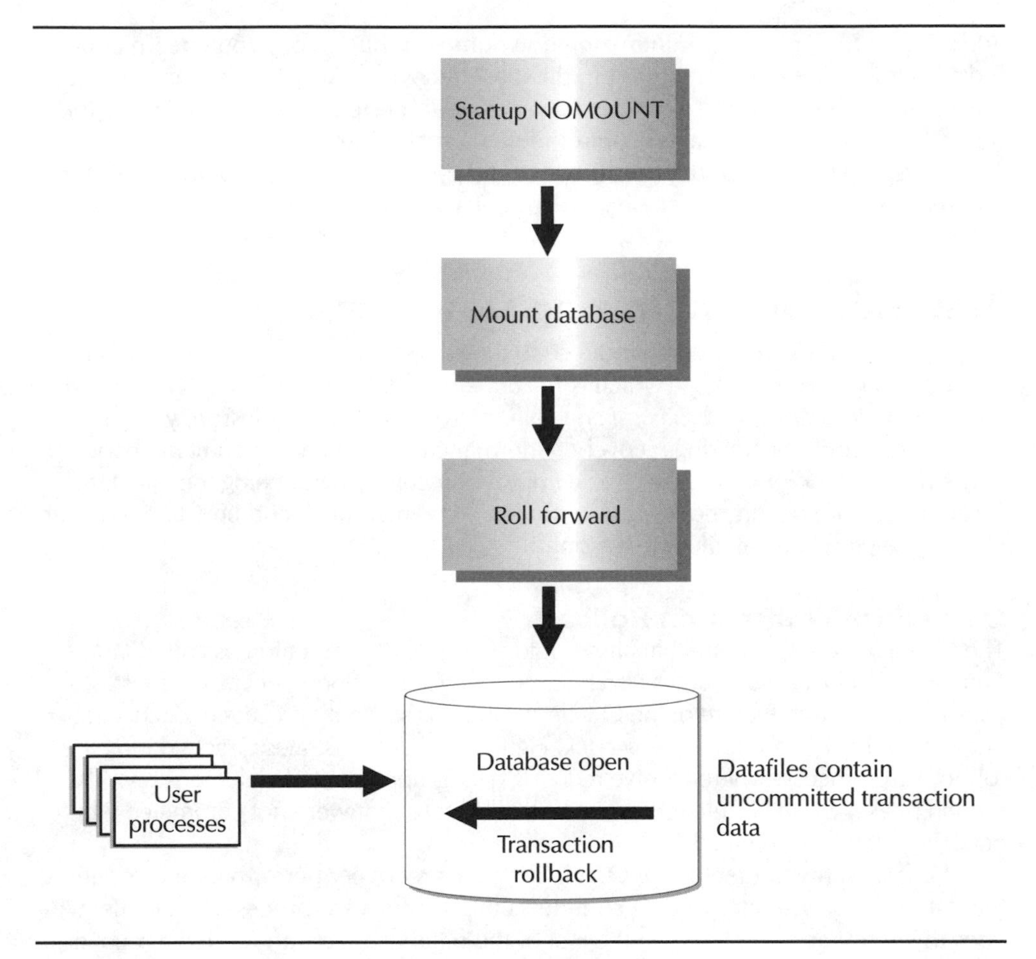

FIGURE 15-1. *Database startup after media failure*

should remain unaffected, even though the tablespaces on the failed disk will be inaccessible. Also, unless you recover those lost tablespace datafiles before shutting down Oracle, you will not be able to start the database again. Here's how to open a database that is missing some of its datafiles, or even entire tablespaces, so that it is available for use while the DBA performs recovery:

1. While the database is open, identify the datafiles that are not available by investigating the contents of the STATUS column in the V$DATAFILE view. If the database is already closed, skip ahead to step 3.

2. Shut down Oracle using the `shutdown immediate` command.
3. Start the instance, mount, but do not open, the database, with the `startup mount` command.
4. Take missing datafile(s) offline using the `alter database datafile` *`filename`* `offline immediate` statement. If all datafiles in one tablespace are missing, you should use this command to take the datafiles offline, one at a time, before bringing the tablespace offline.
5. Give the users of unaffected applications access to the database by opening it with the `alter database open` command.
6. Restore the datafile from a backup.
7. Perform either tablespace or datafile recovery, whichever is appropriate.
8. Bring the tablespace or datafiles online with `alter tablespace` *`tablespace`* `online.`

Using Parallel Recovery

A final method you may use to improve database-recovery performance is the parallel recovery feature. You can run a recovery in parallel to dedicate more processing power and database resources to accomplish the database recovery faster, thus minimizing downtime while also taking better advantage of the resources of the host machine running Oracle. Parallel recovery has several benefits. It works best in situations in which the media failure damaged information on two or more disks. In this way, recovery operates on the disks in parallel. However, the real performance benefit of parallel recovery depends on the operating system's ability to have two or more processes writing I/O to the same disk, or to different disks, at the same time. If the operating system on the machine hosting Oracle does not support this function, then the performance gain made by parallel recovery may be limited.

Parallel recovery requires the Parallel Server Option to be used. You can recover the entire database, a tablespace, or a datafile using parallel recovery. When parallel recovery is used, a master process coordinates the recovery. Oracle will allow the master process to create several slaves that execute the recovery in parallel, according to several different parameters. To execute a parallel recovery, issue the `recover parallel` statement from Server Manager, with several options specified:

```
SVRMGR> RECOVER DATABASE PARALLEL (DEGREE 3 INSTANCES 2);
```

- **`degree`** When you issue the `recover parallel` command, you specify the degree of parallelism to which the recovery should be executed. This defines how many processes will operate in tandem to recover the database.

The `degree` clause of the recovery operation represents the number of processes that will execute the recovery operation at the same time.

- **`instances`** When the DBA issues the parallel recovery command, the instances that will be dedicated to the task of database recovery can be specified. This only works when Parallel Server Option is used. In order to use the `instances` clause, the database must be mounted and opened in parallel by more than one instance. The `instances` clause acts as a multiplier for the `degree` clause, allowing the DBA to apply a specified `degree` number of processes or degrees to database recovery for every instance specified for the `instances` clause. The total number of processes that can be applied to the database recovery equals `degree` times `instances`.
- **`RECOVERY_PARALLELISM`** The parallel processes used to execute a parallel recovery can be set to a default using an `init`*`sid`*`.ora` parameter called `RECOVERY_PARALLELISM`. The value for this parameter cannot exceed the value specified in another init*sid*.ora parameter set for parallelism, `PARALLEL_MAX_SERVERS`. However, if you specify values for `degree` and `instances` above, any value set for `RECOVERY_PARALLELISM` will not be used.

More Frequent Backups

Probably the best method for improving database recovery time is taking more frequent backups. This method is particularly effective on OLTP systems with large transaction processing volumes. By having backups that are more recent, you reduce the amount of time you spend applying archived redo to the backup datafiles, because your backups have more of the changes stored in them already. By taking more frequent backups during periods of intense activity, you will improve your overall recovery time later. However, this method is often at the expense of strong performance for online transaction-processing volumes, because it takes Oracle longer to process those transactions while simultaneously taking an online backup. In addition, you may not be able to take more frequent backups if your strategy is to use offline backups, because your users may not be able to handle the periods of database unavailability.

Exercises

1. What is parallel recovery? What are the `init`*`sid`*`.ora` parameters that must be used in conjunction with parallel recovery? What may limit the performance benefits granted by parallel recovery?

2. What options must be used to start a database that has datafiles missing? When might it be useful to do this?
3. What database feature enables Oracle to start more quickly after a database has experienced media failure? How does this feature accomplish its goals?
4. After a database failure occurs, what potential limitations may database users experience if they access the database soon after it opens?

Diagnosing and Recovering from Database Corruption Errors

Database corruption may one day occur in one of your Oracle datafiles. You can detect block corruption in datafiles using the DBVERIFY command, covered in Chapter 14. Oracle will also give you the `ORA-01578: Oracle data block corrupted (file # num, block # num)` error.

There are a few different ways to fix database corruption. The first, and by far the most effective method is to recover your datafiles from backup and apply archived redo log information.

Alternatively, you can determine exactly where the datafile corruption exists in the file using the error message output or the DBVERIFY utility. After doing so, you can either continue using the table by selecting the corrupted data from the table using index range scans, or `select` data out of the table above and below the corrupted blocks, moving it into another table, and then drop the corrupted table.

Exercises

1. Identify two methods you can use to determine whether data-block corruption exists on the Oracle database.
2. What options must be used to fix the corruption problem? Which is the most effective?

Reconstructing Lost or Damaged Control Files

You may encounter situations requiring you to reconstruct or replace a lost or damaged control file on your Oracle database. Several situations indicate this need, including loss of all control files for your database due to media failure, needing to change option settings specified in your `create database` statement (`maxlogfiles`, `maxdatafiles`, `maxlogmembers`, and others), and wanting to change the name of the database.

You can recover your lost or damaged Oracle control files in several different ways. The first is by using a copy of your control file that may have been multiplexed. This is technically cheating, because you don't have to recover anything. In the strictest sense, you didn't even lose all your control files. Simply shut down the database using the `normal` or `immediate` option, copy your control file, and start the database again.

A real loss of control files can be solved using the `create controlfile` command, so long as the database is still open. You can facilitate this process with the script produced by running the `alter database backup controlfile to trace` command, first introduced in Chapter 12. The script will contain a `create controlfile` command that you can use to recreate the control file on your database. You may want to supplement your backup strategy by including control file backups, particularly if you do not multiplex your control files.

You can also recover from losing control files by using backup binary copies of your controlfile—backups made with the `alter database backup controlfile to` *`filename`* command, where *`filename`* identifies the name of a file to which Oracle will write a binary copy of the control file. The `ORA-01207: file is more recent than control file - old control file` error message indicates that you need to recover your database using a backup control file. To recover, follow these steps:

1. Copy your binary control file copy to the location of your lost control file (or change the `CONTROL_FILES` `init`*`sid`*`.ora` parameter).
2. Run a database recovery using the `recover database using backup controlfile` command to get the control file current with the current redo log sequence.
3. Issue the `alter database open resetlogs` command to reset the redo log sequence number in your control file to zero.

Exercises

1. Identify three ways you can ensure that you have more than one copy of a control file on your database. In which one will that additional copy be maintained?
2. What is the command used to create a script containing the `create controlfile` statement that can be used to create your control file? What command is used to create a backup binary copy of your control file?
3. What function does the `using backup controlfile` clause serve?

Recovery Issues for Offline and Read-Only Tablespaces

Static data needs less backup and recovery attention from you than other types of data. Static data includes special valid-values data kept in lookup tables, and this data can be placed into read-only tablespaces. Data in read-only tablespaces needs to be backed up only in two cases—either when the status of the tablespace changes from read-only to read-write, or when the data is changed.

There is only one complex recovery situation for read-only tablespaces. This is when your read-only tablespace experiences media failure, and the backup you have was taken when the tablespace was in a read-write state. In order to manage this recovery, you must first recover the tablespace from backups taken when it was a writable tablespace and apply redo logs to update the objects in that tablespace up to the point when the tablespace was made read-only. Then, you can change the tablespace state to read-only. In the converse situation, you may have a tablespace that was set to read-only in the last backup, but which is now set to read-write. In this case, simply restore the backup copy of the read-only tablespace and apply redo logs to change the tablespace status and all data changes made.

There may be situations where you cannot restore your read-only tablespace datafiles to the proper location, perhaps because a failed disk cannot be replaced before the users need the database back online. In this case, you can use the `alter database rename file` command to move the file.

Recovery when you need to re-create the control file is slightly trickier than for normal read-write tablespaces. If you look in the file produced by the `alter database backup controlfile to trace` statement, you will find the procedures required for handling this recovery operation. The following code block shows an excerpt from a trace script generated from a database in which a read-only tablespace exists:

```
# Recovery is required if any of the datafiles are restored backups,
# or if the last shutdown was not normal or immediate.
RECOVER DATABASE
# Database can now be opened normally.
ALTER DATABASE OPEN;
# Files in read only tablespaces are now named.
ALTER DATABASE RENAME FILE 'MISSING00003'
  TO 'D:\ORANT\DATABASE\USR1JSC.ORA';
# Online the files in read only tablespaces.
ALTER TABLESPACE "USR" ONLINE;
```

Exercise

Identify some of the issues surrounding the recovery of read-only tablespaces.

Recovering from Recovery Catalog Loss

As you learned in Chapter 13, the recovery catalog is an important feature in Oracle8 database backup and recovery. If this database is damaged or destroyed, you should take backups of it in the same way that you'd back up your primary database. However, if you cannot recover the recovery catalog, you can still resume normal processing by using the `catalog` command in RMAN to catalog all the datafile backups, archived redo logs, and the backup control files you have available on your machine. This process is the same as the process you would use if you had taken operating system backups not using RMAN, and then wanted to incorporate them into the recovery catalog later.

Another option is to use the `resync catalog from backup controlfile` command within RMAN. This command will glean the recovery catalog information from a backup control file copy. Unfortunately, there is no way for RMAN to verify that the files it finds listed in the control file backup actually exist. Thus, in the end you may have a recovery catalog containing many items that don't exist. To remove those items later, simply use the `uncatalog` command in RMAN.

Exercise

What happens when you lose your recovery catalog in Oracle? What are some ways you can get it back?

Oracle EXPORT and IMPORT Utilities

In this section, you will cover the following topics concerning Oracle's EXPORT and IMPORT utilities:

- Using EXPORT to create complete logical backups
- Using EXPORT to create incremental logical backups
- Invoking EXPORT on the direct path
- Using IMPORT to recover database objects

Unit II introduced you to the use of IMPORT and EXPORT for making copies of your data for tablespace reorganization and other purposes. In this section, you will take another look at these tools from the perspective of doing a logical database backup. This means making a copy of your logical Oracle data structures, not of the physical database files. The areas you will cover include using EXPORT to create complete, cumulative, and incremental logical backups of your files, using EXPORT direct path, and using IMPORT to recover database objects.

Using EXPORT to Create Complete Logical Backups

Recall from Unit II that you can run EXPORT in three modes: `full`, `user`, and `table`. In this section, you will be primarily concerned with running EXPORT in `full` mode in order to make logical backups of your entire database. This mode will export all tables from all user schemas. In order to use `full` mode, the `FULL` parameter must be set to Y, either at the command line or in the parameter file.

Several types of exports can be executed when EXPORT runs in `full` mode. The types of exports that can be used are *complete*, *cumulative*, and *incremental*, specified by setting the `INCTYPE` parameter to `complete`, `cumulative`, or `incremental`. Together, these exports can operate in a plan to provide the complete backup solution required for databases.

TIP
Review how to operate EXPORT using command line parameters, as shown in Unit II, before taking OCP Exam 3!

Taking Complete Exports

A complete export produces a dump file containing all objects in the database. You can make a complete recovery on the database using that export file as well. Complete exports are handy for recovering from user errors, such as dropped or truncated tables. In order to take a complete export in `full` mode, the DBA should use the `INCTYPE` parameter either at the EXPORT command line or in a parameter file. The following code block demonstrates the use of EXPORT in Windows:

```
D:\orant\bin> exp80 userid=sys/jason full=Y inctype=complete
file='010199cmpl.dmp' log=junk.log
Connected to: Oracle8 Enterprise Edition Release 8.0.5.0.0
With the Partitioning and Objects options
PL/SQL Release 8.0.5.0.0 ... Production
Export done in WE8ISO8859P1 character set
About to export the entire database ...
. exporting tablespace definitions
. exporting profiles
```

```
. exporting user definitions
. exporting roles
. exporting resource costs
. exporting rollback segment definitions
. exporting database links
. exporting sequence numbers
. exporting directory aliases
. exporting foreign function library names
. exporting object type definitions
. exporting cluster definitions
. about to export SYSTEM's tables via Conventional Path ...
. . exporting table            DEF$_AQCALL       0 rows exported
. . exporting table           DEF$_AQERROR       0 rows exported
. . exporting table          DEF$_CALLDEST       0 rows exported
. . exporting table       DEF$_DEFAULTDEST       0 rows exported
. . exporting table       DEF$_DESTINATION       0 rows exported
. . exporting table             DEF$_ERROR       0 rows exported
. . exporting table               DEF$_LOB       0 rows exported
. . exporting table            DEF$_ORIGIN       0 rows exported

...

. . exporting table                 MD$LER       0 rows exported
. . exporting table                MD$PTAB       0 rows exported
. . exporting table                 MD$PTS       0 rows exported
. . exporting table              MD$RELATE      75 rows exported
. . exporting table                 MD$TAB       0 rows exported
. exporting referential integrity constraints
. exporting posttables actions
. exporting synonyms
. exporting views
. exporting stored procedures
. exporting triggers
. exporting snapshots
. exporting snapshot logs
. exporting job queues
. exporting refresh groups and children
. exporting user history table
. exporting default and system auditing options
Export terminated successfully without warnings.
```

To use EXPORT as a full-service logical backup-and-recovery solution, you must first create a complete export as a benchmark, such as the one produced in the preceding code block.

The EXPORT tool is useful for devising a backup strategy based on the logical view of the database. The three types of `full` exports are most effective for an overall export backup strategy, while the `user` and `table` modes allow for highly specialized data storage for recovery purposes. It is important to note, however, that it is only possible to recover the database to the point in time that the most recent export dump was taken. If a situation arises in which the recovery of data that was entered after the most recent export was performed is required, then the users must reenter the data manually.

Exercises

1. Explain how to take a complete backup using EXPORT.
2. What are the three modes for full database backup, and which command line parameter is used to identify them?

Using EXPORT to Create Incremental Logical Backups

A sample EXPORT backup schedule using all `full` export options presented in this discussion appears in Figure 15-2. There are several reasons for not wanting to take a complete export of all your data every time you handle database recovery. For one, there might be a limit on the maximum file size in your operating system that EXPORT would exceed if it dumped all your table data. A complete export may also take a long time, meaning that you may prefer to run complete exports only on the weekends, when other database activity may be low or nonexistent.

Running Incremental Exports

EXPORT allows you to make incremental exports of your database—exports containing only the data that experienced changes since the last time a complete export was run. An incremental export consists of all database objects that have changed since the last cumulative, complete, or incremental export was run on the database. In other words, an incremental export saves all database objects (not just changed row data) that changed since the last backup of any type. An example of using EXPORT and specifying an incremental export appears in the following code block:

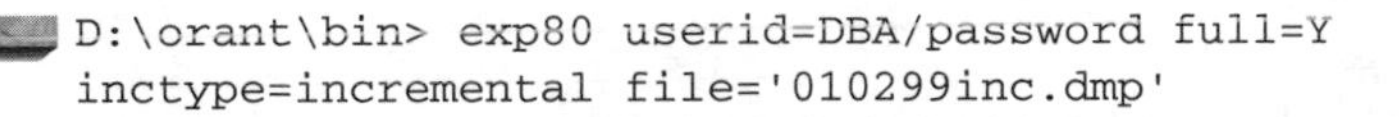

```
D:\orant\bin> exp80 userid=DBA/password full=Y
inctype=incremental file='010299inc.dmp'
```

Running Cumulative Exports

Incremental exports can also be rolled up into a cumulative export. If a cumulative export has been run, a later incremental export will only make copies of the data that changed since the last cumulative or incremental export ran. Although a cumulative export can be considered redundant work, it serves some value because

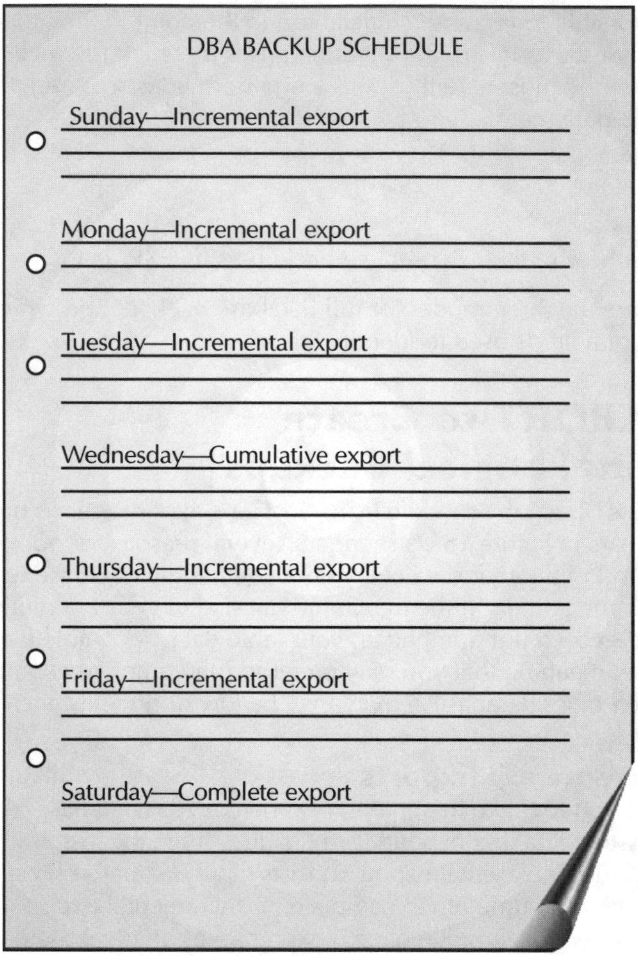

DBA BACKUP SCHEDULE

Sunday—Incremental export

Monday—Incremental export

Tuesday—Incremental export

Wednesday—Cumulative export

Thursday—Incremental export

Friday—Incremental export

Saturday—Complete export

FIGURE 15-2. *Sample backup strategy using* `export`

the cumulative export reduces the number of imports required for recovery. Unlike the complete export, which creates an export of every logical database object in the database, the cumulative export creates a copy of only the database objects that have been changed in the database since the last time a cumulative or complete database export was taken.

```
/home/oracle/app/oracle/8.0.5/bin> exp userid=DBA/password \
full=Y inctype=cumulative file='010399cml.dmp'
```

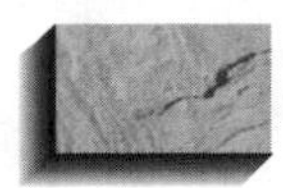

TIP
The benefits of cumulative and incremental exports include smaller export dump files, shorter duration exports, and the ability to recover from user errors, such as `drop table` *or* `truncate table`.

Exercises

1. What are the three types of exports made in `full` mode? What is the name of the parameter where the type of full export is determined?
2. What are the primary benefits of cumulative and incremental exports over complete exports?

Invoking EXPORT on the Direct Path

In Unit II, you learned that there are two unload paths for EXPORT to use: the conventional path and the direct path. The conventional path export uses much the same mechanisms for extracting data as a SQL `select` statement would use. Data is read into the buffer cache from disk, evaluated, passed over to a user process (the EXPORT client, in this case), and written to file. Direct path exports, on the other hand, run faster because the data is extracted from Oracle datafiles and passed directly to the EXPORT client for processing, bypassing the buffer cache entirely. The IMPORT tool has no problem with data extracted using either the conventional or direct path EXPORT.

TIP
You can find out whether an export dump file was created using the direct or conventional path by looking in the log file produced by the EXPORT run, either on the screen while EXPORT is running or when the dump file is imported later.

Running EXPORT with the direct path has a few drawbacks. For one, you cannot use it when your tables contain columns defined with Oracle8-specific datatypes, such as LOB, BFILE, REF, TABLE, VARRAY, or other object types. This is because

Oracle didn't do too much revision on the EXPORT tool when Oracle8 was released—in fact, neither EXPORT nor IMPORT have changed much at all since Oracle7. Another drawback is that you cannot specify direct path EXPORT when running the tool interactively. You must use the command line `DIRECT` parameter. The `BUFFER` parameter, used to define the buffer size EXPORT uses when dumping data on the conventional path, is not used on direct path EXPORT either. Finally, when using EXPORT direct path, the character set on the client machine must match that on the host server, because no character-set conversion will be performed.

EXPORT has some compatibility restrictions you should be aware of, as well. First, you can't run the version of EXPORT from Oracle6 against an Oracle8 database. However, you can use Oracle7's EXPORT against an Oracle8 database, with the limitation that the dump file is in Oracle7's format, not Oracle8's, and it won't contain objects that did not exist in Oracle7 (index-organized tables, for example). Finally, you can run later versions of IMPORT against a dump file produced by earlier versions of EXPORT, but you should avoid using later versions of EXPORT and IMPORT against earlier versions of the database, because doing so will likely result in an error.

Exercises

1. What are the benefits of performing exports using the EXPORT direct path? How is the direct path specified?
2. What parameters used for EXPORT's conventional path have no meaning on the EXPORT direct path?

Using IMPORT to Recover Database Objects

Once you have a dump file produced by EXPORT, the only program that can do anything with it is IMPORT. You learned about using IMPORT in Unit II, so the general use of IMPORT will not be repeated here. But, take heed—do not go into OCP Exam 3 without knowing exactly how to use IMPORT.

As you may already have gathered, IMPORT has several uses, from assisting in overcoming user errors like accidental `drop table` or `truncate table` statements to making copies of table structures (with or without row data). Like EXPORT, IMPORT runs in `table`, `user`, and `full` mode. However, `full` mode has the limitation that you cannot load SYS-owned database objects, such as the tables in the data dictionary. Thus, EXPORT and IMPORT do not provide as robust a backup and recovery strategy that some other options you learned about in this unit provide. As with EXPORT, there are different types of full imports, set with the

`INCTYPE` parameter. They are `system` and `restore`. When `INCTYPE` is set to `system`, IMPORT imports tables and related data from objects owned by SYSTEM (but not SYS). When `INCTYPE` is set to `restore`, everyone else's database objects (except SYS) in the export file are imported.

Database Recovery with IMPORT

Database recovery with `import` occurs in the following way. First, you take the most recent database export and re-create the data dictionary and other database internals by using IMPORT running with the `FULL=Y` and `INCTYPE=system` parameters set. Then, you run IMPORT against the most recent complete database export with `FULL=Y` and `INCTYPE=restore` parameters set. After that, you import all cumulative exports taken since the most recent complete export. After all *cumulative* exports are applied to the database, in order, you then apply all *incremental* exports, in order.

Given the backup strategy indicated in Figure 15-2 and a database failure on Friday morning that requires media recovery, the following procedure might be followed:

1. The Thursday night incremental export is the first that should be applied, in order to recover database objects owned by the SYSTEM user. The DBA uses the following command:

   ```
   D:\orant>imp80 file='thursdayinc.dmp' userid=DBA/password
    full=y inctype=system
   ```

2. The next step the DBA must accomplish is to apply the most recent complete export. In this backup strategy, complete backups are taken Saturday nights.

   ```
   D:\orant> imp80 file='saturdaycmpl.dmp' userid=DBA/password
   full=y inctype=restore
   ```

3. Only one cumulative export is taken in this backup strategy, on Wednesday evenings. This is the next backup to be applied.

   ```
   D:\orant> imp80 file='wednesdaycmlt.dmp' userid=DBA/password
   full=y inctype=restore
   ```

4. Since the problem occurred Friday morning, only one incremental export has taken place. Therefore, only one incremental must be applied. The following code block illustrates this:

   ```
   D:\orant> imp80 file='thursdayinc.dmp' userid=DBA/password
   full=y inctype=restore
   ```

TIP
Ensure that you understand how IMPORT works, and that you understand the command line IMPORT parameters, the order in which IMPORT loads data into Oracle, and the National Language Support (NLS) considerations of loading data into Oracle. You can find this information in Chapter 11. This information is critical for OCP Exam 3, so make sure you understand it!

Exercises

1. What are the three modes that IMPORT runs in? How is the mode of an IMPORT run determined? What two options are available for parameter-passing for IMPORT?
2. What are the two types of `full` import? What database information does each one import? Which parameter determines the type of import taken?
3. What parameters determine which types of database objects are imported? Identify a recovery strategy that uses IMPORT. How is the overall recovery performed? What are some of the overall limitations of a recovery strategy that uses IMPORT?

Chapter Summary

This chapter wrapped up the coverage of backup and recovery topics for OCP Exam 3. It covered three basic topics: the incomplete recovery of an Oracle database with and without the use of RMAN and the recovery catalog, advanced recovery issues in the Oracle database, and the use of EXPORT and IMPORT as tools for logical database backup and recovery. These topics covered 20 percent of OCP Exam 3 test content.

First, you learned how and when to use incomplete recovery to recover an Oracle database system. The section covered the actual steps involved in performing incomplete database recovery on an Oracle database from the operating system prompt or from RMAN. Following that, you learned how to recover when you lose redo log files currently being written by your LGWR process. Finally, some coverage of incomplete tablespace recovery—a tricky subject—was offered.

The second section discussed additional database recovery issues in Oracle. Several methods for minimizing downtime were introduced, including fast warmstart, parallel recovery, and starting the database with missing datafiles. You also learned about the methods used to diagnose and recover from corruption issues in your datafiles. The role of DBVERIFY was touched on, as well as the error Oracle produces (1578) when corruption is identified. The methods for reconstructing a lost or damaged control file were covered in some depth, as well. Recovery of read-only tablespaces was another area described in the section, as was recovering from the loss of a recovery catalog.

Finally, the use of EXPORT and IMPORT as a logical database backup and recovery option was covered. Actually, "backup and recovery" is an overstatement of the capabilities of EXPORT and IMPORT, because you cannot actually recover your entire database using this option. However, you can achieve some form of data storage and recovery. Toward this end, you learned how to use EXPORT to take a complete logical backup of your database objects (excluding those owned by SYS). You also learned how EXPORT can be used to take incremental backups of only those database objects that experienced changes since the last EXPORT was taken. You reviewed the use of the EXPORT direct path, as well. Finally, the use of IMPORT to recover database objects from the export dump file produced by the EXPORT utility was covered.

Two-Minute Drill

- There are three types of incomplete recovery: time-based, change-based, and cancel-based. They are differentiated in the `recover database` option by what follows the `until` clause. Cancel-based incomplete recovery uses `until cancel`, change-based incomplete recovery uses `until change` *`scn`*, and time-based incomplete recovery uses `until` *`'yyyy-mm-dd:hh24:mi:ss'`*.
- You need to use incomplete recovery when tables get dropped or when incorrect data is committed to a table by someone.
- Incomplete recovery might be your only choice if you do not have all your archived redo logs, when you have to use a backup control file, or when you lose all unarchived redo logs and one or more datafiles.
- The `automatic` keyword reduces the amount of interaction between Oracle and the DBA by having Oracle automatically apply redo logs to the database. You cannot use this option with the `recover until cancel` command. The logs Oracle uses are based on the contents of V$LOG_HISTORY and on the settings for two `init`*`sid`*`.ora` parameters, `LOG_ARCHIVE_DEST` and `LOG_ARCHIVE_FORMAT`.
- Information about the SCN range contained in archived redo logs is in V$LOG_HISTORY.

- For complete or incomplete recovery, the database cannot be available for users. For complete recovery of a tablespace only, the undamaged or unaffected parts of the database can be available for use.
- In some cases, it may be necessary to move datafiles as part of recovery. If this is required, the control file must be modified with the `alter database rename file` statement.
- Incomplete recovery may be required when the DBA loses an archived redo log file. For example, suppose there are three archived redo logs for a database, numbered 1, 2, and 3. Each archive contains information for 10 transactions (SCN 0–9, 10–19, and 20–29), for a total of 30 transactions. If archive sequence 3 is lost, the DBA can only recover the database through SCN 19, or archive sequence 2. If 2 is lost, then the DBA can only recover the database through SCN 9, and if archive sequence 1 is lost, then *no* archived redo log information can be applied.
- Incomplete recovery from offline backups is accomplished with the following steps. Don't omit any steps, or you will have to go through an even more lengthy process to recover to the point at which you reset the logs and after that point as well.
  1. Do a `shutdown abort` operation.
  2. Restore all backup copies of datafiles.
  3. Start up and mount, but do not open, the database.
  4. Execute a `recover database` operation, applying appropriate archived redo logs. Use the appropriate incomplete recovery option: cancel-based incomplete recovery uses `until cancel`, change-based incomplete recovery uses `until change` *`scn`*, time-based incomplete recovery uses `until '`*`yyyy-mm-dd:hh24:mi:ss`*`'`.
  5. Open the database using the `resetlogs` option to discard archives and reset sequence numbers. Investigate to see if your recovery was successful—don't just assume it was.
  6. Shut down with `transactional, immediate,` or `normal` options.
  7. Back up your database
  8. Open the database and make it available to users
- Create a new control file, if required, by using the `create controlfile` statement before initiating recovery. Be sure to specify `resetlogs` and

`archivelog`. If available, use the control file script created when the `trace` option is used in backing up the control file.

- Back up your control file regularly using the `alter database backup controlfile to [trace|filename]` statement.
- You can recover your database with the `alter database recover` command or simply with the `recover` command.
- Always make sure to periodically clear your ALERT log, because it will continue to grow in size when the database is operational. However, ensure that you save what you clear out, because you might need it later for database recovery.
- If you don't take a backup after you finish your recovery, and your database fails again, you will have to do a lot of work to recover. First, you'll have to recover to the point at which you reset your log sequence number, and then you will have to recover using the sequence number for the current control file.
- Incomplete recovery with RMAN takes much the same form as using operating system commands, except that all commands are put into a `run` script, not executed interactively. Also, archive logs and datafiles must be registered in the recovery catalog.
- There are several methods for minimizing downtime on your database, including:
  - **Fast warmstart** The database will start quickly after recovery because recovery ends at the end of the roll-forward process, and user processes implicitly roll back any uncommitted changes before manipulating recovered blocks.
  - **Parallel recovery** Oracle allows multiple processes to handle recovery at once, though this requires support from the host for multiple processes writing to the same or different disks at the same time. Review the chapter to see the `init`*`sid`*`.ora` parameters and `recover parallel` command options used for parallel recovery.
  - **Start with missing datafiles** You can do this when the database supports multiple applications using datafiles of different tablespaces. Starting your database in this way increases the availability of unaffected applications while allowing you to recover the damaged parts.

- You need to back up read-only tablespaces after their read/write status changes to read-only, or after the data in a read-only tablespace is changed. If you lose datafiles in read-only tablespaces and your only backup is from a time when the tablespace was not read-only, you will have to restore the file, apply archive logs, and change the tablespace status accordingly, after it is restored.
- You need to recreate your database control files in three situations: when all control files are lost due to media failure, when the name of the database must be changed, and when you want to change option settings for your database in the control file (using the `create database` statement). Option settings that can be set with the `create database` statement include `maxdatafiles, maxlogfiles, maxlogmembers,` among others.
- There are two ways to recover a control file. One is to use a backup control file created with the `alter database backup controlfile to` *`filename`* statement. Another is to re-create the control file using a `create controlfile` statement, which can be found in a script generated by the `alter database backup controlfile to trace` command.
- `ORA-1578`, RMAN, or the use of the DBVERIFY command, indicates when there is corruption in data blocks of a datafile. The most effective way to correct the problem is to recover the corrupted datafiles as though they were lost in media failure.
- The loss of your recovery catalog can be remedied by using the `catalog` command to reregister all the datafiles, back up control files, and archive redo logs. Alternatively, you can use the `resync catalog` command to draw this information from the control file, but the problem is that all the files listed there may not exist anymore, so you may need to use the `uncatalog` command.
- EXPORT and IMPORT can be used for a logical data-backup strategy. However, you will not be able to plan a full-fledged recovery strategy using EXPORT and IMPORT alone, because these tools do not save or restore SYS-owned objects.
- If you lost the SYSTEM tablespace on a database that you only backed up with exports, you would first have to drop and re-create the database, and

then create the tablespaces and users needed. After that, you could start loading the database objects from the EXPORT dump file using IMPORT.

- You learned the basics of EXPORT and IMPORT in Chapter 11. You can use EXPORT for logical backup, running it in `full` mode.
- Three types of full exports can be run: `complete` (which exports all database objects except those owned by SYS), `cumulative` (which exports all changed objects since the last `complete` export, rolling up all `incremental` runs), and `incremental` (which exports all changed objects since the last time any type of EXPORT run was taken).
- Review EXPORT command line parameters from Chapter 11 before taking OCP Exam 3!
- The benefits of `cumulative` and `incremental` exports is that they take less space and less time to generate because they only contain the objects that changed since the last `complete` or an EXPORT, respectively.
- EXPORT can run in the direct path when the DIRECT parameter on the command line or, when the parameter file is set to `true`. In this way, blocks read from the database will skip most stages of SQL statement processing and get written to the dump file quickly.
- EXPORT direct path has several restrictions:
  - It cannot be invoked interactively
  - Character sets for the client and server must be the same
  - The `BUFFER` parameter has no impact on performance (it does for conventional path)
  - No datatypes introduced in Oracle8 can be exported in EXPORT direct path.
  - You can use earlier versions of EXPORT on later versions of Oracle, or later versions of IMPORT on files produced by earlier versions of EXPORT. You should avoid using later versions of EXPORT and IMPORT against earlier versions of the Oracle database.
- Review the use of IMPORT command line parameters, IMPORT object sequence, and NLS considerations from Chapter 11 before taking OCP Exam 3!

Chapter Questions

1. **The DBA must perform an incomplete recovery. Characteristics of a change-based recovery include**

   A. Recovery to the point in time of a database failure

   B. Use of the `recover tablespace` option

   C. Recovery by system change number

   D. Availability of the database during recovery

2. **The DBA takes a daily backup of the control file. A situation arises that requires the recovery of the control file. To do this, the DBA uses the `create controlfile` statement in conjunction with her backup. Which of the following correctly describes her control-file backup methods?**

   A. The DBA's backup method for control files puts the backup in a trace directory.

   B. The DBA's backup method for control files creates a binary control file.

   C. The DBA's backup method for control files uses an `alter tablespace` statement.

   D. The DBA's backup method for control files uses the `alter database backup controlfile to dbase.ctl` statement.

3. **In order to execute an incomplete recovery using a full backup, the DBA should first**

   A. Open the database in `restricted session` mode

   B. Restore only the damaged datafiles from backup

   C. Use `resetlogs` to reset the redo log sequence

   D. Mount but not open the database

4. **The DBA must perform incomplete recovery. Characteristics of a cancel-based recovery include**

   A. Automatic application of Oracle's archive redo suggestions

B. Use of the `alter database recover database until cancel` statement

C. Tablespace recovery with online backups

D. Availability of the database during the recovery process

5. An error in batch job processing last night has caused several million transactions to be processed in error on a 24 × 7 database. In addition, a disk containing two datafiles was lost. What type of database recovery is most appropriate for this situation?

A. Recovery using IMPORT

B. Cancel-based recovery

C. Complete recovery from offline backups

D. Complete recovery from online backups

6. The DBA is conducting a closed database recovery using full offline backups. The DBA realizes that archived redo log sequence #34 is missing. What can the DBA do to execute the proper recovery?

A. Check the V$LOG view to find the beginning SCN for log sequence 34, and then issue the `alter database recover tablespace until change 34` statement.

B. Issue the `alter database recover database using backup controlfile` statement.

C. Check V$LOG_HISTORY for the beginning SCN of log 34, issue `alter database recover database until change N`, where *N* equals the beginning SCN minus 1 for log 34.

D. Use IMPORT to recover the database from the most recent database export.

7. Which of the following `recover database` statements should *not* use the `automatic` option?

A. `until change 495893`

B. `until '2000-01-31:22:34:00'`

C. `until cancel`

8. The `recover database` method running in conjunction with a change-based recovery requires which of the following choices to be true about database availability?

A. The database can be available but the tablespace must be offline.

B. The database should not be available.

C. The database and tablespace can be available, but not the damaged datafile.

D. All aspects of the database should be available and online.

9. Archiving is enabled on the database. Which of the following choices are incompatible with the use of incomplete recovery?

A. EXPORT dump files

B. Archived redo logs available on the database

C. Offline backup copies of datafiles

D. Online backup copies of datafiles

10. If the DBA must re-create the control file as part of database recovery, in which of the following ways should it be done?

A. Using the script containing the `create controlfile` command in the trace directory

B. After backup datafile restoration

C. Between restoring backups and applying redo logs

D. Before closing the database to user access

11. The DBA is trying to improve the availability and the performance of database recovery. Which of the following methods shouldn't or can't be used for this purpose?

A. Take less frequent backups

B. Use the `recover parallel` keyword

C. Open the database when datafiles are missing

D. Faster warmstart

12. In order to prevent object-dependency errors when triggers are imported, the IMPORT tool loads which of the following objects before all the other choices?

A. table definitions

B. stored procedures

C. primary keys

D. indexes

13. Which of the following choices best describes a situation in which you would use change-based recovery to resolve a situation where bad data entered the database?

A. Recovery when you know approximately what time the bad data entered the database

B. Recovery when you want maximum control over the duration

C. Recovery when you don't have archived redo logs

D. Recovery in distributed-database environments

14. Which of the following choices best describes the main difference between incomplete recovery using operating system commands and incomplete recovery using RMAN?

A. RMAN is faster than operating system commands for database recovery.

B. RMAN cannot perform operating system procedures such as restoring datafiles.

C. Operating system commands are not as effectively processed as those issued from RMAN.

D. RMAN offers built-in features, such as reports and lists, to help you determine the recoverability of your Oracle database.

15. All of the following types of incomplete recovery require archiving to be used in your database, except one. Which is it?

A. Recovery from full offline backup

B. Cancel-based recovery

C. Complete recovery

D. Change-based recovery

Answers to Chapter Questions

1. C. Recovery by system change number

Explanation Change-based recovery is an incomplete recovery option, and all incomplete recoveries are database recoveries in order to prevent problems with read consistency. Hence, Choices A and B are incorrect, because incomplete recovery by definition does not handle recovery to the point of failure, and tablespace recovery is not used. Choice D is incorrect because incomplete recovery is a "closed database" recovery, meaning that the database is unavailable to users.

2. A. The DBA's backup method for control files puts the backup in a trace directory.

Explanation The tip-off in this question is the use of `create controlfile` to restore the control file to the database. There are two ways to back up the control file—one that creates a copy of the control file, and the other that creates a script that can be used to create the control file. The method of creating a script for creating a control file is the `alter database backup controlfile to trace` statement. This operation alone puts the backup control file creation script in the trace directory of the database. Therefore, choice A is correct.

3. D. Mount but not open the database

Explanation Complete recovery from full backup means that the database cannot be available for users during recovery. Choice A is incorrect because `restricted session` mode is used generally when taking backups of a database using the EXPORT tool. Choice B is incorrect because a database recovery using full backups would restore all datafiles, not just damaged ones. Choice C is incorrect because `resetlogs` is not a factor at this stage of database recovery. Note one important thing not mentioned in this question: In an actual situation, you would most likely take a backup of the database before attempting incomplete recovery. This type of question—where the correct answer is not the thing you would necessarily do first—is commonly found on OCP exams. In situations like this, you should choose the option that best answers the question from the choices given.

4. B. Use of the `alter database recover database until cancel` statement

Explanation Cancel-based recovery is a type of incomplete database recovery, not tablespace recovery, and since database recovery means that the users cannot access the database, choices C and D are incorrect. Choice A is wrong because the DBA cannot use automatic recovery in conjunction with the cancel-based option, because the DBA needs to interact with Oracle to notify the database when the recovery should end.

5. B. Cancel-based recovery

Explanation Of the two types of recovery required in this situation, the incomplete recovery wins out, because even though you could use complete recovery to address the media failure, there is still the issue of the millions of rows of data processing that was performed in error. Incomplete recovery can be used to recover the database to the point in time just prior to the batch job starting. This will implicitly resolve the media failure. The fact that your database contains bad data means you don't want to perform complete recovery, eliminating choices C and D. Choice A is incorrect because logical database backup and recovery is incompatible with any recovery strategy associated with archiving redo logs.

6. C. Check V$LOG_HISTORY for the beginning SCN of log 34, issue `alter database recover database until change` *N*, where *N* equals the beginning SCN minus 1 for log 34.

Explanation In general, it helps to read each answer choice to a question carefully in order to eliminate wrong answers. This question is a good example. This question boils down to one about incomplete recovery. Choice A is incorrect because incomplete recovery cannot be conducted on a tablespace, only on an entire database. Choice B is incorrect because there was no mention of the need to recover from a backup control file. Choice D is grossly incorrect because it refers to logical backup and recovery, a topic covered elsewhere.

7. C. `until cancel`

Explanation The rule is plain and simple—never use the `recover automatic` option to limit interaction between the DBA and Oracle if the DBA wants to execute cancel-based recovery. To execute this incomplete recovery method, the DBA has to interact with Oracle to tell it when to stop the recovery. Automatic recovery minimizes the interaction, and therefore shouldn't be used. However, you can perform incomplete time-based or change-based recovery using the `automatic` option.

8. B. The database should not be available.

Explanation The database shouldn't be open or available in any way during incomplete recovery, which means choice C is correct and choice D should be eliminated. Choices A and C are incorrect for this situation, because the database can only be open if you are performing tablespace and datafile recovery, both of which are complete recovery options.

9. A. EXPORT dump files

Explanation Dump files produced by the EXPORT tool are not usable in conjunction with any recovery that involves applying archived redo logs. The other choices given are fair game, however. You can use backup datafiles taken while the database is online or offline, and you must use archived redo logs. Thus, choices B, C, and D are all incorrect.

10. A. Using the script containing the `create controlfile` command in the trace directory

Explanation This question is tricky, and requires careful reading of the question as well as thorough knowledge of the Oracle database recovery process. Creation of a control file for the database recovery process should be accomplished *first.* Choices A, B, and C are all incorrect because they place the creation of control files later in the recovery process.

11. A. Take less frequent backups

Explanation By backing up your database less frequently, your recovery of the database will take longer because more archived redo information will need to be applied in order to complete the recovery. The other choices offered, namely parallel recovery, faster warmstart, and opening the database when datafiles are missing, actually improve the performance of your database recovery.

12. A. table definitions

Explanation Table definitions are loaded first when IMPORT executes, followed by index definitions, table data, constraints, and triggers. After that, stored procedures are loaded, along with some other types of database objects. This mechanism reduces the chance that a stored procedure will be loaded into Oracle that uses tables that haven't been loaded yet. It prevents other types of object-dependency failures as well, such as indexes with no tables, triggers with no tables, and so on.

13. D. Recovery in distributed-database environments

Explanation You would choose change-based recovery based on whether your database operated in a distributed environment. Time-based recovery is useful mainly when you know the approximate time the problem occurred, eliminating choice A. Choice B is incorrect because cancel-based recovery gives you the maximum control over the recovery stop time, not change-based recovery. Choice C is incorrect because the type of incomplete recovery described here is recovery to the point in time of the most recent backup. Though this type of recovery is incomplete in terms of data recovered, it is not a form of incomplete recovery per se.

14. D. RMAN offers built-in features, such as reports and lists, to help you determine the recoverability of your Oracle database.

Explanation The biggest difference between RMAN and the operating system recovery methods in the choices given is that RMAN offers built-in features, such as reports and lists, to help you determine the recoverability of the database. No operating system offers you this built-in functionality. There is no substantial performance difference between recovery using RMAN and recovery that only uses operating system commands, eliminating choice A. Nor is choice B correct, because RMAN can allocate channels for restoring datafiles to their proper location. RMAN is neither more or less effective at issuing commands for the operating system to process for handling recovery, but stands heads and shoulders above operating systems in telling you a great deal about the recoverability of your database at any point in time.

15. A. Recovery from full offline backup

Explanation Recovery from full offline backup is the only choice that can be performed without archiving enabled on the database. The other three options are simply variants on complete or incomplete recovery, all of which require archiving to be enabled on your database.

UNIT IV

Preparing for OCP DBA Exam 4: Performance Tuning Workshop

CHAPTER 16

Introducing Database Tuning

n this chapter, you will learn about and demonstrate knowledge in the following areas:

- Business requirements and tuning
- Oracle ALERT logs, trace files, and events
- Utilities and dynamic performance views

This chapter introduces aspects of tuning tested in OCP Exam 4. You will cover many areas of tuning on the Oracle database, setting the stage for high-level understanding of the Oracle tuning process and for the material that will come in the rest of Unit IV. This chapter begins with an exploration of tuning from the business perspective, and then moves on to explore tuning the Oracle database and the applications that use the Oracle database. The use of the ALERT log, trace files, and events are covered in detail. Finally, the tools for executing the tuning process will be discussed. The material in this chapter comprises about 20 percent of the test questions asked on OCP Exam 4.

Business Requirements and Tuning

In this section, you will cover the following points on business requirements and tuning:

- Roles associated with tuning
- Steps associated with tuning
- Different tuning goals

The Oracle database server is designed to meet the needs of different applications, including those that have large user populations executing transactions that add data to the database and that modify existing data in the database. Oracle also serves the needs of organizations that require large amounts of data to be available in a *data warehouse*, an application that contains vast amounts of data available primarily for read access and reporting. In order to meet the needs of these different types of applications, Oracle offers a great deal of flexibility in the way it can be configured. The ongoing tuning process is used by DBAs to improve query performance, storage management, and resource usage according to the needs of the application. This section will begin the discussion of tuning, allowing you to make the most of Oracle.

Roles Associated with Tuning

Tuning is done for many reasons on an Oracle database. Users often want their online applications to run faster, and developers may want batch processes to run faster, as well. Management in the organization often recognizes the need for faster applications and batch processing on their Oracle databases. One solution to the problem of performance is to invest in the latest hardware containing faster processors, more memory, and more disk space. To be sure, this is often an effective solution, and methods for maximizing the hardware on the machine hosting the Oracle database will be presented in this unit. However, the latest and greatest machines are also the most expensive. Organizations generally need to plan their hardware purchases some time in advance, which means that acute problems with performance are not usually resolved by purchasing new hardware. Instead, the DBA must determine other ways to improve performance.

Many people in an organization will be involved with database tuning, to a greater or lesser extent. These people include users, developers, the DBA, and management. The first role is that of the user. This is the person most likely to identify the problem (hopefully in a not-too-irate way) to the developers, the DBA, or management. In many environments, users have a contact person on the development team who is notified if there is a problem. The developer may or may not involve a DBA in resolving the performance problem. In most situations, the onus of correcting performance problems falls on the developer because most performance issues are programmatic in nature.

However, with the advent of enterprise resource planning (ERP) software such as Oracle Applications and other packaged applications designed to replace those developed and maintained in-house, correcting a performance issue through programmatic changes is becoming less and less an option. Instead, organizations have shifted more of the responsibility for correcting performance problems onto the DBA, and onto management for allocating money for substantial hardware and network upgrades to run the Oracle server.

A business decision must be made very early in the tuning process. The organization must decide how much attention to give each specific performance problem. An unscientific look at tuning in most business organizations indicates that the amount of attention paid to application performance is directly proportional to two factors—the organization's level of dependence on that application, and the severity of the performance problem. Figure 16-1 shows a simple chart with these two factors on the two axes. The chart has also been divided into four quadrants to categorize the types of applications.

Quadrant I consists of applications that are not critical and that have low to average performance problems. Very few applications in this category fall into the "maybe" band for performance-tuning resolution, and none of them fall into the

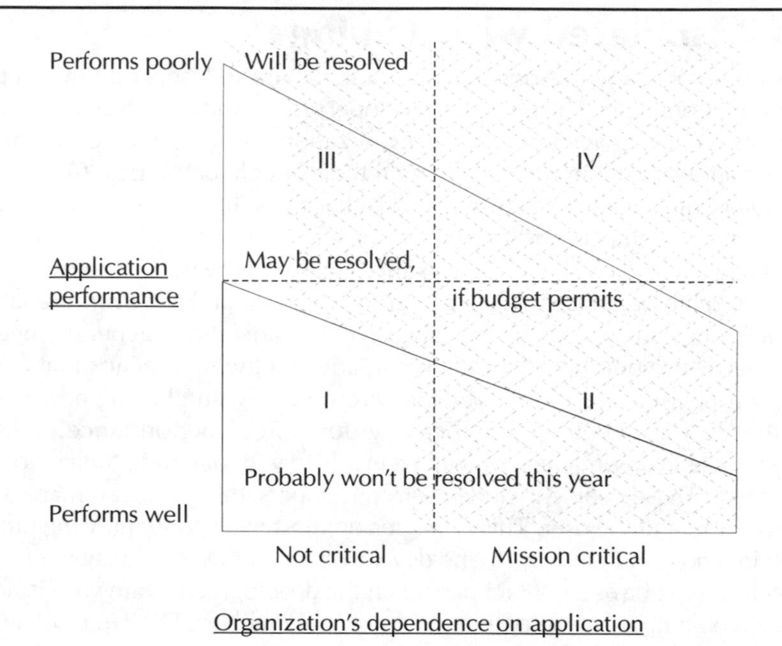

FIGURE 16-1. *A performance versus dependency chart for assessing an organization's tuning budget*

"must resolve" band. Quadrant II consists of applications that are critical and that have low to average performance problems. More of these applications fall into the "maybe" band than applications in Quadrant I, but notice something interesting about these problems. A small sliver of the "must resolve" band falls into Quadrant II, showing that an organization's most critical applications don't necessarily need to have dreadful performance to attract attention. Quadrant III shows the converse of Quadrant II—even if the performance issue is severe, the organization must have some dependence on the application in order for the problem to get resolved immediately. Quadrant IV is where most of the IT budget goes each year—to the mission-critical applications with average or poor performance.

Exercises

1. What are the two factors that determine the severity of a tuning issue? What sort of priority gets placed on a mission-critical system experiencing severe performance issues? What about a system that is not mission-critical, but that has severe performance issues?

2. Identify the role of user, developer, and DBA in resolving performance issues. When might it be more appropriate for a programmer to resolve performance issues? When would it be more appropriate for the DBA to do so?

Steps Associated with Tuning

Oracle has its own five-step process that every DBA should use for performance tuning. In general, it is best to start with step 1 in every situation, in order to avoid creating problems as you attempt to solve them. Also, notice that progressing from step to step directly translates to an increase in the scope and impact of the proposed change. This step-by-step process begins with tuning the performance of applications using the Oracle database, and then moves to tuning the OS. Next is tuning memory usage of the Oracle database. If there are still problems, the DBA can tune the disk I/O and utilization of the Oracle database, and finally, the DBA can tune locks and other contention issues. A more detailed presentation of the process follows.

Step 1: Tune the Application

The importance of tuning the application SQL statements and PL/SQL code cannot be overstated. Most often, poorly written queries are the source of poor performance. DBAs should play an active part in encouraging developers to tune the application queries before engaging in other steps of the tuning process. Some of the tools available for developers are described in this chapter, including SQL Trace and the `explain plan` command. More detailed information about application tuning appears in Chapter 17.

Step 2: Tune the OS Configuration

Oracle does not exist in a vacuum; its performance is affected by the performance of the machine hosting it. If you have a powerful server running your database, you usually won't have problems, except perhaps when use is heavy. However, a poorly tuned host machine can make even a well-tuned database run poorly.

Step 3: Tune Memory Structures

After application tuning, appropriate configuration and tuning of memory structures can have a sizable impact on application and database performance. Oracle should have enough space allocated for the SQL and PL/SQL areas, data dictionary cache, database buffer cache, and log buffer to yield performance improvement. These improvements will include the following:

- Quicker retrieval of database data already in memory
- Reduction in SQL parsing by the RDBMS

- Elimination of OS paging and swapping, which is copying data in memory onto disk.

These points are covered in more detail in Chapter 18.

Step 4: Tune Disk I/O Usage

Oracle is designed to prevent I/O from adversely affecting application performance. Features such as the server, DBW0, LGWR, CKPT, and SMON background process contribute to the effective management of disk usage, and are designed to reduce an application's dependency on fast writes to disk for good performance. However, there are situations in which disk usage can adversely affect an application. Tuning disk usage generally means distributing I/O over several disks to avoid contention, storing data in blocks to facilitate data retrieval, and creating properly sized extents for data storage. More information about disk I/O tuning appears in Chapter 19.

Step 5: Detect and Eliminate Resource Contention

As in the case of tuning disk I/O, Oracle server is designed in such a way as to minimize resource contention. For example, Oracle can detect and eliminate deadlocks. However, there are times when many users contend for resources such as rollback segments, dispatchers, or other processes in the multithreaded architecture of Oracle server, or redo log buffer latches. Though infrequent, these situations are extremely detrimental to the performance of the application. More information about resource-contention tuning appears in Chapter 20.

Proactive Tuning

As stated earlier, the preceding five steps should be used in order in the event of a tuning emergency. However, a proactive DBA should attempt to tune the database even when everything appears to be running well. The reason proactive tuning is necessary is that it reduces the amount of time the DBA needs to spend in production support situations. However, the DBA usually plays production support role, so an obvious dichotomy arises—you need to take time up front to reduce time later, but your time up front is limited because you are constantly correcting earlier problems. Despite this problem, you should, at some point, attempt to take the time to do some proactive work. Proactive tuning also increases your knowledge of the applications, thereby reducing the effort required when the inevitable production emergency arises.

Exercises

1. What are the steps for performance tuning?

2. In what order should the DBA engage in these steps? How does scope relate to this order?

Different Tuning Goals

Before tuning Oracle, you should have an appropriate tuning methodology outlined. This methodology should correspond directly to the goals you are attempting to reach, as defined by the use of each application and by the needs identified by the organization. Some common goals include allowing an application to accept high-volume transaction processing at certain times of the day, returning frequently requested data quickly, and allowing users to create and execute ad hoc reports without adversely affecting online transaction processing. These goals, as well as the many other performance goals set before you, fall into three general categories:

- To improve performance of specific SQL statements running against the Oracle database
- To improve performance of specific applications running within the Oracle database
- To improve overall performance for all users and applications within the Oracle database

In order to meet the needs of an ongoing application that sometimes encounters performance problems, you must know how to resolve those issues. Many problems with performance on an Oracle database can be resolved with three methods, the first being the purchase of new hardware. The second is effective database configuration and the third is effective application design. It should be understood by all people who use Oracle databases that the greatest number of problems with performance are caused by the application—not by the Oracle database. Poorly written SQL statements, the use of multiple SQL statements where one would suffice, and other problems within an application are the source of most performance problems. You should always place the responsibility of performing the first step in any performance investigation on the application developers to see if they can rewrite the code of the application to utilize the database more effectively.

Only after all possibility of resolving the performance problem by redeveloping the application is exhausted should you attempt any changes to the configuration of the Oracle database. This prevents the impromptu reconfiguration of the Oracle database to satisfy a performance need in one area, only to create a performance problem in another area. Any change to the configuration of the Oracle database should be considered carefully, weighing the trade-offs you might need to make in order to improve performance in one area. For example, when changing the memory management configuration for the Oracle database without buying and installing more memory, you must be careful not to size any part of the Oracle SGA out of real memory. Also, if the Oracle SGA takes up more existing memory, other applications that might be running on the same machine may suffer. You may need to work with the systems administrator of the machine to decide how to make the trade-off.

Exercises

1. Why must a database be tuned?
2. What is the cause of most performance problems on Oracle databases?
3. What are some of the goals for performance tuning on a database?

Oracle ALERT Logs, Trace Files, and Events

In this section, you will cover the following topics on Oracle ALERT logs, trace files, and events:

- Location and use of the ALERT log
- Location and use of trace files
- Retrieving and displaying wait events
- Setting predefined events using OEM

Oracle has a host of methods for telling you when there is a problem with performance on your Oracle database. Files such as ALERT logs, user process trace files, and background process trace files all combine to give you an image of how Oracle is running behind the scenes. In this section, you will learn about the location and use of these three types of files. You will also learn some things about events, such as what constitutes an event, how to retrieve and display them, and how to set event alerts using the Oracle Enterprise Manager (OEM) tool.

Location and Use of the ALERT Log

The ALERT log, as explained in Units II and III, is a log file maintained by Oracle to capture information about database-wide events. The information about ALERT logs explained here can also be found in Chapter 6, but as a review of this fundamental area of Oracle database administration from a tuning perspective, consider the following exploration of the ALERT log.

Oracle writes to the ALERT log whenever the database is started or shut down, whenever the control file is modified (for example, by creating a new tablespace), whenever a severe error occurs or an Oracle internal error occurs, and when Oracle starts writing to a new online redo log file.

There are other times in Oracle execution when the ALERT log is written to, as well. The ALERT log can grow quite large, so it makes sense to clear it out once in a while and allow Oracle to start generating a new one, particularly if nothing eventful has happened on your database in a long time. Sometimes, when the ALERT log is written to, the message must be addressed. For this reason, it is important for you as the DBA to check the ALERT log regularly for problems such as internal errors or other anomalies in database behavior. If you have some kind of problem with your Oracle software and need to open a trouble ticket with Oracle Support, you may be requested to supply them with a copy of your ALERT log.

The location of your ALERT log and background trace files depends on the directory specified for the `BACKGROUND_DUMP_DEST` parameter for your instance. Both the background process trace files and the ALERT log will be found in this directory. If you are unsure of the location of your ALERT log, simply use the methods defined for getting parameter values, and look up the value for `BACKGROUND_DUMP_DEST`. The following code block contains the contents of an ALERT log for Oracle running on Windows, with entries generated by a `shutdown immediate` command followed by a `startup open` command:

```
Dump file D:\orant\rdbms80\trace\jscALRT.LOG
Mon Apr 19 14:08:43 1999
ORACLE V8.0.5.0.0 - Production vsnsta=0
vsnsql=c vsnxtr=3
Windows NT V4.0, OS V5.101, CPU type 586
Mon Apr 19 14:08:43 1999
Shutting down instance (immediate)
License high water mark = 2
Mon Apr 19 14:08:43 1999
ALTER DATABASE CLOSE NORMAL
Mon Apr 19 14:08:43 1999
SMON: disabling tx recovery
SMON: disabling cache recovery
Mon Apr 19 14:08:43 1999
Thread 1 closed at log sequence 100
Mon Apr 19 14:08:43 1999
Completed: ALTER DATABASE CLOSE NORMAL
Mon Apr 19 14:08:43 1999
ALTER DATABASE DISMOUNT
Completed: ALTER DATABASE DISMOUNT
```

```
Starting up ORACLE RDBMS Version: 8.0.5.0.0.
System parameters with non-default values:
  processes                = 100
  shared_pool_size         = 11534336
  control_files            =
(D:\orant\database\ctl1jsc.ora,
D:\orant\database\ctl2jsc.ora)
  db_block_buffers         = 550
  db_block_size            = 2048
  compatible               = 8.0.5.0.0
  log_archive_start        = TRUE
  log_buffer               = 32768
  log_checkpoint_interval  = 8000
  log_checkpoint_timeout   = 0
  db_files                 = 1020
  db_file_multiblock_read_count= 16
  dml_locks                = 200
  sequence_cache_entries   = 30
  sequence_cache_hash_buckets= 23
  remote_login_passwordfile= SHARED
  sort_area_size           = 65536
  db_name                  = jason
  text_enable              = TRUE
  utl_file_dir             = D:\FTP
  background_dump_dest     = D:\orant\rdbms80\trace
  user_dump_dest           = D:\orant\rdbms80\trace
  max_dump_file_size       = 10240
PMON started with pid=2
DBW0 started with pid=3
ARCH started with pid=4
LGWR started with pid=5
CKPT started with pid=6
SMON started with pid=7
RECO started with pid=8
Mon Apr 19 14:09:06 1999
alter database  mount
Mon Apr 19 14:09:10 1999
Successful mount of redo thread 1, with mount id 158736909
Mon Apr 19 14:09:10 1999
Database mounted in Exclusive Mode.
Completed: alter database  mount
Mon Apr 19 14:09:10 1999
alter database open
Picked broadcast on commit scheme to generate SCNs
Mon Apr 19 14:09:11 1999
Thread 1 opened at log sequence 100
  Current log# 2 seq# 100 mem# 0: D:\ORANT\DATABASE\LOGJSC2.ORA
```

```
Successful open of redo thread 1.
Mon Apr 19 14:09:11 1999
SMON: enabling cache recovery
SMON: enabling tx recovery
Mon Apr 19 14:09:14 1999
Completed: alter database open
```

Note that in all this discussion, there is scant mention of the ALERT log with respect to performance tuning. This is because the ALERT log is primarily designed to detect errors in database execution; it is not a performance-tuning device. However, you may find a use for the ALERT log in identifying errors that arise as the result of your attempts at tuning. You will learn about some other tools in Oracle designed to help in the tuning effort shortly.

Exercises

1. What is the ALERT log? What sorts of information does the ALERT log store about your Oracle database?
2. Where are ALERT logs stored in Oracle?

Location and Use of Trace Files

There are two basic types of trace files in the Oracle database. The first type of trace file is the file that individual background processes in Oracle, such as DBW0 and LGWR, generate only if they experience an error that causes the process to terminate. (You have already learned a bit about background trace files in Chapter 6.) These files are primarily useful for debugging the error that caused the process to terminate, so you're probably not going to care too much about these files for performance-tuning purposes. This type of trace file is found in the host system under the directory you assigned to your `BACKGROUND_DUMP_DEST` `init`*`sid`*`.ora` parameter.

Using SQL TRACE and TKPROF

Another important type of trace file exists in Oracle, and that is the trace file that is optionally produced by a user session running against the database. This user-session trace file does contain lots of relevant information for performance tuning. Some examples of this information include an explanation of the execution plan Oracle takes for each SQL statement run in your session, along with I/O, CPU, and other statistics Oracle generates while obtaining or processing the data requested in the session. A user-session trace file is produced when you issue the `alter session set SQL_TRACE = TRUE` statement in your session. Every user session that connects to Oracle will produce a trace file if the `SQL_TRACE` `init`*`sid`*`.ora` parameter is set to

TRUE and the database is restarted. The following code block shows how to enable tracing in your session:

```
D:\orant\RDBMS80\TRACE> plus80 jason/jason@orgdb01
SQL*Plus: Release 8.0.5.0.0 - Production on Wed Apr 7 22:13:6 1999
With the Partitioning and Objects options
PL/SQL Release 8.0.5.0.0 - Production
SQL> alter session set sql_trace = true;
Session altered.
```

The following code block demonstrates the generation of trace data from within SQL*Plus on a Windows machine:

```
SQL> select * from baseball_bat;
OWNER         LENGTH
---------- ---------
Mattingly         28
Boggs             32
Strawberry        33
```

Session trace files can be found in the host system under the directory you assigned to your `USER_DUMP_DEST` `init`*`sid`*`.ora` parameter. The following code block shows a user leaving SQL*Plus and then viewing the contents of this directory:

```
SQL> exit;
D:\orant\RDBMS80\TRACE> dir
04/07/99  09:24p       <DIR>          .
04/07/99  09:24p       <DIR>          ..
04/07/99  09:23p             1,294 ORA00152.TRC
              11 File(s)     1,294 bytes
                   2,251,091,968 bytes free
```

You can look at the contents of your trace file after the user session ends, but the data in the file probably won't make much sense. This is because you are supposed to execute a utility Oracle provides, called TKPROF, on the trace file. TKPROF produces a more readable output file displaying the activity from the session. Here is how you process the trace file through TKPROF using Windows:

```
D:\orant\RDBMS80\TRACE> tkprof80 ora00152.trc jason.out
TKPROF: Release 8.0.5.0.0 - Production on Wed Apr 7 22:21:35 1999
D:\orant\RDBMS80\TRACE>
```

You now have some output you can use for performance-tuning purposes. You will see a real example of the contents of a TKPROF-generated file and learn more about using this tool in Chapter 17.

Exercises

1. What is a trace file? What are the two types of trace files in the Oracle database? Where in the file system of your host machine will you find each type of trace file? What `initsid.ora` parameters are useful for locating each type of trace file?
2. Which trace file is used for performance tuning? What are some of the contents you will find in user trace files? What utility do you need to use to process the trace file in order to make it more readable?

Retrieving and Displaying Wait Events

An interesting concept in Oracle is that of the *event*. An event in Oracle is an occurrence that substantially alters the way your database executes or performs. There are two different categories of events in the Oracle database. One type is a wait event, which occurs when some user process is kept waiting because of a problem, such as an I/O bottleneck, a busy CPU, or a lack of free memory. System-wide wait events are stored internally within Oracle in the V$SYSTEM_WAIT view, while wait events experienced by specific sessions are stored in the V$SESSION_WAIT view according to session ID. The other type of event, the OEM-defined event, will be covered in the next lesson.

Looking at V$SYSTEM_EVENT

You can analyze the different types of system-wide events tracked in V$SYSTEM_EVENT. This view tracks several categories of wait events, including waits surrounding datafiles, redo logs, networking, and background processes. Statistics are kept detailing the total number of waits that occurred and the total number of times that the wait lasted before the waiting process timed out. The following code block displays the contents of V$SYSTEM_EVENT:

```
SQL> select event, total_waits as waits,
  2  total_timeouts as timeouts,
  3  time_waited as totalwait,
  4  average_wait as avgwait
  5  from v$system_event;
```

```
EVENT                          WAITS TIMEOUTS TOTALWAIT   AVGWAIT
------------------------------ ----- -------- --------- ---------
Null event                         1        1       401       401
pmon timer                      5904     5904   1773884 300.45461
process startup                    7        0        15 2.1428571
rdbms ipc reply                   10        0       166      16.6
rdbms ipc message              17844    17778   8717185 488.52191
control file sequential read     111        0       254 2.2882883
control file parallel write     5930        0       316 .05328836
refresh controlfile command        1        0         4         4
checkpoint completed               1        0        10        10
log file sequential read          13        0        59 4.5384615
log file single write              6        0         1 .16666667
log file parallel write           50        0        20        .4
log file sync                     21        0         7 .33333333
db file sequential read         1092        0      1021 .93498168
db file scattered read           202        0       237 1.1732673
db file single write               9        0         0         0
db file parallel write             9        0        16 1.7777778
db file parallel read              1        0        35        35
direct path read                  36        0         5 .13888889
direct path write                 18        0         0         0
instance state change              2        0         0         0
smon timer                        63       58   1764358 28005.683
file identify                     30        0        62 2.0666667
file open                         78        0         0         0
SQL*Net message to client        760        0         0         0
SQL*Net more data to client        1        0         0         0
SQL*Net message from client      758        0   3382408 4462.2797
SQL*Net break/reset to client     22        0         1 .04545455
```

Looking at V$SESSION_WAIT

In the V$SESSION_WAIT view, you can find information about waits that are specific to particular sessions. Since wait information for all sessions is stored in this view by session ID (SID), it helps if you order the output from this view by the SID column. Note also that, since every background process connected to Oracle will also have a SID, you can use this view to see what sorts of waits are occurring for background processes as well as user processes. You can use OEM Instance Manager to determine whether a SID corresponds to a user or background process. The contents of V$SESSION_WAIT are shown in the following output:

```
SQL> select sid, event, total_waits as waits,
  2  total_timeouts as timeouts, time_waited as totalwait,
  3  average_wait as avgwait
  4  from v$session_event
  5  order by sid;
```

```
SID     EVENT                        WAITS  TIMEOUTS TOTALWAIT   AVGWAIT
--- ---------------------------- ----- --------- --------- ---------
  1 pmon timer                    6324      6324   1900101 300.45873
  2 rdbms ipc message             6344      6323   1900098 299.51103
  2 control file sequential read    32         0        49   1.53125
  2 file identify                    9         0        16 1.7777778
  2 file open                       13         0         0         0
  2 direct path read                18         0         0         0
  2 db file parallel write           9         0        16 1.7777778
  3 rdbms ipc message               65        64   1890152 29079.262
  3 log file sequential read         6         0        34 5.6666667
  3 control file parallel write      4         0         7      1.75
  3 file identify                    5         0        10         2
  3 file open                        5         0         0         0
  3 control file sequential read    15         0        51       3.4
  4 rdbms ipc message             6363      6323   1900067 298.61182
  4 control file parallel write     14         0        14         1
  4 file open                       16         0         0         0
  4 file identify                    5         0        16       3.2
  4 direct path write                9         0         0         0
  4 direct path read                 9         0         0         0
  4 log file parallel write         50         0        20        .4
  4 log file single write            5         0         1        .2
  4 log file sequential read         4         0         0         0
  4 control file sequential read    25         0        58      2.32
  5 rdbms ipc message             6327      6323   1899812 300.27059
  5 control file parallel write   6322         0       324  .0512496
  5 file open                        6         0         0         0
  5 file identify                    4         0         7      1.75
  5 control file sequential read     6         0         2 .33333333
  6 rdbms ipc reply                  1         0         2         2
  6 file open                       12         0         0         0
  6 smon timer                      67        62   1884359 28124.761
  6 db file sequential read         69         0        47 .68115942
  6 db file scattered read          46         0        74 1.6086957
  7 rdbms ipc message               12        12   1806310 150525.83
  7 db file sequential read          6         0        11 1.8333333
  7 file open                        1         0         0         0
  8 rdbms ipc reply                  2         0         0         0
  8 SQL*Net break/reset to client   22         0         1 .04545455
  8 log file sync                   19         0         2 .10526316
  8 file open                        3         0         0         0
  8 SQL*Net message to client      128         0         0         0
  8 SQL*Net message from client    127         0   1739107 13693.756
  8 SQL*Net more data to client      1         0         0         0
  8 db file scattered read         110         0       111 1.0090909
  8 db file sequential read        692         0       467 .67485549
 11 db file sequential read         42         0       278 6.6190476
```

```
11 SQL*Net message from client     55          0    1895598 2894.0427
11 SQL*Net message to client      656          0          0         0
11 file open                        1          0          0         0
```

Exercises

1. Identify what is meant by an *event* in Oracle. What is the difference between a session event and a system event?
2. What view can be used to identify system events in Oracle?
3. What view can be used to identify session events in Oracle? What OEM tool can be used to determine whether a session is a user session or background process session?

Setting Predefined Events Using OEM

The second category of event in Oracle is the set of events that can be tracked using Oracle Enterprise Manager (OEM). These event categories, along with a few examples of each event considered part of this category, are listed here:

- **Database fault management events** These events include ARCH process hangs, corrupted data blocks, terminated sessions, and failed DBMS_JOB processes.
- **Space management events** These events include filled tablespaces, filled archive log destinations, and tables that have allocated numerous extents.
- **Database resource management events** These events include hitting the process limit, session limit, or user limit on the Oracle database.
- **Performance management events** These events include performance monitoring of memory areas such as the buffer cache, shared pool, redo allocation, and copy latches.
- **Database auditing events** These events include various types of audits.
- **Node fault, space, and performance events** These events include several different aspects of host-machine monitoring.
- **Listener fault events** These events include detecting whether the listener is up or down.

Retrieving Wait Events

Oracle keeps track of events that can be tracked with Oracle Enterprise Manager by using several options under the Event menu. In the lower-right window, there is a display area for events that have occurred on the Oracle database. Within that window, there are four tabs. These tabs are explained in the following set of subtopics.

OUTSTANDING EVENTS This tab identifies all the events that have been registered on a destination where event conditions have occurred. The information in the tab includes the name of the event, the severity (alert is red, warning is yellow, and all clear is green), the host machine or node where the event was detected, and the event type, such as the types in the prior bullet list. You also get the date of the event and a meaningful message about the event. You can acknowledge the event by double-clicking it in the list and then clicking the Move to History button. You can also use the Event | Acknowledge menu option to perform this task.

EVENT SET LIBRARY This tab identifies the various predefined event sets for your machine, along with a short description of each. If you double-click a particular event in the event set, a window will appear that you can use to edit aspects of the predefined event set.

EVENT HISTORY This tab identifies all the events that have occurred and been acknowledged by an administrator or cleared by an agent. The Event History page contains the same columns as the Outstanding Events page, plus the name of the user that cleared the event, the date the event was acknowledged, and any comments entered when the event was acknowledged. You can save the events from the Event History page to a text file and clear the events from the Event History window. This prevents the Event History page from being overloaded with obsolete events that occurred on previous days.

REGISTRATIONS This tab displays event sets applied and registered to monitor events on any network objects. The Registrations tab shows a specific icon according to the type of event set, such as Database, Node, or Listener, the service monitored by the event, the name of the registered event set, and event status (Pending, Successful, or Failed).

The Importance of Running Intelligent Agent

Note that in order to work with events in Oracle Enterprise Manager, you must have Oracle Intelligent Agent running in support of your Oracle database. You most likely will want to run Intelligent Agent on the same machine that hosts your Oracle database.

How you start Intelligent Agent depends on your operating system. For Windows, Intelligent Agent is set up as a service, so all you need to do is click on Start | Control Panel | Services, and then choose the OracleAgent service and click the Start button. In both NT and Unix, you can also use the LSNRCTL utility to start and stop Intelligent Agent. Chapter 22 contains more information on this tool.

Once you set up Intelligent Agent on your host machine, you must allow OEM to discover the service. OEM can automatically detect Intelligent Agent running on the host when you run the Service Discovery Wizard by clicking on the Navigator | Service Discovery | Discover New Services menu option. Keep in mind that, to set up and use the performance management events, you must have the OEM Tuning Pack installed on your database.

Setting Up Events in OEM

The simplest event to set up in Enterprise Manager is the UpDown event, which simply tells you when the resource was started or stopped. If you click on the Event Set Library, you will see a series of resources. Note that the resources listed in the figure are the basic resources provided with Intelligent Agent and Enterprise Manager. Specifically, if you want to configure and use the performance management events, you will need to install the OEM Tuning Pack.

Assuming you have already started Intelligent Agent on the appropriate host machines and discovered your Oracle databases, double-click the listing of your database in the Event window on the OEM console. The Quick Edit Event Set window will appear. Then click on the Events tab in the window. On the right side, a list of available events will appear. Unless you have installed Tuning Pack, this list will be quite basic, mainly consisting of events like UpDown that determine whether the database is available or not. Click on the UpDown event at the top, and click on the arrow button in the center of the interface to select this event. Then click OK. Oracle Enterprise Manager will now display event information it receives from Intelligent Agent when your database is started or stopped.

Configuring Paging and Mail Services

In addition to simply retrieving or displaying wait events or other events from within the OEM console, you can set up event alerts in OEM that will send you an e-mail message or even page you automatically when a problem arises. These actions are accomplished using the Event | Configure Services | Mail, or Event | Configure Services | Paging, menus. Note that you will need to configure OEM to either connect to a mail server on the LAN for e-mail services or to dial a phone number via modem to use paging, and you will also have to subscribe to a pager service.

Exercises

1. Describe the process for configuring a predefined event in Oracle Enterprise Manager. Explain why Tuning Pack plays a vital role in configuring predefined events in OEM.
2. What menu would you use if you wanted to configure OEM to page you if the database instance aborted?

Utilities and Dynamic Performance Views

In this section, you will cover the following topics related to utilities and dynamic performance views:

- Using dynamic performance views
- Using the UTLBSTAT/UTLESTAT output report
- Using appropriate OEM tools

The most important step in solving performance issues is discovering them. While the easiest way to discover performance issues is to wait for developers or users to call and complain, this method is not very customer-oriented, and has proved very detrimental to the reputation of many information technology departments. The approach of taking performance problems on the chin is not required, given the availability of tools to help monitor and eliminate Oracle performance problems.

Using Dynamic Performance Views

Dynamic performance views are views against several memory structures created by the Oracle SGA at instance startup. These views contain database performance information that is useful to both DBAs and Oracle for determining the current status of the database. Performance tuning tools, such as those in the Oracle Enterprise Manager Tuning Pack, as well as utilities available from third-party vendors, use the underlying V$ performance views as their basis for information. The next four chapters on performance tuning that comprise this unit use information from dynamic performance views on the Oracle database. These views are the cornerstone of statistics collection for the Oracle database and are used by performance monitoring tools such as Enterprise Manager. Access to these views, whose names generally start with V$, is given to users who have the `select any table` privilege, to users with the SELECT_CATALOG_ROLE role, or to user SYS.

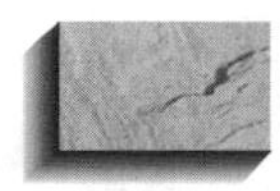

TIP
The `select any table` privilege doesn't have to give access to V$ views in Oracle8. Instead, to access those views you must have the SELECT_CATALOG_ROLE role granted to you. X$ views are accessed only by user SYS.

Instance-Wide Dynamic Performance Views in Oracle

Table 16-1 lists some important dynamic performance views in Oracle. Some of these views may have already been introduced, so consider this material a refresher on these important areas of the Oracle database. These views are used for instance-wide tuning.

Although other views listed give actual statistical information about the performance of your database, perhaps the most important view in this set is V$SYSSTAT. V$SYSSTAT contains the names of many statistics Oracle tracks, in addition to the lookup code for a given statistic. Values and tuning categories are displayed, as well. The following code block illustrates the use of V$SYSSTAT to find performance information for every statistic related to the database writer (DBW0DBW0) process:

```
SQL> select * from v$sysstat where name like '%DBWR%';
STATISTIC# NAME                                   CLASS VALUE
---------- -------------------------------------- ----- -----
        61 DBWR skip hot writes                       8     0
        62 DBWR checkpoint buffers written            8     0
        63 DBWR transaction table writes              8     6
        64 DBWR undo block writes                     8    15
        65 DBWR checkpoint write requests             8     0
        66 DBWR incr. ckpt. write requests            8     0
        67 DBWR revisited being-written buffer        8     0
        68 DBWR timeouts                              8     0
        69 DBWR make free requests                    8    24
        70 DBWR free buffers found                    8  3262
        71 DBWR lru scans                             8    24
        72 DBWR summed scan depth                     8  3312
        73 DBWR buffers scanned                       8  3311
        74 DBWR checkpoints                           8     0
        75 DBWR Flush object cross instance calls     8     0
        76 DBWR Flush object call found no dirty      8     0
        77 DBWR cross instance writes                40     0
```

View Name	Description
V$FIXED_TABLE	Lists all the V$ and X$ views present in the release.
V$INSTANCE	Shows the state of the current instance.
V$LATCH	Lists statistics for latches on the database.
V$LIBRARYCACHE	Contains statistics about library cache performance and activity.
V$ROLLNAME	Lists the names of all online rollback segments and associated USNs (undo segment numbers).
V$ROLLSTAT	Contains statistics about all rollback segment activities, by USN.
V$ROWCACHE	Shows statistics for data dictionary activity.
V$SGA	Contains summary information on the system global area.
V$SGASTAT	Contains detailed information on the system global area.
V$SORT_USAGE	Shows the size of the temporary segments and the session creating them; this information can help you identify which processes are doing disk sorts.
V$SQLAREA	Lists statistics on shared SQL area; contains one row per SQL string. Provides statistics on SQL statements that are in memory, parsed, and ready for execution. Text limited to 1,000 characters; full text is available in 64-byte chunks from V$SQLTEXT.
V$SQLTEXT	Contains the text of SQL statements belonging to shared SQL cursors in the SGA.
V$SYSSTAT	Contains general statistics for the instance by name.
V$SYSTEM_EVENT	Contains information on total waits for an event.
V$WAITSTAT	Lists block contention statistics; updated only when timed statistics are enabled.

TABLE 16-1. *Instance-Wide Tuning Views*

Dynamic Performance Views for Session-Level Tuning

Table 16-2 lists some important dynamic performance views in Oracle. Some of these views may have already been introduced, so consider this a refresher on these important areas of the Oracle database. These views are used for session-level tuning. Later, you will see how to use some of these views to determine various

View	Description
V$LOCK	Lists the locks currently held by the Oracle8 Server and outstanding requests for a lock or latch.
V$MYSTAT	Shows statistics from your current session.
V$PROCESS	Contains information about the currently active processes.
V$SESSION	Lists session information for each current session. Links SID to other session attributes. Contains row lock information.
V$SESSION_EVENT	Lists information on waits for an event by a session.
V$SESSION_WAIT	Lists the resources or events for which active sessions are waiting, where WAIT_TIME = 0 for current events.
V$SESSTAT	Lists user session statistics. Requires join to V$STATNAME, V$SESSION.

TABLE 16-2. *Session-Level Dynamic Performance Views*

conditions on your database, such as users waiting for other users to relinquish locks on rows or tables.

Exercises

1. Describe the general use of V$ views. Where is the information in these views stored? What role is required if you want to view the data in dynamic performance views?
2. Identify the use of the V$SYSSTAT view. What are some of the elements it contains? Describe the contents of the V$SESSION view.

Using the UTLBSTAT/UTLESTAT Output Report

The UTLBSTAT utility creates tables to store dynamic performance statistics for the Oracle database. Execution of this script also begins the statistics collection process. In order to make statistics collection more effective, the DBA should not run UTLBSTAT until after the database has been running for several hours or days. This utility uses underlying V$ performance views such as those listed in Tables 16-1 and 16-2 to find information about the performance of the Oracle database, and the accumulation of useful data in these views may take some time.

Statistics collection for the instance is ended with the UTLESTAT utility. An output file called `report.txt` containing a report of the statistics is generated by UTLESTAT. To maximize the effectiveness of these two utilities, it is important that UTLBSTAT be allowed to run for a long time, under a variety of circumstances, before ending statistics collection. These circumstances include batch processing, online transaction processing, backups, and periods of inactivity. This wide variety of database activity will give the DBA a more complete idea about the level of use the database experiences under normal circumstances.

These two utilities provide the functionality required to maintain a history of performance information. Typically, the script containing the UTLBSTAT utility is called `utlbstat.sql`, is found in the `rdbms/admin` directory under the Oracle software home directory, and is executed from within Server Manager. You will have to issue the `connect internal` command to connect to the database as the INTERNAL user from Server Manager in order to run UTLBSTAT, because the utility requires privileges granted to INTERNAL in order to run. The database overhead used for collecting these statistics can be substantial, with an impact on the system as high as 10 percent. UTLBSTAT creates tables to store data from several V$ performance views. Assuming `TIMED_STATISTICS` is already set (see the tip following this code block), the following code block demonstrates how to start UTLBSTAT running, using Server Manager:

```
D:\ORANT\RDBMS80\ADMIN\> svrmgr30
Oracle Server Manager Release 3.0.5.0.0 - Production
(c) Copyright 1997, Oracle Corporation. All Rights Reserved.
Oracle8 Enterprise Edition Release 8.0.5.0.0 - Production
With the Partitioning and Objects options
PL/SQL Release 8.0.5.0.0 - Production
SVRMGR> @D:\ORANT\RDBMS80\ADMIN\UTLBSTAT
SVRMGR> set echo on;
ECHO                         ON
SVRMGR> Connect internal
Password:
...
```

You will normally see several `create table as select` statements after issuing the command to execute UTLBSTAT and `connect internal`. If these table-creation statements encounter errors, you will have to correct the errors before relying on the output from this utility for statistics collection.

TIP
In order to execute UTLBSTAT, the `TIMED_STATISTICS` `initsid.ora` parameter must be set to TRUE for the Oracle instance. Certain information will not be captured by the utility if this parameter is not correctly set. Also, do not run this utility against a database that has not been running for several hours or more, as it relies on dynamic performance views that will not contain useful information if the database has not been running for some time.

UTLESTAT ends the collection of performance statistics from the views named previously. Typically, the script is called `utlestat.sql` and is found in the same location as UTLBSTAT, in the `rdbms/admin` directory under the Oracle software home directory. It is executed from Server Manager. You will have to use the `connect internal` command to run UTLESTAT from Server Manager, for reasons explained earlier. This utility will gather all statistics collected and use them to generate an output file called `report.txt`. After generating `report.txt`, the utility will remove the statistics tables it used to store the performance history of the database. The contents of `report.txt` will be discussed shortly.

```
SVRMGR> @D:\ORANT\RDBMS80\ADMIN\UTLESTAT
...
SVRMGR> set echo on;
ECHO                           ON
SVRMGR> Connect internal
Password:
...
```

You will normally see several `drop table` statements as output while this script runs. If you see `ORA-00942` errors, telling you that tables, or views that UTLESTAT is attempting to drop, don't exist, you may not have run UTLBSTAT prior to running UTLESTAT, and thus you will have no statistics collected. Also, don't shut down the database while UTLBSTAT is running. If you do, there could be problems interpreting the data, and since the database must be running for several hours in order for the V$ views that UTLBSTAT depends on to contain useful data, all work done by UTLBSTAT will be useless. The best thing to do in this situation is to run UTLESTAT as soon as possible to clear out all data from the prior run, and wait until the database has been up long enough to attempt a second execution.

Contents of report.txt

The `report.txt` file provides a great deal of useful information in the following areas. First, it provides statistics for file I/O by tablespace and datafile. This information is useful in distributing files across many disks to reduce I/O contention. The `report.txt` file also provides information about SGA, shared area, dictionary area, table/procedure, trigger, pipe, and other cache statistics. The `report.txt` file is also used to determine whether there is contention for any of several different resources. This report gives latch wait statistics for the instance and shows whether there is contention for resources using latches. A latch is an internal resource that is used to manage access to various important Oracle resources, such as the redo log buffer, buffer cache, shared pool, and other items.

Statistics are also given for how often user processes wait for rollback segments, which can be used to determine whether more rollback segments should be added. The average length of a dirty buffer write queue is also shown, which the DBA can use to determine whether DBW0 is having difficulty writing blocks to the database. The dirty buffer write queue is an area in the Oracle buffer cache that lists all the buffers in the buffer cache that have been modified but not written to disk. Finally, `report.txt` contains a listing of all `init`*`sid`*`.ora` parameters for the database and the start and stop time for statistics collection. An example of `report.txt`, slightly modified and consolidated for readability, is listed here:

```
SVRMGR> Rem Select Library cache statistics. Pin hit rate
SVRMGR> Rem should be high.
SVRMGR> select namespace library, gets,
   2>      round(decode(gethits,0,1,gethits)/decode(gets,0,1,gets),3)
   3>       gethitratio, pins,
   4>      round(decode(pinhits,0,1,pinhits)/decode(pins,0,1,pins),3)
   5>       pinhitratio, reloads, invalidations from stats$lib;

LIBRARY         GETS    GETHITRATI     PINS     PINHITRATI  RELOADS  INVALID
--------- ---------- ---------- -------- ---------- ---------- -------
BODY               2          1        2          1          0       0
CLUSTER            0          1        0          1          0       0
INDEX              0          1        0          1          0       0
OBJECT             0          1        0          1          0       0
PIPE               0          1        0          1          0       0
SQL AREA        5098       .605    18740       .772        185       0
TABLE/PROCED    7762       .989    15138       .982        186       0
TRIGGER            0          1        0          1          0       0

SVRMGR> Rem The total is the total value of the statistic between
SVRMGR> Rem the time bstat was run and the time estat was run. Note
SVRMGR> Rem that the estat script logs on as "internal" so the
```

```
SVRMGR> Rem per_logon statistics will always be based on at least
SVRMGR> Rem one logon.
SVRMGR> select n1.name "Statistic", n1.change "Total",
     2>        round(n1.change/trans.change,2) "Per Transaction",
     3>        round(n1.change/logs.change,2)  "Per Logon"
     4>    from stats$stats n1, stats$stats trans, stats$stats logs
     5>    where trans.name='user commits'
     6>     and  logs.name='logons' and  n1.change != 0
     7>    order by n1.name;

 0 rows selected.

SVRMGR> Rem Average length of the dirty buffer write queue. If larger
SVRMGR> Rem than the value of db_block_write_batch init.ora parameter,
SVRMGR> Rem consider increasing db_block_write_batch and check for
SVRMGR> Rem disks that are doing many more IOs than other disks.
SVRMGR> select queue.change/writes.change "Average Write Queue Length"
     2>   from stats$stats queue, stats$stats writes
     3>  where queue.name  = 'summed write queue length'
     4>   and  writes.name = 'write requests';

 0 rows selected.

SVRMGR> Rem I/O should be spread across drives. A big difference
SVRMGR> Rem between phys_reads and phys_blks_rd implies table
SVRMGR> Rem scans are going on.
SVRMGR> select * from stats$files order by table_space, file_name;

TABLE_SPACE  FILE_NAME
------------ ------------------------------------------------
PHYS_READS   PHYS_BLKS_RD PHYS_RD_TIME PHYS_WRT PHYS_BLKS_WR PHYS_WRT_T
------------ ------------ ------------ ------------ ------------ -----
DATA          /u01/oradata/norm/data01.dbf
         303          405            0          108          108     0
INDEX         /u03/oradata/norm/index01.dbf
         200          189            0           56           56     0
RBS           /u04/oradata/norm/rbs01.dbf
           7            7            0          202          202     0
SYSTEM        /u02/oradata/norm/system01.dbf
        1072         3731            0          367          367     0
TEMP          /u05/oradata/norm/temp01.dbf
           3           34            0          280          280     0
USERS         /u05/oradata/norm/users01.dbf
           0            0            0            0            0     0

SVRMGR> Rem sum over tablespaces
SVRMGR> select table_space, sum(phys_reads) phys_reads,
     2>  sum(phys_blks_rd) phys_blks_rd,
```

```
     3>   sum(phys_rd_time) phys_rd_time,sum(phys_writes) phys_writes,
     4>   sum(phys_blks_wr) phys_blks_wr,  sum(phys_wrt_tim) phys_wrt
     5>  from stats$files group by table_space order by table_space;

TBLE_SPACE PHYS_READS PHYS_BLKS_RD PH PHYS_WRITES PHYS_BLKS_WR PH
---------- ---------- ------------ -- ----------- ------------ --
DATA       303        405           0 108         108           0
INDEX      200        189           0 56          56            0
RBS        7          7             0 202         202           0
SYSTEM     1072       3731          0 367         367           0
TEMP       3          34            0 280         280           0
TOOLS      1          1             0 0           0             0
USERS      0          0             0 0           0             0

SVRMGR> Rem Sleeps should be low. The hit_ratio should be high.
SVRMGR> select name latch_name, gets, misses,
  2> round(decode(gets-misses,0,1,gets-misses)/decode(gets,0,1,gets),3)
  3> hit_ratio, sleeps, round(sleeps/decode(misses,0,1,misses),3)
  4> "SLEEPS/MISS" from stats$latches where gets != 0 order by name;

LATCH_NAME                GETS   MISSES  HIT_RATIO SLEEPS  SLEEPS/MI
------------------ ----------- ------ --------- ------    --------
cache buffer handl         532      0          1      0          0
cache buffers chai     1193540    203          1    514      2.532
cache buffers lru        20200    145       .993    332       2.29
dml lock allocatio        1016      0          1      0          0
enqueues                  3601      0          1      0          0
library cache           133513    853       .994   1887      2.212
messages                  1998      0          1      0          0
multiblock read ob        5265      0          1      0          0
process allocation          14      0          1      0          0
redo allocation           3776      4       .999     15       3.75
row cache objects       150451    266       .998    633       2.38
sequence cache             170      0          1      0          0
session allocation        1430      1       .999      1          1
session idle bit         37204      7          1     11      1.571
shared pool              87978    447       .995    931      2.083
system commit numb        7702      4       .999      9       2.25
transaction alloca         578      0          1      0          0
undo global data           442      0          1      0          0
user lock                   30      0          1      0          0

SVRMGR> Rem Statistics on no_wait latch gets. No_wait get does not
SVRMGR> Rem wait for latch to become free, it immediately times out.
SVRMGR> select name latch_name,
     2>     immed_gets nowait_gets,
     3>     immed_miss nowait_misses,
     4>     round(decode(immed_gets-immed_miss,0,1,
```

```
    5>     immed_gets-immed_miss)/
    6>     decode(immed_gets,0,1,immed_gets),3)
    7>     nowait_hit_ratio from stats$latches
    8> where immed_gets != 0 order by name;

LATCH_NAME         NOWAIT_GETS NOWAIT_MISSES NOWAIT_HIT_RATIO
------------------ ----------- ------------- ----------------
cache buffers chai       87850           109             .999
cache buffers lru       580277         18656             .968
library cache              555            45             .919
row cache objects          649            60             .908

SVRMGR> Rem Waits_for_trans_tbl high implies add rollback segments.
SVRMGR> select * from stats$roll;

UN TRANS_T_G TRANS_T_W UNDO_BYT_WR SEGMENT_ XACTS SHRINKS WRA
-- --------- --------- ----------- -------- ----- ------- ---
 0         6         0           0   180224     0       0   0
 2        68         0       10915 10645504     0       0   0
 3        28         0        4857 10645504     0       0   0
 4        65         0       14027 10645504     0       0   0
 5        18         0        1786 10645504     0       0   0
 6        10         0        1530 10645504    -1       0   0
 7        58         0       18306 10645504     1       0   0
 8        50         0        8018 10645504    -1       0   0
 9        39         0       13020 10645504     0       0   0
10         6         0           0 10645504     0       0   0
11         6         0           0 10645504     0       0   0
12        51         0       12555 10645504     0       0   0
13        61         0       10194 10645504     0       0   0
14        57         0       10081 10645504    -1       0   0
15         8         0         938 10645504    -1       0   0
16        29         0        3369 10645504    -1       0   0
17        20         0        3267 10645504     0       0   0
18        68         0       58861 10645504     0       0   0
19        12         0        6187 10645504     0       0   0
20         6         0           0 10645504     0       0   0
21         6         0           0 10645504     0       0   0

SVRMGR> Rem The init.ora parameters currently in effect:
SVRMGR> select name, value from v$parameter where isdefault = 'FALSE'
     2> order by name;

NAME                                    VALUE
--------------------------------------- ------------------------------
audit_trail                             NONE
background_dump_dest                    $ORACLE_BASE/admin/norm/bdump
control_files                           /u02/oradata/norm/control.ctl
```

```
core_dump_dest                        $ORACLE_BASE/admin/norm/cdump
db_block_buffers                      6000
db_block_size                         4096
db_file_multiblock_read_count         8
db_file_simultaneous_writes           8
db_files                              200
db_name                               norm
distributed_transactions              61
dml_locks                             750
enqueue_resources                     5000
gc_db_locks                           6000
ifile                     /u07/app/oracle/admin/norm/pfile/co
log_archive_dest          $ORACLE_BASE/admin/norm/arch/arch.l
log_archive_format        'log%S%T.arch'
log_checkpoint_interval   4096
log_checkpoints_to_alert  TRUE
log_simultaneous_copies   0
max_dump_file_size        10240
max_enabled_roles         22
mts_servers               0
nls_sort                  BINARY
open_cursors              255
optimizer_mode            RULE
pre_page_sga              TRUE
processes                 200
resource_limit            TRUE
rollback_segments         r01, r02, r03, r04, r05
row_locking               ALWAYS
sequence_cache_entries    30
sequence_cache_hash_bucke 23
sessions                  225
shared_pool_size          31457280
sort_area_retained_size   131072
sort_area_size            131072
temporary_table_locks     225
transactions              206
transactions_per_rollback 42
user_dump_dest            $ORACLE_BASE/admin/norm/udump

SVRMGR> Rem get_miss and scan_miss should be very low compared
SVRMGR> Rem to requests.cur_usage is the number of entries in the
SVRMGR> Rem cache being used.
SVRMGR> select * from stats$dc
     2>  where get_reqs != 0 or scan_reqs != 0 or mod_reqs != 0;

NAME            GET_REQS GET_ SCAN_REQ SCAN_MIS MOD COUNT    CUR_U
--------------- -------- ---- -------- -------- --- -------- -----
dc_tablespaces        45    0        0        0   0       15    12
```

```
dc_free_extents        1300   53         64          0 133      311    302
dc_segments            2789   21          0          0  51      315    310
dc_rollback_seg         264    0          0          0   0       24     23
dc_used_extents          65   40          0          0  65       62     54
dc_users                134    0          0          0   0       36     24
dc_user_grants           59    0          0          0   0       58     19
dc_objects             7837  109          0          0   0      984    983
dc_tables             21636   15          0          0   0      415    412
dc_columns            62063 2272       3001        522   0    11106    100
dc_table_grants       18080  113          0          0   0      956    938
dc_indexes             3620   39       2742         12   0      849    848
dc_constraint_d         554   82         61          9   0      536    535
dc_constraint_d           0    0         41          2   0        1      0
dc_synonyms            2524   85          0          0   0      510    509
dc_usernames           3010    0          0          0   0       44     40
dc_sequences            156    3          0          0  24       46     43
dc_sequence_gra          98    4          0          0   0      124    123
dc_tablespaces           38    0          0          0  38       16      8
dc_profiles              14    0          0          0   0        8      1

SVRMGR> Rem The times that bstat and estat were run.
SVRMGR> select * from stats$dates;

STATS_GATHER_TIMES
--------------------
28-JUN-99 15:20:42
28-JUN-99 16:30:40
```

Exercises

1. The output for the `report.txt` file shows a great deal of *hit* and *wait* information. What do you think this information means? What sorts of values (high or low) for hits and waits do you think indicate good or poor database performance?

2. You are the DBA on a database experiencing performance problems accessing information from many dictionary views. The database has been running for a while. You use the UTLBSTAT and UTLESTAT utilities to pinpoint the cause of the performance degradation. In what area might you look in the output file to see if there is a problem?

3. Name the sections of the `report.txt` file, and identify uses for each.

Using Appropriate OEM Tools

The set of utilities comprising the Oracle Enterprise Manager Tuning Pack contains products that will help the DBA identify performance issues. You can run Tuning Pack in Windows operating systems in conjunction with Oracle Enterprise Manager. This tuning tool can be used in conjunction with Oracle databases running on Windows and Unix (so long as Intelligent Agent is running and monitoring those databases) as well, so this tool set is useful and versatile for diagnosing your performance issues in Oracle on both platforms, along with many others. The purpose of this section is to acquaint you with the tools comprising Oracle Enterprise Manager for tuning and monitoring your database.

Other Tools for Performance-Tuning Diagnosis

The `explain plan` command enables the DBA or developer to determine the execution path of a block of SQL code. The execution plan is generated by the SQL statement-processing mechanism. This command can be executed by entering `explain plan set statement_id = 'name' into plan_table for SQL_statement` at the SQL*Plus prompt. The execution plan shows the step-by-step operations that Oracle will undertake in order to obtain data from the tables comprising the Oracle database. This option is provided mainly so that developers and users who write SQL statements and run them against the database can avoid running inefficient SQL. The output of this command is placed into a special table created by running the `utlxplan.sql` script found in the rdbms/admin subdirectory under the Oracle software home directory. This table is called PLAN_TABLE. The following code block shows a typical execution plan.

```
QUERY_PLAN
------------------------------------------------------------
  SORT AGGREGATE
    NESTED LOOPS
      NESTED LOOPS
        MERGE JOIN
          TABLE ACCESS BY INDEX ROWID TIME_LOOKUP
            INDEX UNIQUE SCAN SYS_C001907
          FILTER
            TABLE ACCESS FULL SALES_FACT_TABLE
        TABLE ACCESS BY INDEX ROWID STORE_REGION_LOOKUP
          INDEX UNIQUE SCAN SYS_C001906
      TABLE ACCESS BY INDEX ROWID PRODUCT_LOOKUP
        INDEX UNIQUE SCAN SYS_C001905
```

In Chapter 17, you will learn more about generating an execution plan. For now, understand that the course of action Oracle takes is based on reading the execution plan from the inside out first, then from the top down. Thus, the index unique scan on the SYS_C001907 index and the full table scan on the SALES_FACT_TABLE are the first actions the Oracle RDBMS performs, while the sorting operation is the last. You will learn more about what these actions mean in Chapter 17.

Exercises

1. Identify the tool that identifies the execution plan of a given SQL query. In what step of Oracle's recommended tuning methodology might this information be useful? How do you read an execution plan?
2. What is Oracle Enterprise Manager? How is it used for tuning?

Chapter Summary

You learned several things in this chapter that will form the basis of your understanding of Oracle performance tuning for OCP Exam 4. The areas covered include business requirements and tuning, ALERT and trace files and events in OEM, utilities for performance tuning, and dynamic performance views. These areas comprise 20 percent of OCP Exam 4 test content.

The first topic you covered was the area of business requirements and tuning. You learned about the different roles people in an organization play in the tuning process. You also learned about the steps associated with the tuning process, and covered each of them in some detail. Finally, you identified the different tuning goals you might have as a DBA.

The use of the Oracle ALERT log was also discussed. You learned where to locate this special trace file for database-wide events, identifying the location and usefulness of the ALERT log file. Next, you learned where to find background and user trace files, and how to use user trace files for performance-tuning purposes. The special role of SQL Trace and TKPROF for this purpose was covered in some detail. The use of OEM for displaying and retrieving wait events in conjunction with Oracle Intelligent Agent and Tuning Pack was covered in some detail as well. Finally, you learned how to set events using OEM, so that you can be alerted about predefined situations.

In the final section, you covered the use of utilities and dynamic performance views in the task of database tuning. The special role of V$ views for collecting statistics about how Oracle is running was discussed, and the information these different views actually capture was identified. You learned about the statistics-diagnosis process using UTLBSTAT and UTLESTAT, two trusty standby utilities that have been a part of the Oracle database for a long time. How you read the resultant file `report.txt` was covered, as well. Finally, you learned about the OEM Tuning Pack and how it is used for database tuning.

Two-Minute Drill

- Three goals of performance tuning are: improving the performance of particular SQL queries, improving the performance of applications, and improving the performance of the entire database.
- The steps for performance tuning are as follows:
  1. Tune application configuration
  2. Tune operating system structures
  3. Tune memory structures
  4. Tune I/O
  5. Detect and resolve contention
- The preceding performance-tuning steps should be executed in the order given, to avoid making sweeping database changes that could cause things to break in unanticipated ways.
- Oracle maintains several log files for user and background processes, and for system-wide events. The log files for user and background processes are called trace files, and they can be found in the directories specified by `USER_DUMP_DEST` and `BACKGROUND_DUMP_DEST` `init`*`sid`*`.ora` parameters.
- Background trace files are created when background processes fail. They offer little value in the goal of tuning an Oracle database.
- The system-wide event log file is called the ALERT log. This file can be found in the directory identified by the `BACKGROUND_DUMP_DEST` parameter.
- The ALERT log doesn't offer much information for database tuning, but it will help to identify system-wide events.
- Events are occurrences in Oracle that substantially alter the behavior or performance of the database.
- If you are running Oracle Intelligent Agent, you can track events using the Oracle Enterprise Manager console.

- V$ performance views are used in Oracle to collect and review statistics for database performance and operation. These views are owned by SYS and are accessible to users who have the SELECT_CATALOG_ROLE role granted to them.
- Review Tables 16-1 and 16-2 to become familiar with various V$ performance views before taking OCP Exam 4.
- System events and their statistics in Oracle can be identified using the V$SYSTEM_EVENT view. Session events and their statistics in Oracle can be identified using the V$SESSION_EVENT view.
- The UTLBSTAT and UTLESTAT utilities are frequently used by DBAs to identify performance issues on the Oracle database.
- The UTLBSTAT and UTLESTAT utilities require the user executing these scripts to be connected to Oracle as the `internal` user.
- UTLBSTAT is the utility that begins statistics collection. Executing this file creates special tables for database-performance statistics collection and begins the collection process.
- UTLESTAT is the utility that ends statistics collection. It concludes the statistics-collection activity started by UTLBSTAT and produces a report of database activity called `report.txt`.
- The `report.txt` file consists of the following components:
  - Statistics for file I/O by tablespace and datafiles. This information is useful in distributing files across many disks to reduce I/O contention.
  - SGA, shared pool, table/procedure, trigger, pipe, and other cache statistics used to determine whether there is contention for any of the listed resources.
  - Latch wait statistics for the database instance, used to determine whether there is contention for resources using latches.
  - Statistics for how often user processes wait for rollback segments, which is used to determine whether more rollback segments should be added.
  - Average length of dirty buffer write queue, which is used to determine whether DBW0 is having difficulty writing blocks to the database.
  - Initialization parameters for the database, including defaults.
  - Start time and stop time for statistics collection.

- OEM Tuning Pack is a tool that can be used for advanced tuning and event detection in Oracle using Enterprise Manager.

Chapter Questions

1. **The DBA is about to begin performance tuning. Which utility script can be run by the DBA in order to begin tracking performance statistics on the database instance?**

   A. UTLESTAT

   B. UTLBSTAT

   C. UTLMONTR

   D. UTLLOCKT

2. **You are attempting to tune overall performance of your Oracle database. Which of the following is not part of `report.txt`?**

   A. Redo log and rollback segment entries

   B. Database instance initialization parameters

   C. Dirty buffer write queue statistics

   D. Statistics collection start and stop times

3. **The DBA is about to begin performance tuning. What area of the database should the DBA tune before tuning memory structures?**

   A. Disk I/O

   B. Contention

   C. SQL statements

   D. Latches and locks

   E. Dispatchers and shared servers

4. **You are analyzing SQL statement execution plans. Output for the `explain plan` command is stored in which of the following choices?**

   A. PLAN_TABLE

   B. `report.txt`

C. TRACE files

D. `initsid.ora`

E. Nowhere

5. The DBA is preparing to analyze database performance statistics using UTLBSTAT and UTLESTAT. In order to increase the likelihood that UTLBSTAT will capture meaningful statistics,

A. the instance name should be fewer than eight characters.

B. the instance should be running for several hours before starting UTLBSTAT.

C. the shared pool should be flushed.

D. the SYSTEM tablespace should be reorganized to reduce fragmentation.

6. You are trying to determine the value of an initialization parameter that you did not set prior to database startup. The most efficient and effective way to find out the database instance parameters is to

A. run UTLBSTAT and UTLESTAT

B. read the `initsid.ora` file

C. execute the `show parameter` command

D. read `report.txt`

7. You are tuning performance on your Oracle database using tuning tools. Which of the following is *not* a tool used for diagnosing tuning problems on the Oracle instance?

A. Server Manager

B. V$ performance views

C. SQL*Loader

D. TKPROF

E. Oracle Enterprise Manager

8. You are attempting to track latch performance statistics. Which two views are used to track latch performance statistics? (Choose two)

A. V$LATCH

B. V$LATCHWAIT

C. V$LATCHNAME

D. V$LATCHHOLDER

E. V$LATCHLOG

9. SQL operations are listed as output from `explain plan` in which of the following ways?

A. from top to bottom, from outside in

B. from bottom to top, from outside in

C. from top to bottom, from inside out

D. from bottom to top, from inside out

10. Dynamic performance views in the Oracle instance are owned by

A. SYSTEM

B. `sysdba`

C. `osdba`

D. SYS

Answers to Chapter Questions

1. B. UTLBSTAT

Explanation UTLBSTAT is the utility that begins statistics collection. Choice A is incorrect because UTLESTAT is the script run to end statistics collection on the database. Choice C is incorrect because the UTLMONTR script is incorporated in the installation of Oracle. Choice D is incorrect because UTLLOCKT creates a package used to manage locks. Review the discussion of the UTLBSTAT and UTLESTAT utilities in the "Using the UTLBSTAT/UTLESTAT Output Report" section of the chapter.

2. A. Redo log and rollback segment entries

Explanation All other choices are contained in `report.txt.` Redo log entries are contained in the redo log, and rollback segment entries are contained in the rollback segments. Review the tour of `report.txt` in the "Using the UTLBSTAT/UTLESTAT Output Report" section of the chapter.

3. C. SQL statements

Explanation SQL statements are the first area the DBA should tune on the database. Choice A is incorrect because disk I/O is tuned after memory usage, according to the tuning methodology. The same is true of contention, choice B. Choices D and E are both tuned as part of tuning memory usage. Review the discussion of tuning methodology.

4. A. PLAN_TABLE

Explanation PLAN_TABLE stores all execution plan information generated by the `explain plan` command. Choice B is incorrect because `report.txt` contains output from the UTLBSTAT/UTLESTAT statistics collection utilities. Choice C is partly correct because trace files contain the execution plan for statements executed during the traced session, but user session trace files are not the only type of trace file on the database. Review the discussion of available diagnostic tools.

5. B. The instance should be running for several hours before starting UTLBSTAT.

Explanation The database must be running for several hours in order for the performance views that feed UTLBSTAT to contain meaningful information. Choice

A is incorrect because, although the instance name should be eight characters or fewer, it does not improve performance to have that instance name under eight characters. Choice C is incorrect because the shared pool does not need to be flushed to improve statistics-collection performance. Choice D is incorrect because correcting tablespace fragmentation defeats the purpose of gathering statistics to determine the problem. Review the discussion of UTLBSTAT and UTLESTAT.

6. C. Execute the `show parameter` command

Explanation The `show parameter` command from Server Manager is the easiest and fastest way to obtain all initialization parameters, including defaults. Running UTLBSTAT and UTLESTAT to generate initialization parameters in `report.txt` will work, but it takes longer to execute than showing the parameter block; therefore, choices A and D are incorrect. Choice B is incorrect because `init`*`sid`*`.ora` only shows the parameters that the DBA sets for the instance, not all initialization parameters. Review the discussion of `report.txt`.

7. C. SQL*Loader

Explanation Server Manager gives a graphical interface to the V$ performance views, so choices A and B are not correct. Choice D is incorrect because TKPROF produces a report on SQL performance based on trace file statistics. Choice E is incorrect because Oracle Enterprise Manager is used to manage and administer the Oracle database through a GUI interface.

8. A. *and* D. V$LATCH *and* V$LATCHHOLDER

Explanation V$LATCH tracks the statistics used to calculate hit ratios for latches, while V$LATCHHOLDER identifies processes that are holding latches and the processes that are waiting for the latches to become free. The V$LATCHNAME view associates a descriptive name for a latch with its latch number and tracks no pertinent statistics for performance tuning; therefore, choice C is incorrect. V$LATCHWAIT and V$LATCHLOG are not performance views in the Oracle instance; therefore, choices B and E are incorrect. Review the discussion of latch contention.

9. C. From top to bottom, from inside out

Explanation When the execution plan is pulled from the PLAN_TABLE using the script Oracle provides, the user must read the results from top to bottom, with output from inner operations feeding as input into outer operations. Review the explanation of `explain plan` in the available diagnostic tools section.

10. D. SYS

Explanation SYS owns all dynamic performance views in the Oracle database. SYSTEM can access the performance views, but does not own the views; therefore, choice A is incorrect. `sysdba` and `osdba` are privileges granted on the database to the DBA that allow access to the views, but again, access does not mean ownership. Therefore, choices B and C are also incorrect. Review the concluding points from the tour of `report.txt`.

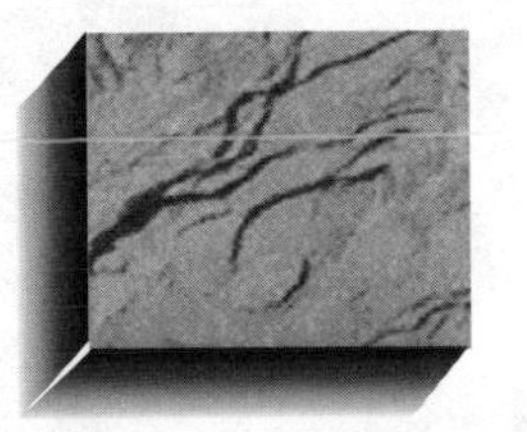

CHAPTER 17

Tuning Database Applications

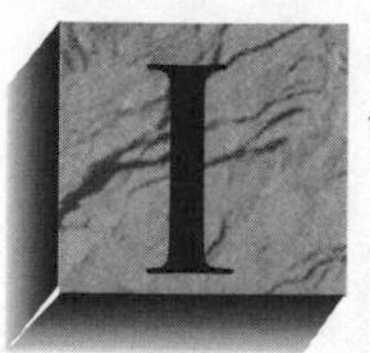

n this chapter, you will learn about and demonstrate knowledge in the following areas:

- Tuning for differing application requirements
- SQL tuning

The first areas of any database that require tuning, in most cases, are the queries and applications that access the database. By far, the greatest improvement to performance can be made through this critical tuning step. Other areas of tuning, such as memory and disk usage, though beneficial to the database as a whole, don't have as dramatic results as a change in the SQL statements of an application. When there is a performance issue on the machine, the DBA's first inclination should be to work with the application developer. In fact, this material may actually be of more use to developers than DBAs. However, the DBA should grow accustomed to serving as an Oracle guru around the office. And, of course, the OCP certification series for DBAs requires that the DBA know how to tune applications—about 15 percent of OCP Exam 4 content will be on performance tuning.

Tuning for Differing Application Requirements

In this section, you will cover the following topics related to tuning for different application requirements:

- Using data-access methods to tune logical database design
- Demands of online transaction processing systems
- Demands of decision support systems
- Configuring systems temporarily for particular needs

The design of a database should take into consideration as many aspects of how the production system will work as possible. This discussion will focus on the design characteristics of different types of databases that facilitate those strategies already covered. First, you will learn how to use data-access methods to tune logical database design. Next, some different types of applications that organizations use in conjunction with Oracle will be described, including online transaction-processing (OLTP) applications and decision support systems (DSS). Last, you will learn how to use `initsid.ora` and other methods to reconfigure your system temporarily for particular needs.

Using Data-Access Methods to Tune Logical Database Design

From an application standpoint, a first step you will want to take for tuning is to ensure that there is efficient access to your data. Two perspectives exist for this analysis. The first is to evaluate the use of performance-adding objects in your database's physical design. These objects include all kinds of indexes, clustered tables, and index-organized tables. To use these objects effectively in tuning your database, be sure you understand how these objects add value to database performance. The second way to approach database tuning is to tune the logical data model to ensure proper *normalization*. The following set of short explanations will give you a basic sense of how these techniques improve performance, and when it might be appropriate to use them.

Using Clustered Tables, Hash Clusters

Recall that a cluster is a special type of segment in Oracle that stores data from different tables together in close physical proximity on disk. This configuration can be useful, particularly when your application joins data from those tables frequently. The goal of this configuration is to obtain rows from several different tables using only one disk read, because the common rows are stored in the same block. Hash clusters can take performance one step higher by using a hash function to derive the location of the requested data on disk using the data itself as input. However, these two configurations require that the growth of your data be relatively static, or the configuration could be disrupted.

Using B-Tree Indexes

If your SQL application consistently uses particular columns in the `where` clause as selection criteria, you should ensure that those columns are indexed properly. If your indexes only contain one column, ensure that an index exists on the columns employed by your `where` clauses. If you use composite indexes, be sure the leading column (the column where position equals 1 in the row for that composite index in the USER_IND_COLUMNS view) is used somewhere in the `where` clause. Furthermore, you may need to pay attention to column order, particularly if you have set up your database to use rule-based optimization, but not when using cost-based optimization. You will learn more about the use of composite indexes for improved performance later in the section. Finally, when deciding on how to index a column, be sure that you understand the cardinality of its data. If the column contains mostly distinct, and few NULL values, and the data in each row for that column frequently changes, you can use B-tree indexes to tune your application effectively.

Using Bitmap Indexes

When all of the following conditions are met, you can use bitmap indexes to speed access to your table data to improve performance. The conditions are:

- The table is large
- The column you want to index contains few distinct values
- The data in each row for that column rarely changes
- You use the `and` and `or` operations in the `where` clauses of queries on the table

Using Normalized Data and IOTs

Normalization is the process detailed by E.F. Codd in the original work on relational database design—columns are placed in a table only if they are functionally dependent on the primary key. Functional dependence means that the value in the dependent key modifies or refines the data stored in the primary key. Data in dependent columns has no meaning standing on its own. If a column is not functionally dependent on the primary key for that table, the column either belongs in another table where it is functionally dependent on the primary key, or the column needs to be the primary key of a new table. The goal of data normalization is to ensure that every column in every table depends on the *key*, the *whole key*, and *nothing but the key* (so help me Codd!).

What's more, in order for true data normalization to take place, the process of breaking tables into smaller tables with columns functionally dependent on their primary keys must result in no loss of data, therefore making the process reversible. In highly normalized databases, you may find it useful to employ index-organized tables (IOTs) heavily. Since efficient access to all data is governed by proper use of the primary key, the IOT allows you to represent your data physically in an object that accurately reflects the logical design of your application.

TIP

Real-world applications rarely take data normalization to the extremes that E.F. Codd took them. Instead, many application designers use a balance of normalized and de-normalized data modeling in OLTP applications, as appropriate. Data warehouses are known for their extensive use of de-normalized data modeling, however!

Exercises

1. What are two approaches to data-access methods you can use to tune database design?
2. What is normalization? If you have successfully normalized your data model, what database object might you find useful for physical representation of a normalized table?

Demands of Online Transaction Processing Systems

Online transaction processing (OLTP) is a common system in many organizations. When you think about data entry, you are thinking about OLTP. These types of applications are characterized by high data-change activity, such as inserts or updates, usually performed by a large user base. Some examples of this type of system include order-entry systems, ticketing systems, timesheet-entry systems, payments-received systems, and other systems representing the entry and change of mass amounts of data. Figure 17-1 shows information about data volume and direction on OLTP systems.

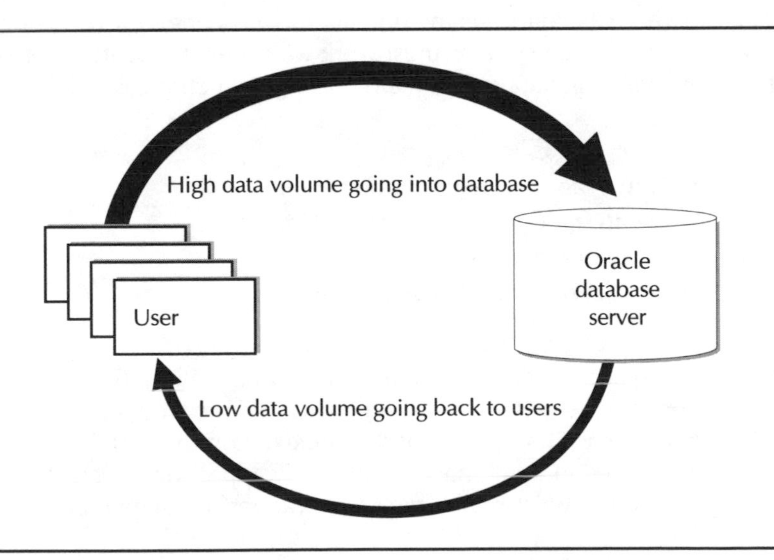

FIGURE 17-1. *Data volume and direction in OLTP systems*

Data in these systems is highly volatile. Because data changes quickly and frequently, one design goal for OLTP systems is the ability to enter, change, and correct data quickly without sacrificing accuracy. Since many users of the system may manipulate the same pieces or areas of data, mechanisms must exist to prevent users from overwriting one another's data. Finally, because users can make changes or additions to the database based on existing data, there must be mechanisms to show changes online quickly.

There are several design paradoxes inherent in OLTP systems. First, OLTP systems need to be designed to facilitate fast data entry without sacrificing accuracy. Any mechanism that checks the data being entered will cause some performance degradation. Oracle provides a good structure for checking data entry in the form of integrity constraints, such as `CHECK` and `FOREIGN-KEY` constraints. Since these mechanisms are built into the data-definition language, they are more efficient than using table triggers to enforce integrity. Constraints thus solve this paradox for all but the most complex business rules, which must be enforced with triggers.

Typically, OLTP systems have a need to see the data in real time, which creates one of the largest design paradoxes in OLTP systems. Oracle uses index and cluster mechanisms to facilitate data retrieval. Indexes and clusters work better on tables that experience less frequent data change. This is true for indexes, because every data change on an indexed column means a required change to the index. In the case of clusters, since the cluster must be carefully sized to allow so much data to hang off the cluster index, data changes in clustered tables can lead to row migration and chaining—two effects that will kill any performance gains the cluster may give. However, data change is the primary function of an OLTP system. The designers and DBAs of such systems must work with users to create an effective trade-off between viewing data quickly and making data changes quickly.

TIP
Indexes slow down table `insert`, `update`, and `delete` statements; therefore, on OLTP systems, there should be as few indexes as possible to minimize the impact on data-change activity.

This goal can be accomplished through data normalization. By reducing functional dependency between pieces of information as part of the normalization process, the database can store pieces of data indexed on the table's primary key. This design feature, used in combination with a few appropriately created foreign keys to speed table joins, will provide data-retrieval performance that is acceptable in most cases.

If possible, DBAs should participate in the data-modeling process to better understand which tables are frequently updated. In general, it is wise for the DBA to put tables that are frequently updated in a special data tablespace that is backed up frequently. Also, that tablespace can have default settings for data blocks with a high `pctfree` and a low `pctused` to reduce the chances of data migration and row chaining. You will cover other aspects of space utilization in Chapter 19. Although configuring data blocks with high `pctfree` can waste disk space, the desired effect of preventing row migration is obtained because more space is kept free for row growth. Finally, keep the use of indexes as low as possible to minimize the overhead involved in updating both the table and the index. More index-tuning methods are presented in Chapter 19.

Exercises

1. What is online transaction processing?
2. What are some of the requirements for an OLTP system? What are some of the paradoxes inherent in the design requirements of an OLTP system?

Demands of Decision Support Systems

Decision support systems (DSS), offer some challenges that are different from OLTP systems. Decision support systems are used to generate meaningful report information from large volumes of data. A DSS application may often be used in conjunction with an OLTP system, but since their design needs differ greatly, it is often a bad idea to use an OLTP system for decision support needs. Whereas the user population for an OLTP system may be large, the user population for a DSS application is usually limited to a small group. Some decision support system examples include cash-flow forecasting tools that work in conjunction with order-entry systems that help an organization determine how large a cash reserve they should hold against anticipated returns. Another example is a marketing tool working in conjunction with an order-entry system.

The key feature of a decision support system is fast access to large amounts of data. The trade-off between accessing data quickly and updating it quickly (mentioned in the discussion of OLTP systems) needs to be discussed here. The mechanisms that will update the data in the decision support system should be determined as part of the design process. Usually, data flows from the OLTP system (or some other source) into the decision support system on a batch schedule. Users of the decision support system rarely, if ever, `update` or `insert` new data into the system, because it is designed for query access only. Figure 17-2 illustrates data volume and direction in DSS applications.

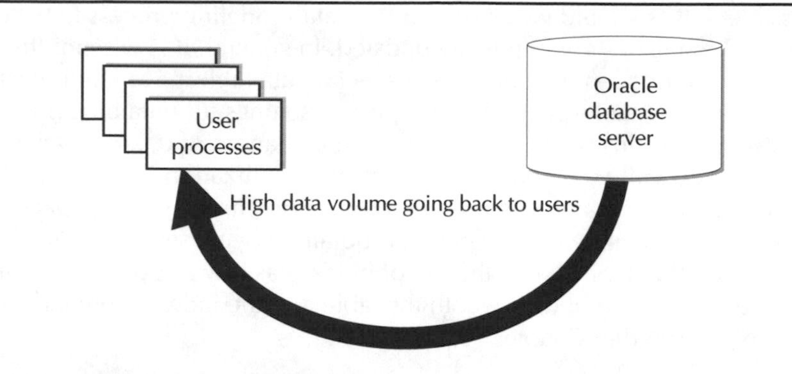

FIGURE 17-2. *Data volume and direction in DSS applications*

Since the decision support system data is updated on a regular batch schedule, the DBA has more options available for performance tuning. Heavy use of indexes and clusters are both options, because data updates happen less often. A process for re-creating indexes and clusters can be designed in conjunction with the batch `update` so as to prevent the ill effects of updating indexed or clustered data. In some cases, the DBA may find that some tables never change. If this is the case, the DBA may assess that it makes sense to gather those tables into a special tablespace and make the tablespace access read-only.

Exercises

1. What is a decision support system?
2. What are the design requirements for decision support systems?

Configuring Systems Temporarily for Particular Needs

In general, the DBA will focus most of his or her tuning energy on tuning the production needs for a particular application. Sometimes, however, those systems will require some special tuning or configuration based on a temporary need. That need may take many forms. For example, an OLTP application may expect that there will be a window of time when use will be particularly heavy. In this case, the DBA may plan in advance for anticipated increase in user activity. Some steps the DBA might take include increasing the number of rollback segments available on the system, reconfiguring some initialization parameters related to redo log use, and so on.

One approach the DBA might take in preparing for the increase in database use is altering the `initsid.ora` file to reflect the necessary parameters for the configuration change. However, making some changes to the database to suit anticipated needs of the system may not be in the best interests of the current needs of that system. In some cases, the DBA is better off waiting until the last possible moment to make the changes to suit a particular need.

To suit the different needs of the applications at different times, the DBA might place any DDL changes that need to happen into a script to be run when the time is right to make the changes, keeping another set of scripts on hand that will reverse the changes. This plan may include having a few different copies of the initialization script `initsid.ora` on hand, each with different settings appropriate to different usage situations, in order to facilitate the process of reconfiguring the database on short notice.

In order to reconfigure the database with a new set of parameters, the parameters should be placed in another version of `initsid.ora` that contains the specifications that must stay the same, such as `DB_NAME, CONTROL_FILES, DB_BLOCK_SIZE`, and other parameters that identify a unique database. When the database must be altered to handle a particular situation, the DBA can bring down the database instance and restart it using the copy of `initsid.ora` especially designed for the situation. Additionally, the DBA can execute the scripts prepared for altering other aspects of the database for the particular situation. When the need passes, the DBA can set the database to run as it did before by executing the scripts designed to reverse whatever alterations took place, bringing down the database, and restarting with the old `initsid.ora` file.

Having special `initsid.ora` files on hand to configure the database for specific needs is also useful when the DBA needs to set up the database for maintenance. Since having the database tuned to handle online transaction processing, decision support, and other application needs could interfere with the upgrade or maintenance activities a DBA must perform, it is advisable to have a mechanism that easily reconfigures the database in such a way as to allow the DBA to perform maintenance quickly. Usually, DBAs have only a short time to perform maintenance activities, such as reorganizing tablespaces or distributing file I/O. The DBA should configure the database to make maintenance go quickly.

Using Instance Manager Configuration Settings

You can reconfigure your database operation in various ways using Instance Manager in OEM. In Windows, you can open Instance Manager using the Start | Programs | Oracle Enterprise Manager | Instance Manager menu option. You should log in as `internal` or as another user with the `sysdba` privilege. Figure 17-3

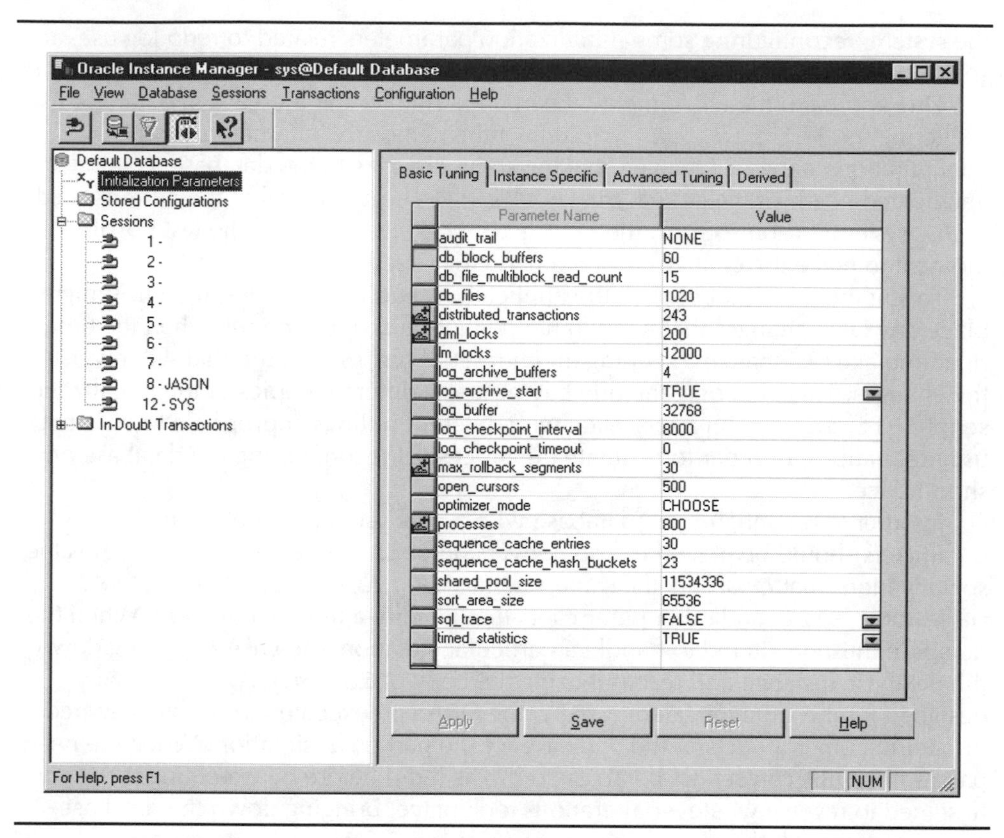

FIGURE 17-3. *Instance Manager interface*

shows the Instance Manager interface. When connected to Oracle, Instance Manager allows you to alter certain `initsid.ora` parameters dynamically and apply them using the Apply button at the bottom of the window. You may want to save your configurations locally if they allow you to accomplish certain goals, such as reorganizing the database or tuning operation. To do so, click the Save button at the bottom of the Instance Manager interface. Enterprise Manager then stores your `initsid.ora` configuration locally. You can use this local configuration later when you restart your instance using different sets of `initsid.ora` parameter values.

Exercises

1. What are some ways the DBA can reconfigure the instance on a temporary basis for different needs?

2. Identify some of the parameters in the `initsid.ora` file that uniquely identify a database.

SQL Tuning

In this section, you will cover the following topics related to tuning applications:

- Role of the DBA in application tuning
- Using Oracle tools to diagnose SQL performance
- Using different optimizer modes
- Using star queries and hash joins
- Tracking and registering module use for PL/SQL blocks
- Identifying alternative SQL statements to enhance performance

To highlight the importance of tuning applications, consider the following situation that actually happened to a Fortune 500 company that used Oracle. One of their applications was used by nearly two-thirds of the company's over 70,000 employees, and it had several batch processes feeding data into it. Over the course of several weeks, during which time several thousand employees were added to the system, the execution of one batch process went from taking 4 hours to 26 hours. The company had grown accustomed to long-running batch processes, but this process ran so long that it couldn't be considered a daily job anymore. Apparently there were some poor comparison operations specified that caused a table to be joined to itself about 15 times before any results could be obtained. The solution wasn't a famous "one-line code fix," but it didn't take long to figure out what the solution was, and once implemented, the 26-hour process became a 30-minute one. One year later, the organization doubled its user base, as well as the amount of data being fed through this batch process, and it still ran in under 40 minutes. Such is the power of application tuning.

Role of the DBA in Application Tuning

The role of the DBA in application tuning is as unique as the corporate IT organization, itself. Since every organization is different, the role of the DBA in application tuning may differ. However, that role has some definite characteristics that are influenced by a number of factors, such as the number of applications housed in a production Oracle instance, the size of the IT developer and DBA organizations, and whether the DBA team is more a team of peers or a team of specialists. This last factor is a relative newcomer to the world of database administration; many organizations have specialists in areas such as backup and recovery, data warehousing, performance tuning, and enterprise resource planning (ERP) installation management, instead of simply having each DBA be a jack-of-all-trades, competent in each of the areas. This trend will no doubt continue, as more ERP applications come online and as corporate database use gets more complicated in general.

Application Tuning and the DBA in a Large Organization

In large and complex database environments where several applications' data are all housed on one instance or a few production instances, the DBA's first loyalty will be to keep that instance up and running. Although the DBA may be involved in enterprise-wide efforts to tune the database, these efforts may also involve hardware upgrades, memory tuning, I/O tuning, and general back-office tuning efforts that will affect every application with data on a production Oracle instance. Thus, it may be difficult, if not impossible, for a DBA to understand the intricacies of every application, including how it acquires locks, and when the batch-processing load kicks in.

In these larger organizations, the efforts to tune the database must fall on the shoulders of the application developer. Many IT organizations structure their teams around applications so that a group of developers share production support and enhancement responsibilities for an existing application. These people bear the primary responsibility for tuning SQL statements, the subject of this section. That said, one way the DBA can support developers is by providing them with good SQL-tuning tools.

This support may take the form of a software-purchase suggestion to management. As the office guru on Oracle technology, the DBA may be called on from time to time to provide informal tutorials on how to tune SQL statements using Oracle's built-in tools, like SQL Trace, TKPROF, and `explain plan`. Since many of these tools require altering `init`*`sid`*`.ora` parameters, the DBA will need to be involved in the effort to change `TIMED_STATISTICS` to TRUE and other parameters.

Finally, sometimes the DBA will regrettably take on the role of "bad cop" in application tuning, particularly if poorly tuned reports or queries are deployed that seriously degrade overall performance. The role of the DBA in this case may involve disconnecting user sessions, identifying problem code blocks, and recommending that changes be made.

Application Tuning and the DBA in Smaller Organizations

Smaller organizations with less complex database applications may run their IT shops differently. An Oracle instance may house only one application in these environments, and the organization may have only a few databases overall. In this situation, the DBA may assume the role of part-time (or even full-time) application developer in addition to production DBA. Where this situation exists, the role of application tuning still falls on the developer, but since the DBA is also the developer, the DBA winds up with all the work.

Exercises

1. Identify some factors that shape the role of the DBA in application-performance tuning. What factors may cause the DBA to handle a great deal of application tuning?
2. Describe areas of responsibility the DBA might have in a large organization. Now, picture yourself as a DBA in a large organization. A meeting has been called regarding the recent poor performance of several applications on one production instance. If DBA application-tuning responsibilities are divided as described in the lesson, what are some recommendations you might make at this meeting?

Using Oracle Tools to Diagnose SQL Performance

There are several tools that help in the performance-tuning process. These tools can be used to identify how the Oracle optimizer handles certain queries based on several criteria, such as the existence of indexes that can be used, whether the table is clustered, whether there are table-performance statistics available, or whether rule-based or cost-based optimization is in use. One of the tools the DBA can use to tune Oracle queries has already been identified: the `explain plan` statement. In this section, more details about interpreting execution plans, along with common tuning techniques will be presented.

Explaining the Execution Plan

DBAs can use the `explain plan` statement to determine how the optimizer will execute the query in question. The DBA or developer can submit a query to the database using `explain plan`, and the database will list the plan of execution it determines it will take, based on the many different factors listed previously. To use `explain plan`, a special PLAN_TABLE table must exist in the user's schema. This table can be created in the user's schema with the `utlxplan.sql` script provided in the `rdbms/admin` directory under the Oracle software home directory. Once the PLAN_TABLE table is in place, the DBA is ready to begin using `explain plan` to optimize query performance.

The syntax requirements for `explain plan` are as follows. First, the `explain plan` clause identifies the statement as one that should have the execution plan created. The following clause is the `set statement_id` clause. It is used to identify the plan for later review. Neglecting to specify a `STATEMENT_ID` for the execution plan will make it difficult to obtain the plan. Finally, the `into table_name for` clause identifies the table into which `explain plan` will put the information. The `explain plan` statement needn't use the PLAN_TABLE, so long as an alternative table is specified that contains the same columns as PLAN_TABLE.

```
SQL> EXPLAIN PLAN
  2 SET STATEMENT_ID = 'your_statement_id'
  3 INTO plan_table FOR
  4 SELECT *
  5 FROM emp
  6 WHERE empid = '43355';
Explained.
```

TIP
If PLAN_TABLE exists already, you may omit the `into PLAN_TABLE for` clause, and Oracle will assume it should put the execution plan information into PLAN_TABLE.

After executing the `explain plan` statement, the DBA can recall the execution plan from the PLAN_TABLE (or other appropriately defined location) using a query similar to the following, modified from a utility provided in the Oracle release software:

```
SQL> SELECT LPAD(' ',2*level) || operation || ' '
  2 || options || ' ' || object_name AS query_plan
  3 FROM plan_table
  4 WHERE statement_id = 'your_statement_id'
  5 CONNECT BY PRIOR ID = parent_id
  6 and statement_id = 'your_statement_id'
  7 START WITH ID=1;
```

This query will produce the plan for the query just explained. The `connect by` clause joins the retrieved rows to the user in a hierarchical format. In the preceding example, the resulting set that will come out of PLAN_TABLE when the retrieval query is executed will be similar in content to the following listing:

```
QUERY_PLAN
--------------------------------------------------------
 TABLE ACCESS BY INDEX ROWID EMP
  INDEX RANGE SCAN PK_EMP_01
```

The execution plan is interpreted in the following way. Innermost rows are the first events taking place in the execution plan. From there, the plan is evaluated from the inside out, with the result sets from inner operations feeding as input to the outer operations. For multiple hierarchies, indicated by an additional series of inserts and often appearing in execution plans for join queries, the resulting execution plan is also read from top to bottom. In the preceding example, we have good use of an index driving the overall table-access operation that will produce the data the query has asked for. If the query had not used an index, however, the execution plan would have consisted of one statement—a full table scan on table EMP.

Common SQL Operations and Their Meanings

Your execution plan will contain a listing of several internal operations, many of which you may not have seen before. To understand some other SQL statement-processing operations that may appear in an execution plan, you must understand what work the RDBMS performs as part of each of these operations. Table 17-1 describes several common execution-plan operations and what they mean.

Operation	Meaning
TABLE ACCESS FULL	Oracle will look at every row in the table to find the requested information. This is usually the slowest way to access large tables, but for small tables, the operation is fast.
TABLE ACCESS BY INDEX	Oracle will use the ROWID method to find a row in the table. ROWID is a special column detailing an exact Oracle block where the row can be found. Provided the index is properly configured, this is usually the fastest way to access a table.

TABLE 17-1. *Execution-Plan Operations*

Operation	Meaning
INDEX RANGE SCAN	Oracle will search an index for a range of values. Usually, this event occurs when a `between` operation is specified by the query or when only the leading columns in a composite index are specified by the `where` clause. It can perform well or poorly, based on the size of the range and the fragmentation of the index.
INDEX UNIQUE SCAN	Oracle will perform this operation when the table's primary key or a unique key is part of the `where` clause. This is the most efficient way to search an index.
NESTED LOOPS	This indicates that a join operation is occurring. It can perform well or poorly, depending on performance on the index and table operations of the individual tables being joined. It usually returns the first rows of data to the user quickly, but may not have the best overall performance.
MERGE JOIN	This indicates that a join operation is occurring. It usually returns the entire set of data requested more quickly than the `NESTED LOOPS` operation, although `NESTED LOOPS` may return the first few rows of data more quickly.
FILTER	This is an operation that adds selectivity to a `TABLE ACCESS FULL` operation, based on the contents of the `where` clause.
SORT AGGREGATE	Oracle performs a sort on the data obtained for the user. This is usually the last operation the RDBMS performs in an execution plan. It could result in a disk sort, if enough space is not available in memory.

TABLE 17-1. *Execution-Plan Operations* (continued)

Using SQL Trace and TKPROF

The database provides a pair of tools called SQL Trace and TKPROF that monitor query performance for tuning purposes. SQL Trace puts hard numbers next to the execution plan of SQL statements to identify other problem areas in the system, creating a file detailing the appropriate statistical raw data. TKPROF is then executed on the output file, turning raw data into formatted output. The informational components offered by a trace file generated by SQL Trace are shown in Table 17-2. The following code block demonstrates the contents of a trace file:

```
TKPROF: Release 8.0.5.0.0 - Production on Wed Apr 7 22:21:35 1999
(c) Copyright 1998 Oracle Corporation. All rights reserved.
Trace file: ora00152.trc
Sort options: default
****************************************************************
count   = number of times OCI procedure was executed
cpu     = cpu time in seconds executing
elapsed = elapsed time in seconds executing
disk    = number of physical reads of buffers from disk
query   = number of buffers gotten for consistent read
current = number of buffers gotten in current mode (usually for update)
rows    = number of rows processed by the fetch or execute call
****************************************************************
alter session set sql_trace = true
call  count cpu elapsed disk query current rows
------- ----- ---- ------- ---- ----- -------- -----
Parse    0 0.00  0.00  0   0    0   0
Execute   1 0.00  0.00  0   0    0   0
Fetch    0 0.00  0.00  0   0    0   0
total    1 0.00  0.00  0   0    0   0
Misses in library cache during parse: 0
Misses in library cache during execute: 1
Optimizer goal: CHOOSE
Parsing user id: 25
****************************************************************
select * from junk
call  count cpu elapsed disk query current rows
------- ----- ---- ------- ---- ----- -------- -----
Parse    1 0.00  0.00  0   0    0   0
Execute   1 0.00  0.00  0   0    0   0
Fetch    2 0.02  0.02  0   2    3   6
total    4 0.00  0.00  0   2    3   6
Misses in library cache during parse: 1
Optimizer goal: CHOOSE
Parsing user id: 25
****************************************************************
OVERALL TOTALS FOR ALL NON-RECURSIVE STATEMENTS
call  count cpu elapsed disk query current rows
------- ----- ---- ------- ---- ----- -------- -----
Parse    1 0.00  0.00  0   0    0   0
Execute   2 0.00  0.00  0   0    0   0
Fetch    2 0.00  0.00  0   2    3   6
total    5 0.00  0.00  0   2    3   6
Misses in library cache during parse: 1
Misses in library cache during execute: 1
OVERALL TOTALS FOR ALL RECURSIVE STATEMENTS
```

```
call  count cpu elapsed disk query current rows
------- ----- ---- ------- ---- ----- -------- -----
Parse     0 0.00  0.00  0    0     0    0
Execute    0 0.00  0.00  0    0     0    0
Fetch     0 0.02  0.02  0    0     0    0
total     0 0.00  0.00  0    0     0    0
Misses in library cache during parse: 0
  2 user SQL statements in session.
  0 internal SQL statements in session.
  2 SQL statements in session.
****************************************************************
Trace file: ora00152.trc
Trace file compatibility: 7.03.02
Sort options: default
    1 session in tracefile.
    2 user SQL statements in trace file.
    0 internal SQL statements in trace file.
    2 SQL statements in trace file.
    2 unique SQL statements in trace file.
   36 lines in trace file.
```

Three `init`*`sid`*`.ora` parameters should be set to run SQL Trace. The first parameter is `TIMED_STATISTICS`. This parameter must be set to TRUE to use SQL Trace. If not, the collection of CPU statistics and elapsed time will not happen.

Operation Name	Operation Description
Parse, execute, fetch counts	Number of times the `parse`, `execute`, and `fetch` operations were processed in Oracle's handling of this query
Processor time/elapsed query time	The CPU and real elapsed time for execution of this statement
Physical/logical reads	Total number of data blocks read from the datafiles on disks for `parse`, `execute`, and `fetch` portions of the query
Rows processed	Total number of rows processed by Oracle to produce the result set, excluding rows processed as part of subqueries
Library cache misses	Number of times the parsed statement had to be loaded into the library cache for use

TABLE 17-2. *Operations Identified in a Trace File*

Setting this statistic to TRUE causes some additional overhead at the processor level, so only set this parameter to TRUE when statistics collection is necessary.

The next parameter is `MAX_DUMP_FILE_SIZE`, used to determine trace-file output file size in operating system blocks. The default value for this setting is 500, which translates to 500 operating system blocks' worth of data stored in a trace file. If the desired trace data isn't present, or the file itself looks truncated, adjust `MAX_DUMP_FILE_SIZE` and trace again.

The last parameter is `USER_DUMP_DEST`, which tells Oracle where to put the trace file on the machine's file system. The value specified should be an absolute pathname.

SQL Trace can analyze SQL statements on a session-wide and instance-wide basis. To enable tracing instance-wide, set the `SQL_TRACE` parameter to TRUE in the `init`*`sid`*`.ora` file, and restart the instance. Setting up SQL Trace on a session-wide level overrides the instance-wide trace specification, and it can be done in several ways. The first way utilizes the `alter session set SQL_TRACE=TRUE` statement. The second method uses a special package called DBMS_SESSION. Within this package is a special procedure called `set_sql_trace( )`. The user can execute this procedure in order to start tracing statistics on SQL statements in the session, as well. Another method to set tracing in the current session, and the only non-instance-wide way to set tracing for sessions other than the current one is to execute another procedure in a different package, called DBMS_SYSTEM, the `set_sql_trace_in_session( )` procedure. The user executing this process should obtain the appropriate values in the SID and SERIAL# columns from the V$SESSION view for the session to have tracing enabled. These two values must be passed into the procedure, along with the `SQL_TRACE` setting (TRUE or FALSE).

Using AUTOTRACE

Another tool you can use for statement and application tuning is AUTOTRACE. In your SQL*Plus session, you can issue the `set autotrace on` command to begin using AUTOTRACE. To use this tool, you will need to have created the PLAN_TABLE table beforehand, and you 'll need special privileges on V$ views. A role called PLUSTRACE will be created with these privileges by running the `plustrce.sql` script as the SYS user. The `plustrce.sql` script can be found in the `sqlplus` or `plus80` subdirectory beneath your Oracle software home directory. After running `plustrce.sql`, you can grant the PLUSTRACE role to the user who will use the AUTOTRACE tool. Oracle will then generate and display execution plans and trace statistics for every SQL statement issued in the session for the rest of the session or until you issue the `set autotrace off` command. The following code block demonstrates the use of AUTOTRACE in a session.

```
SQL> set autotrace on
SQL> select * from emp;
EMPID LASTNAME  FIRSTNAME SALARY
----- ---------- --------- ------
02039 WALLA    RAJENDRA  60000
39334 SMITH    GINA     75000
60403 HARPER    ROD     45000
49539 QIAN     LEE    90000
49392 SPANKY    STACY   100000
Execution Plan
----------------------------------------------------------
  0    SELECT STATEMENT Optimizer=CHOOSE
  1  0  TABLE ACCESS (FULL) OF 'EMP'
Statistics
----------------------------------------------------------
     0 recursive calls
     3 db block gets
     2 consistent gets
     2 physical reads
     0 redo size
    1004 bytes sent via SQL*Net to client
    645 bytes received via SQL*Net from client
     4 SQL*Net roundtrips to/from client
     1 sorts (memory)
     0 sorts (disk)
     5 rows processed
```

Other Tools for Diagnosing Tuning Problems

The following list identifies several other tools you can use to diagnose and correct tuning problems. Please note that these tools require the use of Oracle Enterprise Manager in your administration of the Oracle database:

- **Performance Manager** This tool collects and displays information about the performance of your database, allowing you to tune memory, minimize disk I/O, and avoid resource contention. It is a graphical tool with drill-down capability that allows both real-time monitoring and recording of statistics over time for replay later.
- **TopSessions** This tool allows you to quickly gather information about the top Oracle user sessions, such as file I/O, CPU, and other metrics. With this information, you can determine which users are utilizing the most Oracle resources.

- **Oracle Trace** This tool allows a detailed level of performance-data collection at the level of every server, network, and host machine activity associated with an application. (This is not the same as SQL Trace, which provides the ability to trace SQL processing in a SQL*Plus session.)
- **Tablespace Manager** This tool allows you to analyze block usage in tablespaces and to perform tablespace defragmentation dynamically.
- **Oracle Expert** This tool provides performance-tuning handled automatically by Oracle. Problems detected via Performance Manager, TopSessions, and Oracle Trace are analyzed and solved, including problems involving access methods, `init`*`sid`*`.ora` parameters, and object sizing and placement. You will explore the use of Oracle Expert in Chapter 20.

Exercises

1. Where does `explain plan` put the execution plan for a query?
2. What are the ways a user can invoke SQL Trace for their session? For the entire database?
3. What initialization parameters are associated with setting up trace? In what way is TKPROF used in conjunction with SQL Trace?

Using Different Optimizer Modes

Since Oracle7, Oracle has provided two different RDBMS engine modes for optimizing the SQL statements users issue in their sessions. An optimizer mode is a mode in which the RDBMS will determine how to access your data. The first of the two available optimization modes is *cost-based* optimization. Cost-based optimization is activated by setting the `OPTIMIZER_MODE init`*`sid`*`.ora` parameter to `all_rows, first_rows`, or `choose`, and restarting the instance. Setting this parameter to `choose` is recommended by Oracle, and it is the default value Oracle uses if you do not specify another value. (The other optimizer modes will be described shortly.)

The cost-based optimizer allows the RDBMS to determine the method it will use to obtain user data, based on statistics that are generated using the `analyze` command. You must run the `analyze` command on all database objects the application will use in order for cost-based optimization to be effective. The basic syntax for this command is `analyze` *`object object_name`* `[compute|estimate] statistics`, and its use is shown in the following code block:

```
SQL> analyze table survey compute statistics;
Table analyzed.
SQL> analyze table signup estimate statistics;
Table analyzed.
```

This command generates statistics on individual tables based on recent data changes, and therefore should be executed regularly to ensure that the cost-based optimizer operates in the most efficient manner, using the most current statistics.

You can run this command to determine statistics based on all data in the table using the `compute` keyword, which can take a little extra time because Oracle must perform processing on every row in the table in order to compute statistics. Or, you can run this command to determine statistics based on a random sampling of data from the table using the `estimate` keyword, which takes less time because Oracle only analyzes statistics for a sample of the table data. The default number of rows Oracle will sample when `estimate` is used is 1064, but you can change this by using the `estimate sample` *n* `[rows|percent]` syntax instead of using `estimate` by itself, as shown here:

```
SQL> analyze table emp estimate sample 80 rows statistics;
```

TIP
For tables with hundreds of thousands or millions of rows, I recommend estimating your statistics rather than computing them.

Setting the Session-Wide Cost-Optimizer Goal

After using `analyze` to set up and maintain statistics for your cost-based optimization, the next thing you need to consider is setting an optimization goal for the Oracle RDBMS. The optimization goal is a configuration setting that determines whether the optimizer should determine its execution plans based on getting the first row of return data to the user as quickly as possible, or getting the entire query result to your users as quickly as possible. This feature is set in a user session using the `alter session set OPTIMIZER_MODE =` *mode* command, as shown here:

```
SQL> alter session set optimizer_mode = first_rows;
Session altered.
SQL> alter session set optimizer_mode = all_rows;
Session altered.
```

If the `initsid.ora` value for `OPTIMIZER_MODE` is `choose`, Oracle will choose the most efficient optimizer mode to use dynamically. The first optimizer goal of getting the first row of return data to the user as quickly as possible is known as `first_rows`. This goal optimizes Oracle to give the best response time for online applications, such as Oracle Forms, other GUI tools, or SQL*Plus queries where users are waiting to see some data, but don't necessarily need the best overall time for returning all rows of output from the query. With this setting, the RDBMS will prefer to use full table scans and nested loop join operations in the execution plan.

The other optimizer goal is called `all_rows`. When it is used, the RDBMS will optimize its query execution plans to return the entire set of data requested as quickly as possible, for best overall process throughput. However, the RDBMS may need more time up front in order to obtain the data requested most efficiently. Thus, you will optimize for best throughput in batch processes or Oracle Reports because users care more about the overall time it takes the job to execute, and not about seeing the first row result from any particular query in the process.

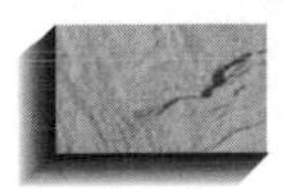

TIP
You can set a cost optimizer goal at the SQL-statement level, as well, using the `/*+ all_rows */` or `/*+first_rows */` hints in individual queries.

Using Rule-Based Optimization

Rule-based optimization is the other method the RDBMS can use to optimize queries. This method is prevalent in many existing Oracle applications developed in Oracle7 and migrated to Oracle8. Thus, Oracle8 supplies the rule-based optimizer for backward compatibility. Rule-based optimization is set up by changing the `OPTIMIZER_MODE initsid.ora` parameter to `rule`, and restarting the instance. Given the strength of cost-based optimization and the abundance of new features, however, Oracle recommends using cost-based optimization when developing new applications and when enhancing existing applications to take advantage of new features. In particular, the following new features require cost-based optimization to be in place on your Oracle database:

- Partitioned and index-only tables
- Reverse-key indexes
- Parallel queries, star queries, and star transformations

Exercises

1. What is optimization? Identify the two main types of query optimization. How are these methods of query optimization set?
2. What are the meanings of the `all_rows` and `first_rows` optimization goals? What is the difference between the two? Identify some situations in which you would use each.

Using Star Queries and Hash Joins

Many organizations are turning to data warehouses as a solution for business intelligence involving Oracle products. A common feature of data warehouse application design is the *star schema*. It consists of one or more large *fact* tables and a number of much smaller *dimension* (sometimes also called lookup or reference) tables. A star query is one that joins several of the dimension tables, usually by predicates in the query, to one of the fact tables. For example, a data warehouse managed by a large computer reseller may consist of a fact table listing all the sales made over a five-year period. The columns in the fact table have foreign key relationships to primary keys of the dimension tables. There might be several dimension tables associated with a particular fact table, so that when the data model is laid out on paper it looks like a star, hence the name. Figure 17-4 illustrates a star schema, with ordinality and primary-key and foreign-key relationships defined.

Oracle cost-based optimization can generate efficient execution plans for star queries, while rule-based optimization cannot. Thus, you must use cost-based optimization to get efficient star-query execution. The following code block contains a star query using the tables identified in Figure 17-4:

```
SQL> SELECT sum(s.total_amt)
 2 FROM
 3  sales_fact_table s,
 4  product_lookup p,
 5  store_region_lookup l,
 6  time_lookup t
 7 WHERE
 8  /* selection criteria */
 9    p.product_owner = 'Bob Misty'
 10  AND t.market_condition = 'Hurricane Season'
 11  AND l.region = 'Southeast USA'
 12  AND t.quarter_code = 'FY3Q1999'
 13  /* join conditions */
 14  AND t.quarter_code = s.quarter_code
 15  AND p.product_id = s.product_id
 16  AND l.store_loc_code = s.store_loc_code;
```

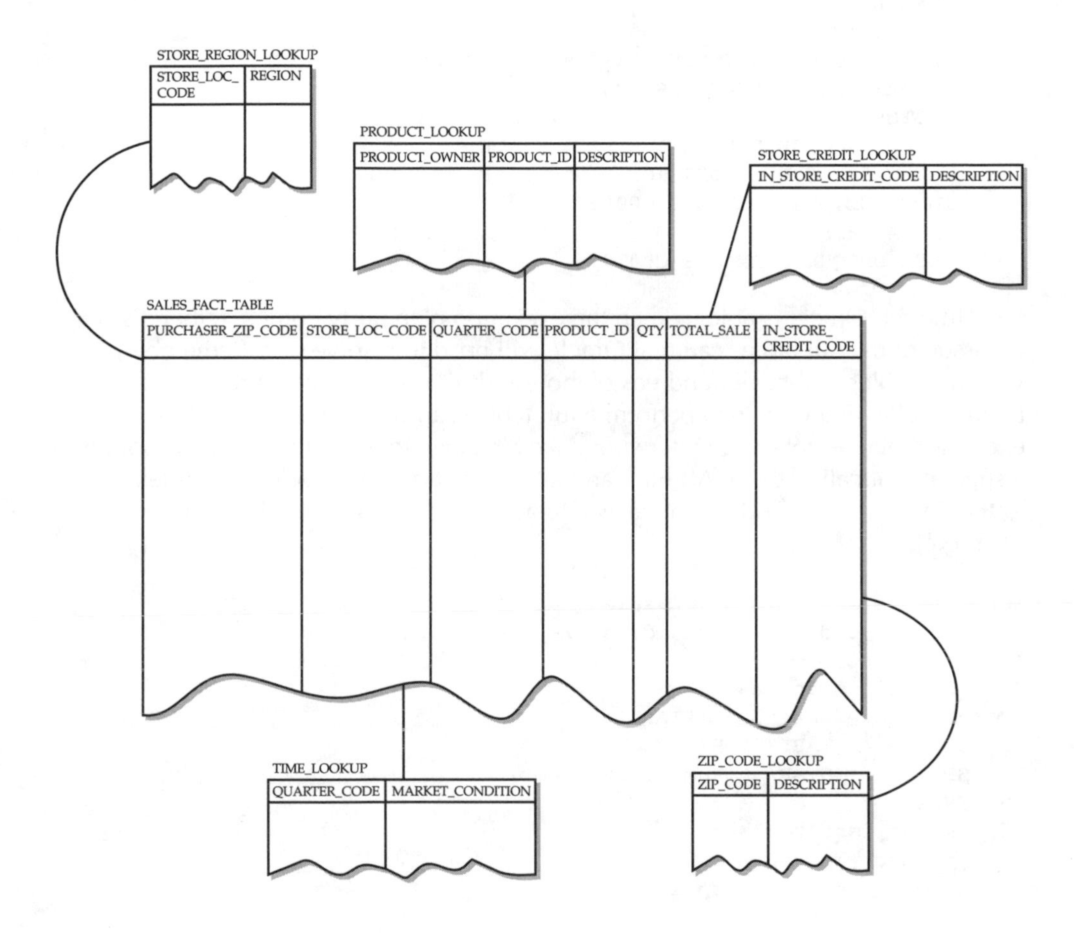

FIGURE 17-4. *A star schema*

This is a complicated query; many tables are being joined to many other tables. If indexes are not constructed properly on the fact table, you may run into some performance problems. For example, the preceding query generates the following execution plan when no indexes are present on the fact table SALES_FACT_TABLE:

```
QUERY_PLAN
------------------------------------------------------------
 SORT AGGREGATE
```

```
NESTED LOOPS
 NESTED LOOPS
  MERGE JOIN
   TABLE ACCESS BY INDEX ROWID TIME_LOOKUP
    INDEX UNIQUE SCAN SYS_C001907
   FILTER
    TABLE ACCESS FULL SALES_FACT_TABLE
  TABLE ACCESS BY INDEX ROWID STORE_REGION_LOOKUP
   INDEX UNIQUE SCAN SYS_C001906
 TABLE ACCESS BY INDEX ROWID PRODUCT_LOOKUP
  INDEX UNIQUE SCAN SYS_C001905
```

Although Oracle is able to keep the execution plan fairly compact, there is the issue of the full table scan that Oracle will need to resolve first. Remember, your fact tables will have hundreds of thousands (if not millions) of rows in them, so allowing Oracle to perform a full table scan will not do. The following execution plan is generated after you make a change to your query to incorporate a special hint called the STAR hint, and after you add a new composite index to the SALES_FACT_TABLE that takes into account the order of columns in your where clause:

```
SQL> create index idx_1 on sales_fact_table
 2 (quarter_code, product_id, store_loc_code);
Index created.
SQL> explain plan
 2  set statement_id = 'STAR_1'
 3  INTO PLAN_TABLE FOR
 4  SELECT /*+STAR */ sum(s.total_amt)
 5  FROM
 6   sales_fact_table s,
 7   product_lookup p,
 8   store_region_lookup l,
 9   time_lookup t
 10  WHERE
 11    /* selection criteria */
 12      p.product_owner = 'Bob Misty'
 13   AND t.market_condition = 'Hurricane Sea'
 14   AND l.region = 'Southeast USA'
 15   AND t.quarter_code = 'FY3Q1999'
 16    /* join conditions */
 17   AND t.quarter_code = s.quarter_code
 18   AND p.product_id = s.product_id
 19   AND l.store_loc_code = s.store_loc_code;
Explained.
SQL> SELECT LPAD(' ',2*level) || operation || ' '
 2   || options || ' ' || object_name AS query_plan
 3   FROM plan_table
```

```
 4   WHERE statement_id = 'STAR_1'
 5   CONNECT BY PRIOR ID = parent_id and statement_id = 'STAR_1'
 6  START WITH ID=1;
QUERY_PLAN
----------------------------------------------------
 NESTED LOOPS
  NESTED LOOPS
   NESTED LOOPS
    NESTED LOOPS
     TABLE ACCESS FULL SCAN PRODUCT_LOOKUP
    TABLE ACCESS FULL SCAN STORE_REGION_LOOKUP
   TABLE ACCESS FULL SCAN TIME_LOOKUP
  TABLE ACCESS BY ROWID SALES_FACT_TABLE
   INDEX RANGE SCAN SFT_IDX_01
```

Star queries are unusual, and difficult for query optimizers, because the optimal strategy requires that the smaller tables (PRODUCT_LOOKUP, STORE_REGION_LOOKUP, TIME_LOOKUP) undergo Cartesian product joins. That is, these smaller tables are joined together despite the fact that there are no join predicates between them. In general, Cartesian product joins are expensive and should be avoided. However, for star queries, it is more efficient to use Cartesian product joins on your dimension tables than to repeatedly access the data from the fact table.

Using Hash Joins

Hash joins are special execution-plan operations that Oracle can use in certain situations involving equijoin operations. Recall that an equijoin is a join operation involving two or more tables in which data from one table will be returned only if there is corresponding data in the other table in the join. Oracle will never use hash joins if rule-based optimization is specified for the database. Hash joins can be useful when you want to `select` all data from two or more tables and want to join those results together correctly. For example, the following code block shows the plan Oracle will use to execute without hash joins, using the `NESTED LOOPS` operation instead:

```
SQL> explain plan
 2 set statement_id = 'HASH_1'
 3 into PLAN_TABLE for
 4 select a.market_condition,
 5 b. product_id
 6 from time_lookup a,
 7 sales_fact_table b
 8 where a.quarter_code = b.quarter_code;
Explained.
SQL> SELECT LPAD(' ',2*level) || operation || ' '
```

```
 2    || options || ' ' || object_name AS query_plan
 3    FROM plan_table
 4    WHERE statement_id = 'HASH_1'
 5    CONNECT BY PRIOR ID = parent_id and statement_id = 'HASH_1'
 6    START WITH ID=1;
QUERY_PLAN
-------------------------------------------------------
 NESTED LOOPS
  TABLE ACCESS FULL SALES_FACT_TABLE
  TABLE ACCESS FULL TIME_LOOKUP
```

To force Oracle to use hash joins, you should set the HASH_JOIN_ENABLED init*sid*.ora parameter to TRUE, either before starting Oracle for enabling instance-wide hash join operations, or by simply setting that parameter to TRUE for the session. To perform a hash join, Oracle performs a full table scan on each table and splits the data for each into as many partitions as possible, given limited available memory. Then, Oracle builds a hash table from one of the partitions that fits into available memory. Oracle then uses the corresponding partition in the other table to probe the hash table. All partition pairs that do not fit into memory are placed onto disk.

For each pair of partitions from each table, Oracle uses the smaller one to build a hash table and the larger one to probe the hash table. The initialization parameter HASH_AREA_SIZE controls the amount of memory used for hash join operations, and HASH_MULTIBLOCK_IO_COUNT controls the number of blocks a hash join operation should read and write concurrently. When a hash join operation is part of the execution plan, Oracle will divide the tables on which it performs full table scans into partitions in memory, as follows:

```
SQL> alter session set hash_join_enabled = TRUE;
Session altered.
SQL> explain plan
 2 set statement_id = 'HASH_2'
 3 into PLAN_TABLE for
 4 select /*+ USE_HASH */
 5  a.market_condition,
 6  b. product_id
 7 from time_lookup a,
 8 sales_fact_table b
 9 where a.quarter_code = b.quarter_code;
Explained.
SQL> SELECT LPAD(' ',2*level) || operation || ' '
 2    || options || ' ' || object_name AS query_plan
 3    FROM plan_table
 4    WHERE statement_id = 'HASH_2'
 5    CONNECT BY PRIOR ID = parent_id and statement_id = 'HASH_2'
```

```
 6   START WITH ID=1;
QUERY_PLAN
-----------------------------------------------------
 HASH JOIN
  TABLE ACCESS FULL SALES_FACT_TABLE
  TABLE ACCESS FULL TIME_LOOKUP
```

Exercises

1. What is a star schema? What is a star query? Which optimizer mode must the Oracle RDBMS use in order to run star queries efficiently? Which database objects might also be required to enhance the performance of a star query?
2. What is a hash join? Which optimizer mode must the Oracle RDBMS use in order to run hash joins?

Tracking and Registering Module Use for PL/SQL Blocks

In complex large applications, it can sometimes be hard to track the activities of individual procedural components using conventional methods for performance tuning, such as `explain plan` and SQL Trace. Oracle provides a package called DBMS_APPLICATION_INFO that gives the ability to track performance of application components using the V$SESSION and V$SQLAREA dynamic performance views. Using DBMS_APPLICATION_INFO features is also known as registering the application with Oracle. Once you have registered one or more applications, you can use the registration information to track the performance of registered applications and recommend areas for tuning improvement.

Table 17-3 gives the names of each DBMS_APPLICATION_INFO procedure, along with a short description of its use, and the accepted parameters. The source code for the DBMS_APPLICATION_INFO package description, where these descriptions can also be found, is located in your database. In Schema Manager, you can drill down into the Schema Objects | Packages | SYS | DBMS_APPLICATION_INFO node for further reference.

DBMS_APPLICATION_INFO in Action

Assume you have a large application that handles currency trading, and that has many PL/SQL procedures. You may have one procedure called `convert_money( )` in this application that performs the work of converting a sum of money from one currency to another, based on a table of daily exchange rates. Since this procedure is called hundreds of thousands of times a day, you have identified that a

DBMS_APPLICATION_INFO Module	Description
set_module(*module_name*, *action_name*)	This procedure sets the name of the module that is currently running to a new module. Input arguments for this procedure include *module_name*, the name of the module that will now be running (max. 48 bytes), and *action_name*, the name of the action that will now be running (max. 32 bytes).
set_action(*action_name*)	Sets the name of the current action within the current module. Input argument is *action_name*, the name of the action that will now be running (max. 32 bytes).
set_client_info(*client_info*)	Sets the client info field of the session. Input argument is *client_info*, which is any character data you want to store, up to a maximum of 64 bytes. After being set, the client info field can be queried from V$SESSION.
read_module(*module_name*, *action_name*)	Reads the values of the module and action fields of the current session. Output arguments include *module_name* and *action_name*.
read_client_info(*client_info*)	Reads the value of the *client_info* field of the current session.
set_session_longops(*options*)	Sets a row in the V$SESSION_LONGOPS view, used to indicate the ongoing progress of a long-running operation. Input options include all columns in the V$SESSION_LONGOPS view.

TABLE 17-3. *DBMS_APPLICATION_INFO Procedures and Functions*

performance improvement made here would provide immense performance benefits and user satisfaction. The following code block illustrates your procedure:

```
create or replace function convert_money
( p_old_currency in varchar2,
 p_new_currency in varchar2,
 p_old_amt in number
) return number is
 my_conversion_rate number;
```

```
begin
 select conversion_rate
 into my_conversion_rate
 from currency_convert
 where old_currency = p_old_currency
 and new_currency = p_new_currency
 and trunc(currency_valid_date) = trunc(sysdate);
 return ( p_old_amt * my_conversion_rate);
exception
 when no_data_found then
 dbms_output.put_line('NO CONVERSION FACTOR FOR THIS CURRENCY');
end;
```

You would make the following enhancements to this procedure in order to register it for tracking on the Oracle database. Assume in this situation that you want to keep track of how `convert_money( )` performs, taking into consideration in the analysis which program module called it:

```
create or replace function convert_money
( p_old_currency in varchar2,
 p_new_currency in varchar2,
 p_old_amt in number
) return number is
 my_conversion_rate number;
begin
 dbms_application_info.set_module('convert_money','start');
 select conversion_rate
 into my_conversion_rate
 from currency_convert
 where old_currency = p_old_currency
 and new_currency = p_new_currency
 and trunc(currency_valid_date) = trunc(sysdate);
 dbms_application_info.set_action('returning new rate');
 return ( p_old_amt * my_conversion_rate);
exception
 when no_data_found then
  dbms_output.put_line('NO CONVERSION FACTOR FOR CURRENCY');
end;
```

You would then execute another PL/SQL block that calls `convert_money( )`, as shown in the following code block:

```
SQL> set serveroutput on
SQL> declare
 2 my_new_amt number;
 3 begin
 4  my_new_amt := convert_money('USDOLLAR','DEUTSCHMARK',120394.45);
```

```
 5  dbms_output.put_line('New amount = ' || to_char(my_new_amt));
 6 end;
 7 /
New amount = 174571.9525
PL/SQL procedure successfully completed.
```

You can now easily look for your code in V$SQLAREA and V$SESSION by referencing the MODULE column. Here is an example using V$SESSION to illustrate this:

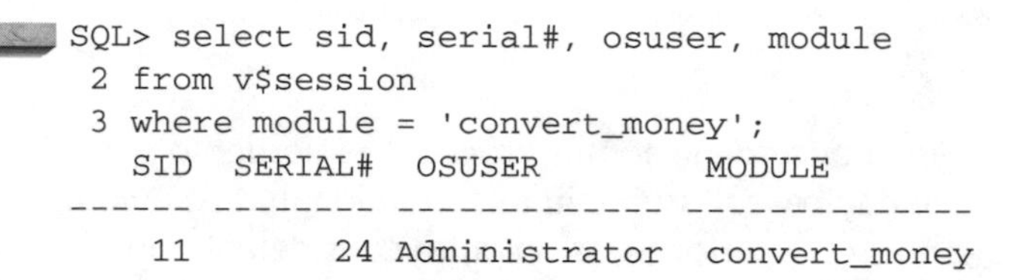

```
SQL> select sid, serial#, osuser, module
 2 from v$session
 3 where module = 'convert_money';
   SID  SERIAL#  OSUSER         MODULE
------ -------- ------------- --------------
    11       24 Administrator  convert_money
```

Exercises

1. What functionality is provided by DBMS_APPLICATION_INFO? How does it relate to performance tuning?
2. What are the functions available in DBMS_APPLICATION_INFO?

Identifying Alternative SQL Statements to Enhance Performance

No discussion of SQL or application tuning is complete without a discussion of alternative SQL syntax for variation and improvement in application performance. SQL is flexible, and your application needs can often be met with SQL statements that produce the same results but that Oracle can process more quickly. The `explain plan` statement has already shown its utility in distinguishing efficient SQL from inefficient SQL. This section will show you some rules for formulating your SQL statements, as well as the execution plans for several alternative SQL statements.

TIP
*There are several `explain plan` code block examples in this section. If you try to run these code blocks in SQL*Plus, make sure you `delete` all data from your PLAN_TABLE between each code block. If you don't, your execution plans won't be correct, because Oracle appends every additional execution plan to the PLAN_TABLE.*

Using exists Instead of in

Queries containing `where` *`column`* `in (`*`dataset_generated_by_subquery`*`)` or `where` *`column`* `not in (`*`dataset_generated_by_subquery`*`)` can be rewritten using `exists` or `not exists` if *`column`* has an associated index and the subquery can be rewritten including a `where` clause that uses the index. The following code block illustrates how Oracle processes a SQL statement containing the in operation. Assume the LASTNAME column of the EMP table has an index on it called IDX_2:

```
SQL> explain plan
 2  set statement_id = 'JASON'
 3  into plan_table for
 4  select last_name, first_name
 5  from survey
 6  where last_name in
 7  (select lastname from emp);
Explained.
SQL> SELECT LPAD(' ',2*level) || operation || ' '
 2    || options || ' ' || object_name AS query_plan
 3    FROM plan_table
 4    WHERE statement_id = 'JASON'
 5    CONNECT BY PRIOR ID = parent_id and statement_id = 'JASON'
 6    START WITH ID=1;
QUERY_PLAN
---------------------------------------------------
 MERGE JOIN
  SORT JOIN
   TABLE ACCESS FULL SURVEY
  SORT JOIN
   VIEW
    SORT UNIQUE
     TABLE ACCESS FULL EMP
```

Two full table scans are produced as part of this execution plan, causing performance nightmares if both these tables are large. In addition, the RDBMS reworks the subquery into three separate join operations, performs some sort operations, and even creates a dynamic view. This activity is terribly inefficient. Consider a statement rewrite using the `exists` clause as an alternative. The following rewrite will make the RDBMS process the query more efficiently:

```
SQL> explain plan
 2  set statement_id = 'JASON'
 3  into plan_table for
 4  select a.last_name, a.first_name
 5  from survey a
```

```
 6  where exists
 7  (select b.lastname from emp b
 8   where a.last_name = b.lastname);
Explained.
SQL> SELECT LPAD(' ',2*level) || operation || ' '
 2     || options || ' ' || object_name AS query_plan
 3     FROM plan_table
 4     WHERE statement_id = 'JASON'
 5     CONNECT BY PRIOR ID = parent_id and statement_id = 'JASON'
 6     START WITH ID=1;
QUERY_PLAN
-------------------------------------------------
 FILTER
  TABLE ACCESS FULL SURVEY
  INDEX RANGE SCAN IDX_2
```

By using this alternative, you eliminate several extraneous join operations. You also replace one of the two full table scans with an index scan on IDX_2. The dynamic view and the sort operations are gone, as well. The result is a faster SQL statement that won't keep your users waiting if the tables are enormous. Thus, you can see it is important to use `explain plan` to compare execution plans of various SQL statements before deploying them in production.

Avoiding Functions on Indexed Columns in where Clauses

SQL functions on indexed columns do not belong in `where` clauses because they force Oracle not to use an index it might have otherwise used. In the following example, table EMP has an index on column SALARY that the RDBMS doesn't use because of the presence of `to_char( )` in the `where` clause:

```
SQL> explain plan set statement_id = 'TEST'
 2 into plan_table for
 3 select * from emp
 4 where to_char(salary) = '12500';
Explained.
SQL> SELECT LPAD(' ',2*level) || operation || ' '
 2      || options || ' ' || object_name AS query_plan
 3      FROM plan_table
 4      WHERE statement_id = 'TEST'
 5      CONNECT BY PRIOR ID = parent_id and statement_id = 'TEST'
 6      START WITH ID=1;
QUERY_PLAN
-------------------------------------------------
 TABLE ACCESS FULL EMP
```

Oracle can perform implicit datatype conversions in certain situations, such as in `where` clause equality comparisons when the column datatype doesn't match the expression datatype. Given this fact, you may wonder whether Oracle's implicit datatype conversions impede the use of indexes by the RDBMS. The answer is sometimes they do, and sometimes they don't. For example, when Oracle implicitly converts a NUMBER value to VARCHAR2 to match the expression in the `where` clause, the RDBMS will still use index IDX_3 on column SALARY. The following code block illustrates this:

```
SQL> explain plan set statement_id = 'TEST'
 2 into plan_table for
 3 select * from emp
 4 where salary = '12500';
Explained.
SQL> SELECT LPAD(' ',2*level) || operation || ' '
 2      || options || ' ' || object_name AS query_plan
 3      FROM plan_table
 4      WHERE statement_id = 'TEST'
 5      CONNECT BY PRIOR ID = parent_id and statement_id = 'TEST'
 6      START WITH ID=1;
QUERY_PLAN
-----------------------------------------------------
 TABLE ACCESS BY INDEX ROWID EMP
  INDEX RANGE SCAN IDX_3
```

However, when Oracle performs other implicit datatype conversions, such as a VARCHAR2 value to a NUMBER, the RDBMS will not use the index. Consider the following example, where the RDBMS will not use index IDX_2 on column LASTNAME in table EMP because Oracle implicitly converts LASTNAME from VARCHAR2 to NUMBER:

```
SQL> explain plan
 2 set statement_id = 'TEST'
 3 into plan_table for
 4 select * from emp
 5 where lastname = 903;
Explained.
SQL> SELECT LPAD(' ',2*level) || operation || ' '
 2      || options || ' ' || object_name AS query_plan
 3      FROM plan_table
 4      WHERE statement_id = 'TEST'
 5      CONNECT BY PRIOR ID = parent_id and statement_id = 'TEST'
 6      START WITH ID=1;
QUERY_PLAN
-----------------------------------------------------
 TABLE ACCESS FULL EMP
```

Using Composite Indexes Properly

Recall that a composite index contains two or more columns of a table. The Oracle RDBMS uses a composite index in execution plans only when you reference the composite index's leading column in the `where` clause of your query. In the following examples, table EMP has a composite index called IDX_2 on columns LASTNAME, FIRSTNAME, and SALARY, in that order. In the first example, reference is made to the leading column LASTNAME only. The RDBMS uses the index:

```
SQL> explain plan
  2 set statement_id = 'TEST'
  3 into plan_table for
  4 select * from emp
  5 where lastname = 'COUCHMAN';
Explained.
SQL> SELECT LPAD(' ',2*level) || operation || ' '
  2      || options || ' ' || object_name AS query_plan
  3      FROM plan_table
  4      WHERE statement_id = 'TEST'
  5      CONNECT BY PRIOR ID = parent_id and statement_id = 'TEST'
  6      START WITH ID=1;
QUERY_PLAN
------------------------------------------------------------
  TABLE ACCESS BY INDEX ROWID EMP
   INDEX RANGE SCAN IDX_2
```

The order in which you reference composite index columns in the `where` clause of your SQL statement doesn't matter if you are using cost-based or rule-based optimization. This example references the SALARY column first, followed by FIRSTNAME, followed by LASTNAME (the leading column in the composite index). Oracle still uses the composite index:

```
SQL> explain plan
  2 set statement_id = 'TEST'
  3 into plan_table for
  4 select * from emp
  5 where salary = 50000
  6 and firstname = 'JASON'
  7 and lastname = 'COUCHMAN';
Explained.
SQL> SELECT LPAD(' ',2*level) || operation || ' '
  2       || options || ' ' || object_name AS query_plan
  3       FROM plan_table
  4       WHERE statement_id = 'TEST'
  5       CONNECT BY PRIOR ID = parent_id and statement_id = 'TEST'
  6       START WITH ID=1;
```

```
QUERY_PLAN
-----------------------------------------------------
 TABLE ACCESS BY INDEX ROWID EMP
  INDEX RANGE SCAN IDX_2
```

You can even skip reference to middle columns in the `where` clause of your query. In the next example, the `where` clause references SALARY and LASTNAME, but not FIRSTNAME. Oracle still uses the composite index:

```
SQL> explain plan
 2 set statement_id = 'TEST'
 3 into plan_table for
 4 select * from emp
 5 where salary = 50000
 6 and lastname = 'COUCHMAN';
Explained.
SQL> SELECT LPAD(' ',2*level) || operation || ' '
 2      || options || ' ' || object_name AS query_plan
 3      FROM plan_table
 4      WHERE statement_id = 'TEST'
 5      CONNECT BY PRIOR ID = parent_id and statement_id = 'TEST'
 6      START WITH ID=1;
QUERY_PLAN
------------------------------------------------------------
 TABLE ACCESS BY INDEX ROWID EMP
  INDEX RANGE SCAN IDX_2
```

However, in this last example, the RDBMS will not use the composite index IDX_2 because the query doesn't reference the leading column of the index anywhere in the `where` clause:

```
SQL> explain plan
 2 set statement_id = 'TEST'
 3 into plan_table for
 4 select * from emp
 5 where firstname = 'JASON'
 6 and salary = 50000;
Explained.
SQL> SELECT LPAD(' ',2*level) || operation || ' '
 2     || options || ' ' || object_name AS query_plan
 3     FROM plan_table
 4     WHERE statement_id = 'TEST'
 5     CONNECT BY PRIOR ID = parent_id and statement_id = 'TEST'
 6     START WITH ID=1;
QUERY_PLAN
--------------------------------------------------
 TABLE ACCESS FULL EMP
```

Properly Constructing Join Operations

Enhancing performance is often a matter of setting up properly formed join statements. Tricks and rules for formulating good join statements are described here:

- **Use equijoins whenever possible** The most basic rule for developing join statements is to use equijoins where possible. An equijoin is formed with equality comparisons and `and` operations, as in `where` *`table.column`* `=` *`table.column`* `and` *`table.column`* `=` *`table.column`*.
- **Just say no to full table scans** Avoid join statements that force Oracle to process a full table scan. The performance of these statements will get worse as the table Oracle scans gets larger. Instead, compare different SQL statements that yield the same results, using `explain plan` to devise join statements that utilize indexes. You can either restructure your SQL to use existing indexes or create new ones.
- **Use indexes from driving tables that are small** A *driving table* is the table that appears to the left of the equality comparisons in a join clause, as in `where` *`driving_table.column`* `=` *`other_table.column`*. The *`driving_table.column`* should have an index that fetches a much smaller number of rows than the index on *`other_table.column`*. For example, in data warehouses where you join dimension tables with fact tables, your dimension tables should always be the driving tables. You must have at least an index on the inner-join table, because this will be scanned in a loop.
- **Set up join order to discard most rows early** Join statements should be configured so that the most selective operations occur earliest, to eliminate most rows. This way, later operations that are not as selective won't take as long to run, because the candidate pool of data will be much smaller. Your choice of driving table and index should be based on your understanding of the data in the tables being joined.

Setting Up Join Order: Example

The following code block illustrates a sample join statement that might be used to identify employee ID, office location, and work telephone number in a global corporation headquartered in the United States.

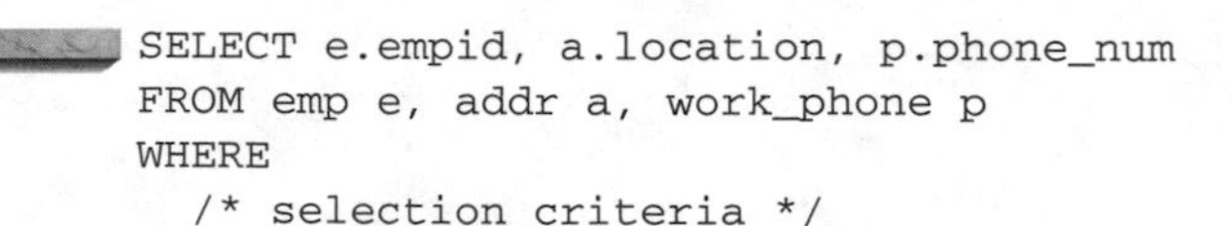

```
SELECT e.empid, a.location, p.phone_num
FROM emp e, addr a, work_phone p
WHERE
   /* selection criteria */
```

```
AND a.region = 'Southeast Asia'
AND e.lastname = 'SMITH'
AND p.phone_num_type = 'OFFICE SITE'
  /* join conditions */
AND a.empid = e.empid
AND a.empid = p.empid;
```

The rules for structuring the `where` clause of this join query are as follows:

- Filter conditions belong at the beginning of the `where` clause, since single table filters usually discard far more data than join conditions. The first three conditions in the code block filter single tables, while the last two conditions are join conditions.
- Put the filter condition you believe will eliminate the most data first, followed by progressively less-selective filters. In this case, you need to know your data. For instance, you may know that the Southeast Asia offices are mainly for a handful of salespeople, making this condition highly selective. In contrast, the last name "Smith" is common in the United States, and every employee in the company has a phone number at an office site. Thus, these other conditions are less selective.
- Make the table whose filter condition is most restrictive (resulting in the smallest set of rows) the driving table. Thus, even though all three tables in this example might have about the same number of rows overall, table ADDR should be the driving table because it will have the fewest rows left over when Oracle completes the filter operation.
- Choose the most selective indexed column(s) from the driving table that is (are) shared with other tables in the join. In this situation, the EMPID column is common to all three tables, but in other situations you may not always have one shared column.
- Order your join conditions according to the filter condition that discarded more rows earlier. In this case, you'd join ADDR with EMP first because more people will have a last name other than "Smith" than there are non-work telephone numbers, such as cellular numbers, in the EMP_PHONE table. Thus, by placing the join between ADDR and EMP first, you will reduce Oracle's effort in joining ADDR and WORK_PHONE after.

Avoiding Misuse of Views

Although Oracle is optimized to work well with queries directly against views, you should avoid queries that join tables with views and joins between complex views. Remember, a complex view already contains an implicit join operation, so you are actually loading joins on top of joins. Generally speaking, you should also avoid outer joins that use views, particularly if the view itself also contains an outer join. Instead, construct the outer join to the underlying table, or eliminate the outer join entirely. Finally, do not use a view for a different purpose than it was intended. Instead, you should create views that have special purposes and then use them only for that purpose.

Miscellaneous Tips

Finally, consider a few more tips.

- One-size-fits-all SQL statements don't perform very well. Instead, you should develop many different SQL statements for each individual query purpose, and resize the shared pool to accommodate more execution plans. More about the shared pool and memory tuning will appear in Chapter 18.
- Use optimizer hints to improve performance when you believe Oracle will execute the statement one way but you think the statement will execute faster another way.
- Use the `distinct` keyword as little as possible, because it forces Oracle to perform a sort operation, and these operations require extra effort. If you must use the `distinct` keyword in a SQL statement in your application, you can force Oracle to use an index by using hints. See Chapter 20 for more information on sorts.
- If you can reduce the number of calls to the database by structuring DML operations that use well-formed subqueries, do so, because the fewer calls you make to Oracle (particularly over a network connection) the better your application will perform.

Exercises

1. Identify some of the rules for determining how to formulate your `where` clause to process join operations efficiently.
2. Describe the process for determining alternatives for SQL statements that are inefficient.

Chapter Summary

This chapter covers two important topics related to application tuning. They include tuning considerations for different types of applications, and how to perform SQL-statement tuning that works. These two topics comprise about 15 percent of OCP Exam 4. In the first section, you learned how to use available data-access methods to tune the logical design of your Oracle database. You also learned how to identify the demands of online transaction processing (OLTP) systems. The special characteristics of these systems were discussed, along with the basic tuning techniques that should be applied to these systems. The requirements of decision support systems was also covered in this section. Concluding the section on application tuning considerations was a discussion of how to reconfigure your database temporarily, based on particular needs, using multiple `init`*`sid`*`.ora` files or stored configurations in Instance Manager.

The second section of this chapter covered SQL-statement tuning. At the start of this section, you identified the roles of the DBA in application tuning. You learned that the role of the DBA in application tuning often depends on the size of the IT organization and the number of applications the organization uses. In large organizations, DBAs focus on keeping the instance operative, perhaps acting as a mentor to developers, who are the real tuning people. In smaller organizations, where the developer might also be the DBA, the responsibility is shared accordingly.

In this second section, you also learned about Oracle's different optimizer modes. The available choices are cost-based and rule-based optimization. Within cost-based optimization, Oracle offers optimizer goals that have better application response time or better throughput. The use of star queries in data warehouse applications was explained in some detail, as well, along with Oracle's ability to identify and optimize star queries when cost optimization is in place. You also learned the use of the PLAN_TABLE table and the `explain plan` command, as well as the use of SQL Trace and TKPROF for SQL-statement tuning. Several other tools available in Oracle Enterprise Manager and in Oracle Management Packs for tuning were identified, as well. You learned how to track and register stored procedures, packages, and triggers using the DBMS_APPLICATION_INFO package, an Oracle-supplied package that enables the V$SESSION and V$SQLAREA views to capture statistics for application execution.

The final area covered was identifying and comparing execution plans for alternative SQL statements that produce the same data results. You covered several different rules for formulating your SQL statements, ranging from join statements to statements using views to rules for Oracle using composite indexes. Make sure you understand how to use `explain plan` to compare alternative SQL statements, and how to read an execution plan. Different operations you might see in an execution plan were also explained.

Two-Minute Drill

- Online transaction processing (OLTP) applications are systems generally used by large user populations, and these databases have frequently updated data and constantly changing data volume.

- OLTP application performance is adversely affected by increases in processing overhead for data changes. This includes excessive use of indexes and clusters.
- Decision-support systems (DSS) are systems that store large volumes of data for generating reports for users.
- DSS system performance is adversely affected by processing overhead associated with complex `select` statements. This may include a lack of proper indexing, clustering, data migration, or chaining.
- Systems can be reconfigured on a temporary basis for application requirements.
- Multiple copies of initialization parameter files (`init`*`sid`*`.ora`) can be used to manage this need for on-the-fly reconfiguration.
- You can also store multiple parameter configurations in Instance Manager for reconfiguring the database temporarily.
- SQL tuning is the most important step in all database performance tuning, and it should always happen as the first step in that tuning process.
- The DBA's role in tuning depends on how large the IT organization is and how many applications the DBA administers. The larger the organization or DBA instance workload, the more likely that application tuning falls into the hands of developers.
- There are several tools available for diagnosing tuning problems in SQL*Plus, the command line, and Enterprise Manager, including the following:
  - **`explain plan`** Used to determine the execution plan for SQL statements.
  - **SQL Trace and TKPROF** Used to determine execution statistics for SQL statements.
  - **AUTOTRACE** Offers execution plan and execution statistics for statements in SQL*Plus sessions as they are executed.
  - **Performance Manager** This tool collects and displays information about the performance of your database, allowing you to tune memory, minimize disk I/O, and avoid resource contention. It is a graphical tool with drill-down capability that allows both real-time monitoring and recording of statistics over time for replay later.

- **TopSessions** This tool allows you to gather information about the top Oracle user sessions quickly, such as file I/O, CPU, and other metrics, allowing you to determine which users are utilizing the most Oracle resources.
- **Oracle Trace** This tool allows a detailed level of performance-data collection at the level of every server, network, and host machine activity associated with an application. (This is not the same as SQL Trace, which offers the ability to trace SQL processing in a SQL*Plus session.)
- **Tablespace Manager** This tool allows you to analyze block usage in tablespaces, and to perform tablespace defragmentation dynamically.
- **Oracle Expert** This tool provides performance-tuning handled automatically by Oracle. Oracle Expert analyzes and solves problems detected via Performance Manager, TopSessions, and Oracle Trace in areas of access methods, `init`*`sid`*`.ora` parameters, and object sizing and placement. You will explore further use of Oracle Expert in Chapter 20.

- There are two optimizer modes in Oracle: rule-based and cost-based optimization. Optimizer mode is set with the `OPTIMIZER_MODE` parameter. Within cost-based optimization, there are two different optimizer goals: `all_rows` for maximizing throughput, and `first_rows` for minimizing response time. The default setting for `OPTIMIZER_MODE` is `choose`, allowing Oracle to determine dynamically what the goal will be. Rule-based optimization is provided for backward compatibility.
- Use of the following new features in Oracle require cost-based optimization:
  - Partitioned and index-only tables
  - Reverse-key indexes
  - Parallel queries, star queries, and star transformations
- Star queries, star transformations, and star schemas relate to data warehouse applications. Oracle can optimize star queries to run efficiently when cost-based optimization is in place.
- Hash joins are special operations the RDBMS can perform where two tables are joined together using dynamic partitions in memory, where Oracle will use the smaller partition to probe data in the larger one.

- To permit hash joins, the `HASH_JOIN_ENABLED` `init`*`sid`*`.ora` parameter must be set to TRUE, or the /*+`HASH` */ hint must be included in the SQL statement.
- SQL Trace can be enabled at the instance level by setting the `SQL_TRACE` parameter to TRUE and starting the instance.
- SQL Trace can be enabled at the session level with the `alter session set sql_trace=true` statement.
- SQL Trace tracks the following statistics for SQL statements: CPU time and real elapsed time; `parse`, `execute`, and `fetch` counts; library cache misses; data block reads; and number of rows processed.
- To use SQL Trace properly, several initialization parameters should be set in the `init`*`sid`*`.ora` file:
  - `TIMED_STATISTICS` = `TRUE`
  - `MAX_DUMP_FILE_SIZE=(`*`appropriate size to capture all contents, default 500, expressed in operation system size blocks`*`)` (optional)
  - `USER_DUMP_DEST=`*`absolute_pathname_on_your_system`* (optional)
- TKPROF takes as input the trace file produced by SQL Trace and produces a readable report summarizing trace information for the query.
- DBMS_APPLICATION_INFO is used to register various blocks of code with the database for performance-tuning purposes. When the code is registered, you can find performance information for procedures, functions, packages, and triggers in the V$SESSION and V$SQLAREA views.
- SQL is a flexible language in which the same data result can be generated from different statements. There is usually an efficient and an inefficient way to construct your SQL statements. The following rules offer a methodology for optimizing SQL statements:
  - Use `(not) exists` instead of `(not) in`.
  - Avoid functions on indexed columns in `where` clauses if you want Oracle to use the index on that column.
  - Include leading columns from composite indexes in `where` clauses if you want Oracle to utilize the index.

- Avoid the misuse of views, such as using views where they weren't intended to be used and constructing joins using views.
- Construct separate SQL statements for different purposes.
- Use hints where appropriate.
- Avoid the `distinct` keyword.

- When tuning join statements, observe the following rules:
  - Construct joins with equality comparisons and `and` operations.
  - Avoid full table scans.
  - Construct `where` clauses that use small tables as driving tables. If you need to, review the chapter to understand what a driving table is.
  - Put the most selective comparison operations first in `where` clauses.
  - Filter operations on single tables belong before join operations.

Chapter Questions

1. You are tuning application SQL statements on table EMP, which has one index on column EMPID, declared as VARCHAR2(20). Which of the following SQL statements has an execution plan that will not use the index?

A. `select EMPID from EMP where EMPID = '604';`

B. select `nvl(EMPID,0) from EMP where EMPID = '604';`

C. select `ROWID from EMP WHERE EMPID = '604';`

D. select `* from EMP where EMPID = 604;`

2. You have registered modules of code in your application using the appropriate methods. In order to track application performance, which of the following SQL statements might be used?

A. `select * from V$SYSSTAT;`

B. `select * from V$SESSION;`

C. `select * from V$PROCESS;`

D. `select * from V$PACKAGE;`

3. **The DBA is tuning application performance. In order to obtain statistics for actual database processing associated with specific SQL statements running in a session, which of the following tuning tools would not be used?**

   A. `explain plan`

   B. AUTOTRACE

   C. TKPROF

   D. Performance Manager

   E. Oracle Expert

4. **You are developing system requirements for an OLTP application. Two of the primary performance goals in OLTP systems that you might include are which of the following choices? (Choose two)**

   A. Fast report execution

   B. Fast `update` capability

   C. Fast `insert` capability

   D. Fast ad hoc queries

   E. Fast online access to data

5. **You are examining the plan for a SQL statement running against a large table. The statement contains the operations indicated in the choices for this question. In order to improve performance on SQL statements, which of the following operations should be avoided?**

   A. `INDEX RANGE SCAN`

   B. `TABLE ACCESS FULL`

   C. `FILTER`

   D. `MERGE-JOIN`

   E. `NESTED LOOPS`

   F. `TABLE ACCESS BY ROWID`

6. **Table EMP has an index on one of its columns. You determine that the execution plan for a SQL statement will utilize this index. One reason for poor performance on a `select` statement using this index may be due to which of the following causes?**

   A. The query causes a `TABLE ACCESS FULL` to be performed.

   B. The query uses an `INDEX RANGE SCAN`.

   C. The index has only one extent.

   D. The index has low cardinality.

7. **You are determining the application requirements for a decision-support system. Which of the following features are generally *not* found in decision support systems?**

   A. Frequent updates made by users

   B. Frequent reports generated by users

   C. Use of indexes

   D. Use of clusters

   E. Low data volatility

8. **You are about to reorganize the segment and extent allocation of several tables in a database. Which of the following options makes preventing users from accessing the database and reconfiguring general instance startup and operation easier?**

   A. Many change processes done manually

   B. Use of multiple `init`*`sid`*`.ora` files

   C. The `parallel query` option

   D. Use of SQL Trace and TKPROF to track statistics

   E. Multiple tablespaces to store index data

9. **You are trying to determine the statistics generated by SQL statements in a user session using TKPROF. This utility accepts as input which of the following choices?**

A. The output from `UTLESTAT`

B. The output from `select * from DBA_IND_COLUMNS`

C. A file in a directory specified by the `USER_DUMP_DEST` parameter

D. The output from `EXPORT`

10. You have a table in a heavily updated OLTP system. Which of the following choices indicate the situation that will occur when you add several indexes to this table?

A. Decreases performance for reports, and therefore shouldn't be used

B. Decreases performance of online viewing, and therefore shouldn't be used

C. Decreases performance of ad hoc queries, and therefore shouldn't be used

D. Decreases performance of database updates, and therefore shouldn't be used

11. You are incorporating use of the DBMS_APPLICATION_INFO package in your application for performance tuning. Which of the following choices is not a procedure in that package?

A. `read_action( )`

B. `set_client_info( )`

C. `read_client_info( )`

D. `set_module( )`

12. The DBA runs SQL Trace, but the output file contains only about half of the information from the session. What should the DBA do to correct the problem?

A. Increase the value of `TIMED_STATISTICS`

B. Increase the value of `MAX_DUMP_FILE_SIZE`

C. Run UTLBSTAT/UTLESTAT again

D. Flush the shared pool

Answers to Chapter Questions

1. D. `select * from EMP where EMPID = 604;`

Explanation In Choice D, Oracle uses an implicit datatype conversion from VARCHAR2 to NUMBER that prevents the RDBMS from using the index on the EMPID column. All queries for choices A, B, and C will use the index on EMPID because of how the `where` clauses are constructed. The use of functions in the `select` clause will not cause Oracle to not use the index, either.

2. B. `select * from V$SESSION;`

Explanation When applications are registered in Oracle, you can find performance statistics for their operation in two views, V$SESSION and V$SQLAREA. The V$PACKAGE view does not exist in Oracle, so choice D is incorrect. V$SYSSTAT and V$PROCESS track statistics for other database resources, so choices A and C are incorrect. Review the discussion on DBMS_APPLICATION_INFO for more information.

3. A. `explain plan`

Explanation The `explain plan` utility merely gives the statement execution plan for SQL statements, while the other choices will offer statistics for SQL statement operation and/or an execution plan. Some of the choices given work in conjunction with Oracle Enterprise Manager, which offers a visually appealing alternative to the command-line options.

4. B *and* C. Fast `update` capability *and* fast `insert` capability

Explanation For online transaction processing (OLTP) systems, you will want users to be able to add new records quickly, and change those records quickly, as well. OLTP systems are generally designed for fast data entry and maintenance. Choices A, D, and E all indicate the need for and use of indexes, all of which cause processing overhead on inserts and updates, the primary function of OLTP applications. Therefore, A, D, and E are incorrect. Review the discussion of OLTP system requirements for more information.

5. B. `TABLE ACCESS FULL`

Explanation The `FILTER` operation usually occurs in conjunction with a `TABLE ACCESS FULL` operation when SQL statements are issued that have where clauses refer to non-indexed columns as their filter criteria. `INDEX RANGE SCAN` operations usually occur in conjunction with `TABLE ACCESS BY ROWID` operations, both of which perform better than `FILTER` operations. `MERGE-JOIN` and `NESTED LOOPS` operations indicate joins, which may or may not perform well, depending how the tables being joined are indexed.

6. D. The index has low cardinality.

Explanation Choice D indicates the most plausible choice given, because an index with low cardinality won't necessarily improve SQL statement performance even if the query uses the index. Given the information in the question, choice A is untrue. The SQL processing mechanism will not perform a full table scan when an index is available and the statement does not force it to avoid the index. Similarly, using an `INDEX RANGE SCAN` alone does not imply poor performance; in fact, quite the opposite is true. Therefore, choices A and B are incorrect. Choice C indicates that performance on the index scan will be impressive, given a lack of dynamically allocated extents to fragment the index data. Cardinality, on the other hand, is the key to good index performance. If an index has few unique values, queries using it will perform badly. Therefore, only choice D is correct. Review the discussion of causes for inefficient SQL.

7. A. Frequent updates made by users

Explanation Choice A is not generally a feature on DSS systems because frequent updates can disrupt DSS operation in several ways. Those ways include index fragmentation and cluster disruption. DSS systems are typically used for heavy reporting or ad hoc queries, thus eliminating those choices. Indexes and clusters typically improve performance for those operations, discarding those choices as well.

8. B. Use of multiple `init`*`sid`*`.ora` files

Explanation By employing multiple `init`*`sid`*`.ora` files, you can alter the operation of your database quickly and easily by simply shutting down and restarting with a different value set for the `PFILE` parameter in `startup open` in Server Manager or using a different stored configuration in Instance Manager. Therefore, choice B is correct. Choice A makes the process of reconfiguring the database on a temporary basis more difficult, not easier. Choices C, D, and E have little bearing on the reconfiguration of the Oracle instance. Review the discussion of reconfiguring systems on a temporary basis for particular needs.

9. C. A file in a directory specified by the `USER_DUMP_DEST` parameter

Explanation The parameter `USER_DUMP_DEST` indicates where user session trace files are located on your host machine. Since trace files are the input for TKPROF, choice C is the correct answer. Choice A is incorrect because the output from UTLBSTAT/UTLESTAT is `report.txt`, which provides its own performance statistics for the instance. Choice B is incorrect as well. DBA_IND_COLUMNS is a listing of all indexed columns in the database. It can be helpful for tuning SQL queries because it identifies which columns on a table are indexed, but it gives no relevant information to TKPROF. Finally, choice D is incorrect because the output from EXPORT can only be read by IMPORT.

10. D. Decreases performance of database updates, and therefore shouldn't be used

Explanation Choices A, B, and C are all incorrect statements. In every case, an index improves performance of the operation. However, indexes also increase overhead on inserts and updates, which are the key functionality of the OLTP system. Review the discussion of the demands of OLTP systems.

11. A. `read_action( )`

Explanation The procedure `read_action( )` is not from the DBMS_APPLICATION_INFO package. All other choices are actual procedures from the DBMS_APPLICATION_INFO package. Review discussion of this package.

12. B. Increase the value of `MAX_DUMP_FILE_SIZE`

Explanation `MAX_DUMP_FILE_SIZE` is the maximum size permitted for trace files. If the output of a trace file is cut off, this value should be increased. Choice A is incorrect because TIMED_STATISTICS is a parameter that usually has TRUE or FALSE assigned to it. Choice C is incorrect because UTLBSTAT/UTLESTAT were not run at this point to produce a trace file. Choice D is incorrect because the shared pool does not need to be flushed in order to run traces. See the discussion on SQL Trace and TKPROF as part of the section on diagnosing application performance problems.

CHAPTER 18

Tuning Memory and Operating System Use

n this chapter, you will learn about and demonstrate knowledge in the following areas:

- Generic operating system tuning
- Tuning the shared pool
- Tuning the buffer cache
- Tuning the redo log buffer

After tuning SQL statements and the applications that use them, tuning operating system (OS) configuration and memory can yield great performance benefits for the database. Unfortunately, upon leaving the insulated world of SQL tuning for the adventure of exploring the host system and SGA, the DBA leaves behind the advantage of knowing that the changes he or she makes won't adversely affect another area of the database. Tuning memory utilization on the Oracle database is tricky because memory (and disk I/O) resources are a global need—and if that global need is changed in a way that doesn't work, it is a problem for everyone using the Oracle database. Understanding how to tune memory utilization represents a major component of the DBA's skills, and it is also the largest performance-tuning component of Oracle certification. The material in this chapter covers about 20 percent of OCP Exam 4.

Generic Operating System Tuning

In this section, you will cover the following points on generic OS tuning issues and Oracle:

- The primary steps for OS tuning
- Similarities between OS and database tuning
- The difference between processes and threads
- Describing paging and swapping

There are several different things that you can do as the Oracle DBA to tune host machine operation so that Oracle database processing is optimized. Many major hardware vendors are working with Oracle to ensure that the Oracle database can easily be configured to run efficiently on their platforms. Advances in everything, including CPU processing speed, disk controller caches, memory, solid state storage media, and disk spindle speed, make tuning an Oracle database from the host-system perspective more complicated than ever before.

DBAs used to have the luxury of passing these issues off to infrastructure specialists or hardware-system administrators. Not anymore. DBAs emphasizing SQL-statement optimization in proprietary applications developed in-house must change their paradigm in light of the fact that many organizations now use packaged products, such as Oracle Financials, to manage their corporate information, and developers usually aren't able to modify the application. It is more important than ever that the DBA understand how to tune Oracle from the host-system perspective.

The Primary Steps for OS Tuning

It has usually been beyond the scope of documentation on Oracle products to discuss how to tune the operating system. Typically, Oracle-centric documents have referred you to operating system–specific Oracle manuals or to manuals on the operating systems themselves. This was with good reason, because operating systems can be vastly different. For example, many operating systems function mainly through the command line, such as the many flavors of Unix and VMS. Others are mainframe operating systems that operate via terminals or terminal emulators, like MVS. With the advances of Windows (from DOS add-on to a multithreaded operating system capable of ever-increasing workloads), a new breed of GUI-based operating system has also emerged. Each of these platforms has its own quirks with respect to running Oracle efficiently.

Even within the world of Unix, there is a spectrum of products to choose from. Despite a similar "look and feel" provided from familiar tools like `grep` and `awk`, each version of Unix built by a different vendor represents a different approach to system administration. Despite these differences, there is a common set of steps you can take for primary operating system tuning to ensure Oracle's ability to run efficiently. The actual execution of these steps may vary, but the principles they represent are fairly universal. These principles include tuning memory and hardware caching, I/O and disk usage, and background-process prioritization and scheduling.

Tuning Memory and Hardware Caching

Tuning operating system and hardware caches that may be in use on your disk controllers and/or memory on the host machine is a tuning step you might engage in after you have exhausted your options tuning the application. An important area of host-machine tuning involves ensuring that no paging or swapping occurs in memory. This is highly important, and it will be covered shortly, in the section titled "Describing Paging and Swapping."

In the area of hardware caching, many large machines built nowadays have disk controllers that manage access to disk devices. Several of these controllers offer a cache that allows Oracle background processes to write data changes to the controller cache instead of to disk. The controller then sends a signal back to the process telling it that the change was written to disk and that the process should continue with its other work. The change was actually written to the disk controller cache, not to disk. The controller will write the change to disk asynchronously, when the controller needs to do so, either because of I/O load or because the cache is full. From the time the controller tells Oracle that the change is saved to disk, to the time that the controller actually writes it to disk, your database is at risk. If the controller fails to operate, or if there is a power loss to the machine, Oracle may not be recoverable because the data Oracle was told is on disk isn't actually there. Disk controller caches may or may not improve I/O write performance, but their use can have a nasty effect on recoverability when disaster strikes. If one is available, you should use a "write-through" option so that Oracle data will not be held in the cache. This option may be available in Unix, depending on the version; the write-though option is always available in Windows.

Tuning I/O and Disk Usage

The first step in this type of tuning is to evaluate the management of I/O on the host machine. This process includes considering the use of *raw devices* managed by Oracle as an alternative to files managed by the Unix-specific file-system manager. A raw device is basically raw disk space allocated to Oracle—the database manages formatting and storage allocation. Raw devices are commonly found on Oracle Parallel Server installations and in Oracle running on Unix machines. Raw devices can serve as an alternative in situations where the write-though option isn't available on the host machine. However, it is complicated to manage and doesn't work well when Oracle must perform `table access full` operations, which gives you even more incentive to ensure your application uses indexing properly.

I/O tuning from the operating system perspective may also involve the evaluation and use of RAID technology or solid-state storage media. The RAID level you use on your host machine may have an impact on how Oracle performs. For example, storage of redo log files on a disk resource using RAID-5 may not perform well. This is because RAID-5 stripes redo log data over several different disks in the array. As you know, Oracle is constantly writing redo, which means the disk controller would constantly be writing information striped across several different disks. In many cases, redo logs stored in RAID-5 configurations will cause the entire Oracle database to perform poorly during times of heavy use because the redo log buffer backs up, making processes wait to write their redo in memory. Instead, you may want to consider a RAID level that allows LGWR to write sequentially on one or two disks using mirroring, or invest in solid-state disk hardware.

Tuning Background Process Prioritization and Scheduling

The next step is to optimize how the operating system schedules and prioritizes background processes to execute on the host machine. Your Oracle database has several background processes that perform specialized functions, such as writing data blocks and redo information to disk. It is important for overall database operation that all Oracle background and user processes be assigned the same priority by the operating system, so that the CPU scheduler does not consistently put one process or set of processes on hold. Assigning different priorities to background and user processes prevents one area of database operation from functioning as efficiently as another. Background and user processes are interdependent. For example, if you assigned LGWR lower priority than user processes, then the redo log buffer would fill quickly and not be cleared out efficiently. This would lead to long wait times for users, because the only time the log buffer would get cleared out is when user processing gets backed up and has to wait, thus giving LGWR some CPU time.

Exercises

1. Identify some steps in tuning the operating system. Why is tuning the operating system important?
2. What are some of the adverse effects of using hardware caching on your host machine? What about adverse impacts from the perspective of process prioritization and scheduling?

Similarities Between OS and Database Tuning

Although the only topic discussed from the perspective of Oracle tuning thus far has been application SQL tuning, several discussions of memory, I/O, and Oracle internals tuning are coming up. There are many similarities between database tuning and operating system tuning in that Oracle is like any other application running on your host machine. It uses host-system memory, CPU resources, and space on disk. Later in this chapter, and in Chapters 19 and 20, you will learn about methods within Oracle for tuning host-machine use. Obviously, if there is something you can do outside of Oracle to improve the host machine in any of these areas, the database will benefit, too. For example, if you upgrade the CPU, add processors on the host machine, or use an operating system feature that maximizes CPU throughput, such as asynchronous I/O, Oracle stands to benefit as well.

Similarly, if you tune Oracle in areas like memory, disk I/O, or CPU usage so that Oracle runs more efficiently, then the processing load Oracle places on the operating system becomes easier to manage, as well. For example, suppose 95 percent of available memory on the host machine is allocated to Oracle, and you determine that Oracle could provide substantially the same performance using only 65 percent of available memory. You could return some memory to the operating system that it could use to handle other things, such as system calls, making overall processing more efficient for both Oracle and the operating system.

Generally, a careful balance between Oracle and the operating system must be found in resource usage areas, such as the CPU. For example, if operating system calls receive more attention from the CPU scheduler than Oracle processes do, then Oracle will have to wait until it gets some processor attention. However, if Oracle gets most of the CPU's attention (90 percent, for example), then Oracle may still have to wait because some system calls (disk reads, for example) may need to be processed in order for Oracle to function properly. In general, Oracle should receive about 2/3 (about 67 percent) of the processor's attention, and the OS should get about 1/3 (about 33 percent), give or take about 10 percent, in order for Oracle to execute properly.

Exercises

1. Describe similarities between Oracle tuning and OS tuning. What overlaps exist between these two areas of overall system tuning?
2. Why is it important to have a proper balance between Oracle and the OS with respect to CPU usage?

The Difference Between Processes and Threads

Thus far, discussion of executable components of the Oracle database, such as the server process, LGWR, DBW0, and CKPT, have been referred to as exactly that—*processes.* A process is an individual executable program or job that runs on a computer, using resources such as memory, CPU, and I/O. Oracle on Unix-based systems uses a separate executable for each background, user, and server process identified so far in the book. In other words, if you issued `ps -elf | grep -i ORA` in your Unix command shell, you would receive a list of all the individual processes currently running on your host machine that have "ORA" or "ora" somewhere in their name, thus denoting themselves as Oracle processes. The list will be extensive, even if no users are currently connected, because Oracle in Unix environments runs its background operations as individual processes—one for LGWR, one for CKPT, and so on, as Figure 18-1 illustrates.

This is in contrast to Oracle running on the Windows platform. On Windows, the Oracle server runs as only one process, called `oracle80.exe`. This one process in Windows performs the work of many processes in Unix. The individual activities of CKPT, LGWR, and DBW0 are handled as *threads* in Windows. A thread is an object within a process that runs program instructions. Threads allow concurrent operations within a process and enable one process to run different parts of its program on different processors simultaneously. Thus, when this book refers to background processes such as CKPT and DBW0, it is specifically referring to those individual activities that are handled as processes in Unix. If you run Oracle on Windows, substitute "thread" for "process" and you will have the same

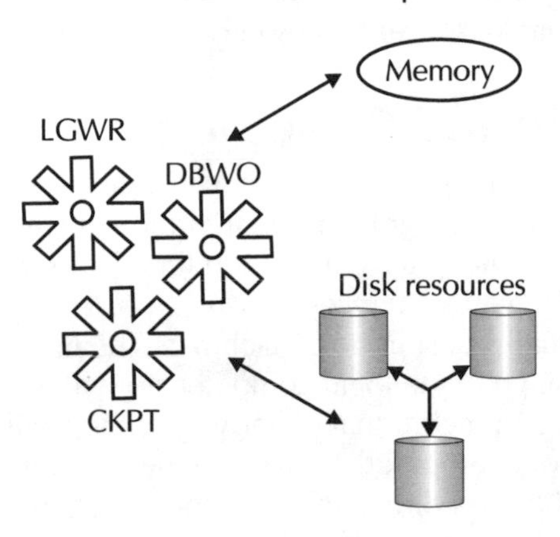

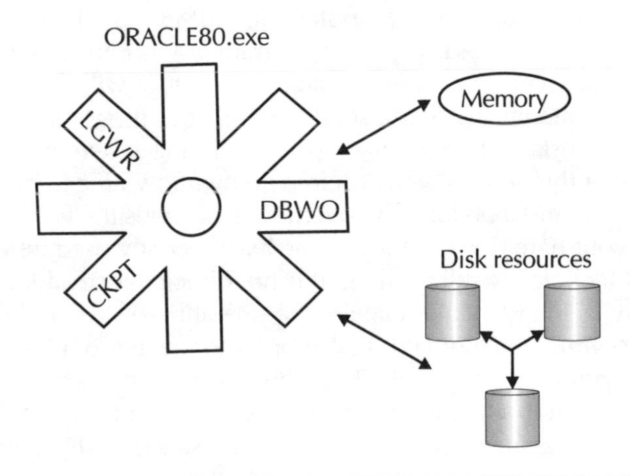

FIGURE 18-1. *Oracle on Unix and Windows platforms*

meaning. Figure 18-1 illustrates Oracle processes and threads in Windows environments, as well.

Exercises

1. Describe what is meant by the term "process." How many processes run in association with the Oracle database in Unix environments?

2. Describe what is meant by the term "thread." How many processes run in association with the Oracle database in Windows environments? What threads are part of that (or those) processes?

Describing Paging and Swapping

It was mentioned earlier that keeping the size of Oracle's memory use low so that it can always reside in real memory is highly important in the operation of your Oracle database, regardless of what platform you run Oracle on. This point raises the need to explain basic OS memory management.

Two types of memory usually exist in host machines. The first kind of memory is known as *real memory*. If you go to the local computer store and ask for a memory upgrade, they give you a long, thin chip that either you or they will place into a slot on the motherboard inside your computer. This is real memory, and it increases the amount of space your computer has direct access to for storing information from a program in action.

Many operating systems have another kind of memory designed within them, called *virtual memory*. This kind of memory is designed to act as an overflow area. For example, suppose you have a computer with 48MB of real memory available on it. Four instantiations of a word processor program are running at the same time on your computer, each requiring 10MB of memory. All four will fit comfortably in real memory. You then attempt another instantiation of your program. To accommodate the 10MB this fifth instantiation requires, your operating system may put information from the least recently used instantiation into an overflow area to make room in real memory for the new instantiation. The overflow area takes the form of a *paging file* or *swap file* on your hard drive. Although the least recently used instantiation of your program is technically still running, it is not directly accessible. If you try to use the least recently used instantiation again, the operating system will first put another instantiation into virtual memory on disk in order to make room in real memory for the instantiation you just referenced. Then, the operating system will load the instantiation you want to use into real memory so you can access it directly. This activity is known as *paging* or *swapping*, and it can substantially degrade application performance.

CAUTION
For the sake of performance, you will want to prevent the operating system from ever paging or swapping your Oracle SGA from real memory into virtual memory! The rest of the chapter will discuss how to handle this task.

Exercises

1. What is real memory? What is virtual memory? What is the difference between the two?
2. What performance impact will occur on your Oracle database if you allow the SGA to be swapped into virtual memory?

Tuning the Shared Pool

In this section, you will cover the following topics related to tuning the shared pool:

- Tuning the library cache and dictionary cache
- Measuring shared-pool hit percentage
- Sizing the shared pool
- Pinning objects in the shared pool
- Tuning shared-pool reserved space
- Listing the UGA and session memory

This section covers several different topics related to tuning the shared pool. The first is tuning the dictionary cache and the library cache. Next is measuring hit ratios, or percentages, on the shared pool. A *hit ratio* is the frequency with which a process looking for a resource finds that resource already loaded into memory. High hit ratios are good, and this section will tell you why. After that, you'll cover how to size the shared pool appropriately. You'll also learn how to make objects persist in the shared pool, even when Oracle would ordinarily eliminate them. Sometimes, this is referred to as *pinning* objects. The two last topics covered in this chapter are tuning the shared-pool reserved space and listing UGA and session memory considerations as part of tuning the shared pool.

Tuning the Library Cache and Dictionary Cache

In Unit II, you became acquainted with the components of the SGA, illustrated in Figure 18-2. One of those components is the shared pool. The shared pool contains three main areas. The first is the *library cache*. The library cache is further divided into components. One of those components is the *shared SQL area*, which is where SQL statements are turned into the execution plans you learned about in Chapter

17. The library cache also contains PL/SQL programs in their compiled form. Finally, the library cache also contains certain *control structures,* such as locks, which are designed to prevent two processes from manipulating the same resource at the same time. A good example of locks in action involves transaction processing. If user SPANKY tries to `update` a row that is currently being changed by user ATHENA, then Oracle will force SPANKY to wait until ATHENA has finished the change and ended the transaction.

The second main area of the shared pool is the *dictionary cache,* sometimes also known as the *row cache.* The dictionary cache stores rows of information from the data dictionary in memory for faster access by Oracle and user processes. Since the data dictionary is used quite heavily in support of other activities, the dictionary cache improves overall database performance by giving fast access to recently used dictionary data contents. As long as this data is available in the dictionary cache, database users can access the information more quickly than if Oracle had to read the data from disk.

Methods for Improving Dictionary-Cache Performance

To improve dictionary-cache or library-cache performance, you should increase the overall amount of memory used by the SGA by adding memory to the shared pool. This is accomplished by increasing the value set for the `initsid.ora` parameter `SHARED_POOL_SIZE`. This method increases the amount of dictionary data and SQL-statement execution-plan information that can be stored in memory. When a process looking for SQL-statement execution-plan or dictionary information finds that information in memory, this situation is called a *library cache hit* or a *dictionary cache hit,* respectively. Since each of these areas in the shared pool are sized

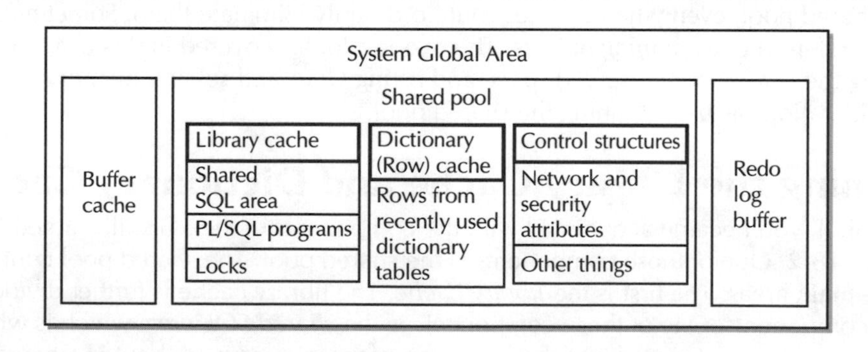

FIGURE 18-2. *Contents of the Oracle SGA*

dynamically according to need, increasing SHARED_POOL_SIZE is not precise enough to add space specifically to one cache or the other. Care should be taken in determining how much space to add. The SGA usually takes up most of the memory available on the host machine. Make sure that allocating more real memory to the shared pool does not cause the host machine to page the SGA out of real memory.

Methods for Improving Library-Cache Performance

In addition to resizing the shared pool, other methods are available for improving library cache performance on the database. If applications accessing the database execute many identical SQL statements, then Oracle will be able to share more SQL statement parse information, thus increasing library cache hits. A SQL statement must be identical to the one the user process wants to execute in order for Oracle to permit sharing. When Oracle says that two SQL statements must be identical for parse-tree sharing to occur, Oracle means *identical*—character for character, space for space—*including case sensitivity*!

Another method for improving library-cache performance involves understanding how Oracle manages the library cache. The CURSOR_SPACE_FOR_TIME init*sid*.ora parameter influences this activity. When a user process needs to parse and execute a SQL statement, Oracle may eliminate an existing SQL execution plan from the library cache to make room for the new one if CURSOR_SPACE_FOR_TIME is set to FALSE, the default. However, the problem here is that another process may need the execution plan to be eliminated to make room. If you set CURSOR_SPACE_FOR_TIME to TRUE, Oracle will not eliminate a parsed execution plan from the library cache until all open cursor user processes and applications that use the execution plan have been closed. Library cache performance can be improved by setting CURSOR_SPACE_FOR_TIME to TRUE. However, you must be careful only to do so when your library-cache hit ratio is 100 percent. If an execution miss occurs on your database when this parameter is set to TRUE and all execution plans in the library cache are associated with open cursors, your users will receive errors saying there is not enough shared memory in your database.

Exercises

1. To what area of the SGA do the library cache and the dictionary cache belong?
2. What structures does the library cache contain? What does the dictionary cache contain?
3. How can performance be improved on the library or dictionary cache?

Measuring Shared-Pool Hit Percentage

As mentioned, the performance on either cache of the shared pool can be measured using hit ratios. The hit ratio is calculated as a percentage: the number of times a user process found what it was looking for in memory divided by the number of times the process attempted to find something in memory, multiplied by 100. This performance information can be found in certain dynamic performance views whose names are prefixed with V$ in Oracle. This discussion will present the views used for calculating hit ratios, along with appropriate formulas.

Hits on the Dictionary Cache

Dictionary-cache performance is monitored by Oracle, and the performance statistics are stored in a dynamic performance view called V$ROWCACHE. This dynamic performance view is accessible only by those users granted the SELECT_CATALOG_ROLE role or the `select any table` privilege, or by user SYS. The hit ratio for the dictionary cache is collected by treating data in V$ROWCACHE as an aggregate. Relevant columns for calculating the hit ratio on the dictionary cache from V$ROWCACHE include GETS and GETMISSES. Another column, PARAMETER, identifies a type of object whose dictionary information has been requested. For each row in V$ROWCACHE, statistics in the GETS column represent the total number of times a process or Oracle asked for the item named in column PARAMETER. Notice that this definition says *total number*, not just the ones that ended with Oracle successfully finding the data in the dictionary cache. The other column, GETMISSES is the number of times a request for dictionary information couldn't find that information in the dictionary cache, and instead had to go out to the SYSTEM tablespace to retrieve the information. Retrieving data from disk decreases system performance and creates additional I/O overhead. You calculate the hit ratio using the formula

```
sum(GETS - GETMISSES) / sum(GETS) * 100
```

The following code block includes use of the `round( )` function to make output more readable:

```
SQL> select sum(gets-getmisses) as hits,
  2  sum(getmisses) as misses,
  3  round((sum(gets-getmisses)/sum(gets))*100,2) as hit_ratio
  4  from v$rowcache;
     HITS    MISSES HIT_RATIO
--------- --------- ---------
     2313       187     92.45
```

An ideal hit ratio for dictionary-cache activity is 99 percent or higher, so the hit ratio shown in this code block is probably not acceptable. Some potential causes for an unacceptably low hit ratio include the shared pool being too small and statistical collection being taken too early in the life of the current instance to have any meaning. You have already learned how to correct the former case. To avoid the latter, do not start calculating hit ratios using output from V$ROWCACHE until the database has been running awhile.

Hits on the Library Cache

Key to ensuring the performance of the Oracle library cache is monitoring library-cache activity. The view used for monitoring statistics on the library cache is V$LIBRARYCACHE. As with other V$ views, access to the V$LIBRARYCACHE is limited to those users with `select any table` privileges, the SELECT_CATALOG_ROLE role, or the owner of the view, SYS. Each row contains statistics associated with different types of SQL code blocks. As with V$ROWCACHE, you should treat the rows in V$LIBRARYCACHE as an aggregate when calculating the overall hit ratio for this resource. The three useful columns for obtaining library-cache hit ratio are NAMESPACE, PINS, and RELOADS. NAMESPACE identifies different types of library cache activity associated with SQL statements and other structures. The PINS column value corresponds to the number of times a parsed object in the library cache was executed. The RELOADS column tracks the number of times a user attempted to execute a previously parsed statement, only to find it had been flushed from the cache. This is known as an *execution miss*. The library cache hit ratio is calculated as

```
(sum(PINS - RELOADS) / sum(PINS)) * 100
```

using data from that view. The following code block includes use of the `round( )` function to make output more readable:

```
SQL> select sum(pins) as hits,
  2  sum(reloads) as misses,
  3  round((sum(pins-reloads)/sum(pins))*100,2) as hit_ratio
  4  from v$librarycache;
     HITS    MISSES HIT_RATIO
--------- --------- ---------
     2994        16     99.47
```

Ideally, the library-cache hit ratio should be 99 percent or higher, so the hit ratio shown in this code block is acceptable. Some potential causes for an unacceptably low hit ratio include the shared pool being too small and statistical collection being taken too early in the life of the current instance to have any meaning. You have already learned how to correct the former case. To avoid the latter, do not start calculating hit ratios using output from V$LIBRARYCACHE until the database has been running awhile.

Exercises

1. What dynamic performance views are used to collect statistics on the components of the shared pool? How is performance measured on each component?
2. What does an execution miss mean? What dynamic performance view and statistic is used to reflect execution misses? How might performance be improved if too many execution misses are occurring?

Sizing the Shared Pool

Increasing `SHARED_POOL_SIZE` has the potential to impact overall performance if the SGA is sized larger than host machine real memory can accommodate. The most effective way to add memory to the shared pool without adversely impacting performance is to add real memory to the machine hosting Oracle. However, real memory costs real money and funds can be in short supply. The DBA sometimes must juggle the available memory between different components of the SGA or from user private global areas in order to give it to the shared pool.

Another aspect of appropriate sizing for the shared pool with the `SHARED_POOL_SIZE` parameter involves the relationship between the library cache and the dictionary cache. Since data in the dictionary cache is more static and tends to persist in memory longer than information in the library cache will, you might find that by sizing `SHARED_POOL_SIZE` so the library cache can operate precisely, you can successfully tuned the dictionary cache, as well. Tuning the library cache depends on several factors:

- *Ability of users to execute SQL ad hoc versus using "canned" SQL.* If users can enter queries for themselves, there may be little SQL sharing, because statements in the library cache are flushed from memory faster than if everyone accessed the same limited selection of stored procedures or SQL embedded in a front end. Use stored procedures and applications to access data where possible.
- *Size and number of applications permitted access to the database.* A large number of applications that execute different SQL or PL/SQL code against the database, written by developers who don't have established standards

for accessing data, uniformly diminishes potential for SQL sharing in the library cache. Conversely, small applications containing limited numbers of SQL and PL/SQL blocks can share SQL execution plans to a high degree.

- *Associated transaction volumes on the system.* Large systems with many users running different applications may have little opportunity to reuse or share SQL because execution plans are eliminated quickly. There may be a problem with reloads taking place in this situation, as well.

In some cases, however, you actually may want to decrease the size of the shared pool. The V$SGASTAT performance view tracks several statistics about your SGA, including free memory in the shared pool. If you issue `select VALUE` from `V$SGASTAT` where `POOL = 'shared pool'` and `NAME = 'free memory'`, you will see the amount of memory currently free in the shared pool. If this value is consistently high over time, another area of the SGA needs memory, and if real memory on the machine is limited, you may want to decrease `SHARED_POOL_SIZE`.

Exercises

1. Identify some issues associated with sizing the shared pool. What performance view is useful in decreasing the size of the shared pool?
2. How can library-cache usage be managed to reduce the need for a large shared pool?

Pinning Objects in the Shared Pool

Performance may be crucial for a certain block of code. You may have a mission-critical data feed that needs to run quickly. There may also be problems with fitting large PL/SQL blocks into contiguous blocks of shared memory in order to even parse and execute the code. It may be necessary to place objects into the library cache so the shared SQL will not be paged out of the shared pool. This is known as *pinning* and is accomplished using the `keep( )` procedure in the Oracle-supplied package DBMS_SHARED_POOL.

Check to make sure this package exists before you use it by drilling into the Schema Objects | Packages | SYS node and looking for a node with the name DBMS_SHARED_POOL. If this package does not exist, you must create it using Server Manager. To do so, connect to the database as `internal` or as another user with `sysdba` privileges. Then, execute the `dbmspool.sql` and `prvtpool.plb` scripts located in the `rdbms/admin` subdirectory of the Oracle software home directory, as the following code shows.

```
SVRMGR> connect internal
Password:
Connected.
SVRMGR> @d:\orant\rdbms80\admin\dbmspool
Statement processed.
Statement processed.
Statement processed.
Statement processed.
SVRMGR> @d:\orant\rdbms80\admin\prvtpool.plb
Statement processed.
Statement processed.
```

If the object you want to pin in the shared pool is not already present in the shared pool, you may need to flush (clear) all information currently stored in the shared pool, or restart the instance, before pinning the object. You will need to do this when you are trying to pin an object into the shared pool that Oracle is unable to load. When you flush the shared pool, all space in the shared pool is then freed temporarily for new SQL statements to parse, which temporarily reduces performance for other statements running on the system. You can flush the shared pool with the `alter system flush shared_pool` statement:

```
SVRMGR> ALTER SYSTEM FLUSH SHARED_POOL;
Statement processed.
```

You should then make reference to the object you want to pin by executing all or some portion of it. This execution causes Oracle to parse the code—either a cursor, procedure, or trigger—which places the code in shared memory. *Only code in shared memory can be pinned.* The following code block will cause Oracle to load the STANDARD package into memory:

```
SVRMGR> select to_char(10) from dual;
TO_CHAR(10)
-----------
10
```

Once the shared SQL code is referenced, you should take a moment to look and see if the procedure is there. The `sizes( )` procedure in DBMS_SHARED_POOL accepts one parameter of type NUMBER and allows you to list the objects in the shared pool that are greater than the NUMBER you passed into the procedure. You should issue the `set serveroutput` on command to ensure you will see the result from this procedure:

```
SVRMGR> set serveroutput on size 15000;
Server Output                     ON
```

```
SVRMGR> execute dbms_shared_pool.sizes(150);
SIZE(K) KEPT NAME
------- ---- ---------------------------------------------
    165      SYS.STANDARD
```

To pin the object, execute the `keep( )` procedure, passing both the name of the object to be pinned, as it appears in the NAME column of the `DBMS_SHARED_POOL.sizes( )` procedure, and a character indicating what sort of object it is. Acceptable values for the *type* variable are P (procedure), C (cursor), Q (sequence), and R (trigger). When finished, you can view the output from `DBMS_SHARED_POOL.sizes( )` to ensure that the object is now pinned in the shared pool:

```
SVRMGR> execute DBMS_SHARED_POOL.KEEP('SYS.STANDARD','P');
Statement processed.
SVRMGR> execute dbms_shared_pool.sizes(150);
SIZE(K) KEPT NAME
------- ---- ---------------------------------------------
    165 YES  SYS.STANDARD
```

Determining When to Flush the Shared Pool

Whether you need to flush the shared pool before attempting to pin an object in it or not depends on whether the object you want to pin in the shared pool can actually be loaded into the shared pool. In some cases, you may have a large object, such as a PL/SQL package that Oracle is unable to load into shared memory. In this case, you will either need to flush the shared pool or restart the instance, and then load the package by referencing it in some way, and pin it so Oracle will never eliminate it. However, if the object you want to pin in shared memory already resides there, you needn't flush the shared pool or reload it.

Exercises

1. What procedure is taken by the DBA if it is important to keep a parsed shareable copy of a SQL or PL/SQL code block in memory? What is flushing the shared pool?
2. What is DBMS_SHARED_POOL? How is it created?

Tuning Shared-Pool Reserved Space

Pinning objects in the shared pool is one solution to the challenge of managing large blocks of PL/SQL and their presence in the shared pool. Another is reserving space in the shared pool. Oracle can be configured to keep some space aside in the shared pool that it will prevent from becoming fragmented by requests for smaller amounts of space. This feature may be useful when you are compiling large PL/SQL packages or triggers. The space held in reserve by Oracle when this feature is used is called the *reserved list*.

Configuring a reserved list in Oracle requires setting values for two `initsid.ora` parameters. The first is `SHARED_POOL_RESERVED_SIZE`, and it is expressed in bytes. This parameter represents the amount of space that is set apart in the shared pool for the reserved list The value you set for this parameter should be less than the value set for `SHARED_POOL_SIZE`. The second parameter that must be set is `SHARED_POOL_RESERVED_MIN_ALLOC`, which is set to a value less than `SHARED_POOL_RESERVED_SIZE`. In order for Oracle to allocate space from the reserved list in the shared pool, the allocation must be greater than or equal to the value set for `SHARED_POOL_RESERVED_MIN_ALLOC`.

The V$SHARED_POOL_RESERVED dynamic performance view is designed to assist in tuning shared-pool reserved-list configuration. An important column is REQUEST_FAILURES, indicating the number of shared pool space requests that weren't granted. If this value is greater than zero, you should examine three other columns in this view: LAST_FAILURE_SIZE, MAX_FREE_SIZE, and FREE_SPACE. If `SHARED_POOL_RESERVED_MIN_ALLOC` is less than LAST_FAILURE_SIZE or greater than MAX_FREE_SIZE or FREE_SPACE, you should either increase both `SHARED_POOL_RESERVED_SIZE` and `SHARED_POOL_SIZE` by the difference between the two, or increase `SHARED_POOL_RESERVED_MIN_ALLOC` and `SHARED_POOL_SIZE` by the difference between the two.

Exercises

1. What is the reserved list? What two parameters handle configuring the reserved list?
2. What view is used to tune the reserved list? Under what circumstances should you increase the size of the reserved list?

Listing the UGA and Session Memory

UGA stands for User Global Area, and it represents the amount of memory allocated in Oracle for a user session. User session information is stored in one of two places, depending on whether you are using dedicated server processes or the MTS architecture to support user requests for data. When dedicated servers are in use, session information, such as a private SQL area, is stored in the memory allocated to the user processes. This is called the PGA, or Program Global Area. However, if you are using the multithreaded server (MTS) architecture, session information will be stored in the shared pool. In that case, you may need to increase

SHARED_POOL_SIZE when switching from dedicated servers to MTS, all other things being equal.

You can determine the total UGA allocation for sessions currently connected to Oracle using the V$SESSTAT and V$STATNAME dynamic performance views. Two statistics are relevant to your understanding. They are session UGA memory, which is the amount of memory in bytes allocated to all active sessions, and session UGA memory max, which is the most amount of memory ever allocated to sessions, total. Both these values are expressed in bytes and can be obtained with the following query, and you can then use the values returned to determine how much memory you need to add to your shared pool:

```
SQL> select n.name, trunc(sum(s.value)/1024) as KB
  2  from v$sesstat s, v$statname n
  3  where n.name in ('session uga memory',
  4                   'session uga memory max')
  5  and s.statistic# = n.statistic#
  6  group by n.name;
NAME                                    KB
------------------------------- ---------
session uga memory                     316
session uga memory max                 499
```

Exercises

1. Where is session information stored when dedicated servers are being used? What about when multithreaded server architecture is being used?
2. What is the session UGA? What views are available to help you find the session UGA?

Tuning the Buffer Cache

In this section, you will cover the following topics related to tuning the buffer cache:

- How Oracle manages the buffer cache
- Calculating the buffer-cache hit ratio
- Assessing the impact of adding or removing buffers
- Creating multiple buffer pools
- Sizing multiple buffer pools
- Monitoring the buffer cache
- Using table caching

The buffer cache consists of memory buffers, each of which is the same size as the `initsid.ora` parameter `DB_BLOCK_SIZE`. This section will discuss how to tune the database buffer cache. You will learn how Oracle manages the buffer cache, how to calculate the buffer-cache hit ratio, and how to assess the impact of adding or removing buffers. You will also learn what Multiple Buffer Pools are, and how to create and size them. Techniques for overall monitoring of the buffer cache will also be presented, along with an explanation of the use of table caching.

How Oracle Manages the Buffer Cache

Information in memory can be accessed faster than data in datafiles on disks. It makes sense from a performance perspective for Oracle to keep as many data blocks stored in memory as it can, without exceeding the amount of physical memory available on the host machine. Hence, Oracle has the database buffer cache. However, simply having the space to store thousands of data blocks isn't enough. Oracle attempts to store the right data blocks—those blocks used most frequently by user processes. Some tuning methodologies suggest that OLTP systems suffer from poor buffer-cache management. Buffer caches are sized too large on those systems, where activity typically consists of a block being loaded into memory for use once or twice. Therefore, it makes sense for you to learn as much about buffer-cache tuning as possible, both for certification and for the real world.

The size of the database buffer cache is determined by the `DB_BLOCK_BUFFERS` initialization parameter. To change the size of the buffer cache, alter the value for this parameter and restart the instance. The size of each buffer depends on the size of blocks in the database, determined by the `DB_BLOCK_SIZE` parameter. Blocks enter the buffer cache by means of server processes acting on behalf of user processes. The DBW0 process writes changed buffers back to disk and eliminates other unnecessary blocks. DBWR writes changed, or "dirty," buffers to disk when one of the three following conditions is TRUE:

- The DBWR time-out occurs (every three seconds)
- A checkpoint occurs
- When a scan of the buffer cache shows that there are no free buffers

When a scan of the buffer cache shows that there are no free buffers, DBWR determines which blocks to eliminate, based on a least-recently-used algorithm (LRU). The LRU is based on the idea that blocks recently accessed are more likely to be used repeatedly than blocks that haven't been accessed in a while. This algorithm is slightly modified to place blocks that have been read into memory by

TABLE ACCESS FULL operations at the end of the LRU list so that full table scans don't disrupt other user processes by eliminating other blocks from the buffer cache.

Exercises

1. What process reads information into the buffer cache? What process writes changed buffers out of the cache? When does this latter action occur?
2. What is the algorithm used to determine how to eliminate buffers from the buffer cache when more room is needed? How has this algorithm been modified?

Calculating the Buffer-Cache Hit Ratio

Having a block required by a user process in the buffer cache is called a *buffer-cache hit*. Hits are good because they reduce the amount of disk I/O required for the user process. To determine buffer-cache hits, the DBA can use the V$SYSSTAT dynamic performance view to calculate the *buffer-cache hit ratio*. The V$SYSSTAT dynamic performance view is available only to users with `select any table` privileges or the SELECT_CATALOG_ROLE role, or to the SYS user. There are three statistics tracked in that performance view that are of use in calculating hit statistics: database block gets, consistent gets, and physical reads.

```
SQL> select name, value
  2  from v$sysstat
  3  where name in ('db block gets',
  4  'consistent gets','physical reads');
NAME                     VALUE
-------------------- ---------
db block gets             1333
consistent gets           9622
physical reads            1948
```

The hit ratio is determined by the total number of instance data requests (the sum of the two "get" statistics) minus physical reads, divided by the total number of instance data requests, multiplied by 100. The formula is as follows:

```
((db block gets + consistent gets - physical reads) / (db block gets + consistent
gets)) * 100
```

Sometimes, you might see it simplified with the formula

```
1- (physical reads/(db_block gets + consistent gets)
```

The following code block identifies a function used to calculate the buffer-cache hit ratio and an anonymous block used to obtain a value from the function. You should generate the function as SYS or as a user with `select any table` granted directly to the user, not via a role:

```
SQL> connect sys/jason
Connected.
SQL> create or replace function calc_bc_hitratio
  2  return number
  3  is
  4   my_blockgets number;
  5   my_consgets  number;
  6   my_physreads number;
  7   my_upper     number;
  8   my_lower     number;
  9  begin
 10   select value
 11   into my_blockgets
 12   from v$sysstat
 13   where name = 'db block gets';
 14   select value
 15   into my_consgets
 16   from v$sysstat
 17   where name = 'consistent gets';
 18   select value
 19   into my_physreads
 20   from v$sysstat
 21   where name = 'physical reads';
 22   my_upper := my_blockgets+my_consgets-my_physreads;
 23   my_lower := my_blockgets+my_consgets;
 24   return (my_upper/my_lower)*100;
 25  end;
 26  /
Function created.
SQL> set serveroutput on
SQL> declare
  2   myhitratio number;
  3  begin
  4   myhitratio := calc_bc_hitratio;
  5   dbms_output.put_line('hit ratio');
  6   dbms_output.put_line('---------');
  7   dbms_output.put_line(to_char(round(myhitratio,2)));
  6  end;
  7  /
hit ratio
---------
82.22
PL/SQL procedure successfully completed.
```

A higher hit ratio according to this formula means the database is accessing a high number of data blocks in memory, performing few physical reads. A low hit ratio means that the database is not storing many blocks in memory that it requires for SQL statements being processed, which requires it to perform many physical reads of data blocks into the buffer cache. The breakdown of value ranges for database buffer-cache hit ratios and their meanings are listed here:

90–100%	Buffer cache is experiencing few physical reads. Current size is optimal, if a bit high. It should be okay to remove buffers from the buffer cache if memory is needed elsewhere.
70–89%	Buffer cache is experiencing a low to moderate number of physical reads required to access data blocks. The DBA may want to resize only if there is a serious problem with memory on the Oracle database.
60–69% or less	Buffer cache is experiencing a moderate to high number of physical reads. The DBA should consider adding more buffers to the database buffer cache to improve the hit ratio.

Exercises

1. Which performance view contains statistics required to calculate the buffer-cache hit ratio? What is the formula for calculating that ratio?
2. What are some appropriate measures to take when the buffer-cache hit ratio falls below 65 percent? What action might a DBA consider if the hit ratio was 96 percent?
3. Name the parameter used to determine the size of the database buffer cache. What would happen if this parameter were sized such that Oracle's memory structures no longer fit into real memory?

Assessing the Impact of Adding or Removing Buffers

If the buffer-cache hit ratio is extremely high or low, or if there is a problem with memory allocation on the database, you may need to resize the buffer cache. In which case you'll need a way to assess the way that adding or subtracting buffers will affect the buffer-cache hit ratio for your database. Such a means of comparison would help you weigh the trade-off of juggling available memory or swallowing the expense of adding real memory to the host machine.

Raising Buffer-Hit Ratio with V$RECENT_BUCKET

Oracle can collect statistics for estimating the performance gain from adding space to the buffer cache in a special performance view called V$RECENT_BUCKET, owned by user SYS. Like other performance views, V$RECENT_BUCKET can be accessed by users with the `select any table` privilege, the SELECT_CATALOG_ROLE role, or by user SYS. Each row in the view V$RECENT_BUCKET shows the relative performance gain of adding one more block to the buffer cache. Setting the `DB_BLOCK_LRU_EXTENDED_STATISTICS` `init`*`sid`*`.ora` parameter to a nonzero value enables collection of V$RECENT_BUCKET statistics from V$SYSSTAT. The number of rows V$RECENT_BUCKET contains will equal the value set for this `init`*`sid`*`.ora` parameter. V$RECENT_BUCKET has one column, called COUNT. This column stores an estimate of cache hits gained by adding buffers to the buffer cache.

```
SQL> select rownum, count
  2  from v$recent_bucket
  3  where ROWNUM < 11;
ROWNUM COUNT
------ -----
     1   314
     2   358
     3   394
     4   505
     5   210
     6    15
     7     4
     8     0
     9     0
    10     1
```

Interpret the output as follows: "buffer #1 adds 314 hits, buffer #2 adds 358 more hits," and so on, not as "1 buffer adds a total of 314 hits, 2 buffers add a total of 358 hits," and so on. Thus, as ROWNUM increases, COUNT also increases, but only to a certain point, after which COUNT decreases again. This is a curious twist on the principle of diminishing marginal utility. There is a threshold after which it doesn't matter how many buffers you add—the hit ratio simply won't increase appreciably.

You can also use that information to determine how many additional hits will occur if you add many buffers:

```
SQL> SELECT SUM(count) additional_hits
  2  FROM V$RECENT_BUCKET
  3  WHERE ROWNUM < 11;
ADDITIONAL_HITS
```

```
---------------
           1801
```

You may also want to consider how these additional hits affect your hit ratio, as well. The formula for doing so is

```
((db block gets + consistent gets - physical reads + additional hits) /
  (db block gets + consistent gets)) * 100
```

You may not have enough memory to add 10 buffers, however. So, instead you'll want to determine the improvement gains according to each level of addition you make. The data in V$RECENT_BUCKET can also be grouped together to provide you with the number of hits that would be the result of adding different ranges of buffers to the buffer cache. The following query demonstrates how the statistics in this view can be better manipulated to make an informed decision about adding buffers to the buffer cache without the stepwise refinement that is inherent in the process previously outlined:

```
SQL> SELECT 3*TRUNC(rownum/3)+1|| '-'||
  2         3*(TRUNC(rownum/3)+1) range,
  3         SUM(count) additional_hits
  4  FROM v$recent_bucket
  5  GROUP BY TRUNC(rownum/3);
RANGE          ADDITIONAL_HITS
-------------- ---------------
1-3                        672
4-6                       1109
7-9                         19
10-12                        1
```

Each row in the output above indicates the increased hits resulting from adding 1–3 buffers, 4–6 buffers, and so on. You can substitute a different number wherever you see 3 in the query to display data according to a different range. Notice in this example that adding 6 buffers gives you a performance gain of 1781 more hits—almost as high as the gain made by adding 10 buffers. Thus, you can add 6 buffers instead of 10 and still get nearly the same result.

Reducing Buffer-Hit Ratio with V$CURRENT_BUCKET

In some cases, you may want to make a memory allocation trade-off. Perhaps the buffer-cache hit ratio is 96 percent, while shared pool hit ratios are too low. If real memory is an issue, you can take some memory away from the buffer cache and allocate it to the shared pool. The V$CURRENT_BUCKET view assists your effort. V$CURRENT_BUCKET has one column, called COUNT, that stores the number of hits gained by each individual buffer already in the buffer cache.

V$CURRENT_BUCKET is populated with statistics from V$SYSSTAT when DB_BLOCK_LRU_STATISTICS is set to TRUE. You should use a range query similar to the one listed previously to interpret the statistics collected in V$CURRENT_BUCKET. The following code block demonstrates this:

```
SQL> SELECT 100*TRUNC(ROWNUM/100)+1|| '-'||
  2  100*(TRUNC(ROWNUM/100)+1) range,
  3    SUM(count) additional_reads
  4  FROM V$CURRENT_BUCKET
  5  WHERE ROWNUM > 0
  6  GROUP BY TRUNC(ROWNUM/100);
RANGE                      ADDITIONAL_READS
-------------------------- ----------------
1-100                                  9646
101-200                                 773
201-300                                 286
301-400                                  77
401-500                                 148
501-600                                  25
```

Based on this example, you can then determine whether it is appropriate to remove buffers. In this case, the first 200 buffers contribute the highest number of hits overall, 10419. All other ranges combined add only 536 more hits. If you need to allocate more space to the shared pool, and overall host-system real memory is an issue, you could eliminate all but the first 200 buffers from your buffer cache. This action adds 536 additional physical reads. Using the V$SYSSTAT statistics from earlier in the section, your resulting buffer cache hit ratio as calculated by the formula

```
((db block gets + consistent gets - physical reads
  - additional physical reads) / (db block gets + consistent gets)) * 100
```

would be 77.32 percent, only about 5 percent lower than the current hit ratio.

Exercises

1. Which view is used to determine the impact of adding more buffers to the buffer cache? Which parameter controls the use of that view?
2. Which view is used to determine the impact of removing buffers from the buffer cache? Which parameter controls the use of that view?
3. You are considering adding buffers to the buffer cache. According to the following information, how many buffers are appropriate to add for the maximum cache-hit increase for the least amount of memory?

```
RANGE     ADDITIONAL_HITS
-------   ---------------
1-50                  506
51-100               1179
101-150               214
151-200                95
```

Creating Multiple Buffer Pools

In Oracle8, the buffer cache has been refined a great deal in order to accommodate the different needs of different user processes accessing different database objects. In prior versions of Oracle, all data blocks requested by user processes were stored for use in the same buffer cache. Objects that persisted in the buffer cache for a long time were stored in the same overall cache as objects that were used and then quickly forgotten. Recall that the buffer cache uses a least-recently-used (LRU) algorithm to determine what buffers to recycle when user processes need to allocate space and the buffer cache is full. Oracle8 takes this functionality even further by introducing the concept of having *multiple* buffer pools for separately storing objects that persist and objects that recycle. By properly allocating objects to appropriate buffer pools, you can reduce or eliminate I/O, isolate an object in the buffer cache, and restrict or limit an object to a part of the cache.

Oracle allows you to configure your buffer cache into multiple buffer pools of three different types. The first type is a *keep pool*. A keep pool is used for storing buffers for database objects you definitely want to have persist in your buffer cache. A later discussion, called "Using Table Caching," explains how to force Oracle to keep blocks from certain tables in the buffer cache. Objects in the keep pool will not be eliminated from memory, meaning that references to objects in the keep pool will not result in a physical read.

The second type is a *recycle pool*. The recycle pool is used for storing buffers for database objects you want Oracle to discard quickly. These might include blocks read in as part of full table scans or blocks read in order to `update` a row, followed quickly by a `commit`.

The final type is the *default pool*. This pool will contain all buffers not explicitly assigned to the keep or recycle pools.

Figure 18-3 illustrates the difference between a buffer cache that does not use multiple buffer pools.

Creating Keep and Recycle Pools from the Default Pool

As you've just learned, Oracle8 makes three buffer pools in the buffer cache for every instance: the keep pool, the recycle pool, and the default pool. The overall buffer cache storage and LRU latch allocation is set at instance startup using the `DB_BLOCK_BUFFERS` and `DB_BLOCK_LRU_LATCHES` `init`*`sid`*`.ora` parameters.

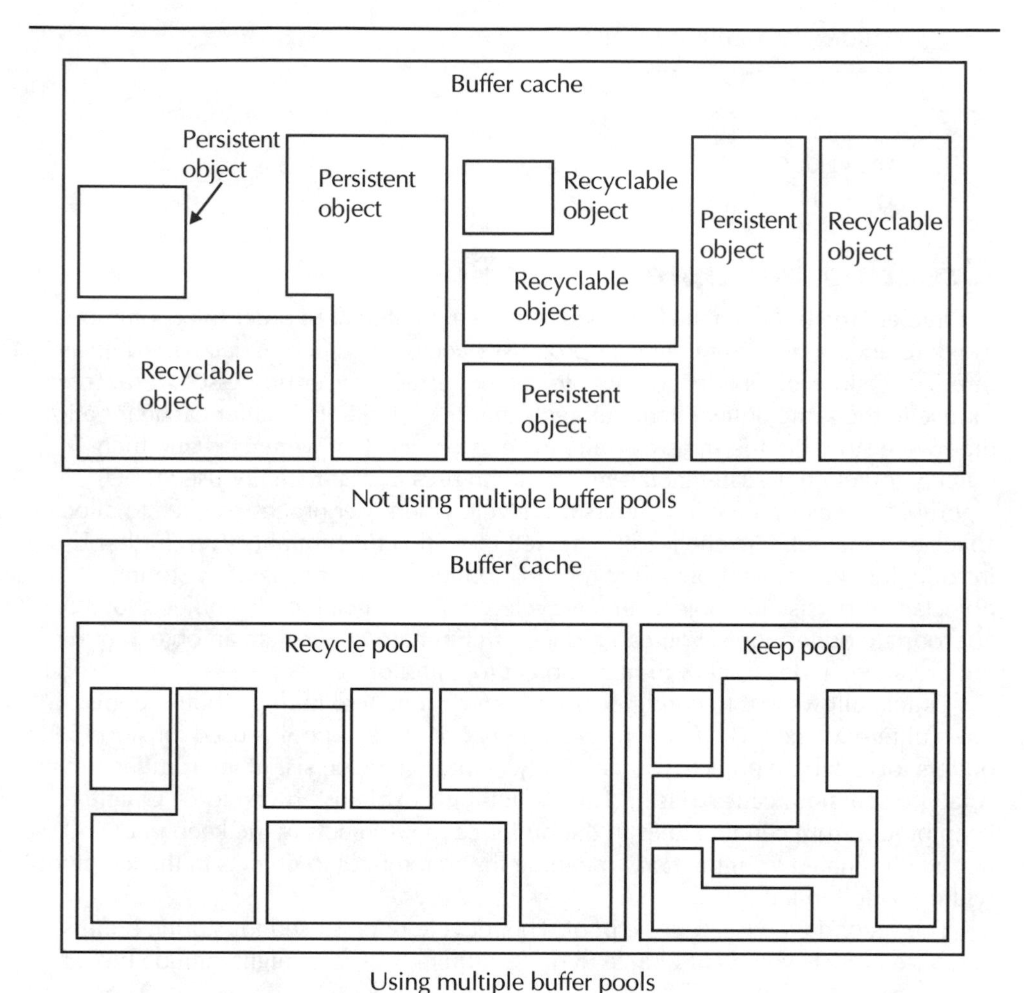

FIGURE 18-3. *Buffer cache and multiple buffer-pool use*

A *latch* is an Oracle internal resource that governs access to other resources. In this case, the LRU latch governs access to load data blocks into the buffer cache by server processes acting on behalf of user processes. The number of latches you can specify for the instance must be proportional to the number of buffers in the buffer cache. There must be at least 50 block buffers for every LRU latch you allocate to your buffer cache. You will learn more about latches later this chapter and in Chapter 20.

The keep and recycle buffer pools are sized from the overall allocation of your buffer cache using the `BUFFER_POOL_KEEP` and `BUFFER_POOL_RECYCLE` parameters. These parameters each accept two elements, `BUFFERS` and `LRU_LATCHES`, to determine the size of the pool and the number of latches dedicated to managing access to the pool, respectively. Your buffer pool configurations cannot exceed the overall buffer cache allocation, and the proportion of block buffers to LRU latches must be 50 to 1 or greater, or else the Oracle instance will not start. The following code block displays an excerpt from the `init`*`sid`*`.ora` file containing assignments for each of these parameters:

```
DB_BLOCK_BUFFERS = 500
DB_BLOCK_LRU_LATCHES = 10
BUFFER_POOL_KEEP = (buffers:100, lru_latches:2)
BUFFER_POOL_RECYCLE = (buffers:250, lru_latches:5)
```

Whatever space is left over from configuring the keep and recycle pools goes to the buffer-cache default pool. Thus, in this example, the default pool has the remaining 150 buffers and 3 LRU latches allocated to the buffer cache overall, while the keep pool has 100 buffers and 2 LRU latches and the recycle pool has 250 buffers and 5 LRU latches.

Assigning Database Objects to Buffer Pools

Your efforts regarding the use of multiple buffer pools doesn't stop there. You must further refine your use of buffer pools by assigning objects to use them in the `storage` clause of the `create` *`object`* and `alter` *`object`* statements, where *`object`* can be any object that accepts the `storage` clause, such as tables, indexes, clusters, and partitions. Since each partition of a partitioned object can have its own storage clause, you can also assign each partition to different buffer pools. The syntax for assigning an object to a buffer pool is `storage (buffer_pool` *`pool`*`)`, where *`pool`* can be set to `keep`, `recycle`, or `default`, depending on which buffer pool you want blocks from this object to be part of. Note that this task only assigns objects to a particular buffer pool by default. You are not actually loading data from those objects into memory by executing this statement. The following code block assigns the EMP table to the keep pool:

```
SQL> alter table emp storage (buffer_pool keep);
Table altered.
SQL> select table_name, buffer_pool
  2  from user_tables
  3  where table_name = 'EMP';
TABLE_NAME                     BUFFER_
------------------------------ -------
EMP                            KEEP
```

TIP

In Oracle8, dictionary views supporting database objects that can be assigned to buffer pools have a column called BUFFER_POOL that indicates the buffer pool in which an object will be stored. The default value for this column is DEFAULT, meaning that the object will be stored in the default pool.

Exercises

1. Explain the concept of multiple buffer pools. Which pools are available in the buffer cache?
2. Which parameters are used to configure the buffer cache's multiple buffer pools? What are the constraints for configuring multiple buffer pools?
3. How do you assign objects to multiple buffer pools? Does this action actually place those objects into the buffer pool? Why or why not?

Sizing Multiple Buffer Pools

Now that you understand the concept of multiple buffer pools and the mechanics of configuring them, you need to understand how to size them according to their different goals. You want to size the keep pool so it is large enough to store all database objects you want kept in memory. You also want to ensure the keep pool is large enough to accommodate growth of the objects it keeps. However, make sure that the keep pool is small enough in the context of the overall buffer cache. If you make your keep pool too large, you may wind up keeping infrequently used objects at the expense of more frequently used objects being unnecessarily eliminated from the default and recycle pools. Similarly, you should size the recycle pool to ensure that objects don't get eliminated from that pool so quickly that Oracle has to perform extra I/O to load, unload, and reload data to memory.

Sizing the Keep Pool

The basic rules for sizing the keep pool are as follows. For each object you plan to store in the keep pool, issue the `analyze` *`object name`* `compute statistics` command, where *`object`* is the type of object you are analyzing, and *`name`* is the name of that object. Then, issue the `alter` *`object name`* `storage (buffer_pool keep)` command to set the object to be stored in the keep pool. Finally, issue a command based on the following example:

```
select sum(BLOCKS) as BUFFERS,
  decode(floor(sum(BLOCKS)/50), 0, 1, floor(sum(BLOCKS)/50))
  as LRU_LATCHES from dictionary_view
  where BUFFER_POOL = 'KEEP'
```

In this code block, `dictionary_view` is the dictionary view containing a listing of the objects being kept in the keep pool, and 50 is the minimum number of buffers an LRU latch is designed to handle. Of course, an LRU latch can handle more than that, so this formula is actually telling you the maximum number of latches you need for the pool. You may need to run this statement several times using different dictionary views in order to get the block allocations for all types of objects being kept.

The following statement illustrates the preceding example in action on the USER_TABLES view containing table EMP, which is to be housed in the keep pool:

```
SQL> select sum(blocks) as buffers,
  2  decode(floor(sum(blocks)/50),0,1,floor(sum(blocks)/50))
  3  as lru_latches   4  from user_tables
  5  where buffer_pool = 'KEEP';
  BUFFERS LRU_LATCHES
--------- -----------
        1           1
```

TIP
While 50 buffers is the lowest limit for a latch to handle, a latch can handle many more buffers.

The keep pool will reduce the physical reads associated with use of the objects in this pool but will not eliminate them entirely. Remember, the object will need to be read into memory initially before Oracle will keep it there. Thus, you may find that buffer-cache hit ratios in the keep pool approach, but do not achieve, 100 percent. Also, if an object grows in size, then it may no longer fit in the keep buffer pool. In this case, you will begin to lose blocks out of the cache.

TIP
You can determine hit ratios for objects in your buffer pools using the performance view V$BUFFER_POOL_STATISTICS. This view is created when you run the `catperf.sql` *script found in the* `rdbms/admin` *directory under your Oracle software home directory.*

Sizing the Recycle Pool

Sizing the recycle pool is done through stepwise refinement. TKPROF and SQL Trace can be used to help determine the size of the recycle pool. First, perform the appropriate statement to assign objects to the recycle pool. Then run SQL statements on those objects that your application would typically run, with SQL Trace enabled for the session. Process the trace file through TKPROF and open the output file. Look at the total number of data blocks physically read from disk, which is the DISK column in the TKPROF output file. Then repeat this entire process, only this time, don't assign the object to the recycle pool. Rerun SQL Trace and TKPROF as necessary. Compare the number in the DISK column for the second run to the value in that same column when SQL Trace and TKPROF are run on the same statement when the object is not assigned to the recycle pool for the first run. If the first run (with the object in the recycle pool) produced a higher number, you should decrease the size chosen for your recycle pool, because Oracle is eliminating and reloading buffers before the SQL statement has a chance to finish.

Exercises

1. What actions are involved in sizing the keep pool? What about for sizing the recycle pool?
2. What considerations should you evaluate when sizing the keep pool? What about when sizing the recycle pool?

Monitoring the Buffer Cache

The best indicator of buffer-cache performance is the buffer cache hit ratio. Determining the buffer-cache hit ratio depends on the proper use of the performance view V$SYSSTAT. The main statistics to refer to on this view are the db block gets, consistent gets, and physical reads. The DBA needs to remember that the buffer-cache hit ratio will *never* be 100. Even if your host machine has gigabytes of memory allocation, or more, there will probably still be far more space available on disk. You can also ensure your buffer-cache monitoring by using the performance view V$BUFFER_POOL_STATISTICS. You can use this view to calculate buffer-cache hit ratios for your multiple buffer pools. Oracle Enterprise Manager Tuning Pack can be used in monitoring the buffer cache to ensure that hit ratios fall within appropriate boundaries. You can configure Intelligent Agent to signal buffer-cache events to the event window of the Enterprise Manager console. You can configure Oracle Trace to assist with buffer-cache monitoring, as well.

Exercises

1. Identify views that are used in monitoring the buffer cache.

2. Identify components of Enterprise Manager used in monitoring the buffer cache.

Using Table Caching

You can use table caching to prevent the table from being eliminated from the buffer cache. This is essentially the same thing as assigning the table to the keep pool, except that by caching the table, you can store it in either the recycle or default pool. Oracle will not store a cached table in the keep pool unless you assign that object to the keep pool in addition to caching it. When Oracle performs a `TABLE ACCESS FULL` operation, the blocks loaded into memory as part of the full table scan are placed at the end of the LRU list and eliminated almost immediately. However, if you issue the `alter table` *`tablename`* `cache` statement, Oracle keeps these blocks in memory for as long as it would keep any other block loaded into the buffer cache.

As when assigning a table to the keep pool, you do not actually load the table data into memory when you issue the `alter table cache` statement. You must reference the table in a query or DML operation for the data actually to be cached. Keep in mind that it is not appropriate to cache tables with large numbers of rows, and if you plan to cache a table, you should assign it to the keep pool in order to leave space available in other pools for objects that may be loaded and then eliminated.

Exercises

1. What is table caching? When might it be appropriate to cache a table?
2. What statement can be used to set up table caching? After issuing this statement, is the table cached in memory? Explain.

Tuning Redo Mechanisms

In this section, you will cover the following topics related to tuning redo mechanisms:

- Determining contention for the redo log buffer
- Sizing the redo log buffer
- Reducing redo operations

Every SQL change operation on the database requires the online redo-log resource in order to complete its transaction. The pressure on availability for the online redo log is in direct proportion to the number of users making changes to the database at any given time. Contention for redo-log resources is particularly detrimental to the system as a whole because of the heavy dependence every process has on redo logs. This section will introduce you to determining whether contention exists for the redo log buffer. You will also learn how to size the redo log buffer. Finally, you will learn how to reduce redo-log operations as a way to reduce contention or the buffer.

Determining Contention for the Redo Log Buffer

Every user process making changes in the database must write redo information to the redo log buffer. In order to write that redo information, the user process must acquire the redo allocation latch. There is only one redo allocation latch in Oracle, so you might imagine that there is a potential for bottlenecks when it comes to writing redo, particularly during periods of high transaction activity. (You will learn more about latches in Chapter 20.)

The LGWR process writes information from the redo log buffer to online redo logs constantly. If the redo log buffer fills before LGWR has a chance to clear the buffer, then user processes will have to wait for space in the redo log buffer. When the active log file is full and Oracle is waiting for disk space to be allocated for the redo-log entries, more redo space is created by performing a log switch. Small log files in relation to the size of the SGA or the commit rate of the workload can cause problems. When the log switch occurs, Oracle must ensure that all committed dirty buffers are written to disk before switching to a new log file. If you have a large SGA full of dirty buffers and small redo log files, a log switch must wait for DBWR to write dirty buffers to disk before continuing.

The REDO BUFFER ALLOCATION RETRIES statistic reflects the number of times a user process waits for space in the redo log buffer. This statistic is available through the dynamic performance table V$SYSSTAT.

```
SQL> SELECT name, value
  2  FROM v$sysstat
  3* WHERE name = 'redo buffer allocation retries'
NAME                                        VALUE
------------------------------------ ---------
redo buffer allocation retries                  0
```

The value of REDO BUFFER ALLOCATION RETRIES should be near 0. If this value increments consistently, it means that processes have had to wait for space in the buffer. The wait may be caused by the log buffer being too small or because checkpoints or log switches occur too frequently. Increase the size of the redo log buffer, if necessary, by changing the value of the initialization parameter `LOG_BUFFER`. The value of this parameter, expressed in bytes, must be a multiple of `DB_BLOCK_SIZE`. This will also cause the ARCH process to run less frequently, because there will be fewer log switches. You may also want to reduce the number of checkpoints by changing the LOG_CHECKPOINT_INTERVAL and LOG_CHECKPOINT_TIMEOUT init*sid*.ora parameters.

Exercises

1. When is data written from the redo log buffer to the online redo log? What happens if the redo log buffer is full?
2. Which dynamic performance view is used to detect whether processes are waiting for space in the redo log buffer? How can that view be queried?

Sizing the Redo Log Buffer

The size of the redo log buffer is assigned at instance startup by the LOG_BUFFER init*sid*.ora parameter. The value specified is interpreted by Oracle in bytes, and must be a multiple of DB_BLOCK_SIZE. As with any increase in the size of a portion of memory, care should be taken in order to avoid sizing the SGA out of real memory. If the SGA uses any virtual memory at all, the system can take a major performance dive as Oracle attempts to page blocks into memory and onto swap disk space while it attempts to update blocks. The result is that the database will spend a great deal of time "thrashing" data between memory and swap space, creating a major performance problem.

Exercise

Which parameter is used to change the size of the redo log buffer?

Reducing Redo Operations

As discussed earlier, access to write redo to the redo log buffer is governed by the *redo allocation latch*. The user process must first obtain this latch to write redo in the buffer. There is only one redo allocation latch in the Oracle instance. This design choice was made to ensure sequential database redo for database recovery. After obtaining the latch, the user process updates the redo log buffer. The amount of space a user process is allowed to write in the redo log buffer is determined in bytes by the LOG_SMALL_ENTRY_MAX_SIZE init*sid*.ora parameter. If the user process attempts to write more redo than is permitted by this parameter, the user process must acquire another latch called the *redo copy latch* to finish writing the redo entry.

Since there is only one redo allocation latch on the database, to avoid contention problems you should configure Oracle to minimize the time a user process can hold this latch by setting the value for LOG_SMALL_ENTRY_MAX_SIZE as small as possible. You can also reduce the time each user spends writing redo log information while it holds the redo allocation latch by setting LOG_ENTRY_PREBUILD_THRESHOLD to a value greater than zero. This setting forces user processes to build their redo-log entries before attempting to acquire the redo allocation latch, if the size of their redo entry in bytes is greater than LOG_ENTRY_PREBUILD_THRESHOLD.

TIP
Consider setting the LOG_SMALL_ENTRY_MAX_SIZE to be the same value as the one you set for LOG_ENTRY_PREBUILD_THRESHOLD. That way, user processes will have to prebuild redo entries they want to copy to the redo log buffer on the redo allocation latch. Otherwise they will have to acquire the redo copy latch, as well.

Exercises

1. How many redo allocation latches are available on the Oracle database?
2. Which parameter determines how long a process will hold onto the redo allocation latch?
3. How can the amount of time that each process holds the redo allocation latch be changed?

Chapter Summary

The contents of this chapter cover the tuning of operating system and memory structures in the Oracle database. This discussion covers aspects of performance tuning for your host system, the shared pool, the redo log buffer, and the buffer cache. These topics are important ones on OCP Exam 4, so care should be taken to review the material and answer the questions. This chapter covers 20 percent of the material on OCP Exam 4.

The first topic you covered was generic operating-system tuning. You learned about the primary steps for tuning the host machine, along with the similarities between host-system tuning and Oracle tuning. The difference between a process in Oracle running on Unix and a thread in the oracle80.exe process running on Windows was discussed, as well. Finally, you learned about paging and swapping, and why it is important to configure your machine so the Oracle SGA always resides in real memory.

The next topic you studied in this chapter was tuning the shared pool. This is probably the most important memory resource in Oracle, so ensuring that it is properly tuned is very important. You learned how to tune the dictionary cache and the library cache, and the special challenges of tuning each of these important areas in shared memory. You also learned about measuring hit percentages or hit ratios for the different areas of your shared pool. The `init`*`sid`*`.ora` parameters available for sizing the shared pool and the techniques used to determine appropriate values for those parameters were covered, as well. Finally, you learned how to pin objects in the shared pool, how to tune reserved space in the shared pool, and how to determine the size of the User Global Area (UGA) when multithreaded server (MTS) is being used, thus meaning that UGA information is stored in the shared pool.

The next section covered how to tune the buffer cache. You learned that Oracle manages access to the buffer cache using LRU latches. The performance of the buffer cache is measured by the buffer-cache hit ratio, and you learned how to measure that statistic using statistics from the V$SYSSTAT performance view. The impact of adding and removing buffers was also covered, along with using the appropriate `init`*`sid`*`.ora` parameters identified in the text and the dynamic performance views V$RECENT_BUCKET and V$CURRENT_BUCKET. You also covered a new feature of the Oracle8 buffer cache: multiple buffer pools. You learned about the keep pool and the recycle pool, and the `init`*`sid`*`.ora` parameters used for configuring those pools. The techniques for sizing those two areas in memory were covered, as well. Finally, you learned how to use table caching appropriately.

The last section of this chapter briefly covered how to size the redo log buffer. Access to the redo log buffer via the redo allocation latch was explained. The statistics available in the V$SYSSTAT view used for determining whether user processes were waiting for space in the redo log buffer were covered. You also learned how to decide whether to increase the size allocation for the redo log buffer. Finally, the text covered how you can configure Oracle to reduce redo operation by reducing the amount of time a process can hold the redo allocation latch. Reducing the maximum size for redo log buffer entries that can be made while holding the redo allocation latch was covered, along with the `init`*`sid`*`.ora` parameters you need to set in either case. Setting the redo log buffer entry's prebuild threshold so that user processes assemble their redo log entries before acquiring the redo allocation latch was also explained.

Two-Minute Drill

- Oracle performance often depends on the capabilities of the host machine.
- You tune your host machine in three areas: memory configuration, I/O, and process scheduling.

- Memory tuning consists of ensuring that the Oracle SGA always resides in real memory.
- I/O configuration consists of enabling I/O cache write-through on the operating system or hardware level, using I/O devices with rapid read/write capability, such as fast disk spindles or solid-state disk media, and using hardware mirroring instead of striping for Oracle resources, particularly redo logs.
- Process-schedule tuning means that all Oracle processes should have the same priority at the OS level so that no Oracle process gets less or more attention from the CPU scheduler than another.
- A process is a program currently executing on a machine that handles a defined task. CKPT, LGWR, and other background operations are handled as processes in Unix.
- In Windows, all these operations are handled in one process called `oracle80.exe`. Each individual operation is handled as a thread within that process.
- Many machines that run Oracle support both real and virtual memory. Real memory is directly accessible by a process or thread at any given time, while virtual memory is an area or file on disk storing information that hasn't been used by an executing process in a while.
- Oracle SGA consists of three parts: the shared pool, the redo log buffer, and the buffer cache.
- The shared pool contains the dictionary (row) cache and the library cache.
- The dictionary cache stores row data from the Oracle data dictionary in memory to improve performance when users select dictionary information.
- Performance on the dictionary cache is measured by the hit ratio calculated from data in the V$ROWCACHE view, using the formula `SUM(GETS - GETMISSES) / SUM(GETS) * 100`. Be sure you understand what each of the referenced columns means in the V$ROWCACHE view.
- Row-cache hit ratio should be 99 percent or more, or else there could be a performance problem on the database. This ratio is improved by increasing the `SHARED_POOL_SIZE` init*sid*.ora parameter.
- The library cache stores parse information for SQL statements executing in the Oracle database for sharing purposes.
- Library cache performance is measured by the library-cache hit ratio, calculated from data in the V$LIBRARYCACHE view using the formula

SUM(PINS - RELOADS) / SUM(PINS) * 100. Be sure you understand what each of the referenced columns means in the V$LIBRARYCACHE view.

- The library-cache hit ratio should be 99 percent or more, or else a performance problem may exist on the database. This ratio is improved by increasing the SHARED_POOL_SIZE parameter, using more identical SQL queries in the database, or pinning objects in the shared pool.
- The size of your buffer cache is configured in Oracle using the DB_BLOCK_BUFFERS parameter.
- Access to the buffer cache is managed by LRU latches. Set the number of latches managing the buffer cache with the DB_BLOCK_LRU_LATCHES parameter so that the ratio of buffers to latches is 50 to 1 or greater.
- Performance on the buffer cache is measured by the buffer-cache hit ratio, calculated from the statistics in the VALUE column of the V$SYSSTAT view where NAME is db block gets, consistent gets, and physical reads.
- Buffer cache hit ratio is calculated as (db block gets + consistent gets - physical reads) / (db block gets + consistent gets) * 100. The result should be at least 70 percent for effective database performance.
- You can assess the impact of adding buffers to the buffer cache using the V$RECENT_BUCKET view. Statistics will be collected in this view from the V$SYSSTAT view if the DB_BLOCK_LRU_EXTENDED_STATISTICS parameter is greater than 0.
- You can assess the impact of removing buffers from the buffer cache by using the V$CURRENT_BUCKET view. Statistics will be collected in this view from the V$SYSSTAT view if the DB_BLOCK_EXTENDED_STATISTICS parameter is set to TRUE.
- Oracle8 allows you to configure your buffer cache to have multiple buffer pools. A keep pool contains object blocks you want to persist in memory, a recycle pool contains object blocks you want eliminated from memory as quickly as possible.
- Multiple buffer pools are configured using init*sid*.ora parameters, allocating their space and dedicated latches from the overall totals set for the buffer cache:
  - BUFFER_POOL_KEEP configures the keep pool. You set it as follows: BUFFER_POOL_KEEP = (buffers:*n*, lru_latches:*n*).

- BUFFER_POOL_RECYCLE configures the recycle pool. You set it as follows: BUFFER_POOL_RECYCLE = (buffers:*n*, lru_latches:*n*).
- The total allocation for buffers and latches in both pools cannot exceed the overall allocation for space and latches for the buffer cache. All space left over in the buffer cache configuration goes to the default pool.

- Table caching is done using the alter table *name* cache statement.
- Blocks are stored in either pool depending on which one you assign the block to be stored in by using the alter *object name* storage (buffer_pool *pool*) command, where *object* is the type of object that permits a storage clause, such as table, index, cluster, or partition. The *name* variable indicates the name of the object you are assigning to one of the buffer pools, and *pool* is the name of the pool you want to assign the object to (keep, recycle, or default).
- The redo log buffer stores redo entries in memory until LGWR can write them to disk.
- If the redo log buffer fills with redo information faster than LGWR can write it to online redo logs, user processes will have to wait for space to write redo to the redo log buffer.
- You can identify whether user processes are waiting for redo log buffer space by using the V$SYSSTAT view. Select the VALUE column where the NAME column is redo space allocation retries, and if this statistic is not 0 and it increases regularly, increase the size of the redo log buffer using the LOG_BUFFER parameter.
- If the value for redo log space requests is not near zero, the DBA should increase the redo log buffer cache by 3–5 percent, until redo log space requests are near zero. The redo log buffer-cache size is determined by the parameter LOG_BUFFERS.
- There is only one redo allocation latch in your database, and it must be acquired by a user process so that process can write to the redo log buffer. You can reduce contention for the redo allocation latch by decreasing the setting for LOG_SMALL_ENTRY_MAX_SIZE to a smaller value.
- You can also set LOG_ENTRY_PREBUILD_THRESHOLD equal to LOG_SMALL_ENTRY_MAX_SIZE to ensure that all processes prebuild their redo-log entries before attempting to acquire the redo allocation latch.

Chapter Questions

1. **The database is experiencing problems with performance. A query against the appropriate view determines that users are waiting for space in the redo buffer in memory. To alleviate this problem, which of the following initialization parameters would you change?**

   A. DB_BLOCK_LRU_LATCHES

   B. LOG_SMALL_ENTRY_MAX_SIZE

   C. DB_BLOCK_BUFFERS

   D. DB_BLOCK_LRU_EXTENDED_STATISTICS

2. **You are considering an increase to the number of buffers in the buffer cache. Which of the following views will contain appropriate statistics for determining the right number of buffers to add, if any?**

   A. V$SYSSTAT

   B. V$RECENT_BUCKET

   C. V$CURRENT_BUCKET

   D. V$BUFFER_POOL_STATISTICS

3. **The DBA is about to begin performance tuning. Queries on the appropriate view indicate that the problem has to do with memory allocation. Which of the following items will she most likely not tune?**

   A. I/O file-system or hardware-cache usage

   B. Library cache pin and reload usage

   C. Row cache gets and getmisses usage

   D. Buffer cache multiple buffer-pool usage

4. **An application has experienced poor performance due to frequent reloads over the past several months. To address the problem, the DBA is considering the following approaches. Which of these approaches should the DBA discard immediately?**

   A. Adopting standards for uniform SQL-statement development

   B. Increase the value set for SHARED_POOL_SIZE

   C. Increase the value set for DB_BLOCK_BUFFERS

   D. Set CURSOR_SPACE_FOR_TIME to FALSE

5. **You are developing a script that automates the calculation of all actual-hit statistics for your database. Which two of the following views would not be referenced at all in that script? (Choose two)**

   A. V$LIBRARYCACHE

   B. V$ROWCACHE

   C. V$RECENT_BUCKET

   D. V$SYSSTAT

   E. V$BUFFER_POOL_STATISTICS

   F. V$LATCH

6. **You are developing an administrative script to assist in pinning an object in the shared pool that Oracle is currently unable to load into shared memory. Which of the following statements should not be used in that script?**

   A. `shutdown immediate`

   B. `DBMS_SHARED_POOL.keep( )`

   C. `DBMS_SHARED_POOL.sizes( )`

   D. `shutdown abort`

   E. `startup open`

   F. `alter system flush shared_pool;`

7. **You have just issued a query on the V$CURRENT_BUCKET view. Which of the following activities are you most likely engaged in?**

   A. Increasing the size of the buffer cache

   B. Increasing the size of the shared pool

   C. Tuning file system I/O

   D. Adding real memory to your host machine

   E. Porting to Parallel Server

8. **By setting the `LOG_SMALL_ENTRY_MAX_SIZE` to the same value as you have set for the `LOG_ENTRY_PREBUILD_THRESHOLD` parameter, which of the following things will most likely happen?**

   A. Buffer-cache hit ratio will decrease

   B. User processes will wait less time for log-buffer space

C. Paging and swapping will increase

D. Oracle will crash

E. You will increase the number of redo allocation latches

F. Buffer-cache hit ratio will increase

9. **In order to improve the hit ratio on your library cache, you will want to configure Oracle in such a way that which of the following statistics decreases?**

A. reloads

B. physical reads

C. gets

D. getmisses

E. consistent gets

F. pins

G. db block gets

10. **You have decided that, to improve performance on your database, you must keep a small lookup table called LOOKUP_VALUES in memory. Which of the following statements will cause Oracle to load data from that table into memory?**

A. `alter table LOOKUP_VALUES cache;`

B. `alter table LOOKUP_VALUES storage (buffer_pool keep);`

C. `select * from LOOKUP_VALUES;`

D. `alter table LOOKUP_VALUES storage (buffer_pool recycle);`

11. **After configuring MTS, the DBA notices a severe decline in the hit ratios of both the dictionary and the library cache. Assuming no other `init`*`sid`*`.ora` changes were made, which of the following may be the cause?**

A. The SGA has been sized out of real memory.

B. There are not enough LRU latches active on the system.

C. The shared server processes have been given a lower priority than LGWR.

D. Session information is now being stored in the shared pool.

E. The value for LOG_BUFFER is set too low.

12. The DBA is evaluating an increase in the size of the buffer cache. Statistics returned from the appropriate view show the following information:

```
RANGE      HITS
---------------------------
1-100      45039
101-200    9002
201-300    901
301-400    602
401-500    120
```

Based on this information, which of the following choices identifies the best number of buffers to add to the buffer cache?

A. 100

B. 200

C. 300

D. 400

E. 500

13. You have assigned three tables to the keep pool. How should you determine the appropriate size for the keep pool?

A. Based on the size of your shared pool

B. Based on the number of blocks in the table only

C. Based on the number of blocks in the table plus blocks in associated indexes

D. Based on the number of blocks in associated indexes only

E. None of the above

14. You test an application's SQL statements in a session using TKPROF and find that the total blocks read from disk is 40,394. You then assign the tables referenced by this application to the recycle pool. When rerunning TKPROF, you find that your total blocks read from disk is now 50,345. How should you tune your database? (Choose two)

A. Increase your keep pool

B. Increase your buffer cache

C. Decrease your recycle pool

D. Assign the tables referenced by the application to the default pool

E. Increase your library cache

F. Issue the `analyze table compute statistics` command

Answers to Chapter Questions

1. B. LOG_SMALL_ENTRY_MAX_SIZE

Explanation LOG_SMALL_ENTRY_MAX_SIZE is the only parameter that affects the redo log buffer. It reduces the size of redo-log entry that user processes are allowed to write when they acquire the redo allocation latch. DB_BLOCK_LRU_EXTENDED_STATISTICS is used as part of sizing the buffer cache and is wrong, while DB_BLOCK_BUFFERS actually determines the size of that cache and is wrong. DB_BLOCK_LRU_LATCHES determines how many LRU latches are available for access to the buffer cache and is wrong.

2. B. V$RECENT_BUCKET

Explanation If you are trying to determine the appropriate increase of buffers to the buffer cache, you should enable the V$RECENT_BUCKET view. Although the statistics put into that view come from V$SYSSTAT, it is difficult to extrapolate the appropriate statistics yourself. V$CURRENT_BUCKET is incorrect because this view helps to determine whether to decrease the size of the buffer cache, not increase it. Finally, the V$BUFFER_POOL_STATISTICS view is used to determine multiple buffer-pool hit ratios, and should be discarded mainly for the same reason as V$SYSSTAT.

3. A. I/O file-system or hardware-cache usage

Explanation If the problem has to do with memory allocation, then tuning I/O won't help, thus making the choice identifying I/O file-system or hardware-cache usage your answer. All other choices identify methods for tuning memory, which would address the need identified in the question.

4. C. Increase the value set for DB_BLOCK_BUFFERS

Explanation Reload statistics are a measurement of the shared pool's size, while DB_BLOCK_BUFFERS is designed to affect the buffer cache. If too many reloads occur, your shared pool may be too small or else execution plans in the shared pool are not being retained long enough. You can improve reload statistics by increasing the size of your shared pool, setting CURSOR_SPACE_FOR_TIME to TRUE, or adopting standards for SQL-statement development, allowing Oracle to reuse more execution plans.

5. C *and* F. V$RECENT_BUCKET *and* V$LATCH

Explanation You must generate current- and actual-hit ratios in the script. These statistics don't come from V$RECENT_BUCKET or V$LATCH. Recall that shared-pool hit ratios are calculated from V$LIBRARYCACHE and V$ROWCACHE views, while buffer-cache hit ratios can be calculated from both V$SYSSTAT and V$BUFFER_POOL_STATISTICS views.

6. D. `shutdown abort`

Explanation You never want to abort database operation unless there has been a media failure on your host system. You can both determine which objects are in the shared pool and pin an object in that pool using the functions identified as choices from the DBMS_SHARED_POOL package. Now, because Oracle is currently unable to load the object into shared memory, you need to either flush the shared pool using the statement `alter system flush shared_pool` or `shutdown` (using any shutdown option besides shutdown abort to save time) and restart the database.

7. B. Increasing the size of the shared pool

Explanation Given that V$CURRENT_BUCKET is used to estimate the effects of reducing the size of the buffer cache, not increasing it, you are probably trying to determine how to decrease the size of the buffer cache in order to allocate space to another area of the SGA. You wouldn't be tuning I/O, because I/O-tuning improvements are not made by resizing SGA. Nor is it likely that you are adding real memory, for if you were, you might consider an increase to the buffer cache instead. Finally, there is no information indicating that you are porting to Parallel Server in this situation.

8. B. User processes will wait less time for log-buffer space

Explanation Setting these two log-buffer management parameters to the same value will most likely affect the amount of time user processes wait for space in that buffer. Choices A and F refer to the buffer cache, an area of memory not affected by these parameters, so these choices are wrong. These parameters do not, in fact, resize any areas of the SGA, so there shouldn't be any effect on paging and swapping, nor will Oracle crash, eliminating those choices. The number of redo allocation latches is fixed at 1, making that choice also incorrect.

9. A. reloads

Explanation By decreasing reloads, you will improve the overall hit ratio and performance on your library cache. Although pins is also a measurement of the library cache, simply increasing pins won't necessarily improve or worsen the overall hit ratio for the library cache. Physical reads, consistent gets, and db block gets are all measurements of buffer-cache performance. Gets and getmisses are measurements of the dictionary-cache hit ratio and performance.

10. C. `select * from LOOKUP_VALUES;`

Explanation Buffers are only loaded into the buffer cache when users `select` data from objects, not when DDL statements, such as `alter table`, are made. Although choices B and D both enable Oracle to place the LOOKUP_VALUES table into different multiple buffer pools, these statements don't actually cause Oracle to do so at the time the alter table statement is issued. The same condition applies to `alter table LOOKUP_VALUES cache`, even though issuing that statement forces Oracle to make blocks from that table persist in the buffer cache.

11. D. Session information is now being stored in the shared pool.

Explanation When the multithreaded server architecture is used, Oracle keeps session UGA information in the shared pool, which decreases the amount of space available for other items, such as the library and dictionary cache. Thus, you have a loss of performance. Since no other init*sid*.ora parameters have changed, there is no basis for the SGA being sized out of real memory. Also, you don't really have enough information to judge whether CPU scheduling is the real issue. Finally, the problem lies in the shared pool, not the buffer cache or redo log buffer, making choices that refer to those other SGA components incorrect.

12. B. 200

Explanation It would not be wise to add more than 200 buffers to the buffer cache because with that number you will enjoy 54,041 more hits in your buffer cache. In contrast, only 1,623 more hits are added by adding 300–500 buffers, or about a 3 percent improvement over adding the first 200 buffers. You would see better value by simply adding the 200 buffers and making the rest of the real memory available to some other SGA resource, such as the shared pool. Thus, choice B is the correct answer.

13. C. Based on the number of blocks in the table plus blocks in associated indexes

Explanation When sizing the keep pool, ensure that there is enough room for the entire table plus all associated indexes. If one or the other are omitted, you may size the keep pool too small and lose blocks, resulting in I/O operations later to read either table or index data back into memory. You wouldn't base the size of the keep pool on anything from your shared pool.

14. C *and* D. Decrease your recycle pool, *and* assign the tables referenced by the application to the default pool

Explanation Use of the recycle pool in this situation actually increases disk-read activities, thereby worsening performance, because buffers are being eliminated before SQL statements or transactions complete. Thus, you should assign the tables referenced back to the default pool where they won't be eliminated, and you should decrease the size of your recycle pool.

CHAPTER 19

Tuning Disk Utilization

n this chapter, you will learn about and demonstrate knowledge in the following areas:

- Database configuration and I/O issues
- Tuning Oracle block usage
- Tuning rollback segments

Oracle uses background processes and memory areas for moving data from memory to disk to reduce user dependence on disk I/O. This configuration frees user processes from being bound by I/O constraints on all but the most transaction-intensive OLTP systems with large numbers of users. This chapter will focus on several areas of Oracle disk-usage tuning, including database configuration, Oracle block usage, and tuning rollback segments. These areas comprise 25 percent of the material tested by OCP Exam 4.

Database Configuration and I/O Issues

In this section, you will cover the following areas of database configuration:

- Identifying inappropriate use of different tablespaces
- Detecting I/O problems
- Distributing files to reduce I/O contention
- Using striping where appropriate
- Tuning checkpoints
- Tuning background-process I/O

The foundation of a well-tuned database is a well-configured database. Since many performance issues stem from improper configuration, this section is designed to explain Oracle's recommendations on database configuration. The OCP examination for performance tuning also focuses on this area.

Good database configuration starts with the effective use of the tablespaces that are part of the instance, so you will learn how to detect inappropriate use of different tablespaces in Oracle. After that, you will learn how to detect I/O problems that may occur on Oracle. You will learn some basic file-distribution strategies to reduce contention, as well. The topic of striping will be defined and described, along with how to tune checkpoints. Finally, you will learn how to tune background-process I/O for maximum performance.

Identifying Inappropriate Use of Different Tablespaces

A typical database might have five basic categories of tablespaces in use to store its objects: SYSTEM, ROLLBACK, DATA, INDEX, and TEMP. Actual tablespaces must be created by the DBA before they are available for use.

The SYSTEM tablespace is created when you issue the `create database` statement. It contains SYS-owned database objects that are vital to the Oracle instance, such as the data dictionary and the SYSTEM rollback segment. The SYSTEM tablespace should not be used for storing database objects owned by users other than SYS. As soon as other objects are placed in the SYSTEM tablespace, there can be problems. For example, a frequently used table in the SYSTEM tablespace could cause I/O contention every time users access the data dictionary and that table simultaneously. After detecting the problem, you could then use the `create table as select` and `rename` commands to correct it. The following code block illustrates a simple way of detecting user objects placed in the SYSTEM tablespace:

```
SQL> select owner, segment_name, segment_type
  2  from dba_segments where owner <> 'SYS'
  3  and tablespace_name = 'SYSTEM';
OWNER   SEGMENT_NAME SEGMENT_TYPE
------- ------------ ------------
JASON   EMP          TABLE
JASON   PK_EMP_01    INDEX
```

Next, consider the ROLLBACK tablespace. ROLLBACK is short for *rollback segment*. As discussed in Unit II, rollback segments contain changed and original versions of data from uncommitted transactions. Since rollback segments frequently acquire and relinquish additional extents, they have a tendency to fragment a tablespace. They can be disruptive to other objects in the tablespace, such as tables and indexes, which also require contiguous blocks of free space for extents. Placing rollback segments in their own tablespace can alleviate some of the disruptions they create for other objects. You should also remember that you cannot take the ROLLBACK tablespace offline if there are active rollback segments in the tablespace. You can use the following statement to detect user objects in the ROLLBACK tablespace:

```
SQL> select owner, segment_name, segment_type
  2  from DBA_SEGMENTS
```

```
  3  where tablespace_name = 'ROLLBACK'
  4  and segment_type <> 'ROLLBACK';
OWNER   SEGMENT_NAME   SEGMENT_TYPE
------- -------------- ------------
JASON   PRODUCTS       TABLE
JASON   PK_PRODUCTS_01 INDEX
```

Two other important types of tablespaces are the DATA and INDEX tablespaces. The DATA tablespace can be used to store table data. Typically, the DBA creates several different DATA tablespaces, each containing database tables. If the database contains objects supporting multiple applications, the database tables for each of those applications may be placed in different tablespaces. The INDEX tablespace contains indexes that correspond to the tables stored in the DATA tablespaces. There are benefits to having separate tablespaces for data objects and indexes. Separate DATA and INDEX tablespaces on different disks can speed retrieval of information. You can use the following queries to detect where your indexes are in DATA tablespaces, and vice-versa:

```
SQL> select owner, segment_name, segment_type
  2  from DBA_SEGMENTS
  3  where tablespace_name = 'DATA1'
  4  and segment_type <> 'TABLE';
OWNER   SEGMENT_NAME   SEGMENT_TYPE
------- -------------- ------------
JASON   PK_TEST_01     INDEX
SQL> select owner, segment_name, segment_type
  2  from DBA_SEGMENTS
  3  where tablespace_name = 'INDEX'
  4  and segment_type <> 'INDEX';
OWNER   SEGMENT_NAME   SEGMENT_TYPE
------- -------------- ------------
JASON   TEST           TABLE
```

The final tablespace considered here is the TEMPORARY tablespace. This tablespace is used for temporary storage of sort information being manipulated by a user process. A user process trying to manage a large sort or a `select` statement containing the `order by` clause might utilize temporary storage. Since this type of data is very dynamic, the DBA is again confronted with the issue of a fragmented tablespace, which can be disruptive to other objects as they attempt to allocate additional extents. Here is a query that you can use to detect when temporary segments are stored in non-TEMPORARY tablespaces, and another query for determining when TEMPORARY tablespaces contain permanent objects:

```
SQL> select owner, segment_name, segment_type
  2  from DBA_SEGMENTS
  3  where tablespace_name <> 'TEMP'
  4  and segment_type = 'TEMPORARY';
No rows selected.
SQL> select owner, segment_name, segment_type
  2  from DBA_SEGMENTS
  3  where tablespace_name = 'TEMP'
  4  and segment_type <> 'TEMPORARY';
No rows selected.
```

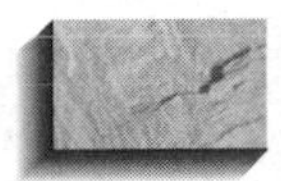

TIP
In Oracle8, you can now designate a temporary tablespace using the `create tablespace temporary` or `alter tablespace temporary` commands to force Oracle to prevent users from creating permanent objects in tablespaces containing temporary segments. How temporary tablespaces work in Oracle8 is explained in more detail in Chapter 7.

Creating Users Properly

Proper tablespace use often comes down to configuring users properly. By default, a user's temporary-storage areas are set as the SYSTEM tablespace. You can head off performance issues before they occur by creating all users with different default and temporary tablespaces. Proper configuration reduces the chance of user tables or temporary segments finding their way into SYSTEM, where they may cause problems later. Figure 19-1 indicates proper protocol for user creation.

Wrong

```
CREATE USER smith
IDENTIFIED BY sally
DEFAULT TABLESPACE data01
TEMPORARY TABLESPACE temp01;
```

Right

FIGURE 19-1. *Protocol for user creation*

Exercises

1. Identify the contents of the ROLLBACK and TEMP tablespaces. Why is it inappropriate to place tables and indexes in ROLLBACK and TEMP tablespaces? Why is it inappropriate to place the contents of ROLLBACK and TEMP tablespaces in other tablespaces?
2. What are some reasons not to store data objects, such as tables, in the SYSTEM tablespace? Why not store them in a tablespace earmarked for rollback segments?
3. When creating users, how can you avoid inappropriate use of the SYSTEM tablespace related to default and temporary tablespace assignment.

Detecting I/O Problems

You will want to know how to detect I/O problems in order to solve them. There are two areas where you must monitor I/O performance—Oracle-generated I/O and non-Oracle-generated I/O. Since both Oracle and other processes' disk activity have the potential to create I/O problems with the host system, you must be able to detect both in order to really know what the problem is, with regard to I/O activity. Many Unix systems have commands like `sar`, `iostat`, and `top`, which can be executed from the host-system command prompt to show you what processes are generating a lot of I/O activity. In Windows, the `perfmon` (Performance Monitor) utility allows you to visually plot system performance on a graph. Performance Monitor can be run using the Start | Programs | Administrative Tools | Performance Monitor menu option. You can use the Oracle extension to Performance Monitor for tracking Oracle-specific statistics with the Start | Programs | Oracle for Windows | Oracle Performance Monitor menu item, as well.

Several options exist within Oracle to detect I/O waits experienced by Oracle processes or sessions. These options mainly take the form of dynamic performance views. You will use different performance views depending on whether you want to check the performance information for datafiles, online redo logs, control files, or archive logs. You have already learned how to check the V$SYSTEM_EVENT and V$SESSION_EVENT views to detect wait events occurring in conjunction with redo or archive logs and control files. The view you will use to check I/O bottlenecks on datafiles is V$FILESTAT. The key elements from this view that you will want to know are: the number of times a datafile has been read or written to, how many blocks have been read or written, and the amount of time it takes Oracle to perform these tasks. Table 19-1 shows names and descriptions for columns you might care about in the V$FILESTAT view.

Column	Description
FILE#	Datafile number, used for joining V$FILESTAT with V$DATAFILE to get actual file and path name
PHYRDS	Number of physical reads on your datafile, occurring when user processes want data not already stored in the buffer cache
PHYWRTS	Number of physical writes on your datafile, occurring when data changes are written to disk by database writers
PHYBLKRD	Total number of blocks read from disk by server processes
PHYBLKWRT	Total number of blocks written to disk by database writers
READTIM	Total time all server processes have spent reading data, measured in milliseconds
WRITETIM	Total time all database writers have spent writing data, measured in milliseconds
AVGIOTIM	Average amount of time spent performing I/O, measured in milliseconds
LSTIOTIM	Amount of time the last I/O operation took to complete, measured in milliseconds
MINIOTIM	Shortest amount of time any I/O operation took to complete, measured in milliseconds
MAXIOWTM	Longest amount of time a write operation took to complete, measured in milliseconds
MAXIORTM	Longest amount of time a read operation took to complete, measured in milliseconds

TABLE 19-1. *Columns in the V$FILESTAT View*

V$FILESTAT in Action

Now you will see how to use V$FILESTAT to diagnose an I/O problem in a Windows environment. The following code block shows a query that displays whether a datafile on your database is a *hotspot*. A hotspot is an area on disk that is frequently accessed either for reading or writing. You will want to distribute datafiles across as many disk resources as possible to avoid these performance bottlenecks. Notice that on drive E, you have a great deal of I/O activity, leading to a much higher average I/O time than any of the other drives:

```
SQL> select d.name, a.phyrds, a.phywrts, a.avgiotim
  2  from v$datafile d, v$filestat a
  3  where a.file# = d.file#;
```

```
NAME                                PHYRDS PHYWRTS AVGIOTIM
----------------------------------- ------ ------- --------
D:\ORANT\DATABASE\SYSJSC1.ORA         1707       8        1
E:\ORANT\DATABASE\ROLLBACK1.ORA      35004   65030       11
E:\ORANT\DATABASE\USR1JSC.ORA        20399    2305        9
G:\ORANT\DATABASE\TEMP1JSC.ORA         304      45        4
H:\ORANT\DATABASE\INDX1JSC.ORA        4059    1023        5
I:\ORANT\DATABASE\DRJSC.ORA             29      24        0
J:\ORANT\DATABASE\RMAN01.DBF             4       2        5
K:\ORANT\DATABASE\TBLSPC.DBF             4       2        5
```

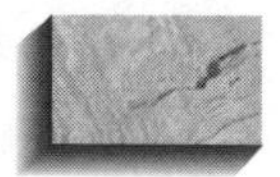

TIP

Several of the wait events in the V$SYSTEM_EVENT and V$SESSION_EVENT views with values in column EVENT beginning with "db" (shown in Chapter 16) are related to I/O bottlenecks. You should be sure you understand how to use these views and the V$FILESTAT and V$DATAFILE views to detect I/O wait events.

Exercises

1. Describe what is meant by a *hotspot*? What views can you use to detect what datafiles may be creating hotspots on your machine?
2. Identify some of the information that is part of the views that allow you to detect I/O activity on your datafiles.

Distributing Files to Reduce I/O Contention

When you have a hotspot because resources heavily used by Oracle are placed on the same disk, you must distribute these files to reduce or eliminate I/O contention. The underlying principle of distributing files to reduce I/O contention is that several Oracle database resources are used at the same time to support database activity. To eliminate contention for those resources at a hardware level, the DBA should determine which resources contend and then place those resources on different disks. There is a financial constraint for obtaining contention-free databases—you need to have several independent disk resources—not merely large disks, but actual separate disk drives. This is a financial decision, and sometimes trade-offs must be made. A factor in making the trade-off is that some resources don't take up much room on disk, such as control files.

Combos to Attempt

A good balance is achieved when noncontending resources are placed on the same disk drives, and potential I/O contenders are placed on their own drives. Placing control files on the same drives as redo logs and/or datafiles reduces the number of disks necessary. This configuration also improves recoverability, while adding only trace amounts of additional I/O processing. Another placement strategy is to put ROLLBACK tablespaces together on the same disk, and away from redo logs and DATA and INDEX tablespaces. In general, all TEMP tablespaces can be placed on their own disk, as well. However, on host systems where separate disk resources are in short supply, you can place TEMP tablespaces on the same disk as other tablespaces. One caveat to this approach is that you should either provide a lot of memory for `SORT_AREA_SIZE` so Oracle does its big sorts in memory, or else make the other tablespace on that disk read-only. Other recommended combinations appear in Figure 19-2.

Combos to Avoid

Several *don'ts* also exist when distributing disk resources to minimize I/O contention. To minimize dependence on any one disk in the host machine and to minimize contention between ARCH and LGWR during log switches, the recovery-minded DBA should ensure that export dumps, backup files, and archived redo logs don't appear on the same disks as their live production counterparts. You will learn more about tuning checkpoints and log switches later in the section, in a discussion titled "Tuning Checkpoints."

Typically, you should not put rollback segments on the same disks as redo logs, either. On busy systems, Oracle will write to both resources almost constantly, so having both on the same disk is a performance and recovery headache. Another combination to avoid is having DATA tablespaces and INDEX tablespaces on the same disk. The database can run into I/O contention when a query is issued against an indexed table. Having tables and indexes on separate disks allows the database to search the index and retrieve data from the table almost in parallel, whereas having both tablespaces on the same disk can create some friction.

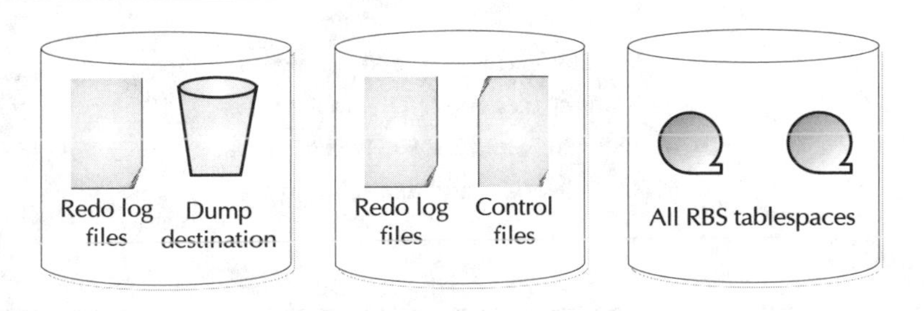

FIGURE 19-2. *Appropriate combinations for resources on the same disk*

You should also avoid having the SYSTEM and DATA tablespaces on the same disk. The SYSTEM tablespace contains the data dictionary, and `select` statements frequently require Oracle to perform a lookup of dictionary information for the table columns. If a user table on the same disk was accessed frequently, the user-table accesses might contend with dictionary access, leading to overall performance degradation in your Oracle database. Combinations of disk resources *not* recommended appear in Figure 19-3.

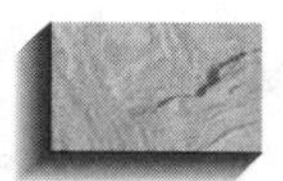

TIP
Another way to reduce contention is to reduce the amount of processing the host machine performs that is not related to the Oracle database. If your IT budget allows additional hardware purchases, try to give every Oracle database its own host machine, and try to run only Oracle on each host machine.

Exercises

1. What constraints exist in organizations that prevent you from placing every Oracle database resource on a separate disk?
2. What are some good combinations of resources on disks that will not produce I/O contention? What are some bad combinations of resources on disks that will produce I/O contention?
3. What factors determine whether a combination of disk resources on the same disk drive will be good or bad?

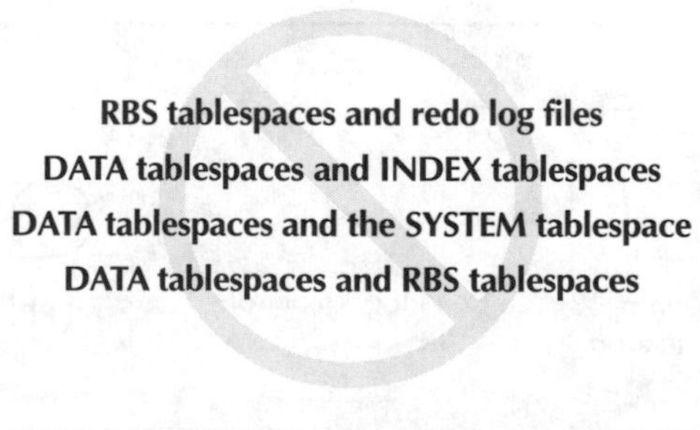

RBS tablespaces and redo log files
DATA tablespaces and INDEX tablespaces
DATA tablespaces and the SYSTEM tablespace
DATA tablespaces and RBS tablespaces

FIGURE 19-3. *Poor combinations for resources on the same disk*

Using Striping Where Appropriate

You may also want to use striping to reduce I/O contention on your database. Two methods exist for doing so. The first is *object striping,* and this method employs Oracle8 partitioning. If you have large tables or indexes accessed heavily by your application, you may want to partition those objects and place the partitions on different physical disk resources. More information about how to configure and use partitioning appears in Chapter 28. This option is particularly useful for situations where a datafile has been identified to be a hotspot on your system, and you know that datafile contains only one table or index. Partitioning tables has some recoverability and data-availability advantages that are also covered in Chapter 28.

The other method for striping is *disk striping*. The options you have available for disk striping are operating system- and hardware-dependent. Using these methods often involves making a separate hardware purchase in addition to your basic host system. You should have a strong understanding of the options provided by different hardware vendors for disk striping.

Many vendors provide data-striping products that utilize RAID (redundant array of independent disks) technology. RAID allows file I/O distribution over several disks in an array by striping data across those disks. RAID technology can also be used for mirroring drives. RAID and other similar hardware options have a distinct advantage over partitioning in that configuring RAID is managed at the OS level, and data reads and writes in RAID are managed at the hardware level, outside of Oracle.

Still, table striping in Oracle offers the advantage of controlling what data gets placed on which drives, which is not typically a feature offered by RAID technology. Object striping methods may be used instead of RAID in many situations where RAID would be more expensive than supporting partitions, or when few tables are large enough to require striping.

Exercises

1. Explain the concept of striping. How does it reduce I/O contention?
2. Which Oracle option should be used in conjunction with striping to better utilize multiple disk controllers? On what type of query will striping produce the greatest performance improvement?
3. Compare striping in the Oracle database to hardware options for data striping. What things can using hardware solutions for data striping accomplish that striping in Oracle cannot? When might it still be a good idea to use table striping in Oracle?

Tuning Checkpoints

When a checkpoint occurs, several things are done by LGWR. First, CKPT writes the last system change number in the redo log to the datafile headers and to the control files of the database. Also, LGWR tells DBWR to write the blocks in the dirty-buffer write queue to the appropriate datafiles of the database. More frequent checkpoint intervals decrease the recovery time of the database because dirty buffers in the buffer cache are written to disk more frequently. In the event of an instance failure, the dirty buffers that are still in the buffer cache are lost by Oracle, and must be recovered from online redo-log information. More frequent checkpoints means that fewer of these dirty blocks must be recovered during instance recovery, thus improving recovery time. But, more frequent checkpoints can degrade performance in periods of high-transaction activity.

On one hand, users want their transactions to run quickly, particularly on OLTP systems. The frequency of checkpoints can be altered using the `LOG_CHECKPOINT_INTERVAL` and `LOG_CHECKPOINT_TIMEOUT` `init`*`sid`*`.ora` parameters. Less frequent checkpoint intervals may be used to reduce the burden on LGWR. But, on the other hand, users want fast recovery in the event of system failure. The more frequent the checkpoint intervals, the more efficient the database recovery. However, the application has to wait until the recovery information is saved before continuing. Such is the trade-off between the reliability of having many checkpoints and poor online performance while those checkpoints happen. This trade-off may be particularly painful on OLTP systems, giving rise to a certain paradox. Users want maximum online performance, pushing DBAs to reduce the number of checkpoints performed. But, users also want maximum database availability, pushing DBAs to increase the number of checkpoints performed in order to minimize downtime.

You may also find that contention exists between your ARCH and LGWR processes during checkpoints at log switches. To resolve this performance problem, you must do the following. Place your redo log files on separate disk resources so that ARCH can copy the recently filled online log to the archive destination. Also, place your archive destination on yet another separate disk resource, away from all the online redo logs. This way, LGWR can continue writing to the new online redo log without contending with ARCH.

Exercises

1. What performance impact do frequent checkpoints have on the Oracle database? What benefit do frequent checkpoints provide? How can the number of checkpoints be reduced?
2. What contention potential exists between ARCH and LGWR with respect to checkpoints occurring at log switches?

Tuning Background Process I/O

Oracle has several background processes that are always running to handle various sorts of activities. You will need to tune these background processes if they become an I/O bottleneck for any reason. The following discussions cover some performance-tuning techniques for important background processes that may experience I/O problems.

DBW0 Performance

Your database writer process has a role in checkpoint performance. CKPT tells DBW0 to write dirty buffers at a checkpoint. If DBW0 has not written a substantial amount of dirty blocks between checkpoints, your overall performance could degrade because DBW0 will have fallen behind in processing its dirty block writes and needs to catch up. If performance was charted over time in this situation, you might see DBW0 activity resembling a wave with high crests and low troughs, such as in Figure 19-4.

To correct the problem, you must smooth out the wave by forcing DBW0 to write dirty buffers consistently between checkpoints. `DB_BLOCK_CHECKPOINT_BATCH` is an `init`*`sid`*`.ora` parameter that specifies the number of blocks that DBW0 can process in one batch as part of a checkpoint, and it defaults to eight. The overall amount of data written during a checkpoint will depend on the setting for this parameter and on what Oracle determines as its internal write-batch size. This internal write-batch size depends on what you set for the `DB_FILES` and `DB_FILE_SIMULTANEOUS_WRITES` init*sid*.ora parameters. You should consider increasing your value set for `DB_BLOCK_CHECKPOINT_BATCH` to speed up checkpoints by forcing DBW0 to write more than eight blocks at a time.

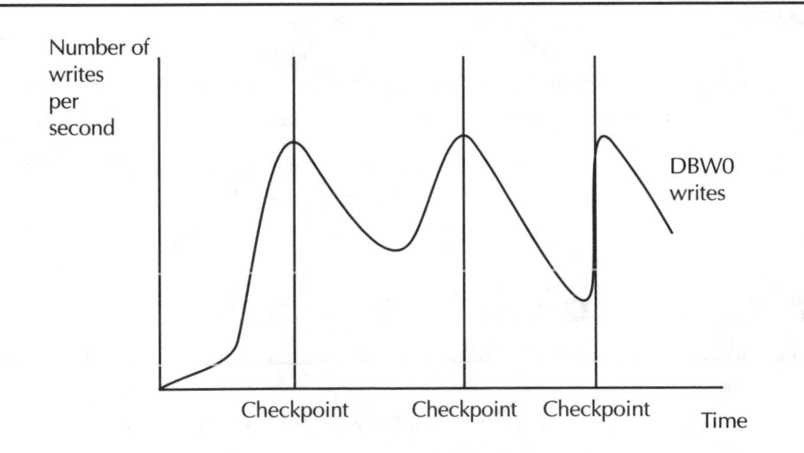

FIGURE 19-4. *DBW0 performance*

Also, you can improve performance in Oracle8 by using multiple database writers, particularly if you have multiple CPUs available on your host system. Setting the `initsid.ora` parameter `DB_WRITER_PROCESSES` to a value between two and nine enacts multiple database writers, called DBW0, DBW1, DBW2, and so on. Using multiple database writers also takes advantage of an increased number of latches you set when you use multiple buffer pools or configure your buffer cache parameter `DB_BLOCK_LRU_LATCHES`. In general, you should ensure that the number of database writers and CPUs are equal, and that LRU latches are either equal to, or a multiple of, the number of database writers, to ensure that each database writer takes an equal share of the load.

LGWR Performance Tuning

Applications with high `insert` activity or that use LONG or RAW datatypes in tables need a redo log buffer to be sized appropriately. LGWR will write data to an online redo log as soon as the redo log buffer is 1/3 full, or when a user issues a `commit` statement. You don't want the log buffer to be too small, because user processes may have to wait for space in the buffer. But, you don't want the buffer to be too large either, because then your redo-log writes to disk could get delayed.

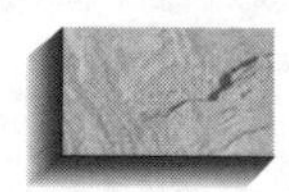

TIP
The CKPT process is always running in Oracle8. It is enabled automatically at startup in Oracle8—you don't need to specify the `CHECKPOINT_PROCESS` to start CKPT anymore.

Exercises

1. Identify some tuning techniques for the DBW0 process. Which parameter is used to configure multiple database writers?
2. Identify some tuning techniques for the LGWR process. When will LGWR write redo information from memory to disk?

Tuning Rollback Segments

In this section, you will cover the following topics related to tuning rollback segments:

- Using V$ views to monitor rollback-segment performance
- Modifying rollback-segment configuration

- Determining the number and size of rollback segments
- Allocating rollback segments to transactions

Every `update`, `insert`, and `delete` statement executed on a table produces rollback segment entries, thus making rollback segments an important and heavily used resource. Configuring rollback segments properly allows user processes to operate smoothly. If these resources are not configured to run at an optimum level, the backlog of processes needing to write rollback entries will grow quickly, causing a problem for all users on the database. This section introduces you to the V$ views that help you monitor rollback-segment performance. You will learn how to modify rollback-segment configuration and how to size rollback segments properly. You will learn how to allocate a specific rollback segment to a particular transaction, as well.

Using V$ Views to Monitor Rollback-Segment Performance

Contention for the rollback-segment resource is indicated by contention in memory for the buffers containing blocks of rollback-segment information. The V$WAITSTAT view can be used to detect this type of contention. This view is available to users with `select any table` privileges or the SELECT_CATALOG_ROLE role, or to user SYS. Four types of blocks exist in rollback segments, and it is important to monitor for them to detect contention on rollback segments. These block types are *system undo header, system undo block, undo header,* and *undo block*. The names and descriptions of these four block types are given in Table 19-2.

Statistics for these rollback-segment block types should be monitored to ensure that no processes are contending for rollback segments. You can calculate rollback-segment performance as a hit ratio using the following equation:

```
(db block gets + consistent gets - undo segment waits /
  db block gets + consistent gets) * 100
```

Block Type	Description
SYSTEM undo header	Header block for the SYSTEM rollback segment
SYSTEM undo block	Block for storing SYSTEM rollback-segment information
Undo header	Header block for non-SYSTEM rollback segment
Undo block	Block for storing non-SYSTEM rollback-segment information

TABLE 19-2. *Rollback segment block types and their descriptions*

Four *undo segment waits* substitute the value in column COUNT from V$WAITSTAT, where the value in column CLASS is `system undo header`, `system undo block`, `undo header`, or `undo block`, depending on the hit ratio you are calculating. The resulting hit ratio should be 99 percent or more, or else you may have a problem on your system with rollback-segment contention. Recall that you get the other information in this equation from the V$SYSSTAT view. You obtain the statistics for this equation using the following statements:

```
SQL> select class, count from v$waitstat
  2  where class in ('system undo header',
  3                 'system undo block',
  4                 'undo header',
  5                 'undo block');
CLASS                  COUNT
------------------ ---------
system undo header         0
system undo block          0
undo header              218
undo block                 0
SQL> select name, value from v$sysstat
  2  where name in ('db block gets','consistent gets');
NAME                          VALUE
------------------------ ---------
db block gets                   826
consistent gets               14383
```

In this example, you see that only the undo header block class could possibly have a hit ratio of less than 100 percent. Using the statistics in the example, you calculate that the hit ratio for that block class is (14383 + 826 - 218) / (14383 + 826), or 98.56 percent. Therefore, there is a problem with contention on the undo-header block class for your rollback segments. To resolve the problem, you must add more rollback segments, either by putting ones that are offline back online with the `alter rollback segment` *name* `online` command, or by creating new rollback segments with the `create rollback segments` command, and then taking it online.

If you have an adequate number of private rollback segments created on your database, you may still have contention. If Oracle seems to be using a few rollback segments almost to exclusion, you can tune using the `TRANSACTIONS_PER_ROLLBACK_SEGMENT` and `TRANSACTIONS` parameters. Oracle tends to use the number of rollback segments determined by dividing `TRANSACTIONS` by `TRANSACTIONS_PER_ROLLBACK_SEGMENT`. Thus, if `TRANSACTIONS` is 200 and `TRANSACTIONS_PER_ROLLBACK_SEGMENT` is set to 65, Oracle will tend to use only 3 rollback segments, even if your database has 30. To distribute rollback segment usage more evenly, set `TRANSACTIONS_PER_ROLLBACK_SEGMENT` and `TRANSACTIONS` so that when you divide `TRANSACTIONS_PER_ROLLBACK_`

SEGMENT by TRANSACTIONS, you wind up with approximately the number of rollback segments available in your database.

Exercises

1. Describe how to identify contention for rollback segments. What views are involved in discovering contention for rollback segments?
2. Name four rollback-block classes. How do you resolve contention for rollback segments?

Modifying Rollback-Segment Configuration

The `storage` clause of the `create rollback segment` statement is unique in that you can specify an optimal size for your rollback segment. If you do so, Oracle will periodically deallocate extents from the rollback segment to reduce it to the specified optimal size if transactions have caused the rollback segment to get stretched out of shape. You should use the number of active transactions that use particular rollback segments to determine that rollback segment's optimal size.

The current allocation for all rollback segments can be determined from V$ROLLSTAT. This view is accessed by users with the `select any table` privilege or the SELECT_CATALOG_ROLE role, or by user SYS. The V$ROLLSTAT view can be joined with V$ROLLNAME to determine rollback-segment names associated with a particular "undo," or rollback-segment number, or USN in V$ROLLSTAT. The following code block illustrates the appropriate query (Table 19-3 identifies the meaning of the columns in the V$ROLLSTAT view from the query):

```
SQL> select a.name, b.extents, b.rssize,
  2  b.optsize, b.shrinks, b.aveshrink,
  3  b.aveactive, b.wraps, b.extends, b.status
  4  from v$rollname a, v$rollstat b
  5  where a.usn = b.usn;
NAME   EXTENTS  RSSIZE OPTSIZE WRAPS EXTENDS SHRINKS AVESHRINK
------ ------- ------- ------- ----- ------- ------- ---------
AVEACTIVE STATUS
--------- ------
SYSTEM       8  407552       0     0       0       0         0
        0 ONLINE
RB0         17  868352       0     0       0       0         0
        0 ONLINE
RB1         25 1277952       0     0       0       0         0
        0 ONLINE
CTXROL     444 4540416       0     0       0       0         0
        0 ONLINE
```

Column Name	Description
NAME	Name of the rollback segment from V$ROLLNAME
EXTENTS	Number of extents currently allocated to the rollback segment
RSSIZE	Size of the rollback segment in bytes
OPTSIZE	Optimal size for the rollback segment; 0 if `optimal` is not defined
EXTENDS	Number of times the rollback segment obtained an extent
SHRINKS	Number of times the rollback segment deallocated extents to return to `optimal` size
AVESHRINK	Average amount of space shed by the rollback segment in each shrink
AVEACTIVE	Average number of bytes for the rollback segment that are part of uncommitted transactions, or that are committed but not shrunk together
STATUS	The current status of the rollback segment

TABLE 19-3. *Significant Columns in V$ROLLNAME and V$ROLLSTAT*

Notice that the CTXROL rollback segment is stretched horrendously out of shape—and it doesn't even have an optimal size set. Furthermore, all your rollback segments are different sizes. You can do a lot of tuning on rollback segments to get them all to have the same size, number of extents, and optimal size. You could set it so that every rollback segment had 10 extents, each 100K in size, with each extent taking 1MB of the segment. The following query shows how to use the DBA_ROLLBACK_SEGS dictionary view to determine the size of each extent in each rollback segment:

```
SQL> select segment_name, initial_extent, next_extent
  2  from dba_rollback_segs;
SEGMENT_NAME                   INITIAL_EXTENT NEXT_EXTENT
------------------------------ -------------- -----------
SYSTEM                                  51200       51200
SYSROL                                 102400      102400
RB0                                     51200       51200
RB1                                     51200       51200
CTXROL                                  10240       10240
```

As you can see, all your rollback segments have different-sized extents, too. To correct this problem, you will most likely want to create an entirely new set of rollback segments, each with the same number of like-sized extents, and set `optimal` so that Oracle will reduce the excess capacity occasionally. You can also accomplish the task of shrinking your rollback segments manually (if `optimal` is set) using the `alter rollback segment shrink` statement.

Excessive rollback-segment shrinkage is an indication of a larger problem—that the rollback segment is improperly sized. If a small rollback segment routinely handles large transactions, that rollback segment will extend to the size required by the query. The more frequently Oracle tries to shrink the rollback segment to optimal size, the worse your database performance will be. Compare values in the SHRINKS and AVESHRINK columns, and also look at the value in the AVEACTIVE column. Table 19-4 indicates the relationships between the various columns of the V$ROLLSTAT view and their meanings.

Exercises

1. What dynamic performance view carries rollback-segment performance information?
2. How does the DBA identify whether dynamic extension and shrinks are causing a performance problem on the rollback segments? What storage parameter is changed if the DBA determines that there are too many shrinks occurring on the rollback segment?

Determining Number and Size of Rollback Segments

In Chapter 8, you were introduced to the method for determining the number and size of rollback segments. For a refresher, at instance startup, Oracle will attempt to acquire at least two rollback segments if there are more tablespaces than just SYSTEM existing on the database. There are two types of database rollback segments: *public* and *private*. If you use Oracle Parallel Server, public rollback segments are available to every instance connecting to the database, while private rollback segments are available to only the instance in which the rollback segment was created. If you don't use Parallel Server, public

SHRINKS	AVESIZE	OPTSIZE
High	High	Too low, increase `optimal`
High	Low	Too low, increase `optimal`
Low	Low	Too high, reduce `optimal` (unless nearly equal to AVEACTIVE)
Low	High	OK

TABLE 19-4. *V$ROLLSTAT Settings and Their Meanings*

and private rollback segments are the same. To understand how Oracle acquires rollback segments at startup, review Chapter 8.

Determining Rollback Segment Number: The Rule of Four

To determine how many rollback segments are appropriate for your Oracle database, use the *Rule of Four*, illustrated in Figure 19-5. Here is an example of the Rule of Four: Assume the database handles 133 transactions concurrently, on average. By applying the first part of the Rule of Four, the DBA knows that 133 / 4 = 33¼, or 34. Since this result is greater than 4 + 4, the DBA knows that 34 rollback segments are appropriate for the instance. If that number of concurrent transactions was only 10, however, 10 / 4 = 2½, or 3, which should be rounded up to the nearest multiple of 4, which is 4.

TIP

Use the Rule of Four to determine the appropriate number of rollback segments for your Oracle instance—divide concurrent transactions by 4. If the result is less than 4 + 4, round up to the nearest multiple of 4.

Sizing Extents by Monitoring WRAPS and EXTENDS

To determine what the optimum size is for each extent on a rollback segment, you should also monitor the number of times transaction information will be wrapped from extent to extent in a rollback segment. When wraps occur, it means that the current extent handling the transaction is not large enough to hold the undo for that transaction. In some cases, this might be acceptable, particularly if the transaction undo is always wrapping into an inactive extent, given evidence by a high WRAPS and a low EXTENDS statistic. But, if WRAPS and EXTENDS are both high, then many transactions on the database don't fit into your rollback-segment extents, and you should probably try to reduce wrapping by increasing the size of rollback-segment extents.

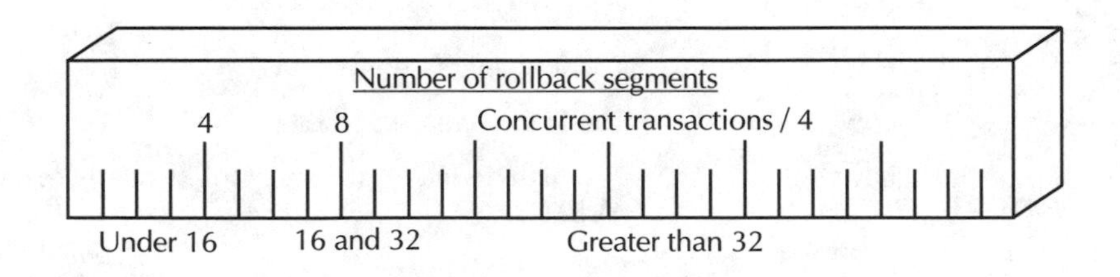

FIGURE 19-5. *Typical transaction to rollback segment ratios*

Exercises

1. How does Oracle determine the number of rollback segments to acquire at startup? How can the DBA specify certain rollback segments that must be acquired at startup?
2. You are trying to determine the appropriate number of rollback segments to put on a database with an average of 97 concurrent users. Use the Rule of Four to calculate the number of rollback segments your database needs.
3. What are wraps? When might they indicate a problem on the rollback segment?

Allocating Rollback Segments to Transactions

Allocating rollback segments directly to transactions is only a good idea in a few situations. One situation is where you have a marathon batch job that only runs occasionally and cannot fit into the average rollback segment available on the database. In this situation, you may want to create an unusually large rollback segment for handling rollback from that batch job that you bring online for the specific purpose of running that job. To assign the batch job to the large rollback segment, issue the statement `set transaction use rollback segment` *`rollback_segment`* at the beginning of the transaction.

It is not a good idea to assign every transaction explicitly to a rollback segment. In order to assign transactions to rollback segments en masse throughout the database, each process must have a complete idea of the processes running at that time, as well as the knowledge of which rollback segments are online. If too many transactions request the same rollback segment, that could cause the rollback segment to extend and shrink unnecessarily while other rollback segments remain inactive. Oracle itself can do an appropriate job of finding rollback segments for most short- and medium-duration transactions.

Exercises

1. What statement is used to assign transactions to a rollback segment?
2. When is it a good idea to assign transactions to rollback segments? When is it not a good idea to do so?

Using Oracle Blocks Efficiently

In this section, you will cover the following topics related to using Oracle blocks:

- Determining appropriate block size

- Optimizing space usage within blocks
- Detecting and resolving row migration
- Monitoring and tuning indexes
- Sizing extents appropriately

The foundation of all I/O activity in the Oracle database is the Oracle block. Row data for indexes and columns, rollback-segment information, data-dictionary information, and every other database component stored in a tablespace is stored in an Oracle block. Proper use of Oracle at the block level will go a long way in enhancing the performance of Oracle. In this section, you will learn how to determine appropriate block size, and how to optimize space usage in blocks. You will also learn how to detect and resolve row migration. The topics of monitoring and tuning indexes and sizing extents appropriately will also be covered.

Determining Appropriate Block Size

The size of Oracle blocks is determined at database creation with the `DB_BLOCK_SIZE` `init`*`sid`*`.ora` parameter. It should be based on a few different factors. First, Oracle block size should be a multiple of operating-system block size. This allows the operating system to handle I/O use by Oracle processes in a manner consistent with its own methods for reading operating-system blocks from the file system. Most operating systems have a block size of 512 or 1,024 bytes. Usually, Oracle block size is a multiple of that. Many times, it is 2K or based on a multiple of 2K—either 4K or 8K. On certain large systems, the Oracle block size can be 16K, 32K, or even higher. Oracle's default size for blocks is specific to the operating system hosting Oracle, and should always be set higher than the size of operating-system blocks to reduce the number of physical reads Oracle has to perform.

Once `DB_BLOCK_SIZE` is specified at database creation, it cannot be changed without first re-creating the database. Determining the value for `DB_BLOCK_SIZE` depends largely on the type of application you plan to use with your Oracle database. OLTP applications typically work best with smaller block sizes. In these applications, you may find the 2–4K size works best, because block contention is reduced when blocks are small; small blocks hold small rows of normalized table information well, and small blocks perform well for random access, which is common on OLTP systems. If your OLTP system commonly stores larger rows of slightly denormalized data, your needs may be served well with 8K blocks. However, you run the risk of wasting space in both memory and on disk if only a few rows in your database are large enough to warrant the use of an 8K block size. You would almost be better off suffering with the inevitable small amount of chaining or row migration than wasting large amounts of space.

For DSS systems or data warehouses, you should consider moving beyond 8K block sizes, perhaps to 16K, 32K, or even 64K. The larger block size allows you to bring more rows of data into memory with less I/O overhead. You'd have fewer block headers in your datafiles as well, which reduces the amount of storage overhead, leaving more room on disk to store large amounts of data. If your rows are large, perhaps containing large objects, or you need to access your data sequentially, large blocks allow you to store more and retrieve more information per block. But beware of a large block size on an OLTP application. Large block size is bad for indexes, because their size increases block contention on index leaf blocks.

Exercises

1. What is the name of the variable that determines block size for the Oracle database?
2. Identify some factors upon which the database block size depends. What application considerations should determine block size?

Optimizing Space Usage Within Blocks

The use of space in data blocks is determined by values assigned to `pctfree` and `pctused` clauses in the `create` *`object`* statement. You first learned about space usage in Chapter 7. Space within each block must be managed in a way consistent with the needs of the data being stored. The needs of an OLTP application, with thousands of users entering new information daily, are not the same as a DSS system with few users. The values set for `pctfree` and `pctused` in tables for those two types of applications should not be the same, either. (To understand how these clauses affect Oracle's storage of data in blocks, review Chapter 7.) These two options are configured in relation to one another to manage space utilization in data blocks effectively.

The range allowed for specifying `pctfree` and `pctused` is between 0 and 99. The sum of the values for these two options should not exceed 100. When set up properly, `pctfree` and `pctused` can have many positive effects on the I/O usage of the Oracle database. However, the key to configuring `pctfree` and `pctused` properly is knowing about a few different aspects of how the application intends to use the object whose rows are in the block. Some of the important questions that need to be answered by the DBA before configuring `pctfree` and `pctused` are:

- What kind of data object is using these blocks?
- How often will the data in this object be updated?
- Will updates to each row in the object increase the size of the row in bytes?

Examples of pctfree and pctused Use

It is usually not wise to set `pctfree` and `pctused` to values that add up to exactly 100. When these two options add up to 100, Oracle will work very hard to ensure that no data block keeps more free space than is specified by `pctfree`. This additional work keeps Oracle's processing costs unnecessarily high because of `insert` activity. For example, if you update a row and make the row one byte shorter, then you have a block on your freelist that cannot be used for most inserts. If you provided a gap of 20 percent, for example, between `pctfree` and `pctused`, then you could use the block for many more `insert` statements, because you have one byte plus 20 percent free space available before exceeding the `pctfree` limit. Oracle's default settings for `pctfree` and `pctused` are 10 and 40, respectively, making for a total of 50.

Consider some other examples of `pctfree` and `pctused` settings and what they mean:

`pctfree=25, pctused=50` This combination might be used on high-transaction-volume OLTP systems with some anticipated growth in row size as a result of updates to existing rows. The value for `pctfree` should accommodate the increase in row size, although it is important to assess as closely as possible the anticipated growth of each row as part of updates, in order to maximize the storage of data. The value for `pctused` prevents a block from being added to the freelist until there is 50 percent of space used in the block, allowing many rows to be added to the block before it is taken off the freelist.

`pctfree=5, pctused=85` This combination of values may be useful for systems such as data warehouses or DSS applications. The setting for `pctfree` leaves a small amount of room for each row size to increase. The `pctused` value is high in order to maximize data storage within each block. Since data warehouses typically store mass amounts of data for query access only, these settings should manage storage well.

Exercises

1. What is the meaning of the `pctfree` storage option? What is the meaning of the `pctused` option? How are they specified? What are the ranges for these values? What should the sum of these values add up to?
2. The DBA is considering a change to the values for `pctfree` and `pctused` for a table used by an OLTP application that experiences high `insert` activity. Existing records in the database are updated frequently, and the size of the row is rarely affected by those updates. Should the value for `pctfree` be high or low? Should the value for `pctused` be high or low?

Detecting and Resolving Row Migration

Higher pctfree values represent a proactive solution to row chaining and migration. Row migration occurs when a user process updates a row in an already crowded data block, forcing Oracle to move the row out of that block and into another one that can accommodate the row. Chaining occurs when Oracle attempts to migrate the row but cannot find a block large enough to fit the entire row, so it breaks the row into two or more parts and stores the parts separately. The DBA should avoid allowing Oracle to migrate or chain rows, because performance can drop significantly if many rows are chained or migrated in the table. The importance of avoiding row migration and chaining is demonstrated in Figure 19-6. The case in which the problem arises is when Oracle attempts index access to the migrated row. Oracle looks up a row in the index and obtains its ROWID, only to look in the table for that ROWID and be referred to another ROWID indicating where the row migrated to.

The analyze *object name* list chained rows into CHAINED_ROWS command is used to determine whether there are chained rows in the database. The *object* and *name* in this context are the type of object (table or cluster) and the name of the object being analyzed for chained rows, while CHAINED_ROWS is the name of the table into which analyze places the results of its execution. The DBA can then query the CHAINED_ROWS table to determine whether there is an issue with row chaining on the database.

This table is not automatically created as part of database creation. Instead, the DBA must run the utlchain.sql script that is included with the distribution. Usually, this file is found in the rdbms/admin directory under the Oracle software home directory. CHAINED_ROWS is owned by the user that creates it. After running analyze, the original ROWID for each chained row will appear in the CHAINED_ROWS table.

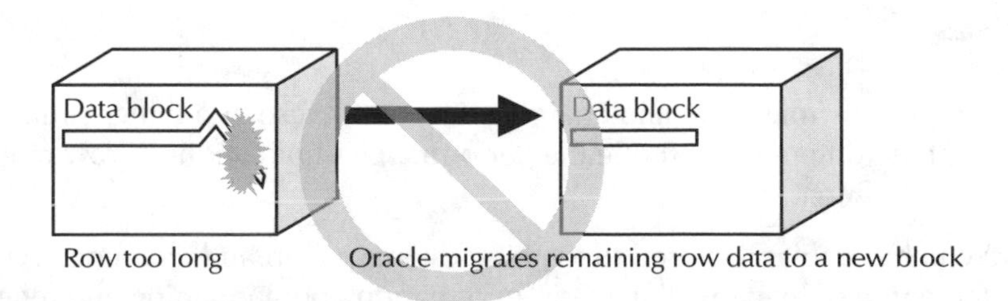

FIGURE 19-6. *Avoid row migration and chaining*

To determine the extent of chaining or row migration in a database table or cluster, the DBA can execute the following statements:

```
SQL> analyze table emp
  2  list chained rows into chained_rows;
Table analyzed.
SQL> select count(*) from chained_rows;
 COUNT(*)
---------
        0
```

If row migration for the table seems too high, and the migrated rows are typically accessed via indexes, you should resize `pctfree` and `pctused` for that table. This is done in one of two ways. You can run EXPORT to get an export dump of the data in the table. Then, drop and recreate the table using new `pctfree` and `pctused` values. After that, load the data again using IMPORT with `IGNORE=Y` to load the data from the table without having IMPORT return errors because the table definition already exists. More information about what happens when you set `IGNORE=Y` can be found in Chapters 11 and 19. Or, you could use the SQL*Plus `spool` *`filename`* command to set up an output file in your session. Then, `select` your data using some character delimiter, such as a comma. Then, drop and re-create the table. Finally, load the data from the flat file using SQL*Loader. You can find more information about SQL*Loader in Chapter 11.

TIP
You need not drop and re-create the table to change `pctfree` and `pctused` options on that table, but if you don't, the changes will only be applied to new data entering the table.

Exercises

1. Define row migration and chaining. How are these two things similar? How are they different? Describe the performance implications of row migration and chaining.
2. Which command is used to identify row migration and chaining? What is the name of the table that stores information about chaining and migration?

Monitoring and Tuning Indexes

You have already learned most of what you need to know about tuning indexes, so this is a good time for review. Following these points, you will cover some techniques for monitoring and tuning indexes.

- Indexes improve performance on queries only when reference is made to the indexed column in the query's `where` clause. Thus, if column EMPID in table EMP has an index on it, the statement `select * from EMP where EMPID = '50694'` uses the index, but `select * from EMP` does not. When you want to use composite indexes, be sure the `where` clause of your query references the leading column at the very least.
- B-tree indexes work best when the column indexed has mostly distinct and few NULL values, and the data can change frequently.
- A bitmap index works best when there are only a few distinct values in the column, and the data in the indexed column changes very infrequently.

Monitoring Use of Indexes: Technique 1

One new concept to be introduced regarding monitoring the use of indexes on your database relies on your ability to read statistics from the V$SYSSTAT view. You will want to determine whether or not your users are obtaining their requested data via `TABLE ACCESS FULL` operations (meaning no index was used) or via `TABLE ACCESS BY ROWID` (meaning an index was used for the query). The following code block shows a set of statistics from V$SYSSTAT that can help you determine this information:

```
SQL> select name, value from v$sysstat
  2  where name in ('table scans (short tables)',
  3                 'table scans (long tables)',
  4                 'table scan rows gotten',
  5                 'table fetch by rowid');
NAME                                      VALUE
---------------------------------------- --------
table scans (short tables)                    40
table scans (long tables)                     33
table scan rows gotten                     33600
table fetch by rowid                        2201
```

The output from this query gives you all the statistics related to full table scans on small and large tables. It also shows the total number of rows obtained from table scans, and then the number of times Oracle performed a fetch of data from tables using ROWID, which means that an index was involved. There is no hard-and-fast formula for determining whether your application uses indexes frequently enough. But, if you look at these statistics and see that full table scans on short or long tables is very high, and table fetches by ROWID is very low, then you might have a problem with the use of indexes on your database.

Monitoring Use of Indexes: Technique 2

Another method for determining whether your application is using indexes available on the system is to return to the use of `explain plan`, detailed in Chapter 17. To get a thorough idea of your application's use of indexes, you should test every SQL statement used in the application to ensure that no `TABLE ACCESS FULL` operations are being performed. However, this is very time-consuming. A better approach would be to register the application using the Oracle-supplied package DBMS_APPLICATION_INFO, also explained in Chapter 17, to determine which areas of the application seem to take the longest to execute. Then, go through the SQL operations in that area of the application with the `explain plan` command to see if full table scans are the culprit.

Exercises

1. What rules should you follow when tuning indexes?
2. Which two techniques are described here to help you determine whether indexes are being used effectively on your database?

Sizing Extents Appropriately

Excluding situations in which you are using parallel DML and parallel query in Oracle8, database objects such as clusters, indexes, and tables should be sized so that all data in the object fits into one extent or a few extents. In DSS applications where data is static, it should not be too hard to ensure that the entire object fits into one extent. You simply must obtain the average size for each row, determine how many rows fit into a block, and then ensure that your initial extent has that many blocks allocated to it. For OLTP applications, on the other hand, you cannot know beforehand how much data the object might store, because new records are added by users all the time. Thus, you will have to ensure there is extra space in the initial extent available for growth. In addition, you will have to monitor the growth of the object and periodically resize the initial extent so that all data added fits into that extent.

Process for Table-Extent Resizing

The task of reorganizing table-extent sizes is something that should be reserved for when database activities are lightest. Many DBAs schedule a day or weekend of downtime regularly to handle routine maintenance, such as table and extent resizing. You can save time by determining appropriate values for `initial` a day or two ahead of time. The process for determining the size of the first extent on a table is as follows:

1. Determine which tables have too many extents allocated to them, and thus need to be resized. Note that in the following query, you don't use 1 in the `where` clause's second comparison operation because you would get too many objects, and if you use parallel query you probably want as many extents as your parallel processing can access simultaneously without degrading performance.

```
SQL> select segment_name
  2  from dba_segments
  3  where segment_type = 'TABLE'
  4  and extents > 5;
SEGMENT_NAME
----------------------------------------
EMP
```

2. Determine the average size of rows in the table you are resizing, adding in your row header and the length byte stored for non-NULL column values, which is 1 for columns less than 250 bytes wide, 3 for columns greater than or equal to 250 bytes wide. The following code block contains a sample query to show you how:

```
SQL> select 3 + avg(vsize(empid) +
  2                       1 + vsize(lastname) +
  3                       1 + vsize(firstname) +
  4                       1 + vsize(salary) +
  5                       1 + vsize(dept)) as AVGSIZE
  6  from emp;
AVGSIZE
-------
   27.2
```

3. Use the formula `DB_BLOCK_SIZE - (DB_BLOCK_SIZE * (1 / pctfree)) -` *`fixed block header size - variable block header size`* to determine free space in your block for data rows. If DB_BLOCK_SIZE is 4,096, and `pctfree` is 10, then you will lose 410 bytes off the top.

4. Your total fixed block header for tables is 52, and your variable block header size is 4 * *number_of_rows_in_block*. You can then estimate the amount of space after fixed header and `pctfree` space is factored out as (4,096 – 410 – 52), or 3634. You then want to divide that result by the number of bytes required to store an average sized row, to get the approximate number of rows that fit in a block, or 3634/ 27.2 bytes per row, which gives you approximately 133 rows per block. However, the variable block header size in this situation would be 4 * 133 rows per block, or 532 bytes more in each block for the block header, which means that 532 / 27.2, or 20 additional rows will be displaced, for 113 rows per block. Checking the math, you have:
   - 4,096 – (4,096 * (1 / 10)) – 52 – (4 * 113) = 3,182 bytes free for row data in a block
   - 3,182 bytes / 27.2 bytes per row = 116 rows per block
   - 116 > 113, so you have plenty of room for 113 rows in each block
5. Determine the appropriate size for your initial extent in table EMP. First, get your current row count from the table. Then, divide that number by the result from step 3. For the example, 240,239 rows in EMP / 113 rows per block = 2,126 blocks, or 8,708,096 bytes for the initial extent. For an OLTP system, you may even want to round up and make the first extent an even 10MB.

```
SQL> select count(*) from EMP;
COUNT(*)
--------
  240239
```

Process for Reorganizing Table Extent Allocation

Once the appropriate setting for `initial` is determined, you should resize the object on your DBA maintenance day. Use the following steps to do so:

1. Restrict access to Oracle so that only you can connect. The database must be open.
2. Use EXPORT to get a dump file containing all data for the table being resized. The parameters you might use for the task are `TABLES=`*`tablename`* and `COMPRESS=Y`.
3. Drop the table in your database.
4. Recreate the table with the appropriate setting for `initial` in your `storage` clause.

5. Use IMPORT with parameters `IGNORE=Y` and `ROWS=Y` to load only row data from EMP in the dump file into your new table (not the table definition, which is also in the dump file). You are left with a table that has all data stored in only one extent.

Exercises

1. What two processes are involved in determining the appropriate size for initial extents on a table?
2. You have a table whose average row size is 36 bytes. The number of rows in the table is 40,593,405. `DB_BLOCK_SIZE` is set to 2,048, and `pctfree` is 8. What should the size of `initial` be for this table?

Chapter Summary

This chapter discussed the many facets of tuning Oracle disk usage. The three topics in this section—database configuration, tuning rollback segments, and using Oracle blocks efficiently—comprise nearly 25 percent of OCP Exam 4. The first section you covered in this chapter was database configuration and I/O issues. You learned how to use the DBA_SEGMENTS view to diagnose inappropriate use of various types of tablespaces that should exist on your database. You learned about the methods for detecting I/O problems in your database using V$SESSION_WAIT, V$SYSTEM_WAIT, and V$FILESTAT performance views. After that, you learned about file distribution for an Oracle database system. Appropriate and inappropriate combinations of disk resources were presented. You learned about object striping using table and index partitions to eliminate hotspots, and also covered the use of striping and mirroring at the hardware level to improve performance. Finally, you learned about tuning checkpoints by reducing their frequency and about tuning background process I/O to improve overall performance for your database.

The next section of the chapter covered tuning rollback segments. You learned about the V$ROLLSTAT and V$ROLLNAME dynamic performance views and how they can be used to check rollback-segment performance. The different columns in V$ROLLSTAT were covered, along with their meanings. You also learned how to reconfigure a rollback segment so that Oracle can reduce the size of the segment when it gets stretched out of shape by long-running transactions. You learned how to determine the appropriate number of rollback segments for a database, and also about the importance of sizing extents so that undo information for entire transactions fits into one extent. Last, you covered how to allocate a rollback segment to a specific transaction, and which situations are appropriate for this sort of setup.

The last section in this chapter covered the efficient use of Oracle blocks. You learned a few things about determining the appropriate block size for OLTP and DSS systems, and why it is important for Oracle blocks to be sized as a multiple of operating system blocks. You learned more about using `pctfree` and `pctused` to optimize data storage space in a block for a database object. Some examples of different possible settings for these storage options were covered, along with their effects. You learned how to use the `analyze` command to detect row migration, and how to resolve row migration using the `pctfree` storage option. This section wrapped up with techniques for monitoring and tuning indexes, and how to size extents appropriately.

Two-Minute Drill

- Five types of tablespaces commonly found on the Oracle database are SYSTEM, DATA, INDEX, ROLLBACK, and TEMP. You can use the DBA_SEGMENTS view to determine if objects are inappropriately placed in various tablespaces.
- The SYSTEM tablespace should contain data dictionary tables and initial rollback segments only. It is inappropriate to place any other objects in them as they may fill the SYSTEM tablespace, causing maintenance problems.
- The DATA tablespaces should contain table data only. Other types of segments, such as rollback segments or temporary segments, could cause tablespace fragmentation, making it hard for the tables to acquire extents.
- The INDEX tablespaces should contain indexes to table data only.
- The ROLLBACK tablespaces should contain rollback segments only.
- The TEMP tablespaces should be available for the creation of temporary segments for user queries. No other objects should be placed in this tablespace.
- Detecting I/O problems with datafiles is handled with the V$FILESTAT view. Look for high values in the PHYRDS, PHYWRTS, and AVGIOTIM columns of this view to identify hotspots and I/O issues.
- V$SYSTEM_WAIT and V$SESSION_WAIT can both be used to identify I/O problems with online redo logs and control files, as well.
- Files should be distributed to reduce I/O contention:
  - Acceptable combinations of resources on the same disk include the following: multiple control files can be on the same disks as online

redo logs or datafiles; temporary tablespace datafiles can be combined with other disk resources only when enough memory is available to ensure that all sorts occur in memory.

- Unacceptable combinations of resources on the same disk include the following: DATA and INDEX tablespace datafiles; ROLLBACK tablespace datafiles and any other tablespace datafiles; DATA or INDEX tablespace datafiles and the SYSTEM tablespace; and online redo logs and any other tablespace datafiles.

- You can stripe in two ways:
  - Object striping is taking a large table, dividing it into partitions, and putting the partitions on separate disks.
  - Hardware striping is configured at the OS level, and it involves copying identical segments or stripes of information across several different disks to avoid dependence on any single disk.
- Checkpoints occur at least as frequently as log switches, but can occur more frequently in two cases:
  - `LOG_CHECKPOINT_INTERVAL` is set to a number representing the number of blocks that can be written to an online redo log before the checkpoint occurs.
  - `LOG_CHECKPOINT_TIMEOUT` is set to a number representing the number of seconds between checkpoints.
- More frequent checkpoints improve database recoverability by copying dirty buffers to disk more frequently, but can reduce online performance because LGWR stops clearing out the log buffer more frequently to handle checkpoint processing.
- You can improve process I/O on the DBW0 background processes by using the same number of database writers as CPUs on the machine by changing `DB_WRITER_PROCESSES` to a value from 2 to 9. Be sure the number of LRU latches set with the `init`*`sid`*`.ora` parameter `DB_BLOCK_LRU_LATCHES` in the buffer cache is set to a multiple of the number of `DB_WRITER_PROCESSES` on the system.
- Rollback segments acquire a number of public rollback segments in Oracle Parallel Server calculated by `TRANSACTIONS` divided by `TRANSACTIONS_PER_ROLLBACK_SEGMENT` `init`*`sid`*`.ora` parameters. These parameters also determine how many private rollback segments Oracle tends to use when Parallel Server isn't being used.

- The DBA can specify that the instance acquire certain private rollback segments at startup by using the `ROLLBACK_SEGMENTS` initialization parameter.
- All extents of a rollback segment are the same size. This is enforced by Oracle with the removal of the `pctincrease` storage clause in `the create rollback segment` syntax.
- Rollback segments should have an `optimal` size specified by the `optimal` storage clause.
- If a data transaction forces the rollback segment to grow more than one extent past its `optimal` setting, Oracle will shrink the rollback segment automatically at some point in time after the transaction commits.
- Shrinks and extends cause additional processing overhead on the Oracle instance.
- The DBA can query the V$ROLLSTAT dynamic performance view to determine whether a high number of extends and shrinks are happening to the rollback segment.
- If a high number of shrinks are occurring, as reflected by the SHRINKS column of V$ROLLSTAT, the DBA should increase the `optimal` storage clause for that rollback segment.
- Block size is determined by the `DB_BLOCK_SIZE` initialization parameter.
- Block size cannot be changed once the database is created.
- Oracle block size should be a multiple of operating-system block size.
- The use of space within a block to store row data is determined by `pctfree` and `pctused`. The `pctfree` option is the amount of space Oracle leaves free in each block for row growth. The `pctused` option is the amount of space that must be freed after the block initially fills in order for Oracle to add that block to the freelist.
- A high `pctfree` means the block leaves a lot of room for rows to grow. This is good for high-volume transaction systems with row growth, but has the potential to waste disk space.
- A low `pctfree` maximizes disk space by leaving little room for rows to grow. Space is well utilized but potential is there for chaining and row migration.
- Row migration occurs when a row has grown too large for the block it is currently in, and Oracle moves it to another block.

- Chaining occurs when Oracle tries to migrate a row, but no block in the freelist can fit the entire row because the row is larger than the entire block size (for example, one of the columns in the table is type LONG), and Oracle breaks it up and stores the pieces where it can find room in several blocks).
- The `analyze` command places ROWIDs for chained rows in the CHAINED_ROWS table created by `utlchain.sql`. This table must be present for `analyze` to work.
- Index use in retrieving table data can be monitored using the V$SYSSTAT view or by executing `explain plan` on every SQL statement in an application.
- Database objects should be sized so that all data in the object fits into one extent or a few extents.

Chapter Questions

1. **You are determining appropriate space usage for your application, an OLTP system on which data is highly volatile. Keeping a high `pctfree` for that system has which of the following effects?**

   A. Keeps the data blocks filled to capacity with table or index data

   B. Works well for both OLTP and decision support systems

   C. Maximizes performance on the database buffer cache

   D. Reduces the possibility of row chaining and data migration

2. **In your initialization file, you have `TRANSACTIONS` set to 150 and the parameter `TRANSACTIONS_PER_ROLLBACK_SEGMENT` set to 1,000. If, after database startup, your database has 15 rollback segments and 12 of them are online, how many rollback segments will Oracle tend to use on your database?**

   A. 7

   B. 10

   C. 12

   D. 15

3. You are about to attempt to detect whether row migration is the source of a performance problem on your database. Which of the following will you do first?

A. Look at the contents of `report.txt`

B. Use the `analyze` command

C. Increase the value of `pctfree`

D. Decrease the value of `pctused`

4. You are analyzing the output of the V$ROLLSTAT view. Which of the following combinations would most likely make you believe you should increase the size of the extents within your rollback segments?

A. Low WRAPS, low EXTENDS

B. High WRAPS, low EXTENDS

C. High WRAPS, high EXTENDS

D. Low WRAPS, high EXTENDS

5. You are trying to reduce I/O bottlenecks by distributing disk resources. A query on V$SYSSTAT yields that disk sorts equals 0 for the database. Which of the following is an appropriate combination of resources on one disk?

A. Redo logs and ROLLBACK tablespace

B. DATA tablespace and TEMP tablespace

C. DATA tablespace and INDEX tablespace

D. SYSTEM tablespace and DATA tablespace

6. You are planning the design and use of rollback segments for your application. Which of the following is an appropriate use of rollback segments explicitly assigned to transactions?

A. Assigning rollback segments to every transaction on your system

B. Assigning short transactions to small rollback segments brought online for that purpose

C. Assigning long transactions to large rollback segments brought online for that purpose

D. Assigning long transactions to small rollback segments brought online for that purpose

7. You are designing a decision support system with 250 users. The system requires 24-hour uptime, because users are spread across the US and Japan. Which of the following choices identifies a proper block size for the database supporting this application?

A. 2K

B. 4K

C. 8K

D. 32K

8. The DBA is trying to tune disk-write operations to datafiles. Which three choices identify ways to tune performance of disk writes? (Choose three)

A. Changing the value for LOG_BUFFER

B. Increasing DB_WRITER_PROCESSES

C. Increasing DB_BLOCK_CHECKPOINT_BATCH

D. Making DB_BLOCK_LRU_LATCHES a multiple of DB_WRITER_PROCESSES

E. Decreasing the value set for LOG_SMALL_ENTRY_MAX_SIZE

9. Online application performance during checkpoints has become an issue. Which of the following choices is not used to address the issue of online performance during checkpoints?

A. Changing LOG_CHECKPOINT_INTERVAL

B. Increasing the number of online redo logs

C. Increasing the size of existing online redo logs

D. Changing LOG_CHECKPOINT_TIMEOUT

10. The needs of the applications using the Oracle database have changed from primarily DSS to primarily OLTP. The value of `DB_BLOCK_SIZE` can be changed by which of the following methods?

A. Resetting the `DB_BLOCK_SIZE` parameter

B. Re-creating the database

C. Resetting the value in the `next` storage option in the table

D. Resizing the value in the `pctincrease` storage clause for the tablespace

11. The number of times a rollback segment resizes itself according to the `optimal` clause is collected in which performance view?

A. V$ROLLSTAT

B. V$WAITSTAT

C. V$SYSSTAT

D. V$SESSTAT

12. The DBA creates a database and issues a `create tablespace data_01 online` statement. The minimum number of rollback segments Oracle must allocate in order for the instance to start is

A. 2

B. 3

C. 4

D. 5

Answers to Chapter Questions

1. D. Reduces the possibility of row chaining and data migration

Explanation High `pctfree` means that much space will be left empty in each data block. This doesn't keep the block filled to capacity, as choice A suggests, nor is it a good setting for decision support systems that attempt to maximize their storage capacity, as choice B suggests. A high `pctfree` has little bearing on effective use of the database buffer cache; if anything, it reduces performance because fewer rows are stored per buffer in the buffer cache. Refer to the discussion of setting `pctfree` and `pctused`.

2. A. 7

Explanation Even when you are not using Oracle Parallel Server, the `TRANSACTIONS` and `TRANSACTIONS_PER_ROLLBACK_SEGMENT` parameters have some role in determining how effectively Oracle distributes transactions between available rollback segments. 1,000 / 150 equals approximately 7. Be careful of seeing the same number in the question and in the answer, as is the case with two choices in this question.

3. B. Use the `analyze` command

Explanation The `analyze` command is used to determine which rows are chained and/or migrated in the table being analyzed. You would use `report.txt` for overall performance-tuning purposes after running UTLBSTAT and UTLESTAT, eliminating that choice. Although you would increase the value set for `pctfree` to resolve migration and chaining issues, this is not the method you would use for detecting the problem. The `pctused` option plays no role in chaining and row migration.

4. C. High WRAPS, high EXTENDS

Explanation If the value in WRAPS is high, then transaction undo information does not fit into a single extent on your rollback segments, thus meaning you should probably increase the size of the extents in the rollback segments. All other choices are incorrect because low or zero WRAPS means that transaction undo information fits comfortably into a single rollback segment extent. The use of EXTENDS in this question is a bit misleading, because the question talks only about increasing the *size* of extents in a rollback segment, not increasing the *number* of extents in the rollback segment.

5. B. DATA tablespace and TEMP tablespace

Explanation Because no disk sorts are occurring in the Oracle database, the TEMP tablespace is not being used very much, and therefore presents little risk for I/O contention when combined with another resource on disk. All other choices identify bad combinations of resources for the same disk.

6. C. Assigning long transactions to large rollback segments brought online for that purpose.

Explanation Explicitly assigning a transaction to a rollback segment is recommended only when you have a few long-running transactions (such as batch processes) that need rollback segments that are substantially longer than those usually available in Oracle. In this case, it is best to keep the larger rollback segment offline, and only bring it online when you need to run the long transaction. Thus, choice C is correct.

7. D. 32K

Explanation DSS applications typically use larger block sizes than OLTP applications. Choices A, B, and C all identify block sizes that work well for OLTP applications. Choice D, or an even larger block size, would work well for DSS applications, where reading large amounts of data quickly is the processing goal. The point made about uptime in the question is a bit misleading. Be careful not to be distracted by its presence.

8. B, C, *and* D. Increasing `DB_WRITER_PROCESSES`, increasing `DB_BLOCK_CKECKPOINT_BATCH`, *and* making `DB_BLOCK_LRU_LATCHES` a -multiple of `DB_WRITER_PROCESSES`

Explanation Choices B, C, and D can all be used to optimize how DBW0 processes. Increasing the number of database writers improves performance overall, while increasing the value set for `DB_BLOCK_CHECKPOINT_BATCH` improves performance during checkpoints. Finally, making `DB_BLOCK_LRU_LATCHES` a multiple of `DB_WRITER_PROCESSES` helps distribute the load between multiple database writers.

9. B. Increasing the number of online redo logs

Explanation Adding new online redo logs will have no effect on the frequency with which checkpoints are performed in Oracle over time. Changing the setting for `LOG_CHECKPOINT_TIMEOUT` and `LOG_CHECKPOINT_INTERVAL` will change the frequency of checkpoints that occur outside of log switches. Increasing the size of existing online redo logs will change the frequency of log switches, and thus the frequency of checkpoints that occur at those log switches.

10. B. Re-creating the database

Explanation This option is the only way to change the `DB_BLOCK_SIZE` for the database. Any other option either doesn't relate to block size or will corrupt the database if enacted. Refer to the discussion of using Oracle blocks efficiently.

11. A. V$ROLLSTAT

Explanation This V$ performance table tracks statistics about rollback-segment performance related to the rollback segment maintaining its `optimal` size. The other performance views mentioned track statistics for other areas of the database. Refer to the discussion of configuring rollback segments.

12. A. 2

Explanation The minimum number of rollback segments required by Oracle to start the instance is two when the database has more tablespaces than just SYSTEM. If the database has only a SYSTEM tablespace, the minimum number of rollback segments that must be acquired by Oracle is 1.

CHAPTER 20

Tuning Other Areas of the Oracle Database

n this chapter, you will learn about and demonstrate knowledge in the following areas:

- Monitoring and detecting lock contention
- Resolving latch and contention issues
- Tuning sort operations
- Tuning with Oracle Expert

This chapter covers the final areas of tuning the Oracle database. The first area you will cover is monitoring and detecting lock contention. You will then learn how to manage latches and contention issues arising from them. From there, you will move on to optimizing sort operations in Oracle. Last, you'll learn how to perform tuning with Oracle Expert. Each of these areas is important to understand from the perspective of the day-to-day activities of an Oracle DBA. All told, the materials in this chapter comprise about 20 percent of the material covered in OCP Exam 4 test questions.

Monitoring and Detecting Lock Contention

In this section, you will cover the following topics concerning monitoring and detecting lock contention:

- Levels of locking in Oracle
- Identifying possible causes for contention
- Using tools to detect lock contention
- Resolving contention in an emergency
- Preventing locking problems
- Identifying and preventing deadlocks

There are two objects in the Oracle architecture that manage control of access to the resources of an Oracle database: locks and latches. Locks are used to manage access to user-defined resources, such as tables and their contents. Latches are used for control on Oracle internal resources, and will be discussed in the second section of this chapter. In this section, you will learn about the levels of locking available in Oracle. You will also learn how to identify possible causes of contention on your

Oracle database, and how to use tools available in Oracle for this purpose. You will learn how to resolve contention in emergency situations, and how to prevent locking problems. Finally, you will learn how to identify and prevent deadlocks from occurring on your Oracle database.

Levels of Locking in Oracle

Locks help maintain transaction consistency on the Oracle database. A lock prevents one user from overwriting changes to the database made by another user. If two user processes are executing a series of procedures in order to make updates to the database system with no transaction consistency, there is no guarantee that the data being updated by each user will remain the same for the life of that user's transaction. However, lock mechanisms provide the ability to perform transaction processing. Locking allows users to manipulate data freely during the transaction without worry that someone else will change the data before they are done changing it.

Lock Categories and Scope

There are six different types of table locks in Oracle: *exclusive, share, share row exclusive, row share, share update,* and *row exclusive.* All locks in Oracle are table locks because the lock is acquired on the table. However, there are two different levels of locking offered by the six different types of locks. Those levels of locking are *table-level* and *row-level* locking. Table-level locking is when other locks are restricted from gaining access to change data in an entire table. Row-level locking is when a table lock allows other table locks to be acquired on a resource while preventing those locks from acquiring certain records or rows within a table to make data changes. Figure 20-1 indicates the scope of table-level locks and row-level locks.

Locks in Oracle are used for two basic purposes. The first purpose is for data-definition language (DDL) operations. DDL statements are those used in the Oracle architecture for defining tables, indexes, sequences, and other user-defined objects. Locks must be acquired to complete `create` or `alter` operations on database objects. The second purpose is for data-manipulation language (DML) operations. DML locks are acquired by user processes to make changes to object data. They allow transaction processing to take place within Oracle.

Related to the subject of transaction processing is the discussion of transaction-level read consistency. This term means that as a process executes a series of data-change statements that constitute a transaction, the process should have a version of the data that is consistent throughout the entire transaction. Locks support transaction-level read consistency by preventing two transactions from making changes to the same data in a table at the same time, without the other transaction knowing about the change. The following explanations present more

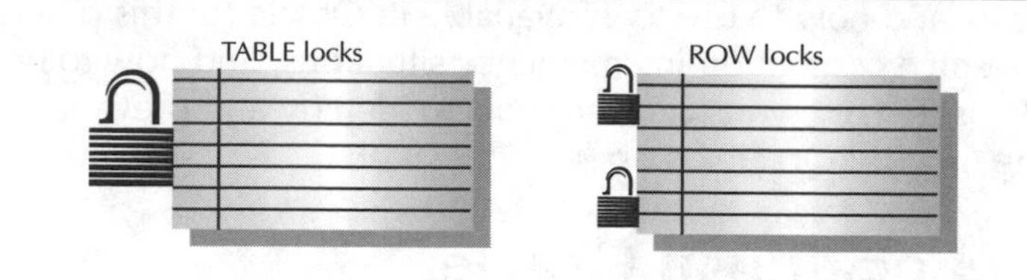

FIGURE 20-1. *Scope of table and row locks on tables*

information about each type of lock in Oracle. It is imperative that you understand how lock mechanisms work in Oracle before taking OCP Exam 4.

EXCLUSIVE During the time an exclusive lock is held, the lock holder has exclusive access to change the table and its data. Other users may `select` data, but no other transaction can acquire any type of lock on the table or `insert`, `delete`, or `update` data in the table until the exclusive lock is released by the holder of that lock.

SHARE When one transaction has a share lock on a table, other transactions can also acquire a share, share-row, or share-update lock on that same table. However, other transactions will usually have to wait until the transaction holding a share lock completes in order to complete their own transactions. No transaction can acquire exclusive, row-exclusive, or share-row-exclusive locks on a table when another transaction already holds a share lock on that table. If two transactions hold a share lock on the same table, neither transaction can change data in the table until the other transaction gives up its lock. A transaction holding the only share lock on a table can make changes to that table that Oracle will process immediately. If other transactions hold share-row or share-update locks on the same table as a transaction holding a share lock, then data changes made by the transactions holding the share-row or share-update locks will have to wait until the transaction holding the share lock commits.

ROW EXCLUSIVE A row-exclusive lock held by a transaction allows other transactions to query any rows or `insert` new rows on the table while the row-exclusive lock is being held. In addition, transactions can concurrently process `update` or `delete` statements on rows other than those held under the row-exclusive lock in the same table. Therefore, row-exclusive locks allow multiple transactions to obtain simultaneous row-exclusive, share-row, or share-update locks for different rows in the same table. However, while one transaction holds a row-exclusive lock, no other transaction can make changes to rows that the first transaction has changed until the first transaction completes. Additionally, no transaction may obtain an exclusive, share, or share-row-exclusive lock on a table while another transaction holds a row-exclusive lock on that same table.

ROW SHARE A row-share lock held by a transaction allows others to query any rows or `insert` new rows on the table while the row-share lock is being held. In addition, transactions can process `update` or `delete` statements on rows other than those held under a row-share lock concurrently in the same table. Therefore, two or more transactions can make data changes to different rows in the same table at the same time, using row-share, row-exclusive, share-update, and share-row-exclusive locks. Other transactions can acquire share locks on a table when a transaction already has a row-share lock on that table. In this case, the transaction holding the row-share lock will now have to wait until the transaction holding the share lock completes before being able to proceed with its own changes. A transaction cannot acquire an exclusive lock on a table if another transaction has already acquired the row-share lock on that table.

SHARE ROW EXCLUSIVE A share-row-exclusive lock held by a transaction allows others to query rows while the share-row-exclusive lock is being held. Transactions can acquire share-row or share-update locks on the table while a transaction holds the share-row-exclusive lock, but any transaction that attempts to `insert`, `update`, or `delete` data will have to wait until the transaction holding the share-row-exclusive lock completes. No exclusive, share, share-row-exclusive, or row-exclusive locks can be acquired on a table until the transaction holding the share-row-exclusive lock completes. A share-row-exclusive table lock held by a transaction allows other transactions to query or lock specific rows using the `select for update` clause, but not to update the table.

SHARE UPDATE A share-update lock is acquired for making changes to data in table rows. When a transaction holds this lock, any other transaction can acquire any other type of lock on a table except for the exclusive lock. A share-update lock held by a transaction allows others to query any rows or `insert` new rows on the table while the share-update lock is being held. In addition, transactions can concurrently process `update` or `delete` statements on rows other than those held under share-update locks in the same table. Therefore, two or more transactions can make data changes to different rows in the same table at the same time using row-share, row-exclusive, share-update, and share-row-exclusive locks. Other transactions can acquire share locks on a table when a transaction already has a share-update lock on that table. In this case, the transaction holding the share-update lock will have to wait until the transaction holding the share lock completes before being able to proceed with its own changes.

Acquiring Locks in Oracle

There are three different methods for acquiring locks. The first method is to let Oracle implicitly acquire the row lock you require as part of the overall use of the `select for update` or `update` statements. The `select for update` statement selects rows and places those rows under a row-share lock. The `update` statement places all rows affected by the `update` under a row-exclusive lock. Note that these two statements are able to acquire row-level locks only. The second method is through the use of the `request( )` procedure in the DBMS_LOCK Oracle-supplied package. The third method for acquiring locks is through the use of the `lock table` *`name`* `in` *`lock`* `mode [nowait]` command, where *`name`* is the name of the table and *`lock`* is the table lock mode you want to lock the table in. Valid values for *`lock`* include the lock types described previously.

```
SQL> lock table survey in share update mode nowait;
Table(s) Locked.
SQL> lock table emp in exclusive mode;
Table(s) Locked.
```

Locks Are Held Until the Transaction Completes

Note that your session will hold these locks from the time you acquire them until you end your transaction with `commit`, `rollback`, or by ending the session. Note also that if your locks were acquired as part of a PL/SQL block, the end of the block's execution does *not* implicitly end the transaction. Finally, note that the `savepoint` command does not end a transaction, either, so no locks will be released when you issue this command.

Exercises

1. What is a lock? How do locks facilitate the use of transaction processing?
2. Describe the meaning of a share lock and an exclusive lock. What are the two available scopes of locking within the Oracle architecture?
3. What is the name of the Oracle package that provides several different lock functions? What are the six types of locks available in Oracle? How are these locks obtained?

Identifying Possible Causes for Contention

Users sometimes have to wait to acquire locks on the database system, or wait to see data on the database that is held by a lock. This process of waiting for a lock itself is not contention, because many times a process will have to wait until another process completes its changes. However, excessive waiting for locks to be released could be a sign of contention. For example, if you `update` data in an area of the application where users expect to perform queries against the database, you might wind up holding a lock that causes contention. This is because the application probably won't issue a commit any time soon, to release the acquired lock. The effects can be damaging—hundreds of locks may pile up on a table, causing performance to reduce drastically. The cleanup will take a long time, as well, because you will have to correct the application, put it into production, and also kill all sessions holding locks that other users are waiting for; it may even require downtime.

Other sources of contention abound. If a process holds an exclusive lock on a table and does not relinquish that lock, then other processes will contend in their attempt to change the same data in the table. The same effect is seen with row-exclusive locks, though the effects are not as great because row locks have more limited scope than table locks. As another general rule, don't start batch processes during times of heavy OLTP use on the database because of the potential for lock contention. Figure 20-2 illustrates contention for tables that are held by table locks.

Another possibility for contention exists with the use of the share-row-exclusive lock. Although this lock is a table lock, it allows access to the table by other processes that also have the ability to acquire row locks on the table and change data. This situation means that the holder of the original share-row-exclusive lock may have to wait for other processes that acquire row-exclusive locks on the table to complete their changes and relinquish the lock before the original process can proceed.

A final possibility for contention exists on client/server systems. In this environment, it is possible for network problems or process errors on the client side

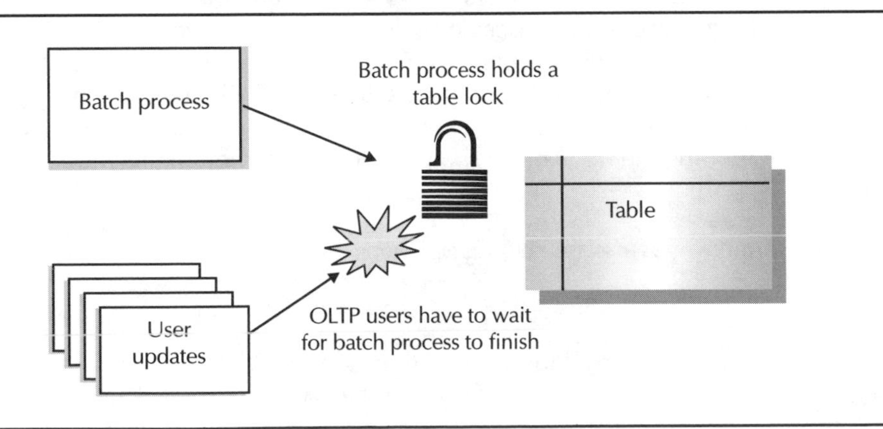

FIGURE 20-2. *Contention for tables held by table locks*

to cause a process failure on the client. In some situations, there may occur times when the user is in the process of updating a table via a row-exclusive or share lock, and the client process or Net8 network transportation layer fails. In this situation, although the process has terminated, the lock and the `update` have not. After a short period, Oracle will catch up to the *zombie* process and handle the cleanup and rollback portion of that process. But, in some cases, there could be contention if the user does not understand that some time needs to pass before the lock they just let go actually relinquishes the resource on the table. In this situation, the user may simply restart their client process immediately after killing it and attempt to perform the same data-change operation they just tried, placing a request for the same lock they still hold on another session, and *lock-wait* their own database activities.

Exercises

1. Identify a situation involving PL/SQL where lock contention might be produced. How can the contention issue be resolved?
2. Identify a situation involving Net8 where lock contention might be produced.

Using Tools to Detect Lock Contention

Once contention starts occurring on the database, it can be hard to stop without having utilities and views at your disposal. One commonly used tool for identifying contention is UTLLOCKT, a script utility provided in the Oracle distribution software. On most systems, this utility SQL script can be found in the `rdbms/admin` directory under the Oracle software home directory, called `utllockt.sql`. UTLLOCKT queries the V$ACCESS and the V$SESSION_WAIT views to find the sessions and processes holding and waiting for locks. UTLLOCKT places output in a readable tree-graph form. This script should be run while logged on as SYS. Before using this script for the first time, you will need to run `catblock.sql` to generate some dictionary views required for UTLLOCKT. The output from running the `utllockt.sql` script looks something like the following code block:

```
WAITING_SESSION TYPE MODE REQUESTED MODE HELD      LOCK ID1 LOCK ID2
--------------- ---- -------------- ---------      -------- --------
8               NONE None           None                  0        0
9               TX   Share (S)      Exclusive (X)       604      302
7               RW   Exclusive (X)  S/Row-X(SSX) 50304040       19
10              RW   Exclusive (X)  S/Row-X(SSX) 50304040       19
```

A potential drawback to this utility is that, to demonstrate the locks being held on the system, the script itself has to acquire some locks. Thus, the utility could potentially get caught in the locking situation you want to resolve. An alternative for determining whether there are contention issues that doesn't require logging into the database as user SYS, is to use the OEM Tuning Pack. Utilities, such as Lock Manager, that are part of the Tuning Pack help you to quickly identify locks acquired on the system.

There is a method for determining whether there are locking issues on the database. The method is to `select` information from V$SESSION where the value in the LOCKWAIT column is not NULL. This query obtains the processes on the database that are contending, and also identifies which operation is active, based on the value stored in the COMMAND column for sessions that are currently experiencing a lock wait.

Exercises

1. Identify the uses for the UTLLOCKT utility. Which script must be run in order to use UTLLOCKT? Which two views are used by this utility? What potential downfall does the UTLLOCKT utility have?
2. What other database view can provide information about lock contention on the database?

Resolving Contention in an Emergency

One of the few guarantees a DBA will have in the course of regular production support on the Oracle database is that emergencies will arise that require immediate resolution of locking and contention issues. There are several ways for a DBA to combat the problem of lock contention. This section will detail some of them.

One blanket solution to resolving contention is to determine which session is holding the locks that make the whole database wait, and to kill that session. The DBA can execute the query listed on the V$SESSION view to determine the session ID (SID) of the process holding the lock. The other component required for killing a session is the serial number for that session. This information can be obtained from the V$SESSION dynamic performance view with the following query:

```
SELECT sid, serial#
FROM v$session
WHERE sid in (SELECT SID FROM V$SESSION_WAIT);

ALTER SYSTEM
KILL SESSION 'sid,serial#';
```

Once the SERIAL# and SID are obtained from V$SESSION, the DBA can issue the `alter system kill session` statement. Please note, however, that this method is a blanket solution that, at the very least, does not address the underlying problem of the locking situation. However, it is important to at least know how the "solution of last resort" works.

Exercises

1. Which statement can be used to resolve lock contention in an emergency?
2. Which two pieces of information does this statement require?
3. From which performance view can the DBA obtain this data?

Preventing Locking Problems

The better and more effective solution lies in the use of the DBMS_LOCK package, which was mentioned earlier in the chapter. This set of procedures allows the application to do many things. In addition to obtaining special table locks, this package has utilities that change the status of locks being held by user processes, and it also has a tool that allows the DBA to force a session to relinquish a lock. These procedures are used for resolving contention in emergency situations and should not be undertaken lightly. At the very least, the DBA should either try to contact users or management before pursuing the `alter system kill session` approach in production environments. The DBA should also ensure that the application developer follows up with a solution that ensures the locking issue will not arise in the future.

The two procedures that may be of greatest use in lock management are the `convert( )` and `release( )` procedures of the DBMS_LOCK package. The first procedure takes a lock of one type and converts it to another. For example, a process may be holding an exclusive lock on a table, in order to `update` several rows in a read-consistent manner. It may be possible to obtain the same data-change information with a share lock, and by having the lock in that state, several SQL selects will not have to wait for the process to relinquish its lock in order to simply select data. Or, if the application developer does not want other processes to see the changes it makes until the transaction completes, perhaps a reduction in lock scope from table to row is in order.

By default, Oracle acquires the lowest level of locking for `select for update` and `update` statements—the share-row or exclusive-row lock, respectively. For acquiring all other locks, the application developer must use the `allocate_unique( )` procedure from DBMS_LOCK, which identifies the lock with a lock ID consisting of a unique numeric value, or the `lock table` command.

For the OCP exam, you should be sure that you can at least identify the package containing these functions, though the exam most likely will not test you extensively on their usage. (For this reason, you will not be given an example of the functions here.) For the `convert( )` function, that lock ID must be passed to the procedure, as well as a numeric identifier for the lock mode requested and a time-out value identifying the period of time after which the `convert( )` function will no longer attempt to change the lock mode. The `convert( )` function will return an integer value that details how the processing went for that execution. The `release( )` function simply takes the lock ID generated by `allocate_unique( )` and releases the lock.

The preceding information about DBMS_LOCK is provided as an outline for the discussion between the DBA and the developer that must take place in order to prevent contention issues from occurring. Other functionality that DBMS_LOCK can provide is to ensure that all processes on the system use the Oracle default locking mechanisms used in the `select for update` or `update` statement, rather than using higher levels of locking if those higher levels are not absolutely critical to the application.

Exercises

1. Identify the package that can be used to change lock status.
2. What is the lock acquired by an `update` statement? What about by a `select for update` statement?

Identifying and Preventing Deadlocks

Deadlocks are situations that cause serious performance problems on the Oracle database. Situations sometimes arise in which one process holds a lock on a resource while trying to obtain a lock for a second resource. A second process holds the lock for that second resource, but needs to obtain the lock for the first resource in order to release the lock on the second. This catch-22 is known as a deadlock, and this situation can involve more than two processes. Figure 20-3 illustrates a simple deadlocking situation where both processes in the diagram hold a lock, but they each need the other's lock to relinquish their own. Since neither process can proceed without the other giving up its lock, both processes are considered to be deadlocked.

The figure is provided for information only, and does not illustrate a particular situation on the database that the DBA must watch out for. In fact, the Oracle database has several features built into it that prevent the occurrence of certain deadlocks, including the one illustrated in Figure 20-3. In reality, the DBA will have to identify and resolve far more challenging deadlock situations on the database than the one in the figure.

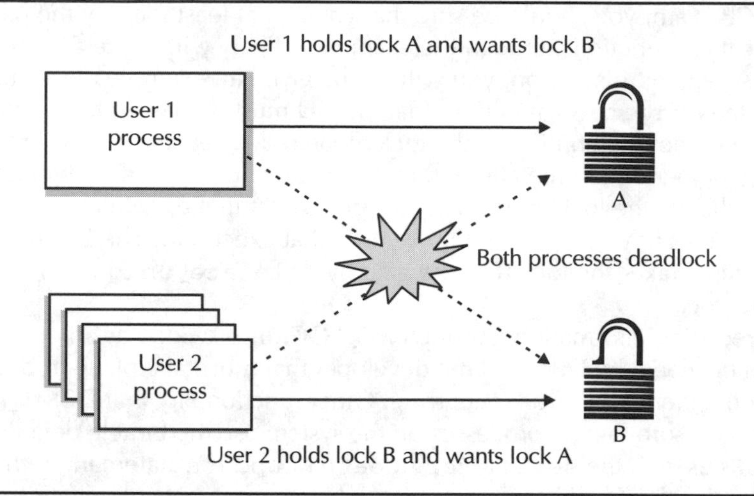

FIGURE 20-3. *Deadlocking in action*

There is only one solution for a deadlock situation, and it is the solution of last resort. The DBA must kill one or both processes in a deadlock, as explained earlier in this chapter. When Oracle's deadlock detection mechanisms discover a deadlocking situation on the database, they write a message to the ALERT log for the Oracle instance. This special trace file, which is maintained by the database, contains all error messages, along with some other meaningful information about the instance. The DBA should take note of the `"deadlock detected while waiting for a resource"` error messages, and any included process information from the ALERT log sent to assist the DBA in determining the cause of the deadlock.

There are three final points to make on preventing deadlocks. The DBA should recommend to developers that they try to set their processes up such that all processes acquire locks in the same order. This will prevent situations in which processes acquire locks on resources that others need in reversed order, which has a high probability of creating deadlock situations. The second point is for applications to always specify the lowest level of locking provided by Oracle in `select for update` and `update` statements. The locking mechanisms provided by Oracle in those two data-change statements should be sufficient for almost all application-development needs. Finally, in the interest of preventing lock contention in OLTP systems, all long-running batch updates should be scheduled to happen outside of the normal business day's data processing time.

Exercises

1. What is a deadlock? Where should the DBA look to see if deadlocking is present on the database?
2. How does the DBA resolve lock-contention issues on the database in emergencies?
3. What should the DBA do in order to prevent locking problems on the database?

Resolving Latch and Contention Issues

In this section, you will cover the following points regarding latch and contention issues:

- Using Oracle tools to resolve freelist contention
- Identifying latch-contention situations
- Resolving redo allocation-latch and copy-latch contention
- Resolving LRU-latch contention

There are two items in Oracle designed to govern access to database resources: locks and latches. Locks, which manage access to user-defined resources, were explained in the preceding section. Latches are used to provide control on Oracle internal resources, like redo logs, shared SQL buffers, the LRU list of buffers in the buffer cache, and other items that manage Oracle behind the scenes. In this section, you will learn how to use Oracle tools to resolve freelist contention. You will also learn how to identify latch-contention situations, and the special topic of resolving contention for redo allocation and copy latches will be presented. Finally, you will learn how to resolve LRU-latch contention.

Using Oracle Tools to Resolve Freelist Contention

When a data block's utilized space hits the limit specified by `pctfree` as the result of row inserts, no more rows can be inserted into it. When the amount of data stored in a block falls below `pctused`, the block is again available for new rows. Oracle maintains lists of blocks that have space available for data insertion for all tables, called *freelists*. When Oracle needs to `insert` a new row into a block, it looks at the freelist for that table in memory to find some blocks in which to put the new record. Contention can arise when more processes attempt to concurrently add data to a table than there are freelists available for that table. The DBA can identify freelist contention in the Oracle database by looking for contention for free data blocks within the buffer cache. This information is contained in the V$WAITSTAT performance view.

You can figure out freelist contention in the following way. Within V$WAITSTAT are columns CLASS and COUNT. Column CLASS contains the names of various classes of statistics Oracle maintains in this view. In this case, you will use the information in V$WAITSTAT where CLASS equals `'free list'` or `'data blocks'`. The value in column COUNT identifies freelist contention, which is how often a server process waited for free blocks in the buffer cache. The following code block illustrates retrieving this information:

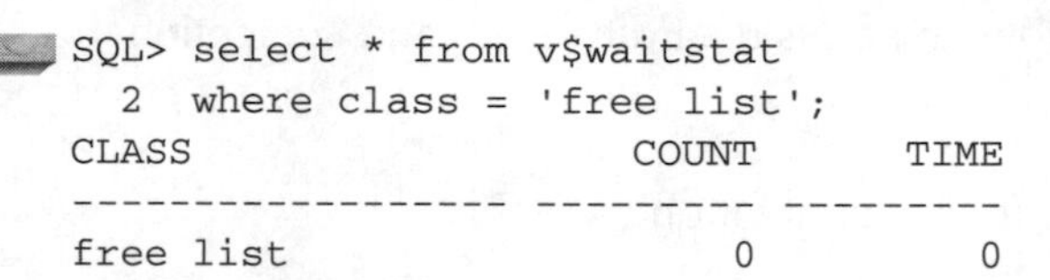

```
SQL> select * from v$waitstat
  2  where class = 'free list';
CLASS                  COUNT       TIME
------------------ --------- ---------
free list                  0         0
```

You can also look for freelist contention in the V$SYSTEM_EVENT view by searching for information where column EVENT equals `'buffer busy waits'`:

```
SQL> select * from v$system_event
  2  where event = 'buffer busy waits';
no rows selected
```

In this example, there is no contention for a freelist, but if the value for COUNT had been high, you would have had to determine which freelists for what objects were actually involved in the contention. The resolution for freelist contention on the database for that table is to add more freelists. Unfortunately, changing the number of freelists for a table is much easier said than done. The only way to add more freelists for a table is to re-create the table with a higher value specified for the `freelists` storage clause. Depending on the number of rows in the table, you may need to use EXPORT to store an intermediate copy of the data.

To choose an appropriate value for the `freelists` storage clause, in the event of detecting freelist contention for a table, first determine how many processes concurrently add data to the table. The `freelists` clause can then be set to that number of processes that are looking for free blocks to add their data in memory. With the number of freelists set to the number of processes adding row entries to that table, there should be little if any contention for freelists on that table.

Exercises

1. What are the two performance views used to determine the wait ratio for freelist contention?
2. How is freelist contention resolved?

Identifying Latch-Contention Situations

Latches limit the amount of time and space any single process can command the resource at any given time. Monitoring the latch that controls access to the resource is the method used to determine whether there is a problem with contention for the resource. A latch is simply an object in the Oracle database that a process must obtain access to in order to conduct a certain type of activity.

Latches Available in Oracle

Two V$ dynamic performance views are provided by Oracle to assist in the task of observing latch contention. They are V$LATCHHOLDER and V$LATCH. V$LATCH gives statistical information about each latch in the system, like the number of times a process waited for and obtained the latch. There are dozens of different latches in Oracle (possibly more, depending on the options installed and used). V$LATCHHOLDER tells the DBA which latches are being held at the moment and identifies the processes that are holding those latches. Unfortunately, this information is stored in V$LATCHHOLDER and V$LATCH according to latch number, while the actual names of the latches corresponding to latch number are stored only in V$LATCHNAME.

Latch Categories

Latches manage many different resources on the Oracle database. Those resources, along with some of the latches mentioned previously that handle management of that resource, are listed below:

- **Buffer cache** Cache-buffers chain, cache-buffers LRU chain, cache-buffer handle, multiblock-read objects, cache-protection latch, checkpoint-queue latch
- **Redo log** Redo allocation, redo copy, archiving control
- **Shared pool** Shared pool, library cache, library-cache load lock, row-cache objects

- **Parallel query** Parallel-query stats, parallel-query alloc buffer
- **User processes and sessions** Process allocation, session allocation, session switching, session-idle bit

Available Latches

In Oracle8 Enterprise Edition for Windows, version 8.0.5.0.0, there are over 80 latches available. Your installation of Oracle8 may have more or fewer latches available. You can determine the latches that are available on your system using the query in the following code block:

```
SQL> select * from v$latchname;
   LATCH# NAME
--------- ----------------------------------------------
        0 latch wait list
        1 process allocation
        2 session allocation
        3 session switching
        4 session idle bit
        5 cached attr list
        6 GDS latch
        7 modify parameter values
        8 messages
        9 enqueues
       10 enqueue hash chains
       11 trace latch
       12 KSFQ
       13 i/o slave adaptor
       14 ksfv message
       15 msg queue latch
       16 done queue latch
       17 session queue latch
       18 direct msg latch
       19 vecio buf des
       20 ksfv subheap
       21 first spare latch
       22 second spare latch
       23 file number translation table
       24 mostly latch-free SCN
       25 batching SCNs
       26 cache buffers chains
       27 cache buffer handles
       28 multiblock read objects
       29 cache protection latch
       30 large memory latch
       31 cache buffers lru chain
       32 Active checkpoint queue latch
```

```
33 Checkpoint queue latch
34 system commit number
35 archive control
36 redo allocation
37 redo copy
38 redo writing
39 KCL instance latch
40 KCL lock element parent latch
41 KCL name table latch
42 KCL freelist latch
43 loader state object freelist
44 begin backup scn array
45 dml lock allocation
46 list of block allocation
47 transaction allocation
48 transaction branch allocation
49 sort extent pool
50 undo global data
51 ktm global data
52 sequence cache
53 row cache objects
54 cost function
55 user lock
56 global tx free list
57 global transaction
58 global tx hash mapping
59 shared pool
60 library cache
61 library cache load lock
62 Token Manager
63 Direct I/O Adaptor
64 dispatcher configuration
65 virtual circuit buffers
66 virtual circuit queues
67 virtual circuits
68 ncodef allocation latch
69 NLS data objects
70 query server process
71 query server freelists
72 error message lists
73 process queue
74 process queue reference
75 parallel query stats
76 parallel query alloc buffer
77 constraint object allocation
78 device information
79 SGA variable
80 AQ statistics
```

Obtaining Latches

To obtain Oracle internal resources, a user or background process must first acquire the appropriate latch. Processes that request latches to perform activities using Oracle resources do not always obtain the latch the first time they request it. Some processes will wait for the latch to become available for the process's use. Other processes will not wait for the latch to become available, but instead will move on within their own process. Thus, processes holding latches may be causing waits on the system. V$LATCHHOLDER can be used to identify processes holding latches on the database. The period of time that any process will hold a latch is usually very brief—the task of identifying waits on the system, as discussed earlier, can be accomplished by continuously monitoring V$LATCHHOLDER to see which users are holding latches excessively. If there are processes that are holding latches for a long while, those processes will appear again and again. Performance for all processes that are waiting for the latch to be free will wait as well.

Unfortunately, these views use a cryptic method of identifying latches currently held. A listing of the columns in each table can be found in Figure 20-4. One solution to the problem is to use V$LATCHNAME. This view maps the latch number to a more readable name that the DBA can associate with a latch. Here is a sample query that lists the latches currently held by a process, as well as the name of the held latch:

```
SQL> SELECT h.pid, n.name
  2  FROM v$latchholder h, v$latchname n, v$latch l
  3  WHERE h.laddr = l.addr
  4 AND l.latch# = n.latch#;
PID       NAME
--------- -----------------------
34        redo allocation
12        library cache
```

This query performs a join through V$LATCH because the link from latch name in V$LATCHNAME to latch address that is given in V$LATCHHOLDER can only be made through the latch number in V$LATCH.

Exercises

1. Identify several different latches in the database. What resource do the redo allocation and copy latch handle resource management for?
2. What are two different ways a process may request access to a latch?
3. What are three dynamic performance views showing information about latches?

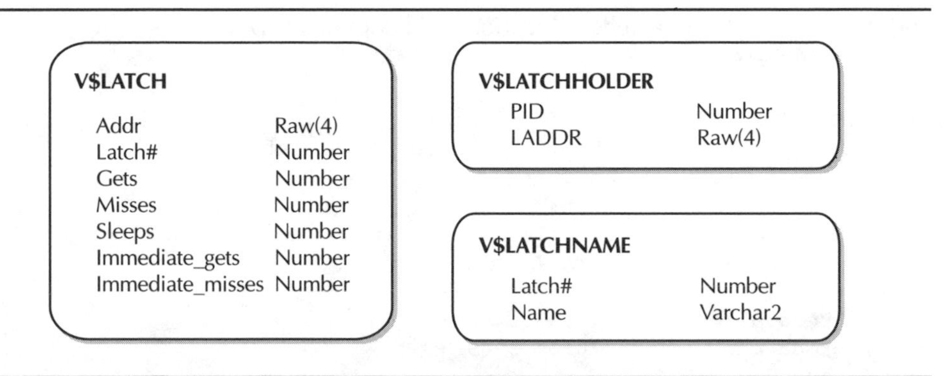

FIGURE 20-4. *V$ performance views storing latch statistics*

Resolving Redo Allocation-Latch and Copy-Latch Contention

There are two special latches in Oracle that govern access to the redo log buffer. They are the redo-allocation latch and the redo-copy latch. The redo-allocation latch must be acquired by any user process making data changes so that the user process can write a redo entry to the buffer. There is only one redo-allocation latch in Oracle. The redo-copy latch is used to write large entries to the redo log buffer. If the redo entry being made by a user process is greater than the value set for `LOG_SMALL_ENTRY_MAX_SIZE`, then the user process must acquire a redo-copy latch after acquiring the redo-allocation latch to finish writing the large entry to the buffer. There are at least as many redo-copy latches in Oracle as there are CPUs on the host machine, set automatically by Oracle by setting `LOG_SIMULTANEOUS_COPIES` equal to the value of `CPU_COUNT`. You can configure up to twice as many redo-copy latches as there are CPUs by increasing the value for `LOG_SIMULTANEOUS_COPIES` in `init`*`sid`*`.ora` and restarting the instance.

Detecting Allocation- and Copy-Latch Contention

V$LATCH is used to link different latch views to obtain latch numbers corresponding with latch addresses. This link is useful for tying in another important piece of information related to latches, the *latch wait ratio* or the number of times processes waited for latch access in proportion to the overall number of times processes requested the latch. This wait ratio helps determine whether a more serious problem with latch waits exists on the system. The following code block shows how to obtain the redo allocation- and copy-latch wait ratios using appropriate views:

```
SQL> SELECT h.pid, n.name, (l.misses/l.gets)*100 wait_ratio
  2  FROM v$latchholder h, v$latchname n, v$latch l
  3  WHERE h.laddr = l.addr
  4  AND l.latch# = n.latch#
  5  AND n.name in ('redo allocation', 'redo copy');
H.PID  N.NAME             WAIT_RATIO
------ ------------------ -------------
    34 redo allocation    1.0304495
    12 redo copy          0.0403949
```

This query compares the number of times a process did not obtain the latch to the total number of times the latch was requested. Consistent monitoring helps to determine whether the same process holds a latch over a long period of time. If other processes have to wait for that latch, there could be a problem with an event causing a wait on the system.

The V$PROCESS view has a special column called LATCHWAIT that identifies the address of a latch for which that process is currently waiting. If the LATCHWAIT column is not NULL, a wait is happening. Associating the latch name and wait ratio can be accomplished with an extension of the query already identified. The following code block demonstrates how to do this:

```
SQL> SELECT p.pid, n.name, (l.misses/l.gets)*100 wait_ratio
  2  FROM v$process p, v$latchname n, v$latch l
  3  WHERE p.latchwait is not null
  4  AND p.latchwait = l.addr
  5  AND l.latch# = n.latch#
  6  AND n.name in ('redo allocation', 'redo copy');
P.PID   N.NAME           WAIT_RATIO
------- ---------------- -------------
     34 redo allocation  1.0304495
```

Types of Requests for Redo-Allocation Latch

There are two types of requests for the redo-allocation latch. The distinction between each type of request is based on whether the requestor will continue to run if the latch is not available to that process. Some processes are willing to wait for the latch, while others are not. If a process will wait for the latch, the following series of events will take place:

1. The process will request the latch.
2. If the latch is available, the process will obtain it.

3. If the latch is unavailable, the process will wait a short period of time and ask for the latch again. This period of wait time is called a *sleep*. The process will continue its cycle of asking and sleeping until the latch becomes available.

Unlike those processes that are willing to wait until a latch becomes available, there are other processes that will not wait until the latch is free to continue. These processes require the latch immediately or they move on. The V$LATCH dynamic performance view captures statistics on both types of latch requests. Table 20-1 shows the columns of V$LATCH, an explanation of the column, and the corresponding type of request it reflects.

Consider an examples of obtaining latches. Assume a user process puts forth an immediate request to obtain a latch. The latch is available, so the request is granted and the user process obtains the latch. The IMMEDIATE_GETS column on V$LATCH corresponding to the row entry for that latch will be incremented by one. Using that same example, let's say now that the latch was busy. In that case, Oracle would increment the IMMEDIATE_MISSES column on the corresponding row entry in V$LATCH for that latch. This example illustrates that the statistics compilation process for immediate requests for latches is straightforward.

Determining Contention for Redo Allocation and Copy Latches, Revisited

Now, consider the more involved process of compiling statistics for requests that are willing to wait. A user process makes a willing-to-wait request for a latch. The latch

Column	Request Type	Explanation
GETS	Willing to wait	The number of latch requests that resulted in actually obtaining the latch
MISSES	Willing to wait	The number of latch requests that did not result in actually obtaining a latch
SLEEPS	Willing to wait	The number of times a process waited for the latch, and then requested to obtain it again
IMMEDIATE_GETS	Immediate	The number of latch requests that resulted in immediately obtaining the latch
IMMEDIATE_MISSES	Immediate	The number of latch requests that were unsuccessful in obtaining the latch

TABLE 20-1. *Types of Latch Requests and Their Meanings*

is available, so the process obtains the latch. The GETS column from V$LATCH is incremented by one. Using the same example, the user process requests a latch, but this time the latch is unavailable. The user process has to wait. So, the user process goes to sleep. The MISSES column is incremented and the SLEEP column is incremented, and the process doesn't get its latch. After a short period, the process wakes up and asks for the latch again. The latch is now available, so the GETS column in V$LATCH for that latch is incremented, as well. One can see that the numbers will add up on those columns corresponding to willing-to-wait requests if latches become tough to obtain.

The next important aspect of latches is the calculation of the wait ratio for a latch. The DBA can obtain the wait ratio for a given latch by executing the following query against Oracle:

```
SQL> SELECT n.name,
  2  (l.misses/l.gets)*100 w2wait_ratio,
  3  (l.immediate_misses/l.immediate_gets)*100 immed_ratio,
  4  FROM v$latch l, v$latchname n
  5  WHERE n.name in ('redo copy','redo allocation')
  6  AND n.latch# = l.latch#;
N.NAME              W2WAIT_RATIO   IMMED_RATIO
------------------- -------------- --------------
redo allocation     1.0304495      2.9405949
```

Any of the names for latches listed in the code block displaying the contents of V$LATCHNAME can be used as part of the `in` clause in this statement. However, as you will learn in this unit, the latches that manage access to the redo log resources are particularly important because there are few of them, and every process that makes changes to data needs access to them. If either the wait ratio on the willing-to-wait or immediate latch requests for the latch named by the DBA in the query are greater than 1, then there is a problem with latch contention in the database.

Resolving the Problem

To resolve the problem of redo allocation- and copy-latch contention, you must decrease the value set for `LOG_SMALL_ENTRY_MAX_SIZE` so that user processes hold the redo-allocation latch for only a short time. You can also set the `LOG_ENTRY_PREBUILD_THRESHOLD` to the same value as `LOG_SMALL_ENTRY_MAX_SIZE` so that all user processes have to prebuild their redo entries that will be written while holding the redo-allocation latch. You can further reduce contention for the redo-copy latch by setting the `LOG_SIMULTANEOUS_COPIES` parameter to twice the number of CPUs available on the system. These efforts should reduce or eliminate contention for the redo copy and allocation latches.

Exercises

1. What is a willing-to-wait request for a latch? How does it differ from an immediate request for a latch?
2. What is a wait ratio? What are the two types of wait ratios associated with latches? How can the DBA find out what the wait ratio is? If the wait ratio is 6, is there an issue with latch contention in the database?
3. How do you resolve contention for the redo allocation and copy latches?

Resolving LRU Latch Contention

The LRU (least-recently-used) latch controls the server process's access to write new buffers into the buffer cache. Oracle automatically sets the number of LRU latches to be one-half the number of CPUs on the system. When your host machine has only one processor, one LRU latch is sufficient. Contention for the LRU latch can impede database performance when a large number of CPUs are available on the host system, when only one DBW0 process is available on the database, or when the load between multiple DBW0 processes is unequally distributed. You can detect LRU-latch contention by querying V$LATCH in the following way:

```
SQL> SELECT p.pid, n.name, (l.misses/l.gets)*100 wait_ratio
  2  FROM v$process p, v$latchname n, v$latch l
  3  WHERE p.latchwait is not null
  4  AND p.latchwait = l.addr
  5  AND l.latch# = n.latch#
  6  AND n.name = 'cache buffers lru chain');
P.PID   N.NAME                    WAIT_RATIO
------- ------------------------- -------------
     31 cache buffers lru chain  1.0304495
```

You can also query V$SYSTEM_EVENT to determine LRU latch contention in the following way:

```
SQL> select * from v$system_event
  2  where event = 'buffer latch';
no rows selected
```

Reducing LRU-Latch Contention

You can specify the number of LRU latches on your system with the initialization parameter DB_BLOCK_LRU_LATCHES to reduce LRU-latch contention. This parameter sets the maximum number of LRU latches for your database buffer cache. Each LRU latch controls access to a set of buffers within the buffer cache. The following factors should be weighed when setting the appropriate value for DB_BLOCK_LRU_LATCHES:

- The maximum number of latches is twice the number of CPUs in the system. An appropriate setting for DB_BLOCK_LRU_LATCHES is between half the number of CPUs and the actual number of CPUs in your host system.
- A latch should have no less than 50 buffers in its set
- Do not create multiple latches when Oracle runs in single-process mode. Oracle automatically uses only one LRU latch in single-process mode.
- The higher the workload, the more latches you need.

TIP
To change the number of LRU latches on your database, you must adjust the DB_BLOCK_LRU_LATCHES parameter and restart the instance.

Exercises

1. Which parameter is used to determine the number of LRU latches on your database? How do you determine whether contention is occurring for LRU latches?
2. What are some guidelines for setting LRU latches on your system?

Tuning Sort Operations

In this section, you will cover the following topics related to tuning sort operations:

- Identifying SQL operations that use sorts
- Ensuring that sorts happen in memory
- Allocating temporary disk space for sorts
- Using direct writes for sorts

Sort operations are the final area of tuning covered in this unit. Oracle can require a great deal of overhead to impose order on your data, because relational databases do not store data in any particular order. In this section, you will first learn which SQL operations require sorts to be performed. Then, you will learn how to ensure that sorts happen in memory rather than in your TEMPORARY tablespaces. After that, you'll learn how to properly allocate temporary disk space for sorts. Last, you'll cover how to use direct writes for disk sort operations.

Identifying SQL Operations That Use Sorts

Since the rows in the Oracle database usually aren't stored in any particular order, the user may want to force some order upon them. This type of operation may be used in reports or online, or within the B-tree index-creation mechanism where the indexed column on the database is stored in a particular order with the intent of allowing fast access to the table on that sorted column. Hence, in the absence of storing Oracle data in a special order, often there is a need for sorting data on the database (see Figure 20-5).

Several data-manipulation activities will require sorts. One example is the `order by` operation. The `order by` option improves readability of data for the purposes of providing a more meaningful report. For example, a table dump for all employee data contains the information needed to produce a comparison report to find out who the 65 highest-paid employees are. However, since the data is provided in a haphazard format, through which the reader has to search intensively for several minutes or hours to find those 65 highly paid employees, the data really has no meaning. Instead, the report could be designed to list every employee and their salary in a department, in descending order on the SALARY column on the relevant table, using the `order by` clause of the `select` statement.

Another SQL operation that utilizes sorts is the `group by` clause. This operation is used to collect data into groups based on a column or columns. This function can be useful in various reporting situations where a set of distinct column values may appear several times, mapped with unique values in other columns.

Sorts are used in several other situations on the Oracle database. Sorts are conducted as part of `select distinct`, `minus`, `intersect`, and `union` statements, as well as in the `min( )`, `max( )`, and `count( )` operations. The *sort merge join* internal Oracle operation running behind the scenes when a user executes a `select` statement to create a join also uses sorts, as does the creation of indexes.

Exercises

1. What is a sort operation?
2. Which SQL operations use sorts?

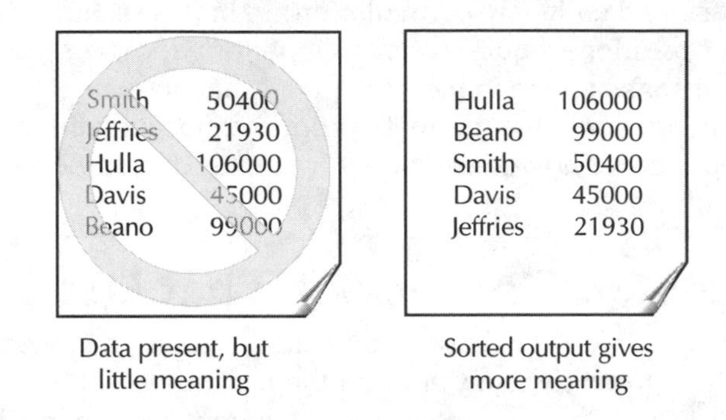

FIGURE 20-5. *Using sorts to give data meaning*

Ensuring That Sorts Happen in Memory

Oracle requires some temporary space, either in memory or on disk, in order to perform a sort. If Oracle cannot get enough space in memory to perform the sort, then it must obtain space in a TEMPORARY tablespace on disk. In most cases, the default size for the area in memory used for sorting is enough to store the entire sort; however, there can be situations in which a large sort will require space on disk. Since data in memory can be accessed faster than data on a disk, it benefits the performance of sorts to keep all aspects of the sort within memory.

The DBA should monitor sort activities. The dynamic performance view that stores information about how frequently Oracle needs to access disk space to perform a sort is called V$SYSSTAT. To find the number of sorts occurring in memory versus the number of sorts occurring on disk, the DBA can select the NAME and VALUE from V$SYSSTAT where the name is either `'sorts(memory)'` or `'sorts(disk)'`. In the output from this query, a high value for memory sorts is desirable, while the desired value for disk sorts is as close to zero as possible.

Sizing the Memory Area Used for Sorting

If there is a consistently high number of disk sorts, or if the number of disk sorts taking place on the database is increasing, then the DBA may want to consider increasing the space allocated for sorts in memory. This task is accomplished by increasing the value for the initialization parameter `SORT_AREA_SIZE`. This initialization parameter represents the greatest amount of memory a user process can obtain in order to perform a sort. Setting this value high allows the process to sort more data in fewer operations. However, as with increasing the size of any memory structure, the DBA will want to spend some time making sure that the additional size added to the sort area does not interfere with the amount of real memory available for the SGA. If the machine hosting Oracle starts paging the SGA into virtual memory on disk, there will be a bigger memory performance issue at hand associated with swapping information in real memory out to disk.

One way the DBA can avoid problems with memory management as a result of increasing SORT_AREA_SIZE is to decrease another parameter associated with sorts, the SORT_AREA_RETAINED_SIZE. This initialization parameter represents the smallest amount of space Oracle will retain in a process's sort area when the process is through using the data that was sorted. This may help memory, but at the expense of creating some additional disk utilization to move data around in temporary segments on disk. The DBA and application administrators may also improve database performance by ensuring that batch processing does not interfere with OLTP data usage during the normal business day.

Avoiding Sorts in Index Creation

Another way to improve performance with respect to sorting is to avoid sorts entirely. This method is particularly useful when creating indexes. As stated earlier, indexes use sorts to create the B-tree structure that is then used to find a particular value in the indexed column and its corresponding ROWID quickly. Sorts in index creation can only be avoided if the data in the table is already sorted in appropriate order on the column that needs to be indexed. This option is useful if the operating system on the machine hosting Oracle has a particularly efficient sorting algorithm, or if there is only a tight window available for the DBA to create the index. The nosort clause allows the DBA to create an index based on table data that is already sorted properly. In this scenario it is important to remember that the table data needs to be sorted on the column being indexed in order for nosort to work. If the data in the table whose column is being indexed is not sorted, then the index-creation process will fail.

```
SQL> CREATE INDEX uk_emp_01
  2  ON emp (empid)
  3  NOSORT;
Index created.
```

Exercises

1. For better performance, on which part of the system should sorts take place?
2. Which dynamic performance view can be used to determine how frequently sorts are using the various resources of the machine hosting Oracle?

Allocating Temporary Disk Space for Sorts

When a sort operation takes place that requires disk space to complete successfully, the disk space it uses is temporary. The appropriate tablespace for this space is the TEMPORARY tablespace. (For more information on how TEMPORARY tablespaces work in Oracle8, consult Chapter 7.) The TEMPORARY tablespace is used for user processes that require allocating temporary segments in order to process certain SQL statements. Sorts are one type of operation that may require temporary disk storage. The `group by` and `order by` clauses are two types of SQL statements that require sorts, which may, in turn, allocate space in the user's temporary tablespace for the purpose of sorting.

Care should be taken to ensure that the user's temporary tablespace is not set to default to the SYSTEM tablespace, because temporary allocation of segments for operations like sorts can contribute to fragmenting a tablespace. Both the default and temporary tablespaces for a user are set in the `create user` or `alter user` statement. If the tablespaces are not set in either of those statements, the user will place temporary segments used for sorts in the SYSTEM tablespace. Given the importance of SYSTEM to the integrity of the database, it is important that the DBA minimize any problems that may occur with space management.

```
SQL> CREATE USER stacy
  2  IDENTIFIED BY spanky
  3  DEFAULT TABLESPACE users_01
  4  TEMPORARY TABLESPACE temp_01;
User created.
SQL> ALTER USER DINAH
  2  TEMPORARY TABLESPACE temp_02;
User altered.
```

Exercises

1. How can the DBA ensure that users utilize the TEMP tablespace for sorts requiring temporary segments?
2. Which tablespace should never be used to store temporary segments?

Using Direct Writes for Sorts

In some situations, the machine hosting the Oracle database may have extensive disk and memory resources available for effective performance on data sorts that the use of direct writes for sorting provides. A *direct write* is when Oracle avoids use of the buffer cache for writing blocks of temporary information required for a sort, instead writing them directly to disk. This option is set up using three parameters from the Oracle initialization parameter file. The parameters, along with an explanation of their use, are as follows:

- **SORT_DIRECT_WRITES** Should be TRUE or AUTO. When TRUE, Oracle will obtain buffers in memory that are designed to handle disk writes as part of the sort.
- **SORT_WRITE_BUFFERS** Specified as an integer. When SORT_DIRECT_WRITES is TRUE, Oracle will obtain this number of buffers to handle disk I/O on sorts.
- **SORT_WRITE_BUFFER_SIZE** Value specified as an integer in bytes. When SORT_DIRECT_WRITES is TRUE, Oracle will size each buffer obtained for disk writes to be the value specified for this parameter.

It is important to remember that using SORT_DIRECT_WRITES represents a large memory and disk-resource commitment for the purpose of sorting data. Specifically, in addition to whatever sort area has been allocated as part of the SGA, this option will require memory in the amount of SORT_WRITE_BUFFERS times SORT_WRITE_BUFFER_SIZE. The DBA should use extreme care in order to make sure that this additional memory requirement does not cause a shortage of available real memory and cause the host machine to page the SGA out into virtual memory on disk. By reducing the amount of memory allocated for SORT_AREA_SIZE to the same amount that the SORT_DIRECT_WRITES parameter will consume as calculated by the preceding formula, the DBA alleviates some of the burden on real memory that is produced by increasing SORT_DIRECT_WRITES. Oracle recommends that SORT_DIRECT_WRITES be used only in the event that the above formula is 1/10 the value specified for SORT_AREA_SIZE. If the space allocated for direct writes is any larger than 10 percent of the SORT_AREA_SIZE, then this option should not be used.

Exercises

1. Explain how direct writes boost performance on sorts.
2. What are the hardware considerations of using that option?
3. What are the three initialization parameters used to configure that option?

Tuning with Oracle Expert

In this section, you will cover the following points on tuning with Oracle Expert:

- Oracle Expert features

- Creating a tuning session
- Gathering, viewing, and editing input data
- Analyzing collected data using rules
- Reviewing tuning recommendations
- Implementing tuning recommendations

Oracle Expert is a new tool that helps you monitor and tune your Oracle database. Perhaps the most distinguishing feature about this tool is its ability to correct many routine tuning problems experienced by Oracle databases without intervention from the DBA. In this section, you will cover the features of Oracle Expert. You will learn how to create a tuning session with Oracle Expert to identify the tuning issues currently active on your database. You will also learn how to gather, view, and edit input data for your tuning session, and how to analyze data collected from a tuning session using rules. You will learn how to review and implement Oracle Expert's tuning recommendations, as well.

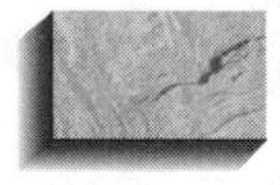

TIP
Oracle Expert is a tool with more features than there is room to discuss in this section. For brevity's sake, the discussion focuses on the areas of this tool that will most likely be tested on OCP Exam 4. For a thorough treatment on this tool, you should review the Oracle Enterprise Manager & Management Packs Demo CD-ROM, available from the Oracle Corporation at http://www.oracle.com.

Oracle Expert Features

Oracle Expert is designed to assist both with the assessment of tuning issues and the implementation of tuning solutions on your Oracle database. To use Oracle Expert effectively, you should have an understanding of how this tool approaches tuning. First, Oracle Expert allows you to define how it should monitor database activity to focus its assessments on areas you want to tune. For example, if you want to tune database operation, and you want to make necessary changes to the layout of datafiles in the host file system, you can specify this as a structural tuning session and Oracle Expert will focus on structural changes that could be made to improve performance. Oracle Expert then collects data in many different areas, such as the application, instance configuration, and overall workload on the production machine hosting Oracle.

After Oracle Expert completes its effort, you can view the data it collected and tell Oracle Expert to apply certain rules to that data. Returning to the structural change example, you can optimize how Oracle Expert interprets the information gathered. Based on how you tell Oracle Expert you want to tune your database, the tool will generate some recommendations on how to improve system performance. You can then review Oracle Expert's suggestions, and either accept or reject the changes. If you accept, Oracle Expert can then generate scripts, `init`*`sid`*`.ora` files, and other means to implement the changes it has suggested.

Oracle Expert supports several different methods of tuning, as well. For example, as part of your ongoing maintenance of your Oracle database, you may run Oracle Expert periodically to assess whether any issues have surfaced that may affect system performance. You might tune in this way after adding new hardware designed to improve system performance, such as faster disk controllers or more CPUs. Your tuning needs may encompass emergency situations, as well. There may be some problem with overall database operation that needs to be resolved right away.

You may find it useful to use Oracle Performance Manager in addition to Oracle Expert. Oracle Performance Manager is another component of the Oracle Tuning Pack. In some situations, such as when designing an application for production needs, you may even want to find information about how Oracle might run in different scenarios, such as during peak load times, or if you substantially increased the number of users of a system. Oracle Expert can help you in such experimental tuning situations, as well.

TIP
You must have Oracle Tuning Pack in order to use Oracle Expert! The basic Oracle Enterprise Manager software that comes with Oracle8 or Oracle8i Enterprise or client will not contain the Tuning Packs.

Exercises

1. Identify some uses for Oracle Expert. What is the general procedure for utilizing this tool?
2. In what tuning situations might you use Oracle Expert? When might you use other tools in addition to Oracle Expert?

Creating a Tuning Session

To create a tuning session, you must first start Oracle Expert. In Windows, you can run Oracle Expert on its own by selecting Start | Programs | Oracle Enterprise Manager | Oracle Expert, or from within the OEM console you can click the Oracle Expert button in the OEM Tuning Pack toolbar. You will then have to connect to your Oracle database as a user with the `select any table` privilege. If this is your first time using Oracle Expert, you may first want to create a username for Oracle Expert to use when logging into your Oracle database. It may also be beneficial to create a small tablespace for that user in Tablespace Manager, because Oracle Expert will want to create a repository to store tuning information.

The Oracle Expert interface is similar to interfaces in other OEM tools, with a menu bar across the top, the drill-down nodes on the left side, and the work area on the right. After starting Oracle Expert and connecting as your privileged user, you can create a tuning session by selecting the File | New menu option to create a new tuning session. You will then work through a small wizard that prompts you to name your tuning session for future reference and use. If you already have tuning sessions you have used for that database, you can use those sessions by drilling down to the appropriate Databases | *Your Database* | Tuning Session | *Your Tuning Session* node.

A tab interface will appear in the work area of your Oracle Expert window after you open a tuning session. The tabs, from left to right, are Scope, Collect, View/Edit, Analyze, Review Recommendations, and Implement. These tabs show, sequentially, the activities you will engage in for tuning your database with Oracle Expert. In the next section, you will learn how to use the first three tabs to tune with Oracle Expert.

Exercises

1. What are two ways to start Oracle Expert?
2. What are the actions Oracle Expert will perform the first time you log into Oracle using that tool? What are Oracle Expert's requirements of the username you use to connect to Oracle?

Gathering, Viewing, and Editing Input Data

You must begin your tuning session by defining the scope. Available scopes for Oracle Expert include instance tuning, application tuning, and structural tuning. Instance tuning is used to tune the `init`*`sid`*`.ora` parameters you have set for your instance in the areas of SGA, I/O, sorting, parallel query, Parallel Server, and any parameters that are specific to your operating system. Application tuning covers SQL statement tuning, as well as access methods. You can review Chapter 17 for more information on what those two areas encompass. Finally, structural tuning is tuning that checks the layout of Oracle file resources on disks to identify any resource-contention issues that may arise from placement. Structural tuning is also good at verifying segment and extent sizing to ensure that database objects are properly sized. In addition to choice of tuning scope, you will need to choose values for your control parameters. These include workload class (OLTP, batch, or DSS), amount of unscheduled downtime that occurs for this database, the peak logical write rate (low, medium, or high), and whether forms applications will be used on this database.

Input Data Collection

Once you set your scope, you can click on the Collect tab to determine which data classes you want Oracle Expert to collect. The classes are Database, Instance, Schema, Environment, and Workload. This data is then stored in the Oracle Expert repository. The more data you collect, the longer your tuning session will last, so if you are short on time or need answers fast, you should only collect the minimum amount of data required for the tuning scope you chose in the previous tab. Each class of data has a number of subclasses, which you can view and select, using the interface that appears when you click the Options button to the far right on the row where the checkbox for that class appears.

Collecting Input Data About Workload

The only aspect of data collection Oracle Expert cannot collect automatically is workload class data. This is data that gives Oracle Expert the "big picture" of the regular application workload for this database. You must collect this data when the activity is occurring, using Oracle Trace (another component of the Oracle Tuning Pack). This information can also be collected using an Oracle Expert tuning session run during the time of the application workload you want to tune, or you can enter this data manually using the View/Edit tab, which will be covered shortly. Oracle Expert can also collect this information from the library cache of your database.

Viewing and Editing Input Data

Once you have set the collection information, you can view and edit the input data using the View/Edit tab of the Oracle Expert interface window. The input data for your tuning session will be shown as a drill-down hierarchy in the View/Edit tab, and if you click on any of the nodes, a property sheet with relevant information about each of those input areas will appear. You can make changes to the input data within the property sheet for that input data.

Exercises

1. Explain the function and use of the Scope tab. Which scopes are available in Oracle Expert?
2. Explain the function and use of the Collect tab. What are classes of the data from which you can collect input?
3. Explain the use and function of the View/Edit tab. How can you edit input information using this interface?

Analyzing Collected Data Using Rules

In addition to editing data, you can modify the rules Oracle Expert uses to evaluate information gathered in the tuning session. In the property sheet, notice the Rules tab. If you have Oracle Expert on your machine, you can click the Rules tab and view or modify any of the basic rules displayed in the window. By modifying rules, you can affect the tuning recommendations made by Oracle Expert to override, influence, or otherwise modify the feedback this tool gives you. You can modify rules in several different areas, as denoted by the tabs available in the Rules interface.

TIP
Your own knowledge of performance tuning should indicate to you whether you should feel comfortable changing rules in Oracle Expert. If you have tuned successfully without using Oracle Expert, you might want to design your own rules for use by your team members.

Analyzing Your Database

Once you enter the information you need to enter in the Scope, View/Edit, and Collect tabs, you are ready to have Oracle Expert analyze your database. This can take a while, particularly if you are collecting statistics from many different classes. Click on the Analyze tab, and you will see an interactive message window along with some buttons on the bottom of the interface. Click on the Perform Analysis button at the bottom center of the Analyze tab to start Oracle Expert's analysis of your database.

Exercises

1. What are rules? How do you view and modify rules? What effect does changing these rules have on the results?
2. How do you perform the analysis of your database?

Reviewing Tuning Recommendations

When analysis is complete, you can review Oracle Expert's recommendations in two ways. The first is online, by clicking the Review Recommendations tab. You will see a drill-down interface listing all the recommendations Oracle Expert can offer for tuning your database. You can double-click any of these recommendations to view detailed explanations about the recommendations made by Oracle Expert.

The second method is to have Oracle Expert generate a report containing its findings. Available reports can be found under the Reports menu in the main window of Oracle Expert. You can specify the sections to be included in these reports, the filenames, and where the reports should be saved.

Exercise

What are the two ways you can review tuning recommendations from Oracle Expert?

Implementing Tuning Recommendations

After you've reviewed the Oracle Expert suggestions, you can implement the recommendations Oracle Expert makes by having Oracle Expert generate scripts, parameter files, or other methods of implementation for the changes suggested. Oracle Expert will offer suggestions in the areas of application tuning, `init`*`sid`*`.ora` parameters, changes to the structural layout of Oracle disk resources on the host, and Parallel Server recommendations if you are using that product. One important thing to be aware of is that Oracle Expert makes overlapping or interdependent suggestions to solve certain performance problems. A simple example is when you are tuning checkpoint processing, Oracle Expert may suggest increasing the size of your redo logs (structural) and setting LOG_CHECKPOINT_ TIMEOUT to 0 (parametric). If you implement only one of these suggestions, you may not see a full improvement on performance. If there is one category of changes you do not wish to make, such as structural changes, you should include this in your Oracle Expert preferences and analyze again.

On the far right-hand side of the Oracle Expert is the Implement tab. Clicking it will reveal a list of files that Oracle Expert can generate to help you implement its suggestions. Click on the Generate Files button at the bottom of the window to have Oracle Expert generate those files.

Exercise

Describe the procedure for implementing Oracle Expert's recommendations.

Chapter Summary

This chapter covered some miscellaneous aspects of tuning the Oracle instance, including tuning lock contention, tuning latch contention, tuning sorts, and using Oracle Expert. These topics cover material that comprises 20 percent of the questions asked on OCP Exam 4.

The first topic covered in this chapter was monitoring and detecting lock contention. You learned about the different levels of locking available in Oracle, along with the possible causes of lock contention. The use of Oracle utilities for detecting lock contention was also covered in some detail. You learned how to resolve contention in an emergency by killing a user session, how to prevent locking problems on your application, and how to recognize Oracle errors that arise from deadlocks.

The next section of this chapter explained latches and the contention issues that arise from their use. You learned how to use Oracle tools and views to detect contention for freelists in your Oracle database. You also learned about the different types of latches and when contention might occur for these latches. The special situation of detecting contention for the redo allocation and copy latch was covered in some detail. Finally, you learned how to detect and resolve problems with contention for the LRU latch in the database buffer cache.

The third section of this chapter covered tuning and optimizing sort operations. You learned which SQL operations in Oracle require performing sorts. The distinction between a memory sort and a disk sort was made, and you learned how to size memory in order to ensure that sorts happen in memory as often as possible. You learned the importance of properly allocating temporary space on disk for sorts, and also how to set Oracle so that it uses direct writes for disk sorts to enhance performance.

The last section of this chapter covered tuning your database with Oracle Expert. You learned what the features of Oracle Expert are, along with how to create a tuning session. You also learned how to gather, view, and edit input data for your tuning session. The techniques for analyzing collected data using rules was explained, as well. Finally, you learned how to review and implement the tuning recommendations made by Oracle Expert.

Two-Minute Drill

- Levels of locking include row share, row exclusive, share, exclusive, and share row exclusive.
- Lock contention occurs when a process doesn't relinquish a lock it holds, when a process holds a higher level of lock than it really needs, and when a user process drops while holding a lock in the client/server architecture.
- The UTLLOCKT procedure is used to detect lock contention.
- The method used to eliminate contention is to kill sessions that are deadlocked. The Session ID and serial number from V$SESSION are required for this activity. To kill a session, execute `alter system kill session`.
- Preventing deadlocks is done at the application level by changing the application to relinquish locks it obtains or using locks with the least amount of scope required to complete the transaction.
- Oracle errors arising from deadlocks can be found in the `alert` log, a special file the Oracle database uses to track all errors on that instance. The error `"deadlock detected while waiting for a resource"` corresponds to a deadlock.
- Application developers can also prevent deadlocks by designing the application to acquire locks in the same order in all processes, and to use the minimum locking capability required to complete the transaction.
- Latches are similar to locks in that they are used to control access to a database resource. Latch contention occurs when two (or more) processes are attempting to acquire a latch at the same time.
- There are dozens of different latches available in the Oracle database.
- Latches are used in conjunction with restricting write access to online redo logs, among other things. The two types of latches for this purpose are redo-allocation latches and redo-copy latches.
- Some processes that make requests for latches are willing to wait for the latch to be free. Other processes move on if they cannot obtain immediate access to a latch.

- V$LATCH is used for latch-performance monitoring. It contains the GETS, MISSES, SLEEPS, IMMEDIATE_GETS, and IMMEDIATE_MISSES statistics required for calculating wait ratios.
- V$LATCHNAME holds a readable identification name corresponding to each latch number listed in V$LATCH.
- V$LATCHHOLDER lists the processes that are currently holding latches on the system. This is useful for finding the processes that may be causing waits on the system.
- V$LOCK lists the processes that are holding object locks on the system. This is useful for finding processes that may be causing waits on the system.
- Latch performance is measured by the wait ratio. For processes willing to wait, the wait ratio is calculated as MISSES / GETS * 100.
- For processes wanting immediate latch access, the wait ratio is calculated as IMMEDIATE_MISSES / IMMEDIATE_GETS * 100.
- SQL operations that use sorts include `group by`, `order by`, `select distinct`, `minus`, `intersect`, `union`, `min( )`, `max( )`, `count( )`, `create index`, *sort merge join* RDBMS operations, and the creation of indexes.
- Sorting should be done in memory. The V$SYSSTAT view can be queried to find the number of sorts done in memory versus the number of sorts done using disk space.
- To increase the number of sorts taking place in memory, increase the value set for the `SORT_AREA_SIZE` initialization parameter.
- If a disk sort is performed, the DBA should ensure that all temporary segments allocated for that sort are placed in a temporary tablespace. This is ensured by creating users with a temporary tablespace named in `create user`.
- If no temporary tablespace is named, the default tablespace used for storing temporary segments will be SYSTEM—this can lead to problems, because temporary segments fragment tablespaces and SYSTEM is critical to the proper functioning of the database.
- If memory and disk resources permit, set the database to use `SORT_DIRECT_WRITES`. This parameter is set to TRUE if the database is to use direct writes to the database for sorting.

- The SORT_WRITE_BUFFERS parameter determines the number of buffers that will be used for direct writes, and the SORT_WRITE_BUFFER_SIZE parameter will be used to determine the size of the buffers.
- Oracle Expert is a tool that helps to diagnose and resolve tuning problems on your Oracle database. You should understand basic usage of this tool, as covered in this chapter, before taking OCP Exam 4.

Chapter Questions

1. Users are complaining of poor performance on the Oracle database. You are trying to determine the source of the problem. Which of the following choices is not a method you could use to determine whether the problem is related to users waiting for space in the redo log buffer?

A. A query on V$WAITSTAT

B. A query on V$SYSSTAT

C. A query on V$SYSTEM_EVENT

D. A query on V$LATCH

2. You determine that 35 users, on average, experience contention when concurrently attempting to add data to one table. In order to correct the problem, you have to change which of the following?

A. Latches

B. Freelists

C. Redo log buffer

D. LOG_SMALL_ENTRY_MAX_SIZE

3. You are about to configure sorting operations on your database. Before using sort direct writes, you should first ensure that which of the following conditions are met?

A. SORT_AREA_SIZE is larger than DB_BLOCK_BUFFERS

B. SORT_DIRECT_WRITES is greater than 10

C. SORT_TEMP_TABLESPACES contains the name of the tablespaces holding temporary segments

D. All temporary segments are placed in the SYSTEM tablespace

E. There is enough real memory to store a number of bytes equal to or greater than `SORT_WRITE_BUFFERS * SORT_WRITE_BUFFER_SIZE`

4. You are about to start tuning sort operations on your database. Increasing `SORT_AREA_SIZE` has which of the following effects?

A. The potential to size the PGA beyond real memory capacity

B. Improves the performance of sort direct writes

C. Increases the size of redo-log entries produced by sorts

D. Alters the location of the ALERT log to the sort location

5. Two user processes are contending for a resource held by another process. Killing a user session requires which two pieces of information about the session?

A. Username and session ID

B. Username and SQL operation

C. Session ID and SERIAL#

D. SERIAL# and process address

E. Username and process address

6. You are attempting to tune sort operations on your Oracle database. What is the name of the row in V$SYSSTAT that identifies the number of sorts occurring in memory?

A. sorts (disk)

B. sorts (memory)

C. sorts (rows)

D. table scans (long tables)

E. table scans (ROWID ranges)

F. table scans (short tables)

7. **You are designing an application's data change operations and trying to determine which changes would be the least invasive for concurrency purposes. The type of lock obtained by an `update` process is which of the following?**

   A. Share lock

   B. Exclusive lock

   C. Share-row-exclusive lock

   D. Row-share lock

   E. Row-exclusive lock

8. **You are tuning your application's use of sorting. Which of the following SQL operations does not use sorts?**

   A. `group by`

   B. `select * from EMP;`

   C. `order by`

   D. `select count(*)`

   E. `create index`

9. **You are working with developers to tune the application design. What two recommendations can you make to the developers to avoid deadlocks?**

   A. Use exclusive locks for all data-change operations.

   B. Give different priorities to different background processes.

   C. Set all processes to acquire locks in the same order.

   D. Assign long-running transactions to large rollback segments.

   E. Set all processes to use the lowest level of locking necessary.

10. **You are attempting to resolve a lock situation. A listing of processes holding locks and processes waiting for those locks can be found in the output of which utility?**

    A. UTLBSTAT/UTLESTAT

    B. EXPORT

    C. DBMS_APPLICATION_INFO

    D. UTLLOCKT

Answers to Chapter Questions

1. A. A query on V$WAITSTAT

Explanation The V$WAITSTAT view will not provide information about waits on online redo logs, because this view focuses primarily on tuning index, table, and rollback segment use by your application. The V$SYSSTAT view will allow you to determine whether users are waiting for space in the redo log buffer, as will the V$SYSTEM_EVENT view. The V$LATCH view will also assist in this purpose if you monitor contention on the redo-allocation latch. A careful review of Chapter 17 should round out your understanding for this and similar questions.

2. B. Freelists

Explanation Freelists help to govern access to data blocks associated with an object for data changes, such as updates to existing rows. Since the problem stated in the question is that concurrent users are contending with one another to make changes, the answer is to increase the number of freelists on that object. Changing aspects of redo log handling, as indicated by choices C and D, are incorrect. The problem also has little to do with any of the latches you have studied thus far.

3. E. There is enough real memory to store a number of bytes equal to or greater than `SORT_WRITE_BUFFERS * SORT_WRITE_BUFFER_SIZE`

Explanation Choice A is incorrect because there really is no relationship between `SORT_AREA_SIZE` and `DB_BLOCK_BUFFERS`. `SORT_DIRECT_WRITES` is a TRUE/FALSE variable, so choice B is also incorrect. User temporary tablespaces are set in the `create user` statement, not in an initialization parameter for the instance, so choice C is wrong. Due to the fragmentation that temporary-segment allocation causes, it is not advisable to put temporary segments in the SYSTEM tablespace, so choice D is also wrong. Refer to the discussion of sort direct writes in the tuning sorts section.

4. A. Has the potential to size the PGA beyond real memory capacity

Explanation The `SORT_AREA_SIZE` parameter has little to do with redo log buffers or the location of the ALERT log, which eliminates choices C and D. The performance of direct writes depends first on setting `SORT_DIRECT_WRITES` to TRUE, and then properly setting values for `SORT_WRITE_BUFFERS` and `SORT_WRITE_BUFFER_SIZE`. In fact, direct write performance can be improved more by decreasing the `SORT_AREA_SIZE`. Refer to the discussion of tuning sorts.

5. C. Session ID and SERIAL#

Explanation This question is a classic bit of Oracle trivia and is worth remembering. The username for the session to be killed is not needed, which eliminates choices A, B, and E. The process address in memory is also not required, thereby eliminating choice D. Refer to the discussion of resolving lock contention in an emergency.

6. B. sorts (memory)

Explanation All row names corresponding to sorts in V$SYSSTAT are called sorts (something), and remember that sorts can be performed in two places: memory and disk. Therefore, choice C is the only one that can be correct. Refer to the discussion of keeping sorts in memory.

7. E. Row-exclusive lock

Explanation There are two statements in the Oracle database that obtain locks automatically when they are executed. The `update` statement obtains a row-exclusive lock while the `select for update` statement obtains a row-share lock. All other locks are obtained through executing a statement specifically for acquiring the lock, and then processing the transaction.

8. B. `select * from EMP;`

Explanation Many statements use sorts, but statements that cause Oracle to execute *full table scans* and do not have `where` clauses or any other type of clause, such as the statement listed for choice B, usually do not perform sorts. All other options will cause a sort to occur.

9. C and E. Set all processes to acquire locks in the same order *and* set all processes to use the lowest level of locking necessary.

Explanation Choice A is inappropriate because exclusive locks are the highest level of locking available on the instance and generally cause lock-contention problems, not solve them. Choice B is entirely inappropriate, because background processes are managed by DBAs (not developers) and assigning execution priorities that are not equal to background processes will cause performance problems in other areas. Choice D is a good idea as a way for developers to avoid the `"snapshot too old"` error, but will do little to prevent a deadlock. Choices C and E are the answers. Refer to the discussion of preventing deadlocks for more information.

10. D. UTLLOCKT

Explanation UTLBSTAT/UTLESTAT gives a great deal of performance information about the database, but locked processes is not an item it covers. DBMS_APPLICATION_INFO tracks module performance and may identify the time periods when a process slowed down, but these options don't show exactly which process caused the poor performance. EXPORT is a method for backing up the database structure and has no usage for lock detection. Refer to the discussion of detecting lock contention.

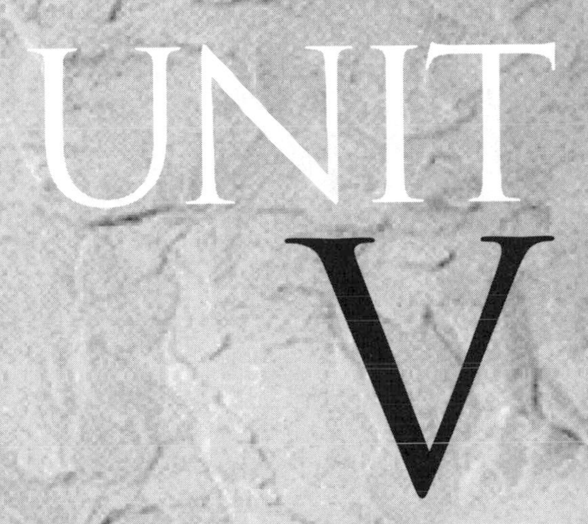

Preparing for OCP Exam 5: Network Administration

CHAPTER 21

Overview of Net8 for Client and Server

n this chapter, you will cover the following topics, which give an overview of Net8 for clients and servers:

- Net8 overview
- Basic Net8 architecture
- Basic Net8 server-side configuration
- Basic Net8 client-side configuration

In the previous edition of this book, several components of Oracle's software networking architecture were covered as part of performance tuning. I felt that this topic merited its own discussion, and am glad to see Oracle take it one step further by giving a complete exam around the subject of Oracle networking. Understanding how the Oracle networking software works is important for every DBA. This chapter provides an overview of Net8, and an explanation of the basic Net8 architecture. You will learn about the configuration needs for Net8 on both the client and server side. This chapter contains about 33% of the material you need to know for OCP DBA Exam 5.

Net8 Overview

In this section, you will cover the following topics on Net8:

- Identifying networking trends and problems
- Describing Oracle networking solutions

Whatever your network, Net8 can help you connect users to the Oracle database. There are versions of Net8 that run on TCP/IP, DECnet, IPX, and many other LAN or WAN products. Moreover, it is possible for Net8 to handle users on multiple networks attempting to connect to the same Oracle database. In this section, you will cover some common networking trends and the problems related to those trends being experienced by organizations. You will also learn about Oracle's Net8 networking solution.

Identifying Networking Trends and Problems

Networked computing has seen three distinct trends in the last 40 years of the organizational use of computers. The first trend can be categorized as one of monolithic centralization in computer networking. The second trend was toward attractive but decentralized computing. The third trend attempts to solve the problems of prior trends while adding some desirable new features, such as universal accessibility. Figure 21-1 illustrates these three network trends.

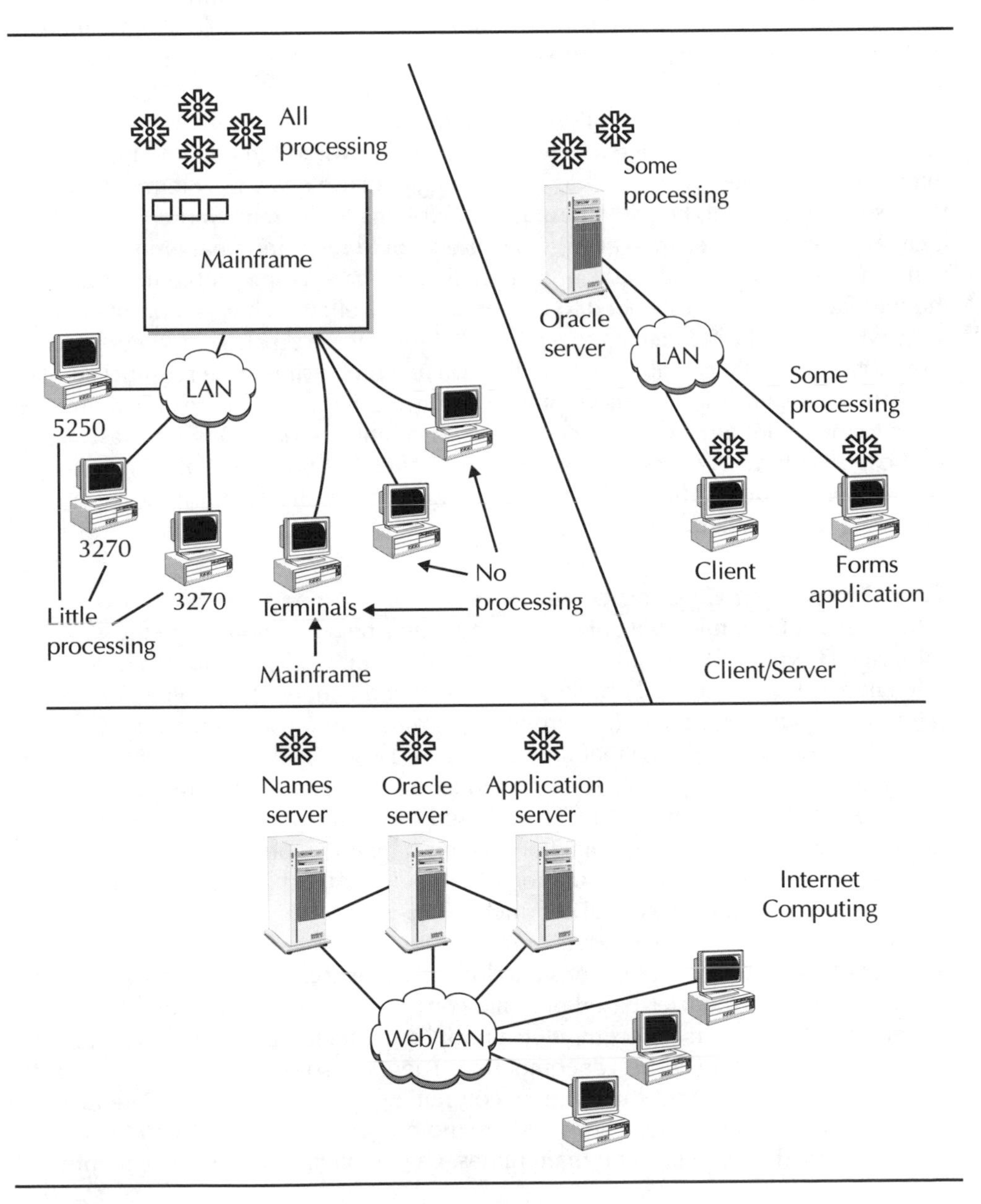

FIGURE 21-1. *Various trends in networking*

The Mainframe Computing Paradigm

The monoliths at the center of the mainframe computing paradigm were, of course, mainframes. These powerful computers had many advantages, including the ability to handle multiple users concurrently. Mainframes can process complex operations very quickly. They also offered simple code management and deployment. Since all code was managed and run on the one machine, a code change in one place was available everywhere.

However, there were several drawbacks to mainframe computing. The earliest mainframe "networks" were really just terminals hardwired directly into the mainframes themselves, which was a drawback because every new terminal added to a user's desk had to be wired through the building to the mainframe. Later, when local area networks began to emerge, PC users could run a terminal emulator and connect to the mainframe that way, eliminating the hardwiring problem. However, the interfaces themselves tended to be primitive as well, which was a problem for users who needed extra training to navigate the interface. You also could not perform more than one activity within one application at a time using these terminals, unless you ran two separate instantiations of your terminal emulator program and connected twice to the mainframe. Finally, the software available for designing database applications on mainframes was complex, and often did not use relational concepts the way Oracle does. Thus, building and maintaining applications on these machines was cumbersome.

The Growth of Client/Server

In the late 1980s to mid 1990s, PC-based networks began to flourish in the corporate IT world. One popular early use for these networks was to combine an office network with terminal-emulation software and connection pooling on the mainframe, as a replacement for hardwiring terminals to those mainframes. Two things were occurring during that time that caused organizations to move away from mainframe-centric computing. The first had to do with network hardware. Ethernet technology began to outpace token ring–based networks in terms of the network bandwidth available to an organization. As this happened, organizations began to take advantage of collaborative solutions that could be used in a network-friendly environment, the most successful of which was e-mail.

At the same time, many products such as Oracle Forms emerged, allowing corporate IT to develop applications that looked more appealing to users and were easier to use than character-based programs on mainframes. The explosion of power available on personal computers undoubtedly fueled the growth of this new form of computing—*client/server* computing. There are some definite advantages to client/server computing over mainframe computing. The graphical user interface (GUI) applications are easier to use and are more visually appealing than their character-based counterparts on mainframes. GUI applications make excellent use of the expanded power of the personal computer. Often, these applications make distributed copies of information more widely available to people in an organization, which empowers users to make better decisions.

However, there is also a downside to client/server computing. More distributed copies of data floating around means that more copies of the data have to be kept in sync, which leads some to wonder if the data they have is actually the most current. There are high software-development costs associated with client/server computing, as well. It is rare for an organization to have exactly the same hardware platform on everyone's desk in an organization. So, developers have to ensure that the GUI applications they write are compatible with every platform they have to run on, which can take a significant amount of testing and overhead on a project plan. Even when development is complete, there is still a large cost associated with distributing client applications to the desktop of everyone who needs it. Either users must download software themselves, using large amounts of network resources and often requiring telephone support, or microcomputer support technicians must go to everyone's desk and install the software for users.

Emergence of Internet Computing

Although client/server computing solved the problem of making an application more user-friendly and used powerful personal computers effectively, there were still some problems with software distribution, scalability, and platform dependence. The Internet computing architecture is designed to change that. The basic principle behind Internet computing is a multi-tiered architecture. The Oracle database server is one tier in that architecture. The second tier is the application server. This tier may contain any type of application, from general ledger to sales-force automation. There is still a client component, but that client is a generic Web browser. The real logic of the application is stored centrally, either on the database server or the application server.

Internet computing solves several problems associated with both mainframe and client/server computing while also utilizing the best features of each. The Internet application is user-friendly, allowing for point-and-click ease of use, just like a client/server application. Application code is centralized, and therefore there is no need for incurring high distribution costs. Web-based browsing allows for high scalability.

Exercises

1. Identify the best features and problems associated with mainframe and client/server computing.
2. How does network computing address the issues raised by mainframe and client/server computing?

Describing Oracle Networking Solutions

Net8 is Oracle's networking solution, and it allows for both Internet computing and client/server architecture to be used in your database applications. You can configure your Oracle networking software to support client/server architecture by maintaining local copies of all Oracle database-connection and naming information on the client side, and all Oracle Net8 listener-operation information on the server side. In this case, Net8 is used as a basic protocol for transporting SQL statements from client to server, and the results of these statements from the server back to the client. This architecture is very much in line with the traditional use of SQL*Net, Net8's predecessor.

Net8 supports many other architectures besides client/server. One step up from the basic client/server layout is to store database-naming and connection information away from the client machine, using Oracle Names, a tool for managing host naming for your Oracle resources on the network. In this way, you avoid situations where your database is called something different by all your users, and each user has his or her own naming convention or setup. Such decentralization is a support nightmare for offices with more than a few users connecting to Oracle. So, this basic step toward adding another tier to your internet-computing architecture reduces support burdens by centralizing the management of all Oracle database resources.

Another major feature of the Net8 networking solution is security. Many complementary products are available that integrate with Net8 for enhanced security. Integration of these products is managed by the Advanced Networking Option, renamed the Advanced Security Option for Oracle8*i*. Depending on the level of security your organization requires, you may want to consider adding these products to your existing Oracle installation. The Advanced Networking Option supports strong levels of user authentication with the use of third-party tools for user identification. You will learn more about managing security with these features and options in Chapter 23.

Other Features of Net8

Net8 also offers several other features, as identified by the following points:

- Application scalability is offered with features in Net8 such as connection pooling and connection concentration.
- Net8 offers independence from standard networking protocols with the use of Oracle Protocol Adapters.
- Net8 has the ability to handle connections from multiple network protocols for the same Oracle server using Oracle Connection Manager.

- Network administration is simpler via Net8 Assistant than it was with SQL*Net.
- Net8 relies less on locally maintained `tnsnames.ora` files than prior versions of Oracle networking products like SQL*Net, through the use of host naming.
- Improved management of locally maintained `tnsnames.ora` files including specification of listener ports other than the Oracle default is possible using Net8 Assistant, but not with prior versions of SQL*Net Easy Config, though the latter utility still provides for backward compatibility but will eventually be phased out.
- Manual detection and diagnosis of network performance using Oracle Trace Assistant is possible with Net8.
- Interconnectivity with third-party vendor standard name services with Native Naming Adapters is possible with Net8.

Exercises

1. Identify Net8 add-on utilities that enhance security features available for your Oracle database.
2. What is Oracle Names, and what purpose does it serve?
3. Identify some other features of Net8 for scalability, network protocol independence, multiple network environments, administration, and performance.

Basic Net8 Architecture

In this section, you will cover the following points on basic Net8 architecture:

- The procedure Net8 uses to establish server connections
- Components of Net8 architecture

To use Net8 effectively, you must understand the Net8 architecture. This section will cover how Net8 establishes and terminates connections between user processes and the Oracle server. You will also learn more about the components of the Net8 architecture that have already been identified, and how those components interact to create a networking environment for your Oracle installation. These concepts are central to understanding the rest of the material presented in this unit.

The Procedure Net8 Uses to Establish Server Connections

The first thing you should understand about Net8 is how it connects user processes to Oracle. (The process described here is illustrated in Figure 21-2.) There are two operations involved in a connection: *open* and *close*. When you want to open a connection to Oracle, for example, when you start SQL*Plus, you must supply a username, password, and a *connect string*. The connect string is usually a short name that uniquely identifies the database you want to connect to.

In order for Net8 to recognize the connect string you provide as a valid representation for a database somewhere on the network, your connect string must map to a *connect descriptor*, which is a description of the Oracle service you want to connect to. A connect descriptor has several components that are network-specific, including a host machine name/address, Oracle SID, and specific port number for connecting to Oracle. The mapping of the connect string to connect to the descriptor can be found in one of four places on your network. The first place is locally, in the `tnsnames.ora` file on your client machine running SQL*Plus.

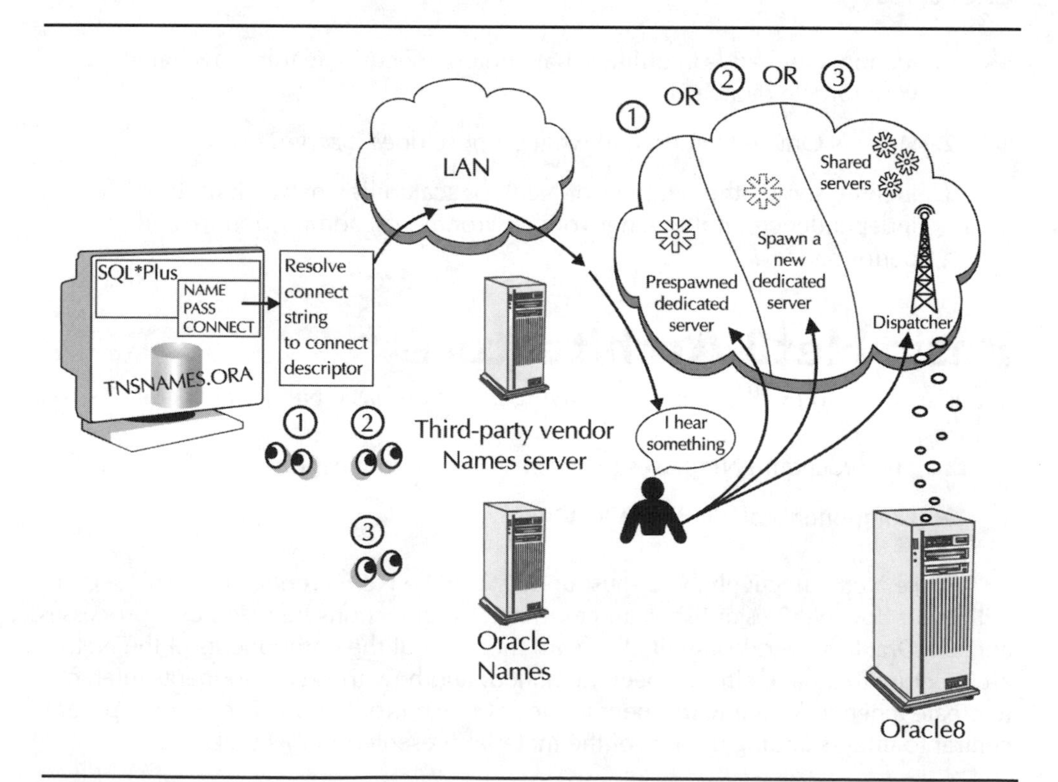

FIGURE 21-2. *Net8 connecting a client to server*

The second place is on a Names server running somewhere on your computer network. The third place is on another kind of naming service that may be operating-system dependent. Finally, you can use host naming, which requires no configuration if the name of your Oracle database is identical to the name of the machine hosting it.

Net8 then travels the network, looking for the host machine named in the descriptor. Once found, Net8 calls on that host machine using the specific port identified in the connect descriptor. A *listener* process should be running on the server, tuned into that particular port, waiting for user processes to call. The listener process knows what port to listen to because that port is identified in the connect descriptor. When the listener hears the incoming connection, the listener will either refuse the connection or allow the connection. A listener will refuse a connection if the user process requests a connection to an Oracle database that this listener does not listen for, if the user authentication information provided isn't valid, or if the Oracle database is not available.

Once a Connection Is Established

If the connection is allowed, one of three things occur, depending on whether you are using shared or dedicated servers to handle user-process data requests. (Some of these concepts should look familiar from Chapter 6.) If you are using dedicated server processes to handle user requests for data, the listener generates or *spawns* a new dedicated server for that user process to use and then hands or *bequeaths* the user process to that dedicated server. The user process then requests the dedicated server to obtain data on its behalf, and the dedicated server does what it is told. When the user process ends, the dedicated server also ends.

In some cases, you may have prespawned dedicated server processes running on the machine hosting the Oracle database, as well. If this is the case, the listener gives the address in memory of the prespawned dedicated server back to the user process, which then establishes a connection to that dedicated server process directly. The listener process also keeps track of which prespawned dedicated servers are active and idle at any given time. The listener process may also prespawn a new dedicated server process to replace the one that was just assigned a user process. This happens when the value for the `listener.ora` parameter `PRESPAWN_MAX` is not exceeded by the number of prespawned dedicated servers already running on the host. For both types of dedicated-server processing, Net8 supports synchronous data transfer of SQL statements from client to server, and data returned from server to client.

If the multithreaded server (MTS) architecture is being used, the listener process replies to the user process with the address in memory of the least busy *dispatcher* process, and the user process then establishes a connection with the dispatcher directly. The dispatcher process maintains a queue for user processes to place their data requests on. The least busy dispatcher process is the one with the shortest queue.

There may be more than one dispatcher process running on the host machine. The dispatcher has a number of *shared-server* processes working with it that pull requests off the queue in *first in, first out* order and process the request to return data to the user process. The dispatchers and shared servers will keep running even after user processes finish. For shared-server processing, Net8 supports asynchronous data transfer of SQL requests from client to dispatcher queue and then transfers the results from server to client.

Ending a Connection to a Server Process

Ending a connection to a server process can happen voluntarily or involuntarily. For example, you may terminate your SQL*Plus session by typing `exit`, and your connection with the shared or dedicated server process will be severed. If you are connected to Oracle via OEM, SQL*Plus, or another tool, and you attempt to establish a new connection to Oracle as a different user, the tool you are using will usually disconnect your current session before establishing a new one. This explains why you are disconnected from Oracle after failing to attempt another connection, as shown in the following code block:

```
SQL> connect jason/jason
Connected.
SQL> connect jason/jasoin
ERROR:
ORA-01017: invalid username/password; logon denied
Warning: You are no longer connected to ORACLE.
```

Your session may also be ended involuntarily, usually because some process died. For example, if your client machine hangs and you reboot, then your session has been ended involuntarily. Also, if your dedicated server fails for some reason, your session is disconnected involuntarily. Note that if you have already established a connection to a dispatcher or dedicated server, and the listener process fails, Net8 and Oracle behavior for connected users may become highly erratic—user connections may be terminated, and you may be unable to restart the listener until all connected users have been disconnected.

Exercises

1. Describe how a user process establishes a connection with a shared or dedicated server via Net8. What is a listener process, and what file is involved in its configuration?
2. What is a connect string? What is a connect descriptor? What are three locations where the mapping between the two can be found?
3. How are user processes disconnected from their servers?

Components of Net8 Architecture

Net8, like its SQL*Net predecessor, uses the Transparent Network Substrate (TNS) Oracle protocol in order to form connections between clients and servers. TNS allows Net8 to communicate with many different network protocols using a uniform interface. Using the Oracle Connection Manager, TNS also allows for connectivity between Oracle clients and servers on different network types (such as TCP/IP and DECnet), even where no lower level of connectivity exists. TNS also allows for client software such as SQL*Plus and Oracle8 Enterprise to run and connect with one another on the same machine. The connectivity provided by TNS allows for communication between client processes and server processes, and it also allows communication between two servers.

The OSI Network Model

To understand how the Net8 architecture works, take a moment to review the open systems interface (OSI) network model. There are seven layers of abstraction in the basic OSI network model, all building on the work of each other to connect processes on different machines with one another. These layers are shown in Figure 21-3. The following points explain each level in the OSI network model, from bottom to top:

1. **Physical layer** This is your network protocol, such as TCP/IP.
2. **Link layer** In Net8, this is the specific Protocol Adapter for Net8 to your network protocol.
3. **Network layer** This is the Transparent Network Substrate.
4. **Transport layer** At this level, data is routed from client to server across the network, connect strings are translated to connect descriptors, and security authentication takes place.
5. **Session layer** Net8 Network Interface allows different Oracle programs to communicate basic messages back and forth.
6. **Presentation layer** This is the Oracle RDBMS layer, where activities like character and datatype conversions are handled by "Two-Task Common," and SQL or PL/SQL are handled by Oracle Call Interface (OCI). The server-side counterpart is the Oracle Program interface.
7. **Application layer** Closest to the user, this layer may be represented by a GUI program, such as Oracle Reports.

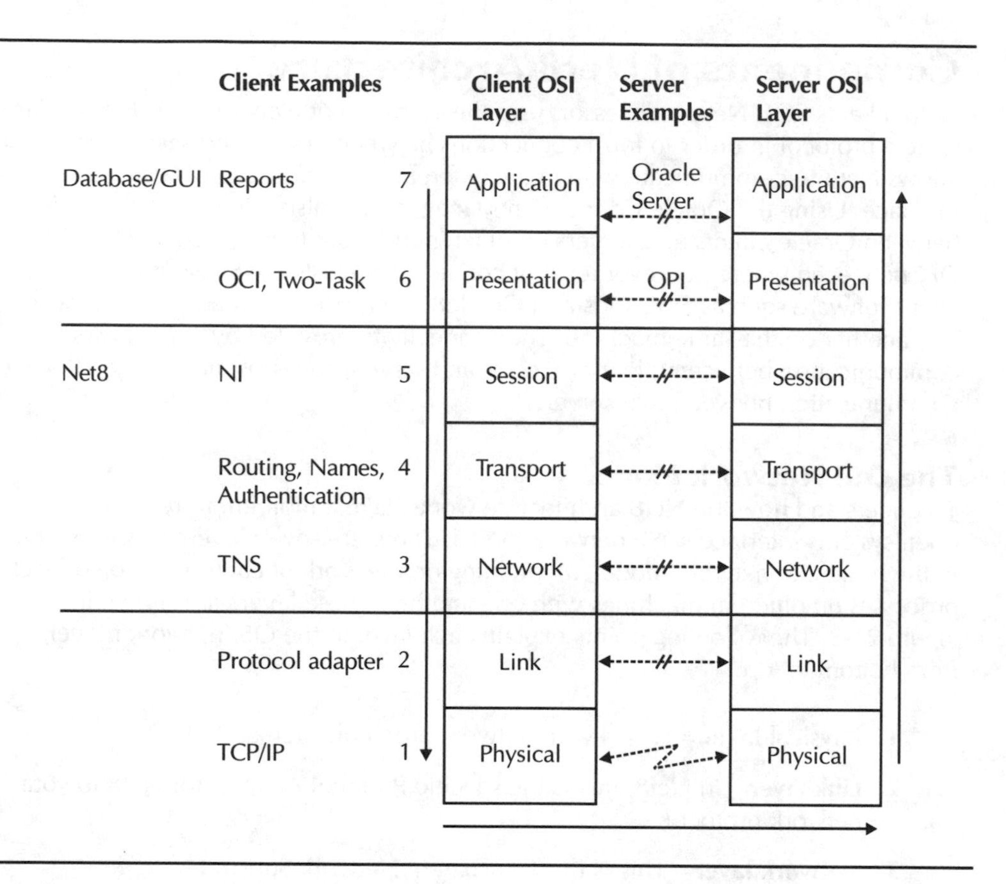

FIGURE 21-3. *OSI network model between client and server*

Note something very interesting about Figure 21-3. The figure shows that messages on the client side must traverse the different layers of the OSI model to get to the server side. So, messages for data from Oracle Reports' application layer get sent to the presentation layer as SQL. From there, they go to Net8, which handles opening and closing the connection, routing, naming, and authentication. After that, the message passes through the Oracle Protocol adapter to be converted into the network-specific commands and operations. The message then moves across the physical layer according to that protocol. At the server side, the reverse process occurs, and the message is reassembled into something meaningful by Net8, the Oracle Protocol Adapter, and so on.

Notice also, that another level of connectivity is present on both client and server. For a client-side component, there must also be a server-side component. For example, to establish the session layer, Net8 needs to be present on both sides.

Net8 doesn't care if you use TCP/IP; it communicates directly with Net8 on the other machine. This level of abstraction means that each layer only needs to have a limited amount of knowledge about the levels above and below it, and it doesn't need knowledge of anything beyond its most immediate neighbors.

Exercises

1. Describe the seven layers of the OSI network model. How do these layers simplify transport between client and server?
2. Identify the areas in the OSI model where each of the following items are active: "Two-Task Common," TNS, OCI, authentication, protocol adapters, and GUI application.

Basic Net8 Server-Side Configuration

In this section, you will cover basic Net8 server-side configuration:

- Configuring the listener with Net8 Assistant
- Starting the listener using LSNRCTL
- Stopping the listener using LSNRCTL
- Additional LSNRCTL commands
- Setting up multiple listeners on the same node

So much for theory; now you will learn about actual implementation. This section covers a lot of ground on setting up Net8 on the machine hosting your Oracle database. The first topic you will learn about is configuring the listener with Net8 Assistant. Then you'll learn how to start your Net8 listener process by using Oracle's command-line utility for Net8 administration, LSNRCTL. You will also learn how to stop your listener using that same utility. LSNRCTL is not just for starting and stopping the Net8 listener, however. You will also learn about some of the other commands available using this utility. Finally, you will learn how to set up multiple listeners on the same node, and when doing so might be appropriate.

Configuring the Listener with Net8 Assistant

To configure the Net8 listener on your host machine, you must first start Net8 Assistant. When Oracle is running on Windows, this is accomplished by clicking on Start | Programs | Oracle for Windows | Oracle Net8 Assistant. You may be asked whether it is okay to continue due to comment information being detected in your network configuration file. Click Yes, and you will then see the Net8 Assistant window, shown in Figure 21-4. As you can see from the figure, this utility is laid out like most Oracle utilities, with the drill-down interface on the left and the work area on the right.

The default name for your network listener process is LISTENER. You can configure the default listener by drilling down to the Network | Listeners | LISTENER node. In the work area on the right, you should see the listener configuration interface shown in Figure 21-4. You can configure your Net8 listener in four different areas, specified by the drop-down list box in the upper-left corner of the Net8 Assistant work area. These four areas are General Parameters, Listening Locations, Database Services, and Other Services. These areas will each be explained in some detail.

Configuring General Parameters

The General Parameters configuration area allows you to configure general listener properties, including delay on startup, saving configuration on shutdown, logging and tracing properties such as log and trace files, and whether authentication is

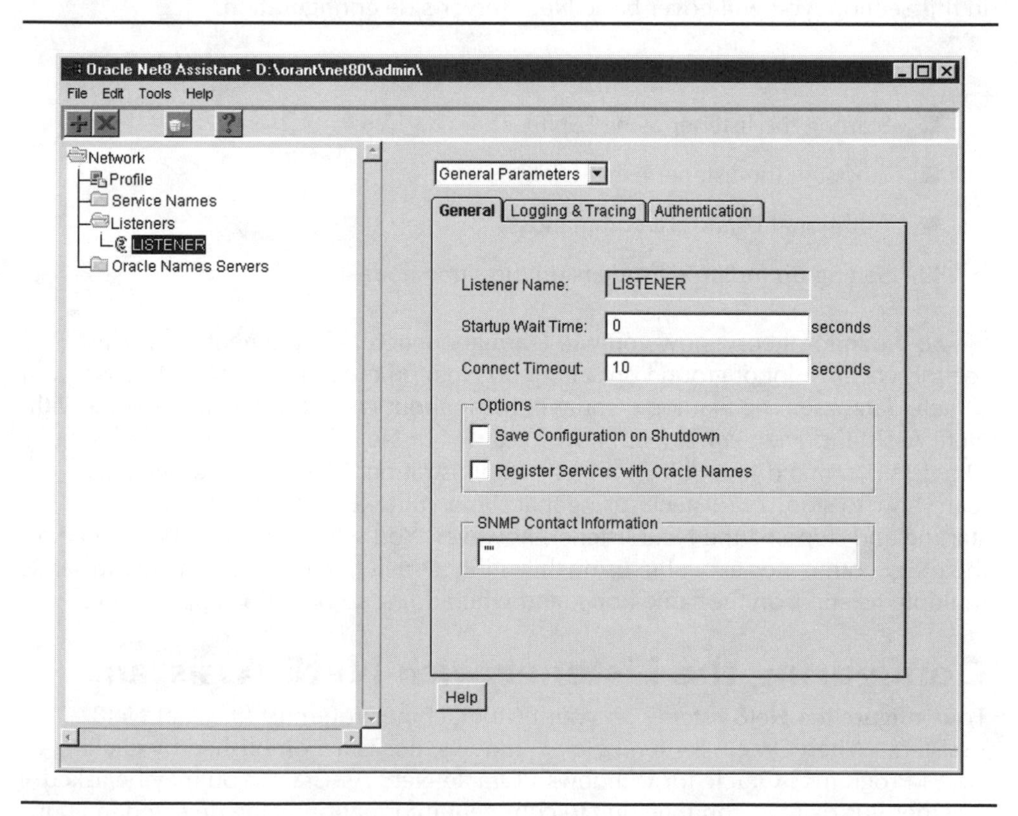

FIGURE 21-4. *Net8 Assistant interface*

required to perform listener startup and shutdown. There are three tab interfaces: General, Logging & Tracing, and Authentication (shown in Figure 21-4).

The General tab has several text boxes where you can set values for Startup Wait Time, Connect Timeout, and SNMP Contact Information. There is also a pair of checkboxes where you can indicate whether you want your configuration saved on listener-process shutdown and whether any of the services this listener tunes in for should be registered with Oracle Names. If you are running Names, you should click this checkbox.

Many operations performed by LSNRCTL, such as stopping the listener, require a password by default. You may find it easier if you configure the listener not to require a password. This is accomplished by clicking on the Authentication tab in the General Parameters work area for your listener. In the Authentication tab, click on the Do Not Require a Password for Listener Operations radio button, as shown in Figure 21-5. Then, select the File | Save Network Configuration menu option to save this setup.

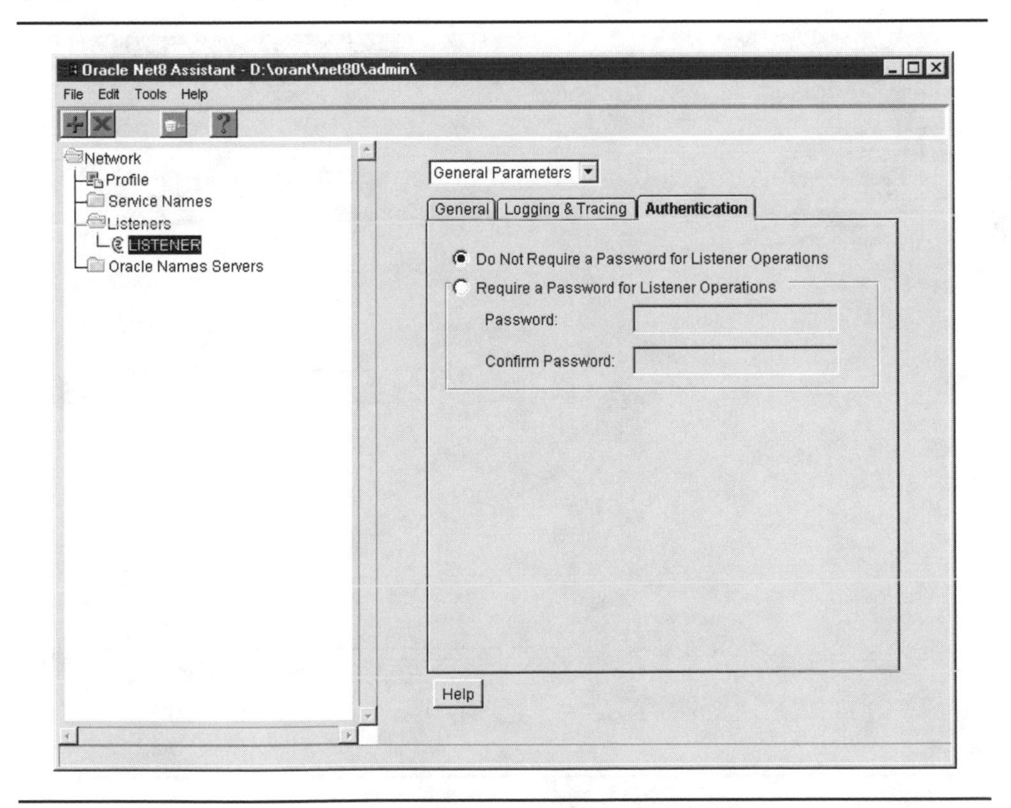

FIGURE 21-5. *Net8 Assistant Authentication tab*

Configuring Listening Locations

The Listening Locations configuration area allows you to specify where this listener will listen for connections. Available addresses are listed as tab interfaces, as shown in Figure 21-6, and in each tab you select a protocol for the location and either host/port or key information. Buttons at the bottom of the window allow you to add or remove listening locations. You can include setups for all the networks from which users may attempt to access Oracle, each as a separate address in this interface.

Each Address tab has a Protocol drop-down list box, where you can select from available protocols. The appearance of any other text boxes in this interface depends on the protocol you choose. If you choose TCP, you will see Host and Port text boxes for setting the hostname/IP address, and the port the listener should tune into. If you choose NMP (named pipes), you will see Machine Name and Pipe Name text boxes. If you choose IPC (interprocess communication, used when client and server run on the same node), you will see a Key text box. If you choose SPX,

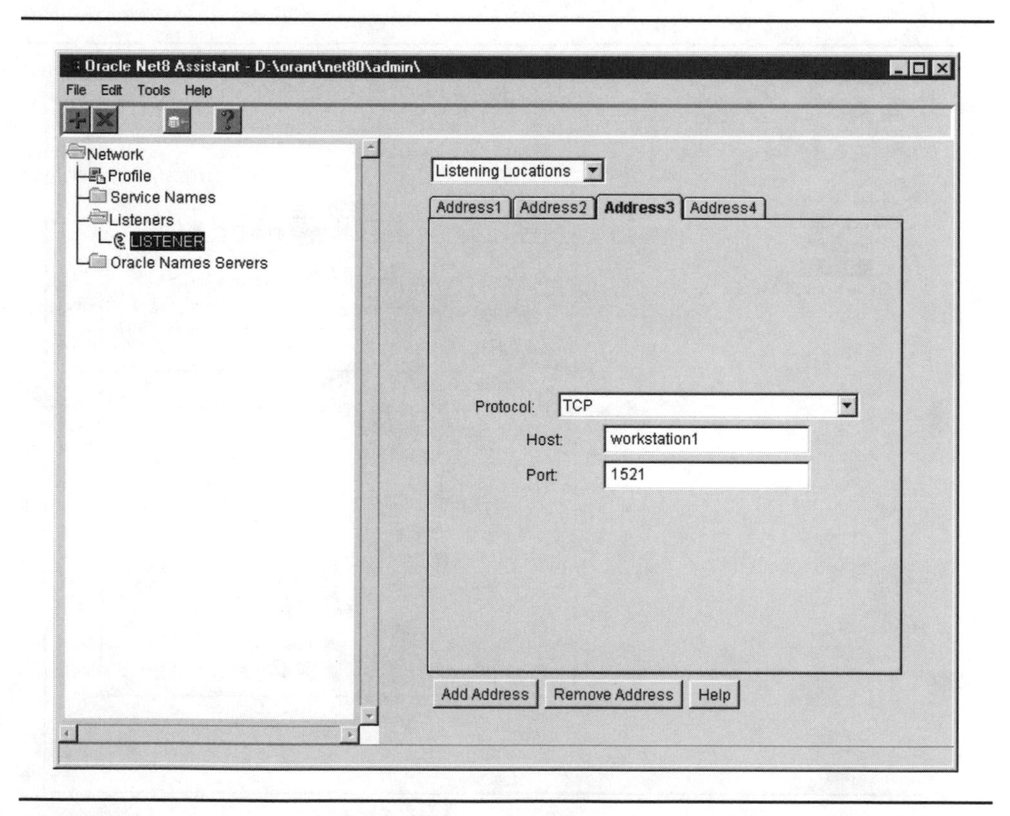

FIGURE 21-6. *Listening Locations tab interface*

you will see a Service Name text box. Selecting other protocols will cause other text boxes to appear that capture relevant information for establishing how the listener process tunes into incoming user sessions.

Configuring Database Services

The Database Services tab is where you configure which database this listener will listen for connections. (Figure 21-7 shows you the Database Services tab interface.) Many organizations run only one Oracle database on a host machine, meaning that a listener will listen for connections to only one database. But, if you plan to run multiple Oracle8 databases on one host, you may need to manipulate the number of databases listener will listen for, using the Add Database and Remove Database buttons.

For each database your listener serves, you will define a Global Database Name, Oracle Home Directory, and SID, all in the appropriate text boxes in the

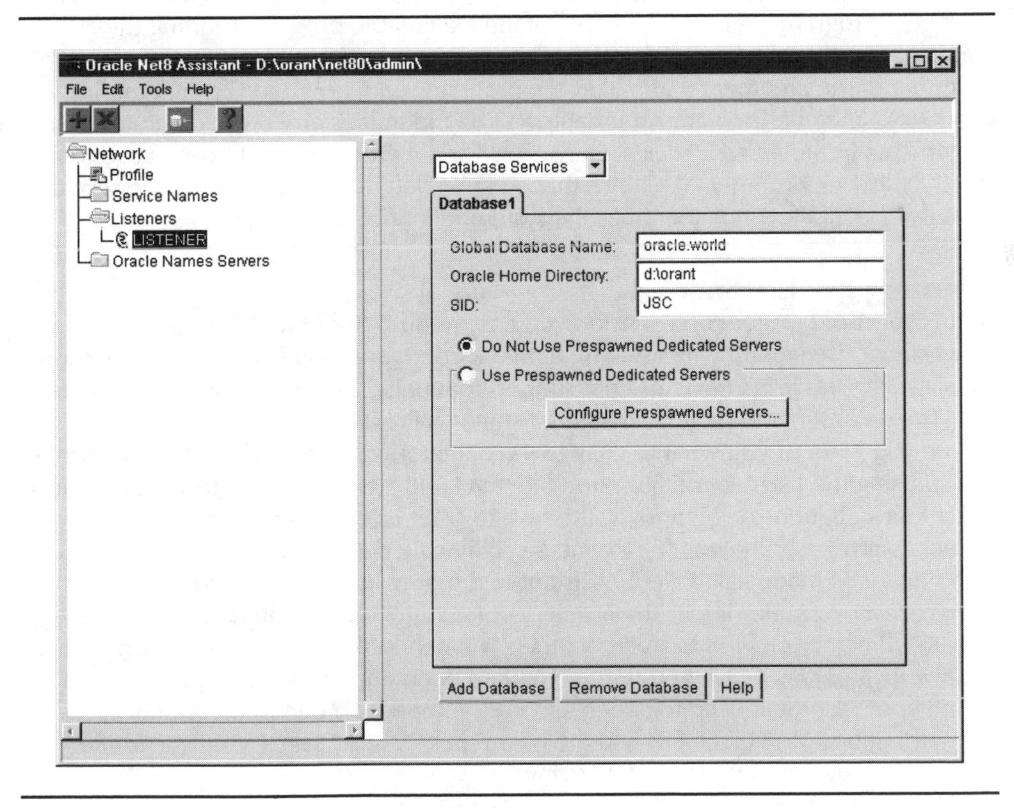

FIGURE 21-7. *Database Services tab interface*

interface. You can also choose to have the listener prespawn or not prespawn dedicated servers for this database by clicking on the appropriate radio button. If you choose to prespawn, you will need to select the number of dedicated servers that the listener should prespawn for each of the network protocols the listener tunes in to; to do this, click the Configure Prespawned Servers button and enter the appropriate values in the Configure Prespawned Servers interface.

Configuring Other Services

The Other Services area is where you configure the Net8 listener to listen for services other than databases that might have users connecting to them. Figure 21-8 shows this interface. The most common example of another service that your listener might listen for connections to is EXTPROC. Other examples include Web and other application servers.

For each service you configure, you will need to enter several pieces of information in the text boxes in the interface. The first text box, Global Service Name, is the global name for this service. Any valid service name is okay. The next text box, Program Name, is the name of the executable program running the service. The third text box, Program Argument Zero, is the internal first argument or command line argument that makes the program run (known in C programming as *argv0*). Next, the Program Arguments text box identifies any other command-line arguments in the form *argument=value*. The Environment text box is used to identify any environment variables that must be defined before starting the service. Finally, the SID text box identifies the system identifier for this service.

Naming the Listener

One aspect of listener configuration you can do outside of Net8 Assistant is to name the listener. Be careful when editing network configuration files manually. For some releases of Oracle7, Oracle did not support manually changed configuration files.

The default name for your network listener is LISTENER, but it can have any name you want. If you want to change the name of your network listener, you must do so using the listener configuration file that Net8 Assistant helps to write. In most Oracle installations on Windows, the `net80/admin` subdirectory under your Oracle software home directory contains a file called `listener.ora`. The modifications made using Net8 Assistant in the previous section were made to the `listener.ora` file. This is the listener configuration file. If you do not find the `net80` directory on your installation, then you can look in other directories, such as `network/admin`. Once you find it, you can open and modify `listener.ora` using your favorite text editor, such as VI or Notepad. To name the listener something besides LISTENER, add the parameter `MYLISTENER` = *name*, where *name* is a small alphanumeric text string.

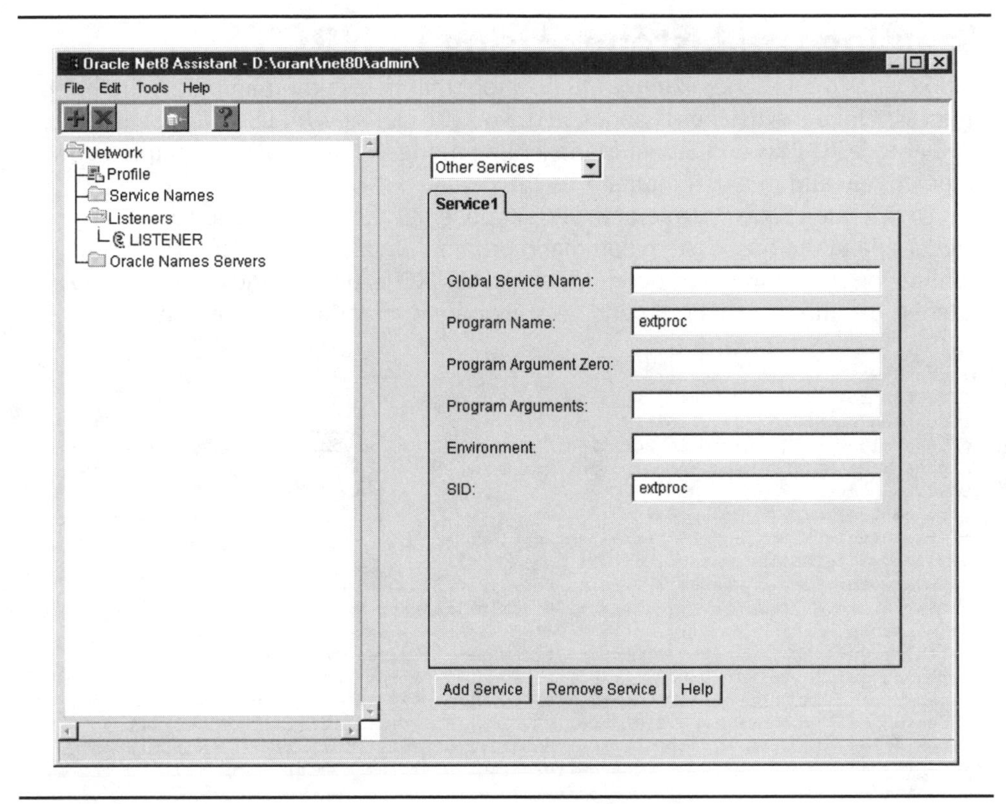

FIGURE 21-8. *Other Services tab interface*

Exercises

1. What are the four areas for configuring your Net8 listener in the Net8 Assistant?
2. Identify the method of navigating through the Net8 Assistant interface to configure the listener.
3. What is the name of the listener configuration file? What is the default name for your listener? How do you name the listener something besides its default name?

Starting the Listener Using LSNRCTL

LSNRCTL is the Listener Control utility, a tool that helps you manipulate the listener process. Once the listener is configured, you can start it with LSNRCTL. LSNRCTL is similar to SQL*Plus and Server Manager line mode in that you can run this utility interactively and in batch mode.

To operate LSNRCTL interactively, simply enter the name of the LSNRCTL executable at the host-system command prompt. Once in the LSNRCTL interactive application, you can enter a command that LSNRCTL understands. To start your listener, use the `start` command, as shown here for Windows environments:

```
D:\orant\NET80\ADMIN> lsnrctl80
LSNRCTL80 for 32-bit Windows: Version 8.0.5.0.0
Production on 05-MAY-99 11:58:39
(c) Copyright 1997 Oracle Corporation.  All rights reserved.
Welcome to LSNRCTL, type help for information.
LSNRCTL> start
Starting tnslsnr80: please wait
Service OracleTNSListener80 start pending.
Service OracleTNSListener80 started.
TNSLSNR80 for 32-bit Windows: Version 8.0.5.0.0 Production
System parameter file is D:\orant\NET80\admin\listener.ora
Log messages written to D:\orant\NET80\log\listener.log
Listening on: (ADDRESS=(PROTOCOL=ipc)(PIPENAME=\\.\pipe\oracle.worldipc))
Listening on: (ADDRESS=(PROTOCOL=ipc)(PIPENAME=\\.\pipe\EXTPROC0ipc))
Listening on: (ADDRESS=(PROTOCOL=nmp)(PIPENAME=\\WORKSTATION1\pipe\ORAPIPE))
Listening on: (ADDRESS=(PROTOCOL=tcp)(DEV=164)(HOST=11.11.11.11)(PORT=1521))
Listening on: (ADDRESS=(PROTOCOL=tcp)(DEV=124)(HOST=11.11.11.11)(PORT=1526))
Listening on: (ADDRESS=(PROTOCOL=tcp)(DEV=140)(HOST=127.0.0.1)(PORT=1521))
Listening on: (ADDRESS=(PROTOCOL=ipc)(PIPENAME=\\.\pipe\JSCipc))
Connecting to (ADDRESS=(PROTOCOL=IPC)(KEY=oracle.world))
STATUS of the LISTENER
----------------------
Alias                     LISTENER
Version                   TNSLSNR80 for 32-bit Windows: Version 8.0.5.0.0 Production
Start Date                05-MAY-99 11:58:47
Uptime                    0 days 0 hr. 0 min. 2 sec
Trace Level               off
Security                  ON
SNMP                      OFF
Listener Parameter File   D:\orant\NET80\admin\listener.ora
Listener Log File         D:\orant\NET80\log\listener.log
Services Summary
  JSC          has 1 service handler(s)
  extproc      has 1 service handler(s)
The command completed successfully
LSNRCTL>
```

To operate LSNRCTL in batch, you issue the name of the Listener Control utility executable, followed by the command you want executed on your listener, followed by the listener name. If you have not renamed your listener, you needn't include the name of your listener, because LSNRCTL will assume LISTENER is the name of your listener. For example, to start the listener on Unix, issue `lsnrctl start`. For

Windows, the name of the LSNRCTL executable is `lsnrctl80`, as shown in the following code block:

```
D:\orant\NET80\ADMIN> lsnrctl80 start
LSNRCTL80 for 32-bit Windows: Version 8.0.5.0.0
Production on 05-MAY-99 12:00:39
(c) Copyright 1997 Oracle Corporation.  All rights reserved.
Starting tnslsnr80: please wait
Service OracleTNSListener80 start pending.
Service OracleTNSListener80 started.
TNSLSNR80 for 32-bit Windows: Version 8.0.5.0.0 Production
System parameter file is D:\orant\NET80\admin\listener.ora
Log messages written to D:\orant\NET80\log\listener.log
Listening on: (ADDRESS=(PROTOCOL=ipc)(PIPENAME=\\.\pipe\oracle.worldipc))
Listening on: (ADDRESS=(PROTOCOL=ipc)(PIPENAME=\\.\pipe\EXTPROC0ipc))
Listening on: (ADDRESS=(PROTOCOL=nmp)(PIPENAME=\\WORKSTATION1\pipe\ORAPIPE))
Listening on: (ADDRESS=(PROTOCOL=tcp)(DEV=164)(HOST=11.11.11.11)(PORT=1521))
Listening on: (ADDRESS=(PROTOCOL=tcp)(DEV=124)(HOST=11.11.11.11)(PORT=1526))
Listening on: (ADDRESS=(PROTOCOL=tcp)(DEV=140)(HOST=127.0.0.1)(PORT=1521))
Listening on: (ADDRESS=(PROTOCOL=ipc)(PIPENAME=\\.\pipe\JSCipc))
Connecting to (ADDRESS=(PROTOCOL=IPC)(KEY=oracle.world))
STATUS of the LISTENER
----------------------
Alias                     LISTENER
Version                   TNSLSNR80 for 32-bit Windows: Version 8.0.5.0.0 Production
Start Date                05-MAY-99 12:01:07
Uptime                    0 days 0 hr. 0 min. 2 sec
Trace Level               off
Security                  ON
SNMP                      OFF
Listener Parameter File   D:\orant\NET80\admin\listener.ora
Listener Log File         D:\orant\NET80\log\listener.log
Services Summary
  JSC           has 1 service handler(s)
  extproc       has 1 service handler(s)
The command completed successfully
D:\orant\NET80\ADMIN>
```

Exercises

1. What is LSNRCTL? How is it used? What is it used for?
2. What are the three arguments for running LSNRCTL from the command line? Which of these arguments is optional, and under what circumstances?

Stopping the Listener Using LSNRCTL

Stopping your listener using LSNRCTL is best accomplished with LSNRCTL running in interactive mode, because this operation requires a password by default. To stop the listener interactively in Windows, start LSNRCTL using the `lsnrctl80` command, set the password for the session using `set password`, and then issue the `stop` *name* command, where *name* is the name of your listener and is optional if your listener name is LISTENER. The following code block illustrates stopping the listener:

```
D:\orant\NET80\ADMIN> lsnrctl80
LSNRCTL80 for 32-bit Windows: Version 8.0.5.0.0
Production on 05-MAY-99 12:05:39
(c) Copyright 1997 Oracle Corporation.  All rights reserved.
Welcome to LSNRCTL, type help for information.
LSNRCTL> set password
Password:
The command completed successfully
LSNRCTL> stop
Connecting to (ADDRESS=(PROTOCOL=IPC)(KEY=oracle.world))
The command completed successfully
LSNRCTL>
```

Troubleshooting Listener Shutdown

If you want to start and stop your listener in batch mode, you may find it easier to do so if you configure the listener not to require password authentication using Net8 Assistant. To configure the listener not to require password authentication for startup and shutdown, you can do so within Net8 Assistant by selecting the Do Not Require a Password for Listener Operations radio button, in the General Parameters menu, on the Authentication tab.

You may experience some problems with stopping your network listener process in batch if you use the default password authentication requirement, as shown in the following code block:

```
D:\orant\NET80\ADMIN> lsnrctl80 stop
LSNRCTL80 for 32-bit Windows: Version 8.0.5.0.0 -
Production on 05-MAY-99 12:10:03
(c) Copyright 1997 Oracle Corporation.  All rights reserved.
Connecting to (ADDRESS=(PROTOCOL=IPC)(KEY=oracle.world))
TNS-01169: The listener has not recognized the password
```

A `TNS-01169` error simply means you should run LSNRCTL interactively, issue the `set password` command for the LSNRCTL session, then issue the `stop` command. If running LSNRCTL interactively seems too frustrating, you should set up your listener not to require password authentication at all using Net8 Assistant.

Finally, if your listener is not running when you attempt to stop it, you will receive a long set of output. Don't worry, you simply need to remember that you must have your listener started before you stop it. The output that will result when you try to stop a stopped listener looks approximately like the following code block:

```
D:\orant\NET80\ADMIN> lsnrctl80
LSNRCTL80 for 32-bit Windows: Version 8.0.5.0.0
Production on 05-MAY-99 12:20:39
(c) Copyright 1997 Oracle Corporation.  All rights reserved.
Welcome to LSNRCTL, type help for information.
LSNRCTL> set password jason
The command completed successfully
LSNRCTL> stop
Connecting to (ADDRESS=(PROTOCOL=IPC)(KEY=oracle.world))
TNS-12224: TNS:no listener
 TNS-12541: TNS:no listener
  TNS-12560: TNS:protocol adapter error
   TNS-00511: No listener
    32-bit Windows Error: 2: No such file or directory
```

Exercises

1. How do you stop your network listener process? How can you change the authentication requirement for stopping the listener?
2. Which command is used to identify a password for LSNRCTL operations?

Additional LSNRCTL Commands

Although your use of LSNRCTL will be primarily for starting and stopping the listener, there are several other listener-management tasks you can accomplish with it. The basic format for all commands is `lsnrctl` *command name*, where *command* is replaced by the command you want to use, and *name* is replaced with the name of the listener you wish to administer. If you want to work on the default listener named LISTENER, *name* is optional.

Table 21-1 shows the available LSNRCTL commands. Note that, by default, these operations require you to supply a password. The following code block gives an example of using LSNRCTL commands:

```
D:\orant\NET80\ADMIN> lsnrctl80
LSNRCTL80 for 32-bit Windows: Version 8.0.5.0.0
Production on 05-MAY-99 12:30:39
(c) Copyright 1997 Oracle Corporation.  All rights reserved.
Welcome to LSNRCTL, type help for information.
LSNRCTL> services
Connecting to (ADDRESS=(PROTOCOL=IPC)(KEY=oracle.world))
```

```
Services Summary...
  JSC           has 1 service handler(s)
    DEDICATED SERVER established:0 refused:0
      LOCAL SERVER
  extproc       has 1 service handler(s)
    DEDICATED SERVER established:0 refused:0
      LOCAL SERVER
The command completed successfully
```

LSNRCTL Command	Description
change_password	Changes the password required for authenticated listener activities, such as stopping the listener
dbsnmp_start	Starts the Simple Network Management Protocol agent for Oracle running on that host machine
dbsnmp_status	Returns current status for the Simple Network Management Protocol agent for Oracle running on that host machine
dbsnmp_stop	Stops the Simple Network Management Protocol agent for Oracle running on that host machine
help	Lists all the commands available; use the help command to get specific information about a particular LSNRCTL command.
quit exit	Terminates this session with LSNRCTL; only used when LSNRCTL is run in interactive mode
reload	Reconfigures your listener without stopping it, by shutting down all aspects of your listener except listener addresses, then reloading listener.ora
save_config	Updates listener.ora with any configuration changes made in the LSNRCTL interactive session, and also makes a copy of your configuration file called listener.bak
services	Shows information about connections established and refused for dedicated servers, prespawned servers, and dispatchers that listener works with
spawn *program* (*arguments*)	Starts the *program* named as a parameter to this command. The *program* should correspond to an alias defined by settings for the SID_LIST_LISTENER parameter in the listener.ora file
status	Displays listener version, start time, run duration, trace enabled, and listener.ora file used for startup
trace (*option*)	Starts tracing for the listener; valid values for *option* include off, user, admin, and support
version	Displays listener and Oracle Protocol Adapter versions

TABLE 21-1. *Available LSNRCTL Commands*

Available LSNRCTL set and show Commands

The `set` and `show` commands allow you to establish and display LSNRCTL session-wide values for various options. You have already seen one example of a `set` command, and that was `set password`. Every option you can specify for the `set` command has an equivalent `show` command option, except for `set password`.

The syntax for `set` and `show` commands are `set` *`option`* and `show` *`option`*, respectively. Available `set` and `show` options are given in Table 21-2. An example of using `set` and `show` are given in the following code block:

```
D:\orant\NET80\ADMIN> lsnrctl80
LSNRCTL80 for 32-bit Windows: Version 8.0.5.0.0
Production on 05-MAY-99 12:58:39
(c) Copyright 1997 Oracle Corporation.  All rights reserved.
Welcome to LSNRCTL, type help for information.
LSNRCTL> set log_file logfile1;
Connecting to (ADDRESS=(PROTOCOL=IPC)(KEY=oracle.world))
LISTENER parameter "log_file" set to logfile1.log
The command completed successfully
LSNRCTL> show log_file
Connecting to (ADDRESS=(PROTOCOL=IPC)(KEY=oracle.world))
LISTENER parameter "log_file" set to logfile1.log
The command completed successfully
```

Exercises

1. Identify the commands that can be used to determine the current listener version running on a machine. What are some other commands that can be used with LSNRCTL?
2. What are `set` and `show` commands? Identify some different options that can be defined and displayed with `set` and `show` commands.

Setting Up Multiple Listeners on the Same Node

You have already seen how to configure a single listener to listen for multiple databases on the same node. In certain situations, you may want to run multiple listeners on the same node, each listening for one database. This is useful particularly when you are moving between different versions of Oracle and you are running two databases at the same time. You may also want to use multiple listeners on the same node in order to prevent your listener from becoming a performance bottleneck. You could, for example, set up one listener to handle database service requests, and another to handle EXTPROC service requests.

set/show Option	Description
`connect_timeout` *seconds*	Specifies *seconds* to be the amount of time that the listener will wait for connection request after the connection is started
`current_listener` *name*	Specifies *name* to be the listener being manipulated during this LSNRCTL session; useful when multiple listeners are available on the machine
`log_directory` *path*	Sets *path* to be the default log directory where listener process logs are written
`log_file` *filename*	Changes the default log filename to *filename*
`log_status` *status*	Changes logging status, where *status* can be on or `off`
`save_config_on_stop` *status*	Defines whether LSNRCTL should save listener configuration changes made this session to `listener.ora`; valid values for *status* are `on` and `off`
`startup_waittime` *seconds*	Specifies *seconds* to be how long the listener will wait before responding to a `start command`
`trc_directory` *path*	Specifies *path* to be the default directory where trace files for this listener will be written
`trc_file` *filename*	Changes the default trace filename for this listener to *filename*
`trc_level` *option*	Sets tracing for this listener; valid values for *option* are `off`, `user`, `admin`, and `support`
`use_plug_and_play` *status*	Tells the current listener to register with a Names server running on the network, and the listener will look for Names servers on established ports; valid values for *status* are on and `off`.

TABLE 21-2. *set and show Command Options*

Step 1: Configuring a Second Listener

To set up multiple listeners on the same host machine, you must first configure the second listener. In Windows, start Net8 Assistant by clicking Start | Programs | Oracle for Windows | Oracle Net8 Assistant. Once in Net8 Assistant, drill down to the Network | Listeners node and then click the Create button, just below the menu bar with a green plus sign (+) on it. (Look ahead to Figure 21-10 where the location of this button is pointed out.) You will be prompted to define a name for your listener. For this example, the second listener's name will be JSCLSNR, as shown in Figure 21-9. After setting the second listener's name, click OK.

You will then be prompted to enter Listening Locations information for your new listener in the work area on the right of the Net8 Assistant interface. Click on the Add Addresses button at the bottom of the work area, and then enter the network protocol and related information the listener must use for that protocol. Since these two listeners will exist on the same node, you must be sure that the second listener does not conflict with the first one in terms of how or where it listens for new connections. For example, if you were configuring the second listener to listen for EXTPROC, you would use IPC as the protocol (see the second tip below for more information on EXTPROC). You should enter EXTPROC0 in the Key text box because you may have more than one EXTPROC running for your database. Figure 21-10 shows Net8 Assistant with the appropriate information set for Listening Locations.

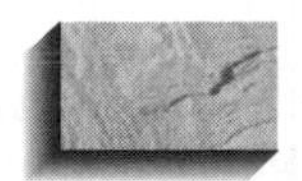

TIP

If you are configuring your Net8 listener to handle connections to a second database running on a single host, you must ensure that the service, port, pipe, or key information specified for the second listener is different than that used for the first. For example, if you are setting up a listener to listen for TCP/IP connections to your second database on the same node, use the same host as your first listener, but a different port, such as 1522.

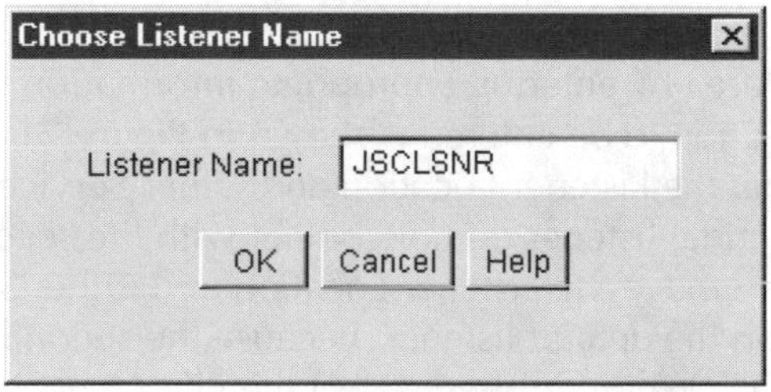

Choose Listener Name

Listener Name: JSCLSNR

OK | Cancel | Help

FIGURE 21-9. *Defining the name of your new listener*

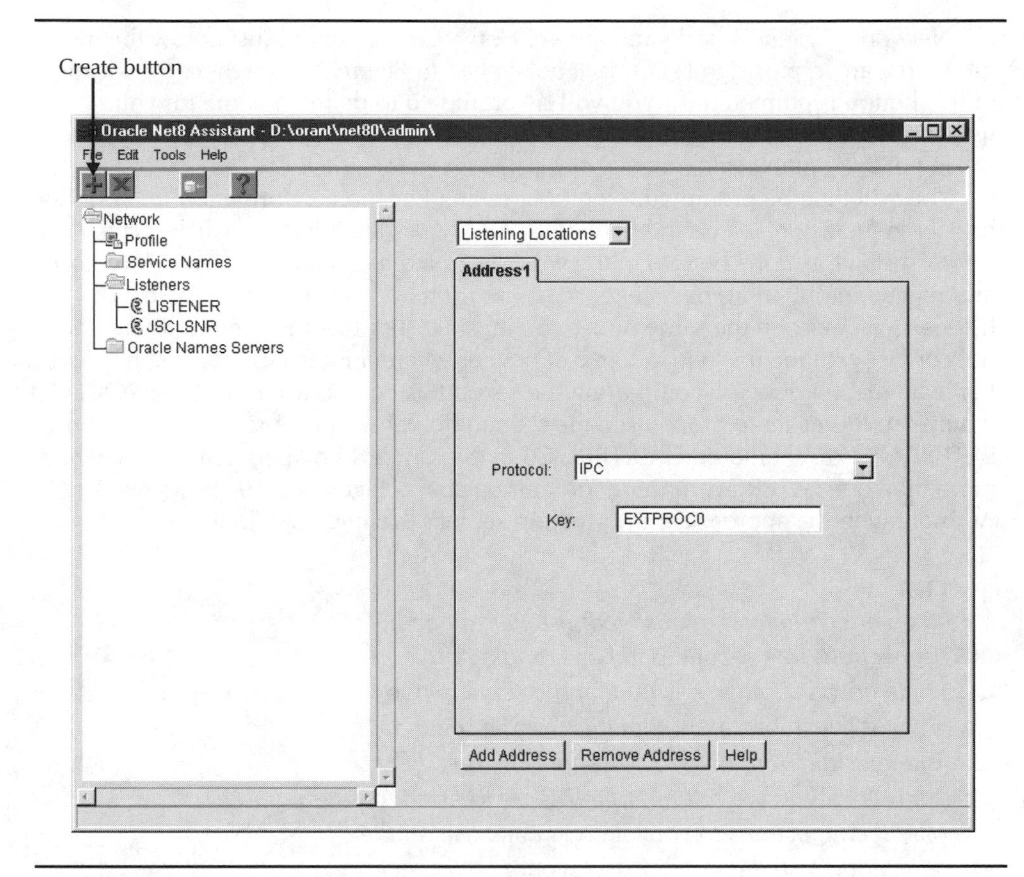

FIGURE 21-10. *Net8 Assistant with Listening Location info set for the second listener*

When you are finished setting up the listening location, you must then configure a database or other service for your listener to listen for. In this example, the second listener is set to tune in for EXTPROC connections, so this must be set up in the Other Services work area by entering appropriate information in the text boxes for that area. The information to be entered is shown in Figure 21-11. Also, you would need to make sure that the Listener Location and Other Services information configured for the original listener do not conflict with the second listener. In this example, you would remove the Listener Location and Other Services information setup for EXTPROC on the default listener, because the second listener will be dedicated to EXTPROC. When finished, select the File | Save Network Configuration menu option.

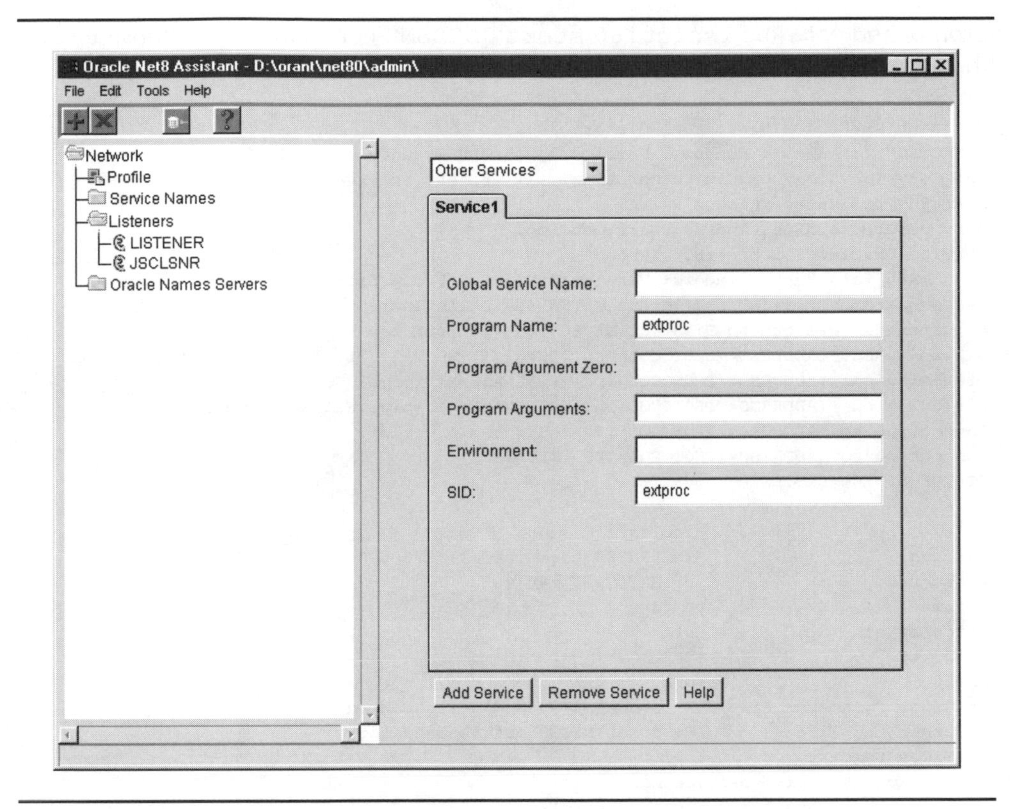

FIGURE 21-11. *Net8 Assistant with Other Services info set for second listener*

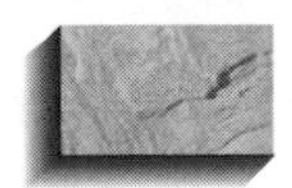

TIP

EXTPROC is a component of Oracle8 and later releases of the Oracle database that gives you the ability to create libraries of procedures written in the C programming language that are callable from PL/SQL. Don't worry about understanding the details of how EXTPROC works, it's not covered on OCP Network Administration Exam 5.

Step 2: Starting the Second Listener

After you complete the configuration of your second listener, you must start the second listener on your host machine. In Windows, return to your command prompt and enter the `lsnrctl80 start JSCLSNR` command, as demonstrated in the following code block:

```
D:\orant\NET80\ADMIN> lsnrctl80 start jsclsnr
LSNRCTL80 for 32-bit Windows: Version 8.0.5.0.0 Production 17:40:00
(c) Copyright 1997 Oracle Corporation.  All rights reserved.
Starting tnslsnr80: please wait
Service OracleTNSListener80 start pending.
Service OracleTNSListener80 started.
TNSLSNR80 for 32-bit Windows: Version 8.0.5.0.0 Production
System parameter file is D:\orant\NET80\admin\listener.ora
Log messages written to D:\orant\NET80\log\\jsclsnr.log
Listening on: (ADDRESS=(PROTOCOL=tcp)(DEV=144)(HOST=11.11.11.11)(PORT=1521))
Listening on: (ADDRESS=(PROTOCOL=ipc)(PIPENAME=\\.\pipe\JSCipc))
Listening on: (ADDRESS=(PROTOCOL=ipc)(PIPENAME=\\.\pipe\EXTPROC0ipc))
Connecting to (ADDRESS=(PROTOCOL=IPC)(KEY=oracle.world))
Connecting to (ADDRESS=(PROTOCOL=IPC)(KEY=JSC))
STATUS of the LISTENER
------------------------
Alias                     jsclsnr
Version                   TNSLSNR80 for Windows: 8.0.5.0.0 Production
Start Date                05-MAY-99 17:40:08
Uptime                    0 days 0 hr. 0 min. 2 sec
Trace Level               off
Security                  OFF
SNMP                      OFF
Listener Parameter File   D:\orant\NET80\admin\listener.ora
Listener Log File         D:\orant\NET80\log\jsclsnr.log
Services Summary...
  extproc       has 1 service handler(s)
  jsc           has 1 service handler(s)
The command completed successfully
D:\orant\NET80\ADMIN>
```

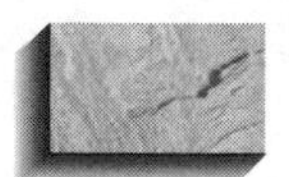

TIP

The TNS_ADMIN environment variable is used to define the file-system location of important configuration files, such as `sqlnet.ora`, `listener.ora`, or `tnsnames.ora`.

Exercises

1. Describe the process of configuring a second listener for a node already running one listener.
2. How do you start the second listener on your machine.

Basic Net8 Client-Side Configuration

In this section, you will cover basic Net8 client-side configuration:

- Establishing connections using host naming method
- Configuring Net8 files using local naming method
- Using Net8 Assistant to identify client preferences

Once listener configuration on your server is complete, you must then configure how your clients will connect to Oracle. Net8 operates on the client side to locate your servers in three ways, two of which are covered in this section. You can either use the host naming method or a locally maintained naming method. The third method, using Oracle Names, is covered in Chapter 22. You will learn how to configure the host naming method using Oracle Names in this section. You will also learn how to configure local naming with your `tnsnames.ora` file. Finally, you will learn how to identify client preferences with Net8 Assistant.

Establishing Connections Using Host Naming Method

Net8 makes it possible to configure your clients so that you don't need to rely on locally configured client `tnsnames.ora` files or Oracle Names servers to connect those clients to the Oracle server. Instead, Net8 offers a feature called host naming. This feature takes advantage of any naming services that are already available on the network to identify the machine that hosts Oracle to the client. Once a connection with that machine is established, Net8 client attempts to connect to Net8 server using the established methods for Oracle connections. In TCP/IP, which is the environment where host naming can be used, this consists of the Net8 client attempting to locate the listener on the well-known port an Oracle listener listens on, `1521`.

Host naming works well for smaller database environments. It supports multiple databases running on one host by matching listener global database names with host machine names. Furthermore, it requires little or no configuration of any files other than the domain naming files or DNS directory used to track all the server hostnames available on the network. When Oracle is installed on the server, Oracle creates a `listener.ora` file with the basic hostname configuration information Oracle receives from the host machine. At that time the listener is configured to listen for connections to a database with the same name as the hostname. When Oracle is installed on the client, all you must supply is the name of the machine hosting the Oracle database you are trying to reach, and you should be able to connect. If not, then the host information for the server was probably configured incorrectly, perhaps because the database name is not the same as the hostname.

Connection Process Using Host Naming

When a client attempts to connect to the server, host naming establishes a connection in the following way. On the client side, you specify your username, password, and connect-string information. The connect string is either the hostname, an established alias to the hostname, or the IP address for the machine on the network. Net8 then looks for the host using regular network hostname-resolution methods, and attempts to connect to the Net8 listener on that machine by assuming there is a listener on port 1521. The listener at the established port hears the request, formulates the appropriate response by either passing the request to a dispatcher or dedicated server, and a connection is made. This process is shown in Figure 21-12.

For example, you can use naming resolution in your `/etc/hosts` file on the Unix platform:

```
#IP address of server      host name   alias
#--------------------      ----------- ---------
144.15.129.6               sales-pc    sales.com
```

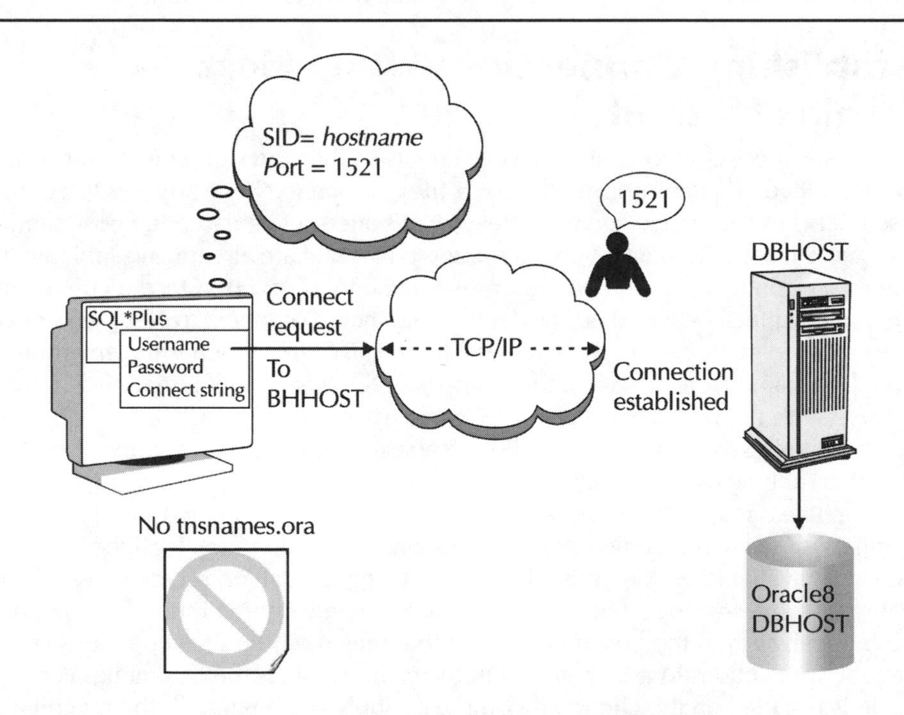

FIGURE 21-12. *Connecting client to server using host naming*

Then, you would define the required information in the `SID_LIST_LISTENER` section of your `listener.ora` file:

```
sid_list_listener=(sid_list=
(sid_desc=
 (global_dbname=sales.com)
 (sid_name=db1)
 (oracle_home=/u01/app/oracle/8.0.5)
)
```

Exercises

1. Describe how a connection request is made using host naming. What assumptions does the client make about the server?
2. How is host naming configured on the client and the server? What limitations does this configuration create?

Configuring Net8 Files and Using the Local Naming Method

You can continue to use locally configured and maintained `tnsnames.ora` files. Net8 has the Net8 Assistant utility to improve your ability to configure this file. The following discussion covers how to use Net8 Assistant for this purpose. Please also note that you can use Net8 Easy Config to configure your local names file, as you might have done with SQL*Net 2.3. However Oracle has not committed to supporting Net8 Easy Config, given that Net8 Assistant also provides this functionality.

TNSNAMES Setup Using Net8 Assistant

To set up your `tnsnames.ora` file using Net8 Assistant, follow these steps.

1. Start Net8 Assistant on your client. In Windows, do this by clicking Start | Programs | Oracle for Windows | Oracle Net8 Assistant. You may be informed that there is comment information in your file that may be overwritten. Click Yes to specify that it is okay to do so.
2. Drill down to the Network | Services node, and click on the Add button, which has the small plus sign (+) on it at the top of the interface. You will then see the Net8 Assistant Service Name Wizard. First, you will define your service name, which is the same as the connect string used to logically identify the database. Figure 21-13 displays the Net8 Assistant Service Name Wizard window with a new service being configured. To proceed to the next screen, click Next.

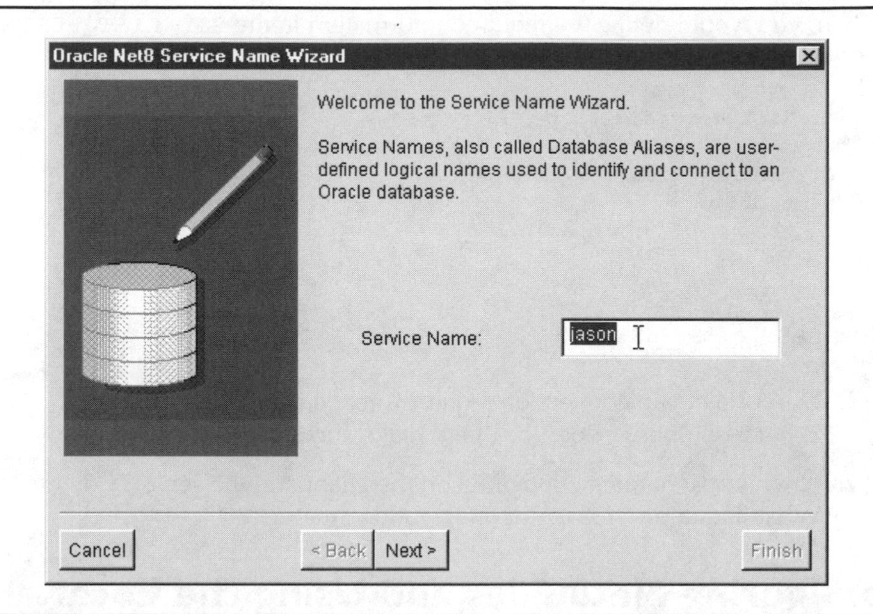

FIGURE 21-13. *Net8 Assistant with new service being configured*

3. The next screen is where you select the networking protocol to be used in support of the new service being configured. The list box in the center of the screen will reflect all the protocols installed on your client, such as TCP/IP, SPX, or Named Pipes. You may have additional network protocols on your own machine, as well. There are two other protocols you should always see listed; Bequeath for local Oracle databases, and IPC (interprocess communication) for other local processes, such as EXTPROC. Figure 21-14 shows the networking-protocol selection screen in Net8 Assistant Service Name Wizard.

4. You can select your networking protocol for this connect string and then click Next to move to the next screen, where you define the network-specific information for connecting to your host using this protocol. For example, if you selected TCP/IP as the networking protocol, the next screen would ask that you define the name of the machine hosting Oracle and the port number on which the listener exists. After configuring this information, click Next.

5. The screen after that is where you define the SID for your Oracle database on that host. Enter your SID in the text box provided, and click Next.

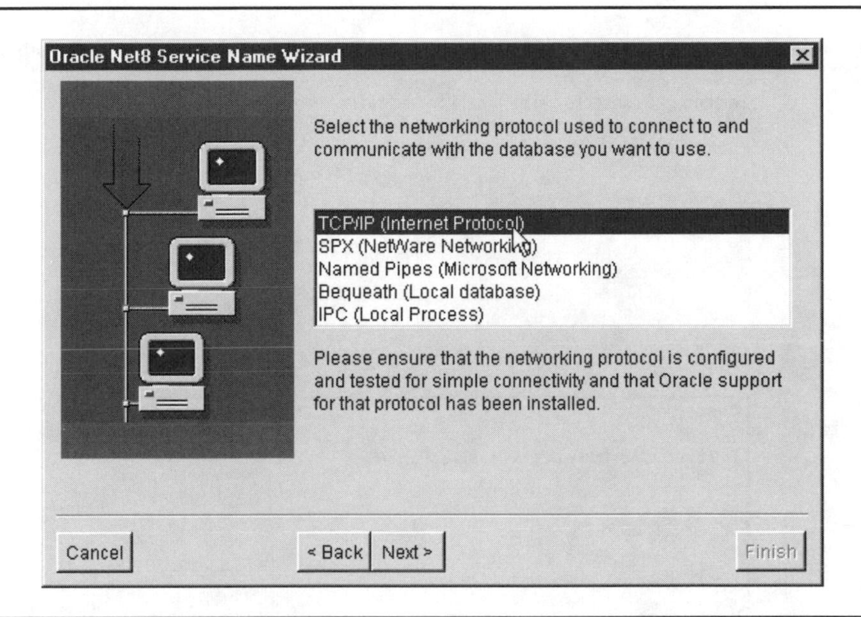

FIGURE 21-14. *Net8 Assistant with networking protocol being configured*

6. The following screen is where you can test your service configuration. Click the Test button to do so, and a new screen will appear where Net8 Assistant will attempt to execute a test connection to the listener. Enter a username and password for Net8 to use, and click Test. The results of your test will be shown in the text box, as shown in Figure 21-15. When testing is finished, click Done.
7. You will now be back to the screen you saw in step 6. If the test succeeded, proceed to the next screen by clicking the Next button, and skip ahead to step 8. If the test didn't succeed, click the Back button to return to steps 3, 4, and 5, where you can reconfigure your network or Oracle SID information to correct the problem. After that, return to step 6 and retest. Keep doing this until your test succeeds.
8. At this point, your configuration is finished, so click the Finish button.

Net8 Client Configuration Files

The Net8 Assistant tool helps you manage the `tnsnames.ora` file, which, as you know, is the cornerstone for locally configured networking. In addition to the `tnsnames.ora` file, another file is used to specify whether client-side tracing is

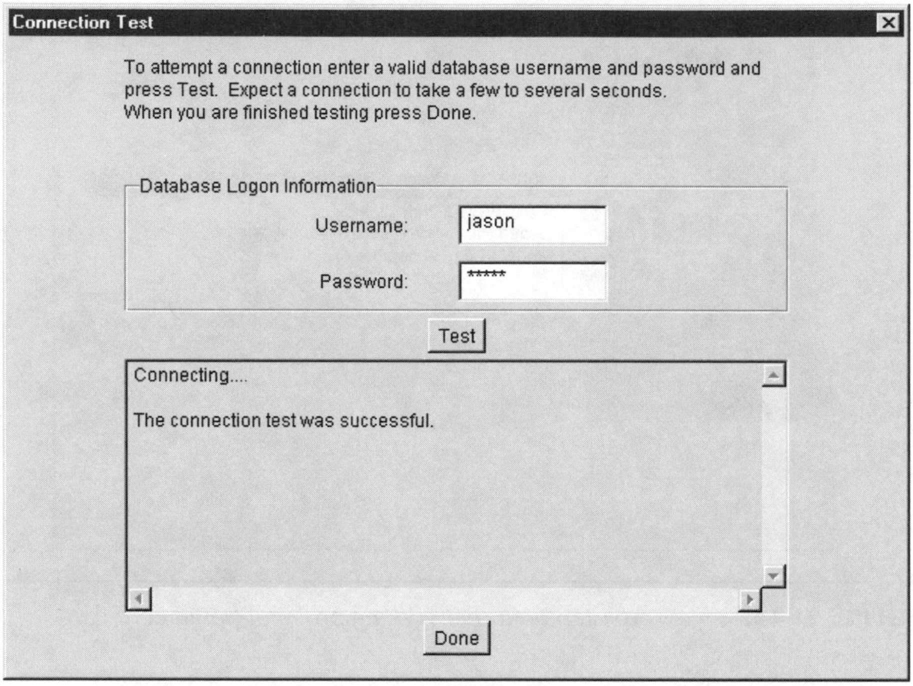

Connection Test

To attempt a connection enter a valid database username and password and press Test. Expect a connection to take a few to several seconds.
When you are finished testing press Done.

Database Logon Information

Username: jason

Password: *****

Test

Connecting....

The connection test was successful.

Done

FIGURE 21-15. *Net8 Assistant test interface*

enabled, and what the default naming conventions are for database domain and directory path. This file is called `sqlnet.ora`. These two files can be found in the `network/admin` subdirectory under your Oracle software home directory on your client machine.

The following code block shows what the `tnsnames.ora` file typically looks like:

```
#This is Net8 Assistant file generated by Net8 Assistant.
#Attention: Do not modify this file yourself.

Beq-local.world =
  (DESCRIPTION =
    (ADDRESS_LIST =
        (ADDRESS =
          (COMMUNITY = beq.world)
          (PROTOCOL = BEQ)
```

```
          (PROGRAM = oracle73)
          (ARGV0 = oracle73ORCL)
          (ARGS = '(DESCRIPTION=(LOCAL=YES)(ADDRESS=(PROTOCOL=beq)))')
        )
    )
    (CONNECT_DATA = (SID = ORCL)
    )
  )
Tcp-loopback.world =
  (DESCRIPTION =
    (ADDRESS_LIST =
        (ADDRESS =
          (COMMUNITY = tcp.world)
          (PROTOCOL = TCP)
          (Host = 127.0.0.1)
          (Port = 1521)
        )
    )
    (CONNECT_DATA = (SID = ORCL)
    )
  )
Example2.world =
  (DESCRIPTION =
    (ADDRESS_LIST =
        (ADDRESS =
          (COMMUNITY = spx.world)
          (PROTOCOL = SPX)
          (Service = Server_lsnr)
        )
    )
    (CONNECT_DATA = (SID = ORCL)
    )
  )
Example3.world =
  (DESCRIPTION =
    (ADDRESS_LIST =
        (ADDRESS =
          (COMMUNITY = nmp.world)
          (PROTOCOL = NMP)
          (Server = FinanceServer1)
          (Pipe = ORAPIPE)
        )
    )
    (CONNECT_DATA = (SID = ORCL)
    )
  )
```

The following code block shows what a typical `sqlnet.ora` file might look like: x

```
AUTOMATIC_IPC = OFF
TRACE_LEVEL_CLIENT = OFF
names.directory_path = (TNSNAMES)
names.default_domain = world
name.default_zone = world
names.default_domain=world
```

You will learn more about how to modify the `sqlnet.ora` file using Net8 Assistant in the section, "Using Net8 Assistant to Identify Client Preferences."

Connection Procedure When TNSNAMES Is Used

At some point when operating your application, you need to supply a username, password, and connect string to connect to the Oracle database. When local naming is used for clients connecting to servers, the Net8 connects you to Oracle as follows:

1. Net8 takes the connect string you provided in your login attempt and looks in the local `tnsnames.ora` file for a match. If no connect string in the `tnsnames.ora` file matches what you provided, Net8 returns the `ORA-12154: TNS: could not resolve service name` error. If there is a match for the connect string, proceed to step 2.
2. Net8 attempts to find the host machine using the information in the connect descriptor from your `tnsnames.ora` file. If the connect descriptor contains an invalid hostname, Net8 returns the `ORA-12545: Connect failed because target host or object does not exist` error. If the hostname is validated, proceed to step 3.
3. Net8 attempts to find the listener using the information in the connect descriptor from your `tnsnames.ora` file. In TCP/IP, Net8 will check the port specified in the connect descriptor to see if a listener exists on that port. If there is one, proceed to step 4. If not, Net8 returns the `ORA-12224: TNS: no listener` error.
4. Net8 attempts to establish connection to the Oracle SID given in the connect descriptor from your `tnsnames.ora` file. If there is no Oracle database with that SID, Net8 returns the `ORA-12505: TNS: listener could not resolve SID given in connect descriptor` error. If the SID exists on that machine, you proceed to step 5.
5. Net8 then asks Oracle to authenticate the username/password combination provided. If either the username or password is incorrect, Oracle returns the `ORA-01017: invalid username/password; logon denied` error. If the username/password combination is valid, a connection to Oracle is established.

If Net8 Returns Errors While Connecting

If Net8 encounters an error at any point during this process, you have to start again from scratch with a suitable alternative username, password, or connect string, depending on the error Net8 returns. You may also have to correct the connect string and connect descriptor information in your `tnsnames.ora` file. To do so, open Net8 Assistant, choose the Modify radio button, and proceed through the wizard to make the corrections.

Exercises

1. Describe in detail the process for adding new connection information to the `tnsnames.ora` file using Net8 Assistant.
2. What is `sqlnet.ora`, and what does it contain?
3. What is the process Net8 uses to connect clients to servers when `tnsnames.ora` is present on the local machine? What happens if Net8 encounters an error when trying to connect? What are some of the errors you might encounter?

Using Net8 Assistant to Identify Client Preferences

The final area you need to understand in this chapter is how to use Net8 Assistant to identify client preferences for connecting to your database. In Net8 Assistant, there is a node you can drill down into called Profiles, where you can define how your client will attempt to connect to the Oracle server. You can open this node by clicking Network | Profiles in the drill-down area on the left side of Net8 Assistant. When you do so, the work area on the right will show a drop-down list box where you can set up different profile areas for your client. Available areas in the list box are Naming, General, Preferred Oracle Names Servers, Oracle Security Server, and Advanced Networking Options.

Figure 21-16 shows you what you should see in the work area if you select Naming from the drop-down list box. Three tabs are available, representing the three ways you can set up clients to find servers in the Oracle network: Methods, Oracle Names, and External. The Methods tab is where you set all the methods you want available to your client. The available methods are shown in Figure 21-16, and should be self-explanatory. The Selected Methods window on the left shows you what methods your client will attempt to use in order to connect to Oracle. You can add or take away methods from the Available Methods window on the right by selecting a method and clicking one of the arrow buttons between the two windows.

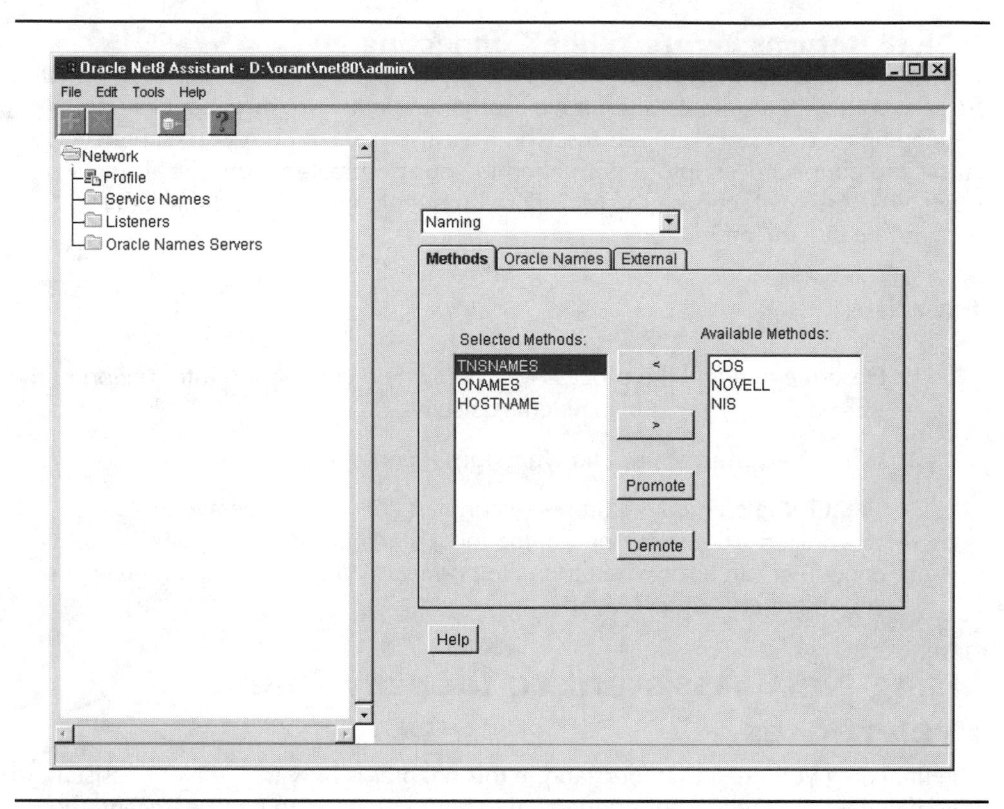

FIGURE 21-16. *The Net8 Assistant Naming work area with Methods tab shown*

Setting Order of Preference for Naming Methods

The list of Selected Methods also indicates the order of preference your client will use in attempting to locate a host. In Figure 21-16, you can see that this client will attempt to use local naming first. If the client cannot find a local `tnsnames.ora` file, it will attempt to use Oracle Names. If the client cannot find `tnsnames.ora` or an Oracle Names server, the client will attempt to use host naming. You can set the order of preference you want your client to use when attempting to find a host by clicking on a method in the Selected Methods window to select it, and then clicking on Promote to move the method up or Demote to move the method down in the list. By doing so, you change the sequence of methods that Net8 uses to determine the location of Oracle databases on the network for this client.

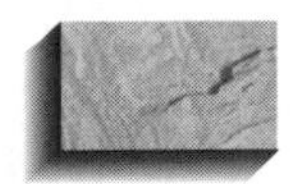

TIP

By default, Net8 will attempt to resolve a service-name lookup using the following methods in the following order: local naming with `tnsnames.ora`, Oracle Names, and then host naming.

Setting Client General Preferences in Net8 Assistant

The other Net8 Assistant topic you need to know about is setting client general preferences. Setting general preferences for your client is accomplished by selecting General in the drop-down list in the Profiles work area. When you do so, you will see four new tabs in that work area: Tracing, Logging, Routing, and Advanced. Figure 21-17 shows the Net8 Assistant Tracing tab. The Tracing tab handles the

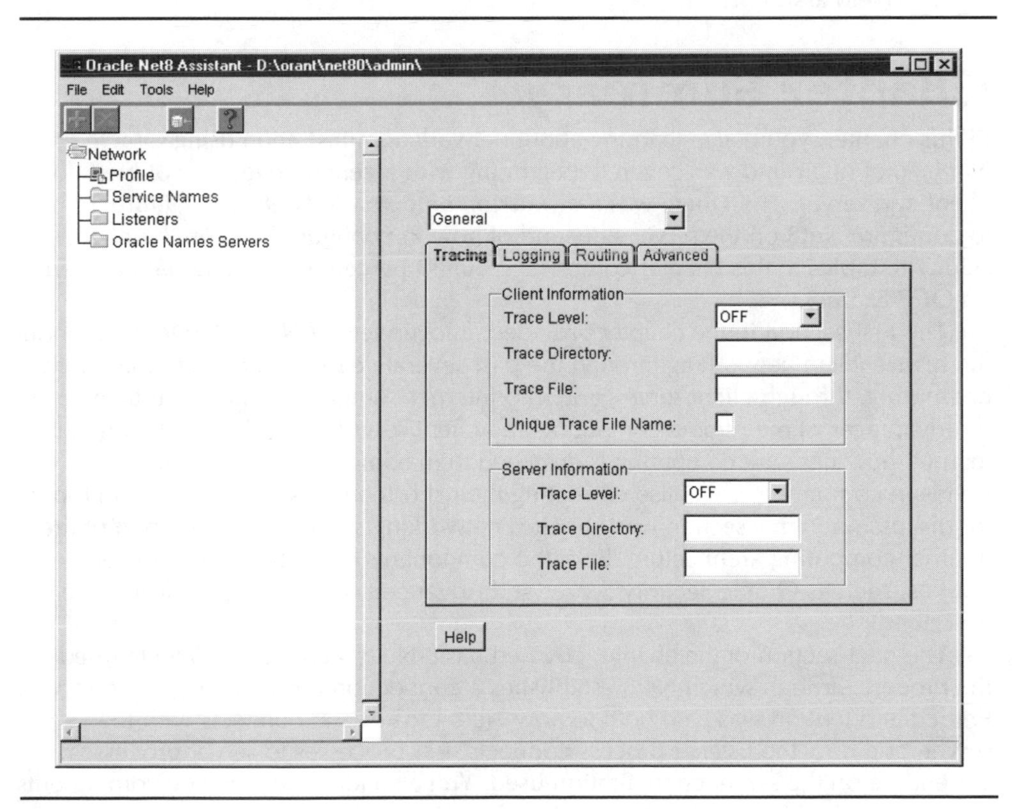

FIGURE 21-17. *Net8 Assistant Tracing tab*

setup of client-side and server-side trace file, directory, and level information, while the Logging tab handles the setup of client-side log file/directory and server-side log directory information. The Routing tab has checkboxes where you can specify whether this client wants to use dedicated servers, IPC addresses, or source routing addresses. Finally, the Advanced tab allows you to configure advanced features, such as a client registration ID and TNS timeout, in seconds.

Exercises

1. Describe the configuration of client-naming preferences with Net8 Assistant. How do you define the naming methods your client will use to locate Oracle databases on the network? How do you define the order of preference your client will use when multiple naming methods are present?
2. What are some general preferences you can define for your clients using Net8 assistant?

Chapter Summary

In this chapter, you began learning about network administration using Oracle Net8. A lot of ground was covered, beginning with a general overview of Net8 for client and server. Then there was a discussion of the basic Net8 architecture, of how to configure Net8 on the server side, and of how to configure Net8 on the client side. The topics in this chapter comprise about 33 percent of the material covered on OCP Exam 5.

The first section in the chapter provided an overview of Net8. You learned about the big trends in networking through the past several years, starting with mainframe computing, through client/server, and into Internet computing. The advantages and disadvantages of mainframe computing and client/server were identified, and you learned how network computing is designed to maximize the benefits of other trends in computing while also correcting their shortcomings. The other main topic for discussion in this section was Oracle's networking solutions that are part of the Internet computing architecture. Both the components of Net8 and the add-on utilities, such as Oracle Security Server and Advanced Networking Option, were described.

The next section of the chapter covered basic Net8 architecture. You learned the process through which Net8 establishes a connection between client and server. Particular attention was paid both to how Net8 locates and connects with the server, and how the listener process connects user processes to server processes depending on the server configuration used. You also identified the key components of the Net8 networking layers and Oracle RDBMS architecture and their interaction. For review, the Net8 components include Network Interface, Network Routing, Network Names, Network Authentication, the Transparent Network Substrate, and Oracle Protocol Adapters for your specific network protocol being used. The RDBMS components include the Oracle Call Interface for client side, and the Oracle Processing Interface for server side, and Two-Task Common for converting between datatypes and character sets.

The third section of this chapter focused on configuring the Net8 listener on your host machine using the Net8 Assistant tool. You learned how to define listener addresses, database services, and other services the listener will operate for, along with some general parameters for listener-process operation. You also learned how to manage the listener using LSNRCTL, a utility provided by Oracle that runs from your host system's command line interactively and in batch. Both starting and stopping the listener with LSNRCTL were covered, along with a host of other commands for managing the listener and setting and showing values for LSNRCTL session and listener configuration options. This section concluded by showing you how to configure multiple listeners running on the same node.

The last section of this chapter covered how to configure the Net8 listener for your client using Net8 Assistant. You learned how Oracle establishes a connection between client and server using the host-naming method. Special attention was paid to the capabilities and limits for host naming with respect to the fact that the hostname and the database name need to be the same in this setup. You also learned how to configure the `tnsnames.ora` file for local management of connection and name information. The use of Net8 Assistant for this purpose was explained and demonstrated. You also covered in-depth the process Net8 uses to establish connections between client and server when local naming is used. Particular attention was paid to the errors you might encounter when attempting to establish a connection, and what the cause of those errors is. Finally, you covered how to use Net8 Assistant to define preferences for the client side. Both general preferences and naming-method preferences were covered.

Two Minute Drill

- Internet computing combines centralized code location with scalability, ease-of-use, low distribution costs, and widespread dissemination of content.
- Net8 base and add-on components offer many features for network and client/server computing, including:
  - Enhanced security with Oracle Security Server and Advanced Networking Option
  - Centralized management of database naming with Oracle Names Server

- Scalability with connection pooling and connection concentration
- Independence from standard networking protocols with the use of Oracle Protocol Adapters
- Ability to handle connections from multiple network protocols for the same Oracle server using Oracle Connection Manager
- Simplified network administration via Net8 Assistant, running stand-alone or from the OEM console.
- Reduced reliance on locally maintained `tnsnames.ora` files through the use of host naming
- Diagnosis of network performance using Oracle Trace Assistant
- Interconnectivity with third-party vendor standard name services with Native Naming Adapters

- The basic procedure Net8 uses to connect client and server is as follows:
    1. You provide username, password, and connect string via a database tool.
    2. Net8 looks in `tnsnames.ora`, Oracle Names, or uses the host-naming method to resolve the connect string into a connect descriptor.
    3. Net8 looks for the machine specified. When it is found, Net8 attempts to connect to the listener and Oracle SID using the information specified or using established assumption patterns if the host-naming method is used.
    4. The listener either accepts the connection or refuses it, depending on database availability and the correctness of the connect descriptor information.
    5. If the connection is accepted, the listener passes the user process either to a dispatcher process or a preexisting dedicated server, or the listener generates a dedicated server for that process and passes the process to that server.
- User connections are ended voluntarily with the appropriate command or by attempting to establish a new connection.
- User connections may end involuntarily when a listener, shared server, dispatcher, or dedicated server fails to operate properly.

- The components of the Net8 architecture for supporting network connections are congruent with the OSI network model, described in the book, and include the following components:
  - Oracle Protocol Adapter for your network protocol (link layer)
  - Transparent Network Substrate (network layer)
  - Network Routing, Network Authentication, and Network Names (transport layer)
  - Network Interface (session layer)
- The components of the Oracle RDBMS that are also mapped to the OSI network model include the following:
  - Two-Task Common and OCI/OPI (presentation layer)
  - Forms, Reports, SQL*Plus, OEM, Tuning Pack, and others (application layer)
- The remaining layer of the OSI model is the physical layer. Your network protocol, such as TCP/IP, resides at that level.
- Connections between client and server travel from the application layer down through other layers, across the physical layer of your network, and then back up through the layers of the OSI model in reverse, in order to be processed on your Oracle database.
- Net8 Assistant can be used to configure your network listeners in the following areas:
  - **General Parameters** General, Logging and Tracing, and Authentication
  - **Listening Locations** Addresses this listener will receive connection requests from on your host machine
  - **Database Services** Oracle databases this listener will manage user connections for
  - **Other Services** Other Oracle services, such as Oracle Application Server or EXTPROC, that this listener will manage user connections for
- The name of your listener is LISTENER by default, but can be changed by changing the parameter `MYLISTENER = `*name* to your `listener.ora` file, where *name* is a short alphanumeric text string.

- The LSNRCTL utility is also used to configure and manage your Net8 listener processes. This tool is run either interactively or in batch from the host system command line of your application.
- Starting and stopping the listener process using LSNRCTL is handled with the `start` and `stop` commands.
- Review Table 21-2 for more LSNRCTL commands, and Table 21-2 for LSNRCTL `set` and `show` commands. The latter set of commands can be used for configuring the listener or session options and displaying those listener/session configuration settings.
- Net8 listener configuration information is stored in the `listener.ora` configuration file, found in the `network/admin` subdirectory under your Oracle software home directory on the machine hosting the Oracle database.
- Recall the need to provide password information to shut down the listener by default. You can change this requirement in Net8 Assistant.
- Host naming allows a connection to be made between client and server without a `tnsnames.ora` file or Oracle Names server being present. Net8 assumes the following about the server it attempts to connect to when host naming is specified:
    - The host system name is the same as the global database name.
    - The listener is tuned to a well-known network protocol-specific service or port location of TCP and 1521 for Net8 client connections.

  If these conditions are not met, then host naming shouldn't be used.
- The local naming method is handled with the `tnsnames.ora` file stored and managed locally on your client machine. This file is configured with the Net8 Assistant tool.
- The other client-side configuration file, `sqlnet.ora`, contains settings for default network-database naming conventions and for whether client-side tracing is enabled. This file can be managed with Net8 Assistant
- Both `tnsnames.ora` and `sqlnet.ora` can be found in the `network/admin` directory under the Oracle software home directory on your client machine.

- When you use local naming on your client, Net8 engages in the following process for connecting to Oracle when you provide a username, password, and connect string:
  - Looks in `tnsnames.ora` for the connect string that is provided.
  - Finds the host machine defined in the associated connect descriptor.
  - Finds the listener defined in the associated connect descriptor on that host.
  - Finds the SID defined in the associated connect descriptor associated with that listener on that host.
  - Oracle authenticates user and password information.
- You can define client-side preferences in areas of general preferences, naming methods used, and referential order.

Chapter Questions

1. **You are analyzing project requirements in order to develop the appropriate Oracle networking implementation. Which two of the following choices do not indicate a benefit of a client/server system? (Choose two)**

   A. Ease of application use

   B. Low distribution cost

   C. Use of client machine processing power

   D. Scalability

   E. Centralized code management

2. **A design diagram for one application system shows several different nodes acting as servers. This "N-tier" implementation is most likely a model for which of the following types of architectures?**

   A. Client/Server

   B. Uniprocessor

C. Internet computing

D. Mainframe

3. **Net8's ability to manage connectivity between client and server through a uniform interface, independent of the underlying network protocol used to manage a network, is provided by which of the following components?**

   A. Oracle Call Interface

   B. Transparent Network Substrate

   C. Oracle Processing Interface

   D. Network Interface

   E. Oracle Protocol Adapter

4. **An Oracle Forms application has just issued a `select` statement to the Oracle database. Which of the following components will be handled on the server within the RDBMS, rather than by Net8?**

   A. Two-Task Common

   B. Transparent Network Substrate

   C. Network Interface

   D. Oracle Protocol Adapter

   E. Oracle Call Interface

5. **You are explaining the benefits of Net8 to a project manager as part of the rationale for converting corporate IT to an Oracle platform. Which of the following choices best describes the role of Oracle Connection Manager?**

   A. Centralizes management of naming services

   B. Offers independence from standard networking protocols

   C. Provides the ability to handle connections to one Oracle server from multiple networks

   D. Implements high application scalability

   E. Allows interconnectivity with external naming services

6. After establishing that a host exists using connect-descriptor information, Net8 encounters an error attempting to locate the Oracle database with SID information given. Which of the following choices identifies the stage of processing where the connection failed?

A. Hostname resolution

B. Password authentication

C. Connect-string lookup

D. Listener-availability check

E. Oracle SID resolution

7. Prespawned servers are being used on Oracle to manage user process requests. After Net8 establishes a connection, which of the following processes will connect users to a prespawned server?

A. Listener

B. Dispatcher

C. Assistant

D. DBWR

8. The Network Routing component of Net8 handles routing data from client to server across a network. Which of the following OSI layers represents where this component resides in the Net8 architecture?

A. Physical

B. Link

C. Network

D. Transport

E. Session

9. Your attempt to shut down a running Net8 listener in batch results in an error. Which of the following commands would result in successful completion of the shutdown operation?

A. `lsnrctl start`, followed by `lsnrctl services`

B. `lsnrctl`, followed by `services`

C. `lsnrctl`, followed by `set password`, followed by `stop`

D. `lsnrctl set password`, followed by `lsnrctl stop`

E. `lsnrctl`, followed by `stop`, followed by `change_password`

10. You want to define a non-default trace directory for your Net8 listener process. Using Net8 Assistant, in which of the following areas would you make the necessary changes?

A. General Parameters

B. Listening Locations

C. Database Services

D. Other Services

11. Your only listener on the host system is called SPACEMAN. You defined the name for the Net8 listener in which of the following areas?

A. `tnsnames.ora`

B. `sqlnet.ora`

C. `listener.ora`

D. Net8 Assistant

12. Issuing `LSNRCTL start` from the command line indicates you are running the utility in which of the following modes?

A. Interactive

B. Batch

C. Read-only

D. Write-protected

13. Your attempt to shut down the listener is met with "protocol adapter error" and "no listener" messages. This is most likely due to which of the following causes?

A. The listener is running in protected mode

B. You didn't supply a password for this privileged operation

C. The version of LSNRCTL you are using is incompatible with the listener

D. The listener you attempted to stop isn't running

14. You use LSNRCTL to issue a command that allows you to determine how many connections have been refused by the listener on every protocol the listener tunes in to. Which of the following commands is the one you issued?

A. `help`

B. `services`

C. `reload`

D. `spawn`

E. `status`

15. Net8 host-naming services makes several assumptions about your network environment. Which of the following choices is *not* an assumption Net8 host-naming services makes?

A. Your network protocol is TCP/IP

B. Your listener is listening to port 1521

C. Your database is using dedicated servers

D. Your global database name is the same as your hostname

16. You are using local naming in your Oracle network. Which of the following contains connection information for databases available to your client?

A. `tnsnames.ora`

B. `sqlnet.ora`

C. `listener.ora`

D. Net8 Assistant

Answers to Chapter Questions

1. B *and* E. Low distribution cost *and* centralized code management

Explanation Choices A, C, and D all describe features of client/server applications. Their visual design makes them easy to use, their substantial application size puts client machine resources to work, and their use of networking makes them as scalable as the server side can handle. They are not inexpensive to distribute to your user populations, however, and the code is distributed over every single client machine, making code management difficult, if not impossible, to centralize.

2. C. Internet computing

Explanation N-tier applications with multiple application servers all handling specialized tasks reserved for clients in client/server or 2-tier architecture are part of the Oracle Internet computer architecture. Mainframes make sure all processing happens on one centralized machine, while, as noted, client/server is typically referred to as 2-tier architecture. Uniprocessor architecture usually denotes that clients and servers all run on the same machine.

3. B. Transparent Network Substrate

Explanation The ability Net8 has to manage connections independent of any network protocol other than its own is gained with the Transparent Network Substrate, or TNS. Oracle Call Interface is part of the client side that applications call to handle data processing operations. Oracle Processing Interface is part of the server side that handles RDBMS operations. Network Interface is part of Net8 that establishes the session layer and accepts information from the client OCI or server OPI and passes that information to the transport layer. Oracle Protocol Adapters are at the link layer, and pass data transmission requests from the Transparent Network Substrate to the network protocol on the physical layer.

4. A. Two-Task Common

Explanation The Two-Task Common process handles converting character-set and datatype information at the presentation layer, within the RDBMS rather than by Net8. Choices B, C, and D all identify components from Net8, which you were supposed to exclude, according to the question. Also, because the question mentions server-side, not client-side, processing, you should eliminate choice E, because the Oracle Call Interface is part of client-side application processing.

5. C. Provides the ability to handle connections to one Oracle server from multiple networks

Explanation The Oracle Connection Manager utility in Net8 provides the ability to handle connections for one Oracle server that come in from multiple networks. Oracle Names is used to centralize management of naming services, eliminating choice A. TNS offers independence from standard networking protocols, eliminating choice B. High application scalability can be implemented with connection pooling and concentration, eliminating choice D. Native Naming Adapters are meant to allow interconnectivity between Oracle and external naming services, eliminating choice E.

6. E. Oracle SID resolution

Explanation Since the question basically says that the error was encountered while trying to resolve the Oracle SID, the answer has to be Oracle SID resolution. The question states that the hostname resolved successfully, eliminating choice A. Because connect-string lookup happens before hostname resolution, choice C must be eliminated, as well. Since the Oracle SID has not been resolved, no password authentication has taken place, eliminating Choice B. And because listener availability is checked before the SID is resolved, and the failure was with the SID, you can assume there was a listener available on the specified port, eliminating choice D.

7. A. Listener

Explanation The listener process connects user processes with prespawned servers. A dispatcher is only used when the multithreaded server architecture is in place, eliminating choice B. The DBWR process is not involved in networking, eliminating choice D, while the Assistant process is fiction, eliminating choice C.

8. D. Transport

Explanation The Network Routing component of Net8 resides at the transport layer of the OSI network model. No Net8 component resides at the physical layer, eliminating choice A. Oracle Protocol Adapters handle tasks at the link layer, eliminating choice B. TNS handles things at the network layer, eliminating choice C. The Network Interface completes tasks at the session layer, eliminating choice E.

9. C. `lsnrctl`, followed by `set password`, followed by `stop`

Explanation By issuing only the `lsnrctl` command by itself on the command prompt, you run LSNRCTL in interactive mode, which is required to stop the listener because of the password requirement. First, you issue the `set password` command, and then you issue the `stop` command. Choice A starts a listener, and therefore is incorrect. Choice B simply lists the running services, and therefore is incorrect. Choice D is almost correct, but because you run both commands in batch mode, your second iteration doesn't actually have the password you set available to it, because the `set password` command sets it only session-wide.

10. A. General Parameters

Explanation Trace directory and filename information are both set in the General Parameters list box of Net8 Assistant. Listening Locations is used to determine what host machine addresses the listener will tune in to for connection requests, and therefore is incorrect. Database Services is used to determine the databases this listener will connect users to, while Other Services is used to determine what non-database services, such as application servers, the listener will connect users to.

11. C. `listener.ora`

Explanation Since the default listener name is LISTENER, having your only listener named SPACEMAN means you changed the name of the listener. The way to do so is to set the `MYLISTENER` parameter equal to something in your `listener.ora` file. Neither the `tnsnames.ora` nor the `sqlnet.ora` files will assist in setting the listener name, because these files handle client configuration while the listener resides on the server side. Likewise, Net8 Assistant is used to set up your `tnsnames.ora` file, a client file.

12. B. Batch

Explanation When you issue the LSNRCTL command from the command line, along with the name of the LSNRCTL executable, you are running LSNRCTL in batch. Interactive execution means you issued the executable from the command line only, and are now at a LSNRCTL prompt. Choices C and D are not valid modes of LSNRCTL operation.

13. D. The listener you attempted to stop isn't running

Explanation "No listener" messages mean only one thing—there is no listener running by the name of the one you just tried to stop. Choice A is incorrect because there really is no such thing as protected mode when it comes to the listener. Choice B is incorrect because if you didn't supply a password, the errors would state that the addresses associated with that listener didn't recognize the password. You wouldn't receive "no listener" errors if the LSNRCTL and listener versions were incompatible.

14. B. `services`

Explanation The `services` command gives you information about the connections that were successful and the ones refused for each address. The `help` command lists all LSNRCTL commands and gives basic syntax for each, eliminating choice A. The `reload` command reloads `listener.ora` information without stopping the listener, eliminating choice C. The `spawn` command starts another process, such as a dedicated server, eliminating choice D. The `status` command gives listener version, start time, run duration, trace enabled, and the name of the file used to initialize the listener, but no information about connections accepted and refused, eliminating choice E.

15. C. Your database is using dedicated servers

Explanation Host naming makes no assumptions about whether you are using MTS or dedicated servers. Choices A, B, and D, however, are all things that host naming does make assumptions about.

16. A. `tnsnames.ora`

Explanation Whenever local naming is used, all Oracle database host names are stored in the `tnsnames.ora` file on the client machine. The `listener.ora` file is used for configuration on the server, eliminating choice C, while `sqlnet.ora` is used to configure client preferences, eliminating choice B. Choice D is wrong because Net8 Assistant is used to configure client preferences and listener services, but not local client hostname-lookup information. Net8 Assistant is used for that purpose.

CHAPTER 22

Names, Intelligent Agent, and MTS

n this chapter, you will cover the following topics on using Names, Intelligent Agent, and MTS:

- Use and configuration of Oracle Names
- Use and configuration of Oracle Intelligent Agent for OEM
- Use and configuration of multithreaded Server (MTS)

This chapter covers several areas of administering your Oracle network. You already have learned how to configure your Net8 listener on the host server for your Oracle database, and how to use host-naming and local-naming methods for your clients to connect to those servers. This chapter starts off by showing you how to manage your Oracle network naming centrally by using the Oracle Names server. You will also learn how to configure the Oracle Intelligent Agent for Oracle Enterprise Manager, a topic that was touched on in Chapter 16. Finally, you will delve into the topic of the Oracle multithreaded server architecture (MTS), a topic mentioned in both the preceding chapter and in Chapter 6. The content of this chapter represents about 33 percent of OCP Exam 5 test content.

Use and Configuration of Oracle Names

In this section, you will cover the following topics on using and configuring Oracle Names:

- Using Net8 Assistant to configure centralized naming
- Storing network configuration on the local file system
- Storing network configuration on a regional database
- Managing the Names server with NAMESCTL

The first section of this chapter discusses how to centrally and efficiently manage your Oracle network naming using Oracle Names. This tool acts as an additional tier to your Oracle network by providing name-lookup services for Oracle network resources in a location that is independent of both client and server. In this section, you will learn how to use Net8 Assistant to configure centralized naming via Oracle Names. You will also learn how to store the network configuration in a local area network (LAN) file system, and how to store that information in a regional database when a wide area network (WAN) is being used. Finally, you will cover the use of the Names Control utility, or NAMESCTL, to start and stop the Names server.

Using Net8 Assistant to Configure Centralized Naming

In Chapter 21, you learned how to use Net8 Assistant for configuring your listener and client preferences. Here, you will learn that Net8 Assistant has yet another ability, the ability to configure centralized naming using the Oracle Names server. Oracle Names is a server that runs on your network to handle host-naming resolution in one central location, rather than on local client machines in multiple `tnsnames.ora` files.

To configure Oracle Names, first start Net8 Assistant if it is not open already on the machine hosting the Names server. You can start it in Windows by selecting Start | Program Files | Oracle for Windows | Net8 Assistant. You may be prompted about comment information that might be displaced by Net8 Assistant if you make some changes. Click Yes, and even before you do that, you may want to click the checkbox for the Don't Show This Warning Again option.

TIP

You don't have to run Oracle Names on a different machine than the machine hosting your Oracle database unless you anticipate that your Names server will get a lot of activity, or if the Oracle database will have a lot of activity. In this case, you would be wise to put Oracle Names on its own server.

Establishing a Connection with the Names Server

The process for establishing a client session using the centralized naming option is as follows:

1. The client initiates a connect request providing a net service name.
2. The connect request is forwarded to an Oracle Names server where the net service name is resolved to a network address. This address is returned to the client.
3. Net8 makes the connect request to the address provided.
4. A listener receives the request and redirects it to the database it is servicing.
5. The connection is accepted by the server.

Configuring Centralized Naming

Centralized naming is configured in the Profiles work area of the Net8 Assistant. Drill down to the Network | Profile node on the left side of the Net8 Assistant interface, and choose the Naming menu item from the list box in the top corner of the right side of the Net8 Assistant interface. The ONAMES method must be in the Selected Methods window. If this method is not in that window, click ONAMES once in the Available Methods window and then click on the Left Arrow button to make ONAMES a selected method. Once ONAMES is a selected method, you may also want to promote it so that Oracle Names is the first method used by clients on the Oracle network for finding servers. To do so, click once on ONAMES in the Selected Methods window, and click the Promote button until ONAMES is at the top of the list. You may even want to take this one step further by selecting the HOSTNAME and TNSNAMES options and clicking the Right Arrow button to make Oracle Names the *only* way for connect strings to get resolved. Figure 22-1 shows Net8 Assistant with Oracle Names usage configured.

You will also want to verify the settings in the Oracle Names tab in the Naming work area of Net8 Assistant. Do so by clicking the Oracle Names tab and reviewing

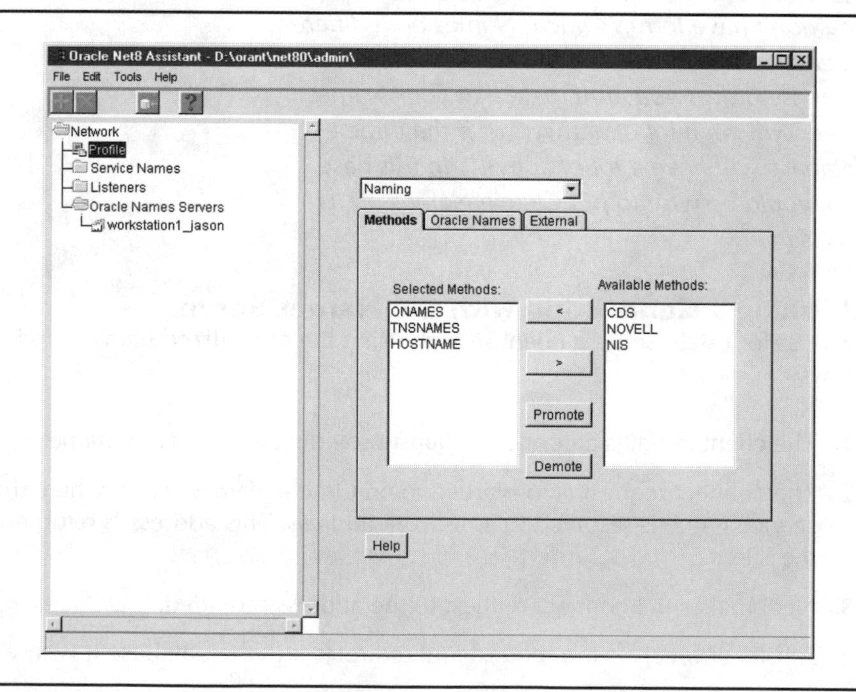

FIGURE 22-1. *Net8 Assistant with Oracle Names usage configured*

the contents of text boxes which fall into three main areas: Default Domain, Resolution Persistence, and Performance. You should probably stick with the default settings for these areas of network naming.

If you are satisfied with the configuration, you should save it. To save this new configuration, select File | Save Network Configuration from the menus.

Defining the Names-Server Location

Oracle Names can be run on any machine on your network where Net8 is installed. In addition to configuring your clients to prefer using Oracle Names, you must identify the Names servers on the network to your clients. In order to identify your Names server, Oracle Names must be running. (For details about starting and stopping the Names server, see the discussion, "Managing the Names Server Using NAMESCTL," later in this chapter.) For now, assume that somewhere on your LAN, Oracle Names is running. Net8 Assistant can be used to make your clients aware of the presence of an Oracle Names server as follows:

1. Drill down to the Network | Oracle Names Servers node in the left side of your Net8 Assistant interface.
2. Click the Create button to enter the Names Wizard, and click Next to continue.
3. The next screen explains some information you need to have on hand if you plan to use a regional database to store the Names configuration. You will learn more about configuring regional databases to store networking information in the next discussion, "Storing Network Configuration on a Regional Database." For now, click Next to continue.
4. Identify a name for your Oracle Names server. This name should be a complete name with the domain specified. The default domain is called WORLD. If you want your Names server to be called WORKSTATION1_JASON, you will specify the Names server name plus the domain name: WORKSTATION1_JASON.WORLD. Figure 22-2 illustrates this setting. Then, click Next to continue.
5. You now need to specify the location of your Oracle Names server on your network. First, select the network protocol where Oracle Names can be found from the Protocol drop-down list box in the middle of the wizard. Then, fill out the protocol-specific information for the machine hosting your Names server. Figure 22-3 illustrates an example of configuring your Oracle Names server to run on a machine called WORKSTATION1 located on a TCP/IP network. The well-established port for Oracle Names to listen to in this network protocol is 1575. When you have specified the protocol settings, click Next to continue.

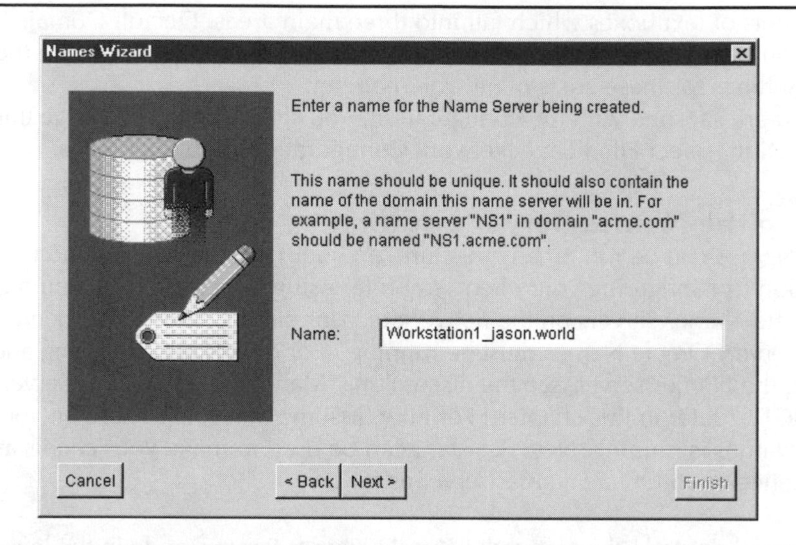

FIGURE 22-2. *Defining Names server name information*

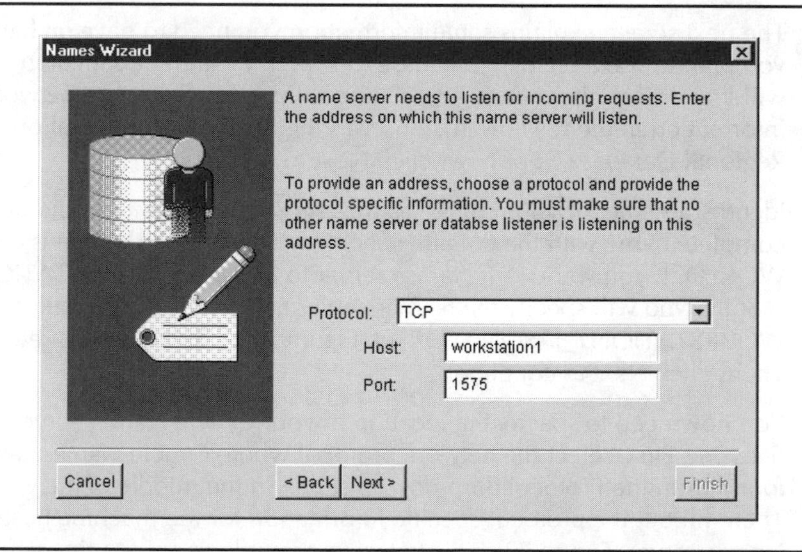

FIGURE 22-3. *Defining Names server network location*

6. At this point, you have to configure some regional domain-specific information. As mentioned in step 3, you will see how to set the Names server up as a non-regional Names server first, and then learn about regional Names server configuration in a later section. When you are finished entering your values, click Next to continue.
7. The Wizard will prompt you for more specific information about the setup of your Names server using a regional database. Click the Don't Use a Region Database, radio button, and click Next to continue.
8. You will need to configure a region for this Names server to operate in. For this example, assume you are configuring Oracle Names to operate in an office workgroup setting where you are installing a Names server for the first time. You will want to set this Names server as the primary server for the region. Click Next to continue.
9. In this example, the next screen of the wizard asks you to identify the root region. A region is the network area of your Oracle network where the Oracle Names server will manage naming resolution for clients to connect to servers. Since this is your first Names server, you are configuring it in the root region. Later regions will be treated as subregions, and you can define another Names server to manage those regions in order to improve name resolution performance. Click the Yes radio button, and click Next to continue.
10. You are finished with your Names server setup. Click the Finish button.

You can now view the configuration for your Names server in Net8 Assistant by drilling down to Network | Oracle Names Servers | Workstation1_jason (though you might have named your Names server differently). The work area to the right will have three areas available through the drop-down list box: Manage Server, Manage Data, and Configure Server. Figure 22-4 shows Net8 Assistant with the new Names server configured. When you are done, select the File | Save Network Configuration menu item to save this configuration.

Setting a Preferred Names Server for Clients

At this point, you will also have to set the preferred Names server for your client machines if you want those clients to use Oracle Names. This process is actually done on client machines. Otherwise, name resolution will take longer, because you've set up Oracle Names as the preferred method for name resolution. It will take a few moments each time you try to connect for the client to figure out that

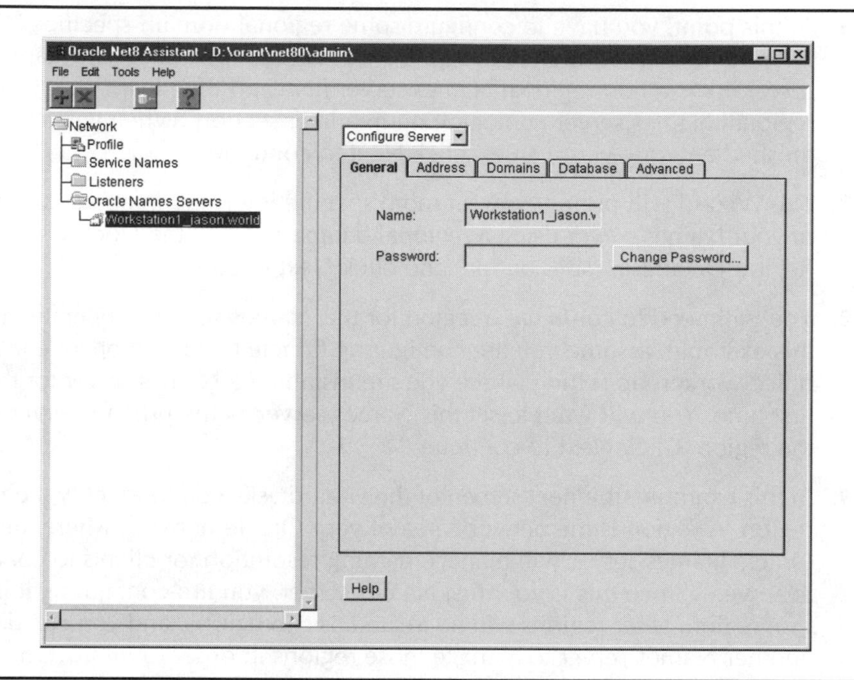

FIGURE 22-4. *Net8 Assistant with Names server configured*

there is no Names server before it will attempt to use its `tnsnames.ora` file for local name resolution. Configure your preferred Names server in the following way:

1. Drill down to the Network | Profile node on the left side of the Net8 Assistant interface.
2. Select Preferred Oracle Names Servers from the drop-down list box in the work area on the right-hand side.
3. Enter the network protocol and location information for the machine hosting your Oracle Names server. Figure 22-5 shows this information set up for the Names server defined earlier in the chapter.
4. When you're finished, select the File | Save Network Configuration menu item to save this configuration.

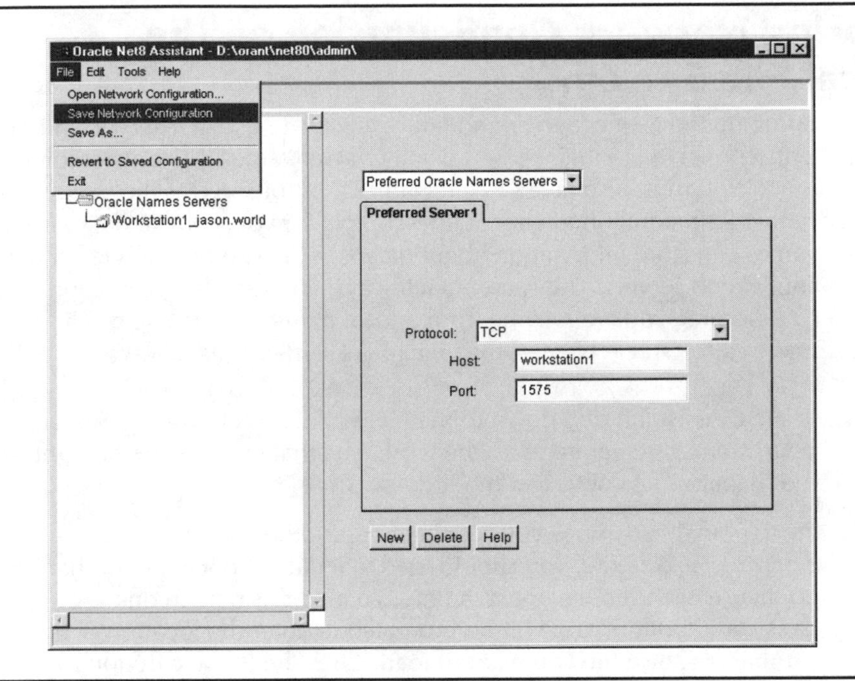

FIGURE 22-5. *Network location information for preferred Names server*

Exercises

1. Explain the process for using Net8 Assistant to configure clients for exclusive use of centralized naming on your Oracle network.
2. Describe how to use Net8 Assistant to set up Oracle Names on your network. In TCP/IP, what is the default and well-established port for Oracle Names to use?
3. What are the factors that influence your decision to place Oracle Names on the same server as the one running the Oracle database or some other server software? What factors would make you put Oracle Names on its own machine?
4. What is a region?

Storing Network Configuration on the Local File System

Simply setting up the Names server and telling clients to use that server isn't enough to get clients connected to their servers using Oracle Names for name-resolution on your network. You must also give Oracle Names a list of services that are available on your network. In addition to connect descriptors for your Oracle databases, Oracle Names can store information about database links, other Oracle services such as application servers, Transparent Gateways, and Oracle Connection Managers. Assuming you are moving from a local naming setup using `tnsnames.ora` to Oracle Names, the way to get started is as follows:

1. In Net8 Assistant, drill down to the Network | Oracle Names Servers | *your_Names_server* node. In the work area that appears on the right, select the Manage Data option in the drop-down list box.
2. Since you already have your connect descriptors available in a `tnsnames.ora` file, you should load that data at once, rather than configure each service one at a time. To load this data in one shot, click the Load radio button. You will be prompted to enter the location of the `tnsnames.ora` file you want to load. Click the Browse button to search on the local file system or on a network directory to find the names file to use. You should now see what's shown in Figure 22-6.
3. Click the Execute button. Net8 Assistant will load the contents of the selected `tnsnames.ora` file into your Names server. You will know how many connect descriptors were loaded because a dialogue box will tell you, when the operation is complete. Click OK in that box to continue.
4. You can then view the connection information by clicking the Network | Service Names node in Net8 Assistant. When finished, click the File | Save Network Configuration menu item.

Maintaining Names Service Information

As new databases are added to the network, their associated listeners can be set up to automatically maintain Names service information using Net8 Assistant. If you don't configure your listeners to do so, you will have to maintain Oracle Names yourself, by manually entering data into Oracle Names. You set up your listeners to update Oracle Names with vital contact information in the following way:

1. Drill down to the Network | Listeners | *listener_name* node for the listener you want to automatically update Oracle Names with.

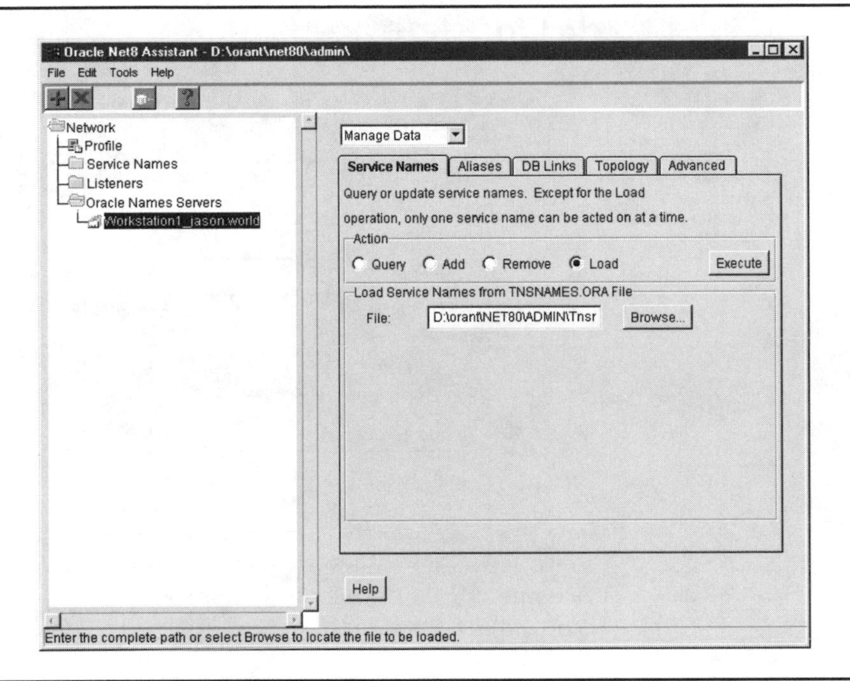

FIGURE 22-6. *The Net8 Assistant Manage Data work area*

2. Choose the General Parameters option from the drop-down list box.
3. Click the General tab.
4. Click the Register Services with Oracle Names checkbox on the General tab. Figure 22-7 shows Net8 Assistant when this is set up.
5. Select the File | Save Network Configuration menu option to save this network configuration information.

The names.ora Configuration File

Like network listeners, Names servers have a configuration file that supports their activities, called `names.ora`. This file can be found in the `net80/admin` subdirectory under the Oracle software home directory on the machine hosting Oracle Names. This configuration file identifies vital information about the Names

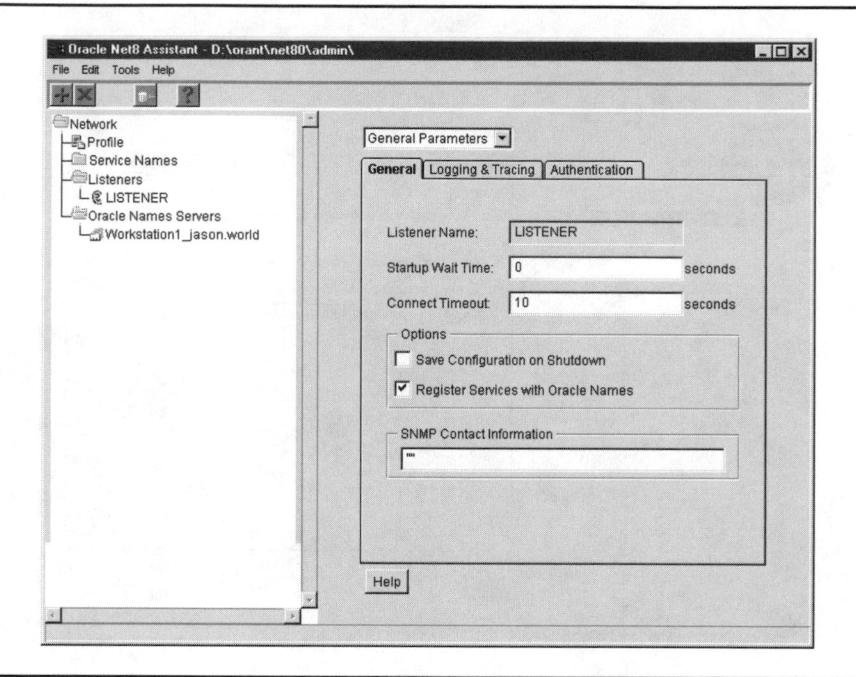

FIGURE 22-7. *Net8 Assistant with Register Services checkbox selected*

server itself, including its name and its location on the network. The following code block shows a sample `names.ora` file:

```
# D:\ORANT\NET80\ADMIN\NAMES.ORA Configuration
# File:D:\orant\net80\admin\names.ora
# Generated by Oracle Net8 Assistant
NAMES.SERVER_NAME = workstation1_jason
NAMES.ADDRESSES =
  (ADDRESS = (PROTOCOL = TCP)(HOST = workstation1)(PORT = 1575))
```

Exercises

1. Describe how to configure Oracle Names lookup information. How can Net8 Assistant be used to set up new listeners so that they maintain Oracle Names automatically?
2. What are the contents of the `names.ora` file, and how are they used?

Storing Network Configuration on a Regional Database

You may have trouble maintaining Names information when you add more Names servers to handle increased name-resolution traffic for many Oracle databases on the network. You may find it effective to store your hostname lookup information within the Oracle database, because then the Names information is available to all Names servers. If one Names server becomes unavailable, others can pick up the slack. Oracle Names can be configured to automatically write new entries to the Names repository with the following steps.

Step 1: Preparing the Oracle Database

Your first order of business is to set up your Oracle database to accommodate another repository. This requires a username and password for Oracle Names to log in to Oracle to store the information. It may benefit you to create a small tablespace to hold this user's data, as well, in order to avoid any space problems later. The following steps may be used to prepare Oracle:

1. Log into Oracle as the DBA, either through SQL*Plus or Server Manager.
2. Create a small tablespace for this repository with the `create tablespace` command. A size of 5–10MB should suffice.
3. Create a new user and assign the user's default tablespace to the tablespace you just created.
4. Using SQL*Plus, SQL*Worksheet, or Server Manager, login to your Oracle database and process the `namesini.sql` script found in the `net80/names` subdirectory on Windows, or `network/admin` on Unix, for the machine hosting Oracle Names.

Step 2: Configuring the Names Server

After database preparation is complete, you must finish the task by configuring some aspects of your Names server via Net8 Assistant. The following steps identify what you need to do:

1. Start Net8 Assistant if it hasn't been started already. In Windows, this is done by clicking Start | Programs | Oracle for Windows | Oracle Net8 Assistant.
2. Drill down to the Network | Oracle Names Servers | *your_Names_server* node. Select the Configure Server option in the drop-down list box in the Net8 Assistant work area.

3. Click the Database tab in the Configure Server work area. This is where you will do your configuring.
4. Click the Region Database radio button to tell Oracle Names you want it to get information from the database.
5. Define the network protocol and specific location of the machine hosting your Oracle database in the appropriate text boxes.
6. Define the Oracle SID and whether Oracle Names will use shared or dedicated servers when connecting to the database in the appropriate text box and list box, respectively.
7. Enter the username and password you created in the database-preparation steps above, so Oracle Names can connect to the database. Figure 22-8 shows an example of how to configure your regional-database information.
8. You can click the Optional button and define properties for how often Oracle Names will refresh itself and the database, and how long and often Oracle Names will repeat its attempts to connect to Oracle if the connection should fail because the database is not available. Figure 22-9 shows how you configure Optional regional-database parameters.

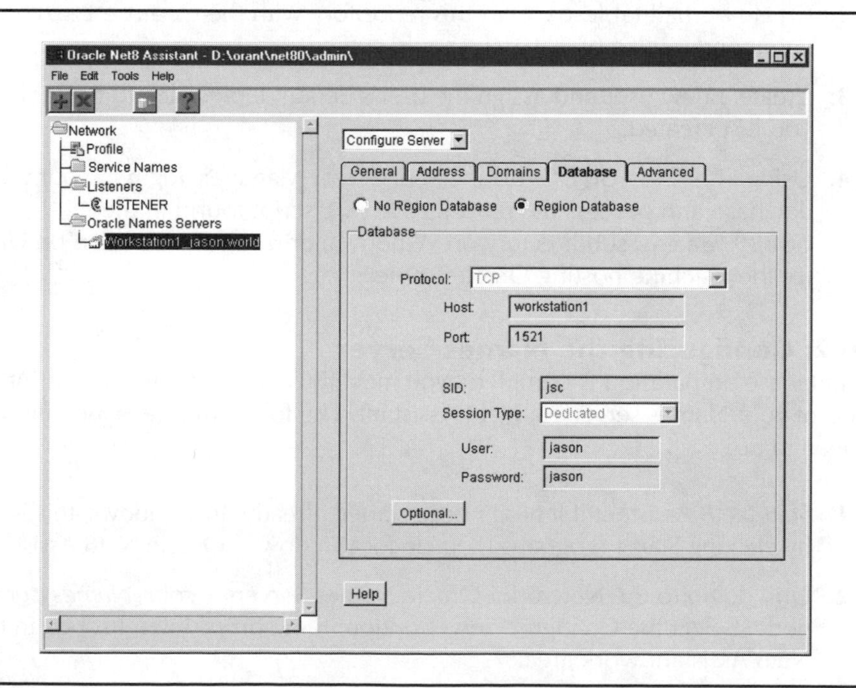

FIGURE 22-8. *Net8 Assistant with regional-database configuration set*

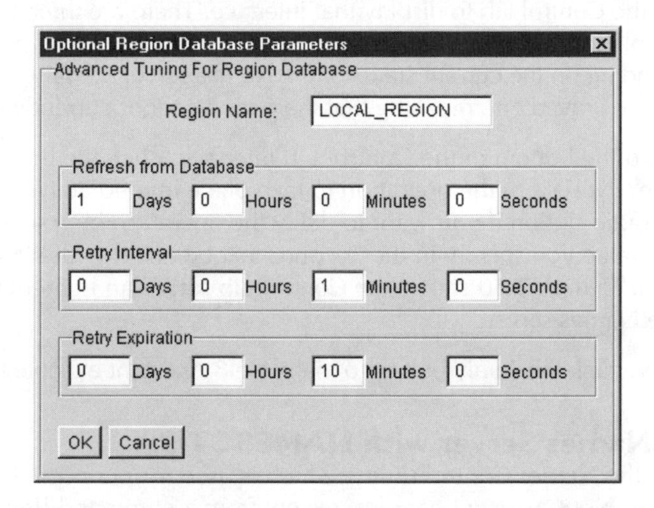

FIGURE 22-9. *Configuring optional regional-database parameters*

Exercises

1. What is the first step in configuring a regional database for use with Oracle Names? Which script is instrumental for doing so?
2. What is the second step?

Managing the Names Server with NAMESCTL

Finally, you will need to understand how to start and stop your Names server. There are a few different methods for doing so. If you are running your Names server on Windows platforms, Oracle Names is set up as a service, so if you are familiar with how to start and stop a service, you can use this method to start and stop your Names server.

Another method for starting and stopping Oracle Names involves Net8 Assistant. You can shut down, start, and restart your Names server in the following way using this tool:

1. Drill down to the Network | Oracle Names Servers | *your_Names_server* node.
2. Select the Manage Server option in the drop-down list box in Net8 Assistant to display the Manage Server work area.

3. Click the Control tab to display that interface. There are three radio buttons available for changing Names server status: Start, Shutdown, and Restart. Depending on the current status of the Names server, certain radio buttons might be grayed out, meaning that the option cannot currently be used.
4. Toward the bottom of the Control tab interface, click the Immediately radio button if you want the operation to take place immediately. Or, click the Wait radio button if you want to delay the operation by *n* seconds, where *n* is the value you specify in the Seconds text box next to the Wait radio button. Figure 22-10 shows the Control tab set for an immediate shutdown of the Names server.
5. Finally, click the Apply button to make Net8 Assistant execute the operation.

Starting a Names Server with NAMESCTL

NAMESCTL is the Names Control utility, which is used for performing many of the same operations Net8 Assistant handles, except from a command-line interface. NAMESCTL operates in much the same way as LSNRCTL, both interactively and in batch. NAMESCTL has several commands that it accepts.

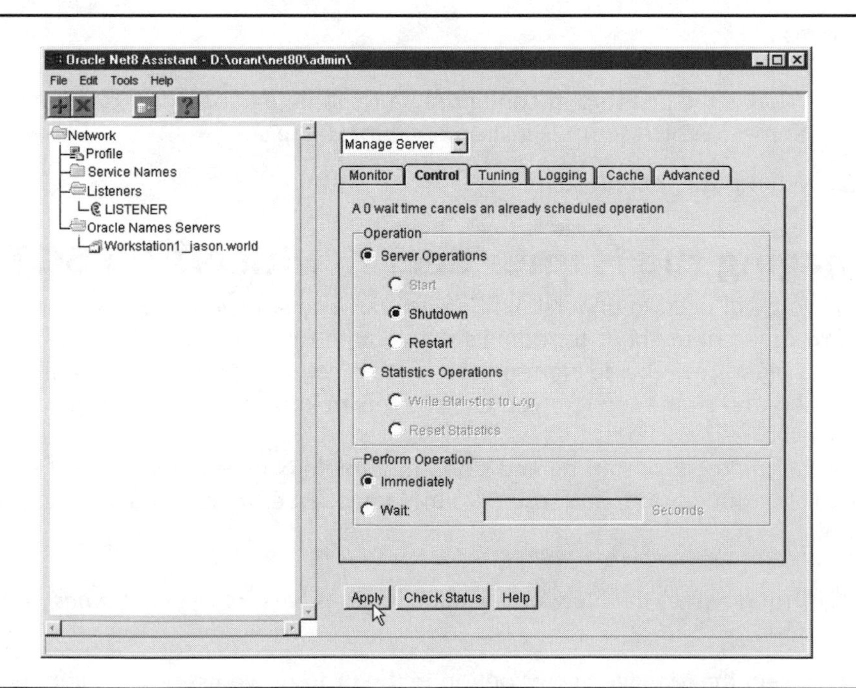

FIGURE 22-10. *Net8 Assistant with immediate shutdown configured*

The command you will focus on for starting your Names server with NAMESCTL interactively from the command line of the machine hosting your Names server is `start`. Note that the `startup` command can also be executed in NAMESCTL for the same results. The interactive method for starting your Names server with this utility is shown in the following code block:

```
D:\orant\bin> namesctl80
Oracle Names Control for 32-bit Windows: Version 8.0.5.0.0
 - Production on 08-MAY-99 18:51:31
(c) Copyright 1997 Oracle Corporation.  All rights reserved.
NNL-00018: warning: could not contact default name server
Welcome to NAMESCTL, type help for information
NAMESCTL> start
Starting "names80.exe"...Service
OracleNamesService80workstation1_jason start pending.
Service OracleNamesService80workstation1_jason started.
server successfully started
Currently managing name server "workstation1_jason"
Version banner is "Oracle Names for 32-bit Windows:
Version 8.0.5.0.0 - Production"
Server name:                                  workstation1_jason
Server has been running for:                  2.81 seconds
Request processing enabled:                   yes
Request forwarding enabled:                   yes
Requests received:                            0
Requests forwarded:                           0
Foreign data items cached:                    0
Region data next checked for reload in:
 23 hours 59 minutes 58.15 seconds
Region data reload check failures:            0
Cache next checkpointed in:                   not set
Cache checkpoint interval:                    not set
Cache checkpoint file name:
 D:\orant\NET80\names\ckpcch.ora
Statistic counters next reset in:             not set
Statistic counter reset interval:             not set
Statistic counters next logged in:            not set
Statistic counter logging interval:           not set
Trace level:                                  0
Trace file name:
 D:\orant\NET80\trace\names125.trc
Log file name:                                D:\orant\NET80\log\names.log
System parameter file name:
 D:\orant\NET80\admin\names.ora
Command-line parameter file name:             ""
Administrative region name:                   root
Administrative region description:(DESCRIPTION=(ADDRESS=(PROTOCOL=TCP)
```

```
(HOST=workstation1)(PORT=1521))
(CONNECT_DATA=(SID=jsc)(Server=Dedicated)))
ApplTable Index:                          0
Contact                                   ""
Operational Status                        0
Save Config on Stop                       no
NAMESCTL> quit
```

To start your Names server in batch, you simply issue the command for running NAMESCTL followed by the `start` command from the command-line interface for the host machine, and press ENTER. You have already seen that, in Windows, the command for NAMESCTL is `namesctl80`, while for Unix, it is simply `namesctl`.

```
D:\orant\bin> namesctl80 start
Oracle Names Control for 32-bit Windows: Version 8.0.5.0.0
- Production on 08-MAY-99 18:51:31
(c) Copyright 1997 Oracle Corporation.  All rights reserved.
NNL-00018: warning: could not contact default name server
Starting "names80.exe"...
Service OracleNamesService80workstation1_jason
start pending.
Service OracleNamesService80workstation1_jason started.
server successfully started
Currently managing name server "workstation1_jason"
Version banner is "Oracle Names for 32-bit Windows:
 Version 8.0.5.0.0 - Production"
Server name:                              workstation1_jason
Server has been running for:              2.81 seconds
Request processing enabled:               yes
Request forwarding enabled:               yes
Requests received:                        0
Requests forwarded:                       0
Foreign data items cached:                0
Region data next checked for reload in:
23 hours 59 minutes 58.15 seconds
Region data reload check failures:        0
Cache next checkpointed in:               not set
Cache checkpoint interval:                not set
Cache checkpoint file name:
D:\orant\NET80\names\ckpcch.ora
Statistic counters next reset in:         not set
Statistic counter reset interval:         not set
Statistic counters next logged in:        not set
Statistic counter logging interval:       not set
Trace level:                              0
Trace file name:
D:\orant\NET80\trace\names125.trc
Log file name:                            D:\orant\NET80\log\names.log
```

```
System parameter file name:
D:\orant\NET80\admin\names.ora
Command-line parameter file name:         ""
Administrative region name:               root
Administrative region description:(DESCRIPTION=(ADDRESS=(PROTOCOL=TCP)
(HOST=workstation1)(PORT=1521))
(CONNECT_DATA=(SID=jsc)(Server=Dedicated)))
ApplTable Index:                          0
Contact                                   ""
Operational Status                        0
Save Config on Stop                       no
D:\orant\bin>
```

Stopping a Names Server

Ending the execution of your Names server is easy. You simply have to issue the NAMESCTL executable, either followed immediately by the `stop` command on the command line (batch), or at the NAMESCTL prompt (interactive). Note that the `shutdown` command in NAMESCTL can be executed for exactly the same results. The following code block shows how to stop a Names server running in Windows in batch. Note that NAMESCTL asks you to confirm the action:

```
D:\orant\bin> namesctl80 stop
Oracle Names Control for 32-bit Windows:
Version 8.0.5.0.0 - Production on 08-MAY-99 19:03:15
(c) Copyright 1997 Oracle Corporation.  All rights reserved.
Currently managing name server "workstation1_jason"
Version banner is "Oracle Names for 32-bit Windows:
Version 8.0.5.0.0 - Production"
Confirm [yes or no]: yes
Server shutting down
D:\orant\bin>
```

The following code block shows NAMESCTL shutting down your Names server interactively:

```
D:\orant\bin> namesctl80
Oracle Names Control for 32-bit Windows:
Version 8.0.5.0.0 - Production on 08-MAY-99 19:03:15
(c) Copyright 1997 Oracle Corporation.  All rights reserved.
Currently managing name server "workstation1_jason"
Version banner is "Oracle Names for 32-bit Windows:
 Version 8.0.5.0.0 - Production"
Welcome to NAMESCTL, type help for information
NAMESCTL> stop
Confirm [yes or no]: yes
Server shutting down
NAMESCTL> quit
```

NAMESCTL General Commands

As with LSNRCTL, there are several commands available with NAMESCTL, falling into the same categories. The first of these categories is that of general commands for performing regular activities. Table 22-1 shows the general commands, which are executed either by issuing the command from the NAMESCTL prompt, or by issuing `namesctl` *command* from the operating-system command prompt.

NAMESCTL Command	Description
`delegate_domain`	Defines a domain as the start of a subregion within the current region.
`domain_hint`	Lists Names servers in different regions to Names servers in current region.
`exit` `quit`	Ends the NAMESCTL interactive session.
`flush` *server*	Eliminates connect descriptors for other subregions from the Names server cache whose name is used in this command instead of *server*. This command is only used when your Oracle network is divided into subregions, and even then only on Names servers assigned to those subregions.
`flush_name` *name*	Eliminates specific connect descriptor for *name* from the Names server cache. This command is only used when your Oracle network is divided into subregions, and even then only on Names servers assigned to those subregions.
`help` *command*	When followed by a *command*, this lists basic syntax for that command. If *command* is not entered, `help` lists all NAMESCTL commands.
`log_stats` *server*	Records Names server statistics to the log file for *server*.
`password` *password*	Allows you to identify the password to be used for authenticating privileged operations. This command does not actually set the Names server password, it only identifies it for the session.

TABLE 22-1. *NAMESCTL Commands*

NAMESCTL Command	Description
`ping` *`server`*	Allows you to determine whether *`server`* is connected to the Oracle network, and how long it takes for that server to respond.
`query` *`service options`*	Retrieves information stored in Names for a service on the Oracle network.
`register` *`service options`*	Lists the connection information for a service joining an Oracle network.
`reload` *`server`*	Forces a check for data changes and reloads new information, if any.
`reorder_ns`	Creates a file listing local Names servers and their addresses.
`repeat` *`n command options`*	Allows you to calculate performance for another *`command`* by repeating the command *`n`* times.
`reset_stats` *`server`*	Returns Names server statistics to their original values when Names server was started.
`restart` *`server`*	Re-initialize a Names server.
`start_client_cache`	Starts the client cache process, where all Names server information will be stored.
`status` *`server`*	Returns status information for the Names server.
`timed_query`	Shows all registered data in the Names server cache.
`unregister` *`service`*	Eliminates information about a service on the Oracle network from the Names server.
`version` *`server`*	Shows the version information for the Names server.

TABLE 22-1. *NAMESCTL Commands* (continued)

NAMESCTL set and show Commands

Table 22-2 shows the options available for the `set` and `show` commands. The `set` commands are used to define values for the NAMESCTL session or for the Names server configuration. The `show` commands are used to display the settings defined with the `set` commands. The syntax for set and show commands from the NAMESCTL interactive prompt is `set` *`option`* or `show` *`option`*. From the operating-system command prompt, issue the `namesctl set` *`option`* or `namesctl show` *`option`* command. Note that the `password` option is only available to the `set` command.

set/show Option	Description
`cache_checkpoint_interval` *seconds*	How many *seconds* before Names server updates all service information on non-local Oracle regions in the cache file.
`default_domain` *name*	The default domain acted upon by this NAMESCTL session.
`forwarding_available` *flag*	Whether name-request forwarding is on or off, where *flag* can be `yes` or `no`.
`log_file_name` *filename*	The non-default log *filename* for a Names server.
`log_stats_interval` *seconds*	The frequency in *seconds* of when statistics are written to the Names server log file.
`namesctl_trace_level` *level*	The tracing level for the NAMESCTL program, where valid values for *level* include `off`, `user`, `admin`, or `support`.
`password` *password*	Register the password for this session, used to authenticate privileged Names server operations. This command does not actually change the password and is only available to the `set` command.
`requests_enabled` *flag*	Whether Names server will respond to requests, where *flag* can be `yes` or `no`.
`reset_stats_interval` *seconds*	The time between statistics being reset to 0 or initial values in the Names server in *seconds*.
`server` *server*	The current Names server being managed.
`trace_file_name` *filename*	The default name of the trace file for the current Names server to *filename*.

TABLE 22-2. *NAMESCTL `set` and `show` Options*

Exercises

1. Describe the process for starting and stopping your Names server using Net8 Assistant.
2. Describe the process for starting and stopping your Names server using NAMESCTL. How does it differ from the process used for Net8 Assistant?

Use and Configuration of Oracle Intelligent Agent for OEM

In this section, you will cover the following topics on the use and configuration of Intelligent Agent:

- The purpose of Intelligent Agent
- Using LSNRCTL to start and stop Intelligent Agent
- Intelligent Agent configuration files

The functionality of Oracle Enterprise Manager is greatly enhanced by using Intelligent Agent. You have already seen a glimpse of Intelligent Agent in Chapter 16, where it was discussed in the context of detecting system events. In this chapter, you will become better acquainted with the purpose of Intelligent Agent. You will also review some LSNRCTL (presented in Chapter 21) that enable you to start and stop the Oracle Intelligent Agent. Finally, you will learn more about the configuration files of Intelligent Agent, and their contents.

The Purpose of Intelligent Agent

Intelligent Agent is a utility that runs on the same machine as your Oracle database and is designed to help you administer your Oracle database by detecting when certain occurrences or events arise that may change the performance of your Oracle database. When Intelligent Agent is running, you can view events detected by the agent in the Oracle Enterprise Manager (OEM) console window. With Intelligent Agent, you can detect Oracle waits and other system-wide database events without having to review the ALERT log or V$ views directly from your host. Instead, you can see the events that have occurred in your database since the last time you looked in the OEM console.

Intelligent Agent also assigns a severity level to the events that occur on your system. These severity levels will appear as flags next to the events listed in the

OEM console. Highest severity issues are marked with a red flag. These include database startups and other items that prevent users from gaining access to Oracle. The next highest level issues are marked with a yellow flag. Other events are marked with green flags.

Intelligent Agent can also be used to manage SNMP on the machine hosting your Oracle database. SNMP stands for *simple network management protocol*, and it can be used for managing nodes on a network from one location or console. However, Oracle Enterprise Manager does not use SNMP to communicate with Intelligent Agent. Instead, the OEM console communicates with the Intelligent Agent using its own communication method. Thus, OEM works with Intelligent Agent even when the host machine does not support SNMP.

Exercises

1. What is Intelligent Agent? How can it be used?
2. How is Oracle Enterprise Manager used in conjunction with Intelligent Agent? How does the agent communicate with the console?

Using LSNRCTL to Start and Stop Intelligent Agent

To start and stop Intelligent Agent running on your machine, you can use any one of a few different methods. The primary method is with LSNRCTL, the same utility you use to start and stop your database listener process. The command in LSNRCTL to start Intelligent Agent is `dbsnmp_start`. There are no arguments that you need to pass along with this command, and you can issue it interactively from LSNRCTL, or from the operating-system command line. The following code block shows how to start Intelligent Agent from within LSNRCTL in Windows:

```
D:\orant\BIN> lsnrctl80
LSNRCTL80 for 32-bit Windows: Version 8.0.5.0.0
Production on 05-MAY-99 12:20:39
(c) Copyright 1997 Oracle Corporation.  All rights reserved.
Welcome to LSNRCTL, type help for information.
LSNRCTL> dbsnmp_start
```

You can also simply execute LSNRCTL from the command line to start your Intelligent Agent, as follows:

```
D:\orant\BIN> lsnrctl80 dbsnmp_start
```

Stopping the listener can also be done with the LSNRCTL utility, using the dbsnmp_stop command. The following code block demonstrates how you would interactively stop the listener:

```
D:\orant\BIN> lsnrctl80
LSNRCTL80 for 32-bit Windows: Version 8.0.5.0.0
Production on 05-MAY-99 12:20:39
(c) Copyright 1997 Oracle Corporation.  All rights reserved.
Welcome to LSNRCTL, type help for information.
LSNRCTL> dbsnmp_stop
```

You can also simply execute LSNRCTL from the command line to stop Intelligent Agent, as shown in the following block:

```
D:\orant\BIN> lsnrctl80 dbsnmp_start
```

Finally, to display the current status of Intelligent Agent, you need to use the dbsnmp_status command. The syntax for this command is shown in the following code block:

```
D:\orant\BIN> lsnrctl80
LSNRCTL80 for 32-bit Windows: Version 8.0.5.0.0
Production on 05-MAY-99 12:20:39
© Copyright 1997 Oracle Corporation.  All rights reserved.
Welcome to LSNRCTL, type help for information.
LSNRCTL> status
```

Other Ways to Manage Intelligent Agent

There are other ways to manage Intelligent Agent, depending on your operating system. You may, for example, be able to use the Services control panel in Windows to start and stop your listener if you are running Oracle in that environment. Or, for Unix, you can incorporate the agent into your inetd.conf file so that the agent gets started automatically when the Unix server reboots. However, the availability of these methods is going to depend on the operating system.

Exercises

1. Identify the command used to start Intelligent Agent. Which utility is used to start the agent?
2. Identify the commands used to stop and determine Intelligent Agent status.

Intelligent Agent Configuration Files

There is one basic configuration file for Intelligent Agent you should be aware of—`snmp.ora`. This file contains information that can be used to configure Intelligent Agent to use Oracle Names for lookup information, and will register the agent with the Names server to keep track of the resources available on your Oracle network. The following code block displays the sample `snmp.ora` file that you can find in your `net80/admin/sample` directory under the Oracle software home directory.

```
################## Filename......: snmp.ora ###################
#                                                             #
# NOTE: This Intelligent Agent Configuration File is          #
# ONLY needed if you are registering with the                 #
#   Oracle Names Server.                                      #
# The Agent will only identify this file if you               #
# edit the line....                                           #
# nmi.register_with_names=TRUE                                #
#                                                             #
###############################################################
snmp.visibleservices = (db_name.world, host_name_lsnr.world)
snmp.index.db_name.world = 1
snmp.index.host_name_lsnr.world = 2
snmp.contact.db_name.world = contact_info
snmp.contact.host_name_lsnr.world = contact_info
snmp.sid.db_name.world = server_id
snmp.oraclehome.db_name.world=$ORACLE_HOME
# ****do not register with names (if names server is not installed).
nmi.register_with_names=true
nmi.trace_level = 0
nmi.trace_mask = (106)
nmi.trace_directory = $ORACLE_HOME\network\trace
dbsnmp.address = (DESCRIPTION=(ADDRESS=(PROTOCOL=tcp)
(HOST=host_name)
(PORT=1748)))
dbsnmp.spawnaddress =
(DESCRIPTION=(ADDRESS=(PROTOCOL=tcp)(HOST=host_name)(PORT=1754)))
###############################################################
```

The configuration file defines agent characteristics in a few different areas. The first area is the SNMP descriptive information used for managing your network via an SNMP console. These characteristics are prefixed by the `snmp` keyword in the listing above. The next set of characteristics define tracing characteristics for Intelligent Agent and whether the agent will register with the Names server. These characteristics are prefixed with the `nmi` keyword in the listing. The final set of characteristics in this listing are the Intelligent Agent address information the listener will use to find the agent. These characteristics are prefixed with the `dbsnmp` keyword in the listing.

Exercises

1. Describe the contents of the `snmp.ora` file. Which three sets of information are configured by this file?
2. For Intelligent Agent to use the `snmp.ora` file, what must happen with regard to Intelligent Agent and the Names server?

Use and Configuration of Multithreaded Server (MTS)

In this section, you will cover the following topics on using and configuring MTS:

- The components of MTS
- Configuring dispatchers using init*sid*.ora
- Configuring shared servers using init*sid*.ora
- Specifying a listener address for MTS
- Setting up connection pooling using MTS

In Chapter 6 there was an explanation of the difference between dedicated-server and shared-server configuration. In this section, you will cover the use of the multithreaded-server architecture in more detail. The first area of this section covers the components of MTS, including the conceptual explanation of shared servers, dispatchers, and all the rest. The next two areas covered are how to configure dispatchers and shared servers using parameters in the init*sid*.ora file. After that, you'll cover how to specify a listener address for MTS. The last area of this section describes setting up connection pooling using the multithreaded server architecture.

The Components of MTS

The multithreaded-server (MTS) architecture has several components. These components consist of different background processes, management of server processes, and the use of the Oracle SGA. The background processes involved with the MTS architecture include *listeners, dispatchers,* and *shared servers.* In addition, session information is stored in the shared pool of the Oracle SGA when MTS is in use.

You should begin your understanding of MTS by understanding all the background processes involved. From Chapter 21, you already know that a listener is the process that tunes in to the network for user sessions attempting to connect with the Oracle database. When a connection is heard by the listener, the listener passes that connection to another process. When dedicated servers are being used, the listener passes the user process to either a prespawned dedicated server, or it spawns a new dedicated server and passes the user process to that new server.

When MTS is being used, the listener passes the user process to another process called a *dispatcher*. The user process will be handed off by the listener to the least busy dispatcher process. The dispatcher process maintains two queues, called a *request queue* and a *response queue*. The longer the request queue is at any given time, the more work a dispatcher has to accomplish on behalf of the user processes assigned to it. Dispatcher processes work with shared-server processes to accomplish the work that is in the request queue. A shared server will grab the request at the beginning of the queue and process the work requested. When the shared server is finished, it puts the information obtained from the Oracle database onto the *response queue*, where the user process that made the request can pick up the results. Figure 22-11 displays a conceptual model of what happens in the MTS configuration.

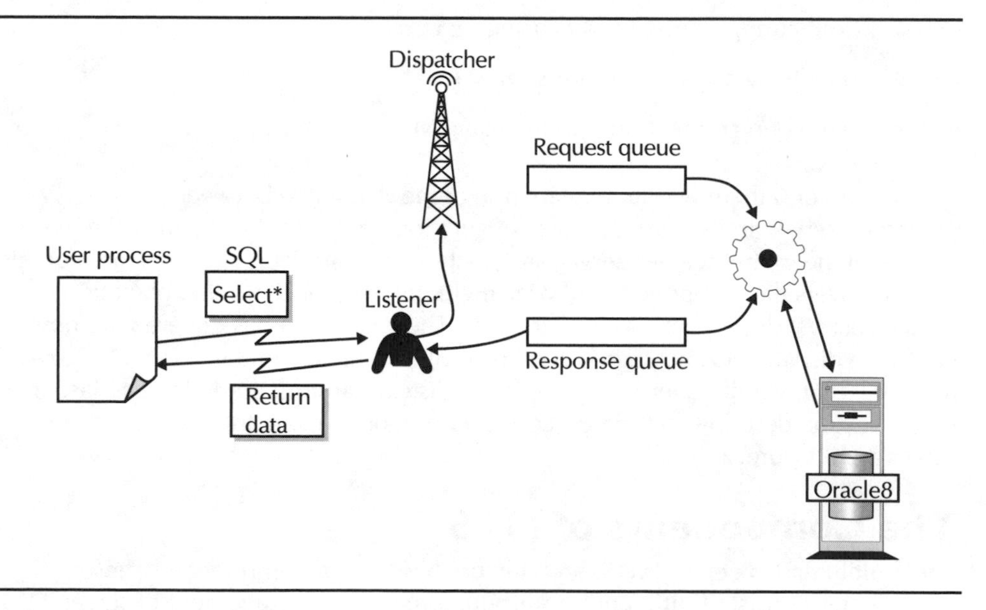

FIGURE 22-11. *Process interaction in the MTS configuration*

Exercises

1. What is a dispatcher? What is a shared server? How does Oracle manage user-process access to shared servers?
2. Describe the functionality provided by the request and response queues in the MTS architecture.

Configuring Dispatchers Using init*sid*.ora

Dispatcher configuration in Oracle consists of several `init`*`sid`*`.ora` parameters. The first one is called `MTS_DISPATCHERS`. This parameter defines the number of dispatchers that handle connections to Oracle from user processes for each network protocol that accesses this server. You need to configure `MTS_DISPATCHERS` in your `init`*`sid`*`.ora` file and then restart the instance. This parameter can be used with a bare syntax of `MTS_DISPATCHERS` = "*`protocol`*, *n*" established in earlier versions of Oracle and which is still supported:

```
MTS_DISPATCHERS = "TCP, 3"
```

You can also use the more elaborate *`name=value`* syntax, which enhances the amount of information that can be configured for your dispatchers using this parameter:

```
MTS_DISPATCHERS = "(procotol=TCP)(dispatchers=3)"
```

Note that you can define this parameter more than once in your `init`*`sid`*`.ora` file to generate dispatchers for each network protocol connected to the machine hosting Oracle, as well.

```
MTS_DISPATCHERS = "(protocol=NMP)(dispatchers=1)"
MTS_DISPATCHERS = "(procotol=TCP)(dispatchers=3)"
```

You can even use the more complex `address` option to force dispatchers to listen to specific addresses and/or ports on the host machine:

```
MTS_DISPATCHERS = "(ADDRESS=(PARTIAL=TRUE)(PROTOCOL=TCP)\
(HOST=workstation1)(PORT=5000))(DISPATCHERS=1)"
MTS_DISPATCHERS = "(ADDRESS=(PARTIAL=TRUE)(PROTOCOL=TCP)\
(HOST=workstation1)(PORT=5001))(DISPATCHERS=1)"
MTS_DISPATCHERS = "(ADDRESS=(PARTIAL=TRUE)(PROTOCOL=TCP)\
(HOST=workstation1)(PORT=5002))(DISPATCHERS=1)"
```

You can also use the *name=value* syntax at the SQL prompt to dynamically change the number of dispatchers on your system, or to accomplish other reconfiguration tasks.

```
SQL> alter system set MTS_DISPATCHERS =
  2  '(procotol=TCP)(dispatchers=3)';
System altered.
```

The available options for configuring your dispatcher using the MTS_DISPATCHERS parameter are listed in Table 22-3. You specify values for the options using the same *option=value* syntax. In general, be sure you configure enough dispatchers to handle the number of concurrent users connected to your Oracle database. More dispatchers available on your database will improve user performance. There should be enough dispatchers running to ensure that all concurrent users receive adequate performance in connecting to dispatchers.

Configuring MTS_MAX_DISPATCHERS

When adding dispatchers, you should ensure that you don't add too many. Every operating system has a limit to the number of processes that can be running at the same time. The parameter MTS_MAX_DISPATCHERS is set to a number that represents the maximum number of dispatcher processes for all network protocols combined that can be started for the duration of an instance. This parameter can help you limit the number of dispatcher processes created so that the total number

Configuration Option	Description
connection	The maximum number of network connections to allow for each dispatcher. Default is platform-specific.
dispatcher	The initial number of dispatchers to start. Default is 1.
listener	The network name of an address or address list of the Net8 listeners with which the dispatchers will register.
multiplex	Used to enable the Net8 network session multiplex feature.
pool	Used to enable the Net8 connection pooling feature.
service	The service name that the dispatchers register with the Net8 listeners, overriding the MTS_SERVICE parameter.
sessions	The maximum number of network sessions to allow for each dispatcher.
ticks	Used to determine the size of a network tick, in seconds.

TABLE 22-3. MTS_DISPATCHERS Configuration Options

of processes, including dispatchers, does not exceed the host operating system's limit on the number of running processes at one time. The following code block shows how you might set this parameter in your initsid.ora file:

```
MTS_MAX_DISPATCHERS = 8
```

Associating a Dispatcher with a Service

The MTS_SERVICE parameter defines the service name you want to associate with a dispatcher. Users employing the service name in the connect string will connect to the instance through the dispatcher associated with that service. Oracle always checks for such a service before establishing a normal database connection. The name specified with a service must be unique. One suggestion for defining MTS_SERVICE is to make it the same as the instance name. If the dispatcher you try to go to is unavailable, Net8 will then still be able to connect the user. If no value is specified for MTS_SERVICE, the value defaults to DB_NAME anyway.

Exercises

1. Explain how to configure the MTS_DISPATCHERS initsid.ora parameter to define your dispatchers. In TCP/IP, which options would you use if you wanted to explicitly assign a dispatcher to a hostname or port?
2. What purpose does the MTS_SERVICE parameter fulfill? What is the purpose of the MTS_MAX_DISPATCHERS parameter?

Configuring Shared Servers Using init*sid*.ora

After setting up your dispatchers, you will also need to configure your shared servers using initsid.ora parameters. The first and most important parameter for configuring your shared servers is the MTS_SERVERS parameter. You specify an integer value for this parameter according to the number of shared servers you want available on your machine. You should set this value to be at least as large as the value set for the dispatchers option in the MTS_DISPATCHERS parameter, so that every dispatcher has at least one shared server handling work on the dispatcher's request queue.

Obviously, having more than one shared server per dispatcher will improve performance because throughput of work between request and response queues will be higher if more servers are available to do the work. In a typical OLTP environment, where users connecting to Oracle may only execute a small amount of processing, you may want to set MTS_SERVERS to a value that allows one server to handle 10–20 concurrent user processes. For DSS systems, data warehouses, or batch processing systems, you may want a smaller ratio of servers to concurrent user processes, perhaps one server for every five processes.

However, it is wise to specify a smaller number of shared-server processes. This is because Oracle will automatically start more shared servers during periods of high load volume, up to a maximum number of shared servers set by the `initsid.ora` parameter `MTS_MAX_SERVERS`. When the load decreases, Oracle will kill the shared servers it started if they sit idle for too long, as well. However, Oracle will never kill the shared servers started at instance startup as specified by the `MTS_SERVERS` parameter.

```
MTS_SERVERS = 3
MTS_MAX_SERVERS = 8
```

Exercises

1. Which parameter defines the number of shared servers created at instance startup for your database?
2. How do you limit the number of shared servers Oracle creates when database load increases?

Specifying a Listener Address for MTS

If you are using a multithreaded server, you should specify the address where your MTS listener is tuned in for user connections by specifying the listener address in `initsid.ora` for the `MTS_LISTENER_ADDRESS` parameter. This parameter is being phased out, starting in Oracle8, but you can use `LOCAL_LISTENER` instead. To determine the value you should specify for this parameter, you can look in the `listener.ora` file for the listener. Recall that you looked at this file in Chapter 21, as part of learning how to configure your network listener. Now, you can use the file to configure your `initsid.ora` file, as well. The following code block shows the contents of a `listener.ora` file where the network listener has been configured:

```
# D:\ORANT\NET80\ADMIN\LISTENER.ORA Configuration
File:D:\orant\net80\admin\listener.ora
# Generated by Oracle Net8 Assistant
USE_PLUG_AND_PLAY_LISTENER = ON
LISTENER =
  (ADDRESS_LIST =
    (ADDRESS = (PROTOCOL = IPC)(KEY = EXTPROC0))
    (ADDRESS = (PROTOCOL = NMP)(SERVER = WORKSTATION1)(PIPE = ORAPIPE))
    (ADDRESS = (PROTOCOL = TCP)(HOST = workstation1)(PORT = 1521))
    (ADDRESS = (PROTOCOL = TCP)(HOST = workstation1)(PORT = 1526))
  )
SID_LIST_LISTENER =
```

```
(SID_LIST =
  (SID_DESC =
    (SID_NAME = extproc)
    (PROGRAM = extproc)
  )
  (SID_DESC =
    (SID_NAME = JSC)
  )
)
```

For setting the MTS_LISTENER_ADDRESS parameter, you can use the values set up in the ADDRESS_LIST component of your listener.ora file. You can also specify multiple listener addresses in your init*sid*.ora file by simply assigning a value to MTS_LISTENER_ADDRESS twice. Both values will then be assigned to this parameter for your instance. The following code block illustrates this:

```
mts_listener_address="(ADDRESS = (PROTOCOL = TCP)\
(HOST = workstation1)(PORT = 1521))"
mts_listener_address="(ADDRESS = (PROTOCOL = TCP)\
(HOST = workstation1)(PORT = 1526))"
```

Registering Dispatchers with a Listener

Dispatchers should register with a listener as part of the configuration for the parameter MTS_DISPATCHERS. This is handled with the listener option, defined previously in Table 22-3. There is another way to specify the address of the listener, using the init*sid*.ora parameter MTS_LISTENER_ADDRESS, but using the listener option in MTS_DISPATCHERS overrides this other method.

Exercises

1. Identify the init*sid*.ora parameter that defines listener addresses for the Oracle database.
2. What other configuration file will you use to define the value for the parameter identified in exercise 1?
3. Describe the process for registering a dispatcher with the Net8 listener process.

Setting Up Connection Pooling Using MTS

In large networks, the connection pooling feature of Oracle can improve scalability by maximizing physical network connections to the multithreaded server. The set of connections made to a dispatcher are shared or pooled between many user processes. Oracle does this by using a time-out mechanism to temporarily release transport connections that have been idle. These physical connections are then available for incoming clients, while the logical session with the previous idle connection is still being maintained. When the idle user process has more work to accomplish, its physical connection is reestablished with the dispatcher, and the process begins all over again.

Connection pooling is configured using the `MTS_DISPATCHERS` `init`*`sid`*`.ora` parameter. Recall that there are several options available for specifying this parameter. To configure connection pooling on a particular dispatcher, you must use the `pool` option in the following way. To turn on connection pooling, set the `pool` option to `on`, `yes`, `true`, or `both`. To leave it off, set the `pool` option to `off`, `no`, or `false`. You can also define connection pooling in either the direction of client to server or vice-versa by setting `pool` to `in` or `out`, respectively. The following code block shows how to set connection pooling to `on` in all cases:

```
MTS_DISPATCHERS = "(ADDRESS=(PROTOCOL=TCP)\
(HOST=workstation1)(PORT=5000))(POOL=ON)(DISPATCHERS=1)(TICKS=3)"
```

TIP
The `ticks` option is used to determine the size of a network tick in seconds. The default is 15 seconds. This parameter is optional for connection pooling.

Exercises

1. Identify the use of connection pooling. What purpose does it serve?
2. Which parameter is used to configure connection pooling? What are some of the different ways you can configure connection pooling to operate?

Chapter Summary

This chapter covered several areas of Oracle networking that involve configuring extended services for Net8. These include Oracle Names, Oracle Intelligent Agent, and the multithreaded server (MTS) processes. These are all server-side configuration processes and account for about 30 percent of the material tested on OCP Exam 5.

The first area you learned about was using and configuring Oracle Names, and the value of using centralized naming from an administrative perspective. You also learned how to configure centralized naming using the Net8 Assistant tool. Storage aspects for Names information were also covered. You learned about the implications and procedures for storing this information on the machine hosting Oracle Names, and you covered the benefits of storing Names information in a Names repository on an Oracle database so that the information is available to many other Names servers, as well. Finally, you learned how to use the NAMESCTL utility to start and stop the Names server. Other commands available in NAMESCTL were discussed, as well.

The next area of this chapter covered using and configuring Oracle Intelligent Agent. This tool works in conjunction with Oracle Enterprise Manager to give you more control over and information about your Oracle database from the OEM console, providing enhanced database management from a centralized location. You learned how to start and stop the agent using LSNRCTL with the appropriate `dbsnmp_start`, `dbsnmp_stop`, and `dbsnmp_status` commands. You also learned about the configuration files associated with Intelligent Agent and how they are used.

The final area covered was using and configuring the multithreaded-server architecture in Oracle, also known as MTS. You learned how to identify the components of MTS, such as the Net8 listener, dispatcher, and shared-server processes. You learned about the init*sid*.ora parameters used to configure dispatchers on your Oracle server, along with the parameters for configuring your shared servers. Specifying the listener address on your machine when MTS is used was covered, as well. Finally, you learned how to set up connection pooling using the `MTS_DISPATCHERS` init*sid*.ora parameter.

Two Minute Drill

- Oracle Names is used as an N-tier server solution for centralized administration of services available on the Oracle network.
- Net8 Assistant is used to configure centralized naming. Client preferences for using Oracle Names is set in the Profiles node of that tool.
- Oracle Names can be run on the same machine hosting the Oracle database, or on a different machine.
- Names server locations can be defined with Net8 Assistant using the wizard available when you create the Names server. Review the chapter to recall the process for doing so.
- When you configure your first Names server on the Oracle network, Oracle calls that network the root region. This is used later for administrative purposes when new subregions are created.

- Review how to define a preferred Names server in the chapter.
- Review the storage of Names information on the local file system, and the use of Net8 Assistant for this purpose.
- You can configure listeners to register their services with Oracle Names using Net8 Assistant. Review the chapter to understand how.
- The `names.ora` configuration file supports Oracle Names by identifying the name of the Names server and its location on the network.
- You can store naming information in a repository on your Oracle database. To configure the database, you must create a user for the Names server to use to login and maintain the repository information, and then run `namesini.sql` to store that information, which is found in the `net80/names` directory on Windows machines, `network/admin` on Unix.
- To set up your Names server to use that regional database, you perform a series of steps using Net8 Assistant. Review the chapter to understand the process.
- NAMESCTL is a utility you can run interactively or from the command line to perform many activities also done using Net8 Assistant.
- To start the Names server, use the `namesctl start` command. For Windows, use `namesctl80 start`.
- To stop the Names server, use the `namesctl stop` command. For Windows, use `namesctl80 stop`.
- Review Tables 22-1 and 22-2 to see the commands available for NAMESCTL.
- Intelligent Agent is used in conjunction with Oracle Enterprise Manager to enhance the DBA's ability to centrally administer multiple Oracle databases and resources on the Oracle network.
- Intelligent Agent runs on the same machine that is hosting your Oracle database and helps you administer that database by detecting when certain occurrences or events arise that may change your database performance.
- LSNRCTL can be used to start Intelligent Agent with the `dbsnmp_start` command.
- LSNRCTL can be used to start Intelligent Agent with the `dbsnmp_stop` command.
- LSNRCTL can be used to determine the current status of Intelligent Agent with the `dbsnmp_status` command.

- The main configuration file for Intelligent Agent is `snmp.ora`, but even this file is only used when you plan on registering Intelligent Agent with Oracle Names on your network.
- The components of Oracle's multithreaded server architecture include dispatchers and shared servers.
- Dispatchers maintain two work queues to handle user processing. User processes place their data-processing requests on the dispatcher request queue for processing by the next available shared server. The shared server places the results of the user-processing request on the response queue.
- Dispatchers are configured with several parameters in `initsid.ora`:
  - `MTS_DISPATCHERS` is used to define the protocol the dispatcher listens to, and the number of dispatchers for that protocol.
  - `MTS_MAX_DISPATCHERS` is used for limiting the number of dispatcher processes on the machine.
  - `MTS_SERVICE` is used to define the service name you want to associate with a dispatcher.
- Shared servers are also configured with `initsid.ora` parameters:
  - `MTS_SERVERS` determines the number of shared servers on the system that will be started when the database starts. Oracle may start more shared servers automatically if the workload for the database gets too large.
  - `MTS_MAX_SERVERS` determines the maximum number of servers Oracle will start automatically.
- You can specify that your MTS network listeners tune into certain addresses by using the `MTS_LISTENER_ADDRESS` parameter. You can also assign dispatchers to certain listeners using the `listener` option in the `MTS_DISPATCHERS` parameter.
- Connection pooling is when Net8 releases transport connections that have been idle to establish a physical connection to a new client connection, while still preserving the logical session with the previous client.
- Connection pooling is configured with the `pool` option in the `MTS_DISPATCHERS` parameter.

Chapter Questions

1. **Your database is configured to run a multithreaded server. The database experienced a heavy transaction load an hour ago, but is now idle. Which of the following parameters most likely identifies how many server processes are running?**

   A. PROCESSES

   B. OPEN_CURSORS

   C. MTS_MAX_SERVERS

   D. MTS_SERVERS

2. **Your TNSNAMES file contains an alias, called DB01, which connects you to a database running on a node called DB01. Another DBA adds a new database on a host machine, the SID for which is DB01, and the listener is configured to automatically register with Oracle Names. The default order of host-naming resolution preference is still in place. When you attempt to connect to Oracle using the DB01 connect string, which database will you connect to, and why?**

   A. The database on node DB01, because Oracle attempts host naming resolution first by default

   B. The database on node DB01, because Oracle attempts local naming resolution first by default

   C. The database whose SID is DB01, because Oracle attempts centralized naming resolution first by default

   D. The database whose SID is DB01, because Oracle attempts external naming resolution first by default

3. **You are determining how to store naming information for your Oracle Names servers. Which of the following choices does not describe a feature of regional database repository usage for this purpose?**

   A. Increased Names server fault tolerance

   B. Higher scalability when subnetworks are configured

   C. Best for Oracle networks consisting of workgroup configurations

   D. Reduced effort for Net8 circulating new Oracle service names

4. **You are attempting to define the location of your Names server on the Oracle network. To do so, which of the following tools would you use?**

   A. Net8 Assistant

   B. LSNRCTL

   C. Oracle Expert

   D. Oracle Enterprise Manager

5. **You are looking for the port on the host machine where the Names server is listening. Which of the following files contains that information?**

   A. `listener.ora`

   B. `tnsnames.ora`

   C. `snmp.ora`

   D. `names.ora`

6. **You are configuring your repository to store naming information within the Oracle database. After creating a user that the Names server will use to connect to the repository, which of the following steps should you undertake?**

   A. Run the `namesini.sql` script.

   B. Make appropriate changes in the Database tab interface of Net8 Assistant.

   C. Click the Optional button to define how Oracle Names refreshes the repository.

   D. Edit the `names.ora` file to define the repository location.

7. **You want to start the Oracle Names server. Which of the following tools enable you to perform this task? (Choose two)**

   A. Oracle Enterprise Manager

   B. NAMESCTL

   C. LSNRCTL

   D. Net8 Assistant

   E. Instance Manager

   F. Server Manager

8. You are attempting to manually add a new service to your Oracle network using the NAMESCTL utility. Which of the following commands will assist you in this purpose?

A. `register`

B. `reorder_ns`

C. `version`

D. `log_stats`

E. `set`

9. You want to change the name of the trace file used by your Names server. Which of the following commands will enable you to do so?

A. `reorder_ns`

B. `reload`

C. `set`

D. `show`

E. `version`

F. `register`

10. You are designing your database administrative configuration for your Oracle network to simplify the management effort. Intelligent Agent would assist in which of the following ways? (Choose three)

A. Increasing system scalability

B. Identifying events occurring on the database

C. Allowing you to stop and restart your Oracle database remotely

D. Allowing you to take backups of your database remotely

E. Managing SNMP on your database host

11. You need to shut down Intelligent Agent. Which of the following utilities will assist you in doing so?

A. Oracle Enterprise Manager

B. NAMESCTL

C. LSNRCTL

D. Net8 Assistant

E. Instance Manager

F. Server Manager

12. Which of the following processes participate in the multithreaded-server architecture. (Choose three)

A. Listeners

B. Dedicated servers

C. Dispatchers

D. Database writers

E. Names servers

F. Shared servers

13. Your dispatcher is configured with the following information:

```
MTS_DISPATCHERS=(protocol=NMP)(dispatchers=4)
MTS_DISPATCHERS=(protocol=TCP)(dispatchers=2)
```

If `MTS_MAX_DISPATCHERS` is set to `8`, and you still need to configure the DECnet protocol, what is the maximum number of dispatchers you can set up for that protocol?

A. 1

B. 2

C. 3

D. 4

14. You are determining how many shared servers to configure for your multithreaded server architecture on your Oracle OLTP database application. You usually have about 500 concurrent users at any given time. How many shared servers should you use?

A. 8

B. 50

C. 200

D. 250

15. You are planning to use connection pooling on your Oracle database. Which of the following `init`*`sid`*`.ora` parameters would you use to configure this feature?

A. `MTS_MAX_SERVERS`

B. `MTS_SERVERS`

C. `MTS_LISTENERS`

D. `MTS_DISPATCHERS`

Answers to Chapter Questions

1. D. `MTS_SERVERS`

Explanation The number of shared servers running when a database is idle returns to the initial number of servers that are automatically started when the instance starts, and this number of servers is determined by the `MTS_SERVERS` parameter. Choice C would have been right an hour before, when the database was experiencing a heavy transaction load, because Oracle automatically starts more servers to handle the work in this situation. The `PROCESSES` and `OPEN_CURSORS` parameters have no bearing on this discussion.

2. B. The database on node DB01, because Oracle attempts local naming resolution first by default

Explanation Choices A and B both get the part about the database on node DB01 right, but only choice B correctly explains why. When the default name-resolution order is used, Net8 attempts local name resolution first, followed by Oracle Names, followed by host naming. Thus, Choice C should be eliminated along with choice A. There is no mention of external naming methods in the question, and external naming is only used if you configure it, never by default.

3. C. Best for Oracle networks consisting of workgroup configurations

Explanation Workgroup configurations are usually small networks in one local office, and these configurations rarely need more than one Names server. Local naming can even replace Oracle Names if the Names server goes down. All other features listed are ones that regional database repositories are useful for.

4. A. Net8 Assistant

Explanation The Net8 Assistant is used for defining the location of your Names server on the Oracle network. LSNRCTL is used for the network listener, as well as for Intelligent Agent, while Oracle Expert is used for tuning. Oracle Enterprise Manager is used as a console for database management activities.

5. D. `names.ora`

Explanation The `names.ora` file is where information about the Names server configuration is stored. The `listener.ora` file is used for configuration of the network listener. The `tnsnames.ora` file is used for local naming resolution on client machines. The `snmp.ora` file is used for configuring Intelligent Agent.

6. A. Run the `namesini.sql` script.

Explanation After creating the repository owner, you create the repository using the `namesini.sql` script. You may optionally want to create a special tablespace to hold this repository, but since this wasn't given as a choice, you should forego the option and choose A instead. Choices B and C both indicate Net8 Assistant tasks, but you do not use Net8 Assistant to configure the Names server to use the database repository until after you have created the repository in Oracle. Choice D is not something you would do, because you don't manually modify the `names.ora` file when you have a GUI that does it for you.

7. B *and* D. NAMESCTL *and* Net8 Assistant

Explanation To start Oracle Names, you can use the Names Control utility (NAMESCTL), or the Net8 Assistant. Oracle Enterprise Manager, Server Manager, and Instance Manager are used for startup and shutdown of the database, while LSNRCTL is used for starting and stopping the Net8 listener process.

8. A. `register`

Explanation The `register` command is used to manually register a service on the Oracle network with your Names server. The `reorder_ns` command is used for changing the order of preferred Names servers in Oracle. The `version` command is used to display the version of the Names server. The `log_stats` command is used for capturing log statistics, and the `set` command is used to define the NAMESCTL session-wide or Names server value for an option.

9. C. `set`

Explanation Changing the name of the trace file is done by using the `set trace_file_name` command, thus making set the right answer. The `reorder_ns` command is used for changing the order of preferred Names servers in Oracle. The `version` command is used to display the version of the Names server. The `show` command is used to display the value you set for various options configured with the `set` command, such as `trace_file_name`. The `register` command is used to manually register a service on the Oracle network with your Names server.

10. B, D, and E. Identifying events occurring on the database, allowing you to take backups of your database remotely, *and* managing SNMP on your database host.

Explanation Oracle Intelligent Agent is used to identify events occurring on your database from the OEM console and to manage SNMP on your database host. It does not increase system scalability. Connection pooling and connection concentration are used for that purpose. Intelligent Agent is also not used for stopping and restarting your Oracle database remotely. Server Manager and Instance Manager are used for that purpose. Finally, backups are managed with Backup Manager or Recovery Manager, which can be scheduled as a job using Oracle Enterprise Manager. Intelligent Agent can then give you event status for that job.

11. C. LSNRCTL

Explanation LSNRCTL is used to start and stop Intelligent Agent and the network listener. To start Oracle Names, you can use the Names Control utility (NAMESCTL), or the Net8 Assistant. Oracle Enterprise Manager, Server Manager, and Instance Manager are used for startup and shutdown of the database. Net8 Assistant is used to configure and manage network services other than Intelligent Agent.

12. A, C, *and* F. Listeners, dispatchers, *and* shared servers

Explanation Listeners, dispatchers, and shared servers are all part of the multithreaded-server architecture in Oracle. Dedicated servers, the DBW0 process, and Names servers are not part of the MTS architecture.

13. B. 2

Explanation Since `MTS_MAX_DISPATCHERS` is set to 8, and you already have 6 dispatchers configured, you can add 2 more for DECnet, and that's it. The number of dispatchers configured for each `protocol` is indicated by the protocol option for `MTS_DISPATCHERS`.

14. B. 50

Explanation In general, you should have one shared server for every 10–20 concurrent users on your database. In this case, 500 divided by 20 would be 25, and 500 divided by 10 is 50. So, since choice B is 50, that must be the right answer. Choices A, C, and D are all far outside the range. Choice A is far too small, while choices C and D are too large. If you are going to run hundreds of shared servers for hundreds of concurrent users, you might as well use dedicated servers.

15.s D. `MTS_DISPATCHERS`

Explanation Connection pooling is configured with the pool option on the `init`*`sid`*`.ora` parameter `MTS_DISPATCHERS`. `MTS_MAX_SERVERS` is used to define the maximum number of multithreaded servers that may be run on Oracle, while `MTS_SERVERS` determines how many shared servers will be started when the database is started. `MTS_LISTENER_ADDRESS` is used to configure listeners on your database.

CHAPTER 23

Connection Manager, Troubleshooting, and Security

n this chapter, you will learn about and demonstrate knowledge in the following areas:

- Using and configuring Connection Manager
- Troubleshooting network environments
- Security in network environments

This is the final chapter covering Net8 topics for OCP Exam 5 on network administration. This chapter covers several important areas, including how to use and configure the Connection Manager tool, which allows you to make your Oracle network available across multiple network protocols residing on your LAN or WAN. You will also cover several tips and techniques for troubleshooting network environments. The final area of this chapter covers an important topic—network security—you'll learn about the risks that are inherent in network environments, the Oracle tools designed to minimize those risks, and how to configure those tools. The content of this chapter comprises about 33 percent of OCP Exam 5 test content.

Using and Configuring Connection Manager

In this section, you will cover topics on using and configuring Connection Manager:

- Connection Manager capabilities
- Configuring connection concentration
- Configuring multiprotocol functionality
- Enabling network access control

This section introduces you to the Connection Manager tool in Net8. Connection Manager is a new tool that replaces some functionality offered through the multiprotocol interchange in SQL*Net version 2 while adding more new features. Connection Manager allows you to integrate two networks connected to the machine hosting Oracle into one larger Oracle network. When used in this way, Net8 can act as a firewall between the two networks in filtering connections to the Oracle database. In this section, you will learn more about Connection Manager's capabilities. You will also learn how to configure connection concentration and how to enable network-access control, two highly important aspects of Connection Manager usage. Finally, you will learn how to configure multiprotocol functionality.

Connection Manager Capabilities

As mentioned, Connection Manager gives Net8 the ability to allow multiple network protocols connected to the machine hosting Oracle to connect to the Oracle database. In a sense, Connection Manager and Net8 transform a collection of separate networks into one logical network for Oracle products. Oracle Connection Manager provides multiple protocol support so that, for example, a client on a Windows network could communicate with an Oracle database on IPX/SPX. This feature replaces the Oracle multiprotocol interchange in SQL*Net version 2. In this way, Connection Manager can merge as many networks as you can install, connect, and support, making the issue of supported networks a hardware issue, not a software issue.

Access between these two networks can be regulated and monitored by the Connection Manager as well. This feature is known as *network-access control.* Connection Manager supports control of client access to designated servers in a TCP/IP network environment by allowing you to define filters to restrict server access by clients according to client hostname/IP address, server hostname/IP address, or by the Oracle SID. In a sense, Connection Manager's network-access control feature can act as a firewall for your Oracle network.

Connection Manager also enhances scalability for your network environment. In Chapter 22, you learned how to configure connection pooling to maximize the number of physical connections that can be made to the Oracle database. Connection Manager takes an additional approach to scalability by providing you with the ability to concentrate many logical client sessions through a single transport connection to the Oracle multithreaded server. With multiple Connection Managers, you can connect thousands of clients to a server concurrently by minimizing the network bandwidth used by Oracle clients. Connection concentration reduces the need to maintain multiple connections between two processes. Since you maintain fewer connection end points for incoming requests, you increase the sessions a server can handle.

How Connection Manager Works

There are three components that work together to provide the functionality of the Connection Manager tool. They are *CMGW, CMADM,* and *CMCTL.* The following subtopics identify these components and discuss their use in Connection Manager; Figure 23-1 illustrates how these three components interact. The actual executables for these processes in Unix are called `cmgw`, `cmadm`, and `cmctl`, while in Windows they are called `cmgw80.exe`, `cmadm80.exe`, and `cmctl80.exe`. CMGW and CMADM are actual processes that run in the background, while CMCTL is the tool you use to control the other two background processes. These three components communicate among themselves using whatever interprocess communication (IPC) protocol is available on the particular platform.

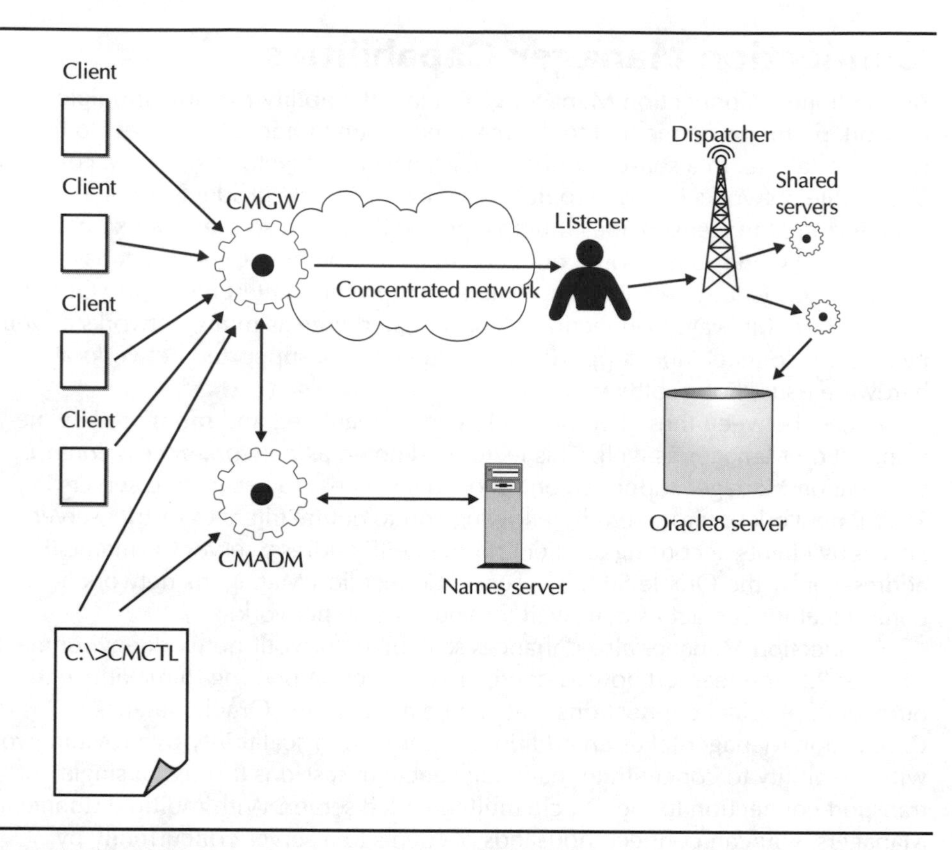

FIGURE 23-1. *Interaction between Connection Manager processes*

Using CMGW

This process is also known as Connection Manager Gateway. As you might have guessed from the name, CMGW is the gateway in Connection Manager through which clients must pass in order to access the Net8 listener. After registering with CMADM on startup, CMGW listens for incoming Oracle client connection requests on a specific port. When it hears a client request, CMGW will initiate a connection request to the Net8 listener for that client, and in general acts as a liaison between client and server. It also has some interaction with CMCTL that will be described shortly.

Using CMADM

This process is also known as Connection Manager Administrator. CMADM is the administrative process in Connection Manager that maintains address information in Oracle Names for clients, and it also processes CMGW address registration. It locates local Names servers and listeners and registers their address information. If an Oracle service is changed or added to the Oracle network, CMADM detects the change and updates the appropriate Names server. CMADM also answers requests initiated by CMCTL.

Using CMCTL

This tool is also known as Connection Manager Control utility. It provides administrative access to CMADM and CMGW. CMCTL is a tool similar to LSNRCTL or NAMESCTL in that you run it from the operating-system prompt to start and control Connection Manager. In Windows, you can run this tool in batch by entering `cmctl80` *`command option`* from the command prompt, where *`command`* is the operation you want CMCTL to perform and *`option`* is the Connection Manager component you want to perform it on. The following code block shows an example:

```
D:\orant\bin> cmctl80 status adm
CMCTL for 32-bit Windows: Version 8.0.5.0.0 -
Production on 12-MAY-99 11:11:05
(c) Copyright 1997 Oracle Corporation.  All rights reserved.
D:\orant\bin>
```

Or, you can run CMCTL interactively by entering `cmctl80` and pressing ENTER, and then entering *`command`* and *`option`* on the CMCTL prompt, as follows:

```
D:\orant\bin> cmctl80
CMCTL for 32-bit Windows: Version 8.0.5.0.0 -
Production on 12-MAY-99 11:11:05
(c) Copyright 1997 Oracle Corporation.  All rights reserved.
CMCTL> status adm
CMCTL>
```

There are a few commands available for the Connection Manager Control utility. Table 23-1 lists these commands, and describes their available options.

Command	**Description and Available Options**
`start` *`option`*	Starts Connection Manager. Replace *`option`* with `cman` to start both CMADM and CMGW, `cm` to start CMGW only, or `adm` to start CMADM only.
`status` *`option`*	Displays version, time started, and up-time for Connection Manager. Replace *`option`* with `cman` for status on both CMADM and CMGW, `cm` for status on CMGW only, or `adm` for status on CMADM only.

TABLE 23-1. *CMCTL Command Set*

Command	Description and Available Options
stats *option*	Display statistics for Connection Manager activity. Replace *option* with cman or cm to display statistics for CMGW.
stop *option*	Stop Connection Manager. Replace *option* with cman to stop both CMADM and CMGW, cm to stop CMGW only, or adm to stop CMADM only.
exit	End the CMCTL interactive session.

TABLE 23-1. *CMCTL Command Set* (continued)

Exercises

1. What is Connection Manager? Identify some of the features of this tool in Net8.
2. Describe the three process components of Connection Manager. Which process manages the other two?

Configuring Connection Concentration

Configuring connection concentration is basically a two-step process. First, you must set up concentration on the server side by telling your dispatchers on a particular network protocol that concentration is enabled for that protocol. The second part of the configuration is to set up your clients to route their connections through Connection Manager.

Configuring Servers for Concentration

You can configure connection concentration on the server side in the following way:

1. In your init*sid*.ora file, set the value for MTS_DISPATCHERS to include the multiplex option for whichever protocols you plan to use connection concentration with. Recall that there was an explanation of this option in Chapter 22, Table 22-3. The following code block illustrates an MTS_DISPATCHERS setting:

```
MTS_DISPATCHERS="(ADDRESS=(PARTIAL=TRUE)(MULTIPLEX=ON) \
(PROTOCOL=TCP)(HOST=workstation1)(PORT=5002))(DISPATCHERS=1)"
```

2. Restart your instance to enable your dispatchers to use connection concentration on the server side.

The following code block demonstrates several different examples of setting the `multiplex` option. Note that you can also specify the `multiplexing` option in the `init`*`sid`*`.ora` parameter `MTS_DISPATCHERS` for virtually the same result. You can also set `multiplex` equal to `1`, `yes`, `both`, or `true` for the same effect. The following code block lists all possible combinations:

```
(MULTIPLEX=1)
(MULTIPLEX=YES)
(MULTIPLEX=TRUE)
(MULTIPLEX=ON)
(MULTIPLEX=BOTH)
(MULTIPLEXING=1)
(MULTIPLEXING=YES)
(MULTIPLEXING=TRUE)
(MULTIPLEXING=ON)
(MULTIPLEXING=BOTH)
```

All the above examples effectively activate or enable connection concentration in both network directions, namely from client to server and server to client. Hence, the `both` option identified above literally means "concentrate connections in both directions." You can optionally enable connection concentration in one direction only. If you want to enable connection concentration from client to server, use the `in` option. If you want to enable connection concentration from server to client, use the `out` option. The following code block illustrates these options:

```
(MULTIPLEX=IN)
(MULTIPLEX=OUT)
```

Configuring Clients for Concentration

To set up your clients to route their connections through Connection Manager, your clients should either use local naming resolution, or preferably Oracle Names. Host naming will not support Connection Manager routing. To configure your clients to route their connections through Connection Manager, you must perform the following steps:

1. Start Net8 Assistant, if it is not running already, by selecting Start | Programs | Oracle for Windows | Oracle Net8 Assistant.
2. Drill down to the Network | Profile node to open that work area. Select the General option from the drop-down list box to view the General work area.

3. Click the Routing tab to view the Routing tab interface. Click the Use Source Route Addresses checkbox. Figure 23-2 shows how the Net8 Assistant should look with this information configured. The following code block shows a `tnsnames.ora` file with `SOURCE_ROUTE` and Connection Manager address configured.

```
Tcp-loopback.world =
  (DESCRIPTION =
    (ADDRESS_LIST =
        (ADDRESS =
          (COMMUNITY = tcp.world)
          (PROTOCOL = TCP)
          (Host = 127.0.0.1)
          (Port = 1521)
        )
    )
    (CONNECT_DATA = (SID = ORCL)
    (SOURCE_ROUTE = YES)
    )
  )
```

4. Save the configuration by selecting the File | Save Network Configuration menu option.

Exercises

1. Describe the process for configuring connection concentration on the server side. What `init`*`sid`*`.ora` parameter is involved?
2. Describe the process for configuring connection concentration on the client side. What role does Net8 Assistant play?

Configuring Multiprotocol Functionality

Multiprotocol functionality requires that you configure Connection Manager to listen on more than one address for connections from different network protocols. By default, Connection Manager uses TCP/IP, and listens on a specified port for incoming connections to concentrate on that protocol. You can extend Connection Manager's functionality into multiprotocol interchange to create a larger Oracle network by having Connection Manager listen on another network. To do so, you will need to manually change the Connection Manager configuration file,

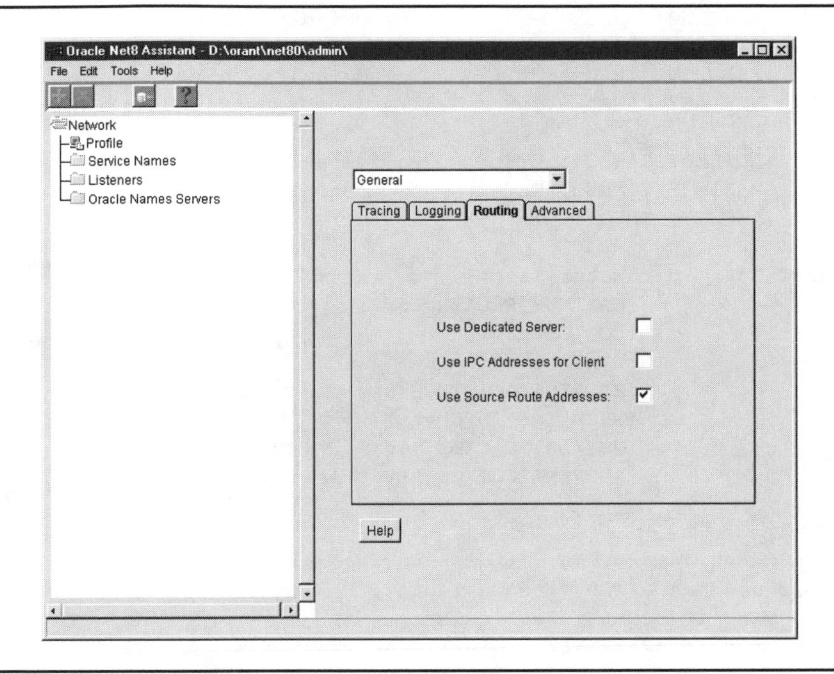

FIGURE 23-2. *Net8 Assistant with connection concentration configured*

cman.ora. This file can be found in the net80/admin directory under the Oracle software home directory. The following code block shows sample output for cman.ora:

```
#
# Connection Manager config file
# cman.ora
#
#
# cman's listening addresses
#
cman = (ADDRESS_LIST=
          (ADDRESS=(PROTOCOL=tcp)(HOST=workstation1)(PORT=1610))
          (ADDRESS=(PROTOCOL=tcp)(HOST=workstation1)(PORT=1620))
       )
#
# cman's configurable params
#
#         MAXIMUM_RELAYS                 defaults to 0
#         LOG_LEVEL                      defaults to 0
```

```
#         TRACING                            defaults to no
#         RELAY_STATISTICS                   defaults to no
#         SHOW_TNS_INFO                      defaults to no
#         USE_ASYNC_CALL (for nscall/nsanswer/nsaccept calls)
#                                            defaults to yes
#         AUTHENTICATION_LEVEL               defaults to 0
#         MAXIMUM_CONNECT_DATA               defaults to 1024
#         ANSWER_TIMEOUT                     defaults to 0
#
cman_profile = (parameter_list=
                    (MAXIMUM_RELAYS=1024)
                    (LOG_LEVEL=1)
                    (TRACING=no)
                    (RELAY_STATISTICS=yes)
                    (SHOW_TNS_INFO=yes)
                    (USE_ASYNC_CALL=yes)
                    (AUTHENTICATION_LEVEL=1)
               )
#
#====================================================
# cman is used as a TCP fire wall proxy
# IF AND ONLY IF "cman_rules" exists
#====================================================
#
#cman_rules = (rule_list=
#                  (rule=(src=spcstn)(dst=x)(srv=x)(act=accept))
#             )
```

Note that there are three basic parameters configured in `cman.ora`. The first is CMAN. As noted in the script above, CMAN is used to configure the address for Connection Manager. The second parameter is CMAN_PROFILE. This parameter is used for general configuration of Connection Manager. The third parameter is called CMAN_RULES, and it is used for configuring Net8 network-access control, covered in more depth in the next discussion.

Configuring Multiprotocol Interchange

In the prior code block, you can see that the CMAN parameter is set to have Connection Manager listening on the TCP/IP protocol only. You can modify the parameter to have Connection Manager listening on the Named Pipes protocol, as well. To do so, add another listener address to the address list, as follows:

```
cman = (ADDRESS_LIST=
          (ADDRESS=(PROTOCOL=tcp)(HOST=workstation1)(PORT=1610))
          (ADDRESS=(PROTOCOL=tcp)(HOST=workstation1)(PORT=1620))
          (ADDRESS=(PROTOCOL=NMP)(Server=workstation1)(Pipe=ORAPIPE))
       )
```

Exercises

1. Name the Connection Manager configuration file. Identify the three parameters that can be set in that file.
2. How do you configure multiprotocol interchange using parameters in the Connection Manager configuration file?

Enabling Network Access Control

The final Connection Manager topic is how to regulate access between two different networks using Net8 as a firewall. This functionality is provided by the network-access control feature in Connection Manager, and can be configured when you have Connection Manager listening on two different network protocols, as was configured in the previous discussion. You use the CMAN_RULES parameter to configure network-access control. Look at the contents of the cman.ora file, presented again in the following code block:

```
#
#==========================================================
# cman is used as a TCP fire wall
# proxy IF AND ONLY IF "cman_rules" exists
#==========================================================
#
#cman_rules = (rule_list=
#               (rule=(src=spcstn)(dst=x)(srv=x)(act=accept))
#          )
```

Configuring network-access control is a two-part process. The first part involves specifying some rules for Connection Manager to follow. The second part involves routing your clients to your Oracle database through Connection Manager.

Configuring Network Access Control: Part I

When configuring network-access control, you first need to specify some rules for Connection Manager to follow, in order to prevent certain clients from accessing certain servers. There are four configurable CMAN_RULES aspects or options to every rule, as highlighted in the preceding code block. You can also specify multiple rules in the rule list, each with its own aspects or options. Table 23-2 identifies each of the rules you can define.

TIP
Network-access control can only be applied on a TCP/IP network.

Rule	Description
src=*client*	Defines the machine hosting the client that the rule applies to. Replace *client* with the machine name or IP address this client resides on.
dst=*server*	Defines the machine hosting the Oracle database that the rule applies to. Replace *server* with the machine name or IP address this client resides on.
srv=*Oracle_SID*	Defines the Oracle server on the machine hosting Oracle that the rule applies to. Replace *Oracle_SID* with the SID for your Oracle server.
act=*action*	Defines the action Connection Manager should respond with if a connection is attempted between the client, server, and Oracle SID specified, where *action* can be set to accept or reject.

TABLE 23-2. *CMAN_RULES Rules Settings and Appropriate Values*

Now you learn how to configure the rules. Say you have user FLUFFY, whose client machine name is also FLUFFY. She is a cat, and you want to keep her out of the FOOD database. This database resides on the machine whose hostname is RFRGRTOR. To configure rules that enforce network-access control, you can define CMAN_RULES in the following way:

```
#
#==========================================
# cman is used as a TCP fire wall
# proxy IF AND ONLY IF "cman_rules" exists
#==========================================
#
cman_rules = (rule_list=
                 (rule=(SRC=FLUFFY)(DST=RFRGRTOR)
                 (SRV=FOOD)(ACT=REJECT))
             )
```

This configuration is fine if you want to restrict FLUFFY from getting to FOOD, but you may also wonder how this configuration affects other users in the Oracle network. If you don't define CMAN_RULES, connections between any client and any server are permitted. If you do define `CMAN_RULES`, you should be aware that Connection Manager will assume it should block any access attempts that are not expressly permitted by the datasets included in `RULE_LIST`.

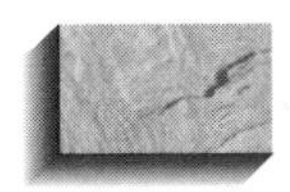

TIP
When `CMAN_RULES` is applied in the `cman.ora` file, you must define all connections you want to accept and reject. If a rule is not defined for a specific client/server combination, Connection Manager will automatically reject the connection. This is Connection Manager's principle of "that which is not expressly permitted is rejected."

Configuring Network Access Control: Part 2

The second part of configuring network access control involves routing your clients to your Oracle database through Connection Manager. To understand this process, refer to the explanation of routing clients to connect to Oracle through Connection Manager in the earlier discussion, "Configuring Connection Concentration."

Exercises

1. Describe the network-access control feature in Connection Manager. What parameter in the `cman.ora` file is used to configure it?
2. Describe the process for configuring network-access control.

Troubleshooting Network Environments

In this section, you will cover the following topics on troubleshooting network environments:

- Setting log and trace parameters
- Analyzing and troubleshooting network problems
- Formatting trace files using Trace Assistant

As a DBA, you face network challenges from performing basic configurations to resolving problems with malfunctioning hubs, or worse. This section will introduce some basic tasks for network troubleshooting. The first area you will cover is setting logging and trace parameters for various processes involved in network processing. By configuring your network processes to record their activities in trace and log files, you take the first step toward solving network problems by providing yourself with evidence to make a diagnosis. The next area you will cover is how to analyze and troubleshoot some common network problems you will face in real life and ones that will be tested for OCP Exam 5. Finally, you will learn how to use Trace Assistant to format trace files for easier reading.

Setting Log and Trace Parameters

The first thing you need to know in order to troubleshoot network problems is how to gather information to diagnose the problem. Information about network component operations is kept in a series of log files. The log file used for storing information for the Net8 components depends on which component you are talking about. Table 23-3 lists Net8 components, their associated log files, and the configuration file where the name and location of the log file can be changed. If you want to set a log filename or location to be different from the default, or define some other log setting, you would either change a log setting in the configuration file (from the settings named in Table 23-3) or use Net8 Assistant.

Changing Log Filenames and Locations in Configuration Files

In order to get the hang of managing your log data using configuration file settings, you should consider the following example involving the Net8 listener. To change

Net8 Component	Default Log Filename	Configuration File for Log Settings
Net8 listener	`listener.log`	`listener.ora`
Oracle Names	`names.log`	`names.ora`
CMGW	`cman.log`	`cman.ora`
CMADM	`cmadm.log`	`cman.ora`
Client/Server Profile	`sqlnet.log`	`sqlnet.ora`

TABLE 23-3. *Network Components and Their Associated Files*

the name of the log file and the location of that file for your network listener, you alter settings in your `listener.ora` file. The following code block shows you the contents of `listener.ora`:

```
USE_PLUG_AND_PLAY_LISTENER = ON
LISTENER =
  (ADDRESS_LIST =
    (ADDRESS = (PROTOCOL = IPC)(KEY = EXTPROC0))
    (ADDRESS = (PROTOCOL = NMP)(SERVER = WORKSTATION1)
               (PIPE = ORAPIPE))
    (ADDRESS = (PROTOCOL = TCP)(HOST = workstation1)(PORT = 1521))
    (ADDRESS = (PROTOCOL = TCP)(HOST = workstation1)(PORT = 1526))
  )
SID_LIST_LISTENER =
  (SID_LIST =
    (SID_DESC =
      (SID_NAME = extproc)
      (PROGRAM = extproc)
    )
    (SID_DESC =
      (SID_NAME = JSC)
    )
  )
```

To change your default log filename and directory, you must set values for the LOG_FILE_*listener* and LOG_DIRECTORY_*listener* parameters, where *listener* is replaced by the name of your listener (LISTENER by default). For log filename, you can omit the `.log extension,` as Oracle will automatically assume log files have a `.log` extension. For log directories, be sure that the value you set for the appropriate parameter conforms to the file system naming conventions in place on your operating system. The following code block shows the `listener.ora` file with your log filename and location modified:

```
LOG_FILE_LISTENER = jasonlsnr
LOG_DIRECTORY_LISTENER = d:\orant\log
USE_PLUG_AND_PLAY_LISTENER = ON
LISTENER =
  (ADDRESS_LIST =
    (ADDRESS = (PROTOCOL = IPC)(KEY = EXTPROC0))
    (ADDRESS = (PROTOCOL = NMP)(SERVER = WORKSTATION1)
               (PIPE = ORAPIPE))
    (ADDRESS = (PROTOCOL = TCP)(HOST = workstation1)(PORT = 1521))
    (ADDRESS = (PROTOCOL = TCP)(HOST = workstation1)(PORT = 1526))
  )
```

```
SID_LIST_LISTENER =
  (SID_LIST =
    (SID_DESC =
      (SID_NAME = extproc)
      (PROGRAM = extproc)
    )
    (SID_DESC =
      (SID_NAME = JSC)
    )
  )
```

Some configuration files use the same parameter naming convention as `listener.ora` does. For example, the `sqlnet.ora` file uses the `init`*`sid`*`.ora` parameters `LOG_DIRECTORY_CLIENT` and `LOG_DIRECTORY_SERVER` to identify the directory locations for each respective log file. The `LOG_FILE_CLIENT` and `LOG_FILE_SERVER` parameters are used to identify the names of those respective files, as well. However, other configuration files may use different configuration parameters. The `names.ora` file, for example, allows you to specify the log filename and directory using `NAMES.LOG_FILE` and `NAMES.LOG_DIRECTORY`, respectively. Finally, Connection Manager only allows you to change the logging level, not the log filename or directory location, in the `cman.ora` file, using the `CMAN_PROFILE` parameter, as follows:

```
#
# LOG_LEVEL valid values are between 1 and 4.
#
cman_profile = (parameter_list=
                    (MAXIMUM_RELAYS=1024)
                    (LOG_LEVEL=1)
                    (TRACING=no)
                    (RELAY_STATISTICS=yes)
                    (SHOW_TNS_INFO=yes)
                    (USE_ASYNC_CALL=yes)
                    (AUTHENTICATION_LEVEL=1)
                )
```

Changing Log Filenames and Locations in Net8 Assistant

If finding the appropriate configuration files and making changes in those files seems complex, you can simplify your efforts using Net8 Assistant. Start Net8 Assistant if it isn't running already. In Windows, you accomplish this by selecting Start | Program Files | Oracle for Windows | Net8 Assistant. You will need to drill down to the node associated with the network component whose log file and location you want to change. Note that by making the change in Net8 Assistant, your GUI interface makes the changes to configuration files for you. The following list gives the details for locating where to make your log file and directory changes in Net8 Assistant:

- **Client and server log file and directory changes** Drill into the Profile node, select the General work area from the drop-down list box, and click the Logging tab.
- **Names server log file and directory changes** Drill into the Oracle Names Servers | *your_Names_server* node. Then, select the Manage Server work area from the drop-down list box, and click the Logging tab.
- **Listener log file and directory changes** Drill into the Listeners | *your_Listener* node. Then, select the General Parameters work area from the drop-down list box, and click the Logging & Tracing tab.
- **`cman.ora` file** Because there are no parameters in this file for changing log location and filename, you cannot make this change using Net8 Assistant, either.

Configuring and Using Trace Features

For diagnosing problems in networking, you may also want to trace the series of actions produced by network listener components on the client and server. You can trace Oracle Connection Manager components, Oracle Names Server, NAMESCTL, and TNSPING utility operations as well. TNSPING is a utility that allows you to chart the amount of time it takes an Oracle service to respond to a request you make. You can also use TNSPING to test whether that service is running or not. Tracing generates a detailed set of instructions Oracle performs, which you can then analyze to uncover problems.

Like logging features, you set up tracing either in the configuration files for each of your Oracle resources listed in Table 23-3, or you can use Net8 Assistant. There are a few basic items to configure when working with tracing. Like the logging configuration, the first two are the trace filename and directory location. For listeners, the parameters you use are `TRACE_FILE_`*`listener`* and `TRACE_DIRECTORY_`*`listener`*, where *`listener`* is replaced with the name of your listener (LISTENER by default). The following code block shows a `listener.ora` file with appropriate values defined for the first two trace parameters:

```
TRACE_FILE_LISTENER = jasontrc
TRACE_DIRECTORY_LISTENER = d:\orant\trc
```

```
USE_PLUG_AND_PLAY_LISTENER = ON
LISTENER =
  (ADDRESS_LIST =
    (ADDRESS = (PROTOCOL = IPC)(KEY = EXTPROC0))
    (ADDRESS = (PROTOCOL = NMP)(SERVER = WORKSTATION1)
               (PIPE = ORAPIPE))
    (ADDRESS = (PROTOCOL = TCP)(HOST = workstation1)(PORT = 1521))
    (ADDRESS = (PROTOCOL = TCP)(HOST = workstation1)(PORT = 1526))
  )
SID_LIST_LISTENER =
  (SID_LIST =
    (SID_DESC =
      (SID_NAME = extproc)
      (PROGRAM = extproc)
    )
    (SID_DESC =
      (SID_NAME = JSC)
    )
  )
```

As with logging configuration, some of the configuration files use the same trace-parameter naming convention as `listener.ora` does. For example, `sqlnet.ora` uses `TRACE_DIRECTORY_CLIENT` and `TRACE_DIRECTORY_SERVER` to identify the directory locations for each respective trace file. The `TRACE_FILE_CLIENT` and `TRACE_FILE_SERVER` parameters are used to identify the names of those respective files, as well. However, other configuration files may use different configuration parameters. The `names.ora` file, for example, allows you to specify the trace filename and directory using `NAMES.TRACE_FILE` and `NAMES.TRACE_DIRECTORY`, respectively. Finally, Connection Manager does not allow you to change trace filename or directory in the `cman.ora` file.

Setting Trace Level for a Network Component

The last area to configure with regard to tracing is the trace level. Setting the trace level indicates how much trace information Oracle will collect in the trace file. There are four tracing levels available, and they are listed in Table 23-4. You set your tracing level using an appropriate trace-level parameter in the configuration file for the network resource. For example, to change the trace settings for your network listener, you will make changes to the `TRACE_LEVEL_`*`listener`* parameter, where *`listener`* is replaced by the name of your listener (LISTENER by

Trace level	Description
off	No trace information will be collected
user	Trace information of interest to users will be collected
admin	Trace information of interest to DBAs will be collected
support	Trace information of use for support calls to Oracle will be collected

TABLE 23-4. *Available Trace Levels and Their Descriptions*

default). The following code block shows your listener.ora file again, with the trace level defined:

```
TRACE_FILE_LISTENER = jasontrc
TRACE_DIRECTORY_LISTENER = d:\orant\trc
TRACE_LEVEL_LISTENER = ADMIN;
USE_PLUG_AND_PLAY_LISTENER = ON
LISTENER =
  (ADDRESS_LIST =
    (ADDRESS = (PROTOCOL = IPC)(KEY = EXTPROC0))
    (ADDRESS = (PROTOCOL = NMP)(SERVER = WORKSTATION1)
               (PIPE = ORAPIPE))
    (ADDRESS = (PROTOCOL = TCP)(HOST = workstation1)(PORT = 1521))
    (ADDRESS = (PROTOCOL = TCP)(HOST = workstation1)(PORT = 1526))
  )
SID_LIST_LISTENER =
  (SID_LIST =
    (SID_DESC =
      (SID_NAME = extproc)
      (PROGRAM = extproc)
    )
    (SID_DESC =
      (SID_NAME = JSC)
    )
  )
```

As with other aspects of trace configuration, some of the configuration files use the same parameter-naming convention as listener.ora does. For example, sqlnet.ora uses TRACE_LEVEL_CLIENT and TRACE_LEVEL_SERVER to identify the trace level for client and server. However, other configuration files may use different configuration parameters. The `names.ora` file, for example, allows you to specify trace level using `NAMES.TRACE_LEVEL`. Finally, Connection Manager allows you to change trace level in the `cman.ora` file with the `CMAN_PROFILE` parameter, as follows:

```
#
# TRACE_LEVEL valid values are between 1 and 4.
#
cman_profile = (parameter_list=
                   (MAXIMUM_RELAYS=1024)
                   (LOG_LEVEL=1)
                   (TRACING=yes)
                   (RELAY_STATISTICS=yes)
                   (SHOW_TNS_INFO=yes)
                   (USE_ASYNC_CALL=yes)
                   (AUTHENTICATION_LEVEL=1)
               )
```

Changing Trace Settings in Net8 Assistant

If finding the appropriate configuration files and making changes in those files seems complex, you can simplify your efforts using Net8 Assistant. Start Net8 Assistant if it isn't running already. In Windows, you can do this by selecting Start | Program Files | Oracle for Windows | Net8 Assistant. You will need to drill down to the node associated with the network component whose trace file, level, and location you want to change. Note that by making the change in Net8 Assistant, your GUI interface makes the changes to configuration files for you. The following bullets give the details for locating where to make your trace file, level, and directory changes in Net8 Assistant:

- **Client and server trace file, level, and directory changes** Drill down to the Profile node, select the General work area from the drop-down list box, and click the Tracing tab.
- **Names server trace file, level, and directory changes** Drill down to the Oracle Names Servers | *your_Names_server* node. Then, select the Manage Server work area from the drop-down list box, and click the Logging tab.
- **Listener trace file, level, and directory changes** Drill into the Listeners | *your_Listener* node. Then, select the General Parameters work area from the drop-down list box, and click the Logging & Tracing tab.
- **Trace file, level, or location information** You cannot change these settings using Net8 Assistant.

A Note About When Changes to Configuration Files Take Hold

Making changes to log filename and directory information in your configuration files (directly or via Net8 Assistant) does not necessarily affect where the network component currently writes log information. The network component only reads the configuration file at startup. If you want to change where the component is actually writing log information, you need to do one of two things. You can restart the network component after changing the configuration file, or you need to make the change dynamically using whatever online control utility is available for that network component. Examples of control utilities include LSNRCTL for the listener, NAMESCTL for Oracle Names, or CMCTL for Connection Manager.

Exercises

1. Describe the process for changing log file and location settings. What are the two ways for reconfiguring this information? Describe the differences between parameters set for this purpose in `listener.ora`, `names.ora`, and `sqlnet.ora`.
2. Describe the process for changing trace file, level, and location settings. What are the two ways for reconfiguring this information? Describe the differences between parameters set for this purpose in `listener.ora`, `names.ora`, and `sqlnet.ora`.
3. When will the actual running network component be reconfigured with the new log or trace information you set up in the configuration file? Is the change immediate? Explain.

Analyzing and Troubleshooting Network Problems

Once your configuration of log and trace levels is complete, and you have gathered information, you must analyze the content of the logging and tracing files to get to the bottom of the network problem. The process for diagnosing problems using log and trace files is outlined in the following basic steps:

1. Review your log file first. It contains a series of error stacks produced whenever the network component receives an error.
2. Look at the error stack at the end of the log file. Usually, the error stack corresponding to the most recent network error is at the end of the log file, with the next most recent network error above it.

3. Diagnose and resolve the problem by reviewing the most recent error stacks in your log file, and looking up the errors in the discussion titled "Identifying and Solving Common Network Problems" that appears later in this section.

4. If you attempt steps 1–3, and still cannot resolve the problem, you should turn tracing on and re-execute the problematic operation. Tracing can consume a lot of machine and network overhead to produce enormous trace files loaded with operational data, so you should only enable tracing when you really need to.

Looking at a Log File Error Stack

A great number of things go on behind the scenes when you log in to your Oracle database. For example, you may receive an error when logging in to Oracle telling you that the Net8 listener couldn't resolve the SID given in the connect descriptor. The following code block illustrates this issue:

```
SQL> connect jason/jason@dbhost
ERROR:
ORA-12505: TNS: listener could not resolve SID given
 in connect descriptor
WARNING: You are no longer connected to Oracle
```

Meanwhile, Net8 will be tracking more information about the error, such as when it occurred and the details of the situation, all behind the scenes in your log file. The following code block contains a log file error stack from the `sqlnet.log` file, slightly modified for readability:

```
***********************************************************************
Fatal NI connect error 12505, connecting to:
(DESCRIPTION_LIST=
  (DESCRIPTION=
    (ADDRESS=
       (PROTOCOL=TCP)
       (HOST=workstation1)
       (PORT=1521)
    )
    (CONNECT_DATA=
       (SID=oracle)
       (Server=Dedicated)
       (CID=
          (PROGRAM=D:\orant\BIN\PLUS80W.EXE)
          (HOST=WORKSTATION1)
          (USER=Administrator)
       )
```

```
      )
    )
    (DESCRIPTION=
      (ADDRESS=
         (PROTOCOL=TCP)
         (HOST=workstation1)
         (PORT=1521)
      )
      (CONNECT_DATA=
         (SID=oracle)
         (Server=Dispatched)
         (CID=
            (PROGRAM=D:\orant\BIN\PLUS80W.EXE)
            (HOST=WORKSTATION1)
            (USER=Administrator)
         )
      )
    )
)
  VERSION INFORMATION:
       TNS for 32-bit Windows: Version 8.0.5.0.0 - Production
       Windows NT TCP/IP NT Protocol Adapter
      for 32-bit Windows: Version 8.0.5.0.0 - Production
  Time: 12-MAY-99 18:20:29
  Tracing not turned on.
  Tns error struct:
    nr err code: 12204
    TNS-12204: TNS:received data refused from an application
    ns main err code: 12564
    TNS-12564: TNS:connection refused
    ns secondary err code: 0
    nt main err code: 0
    nt secondary err code: 0
    nt OS err code: 0
```

You can use this information to assist in your resolution of the issue. Although the issue in this example is relatively straightforward—the Oracle SID in the connect descriptor needs to be changed—you can use this methodology in more complicated situations to record details that might assist in an effective resolution to your problem.

Using TNSPING

In some cases, your troubleshooting efforts will benefit from the use of the TNSPING utility. This tool is similar to the `ping` command in TCP/IP, which allows you to determine whether you can see a machine on the network. TNSPING operates the same way by accepting a connect string as the argument, and seeing if it can resolve the connect descriptor and find the specified machine on the network.

Enabling Tracing

In some situations, you may need to go one step further to find out what the problem is. By enabling network tracing on your network component, you can gather large amounts of information very quickly. Note that in order to enable tracing, you must set the trace level to something besides `off`. For example, if you wanted to enable client-side network tracing, you would configure your `sqlnet.ora` file by adding a reference to the appropriate parameters, as follows:

```
# D:\ORANT\NET80\ADMIN\SQLNET.ORA Configuration
File:D:\orant\net80\admin\sqlnet.ora
# Generated by Oracle Net8 Assistant
TRACE_DIRECTORY_CLIENT = d:\orant\database
NAME.DEFAULT_ZONE = world
NAMES.PREFERRED_SERVERS =
  (ADDRESS_LIST =
    (ADDRESS = (PROTOCOL = TCP)(HOST = workstation1)(PORT = 1575))
  )
NAMES.DEFAULT_DOMAIN = world
TRACE_FILE_CLIENT = sqlnet
TRACE_LEVEL_CLIENT = USER
#sqlnet.authentication_services = (NONE)
USE_CMAN = true
SQLNET.EXPIRE_TIME = 0
SQLNET.ENCRYPTION_SERVER = requested
SQLNET.ENCRYPTION_CLIENT = requested
NAMES.DIRECTORY_PATH= (ONAMES)
```

You may have noticed in the comment header at the top of the code block that the `sqlnet.ora` file was generated by Net8 Assistant—you can configure tracing using that tool. Drill down to the Profile node, and open the General work area using the drop-down list box. Then, click the Tracing tab. Figure 23-3 shows you how the interface should look if you want to set up user-level tracing. Beware, however, because tracing will produce an enormous amount of output, even for user-level tracing, which is the lowest level of network tracing available. You should only use tracing to help you diagnose your network problems when you have a good idea about what you are looking for.

Identifying and Solving Common Network Problems

There are many common network problems that can arise with your use of Oracle. This discussion will cover some of the main errors you will likely see, and explain what the problem is. Further, you will learn some basic methods for resolving the problems, and where to go for help. Some of the following explanations should already look familiar, as they were mentioned in Chapter 21.

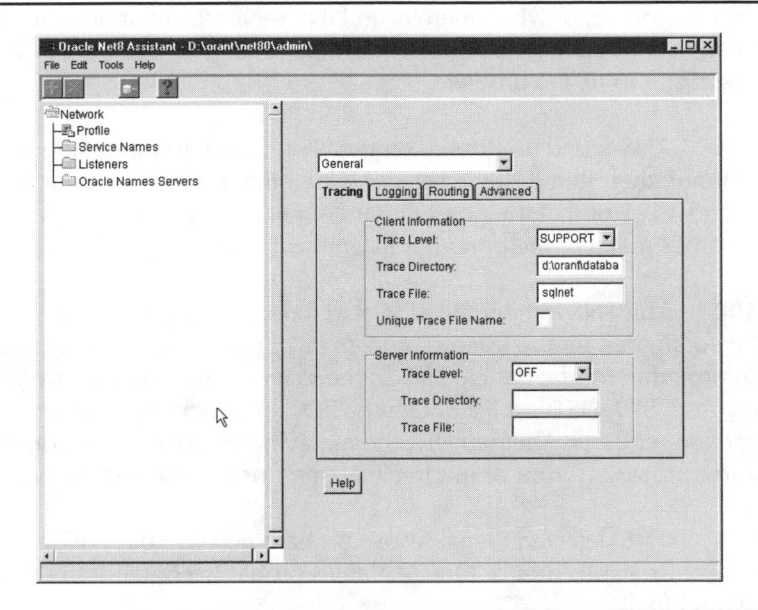

FIGURE 23-3. *Net8 Assistant with trace configuration settings shown*

ORA-3113 End of file on communications channel. This means that you have been disconnected from Oracle unexpectedly. There could be many causes for this error. A network process may have failed, or the Oracle server itself may have failed. To resolve the issue, you must try to reconnect to the database. Your attempt to do so may result in another failure, which will most likely tell you more about the root cause of the problem.

ORA-12154 TNS could not resolve service name. This means that Net8 couldn't resolve your connect string supplied for login. The connect string may have been mistyped, or it may not exist in your local copy of `tnsnames.ora`. If you are using Oracle Names, the connect string may not have a corresponding connect descriptor in the Names server.

ORA-12203 TNS was unable to connect to destination. The name of the machine hosting Oracle configured for the connect descriptor is most likely incorrect. Check it out in your `tnsnames.ora` file or in the Oracle Names server, and correct the hostname. Sometimes, you get this problem in TCP/IP when the domain-names service used to translate hostnames to IP addresses doesn't contain the specified hostname, or when there is no DNS server for your network. In this case, you can usually specify the IP address rather than the hostname in your connect descriptor to fix the problem.

ORA-12224 TNS found no listener on the host. Check to make sure the listener is running. If not, then start it. If the listener is running, ensure that your listener is tuned into port 1521 or that the port in your connect descriptor in `tnsnames.ora` or Oracle Names matches the port your listener is tuned to.

ORA-12500 The TNS listener failed to start a dedicated server process. The `SID_LIST` configured for the listener process in `listener.ora` may not contain the right information for the Oracle SID on the machine hosting the listener and the Oracle database. SID_LIST is a list of Oracle SIDs for which the listener monitors user connection requests. Alternatively, there may be an error in the connect descriptor in `tnsnames.ora` or in Oracle Names for this connect string.

ORA-12533 TNS detected illegal `ADDRESS` parameters. Your connect descriptor in `tnsnames.ora` or Oracle Names probably contains an error. Investigate, and fix it.

ORA-12545 TNS experienced a general lookup failure. The listener may not be running, or else the network may not be available. Make sure the connect descriptor in `tnsnames.ora` or in Oracle Names is valid. Sometimes, you get this problem in TCP/IP when the domain-names service used to translate hostnames to IP addresses doesn't contain the hostname specified, or when there is no DNS server for your network. In this case, you can usually specify the IP address rather than the hostname in your connect descriptor to fix the problem.

ORA-12560 TNS experienced a protocol-adapter error. There could be some problem with the installation of your Oracle Protocol Adapter. To resolve this problem, turn on tracing and review the output to identify the severity of the problem.

Exercises

1. Describe the basic process for diagnosing a network problem. What kind of information does a network-component log file provide in this situation? Describe the contents of a log file error stack.
2. How is tracing enabled? What kind of information does it provide?
3. Describe some common Oracle errors that are network-related, and list some basic steps for correcting each of them.

Formatting Trace Files Using Trace Assistant

As mentioned, a lot of information gets produced by Net8 when you enable tracing for your network component. For example, a single attempt to connect to the Oracle database with admin-level tracing enabled will produce a trace file with over 70K of information! To understand the contents of your trace files without getting saturated with details, you must first understand the information that gets transmitted between clients and servers on the Oracle network.

In general, information is shipped across the network in small increments or chunks called *packets*. Net8 has several different types of packets it transmits, and each packet type has a name. Those names all begin with "NSP." The packet names are: NSPTCN for connect, NSPTAC for accept, NSPTRF for refuse, NSPTRS for resend, NSPTMK for marker, NSPTDA for data, and NSPCNL for control. Notice that the last few characters for all packet types relate to the purpose of that packet type.

Information in the trace files produced by network components is formatted in the following way. Each line starts with the name of a procedure or function currently performing an action, followed by a colon, followed by a description of the action. Sometimes, these code blocks may manipulate a certain type of packet. Note that the first two letters in the names of the procedure calls correspond directly to the Net8 component the procedure belongs to from the OSI network model presented in Chapter 21. For review, the components were NN for network names, NI for network interface, NR for network routing, NS for network session, NT for network transport, and NA for network authentication. The abbreviations identified here are important to know insofar as the procedure calls in trace files will be prefixed with these abbreviations to indicate the network component the procedure belongs to.

The following code block shows some output from the trace file produced by Net8 on the client side with support-level tracing enabled, where you can see some packets being sent and received by a procedure that is part of the network session (NS) component of Net8:

```
nscon: sending NSPTCN packet
nscon: got NSPTAC packet
nsrdr: got NSPTDA packet
nsrdr: NSPTDA flags: 0x0
```

The packet itself will also be displayed when only support-level tracing is enabled, in both hexadecimal and character form. Note in the following code block that the NSPTCN packet sent contains your connect descriptor, because NSPTCN is the connect packet:

```
nspsend: packet dump
nspsend: 00 7E 00 00 01 00 00 00  |.~......|
nspsend: 01 36 01 2C 00 00 08 00  |.6.,....|
```

```
nspsend: 7F FF A3 0A 00 00 01 00  |........|
nspsend: 00 44 00 3A 00 00 08 00  |.D.:....|
nspsend: 00 00 00 00 00 00 00 00  |........|
nspsend: 00 00 00 00 00 F7 00 0A  |........|
nspsend: 4A A8 00 00 00 00 00 00  |J.......|
nspsend: 00 00 28 44 45 53 43 52  |..(DESCR|
nspsend: 49 50 54 49 4F 4E 3D 28  |IPTION=(|
nspsend: 41 44 44 52 45 53 53 3D  |ADDRESS=|
nspsend: 28 50 52 4F 54 4F 43 4F  |(PROTOCO|
nspsend: 4C 3D 54 43 50 29 28 48  |L=TCP)(H|
nspsend: 4F 53 54 3D 77 6F 72 6B  |OST=work|
nspsend: 73 74 61 74 69 6F 6E 31  |station1|
nspsend: 29 28 50 4F 52 54 3D 31  |)(PORT=1|
nspsend: 35 37 35 29 29 29 00 00  |575)))..|
nspsend: normal exit
```

Finding Errors in Your Trace File

If you are looking in your trace file to find information about errors that occurred in processing, you will find the information you need at the end of the file. The most recent activities are appended to the end of the trace file. On some platforms, such as Unix, the output in your trace file will be prefixed with ERROR or FATAL when a network task fails to execute properly. You should also find the error that appeared in your session toward the end of the trace file.

Assume your connection to Oracle in SQL*Plus looked like this:

```
SQL> connect jason/jason@jason
ERROR:
ORA-12224: TNS:no listener
```

The last part of your trace file might look like this:

```
(67e7) nsopen: error exit
(67e7) nscall: error exit
(67e7) nricdt: Call failed.
(67e7) nricfg: entry
(67e7) nricfg: exit
(67e7) nricdt: Call made to destination.
(67e7) nricdt: exit
(67e7) nricall: Failed to copy orig comm name value binding.
(67e7) nricall: Exiting NRICALL with following termination result: -1.
(67e7) nricall: exit
(67e7) nioqper:  error from nricall
(67e7) nioqper:    nr err code: 12224
(67e7) nioqper:    ns main err code: 12541
(67e7) nioqper:    ns (2)  err code: 12560
(67e7) nioqper:    nt main err code: 511
```

```
(67e7) nioqper:    nt (2)   err code: 61
(67e7) nioqper:    nt OS    err code: 0
(67e7) niqme: entry
(67e7) niqme:  reporting nr (1) error: (12224) as rdbms err (12224)
(67e7) niqme: exit
(67e7) niotns: All descriptions exhausted
(67e7) niotns: Couldn't connect, returning 12224
(67e7) nsbfrfl: entry
(67e7) nsbfrfl: normal exit
nigtrm: Count in the NI global area is now 0
nrigbd: entry
nrigbd: exit
nigtrm: Count in the NL global area is now 0
```

You can get information about some of the other error codes produced in the trace file using the OERR utility if your Oracle database runs on the Unix platform. You can call this utility from the command line, using the syntax `oerr` *`chr error`*, replacing *chr* with the three-letter prefix appearing before the error number (such as tns), and replacing *error* with the error number (such as 12224), to obtain a description of the error and how to resolve it. Unfortunately, there is no equivalent utility on Oracle for Windows.

Better Output Using Trace Assistant

You may imagine that it is a pain to slog through hundreds of lines of output to find any meaningful information in your trace files. That's why Oracle provides Trace Assistant. This utility is designed to offer the same type of functionality for reformatting trace file output into something meaningful as does the TKPROF utility described in Chapter 17. Like TKPROF, Trace Assistant operates from the command line, accepting the name of the trace file and several options to determine how you want the output formatted. The command line syntax for Trace Assistant is `trcasst` *`options tracefile`*. You can replace *`options`* on the command line with the options listed in Table 23-5. The *`tracefile`* you specify is the output file produced by enabling tracing for the network component in question. The following code block shows a simple example of Trace Assistant output in Unix environments:

```
/home/oracle/app/oracle/8.0.5/> trcasst -s sample.trc
Trace File Statistics:
----------------------------
SQL*Net:
Total Calls:     73 sent, 109 received, 53 upi
Total Bytes:  8082 sent, 88471 received,
Average Bytes: 110 sent, 811 received,
Maximum Bytes: 504 sent, 2048 received,
GRAND TOTAL PACKETS sent:73 received: 109
```

Command-Line Option	Description
`-o[x]`	Show all connectivity and Two-Task Common information gathered by the trace. You can optionally replace *x* with one or more of the following: `c` for summary connectivity data, `u` for summary Two-Task data, `d` for detailed connectivity data, `t` for detailed Two-Task data, or `q` for SQL commands to put summary Two-Task data into context.
`-e[x]`	Show error information gathered by the trace. You can optionally replace *x* with one of the following: 0 to translate the network-session operation error numbers dumped by function `nserror( )` and all other errors, 1 to translate the network-session operation error numbers dumped by function `nserror( )` only, or 2 to display error numbers with no translation information. If you specify nothing for *x*, `0` is assumed.
`-s`	Display statistics for operations gathered by the trace. Statistics displayed include the number of Two-Task calls and how many packets/bytes were sent and received between network components.

TABLE 23-5. *Trace Assistant Command-Line Options and Their Meanings*

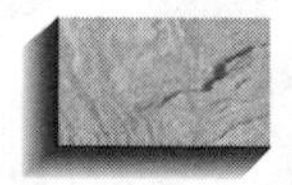

TIP
Specifying command-line options for Trace Assistant is completely optional. If you specify no options for Trace Assistant, then the default options will be used. The default options are `-odt -e -s`. Also, Trace Assistant may not work properly for all operating systems.

Exercises

1. Describe the process by which data travels across the Oracle network. What are the different types of packets you might find information about in your trace file?
2. Describe the contents of a trace file. What are the different components of Net8 with respect to the OSI network model. How are those layers displayed in a trace file?
3. Assume you run Trace Assistant and do not specify any command-line options. What information will be displayed?

Security in Network Environments

In this section, you will cover the following topics on security in network environments:

- Network security risks during data transmission
- Security features in Oracle networking products
- Features of Advanced Networking Option
- Configuring components of Advanced Networking Option

In this last section of the chapter, you'll cover the final area of network administration tested for OCP Exam 5, security in network environments. This section will start you off with a discussion of network security risks inherent during data transmission. Then, you will learn about some of the security features in Oracle networking products. The section will also offer a discussion of the features of the Advanced Networking Option, and conclude with a discussion of how to configure the components of the Advanced Networking Option.

Network Security Risks During Data Transmission

It is often said that the only secure database is one with no users. However, a database with no users defeats the purpose of having a database in the first place. As soon as access is given to users, however, you begin to assume security risks. Some of these risks relate to password authentication, and you already learned how to use Oracle8 password administration features to minimize these risks in Chapter 10. Another area where you assume risks with respect to database access is in your network.

Network security risks come in a few main forms. The first has to do with the authentication of servers on a network. In an open network, such as the Internet, nodes on the network are uniquely identified by means of an IP address, which is four sets of numbers between 0 and 255 taking the form 0.0.0.0. No two machines can have the same IP address, but nothing prevents you from disconnecting one machine and connecting another with the old machine's IP address. Thus, it is possible for someone to disconnect one server and set up a "rogue server" in its place, rerouting traffic to that rogue server.

A situation related to the one just described involves domain names. If you have used the Internet, you know that you don't usually type in an IP address to access a server. Instead, you type in a hostname, such as `www.exampilot.com`, which is then translated into an IP address by the domain-name service (DNS). It might be possible for someone to change the IP address for a hostname, thus causing you to connect to a different server than the one you intended to contact, which again opens the potential for rogue servers.

Another form of network security concern comes from the way the data itself is transported across the network. Some network protocols, such as TCP/IP, transfer information between client and server in plain-text format. While en route, this data is easily read by unauthorized people. Sensitive data, such as trade secrets, e-mail correspondence between executives, and credit-card information could be compromised by this default method of data transport across a network.

A final form of network security concern is also related to the transport of data across a network. Again, some network protocols, such as TCP/IP, use a method of data transport called packet switching. TCP/IP was originally developed with the idea that data should be able to traverse the network even when large portions of that network were damaged and unusable. One feature of packet switching is that one network node will retransmit a packet of data to another network node if the other network node reports that it did not receive the packet in question. This functionality creates the possibility for unauthorized users to intercept packets of data traveling across the network without disrupting service between two network nodes.

In the world of electronic commerce, the effects of network-security lapses are manifold. Intercepted credit information could result in fraudulent card transactions. Intercepted trade secrets or patent information could also result in loss of competitive advantage for a company. And, if a popular Web site disappears overnight because network traffic gets diverted to an illegitimate server, the result could be a ruined reputation for an online content provider.

Exercises

1. Identify the security risks posed by network node identification methods employed in TCP/IP.
2. Describe the format of data transported across a TCP/IP network. What security risks arise from this format?
3. Describe the method used to transport data across a TCP/IP network. What security risks arise from this method?

Security Features in Oracle Networking Products

Oracle networking products are designed to minimize network security risks inherent in the underlying protocols supporting Oracle networks. Although basic Net8 functionality is prone to the same risks inherent in TCP/IP networks, you can add a few important services to your Oracle network that enhance security tremendously. Those services include the Oracle Security Server, the Oracle

Cryptographic Toolkit, and the Advanced Networking Option. The network security tool you choose to add to your Oracle network depends on how secure you want that network to be.

Oracle Security Server Explained

One networking option you may choose to use is the Oracle Security Server. This service provides centralized global user authentication and authorization to control access to data. Oracle Security Server uses X.509 v1 certificates as its authentication mechanism. The X.509 v1 certificate is a standard format for digitally signed certificates that contain information such as user identity, authorizations, and public-key information. Data traveling across the network is also protected by Oracle Security Server through its use of public-key cryptography to encrypt sensitive data. This combination of strong authentication methods and secure data transfer makes Oracle Security Server a great security choice for common business-network needs.

Oracle Cryptographic Toolkit Explained

The Oracle Cryptographic Toolkit is an interface to the cryptographic services provided by Security Server. It unites all cryptographic services, including the use, storage, retrieval, import, and export of credentials into an OCI that can be used to add security enhancements to your application. External customers can use either OCI or PL/SQL to access the Oracle Cryptographic Toolkit.

Oracle Advanced Networking Option Explained

The Oracle Advanced Networking Option (ANO) is another offering that provides enhanced security and authentication functionality to Net8. ANO ensures data integrity by using the MD5 algorithm to calculate cryptographic checksums. Encryption is also used to provide data privacy. ANO supports 40-bit, 56-bit, and 128-bit RSA data encryption, as well as 40-bit and 56-bit encryption using DES algorithms. With ANO, you can configure your Oracle network to permit user access to many different resources at many different levels with a single point of sign-on and authentication, thereby reducing the risk and inconvenience associated with multiple password logon. You will learn more about ANO and how it can be used in conjunction with third-party vendor security products to ensure the highest level of security is used on your Oracle network.

Exercises

1. Identify the security features offered as part of the Oracle Security Server. What technology does Oracle Security Server use to authenticate users?
2. Identify the security features provided by the Oracle Cryptographic Toolkit.
3. Describe the capabilities supported by the Advanced Networking Option.

Features of Advanced Networking Option

A few of the basic features of ANO have already been identified. They are data integrity using MD5 and encryption using RSA or DES technology, and those features ensure that your sensitive data gets from point A to point B without anyone being able to see it or tamper with it without your knowledge. Unlike Oracle Security Server, ANO does not handle authentication by itself. Instead, it offers support for third-party authentication products via adapters. This functionality permits you to use some of the most advanced authentication technologies available for computer networks.

Features for Data Transfer

The data-transfer features in ANO have already been described in a bit of detail. You already know that ANO handles strong data integrity through the use of MD5 checksum algorithms. This feature provides the benefit of knowing that your data cannot be tampered with while en route between network nodes. Without strong data integrity, it is possible for an agent on the network to modify information traveling between clients and servers to produce undesired results. With the use of data-integrity features, your network data transfer can proceed without you worrying about data interception and tampering.

Encryption also solves the problem of data transport across the network in plain-text format. RSA and DES 40-bit encryption is fairly difficult to crack, and only 40-bit encryption is permitted for export outside the United States. Thus, if your organization spans the globe, you can use either of these methods to prevent unauthorized users from seeing trade secrets sent between networks in France and America. If you want a higher level of encryption, you can also use RSA or DES 56-bit or RSA 128-bit encryption with ANO. RSA 128-bit encryption represents the highest level of authentication security available commercially.

Features for Authentication

Oracle Security Server authenticates users via X.509 certificates, which allows strong authentication on your Oracle network environment suitable for most businesses. However, there are some businesses that need powerful, flexible, and open authentication strategies. For example, access to highly sensitive information, such as patents, missile launch codes, or surveillance data, might need to be restricted to only a few users in the entire world, or even only one user. In this case, Oracle can be used in conjunction with highly secure authentication technologies available from other vendors. These technologies include Kerberos and CyberSAFE, and ACE/Server for strong, centralized authentication, SecurID for token cards and one-time use passwords, and Identix biometric authentication adapters for the strongest level of unique authentication using biological evidence, such as fingerprints. If your organization is already using these technologies, it makes sense for you to adopt ANO because of its flexibility for incorporating your existing security solutions into the Oracle network.

Exercises

1. Describe features on ANO that work in the area of data transport. Describe features on ANO that work in the area of authentication.
2. Identify some technologies ANO can integrate in the area of centralized authentication, token cards, and biometric authentication.

Configuring Components of Advanced Networking Option

Configuring authentication and checksum usage requires effort on both the client and server sides. The following discussions explain how to configure components of ANO using both the configuration files and the Net8 Assistant, which simply modifies the configuration files for you.

Configuring Encryption and Checksums: Operational Parameters

To configure encryption and checksums, you will work with the `sqlnet.ora` file for both the server and client by modifying or adding parameters that support those two features. Some of these parameters determine whether encryption or checksums will be used or not. These parameters include:

- **ENCRYPTION_CLIENT** Defines how encryption will be used by the client
- **CRYPTO_CHECKSUM_CLIENT** Defines how checksums will be used by the client
- **ENCRYPTION_SERVER** Defines how encryption will be used by the server
- **CRYPTO_CHECKSUM_SERVER** Defines how checksums will be used by the server

Whether the connection will actually use encryption depends on two components. The first component is the value set for the preceding parameters. Each of these parameters can be set to one of four possible values. The setting determines how encryption or checksums will be employed in connections between the client and the server. The four values and their descriptions are as follows:

- **accepted** This node will use encryption or checksums if the other node wants to use it.
- **rejected** This node will not use encryption or checksums even if the other node wants to use it.
- **requested** This node will use encryption or checksums if the other node permits it.
- **required** This node will use encryption or checksums even if the other node does not want to use it.

The following code block shows some examples of these parameters in `sqlnet.ora` with values set:

```
ENCRYPTION_CLIENT = accepted
CRYPTO_CHECKSUM_CLIENT = rejected
ENCRYPTION_SERVER = requested
CRYPTO_CHECKSUM_SERVER = required
```

Configuring Encryption and Checksums: Technology Parameters

The second component required in determining whether the connection will use encryption and checksums is an examination of the available checksum or encryption methods available in both the nodes. Encryption methods are defined using parameters in the `sqlnet.ora` file, as well. Those parameters are:

- **ENCRYPTION_TYPES_CLIENT** Defines encryption technologies available on the client
- **ENCRYPTION_TYPES_SERVER** Defines encryption technologies available on the server
- **CRYPTO_CHECKSUM_TYPES_CLIENT** Defines checksum technologies available on the client
- **CRYPTO_CHECKSUM_TYPES_SERVER** Defines checksum technologies available on the server

Each of the preceding parameters can have one or more values defined for it. The available values for encryption and checksum technologies on both the client and the server, along with a description of the technology, are as follows:

- **RC4_40** The RSA 40-bit encryption technology
- **DES40** The DES 40-bit encryption technology
- **RC4_56** The RSA 56-bit encryption technology (not available outside the US)
- **DES** The DES 56-bit encryption technology (not available outside the US)
- **RC4_128** The s RSA 128-bit encryption technology (not available outside the US)
- **MD5** The RSA checksum algorithm technology

The following code block shows some examples of these parameters in `sqlnet.ora` with values set:

```
ENCRYPTION_TYPES_CLIENT = (RC4_40, RC4_128)
ENCRYPTION_TYPES_SERVER = (DES, RC4_56)
CRYPTO_CHECKSUM_TYPES_CLIENT = (MD5)
CRYPTO_CHECKSUM_TYPES_SERVER = (MD5)
```

Determining Whether Encryption and Checksums Are Used

Whether encryption and checksums are actually used depends on the settings for both operational and technology parameters. They will be used if both sides can use the technology and want to do so, and if both nodes share at least one encryption and/or checksum method in common. Thus, if a client has `ENCRYPTION_CLIENT` set to `requested` and the server has `ENCRYPTION_SERVER` set to `accepted`, and the `ENCRYPTION_TYPES_CLIENT` and `ENCRYPTION_TYPES_SERVER` parameters both contain `RC4_40`, then the connection will use RSA 40-bit encryption. Table 23-6 shows various combinations of operational parameters and whether that combination will use encryption or checksum technology.

Determining Which Encryption and Checksum Technologies to Use

To determine which technology gets used for encryption, Oracle walks down the list of `ENCRYPTION_TYPES_CLIENT` and `ENCRYPTION_TYPES_SERVER` technologies in the order `RC4_40`, `RC4_56`, `RC4_128`, `DES`, and `DES40`. The first

If the setting for parameter ENCRYPTION_CLIENT is one of the following	If the setting for parameter ENCRYPTION_SERVER is one of the following	How will the connection behave?
accepted requested required	accepted requested required	Connection will be established, and encryption/checksums will be used based on shared technology
accepted requested	rejected	Connection will be established, but encryption/checksums will not be used even if technology is shared
rejected	accepted requested	Connection will be established, but encryption/checksums will not be used even if technology is shared
rejected	required	Connection will not be established
required	rejected	Connection will not be established

TABLE 23-6. *Operational Parameter Value Combinations*

match found between the two nodes attempting to connect will be used as the encryption technology. If a technology from the list is not installed for that client or server, then Oracle skips on to the next technology in the list. If no common technology is shared between the two nodes, then encryption will not be used. Outside the US, only RC4_40 and DES40 are available.

Selecting a checksum technology is a little simpler, because there is only one supported technology, MD5. So, if it is available on both nodes, it will be used. If not, checksum technology won't be used.

Configuring CRYPTO_SEED

CRYPTO_SEED is a special parameter that determines the cryptographic keys used to verify data integrity. You define the value for yourself by entering between 10 and 70 characters for this parameter. Longer and more random character sequences make for stronger cryptographic keys, so try to enter the full 70 characters allowed, in as random an order as possible, to force Oracle to use the strongest key. This parameter is set in `sqlnet.ora`.

Using Net8 Assistant To Configure ANO Options

Net8 Assistant can also help you configure the appropriate parameters for ANO. Open the tool in Windows by selecting Start | Programs | Oracle for Windows | Oracle Net8 Assistant. Drill down to the Network | Profiles node, and select the Advanced Networking Options work area from the drop-down list box. In the Encryption tab, you can configure encryption settings, such as the values for your technology parameters, operational parameters, and encryption seed. Figure 23-4 shows the Encryption tab in Net8 Assistant.

Checksum technology values and behavior are set in the Integrity tab in that same work area, shown in Figure 23-5. You should notice that this tab is less

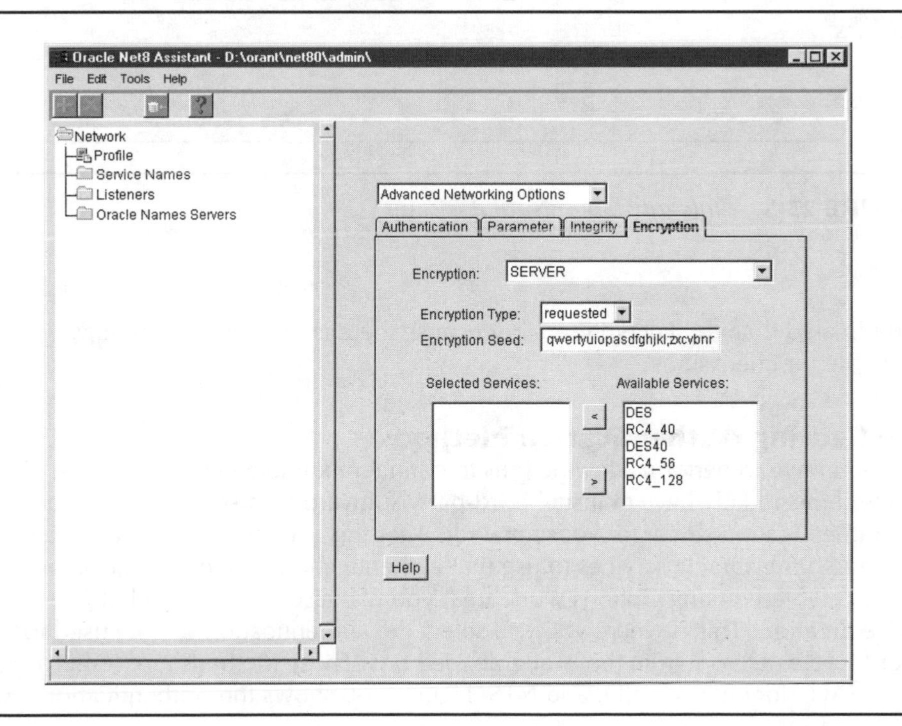

FIGURE 23-4. *Encryption tab in Net8 Assistant*

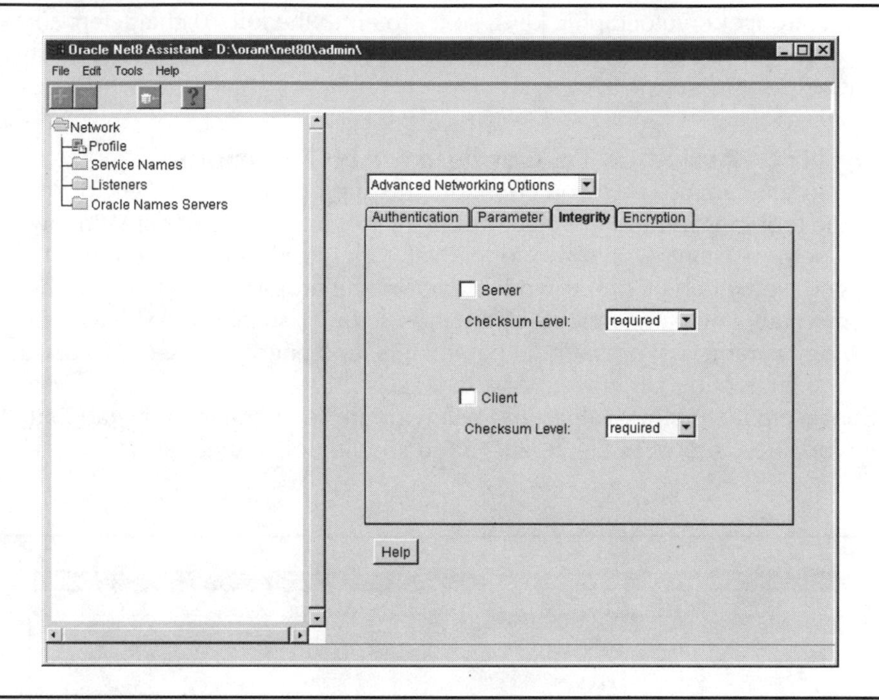

FIGURE 23-5. *Integrity tab in Net8 Assistant*

complicated than the Encryption tab, because there is only one technology available for checksums.

Configuring Authentication Methods

You will have to perform a few actions to configure authentication methods. First, you will most likely have to install third-party software on a server that will act as the authentication server for your network. After this is complete, you will have to configure your Oracle services to use that authentication method. In the same Advanced Networking Options work area, you will also see a tab called Authentication. This is where you will select the authentication service used for your Oracle network from the available methods. Those methods are Kerberos 5, CyberSAFE, Identix, SecurID, and NTS. Figure 23-6 shows the Authentication tab in Net8 Assistant.

TIP

The corresponding `sqlnet.ora` parameter modified by Net8 Assistant for setup of an authentication service is `AUTHENTICATION_SERVICES`. There may also be other authentication parameters to set for various authentication services, in the form `AUTHENTICATION_type_SERVICE`, where `type` is replaced with the name of the specialized parameter corresponding to the authentication service defined for the `AUTHENTICATION_SERVICES` parameter.

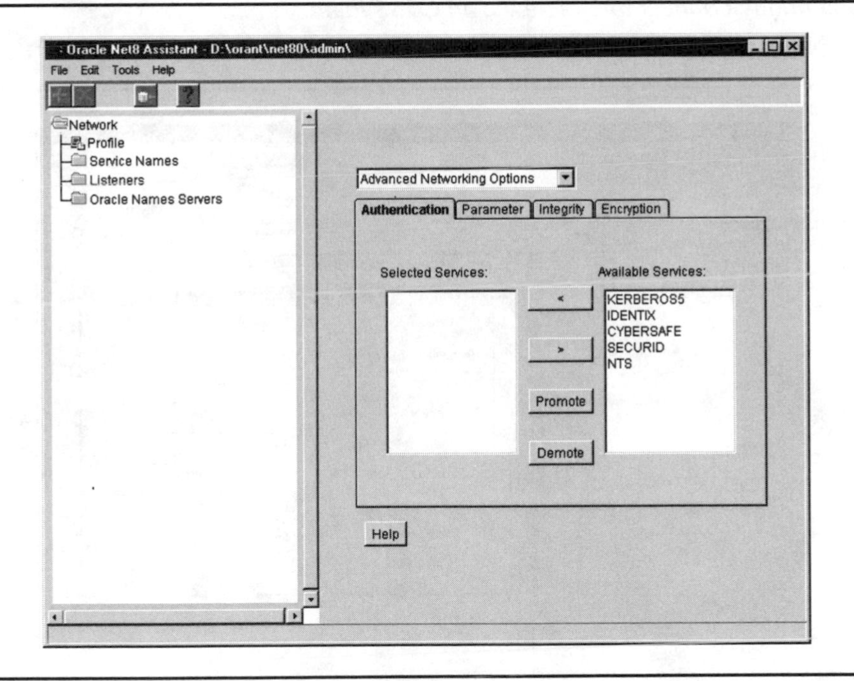

FIGURE 23-6. *Authentication tab in Net8 Assistant*

Some of these services will also require you to configure parameters to refine their use. The services requiring parameters are Kerberos 5, CyberSAFE, and Identix. Both CyberSAFE and Identix require you to define the appropriate server performing authentication on the network, while Kerberos 5 requires you to identify several additional parameters. Figure 23-7 shows the Parameter tab for defining authentication services in Net8 Assistant, with the parameters required for Kerberos 5 on display.

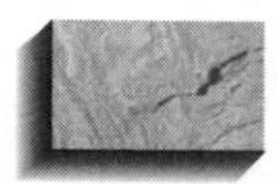

TIP

Although you will not perform Oracle authentication when you configure a third-party authentication service via ANO, you should still set the `initsid.ora` parameter `REMOTE_OS_AUTHENT` to FALSE. Setting this parameter to TRUE allows host machine users to potentially connect to Oracle via an OPS$ login.

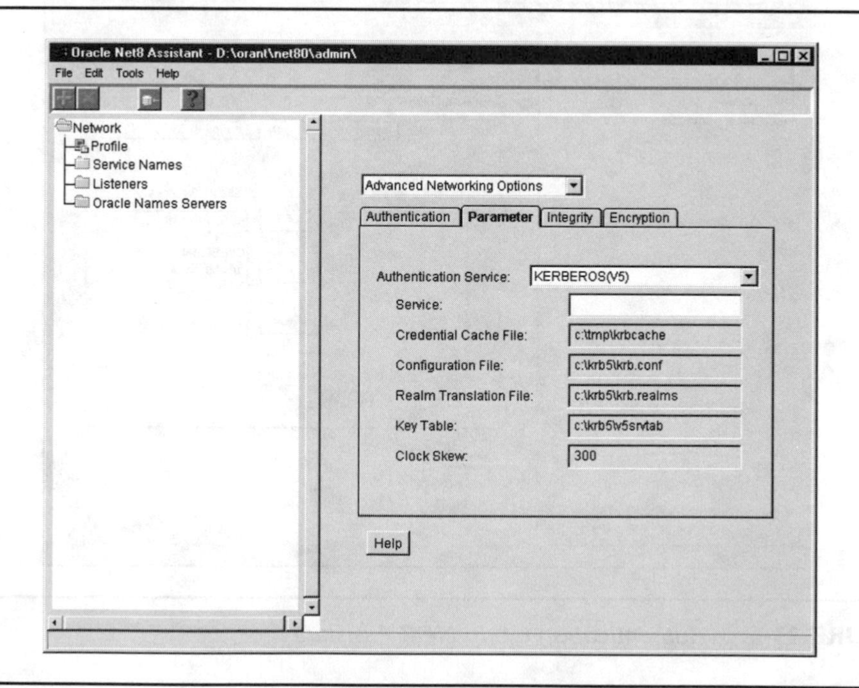

FIGURE 23-7. *Parameter tab in Net8 Assistant*

Exercises

1. Describe the operational and technology parameters used for configuring ANO encryption and checksum features. Which configuration file will these parameters be set in?
2. What are the valid values for ANO encryption and checksum operational parameters? What are the valid values for ANO encryption and checksum technology parameters?
3. How do you configure authentication using Net8 Assistant? Describe the underlying parameters modified by that tool.

Chapter Summary

This chapter concluded your coverage of network administration for OCP Exam 5. You covered three topics: the use and configuration of Connection Manager, troubleshooting the network environment, and security in the network environment. These topic areas comprise about 33 percent of OCP Exam 5 test content.

The first subject you covered was the use and configuration of Connection Manager. You learned about this tool's ability to join multiple underlying network protocols into one logical Oracle network. You also learned how to configure connection concentration as a method for improving the scalability of your Oracle network application. The configuration requirements were described for both multiprotocol functionality and network access control, as well.

The next section covered troubleshooting the network environment. You learned how to set logging and tracing parameters for your various network components so as to gather information to make a diagnosis of the problem. You also learned how to analyze and troubleshoot network problems using the log and trace files generated by network components. Finally, you learned about Trace Assistant and its ability to format the output contained in trace files. An explanation of the contents of a trace file was offered, as well.

The final section of this chapter covered security in the network environment. You learned how to identify network security risks for data during transmission that are inherent in the structure of certain network protocols, such as TCP/IP. You also learned about the security features in Oracle networking products that are designed to minimize the security risks posed by the inherent design of underlying network protocols, such as TCP/IP. The features of Oracle Security Server, Advanced Networking Option, and Cryptographic Toolkit were all explained. Finally, you learned how to set up the features of the Advanced Networking Option.

Two-Minute Drill

- Connection Manager allows Net8 to integrate two or more networks connected to one machine into one logical Oracle network.
- Connection Manager can also filter connections between different clients and servers using network-access control.
- Connection Manager offers connection concentration to connect many logical client sessions through a single transport, thereby increasing scalability for an application.
- There are three components to Connection Manager:
  - **CMGW** The Connection Manager gateway process, which acts as a liaison between clients and the Net8 listener
  - **CMADM** The Connection Manager administrator process, which maintains address information in the Oracle Names server for Net8 clients
  - **CMCTL** The Connection Manager control utility, similar to NAMESCTL or LSNRCTL in that you can set many options for Connection Manager interactively or from the command line using this tool.
- Configuring connection concentration on the server side is handled using the `MTS_DISPATCHERS` parameter in init*sid*.ora using the multiplex or multiplexing option. This option is set to `1, true, yes, on, in, out,` or `both.`
- To configure connection concentration on the client side, you use Net8 Assistant's Routing tab in the General work area in the Profile node. Click the Use Source Route Addresses checkbox to set this up.
- To configure multiprotocol functionality, you must add multiple protocol addresses to the `CMAN` parameter in `cman.ora.`
- Configuring network access control is a two-part process:
  1. Set up the `src`, `dst`, `srv`, and `act` options for the `CMAN_RULES` parameter in `cman.ora`
  2. Use Net8 Assistant's Routing tab in the General work area in the Profile node. Click the Use Source Route Addresses checkbox to set this up.

- If CMAN_RULES is configured in cman.ora, then you must define all client and server connections you want to connect and reject, explicitly. If a client/server combination is not defined in CMAN_RULES, Connection Manager will assume it should reject the combination.
- Log and trace files assist in determining network problems occurring in your Oracle network environment. You configure their use in the configuration file appropriate to the network component you want to monitor:
  - **Net8 listener** listener.ora
  - **Oracle Names** names.ora
  - **Connection Manager** cman.ora
  - **Client/server profile** sqlnet.ora
- The parameters for configuring log and trace filename and location for each of the various configuration files are listed here:
  - **listener.ora** LOG_FILE_LISTENER, LOG_DIRECTORY_LISTENER, TRACE_FILE_LISTENER, TRACE_DIRECTORY_LISTENER
  - **names.ora** NAMES.LOG_FILE, NAMES.LOG_DIRECTORY, NAMES.TRACE_FILE, NAMES.TRACE_DIRECTORY
  - **cman.ora** CMAN_PROFILE permits defining log_level and tracing options
  - **sqlnet.ora** LOG_FILE_SERVER, LOG_DIRECTORY_SERVER, TRACE_FILE_SERVER, TRACE_DIRECTORY_SERVER, LOG_FILE_CLIENT, LOG_DIRECTORY_CLIENT, TRACE_FILE_CLIENT, TRACE_DIRECTORY_CLIENT
- TNSPING is a service that operates in the same way as the ping command in the Unix or Windows operating systems works. It allows you to determine whether an Oracle service is running or not, and how long it takes that service to send a response to a request.
- TRACE_LEVEL is another important parameter for configuring tracing that determines how much trace information is written to the trace file as part of the trace. Valid values for TRACE_LEVEL include off, user, admin, and support.

- You may need to restart your network component in order to have trace settings take hold.
- The four steps for diagnosing network problems include:
  1. Review the log file first.
  2. Look at the error stack at the end of the file.
  3. Diagnose and resolve the problem using the error stack in the log file.
  4. If the log-file error stack doesn't provide enough information, enable tracing and use the trace file for further information.
- Some common network errors and possible causes and resolutions include:
  - **ORA-3113** End of file on communication channel. This means you were disconnected unexpectedly. Attempting to reconnect usually indicates more accurately what the problem is.
  - **ORA-12154** TNS couldn't resolve service name. Ensure that you entered the connect string properly, and that there is an associated connect descriptor in Oracle Names or `tnsnames.ora`.
  - **ORA-12203** TNS was unable to connect to the destination. The host machine information was probably incorrect in the connect descriptor, or else there is no DNS service on your network.
  - **ORA-12224** TNS detected no listener on your host specified. Make sure the listener is running and the port information in the connect descriptor is correct.
  - **ORA-12500** The listener couldn't start a dedicated server on the host. There is probably something wrong with the `SID_LIST` parameter in `listener.ora`, or possibly an error in the connect descriptor.
  - **ORA-12533** There were incorrect parameters in the ADDRESS portion of the connect descriptor specified locally or on the Names server.
  - **ORA-12545** TNS experienced a general lookup failure. Check to see that the connect descriptor is valid, the listener is running, and that the DNS server maps the hostname given to the appropriate network address for the machine hosting Oracle.
  - **ORA-12560** There is a problem with the Oracle Protocol Adapter. Turn on tracing for more info.

- Your trace file tells you a great deal of information about the types of packets that traverse the Oracle network, such as identifying the procedures used by various OSI network components:
  - **NSPTCN** Connect packet
  - **NSPTAC** Accept connection packet
  - **NSPTRF** Refuse connection packet
  - **NSPTRS** Resend data packet
  - **NSPTMK** Marker packet
  - **NSPDA** Data packet
  - **NSPCNL** Control packet
- Your trace file tells you a great deal of information about the functions and procedures doing work in the layers of Net8 corresponding to the OSI Network Model. These functions and procedures are prefixed with two characters to indicate the OSI layer they correspond to. The layers are:
  - **NA** Network authentication
  - **NI** Network interface
  - **NN** Network name resolution
  - **NR** Network routing
  - **NS** Network session
  - **NT** Network transport
- You can identify the trace-error information corresponding to the network error you received in your application (such as SQL*Plus) by looking at the end of your trace file.
- In Unix, the OERR utility gives you more information about how to identify problems. You may use this utility on the Unix command line by entering `oerr` *abc nnnnn*, where *abc* is the three-character sequence at the beginning of the error code you see (such as `ORA`) and *nnnnn* is the error number (such as 12203). This utility is not available in Windows.

- Trace Assistant can be used to format the contents of a trace file into something more readable. The command-line syntax for Trace Assistant is `trcasst` *`options filename`*, where *`filename`* is replaced with the name of your trace file and *`options`* is replaced with zero or more of the following command-line options: `-o, -e, -s`. Each of these options, in turn, has a set of options you can specify. Review the chapter for more information.
- If you specify no options for Trace Assistant, then the default options of `-odt -e -s` are used.
- Some security issues associated with network data transfer include:
  - Sensitive data being transported in plain text, and thus being viewable by third parties
  - Data being intercepted en route by third parties without being discovered by sender or recipient
  - Rogue servers configured either through DNS or by IP address piracy
- Effects of security issues include credit fraud, loss of competitive advantage, or ruined reputation.
- Three Oracle networking products are designed to provide layers of security over network protocols: Security Server, Cryptographic Toolkit, and Advanced Networking Option.
- Oracle Security Server provides an all-in-one solution for most business security needs, using authentication via X.509 certificates and information privacy via public-key encryption.
- Oracle Cryptographic Toolkit allows you to build support for security features used in Oracle Security Server into your application via the Cryptographic Toolkit OCI.
- Oracle Advanced Networking Option (ANO) provides enhanced security and functionality by enabling you to use third-party authentication and encryption technologies to keep data private.
- ANO provides support for the use of the following third-party technologies:
  - RSA 40-bit, 56-bit (US only), and 128-bit (US only) encryption technologies
  - DES 40-bit and 56-bit (US-only) encryption technologies

- RSA MD5 data-integrity checksum algorithm technology
- Kerberos 5, Identix, CyberSAFE, ACE/Server, and SecurID for centralized authentication.

- The `sqlnet.ora` parameters used for configuring encryption/checksum use, and their valid values, include the following:
  - **ENCRYPTION_CLIENT** `accepted, requested, rejected, required`
  - **ENCRYPTION_SERVER** `accepted, requested, rejected, required`
  - **ENCRYPTION_TYPES_CLIENT** RC4_40, RC4_56, RC4_128, DES, DES40
  - **ENCRYPTION_TYPES_SERVER** RC4_40, RC4_56, RC4_128, DES, DES40
  - **CRYPTO_CHECKSUM_CLIENT** `accepted, requested, rejected, required`
  - **CRYPTO_CHECKSUM_SERVER** `accepted, requested, rejected, required`
  - **CRYPTO_CHECKSUM_TYPES_CLIENT** MD5
  - **CRYPTO_CHECKSUM_TYPES_SERVER** MD5

- Review Table 23-6 to understand when Oracle connections will and will not use encryption technology depending on the settings for the preceding list of parameters, and when the connection will not be established at all.

- `CRYPTO_SEED` is a special parameter that defines the 10–70 character cryptographic key used to verify data integrity. Use only random sequences of characters for setting this parameter, and try to make the character sequence as long as possible to ensure Oracle uses the strongest key possible.

- Review the chapter material for how to configure authentication parameters used by ANO in your `sqlnet.ora` file, and how to use Net8 Assistant to configure ANO.

Chapter Questions

1. **You want to enhance scalability for your application through the use of connection concentration. Which of the following parameters will be modified for that purpose?**

   A. MTS_SERVERS

   B. MTS_LISTENER_ADDRESS

   C. MTS_DISPATCHERS

   D. MTS_MAX_SERVERS

2. **You are using Connection Manager in your networking configuration. Which of the following is not a component of that tool?**

   A. CMNS

   B. CMCTL

   C. CMADM

   D. CMGW

3. **You issue the `status adm` command from within the Connection Manager control utility. Which of the following descriptions best identifies the result of this command?**

   A. Returns statistics for all Connection Manager components

   B. Returns statistics for Connection Manager administrative utility only

   C. Returns status of all Connection Manager components

   D. Returns status of Connection Manager administrative utility only

4. **You are configuring connection concentration on your application using the appropriate parameter. Which of the following options for that parameter is appropriate for this purpose?**

   A. protocol

   B. multiplex

   C. concentrate

   D. partial

5. Multiprotocol interchange can be configured so long as Net8 listeners are tuned in to a certain number of network protocols. Which of the following choices indicates a number of protocols that is not acceptable for multiprotocol interchange?

A. 1

B. 2

C. 3

D. 4

6. You want to enable network-access control on your network environment. Which of the following configuration files correctly identifies the file where you would configure network-access control?

A. `listener.ora`

B. `sqlnet.ora`

C. `init.ora`

D. `cman.ora`

E. `names.ora`

F. `access.ora`

7. You are about to begin setup for tracing network activity. Which of the following settings would be appropriate if you planned to process your trace file later using Trace Assistant?

A. `off`

B. `user`

C. `admin`

D. `support`

8. Your users report the following network error message to you: `ORA-12224: No Listener`. To correct the problem, which of the following utilities might you use if you have already set up the listener on your host machine?

A. Net8 Assistant

B. LSNRCTL

C. NAMESCTL

D. CMCTL

9. An excerpt of the contents of a trace file is listed as follows:

```
(c770) nsprecv: packet dump
(c770) nsprecv: 00 72 00 00 06 00 00 00 |.r......|
(c770) nsprecv: 00 00 04 00 00 00 00 F5 |........|
(c770) nsprecv: 03 00 00 00 00 02 00 00 |........|
(c770) nsprecv: 00 18 00 00 00 00 21 00 |......!.|
(c770) nsprecv: 00 00 00 00 00 00 00 00 |........|
(c770) nsprecv: 00 00 00 00 00 00 00 00 |........|
(c770) nsprecv: 00 00 00 00 31 00 00 01 |....1...|
(c770) nsprecv: 00 00 00 36 4F 52 41 2D |...6ORA-|
(c770) nsprecv: 30 31 30 31 33 3A 20 75 |01013: u|
(c770) nsprecv: 73 65 72 20 72 65 71 75 |ser requ|
(c770) nsprecv: 65 73 74 65 64 20 63 61 |ested ca|
(c770) nsprecv: 6E 63 65 6C 20 6F 66 20 |ncel of |
(c770) nsprecv: 63 75 72 72 65 6E 74 20 |current |
(c770) nsprecv: 6F 70 65 72 61 74 69 6F |operatio|
(c770) nsprecv: 6E 0A 00 00 00 00 00 00 |n.......|
(c770) nsprecv: normal exit
```

What Net8 network-layer component produced this output?

A. Two-Task Common

B. Network Interface

C. Network Session

D. Network Transport

E. Network Authentication

10. The output from Trace Assistant displays statistical information from your trace file for the session activity only. Which of the following command-line options were most likely used?

A. `-oq -e`

B. `-e`

C. `-odt -e0 -s`

D. `-s`

E. None, Trace Assistant shows statistical information only by default

11. You are attempting to design the architecture for your Oracle network. Which of the following choices does not describe a feature of the Oracle Advanced Networking Option?

A. Uses X.509 certificates for authentication

B. Uses Identix for authentication

C. Uses Kerberos for authentication

D. Uses SecurID for authentication

12. The following parameters are found in the appropriate configuration file:

```
ENCRYPTION_CLIENT = requested
ENCRYPTION_SERVER = required
ENCRYPTION_TYPE_CLIENT = (RC4_128, DES_40, DES)
ENCRYPTION_TYPE_SERVER = (RC4_40, RC4_56, DES_40)
```

Which of the following choices correctly describes how encryption will be used between the client and server?

A. RC4_128 encryption will be used

B. RC4_56 encryption will be used

C. RC4_40 encryption will be used

D. DES encryption will be used

E. DES40 encryption will be used

F. No encryption will be used

13. You are configuring the mode of authentication used in the Advanced Networking Option. Which of the following files will be modified for this purpose?

A. `listener.ora`

B. `sqlnet.ora`

C. `init.ora`

D. `cman.ora`

E. `names.ora`

F. `access.ora`

14. You are configuring the mode of authentication used in the Advanced Networking Option. Which of the following parameters will be modified for this purpose?

A. `ENCRYPTION_CLIENT`

B. `ENCRYPTION_SERVER`

C. `AUTHENTICATION_SERVICES`

D. `ENCRYPTION_TYPE_CLIENT`

E. `ENCRYPTION_TYPE_SERVER`

F. `CRYPTO_SEED`

Answers to Chapter Questions

1. C. `MTS_DISPATCHERS`

Explanation The `multiplex` option for `MTS_DISPATCHERS` is how connection concentration is configured. `MTS_SERVERS` and `MTS_MAX_SERVERS` are only used to configure the number of shared servers for your database. The initialization parameter `MTS_LISTENER_ADDRESS` is used to configure the addresses on your host machine where listeners will tune in for connections.

2. A. CMNS

Explanation This utility is entirely made-up. The components of Connection Manager include CMCTL, the Connection Manager control utility, CMADM, the Connection Manager administrative utility, and CMGW, the Connection Manager gateway.

3. D. Returns status of Connection Manager administrative utility only

Explanation The command `status adm` is used to return status from CMADM. If status by itself was used, you would obtain status for all Connection Manager components, which eliminates choice C. The `stats` command is used to obtain statistics for Connection Manager components, eliminating choices A and B.

4. B. `multiplex`

Explanation The `multiplex` option for `MTS_DISPATCHERS` is how connection concentration is configured. The `protocol` option defines which network protocol this dispatcher works with, while `concentrate` is not an actual option for this parameter. The `partial` option is not used for this purpose.

5. A. 1

Explanation You need at least two different listeners each tuned to a different network protocol to have multiprotocol interchange taking place. The actual number of networks handled is entirely dependent on the hardware of the network and the machine hosting Oracle. Only one network does not constitute multiprotocol interchange, however, making choice A the correct answer.

6. D. `cman.ora`

Explanation Since Connection Manager is used to manage network access control, the `CMAN_RULES` parameter in `cman.ora` is used to configure network-access control. The listener is not used for this purpose, so `listener.ora` is eliminated. Your instance is not used for this purpose, so `init.ora` must be eliminated, too. The Names server is not involved, so eliminate `names.ora`. Finally, `sqlnet.ora` is not used for this purpose, either.

7. D. `support`

Explanation Support-level tracing is the only level of tracing that can be used in conjunction with Trace Assistant processing. User-level and admin-level tracing cannot be used, nor can no trace level at all. After all, tracing must be enabled in order to obtain a trace file for Trace Assistant to use.

8. B. LSNRCTL

Explanation The LSNRCTL utility is used to restart the listener, which is the source of the problem identified in this question. You know this because the question states you have already set up your listener, thus eliminating the need to use Net8 Assistant to set up the listener, and eliminating choice A along with it. NAMESCTL manages Oracle Names, which is not involved, and CMCTL manages Connection Manager, which also is not involved.

9. C. Network Session

Explanation Recall that the first two letters of every procedure or function listed in the output of a trace file indicates the Net8 network layer component that procedure is called from. In this case, `nsprecv( )` is from the Network Session layer, because the first two letters in the procedure are NS.

10. D. `-s`

Explanation The `-s` option is used to obtain statistics, and when used by itself, Trace Assistant will display statistic information from the trace file only. Though the default set of options will include statistics, that won't be the only thing included, so choice E is eliminated. For this same reason, choice C is eliminated, as well. Finally, choices A and B should be eliminated because they don't even contain `-s`.

11. A. Uses X.509 certificates for authentication

Explanation X.509 certificates are used by Oracle Security Server for authentication, not the Advanced Networking Option. Instead, ANO makes it possible to use third-party authentication services listed for choices B, C, and D.

12. E. DES_40 encryption will be used

Explanation Since both sides will agree to use encryption according to the parameters listed in the question, the only problem becomes which technology to use. ANO determines the answer to this question by finding out which technology is shared between both client and server. In this case, DES 40-bit encryption is the only shared technology, so choice E has to be the answer.

13. B. `sqlnet.ora`

Explanation The parameters for configuring authentication, encryption, and checksums for ANO are all found in `sqlnet.ora`. The listener is not used in configuring ANO, so choice A is eliminated. Your instance is also not used for this purpose, so `init.ora` must be eliminated, too. The Names server is not involved, so eliminate `names.ora`. Connection Manager is not used, so `cman.ora` is eliminated. Finally, `access.ora` is not used for this purpose, either, because this configuration file is made-up.

14. C. `AUTHENTICATION_SERVICES`

Explanation `AUTHENTICATION_SERVICES` is the parameter used to determine the authentication service used by ANO in the `sqlnet.ora` file. All the other choices identify parameters used to configure encryption and checksum technology, not authentication.

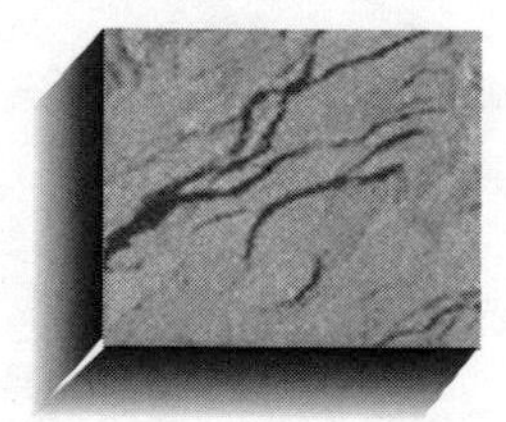

UNIT VI

Preparing for OCP Exam 6: Oracle8*i* New Features for Administrators

CHAPTER 24

Oracle8*i* New Features Topics

In this chapter, you will be introduced to the topics in Unit VI, which covers the new features of Oracle8*i*. The other chapters in Unit VI are as follows:

- Chapter 25: Oracle8*i* Database Management
- Chapter 26: Oracle8*i* Internals
- Chapter 27: Oracle8*i* Object Management I
- Chapter 28: Oracle8*i* Object Management II
- Chapter 29: Oracle8*i* Recoverability
- Chapter 30: Oracle8*i* Advanced New Features

Note that Chapters 25–30 appear only on the CD-ROM that accompanies this book.

This chapter provides an overview of the remaining coverage of Oracle8*i* new features for administrators. The in-depth explanations for these features is provided in the chapters described in the subsequent sections. Oracle8*i* is an extensive new release of the Oracle database, and the content is so lengthy that it cannot all be presented in this book. So, the final six chapters you should use to prepare for the OCP Oracle8*i* upgrade exam are presented in the electronic version of this book on CD-ROM.

The topics fall into six areas. The first topic is database management. The second covers Oracle8*i* database internals. Object management in Oracle8*i* is covered in two parts, as well. You will learn and review features in Oracle8*i* designed to provide high database recoverability and availability. Finally, the unit wraps up with coverage of some of the advanced new features of the Oracle8*i* database environment.

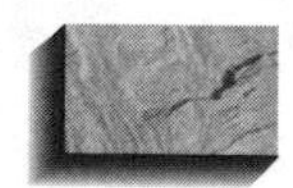

TIP

The technical discussions you need to review in order to understand Oracle8i well enough to pass the OCP Oracle8i upgrade exam are covered only in the electronic version of the book, on the CD-ROM! There are six additional chapters on the CD-ROM (Chapters 25–30) that are not in print, so be sure you review the technical material on the CD before taking this OCP exam.

Chapter 25: Oracle8*i* Database Management

In this chapter, you will cover the following areas related to Oracle8*i* database management:

- Installation and configuration
- Migrating server and applications
- Oracle Enterprise Manager
- ROWID format in Oracle8*i*
- Tablespace management
- Password management
- Other security enhancements

This chapter begins the coverage of Oracle8*i*—the exciting new release of the Oracle database server, capable of integrating your Oracle data with the vast business potential of the Internet. This chapter covers the basic elements of new database-management features offered with Oracle8*i*. The first area covered in this chapter is Oracle8*i* installation and configuration. You will also cover the new features associated with Oracle tablespace management. Another important advance covered by this chapter is the new Java-based Oracle Enterprise Manager, with its N-tier repository of database management information, capable of allowing multiple administrators to manage your Oracle environment. The use of the new Database Resource Manager tool is covered in some detail, as well. You will review the information presented earlier in Unit II with regard to password management in this chapter, and will also learn about some of the new features in Oracle8*i* pertaining to security.

Installation and Configuration

In this section, you will cover the following topics on installing and configuring your Oracle database:

- Using Oracle Universal Installer and Packager
- Installing a pretuned database
- Creating a database using the Database Configuration Assistant

This section covers the Oracle8*i* new features associated with installing and configuring your Oracle8*i* database software. You will learn about the Oracle Universal Installer and Packager, which is Oracle's new installer utility program. You will also learn how to install a pre-tuned database using Oracle Universal Installer and Packager. Finally, you will cover how to use the Database Configuration Assistant, a wizard that assists in creating an Oracle database on your host machine. Note an important thing about this content—it is intentionally not meant to be a step-by-step tutorial about installing Oracle8*i*, because the Universal Installer and Packager itself gives good indications about what you need to do at any given point. Instead, this coverage is meant to instruct you about what's new and different about installing Oracle8*i*, along with any points you need to understand before you begin.

Migrating Server and Applications

In this section, you will cover the following topics on migrating server and applications:

- Migrating from Oracle7 to Oracle8
- Upgrading from Oracle8 to Oracle8*i*

Understanding how to migrate from Oracle7 to Oracle8*i* or to upgrade from Oracle8 to Oracle8*i* is perhaps the most important feature that OCP Exam 6 can present. This section is designed to identify the concepts and steps required for converting Oracle7 applications to Oracle8*i*, and to identify the tools available for the purpose of migrating from Oracle7 to Oracle8. It is also meant to cover how to move from Oracle8 to Oracle8*i*.

Migration from Oracle7 to Oracle8*i* requires that you first migrate to Oracle8, and then upgrade to Oracle8*i*. The first section covers migration from Oracle7 to Oracle8, and the second section covers moving from Oracle8 to Oracle8*i*.

Oracle Enterprise Manager

In this section, you will cover the following topics on new features for Oracle Enterprise Manager:

- Using Java-based console and applications
- Sharing repositories between DBAs
- Changes to OEM components

In addition to overhauling the Oracle utility for installing Oracle software to use Java, Oracle Enterprise Manager has been substantially modified to use both Java and an N-tier architecture to facilitate the centralization of database management tasks between multiple DBAs on the same team. In this section, you will cover several topics related to using Enterprise Manager 2.0. The first topic is the use of the Java-based console and OEM applications. Next, you will learn about scalability in database administration through the sharing of repositories between DBAs. Last, you will cover some of the enhancements made to OEM 2.0 application- and wizard-driven components.

ROWID Format in Oracle8*i*

In this section, you will cover the following new features of ROWID format in Oracle8*i*:

- Differentiating between ROWID types
- Using DBMS_ROWID to Manage ROWIDs

You have already covered several aspects of the new Oracle8 ROWID format in Chapter 8. This section will review the new ROWID format for Oracle8. With new objects and greater size comes the need for accessing those new objects in a new way. In the versions that preceded Oracle8, all access to data in the database is managed with the use of ROWID data consisting of three elements: data block identifier, row number in the block, and datafile identifier. Additional reference information for objects in Oracle8—such as table and index partitions and the increases in the amount of data Oracle8 can store—require that new components be included in the ROWID format. This section will detail those changes.

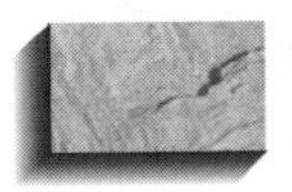

TIP
Although the topic of describing logical ROWIDs is listed under this topic area on the OCP Candidate Guide for this test, logical ROWIDs is a topic best covered in association with index-organized tables (IOTs). For information about logical ROWID formats, review the discussion of IOTs in Chapter 27.

Tablespace Management

In this section, you will cover the following new features involving tablespace management:

- Making a tablespace read-only online
- Transporting tablespaces
- Creating locally managed tablespaces

Oracle8*i* has provided several new features in the area of tablespace management, and you will cover them in this section. The first area of enhanced tablespace management in Oracle8*i* includes how to make a tablespace read-only while the tablespace is still online. The next topic covered is how to transport tablespaces. The last topic area is creating locally managed tablespaces, and what the implications of locally managing tablespaces really means.

Password Management

The topics in this section include:

- Concepts
- Managing passwords using profiles
- Password-complexity checking

Enhanced password management was introduced in Oracle8 and covered extensively in Chapter 10 in this book. With that in mind, you should review the content of Chapter 10 pertaining to the concepts of password management. Nothing new has been added to Oracle8's already powerful enhancement of password administration. Recall from Chapter 10 that password management is configured in conjunction with resource-utilization profiles. You may also configure password-complexity checking to ensure that users do not define passwords that are easily guessed, or recycle their passwords. You can study for this portion of the exam using the discussion of password management appearing in the appropriate section of Chapter 10.

TIP

As of the April 1999 printing of the Oracle Candidate Certification Guide, password management will be covered as a separate topic in OCP Exam 6 for Oracle8i upgrade, separate from the topic of database security, which is about to be covered.

Other Security Enhancements

In this section, you will cover the following database-security enhancements:

- Specifying invoker's rights execution
- Defining fine-grained access control
- Using application context
- Implementing N-tier authentication and global roles

In addition to the password-administration privileges introduced in Oracle8 that were already covered in Chapter 10, Oracle8*i* has added some additional new features to database security overall. This section covers them. The first topic you will cover includes specifying invoker's rights for PL/SQL code execution. Another topic you will cover is using application context. After that, you'll learn how to define fine-grained access control. Implementing N-tier authentication, a topic mentioned in Chapter 23, will be revisited. Finally, some discussion of implementing global roles in conjunction with LDAP will be offered, as well.

Chapter 26: Oracle8*i* Internals

In this chapter, you will cover the following topics concerning Oracle8*i* internals:

- SQL*Plus, PL/SQL, and NLS enhancements
- Memory management
- Parallel query enhancements
- Database resource manager
- Optimizer and query improvements
- Materialized views

Oracle8*i* offers enhancements in several internal areas that you should be aware of. Both the enhancements themselves and the methods used to configure them will be covered in this chapter. The first area you will cover with respect to Oracle8*i* enhancements is enhancements to memory management. Next, you will learn about the enhancements to parallel query operations in Oracle8*i*. After that, you'll cover database resource management, a new feature in Oracle8*i* that helps you control host-machine utilization more strongly than ever before. Following that topic is coverage of the enhancements made to the query optimizer in the Oracle8*i* RDBMS. The last topic of this chapter covers materialized views, another new feature

SQL*Plus, PL/SQL, and NLS Enhancements

In this section, you will cover the following points on SQL, PL/SQL, and NLS enhancements in Oracle8*i*:

- Using SQL*Plus to manage your database
- Using NLS enhancements
- Using PL/SQL enhancements
- Using new triggering events

This chapter covers several areas of Oracle8*i* new features and enhancements related to application development and language constructs. The first area you will learn about in this chapter is how to use SQL*Plus for database management functions instead of Server Manager. You will also learn about support for National Language Support (NLS) enhancements. The chapter covers the use of some of the PL/SQL enhancements not covered already, as well. Finally, you will learn about and use the new triggering events available in Oracle8*i*.

Memory Management

In this section, you will cover the following topics on memory management in Oracle8*i*:

- Using the large pool
- Using multiple buffer pools
- Sizing multiple buffer pools

Memory management has been enhanced for Oracle8 and Oracle8*i* to allow you to operate the multithreaded server (MTS) architecture more efficiently and to manage data stored in your buffer cache with ease. In this section, you will learn about two important topic areas related to memory management. The first involves learning how to configure and manage the large pool. The second is learning how to use multiple buffer pools. If you have already taken Oracle8 OCP Exam 4 on performance tuning, and have read Chapter 18, this content should look familiar. It is provided here for the sake of users on the upgrade path.

Parallel Query Enhancements

In this section, you will cover the following topics on parallel query enhancements in Oracle8*i*:

- Specifying automatic parallel-query optimization
- Monitoring parallel-query performance

Oracle8*i* has provided several enhancements to parallel query processing and optimization that you should understand for certification. This section will explain these new features to you. Some of the improvements include a better default degree of parallelism. In addition, you can use a single parameter to enable database parallelism. Oracle8*i* employs a new method for managing the degree of parallelism based on the current application load. Additional features for load balancing on Oracle Parallel Server are offered, as well. The first topic covered in this section is how to specify automatic parallel-query optimization. The other topic covered in this section is how to monitor parallel-query operations using new dynamic performance views in Oracle8*i*.

Database Resource Manager

In this section, you will cover the following topics on Oracle8*i* Database Resource Manager:

- Configuring database-resource management
- Controlling resource use by user groups

Until Oracle8*i*, the main method available for managing the resources available on the machine hosting the Oracle database was the use of resource profiles. This feature gave granular resource-usage management at the individual user level. Oracle8*i* enhances the DBA's ability to manage database usage of the host machine with the introduction of the database resource manager, a set of Oracle-supplied packages designed to give a complete development environment for managing resource use. In this section, you will learn how to configure database resource management and how to control resource use by user groups.

Optimizer and Query Improvements

In this section, you will cover the following lessons on optimizer and query improvements for Oracle8*i*:

- Controlling plan stability with stored outlines
- Managing statistics with DBMS_STATS
- Optimizing Top-N queries
- Monitoring long-running operations

Oracle8*i* introduces many new internal features that assist with performance tuning and query optimization. This section will cover these features in some detail. The first area you'll learn about is using a stored outline to control the execution-plan stability for your query. The next section will explain how to collect and move statistics on your database using the DBMS_STATS package, a new Oracle-supplied package in Oracle8*i*. Next, you'll learn what Top-N queries are and how to optimize them. Finally, you will learn a few things about monitoring long-running operations in Oracle8*i*.

Materialized Views

In this section, you will cover the following topics on materialized views in Oracle8*i*:

- Controlling refresh of materialized views
- Controlling query rewrite
- Creating summaries
- Materialized views and advisory functions
- Dependencies and materialized-view invalidation
- Controlling rewrites requiring hierarchies

Materialized views in Oracle8*i* are designed to replace read-only snapshots and to allow query rewrite. They store the definition of a view, plus data resulting from the view's execution. Unlike a view, both the definition of the materialized view and the data existing in Oracle8*i* at the time the view was created that conforms to the search criteria are rolled together and stored as a materialized view. You will learn how to create summaries and join indexes. You will also learn how to control refresh of materialized views. This section also explains how to control query rewrite and manage materialized views using advisory functions. You will learn how to manage dependencies and materialized-view invalidation, as well. Finally, you will learn how to control rewrites requiring hierarchies.

Chapter 27: Oracle8*i* Object Management I

In this chapter, you will cover the following topics on Oracle8*i* object administration:

- Constraints
- Other manageability enhancements
- Index enhancements
- Index-organized tables
- Managing large objects
- Object relational databases

Oracle8*i* continues the advances made with Oracle8 in the area of new objects and the enhancement of old objects for use in new and different ways. This chapter covers the new object administration concepts and features for all of Oracle8 and Oracle8*i*'s objects except for those pertaining to the Oracle8*i* Objects Option and partitioned objects. This chapter begins by covering constraints and the new features associated with them. Then, you'll learn about the manageability enhancements offered by Oracle8*i*, such as the ability to drop columns from tables. Oracle8*i* has several enhancements relating to indexes that you will learn about, as well. The chapter covers index-organized tables, and then concludes with some coverage of managing large objects.

Constraints

In this section, you will cover the following points on constraints in Oracle8*i*:

- Using nonunique indexes for primary and unique keys
- Controlling constraint validation

In this section, you will cover several of the new rules for constraint validation and index use. You will learn about the ability to defer constraint validation, introduced in Oracle8 and continued in Oracle8*i*. You will also learn that to defer constraint validation you must use nonunique indexes to support the constraints that enforce uniqueness, namely primary keys and unique constraints. You will also learn how these new features affect data entry, the enabling of disabled constraints, and other aspects of constraint enforcement.

Other Manageability Enhancements

In this section, you will cover the following points on other manageability enhancements:

- Dropping columns
- Creating temporary tables
- Using SQL*Loader's new features

This section covers several of Oracle8*i*'s new manageability enhancements. Oracle8*i* has added several new capabilities to its management of database objects. In this section, you will learn how to drop columns from a table without having to drop and recreate the table. You will also learn how to create temporary tables in Oracle. Finally, you will cover some of the new features added to SQL*Loader.

Index Enhancements

In this section, you will cover the following topics related to index enhancements:

- Combining index creation and statistics generation
- Implementing function-based indexes
- Implementing descending indexes
- Bitmap index improvements
- Using reverse-key indexes
- Building or rebuilding indexes online

Oracle8*i* has made a new set of enhancements in the area of indexes. These enhancements include improvements to existing index types, as well as adding new index types. In this section, you will learn how to combine index creation with the process of generating statistics for cost-based optimization. Next, you will learn about function-based indexes, and then descending indexes. Both these index types are new to Oracle8*i*. The next topic is some improvements to bitmap indexes. There is also a section that will refresh your understanding of reverse-key indexes. Both these index types were explained in Chapter 10. Finally, you'll learn about some internal enhancements to Oracle that make it possible to more efficiently rebuild indexes online.

Index-Organized Tables

In this section, you will cover the following points on index-organized tables:

- Concepts
- Implementing IOTs
- Creating secondary indexes

Index-organized tables were introduced in Oracle8, and have expanded in Oracle8*i* to include new features, functionality, and usage. In this section, you will cover the following topic areas related to index-organized tables. If you need background information on these new features, you can review Chapter 9, where IOTs are also discussed. The first topic discussed in this chapter is the concepts behind index-organized tables. Next, you will cover how to implement IOTs on the Oracle database. The last discussion covers a completely new feature for IOTs in Oracle8*i*, the ability to create secondary indexes on IOTs.

Managing Large Objects

In this section, you will cover the following topics related to LOB datatypes:

- Differentiating between different types of LOBs
- Creating directories
- LOB data management with DBMS_LOB
- Migrating LONGs to LOBs

There are several drawbacks inherent in the use of LONG and LONG RAW datatypes in Oracle7 database tables. First, the use of either datatype is limited to only one column in the database table. If the object is large, the storage of that object inline with other table data almost invariably leads to chaining, which has its own host of performance issues, as previously discussed. Passing LONG and LONG RAW data back and forth between client and server, or between PL/SQL procedures and functions, proves difficult, as well. Oracle has answered these issues by creating new and different datatypes for the storage of large objects—the LOB datatypes. This section will cover the usage and function of each of the LOB datatypes, the benefits and restrictions of each, and also some dictionary views that can be used in order to find information about the LOB datatypes used in the Oracle8*i* database.

Object Relational Databases

In this section, you will cover the following topic areas on object relational databases:

- Defining object types
- Defining object methods
- Creating object tables
- Implementing collections
- Using REF-column referential integrity
- Analyzing dangling references
- Migrating relational databases using object views
- Using `instead of` triggers

Perhaps the most challenging area of Oracle8*i* is the continued use of the object relational database architecture, which has been called Oracle's revolutionary, or at least evolutionary, approach to the future of object-oriented database design. This section will cover several basic areas of Oracle8 object relational database design concepts, including how to define object types and object methods. User-defined abstract datatypes is the cornerstone of object-oriented design methodology. Once you have developed your types, you will learn how to create object tables from them. After that, you'll analyze dangling references and use REF-column referential integrity. The implementation of collection datatypes, such as VARRAY and nested tables, will be covered, as well. Finally, you will cover the migration of your relational databases to object relational databases with object views and `instead of` triggers.

Chapter 28: Oracle8*i* Object Management II

In this chapter, you will cover the following areas of new object administration features on Oracle8*i*:

- Partitioning tables
- Partitioning indexes
- Parallel DML and queries

- Partitioning Techniques
- Partitioned IOTs, LOBs, and objects

Oracle8*i* introduces many new features for the task of managing database objects. Users familiar with Oracle8*i*'s new features should already know that partitioning is an important new feature designed to support increased availability in data warehousing applications. In this chapter, you will learn about the basic concepts behind partitioning tables and indexes. You will cover several techniques for partitioning your database objects, as well. The use of partitioning in large data warehouses makes it possible to use parallelism in your data-change and query operations more effectively, and you will learn more about this topic, as well. Finally, you will cover partitioning index-organized tables, the impact of partitioning when the table contains large objects, and partitioning object tables.

Partitioning Tables

In this section, you will cover the following topics for an overview of partitioning:

- Partitioning definition and rules
- Creating partitioned tables
- Benefits of partitioning
- Restrictions on partitioning
- Altering partitioned tables

This section introduces you to the methods and mechanisms of partitioning database objects. After introducing you to the basic reasons for using the feature, the section will cover the syntax and semantics of creating tables with partitions. Finally, the section will cover the benefits of partitioning database objects. This new feature of Oracle8*i* is relatively complex, but the opportunities and potential for performance improvement certainly outweighs the complexity of the feature.

Partitioning Indexes

In this section, you will cover the following topics related to implementing partitioned indexes:

- Creating partitioned indexes
- Equipartitioning and indexes
- Strategies for partitioning indexes

- Restrictions on partitioning indexes
- Altering partitioned indexes

In addition to tables, indexes on tables may be partitioned. This section will discuss the various topics of partitioning indexes in the Oracle8*i* database. The different types of partitioned indexes will be identified and explained, along with the syntax requirements for creating them. This section will also discuss strategies for using the various types of partitioned indexes available in Oracle8*i*, along with the situations that justify the use of each. Finally, the restrictions on each of the partitioned indexes will be presented in this section. As with partitioning tables, index partitioning is an important new concept in Oracle database administration.

Parallel DML and Queries

In this section, you will cover the following topics related to parallel DML and queries:

- Advantages of using parallel DML
- Enabling and using parallel DML
- Restrictions on using parallel DML
- Dictionary views on parallel DML
- Configuring for partition-wise joins
- Using parallel query on object tables

The overall use of parallelism in Oracle8*i* has increased dramatically in support of large database environments, as given evidence by the treatment of partitioned tables. This increase is due to the increase in database size as a whole, both in data warehouses and in OLTP applications. As Oracle database applications advance in the organization, they also grow. Although most organizations shouldn't ever feel too constrained by the 512 petabyte size limit for Oracle8*i*, even the data warehouse of 20 gigabytes may seem unwieldy with several database objects whose size is measured in hundreds of megabytes. Accessing data in Oracle8*i* offers some relief with partitioning and the new ROWID structure already discussed. Oracle8*i* also improves the ability of users to put data into the database efficiently with parallel DML.

Partitioning Techniques

In this section, you will cover the following points on partitioning techniques in Oracle8*i*:

- Hash partitioning tables and indexes
- Using composite partitioning
- Partitioning operations

In the previous sections, you covered areas of partitioning tables and indexes, and how to set up parallel query and DML operations that use the partitions to speed data access. The type of partitioning you covered thus far is range partitioning. In this section, you will learn about other types of partitioning available in Oracle8*i*. You will cover how to use hash partitioning on your tables and indexes and how to use composite partitioning. Finally, this section will discuss various partitioning operations available for all different types of partitioning techniques.

Partitioned IOTs, LOBs, and Objects

In this section, you will cover the following topics on partitioned IOTs, LOBs, and objects:

- Partitioning index-organized tables
- Partitioning tables with LOBs
- Partitioning object tables

Oracle8*i* provides you with the ability to partition IOTs, tables containing large object columns, and object tables. These options were not provided in prior versions of Oracle. In this section, you will learn how to perform these tasks. You will learn how to partition index-organized tables and how to partition tables containing large objects. Finally, you will learn how to partition object tables. Before proceeding, note an important point about dropping tablespaces that are created by partitioned database objects. You will get errors if you try to drop a tablespace that does not contain all of the components of a partitioned object.

Chapter 29: Oracle8*i* Recoverability Enhancement

In this chapter, you will cover the following topic areas of Oracle8*i* recoverability enhancements:

- Introducing Recovery Manager
- Using RMAN catalog commands and reports
- Using RMAN `run` commands and scripts
- Oracle8*i* availability and recoverability enhancements
- Standby databases

Oracle8*i* offers many features and benefits for database recovery and application development that will be covered in this chapter. You may find the materials on recovery somewhat redundant if you recall the contents of Chapter 13. However, repetition is a good way to learn, especially for new and complex materials like the RMAN command-line programming language. Also, because RMAN is covered as part of the Oracle8*i* exam, you should take another look at this material to foster your understanding. You will learn about RMAN and some of the new features added since RMAN was introduced in Oracle8. You will also learn about automating your standby databases and other recoverability enhancements in Oracle8*i*.

Introducing Recovery Manager

In this section, you will cover the following topics related to introducing Recovery Manager:

- Identifying Recovery Manager architecture and benefits
- Defining the recovery catalog
- Identifying backup types and commands
- Listing associated data dictionary views

RMAN possesses many features to ease the job of backup and recovery. This section will introduce you to the architecture and benefits of RMAN, along with the types of backups that are possible with the tool. The use of the RMAN catalog will also be presented in this section. Finally, the new data dictionary views provided to support RMAN are presented and explained.

Using RMAN Catalog Commands and Reports

In this section, you will cover the following topics related to using catalog commands and reports:

- Starting Recovery Manager
- Maintaining the recovery catalog
- Generating reports and lists from the recovery catalog

In this section, an in-depth discussion of several topics already presented in the overview section will be covered. Starting RMAN and the commands for operating RMAN will be presented in greater detail, along with the details of recovery catalog maintenance. Generating reports and lists will also be covered. This section can be read as the technical specification to the topics presented in the previous section.

Using RMAN run Commands and Scripts

In this section, you will cover the following topics related to using `run` commands and scripts:

- Channels, scripts, and attributes for `run` commands
- Using the `backup` command
- Using the `copy` command
- Using the `restore` command
- Using the `recover` command

The last two sets of commands are those used to operate backup, restoration, and recovery of the Oracle database, and the commands used to define scripts to execute backup, restoration, and recovery. Collectively, the commands for backup and recovery are known as the `run` commands because this keyword precedes each of them when issued in RMAN. These operations map directly to API calls. A more complete explanation of the uses for each of the `run` commands appears as part of this section.

The DBA can execute any of these operations with the `run` command, following the general syntax `run` *`command`*. There are four categories of run commands: `backup`, `copy`, `restore`, and `recover`. There are usually some associated allocate channel and `release channel` commands used to handle manipulation of files at the operating-system level. In addition, the DBA can execute SQL DCL statements. DCL stands for data control language, and it includes statements like `alter database enable restricted session` that set up the availability and runtime status of the database. These commands can be executed interactively within RMAN or, alternatively, they can be put into a script and run with RMAN in batch. This section will cover each of these areas.

Oracle8*i* *Availability and Recoverability Enhancements*

In this section, you will cover the following topics on other availability and recoverability enhancements:

- Specifying multiple archivers and destinations
- Automating standby databases
- Opening your database for read operations
- Using LogMiner
- Specifying bounded recovery time
- Detecting data corruption with DBMS_REPAIR

Oracle8*i* introduces many features designed to promote database availability for your organization. In this section, you will learn about several of the new features designed to enhance database availability. The first discussion will cover specifying multiple archive-log destinations and running multiple ARCH processes. The next discussion covers using LogMiner, a new tool in Oracle that allows you to examine the contents of your online redo logs. Specification of bounded recovery time in Oracle8*i* will be covered, as well. Finally, you will learn how to detect data corruption using the DBMS_REPAIR package.

Standby Databases

In this section, you will cover the following topics related to managing new standby database features in Oracle8*i*:

- Automating standby databases
- Opening standby databases for read-only access

The final area of coverage in this chapter relates to the use of standby databases. This feature was introduced in Oracle7 as a method for maintaining a hot spare database. In the event of there being a problem with your production database, the standby database is available for immediate use. This section covers new features for standby databases in Oracle8*i*. You will learn how to automate many aspects of standby database maintenance. You will also learn how to open standby databases for read-only access.

Chapter 30: Oracle8*i* Advanced New Features

In this chapter, you will cover the following advanced topics in Oracle8*i*:

- Advanced queuing
- Net8
- Java in the database

This is the final chapter covering Oracle8*i* new features. It explains the remaining topics required for passing the OCP Oracle8*i* new features upgrade exam. The first topic covered in this chapter is the use and configuration of the advanced queuing feature of the Oracle database. The chapter also covers Net8 in much detail, explaining the new features of this advanced networking tool. Finally, the most Internet-friendly feature of Oracle8*i*—the use of Java in the Oracle database—will be explained.

Advanced Queuing

In this section, you will cover the following topics related to advanced queuing with DBMS_QUEUE:

- Defining advanced queuing concepts and benefits
- Creating and sending messages with `enqueue( )`
- Processing messages with `dequeue( )`
- Administering the queues and the queue table

Consider the most obvious fact about an online application—you issue a command, and the application executes it immediately. This is known as synchronous, or online, processing because of the synchronization of cause and effect. You say do it, and the application does it—hence, you have an online system. Another concept in data processing is the batch processing system. Instead of the result happening immediately, a batch process happens as an event. Both mainframe and Unix users should be familiar with a similar concept—job scheduling. You take a batch process, schedule it to run at a specific time via CRON or another scheduling utility, and the operating system executes the job at the appropriate time. However, without the right tool to manage scheduling, take note of any runtime errors or exceptions, and notify the appropriate person or process, no developer may ever notice when a batch job has failed until the user notices—and by then it's too late. Oracle has built upon the concepts of job scheduling and sending messages between processes to notify others of progress. The result is advanced queuing—the topic of this section.

Net8

In this section, you will cover the following topics on enhancements to Net8 in Oracle8*i*:

- Automatic instance registration
- Load balancing
- Scalability and non-Net8 connectivity
- Connection Manager, pooling, and concentration
- Using Net8 Assistant

Net8, the powerful connectivity management tool for Oracle networks, has undergone a few significant changes in Oracle8*i*. In addition to covering some basic features that already existed in Net8, you will learn about these enhancements. This section will first cover the use of Connection Manager in Net8. You will learn about multiplexing, also known as connection concentration, and about connection pooling. The way that Net8 accomplishes load-balancing tasks over the Oracle network is a topic you will cover, as well. You will learn how Net8 automatically registers instance information for improved connectivity. Some discussion of how Net8 Assistant is used will be offered, along with some new features for this tool in Oracle8*i*.

Java in the Database

In this section, you will cover the following new features involving the incorporation of Java in the Oracle8*i* database:

- Methods for using Java in Oracle8*i*
- Java virtual-machine architecture
- Loading and publishing Java classes
- Other topics on Java and Oracle8*i*

The extensive use of Java in the database is perhaps the most exciting of the new features available in Oracle8*i*. This section will cover the new features for using Java in your Oracle8*i* applications to enhance the use of your Oracle databases by incorporating them with your corporate intranet or with the Internet. In this section, you will cover several new feature areas of Oracle8*i* for use with Java in your database, the various methods for using Java in Oracle8*i*, the architecture of the Java virtual machine, and how JVM is integrated with Oracle8*i*. You will also cover loading and publishing Java classes.

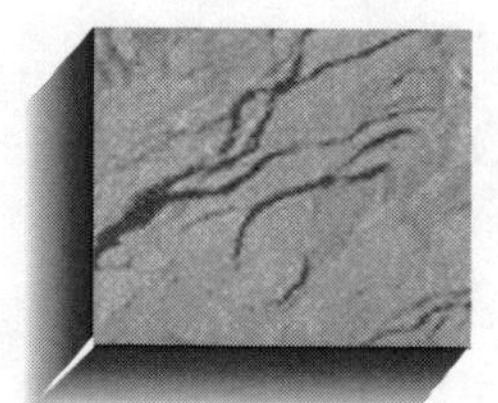

Index

A

Abs ( ) function, 27
Absolute value function, 27
Accept command, 76–78
Access control, user, 177–185
Access, using roles to manage database, 180–182
Account unlock, 467
Accounts
    changing user, 470
    dropping user, 470
    lock status and user sessions, 468
    management, 467, 477
    user, 469
Action, converting data in, 32
Add_months ( ) function, 29–30
Adding
    buffers, 863–867
    columns, 141–143
    database to report command, 626
    new datafiles to tablespaces, 339
    redo logs and members, 331, 573–574
    to storage allocation of tables, 397–398
    tablespace keyword to report command, 626
    tablespaces, 338
Admin apps, identifying in OEM (Oracle Enterprise Manager), 269–271
Admin option, 487
Admin scripts, preparing PL/SQL environment with, 315–317
Administering
    packages, 317–318
    passwords using profiles, 476–480
    stored procedures, 317–318
Administration tools, 267–274
    extrapolating general usage, 274
    identifying admin apps in OEM (Oracle Enterprise Manager), 269–271
    Server Manager line mode, 267–269
Administrative ability, giving along with privileges, 486–489
Administrative authentication, 275
Administrator, DBA and security, 464
Agent
    intelligent, 1035–1036
    running Intelligent, 763–764
Alert files, monitoring, 288–289
ALERT logs, 376, 663–664, 754–757
Aliases, changing column headings with column, 11–13
ALL_CONSTRAINTS view, 118
ALL_views, applying description of, 117
ALL_VIEWS data dictionary, 117
Allocate channel, 623–624
Allocate channel commands, 636
Allocation, 372
    changing user tablespace, 468–469
    See also Deallocation
Alter database add logfile member command, 682
Alter index statement, 424
Alter rollback segment offline statement, issuing, 379
Alter table modify clause, 148
Alter user statement, 492
Altering
    existing users, 468–470
    profiles, 475–476
    roles, 491
Analyze command, 400
Analyzing
    collected data using rules, 966–967
    databases, 966
    network problems, 1101–1106
ANO (advanced network option), configuring components of, 1115–1123
ANO (advanced networking option)
    explained, 1113
    features for authentication, 1114–1115
    features for data transfer, 1114
    using Net8 Assistant to configure, 1119–1120
Application development, 92
Application requirements, tuning different, 790–799
Application tuning, and DBA in large organizations, 800
Application tuning, and DBA in smaller organizations, 800–801
Application tuning, role of DBA in, 799–801
Applications are available for different cartridges, 271
ARCH (archiver process), 331–333, 565
ARCH process, 567–568
Architectural components
    Oracle, 256–267
    stages in processing commitment statements, 266–267
    stages in processing DML statements, 263–265
    stages in processing queries, 261–263
    structures that connect users to Oracle servers, 257–261
Architecture, MTS (multithreaded server), 260
Archive information, obtaining, 325–327
Archived logs, getting information about, 327
Archived redo log files, multiplexing, 583–585
Archived redo logs, displaying information about, 581
Archivelog databases
    opening, 580
    recovering, 674
    recovering after media failure, 675–683
Archivelog mode
    disabling, 580
    enable, 579–580
Archives, 566–568
Archiving
    configuring Oracle for redo log, 577–583
    experiment with, 581
    incomplete recovery with, 702–714
    recovery with, 671–688
    recovery without, 666–671
    turning off, 583
Archiving mode, instance failure in, 672–673
Archiving redo logs, selectively, 581–583
Arithmetic equations, performing, 8–10
Arithmetic, performing on numeric expressions, 9
Assessment, needs, 91–92
Assigning
    database objects to buffer pools, 869–870
    profiles to control resource use, 472–475
Assignments, variable value, 214–215
Astericks (*), 59
@ command, 16
Attributes
    implicit cursor, 222–224
    valid implicit cursor, 224
AUD$ data, 503
AUD$ table, 503
Audit command
    using for object audits, 499
    using for privilege or statement audits, 498–499
Audit configuration, disabling, 500–501
Audit definition shortcuts, 500
Audit information
    managing, 502–503
    protecting, 501
Audit session command, 476
Audit trail information
    DB, 497
    UNIX storing of OS, 497
Auditing
    database, 498–501
    databases, 496–503
    databases and SYSTEM tablespace, 496
    value-based, 497

Auditing information
 maintaining, 502–503
 retrieving, 502–503
Auditing options, viewing enabled, 501–502
Audits, using audit command for object, 499
Authentication
 administrative, 275
 configuring methods, 1120–1122
 controlling password, 489–490
 features for, 1114–1115
 implementation of OS system, 277
 OS, 276–277
 password file, 275–279
 with password file, 277–279
 third-party, 1122
Autoextend, setting up, 339
Automatic indexes, 170
AUTOTRACE, 807–808
Avg ( ) function, 58

B

B-tree index structure, 171–172
B-tree indexes, 791
 and columns, 174
 creating, 421–424
 nonpartitioned, 417–419
Backed up, recovery when datafile is being, 679–681
Background process, 261
Background process I/O, tuning, 903–904
Backing up read-only tablespaces, 593
Backup
 concepts using RMAN, 632–637
 of database, 580
 dictionary views for database, 594–595
 and LOGGING and NOLOGGING modes, 590–591
 OS commands for database, 585–586
Backup of control files, 589
Backup and recovery, 557–607
 architectural components for, 563–565
 business considerations, 559–560
 configuration, 574–585
 considerations, 558–563
 creating level of service, 561
 operational considerations, 559–560
 overview, 557–607
 process evolves with system, 559
 technical considerations, 559–560
Backup and recovery strategy, testing, 561–563
Backup command syntax, 633–635
 specifying options, 633–634
 specifying scope, 634–635
Backup control files
 recovery with, 705–706
 using, 708–709
Backup datafile, recovery without, 678–679
Backup Manager, 683–688
 looking at, 687
 Uses, 614–615
 utility in OEM, 594
Backup prior, database, 708–709
Backup problems, troubleshooting, 639–640
Backup sets, 630–631
Backup sets, datafile, 630
Backups
 creating complete logical, 723–725
 database, 594
 identifying types of RMAN, 629–632
 logical, 586
 more frequent, 718
 not taking after incomplete recovery, 710–711
 offline, 586–587
 online, 586–587
 performing incremental and cumulative, 637–639
 performing offline and online, 587–590
 physical, 585–595, 629–641
 procedure for taking online, 588–590
 Recovery Manager for, 609–651
 types of, 632–633
 using EXPORT to create complete logical, 723–725
 using EXPORT to create incremental logical, 725–727
Backups of control files, taking, 591–593
Bad file, 526
Batch scripts, SQL*Plus, 7
Batch system processing, planning rollback segment numbers for, 373
Behavior, language-dependent, 545–546
Benefits of incremental exports, 727
Bitmap index structure, 173–174
Bitmap indexes, 419–421, 792
Block corruption, checking for, 425
Block defined, 336
Block examples, explain plan code, 820
Block size, determining appropriate, 912–913
Block space utilization parameters, 350–352
Blocking sessions, 381–382
Blocks
 efficient usage of, 911–921
 module use for PL/SQL, 817–820
 optimizing space usage within, 913–914
Bottlenecks, I/O, 898
Buffer
 redo log, 259
 sizing redo log, 875
Buffer cache, 257
 how Oracle manages, 860–861
 monitoring, 872–873
 tuning, 859–873
Buffer-cache hit ratio, calculating, 861–863
Buffer, contention determination for redo log, 874–875
Buffer-hit ratio
 raising with V$RECENT_BUCKET, 864–865
 reducing with V$CURRENT_BUCKET, 865–866
Buffer pools
 assigning database objects to, 869–870
 creating multiple, 867–870
 determing hit ratios for objects in, 871
 sizing multiple, 870–872
BUFFER, setting, 538
BUFFER_POOL column, 870
Buffers
 adding, 863–867
 and latches, 871
 removing, 863–867
Built-in datatypes, 388
Business considerations, backup and recovery, 559–560
Business requirements and tuning, 748–754
Business rules, using triggers to enforce, 431–432
By clause, group, 60–63

C

Cache
 buffer, 257
 dictionary, 257
 hits on dictionary, 852–853
 hits on library, 853–854
 how Oracle manages buffer, 860–861
 library, 257
 monitoring buffer, 872–873
 row, 257, 850
 tuning buffer, 859–873
 tuning dictionary, 849–851
 tuning library, 849–851
Caching
 hardware, 843–844
 table, 873
Calculating buffer-cache hit ratio, 861–863
Call level, 473
Cardinality defined, 176
Cartesian product, 51
Cartridges, applications are available for different, 271
Cascade constraints, 399
Case translators, 26
Catalog
 command, 625
 creating recovery, 617–619
 maintaining recovery, 623–625
 pros and cons of recovery, 617
 resync, 623
 RMAN advantages and recovery, 615–617
Catalog loss, recovering from recovery, 722

Catperf.sql script, 871
Catproc.sql script, 316, 318
CD-ROM, chapters in, 1141
Ceil ( ) function, 27
CHAINED_ROWS table, 915
Chaining, and row migration, 396
Chaining, row, 141
Change command, 624
Changing
  clusters, 446–447
  column headings with column aliases, 11–13
  data in underlying tables, 164
  existing row data, 122–123
  locations in configuration files, 1094–1096
  locations in Net8 Assistant, 1096–1097
  log filenames, 1094–1097
  names of objects, 151–152
  passwords, 182
  storage settings, 340–342
  tablespace sizes, 339–340
  tablespace status, 340–342
  trace settings in Net8 Assistant, 1100
  user accounts, 470
  user tablespace allocation, 468–469
Channel
  allocate, 623–624
  commands, 636
  release, 623–624
Chapters in CD-ROM, 1141
CHAR, 78
CHAR datatype, 108
Character sets
  choosing for databases, 543–545
  databases and national, 544
  EXPORT, 542
  IMPORT, 542
Character strings, converting, 33
Characters
  experimenting with order of, 547
  slash (/), 16
  wildcard (*), 7
CHAR(L), 389
CHECK
  constraints, 104, 429, 435
  integrity constraints, 101
Checking for block corruption, 425
CHECKPOINT_PROCESS, 904
Checkpoints, 566–568
  controlling, 328–330
  specifying frequencies of, 328–329
  synchronizing files, during, 569–571
  tuning, 902
Checksum operations, configuring, 661–663
Checksums
  configuring, 1115–1117
  usage, 1117–1118
Child table, 49
CKPT (checkpoint), 328, 565, 904
Clause
  from, 10
  alter table modify, 148
  DUAL, 10
  explain plan, 801–802
  group by, 60–63
  order by, 18–19
  where, 20–21, 56, 112
Clauses
  having, 70
  where, 822–823
Clearing
  corruption in online redo logs, 662–663
  unarchived redo log, 662
Client configuration files, Net8, 1013–1016
Client preferences, using Net8 Assistant to identify, 1017–1019
Client/servers, growth of, 982–983
Client-side configuration, Net8, 1009–1019
Clients
  configuring for concentration, 1087–1088
  Net8 for, 979–1033
  setting general preferences in Net8 Assistant, 1019
  setting preferred names server for, 1041–1043
Clone defined, 713
Closing databases, 284–285
Cluster-key, defined, 442
Cluster-key index, 445
Cluster segments, 347–348
Clustered tables, 791
Clusters, 440–450
  changing, 446–447
  collisions using hash, 445
  creating, 441–447
  creating hush, 445
  creating index, 443–445
  dictionary information about, 450
  hash, 442, 791
  index, 442–443
  maintaining, 441–447
  removing, 446–447
  tables in, 445
  truncating index, 447
CMADM (Connection Manager Administrator), 1084–1085
CMAN_RULES, 1093
Cman.ora file, 1093
CMCTL (Connection Manager Control utility), 1085–1086
CMGW (Connection Manager Gateway), 1084
Coalescing
  defined, 353
  tablespaces, 353
Code block examples, explain plan, 820
Code in shared memory, pinning, 856
Coding exception handler, 240–241
Collection
  datatypes, 388
  types, 392
Column aliases, changing column headings with, 11–13
Columns in views, 402
Columns, 403
  in, 821
  adding, 141–143
  avoiding functions on indexed, 822–823
  and B-tree indexes, 174
  BUFFER_POOL, 870
  constraint method, 101
  data, 388
  data value for row is NULL, 103
  datatypes of, 435
  DUMMY, 9
  headings with column aliases, 11–13
  and indexes, 174
  modifying, 141–143
  not in, 821
  placing inappropriate data in, 102
  putting together with concatenation, 13–14
  SES$TID, 503
  SESSIONID, 503
  uniqueness of values in, 176
  See also Pseudocolumns
Command
  accept, 76–78
  adding database, to report, 626
  adding tablespace keyword to report, 626
  alter database add logfile member, 682
  analyze, 400
  @, 16
  audit session, 476
  catalog, 625
  change, 624
  copy, 636
  decode ( ), 25
  define, 76
  describe, 402
  NAMESCTL SET, 1055–1056
  NAMESCTL SHOW, 1055–1056
  restore database, 713
  rollback_seg online, 376
Command-line parameters
  for EXPORT, 535
  SQL* loader, 528
Command line parameters, EXPORT, using, 723
Command syntax
  backup, 633–635
  command, 635–636
Commands
  allocate channel, 636
  LSNRCTL SET, 1003
  LSNRCTL show, 1003
  miscellaneous LSNRCTL, 1001–1003
  NAMESCTL general, 1054–1055
  validate structure, 425
Commands for database backup, OS, 585–586
COMMENTS, 315
Commit statements, processing, 266–267
Comparing
  LOB datatypes, 390–391

LONG datatypes, 390–391
LONG RAW datatypes, 390–391
Comparison operations, 51, 215–216
Comparisons
equality, 52
inequality, 52
Composite indexes, 824–825
Composite limits, setting, 474
Composite primary key, 119
Computing, emergence of Internet, 983
Concatenation, putting columns together with, 13–14
Concentration
configuring clients for, 1087–1088
configuring connection, 1086–1088
configuring servers for, 1086–1087
Conditional statement-processing mechanisms, 216
Conditional statements, 215–217
Configuration
of intelligent agent for OEM, 1057–1061
modifying rollback-segment, 907–909
of multithreaded-server (MTS), 1061–1068
Configuration files
changing locations in, 1094–1096
intelligent agent, 1060–1061
Configure ANO options, using Net8 Assistant to, 1119–1120
Configuring
authentication methods, 1120–1122
centralized naming, 1038–1039
checksum operations, 661–663
checksums, 1115–1117
clients for concentration, 1087–1088
components of ANO (advanced network option), 1115–1123
connection concentration, 1086–1088
connection manager, 1082–1093
CRYPTO_SEED, 1118–1119
Database Services, 995–996
dispatchers using initsid.ora, 1063–1065
encryption, 1115–1117
General Parameters, 992–993
listener with Net8 Assistant, 991–997
listening locations, 994–995
mail service in OEM, 764
MTS_MAX_DISPATCHERS, 1064–1065
multiprotocol functionality, 1088–1091
multiprotocol interchange, 1090
names server, 1047–1049
Net8 files, 1011–1017
network access control, 1091–1093
Oracle for redo log archiving, 577–583
paging services in OEM, 764
second listeners, 1004–1007
servers for concentration, 1086–1087
shared servers using initsid.ora, 1065–1066
systems temporarily for particular needs, 796–799
and using trace features, 1097–1098
Connect descriptor defined, 986
Connect string defined, 986
Connection
ending to server process, 988
establishing with names server, 1037
Connection concentration, configuring, 1086–1088
Connection Manager, 1081–1082
capabilities, 1083–1086
configuring, 1082–1093
workings of, 1083–1084
Connection pooling, 1068
Connection pooling using MTS, setting up, 1067–1068
Connection procedure and TNSNAMES, 1016
CONSISTENT parameter, 535
CONSISTENT=Y, 535
Constant declaration, 214
Constraint
deferability, 430–431
enabling disabled, 146
out-of-line, 434
Constraint information, obtaining, 439–440
Constraints, 1150–1151
cascade, 399
CHECK, 104, 429
creating CHECK, 435
creating NOT NULL, 433–434
creating UNIQUE, 435
creating views that enforce, 167
describing integrity, 428–433
disabling, 145–146
enabling, 145–149
implementing data-integrity, 433–436
indexes created by, 110–112
integrity, 100–105
maintaining integrity, 436–439
modifying, 140–153
modifying integrity, 143–145
NOT NULL, 104, 429
NOVALIDATE options for enabling, 148–149
removing, 147–148
rows violating, 438
statuses of, 431
that fail on creation, 144–145
VALIDATE options for enabling, 148–149
Constructing data dictionary views, 313–314
Constructs, logic, 210
Contention, 938-940
detecting allocation latch, 951–952
detecting copy-latch, 951–952
possible causes for, 938–940
reducing LRU-latch, 955–956
resolving copy-latch, 951–955
resolving freelist, 945–947
resolving in emergency, 941–942
resolving LRU latch, 955–956
resolving problem of copy-latch, 954
resolving problem of redo allocation, 954
resolving redo allocation-latch, 951–955
tools to detect lock, 940–941
See also Lock contention
Contention, determining for redo allocation, 953–954
Contention, determining for redo log buffer, 874–875
Contention issues, resolving, 945–956
Control
transaction, 124–127
user access, 177–185
Control files, 522–523
backup of, 589
and combined data, 523–524
data putting in, 524
defined, 522
examining contents, 320–321
for fixed-width data, 524–525
incomplete recovery using backup, 708–709
managing, 318–324
mirroring, 323–324, 572
multiplexing, 323–324, 571–572
new features, 618–619
obtaining information about, 321–323
reconstructing damaged, 719–720
reconstructing lost, 719–720
recovery catalog, gains most information from, 618
recovery with backup, 705–706
taking backups of, 591–593
use of, 319–320
Control resource use, creating and assigning profiles to, 472–475
Control structures, 850
Controlling
availability of roles, 492–493
checkpoints, 328–330
log switches, 328–330
OS, 489–490
password authentication, 489–490
space used by tables, 397–399
Conventional-path data loads, 531–534
Conventional path, EXPORT, 538
Conventional SQL* loader, 522–534
Conventions, table-naming, 105–107
Conversion functions, 31–33
Converting
character strings, 33
data in action, 32
between different ROWID formats, 402–403
ROWID pseudocolumns, 403

Copies in different directories, multiple, 280
Copies, making image, 631
Copy command, 636
Copy command syntax, 635–636
Copy-latch contention
 detecting, 951–952
 resolving, 951–955
 resolving problem of, 954
Copy latches, 953–954
Copy operations, RMAN does not skip blocks in, 636
Copying existing tables, 396
Correlated subqueries, 68–69
Corruption errors
 diagnosing database, 719
 recovering from database, 719
Cost-based optimization, Oracle, 812
Cost-optimizer goal, setting session-wide, 810–811
Costs, setting resource, 474
Count ( ) function, 58–60
Count (*), 59
Count (1), 59
Count (ROWID), 59
Counters
 incrementing, 219
 for loop statements, have built in, 219
Create user, 465
Creating
 B-tree indexes, 421–424
 CHECK constraints, 435
 clusters, 441–447
 complete logical backups, 723–725
 complex views, 162–167
 database objects, 89–137, 466
 database statements, 295
 databases in Oracle, 293–296
 foreign keys, 434–435
 hash clusters, 445
 incremental logical backups, 725–727
 index clusters, 443–445
 indexes, 174–176
 keep pool from default pool, 867–869
 miscellaneous database objects, 139–198
 multiple buffer pools, 867–870
 new database users, 465–467
 NOT NULL constraints, 433–434
 Oracle databases, 289–296
 outer joins, 53–55
 parameter files, 279–281
 primary keys, 433–434
 private synonym, 185
 profiles to control resource use, 472–475
 public synonym, 185
 recovery catalog, 617–619
 recycle pool from default pool, 867–869
 RMAN scripts, 626–627
 roles, 490–492
 rollback segments with storage settings, 374–376
 scripts, 627
 second database, 713
 sequence statement, 154–155
 sequences, 154–156
 simple views, 162–167
 tables of databases, 100–113
 tables with integrity constraints, 100–105
 tables with storage settings, 393–397
 tablespaces, 337–339
 temporary tablespaces, 344–345
 tuning session, 964
 UNIQUE constraints, 435
 users, 895
 views that enforce constraints, 167
CRYPTO_SEED, configuring, 1118–1119
Cryptographic Toolkit explained, Oracle, 1113
CTXROL rollback segment, 908
Cumulative backups, performing incremental and, 637–639
Cumulative exports, benefits of, 727
Cumulative exports, running, 725–727
CURRVAL pseudocolumn, 153–154, 156–157
Cursor attributes
 implicit, 222–224
 valid implicit, 224
Cursor, fetch values from, 262
Cursor for loops, writing, 233–234
Cursor handling, explicit, 225–234
Cursors, 210
 declaring and using explicit, 228–231
 implicit versus explicit, 226–228
 parameters and explicit, 231–233

D

Data
 column, 388
 control file for fixed-width, 524–525
 deleting from Oracle database, 123
 displaying from multiple tables, 48–57
 editing input, 964–966
 gathering input, 964–966
 group, 63
 imported from export dump file, 541
 input, 965
 loading, 520–542
 making changes to existing row, 122–123
 normalization, 98
 normalized, 792
 putting in control file, 524
 putting in order with subqueries, 71–72
 reading from disk for users, 259
 row, 388
 stored in datafile, 522
 viewability of, 66
 viewing input, 964–966
 warehouses, 792
Data-access methods, using, 791–793
Data, analyzing collected, 966–967
Data, AUD$, 503
Data block, managing, 388
Data-change activity, minimizing impact on, 794
Data changes
 moving from memory to disk, 264–265
 referencing sequences in, 157–158
Data, changing in underlying tables, 164
Data dictionary, 275
 ALL_VIEWS, 117
 displaying role information from, 495
 finding information about, 315
 getting index information from, 426–427
 obtaining profile information from, 480
 Oracle, 113–119
 querying the, 116–119
 using, 314–315
 viewing information from, 640–641
Data dictionary information, retrieving about tables, 401–402
Data dictionary views, 160–162, 312–318
 constructing, 313–314
Data in action, converting, 32
Data in columns, placing inappropriate, 102
Data-integrity constraints, implementing, 433–436
Data integrity, managing, 427–440
Data loads, 519–553
 conventional-path, 531–534
 direct-path, 531–534
 performance tuning, 530–531
 problem resolution, 530–531
Data, manipulating, 119–127
 deleting data from Oracle database, 123
 importance of transaction control, 124–127
 inserting new rows into tables, 120–122
 making changes to existing row data, 122–123
Data modeling, 90–100
 basic types of data relationships, 94–95
 de-normalized, 792
 normalized, 792
 reading ERD (entity-relationship diagram), 96–100
 relational database components, 95–96
 stages of system development, 91–94
Data recovery, 701–743
 See also Recovery
Data relationships, basic types of, 94–95

Data, reorganizing, 520–542
Data, reorganizing with EXPORT and IMPORT, 534–542
Data, selecting, 3–44
    limiting selected output, 18–21
    refining selected output, 18–21
    selecting rows, 4–17
    using single-row functions, 21–33
Data selection, advanced, 48–87
DATA tablespace, 354, 894
Data transfer, 1114
Data transmission, network security risks during, 1111–1112
Database
    adding to report command, 626
    auditing, 498–501
    auditing versus value-based auditing, 497
    configuration, 892–904
    creating second, 713
    Java in, 1161–1162
    Net8 listener handling connections to second, 1005
    opening archivelog, 580
    registering, 621–623
    resetting, 621–623
    resynchronizing, 621–623
    security, 93
    shutting down, 580
    tools, 348
    types of failure in, 655–656
Database access, using roles to manage, 180–182
Database applications, tuning, 789–839
Database architecture, 255–309
    basics of, 255–309
    creating Oracle databases, 289–296
    managing Oracle instance, 274–289
    Oracle architectural components, 256–267
    using administration tools, 267–274
Database backups, 580, 594
    dictionary views for, 594–595
    OS commands for, 585–586
Database command, restore, 713
Database components, relational, 95–96
Database corruption errors, diagnosing, 719
Database corruption errors, recovering from, 719
Database datatypes, 211–212
    See also Nondatabase datatypes
Database design, 90–100
    basic types of data relationships, 94–95
    reading ERD (entity-relationship diagram), 96–100
    relational database components, 95–96
    stages of system development, 91–94
    tuning logical, 791–793
Database failure and recovery, 653–699
    troubleshooting, 654–666
    types of failure, 654–666
Database failure situations, human aspects of, 655
Database having host machine, Oracle, 900
Database, interacting with Oracle, 220–225
    SQL statements in PL/SQL, 220–221
    transaction processing in PL/SQL, 225
    using implicit cursor attributes, 222–224
Database management, Oracle8*i*, 1142–1146
Database objects, 367–413
    managing, 415–460
    using IMPORT to recover, 728–730
    view is
    /, 114
Database objects, creating, 89–137, 466
    creating tables of databases, 100–113
    data modeling, 90–100
    database design, 90–100
    manipulating data, 119–127
    Oracle data dictionary, 113–119
Database objects, creating miscellaneous, 139–198
    indexes, 169–176
    modifying constraints, 140–153
    modifying tables, 140–153
    sequences, 153–160
    user access control, 177–185
    views, 160–169
Database objects from dump files, importing, 541
Database password file, users in, 279
Database recovery, 581
    complete procedures, 683–684
    with IMPORT, 729–730
Database Resource Manager, 1148
Database rollback segments, public and private, 909
Database security model, Oracle, 177–178
Database Services, configuring, 995–996
Database statements, create, 295
Database structure, physical, 311–365
    managing, 311–365
Database transparency, using synonyms for, 183–185
Database tuning, 747–786, 845–846
    ALERT logs, 754
    events, 754
    miscellaneous areas of, 933–976
    trace files, 754
    See also Tuning
Database use, managing, 463–516
Database users, creating new, 465–467
    account unlock, 467
    create user, 465
    default tablespace, 466
    identified by, 465
    password expire, 466–467
    profile, 466
    quota, 466
    temporary tablespace, 466
Databases
    analyzing, 966
    auditing, 496–503
    choosing character sets for, 543–545
    closing, 284–285
    creating tables of, 100–113
    logical structures of, 336–337
    maintaining, 324
    and national character, 544
    object relational, 1153
    opening, 281–283
    recovering archivelog, 674
    recovering noarchivelog, 667–668
    standby, 1159–1160
    storing network configuration on regional, 1047–1049
Databases after media failure, recovering archivelog, 675–683
Databases, creating Oracle, 289–296
    preparing OS (operating system), 290–291
    preparing parameter files, 291–293
Databases in Oracle, creating, 293–296
Datafiles, 336, 523–526
    adding to tablespaces, 339
    back up sets, 630
    data stored in, 522
    managing, 335–345
    recovering for ROLLBACK tablespace, 676
    recovering for SYSTEM tablespace, 676
    recovery for damage non-SYSTEM, 676–678
    recovery for damages non-ROLLBACK, 676–678
    recovery for deleted non-ROLLBACK, 676–678
    recovery for deleted non-SYSTEM, 676–678
    recovery for SYSTEM tablespace, 676
    recovery procedures, 685–686
    recovery when backed up, 679–681
    recovery without backup, 678–679
    referring to, 679
Datafiles missing, starting Oracle with, 715–717
Datafiles of SYSTEM tablespaces, 294–295
Datatypes
    built-in, 388
    CHAR, 108
    collection, 388
    and column definitions, 108–110
    of columns, 435
    comparing LOB, 390–391
    comparing LONG, 390–391
    comparing LONG RAW, 390–391
    database, 211–212
    distinguishing Oracle, 388–393
    nondatabase, 212

Oracle8 scalar, 388–390
relationship, 388
scalar, 388
user-defined, 388
VARCHAR2, 108
for variable, 78
DATE, 390
Date format, National Language Set (NLS), 30
Date functions, 29–31
Date, joining from more than one table, 50–53
DB audit trail information, 497
DB_BLOCK_LRU_LATCHES parameter, 956
DBA
in large organizations, 800
role in application turning, 799–801
and security administrator, 464
in smaller organizations, 800–801
DBA_COL_PRIVS, 489
DBA_CONS_COLUMNS, 440
DBA_CONSTRAINTS, 439–440
DBA_SYS_PRIVS, 489
DBA_TAB_PRIVS, 489
DBMS_APPLICATION_INFO, 817–820
DBMS_BACKUP_RESTORE, 613
DBMS_OUTPUT.put_line ( ), 210
DBMS_RCVCAT, 612–613
DBMS_RCVMAN, 613
DBMS_SESSION package, 493
DBVERIFY
parameters, 659–661
tool, 660
utility, 659–661
DBW0 performance, 903–904
DBWR, 328
DBWR (database writer process) role of, 265
DDL (data-definition language), 100, 935–937
De-normalized data modeling, 792
Deadlocks, identifying and preventing, 943–945
Deallocation, extent, 372
Declaration, constant, 214
Decode ( )
command, 25
function, 24
Dedicated servers, 259–260
Default pool
creating keep pool from, 867–869
creating recycle pool from, 867–869
defined, 867
objects stored in, 870
DEFAULT profile, 479
Default role, 492
Default storage options defined, 338
Default tablespace, 466
Default value for size, 444
Define command, 76
Defining prompts, 78
Defining variables, 76–78
See also Undefining variables
Definitions, column, 108–110
Delete statement, indexes slow down table, 794
DELETE_CATALOG_ROLE, 503
Deleting data from Oracle database, 123
Describe command from Server Manager, 402
Describing triggers, 428–433
Descriptor, connect, 986
Detect lock contention, tools to, 940–941
Detecting
allocation latch contention, 951–952
copy-latch contention, 951–952
I/O problems, 896–898
lock contention, 934–945
row migration, 915–916
Development, application, 92
Diagnosing
database corruption, 719
problems, 663–666
tuning problems, 808–809
DICT dictionary view, 315
Dictionary
ALL_VIEWS data, 117
data, 275
displaying role information from data, 495
getting index information from data, 426–427
obtaining profile information from data, 480
querying data, 116–119
using data, 314–315
viewing information from data, 640–641
Dictionary cache, 257
hit, 850
hits on, 852–853
tuning, 849–851
Dictionary-cache performance, improving, 850–851
Dictionary comments, viewing on objects, 152–153
Dictionary information
about clusters, 450
about IOTs, 450
on privileges, 489
Dictionary, Oracle data, 113–119
available dictionary views, 114–116
querying data dictionary, 116–119
Dictionary views, 870
available, 114–116
constructing data, 313–314
containing NLS parameters, 547
data, 160–162, 312–318
for database backup, 594–595
DICT, 315
obtaining rollback segment information from, 378–380
for triggers, 440
V$SESSION, 288
Dimension tables, 812
Direct-path
data loads, 531–534
EXPORT, 538
Direct-path INSERT, loading data using, 520–522
Direct path SQL* loader, 522–534
Direct writes for sorts, 960–961
DIRECT=Y, 538
Directories, multiple copies in different, 280
Disabled constraints, enabling, 146
Disabling
archivelog mode, 580
audit configuration, 500–501
constraints, 145–146
roles, 492–493
triggers, 438
Disaster-recovery plan, components of, 560–561
Discard file defined, 527
Disk
moving data changes from memory to, 264–265
space and sorts, 960
striping, 901
usage, 844
Disk files, how synchronized, 570
Disk utilization, tuning, 891–931
Dispatcher
associating with service, 1065
process, 260–261, 987
registering with listener, 1067
Dispatchers using initsid.ora, configuring, 1063–1065
Displaying
more output, 78
wait events, 759–762
Distinct keyword, 70–71
Dividing concurrent transactions, 910
DML (data-manipulation language), 120, 935–937
parallel, 1155
processing statements, 263–265
Downtime, methods for minimizing, 715–719
more frequent backups, 718
starting Oracle with datafiles missing, 715–717
using fast transaction rollback, 715
using parallel recovery, 717–718
Driving table defined, 826
Dropping
existing users, 468–470
indexes, 425–426
profiles, 475–476
tables, 149–150, 398–399
triggers, 438
user accounts, 470
DSS (decision support systems), 790, 795–796
DUAL clause, 10
DUAL table, 9
DUMMY column, 9
Dump files, 534
data imported from export, 541
export, 727
importing database objects from, 541
Duplex defined, 583

Dynamic performance views, 765–768
instance-wide, 766–767
for session-level tuning, 767–768
and utilities, 765–778

E

Editing input data, 964–966
Employee, 96
EMPLOYEE, select * from, 394
Employer, 96
Enable ARCHIVELOG mode, 579–580
Enabling
disabled constraints, 146
network access control, 1091–1093
resource limits, 474
roles, 492–493
tracing, 1104
triggers, 438
Enabling archivelog mode, 580
Enabling constraints, 145–149
NOVALIDATE options for, 148–149
VALIDATE options for, 148–149
Encryption
configuring, 1115–1117
usage, 1117–1118
Ending connection to server process, 988
Enhancements, 93
index, 1151–1152
parallel query, 1148
Enterprise Manager, 394
Enterprise Manager, Oracle, 335, 1143–1144
Entries, index, 418
Environments
security in network, 1081–1082, 1111–1123
troubleshooting network, 1081–1082, 1093–1110
Equality comparisons, 52
Equality operations, number of, 56
Equations, performing arithmetic, 8–10
Equijoins, 52
ERD (entity-relationship diagram)
from ERD to LDM, 96–98
reading, 96–100
role of ordinality, 98–100
ERP (enterprise resource planning), 800
Error handling, 210, 235–241
Error stack, log file, 1101–1106, 1102–1103
Errors
diagnosing database corruption, 719
ORA-00600, 289
read consistency, 381
recovering from database corruption, 719
trace file, 1108–1109
user, 656
weird, 289
Errors while connecting, Net8, 1017
Event history, 763
Event set library, 763
Events, 754
outstanding, 763
predefined, 762–765
retrieving and displaying wait, 759–762
retrieving wait, 763
setting in OEM, 764
wait, 898
Exception handlers, 209, 235
coding, 240–241
flow control passing, 241
and predefined exceptions, 236
Exceptions
identifying common, 239–240
internal, 237–238
predefined, 235–236
types of, 235–238
user-defined, 236–237
Exceptions in Oracle8, dropping and re-creating, 403
EXCEPTIONS tables, 146–147, 437–438
cleaning up, 438
Oracle, 403
Exclusive table lock mode, 126
Executable section, 209
Execute statement, 262, 264
Executing UTLBSTAT, 770
Execution plan, explaining, 801–803
Exists, using instead of in, 821–822
Expenses, 96
Explain plan clause, 801–802
Explain plan code block examples, 820
Explicit cursors, 226–228
declaring and using, 228–231
handling, 225–234
and parameters, 231–233
EXPORT, 586, 714
best performance of, 538
command-line parameters for, 535
conventional path, 538
direct path, 538
invoking on direct path, 727–728
reorganizing data with, 534–542
running in full mode, 541
runtime modes, 535–538
tools, 470
use of, 534–535
using command line parameters, 723
using to create complete logical backups, 723–725
using to create incremental logical backups, 725–727
utilities, 722–730
EXPORT character sets, 542
Export dump file, 727
Export dump file, data imported from, 541
Exports
benefits of cumulative, 727
benefits of incremental, 727
running cumulative, 725–727
running incremental, 725
taking complete, 723–725
Expressions, performing arithmetic on numeric, 9
EXTENDS, sizing extents by monitoring, 910–911
Extent
deallocation, 372
defined, 336
lifespan, 355
Extent allocation, reorganizing table, 920–921
Extents
controlling use by segments, 348–350
sizing, 910–911, 918–921
sizing by monitoring EXTENDS, 910–911
sizing by monitoring WRAPS, 910–911
EXTPROC defined, 1007

F

Fact tables, 812
Failure
instance, 657, 672–673
media, 576, 658, 666–667
recovering archivelog databases after media, 675–683
statement, 655
user-process, 656
Fast transaction rollback, using, 715
Fetch values from cursor, 262
FIFO (first in, first out), 988
File authentication
password, 275–279
with password, 277–279
File errors, trace, 1108–1109
File system, storing network configuration on local, 1044–1046
Filename location, specifying, 636
Filenames, changing log, 1094–1097
Files
backup of control, 589
bad, 526
changes to configuration, 1101
changing locations in configuration, 1094–1096
cman.ora, 1093
combined data and control, 523–524
configuring Net8, 1011–1017
control, 522–523
creating parameter, 279–281
data imported from export dump, 541
discard, 527
disk, 570
distributing to reduce I/O contention, 898–900
dump, 534
export dump, 727
formatting trace, 1107–1110
incomplete recovery using backup control, 708–709
initsid.ora, 324, 572, 613, 797
intelligent agent configuration, 1060–1061
locations and use of trace, 757–759
log, 527, 1102–1103
log and trace, 663–666

maintaining redo log, 324–335, 330–332
managing control, 318–324
mirroring control, 323–324, 572
monitoring alert, 288–289
monitoring trace, 288–289
moving, 685–686
multiplexing archived redo log, 583–585
multiplexing control, 323–324, 571–572
multiplexing redo log, 330–332
NAMES.ORA configuration, 1045–1046
Net8 client configuration, 1013–1016
online redo log, 325
paging, 848
parameter, 527
planning online redo log, 332–333
preparing parameter, 291–293
reconstructing control, 719–720
reconstructing lost control, 719–720
recovery with backup control, 705–706
restoring to different locations, 668–669
swap, 848
synchronizing during checkpoints, 569–571
taking backups of control, 591–593
trace, 376, 754
users in database password, 279

First in, first out, 988
Fixing views, 168
Flow control passing exception handler, 241
For-loop statements, 219–220
For-loop statements, have built-in counters, 219
Foreign keys, 49, 428–429
creating, 434–435
integrity constraints, 101
referencing columns in parent tables, 435
Formatting trace files, 1107–1110
Four, Rule of, 373
Fragmentation, 353–355
tablespace, 354–355
Freelist contention, resolving, 945–947
From clause, 10
FULL parameters, 538
Functions, 205
abs ( ), 27
absolute value, 27
add_months ( ), 29–30
avg ( ), 58
avoiding on indexed columns, 822–823
ceil ( ), 27
conversion, 31–33
count ( ), 58–60
date, 29–31
decode ( ), 24
defined, 206
hash, 442
last_day ( ), 30
length( ), 26
length ( ), 60
max ( ), 59
min ( ), 59
mod ( ), 28
months_between, 30
new_time ( ), 30
round ( ), 28
sign ( ), 28
single-row, 21–33
sqrt ( ), 28
substr ( ), 26
sum ( ), 60
to_char ( ), 32
to_date ( ), 32
to_number ( ), 32
trunc ( ), 28–29
using in select statements, 24–29
vsize ( ), 29

G

Gathering input data, 964–966
General Parameters, configuring, 992–993
General preferences, client, 1019
Generating
lists, 625–626
reports, 625–626
Global scope defined, 66
Goal, setting session-wide cost-optimizer, 810–811
Granting
object privileges, 182–183
privileges, 485–489
system privileges, 178–179
Group by clause, 60–63
Group data, excluding with having, 63
Group functions
identifying available, 57–58
ignore NULL values by default, 60
and their uses, 57–64
using, 58–60
Group number and status information, 574

H

Hardware caching, 843–844
Hash
function, 442
joins, 815–817
key, 442
Hash clusters, 442, 791
collisions using, 445
creating, 445
Having
clauses and subqueries, 70
excluding group data with, 63
Headings, column, 11–13
Highwatermarks
table, 398
truncating tables and, 151
History, event, 763
Hit ratio
calculating buffer-cache, 861–863
defined, 849
Hit ratios, determining for objects in buffer pools, 871
Hits on library cache, 853–854
Host machine
Oracle having database, 900
running Oracle on, 900
Host machines, users utilizing, 476
Host naming method, connections using, 1009–1011

I

I/O
issues, 892–904
tuning, 844, 903–904
I/O bottlenecks, 898
I/O contention, distributing files to reduce, 898–900
combos to attempt, 898–899
combos to avoid, 899–900
I/O problems, detecting, 896–898
Identifying
deadlocks, 943–945
network problems, 1104–1106
object privileges, 484–485
system privileges, 481–484
Image copies, making, 631
Implementing
data-integrity constraints, 433–436
triggers, 433–436
tuning recommendations, 967–968
Implicit cursor attributes, 222–224
Implicit cursors and SQL statements, 226
Implicit versus explicit cursors, 226–228
IMPORT, 586, 714
character sets, 542
command-line parameters for, 539
database recovery with, 729–730
with FROMUSER and TOUSER parameters, 470
reorganizing data with, 534–542
running in various modes, 539–541
understanding, 730
use of, 534–535
using to recover database objects, 728–730
utilities, 722–730
IMPORT runs, troubleshooting, 541–542
Importing database objects from dump files, 541
Improvements
optimizer, 1149
query, 1149
In
column, 821
column not, 821
using exists instead of, 821–822
Inactive redo log, 681–682
Incomplete recovery
with archiving, 702–714
backups not taking after, 710–711
cancel-based, 705
change-based, 703–704

and losing data, 703
performing, 706–709, 708–709
procedure, 706–707
recover command using for, 707
time-based, 704–705
using backup control files, 708–709
using RMAN in, 711–713
when to use, 703–706
Incremental backups, performing, 637–639
Incremental exports, running, 725
Index
associated, 436
associated unique, 430
cluster-key, 445
enhancements, 1151–1152
entries, 418
entry header, 418
segments, 346
Index clusters, 442–443
creating, 443–445
truncating, 447
Index, corresponding to primary key of table, 112
Index creation, avoiding sorts in, 959
Index-creation issues, sizing and miscellaneous, 423–424
Index information, getting from data dictionary, 426–427
Index-reorganization options, miscellaneous, 424–425
Index statement, alter, 424
Index structure
B-tree, 171–172
bitmap, 173–174
INDEX tablespace, 354, 894
Indexed columns, avoiding functions on, 822–823
Indexes, 169–176
automatic, 170
B-tree, 174, 791
bitmap, 174, 419–421, 792
composite, 824–825
created by constraints, 110–112
creating, 174–175
creating B-tree, 421–424
different types and uses, 417–421
dropping, 425–426
guidelines for creating, 176
managing, 416–427
manual, 170
monitoring, 917–918
monitoring use of, 917–918
nonpartitioned B-tree, 417–419
partitioning, 1154–1155
removing, 175–176
reorganizing, 424–425
reverse-key, 420–421
slow down table delete statement, 794
slow down table insert statement, 794
slow down table update statement, 794
structures and operations, 171–174
tuning, 917–918
uses of, 171
Inequality comparisons, 52
Information
generate redo, 264
Instance Manager not prompting for, 272
managing audit, 502–503
protecting audit, 501
viewing from data dictionary, 640–641
Initsid.ora
configuring dispatchers using, 1063–1065
configuring shared servers using, 1065–1066
file, 324, 572, 613, 797
parameter, 547, 798, 1068, 1122
Inline, storing data, 110
Inner joins, 52, 55
Input data
collecting about workload, 965
collection, 965
editing, 964–966
gathering, 964–966
viewing, 964–966
INSERT, loading data using direct-path, 520–522
Insert statement, indexes slow down table, 794
Inserting new rows into tables, 120–122
Instance
recovering, 657
restarting, 956
shutting down, 284–285
starting, 281–283
Instance and media recovery, structures for, 656–659
Instance failure, 657
Instance failure, in archivelog mode, 672–673
Instance Manager, 271
not prompting for login information, 272
using configuration settings, 797–798
Instance, managing Oracle, 274–289
closing databases, 284–285
creating parameter files, 279–281
getting and setting parameter values, 286–287
managing sessions, 287–288
monitoring alert files, 288–289
monitoring trace files, 288–289
opening databases, 281–283
setting up OS, 275–279
setting up password file authentication, 275–279
shutting down instance, 284–285
starting instance, 281–283
Instance startup, brining rollback segments online at, 376
Instance-wide dynamic performance views, 766–767
Integrity constraints
CHECK, 101
creating tables with, 100–105
describing, 428–433
FOREIGN KEY, 101
maintaining, 436–439
NOT NULL, 101
PRIMARY KEY, 101
and table columns, 102
types of, 102
UNIQUE, 101
Intelligent agent, 1035–1036
configuration files, 1060–1061
miscellaneous ways to manage, 1059
purpose of, 1057–1058
running, 763–764
using LSNRCTL to start and stop, 1058–1059
Intelligent agent for OEM, configuration of, 1057–1061
Internal exceptions, 237–238
Internet computing, emergence of, 983
IOT (index-organized table), segments, 347–348
IOTs (index-organized tables), 368, 388, 416, 440–450, 792, 1152
dictionary information about, 450
partitioned, 1156
and ROWID, 449
using, 447–449
IPC (interprocess communication), 1083

J

Java in database, 1161–1162
Join operations
improving performance for, 443
properly constructing, 826
Join operators, outer, 55
Join order, setting up, 826–827
Join views, updatable, 165–167
Joining
data from more than one table, 50–53
table to itself, 55–56
two tables, 49
Joins, 52
creating outer, 53–55
hash, 812, 815–817
inner, 52, 55
self, 56
See also Equijoins

K

Keep pool
defined, 867
sizing, 870–871
Key-preserved table, 165–167
Keys
cluster, 442
composite primary, 119
creating foreign, 434–435
creating primary, 433–434
foreign, 49, 428–429
hash, 442
primary, 49, 112, 428, 430
unique, 429, 430

Keystrokes, avoiding unnecessary, 527
Keywords, 105
 distinct, 70–71
 %rowtype, 213
 that require subqueries, 69–70
 %type, 212–213

L

Language-dependent behavior, 545–546
Large pool, 567
Last_day ( ) function, 30
Latch
 redo allocation, 875–876
 types of requests for redo-allocation, 952–953
 wait ratio, 951
Latch contention
 detecting, 951–952
 resolving LRU, 955–956
Latch-contention, identifying situations, 947–951
Latch issues, resolving, 945–956
Latches
 available, 948–949
 available in Oracle, 947
 and buffers, 871
 categories of, 947–948
 changing numbers of LRU, 956
 copy, 953–954
 obtaining, 950–951
LDM, from ERD to, 96–98
Leaf nodes, 418
Length ( ) function, 26, 60
LGWR (log writer process), 265, 331–334
 defined, 328
 performance tuning, 904
Library cache, 257
 hits, 850
 hits on, 853–854
 improving performance, 851
 tuning, 849–851
Library, event set, 763
Lifespan, 353–355
Lifespan, extent, 355
Line parameters, EXPORT, using command, 723
List, LRU, 567
Listener address, specifying for MTS, 1066–1067
Listener process, 260–261, 987
Listener shutdown, troubleshooting, 1000–1001
Listeners
 configuring second, 1004–1007
 configuring with Net8 Assistant, 991–997
 handling connections to second database, 1005
 multiple, 1003–1008
 naming, 996
 registering dispatchers with, 1067
 starting second, 1007–1008
 starting using LSNRCTL, 998–999
 stopping using LSNRCTL, 999–1001
Listening locations, configuring, 994–995
Listing
 session memory, 858–859
 UGA (User Global Area), 858–859
Lists, generating, 625–626
Load files at run time, 526–528
Load state, direct, 531
Loading data, 520–542
Loading data, using direct-path INSERT, 520–522
LOB (large object)
 comparing datatypes, 390–391
 partitioned, 1156
 segments, 347–348
Local naming method, 1011–1017
Local scope, 66
Locations in configuration files, changing, 1094–1096
Locations, restoring files to different, 668–669
Lock
 row-exclusive, 127
 share row, 127
Lock categories and scope, 935–937
 exclusive, 936
 row exclusive, 936–937
 row share, 937
 share, 936
 share row exclusive, 937
 share update, 937
Lock contention
 monitoring and detecting, 934–945
 tools to detect lock, 940–941
Locking, levels of, 935–938
Locking problems, preventing, 942–943
Locks, 126–127
 acquiring, 264, 938
 held until transaction completes, 938
Log
 ALERT, 376, 663–664
 clearing unarchived redo, 662
 redo, 705
 and trace files, 663–666
Log archiving, configuring Oracle for redo, 577–583
Log buffer, sizing redo, 875
Log file
 defined, 527
 error stack, 1102–1103
Log file problems, troubleshooting redo, 334–335
Log filenames, changing, 1096–1097
Log files
 maintaining redo, 324–335, 330–332
 multiplexing archived redo, 583–585
 multiplexing redo, 330–332
 online redo, 325
 planning online redo, 332–333
Log groups, online redo, 295
Log, inactive redo, 681–682
Log information, obtaining, 325–327
Log parameters, setting, 1094–1101
Log switches
 controlling, 328–330
 defined, 328
LOG_ARCHIVE_FORMAT examples, 580–581
LOG_ARCHIVE_FORMAT parameter, 581
LOG_ENTRY_PREBUILD_THRESHOLD, 876
LOG_SMALL_ENTRY_MAX_SIZE, 876
Logarithm, mantissa is decimal part of, 390
LOGGING mode, backup implications of, 590–591
Logic constructs and process flow, 210
Logical backups, 586
Logical record, 526
Logical ROWID, 1144
Login information, Instance Manager not prompting for, 272
Logs
 ALERT, 754
 clearing corruption in online redo, 662–663
 displaying information about archived redo, 581
 getting information about archived, 327
 location and use of ALERT, 754–757
 multiplexing online redo, 572–573
 multiplexing redo, 571–574
 online redo, 331, 574
 recovering after losing active redo, 709–711
 recovery implications for not archiving redo, 575–577
 redo, 331–333, 566–568
 selectively archiving redo, 581–583
LONG datatypes, comparing, 390–391
LONG RAW datatypes, comparing, 390–391
Lookup tables, 812
Loop-exit statements, 217–218
Loops
 for-loop statements, 219–220
 using, 217–220
 while-loop statements, 218
 writing cursor for, 233–234
Lpad ( ) operation, 25
LRU-latch contention
 reducing, 955–956
 resolving, 955–956
LRU latches, changing numbers of, 956
LRU list defined, 567
LSNRCTL
 SET commands, 1003
 show commands, 1003
 starting listener using, 998–999
 stopping listener using, 999–1001
 using to start and stop intelligent agent, 1058–1059
LSNRCTL commands, miscellaneous, 1001–1003

M

Machines, users utilizing host, 476
Magic numbers, 214
Magic value in programming, 214
Mail service, configuring in OEM, 764
Mainframe computing paradigm, 982
Maintaining
 auditing information, 502–503
 clusters, 441–447
 databases, 324
 integrity constraints, 436–439
 names service information, 1044–1045
 recovery catalog, 623–625
 redo log files, 324–335, 330–332
 rollback segments, 376–378
 triggers, 436–439
Manage intelligent agent, miscellaneous ways to, 1059
Management
 account, 477
 memory, 1147–1148
 password, 1145
 RMAN and media, 611
 tablespace, 341, 1145
 user-account, 467
Manager
 backup, 683–688
 Connection, 1081–1082
 Database Resource, 1148
 Enterprise, 394
 Instance, 797–798
 Oracle Enterprise, 335, 339, 341, 375, 1143–1144
 Recovery, 609–651, 1157
 RMAN, 683–688
 Schema, 394
 Server, 375, 402
 Storage, 335, 341, 375
 Tablespace, 335
Managing
 audit information, 502–503
 control files, 318–324
 data block, 388
 data integrity, 427–440
 database objects, 367–413, 415–460
 database use, 463–516
 datafiles, 335–345
 indexes, 416–427
 names server with NAMESCTL, 1049–1057
 privileges, 480–490
 resource use, 471–480
 roles, 490–495
 rollback segments, 368–382
 sessions, 287–288
 space within tablespaces, 336
 tables, 387–403
 tablespaces, 335–345
 temporary segments, 383–387
 users, 464–471
Manipulating data, 119–127
Mantissa is decimal part of logarithm, 390
Manual indexes, 170
Max ( ) function, 59
MAXLOGFILES, 333
MAXLOGMEMBERS, 333
Media failure, 576, 658
 in noarchivelog mode, 666–667
 recovering archivelog databases after, 675–683
Media management, RMAN and, 611
Media recovery, structures for instance and, 656–659
Memory
 ensuring they sorts happen in, 958–959
 listing session, 858–859
 management, 1147–1148
 moving data changes from, 264–265
 real, 848
 session, 858–859
 tuning, 841–889, 843–844
 virtual, 848
Memory area
 Oracle user's, 259
 sizing used for sorting, 958–959
Migration
 analyzing tables to check integrity and, 400–401
 row, 141, 400
Min ( ) function, 59
Mirroring control files, 323–324, 572
Mod ( ) function, 28
Mode
 disabling archivelog, 580
 enable ARCHIVELOG, 579–580
 enabling archivelog, 580
 instance failure in archivelog, 672–673
 media failure in noarchivelog, 666–667
 running Oracle, in ARCHIVELOG, 576–577
 running Oracle in NOARCHIVELOG, 575–576
Model, OSI (open systems interface) network, 989–991
Modeling, data, 90–100
Modes
 backup implications of LOGGING, 590–591
 backup implications of LOGGING and NOLOGGING, 590–591
 EXPORT runtime, 535–538
 optimizer, 809–812
 RMAN can run in few different, 613
 running IMPORT in various, 539–541
Modifying
 columns, 141–143
 constraints, 140–153
 integrity constraints, 143–145
 roles, 490–492
 rollback-segment configuration, 907–909
 sequence definitions, 158–159
 tables, 140–153
 views, 168
Modifying sequences, beware of effects of, 159
Modularity, PL/SQL, 204–205
Monitoring
 alert files, 288–289
 buffer cache, 872–873
 indexes, 917–918
 information about existing users, 470–471
 lock contention, 934–945
 trace files, 288–289
Monitoring use of indexes, technique 1, 917–918
Monitoring use of indexes, technique 2, 918
Months_between function, 30
Moving data changes from memory to disk, 264–265
Moving files, 685–686
MTS-DISPATCHERS, parameter, 1067
MTS (multithreaded server), 858, 987, 1035–1036
 specifying listener address for, 1066–1067
MTS (multithreaded server) architecture, 260, 1036
 components of, 1061–1063
 configuration of, 1061–1068
 setting up connection pooling using, 1067–1068
MTS_DISPATCHERS, 1068
MTS_LISTENER_ADDRESS parameter, 1066
MTS_MAX_DISPATCHERS, configuring, 1064–1065
Multiplexing
 archived redo log files, 583–585
 control files, 323–324, 571–572
 online redo logs, 572–573
 redo log files, 330–332
 redo logs, 571–574
Multiprotocol functionality, configuring, 1088–1091
Multiprotocol interchange, configuring, 1090

N

N joined tables, 53
Named pipes, 994
Names, 1035–1036
 running on different machines, 1037
 use and configuration of, 1036–1057
Names of objects, changing, 151–152
Names server for clients, setting preferred, 1041–1043
Names server location defined, 1039–1041
Names servers
 configuring, 1047–1049
 establishing connection with, 1037
 managing with NAMESCTL, 1049–1057
 stopping, 1053

Names service information, maintaining, 1044–1045
NAMESCTL
general commands, 1054–1055
managing names server with, 1049–1057
SET command, 1055–1056
SHOW command, 1055–1056
starting names server with, 1050–1053
NAMES.ORA configuration file, 1045–1046
Naming
configuring centralized, 1038–1039
Net8 Assistant used to configure centralized, 1037–1043
Naming methods
local, 1011–1017
setting order of preference for, 1018
National character sets, databases and, 544
NCHAR(L), 389
Needs
assessment, 91–92
configuring systems temporarily for particular, 796–799
Nested PL/SQL blocks, 213
Nested subqueries, 64–66
Nested table, 392
Net8, 1161
architecture, 985–991
architecture components, 989–991
for client and server, 979–1033
client configuration files, 1013–1016
describing networking solutions, 984–985
emergence of Internet computing, 983
errors while connecting, 1017
establishing server connections procedure, 986–988
growth of client/server, 982–983
identifying networking trends and problems, 980–983
mainframe computing paradigm, 982
miscellaneous features of, 984–985
overview, 980–985
resolving service-name lookup, 1019
server-side configuration, 991–1008
Net8 Assistant
changing locations in, 1096–1097
changing trace settings in, 1100
setting client general preferences in, 1019
sqlnet.ora parameter modified by, 1121
TNSNAMES setup using, 1011–1013
using to configure ANO options, 1119–1120
using to configure centralized naming, 1037–1043
using to identify client preferences, 1017–1019
Net8 Assistant, configuring listener with, 991–997
configuring Database Services, 995–996
configuring General Parameters, 992–993
configuring listening locations, 994–995
configuring miscellaneous services, 996
naming listener, 996
Net8, client-side configuration, 1009–1019
connections using host naming method, 1009–1011
Net8 files, configuring, 1011–1017
Net8 listener, handling connections to second database, 1005
Network access control
configuring, 1091–1093
enabling, 1091–1093
Network-access control, applied only on TCP/IP network, 1091
Network components, setting trace levels for network, 1098–1100
Network configuration
storing on local file system, 1044–1046
storing on regional database, 1047–1049
Network environments
security in, 1081–1082, 1111–1123
troubleshooting, 1081–1082, 1093–1110
Network model, OSI (open systems interface), 989–991
Network, network-access control applied only on TCP/IP, 1091
Network problems
analyzing, 1101–1106
identifying, 1104–1106
solving, 1104–1106
troubleshooting, 1101–1106
Network process, 261
Network security, risks during data transmission, 1111–1112
Network tick, 1068
Networking products, security features in Oracle, 1112–1113
Networking solutions, describing, 984–985
Networking trends and problems, identifying, 980–983
New_time ( ) function, 30
NEXTVAL pseudocolumn, 154
NEXTVAL pseudocolumns, 156–157
NLS (National Language Set), 389
enhancements, 1147
and OCP, 543
NLS (National Language Set) date format, 30
NLS (National Language Support), 519–553, 543–547, 730, 1147
NLS parameters, dictionary vies containing, 547
NLS setting, obtaining information about, 546–547
Nls_date-format, 30
NLS_NUMERIC_CHARACTERS, 547
NMP (named pipes), 994
Noarchivelog databases
recovering, 667–668
recovering with RMAN, 669–671
Noarchivelog mode, media failure in, 666–667
Node, multiple listeners on same, 1003–1008
Nodes, leaf, 418
NOLOGGING mode, backup implications of, 590–591
Non-SYSTEM rollback segments, 369
Nondatabase datatypes, 212
Nonpartitioned B-tree indexes, 417–419
Normalization defined, 98
Normalized data modeling, 792
NOT NULL constraints, 104, 429
NOT NULL constraints, creating, 433–434
NOT NULL integrity constraints, 101
Novalidate, 436
NOVALIDATE options for enabling constraints, 148–149
NS (network session), 1107
NSP, 1107
NULL, column data value for row is, 103
NULL constraints, NOT, 429
NULL values
by default, 60
handling, 10–11
NUMBER(L,P), 390
Numbers
magic, 214
storing binary version of, 390
Numeric expressions, performing arithmetic on, 9
NVARCHAR2(L), 390

O

Object audits, using audit command for, 499
Object management, Oracle8*i*, 1150–1153
Object privileges
available, 179–180
distinguishing between system privilege, 485
granting, 182–183
identifying, 484–485
revoking, 182–183
Object relational databases, 1153
Object striping, 901
Object, view is database, 114
Objects
in buffer pools, 871
creating miscellaneous database, 139–198

database, 367–413, 869–870
managing database, 415–460
managing large, 1152
partitioned, 1156
pinning, 849
pinning in shared pool, 855–857
referencing several, 500
stored in default pool, 870
using IMPORT to recover database, 728–730
viewing dictionary comments on, 152–153
Objects, changing names of, 151–152
Objects, creating database, 89–137, 466
creating tables of databases, 100–113
data modeling, 90–100
database design, 90–100
manipulating data, 119–127
Oracle data dictionary, 113–119
Objects from dump files, importing database, 541
Objects imported, order of, 541
Obtain reimbursement, 96
OCP and NLS, 543
OCP Candidate Guide, 543, 1144
OEM (Oracle Enterprise Manager), 269, 614–615
backup manager utility in, 594
configuration of intelligent agent for, 1057–1061
configuring mail service in, 764
configuring paging services in, 764
identifying admin apps in, 269–271
setting predefined events using, 762–765
setting up events in, 764
tool, 754
using components, 271–274
OEM, setting predefined events, using
event set library, 763
outstanding events, 763
registrations, 763
retrieving wait events, 763
running Intelligent Agent, 763–764
OEM tools, using appropriate, 777–778
Offline
not taking tablespace, 382
rollback_seg, 377
Offline backups
performing, 587–590
recovery, 586–587
Offline statement, 379
Offline statement, issuing alter rollback segment, 379
Offline, tablespace can be taken, 340
Offline tablespace, recovery issues for, 721–722
OLTP (online transaction processing), 257, 373
OLTP (online transaction-processing), 790
systems, 373, 795
systems demand of, 793–795
Online backups
performing, 587–590
procedure for taking, 588–590
recovery of, 586–587
Online command, rollback_seg, 376
Online redo logs, 331, 574
clearing corruption in, 662–663
files, 325, 332–333
groups, 295
multiplexing, 572–573
Online, rollback_seg, 377
Opening archivelog database, 580
Opening databases, 281–283
Operational considerations, backup and recovery, 559–560
Operations
comparison, 51, 215–216
lpad ( ), 25
number of equality, 56
RMAN does not skip blocks in, 636
rpad ( ), 25
Operator, outer join, 55
Optimization
Oracle cost-based, 812
rule-based, 811–812
Optimizer improvements, 1149
Optimizer modes, 809–812
ORA-00600 errors, 289
Oracle
cost-based optimization, 812
creating databases in, 293–296
Cryptographic Toolkit explained, 1113
data dictionary, 113–119
latches available in, 947
managing buffer cache, 860–861
obtaining temporary segment information from, 386–387
physical backups without RMAN, 585–595
recovery structures and processes, 563–574
recovery with archiving, 671–688
running in ARCHIVELOG mode, 576–577
running in NOARCHIVELOG mode, 575–576
running on host machine, 900
starting with datafiles missing, 715–717
Oracle ANO (advanced networking option) explained, 1113
Oracle blocks, efficient usage of, 911–921
Oracle, configuring for redo log archiving, 577–583
close database, shut down instance, 577–578
enable ARCHIVELOG mode, 579–580
opening archivelog database, 580
specifying initialization parameters, 578–579
start up instance, mount database, 579
Oracle database
deleting data, from, 123
having host machine, 900
interacting with, 220–225
preparing, 1047
security model, 177–178
Oracle databases, creating, 289–296
Oracle datatypes, distinguishing, 388–393
Oracle Enterprise Manager, 335, 339, 341, 375, 1143–1144
Oracle EXCEPTIONS table, 403
Oracle Expert
features, 962–963
Oracle Tuning Pack and using, 963
performance tuning and changing rules in, 966
resources, 962
tuning with, 961–968
Oracle instance, managing, 274–289
Oracle networking products, security features in, 1112–1113
Oracle, options for starting, 282–283
Oracle ROWIDs, remembering components of, 392
Oracle security server explained, 1113
Oracle SGA, preventing OS from paging or swapping, 848
Oracle, stopping, 284
shutdown abort, 285
shutdown immediate, 285
shutdown normal, 285
shutdown transactional, 285
Oracle-supplied packages installation of, 318
Oracle-supplied packages not available on server, 316
Oracle tools, 801–809
Oracle tools, using to diagnose SQL performance, 801–809
Oracle Tuning Pack and using Oracle Expert, 963
Oracle, using PL/SQL to access, 203–204
Oracle7 versus Oracle8 ROWIDs, 391–392
Oracle8, EXCEPTIONS in, 403
Oracle8 ROWIDs, Oracle7 versus, 391–392
Oracle8 scalar datatypes, 388–390
Oracle8*i*, availability and recoverability enhancements, 1160
Oracle8*i* advanced new features, 1161–1163
advanced queuing, 1161–1162
Java in database, 1162–1163
Net8, 1162
Oracle8*i* database management, 1143–1147
configuration, 1143–1144
installation, 1143–1144
migrating server, 1144
Oracle Enterprise Manager, 1144–1145
ROWID format in Oracle8*i*, 1145
Oracle8*i* Internals, 1147–1151
Database Resource Manager, 1149
materialized views, 1150–1151
memory management, 1148–1149
NLS enhancements, 1148

optimizer improvements, 1150
parallel query enhancements, 1149
PL/SQL enhancements, 1148
query improvements, 1150
SQL *Plus enhancements, 1148
Oracle8*i*, new features topics, 1141–1163
miscellaneous security enhancements, 1147
password management, 1146
tablespace management, 1146
Oracle8*i* object management, 1151–1154
constraints, 1151–1152
index enhancements, 1152–1153
IOTs (index-organized tables), 1153
managing large objects, 1153
miscellaneous manageability enhancements, 1152
object relational databases, 1154
parallel DML and queries, 1156
partitioned IOTs, 1157
partitioned LOBs, 1157
partitioned objects, 1157
partitioning indexes, 1155–1156
partitioning tables, 1155
partitioning techniques, 1157
Oracle8*i* recoverability, 1158–1161
availability and recoverability enhancements, 1160
introducing Recovery Manager, 1158
standby databases, 1160–1161
using RMAN catalog commands and reports, 1159
using RMAN run commands and scripts, 1159–1160
Oracle8*i*, ROWID format in, 1145
ORAPWD utility, 277
Order by clause, 18–19
Ordinality, role of, 98–100
OS audit trail information, UNIX storing of, 497
OS (operating system), 277
authentication, 276–277
commands for database backup, 585–586
controlling, 489–490
generic tuning, 842–849
preparing, 290–291
setting up, 275–279
OS (operating system) usage, 841–889
and tuning memory, 841–889
OS tuning, 845–846
OS tuning, primary steps for, 843–845
OSI (open systems interface) network model, 989–991
Out-of-line constraint, 434
Outer join operator, 55
Outer joins, creating, 53–55
Output, displaying more, 78
Output, limiting selected, 18–21
order by clause, 18–19
where clause, 20–21
Output, refining output, order by clause, 18–19
Output, refining selected, 18–21
where clause, 20–21
Output report, UTLBSTAT/UTLESTAT, 768–776
OWNER parameters, 538

P

Packages, 205
administering, 317–318
defined, 206–208
standard, 312–318
Packets defined, 1107
Paging described, 848–849
Paging file, 848
Paging services, configuring in OEM, 764
Parallel query enhancements, 1148
Parallel recovery, 717–718
Parameter files, 527
creating, 279–281
preparing, 291–293
Parameter values, getting and setting, 286–287
Parameters
command-line, 528, 535, 539
CONSISTENT, 535
DB_BLOCK_LRU_LATCHES, 956
DBVERIFY, 659–661
dictionary views containing NLS, 547
and explicit cursors, 231–233
EXPORT using command line, 723
FULL, 538
IMPORT with FROMUSER and TOUSER, 470
initsid.ora, 547, 798, 1068, 1122
LOG_ARCHIVE_FORMAT, 581
MTS_DISPATCHERS, 1067
MTS_LISTENER_ADDRESS, 1066
OWNER, 538
setting log, 1094–1101
setting trace, 1094–1101
sqlnet.ora, 1121
TABLE, 538
TIMED_STATISTICS initsid.ora, 770
Parent tables, foreign keys referencing columns in, 435
Parfile defined, 526, 528
Parse statement, 262, 264
Partitioned IOTs, 1156
Partitioned LOBs, 1156
Partitioned objects, 1156
Partitioning
indexes, 1154–1155
tables, 1154
Partitioning techniques, Oracle8*i*, 1156
Password
aging and rotation, 477
complexity verification, 477–479
expiration and user sessions, 468
expire, 466–467
management, 1145
management resource limits, 479
Password files
authentication, 275–279
authentication with, 277–279
users in database, 279
Passwords
changing, 182
and user sessions, 468
Passwords, administering using profiles, 476–480
Path
EXPORT direct, 538
invoking EXPORT on direct, 727–728
Path, EXPORT conventional, 538
Pay, 96
Pctfree, 350, 795
determining values for, 351
options, 916
specifying, 395–396
usage examples, 914
Pctfree=25, 914
Pctfree=5, 914
Pctused, 350
determing value for, 351
options, 916
specifying, 395–396
usage examples, 914
Pctused=50, 914
Pctused=85, 914
Perfmon (Performance Monitor), 896
Performance
DBW0, 903–904
diagnosing SQL, 801–809
See also Dynamic performance
Performance tuning, 93
and changing rules in Oracle Expert, 966
data loads, 530–531
LGWR, 904
Performance tuning diagnosis, miscellaneous tools for, 777–778
Performance views
dynamics, 765–768
instance-wide dynamic, 766–767
utilities and dynamic, 765–778
Performing, arithmetic equations, 8–10
Performing, arithmetic on numeric expressions, 9
Performing, incomplete recovery, 706–709, 708–709
Performing, incremental and cumulative backups, 637–639
Performing, select statements, 502
PGA (Program Global Area), 259, 858
Oracle user's memory area, 259
shared pool or, 260
Physical backups, 629–641
Physical backups, Oracle, 585–595
Physical record defined, 526
Pinning objects defined, 849
Pipes, named, 994
PL/SQL, 201–251
constant declaration, 214
cursors, 210
database datatypes, 211–212
enhancements, 1147
error handling, 210
explicit cursor handling, 225–234
interacting with Oracle database, 220–225
introducing, 201–251

named, 205
nondatabase datatypes, 212
overview of, 202–211
procedure, 500
process flow and logic constructs, 210
%rowtype keyword, 213
SQL statements in, 220–221
transaction processing in, 225
%type keyword, 212–213
using to access Oracle, 203–204
PL/SQL blocks
anonymous, 208–209
components, 209–210
developing, 211–215
module use for, 817–820
nested, 213
unnamed, 208–209
PL/SQL blocks, developing
declaring variables, 211–214
using variables, 211–214
variable value assignments, 214–215
PL/SQL, controlling process flow, 215–220
conditional statements, 215–217
process flow, 215–217
using loops, 217–220
PL/SQL environment, preparing with admin scripts, 315–317
PL/SQL program constructs, 204–211
modularity, 204–205
PLAN_TABLE, 777, 801–802, 820
Planning
number of rollback segments, 369–374
rollback segment numbers, 373
rollback segment numbers for batch system processing, 373
size of rollback segments, 369–374
PMON (process monitor), 565
Point-in-time recovery, tablespace, 713–714
Pooling, connection, 1068
Pools
assigning database objects to buffer, 869–870
creating keep pool from default, 867–869
creating recycle pool from default, 867–869
default, 867
determining hit ratios for objects in buffer, 871
keep, 867
large, 567
objects stored in default, 870
recycle, 867
sizing keep, 870–871
sizing multiple buffer, 870–872
sizing recycle, 872
Prebuilding redo entries, 876
Predefined exceptions, 235–236
Predefined exceptions and exception handlers, 236
Preparing Oracle database, 1047
Preventing deadlocks, 943–945
Primary key, 49, 112
Primary keys, 428, 430
composite, 119
creating, 433–434
integrity constraints, 101
Prioritization, tuning background process, 844–845
Private rollback segments, 369, 909
Private synonym, creating, 185
Privilege audits, using audit command for, 498–499
Privileges
available object, 179–180
dictionary information on, 489
giving administrative ability along with, 486–489
granting, 485–489
granting and revoking
open to public, 489
granting object, 182–183
granting system, 178–179
identifying object, 484–485
identifying system, 481–484
managing, 480–490
revoking, 485–489
revoking object, 182–183
revoking system, 179
select any table, 766
users and system, 487
Proactive tuning, 752
Problems, diagnosing, 663–666
Procedures, 205
administering stored, 317–318
can have subprocedures, 213
defined, 205–206
PL/SQL, 500
Process
ARCH, 567–568
CKPT, 904
dispatcher, 260–261, 987
listener, 260–261, 987
server, 261
SMON (system monitor), 353
Process flow, 215–217
controlling PL/SQL, 215–220
and logic constructs, 210
Processes
background, 261
network, 261
versus threads, 846–848
Processing
commit statements, 266–267
planning rollback segment numbers for batch system, 373
transaction, 225
Processing queries, stages in, 261–263
Product, Cartesian, 51
Profile information, obtaining from data dictionary, 480
Profiles
administering passwords using, 476–480
altering, 475–476
DEFAULT, 479
dropping, 475–476
Programming, magic value in, 214
Prompts, defining, 78
Protecting audit information, 501
Pseudocolumns, 105
converting ROWID, 403
CURRVAL, 153–154, 156–157
NEXTVAL, 154, 156–157
Public rollback segments, 369, 909
Public synonym, creating, 185
PUBLIC user, 489

Q

Queries, 64–66, 1155
improvements, 1149
processing, 261–263
star, 812–817
See also Subqueries
Query enhancements, parallel, 1148
Queuing, advanced, 1160–1161
Quota, 466
Quota 0 on SYSTEM, specifying, 469
Quota for tablespaces, unlimited, 471
Quotas, and tablespaces, 466

R

RAW(L), 390
RDBMS (relational database management system), 50, 141, 261, 522
Read consistency errors, 381
Read-only tablespaces
backing up, 593
recovery issues for, 721–722
Reading
data from disk for users, 259
ERD (entity-relationship diagram), 96–100
Real memory defined, 848
Reconstructing damage control files, 719–720
Reconstructing lost control files, 719–720
Record
logical, 526
physical, 526
Recover command using for incomplete recovery, 707
Recover database objects, using IMPORT to, 728–730
Recoverability
Oracle8*i*, 1157–1160
and tablespaces, 570–571
Recovering
after losing active redo logs, 709–711
archivelog databases, 674
archivelog databases after media failure, 675–683
catalog and RMAN, 711
from database corruption errors, 719
instance, 657
noarchivelog databases, 667–668
noarchivelog databases with RMAN, 669–671
from recovery catalog loss, 722

for ROLLBACK tablespace datafiles, 676
for SYSTEM tablespace datafiles, 676
Recovery catalog
component definitions, 616
creating, 617–619
gains most information from control file, 618
maintaining, 623–625
maintenance, 620–628
pros and cons of, 617
RMAN advantages and, 615–617
Recovery catalog loss, recovering from, 722
Recovery issues, 714–722
diagnosing database corruption errors, 719
methods for minimizing downtime, 715–719
for offline tablespace, 721–722, 721–722
for read-only tablespace, 721–722, 721–722
reconstructing damage control files, 719–720
reconstructing lost control files, 719–720
recovering from database corruption errors, 719
recovering from recovery catalog loss, 722
Recovery Manager, 1157
for backups, 609–651
overview Oracle, 610–620
physical backups using, 629–641
See also RMAN (Recovery Manager)
Recovery operation, complete, 673
Recovery procedures
datafile, 685–686
tablespace, 684–685
Recovery
with archiving, 671–688
and backup, 557–607
with backup control files, 705–706
backups not taking after incomplete, 710–711
cancel-based incomplete, 705
change-based incomplete, 703–704
changed-based incomplete, 703–704
for damage non-SYSTEM datafiles, 676–678
for damages non-ROLLBACK datafiles, 676–678
database, 581
for deleted non-ROLLBACK datafiles, 676–678
for deleted non-SYSTEM datafiles, 676–678
implications for not archiving redo logs, 575–577
implications for offline and online backups, 586–587
incomplete with archiving, 702–714
parallel, 717–718
performing incomplete, 706–709, 708–709
RMAN allows for more robust, 686
RMAN using in incomplete, 711–713
status in progress, 682
structures and processes, 563–574
structures for instance and media, 656–659
for SYSTEM tablespace datafile, 676
tablespace point-in-time, 713–714
time-based incomplete, 704–705
when datafile is being backed up, 679–681
when inactive redo log is lost, 681–682
when to use incomplete, 703–706
without archiving, 666–671
without backup datafile, 678–679
See also Backup and Recovery, Incomplete recovery
Recovery with IMPORT, database, 729–730
Recycle pool, defined, 867
Recycle pool, sizing, 872
Redo allocation
latch, 875–876
resolving problem of, 954
Redo allocation, determining contention for, 953–954
Redo allocation-latch contention, resolving, 951–955
Redo-allocation latch, types of requests for, 952–953
Redo entries, prebuilding, 876
Redo information, generate, 264
Redo log archiving, configuring Oracle for, 577–583
Redo log buffer, 259
determining contention for, 874–875
sizing, 875
Redo log, clearing unarchived, 662
Redo log file problems, troubleshooting, 334–335
Redo log files
maintaining, 324–335, 330–332
multiplexing, 330–332
multiplexing archived, 583–585
online, 325
planning online, 332–333
Redo log groups, online, 295
Redo logs, 566–568
adding and removing, 573–574
can be obtained from V$LOG, 574
clearing corruption in online, 662–663
displaying information about archived, 581
inactive, 681–682
multiplexing, 571–574
multiplexing online, 572–573
online, 331, 574
planning for speedy recovery, 332–333
recovering after losing active, 709–711
recovery implications for not archiving, 575–577
selectively archiving, 581–583
suggestions, 705
Redo logs and members
adding, 331
removing, 331
Redo mechanisms, tuning, 873–876
Redo operations, reducing, 875–876
Reducing redo operations, 875–876
Reference tables, 812
Reference types, 392
Referencing
several objects, 500
several statements, 500
Regional database, storing network configuration on, 1047–1049
Registering
database, 621–623
dispatchers with listener, 1067
module use for PL/SQL blocks, 817–820
Registrations, 763
Reimbursement, obtain, 96
Relational databases
components, 95–96
object, 1153
Relationship
datatypes, 388
role-user, 491
Release channel, 623–624
Relocating tablespaces, 342–343
Remembering components of Oracle ROWIDs, 392
Removing
buffers, 863–867
clusters, 446–447
constraints, 147–148
indexes, 175–176
redo logs and members, 331, 573–574
roles, 493–494
sequences, 159–160
views, 169
Reorganizing
data, 520–542
indexes, 424–425
table extent allocation, 920–921
Report command
adding database to, 626
adding tablespace keyword, 626
adding tablespace keyword to, 626
Report generation, options for, 625–626
Report, UTLBSTAT/UTLESTAT output, 768–776
Reports, generating, 625–626
Report.txt. contents of, 771–776
Resetting database, 621–623
Resizing, table-extent, 919–920
Resolving
contention issues, 945–956
copy-latch contention, 951–955

freelist contention, 945–947
latch issues, 945–956
LRU latch contention, 955–956
redo allocation-latch contention, 951–955
row migration, 915–916
Resource costs, setting, 474
Resource limits
enabling, 474
individual, 473
setting individual, 473
Resource Manager, Database, 1148
Resource use, managing, 471–480
Restarting instance, 956
Restore database command, 713
Restoring files to different locations, 668–669
Resync catalog, 623
Resynchronizing database, 621–623
Retrieving
auditing information, 502–503
wait events, 759–763
Reverse-key indexes, 420–421
Reviewing tuning recommendations, 967
Revoking object privileges, 182–183
Revoking privileges, 485–489
Revoking system privileges, 179
RMAN backups
concepts using, 632–637
identifying types of, 629–632
RMAN, features and components
DBMS_BACKUP_RESTORE, 613
DBMS_RCVCAT, 612–613
DBMS_RCVMAN, 613
RMAN (Recovery Manager), 565, 610, 683–688
advantages and recovery catalog, 615–617
allows for more robust recovery, 686
can run in few different modes, 613
catalog commands and reports, 1158
connecting to, 619–620
determining when to use, 610–614
does not skip blocks in copy operations, 636
features and components, 612–613
and media management, 611
physical backups Oracle without, 585–595
and recovering catalog, 711
recovering noarchivelog databases with, 669–671
run commands and scripts, 1158–1159
setup and modes, 613
using in incomplete recovery, 711–713
when not to use, 612
RMAN scripts
creating, 626–627
running, 626–627
storing, 626–627
Role information, displaying from data dictionary, 495
Role-user relationship, 491
Roles
altering, 491
controlling availability of, 492–493
creating, 490–492
default, 492
disabling, 492–493
enabling, 492–493
managing, 490–495
modifying, 490–492
predefined, 494–495
removing, 493–494
using to manage database access, 180–182
Rollback, 125–126
Rollback segment, 263
allocating, 535
configuration, modifying, 907–909
CTXROL, 908
private, 369
Rollback segment information, obtaining from dictionary views, 378–380
Rollback segment number, determining, 910
Rollback segment numbers, planning, 373
Rollback segment offline statement, issuing alter, 379
Rollback-segment performance, using V$ views to monitor, 905–907
Rollback segment problems, troubleshooting, 380–382
blocking sessions, 381–382
insufficient space for transactions, 380–381
not taking tablespace offline, 382
read consistency errors, 381
Rollback segments, 346–347
acquiring, 399
allocating to transactions, 911
brining online at instance startup, 376
creating with storage settings, 374–376
how transactions use, 369–372
maintaining, 376–378
managing, 368–382
number and size of, 909–911
planning number of, 369–374
planning size of, 369–374
private, 909
public, 369, 909
sizing batch, 373–374
sizing OLTP, 373–374
tuning, 904–911
Rollback-segments, shrinkage, 909
ROLLBACK tablespace, 354, 893
ROLLBACK tablespace datafiles, recovering for, 676
Rollback, using fast transaction, 715
Rollback_seg offline, 377
Rollback_seg online, 377
Rollback_seg online command, 376
Round ( ) function, 28
Row cache, 257
Row cache defined, 850
Row chaining, 141
Row, column data value for, 103
Row data, 388
Row data, making changes to existing, 122–123
Row exclusive able lock mode, 126
Row-exclusive lock, 127
Row migration, 141
and chaining, 396
detecting, 915–916
resolving, 915–916
using analyze command to detect, 400
Row share table lock mode, 126
Row with value of X, 9
ROWID formats
converting between different, 402–403
in Oracle8*i*, 1144
ROWID pseudocolumns, converting, 403
ROWIDs, 105
defined, 59
and IOTs, 1144
logical, 1144
Oracle7 versus Oracle8, 391–392
remembering components of Oracle, 392
rows in IOTs have no, 449
table defined, 172
Rows
inserting into tables, 120–122
in IOTs have no ROWID, 449
tables with many many, 810
violating constraints, 438
Rows, selecting, 4–17
changing column headings with column aliases
> also main, 11–13
editing SQL queries within SQL*Plus, 14–17
handling NULL values, 10–11
performing arithmetic equations, 8–10
putting columns together with concatenation, 13–14
writing select statements, 6–8
%rowtype keyword, 213
Rpad ( ) operation, 25
RS (row share) table lock mode, 126
Rule-based optimization, 811–812
Rule of Four, 373, 910
Rules
analyzing collected data using, 966–967
using triggers to enforce business, 431–432
Running
cumulative exports, 725–727
IMPORT in various modes, 539–541
incremental exports, 725
Intelligent Agent, 763–764
names on different machines, 1037

Oracle in ARCHIVELOG mode, 576–577
Oracle in NOARCHIVELOG mode, 575–576
Oracle on host machine, 900
RMAN scripts, 626–627
scripts, 628
SQL*Loader, 528–530
Runtime, entering variables at, 73–75
Runtime, load files at, 526–528
Runtime modes, EXPORT, 535–538
Runtime variables, 72–78
Runtime variables, automatic definition of, 75–76
RX (row exclusive) table lock mode, 126

S

S (share) table lock mode, 126
SALES_FACT_TABLE, 814
SAVEPOINT, 126
Scalar datatypes, 388
Scalar datatypes, Oracle8, 388–390
Scheduling, tuning background process prioritization and, 844–845
Schema
defined, 6, 8
Manager, 394
SCNs (system change numbers), 266, 570, 703–704
Scopes
global, 66
local, 66
variable, 66–67, 213
Scripts
catperf.sql, 871
catproc.sql, 316, 318
creating, 627
creating RMAN, 626–627
preparing PL/SQL environment with admin, 315–317
putting slash (/) characters on lines before, 16
running, 628
running RMAN, 626–627
running SQL statements from, 16
storing RMAN, 626–627
Security
features in Oracle networking products, 1112–1113
in network environments, 1081–1082, 1111–1123
Security administrator and DBA, 464
Security, database, 93
Security enhancements, miscellaneous, 1146
Security model, Oracle database, 177–178
Security server explained, Oracle, 1113
Segments
acquiring rollback, 399
allocating space for temporary, 385–386
cluster, 347–348
controlling use of extents by, 348–350
defined, 336
how transactions use rollback, 369–372
index, 346
IOT (index-organized table), 347–348
LOB (large object), 347–348
locating, 353–355
maintaining rollback, 376–378
managing rollback, 368–382
managing temporary, 383–387
non-SYSTEM rollback, 369
private rollback, 369
public rollback, 369
rollback, 263, 346–347
sizing batch rollback, 373–374
sizing OLTP rollback, 373–374
table, 346
temporary, 346–347, 386–387
tuning rollback, 904–911
types of temporary, 383–385
Select * from EMPLOYEE, 394
Select any table privilege, 766
Select statements, performing, 502
SELECT_CATALOG_ROLE role, 905
Selecting
data, 3–44
rows, 4–17
Self join, 56
Semicolons, 16
Semicolons, using to end SQL statements, 7
Sequence definitions, modifying, 158–159
Sequence statement, create, 154–155
Sequences, 153–160
beware of effects of modifying, 159
creating, 154–156
referencing in data changes, 157–158
removing, 159–160
role of, 153–154
using, 156–158
Server connections, establishing, 986–988
Server for client, setting preferred names, 1041–1043
Server Manager, 375, 402
Server Manager line mode, 267–269
Server process, 259, 261
ending connection to, 988
think of as genie, 259–260
users connecting to, 260–261
Server-side configuration, Net8, 991–1008
Servers, 982–983
configuring for concentration, 1086–1087
configuring names, 1047–1049
dedicated, 259–260
establishing connection with names, 1037
migrating, 1143
names, 1049–1057, 1050–1053
Net8 for, 979–1033
Oracle-supplied packages not available on, 316
shared, 260
stopping names, 1053
structures that connect users to Oracle, 257–261
See also Client/servers
Service, associating dispatcher with, 1065
Service-name lookup, Net8 resolving, 1019
SES$TID column, 503
Session command, audit, 476
Session level, 473
Session memory, listing, 858–859
Session-wide cost-optimizer goal, setting, 810–811
SESSIONID column, 503
Sessions, managing, 287–288
Set transaction, 124–125
Set_role ( ), 493
Setting
composite limits, 474
log parameters, 1094–1101
order of preference for naming methods, 1018
predefined events using OEM, 762–765
preferred names server for clients, 1041–1043
resource costs, 474
session-wide cost-optimizer goal, 810–811
trace level for network components, 1098–1100
trace parameters, 1094–1101
Setting, client general preferences in Net8 assistant, 1019
Setting parameter values, getting and, 286–287
Setting up
connection pooling using MTS (multithreaded server) architecture, 1067–1068
join order, 826–827
SGA (System Global Area), 257
buffer cache, 257
Oracle's primary memory component, 257
preventing OS from paging or swapping Oracle, 848
redo log buffer, 259
shared pool, 257
Share row exclusive table lock mode, 126
Share row lock, 127
Share table lock mode, 126
Shared memory, pinning code in, 856
Shared pool
flushing, 857
pinning objects in, 855–857
reserved space, tuning, 857–858
sizing, 854–855
tuning, 849–859
Shared pool hit percentage, measuring, 852–854
Shared pool or PGA, locating user session info:, 260
Shared servers, 260
Shared servers, configuring, 1065–1066
Shared SQL area, 849
Shutdown
abort, 285
immediate, 285

normal, 285
transactional, 285
Shutting down
database, 580
instance, 284–285
SID (session ID), 941
Sign ( ) function, 28
Single-row functions, 21–33
conversion functions, 31–33
date functions, 29–31
explained, 22–24
using functions in select statements, 24–29
Size, default value for, 444
Sizing
batch rollback segments, 373–374
extents, 918–921
keep pool, 870–871
memory area used for sorting, 958–959
and miscellaneous index-creation issues, 423–424
multiple buffer pools, 870–872
OLTP rollback segments, 373–374
recycle pools, 872
redo log buffer, 875
shared pool, 854–855
See also Resizing
Slash, 7
Slash (/) character, 16
SMON (system monitor), 328, 336, 565
SMON (system monitor) process, 353
Solving network problems, 1104–1106
Sort operations, tuning, 956–961
Sorting, sizing memory area used for, 958–959
Sorts
avoiding in index creation, 959
direct writes for, 960–961
ensuring they happen in memory, 958–959
SQL operations that use, 957–958
temporary disk space allocation for, 960
Space
managing within tablespaces, 336
for transactions, 380–381
unused, 398
Space quota for tablespaces, unlimited, 471
Space usage, optimizing within blocks, 913–914
Space used by tables, controlling, 397–399
SQL
is functional language, 5
operations and their meanings, 803–804
operations that use sorts, 957–958
SQL * loader
additional load files at run time, 526–528
combined data and control file, 523–524
command-line parameters, 528
control file for fixed-width data, 524–525
datafiles, 525–526
SQL * Plus interface, writing line of output to, 210
SQL *Loader, multiple methods for defining same load using, 528
SQL *Plus, 375
SQL *Plus enhancements, 1147
SQL area, shared, 849
SQL performance, diagnosing, 801–809
SQL queries, editing within SQL*Plus, 14–17
SQL-statement level, setting cost optimizer goal at, 811
SQL statements, 500
enhancing performance, 820–828
and implicit cursors, 226
in PL/SQL, 220–221
running from scripts, 16
using semicolons to, 7
SQL TRACE, 757–759
SQL, trace and TKPROF, 804–807
SQL tuning, 799–828
miscellaneous tips, 828
SQL* loader
conventional, 522–534
direct path, 522–534
running, 528–530
SQL*Plus, 820
batch scripts, 7
editing SQL queries within, 14–17
Sqlnet.ora parameter, 1121
Sqrt ( ) function, 28
SRX (share row exclusive) table lock mode, 126
Stack, log file error, 1101–1106, 1102–1103
Standard packages, 312–318
Standby databases, 1159–1160
STAR hint, 814
Star queries, 812–817
Star schema, 812
Starting
listener using LSNRCTL, 998–999
names server with NAMESCTL, 1050–1053
second listener, 1007–1008
Starting Oracle, options for, 282–283
Startup
brining rollback segments online at instance, 376
force, 283
mount, 283
nomount, 282
open, 283
recovery, 283
restrict, 283
Statement audits, using audit command for privilege or, 498–499
Statements
alter index, 424
alter user, 492
conditional, 215–217
create database, 295
create sequence, 154–155
execute, 262, 264
failure, 655
for-loop, 219–220
issuing alter rollback segment offline, 379
loop-exit, 217–218
parse, 262, 264
performing select, 502
processing commit, 266–267
referencing several, 500
SQL, 220–221, 500, 820–828
stages in processing DML, 263–265
using functions in select, 24–29
using semicolons to end SQL, 7
where clause of select, 112
while-loop, 218
writing select, 6–8
Stopping
listener using LSNRCTL, 999–1001
names server, 1053
Oracle, 284
Storage allocation of tables, adding to, 397–398
Storage Manager, 335, 341
administrative tool, 338–339
administrative utility, 375
Storage, options defined, 338
Storage settings
changing, 340–342
creating rollback segments with, 374–376
creating tables with, 393–397
Storage structures
obtaining information about, 352–353
and relationships, 345–355
Storage structures and relationships, segment types, 345–348
Storing
data inline, 110
network configuration on local file system, 1044–1046
network configuration on regional databases, 1047–1049
RMAN scripts, 626–627
Strings
connect, 986
converting character, 33
Striping
disk, 901
object, 901
Structure commands, validate, 425
Structures, control, 850
Subprocedures, procedure can have, 213
Subqueries, 64–72
correlated, 68–69
to derive valid values, 67–68
having clauses and, 70
keywords that require, 69–70
in miscellaneous situations, 66–71
nested, 64–66
putting data in order with, 71–72
Substitution variables, 74, 76
Substr ( ) function, 26
Sum ( ) function, 60
Swap file, 848
Swapping described, 848–849
Switch, log, 328

Synchronization defined, 658–659
Synchronizing files during checkpoints, 569–571
Synonyms
- creating private, 185
- creating public, 185
- using for database transparency, 183–185

Syntax, backup command, 633–635
Syntax, copy command, 635–636
SYS, 275, 279
Sysdate, 105
Sysdba, 279
Sysoper, 279
System, 275
System development, stages of, 91–94
- application development, 92
- database design, 92
- database security, 93
- enhancements, 93
- needs assessment, 91–92
- performance tuning, 93

System privileges
- distinguishing between object privileges, 485
- granting, 178–179
- identifying, 481–484
- revoking, 179
- and users, 487

System tablespace, 369, 503, 893
- and auditing databases, 496
- datafiles of, 294–295
- defined, 294

System tablespace datafile, recovery for, 676
System tablespace datafiles, recovering for, 676
Systems
- configuring temporarily for particular needs, 796–799
- specifying quota 0 on, 469

T

Table delete statement, indexes slow down, 794
Table extent allocation, reorganizing, 920–921
Table-extent resizing, 919–920
Table insert statement, indexes slow down, 794
Table-naming conventions, 105–107
- avoid keywords, 106–107
- avoid nonalphanumeric characters, 106–107
- avoid quotes, 106–107
- keep names short and descriptive, 105–106
- miscellaneous naming rules, 107
- names in tables, 106
- names of associated objects, 106
- relate names for child tables to parent, 106

TABLE, parameters, 538
Table privilege, select any, 766
Table update statement, indexes slow down, 794
TABLE_NAME, 315
Tables
- adding to storage allocation of, 397–398
- analyzing to check integrity and migration, 400–401
- AUD$, 503
- caching, 873
- CHAINED_ROWS, 915
- changing data in underlying, 164
- child, 49
- cleaning up EXCEPTIONS, 438
- clustered, 791
- in clusters, 445
- columns and integrity constraints, 102
- constraint method, 101
- controlling space used by, 397–399
- copying existing, 396
- creating with data from another, 112–113
- Creation Wizard, 394
- dimension, 812
- displaying data from multiple, 48–57
- driving, 826
- dropping, 149–150, 398–399
- DUAL, 9
- EXCEPTIONS, 146–147, 437–438
- fact, 812
- highwatermarks, 398
- inserting new rows into, 120–122
- joining data from more than one, 50–53
- joining to itself, 55–56
- joining two, 49
- key-preserved, 165–167
- lookup, 812
- managing, 387–403
- with many many rows, 810
- modifying, 140–153
- N joined, 53
- nested, 392
- Oracle EXCEPTIONS, 403
- partitioning, 1154
- PLAN_TABLE, 801
- reference, 812
- retrieving data dictionary information about, 401–402
- ROWID, 172
- segments, 346
- truncating, 151, 398–399
- virtual, 114

Tables, creating
- creating one table with data from another, 112–113
- datatypes and column definitions, 108–110
- indexes created by constraints, 110–112

Tables, creating with integrity constraints, 100–105
Tables, creating with storage settings, 393–397
Tables of databases, creating, 100–113
Tablespace allocation, changing user, 468–469
Tablespace datafile, recovery for SYSTEM, 676
Tablespace keyword, adding to report command, 626
Tablespace sizes, changing, 339–340
Tablespaces
- adding, 338
- adding new datafiles to, 339
- backing up read-only, 593
- can be taken offline, 340
- coalescing, 353
- creating, 337–339
- creating temporary, 344–345
- DATA, 354, 894
- datafiles of SYSTEM, 294–295
- default, 466
- defined, 294, 336
- designating temporary, 895
- fragmentation, 354–355
- INDEX, 354, 894
- management, 341, 1145
- Manager, 335
- managing, 335–345
- managing space within, 336
- not taking offline, 382
- point-in-time recovery, 713–714
- preparing necessary, 343–345
- and quotas, 466
- and recoverability, 570–571
- recovery issues for offline, 721–722
- recovery issues for read-only, 721–722
- recovery procedures, 684–685
- relocating, 342–343
- ROLLBACK, 354, 893
- SYSTEM, 369, 496, 503, 893
- TEMP, 894
- TEMPORARY, 354
- temporary, 466
- temporary segments in permanent, 384
- temporary segments in temporary, 384
- unlimited space quota for, 471
- usage of different, 893–896
- users need quotas on, 466

Tablespaces status, changing, 340–342
Tags, using, 631
TCP/IP network, network-access control applied only on, 1091
Technical considerations, backup and recovery, 559–560
TEMP tablespace, 894
Temporary segment information, obtaining from Oracle, 386–387
Temporary segments, 346–347
- allocating space for, 385–386
- managing, 383–387
- in permanent tablespaces, 384
- in temporary tablespaces, 384
- types of, 383–385

Temporary tablespace, 466
TEMPORARY tablespaces, 354
Temporary tablespaces, designating, 895

Third-party authentication, 1122
Threads, versus processes, 846–848
Tick, network, 1068
Ticks option, 1068
TIMED_STATISTICS initsid.ora parameter, 770
TKPROF, 757–759
TKPROF and SQL trace, 804–807
TNS_ADMIN environment variable, 1008
TNSNAMES, and connection procedure, 1016
TNSNAMES setup using Net8 Assistant, 1011–1013
TNSPING utility, 1103
To_char ( ) function, 32
To_date ( ) function, 32
To_number ( ) function, 32
Tools
 administration, 267–274
 database, 348
 DBVERIFY, 660
 to detect lock contention, 940–941
 for diagnosing tuning problems, 808–809
 EXPORT, 470
 OEM (Oracle Enterprise Manager), 754
 Oracle, 801–809
 Storage Manager administrative, 338–339
 using appropriate OEM, 777–778
Trace Assistant
 better output using, 1109–1110
 specifying command-line options for, 1110
 using, 1107–1110
Trace features, configuring and using, 1097–1098
Trace files, 376, 754
 errors, 1108–1109
 formatting, 1107–1110
 location and use of, 757–759
 log and, 663–666
 monitoring, 288–289
Trace levels, setting for network components, 1098–1100
Trace parameters, setting, 1094–1101
Trace settings, changing in Net8 Assistant, 1100
TRACE, SQL, 757–759
Tracing, enabling, 1104
Tracking module use for PL/SQL blocks, 817–820
Transaction completes, locks, held until, 938
Transaction control, 124–127
 locks, 126–127
 rollback, 125–126
 SAVEPOINT, 126
 set transaction, 124–125
Transaction processing in PL/SQL, 225
Transaction rollback, using fact, 715
Transactions
 allocating rollback segments to, 911
 dividing concurrent, 910
 insufficient space for, 380–381
 set, 124–125
 using rollback segments, 369–372
Translators, case, 26
Transparency, using synonyms for database, 183–185
Triggers, 205
 defined, 208, 428
 describing, 428–433
 dictionary views for, 440
 disabling, 438
 dropping, 438
 enabled or disabled, 433
 enabling, 438
 implementing, 433–436
 maintaining, 436–439
 obtaining information, 439–440
 using to enforce business rules, 431–432
Troubleshooting
 backup problems, 639–640
 IMPORT runs, 541–542
 listener shutdown, 1000–1001
 network environments, 1081–1082, 1093–1110
 network problems, 1101–1106
 rollback segment problems, 380–382
Trunc ( ) function, 28–29
Truncating tables, 151, 398–399
Truncating tables and highwatermarks, 151
Tuning
 background process prioritization and scheduling, 844–845
 buffer cache, 859–873
 and business requirements, 748–754
 checkpoints, 902
 database applications, 789–839
 database versus OS, 845–846
 dictionary cache, 849–851
 different application requirements, 790–799
 disk utilization, 891–931
 generic OS (operating system), 842–849
 goals, 753–754
 I/O, 844
 indexes, 917–918
 LGWR performance, 904
 library cache, 849–851
 logical database design, 791–793
 memory, 843–844
 memory and OS (operating system) usage, 841–889
 miscellaneous areas of database, 933–976
 OS versus, 845–846
 performance, 93
 performing, 530–531
 primary steps for OS, 843–845
 proactive, 752
 redo mechanisms, 873–876
 role of DBA in application, 799–801
 roles associated with, 749–751
 rollback segments, 904–911
 shared pool, 849–859
 shared-pool reserved space, 857–858
 sort operations, 956–961
 SQL, 799–828
Tuning, application
 and DBA in large organizations, 800
 and DBA in smaller organizations, 800–801
Tuning background process I/O, 903–904
Tuning problems, tools for diagnosing, 808–809
Tuning recommendations
 implementing, 967–968
 reviewing, 967
Tuning session, creating, 964
Tuning, session-level, 767–768
Tuning, steps associated with, 751–753
 detect and eliminate resource contention, 752
 tune application, 751
 tune disk I/O usage, 752
 tune memory structures, 751–752
 tune OS configuration, 751
Tuning with Oracle Expert, 961–968
%type keyword, 212–213

U

UGA (User Global Area), listing, 858–859
Unarchived redo log, clearing, 662
Undefining variables, 76
Unique constraints, creating, 435
Unique index, associated, 430
Unique integrity constraints, 101
Unique keys, 429–430
UNIX, storing of OS audit trail information, 497
Updatable join views, 165–167
Updatable join views, examples, 165–167
Update statement, indexes slow down table, 794
Usage, disk, 844
User, 105
User access control, 177–185
User access, privileges and roles for managing, 93
User-account management, 467
User accounts
 changeable by users, 469
 changing, 470
 dropping, 470
User-defined
 datatypes, 388
 exceptions, 236–237
User-defined types, 392
User error, 656
User-process failure, 656
User, PUBLIC, 489
User session info, locating, 260
User sessions
 account lock status and, 468
 and password expiration, 468
 and passwords, 468
 subsequent, 468

User statement, alter, 492
User tablespace allocation, changing, 468–469
Users
- altering existing, 468–470
- connecting to server process, 260–261
- creating, 895
- in database password file, 279
- dropping existing, 468–470
- managing, 464–471
- monitoring information about existing, 470–471
- need quotas on tablespaces, 466
- reading data from disk for, 259
- structure that connect Oracle sewers for, 257–261
- and system privileges, 487
- user accounts changeable by, 469
- utilizing host machines, 476

Utilities
- DBVERIFY, 659–661
- and dynamic performance views, 765–778
- EXPORT, 722–730
- IMPORT, 722–730
- ORAPWD, 277
- TNSPING, 1103

UTLBSTAT, executing, 770
UTLBSTAT/UTLESTAT output report, 768–776

V

V$ views, using to monitor rollback-segment performance, 905–907
V$BUFFER_POOL_STATISTICS, using the performance view, 871
V$CONTROLFILE view, 321
V$CONTROLFILE_RECORD_SECTION view, 322
V$CURRENT_BUCKET, reducing buffer-hit ratio with, 865–866
V$DATAFILE view, 679
V$FILESTAT, 897–898
V$LATCHHOLDER, 950
V$LOG, 331
V$LOGFILE, 326–327
V$LOGFILE view, 334
V$PARAMETER, 286
V$PARAMETER, select VALUE from, 323
V$RECENT_BUCKET, raising buffer-hit ratio with, 865–866
V$ROLLSTAT view, 907
V$ROWCACHE, 852
V$SESSION dictionary view, 288
V$SESSION_EVENT views, 898
V$SESSION_WAIT, 760–762
V$SYSTEM_EVENT, 759–760
V$SYSTEM_EVENT views, 898
V$WAITSTAT view, 905
VALIDATE options for enabling constraints, 148–149
Validate structure commands, 425
Value-based auditing, 497
VARCHAR2 datatype, 108
VARCHAR2, in future releases of Oracle, 109
VARCHAR2(L), 390
Variable declaration section, 209
Variable scopes, 67, 213
Variable scopes defined, 66
Variable value assignments, 214–215
Variables
- automatic definition of runtime, 75–76
- datatype for, 78
- declaring, 211–214
- defining, 76–78
- entering at runtime, 73–75
- runtime, 72–78
- substitution, 74, 76
- TNS_ADMIN environment, 1008
- undefining, 76
- using, 211–214
- wildcard, 59

VARRAY, ordered list of objects, 392
Viewability of data, 66
Viewing
- dictionary comments on objects, 152–153
- enable auditing options, 501–502
- information from data dictionary, 640–641
- input data, 964–966

Views, 160–169
- ALL_CONSTRAINTS, 118
- applying description of ALL_, 117
- available dictionary, 114–116
- avoiding misuse of, 827–828
- changing data in underlying tables and, 164
- columns in, 402
- constructing data dictionary, 313–314
- creating complex, 162–167
- creating simple, 162–167
- creation that enforce constraints, 167
- data dictionary, 160–162, 312–318
- DICT dictionary, 315
- dictionary, 594–595, 870
- dynamic performance, 765–768
- fixing, 168
- instance-wide dynamic performance, 766–767
- is database object, 114
- materialized, 1149–1150
- modifying, 168
- obtaining rollback segment information from dictionary, 378–380
- removing, 169
- updatable join, 165–167
- V$CONTROLFILE, 321
- V$CONTROLFILE_RECORD_SECTION, 322
- V$DATAFILE, 679
- V$LOGFILE, 334
- V$ROLLSTAT, 907
- V$SESSION dictionary, 288
- V$SYSTEM_EVENT, 898
- V$WAITSTAT, 905

Virtual memory, 848
Virtual table, 114
Vsize ( ) function, 29

W

Wait events, 898
- retrieving, 763
- retrieving and displaying, 759–762

WAN (wide area network), 1037
Warehouses, data, 792
Weird errors, 289
Where clauses, 20–21, 56, 822–823
- of select statement, 112

While-loop statements, 218
Wildcard (*) character, 7
Wildcard variables, 59
Wizard, Table Creation, 394
Workload, collecting input data about, 965
WRAPS, sizing extents by monitoring, 910–911
Writing cursor for loops, 233–234
Writing select statements, 6–8

X (exclusive) table lock mode, 126
X, row with value of, 9

http://www.ExamPilot.Com
ExamPilot.Com

Get Your **FREE** Subscription to Oracle Magazine

Stay informed and increase your productivity with every issue of *Oracle Magazine*. Inside each FREE, bimonthly issue you'll get:

- Up-to-date information on Oracle Data Server, Oracle Applications, Network Computing Architecture, and tools
- Third-party news and announcements
- Technical articles on Oracle products and operating environments
- Software tuning tips
- Oracle customer application stories

Three easy ways to subscribe:

1 MAIL Cut out this page, complete the questionnaire on the back, and mail it to: *Oracle Magazine,* P.O. Box 1263, Skokie, IL 60076-8263.

2 FAX Cut out this page, complete the questionnaire on the back, and fax it to **+ 847.647.9735.**

3 WEB Visit our Web site at **www.oramag.com.** You'll find a subscription form there, plus much more!

If there are other Oracle users at your location who would like to receive their own subscription to *Oracle Magazine,* please photocopy the form and pass it along.

☐ **YES! Please send me a FREE subscription to Oracle Magazine.** ☐ **NO, I am not interested at this time.**

If you wish to receive your free bimonthly subscription to *Oracle Magazine,* you must fill out the entire form, sign it, and date it (incomplete forms cannot be processed or acknowledged). You can also subscribe at our Web site at **www.oramag.com/html/subform.html** or fax your application to *Oracle Magazine* at **+847.647.9735.**

SIGNATURE (REQUIRED) ✓ ______ **DATE** ______

NAME ______ TITLE ______

COMPANY ______ E-MAIL ADDRESS ______

STREET/P.O. BOX ______

CITY/STATE/ZIP ______

COUNTRY ______ TELEPHONE ______

You must answer all eight questions below.

1 What is the primary business activity of your firm at this location? *(circle only one)*

- 01 Agriculture, Mining, Natural Resources
- 02 Architecture, Construction
- 03 Communications
- 04 Consulting, Training
- 05 Consumer Packaged Goods
- 06 Data Processing
- 07 Education
- 08 Engineering
- 09 Financial Services
- 10 Government—Federal, Local, State, Other
- 11 Government—Military
- 12 Health Care
- 13 Manufacturing—Aerospace, Defense
- 14 Manufacturing—Computer Hardware
- 15 Manufacturing—Noncomputer Products
- 16 Real Estate, Insurance
- 17 Research & Development
- 18 Human Resources
- 19 Retailing, Wholesaling, Distribution
- 20 Software Development
- 21 Systems Integration, VAR, VAD, OEM
- 22 Transportation
- 23 Utilities (Electric, Gas, Sanitation)
- 24 Other Business and Services ______

2 Which of the following best describes your job function? *(circle only one)*

CORPORATE MANAGEMENT/STAFF

- 01 Executive Management (President, Chair, CEO, CFO, Owner, Partner, Principal)
- 02 Finance/Administrative Management (VP/Director/ Manager/Controller, Purchasing, Administration)
- 03 Sales/Marketing Management (VP/Director/Manager)
- 04 Computer Systems/Operations Management (CIO/VP/Director/ Manager MIS, Operations)
- 05 Other Finance/Administration Staff
- 06 Other Sales/Marketing Staff

IS/IT Staff

- 07 Systems Development/ Programming Management
- 08 Systems Development/ Programming Staff
- 09 Consulting
- 10 DBA/Systems Administrator
- 11 Education/Training
- 12 Engineering/R&D/Science Management
- 13 Engineering/R&D/Science Staff
- 14 Technical Support Director/ Manager
- 15 Webmaster/Internet Specialist
- 16 Other Technical Management/ Staff

3 What is your current primary operating platform? *(circle all that apply)*

- 01 DEC UNIX
- 02 DEC VAX VMS
- 03 Java
- 04 HP UNIX
- 05 IBM AIX
- 06 IBM UNIX
- 07 Macintosh
- 08 MPE-ix
- 09 MS-DOS
- 10 MVS
- 11 NetWare
- 12 Network Computing
- 13 OpenVMS
- 14 SCO UNIX
- 15 Sun Solaris/ SunOS
- 16 SVR4
- 17 Ultrix
- 18 UnixWare
- 19 VM
- 20 Windows
- 21 Windows NT
- 22 Other ______
- 23 Other UNIX ______

4 Do you evaluate, specify, recommend, or authorize the purchase of any of the following? *(circle all that apply)*

- 01 Hardware
- 02 Software
- 03 Application Development Tools
- 04 Database Products
- 05 Internet or Intranet Products

5 In your job, do you use or plan to purchase any of the following products or services? *(check all that apply)*

	Use	Plan to buy
SOFTWARE		
01 Business Graphics	☐	☐
02 CAD/CAE/CAM	☐	☐
03 CASE	☐	☐
04 CIM	☐	☐
05 Communications	☐	☐
06 Database Management	☐	☐
07 File Management	☐	☐
08 Finance	☐	☐
09 Java	☐	☐
10 Materials Resource Planning	☐	☐
11 Multimedia Authoring	☐	☐
12 Networking	☐	☐
13 Office Automation	☐	☐
14 Order Entry/ Inventory Control	☐	☐
15 Programming	☐	☐
16 Project Management	☐	☐
17 Scientific and Engineering	☐	☐
18 Spreadsheets	☐	☐
19 Systems Management	☐	☐
20 Workflow	☐	☐
HARDWARE		
21 Macintosh	☐	☐
22 Mainframe	☐	☐
23 Massively Parallel Processing	☐	☐
24 Minicomputer	☐	☐
25 PC	☐	☐
26 Network Computer	☐	☐
27 Supercomputer	☐	☐
28 Symmetric Multiprocessing	☐	☐
29 Workstation	☐	☐
PERIPHERALS		
30 Bridges/Routers/Hubs/ Gateways	☐	☐
31 CD-ROM Drives	☐	☐
32 Disk Drives/Subsystems	☐	☐
33 Modems	☐	☐
34 Tape Drives/Subsystems	☐	☐
35 Video Boards/Multimedia	☐	☐
SERVICES		
36 Computer-Based Training	☐	☐
37 Consulting	☐	☐
38 Education/Training	☐	☐
39 Maintenance	☐	☐
40 Online Database Services	☐	☐
41 Support	☐	☐
42 **None of the above**	☐	☐

6 What Oracle products are in use at your site? *(circle all that apply)*

SERVER/SOFTWARE

- 01 Oracle8
- 02 Oracle7
- 03 Oracle Application Server
- 04 Oracle Data Mart Suites
- 05 Oracle Internet Commerce Server
- 06 Oracle InterOffice
- 07 Oracle Lite
- 08 Oracle Payment Server
- 09 Oracle Rdb
- 10 Oracle Security Server
- 11 Oracle Video Server
- 12 Oracle Workgroup Server

TOOLS

- 13 Designer/2000
- 14 Developer/2000 (Forms, Reports, Graphics)
- 15 Oracle OLAP Tools
- 16 Oracle Power Object

ORACLE APPLICATIONS

- 17 Oracle Automotive
- 18 Oracle Energy
- 19 Oracle Consumer Packaged Goods
- 20 Oracle Financials
- 21 Oracle Human Resources
- 22 Oracle Manufacturing
- 23 Oracle Projects
- 24 Oracle Sales Force Automation
- 25 Oracle Supply Chain Management
- 26 Other ______
- 27 **None of the above**

7 What other database products are in use at your site? *(circle all that apply)*

- 01 Access
- 02 BAAN
- 03 dbase
- 04 Gupta
- 05 IBM DB2
- 06 Informix
- 07 Ingres
- 08 Microsoft Access
- 09 Microsoft SQL Server
- 10 Peoplesoft
- 11 Progress
- 12 SAP
- 13 Sybase
- 14 VSAM
- 15 **None of the above**

8 During the next 12 months, how much do you anticipate your organization will spend on computer hardware, software, peripherals, and services for your location? *(circle only one)*

- 01 Less than $10,000
- 02 $10,000 to $49,999
- 03 $50,000 to $99,999
- 04 $100,000 to $499,999
- 05 $500,000 to $999,999
- 06 $1,000,000 and over

OMG

WARNING: BEFORE OPENING THE DISC PACKAGE, CAREFULLY READ THE TERMS AND CONDITIONS OF THE FOLLOWING COPYRIGHT STATEMENT AND LIMITED CD-ROM WARRANTY.

Limited Warranty

Osborne/McGraw-Hill warrants the physical compact disc enclosed herein to be free of defects in materials and workmanship for a period of sixty days from the purchase date. If the CD included in your book has defects in materials or workmanship, please call McGraw-Hill at 1-800-217-0059, 9am to 5pm, Monday through Friday, Eastern Standard Time, and McGraw-Hill will replace the defective disc.

The entire and exclusive liability and remedy for breach of this Limited Warranty shall be limited to replacement of the defective disc, and shall not include or extend to any claim for or right to cover any other damages, including but not limited to, loss of profit, data, or use of the software, or special incidental, or consequential damages or other similar claims, even if Osborne/McGraw-Hill has been specifically advised of the possibility of such damages. In no event will Osborne/McGraw-Hill's liability for any damages to you or any other person ever exceed the lower of the suggested list price or actual price paid for the license to use the software, regardless of any form of the claim.

OSBORNE/McGRAW-HILL SPECIFICALLY DISCLAIMS ALL OTHER WARRANTIES, EXPRESS OR IMPLIED, INCLUDING BUT NOT LIMITED TO, ANY IMPLIED WARRANTY OF MERCHANTABILITY OR FITNESS FOR A PARTICULAR PURPOSE. Specifically, Osborne/McGraw-Hill makes no representation or warranty that the software is fit for any particular purpose, and any implied warranty of merchantability is limited to the sixty-day duration of the Limited Warranty covering the physical disc only (and not the software), and is otherwise expressly and specifically disclaimed.

This limited warranty gives you specific legal rights; you may have others which may vary from state to state. Some states do not allow the exclusion of incidental or consequential damages, or the limitation on how long an implied warranty lasts, so some of the above may not apply to you.

This agreement constitutes the entire agreement between the parties relating to use of the Product. The terms of any purchase order shall have no effect on the terms of this Agreement. Failure of Osborne/McGraw-Hill to insist at any time on strict compliance with this Agreement shall not constitute a waiver of any rights under this Agreement. This Agreement shall be construed and governed in accordance with the laws of New York. If any provision of this Agreement is held to be contrary to law, that provision will be enforced to the maximum extent permissible, and the remaining provisions will remain in force and effect.

NO TECHNICAL SUPPORT IS PROVIDED WITH THIS CD-ROM.